Contemporary
Theatre, Film,
and Television

A Note About
Contemporary Theatre, Film, and Television
and
Who's Who in the Theatre

Contemporary Theatre, Film, and Television is a continuation of *Who's Who in the Theatre,* expanded to include film and television personalities. The editors believe this change in coverage of the series makes for a more representative and useful reference tool.

To provide continuity with the last edition of *Who's Who in the Theatre,* the cumulative index at the back of this volume interfiles references to *Who's Who in the Theatre,* 17th Edition, with references to this first volume of *Contemporary Theatre, Film, and Television.*

ISSN 0749-064X

Contemporary Theatre, Film, and Television

A Biographical Guide Featuring Performers, Directors, Writers, Producers, Designers, Managers, Choreographers, Technicians, Composers, Executives, Dancers, and Critics in the United States and Great Britain

A Continuation of
Who's Who in the Theatre

Monica M. O'Donnell, Editor

Volume 1

Includes Cumulative Index Containing References to
Who's Who in the Theatre, **17th Edition**

GALE RESEARCH COMPANY • BOOK TOWER • DETROIT, MICHIGAN 48226

STAFF

Monica M. O'Donnell, *Editor*

J. Peter Bergman, Mel Cobb, James R. Kirkland, *Sketchwriters*
Diane Aronson, Vincent Henry, Linda L. Herr, Edith M. Jaenike,
Mia Perkin-Jensen, Edward R. Sala, Gary Trahan, Gail Weiss, *Editorial Assistants*

Linda S. Hubbard, Peter Ruffner, *Consulting Editors*
Norman MacAfee, *Copy Editor*

Carol Blanchard, *External Production Supervisor*
Vivian Tannenbaum, *Text Layout*
Arthur Chartow, *Art Director*

Special acknowledgment is due to the
Contemporary Authors staff members who
assisted in the preparation of this volume.

Frederick G. Ruffner, *Publisher*
James M. Ethridge, *Executive Vice-President/Editorial*
Dedria Bryfonski, *Editorial Director*
Christine Nasso, *Director, Literature Division*

Copyright © 1984 by
GALE RESEARCH COMPANY
ISBN 0-8103-2064-9
ISSN 0749-064X

Contents

Preface

The worlds of theatre, film, and television hold an undeniable appeal, and the individuals whose careers are devoted to these fields are subjects of great interest. The people both behind the scenes and in front of the lights and cameras—writers, directors, producers, performers, and others—all have a significant impact on our lives, for they enlighten us as they entertain.

Contemporary Theatre, Film, and Television
Continues and Improves
Who's Who in the Theatre

Contemporary Theatre, Film, and Television (CTFT), a comprehensive new biographical guide, is designed to meet the need for information on theatre, film, and television personalities. Existing biographical sources covering entertainment figures are generally limited in scope, focusing only on theatre, for example, as was the case with *Who's Who in the Theatre (WWT).* For more than seventy years *WWT* provided reliable information on theatre people. However, when the editors began reviewing names for inclusion in a proposed supplement to the seventeenth edition of *WWT,* they recognized that they were eliminating large numbers of people who, though not active in the theatre, make significant contributions to other entertainment media. Thus, the editors believe that expanding the scope of *WWT* to encompass not only theatre notables but film and/or television figures as well provides a more useful reference tool.

In addition to its expanded scope, *CTFT* improves upon *WWT* in other important ways. *WWT* was published in *editions,* with the majority of the biographies in every edition being updated and included in subsequent editions. Since entries were dropped from one edition to the next only when listees had been inactive for a sustained period or when active listees died, the number of new entries it was possible to include in each *WWT* edition was governed in part by how many old ones were dropped. *CTFT,* however, will be published annually in *volumes,* and each volume will cover primarily new, entirely different personalities. Thus *CTFT*'s coverage will not be limited by the number of entries that can be listed in a single volume, and cumulative indexes will make the entries in all *CTFT* volumes easily accessible.

Entry format, discussed in greater detail later in this preface, has also been improved in *CTFT.* Instead of presenting information with minimal paragraphing, as was the case in *WWT,* the editors have divided *CTFT* entries into numerous clearly labeled sections to make it easier to locate specific facts quickly. And the inclusion of hundreds of photographs of the personalities listed in *CTFT* adds a useful visual dimension to *CTFT* missing from *WWT.*

Scope

CTFT is a biographical series covering not only performers, directors, writers, and producers but also designers, managers, choreographers, technicians, composers, executives, dancers, and critics from the United States and Great Britain. This premier volume of *CTFT* provides biographies for over 1,100 people involved in all aspects of the theatre, film, and television industries.

Primary emphasis is given to people who are currently active. *CTFT* includes major, established figures whose positions in entertainment history are assured, such as director and screenwriter Peter Bogdanovich, actress Ellen Burstyn, actress and director Lee Grant, and director, actor, and screenwriter John Huston. New and highly promising individuals who are beginning to make their mark are represented in *CTFT* as well—people such as stage actress and singer Shelley Bruce, known for her role in *Annie;* singer and actress Melanie Chartoff, who has appeared on television in *Fridays* and on stage in *Scapino;* actor Ted Danson, known for his role in television's popular *Cheers;* and actor Lonny Price, whose recent credits include the stage play *Master Harold . . . and the Boys* and the film *The Muppets Take Manhattan.*

CTFT also includes sketches on people no longer professionally active who have made significant contributions to their fields and whose work remains of interest today. This first volume, for example, contains entries on singer-actress Kathryn Grayson and actors Harry Carey, Jr., Francis Lederer, and Gary Merrill. Selected sketches also record the achievements of theatre, film, and television personalities deceased since 1960. Among such notables with sketches in this volume are Ingrid Bergman, James Mason, David Niven, Peter Sellers, and Mae West.

With its broad coverage and detailed entries, *CTFT* is designed to assist a variety of users—a student preparing for a class, a teacher drawing up an assignment, a researcher seeking a specific fact, a librarian searching for the answer to a question, or a general reader looking for information about a favorite personality.

Compilation Methods

Every effort is made to secure information directly from biographees. The editors consult industry directories, biographical dictionaries, published interviews, feature stories, and film, television, and theatre reviews to identify people not previously covered in *WWT*. Questionnaires are mailed to prospective listees or, when addresses are unavailable, to their agents, and sketches are compiled from the information they supply. The editors also select major figures included in *WWT* whose entries require updating and send them copies of their previously published entries for revision. *CTFT* sketches are then prepared from the new information submitted by these well-known personalities or their agents. Among the notable figures whose *WWT,* seventeenth edition, entries have been completely revised for this volume of *CTFT* are Dustin Hoffman, Liza Minnelli, Stephen Sondheim, and Tom Stoppard. If people of special interest to *CTFT* users are deceased or fail to reply to requests for information, materials are gathered from reliable secondary sources. Sketches prepared solely through research are clearly marked with an asterisk (*) at the end of the entries.

The emphasis in future volumes will remain on people currently active in theatre, film, and television who are not already covered in *WWT* or *CTFT*. To insure *CTFT*'s timeliness and comprehensiveness, future volumes will continue to include updated *WWT* entries and will also provide revisions of *CTFT* sketches that have become outdated.

Format

CTFT entries, modeled after those in the Gale Research Company's highly regarded *Contemporary Authors* series, are written in a clear, readable style with few abbreviations and no limits set on length. So that a reader needing specific information can quickly focus on the pertinent portion of an entry, typical *CTFT* listings are divided into topical sections with descriptive rubrics, as follows:

Personal—Provides date and place of birth, family data, and information about the listee's education (including professional training), politics, religion, military service, and non-entertainment career items.

Career—Presents a comprehensive listing of principal credits or engagements. The career section lists theatrical debuts (including New York and London debuts), principal stage appearances, and major tours; film debuts and principal films; television debuts and television appearances; and plays, films, and television shows directed and produced. Related career items, such as professorships and lecturing, are also included.

Writings—Lists published and unpublished plays, screenplays, and scripts along with production information. Published books and articles, often with bibliographical data, are also listed.

Awards—Notes theatre, film, and television awards and nominations as well as writing awards, military and civic awards, and fellowships and honorary degrees received.

Sidelights—Cites memberships, recreational activities, and hobbies. Frequently this section provides portions of agent-prepared biographies or personal statements from the listee, and it includes home, office, and agent addresses when available.

Enlivening the text in many instances are large, clear photographs. Often the work of theatrical photographers, these pictures are supplied by the biographees to complement their sketches.

Cumulative Index

To provide easy access to the thousands of sketches in *CTFT* as well as in the last edition of *WWT,* the cumulative index at the back of this volume interfiles references to this first volume of *CTFT* with references to *WWT,* seventeenth edition. Subsequent indexes will cumulate the *CTFT* names and retain the *WWT* references.

Acknowledgments

The editors would like to extend special and sincere thanks to Sir Peter Saunders for recommending British names for inclusion in this volume of *CTFT*.

Suggestions Are Welcome

If readers would like to suggest people to be covered in future *CTFT* volumes, they are encouraged to send these names (along with addresses, if possible) to the editor. Other suggestions and comments are also most welcome and should be addressed to: The Editor, *Contemporary Theatre, Film, and Television,* 150 East 50th St., New York, NY 10022.

Abbreviations

The following abbreviations, acronyms, and initialisms are used in the Sidelights sections of *CTFT* sketches under "Memberships":

AAAS	American Academy of Arts and Sciences
AADA	American Academy of Dramatic Arts
AAUP	American Association of University Professors
ACE	American Cinema Editors
ACLU	American Civil Liberties Union
ACMPS	Academy of Canadian Motion Picture Sciences
ACT	Actor's Conservatory Theatre
ACTRA	Association of Canadian Television and Radio Artists
AEA	Actors' Equity Association
AETA	American Educational Theatre Association
AFI	American Film Institute
AFM	Affiliated Federation of Musicians
AFTRA	American Federation of Television and Radio Artists
AGAC	American Guild of Authors and Composers
AGMA	American Guild of Musical Artists
AGTRA	American Guild of Television and Radio Artists
AGVA	American Guild of Variety Artists
ALA	Academy of Lighting Arts
AMC	American Music Center
AMPAS	Academy of Motion Picture Arts and Sciences
ANTA	American National Theatre and Academy
ASC	American Society of Cinematographers
ASCAP	American Society of Composers, Authors, and Publishers
ASPCA	American Society for the Prevention of Cruelty to Animals
ATA	American Theatre Association
ATA	Association of Talent Agents
ATAS	Academy of Television Arts and Sciences
ATPAM	Association of Theatrical Press Agents and Managers
BMI	Broadcast Music, Inc.
CORD	Congress on Research in Dance
CORE	Congress of Racial Equality
DGA	Directors Guild of America
IATSE & MPMO	International Alliance of Theatrical Stage Employees and Moving Picture Machine Operators of the U.S. and Canada
IFA	International Federation of Actors
IFTR	International Foundation for Theatrical Research
IRTS	International Radio and Television Society
ISPAA	International Society of Performing Arts Administrators
LAMDA	London Academy of Music and Dramatic Arts
MATA	Musical Arena Theatres Association
NAACP	National Association for the Advancement of Colored People
NARAS	National Academy of Recording Arts and Sciences
NATAS	National Academy of Television Arts and Sciences
NEA	National Education Association
NOW	National Organization for Women
PGA	Producers Guild of America
SAG	Screen Actors Guild
SDG	Screen Directors' Guild of America
SDIG	Screen Directors International Guild
SEG	Screen Extras Guild

Continues . . .

SSD&C	Society of Stage Directors and Choreographers
UNICEF	United Nations Children's Fund
UNIMA	Union Internationale de la Marionnette
WAGB	Writers Association of Great Britain
WGA	Writers Guild of America

Contemporary Theatre, Film, and Television

Contemporary Theatre, Film, and Television

* Indicates that a listing has been compiled from secondary sources believed to be reliable.

ABBOT, Rick, playwright

See SHARKEY, Jack

* * *

ABEL, Lionel, educator, critic, writer, translator

PERSONAL: Born November 28, 1910 in Brooklyn, NY; son of Alter (a rabbi and poet) and Anna (a writer; maiden name, Schwartz) Abelson; married Sherry Goldman in 1939 (divorced); married Gloria Becker in 1970; children: Merry (deceased, 1964). EDUCATION: St. Johns University, Brooklyn, NY, 1926–28; University of North Carolina, 1928–29. RELIGION: Jewish.

WRITINGS: PLAYS, PRODUCED—*The Death of Odysseus,* Amato Opera, NY, 1953; *Absalom,* Artists Theatre, NY, 1956, Carl Fisher Concert Hall, 1956; *The Pretender,* Cherry Lane Theatre, NY, 1960; *The Wives,* Stage 73, NY, 1965.

PLAYS TRANSLATED—*Escurial* (Michel de Ghelderode), Gate Theatre, NY, 1960.

BOOKS OF CRITICISM—*Metatheatre,* 1963, *Moderns on Tragedy,* 1967.

TRANSLATIONS—*Letters to His Son Lucien* (Camille Pissarro); *Some Poems of Rimbaud; Georges Seurat* (John Rewald); *The Cubist Painters* (Guillaume Apollinaire); *Three Plays* (Jean-Paul Sartre); *Piet Mondrian: Life and Work* (Michael Seuphor); *Andromaque* (Racine).

THEATRE-RELATED CAREER—Professor of English, State University of New York at Buffalo, 1970; currently professor emeritus. Visiting professor, Pratt Institute, 1962; visiting professor, Columbia University, 1961; visiting professor, Rutgers University, 1964.

AWARDS: Rockefeller Foundation, 1965; Award of the American Academy of Arts and Letters, 1964; Longview, 1963; Guggenheim, 1963; Show Biz Award for the best Off-Broadway play of 1956, *Absalom;* Obie (first Obie awarded) for best play, *Absalom,* 1956.

ADDRESS: Home—207 E. 74th Street, New York, NY 10021. Agent—Bernice Hoffman, 215 W. 75th Street, New York, NY 10023.

* * *

ABRAHAM, F. Murray, actor

PERSONAL: Born October 24. EDUCATION: Attended University of Texas at El Paso, 1959–61; trained for the stage at Herbert Berghof Studio with Uta Hagen.

CAREER: DEBUT—Mr. Shumway, *The Wonderful Ice Cream Suit,* Coronet, Los Angeles, CA, 1965. NEW YORK DEBUT—Santa Claus, Macy's, 1965. PRINCIPAL STAGE APPEARANCES—Old Actor, *Fantasticks,* Sullivan Street, New York, 1966; Player A, *Adaptation Next,* 13th Street, New York, 1967; Jonathan, *To-Nite in Living Color,* Actors Playhouse, New York, 1967; Rudin, *Man in the Glass Booth,* Royale, New York, 1968; Reverend, *Little Murders,* Circle in the Square, New York, 1969; Bummer, *Last Chance Saloon,* La Mama E.T.C., New York, 1970; Monsignor, *The Survival of St. Joan,* Anderson, New York, 1971; Harold, *Scuba Duba,* Studio Arena, Buffalo, NY, 1972; The Men, *Where Has Tommy Flowers Gone?,* Playhouse 74, New York, 1973; Roy Pitt, *Bad Habits,* Booth, New York, 1974; Chris, *The Ritz,* Longacre, New York, 1975–76; Doc, *Legend,* Barrymore, New York, 1977; Detective Hoolihan, *Landscape of the Body,* New York Shakespeare Festival, New York, 1977; Bernie, *Sexual Perversity in Chicago,* Cherry Lane, New York, 1977; Master, *Master and Margarita,* New York Shakespeare Festival, New York, 1978; Demon, *Teibele and Her Demon,* Brooks-Atkinson, New York, 1979–80; Cyrano, *Cyrano de Bergerac,* Studio Arena, Buffalo, NY, 1980; Dorn, *The Seagull,* New York Shakespeare Festival, New York, 1980; Player Man, *Window,* Time and Space Ltd., New York, 1980; Davies, *Caretaker,* Roundabout, New York, 1982; Creon, *Antigone,* New York Shakespeare Festival, New York, 1982; Astrov, *Uncle Vanya,* La Mama E.T.C., New York, 1983. MAJOR TOURS—Father Drobney, *Don't Drink the Water,* Florida, 1966–67; *And Miss Reardon Drinks a Little,* 1972.

FILM DEBUT—Detective Levy, *Serpico.* PRINCIPAL FILMS—Mechanic, *The Sunshine Boys;* Detective Rafferty, *All the*

1

President's Men; Epis, *The Big Fix,* 1978; Omar, *Scarface,* 1983; Salieri, *Amadeus,* 1984; Chris, *The Ritz.* TELEVISION DEBUT—*Love of Life.* PRINCIPAL TELEVISION APPEARANCES— Big Tony, *Kojak;* Jakopo, *Marco Polo; How to Survive a Marriage; All in the Family.*

SIDELIGHTS: MEMBERSHIPS—AEA; SAG; AFTRA.

"For every actor from England who works in New York City, an American must work in London. This is vital!"

ADDRESS: Agent—c/o Clifford Stevens, S.T.E. Representation Ltd., 888 Seventh Avenue, New York, NY 10019.

* * *

ABRAHAMSEN, Daniel Charles, producer, manager

PERSONAL: Born November 27, 1952 in Paterson, NJ; son of John W. (a food products distributor) and Theresa O. (Hagen) Abrahamsen; married Geraldine Perotka (a producer) on June 13, 1983. EDUCATION: William Patterson College, B.A., 1975; studied lighting at the Lester Polakov Forum of Design, in New York.

CAREER: FIRST STAGE WORK—Electrician, National Lampoon's *Lemmings,* Village Gate, NY, 1974. PRINCIPAL STAGE WORK—Designed, sets and lights, *Getting Out,* Theatre de Lys, NY, 1977; produced—*The Great American Backstage Musical,* NY, 1983; *On the Air,* NY, 1983. MAJOR TOURS—Technical Coordinator, *Babes in Toyland,* National Tour.

FILM WORK—Art Director, *Gunmen's Blues,* 1982.

THEATRE-RELATED CAREER—Production coordinator, American Place, NY, 1979–81; President, DCA Design Associates, Inc., NY, 1979–present.

AWARDS: Art Directors Club of New Jersey Award for Best Commercial.

SIDELIGHTS: MEMBERSHIPS—National Academy of Television Arts and Sciences; Illuminating Engineers Society; Association of Theatrical Artists and Crafts People; National Association of Campus Activities. Mr. Abrahamsen also produces cabaret performances in nightclubs.

ADDRESS: Office—437 W. 44th Street, New York, NY 10036.

* * *

ABRAVANEL, Maurice, musical director, conductor and educator

PERSONAL: Born January 6, 1903 in Salonica, Greece; son of Edouard (a pharmacist) and Rachel (Bitty) Abravanel; married Lucy Menassé, September 20, 1947; children: Pierre, Roger. EDUCATION: attended University of Lausanne (Switzerland); studied music with Kurt Weill.

CAREER: DEBUT—Backstage piano, Municipal Theatre, Lausanne (Switzerland). NEW YORK DEBUT—musical director, *Samson and Delilah,* Metropolitan Opera, New York, 1936. PRINCIPAL STAGE WORK—Musical director, *Knickerbocker Holiday,* Ethel Barrymore, New York, 1938; musical director, *Lady in the Dark,* Alvin, New York, 1941; musical director, *One Touch of Venus,* Imperial, New York, 1943; *The Seven Lively Arts,* Ziegfeld, New York, 1944; *The Firebrand of Florence,* Alvin, New York, 1945; *Street Scene,* Adelphi, New York, 1947; *Regina,* 46th Street, New York, 1949. MAJOR TOURS—British National Opera Company, Melbourne, Sydney, 1935; Utah Symphony, four international tours, Berlin Festival, Athens Festival, Barcelona Festival, Hollywood Bowl, Carnegie Hall, London, Washington, D.C. TELEVISION DEBUT—Utah Symphony, PBS.

AWARDS: Gold Baton Award, American Symphony League, 1981; Antoinette Perry Award, Best Musical Direction, 1951: *Street Scene,* 1950: *Regina.*

SIDELIGHTS: MEMBERSHIPS—National Endowment of the Arts, Music Panel NEA; American Arts Alliance, American Symphony Orchestra League.

ADDRESS: 1235 E. Seventh Street, Salt Lake City, UT 84105.

* * *

ABUBA, Ernest (ne Ernest Hawkins Abuba), actor, director, playwright, and screenwriter

PERSONAL: Born August 25, 1947 in Honolulu, HI; son of Domingo Garcia (U.S. Army) and Della Marie (restaurant owner; maiden name, De France) Abuba; married Tisa Chang (a producer and director) on January 25, 1976; children: a son, Auric Kang. EDUCATION: Southwestern College, (2½ years); Washington, DC Theatre of Dramatic Arts, (Ballet); studied with Louise Brandwen at the Actors Stage Studio. MILITARY: U.S. Coast Guard, Seaman/Hospitalman, 1968–71.

CAREER: DEBUT—Aly, *Eh?,* Old Globe Theatre, San Diego, CA, 1969. NEW YORK DEBUT—Young Man, *Hello Out There,* Theatre at St. Clements and American Place, for 20 performances, 1970. PRINCIPAL STAGE APPEARANCES— Wu Chan, *The Legend of Wu Chan,* Buffalo Studio Arena, 1975; Commander Adams, *Pacific Overtures,* Winter Garden, NY, 1976; Dorothy Chandler Pavilion, Los Angeles, 1977; Fisherman, *Loose Ends,* Circle in the Square, NY, 1979; Kadota, *Yellow Fever,* Pan Asian Repertory, NY, 1983; The Singer, *Caucasian Chalk Circle,* La Mama Annex, NY; Pahka, *Dawn Song,* Chelsea Theatre, NY; Priest, *Rashomon,* Equity Library Theatre, NY; Charlie Chan, *Gee Pop,* American Place Workshop, NY; Understudy (Cyrano), *Cyrano de Bergerac,* Santa Fe Theatre; Steve, *F.O.B.,* O'Neill Theatre Center; Balinese Fisherman, *Loose Ends,* Arena Stage, Washington, DC; Hashimoto, *Failure to Zigzag,* Indiana Repertory Theatre; Samurai, *Mockingbird,* New Dramatists; Following roles at Pan Asian Rep/La Mama in NY: Uncle Aki, *Manoa Valley;* Old Actor, *Monkey Music;* Pan, *Sunrise;* Ping, *Thunderstorm;* Lysander, *A Midsummer Night's Dream;* Boniface, *Hotel Paradiso;* Little Big Man,

Crazy Horse Suite, Open Eye Theatre; Lookout, *Christopher Columbus,* Jean Cocteau Rep; Azrael, *Orphee,* Jean Cocteau Rep; Bezano, *He, Who Gets Slapped,* Jean Cocteau Rep; Chet, *Cowboys No. 2,* Theatre Lobby, Washington, DC.

FILM DEBUT—Sato, *The Next Man,* 1978. PRINCIPAL FILM APPEARANCES—Seqouya, *Seqouya,* 1980; Pakistani, *The Last Embrace,* 1981. TELEVISION DEBUT—Florist, *Ryan's Hope.* PRINCIPAL TELEVISION APPEARANCES—Dr. Logan, *Search for Tomorrow,* 1981; Dr. Evns, *Loving,* 1983; narrator, *In Search of Mao; Where the Heart Is.*

WRITINGS: PLAYS, PRODUCED—*The Dowager,* La Mama Annex, 1978: *An American Story,* Pan Asian Repertory, NY, 1980. FILM: DIRECTOR/CO-WRITER—*Vegetable Soup II,* 1979; *Lilac Chen: Asian American Suffragette; Arthur A. Schomburg: Black Historian; Asian American Railroad Strike; Osceola: American Indian Hero; Iroquois Confederacy; Mariana Bracetti: Puerto Rican.* ARTICLES/ESSAYS—*Woodwind,* Washington, DC, 1969. POEMS PUBLISHED—*Hang-Up,* 1967.

THEATRE-RELATED CAREER: Acting teacher, The Basement Workshop, NY, 1977–78.

AWARDS: Obie, Best Actor, *Yellow Fever,* 1983; Outstanding Young Men of America Award, 1981; CAPS Playwriting Fellowship for an American Story, 1979; Best Actor, Focus Press Award, Wu Chang, *The Legend of Wu Chang,* 1975; Best Supporting Actor nomination, Old Globe Theatre, Aly, *Eh?,* 1967; Best Director, Southwestern College, CA, 1981.

SIDELIGHTS: MEMBERSHIPS—AFTRA, SAG, AEA, ACTRA (Canada), Board of Directors, Pan Asian Repertory Theatre; Board of Directors, H. T. Chen Dancers Company. RECREATIONS—Oil painting, fatherhood, yoga, athletics, Shaolin boxing, fencing-rapier, double sword.

ADDRESS: Office—74A East 4th Street, New York, NY. Agent—D.M.I. Talent Agency, 250 W. 57th Street, New York, NY 10107.

* * *

ACKERMAN, Bettye, actress and painter

PERSONAL: Born February 28, 1928, in Cottageville, SC; daughter of Clarence Kilgo (superintendent of schools) and Mary Mildred (a teacher; nee Baker) Ackerman; married Sam Jaffe (an actor), June 7, 1956. EDUCATION: Columbia University, B.A., 1954; prepared for the stage with Louise Gifford, Alexander Kirkland, Stella Adler. POLITICS: Democrat. RELIGION: Methodist.

CAREER: DEBUT—Purity, *Pure as the Driven Snow,* Grace Methodist Church, New York, 1950. NEW YORK DEBUT—Pheelie, *No 'Count Boy,* Theatre de Lys, 1954, 15 performances. PRINCIPAL STAGE APPEARANCES—Elmire, *Tartuffe,* Kaufman Auditorium, New York, 1955; Antigone, *Sophocles' Trilogy,* John Hall Theatre, New York, 1956; Elmire, *Tartuffe,* Theatre Marquee, New York, 1957; Portia, *Merchant of Venice,* Dickinson State College Theatre, Dickinson, ND, 1971. MAJOR TOURS—Wicked Queen, *Snow White*

and the Seven Dwarfs, Clare Tree Major's Children's Theatre, major U.S. cities, 1950.

FILM DEBUT—Grace Prescott, *Face of Fire,* 1958. PRINCIPAL FILMS—Miss Whalen, *Rascal,* 1969. TELEVISION DEBUT—*Crime Photographer,* 1951. TELEVISION APPEARANCES—Maggie Graham, *Ben Casey,* 1961–66; *Bracken's World,* 1969–70; *Medical Center,* 1969–70; Constance MacKenzie, *Return to Peyton Place,* 1972. Guest starred in episodes of many popular television series and specials.

AWARDS: Honorary Doctor of Humane Letters, Drew University, 1983; Southern California Motion Picture Bronze Star Halo Award, 1983; Hollywood Appreciation Society Golden Mask Award, 1982; President's Award, Columbia College, 1971.

SIDELIGHTS: MEMBERSHIPS—Hollywood Motion Picture and Television Museum (secretary, 1976–83), Otis Art Associates (1975–79), Muscular Dystrophy Association (West Coast campaign chairman, 1963–69). Since 1970 has exhibited her paintings in one-woman and group shows in such galleries as The Lambert (Los Angeles), The Sandlapper (Columbia, SC), Gallery Eight (Claremont, CA), Art by Celebrities (Los Angeles), Erskine College (Due West, SC), Galleria Beretich (Claremont, CA), Drew University (Madison, NJ), United States International University (San Diego, CA).

ADDRESS: Agent—c/o Sue Goldin Talent Agency, 119 N. San Vicente Blvd., Beverly Hills, CA 90211.

* * *

ACKROYD, David, actor

PERSONAL: Born: May 30, 1940 in Orange, NJ; son of Arthur Oldfield (an insurance adjustor) and Charlotte Beatrice (Henderson) Ackroyd; married Ruth Liming (a college admissions officer) on March 30, 1963; children: Jessica Lyn, Abigail Ruth. EDUCATION: Bucknell University, A.B., 1962; Rutgers University School of Law, 1962; Yale School of Drama, M.F.A., 1968. RELIGION: Protestant. MILITARY: U.S. Army, lieutenant, 1963–65.

CAREER: DEBUT—Tony, *You Can't Take It with You,* Williamstown Theatre Festival, Williamstown, MA, 1966. NEW YORK DEBUT—Sgt. Marx, *Unlikely Heroes,* Plymouth, 1971, 16 performances. PRINCIPAL STAGE APPEARANCES—3 seasons, Yale Repertory, New Haven, CT, 1968–71; Capt. Korovkin, *Full Circle,* ANTA, New York, 1973; Richard, *Hide and Seek,* Belasco, New York, 1980; James Leeds, *Children of a Lesser God,* Longacre, New York, 1980–81.

FILM DEBUT—Medicine Wolf, *The Mountain Men,* 1979. TELEVISION DEBUT—*Story Theatre,* Theatre in America Series, PBS. TELEVISION APPEARANCES—*Harvest Home, And I Alone Survived, Women in White, A Gun in the House, The Sound of Murder, Cocaine—One Man's Seduction, Deadly Lessons, When Your Lover Leaves, The Sky's No Limit.* (Series): *Kojak, Lou Grant, Dallas, The Paper Chase, Knot's Landing, The Facts of Life, Trapper John, Dynasty, Two Marriages, Whiz Kids.*

ADDRESS: Agent—c/o Alan Iezman, William Morris Agency, 151 El Camino Drive, Beverly Hills, CA 90212.

* * *

ADAM, Ken (ne Klaus), production designer, art director

PERSONAL: Born February 5, 1921 in Berlin, Germany; son of Fritz (businessman) and Lilli (Saalfeld) Adam; married Maria Letizia (an art director), August 16, 1952. EDUCATION: Attended Franzosische Gymnasium (Berlin), St. Paul's School (London), Bartlett School of Architecture, London University. RELIGION: Roman Catholic. MILITARY: Royal Air Force, fighter pilot, flight lieutenant, 1941–46.

CAREER: FIRST FILM WORK—Draughtsman, *This Was a Woman*, 1947. PRINCIPAL FILMS (Production Designer)—*The Rough and the Smooth*, 1959; *In the Nick*, 1959; *Let's Get Married*, 1959; *The Trials of Oscar Wilde*, 1960; *Sodom and Gomorrah*, 1961; *Dr. No*, 1962; *In the Cool of the Day*, 1962; *Dr. Strangelove*, 1963; *Woman of Straw*, 1963; *Goldfinger*, 1964; *The Ipcress File*, 1964; *Thunderball*, 1965; *Funeral in Berlin*, 1965; *You Only Live Twice*, 1966; *Chitty Chitty Bang Bang*, 1967; *Goodbye Mr. Chips*, 1969; *The Owl and the Pussycat*, 1970; *Diamonds Are Forever*, 1971; *Sleuth*, 1972; *The Last of Sheila*, 1972; *Barry Lyndon*, 1974; *Salon Kitty*, 1975; *The Seven Percent Solution*, 1975; *The Spy Who Loved Me*, 1976; *Moonraker*, 1978; *Pennies from Heaven*, 1981. (Art Director)—*The Devils Pass*, 1953; *Soho Incident*, 1955; *Around the World in 80 Days*, 1955; *Child in the House*, 1956; *V.I.*, 1957; *Night of the Demon*, 1957; *Gideons Day*, 1957; *Ten Seconds to Hell*, 1958; *The Angry Hills*, 1958; *Beyond this Place*, 1959. (Special Design Projects)—*Ben Hur*, 1955; *John Paul Jones*, 1956; *The Long Ships*, 1959; *The Hellion*, 1961.

AWARDS: New York Independent Film Critics Award, Best Production Design, 1981: *Pennies from Heaven;* Academy Award, Best Art Direction, 1976: *Barry Lyndon;* Academy Award Nomination, Best Art Direction, 1978: *The Spy Who Loved Me*, 1956: *Around the World in 80 Days;* British Academy Award, Best Art Direction, 1965: *The Ipcress File;* 1963: *Dr. Strangelove;* British Academy Award Nomination, Best Art Direction, 1976: *Barry Lyndon;* 1973: *Sleuth;* 1965: *Goldfinger;* Moscow Film Festival Award, Best Art Direction/Costume Design, 1960: *Trials of Oscar Wilde.*

SIDELIGHTS: MEMBERSHIPS—Academy of Motion Picture Arts and Sciences, American Film Institute, United Scenic Artists (Local 829), ACTT (England).

ADDRESS: Home—34 Montpelier Street, London, SW7, England. Agent—c/o William Morris Agency (UK) Ltd., 147/149 Wardour Street, London W1, England.

* * *

ADAMS, Julie (nee Betty May Adams), actress

PERSONAL: Born October 17; daughter of Ralph Eugene (a cotton buyer) and Esther Gertrude (Beckett) Adams; married Ray Danton 1954 (divorced 1981); children: Steven, Mitchell. EDUCATION: Little Rock Junior College, 1945–46; studied with Florence Enright, George Shdanov, and David Craig.

CAREER: FILM DEBUT—second female lead, *Bright Victory*, 1951. PRINCIPAL FILM APPEARANCES—*Bend of the River*, 1952; *Mississippi Gambler*, 1953; *The Creature from the Black Lagoon*, 1954; *Private War of Major Benson*, 1955; *Tickle Me*, 1964; *Mc Q*, 1975.

STAGE DEBUT—Leading lady, *Dear Sir*, summer stock in Redding, CA, 1960. PRINCIPAL STAGE APPEARANCES—Jean Brodie, *The Prime of Miss Jean Brodie*, El Paso, TX, 1972; Marion, *Father's Day*, Ivanhoe, Chicago, IL; Mary Hadley, *Who's Happy Now*, Forum, Yorba Linda, CA.

PRINCIPAL TELEVISION APPEARANCES—*Marcus Welby; Playhouse 90; Quincy; Capitol; Code Red; The Jimmy Stewart Show;* TV movies—*Go Ask Alice; Six Characters in Search of an Author.*

ADDRESS: Agent—Lew Sherrell Agency, 7060 Hollywood Blvd., Los Angeles, CA 90028.

* * *

ADAMS, Mason, actor

PERSONAL: Married Margot Adams (a writer); children: Betsy, Bil. EDUCATION: University of Wisconsin, B.A., 1940, M.A., 1941; trained for the stage at the Neighborhood Playhouse.

CAREER: DEBUT—Hilltop Theatre, Baltimore, Summer, 1940. NEW YORK DEBUT—Joe Rigga, *Get Away Old Man*, Cort Theatre, New York, 1943. LONDON DEBUT—Playwright, Bed Salesman, Herbert, *You Know I Can't Hear You When the Water's Running*, New Theatre, 1968. PRINCIPAL STAGE APPEARANCES—(Broadway) *Career Angel; Public Relations; Violet; Shadow of My Enemy; Inquest; The Sign in Sidney Brustein's Window; Tall Story; The Trial of the Catonsville Nine; Checking Out;* (Off-Broadway) *The Shortchanged Review*, New York Shakespeare Festival.

FILM DEBUT—President of the United States, *The Final Conflict*, 1980. TELEVISION APPEARANCES—Charlie Hume, *Lou Grant*, 5 seasons; *The Deadliest Season; And Baby Makes Six; The Shining Season; Flamingo Road; The Revenge of the Stepford Wives; The Kid with the Broken Halo; Freedom to Speak; Solomon Northrup's Odyssey.*

AWARDS: 3 Emmy nominations, Charlie Hume, *Lou Grant.*

SIDELIGHTS: MEMBERSHIPS—Players Club, Delta Sigma Rho, Phi Kappa Phi.

An active radio actor during the forties and fifties, Mason Adams played in most of the major radio shows originating in New York; for sixteen years played the title role in the serial, *Pepper Young's Family.*

ADDRESS: Home—49 Owenoke Park, Westport, CT 06880; 2006 Stradella Road, Los Angeles, CA 90077. Agent—c/o

Don Buchwald Associates, 10 E. 44th Street, New York, NY 10017.

* * *

ADAMS, Wayne, producer, actor

PERSONAL: Born December 9, 1930 in Bucyrus, OH; son of Edgar Jacob and Bertha Ann (Gaver) Adams. EDUCATION: Ohio University, B.F.A. 1952. MILITARY: U.S. Air Force, 1st Lieutenant, 1952–54.

CAREER: PRINCIPAL STAGE WORK, PRODUCER—*Jacques Brel Is Alive and Well and Living in Paris*, North American tour, 1972–74; *The Runner Stumbles*, Little Theatre (now the Helen Hayes), NY, 1976; *Say Goodnight Gracie*, Actor's Playhouse, NY, 1979–80; *True West*, Cherry Lane, 1982–84; *And a Nightingale Sang . . .*, Lincoln Center, Mitzi E. Newhouse, 1983–84.

PRINCIPAL STAGE WORK, ACTING—Aegeon/Sorcerer, *Boys from Syracuse*, national tour.

SIDELIGHTS: MEMBERSHIPS—AEA; Association of Off-Broadway Producers.

ADDRESS: Home—53 W. 83rd Street, New York, NY 10024.

* * *

AIDMAN, Betty Linton (nee Betty Hyatt), choreographer, dancer, actress

PERSONAL: Born June 12; daughter of William Green (a business owner) and Lyda (Overall) Hyatt; married Charles Ogilvie; married Bill Linton; married Charles Aidman (an actor), February 9, 1969; children: Charles (Chuck) Ogilvie. EDUCATION: Attended public high school; studied dance at the School of American Ballet, New York; trained for the theatre at the Theatre West Workshop and with Sherman Marks. RELIGION: First Christian Church—Protestant.

CAREER: DEBUT—dancer, *High Button Shoes*, Century, New York, 1947. PRINCIPAL STAGE APPEARANCES—Lady Elizabeth, *Once Upon a Mattress*, St. James, New York, 1959; Sue, *The Conquering Hero*, ANTA, New York, 1961; Violet, *Wonderful Town*, City Center, New York; Adelaide, *Guys and Dolls*, City Center, New York; Hedy LaRue, *How to Succeed in Business*, City Center, New York; Jenny, *Maggie Flynn*, ANTA, New York, 1968; Louella Pringle, *But Seriously*, Henry Miller, New York; Grace, *A Day in Venice*, Theatre West, Los Angeles; *Father's Day*, Huntington Hartford, Los Angeles. PRINCIPAL STAGE WORK (Choreographer)—revival, *Finian's Rainbow*, City Center, New York; revival, *The Music Man*, City Center, New York. MAJOR TOURS—Elsa, *The Desk Set*; Ellie, *Show Boat*; Meg Brockie, *Brigadoon* (with the New York Light Opera Company); Adelaide, *Guys and Dolls*, N.Y. City Center/U.S.O. Tour to Vietnam.

BETTY LINTON AIDMAN

FILM DEBUT—Coral, *Caribbean Adventure*. TELEVISION APPEARANCES—Julia Carson, *Divorce Court;* Donna Jo, *Cops* (CBS Tuesday Night Movies); dancer, *Arthur Godfrey Variety Show;* dancer (guest appearances), *Jackie Gleason Variety Show.* PRINCIPAL TELEVISION WORK (Choreographer)—*Circus of the Stars*, 1982; *Circus of the Stars*, 1983.

AWARDS: Dance study scholarship from George Balanchine.

SIDELIGHTS: MEMBERSHIP—The Magic Castle.

ADDRESS: Agent—c/o The Carey-Phelps-Colvin Agency, 121 N. Robertson Blvd., Suite B, Beverly Hills, CA 90211.

* * *

AIDMAN, Charles, actor, manager, and writer

PERSONAL: Born January 31, 1925 in Indianapolis, IN; son of George (a doctor) and Etta (Kwitny) Aidman; married Betty Hyatt (an actress, choreographer), February 9, 1969; children: Charles (stepson). EDUCATION: Indiana University, B.A., 1942; trained for the stage of the Neighborhood Playhouse in New York with Sanford Meisner. MILITARY: U.S. Navy (Lieutenant), 1946–48.

CAREER: DEBUT—Mark Anthony, *Julius Caesar*, Joseph Papp's Shakespeare in the Park, New York, 1956. PRINCIPAL STAGE APPEARANCES—Sam Lawson, *Career*, Seventh Avenue Theatre, New York, 1957; *Spoon River Anthology*, Booth, New York, 1963; George Shearer, *Zoot Suit*, Mark

CHARLES AIDMAN

Taper Forum, Los Angeles, 1979, Winter Garden, New York, 1980; Dr. Rosenthal, *Nuts*, L.A. Stage Company, Los Angeles, 1982. MAJOR TOURS—Quentin, *After the Fall*, Los Angeles, Washington, Chicago, 1965–66. DIRECTED—*Spoon River Anthology*, Booth, New York, 1963. PRINCIPAL FILMS—*Pork Chop Hill*, 1959; Captain Pratt, *War Hunt*, 1961; *Hour of the Gun*, 1967; *Countdown*, 1968; *Angel, Angel, Down We Go (Cult of the Damned)*, 1970; *Adam at 6 A.M.*, 1970; *Dirty Little Billy*, 1972; *Kotch*, 1971; *Twilight's Last Gleaming; Zoot Suit*, 1981. TELEVISION DEBUT—Lead role, *Before It's Too Late*, Kraft TV Theatre. TELEVISION APPEARANCES—*Spoon River Anthology; Deliver Us from Evil; The Picture of Dorian Gray; The Red Badge of Courage; Amelia Earhart; Prime Suspect; Marian Rose White; Wild Wild West* (replaced Ross Martin for one season); *Magnum, P.I.; Quincy; Bosom Buddies; M*A*S*H; Today's F.B.I.; Little House on the Prairie; Eight Is Enough; Archie Bunker's Place; It Takes Two*.

WRITINGS: PLAYS, PUBLISHED—*Spoon River Anthology*, 1963.

AWARDS: Emmy Nomination, *Spoon River Anthology*.

SIDELIGHTS: MEMBERSHIPS—Oliver Hailey's Writer's Workshop in Los Angeles; The Magic Castle. RECREATION—tennis, cycling, swimming.

One of the founders of Theatre West in Los Angeles.

ADDRESS: Agent—c/o David Shapira & Associates, 15301 Ventura Blvd. Sherman Oaks, CA 91403.

*   *   *

AILEY, Alvin, choreographer, dancer, actor, director

PERSONAL: Born 1931 in Rogers, TX. EDUCATION: Attended UCLA, Los Angeles City College, San Francisco State University; studied modern dance with Martha Graham, Hanya Holm, and Charles Weidman, ballet with Karel Shook, composition with Doris Humphrey and acting with Stella Adler and Milton Katselas, in New York City.

CAREER: DEBUT—Dancer, Lester Horton Dance Company, Los Angeles, CA. NEW YORK DEBUT—Dancer, *House of Flowers*. PRINCIPAL STAGE APPEARANCES—Dancer, *The Carefree Tree*, 1956; dancer, *Sing Man Sing*, 1956; *Show Boat*, 1957; acted in: *Call Me by My Rightful Name; Tiger, Tiger, Burning Bright; Ding Dong Bell; Talking to You;* co-directed: *Jerico-Jim Crow;* choreographed: *Carmen Jones; Dark of the Moon; African Holiday;* staged operas: *Four Saints in Three Acts*, Mini-Metropolitan Opera, NY; *Anthony and Cleopatra*, Metropolitan Opera, NY; Bernstein *Mass* Kennedy Center for the Performing Arts; staged ballet: *Lord Byron*. CREATED AND CHOREOGRAPHED WORKS—*Blues Suite*, 1958; *Revelations*, 1960; *Knoxville: Summer of 1915*, 1961; *Masekela Language*, 1961; *Gymnopédies*, 1970; *Myth*, 1971; *Choral Dances*, 1971; *Cry*, 1971; *Archipelago*, 1971; *Mary Lou's Mass*, 1971; *The Lark Ascending*, 1972; *Love Song's*, 1972; *Hidden Rites*, 1973; *The Mooche*, 1975; *Night Creature*, 1975; *Pas de "Duke,"* 1976; *Memoria*, 1979; *Phases*, 1980; *The River*, 1981; *Landscape*, 1981.

MAJOR TOURS—U.S. State Department, Far East, 1962; The World Festival of Negro Arts at Sakar, Senegal, 1966; East and West Africa, 1967; North Africa, Soviet Union (first modern dance company to perform since Isadora Duncan), 1970; Paris, France, 1974–75; Japan, Far East, Middle East, Africa, Europe, 1978; Latin America, 1980.

CHOREOGRAPHY—The Joffrey Ballet; Harkness Ballet; American Ballet Theatre; Bat-Dor Company of Israel; Ballet Internacional de Caracas; Royal Danish Ballet.

PRINCIPAL TELEVISION WORK—*Memories and Visions*, 1973; *Ailey Celebrates Ellington*, 1974; *Ailey Celebrates Ellington*, 1976 (Bicentennial celebration).

AWARDS: Capezio Award, 1979; Dance Magazine Award, 1975; Proclamation in New York City of Alvin Ailey Dance Theatre Twentieth Anniversary Day, 1979; Mayor's Award (New York City) of Arts and Culture, 1977; First Prize, International Dance Festival in Paris, 1970; Spingarn Medal, NAACP, 1976; Honorary Degrees in Fine Arts from: Princeton University, Bard College, Adelphi University, Cedar Crest College.

SIDELIGHTS: As a child, Ailey attended Sunday school and the Baptist Young People's Union and it is out of these experiences and memories that two of his most popular and critically acclaimed works were inspired: *Blues Suite* and *Revelations*. Created Alvin Ailey American Dance Theatre, 1958.

ADDRESS: c/o The Alvin Ailey American Dance Theatre, 1515 Broadway, New York, NY 10036.

AKROYD, Dan(iel Edward), writer, actor

PERSONAL: Born July 1, 1952, in Ottawa, ON, Canada; son of Peter Hugh and Lorraine G. (Gongeon) Akroyd; married Maureen Lewis, May 10, 1974 (divorced); Donna Dixon, June 1, 1983; children: (first marriage) Mark, Lloyd, Oscar.

CAREER: PRINCIPAL STAGE APPEARANCE—Member, Toronto Co. of Second City Theater; performed with John Belushi as *Blues Brothers.*

PRINCIPAL TELEVISION APPEARANCES—*Coming Up Rosie; Saturday Night Live,* 1975–79; *Beach Boys Special; All You Need Is Cash; Not Ready for Prime Time Players;* host, *Sweet Home Chicago,* 1983.

PRINCIPAL FILM APPEARANCES—*Love at First Sight,* 1975; *Mr. Mike's Mondo Video,* 1979; *1941,* 1979; *The Blues Brothers,* 1980; *Neighbors,* 1981; *Doctor Detroit,* 1983; *Trading Places,* 1983; *Twilight Zone—The Movie,* 1983; *Ghostbusters,* 1984.

RECORDINGS—with John Belushi as Blues Brothers, albums include *Briefcase Full of Blues; Made in America.*

WRITINGS: SCREENPLAYS—*The Blues Brothers,* 1980; *Ghostbusters,* 1984. TELEVISION—*Saturday Night Live,* 1975–79.

AWARDS: Emmy Award, 1976–77.

SIDELIGHTS: MEMBERSHIPS—AFTRA, Writers Guild of America, West.

Mr. Akroyd is part-owner of the Hard Rock Cafe, NY (opened March 1984); regrouped the Blues Brothers Band to finance the John Belushi Memorial Fund, a program that provides scholarships for theater students and supports a number of drug-abuse organizations.

ADDRESS: Office—c/o Atlantic Records, 75 Rockefeller Plaza, New York, NY 10019.*

* * *

ALBERT, Eddie (ne Edward Albert Heimberger), actor

PERSONAL: Born April 22, 1908, in Rock Island, IL; son of Frank Daniel and Julia (Jones) Heimberger; married Margo (nee Margarita Guadalupe Bolado y Castilla; an actress); children: Edward, Maria. EDUCATION: Attended University of Minnesota. MILITARY: U.S. Navy, Lieutenant, World War II.

CAREER: STAGE DEBUT—As a singer and stage manager in Minneapolis, 1933. NEW YORK DEBUT—*O Evening Star,* Empire, 1935. PRINCIPAL STAGE APPEARANCES—Partnered with Grace Bradt in an act called *The Honeymooners,* 1935; Bing Edwards, *Brother Rat,* Biltmore, NY, 1936; Leo Davis, *Room Service,* Cort, NY, 1937; Antipholus, *The Boys from Syracuse,* Alvin, NY, 1938; Horace Miller, *Miss Liberty,* Imperial, NY, 1949; Reuben, *Reuben, Reuben,* Shubert, Boston, 1955; Jack Jordan, *Say, Darling,* ANTA, NY, 1958; Harold Hill, *The Music Man,* Majestic, NY, 1960;

George Bartlett, *No Hard Feelings,* Martin Beck, NY, 1973; Martin Vanderhof, *You Can't Take It with You,* Plymouth, NY, 1983; *Parade of Stars Playing the Palace,* 1983.

FILM DEBUT—*Brother Rat,* 1938. PRINCIPAL FILM APPEARANCES—*On Your Toes,* 1939; *Four Wives; Angel from Texas; Dispatch from Reuters; Rendezvous with Annie; Perfect Marriage; Smash Up; The Story of a Woman; Time Out of Mind; Hit Parade of 1947; Dude Goes West; You Gotta Stay Happy; Fuller Brush Girl; You're in the Navy Now; Meet Me After the Show; Actors and Sin; Roman Holiday,* 1953; *Girl Rush,* 1955; *I'll Cry Tomorrow,* 1955; *Teahouse of the August Moon,* 1956; *Orders to Kill; Oklahoma!,* 1956; *The Sun Also Rises,* 1957; *Attack,* 1958; *Gun Runners,* 1958; *Roots of Heaven,* 1958; *The Young Doctors,* 1961; *The Longest Day,* 1962; *Miracle of the White Stallions,* 1963; *Captain Newman,* 1964; *Seven Women,* 1966; *The Heartbreak Kid,* 1972; *McQ,* 1974; *The Take,* 1974; *The Longest Yard,* 1974; *Escape to Witch Mountain,* 1975; *Devil's Rain,* 1975; *Hustle,* 1975; *Carrie,* 1976; *Birch Interval,* 1976; *Yesterday; The Concorde—Airport '79,* 1979; *Foolin' Around,* 1980; *Ladyfingers; How to Beat the High Cost of Living; Take This Job and Shove It,* 1980; *The Border,* 1982; *Yes, Giorgio,* 1982; *Bless Them All.*

PRINCIPAL TELEVISION APPEARANCES—*Studio One,* 1948–57; *The Outer Limits; Your Show of Shows; Green Acres,* 1965–71; *Switch,* 1975–78.

THEATRE-RELATED CAREER: Organized Eddie Albert Productions for making educational films, 1945; worked in radio on *The Honeymooners; Grace and Eddie;* conducted lecture tour on ecology, 1969–70.

AWARDS: National Film Critics, *The Heartbreak Kid,* 1972. Academy Award Nominations, 1972, *The Heartbreak Kid,* 1953, *Roman Holiday.*

SIDELIGHTS: MEMBERSHIPS—Board of Directors, Film Council; Special World Envoy of Meals for Millions, 1963; Participant, World Hunger Conference, Rome, Italy, 1974; director, U.S. Commission on Refugees; trustee, National Recreation and Parks Association; Alaska-Pacific University; National Arbor Day Foundation; national conservation chairman, Boy Scouts of America; board of directors, Solar Lobby; consumer advisory board; chairman, Eddie Albert World Trees Foundation.

ADDRESS: Agent—c/o ICM, 8899 Beverly Blvd., Los Angeles, CA 90018.*

* * *

ALBERT, Edward Laurence, actor, composer, director, producer, writer

PERSONAL: Born February 20, 1951; son of Eddie (an actor and singer) and Margo (an actress, singer, and dancer) Albert; married Kate Woodville; children: Thais Carmen Woodville. EDUCATION: University California, Los Angeles; Oxford University, England; trained for the theatre in Stratford, England. NON-THEATRICAL CAREER—free-lance writer and photographer in Europe and Southeast Asia; also composer and musician in the pop field.

CAREER: DEBUT—Fortinbras, *Hamlet,* Mark Taper Forum, Los Angeles. NEW YORK DEBUT—Gentleman Caller, *The Glass Menagerie,* Manhattan Theater Club. LONDON DEBUT—Don, *Terribly Strange Bed.* FILM DEBUT—Don Baker, *Butterflies Are Free,* 1974. PRINCIPAL FILM APPEARANCES—*Forty Carats; Midway; Domino Principle; Taxi Mauve; The Greek Tycoon; Seven Graves for Rogan; The Squeeze; Time Ran Out; Where Evil Dwells; Butterfly; The Courageous.* TELEVISION APPEARANCES—*Walking Tall; The Last Convertible; Blood Feud; The Yellow Rose.*

AWARDS: Golden Globe, Best Actor, International Foreign Press; Nosotros Golden Eagle, Highest Career Achievement.

SIDELIGHTS: RECREATION—ranching, raising horses, organic fruits and vegetables.

"Acting is a very personal form of self-revelation. An expression from the heart and for the spirit. It is education in its most intimate form, both for the artist and the audience. That, for me, is the real magic. . . ."

ADDRESS: Office—Tom Masters Company, 120 El Camino Drive, Beverly Hills, CA 90212; Agent—c/o Jay Bernstein, P.O. Box 1148, Beverly Hills, CA 90213.

*   *   *

ALDA, Alan (ne Alphonso D'Abruzzo), actor

PERSONAL: Born January 28, in New York City; son of Alphonso (an actor; stage name, Robert Alda) and Joan (Browne) D'Abruzzo; married Arlene Weiss; children: three daughters. EDUCATION: Fordham University, B.S., 1956; attended Paul Sills Improvisational Workshop.

CAREER: DEBUT—Hollywood Canteen with his father, doing imitations of Abbott and Costello, 1951. NEW YORK DEBUT—understudy, Clarence McShame, *The Hot Corner,* Golden, 1956. PRINCIPAL STAGE APPEARANCES—Jack Chesney, *Charley's Aunt,* Barnesville, PA, 1953; Leo Davis, *Room Service,* Teatro del Eliseo, Rome, Italy, 1955; stock: Wade, *Roger the Sixth,* Artie, *Compulsion,* Irwin Trowbridge, *Three Men on a Horse,* Horace, *The Little Foxes,* 1957, Billy, *Tuck in Nature's Way,* 1958; *The Book of Job* (own adaptation), David Williams, *Who Was That Lady I Saw You With?,* Toni, *To Dorothy, a Son,* Cleveland Playhouse, 1958–59; Sky Masterson, *Guys and Dolls,* stock, 1959; telephone man, *Only in America,* Cort, NY, 1959; title role, *Li'l Abner,* stock, 1960; *Darwin's Theories* (revue), Madison Avenue Playhouse, 1960; David, *The Woman with Red Hair,* Teatro del Servi, Rome, Italy, 1961; Fergie Howard, *Golden Fleecing,* stock, 1961; Fleider, *Anatol,* Boston Arts Center, MA, 1961; Charlie Cotchipee, *Purlie Victorious,* Cort, NY, 1961; Compass Improvsational Revue, Hyannisport, MA, 1962; Howard Mayer, *A Whisper in God's Ear,* Cricket Theatre, 1962; Willie Alvarez, *Memo,* Shubert, New Haven, 1963; *Second City at Square East,* 1963; Benny Bennington, *Fair Game for Lovers,* Cort, NY, 1963; Dr. Gilbert, *Cafe Crown,* Martin Beck, NY, 1964; F. Sherman, *The Owl and the Pussycat,* ANTA, NY, 1964;

Adam/Captain Sanjar/Flip the Prince Charming, *The Apple Tree,* Shubert, NY, 1966.

FILM DEBUT—*Gone Are the Days,* 1963. PRINCIPAL FILM APPEARANCES—*Paper Lion,* 1968; *The Extraordinary Seaman,* 1968; *Jenny,* 1970; *The Moonshine War,* 1970; *The Mephisto Waltz,* 1971; *To Kill a Clown,* 1972; *California Suite,* 1978; *Same Time, Next Year,* 1978; *The Seduction of Joe Tynan,* 1979; *The Four Seasons,* 1981.

PRINCIPAL TELEVISION APPEARANCES—*The Glass House,* 1972; Marlo Thomas and friends in *Free to Be . . . You and Me,* 1974; *6 Rms Riv Vu,* 1974; *Tune in America,* 1975; Hawkeye Pierce, *M*A*S*H,* 1972–82; television movie, *Kill Me If You Can,* 1977.

RELATED CAREER: teacher, Compass School of Improvisation.

WRITINGS: SCREENPLAYS—*The Seduction of Joe Tynan,* 1979; *The Four Seasons,* 1981. TELEPLAYS—episodes of *M*A*S*H,* creator of the television series, *We'll Get By,* 1975.

AWARDS: Emmy Award, Best Actor in a Comedy Series, *M*A*S*H;* Theatre World Award, *Fair Game for Lovers.*

ADDRESS: Office—c/o Twentieth Century Fox TV, P.O. Box 900 Beverly Hills, CA 90213.*

*   *   *

ALDREDGE, Theoni V. (nee Theoni Athanasiou Vashlioti), costume designer

PERSONAL: Born August 22, 1932, Salonika, Greece; daughter of General Athanasios and Meropi (Gregoriades) Vachiotis; married Tom Aldredge (an actor), December 10, 1953. EDUCATION: American School, Athens; Goodman Theatre School, Chicago, 1949–52.

CAREER: FIRST STAGE WORK—Costume designer, *The Distaff Side,* Goodman, Chicago, 1950. PRINCIPAL STAGE WORK—Costume designer: *The Importance of Being Earnest,* stock, 1953; *The Immoralist,* Studebaker, Chicago, 1956; *Much Ado About Nothing, A View from the Bridge, Lysistrata, The Guardsman,* Studebaker, Chicago, 1957; New York: *Heloise, The Golden Six,* 1958; Geraldine Page's costumes for *Sweet Bird of Youth; The Nervous Set, The Saintliness of Margery Kempe, Chic, The Geranium Hat, Flowering Cherry, Silent Night, Lonely Night,* 1959; *A Distant Bell, The Best Man, Measure for Measure, Hedda Gabler, Rosemary, The Alligators,* 1960; *Mary, Mary, Under Milkwood, Smiling the Boy Fell Dead, First Love, Ghosts, A Short Happy Life, Much Ado About Nothing, A Midsummer Night's Dream, The Devil's Advocate,* 1961; *The Umbrella, Rosmersholm, I Can Get It for You Wholesale, Macbeth, King Lear, The Tempest, The Merchant of Venice, Mr. President, Tchin-Tchin, Who's Afraid of Virginia Woolf?,* 1962; Geraldine Page's costumes for *Strange Interlude; The Blue Boy in Black, Memo, The Time of the Barracudas, Anthony and Cleopatra, As You Like It, The Winter's Tale, The Trojan Women,* 1963; *But for Whom Charlie, Anyone Can Whistle,*

The Three Sisters, Hamlet, The Knack, Othello, Electra, Any Wednesday, Luv, Geraldine Page's gowns for *P.S. I Love You, Poor Richard, Ready when You Are CB!,* 1964; *Coriolanus, Troilus and Cressida, Minor Miracle, The Porcelain Year, Skyscraper, The Playroom, Cactus Flower,* 1965; *UTBU, First One Asleep, Whistle, Happily Never After, A Time for Singing, Segeant Musgrave's Dance, All's Well That Ends Well, Measure for Measure, Richard III, A Delicate Balance,* 1966; *You Know I Can't Hear You When the Water's Running, That Summer . . . That Fall, Ilya Darling, Little Murders, The Comedy of Errors, Hamlet, Hair, King John, Titus Andronicus, Daphne in Cottage D, The Trial of Lee Harvey Oswald,* 1967; *Before You Go, I Never Sang for My Father, Portrait of a Queen, Weekend, The Only Game in Town, Ergo, The Memorandum, King Lear, Ballad for a Firing Squad, Huui, Huui, Henry IV,* Parts I and II, *Hamlet, Romeo and Juliet, Don Rodrigo* (opera), 1968; *Zelda, Billy, The Gingham Dog, Cities in Bezique, Invitation to a Beheading, Peer Gynt, Electra, Twelfth Night,* 1969; *The Wars of the Roses,* Parts I and II, *Richard III, The Happiness Cage, Trelawny of the Wells, Colette,* Jack Macgowran in the *Works of Samuel Beckett,* 1970; *Subject to Fits,* (also London), *Blood, Underground, The Basic Training of Pavlo Hummel, Timon of Athens, Two Gentlemen of Verona, The Tale of Cymbeline, The Incomparable Max, Sticks and Bones, The Wedding of Iphigenia, Iphigenia in Concert,* 1971; *The Sign in Sidney Brustein's Window, Voices, That Championship Season, Older People, The Hunter, The Corner, Hamlet, Ti-Jean and His Brothers, Much Ado About Nothing, The Wedding Band, Children,* 1972; *A Village Romeo and Juliet* (Delius's opera for the New York City Opera), *The Three Sisters, No Hard Feelings, The Orphan, Nash at Nine, As You Like It, King Lear, Boom Boom Room, The Au Pair Man, Two Gentlemen of Verona* (London), 1973; *Find Your Way Home, The Killdeer, The Dance of Death, Music! Music!, An American Millionaire, That Championship Season,* (London), *In Praise of Love, Mert & Phil, Kid Champion,* 1974; *A Doll's House, Little Black Sheep, A Chorus Line, Trelawny of the Wells, Souvenir* (Los Angeles), 1975; *Rich and Famous, Mrs. Warren's Profession, The Belle of Amherst, The Baker's Wife, Threepenny Opera, The Eccentricities of a Nightingale,* 1976; *The Dream* (Philadelphia), *Marco Polo Sings a Solo, Annie,* 1977; *Ballroom,* 1978; *The Grand Tour, Break a Leg, The Madwoman of Central Park West,* 1979; *Barnum,* 1980; *Forty-Second Street,* 1980; *Woman of the Year,* 1981; *Dreamgirls,* 1981; *Hamlet,* New York Shakespeare Festival (NYSF), 1982; *Ghosts,* 1982; *A Little Family Business,* 1982; *Merlin,* 1983; *Buried Inside Extra,* NYSF, 1983; *Private Lives,* 1983; *La Cage Aux Folles,* 1983; *The Rink,* 1984.

PRINCIPAL FILM WORK—Costume design: *Girl of the Night,* 1960; *You're a Big Boy Now,* 1967; *No Way to Treat a Lady,* 1968; *Uptight,* 1968; *Last Summer,* 1969; *I Never Sang for My Father,* 1970; *Promise at Dawn,* 1971; *The Great Gatsby,* 1974; *Network,* 1977; *Semi-Tough,* 1977; *The Cheap Detective,* 1978; *Fury!,* 1978; *Eyes of Laura Mars,* 1978; *The Champ,* 1979; *The Rose,* 1979; *Racing with the Moon,* 1983.

AWARDS: Numerous Drama Desk and New York Drama Critics Awards for productions; Antoinette Perry Award, 1984: *La Cage Aux Folles,* 1977: *Annie;* Obie Award for Distinguished Service to the Off-Broadway Theatre, 1976; British Academy of Motion Picture Arts and Sciences

Award, 1976: *The Great Gatsby;* Academy Award, 1975: *The Great Gatsby;* Maharam Award, Peer Gynt.

SIDELIGHTS: MEMBERSHIPS—United Scenic Artists, Costume Designers Guild, Academy of Motion Picture Arts and Sciences.

ADDRESS: Office—425 Lafayette Street, New York, NY 10003.*

* * *

ALDREDGE, Tom (ne Thomas Ernest), actor

PERSONAL: Born February 28, 1928, in Dayton, OH; son of W. J. and Lucienne Juliet (Marcillat) Aldredge; married Theoni Athanasiou Vachlioti (costume designer). EDUCATION: Goodman Memorial School of Theatre, Chicago, B.F.A., 1953.

CAREER: DEBUT—as *Rip Van Winkle,* Belmont High School, Dayton, OH, 1939. NEW YORK DEBUT—Messenger, *Electra,* Jan Hus Playhouse, 1958. LONDON DEBUT—*The Premise,* (improvisational revue) Comedy Theatre, 1962. PRINCIPAL STAGE APPEARANCES—Messenger, *Hamlet,* Goodman, Chicago, 1950; Bud Norton, *Personal Appearance,* stock, 1950; Tower Ranch Tenthouse Theatre, Rhinelander, WI: *The Corn Is Green, Death of a Salesman, The Glass Menagerie, Private Lives, Our Town, The Little Foxes, Blithe Spirit,* 1951–53, *Arms and the Man, The Guardsman, A Streetcar Named Desire, The Heiress, Shadow and Substance,* 1954, *I Am a Camera, Sabrina Fair, Mister Roberts, The Rainmaker,* 1955; Danny, *The Nervous Set,* Henry Miller's, NY, 1959; Trinculo, *The Tempest,* East 74th Street, NY, 1959; David, *Between Two Thieves,* York Playhouse, 1960; Dauphin, *Henry V,* NYSF, Delacorte, 1960; *The Premise* (improvisational revue), Shoreham, Washington, DC, 1962; Boyet, *Love's Labour's Lost,* Delacorte, NY, 1965; Nestor, *Troilus and Cressida,* Delacorte, NY, 1965; Eugene Boyer, *UTBU,* Helen Hayes, NY, 1966; Bernie, *The Mutilated* in double bill with *Slapstick Tragedy,* Longacre, NY, 1966; Angelo, *Measure for Measure,* Delacorte, NY, 1966; a murderer/citizen, *Richard III,* Delacorte, NY, 1966; Jack McClure, *The Butter and Egg Man,* Cherry Lane, NY, 1966; American Shakespeare Festival, Stratford, CT: Chorus, *Antigone,* Gratiano, *The Merchant of Venice,* Macduff, *Macbeth,* 1966; Gilbert, *Everything in the Garden,* Plymouth, NY, 1967; Wurz, *Ergo,* Anspacher, NY, 1968; Tybalt, *Romeo and Juliet,* Sir Andrew, *Twelfth Night,* Delacorte, NY, 1968; Emory, *The Boys in the Band,* Wyndham's, London, 1969; Senator Logan, *Indians,* Brooks Atkinson, NY, 1969; Victor Bard, *The Engagement Baby,* Helen Hayes, NY, 1970; William Detweiler, *How the Other Half Loves,* Royale, NY, 1971; Ozzie, *Sticks and Bones,* Anspacher, NY, 1971, Golden, NY, 1972; second grave digger, *Hamlet,* Delacorte, NY, 1972; Calchas, *The Orphan,* Anspacher, NY, 1973; Fool, *King Lear,* Delacorte, NY, 1973; James Cameron, *The Iceman Cometh,* Circle in the Square, NY, 1973; Mr. Spettigue, *Where's Charley?,* Circle in the Square, NY, 1974; Shaughnessy, *The Leaf People,* Booth, NY, 1975; The Fool, *Rex,* Lunt-Fontanne, NY, 1976; Father, *Canadian Gothic,* Phoenix, NY, 1976; Painter, *Vieux Carre,* St. James, NY, 1977; Archbishop of Rheims,

Saint Joan, Circle in the Square, NY, 1977; Norman Thayer, *On Golden Pond,* Apollo, Century, NY, 1979; Horace, *The Little Foxes,* Martin Beck, NY, 1981; Puget, *The Black Angel,* Circle Repertory Co., NY, 1982; Harmon, *Actors and Actresses,* Hartman, 1983; Sandy, *Getting Along Famously,* Hudson Guild, NY, 1984; Marius, *The Road to Mecca,* Yale Repertory, 1984.

PRINCIPAL STAGE WORK—Directed: *The Fourposter,* Tower Ranch Tenthouse Theatre, Rhinelander, WI, 1954; *Arms and the Man,* Tower Ranch, 1954; *I Am a Camera,* Tower Ranch, 1955; *The Happiness Cage,* Newman, NY, 1970.

PRINCIPAL FILM APPEARANCES—*The Mouse on the Moon,* 1962; *The Troublemaker,* 1964; *The Rain People,* 1969; *Acts of a Young Man,* 1979.

PRINCIPAL TELEVISION APPEARANCES—*The Curious One,* 1956; *Henry Winkler Meets Shakespeare,* 1978.

THEATRE-RELATED CAREER: Producer/director, Chicago Educational TV Association, 1955–57.

AWARDS: Emmy Award, *Henry Winkler Meets Shakespeare,* 1978.

SIDELIGHTS: RECREATIONS—Sailing.

ADDRESS: Home—Rt. #1, Box 547-A, Pine Plains, NY 12567.

* * *

ALETTER, Frank, actor

PERSONAL: Surname accent on second syllable, A-*let*-ter. Born January 14, 1926 in College Point, NY; son of Henry (an ornamental ironworker) and Katherine (Marquardt) Aletter; married: Lee Meriwether, on April 20, 1956 (divorced 1972); children: Kyle Kathleen, Lesley Ann. EDUCATION: Attended public schools in New York; studied at the Dramatic Workshop of the New School for Social Research. MILITARY: U.S. Army Infantry, Sergeant, 3½ years.

CAREER: DEBUT—Conga line sailor, *My Sister Eileen,* Red Cross Show, Wiesbaden, Germany, 1946. NEW YORK DEBUT—Stefanowski, *Mr. Roberts,* Alvin, 210 performances, 1950. PRINCIPAL STAGE APPEARANCES—(New York) Itchy Flexner, *Wish You Were Here,* Imperial, 1952; Sgt. Baker, *Time Limit,* Booth, 1955; Blake Barton, *Bells Are Ringing,* Shubert, 1956. MAJOR TOURS—*Bells Are Ringing.*

FILM DEBUT—Gerhart, *Mr. Roberts,* 1954. TELEVISION DEBUT—*Studio One.* PRINCIPAL TELEVISION APPEARANCES—*Bringing up Buddy; Cara Williams Show; It's About Time.*

SIDELIGHTS: MEMBERSHIPS—Board of Directors, SAG, 10 years. RECREATION—Mr. Aletter is an expert cook, and has worked in an Italian restaurant as Chef. He is also interested in photography and backpacking.

ADDRESS: Agent—Crickett Company, 13455 Ventura Blvd., Sherman Oaks CA 91423.

* * *

ALEXANDER, Jane (ne Quigley), actress

PERSONAL: Born October 28, 1939, in Boston, MA; daughter of Thomas B. (an M.D.) and Ruth Elizabeth (Pearson) Quigley; married Robert Alexander, July 23, 1962 (divorced 1969); Edwin Sherin (a director) March 29, 1975; children: (first marriage) Jason. EDUCATION: Sarah Lawrence College; University of Edinburgh, 1959–60.

CAREER: STAGE DEBUT—Child actress, Long John Silver, *Treasure Island,* Boston, MA. NEW YORK DEBUT—Eleanor Bachman, *The Great White Hope,* 1968. PRINCIPAL STAGE APPEARANCES—Member, Arena Stage acting company, Washington, DC, 1966, playing for three seasons and in fifteen productions; Katrina, *Mother Courage,* Arena Stage, 1970; Mistress Page, *The Merry Wives of Windsor,* American Shakespeare Festival (ASF), Stratford, CT, 1971; La-

JANE ALEXANDER

vinia, *Mourning Becomes Electra*, Stratford, CT, 1971; Kitty Duval, *The Time of Your Life*, Eisenhower, Washington, DC, Huntington Hartford, Los Angeles, CA, 1972; title role, *Major Barbara*, ASF, 1972; Anne Miller, *Six Rms Riv Vu*, Helen Hayes, NY, 1972; Jacqueline Harrison, *Find Your Way Home*, Brooks Atkinson, NY, 1974; Liz Essendine, *Present Laughter*, Eisenhower, Washington, DC, 1974; Gertrude, *Hamlet*, Vivian Beaumont, NY, 1975; Catherine Sloper, *The Heiress*, Broadhurst, NY, 1976; Judge Ruth Loomis, *First Monday in October*, Majestic, NY, 1978; Joanne, *Losing Time*, Manhattan Theatre Club, NY, 1979; *Goodbye Fidel*, NY, 1980; *Antony and Cleopatra*, Alliance, Atlanta, GA, 1981; *Hedda Gabler*, Hartman, Stamford, CT, Boston, 1981; *Monday After the Miracle*, Kennedy Center, Washington, DC, Spoleto Festival, Charleston, SC, NY, 1982; *Old Times*, NY, 1983–84.

FILM DEBUT—Eleanor Bachman, *The Great White Hope*, 1969. PRINCIPAL FILM APPEARANCES—*A Gunfight*, 1971; *The New Centurions*, 1972; *All the President's Men*, 1976; *The Betsy*, 1978; *Losing Time*, 1979; *Kramer vs. Kramer*, 1979; *Brubaker*, 1980; *Night Crossing*, 1982; *Testament*, 1983; *City Heat*, 1984.

PRINCIPAL TELEVISION APPEARANCES—Movies for television: *Welcome Home Johnny Bristol*, 1971; *Miracle on 34th Street*, 1973; *Death Be Not Proud*, 1974; *Eleanor and Franklin*, 1976; *Eleanor and Franklin: The White House Years*, 1977; *A Question of Love*, 1978; *The Time of Your Life*; *Find Your Way Home*; *Playing For Time*; *Calamity Jane: The Diary of a Frontier Woman*, 1981; *Dear Liar*, 1981; *Kennedy's Children*, 1981; *In the Custody of Strangers*, 1983; *When She Says No*, 1984; *Calamity Jane*, 1984; special—*A Circle of Children*, 1977.

WRITINGS: PLAYS TRANSLATED—*The Master Builder* (with Sam Engelstad). BOOKS—*The Bluefish Cookbook* (with Greta Jacobs).

AWARDS: Academy Award Nominations, 1983: *Testament*, 1979: *Kramer vs. Kramer*, 1976: *All the President's Men*, 1969: *The Great White Hope*; Emmy Award: *Playing for Time*; Emmy Award Nomination: *Eleanor and Franklin: The White House Years*; Antoinette Perry Award Nominations: *First Monday in October*, *Find Your Way Home*, *6 Rms Riv Vu*; Television Critics Circle Award, *Eleanor and Franklin*, 1977; Drama Desk Award, Theatre World Award, Antoinette Perry Award, Eleanor Bachman, *The Great White Hope*, 1969; St. Botolph Club Achievement in Dramatic Arts, 1979; Israel Cultural Award, 1982.

SIDELIGHTS: PRODUCTIONS IN DEVELOPMENT—All working titles: Selected Out; The Artist's Story; Paradise Lost; Common Scents.

ADDRESS: Agent—c/o ICM, 40 W. 57th Street, New York, NY 10019.

* * *

ALEXANDER, Jason (ne Jay Scott Greenspan), actor

PERSONAL: Born September 23, 1959 in Newark, NJ; son of Alexander (a bookkeeper) and Ruth Minnie (a registered nurse/nursing educator; maiden name, Simon) Greenspan; married Daena E. Title (a screenwriter), May 31, 1982. EDUCATION: Attended Boston University (Drama) 1977–80; studied musical audition and performance with Larry Moss, Robertson School.

CAREER: NEW YORK DEBUT—Joe Josephson, *Merrily We Roll Along*, Alvin Theatre, New York, 1981. PRINCIPAL STAGE APPEARANCES—Abe/Izzy, *America Kicks Up Its Heels*, Playwrights Horizons, New York, 1982; Alan, *On Hold with Music*, Manhattan Theatre Club, New York, 1982; Baxter, *Fragments*, Troupe Theatre, New York, 1982; Jason, *Forbidden Broadway*, Palssons (cabaret), New York, 1983. FILM DEBUT—Dave, *The Burning*, 1980. TELEVISION DEBUT—Player, Pushcart Players Present: *Feelings/Friends*, 1977; PRINCIPAL TELEVISION APPEARANCES—Pete, *Senior Trip*, (CBS Movie of the Week), 1977.

AWARDS: Boston University, Case Award for Scholastic Achievement, 1980.

SIDELIGHTS: MEMBERSHIPS—AEA, SAG; AFTRA. RECREATION: Composing music and lyrics for pop-songs, magic, flute, roller skating, movie going, singing.

ADDRESS: Agent—c/o Niederlitz/Steele, 250 W. 57th Street, New York, NY 10107.

* * *

ALISON, Dorothy (nee Dorothy Dickson) actress, writer

PERSONAL: Born March 4, 1925; daughter of William Edward (Speaker of Upper House, NSW Parliament) and Alice Cecilia (Cogan) Dickson; married Leslie Linder (a film producer) June 12 1952 (divorced, 1976); children: Seth Edward, Elissa Beth, Toby Genevieve. EDUCATION: Attended public schools in Sydney, Australia. Studied for the theatre at the Independent Theatre of Sydney with Doris Fitton.

CAREER: DEBUT—Manuela, *Children in Uniform*, Independent Theatre, Sydney, Australia, 1940. LONDON DEBUT—Laura, *The Affair*, Strand Theatre, for 11 months, 1961. PRINCIPAL STAGE APPEARANCES—Mrs. Cheveley, *An Ideal Husband*, Northhampton Theatre, 1963; labor councillor, *Have You Any Dirty Washing, Mother Dear?*, Hampstead Theatre Club, 1968; Lady Bountiful, *The Beaux Stratagem*, Royal Exchange Theatre, Manchester, England, 1982. MAJOR TOURS—Sister Anderson, *Whose Life Is It Anyway?*, tour of Australia, Elizabethan Theatre Trust, 1981.

FILM DEBUT—Teacher of Deaf, *Mandy*, 1951. PRINCIPAL FILM APPEARANCES—Nurse Brace, *Reach for the Sky*, 1955; *The Scamp*, 1958; *The Man Upstairs*, 1958; Sister Aurelia, *The Nun's Story*; the Aunt, *Blind Terror*; Mrs. Allen, *Amazing Mrs. Blunder*; *Winds of Jaffa*, Australia, 1983. TELEVISION DEBUT—Policewoman, *Pilgrim Street*. PRINCIPAL TELEVISION APPEARANCES—Mother Superior, *Sister Doren*; Peggy Fawcus, *Forgive Our Foolish Ways*; Mrs. Firth, *A Town Like Alice*.

WRITINGS: TELEVISION PLAYS—*Waters of Babylon*, ATV; *Doubts and Traitors*, BBC; *Dead of Night* series, *Mrs. Smith*, BBC.

AWARDS: Most Promising Newcomer Nomination, B.F.A., *Mandy,* 1952; Nominated for Best Supporting Actress Nomination, B.F.A., *Reach for the Sky,* 1955; Logie Award (Australia) *A Town Like Alice.*

ADDRESS: Home—45 Mabel Street, Willoughby, NSW Australia, 2068. Agent—David Daly, 68 Old Brompton Street, London, England, SW7 3LQ. Agent—International Casting Service, Cornelius Court, 147A. King Street, Sydney, NSW Australia, 2000.

* * *

ALLEN, Billie, actress, director

PERSONAL: Born January 13 in Richmond, VA; daughter of William Roswell (an accountant) and Mamie (an educator; maiden name, Wimbush) Allen; married Luther Henderson (a composer/arranger) on February 8, 1981; children: Duane Harper and Carolyn Jean. EDUCATION: Attended public schools in Richmond, VA; studied at the Hampton Institute and at Barnard College, three years. Studied with Lee Strasberg and Lloyd Richards. RELIGION: Protestant.

CAREER: NEW YORK DEBUT—*A Raisin in the Sun,* 1960. PRINCIPAL STAGE APPEARANCES—Sarah, *Funnyhouse of a Negro,* Theatre Four, New York.

TELEVISION DEBUT—Ada Chandler, *The Edge of Night.*

AWARDS: Directing Fellowship, Women's Project, American Place Theatre.

SIDELIGHTS: MEMBERSHIPS—League of Professional Theatre Women; Black Women in Theatre; Board of Trustees, American Place Theatre; Advisory Board, AMAS Repertory Theatre; 100 Black Women.

ADDRESS: Home—340 W. 57th Street, New York, NY 10019.

* * *

ALLEN, Jay Presson, scriptwriter, producer

PERSONAL: Born March 3, 1922, in Fort Worth, TX; daughter of Albert Jeffrey (a merchant) and May (Miller) Presson; married Lewis M. Allen (a producer), March 12, 1955; children: Anna Brooke. EDUCATION: Miss Hackaday's School in Dallas, TX.

CAREER: FILMS PRODUCED—*Just Tell Me What You Want,* 1980; *Prince of the City,* 1981; *Deathtrap,* 1982; *Stone,* 1984.

WRITINGS: PLAYS, PUBLISHED—*The Prime of Miss Jean Brodie,* 1965; *Forty Carats,* 1968. PLAYS, UNPUBLISHED—*A Little Family Business,* 1982. FILMS—*Marnie,* 1964; *The Prime of Miss Jean Brodie,* 1969; *Travels with My Aunt,* 1972; *Cabaret,* 1972; *Funny Lady,* 1975; *Just Tell Me What*

You Want; 1980; *Prince of the City,* 1981; *Deathtrap,* 1982; *Stone,* 1984.

AWARDS: Donatello Award, Script, 1980: *Just Tell Me What You Want.*

ADDRESS: Agent—c/o I.C.M., 40 W. 57th Street, New York, NY 10019

* * *

ALLEN, Karen, actress

PERSONAL: Born October 5, 1951; daughter of Carroll Thompson (FBI Agent) and Patricia Howell (a teacher) Allen; EDUCATION: Washington University, 1974–76; studied at the Washington Theatre Laboratory with Anthony Abeson.

CAREER: DEBUT—Jane, *The Innocent Party,* Washington Theatre Laboratory, Washington, DC, 1975. NEW YORK DEBUT—Helen Keller, *The Monday After the Miracle,* Eugene O'Neill, New York, 1982. PRINCIPAL STAGE APPEARANCES—Helen Keller, *The Monday After the Miracle,* Kennedy Center for the Performing Arts, Washington, DC, Dock Street Theatre, Spoleto Festival, Charleston, SC; Marjorie, *Extremities,* Westside Arts Theatre, New York, 1983; Laura, Esmerelda, Miriam, *Tennessee Williams: A Celebration,* Williamstown Theatre Festival, Williamstown, MA, 1982; Gittel, *Two for the Seesaw,* Berkshire Theatre Festival, Stockbridge, MA, 1981.

FILM DEBUT—Katy, *Animal House,* 1977. PRINCIPAL FILMS—*The Wanderers,* 1978; *A Small Circle of Friends,* 1978; *Cruising,* 1978; *Raiders of the Lost Ark,* 1981; *Shoot the Moon,* 1982; *Split Image,* 1982; *Until September,* 1983. TELEVISION DEBUT—Abra, *East of Eden,* 1979.

AWARDS: Theatre World, 1983: *Monday After the Miracle,* 1983; Academy of Science Fiction, Fantasy and Horror, Best Actress, 1982: *Raiders of the Lost Ark.*

ADDRESS: Agent—c/o Joan Hyler or John Planco, William Morris Agency, 1350 Ave. of the Americas, New York, NY 10019.

* * *

ALLEN, Vera (nee Klopman), actress

PERSONAL: Born November 27, 1897, in New York City; daughter of William (a business executive) and Lillan (nee Allen) Klopman; married John Malcolm Schloss (an engineer), July 3, 1921; children: one son. EDUCATION: Barnard College, B.A., 1919; studied for the theatre with Maria Ouspenskaya, Howard Barlow, and Laura Elliott at the Neighborhood Playhouse. NON-THEATRICAL CAREER: Worked as a secretary and a researcher.

CAREER: DEBUT—*Grand Street Follies,* Neighborhood Playhouse, New York, June 18, 1925. PRINCIPAL STAGE APPEARANCES—Ann Rigordan, *Slaves All,* Bijou, New

York, 1926; Estelle Pemberton, *Sinner*, Klaw, New York, 1927; *Grand Street Follies*, Booth, 1928; played in the following with the Jessie Bonstelle Stock Company (forty weeks): *Candida, The Constant Wife, Interference, Samson and Delilah, Hedda Gabler, This Thing Called Love, The Queen's Husband, You Never Can Tell, Baby Cyclone, Ghost Train, The Jest, Liliom*, Detroit, 1928–29; with Fritz Leiber Shakespeare Repertory Company as Portia, *The Merchant of Venice*, Rosalind, *As You Like It*, Viola, *Twelfth Night*, Lady Anne, *Richard III*, Goneril, *King Lear*, Emilia, *Othello*, Bianca, *The Taming of the Shrew*, Player Queen, *Hamlet*, Gentlewoman, *Macbeth*, 1929–30; in New York: Celia Hardman, *Lean Harvest*, Forrest, 1931; Penelope, *Money in the Air*, Ritz, 1932; Zillah Carrington, *Strange Gods*, Ritz, 1933; Madeleine, *I Was Waiting for You*, Booth, 1933; *At Home Abroad*, Winter Garden, 1935; *The Show is On*, Winter Garden, 1936; Irene, *Susan and God*, Plymouth, 1936; Christine Foster, *A Woman's a Fool to Be Clever*, National, 1938; Ann, *Glorious Morning*, Mansfield, 1938; Margaret Lord, *The Philadelphia Story*, Schubert, 1939; Cornelia Lauren, *The Burning Deck*, Maxine Elliott's Theatre, 1940; Miss Eloise, *The Moon Vine*, Morosco, 1943; Harriet, *The Two Mrs. Carrolls*, Booth, 1943; Alma Deen, *Strange Fruit*, Royale, 1945; Mrs. Lauterbach, *Ladies of the Corridor*, Longacre, 1953. MAJOR TOURS—Christina, *The Silver Cord*, 1927–28.

RADIO APPEARANCES—with Beatrice Lillie, NBC, 1933–34; with Helen Hayes, CBS, 1941; daytime programs. TELEVISION DEBUT—Peggy O'Neill (lead), *The O'Neills*, September 6, 1949. TELEVISION APPEARANCES—Kass, *From These Roots*, 1958–61; Ida, *Search for Tomorrow*, 1968–72.

AWARDS: Antoinette Perry Award, Special Citation for Services with the American Theatre Wing during and after World War II, 1948; Phi Beta Kappa, Barnard College, 1919.

SIDELIGHTS: MEMBERSHIPS—AEA, council member, 1945–49; SAG; AFTRA, board member, 1947–49; co-founder of the American Theatre Wing, 1940, vice-president, 1940–46, chairman of the board, 1946–47; director of the Speakers Bureau, 1941; founder of the Victory Players, 1942, later the Community Players; vice-chairman of Plays for Living, an outgrowth of Community Plays, now a department of the Family Service Association of America (1962 to date); U.S. National Commission for UNESCO; US Centre of International Theatre Institute, 1948–49. RECREATION—Gardening.

ADDRESS: 510 E. 77th Street, New York, NY 10021.

* * *

ALLEN, Woody (ne Allen Konigsberg), actor, playwright, director

PERSONAL: Born December 1, 1935, in Brooklyn, NY; son of Martin and Netty (Cherry) Konigsberg; married Harlene Rosen (divorced); Louise Lasser (divorced). EDUCATION: Attended City College of New York and New York University.

CAREER: NEW YORK DEBUT—Allan Felix, *Play It Again Sam*, Broadhurst, 1969. PRINCIPAL STAGE APPEARANCES—Stand-up comedian, appeared throughout US and Europe.

PRINCIPAL FILM APPEARANCES—Writer/director/actor: *What's New Pussycat*, 1965; *What's Up Tiger Lily?*, 1966; *Take the Money and Run*, 1969; *Bananas*, 1971; *Everything You Always Wanted to Know About Sex But Were Afraid to Ask*, 1972; *Sleeper*, 1973; *Love and Death*, 1975; *The Front*, 1976; *Annie Hall*, 1977; *Interiors*, 1978; *Manhattan*, 1979; *Stardust Memories*, 1980; *Midsummer Night's Sex Comedy*, 1982; *Zelig*, 1983; *Broadway Danny Rose*, 1984.

WRITINGS: PLAYS, PUBLISHED/PRODUCED—*Don't Drink the Water*, 1966; *Play It Again, Sam*, 1969; *The Floating Lightbulb*, 1981. COMEDY—TV writer for Sid Caesar, 1957, Art Carney, 1958–59, Herb Shriner, 1963. BOOKS—*Getting Even*, 1971; *Without Feathers*, 1975; *Side Effects*, 1980. CONTRIBUTOR TO MAGAZINES—*Playboy, New Yorker*, and others.

AWARDS: New York Film Critics Award, British Academy Award, 1979–80: *Manhattan;* New York Film Critics Award, Best Director and Best Screenplay, 1978: *Annie Hall;* National Society of Film Critics Award for Best Screenwriting, 1977: *Annie Hall;* Special Award, Berlin Film Festival, 1975; Sylvania Award, 1957; Emmy Award Nomination, 1957.

SIDELIGHTS: "Mr. Allen is a noted jazz clarinetist who performs regularly in New York City."

ADDRESS: Agent—c/o Mike Hutner, United Artists, 729 Seventh Avenue, New York, NY 10019.*

* * *

ALLERS, Franz, conductor

PERSONAL: Born August 6, 1905, in Carlsbad; son of Carl (a lawyer) and Paula (a singer; maiden name, Kellner) Allers; married Caroline Shaffer, August 20, 1941 (divorced 1961); married Janne Furch (author, translator), May 30, 1963; children: Carol Hopper. EDUCATION: Prague Conservatory, degree in Violin, 1923; Berlin Academy of Music, degree in conducting, 1926.

CAREER: DEBUT—Conductor, *Der Rosenkavalier*, Opera House, Ruppertal, Germany, October 2, 1927. NEW YORK DEBUT—Conductor, *Ballet Russe de Monte Carlo*, Metropolitan Opera House, October 8, 1939. LONDON DEBUT—Conductor, *Ballet Russe de Monte Carlo*, Drury Lane, September 14, 1938. PRINCIPAL ENGAGEMENT—Conductor, *Brigadoon*, Ziegfeld, New York, 1947; conductor, *Paint Your Wagon*, Shubert, New York, 1951; conductor, *My Fair Lady*, Mark Hellinger, New York, 1956; conductor, *Camelot*, Majestic, New York, 1960; State Opera Comique, Gaertnerplatz Theater, Munich, Germany, 1971–77. MAJOR TOURS—Conductor, *Ballet Russe de Monte Carlo*, six national tours (also South America), 1939–44; conductor, *South Pacific*, national tour, 1950–51; conductor, *Tonkuenstler of Vienna Orchestra*, 1978 and 1980; also tour of U.S.S.R. as part of Presidential Exchange Program, 1960.

TELEVISION DEBUT—Conductor, *Alice in Wonderland*, Hallmark Hall of Fame, 1955. TELEVISION APPEARANCES—Conducting New York Philharmonic, Los Angeles Philharmonic,

Philadelphia Orchestra, Cleveland Orchestra, Chicago Symphony.

AWARDS: Antoinette Perry Award, Musical Director, 1957: *My Fair Lady,* 1961: *Camelot;* Grand Cross of Honor for Arts and Sciences, Federal Republic of Austria, 1981.

SIDELIGHTS: "Having conducted opera, musical theatre, ballet, symphony, television, and recordings, I learned that the conductor's reason to exist is to serve—the composer, author, director or choreographer."

ADDRESS: Agent—c/o Columbia Artists Mgmt., Wilford Dept., 165 W. 57th Street, New York, NY 10019.

* * *

ALLMON, Clinton (ne Clinton James Allmon), actor

PERSONAL: Born June 13, 1941, in Monahans, Texas; son of O. Clinton (in insurance) and Anita Conchita (a landlady; maiden name Clark) Allmon; married Christina Makarvshka (an acting teacher) on October 14, 1971; children: Leandra. EDUCATION: Oklahoma State University, B.A.; studied at the Actors Studio with Lee Strasberg and Allen Miller. POLITICS: World. RELIGION: Oneness. MILITARY: U.S. National Guard and U.S. Army Reserve.

CAREER: DEBUT—Juvenile lead, *Mr. Dooley Jr.,* Com-

CLINTON ALLMON

munity Theatre, Lawton, OK, 1954. NEW YORK DEBUT—Jonathan Jamison/Junebug Jewel, *Lime Green | Khaki Blue,* Provincetown Playhouse, 1978, for 32 performances. PRINCIPAL STAGE SPPEARANCES—Thomas Keffer, *The Caine Mutiny Court Martial,* Circle in the Square, New York; Watchdog/Melvin P. Thorpe, *The Best Little Whorehouse in Texas,* 46th Street Theatre, 1978–82 for 1,669 performances; Chief Joseph, *Indians,* Brooks Atkinson, New York, 1969; David Sigmund, *Brother Gorski,* Astor Place Theatre, New York; Tom Jenson, *The Siamese Connection,* Actors Studio, New York; Zip, *The Silent Partner,* Actors Studio, New York; Reverend Dan Daniels, *The Tommy Allen Show,* Actors Studio, New York; The Man Professor, *Circus,* 4th Street Theatre, New York; Trofimov, *The Cherry Orchard,* Actors Studio, New York; MAJOR TOURS—Chancellor Dullfeet, *The Resistible Rise of Arturo Ui, Boston,* 1975.

FILM DEBUT—Detective O'Leary, *Dog Day Afternoon,* 1975. PRINCIPAL FILM APPEARANCES—David Kemble, *The Rose;* William Smith Sr., *Born on the Fourth of July;* Lee Menthol, *Murphy's Law.* TELEVISION DEBUT—"Richard III," Wayne and Schuster, *The Ed Sullivan Show,* CBS. PRINCIPAL TELEVISION APPEARANCES—Milkman, *Daddy I Don't Like It Like That;* Rudy Winston, *The Doctors;* Dr. McIntosh, *Margaret Sanger Revisited; Nova.*

AWARDS: Best supporting role, Action, *West Side Story,* Oklahoma State University, 1960; membership for life, Actors Studio, 1968.

SIDELIGHTS: MEMBERSHIPS—AEA; SAG; AFTRA; Actors Studio. Allmon's grandmother paid for acting lessons at 13 with John Denny, a New York actor in Oklahoma. Favorite Roles: Rev. Dan Daniels. He wrote and sang a rock song called 'Everyone to God,' at Actors Studio.

EDUCATION: Home—579 W. 21st Street, New York, NY 10034.

* * *

AMBROSE, David, writer

PERSONAL: Born February 21, 1943, in Chorley, England; son of Albert Edwin (an insurance salesman) and Annie Margery (Fairclough) Ambrose; married Laurence Huguette Hammerili (a sculptor), September 21, 1943. EDUCATION: Oxford University, Law Degree, 1965.

CAREER: FILM DEBUT—Writer, *Battle for Rome,* 1968. THEATRE DEBUT—Author, *Five to Six,* Playhouse, Oxford, U.K., 1963. LONDON DEBUT—Author, *Siege,* Cambridge, 1972, 30 performances. TELEVISION DEBUT—Writer, *Public Face,* U.K., 1969.

WRITINGS: FILMS—*Battle for Rome,* 1968; *Passion Flower Hotel,* 1969; *The Pedestrian,* 1972; *The Fifth Musketeer,* 1975; *The Liars; The Final Countdown,* 1980; *The Survivor,* 1981; *The Dangerous Summer,* 1981; *Amityville-3D,* 1983. TELEVISION PLAYS—*Public Face,* 1969; *The Innocent Ceremony,* 1969; *The Undoing,* 1969; *The Professional,* 1972; *When the Music Stops,* 1972; *Reckoning Day,* 1973; *Love Me to Death,* 1974; *Goose with Pepper; A Variety of Passion,* 1975; *Nanny's Boy,* 1977. TELEVISION SPECIALS—*Alternative 3,* 1977. EPISODIC TELEVISION—*Colditz; Hadleigh; Jus-*

tice; Public Eye; Orson Welles Great Mysteries; Oil Strike North.

AWARDS: Sitges Film Festival Award, Best Screenplay, 1981: *The Survivor.*

SIDELIGHTS: MEMBERSHIPS—Writers Guild of America West, Writers Guild of Australia, W.A.G.B., A.C.T.T.

ADDRESS: Agent—c/o Hatton and Baker Ltd., 18 Jermyn Street, London SW1. Agent—c/o Agent for the Performing Arts, 9000 Sunset Blvd., Los Angeles, CA 90069.

* * *

AMRAM, David, composer, musician

PERSONAL: Born November 17, 1930 in Philadelphia, PA; son of Philip and Emily (Weyl) Amram; married Lora Lee Ecobelli (a veterinarian) on January 7, 1979; children: Alana Asha, Adira Alizah. EDUCATION: Attended Oberlin College of Music, 1948, studied French Horn with Martin Morris; George Washington University, B.A. (History), 1952; studied baton technique and score reading with Jonel Perlea; studied French horn with Gunther Shuller. POLITICS: "One world in harmony." RELIGION: Jewish. MILITARY: U.S. Army, (Pfc), 1952–54.

CAREER: FIRST STAGE WORK—composer, *Alcestis,* Howard University Players, Washington, DC, 1949. NEW YORK DEBUT—composer, *Titus Andronicus,* New York Shakespeare Festival, 1956. PRINCIPAL STAGE COMPOSITIONS—Opera—*The Final Ingredient; Twelfth Night.* Incidental music—*After The Fall; All's Well That Ends Well,* New York Shakespeare Festival; *Anthony and Cleopatra,* NYSF; *As You Like It,* American Shakespeare Festival; *The Beaux Stratagem,* Phoenix Theatre, NY; *Caligula,* NY; *Comes a Day,* NY; *Coriolanus,* NYSF; *Death Watch,* NY; *The Family Reunion,* NY; *Far Rockaway; Great God Brown,* Phoenix, NY; *Hamlet,* Phoenix, NY; *Harold and Maude,* Martin Beck, NY; *Henry IV Pt. One,* Phoenix, NY; *Henry V,* NYSF; *Heracles;* JB, NY; *Julius Caesar,* NYSF; *Kataki,* NY; *King Lear,* NYSF; *Lysistrata,* Phoenix, NY; *Macbeth,* American Shakespeare Festival; *Measure for Measure,* NYSF; *Merchant of Venice,* NYSF; *A Midsummer Night's Dream,* NYSF; *Much Ado About Nothing,* NYSF; *Othello,* NYSF; *The Passion of Josef D.,* NY; *Peer Gynt; The Power and the Glory,* Phoenix, NY; *Richard II,* NYSF; *The Rivalry,* NY; *Romeo and Juliet,* NYSF; *The Sign of Winter,* NY; *Summernight's Dream; Taming of the Shrew,* NYSF; *Troilus and Cressida,* NYSF; *Twelfth Night,* NYSF; *Two Gentlemen of Verona,* NYSF; *The Winters Tale,* NYSF.

FILM DEBUT—composer, *Splendor in the Grass,* 1960. PRINCIPAL FILM COMPOSITIONS (scores)—*Pull My Daisy; Young Savages,* 1960; *Manchurian Candidate,* 1962; *The Arrangement,* 1969; *Echo of an Era.* TELEVISION DEBUT—composer, *Turn of the Screw,* 1960. PRINCIPAL TELEVISION COMPOSITIONS (scores)—*Something Special; Cry Vengence; The Fifth Column; The American.*

WRITINGS: Vibrations (autobiography), 1968.

AWARDS: Doctor of Laws, Moravian College, 1979; Obie, Best Music, 1959.

SIDELIGHTS: MEMBERSHIPS—American Federation of Musicians Local 802; B.M.I.; ACTRA (Canada).

Mr. Amram's work includes numerous major compositions for orchestra, chorus, voice, and band as well as jazz quintets and chamber music. He is one of the pioneers in combining classical and jazz music, and has performed with such notables as Dizzy Gillespie and Charlie Parker. "Music is my language, whether it be classical, jazz or folk . . . the one thing people around the world have in common is the beauty that music can bring into our lives. It is meant to be shared."

ADDRESS: Home—Peekskill Hollow Road, R.F.D.#1, Putnam Valley, NY. Agent—Barna Osterag, 501 Fifth Avenue, New York, NY, 10017.

* * *

ANDERSON, Craig, producer and director

CAREER: PRINCIPAL STAGE WORK—PRODUCER: *Da,* Hudson Guild, New York, 1978; *On Golden Pond,* Hudson Guild, New York, 1978; *A Lovely Day for Creve Coeur,* Hudson Guild, New York, 1979; *Devour the Snow,* Hudson Guild, 1979; *The Survivor,* Morosco, New York. PRINCIPAL STAGE WORK—DIRECTOR: *On Golden Pond,* New Apollo, New York, 1979; *A Long Way to Boston,* Goodspeed Opera House, East Haddam, CT, 1980; *The Survivor,* Morosco, New York.

AWARDS: Cue Magazine's Golden Apple for four seasons as Producing Director of the Hudson Guild Theatre; Antoinette Perry Award, Best Play, 1978: *Da.*

* * *

ANDERSON, Richard, actor

PERSONAL: Born August 8, 1926, Long Branch, NJ; son of Harry and Olga (Lurie) Anderson; married Katharine, October 30, 1961; children: Ashley, Brooke Dominique, Deva Justine. EDUCATION: Attended Los Angeles area public schools; trained for the theatre at the Actors Laboratory in Los Angeles. MILITARY: U.S. Army, 1944–45 (T-Sergeant).

CAREER: DEBUT—Spear-Carrier, *Volpone,* Las Palmas Theatre, Hollywood, 1946. NEW YORK DEBUT—Caleb Cornish, *The Highest Tree,* Longacre, 1959, 21 weeks. PRINCIPAL STAGE APPEARANCES—*Kind Lady,* Lobero, Santa Barbara, 1948; *Dear Ruth,* Lobero, Santa Barbara, 1948; Rudolph, *Anna Lucasta,* Laguna Theatre, Laguna Beach, CA, 1949; *Peg Of My Heart,* Laguna, Laguna Beach, 1949.

FILM DEBUT—Dying Soldier, *Twelve O'Clock High,* 1949. PRINCIPAL FILMS—Chief Quinn, *Forbidden Planet,* 1956; Major St. Auban, *Paths of Glory,* 1957; Alan Stewart, *The Long Hot Summer,* 1958; Max Steiner, *Compulsion,* 1959; Lt. Dennis M. Foster, USN, *The Wackiest Ship in the Army,* 1960; Colonel Murdock, *Seven Days in May,* 1964; *Seconds,* 1966; Steve Carson, *The Ride to Hangman's Tree,* 1967;

RICHARD ANDERSON

Capt. John Earle, USN, *Tora! Tora! Tora!*, 1970; Tom Austin, *Dead Men Tell No Tales*, 1971; Randolph, *The Astronaut*, 1972; Harvey Eaton, *The Longest Night*, 1972; Dr. Ben Cole, *Say Goodbye, Maggie Cole*, 1972; Dr. Richard Malcolm, *The Night Strangler*, 1973; Roger Goldsmith, *Partners in Crime*, 1973; George Brubaker, *Murder by Natural Causes*, 1979; Henry Churchbridge, *Condominium*, 1980; also *Payment on Demand*, 1951; *I Love Melvin*, 1952; *Scaramouche*, 1952; *The Student Prince*, 1955; *Hit the Deck*, 1955; *The Search for Bridey Murphey*, 1957; *Johnny Cool*, 1963; *Doctors' Wives*, 1971; *Play It As It Lays*, 1972.

TELEVISION DEBUT—the son, *Mama Rosa*, 1950. TELEVISION APPEARANCES—Glenn Wagner, D.A., *Bus Stop*, 1961–62; Colonel Hiland, USMC, *The Lieutenant*, 1963–64; Lt. Steve Drumm, *Perry Mason*, 1964–65; Chief George Untermeyer, *Dan August*, 1970–71; Oscar Goldman, *The Six-Million-Dollar Man*, *1974–78*, The Bionic Woman, 1976–78; Thomas Seldons, *The Immigrants*, 1978; Commodore John North, USN, *Pearl*, 1978; Terrence Crown, *The French Atlantic Affair*, 1979; also*Alias Smith and Jones; Bracken's World; Barnaby Jones; Bonanza; The Big Valley; Cannon; Charlie's Angels; Checkmate; Death Valley Days; Eleventh Hour; Fantasy Island; Felony Squad; The Fugitive; Gunsmoke; Ironside; The Invaders; Jigsaw; Lobo; Longstreet; The Love Boat; Land of the Giants; Dr. Kildare; My Friend Tony; Thriller; Matt Houston; Owen Marshall, Counsellor at Law; Playhouse 90; Rifleman; Target: The Corrupters; Wagon Train; Wanted: Dead or Alive; Zane Grey Theatre; The Delphi Bureau; The Man from U.N.C.L.E.; Nero Wolfe; The Untouchables; Bring 'em Back Alive; Simon and Simon; Whiz Kids.*

AWARDS: Emmy Nomination, Supporting Actor, 1977–78: *The Bionic Woman*.

SIDELIGHTS: MEMBER—Ephebian Society. RECREATION—travel, tennis, cross-country skiing, working on a 1936 Ford convertible Phaeton.

Mr. Anderson was the first actor ever to star in two TV series at the same time, portraying the same character in both, on different networks. He appeared in 26 feature films while under contract to MGM from 1949 to 1956.

ADDRESS: Agent—c/o William Morris, 151 El Camino, Beverly Hills, CA 90212.

* * *

ANDREWS, George Lee (ne George Lee), actor, singer

PERSONAL: Born October 13, 1942 in Milwaukee WI; son of Robert Edward (a horticulturalist) and Vernonica Catherine (Wettengel) Lee; married Georgia Gray Kirby on May 15, 1965 (divorced 1971); married Martha Alice Morris (an actress and singer) on September 6, 1976; children: (first marriage) Jennifer, (second marriage) Shannon, Robert. EDUCATION: Attended University of Wisconsin at Milwaukee. MILITARY: U.S. Army (Specialist 4th Class), 2 years.

GEORGE LEE ANDREWS

CAREER: DEBUT—Chorus, *Song of Norway,* Fred Miller Theatre, Milwaukee, WI, 1960. NEW YORK DEBUT—Fred, *A Little Night Music,* Shubert, for one year of performances, 1973. PRINCIPAL STAGE APPEARANCES—"Silly People," Sondheim, *A Musical Tribute,* Shubert, NY, 1973; Max, *On the Twentieth Century,* St. James, NY, 1977; Old Merlin, *Merlin,* Mark Hellinger, NY, 1982; Sireno, *Comedy;* Cole Porter, *Red Hot and Cole,* Variety Arts Theatre, L.A.; *Starting Here, Starting Now; Jacques Brel Is Alive and Well and Living in Paris,* Village Gate, NY; El Gallo, *The Fantasticks,* Sullivan Street Playhouse, NY; *Vamps and Rideouts,* Hudson Guild, NY, Berkshire Theatre Festival, John Drew Theatre E. Hampton, Queens Theatre in the Park; Arizona Theatre Company, 1980–81 Season: Sir Lucious O'Trigger, *The Rivals,* Lt. Harrington, *Custer,* Dr. Frederick Treves, *The Elephant Man,* Count Carl-Magnus, *A Little Night Music; Side by Side by Sondheim;* Von Trapp, *The Sound of Music;* Arthur, *Camelot;* Harold Hill, *The Music Man;* Michael, *I Do, I Do;* Curly, *Oklahoma;* Sky, *Guys and Dolls;* Johnny, *The Unsinkable Molly Brown;* Frank, *Annie Get Your Gun;* Albert, *Bye Bye Birdie; Mr. Roberts;* Billy/ Jigger, *Carousel;* Starbuck, *The Rainmaker;* Riff/Action, *West Side Story;* Nestor, *Irma La Douce;* Tony, *The Boyfriend;* Jack, *Charley's Aunt;* Lycus, *A Funny Thing Happened on the Way to the Forum;* MAJOR TOURS—Fredrick, *A Little Night Music,* 1st National Company.

SIDELIGHTS: MEMBERSHIPS—AEA, AFTRA, AGVA.

ADDRESS: Home—110 W. 86th Street, New York, NY. Agent—Dorothy Scott/Marje Fields, Inc. 165 W. 46th Street, New York, NY, 10036.

* * *

ANDREWS, Julie, actress, singer

PERSONAL: Born October 1, 1935, in London, England; daughter of Edward C. and Barbara (Morris) Wells; married Tony Walton (a stage designer) May 10, 1959 (divorced 1968); Blake Edwards (a producer), November 12, 1969; children: Emma, two adopted children. EDUCATION: At Beckenham in Kent, England; studied singing with her step-father, Ted Andrews and with Madame Stiles-Allen.

CAREER: DEBUT—singing operatic arias in the revue, *Starlight Roof,* Hippodrome, London, 1947. NEW YORK DEBUT— Polly, *The Boyfriend,* Royale, 1954. PRINCIPAL STAGE APPEARANCES—Royal Command Performance at the Palladium, 1948; *Humpty Dumpty* (pantomime), Casino, London, 1948; *Red Riding Hood* (pantomime), Theatre Royal, Nottingham, 1950; Princess Balroulbadour, *Aladdin,* Casino, London, 1951; *Jack and the Beanstalk,* Coventry Hippodrome, 1952; *Cinderella* (pantomime), Palladium, London, 1953; Becky Dunbar, *Mountain of Fire,* Royal Court, Liverpool, 1954; Eliza Doolittle, *My Fair Lady,* Shubert, New Haven, CT, 1956, Mark Hellinger, NY, 1956 for two years, Drury Lane Theatre, London, 1958; Guinevere, *Camelot,* Majestic, 1960; solo show at Pallidium, London, 1976.

FILM DEBUT—Mary Poppins, *Mary Poppins,* 1964. PRINCIPAL FILM APPEARANCES—*The Americanization of Emily,* 1964; Maria, *The Sound of Music,* 1965; *Torn Curtain,* 1966; *Hawaii,* 1966; *Thoroughly Modern Millie,* 1967; *Star!,*

1968; *Darling Lili,* 1970; *The Tamarind Seed,* 1974; *"10,"* 1979; *Little Miss Marker,* 1980; *S.O.B.,* 1981; *Victor/ Victoria,* 1982; *The Man Who Loved Women,* 1983.

TELEVISION DEBUT—High Tor, 1956. PRINCIPAL TELEVISION APPEARANCES—*Julie and Carol at Carnegie Hall,* 1961; *The Julie Andrews Show,* 1966; *An Evening with Julie Andrews and Harry Belafonte,* 1969; *The World of Walt Disney,* 1971; *Julie and Carol at Lincoln Center,* 1971; *The Julie Andrews Hour,* 1972–73; *Julie and Dick at Covent Garden,* 1973; *Julie and Jackie: How Sweet It Is,* 1974; *Julie and Perry and the Muppets,* 1974; *My Favorite Things,* 1975; *The Puzzle Children,* 1976; *ABC's Silver Anniversary Celebration,* 1978; *Julie Andrews . . . One Step into Spring,* 1978.

WRITINGS: BOOKS—*Mandy,* 1972; *Last of the Really Great Whangdoodles,* 1973; *Babe* (forthcoming).

AWARDS: Golden Globe, Academy Award Nomination, 1983: *Victor/Victoria;* Harvard University's Hasty Pudding's Woman of the Year, 1983; Golden David, Rome, 1983: *Victor/Victoria;* B'nai B'rith Anti-Defamation League, Woman of the Year, 1983; World Film Favorite, 1967; Golden Globe, 1964–65; Academy Award, 1963: *Mary Poppins;* New York Drama Critics Circle, 1955–56: *My Fair Lady.*

SIDELIGHTS: "One of Julie Andrews' most important priorities is the work she does for numerous charities. She has always been concerned by the plight of the world's less fortunate children. In addition to her work for organizations such as "Save the Children" and UNICEF, the Edwardses are foster parents to several children in the poorer areas of the globe. Their two youngest children at home are adopted Vietnamese orphans. In the summer of 1982, under the auspices of "Operation California," a relief organization of which Miss Andrews is a Board Member, she and Blake Edward's co-producer, Tony Adams, spent ten days in Southeast Asia, visiting Ho Chi Mihn City, Phnom Penh, and the camps of the Thai and Cambodian borders."

ADDRESS: Agent—Creative Artists Agency, 1888 Century Park E., Suite 1400, Los Angeles, CA 90067.

* * *

ANDROS, Douglas (ne Doukas Anastasakis), actor

PERSONAL: Born November 27, 1931, in New York City; son of Paraskevas (an ice-cream parlor proprietor) and Mersina (Haviaris) Anastasakis. EDUCATION: Attended New York City public schools; studied acting with Uta Hagen, Lee Strasberg, and Warren Robertson. POLITICS: Democrat. RELIGION: "Born Greek Orthodox; presently observe all religions." MILITARY: Served in the U.S. Army.

CAREER: DEBUT—Boys' chorus, *Carmen,* Metropolitan Opera House, New York, 1941. PRINCIPAL STAGE APPEARANCES—New York—Unemployed Man, *Good Woman of Setuzan,* H.B. Studio, 1956. Donald, *Shadow of a Gunman;* Husband, *Middle of the Night;* Celestin, Duclos, *In Port;* Woyzeck, *Woyzeck;* Paul, *The Typists;* Zooey, *Franny and Zooey,* H.B. Studio, 1959; Norman, *Wedding Breakfast;* Smirnov, *The Boor;* Tusenbach, *The Three Sisters;* Ferensby, *This Side of Paradise;* Joe, *Waiting for Lefty;* Dr.

DOUGLAS ANDROS

Werner, *Does a Tiger Wear a Necktie?;* Harry, *Born Yesterday;* Barney, *Last of the Red Hot Lovers,* Elysian Playhouse, 1975; Woody, *Smoking Pistols,* Theater Off Park, 1976; Loulou Barrier, *Piaf. . . A Remembrance,* 1977; Izzy Rubin, *Telecast;* Tony Esposito, *The Most Happy Fella,* Citicorp Center Atrium, New York, 1978. Summer Stock: *Dream Girl; Brigadoon; Golden Boy; Her Cardboard Lover; Paris; Anniversary Waltz; Oh Men Oh Women; Fancy Meeting You Again.* Dinner and Regional Theaters: Richard, *Hotline to Heaven,* Alhambra Dinner Theater, Jacksonville, FL, 1977; Candy, *Of Mice and Men,* Stage West Regional Theater, Springfield, MA, 1980; Peter, *The Zoo Story;* Mitch, *A Streetcar Named Desire;* Howard, *Picnic;* Banjo, *The Man Who Came to Dinner.* MAJOR TOURS—Victor Velasco, *Barefoot in the Park,* Indianapolis, St. Louis, 1973.

TELEVISION DEBUT—*Naked City,* 1957. TELEVISION APPEARANCES—*Armstrong Circle Theater; Studio One; East Side, West Side; Edge of Night; Another World.*

SIDELIGHTS: MEMBERSHIPS—AEA; AFTRA; SAG. FAVORITE PARTS—Zooey in *Franny and Zooey;* Barney in *Last of the Red Hot Lovers;* Woody in *Smoking Pistols;* Victor Velasco in *Barefoot in the Park;* Richard in *Hotline to Heaven;* Loulou Barrier in *Piaf. . . A Remembrance;* Candy in *Of Mice and Men;* Tony Esposito in *The Most Happy Fella.*

Mr. Andros has worked as a singer in over 100 night clubs and on radio shows. Enjoys cooking and traveling. Has spent many months on the Greek Islands (speaks Greek fluently).

ADDRESS: Home—63-199 Alderton Street, Forest Hills, NY 11374

* * *

APPLEBAUM, Gertrude H., personal manager

PERSONAL: Born February 20, in Brooklyn, NY; daughter of David (a clothing manufacturer) and Celia (Cohen) Applebaum. EDUCATION: Attended City College, New York. NON-THEATRICAL CAREER: Secretary, literary department, A & S Lyons Agency; worked for Arena Managers Association for two years.

CAREER: Secretary and, in 1936, assistant to Margaret Linley, a casting director; production assistant, third touring company of *State of the Union,* 1946; *Detective Story,* Hudson, New York, 1949, Bucks County Playhouse, New Hope, PA, 1949; *The Liar,* Broadhurst, New York, 1950; *Season in the Sun,* Cort, New York, 1950; *Out West of Eighth,* Ethel Barrymore, New York, 1951; *The Seven Year Itch,* Fulton, 1952; *The Bat,* New York, 1953; *The Warm Peninsula,* Helen Hayes, New York, 1959. Worked on productions for the Cornell-McClintic office. Business manager, Theatre Guild, 1964–65. Formed an investment syndicate for Broadway productions including *Finian's Rainbow,* Forty-Sixth Street Theatre, 1947; *Detective Story; Media; Roomful of Roses; The Happiest Millionaire; The Owl and the Pussycat.* Produced, with Stella Holt, *The World of My America,* Greenwich Mews Theatre, New York, 1965. Manages: Pauline Myers and others.

SIDELIGHTS: MEMBERSHIPS—American Theatre Wing; Actors' Fund; American Jewish Congress. Worked at the Stage Door Canteen and Merchant Seaman Canteen during World War II. Took dictation from Guthrie McClintic for his autobiography.

''I gave Walter Mattau his first Broadway job; also Paul Ford and Pat McVey.''

ADDRESS: 55 Central Park West, New York, NY 10023.

* * *

APTED, Michael, director

PERSONAL: Born February 10, 1941, in London, England; son of Ronald William and Frances Amelia (Thomas) Apted; married Joan, July 9, 1966; children: Paul, James. EDUCATION: City of London School, 1952–60; Downing College, Cambridge, B.A., 1963; special training at Granada Television.

CAREER: PRINCIPAL FILM WORK: Director—*Triple Echo,* 1972; *Stardust,* 1974; *The Squeeze,* 1976; *Agatha,* 1978; *Coalminer's Daughter,* 1980; *Continental Divide,* 1981; *Kipperbang,* 1982; *Gorky Park,* 1983; *First Born,* 1984.

PRINCIPAL TELEVISION WORK: Director—Various work including *Poor Girl, High Kampf, Highway Robbery, Kisses at Fifty, The Collection,* Granada, BBC, London Weekend, and Yorkshire Television, 1963–78.

THEATRE WORK: Director, *Strawberry Fields,* National Theatre of Great Britain, 1978.

AWARDS: Directors Guild of America Nominations, 1980: *Coalminer's Daughter,* 1978: *The Collection;* various awards and nominations from British Academy of Television and Film.

ADDRESS: Agent—Mike Marcus, Creative Artists Agency, 1888 Century Park E., Suite 1400, Los Angeles, CA 90067.

* * *

ARBUS, Allan, actor

PERSONAL: Son of Harry and Rose (Goldberg) Arbus; married Diane E. on April 10, 1941 (divorced 1969); married Mariclare Costello (an actress) in July 1977; children: Doon, Amy, Arin. EDUCATION: City College of New York for 1½ years; studied acting with Mira Rostova in New York. MILITARY: U.S. Army Signal Corps.

CAREER: NEW YORK DEBUT—*Dreyfus in Rehearsal,* Barrymore 1974. PRINCIPAL STAGE APPEARANCES—*Dr. Nuts,* Los Angeles, 1982–83; title role, *In the Matter of J. Robert Oppenheimer,* Los Angeles, 1983. FILM DEBUT—*Hey Let's Twist,* 1959. PRINCIPAL FILM APPEARANCES—*The Electric Horseman; The Last Married Couple in America; Omen II; W. C. Fields and Me; Greaser's Palace; Putney Swope; Cinderella Liberty; Cisco Pike; Law and Disorder.* TELEVISION DEBUT—*Here Come the Brides.* PRINCIPAL TELEVISION APPEARANCES—*M*A*S*H*; Gangster Chronicles; Ethel and Julius Rosenberg; The Law.*

ADDRESS: Office—c/o Benson and Klass Associates, 211 S. Beverly Drive, Beverly Hills, CA 90212.

* * *

ARNAZ, Desi, Jr., actor, writer, singer, record producer

PERSONAL: Born January 19, 1953; son of Desi (an actor/producer) and Lucille (an actress/comedienne; maiden name, Ball) Arnaz; married Linda Purl. EDUCATION: Attended California Institute of the Arts; studied with John Ingle at the Beverly Hills High School.

CAREER: DEBUT—Lead role, *Sunday in New York,* Kenley Players, OH, 1977. PRINCIPAL STAGE APPEARANCES—*Promises, Promises,* Melody Top Theatre; *Grease,* Sacramento Music Theatre.

MAJOR TOURS—*Sunday in New York.*

FILM DEBUT—*Red Sky at Morning,* 1968. PRINCIPAL FILM APPEARANCES—*Billy Two Hats; Joyride; The Wedding; Fake Out; House of Long Shadows.* TELEVISION DEBUT—*Here's Lucy.* PRINCIPAL TELEVISION APPEARANCES—*Mr.*

DESI ARNAZ, JR.

and Mrs. Bojo Jones; Voyage of Yes; She Lives; Marco Polo; Medical Story; Giving Birth; Streets of San Francisco; Police Story; Fantastic Voyage; Trouble Shooters; A Very Dangerous Love; To Kill a Cop; Love Boat; Joshua Tree; Fantasy Island; How to Pick up Girls; Crisis in Mid-Air; Supertrain; The Night the Bridge Fell Down; The Great American Traffic Jam; Advice to the Lovelorn; Whacked Out; I Love Liberty; Automan.

AWARDS: Golden Globe—Most Promising Newcomer, 1968.

SIDELIGHTS: MEMBERSHIPS—AFTRA, SAG, AEA, Musicians Union Local. FAVORITE ROLES—*Red Sky at Morning, Billy Two Hats, She Lives, The Voyage of Yes, Mr. & Mrs. Bojo Jones, Automan.* RECREATION—Tennis, surfing, fencing.

ADDRESS: Office—Automan, c/o 20th Century Fox Studios, Los Angeles, CA. Agent—The Artists Agency, 10000 Santa Monica Boulevard, Los Angeles, CA. 90067.

* * *

ARNAZ, Lucie, actress

PERSONAL: Born July 17, 1951, in Los Angeles, CA; daughter of Desiderio Alberto (actor, bandleader, producer) and Lucille Desiree (an actress; maiden name Ball) Arnaz III;

married Philip Menegaux (divorced); Laurence Luckinbill (an actor). EDUCATION: Attended public schools in California.

CAREER: DEBUT—as a regular on her mother's TV show, *Here's Lucy,* for six seasons. NEW YORK DEBUT—Sonia Walsk, *They're Playing Our Song,* Imperial, 1979. PRINCIPAL STAGE APPEARANCES—*Cabaret,* San Bernardino Civic Light Opera, 1972; Kathy, *Vanities,* Mark Taper Forum, LA, 1977; Annie Oakley, *Annie Get Your Gun,* Jones Beach, NY, 1978; three seasons with the John Kenley Theatres, including *Once Upon a Mattress, Li'l Abner, Bye Bye Birdie,* etc.. MAJOR TOURS—Gittel Mosca, *Seesaw,* national tour, 1974–75.

PRINCIPAL FILM APPEARANCES—*Billy Jack Goes to Washington,* 1977; *The Jazz Singer,* 1980. PRINCIPAL TELEVISION APPEARANCES—*The Black Dahlia,* 1974; *The Sixth Sense; Marcus Welby; Timex Presents Words and Music; Ed Sullivan's Clown Around; Lucie at Walt Disney World; Kraft Music Hall; Death Scream; The Mating Game;* host radio show, *Tune in with Lucie,* Southern California; host, *Southern California Easter Seals Telethon.*

AWARDS: Theatre World 1979: *They're Playing Our Song;* Los Angeles Drama Critics Award.

ADDRESS: c/o Nathan Golden, 9601 Wilshire Blvd., Beverly Hills, CA 90210.*

* * *

ARROWSMITH, William (ne William Ayres Arrowsmith), educator, critic, writer, translator

PERSONAL: Born April 13, 1924, in Orange, NJ; son of Walter Weed and Dorothy (Ayres) Arrowsmith; married Jean Reiser, on January 10, 1945 (divorced 1980); children: Nancy, Beth. EDUCATION: Princeton University, B.A., 1947, Ph.D., 1954; Oxford University, England (Rhodes Scholar), M.A., 1958.

THEATRE-RELATED CAREER: EDUCATION—instructor, classics, Princeton University, 1951–54; instructor, classics and humanities, Wesleyan University, Middletown, CT, 1953–54; assistant professor, classics and humanities, University of California at Riverside, 1954–56; faculty member, University of Texas, 1958–70, professor classics, 1959–70, chairman department, 1964–66; University Professor Arts and Letters, 1965–70; visiting professor of humanities, Massachusetts Institute of Technology, 1971; professor of classics, Boston University, 1971–76; Visiting, Henry McCormick, Professor of Dramatic Literature, Yale School of Drama, 1976–77; professor, writing seminars and classics, Johns Hopkins University, 1977–81. EDUCATIONAL CONSULTATION: Ford Foundation, 1970–71; Leadership Training Institute, Office of Education, 1970–71; visiting professor, MIT, 1971; FELLOWSHIPS: Center, Advanced Studies, Wesleyan University, 1967; Battelle Memorial Institute, Seattle, WA, 1968; Woodrow Wilson, 1947–48; Prix de Rome, Senior research fellow, American Academy of Rome, 1956–57; Guggenheim, 1957–58; Phi Beta Kappa visiting scholar, 1964–65; Rockefeller, in humanities, 1980–81. EDITORIAL: Founding editor, *Chimera,* 1942–44; *Hudson Review,* 1948–60, *Arion,* and *Journal of Classical Culture,* 1962; advisory

editor *Tulane Drama Review,* 1960–67; advisory board, *Mosaic,* 1967; *Image of Italy,* 1961; *Five Modern Italian Novels,* 1964; *The Greek Tragedy in New Translation* Oxford University Press, 33 vols., 1973–.

WRITINGS: TRANSLATIONS—*The Satyricon,* 1959; *The Bacchae, Cyclops, Heracles, Orestes, Hecuba,* 1960; *The Birds,* 1961; *The Clouds,* 1962; *Alcestis,* 1973. BOOKS—*The Craft and Context of Translation* (with R. Shattuck), 1962; *Dialogues with Leucò* (with D. S. Carne, Cesare Pavese), 1965; *Hard Labor* (with Cesare Pavese), 1976.

AWARDS: National Institute of Arts and Letters, 1978; Harbison Award for distinguished teaching, 1971; Piper professor for distinguished teaching, 1966; Morris L. Ernst award for excellence in teaching, 1962; Bromberg Award for excellence in teaching, 1959; Longview award for criticism, 1960; Loyola University, LL.D., 1968; St. Michael's College, Burlington, VT, L.H.D., 1968; Westminster College, Fulton, MO, D.Litt., 1969; Dartmouth College, 1970; Dickinson College, LL.D., 1971; Lebanon Valley College, D.Litt., 1973; University of Detroit, D.L.H., 1973; Grand Valley State College, 1973, Carnegie-Mellon University, L.H.D., 1974.

SIDELIGHTS: MEMBERSHIPS—PEN, Association of American Rhodes Scholars, Acad. Lit. Studies, International Council on Future of the University. Served with AUS, 1943–46. Phi Beta Kappa, Cosmos.

''The essential thing is poetry, dramatic poetry in particular, which I'm prepared to follow across any linguistic or disciplinary boundaries. Hence, my professional interest in teaching and writing about the films of Kurosawa and Antonioni, Greek drama, Marlowe and Shakespeare, T. S. Eliot, Amerindian poetry.''

ADDRESS: 1050 Fifth Avenue, New York, NY 10028.

* * *

ARTHUR, Carol, actress

PERSONAL: Born August 4, 1935, in East Rutherford, NJ; daughter of Peter (a police officer) and Mildred (Foehl) Arata; married Dom DeLuise (an actor), November 23, 1965; children: Peter, Michael, David. EDUCATION: Special Theatre Training—American Academy of Dramatic Arts, 1954 and 1955; summer stock at Dorset Playhouse with Pat and Fred Carmichael.

CAREER: DEBUT—Nightingale of Samarkand and Understudy to Dody Goodman, *Once Upon a Mattress,* Erlanger, Chicago, and national tour, 1960. NEW YORK DEBUT—Edith, *High Spirits,* Alvin, 1964, one year. LONDON DEBUT—Hildy, *On the Town,* Prince of Wales, 1963, six months. PRINCIPAL STAGE APPEARANCES—Miss Marmelstein, *I Can Get If for You Wholesale;* Waitress, *Kicks and Co.;* Luce, *The Boys from Syracuse;* Doris, *Last of the Red Hot Lovers;* Phoebe, *Quality Street;* Widda Paroo, *The Music Man;* Jan, *Woman of the Year.* MAJOR TOURS—*Oh What a Lovely War,* Buffalo Arena, Buffalo, NY, 1965; *Luv,* Kenley Players, Ohio, 1966; *High Spirits,* Dallas Musicals, 1965.

FILM DEBUT—Schoolmarm, *Blazing Saddles.* PRINCIPAL FILMS—Doris, *The Sunshine Boys;* Pregnant Lady, *Silent Movie; Hot Stuff; The World's Greatest Lover; Our Time; Making It.* TELEVISION DEBUT—Arnie's sister, *Arnie.* PRINCIPAL TELEVISION APPEARANCES—*Alice; Rhoda; Sanford and Son; Fernwood 2-Nite; The Cop and The Kid; Emergency; Karen.*

ADDRESS: Agent—c/o The Gage Group, 1650 Broadway, New York, NY 10019

* * *

ASHLEY, Elizabeth (nee Cole), actress

PERSONAL: Born August 30, 1939, in Ocala, FL; daughter of Arthur Kingman and Lucille (Ayer) Cole; married George Peppard (an actor; divorced); James Michael McCarthy; children: Christian (first marriage). EDUCATION: Attended Louisiana State University; prepared for the stage at the Neighborhood Playhouse and with Philip Burton.

CAREER: DEBUT—Esmeralda, *Camino Real,* Neighborhood Playhouse, 1959. NEW YORK DEBUT—(under the name Elizabeth Cole) Jessica, *Dirty Hands,* Actors Playhouse, 1959. PRINCIPAL STAGE APPEARANCES—(as Elizabeth Cole) Louise, *Marcus in the High,* Westport Country Playhouse, CT, 1959; (as Elizabeth Cole), Jane Ashe, *The Highest Tree,* Longacre, NY, 1959; Mollie Michaelson, *Take Her, She's Mine,* Biltmore, NY, 1963; Maggie Train, *Ring Round the Bathtub,* Martin Beck, NY, 1972; Isabel, *The Enchanted,* John F. Kennedy Center, Washington, DC, 1973; Maggie, *Cat on a Hot Tin Roof,* American Shakespeare Festival, Stratford, CT, ANTA, NY, 1974; Sabina, *The Skin of Our Teeth,* Mark Hellinger, NY, 1975; Betsey-No-Name, *Legend,* Barrymore, NY, 1976; Cleopatra, *Caesar and Cleopatra,* Palace, NY, 1977; Mary, *Vanities,* Chicago, 1977; *The Madwoman of Central Park South,* NY; *Agnes of God,* Music Box, NY, 1982–83.

FILM DEBUT—Monica, *The Carpetbaggers,* 1964. PRINCIPAL FILM APPEARANCES—*Ship of Fools,* 1964; *The Third Day,* 1965; *Marriage of a Young Stockbroker,* 1971; *Paperback Hero,* 1974; *Golden Needles,* 1974; *Rancho Deluxe,* 1975; *92 in the Shade,* 1976; *The Great Scout and Cathouse Thursday,* 1976; *Coma,* 1978; *Windows,* 1980; *Captured; Paternity,* 1981; *Split Image,* 1982.

TELEVISION DEBUT—*Du Pont Show of the Month.* PRINCIPAL TELEVISION APPEARANCES—Movies for television, *Second Chance,* 1972; *The Heist,* 1972; *Your Money or Your Wife,* 1972; *The File on Devlin; Hallmark Hall of Fame.*

WRITINGS: AUTOBIOGRAPHY—*Postcards from the Road,* 1978;

AWARDS: Antoinette Perry Award, 1961: *Take Her She's Mine.*

SIDELIGHTS: MEMBERSHIPS—Appointed to the President's Council on the Arts, 1965–69; director, American Film Institute, 1968–72; AEA; SAG; AFTRA.*

ASHMAN, Howard, director, lyricist, librettist

PERSONAL: Born May 17, 1950 in Baltimore, MD; son of Raymond Albert (an ice cream cone manufacturer) and Shirley Thelma (Glass) Ashman. EDUCATION: Goddard College, B.A., 1971; Indiana University, M.A., 1974.

CAREER: LONDON DEBUT—Director, *Little Shop of Horrors,* Comedy Theatre, 1983. PRINCIPAL STAGE WORK—Director, *Little Shop of Horrors,* Orpheum, NY, 1982; *God Bless You Mr. Rosewater,* Entermedia, NY, 1979.

WRITINGS: Plays—*The Confirmation,* 1976; book and lyrics—*God Bless You Mr. Rosewater,* 1979, *Little Shop of Horrors,* 1982.

AWARDS: Drama Desk Award, Outstanding Lyrics, Best Musical, New York Drama Critics Circle, Best Musical, Outer Critics Circle: *Little Shop of Horrors.*

THEATRE-RELATED CAREER: Artistic Director, WPA Theatre, NY, 1977–82.

SIDELIGHTS: MEMBERSHIPS—ASCAP, Writers Guild, Dramatists Guild.

ADDRESS: Agent—Esther Sherman, c/o William Morris Agency, 1350 Avenue of the Americas, New York, NY 10019.

* * *

ASNER, Edward, actor

PERSONAL: Born November 15, 1929, in Kansas City, MO; son of Morris and Lizzie Asner; married Nancy Lou Sykes, March 23, 1959; children: Matthew, Liza, Kathryn. EDUCATION: Attended University of Chicago; trained for the stage with the Playwrights Theatre Club and the Second City. RELIGION: Jewish. MILITARY: U.S. Army, 1951–53.

CAREER: PRINCIPAL TELEVISION APPEARANCES—*Slattery's People,* 1964–65; *The Doomsday Flight,* 1966; *Doug Selby, D.A.,* 1969; *House on Greenapple Road,* 1969; *Daughter of the Mind,* 1969; *The Old Man Who Cried Wolf,* 1970; Lou Grant, *The Mary Tyler Moore Show,* 1970–77; *The Last Child,* 1971; *The Haunts of the Very Rich,* 1972; *Hey, I'm Alive,* 1975; *Twigs,* 1975; *Rich Man, Poor Man,* 1976; *Life and Assassinations of the Kingfish,* 1977; *The Gathering,* 1977; Lou Grant, *Lou Grant,* 1977–82; *Roots,* 1977; *The Family Man,* 1979; *A Small Killing,* 1981; *Anatomy of an Illness.*

PRINCIPAL FILM APPEARANCES—*Kid Gallahad,* 1962; *The Slender Thread,* 1965; *The Satan Bug,* 1965; *The Venetian Affair,* 1967; *Eldorado,* 1967; *Peter Gunn,* 1967; *Change of Habit,* 1969; *Halls of Anger,* 1970; *They Call Me Mister Tibbs,* 1970; *Skin Game,* 1971; *Gus,* 1976; *Fort Apache, the Bronx,* 1980; *O'Hara's Wife,* 1982; *Daniel,* 1983.

PRINCIPAL STAGE APPEARANCES—*Woyzek, Volpone, Widower's Houses, Dybbuk, Red Gloves, Murder in the Cathedral, Miss Julie, The Sea Gull, Peer Gynt, Juno and the Paycock, Oedipus Rex,* Chicago Playwrights Theatre; (Off-Broadway)

Borkin, *Ivanov;* Peachum, *Threepenny Opera;* Dulac, *Legend of Lovers;* Prospero, *The Tempest,* Spinoza, *Venice Preserved;* (Stock) *Born Yesterday; My Three Angels; Goodbye My Fancy;* (Broadway) *Face of a Hero.*

AWARDS: Emmy Awards, 1980, 1978: *Lou Grant;* Emmy Award, 1977: *Roots;* Emmy Award, 1976: *Rich Man, Poor Man;* Emmy Awards, 1975, 1972, 1971: *The Mary Tyler Moore Show;* Foreign Press Award (5); Critics Circle Award, Best Actor in a Drama: *Roots;* Critics Circle Award, Best Actor in a Comedy: *Mary Tyler Moore Show.*

SIDELIGHTS: MEMBERSHIPS—SAG (president).

ADDRESS: Agent—c/o Jack Fields and Associates, 9255 Sunset Blvd., Los Angeles, CA 90069.

* * *

ASTREDO, Humbert Allen, actor

PERSONAL: Born April 4, in Pasadena, CA; son of Humbert Allen and Bess Houston (Alley) Astredo; children: Jennifer. EDUCATION: Pasadena Playhouse. MILITARY: U.S. Army, Special Services, Korea (8th Army).

CAREER: NEW YORK DEBUT—Cassio, *Othello,* Martinique, 1964. LONDON DEBUT—William Marshal, *The Little Foxes,* Victoria Palace, 1982. PRINCIPAL STAGE APPEARANCES (NEW YORK)—DeKoven, *Les Blancs,* Longacre, 1970; *Murderous Angels,* Playhouse, 1972; Gore Vidal, *An Evening with Richard Nixon And. . .,* Shubert, 1972; William Marshal, *The Little Foxes,* 1981. MAJOR TOURS—Frank Strang, *Equus,* Boston, Los Angeles, Chicago, 1975–77; William Marshal, *The Little Foxes,* Los Angeles, London, 1972–82.

TELEVISION DEBUT—*Simon Bolivar, Matinee Theatre,* 1954. PRINCIPAL TELEVISION APPEARANCES—*Dark Shadows; Love of Life; Another World;*

AWARDS: Nominated by Walter Kerr, Most Promising New Actor on Broadway for *Les Blancs,* 1970.

ADDRESS: Agent—Don Buchwald and Associates, 10 E. 44th Street, New York, NY 10017.

* * *

ATLEE, Howard (ne Howard Atlee Heinlen), press representative, manager

PERSONAL: Born May 14, 1926 in Bucyrus, OH; son of Howard Ezra (a miller, cab owner, railroader, real estate broker) and Blanche Lena (Newmann) Heinlen; married Barbara Anne Shumacher (business partner) on November 25, 1977. EDUCATION: Attended Ohio State University, 1944; Emerson College, A.B. 1950. MILITARY: U.S. Navy Reserve, 1944–46.

CAREER: Actor/assistant manager, Olney, MD, 1952; actor/manager/press representative, Mountaintop, Frederick, MD, 1953; production assistant, *By the Beautiful Sea,* Ma-

jestic, NY, 1953; press representative, Oguniquit Playhouse, ME, 1954–55; press assistant, *Wonderful Town,* Winter Garden, NY, 1953; press assistant, *The Seven Year Itch,* Fulton, 1952; assistant press representative, *Pipe Dream,* Shubert, NY, 1955; press representative, The Playhouse, Camden, NJ, 1956; press assistant, *The Happiest Millionaire,* Lyceum, NY, 1956; press assistant, *Speaking of Murder,* Royale, NY, 1956; press assistant for the Irish Players productions, *In the Shadow of the Glen, The Tinkers Wedding, Riders to the Sea,* Theatre East, NY, 1957; press representative, Lakeside Playhouse, Barnesville, PA, 1957.

Press Representative for New York productions, 1958–60— *She Shall Have Music; The Legend of Lizzie; The Playboy of the Western World; Triad; Season of Choice; Shadow and Substance; The Tempest; Krapp's Last Tape; The Zoo Story; Shakespeare in Harlem; Absolutely Time; The Ignorants Abroad; Darwin's Theories; John Brown's Body; Call Me by My Rightful Name; The Sudden End of Annie Cinquefoil; A Banquet for the Moon; The American Dream; Bartleby; The Death of Bessie Smith* and for Circle-in-the-Square. 1961— *Hedda Gabler; A Worm in Horseradish; The Moon in the Yellow River; Happy as Larry; Philoktetes; Women at the Tomb; Young Abe Lincoln; The Sap of Life; The Opening of a Window; The Cockeyed Kite; Ghosts; The Golden Apple; Sharon's Grave; The Cantilevered Terrace; A Stage Affair; Black Nativity; Fly Blackbird.*

1962—*The Theatre of the Absurd; 4x4; Toy for the Clowns; Wretched the Lion Hearted; Anything Goes; Sweet Miami; Who's Afraid of Virginia Woolf?; Whisper into My Good Ear/Mrs. Dally Has a Lover; The Laundry; The Coach with the Six Insides; Brecht on Brecht;* and for the APA Repertory Company and American Savoyards. 1963—*Strange Interlude; Save Me a Place at Forest Lawn; The Last Minstrel; Andorra; Tour de Force; The Ballad of the Sad Cafe; Corruption in the Palace of Justice; The Streets of New York; Play/The Lover.* 1964—*Funnyhouse of a Negro; Dutchman; The Two Executioners; Naughty Marietta; The Brig; Tiny Alice; That Hat; The Giants' Dance.* 1965—*The Fourth Pig; The Fisherman; Friday Night; A Sound of Silence; Do Not Pass Go; That Thing at the Cherry Lane; Troubled Waters; Good Days; The Exhaustion of Our Son's Love; Happy Ending; Day of Absence.*

1966—*Winterset; Malcolm; Laughwind; A Delicate Balance; The Long Christmas Dinner; Queens of France; The Happy Journey to Trenton and Camden; The Butter and Egg Man; America Hurrah; Three Hand Reel; Night of the Dance.* 1967—*The Rimers of Eldritch; The Experiment; The Party on Greenwich Avenue; Johnny No-Trump.* 1968—*Song of the Lusitanian Bogey; The Indian Wants the Bronx; It's Called the Sugar Plum; The Bench; Two Camps; Frère Jacques; Walk Down Mah Street; Another City, Another Land; The Young Master Dante; The Grab Bag; Sweet Eros/Witness; God Is (Guess What); The Firebugs; How To Steal an Election; Yes, Yes, No, No.* 1969—*Get Thee to Canterbury; Adaptation/Next/Ceremonies in Dark Old Men; The Triumph of Robert Emmet;* American Conservatory Theatre revivals, *Tiny Alice, A Flea in Her Ear, Three Sisters; The Front Page; Man Better Man; The Reckoning; The American Hamburger League; Mercy Street; Crimes of Passion; The Harangues.*

1970—*Gloria and Esperanza; The Cherry Orchard; The Memory Bank; Hedda Gabler; Nature of the Crime; End-*

game; Hay Fever; Johnny Johnston; Sunday Dinner; Ododo.
1971—*Ride a Black Horse; In New England Winter; Things
That Almost Happen; Kiss Now; Black Girl; The Sty of the
Blind Pig; Fingernails Blue as Flowers.* 1972—*Uhuruh;
Jamimma; The Contrast; The River Niger.* 1974—*The Great
Mcdaddy; In the Deepest Part of Sleep.* 1975—*Bette Mid-
ler's Clams on the Half Shell Revue; Salome; The First
Breeze of Summer.*

SIDELIGHTS: MEMBERSHIPS—ATPAM. RECREATION—Licensed American Kennel Club Dog Show Judge. Mr.
Atlee raises, breeds and shows pure bred dogs, especially
dachshunds.

ADDRESS: Office—165 W. 46th Street, New York, NY
10036.

* * *

ATTENBOROUGH, Sir Richard, CBE (cr. 1967), actor, producer, director

PERSONAL: Born August 29, 1923, in Cambridge, England; son of Frederick L. (MA) and Mary (Clegg) Attenborough; married Sheila Sim. EDUCATION: Leverhulme
Scholarship, Royal Academy of Dramatic Art, 1942; MILI-
TARY: RAF, 1943, Film Unit.

CAREER: DEBUT—Richard Miller, *Ah! Wilderness,* Intimate
Theatre, Palmer's Green, 1941. PRINCIPAL STAGE APPEAR-
ANCES—Sebastian, *Twelfth Night,* Ralph Berger, *Awake and
Sing,* Arts Theatre, 1942; Andrew, *London W1,* Q Theatre,
1942; Leo Hubbard, *The Little Foxes,* Piccadilly, 1942; Ba,
The Holy Isle, Arts, 1942; Pinkie, *Brighton Rock,* Garrick,
1943; Coney, *The Way Back,* Westminster, 1949; Toni Rigi,
To Dorothy, a Son, 1950; Valentine Crisp, *Sweet Madness,*
Vaudeville, 1952; Detective Trotter, *The Mousetrap,* Am-
bassadors', 1952; David and Julian Fanshaw, *Double Image,*
Savoy, 1956; Theseus, *The Rape of the Belt,* 1957.

FILM DEBUT—*In Which We Serve,* 1942. PRINCIPAL FILM
APPEARANCES—*Journey Together; School for Secrets; The
Man Within; Dancing with Crime; Brighton Rock; London
Belongs to Me; The Guinea Pig; The Lost People; Boys in
Brown; Morning Departure; Hell Is Sold Out; The Magic
Box; Gift Horse; Father's Doing Fine; Eight O'Clock Walk,*
1955; *The Ship that Died of Shame,* 1956; *Private's Prog-
ress,* 1956; *The Baby and the Battleship; Brothers in Law,*
1957; *The Scamp; Dunkirk,* 1958; *The Man Upstairs,* 1959;
The Angry Silence, 1959; *Sea of Sand; Danger Within; I'm
All Right Jack,* 1960; *Jet Storm; S.O.S. Pacific,* 1960; *Only
Two Can Play,* 1962; *All Night Long; The League of Gentle-
men; The Dock Brief; The Great Escape,* 1963; *The Third
Secret,* 1964; *Guns at Batasi,* 1964; *Seance on a Wet
Afternoon,* 1964; *The Flight of the Phoenix,* 1966; *The Sand
Pebbles,* 1966; *Doctor Doolittle,* 1967; *The Bliss of Mrs.
Blossom,* 1968; *Only When I Larf,* 1969; *The Last Grenade,*
1970; *The Magic Christian,* 1970; *A Severed Head,* 1971; *10
Rillington Place,* 1971; *David Copperfield; Young Winston,*
1972; *Loot,* 1972; *Ten Little Indians,* 1975; *Rosebud,* 1975;
Brannigan, 1975; *Conduct Unbecoming,* 1975; *The Chess
Players; The Human Factor,* 1975.

PRINCIPAL FILM WORK—Producer, *The Angry Silence,* 1959;
producer, *The League of Gentlemen;* producer, *Whistle

Down the Wind, 1961; producer, *The L Shaped Room,* 1962;
producer/director, *Oh! What a Lovely War,* 1968; producer,
Seance on a Wet Afternoon, 1964; director, *Young Winston,*
1972; director, *A Bridge Too Far,* 1975; director, *Magic,*
1978; producer/director, *Gandhi,* 1982; *A Chorus Line,*
1985.

RELATED CAREER: Formed own film production company in
1959, Beaver Films; chairman, Royal Academy of Dramatic
Art; chairman, Capital Radio; pro-chancellor of Sussex University and Chairman of its Arts Center Board.

AWARDS: Academy Award, Best Picture, Best Director,
1982: *Gandhi;* Knighted in the New Year Honours, 1976;
Hon. DCL, Newcastle, 1974; D.Litt. Leicester, 1970;
Golden Globe, 1966, 1967, 1969; Best Actor, British Film
Academy, 1965; Best Actor, Variety Club of Great Britain,
1959, 1965; Best Actor, San Sebastian Film Festival, 1961,
1964; Leverhulme scholar and winner Bancroft Medal,
Royal Academy of Dramatic Arts.

SIDELIGHTS: MEMBERSHIPS—British Academy of Film and
Television Arts; Garrick Club; Beefstake Club; Green Room
Club; Arts Council of Great Britain; Governor of the Na-
tional Film School; Cinematograph Films Council; Council,
British Actors' Equity Association, 1949–73; Chairman,
Actors' Charitable Trust; President of the Muscular Dis-
trophy Group of Great Britain. RECREATIONS—Listening to
music, collecting paintings.

ADDRESS: Agent—c/o Creative Artists, 1888 Century Park
E., Los Angeles, CA 90067.*

* * *

ATTLES, Joseph (ne Joseph Egbert Attles), actor

PERSONAL: Born April 7, 1903, on James Island, SC; son
of Joseph Elias and Victoria Attles. EDUCATION: Graduate,
Avery Normal Institute, Charleston, SC, 1924; studied voice
at the Harlem Conservatory in New York City.

CAREER: DEBUT—Member of a quartet giving summer
concerts at Congregational gatherings throughout South
Carolina. NEW YORK DEBUT—Hall Johnson Choir, Lafayette,
1926. PRINCIPAL STAGE APPEARANCES—Porgy, *Blackbirds
of 1928,* Liberty, NY, 1928; Sam/Bad Stacker Lee, *John
Henry,* 44th Street, NY, 1940; understudy, Sportin' Life,
Porgy and Bess, Ziegfeld, NY, 1953; Akufo, *Kamina,* 54th
Street, NY, 1961; Chicken-Crow-for-Day, *Tambourines to
Glory,* Little, NY, 1963; Father, *Jerico-Jim Crow,* Sanc-
tuary, NY, 1964; Brother Green/John Henry, *Cabin in the
Sky,* Greenwich Mews, NY, 1964; Innkeeper, *The Exception
and the Rule,* Greenwich Mews, 1965; Exhorter, *The Prodi-
gal Son,* Greenwich Mews, NY, 1965; Pious, *The Day of
Absence,* St. Marks Playhouse, NY, 1965; *King Lear,* Viv-
ian Beaumont, Lincoln Center, NY, 1968; *A Cry of Players,*
Vivian Beaumont, Lincoln Center, NY, 1968; Josh, *The
Reckoning,* St. Marks Playhouse, NY, 1969; One Man
Show, *The World of Paul Lawrence,* 1970; Sweets, *No Place
to Be Somebody,* Hartford Stage Company, CT, 1971; Pops,
The Duplex, Forum, NY, 1972; Henry, *The Last of Mrs.
Lincoln,* ANTA, NY, 1972.

MAJOR TOURS—*Blackbirds of 1928*, international tour, 1928–29; Sportin Life, *Porgy and Bess*, international tour, 1952–56; Checkers Clark, *Bubbling Brown Sugar*, national tour, 1976.

PRINCIPAL FILM APPEARANCES—*The Swimmer*, 1968; *LBJ*, 1969; *The Liberation of Lord Baron Jones*, 1969; *Pursuit of Happiness*, 1971; *Going Home*, 1971; *The Gang That Couldn't Shoot Straight*, 1971; *Across 110th Street*, 1972; *The Gambler*, 1974; *The Taking of Pelham 1-2-3*, 1974. PRINCIPAL TELEVISION APPEARANCES—*Weddin' Band*, 1974; *Bad Girl*, 1974; *Love's Sweet Song*, 1974; *Harriet Tubman*, 1974; *Beacon Hill*, 1975. PRINCIPAL NIGHT CLUB APPEARANCES—Plantation Club, NY, 1929; Kit Kat Club, NY, 1938; The New Plantation Club, NY, 1938–39; Vecchia Roma, Rome, Italy, 1956; Copacabana, NY, 1960.

AWARDS: Life Member of the Actors Fund, Distinguished Achievement in the Performing Arts, Uptown Musicians N.Y.C.—1975.

SIDELIGHTS: MEMBERSHIPS—AEA; SAG.

"We need more Black producing companies and more Black people interested in putting money behind Black talent, willing to take risks. We don't take enough risks right now, enough chances. . . . In all business, there is chance. We shouldn't lose our Black talent and artistry."

ADDRESS: Home—240 W. 65th Street, New York, NY, 10023.

* * *

AULETTA, Robert, dramatist

PERSONAL: Born March 5, 1940, in New York City; son of Anthony A. (a milkman) and Margaret (a secretary; maiden name Stark) Auletta; married Carol Carey, January 7, 1964 (divorced May 1980); children: Colleen, Deirdre. EDUCATION: Queens College of the City of New York, B.A. (English Literature), 1964; Yale University, School of Drama, M.F.A. (Playwrighting) 1969. POLITICS: Utopian Socialist. RELIGION: Born a Catholic.

WRITINGS: PLAYS PUBLISHED—*The National Guard, Yale Theatre*, vol. 1, #1; *Red Mountain High, Yale Theatre*, vol. 2, #3; *Walk the Dog, Willie, Yale Theatre*, vol. 6, #1; *Foreplay-Doorplay, Yale Theatre*, vol. 6, #3; *Stops, Playwrights for Tomorrow*, University of Minnesota Press, vol. 10; *Rundown, Plays in Process*, Theatre Communications Group, 1981–82.

CAREER: PLAYS PRODUCED—*The National Guard*, Experimental Theatre, Yale School of Drama, 1967; *Red Mountain High*, Studio Theatre, Yale School of Drama, 1969; *Coocooshay*, New York Shakespeare Festival, 1970; *Stops*, Yale Repertory Theatre, 1972; *Foreplay-Doorplay*, St. Peter's Church, New York, 1975; *Walk the Dog, Willie*, Yale Repertory Theatre, 1976; *Wednesday Sharp*, Yale Cabaret, 1976; *Guess Work*, Yale Repertory Theatre, 1978; *Expo 99*, Third Street Music School, New York, 1979; *Joe: A Dramatic Idiocy*, Theatre for the New City, New York, 1980; *Hage: The Sexual History*, Eugene O'Neill Theatre Center,

Waterford, CT, 1981; *The Tobogganists*, Ensemble Studio Theatre, New York, 1981; *Stops and Virgins*, P.S. #122, New York, 1982; *Rundown*, American Repertory Theatre, Cambridge, MA, 1982; *Days in a Can*, Westbank Cabaret, New York, 1983; *Birth*, Cooper Union, New York, 1983.

ARTICLES—"Hello Columbus," *New Catholic World*, 1975; "Political Theatrics," *Courier*, Queens College Alumni publication.

THEATRE-RELATED CAREER: Teacher of playwriting, University of Illinois, Urbana, IL, 1969–74; playwright in residence, Yale Repertory Theatre, 1974–77; teacher of theatre, School of Visual Arts, New York, NY, 1975–present.

AWARDS: National Endowment for the Arts Playwrighting fellowship, for *Rundown*, 1982; *Rundown*, cited by the American Theatre Critics Association as one of the eight outstanding plays produced outside of New York City, 1981–82 season; Village Voice Obie Award for *Stops and Virgins*, 1982; Hazan Foundation Grant as Playwright in Residence at the Yale Divinity School; CBS Fellowship and John Golden Fellowship as Playwright in Residence at Yale Repertory Theatre, 1977; Rockefeller Grant through Office of Advanced Drama Research; John Golden Fellowship, Lemist Esler Fellowship, Mollie Kazan Award for best play at Yale School of Drama; Peter Pauper Press Award for creative writing, Queens College.

SIDELIGHTS: "I keep wrestling with America. You can't walk a step without running into dramatic material. None of us will ever get to the bottom of it, but the attempt has to be made. Journalism can only go so far. Dramatic fiction has the edge over it all, I believe, including movies and novels. The theatre today commands a special perspective on reality. Only the stage can address itself to the multi-dimensional ebb and flow of images that constitute our present day 'realism.' America is a dramatist's dream—if only he is careful not to lose himself amidst the hallucinations of its constantly shifting landscape. England has produced some very good playwrights lately—full of seriousness and style—but they lack the Whitmanesque poetry and tragedy of our best work. If only we could overcome our hyperactive commercialism; if only our regional theatres could regain some of the purity and purpose that first inspired them; if only our most conservative playwrights were not continually encouraged at the expense of the innovators; if only our actors were offered alternatives to 'making it' other than movies and T.V. . . . Still and all, the audiences are out there waiting for the living word, the inspired action, that image of America that offers both pain and pleasure in quick succession."

ADDRESS: Home—161 Prince Street, New York, NY 10012. Office—School of Visual Arts, 209 E. 23rd Street, New York, NY 10010. Agent—Helen Merrill, 337 W. 22nd Street, New York, NY 10011.

* * *

AUSTIN, Lyn (nee Evelyn Page Austin), manager

PERSONAL: Born January 14, 1922 in Upper Montclair, NJ; daughter of Chellis A. (a bank president) and Edna Louise (a community volunteer; maiden name, Page) Austin; EDUCA-

TION: Vassar College, B.A., Drama, 1944; Columbia University, M.A., Dramatic Literature, 1949. POLITICS: Democrat. RELIGION: Episcopalian.

CAREER: Associate Producer with Roger L. Stevens, New York, 1952–63; Founder/Producing Director, Lenox Arts Center, Stockbridge, MA, 1970; Founder/Producing Director, Music-Theatre Group, New York, 1974. FIRST STAGE WORK—Co-producer, *Frogs of Spring,* Music Box, New York, 1953. PRINCIPAL STAGE WORK: ASSOCIATE PRODUCER: *In the Summer House,* Playhouse Theatre; *Tea and Sympathy,* Morosco, New York; *The Best Man,* Morosco, *Mary, Mary,* Morosco, and national tour; *Oh Dad, Poor Dad. . . . ,* 74th Street Theatre and national tour; CO-PRODUCER: Plays—*Take a Giant Step,* Lyceum, New York, 1953. *Indians,* Martin Beck, New York, and national tour; *Adaptation/ Next,* 13th Street Playhouse, and national tour; *Alice in Wonderland,* Manhattan Theatre Project, and International Tour; *Our Late Night,* Public, New York; *The Mother of Us All,* Guggenheim Museum, New York; *Dr. Selavy's Magic Theatre,* Mercer Arts Center, New York; *Mourning Pictures,* Lyceum, New York; *Hotel for Criminals,* Westbeth Arts Center, New York; *The Club,* Circle-in-the-Square Downtown, New York; *Nightclub Cantata,* Village Gate, New York; *Portraits,* Lenox Arts Center, Stockbridge, MA; *The Tennis Game,* South Street Theatre, New York; *Prairie Avenue,* South Street Theatre, New York; *The Brides,* Lenox Arts Center, Stockbridge, MA; *Trio,* Lenox Arts Center; *The Columbine String Quartet Tonight!* Cubiculo/Lenox Arts Center; *A Metamorphosis in Miniature,* Cubiculo, New York; *Poppie Nongena,* Cubiculo/St. Clement's/Douglas Fairbanks, New York; Edinburgh Festival, London, England; PRODUCING DIRECTOR: *The Mother of Us All,* St. Clement's, New York, Wolf Trap Farm Park for the Performing Arts, VA.

AWARDS: Plays produced have garnered 17 Obie Awards, and several Drama Desk Awards.

ADDRESS: c/o Lenox Arts Center/Music Theatre Group, P.O. Box 858, Stockbridge, MA 01262.

* * *

AVEDIS, Howard (ne Hikmet Avedis), director, producer, writer

PERSONAL: Born May 25; married Marlene Schmidt (a producer of feature films). EDUCATION: London School of Film Technique; University of Southern California, M.A. (Cinema), also holds a B.A. in English Literature.

CAREER: PRINCIPAL FILM WORK, DIRECTED—*The Stepmother,* 1972; *The Teacher,* 1974; *Scorchy,* 1976; *Texas Detour,* 1977; *The Fifth Floor,* 1978; *Separate Ways,* 1979; *Mortuary,* 1982; *Playing with Fire,* 1984.

WRITINGS: He has written screenplays for some of his films and has contributed to others.

AWARDS: Academy Award Nomination, 1972: *The Stepmother;* George Cukor Award, USC.

SIDELIGHTS: MEMBERSHIPS—Writers Guild of America,

West. Mr. Avedis speaks seven languages fluently, English, French, Italian, Arabic, Persian, Armenian, and Turkish.

ADDRESS: Home—13521 Rand Drive, Sherman Oaks, CA 91423. Office—Hickmar Productions, Burbank Studios, PB4 Room 105, Burbank, CA 91505. Agent—Mike Greenfield, Charter Management, 9000 Sunset Blvd., Los Angeles, CA 90069.

* * *

AVNI, Ran, artistic director, producer

PERSONAL: Born October 1, 1941, in Israel; son of Avraham (a farmer) and Shulamith (a teacher; maiden name, Goodman) Avni; married Lori S. (Christie's Wine manager) on July 29, 1983; children: Sheerly. EDUCATION: Emerson College, Boston, M.A., 1972; School for the Stage Arts, Israel, graduate; undergraduate studies, Harvard University.

CAREER: DIRECTED—*Incident at Vichy,* Jewish Repertory Theatre (JRT); *Up from Paradise,* JRT; *My Heart Is in the East,* JRT; *Vagabond Stars,* JRT. Over fifty productions at JRT since 1974.

AWARDS: The Villager's Downtown Theatre Award, Outstanding Director, *Vagabond Stars,* 1982.

SIDELIGHTS: Founded the Jewish Repertory Theatre in 1974, to present plays in English that relate to the Jewish experience.

ADDRESS: c/o Jewish Repertory Theatre, 344 E. 14th Street, New York, NY 10003.

* * *

AYERS, David H., actor, director, administrator

PERSONAL: Born February 26, 1924; son of Walter E. (a farmer) and Thelma Clara (Runyon) Ayers; married Jean Yeager (a librarian) on March 23, 1923; children: Carol Jane, Amy, Lisa, Michael. EDUCATION: Ohio State University (OSU), B.A. (Theatre and Radio, Television), 1949, M.A. 1951; Ph.D. (Theatre), 1969; Lessac Institute, Binghamton, NY, post-graduate workshops, 1972–73. MILITARY: Fleet Marine Force, 1944–46.

CAREER: PRINCIPAL STAGE APPEARANCES—Has created leading roles in three new plays by Lawrence and Lee including Henry David Thoreau in *The Night Thoreau Spent in Jail.* Has acted in numerous training films and radio and television commercials, and in two feature films. DIRECTED: Co-director with Paul Baker for the Dallas Theatre Center production of *The Night Thoreau Spent in Jail* in 1971. Director of plays and co-director of musicals for OSU Department of Theatre since 1962. Served as free-lance director for Columbus Players Theatre, the Gallery Players of the Columbus Jewish Center, and Nationwide Insurance Players. THEATRE-RELATED CAREER: Teaching—instructor, Theatre, Ohio State University, 1963–69; assistant professor, Theatre, Ohio State University, 1969–75; associate professor, Theatre, Ohio State University, 1975–. ADMINIS-TRATION: Executive Director, American Playwrights Theatre, 1963–80; manager, Television Programing and Production, OSU, 1958–63; production manager, WOSU Television, OSU, 1956–58; production supervisor, WOSU-AM/FM, 1955–56; producer-director, WOSU AM/FM, 1951–55.

WRITINGS: PUBLISHED ARTICLES—"Toward a New Broadway," 1964; "American Playwrights Theatre—A Progress Report;" "Introduction," *Modern International Drama.*

AWARDS: Columbus Council of the Arts, Outstanding Artist, 1978.

SIDELIGHTS: Chairman of OSU committee that secured the honorary doctorate for Robert E. Lee (playwright), 1979; chairman, OSU committee that successfully raised the money for the establishment of the Roy Bowen Scholarship Fund in the OSU Department of Theatre, 1978; chairman, Undergraduate Committee, OSU Department of Theatre, 1978–81; member, OSU College of the Arts Curriculum Committee, 1983; member, OSU Theatre Department Executive Advisory Committee, 1983.

ADDRESS: c/o Department of Theatre, Ohio State University, 1089 Drake Union, 1849 Cannon Drive, Columbus, OH 43210.

* * *

AZZARA, Candy, actress

PERSONAL: Born May 18, 1947, in Brooklyn, NY; daughter of Sam (a carpenter) and Josephine (Bravo) Azzara.

EDUCATION: Studied acting with Gene Frankel, Hugh Whitfield, and Lee Strasberg; voice with David Craig, Neyneen Pires and Nora Dunfee; dance with Delores Bagley.

CAREER: PRINCIPAL STAGE APPEARANCES—*Any Wednesday,* Lake Placid Playhouse, NY, 1968; *Barefoot in the Park,* Lake Placid Playhouse, 1969; *Cactus Flower,* Bucks County Playhouse, New Hope, PA, 1973; performed with the Gene Frankel Repertory Company, 1971–72; *Lovers and Other Strangers,* NY, 1970–72; *Engagement Baby,* NY, 1970–72; *Detective Story,* Ahmanson, Los Angeles, CA, 1984. MAJOR TOURS—*The Moon Is Blue,* Florida and North Carolina, 1968; *Why I Went Crazy,* 1971–72; *Only the Shadow Knows,* 1971–72.

PRINCIPAL FILM APPEARANCES—*They Might Be Giants,* 1971; *Made for Each Other,* 1971; *Hail,* 1973; *Hearts of the West,* 1975; *Bogart Slept Here,* 1975; *A.F.I. Fatso,* 1976–77; *World's Greatest Lover,* 1976–77; *House Calls,* 1976–77; *Fatso,* 1980; *Pandemonium,* 1982; *Easy Money,* 1983.

PRINCIPAL TELEVISION APPEARANCES—Movies of the week, *Divorce Wars,* 1981, *Million-Dollar In-Field,* 1981, *Love Boat,* 1982; shows, 1978–84, *House Calls, Barney Miller, Trapper John, M.D., The Two of Us, Soap, Diff'rent Strokes, Mama Malone, Chips, Reverend Grady Nutt, One Day at a Time;* pilots, *Ernie and Joan, R.I.P., The Rainbow Girl;* talk shows, *Merv Griffin Show, Dinah Shore;* and *Love Boat II, Kojak, Baretta, Eddie & Herbert, Barney Miller, The Practice, Rhoda, M.T.M. Special Variety Show, The Girl Who Couldn't Lose, Wives, Fay, Montefusco's, The Cop and the Kid, Calucci's Dept., Kraft Music Hall, Secret Storm, Those Were The Days, NYPD.*

ADDRESS: Agent—Abrams, Harris and Goldberg, Ltd., Garden Suite B, 9220 Sunset Blvd., Los Angeles, CA 90069.

B

LAUREN BACALL

BACALL, Lauren (nee Betty Perske), actress

PERSONAL: Born September 16, 1924, in New York City; daughter of William and Natalie (Bacall) Perske; married Humphrey Bogart (deceased); Jason Robards Jr. (an actor, divorced). EDUCATION: Attended public schools in New York City; studied at the American Academy of Dramatic Arts in New York. NON-THEATRICAL CAREER: Fashion model.

CAREER: NEW YORK DEBUT—a walk-on, *Johnny 2 x 4*, Longacre, 1942. LONDON DEBUT—Margo Channing, *Applause*, Her Majesty's Theatre, 1972. PRINCIPAL STAGE APPEARANCES—Ingenue, pre-Broadway tour, *Franklin Street*, 1942; Charlie, *Goodbye Charlie*, Lyceum, NY, 1959; Stephanie, *Cactus Flower*, Royale, NY, 1965; Margo Channing, *Applause*, Palace, NY, 1970, for over a year in Toronto, Civic Auditorium, 1971; *Wonderful Town*, stock, 1977; Tess Harding, *Woman of the Year*, Palace, NY, 1981. MAJOR

TOURS—Margo Channing, *Applause*, 1970; Tess Harding, *Woman of the Year*, 1983–84. FILM DEBUT—*To Have and Have Not*, 1944. PRINCIPAL FILM APPEARANCES—*The Big Sleep; Dark Passage; Key Largo; How to Marry a Millionaire; The Cobweb*, 1955; *Designing Woman*, 1957; *Sex and the Single Girl*, 1965; *Harper*, 1966; *Murder on the Orient Express*, 1974; *The Shootist*, 1976; *Health*, 1980; *The Fan*, 1981.

PRINCIPAL TELEVISION APPEARANCES—*Petrified Forest*, 1955; *Blithe Spirit*, 1956; *A Dozen Deadly Roses*, 1963; *The Light Fantastic*, 1967.

WRITINGS: BOOKS—*By Myself* (autobiography).

AWARDS: Antoinette Perry Award, Best Actress in a Musical, 1981: Tess Harding, *Woman of the Year;* Antoinette Perry Award, 1970: Margo Channing, *Applause;* American Academy of Dramatic Arts Award for Achievement, 1963.

SIDELIGHTS: RECREATIONS—Fashion, tennis, swimming, needlepoint.

ADDRESS: Agent—c/o STE Representation, 888 Seventh Avenue, New York, NY, 10019.

* * *

BACCUS, Stephen, actor, dancer, and singer

PERSONAL: Born February 25, 1969, in Miami, FL; son of James Albert (a lawyer) and Florence Ann (a guidance counselor) Baccus. EDUCATION: New York University, 1981–82; University of Miami, B.S., 1983; currently attending University of Miami Law School; trained for the theatre at Herbert Berghof Studio with Ruth Foreman.

CAREER: DEBUT—Louis, *The King and I*, Royal Palm Dinner Theater, Boca Raton, FL, 1979–80. NEW YORK DEBUT—Donald Fortune, *The House Across the Street*, Ensemble Theater, New York, 1982. PRINCIPAL STAGE APPEARANCES—Patrick, *Mame*, Royal Palm Dinner Theater, Boca Raton, FL, 1981; Klaus, *Three Acts of Recognition*, Public Theater, New York, 1982; Emil Brukner, *Tomorrow the World*, Ruth Foreman Theater, New York, 1983. FILM DEBUT—Peter, *Hardly Working*, 1980.

PRINCIPAL TELEVISION APPEARANCES—*That's Incredible; Good Morning America; The Today Show; Kids Are People Too; David Letterman Show; Jennifer's Journeys; P.M.*

STEPHEN BACCUS

Magazine; Live at Five; CBS 30 Minutes.

AWARDS, HONORS, AND PRIZES: SCHOLARSHIPS—International Thespian; Joston's; National Merit; New York University; University of Miami.

SIDELIGHTS: MEMBERSHIPS—Actors' Equity, Screen Actors' Guild, AFTRA, AGVA. "Stephen is the youngest person ever to graduate from the University of Miami and will be the youngest ever to meet the admission standards of the University of Miami's Law School. He has created his own variety act, which includes singing in five languages, dancing, comedy, and magic routines. He performs in South Florida theaters, hotels, hospitals, and other charitable organizations. Stephen enrolled in law school because he believes it is a good background for any career, but he is not yet sure if he will ultimately become a lawyer. 'Right now, I would choose a career in show business or computer science. But I might eventually decide that I like law best. It's not that important to me to be the youngest student or to finish my degree faster than others. I just want to be busy and make the most of my abilities.'"

ADDRESS: Home—19041 N.W. 5 CT, Miami, FL 33169. Agent—Office of Public Affairs, P.O. Box 248105, University of Miami, Coral Gables, FL 33124.

* * *

BADE, Tom, actor

PERSONAL: Born June 29, 1946, in Brooklyn, NY; son of Louis W. (a packaging engineer) and Kathleen Mary (Wynne)

Bade. EDUCATION: Trained for the stage at the American Academy of Dramatic Arts (graduate), 1965. RELIGION: Roman Catholic. MILITARY: U.S. army, 1966–68.

CAREER: DEBUT—apprentice, Rockland County Playhouse, Blauvelt, NY, 1964. NEW YORK DEBUT—Bernie, *The Perfect Match,* Theatre DeLys, New York, 1970. PRINCIPAL STAGE APPEARANCES—(New York) Duke, *Domino Theory,* Ensemble Studio Theatre, 1977; Kurt, *Play Strindberg,* Impossible Ragtime Theatre, 1977; Hercule Poirot, *Peril at End House,* Impossible Ragtime Theatre, 1978; Linzman/God, *Liliom,* Jewish Repertory, 1979; *My Mother, My Father and Me,* WPA, 1979; Steve, *Nature and Purpose of the Universe,* Wonder Horse, 1979; Regional—Craven, *Sly Fox,* Alaska Repertory, 1980; Lawrence, *Loose Ends,* Alaska Repertory, 1980; *A Christmas Carol,* Indiana Repertory, 1980; Jeff Baird, *Merton of the Movies,* Hartman Theater, Stamford, CT, 1981; Harold, *Maiden Stakes,* White Barn Theater, 1981; Mishkin, *Fools,* Alaska Repertory, 1982; Freddy, *Crossing the Bar,* Baltimore Centre Stage, 1983. MAJOR TOURS—understudy, *Sly Fox,* U.S. cities, 1978.

FILM DEBUT—Tanny, *Some of My Best Friends Are . . . ,* 1972. PRINCIPAL FILM APPEARANCES—*A Mother's Tale,* 1974; *A Tree, a Rock, a Cloud,* 1977; *The Renegade,* 1978; *Soup for One,* 1981; *Sentimental Journey,* 1983. TELEVISION DEBUT—*Ryan's Hope,* 1979. PRINCIPAL TELEVISION APPEARANCES—*O'Malley; Loving; All My Children; Search for Tomorrow; Ryan's Hope; As the World Turns.*

AWARDS: Show Business Publications Award Nomination, Best Newcomer, 1971.

ADDRESS: Phone Service—(212) 581-6470.

* * *

BADHAM, John MacDonald, film director

PERSONAL: Born August 25, 1943, in Luton, England; came to United States in 1945, naturalized in 1950; son of Henry Lee and Mary Iola (Hewitt) Badham; married Bonnie Sue Hughes on December 28, 1967 (divorced, 1979); children Kelly MacDonald. EDUCATION: Yale University, B.A., 1963, M.F.A., 1965. MILITARY: U.S. Army 1963–64.

CAREER: PRINCIPAL FILMS DIRECTED—*The Bingo Long Travelling All Stars and Motor Kings,* 1976; *Saturday Night Fever,* 1977; *Dracula,* 1979; *Whose Life Is It Anyway?,* 1981; *Blue Thunder,* 1983; *War Games,* 1983. TELEVISION PRODUCTION—Associate Producer, *Night Gallery,* 1969, *Neon Ceiling,* 1970; Associate Producer/director, *The Senator,* 1971, numerous episodes, *Night Gallery, Police Story, Streets of San Francisco, The Bold Ones.* TELEVISION MOVIES—*The Impatient Heart,* 1971; *Isn't It Shocking,* 1973; *Reflections of Murder,* 1973; *The Gun,* 1974; *The Law,* 1974; *The Godchild,* 1974. THEATRE-RELATED CAREER: President, John Badham Films, Inc.; chairman of the board, JMB Films, Inc.; guest lecturer, University of California, Loyola Marymount College, University of Alabama, Amherst College, and University of Southern California.

AWARDS: Grand Prize, Paris International Science Fiction and Fantasy Festival, Best Horror Film award Academy

Science Fiction and Fantasy, 1979: *Dracula;* NAACP Image Award Nomination, 1976: *The Bingo Long Travelling All Stars and Motor Kings;* Emmy Nomination, 1974: *The Law;* ARD reihe 'das Film Festival Award, 1975: *The Law;* Southern California Motion Picture Council Award, 1974: *The Gun;* Christopher Award, 1971: *The Impatient Heart;* Emmy Nomination, 1971: *The Senator.*

SIDELIGHTS: MEMBERSHIPS—Directors Guild, American Filmex Society, Academy of Motion Picture Arts and Sciences.

ADDRESS: c/o Adams, Ray and Rosenberg, 9200 Sunset Blvd., Los Angeles, CA 90069

* * *

BAER, Marian, actress

PERSONAL: Born August 18, 1924; daughter of Paul V. (a lawyer) and Liatonia L. (head of Voice Department, University of Missouri; maiden name Leece) Barnett; married George O. Baer on August 24, 1946 (deceased); children: Liatonia, Diana, George, Jr. EDUCATION: American Academy of Dramatic Arts, 2 years. RELIGION: Unitarian.

CAREER: DEBUT—Mop, *As You Desire Me,* Resident Theatre, Kansas City, MO. NEW YORK DEBUT—Mrs. Pearce, *My Fair Lady,* Uris, for four months. PRINCIPAL STAGE APPEARANCES—Ethel, *On Golden Pond,* Chanhassen Dinner Theatre, Minneapolis, MN, 1983; Mildred, *Squabbles,* Waldo Astoria Dinner Theatre, Kansas City, MO, American Stage Festival, Milford, NH, 1982; Kate, *All My Sons,* Advent Theatre, Nashville, TN, 1979; Amanda, *The Glass Menagerie;* Mrs. Muskat, *Liliom;* Marjorie, *Home;* Mrs. Whitefield, *Man and Superman;* Madam Arcati, *Blithe Spirit;* Lady Britommart, *Major Barbara;* Marina, *Uncle Vanya;* Catherine, *Arms and the Man;* Nurse, *Antigone;* Mrs. Boyle, *Mousetrap;* Penny, *You Can't Take It with You;* Aunt Eller, *Oklahoma;* Frau Schmidt, *The Sound of Music;* Sostrata, *Mandragola;* Lady Falconbridge, *King John,* New York Public Theatre; Anna, *A Month in the Country,* Colonnades Theatre, New York; Lady Bracknell, *The Importance of Being Earnest,* National Arts Theatre, New York; Mrs. Purdy, *Daughter-in-Law,* W.P.A. Theatre, New York; Agnes, *A Delicate Balance,* Central Arts Cabaret, New York. REGIONAL COMPANIES—Alaska Repertory Theatre; Advent Theatre, Nashville, TN; Cincinnati Playhouse in the Park, Cincinnati, OH; Carolina Regional Theatre; George Street Playhouse; Theater by the Sea. MAJOR TOURS—Mrs. Pearce, *My Fair Lady,* with Rex Harrison, national company; Helga Tendorp, *Deathtrap,* Bus and Truck Tour; Berthe, *Pippin.*

FILM DEBUT—Maria, *Communal Flat,* 1983. PRINCIPAL TELEVISION APPEARANCES—*Edge of Night; Love of Life; Search for Tomorrow; The Guiding Light; The Doctors; As the World Turns.*

ADDRESS: Home—63 E. Ninth Street, New York, NY 10003. Agent—Marian Ivry, 1650 Broadway, New York, NY 10036.

RONALD BAGDEN

BAGDEN, Ronald, actor

PERSONAL: Born December 26, 1953; son of Stephen Edward (a fireman) and Helen Anita (a secretary; maiden name, Cusick) Bagden. EDUCATION: Royal Academy of Dramatic Art, London, England, 1974–76; Temple University, Philadelphia, 1971–73.

CAREER: DEBUT—Patrice Bombelles, *Ring Round the Moon,* Pennsylvania Stage Company, Allentown, PA, 1977. NEW YORK DEBUT—Pierrot, *Oh What a Lovely War!,* Playwrights Horizons, 1978. PRINCIPAL STAGE APPEARANCES—Valet, *Amadeus,* Broadhurst, New York, 1980–83; Boy, *Waiting for Godot,* Virginia Museum Theatre, Richmond, VA, 1980.

AWARDS: Sherek Memorial Prize, Royal Academy of Dramatic Art; Arthur Talbot Smith Award, RADA; Lord Lurgan's Ivor Novello Memorial Award, RADA, 1976.

SIDELIGHTS: MEMBERSHIPS—Actors Equity.

ADDRESS: 129 Perry Street, New York, NY 10014. Agent—Harris Spylios, 250 W. 57th Street, New York, NY 10019.

* * *

BAILEY, Frederick (ne John Frederick Bailey II), playwright, director, actor

PERSONAL: Born November 7, 1946, in Dallas, TX; son of

John Frederick (a sales engineer) and Elizabeth Aileen (a librarian; maiden name, Watson) Bailey; married Leilani Johnson, September 12, 1967 (divorced, 1971). EDUCATION: Southern Methodist University, B.F.A. (directing and playwrighting) 1967. POLITICS: Liberal Democrat. RELIGION: Protestant/Christian.

CAREER: DEBUT—Al, *Tea and Sympathy,* Theatre Three, Dallas, TX, 1964. NEW YORK DEBUT DIRECTED—*The Garden Of Forking Paths,* New York Theatre Ensemble, 1970. LONDON DEBUT PLAYWRIGHT—*Gringo Planet,* Gate, 1982. FILM DEBUT ACTOR—Small speaking role, *Gasss!,* 1970. THEATRE-RELATED CAREER: Founding member, Canyon Pictures (live theatre, motion picture production company) with partners, Beth Henley, Stephen Tobolowsky, William Utay, Bruce Wright, William B. Steis, and Joe Clark.

DIRECTOR: Staff Associate Director, Forestburgh Summer Theatre, Monticello, NY, 1972; Guest Director, 1973, Resident Director, The Major's Inn, Gilbertsville, NY, 1974; Staff Associate Director, 1968–69, Guest Director, 1974, Managing Director, The Warehouse Theatre, Oklahoma City, Oklahoma, 1974–76; extensive free-lance directing off-off Broadway at The New York Theatre Ensemble, The Playbox, New York, 1970–73.

WRITINGS: PLAYS, PUBLISHED—*The Bridgehead,* 1973; *Gringo Planet,* 1974; *Rio Pork,* 1975; *Lonesome Canyon,* 1978; *Midnight in Topanga,* 1980; *No Scratch,* 1981; *Walkie Talkie,* 1982. ONE ACT PLAYS, PUBLISHED—*Set It Down with Gold on Lasting Pillars,* 1972; *The Hooded Gnome,* 1975; *Dirty Ugly People & Their Stupid Meaningless Lives.*

FILM-DIALOGUE, *Polish Android,* 1970; screenplay, *Vindicator,* (tentative title), 1983. SHORT STORIES PUBLISHED—*Bare-Shouldered Gal,* 1981; *The Drone of Wings,* 1981; *Oswald's Back Alley,* 1981; *The Last White Main Sight,* 1982.

AWARDS: Received four commissions to write plays: South Coast Repertory Theatre, Costa Mesa, CA, Actors Theatre of Louisville; Wurlitzer Foundation Grant, Taos, NM, 1978–79: co-winner, First Prize, Actors Theatre of Louisville, First Annual New Play Festival, *The Bridgehead,* 1977.

SIDELIGHTS: "My wish is to direct primarily my own plays. Up until 1974–75, I never directed my own plays. Usually directed other people's plays (new, revivals, classics including much Shakespeare). If one of my plays was done I recruited another director. In '74, however, working with new plays at The Warehouse Theatre in OKC, there was no other director I could recruit and so I started directing my own work. I discovered how enjoyable this was. I do not feel that I must direct my own plays. There are some of them that I would never wish to direct, such as *The Bridgehead.* I feel most comfortable with my more farcical pieces. In my work, I am interested in studying human behavior, under pressure, in isolation. That is, pure human behavior, removed from outside influences of our modern media age. How people behave when what's internal becomes external. All my plays have this common theme. My purpose would be to demonstrate that there is another life, on this planet, in this dimension of consciousness. I believe that creative, intuitive intelligence gives us the opportunity to alter the destiny of the human species by uplifting and expanding Human Consciousness, Human Awareness, through social mutuality.

Maybe the uplift will be minuscule, infinitesimal, but that is the attempt. The hope is that it will also be fun."

ADDRESS: 1569 N. Topanga Canyon, Topanga, CA 90290

* * *

BAIRD, Mary E., actress

PERSONAL: Born June 26, 1947, in Berkeley, CA; daughter of Cecilia M. (a store clerk) Demenski. EDUCATION: Chabot College, Hayward, CA, A.A.; studied with American Conservatory Theatre in San Francisco.

CAREER: DEBUT—Sleeping Princess, ballet, *Seven Dancing Princes,* Oakland Civic Center, Oakland, CA, 1957. NEW YORK DEBUT—Waitress, *At Sea with Benchley,* American Place Theatre, 1975. PRINCIPAL STAGE APPEARANCES (NEW YORK)—Understudy, *Curse of an Aching Heart,* Little Theatre, 1982; K, Woman, Nurse, *K, The Trial;* Bennett, *Peg o' My Heart,* Theatre Four; Clerk, *Rubbers;* Babs, *A Pair of Hearts,* Manhattan Punchline; Kate, *The Doctor and the Devils,* SoHo Repertory Theatre; Jennie, *The Front Page,* Jill the Ripper, *The Jack the Ripper Review,* victim/housewife, *Flagship/A Slice of Life,* all Manhattan Punchline; nurse/dancer, *Marathon '33;* suffragette, *A Night at the Black Pig;* Gloria, *Blizzard,* Lion Theatre; Phoebe Morris, *Saturday Night Special,* Direct Theatre; Gloria, *The Tiger,* New York Stageworks. REGIONAL—Sarah, *Table Manners,* Capital Repertory Theatre; Eunice, *A Streetcar Named Desire,* Capital Repertory Theatre; Mrs. Frankenstein/Ensemble, *Frankenstein,* Capital Repertory Theatre; Lexington Conservatory Theatre, Lexington, NY—Tom Snout, *A Midsummer Night's Dream,* Gertrude, *The Sea Horse,* Mrs. Kirby, *You Can't Take It with You,* Patty, *Quality Street,* Mrs. Potts, *Picnic,* Old Lady Squeamish, *The Country Wife,* Mrs. Shinn, *Good Woman of Setzuan,* Nurse, *Welcome to Andromeda,* Donna Luna Donna, *Yanks,* Ensemble, *Faustus,* Viola Henderson, *Nursery Land,* Mother, *Nesting,* Housekeeper, *Bedtime Story;* Ask, *Season,* Shady Lane Theatre.

FILM DEBUT—Marina, *Communal Flat,* 1983.

SIDELIGHTS: MEMBERSHIPS—AEA, SAG. "Love out-of-doors life. Spending time in country away from City madness. Finally growing into my age. Starting to work and be recognized as good. Keep laughing, love friends."

* * *

BAKER, Blanche (nee Blanche Garfein), actress

PERSONAL: Born December 20, 1956 in New York; daughter of Jack (a director) and Carroll (an actress; maiden name Baker) Garfein; married Robert Bruce van Dusen (film production company owner) on October 1, 1983. EDUCATION: Wellesley College three years; studied with Uta Hagen.

CAREER: DEBUT—Pauline, *White Marriage,* Yale Repertory Company, New Haven, CT, 1978. NEW YORK DEBUT—Lolita, *Lolita,* Brooks Atkinson, 1981. PRINCIPAL STAGE

BLANCHE BAKER

APPEARANCES—Hedvig, *The Wild Duck*, Yale Repertory, 1979; Laura, *The Glass Menagerie*, Berkshire Theatre Festival, 1980; Claire, *Poor Little Lambs*, 1982; Hannah, *Hannah*, 1983; Young Playwrights Festival, Circle Repertory, 1983; Salome, *Salome*, 1983.

PRINCIPAL FILM APPEARANCES—Janet, *The Seduction of Joe Tynan*, 1978; Laura, *French Postcards*, 1979; Leslie, *Cold Feet*, 1983; Ginny, *Sixteen Candles*, 1983. TELEVISION DEBUT—Anna Weiss, *The Holocaust*, 1977. PRINCIPAL TELEVISION APPEARANCES—Mary, *Mary and Joseph*, 1979; Jolan, *The Day the Bubble Burst*, 1980; Juliet, *Romeo and Juliet*, 1982; Candra, *The Awakening of Candra*, 1982.

AWARDS: Emmy Award, Best Supporting Actress in a Limited Series, *The Holocaust*, 1978; Woman of Achievement Award, Anti-Defamation League, 1978.

SIDELIGHTS: Miss Baker grew up in Italy and Switzerland and speaks French and Italian.

ADDRESS: Agent—Myrna Jacoby, c/o The William Morris Agency, 1350 Ave. of the Americas, New York, NY 10019.

* * *

BAKER, Carroll, actress, writer

PERSONAL: Born May 28, 1931, in Johnstown, PA; daughter of William and Virginia Baker; married Jack Garfein (a director, producer) April 5, 1955 (divorced 1969); married Donald G. Burton (a British actor), March 10, 1982; children: (first marriage) Herschel David, Blanche Baker (an actress); EDUCATION: Studied for the theatre at the Actor's Studio.

CAREER: DEBUT—Magician, *Kemp Time Vaudeville Circuit*, North Carolina. NEW YORK DEBUT—leading role, *All Summer Long*. LONDON DEBUT—Lucy, *Lucy Crown*. PRINCIPAL STAGE APPEARANCES—Lead, *Come On Strong*, New York, 1962; lead, *27 Wagons Full of Cotton*, London; *Motive;* Sadie Thompson, *Rain*, London.

CARROLL BAKER

FILM DEBUT—Title role, *Baby Doll*, 1956. PRINCIPAL FILMS—*Giant*, 1956; *The Big Country*, 1958; *But Not for Me*, 1959; *Bridge to the Sun*, 1960; *Something Wild*, 1962; *Station Six Sahara*, 1963; *The Carpetbaggers*, 1964; *Jean Harlow, Harlow*, 1965; *How the West Was Won*, 1963; *Cheyenne Autumn*, 1964; *Sylvia*, 1965; *Mister Moses*, 1965; *Jack of Diamonds*, 1967; *The Sweet Body of Deborah*, 1968; *Captain Apache*, 1971; *Andy Warhol's "Bad"*, 1977; *Watcher in the Woods*, 1980; *Red Monarch*, 1983; *Star 80*, 1983; *The Secret Diary of Sigmund Freud*, 1983; several dozen foreign films made in the years between 1968 and 1982. TELEVISION DEBUT—in commercials during the 1950's. TELEVISION APPEARANCES—Sadie Thompson, *Rain*, BBC.

WRITINGS: Books—*Baby Doll*, an autobiography, 1983.

AWARDS: Academy Award Nomination, *Baby Doll*, 1956.

SIDELIGHTS: In her early years Miss Baker worked as a nightclub girl, a specialty dancer, and a sleight-of-hand magician.

ADDRESS: Agent—I.C.M., 40 W. 57th Street, New York, NY 10019.

BAKER, Paul, director, producer, manager, educator

PERSONAL: Born July 24, 1911 in Hereford, TX; son of William Morgan (a minister) and Retta C. (Chapman) Baker; married Sallie Kathryn Cardwell (a mathematician) on December 21, 1936; children: Robyn, Retta, Sallie. EDUCATION: Attended University of Wisconsin; Trinity University, B.A. 1932; Yale University, School of Drama, M.F.A. 1939; studied with Elsie Fogarty at the Central School of Speech, London, England, 1932; studied and observed theatre in England, Germany, Russia, Manchuria, Korea, and Japan, 1936. POLITICS: Liberal. RELIGION: Presbyterian. MILITARY: U.S. Army, Major, Chief of Entertainment Branch, ETO, WWII, 1943–45.

CAREER: PRINCIPAL STAGE WORK, DIRECTED—*Othello*, Baylor University, 1953; *A Different Drummer*, Baylor University (and for CBS TV) 1955–56; *Journey to Jefferson*, Théâtre des Nations, Paris, France, 1964.

PRINCIPAL STAGE WORK, PRODUCED—Founder/Artistic Director/Managing Director, The Dallas Theatre Center, 1959–81, directed/produced 435 plays including: *Of Time and the River, The Cross-Eyed Bear, Our Town, The Matchmaker, Waltz in the Afternoon, The Visit, Joshua Bean and God, The Crossing, Naked to Mine Enemies, Journey to Jefferson, Hamlet ESP, Macbeth, The Homecoming, Jack Ruby, All-American Boy; The Texas Trilogy*.

THEATRE-RELATED CAREER: Chairman, Department of Drama, Baylor University, 1934–63; Chairman, Department of Speech and Drama, Trinity University, 1964–76; Theatre Design/Construction, Theatre inside Waco Hall, Baylor University, 1939, Studio I Theatre, Baylor University, 1942, Weston Theatre addition, Baylor Theatre, Baylor University, 1954, consultant, Taylor Theatre, Trinity University.

WRITINGS: PLAYS, PUBLISHED—*Hamlet ESP; Jack Ruby, All-American Boy*, (co-author); BOOKS—*Integration of Abilities; Exercises for Creative Growth*.

AWARDS: San Diego National Shakespeare Festival Award, for Outstanding Contribution to Classic Theatre, 1974; Margo Jones Award for "daring and continuous new play production," 1968; Special Jury Award, Théâtre des Nations, Paris, France, 1964; the first Rodgers and Hammerstein Award for theatrical contribution in the Southwest, 1961; Rockefeller Foundation Study Grant, for study of leisure-time problems as related to the community, 1959; Honorary Doctor of Fine Arts Degree, Trinity University, 1958; a prize at the Brussels World Fair Film Festival for the best short-run fiction film, 1958; The Chris Award (with Eugene McKinney) for production of Baylor University's *Hamlet*, 1957; Rockefeller Foundation Study Grants, to write on his war experiences, 1946, for Baylor Theatre, 1941, for study at Yale University.

SIDELIGHTS: MEMBERSHIPS—Texas Fine Arts Commission, 1967–68, Ad Hoc Committee, Professional-Educational Theatre Relationships; Board of Governors, American Playwrights Theatre; N.T.C.; Southwestern Theatre Conference.

"I firmly believe that American resident theatres should have graduate schools as a vital part of their operations." Mr. Baker founded Dallas Theatre Center with company and school.

ADDRESS: Home—R.F.D. 1 Box 181, Waelder, TX 78959.

* * *

BAKER, Raymond, actor

PERSONAL: Born July 9, 1948, in Omaha, NE; son of Henry L. (a contractor) and Audrey (Peart) Baker; married Avis Alexander, June 7, 1970 (divorced 1978); married Patricia Richardson (an actress), June 20, 1982. EDUCATION: University of Denver, B.A., 1970; studied acting with Stephen Strimpel.

CAREER: DEBUT—Van Dyke Vernon, *The Virginian*, Bob Young's Cabaret, Cascade, CO, 1968. NEW YORK DEBUT—Improvisational actor, *The Proposition*, Mercer Arts Center, 1972, more than 360 performances. PRINCIPAL STAGE APPEARANCES—Larry Parks, *Are You Now . . . ?*, Promenade, New York, 1977–78; Henry, *Swing*, Kennedy Center, Washington, 1979; Doc Porter, *Crimes of the Heart*, Golden, New York, 1981; Barry Austin, *Is There Life After High School?*, Barrymore, New York, 1982; John Landis, *Fifth of July*, Cincinnati Playhouse, 1983.

FILM DEBUT—Marty, *Gloria*, 1980. PRINCIPAL FILMS—Lt. Raymond Johnson, *The Line*, 1982; Pete Dawson, *Silkwood*, 1983. TELEVISION DEBUT—*Easy Does It*, 1976. TELEVISION APPEARANCES—James Roosevelt, *Eleanor and Franklin: The White House Years*, 1977; *Neighborhood*, 1980; *Dream House*, 1982.

RAYMOND BAKER

ADDRESS: Agent—c/o DHKPR, 165 W. 46th Street, New York, NY 10036

* * *

BAKER, Word (ne Charles William), director, dancer, choreographer, producer

PERSONAL: Born March 21, 1923, in Honey Grove, TX; son of Dan (a druggist) and Maggie (a music teacher; maiden name, Word) Baker; married Joanna Alexander, October 24, 1942; children: three daughters. EDUCATION: North Texas State University, 1940–42; University of Texas, B.F.A., 1951. MILITARY: U.S. Army, 1942–48 (three years anti-aircraft artillery; S/Sgt) 1946–48. NON-THEATRICAL CAREER: Bookkeeper.

CAREER: DEBUT—Lear (at age nine), King Lear, School Production, Honey Grove, Texas, 1932. NEW YORK DEBUT—(as designer) The Admirable Bashville and The Dark Lady of the Sonnets, ELT Production at Lenox Hill Playhouse, 1956; (as director) The Crucible, Martinique, 1958. LONDON DEBUT—(as director) The Fantasticks, Apollo, 1961. PRINCIPAL STAGE WORK: Director (w/Julius Monk), Demi-Dozen, Upstairs-at-the-Downstairs, New York, 1958; director, choreographer, Ride a Pink Horse, Crest, Toronto, 1959; director, The Mall, The Gay Apprentice, The Fantasticks, Minor Latham, New York, 1959; director, Pieces of Eight, Upstairs-at-the Downstairs, 1959; director, The Fantastics, Sullivan Street Playhouse, New York, 1960; director, The Tragickal History of Doctor Faustus, Phoenix Theatre Co., East 74th Playhouse, New York, 1961; director, As You Like It, American Shakespeare Festival, Stratford, CT, 1961; director and choreographer, Guys and Dolls, Bradford, Boston, 1962; director and choreographer, Maggie, Paper Mill Playhouse, Millburn, NJ and Westport Country Playhouse, Westport, CT, 1962; directed The American Dream, Rosemary, Ginger Man, The Exhaustion of Our Son's Love, Festival of Two Worlds, Spoleto, Italy, 1962; director, The Pinter Plays, Writers' Stage, New York, 1964; director, Now Is the Time for All Good Men, Theatre de Lys, New York, 1966; director, The Last Sweet Days of Isaac, East 74th Street Theatre, New York, 1970; director and producer, Word Baker's Cabaret Repertory Company in Ragtime & Romance, Once-Upon-a-Stove, New York, 1978; director, I'm Getting My Act Together and Taking It on the Road, New York Shakespeare Festival and Circle-in-the-Square, New York, 1978; director, Pump Boys and Dinettes, 1981; director (w/Rod Kates), R.S.V.P., Theatre East, New York, 1982; director, Booth! Is Back in Town, Pepsico Summerfare, 1983; director (w/Rod Kates), The Amorous Flea (musical), Fairmont Theatre of the Deaf, Cleveland, 1983.

Artistic director, Playhouse-in-the-Park, Cincinnati for two years: directed As Your Like It (all-male version); Caravaggio; Kiss Me, Kate; Lady Audley's Secret; Many Happy Returns—a ReView of Revues; Our Town; Pygmalion; Sensations of the Bitten Partner; The Crucible; The Miser; The Play's the Thing; The Rivals; Shelter; Tobacco Road; produced A Midsummer Morning's Madness; Angel Street; Jacques Brel Is Alive and Well. . . ; Life with Father; Rain; School for Wives; Slow Dance on a Killing Ground; The Blacks; The Innocents; Why Hannah's Skirt Won't Stay Down. Also directed A Comedy of Errors, Milwaukee Rep;

For the Use of the Hall, Jumpers, Lady Audley's Secret, Two Gentlemen of Verona for Trinity Square Repertory Company; The Matchmaker, Seattle Repertory; Medicine Show and The Importance of Being Earnest, Phoenix Little Theatre; The Odd Couple, Pittsburgh Playhouse; The Great American Backstage Musical, Goodspeed Opera House, East Haddam, CT; Mme. Mousse, in stock; Leonard Bernstein's Mass, Cincinnati Symphony's May Festival; Your Basic AllStar Ragtime, Romance, BeBop & Blues Revue in stock; Ingrid & Isaac, and Mme De. . ., Pepsico Summerfare, 1980; workshop productions of Stormin' Norman & Suzy, Red, Hot & Cole, and Cowboy; various regional productions of The Fantasticks and college productions of A Little Night Music; Celebration; Doctor Faustus; Edward II; Mother Courage; and The Golden Apple. As a designer, created sets for productions of Anna Lucasta, No Time for Comedy, Oh, Men, Oh, Women, Sabrina Fair; and costumes for productions of Liliom, The Admirable Bashville, and The Dark Lady of the Sonnets. Assistant stage manager, Happy Hunting, Majestic, New York, 1956.

PRINCIPAL FILM WORK—sixty films designed by Jo Mielziner, A.T.&.T. Pavilion/New York World's Fair, 1964–65. PRINCIPAL TELEVISION WORK—director, The Grass Harp, Play-of-the-Week, 1960; director, New York Scrapbook, Play-of-the-Week, 1961.

AWARDS: Obie, Best Director, The Crucible, 1958; Obie, Best Director, The Pinter Plays, 1964; Obie, Best Director, The Last Sweet Days of Isaac, 1970; Ford Foundation Grant.

SIDELIGHTS: MEMBERSHIPS—S.S.D.&C., A.E.A.

ADDRESS: Home—333 W. 56th Street, New York, NY 10019. Agent—Lucy Baker, S.T.E. Representation, Ltd., 888 Seventh Ave., New York, NY 10106.

* * *

BALABAN, Bob, actor

PERSONAL: Born August 16, 1945, in Chicago, IL; son of Elmer (communications) and Eleanor (Pottasch) Balaban; married Lynn Grossman (a writer), April 1, 1977; children: Mariah. EDUCATION: New York University, B.A.; trained for the stage with Uta Hagen and Viola Spolin.

CAREER: NEW YORK DEBUT—Linus, You're a Good Man Charlie Brown, Theatre 80, 1968. PRINCIPAL STAGE APPEARANCES—Pavlo, The Basic Training of Pavlo Hummel, New York Shakespeare Festival, 1980; The Three Sisters, Manhattan Theatre Club, NY, 1983.

FILM DEBUT—Midnight Cowboy, 1972. PRINCIPAL FILM APPEARANCES—Catch 22; Close Encounters of the Third Kind; Altered States; Prince of the City; Absence of Malice; 2010; Whose Life Is It Anyway? TELEVISION DEBUT—Mod Squad.

WRITINGS: BOOKS—CE3K Diary, 1977.

AWARDS: Antoinette Perry Award Nomination: The Government Inspector.

SIDELIGHTS: MEMBERSHIPS—Astoria Foundation (board of directors).

ADDRESS: Agent—c/o D.H.K.P.R., 165 W. 46th Street, New York, NY 10036.

* * *

BALLARD, Kaye (nee Catherine Gloria Balotta), actress, singer

PERSONAL: Born November 20, 1926, in Cleveland, OH; daughter of Vincent and Lena (Nacarato) Balotta.

CAREER: DEBUT—*Stage Door Canteen,* USO production, Cleveland, OH, 1941. NEW YORK DEBUT—*Three to Make Ready,* vaudeville revue, Aldelphi, 1946. LONDON DEBUT—*Touch and Go,* revue, Prince of Wales's, 1950. PRINCIPAL STAGE APPEARANCES—Vaudeville RKO circuit, 1943; *That's the Ticket,* Shubert Philadelphia, 1948; Helen of Troy, *The Golden Apple,* Phoenix, NY, 1954; Countess, *Reuben, Reuben,* Shubert, Boston, 1955; *The Ziegfeld Follies,* Royal Alexandra, Toronto, Canada, 1957; the Incomparable Rosalie, *Carnival,* Imperial, NY, 1961; Rose, *Gypsy,* State Fair Music Hall, Dallas, TX, 1962; Ruth, *Wonderful Town,* City Center, NY, 1963; *The Beast in Me,* Plymouth, NY, 1963; *The Decline and Fall of the Entire World as Seen Through the Eyes of Cole Porter Revisited,* Square East, 1965; cabaret performance, Mister Kelly's, Chicago, 1972; cabaret performance, St. Regis, NY, 1973; Molly Goldberg, *Molly,* Alvin,

NY, 1973; Lola Delaney, *Sheba,* First Chicago Center, 1974; cabaret performance, Hyatt Regency, Chicago, 1975; *I'll Stake My Life,* Crystal Palace, Dallas, TX, 1975; cabaret performance, Persian Room, Plaza Hotel, NY, 1975–76; Ruth, *The Pirates of Penzance,* Uris, NY, 1981; *Hey Ma. . . ,* Promenade, NY, 1984.

FILM DEBUT—*The Girl Most Likely,* 1956. PRINCIPAL FILM APPEARANCES—*A House Is Not a Home,* 1964; *The Ritz,* 1976; *Freaky Friday,* 1977; *In Love Again.*

TELEVISION DEBUT—*The Mel Torme Show,* 1952. PRINCIPAL TELEVISION APPEARANCES—*The Jack Paar Show; The Johnny Carson Show; Perry Como* shows; *The Mothers-in-Law; Hollywood Squares; The Jerry Lewis Show; The Steve Allen Show; The Doris Day Show; Dinah; Merv Griffin Show; The Montefuscos; The Patty Duke Show; Love American Style; Police Story; What's My Line; Alice; The Muppet Show; Love Boat; Fantasy Island; Hello Kaye Ballard, Welcome to Las Vegas.*

AWARDS: The Italian American award; Dallas State Fair Award: *Gypsy.*

SIDELIGHTS: MEMBERSHIPS—SAG, AEA, AFTRA, AGVA.

ADDRESS: Agent—c/o Roy Gerber, 9200 Sunset Blvd., Suite 620, Los Angeles, CA 90069.*

* * *

BANCROFT, Anne (nee Italiano), actress

PERSONAL: Born September, 17, 1931, in the Bronx, NY; daughter of Michael and Mildred (DiNapoli) Italiano; married Martin A May (divorced); Mel Brooks (writer, producer, director), 1964; children: one son. EDUCATION: Studied at the Actor's Studio and at the American Academy of Dramatic Arts.

CAREER: NEW YORK DEBUT—Gittel Mosca, *Two for the Seesaw,* Booth, 1958. PRINCIPAL STAGE APPEARANCES—Annie Sullivan, *The Miracle Worker,* Playhouse, NY, 1959; title-role, *Mother Courage and Her Children,* Martin Beck, NY, 1963; Prioress, *The Devils,* Broadway, NY, 1965; Regina Giddens, *The Little Foxes,* Vivian Beaumont, NY, 1967; Anne, *A Cry of Players,* Vivian Beaumont, NY, 1968; Golda Meir, *Golda,* Morosco, NY, 1977; *Duet for One,* Royale, NY, 1981.

FILM DEBUT—*Don't Bother to Knock,* 1952. PRINCIPAL FILM APPEARANCES—*Tonight We Sing; Treasure of the Golden Condor,* 1953; *Kid from Left Field; Demitrius and the Gladiators,* 1954; *Gorilla at Large,* 1954; *The Raid,* 1954; *Life in the Balance; New York Confidential,* 1955; *The Brass Ring; Naked Street,* 1955; *Last Frontier,* 1955; *Nightfall,* 1956; *Walk the Proud Land,* 1956; *Girl in the Black Stockings,* 1957; *Restless Breed,* 1957; Annie Sullivan, *The Miracle Worker,* 1962; *The Pumpkin Eater,* 1964; *Slender Thread,* 1966; *Seven Women,* 1966; Mrs. Robinson, *The Graduate,* 1967; Jennie Churchill, *Young Winston,* 1972; *Prisoner of Second Avenue,* 1975; *The Hindenburg,* 1975; *Silent Movie,* 1976; *The Turning Point,* 1977; *Fatso* (also director and writer), 1980; *The Elephant Man,* 1980; *To Be or Not to Be,* 1983.

KAYE BALLARD

ANNE BANCROFT

TELEVISION DEBUT—Anne Marno, *The Goldbergs,* 1950. PRINCIPAL TELEVISION APPEARANCES—*Danger; Suspense; Philco-Goodyear Playhouse; Perry Como Show; Bob Hope Show; Tom Jones Show; Kraft Music Hall;* special, *Annie— The Woman in the Life of Men,* 1970.

AWARDS: Emmy Award, *Annie—The Woman in the Life of Men,* 1970; Academy Award, Best Actress, *The Miracle Worker,* 1962; Antoinette Perry Award, *The Miracle Worker,* 1959; New York Drama Critics Award, Best Performance by a Straight Actress, *The Miracle Worker,* 1959; Antoinette Perry Award, Gittel Mosca, *Two for the Seesaw,* 1958.

ADDRESS: c/o Twentieth Century Fox, P.O. Box 900, Beverly Hills, CA 90213.*

* * *

BANTRY, Bryan, producer

PERSONAL: Born October 12, 1956 in Florida. EDUCATION: Professional Children's School and the Browning School, New York City. NON-THEATRICAL CAREER: Artist representative, fashion photographers, hair and make-up artists, New York, 1973–present; personality editor, Italian *Harpers Bazaar, Mens Bazaar,* and French *Harpers Bazaar,* 1980– present.

CAREER: FIRST STAGE WORK—Co-Produced, *Greater Tuna,* Off-Broadway, 1983. PRINCIPAL STAGE WORK—Co-Producer, *You Can't Take It with You,* Plymouth, New York, 1983; *Hey Ma. . .,* Promenade, New York, 1984. MAJOR TOURS— *Greater Tuna,* scheduled national tours, 1984.

SIDELIGHTS: MEMBERSHIPS—League of New York Theatres and Producers.

''Committed along with co-producer Karl Allison to change royalty and profit participation structures to benefit investors thereby attracting more of them as a step toward changing the viewpoint of theatre as the worst investment.'' Mr. Bantry is one of the subjects chronicled in a new publication, *Young, Gifted and Rich: The Secrets of America's Youngest Entrepreneurs,* to be published by Simon & Schuster, 1984.

ADDRESS: Office—105 W. 55th Street, New York, NY 10019.

* * *

BARANSKI, Christine, actress

PERSONAL: Born May 2, 1952; daughter of Lucien and Virginia (Mazerowski) Baranski; married Matthew Cowles (an actor) on October 15, 1983. EDUCATION: Julliard School, B.A., 1974.

CAREER: DEBUT—Annabella, *'Tis Pity She's a Whore,*

CHRISTINE BARANSKI

McCarter, Princeton, NJ. NEW YORK DEBUT—*Hide and Seek.*

PRINCIPAL STAGE APPEARANCES—*The Real Thing*, NY; Lady Capulet, *Romeo and Juliet*, American Shakespeare Festival, Stratford, CT; Maggie, *Cat on a Hot Tin Roof*, American Shakespeare Festival; Center Stage Company, Baltimore, MD—Constance, *She Stoops to Conquer*, Dunyasha, *The Cherry Orchard*, Lina, *Misalliance*, Dorine, *Tartuffe*, Billie Dawn, *Born Yesterday;* Miss Scoons, *Angel City*, McCarter; Elvira, *Blithe Spirit*, McCarter; *Coming Attractions*, Playwrights Horizons, NY; Miss Harris, *The Undefeated Rumba Champ*, Ensemble Studio Theatre, NY; Marsha, *Sally and Marsha*, Manhattan Theatre Club, NY; *Sunday in the Park with George*, Playwrights Horizons; Helena, *A Midsummer Night's Dream*, New York Shakespeare Festival. MAJOR TOURS—Davina Saunders, *Otherwise Engaged*, National Tour.

FILM DEBUT—*Soup for One*, 1981. PRINCIPAL FILM APPEARANCES—*Crackers; Lovesick.* TELEVISION DEBUT—*The Adams Chronicles.* PRINCIPAL TELEVISION APPEARANCES—*Playing for Time; Murder Ink; All My Children; Texas; Another World.*

AWARDS: Obie, Helena, *A Midsummer Night's Dream*, New York Shakespeare Festival, 1983.

ADDRESS: Agent—Paul Doherty, Schumer-Oubre, 1697 Broadway, New York, NY 10019

* * *

BARBER, John, critic

PERSONAL: Son of Herbert and May (Skinner) Barber; married Roshan Mirza (divorced); married Kathleen Mary Annis; children: Stephen, Anna, Paul, Philippa. EDUCATION: King Edward's School, Birmingham, England; Birmingham University; Merton College Oxford, M.A.

WRITINGS: DRAMA CRITIC, *Oxford Mail; Daily Express*, 1950–59, *Daily Telegraph*, 1968–present. SCRIPT EDITOR, Metro-Goldwyn-Mayer and Arthur Rank Studios. Editor, *Leader* Magazine. STORY EDITOR, BBC, 1964–68. Literary agent, 1959–64.

SIDELIGHTS: RECREATIONS—Music, photography.

ADDRESS: Office—c/o *Daily Telegraph*, 135 Fleet Street, London, EC4, England.

* * *

BARBERA, Joseph R., cartoonist, manager

PERSONAL: Born March 24, in New York City; son of Vincente and Frances Barbera; married Sheila Holden; children: Lynn Meredith, Jayne Earl, Neal Francis. EDUCATION: American Institute of Banking, Pratt Institute, Art Students League and New York University.

CAREER: FIRST FILM WORK—General animation for MGM studios. PRINCIPAL FILM WORK—Producer/cartoonist: with William Hanna created the *Tom and Jerry* Cartoons for MGM, *Puss Gets the Boot*, 1938; creator/co-producer, feature, *Tom & Jerry*, 1957; *Charlotte's Web*, 1973; *Heidi's Song*, 1981; *The Gathering, Parts I and II*, 1979.

PRINCIPAL TELEVISION WORK—Creator/co-producer: *Huckleberry Hound; Yogi Bear; The Flintstones; The Jetsons; Scooby-Doo; The Last of the Curlews; Wait till Your Father Gets Home; The Smurfs.*

RELATED-CAREER: Sketch artist for Van Buren Associates, NYC. President, Hanna-Barbera Productions, 27 years.

AWARDS: Seven Academy Awards for *Tom & Jerry Cartoons;* Christopher Award, 1978; Annie Award, 1978: *Charlotte's Web;* Emmy Award, 1977; Golden Globe, *The Flintstones.*

SIDELIGHTS: MEMBERSHIPS—Academy of Television Arts and Sciences; president, Board of Directors, Huntington-Hartford Theatre; president, Greek Theatre Association; president, Southern California Theatre Association; advisory board, St. Joseph's Medical Center; president, Visitors and Convention Bureau; advisory board, Children's Village; honorary board, Wildlife Waystation.

''Mr. Barbera began cartooning at Terrytoons for 1½ years and then went to New York to work as a sketch artist in the animation department of MGM where he met William Hanna, his life long partner to be. Together they created the Oscar-winning *Tom and Jerry* theatricals and formed their own studio in 1957, Hanna-Barbera Productions, the world's largest animated cartoon studio.''

ADDRESS: Office—3400 Cahuenga Blvd. Hollywood, CA 90068.

* * *

BARNES, Fran (nee Stridinger), actress

PERSONAL: Born February 24, 1931 in Windber, PA; daughter of Fred and Frieda (Kolak) Stridinger; married Robert C. Barnes (a stage designer and associate professor at Florida State University) on April 20, 1958; children: Laura, Jeffery. EDUCATION: Pennsylvania State University, B.A.; studied with Lee Grant at the Herbert Berghof Studios in New York; studied with Richard Edelman. RELIGION: Roman Catholic.

CAREER: NEW YORK DEBUT—Standby, *The Waltz of the Toreadors*, 1958. PRINCIPAL STAGE APPEARANCES—Mrs. Marchmont, *An Ideal Husband*, Royal Playhouse, NY, 1956; Miss Shotgraven, *Solid Gold Cadillac*, Sacandaga, NY, 1956; Poncia, *House of Bernarda Alba*, Pennsylvania Stage Festival, 1971; Regina, *The Little Foxes*, Jennerstown Playhouse, PA, 1972; Angela, *Angela*, Jennerstown Playhouse, 1972; Golde, *Fiddler on the Roof*, Jennerstown Playhouse, 1972; Meg Hardy, *Damn Yankees*, Pennsylvania Stage Festival, 1972; Mother Hare, *The Golden Apple*, Pennsylvania Stage Festival, 1973; Pat Nixon, *Knight Errant*, Intar, NY, 1982; standby, Helen Gallagher, *Tallu-*

lah, TOMI, NY, 1983; Megan Wells/Maxine Stewart, *84 Charing Cross Road*, Westport Country Playhouse, 1983. MAJOR TOURS—*Waltz of the Toreadors*, 1957.

SIDELIGHTS: FAVORITE ROLE—Blanche Dubois in *A Streetcar Named Desire*. RECREATION—piano. Mrs Barnes' husband, Robert, designed the first Off-Off-Broadway theater in Greenwich Village at what is now the Bleeker Street Cinema.

ADDRESS: Home—450 W. 55th Street, New York, NY 10019. Agent—Sheldon R. Lubliner, c/o News & Entertainment Corp., 230 W. 55th Street, New York, NY 10019.

* * *

BARNEY, Jay (ne John Bernhardt Vander Kleine Schmide), actor

PERSONAL: Born March 14, in Chicago, IL; son of Edwin Walter (a businessman) and Evelyn (a pianist and lecturer; maiden name, Stowell) Schmide. EDUCATION: University of Chicago, B.S., 1938; trained for the stage at the American Theatre Wing with Lee Strasberg and Martin Ritt. MILITARY: U.S. Army, 1941–47.

CAREER: STAGE DEBUT—Director, *Merton of the Movies*, Maywood, IL. NEW YORK DEBUT—Inspector Warren, *Many Mansions*, 44th Street Theater, 1937–38, 110 performances. PRINCIPAL STAGE APPEARANCES—Al, *On Borrowed Time*, Longacre, NY, 1938; Father Chu, *Flight into China*, Dr. Levine, *Men in White*, Paper Mill Playhouse, NJ, 1939; Jason, *Jason*, Equity Library, Hudson Park, NY, 1945; Wellborne, *A New Way to Pay Old Debts*, Equity Library, NY, 1945; Rector, *Land's End*, Playhouse, NY, 1946; Tremoille, *Joan of Lorraine*, Ridgefield Playhouse, NJ, 1947; Dr. Cobb, *Shining Threshold*, Falmouth Playhouse, MA, 1947; Cardinal Borgia/Cesare, *Lamp at Midnight*, New Stages, NY, 1947; Reverend Morrell, *Candida*, Equity Library, Lenox Hill Playhouse, NY, 1948; lynch mob leader, *The Respectful Prostitute*, Pa Kirby, *The Happy Journey to Trenton and Camden*, Cort, NY, 1948; Dock, *Hope is the Thing with Feathers*, Cort, NY, 1948; bride's father, *Blood Wedding*, New Stages, NY, 1949; Albert, *Brooklyn, U.S.A.*, Equity Library, Lenox Hill Playhouse, NY, 1949; Bassanio, *The Merchant of Venice*, Equity Library, Lenox Hill Playhouse, NY, 1949; Georgie Porgie, *Don't Go Away Mad*, Master, NY, 1949; Hasdrubal, *The Road to Rome*, Equity Library, Lenox Hill Playhouse, NY, 1951; Franklin, *Southern Wild*, New Stages, NY, 1951; Si, *The Number*, Biltmore, NY, 1951; Postmaster, *The Grass Harp*, Martin Beck, NY, 1952; Dr. Schiller, *The World We Make*, Equity Library, NY, 1952; Judge Cool, *The Grass Harp*, Circle in the Square, NY, 1953; Odysseus, *Death of Odysseus*, Artists and Poets, Amato Theater, NY, 1953; Major, *Stockade*, President, NY, 1954; Michel, *The Immoralist*, Royale, NY, 1954; Anthony, *The Homeward Look*, Theater de Lys, NY, 1954; York, *Henry IV*, Shakespearewrights, NY, 1955; Masters, *Joan of Lorraine*, Equity Library, Lenox Hill Playhouse, NY, 1955; Titorelli, *The Trial*, Provincetown Playhouse, NY, 1955; Mr. Perry, *The Young and the Beautiful*, Longacre, NY, 1955; Professor Sonnenstitch, *Spring's Awakening*, Provincetown Playhouse, NY, 1955.

Robert Acton, *Eugenia*, Ambassador, NY, 1957; Jackson

Thorpe, *Sign of Winter*, Theater 74, NY, 1958; Walter Burns, *The Front Page*, Equity Library, NY, 1961; Reverdy Johnson, *The Story of Mary Surratt*, Equity Library, Lenox Hill Playhouse, NY, 1961; Hiram Griswold, *The Anvil*, Maidman, NY, 1962; Franz, *The Sound of Music*, Lunt-Fontanne, NY, 1964; Reverend Plap, *Blastoma City*, One Sheridan Square Theater, NY, 1964; Mayor Crane, *Never Too Late*, Playhouse, NY, 1962; Claude Dancer, *Anatomy of a Murder*, Mill Run Playhouse, Niles, IL, 1965; Miller, *Enemies*, Theater East, NY, 1965; George Masters, Jr., *The Parasite*, Renate, NY, 1965; Mayor Muller, *Beyond Desire*, Theater Four, NY, 1967; Charlie Danvers, *A Certain Young Man*, Stage 73, NY, 1967; Administrator, *Goa*, Martinique, NY, 1968; Mr. Mittleman, *The Fig Leaves Are Falling*, Broadhurst, NY, 1969; Angel Rodrigues, *All the Girls Came Out to Play*, Cort, NY, 1972; Norman Thayer, *On Golden Pond*, tour.

FILM DEBUT—*711 Ocean Drive*, 1950. PRINCIPAL FILM APPEARANCES—*The Killer That Stalked New York*, 1950; *Convicted*, 1950; *Visa*, 1950; *Spy Hunt*, 1950; *The Fuller Brush Girl*, 1950; *Wyoming Mail*, 1950; *The Return of Jesse James*, 1950; *The Jackpot*, 1950; *Battle Taxi*, 1955; *The Shrike*, 1955; *Mister Rock and Roll*, 1957; *The Big Fisherman*, 1959; *Blueprint for Murder*, 1961.

PRINCIPAL TELEVISION APPEARANCES—*You Be the Jury*, 1949; *Your Witness*, 1950; *Armchair Detective*, 1950; *Ed Wynn Show*, 1950; *My Heart's in the Highlands*, 1950; *State's Attorney*, 1950; *Big Town*, 1950, 1951, 1958; *Hands of Mystery*, 1950; *Billy Rose Show*, 1950; *Macbeth*, 1950; *Plainclothesman*, 1950; *Pilgrim's Progress*, 1950; *Casey, Crime Photographer*, 1951; *Treasury Men in Action*, 1951, 1952; *The Moon and Sixpence*, 1951; *The Greatest Story Ever Told*, 1951; *Armstrong Circle Theater*, "Rodeo," 1951; *Shadow of the Clock*, 1951; *Assignment Manhunt*, 1951; *Police Story*, 1951; *A Date with Judy*, 1951, 1952, 1953; *Rogue's Gallery*, 1951; *Nero Wolfe*, 1951; *Captain Video*, 1951, 1952, 1953, 1954;

Kraft Television Theater, "John Wilkes Booth," 1951; *Madame Liu-Tsong*, 1951; *Studio One*, "Signal 32," 1951; *Flying Tigers*, 1951; *Cameo Theater*, 1952; *Danger*, 1952, 1953; *Suspense*, "Paper Box Kid," 1952; *Crime Syndicated*, 1952; *The Fix*, 1952; *Lamp Unto My Feet*, 1952, 1953, 1954; *The Web*, 1952; *Studio One*, 1952, 1953; *You Are There*, 1953, 1954; *Martin Kane*, 1953; *City Hospital*, 1953; *Johnny Jupiter*, 1953; *Rookie Cop*, 1953; *Revlon Theater*, 1953; *Inner Sanctum*, "Parakeet," 1953; *Doorway to Danger*, 1953; *Kate Smith Show*, 1953; *Philip Morris Playhouse*, 1953; *Sound Stage*, 1953; *Hallmark Hall of Fame*, "John Paul Jones, 1954; *Omnibus*, "Saint Joan," 1955; *Mama*, 1955; *Omnibus*, "The Adams Family," 1955; *Omnibus*, "The Trial of Billy Mitchell," 1956; *Valiant Lady*, 1956; *U.S. Steel Hour*, "Honest in the Rain," 1956; *Ethel and Albert*, 1956; *Robert Montgomery Presents*, "The Janitor," 1956; *Alcoa Presents*, "Election Returns," 1956; *Soldier from the Wars Returning*, 1956; *Frontiers of Faith*, 1957; *Brighter Day*, 1958; *Search for Tomorrow*, 1958; *Love of Life*, 1958; *Ed Sullivan Show*, 1958; *Armstrong Circle Theater*, "Kidnap: Hold for Release," 1958; *New York Confidential*, 1958; *Edge of Night*, 1958; *Ellery Queen*, 1958; *Armstrong Circle Theater*, "Sound of Violence," 1959; *Dupont Show of the Month*, "Body and Soul," 1959; *Armstrong Circle Theater*, "Boy on Page One," 1959;

As the World Turns, 1960; *American Heritage*, "Gentlemen's Agreement," 1961; *American Heritage*, "Andrew Carnegie Story*,*" 1960; *Search for Tomorrow*, 1961; *Lonely Woman*, 1961; *Perry Mason*, 1962, 1964, 1965; *Car 54, Where Are You?*, 1962; *Dupont Show of the Month*, "Mutiny," 1962; *Secret Storm*, 1962–64.

PRINCIPAL RADIO APPEARANCES—*Theater Guild of the Air; Treasury Hour; The March of Time; School of the Air; The Falcon; Believe It or Not; Michael Shayne; Rosemary; House of Glass; Ma Perkins; Inheritance; Doctor's Wife; The Eternal Light; The Romance of Helen Trent; Ave Maria Hour; Five Star Final; True Confessions; The Couple Next Door; My True Story; Voice of America*, "Birthright," "Our Town," "Ethan Frome," "Mr. Roberts," "Beyond the Horizon," "Abe Lincoln in Illinois," "The Heiress."

PRODUCED/DIRECTED: Films—U.S. Army Signal Corps Training Films, 1941–47.

AWARDS: Academy Award Nomination, Best Documentary, 1957: *Shades of Gray;* First Prize Award, International Venice Film Festival, 1947: *Schistosomiasis* (Snail Fever).

SIDELIGHTS: MEMBERSHIPS—AEA, SAG, AFTRA, New Stages, Actors Studio. RECREATION—Reading, scooter riding.

ADDRESS: Agent—c/o Marvin Starkman, 1500 Broadway, New York, NY 10036.

* * *

BARRS, Norman, actor, director

PERSONAL: Born November 6, 1917; son of Percy (a chemist, optician, and magician) Barrs; EDUCATION: Cambridge University, B.A., 1938.

CAREER: DEBUT—Morell, *Candida*, German tour, 1937. NEW YORK DEBUT—Hodson, *John Bull's Other Island*, Mansfield (now Brooks Atkinson), 1948. LONDON DEBUT—Repertory, *Dublin Gate Theatre Co.*, Embassy, 1948. PRINCIPAL STAGE APPEARANCES—Christmas Pantomime, Dublin, 1938; five roles, *1066 and All That*, 1938; Rudd, *A Spot of Bother*, Aldwych Farce, 1938; Billy Blee, *Devonshire Cream*, Phillpotts Farce, 1939; Charley, *Charley's Aunt*, 1939; Henry, *The Shining Hour*, 1939; Jervis, *Daddy-Long-Legs*, 1939; Hector/Statue, *Man and Superman*, 1939; Lorenzo, *The Merchant of Venice*, 1939; Commander Rogers, *French Without Tears*, 1940; performer, *April Fooling*, Queens, Dublin, 1941; Chorus, *Oedipus*, 1941; Bassanio, *The Merchant of Venice*, 1941; Macduff, *Macbeth*, 1941; Dr. Ridgeon, *The Doctor's Dilemma*, 1942; performer, *Of Pastures New*, Gaiety, Dublin, 1943; performer, *Royal Roadhouse Revue*, Olympia, Dublin, 1943; Birnbaum, *The Constant Nymph*, 1943; Randall, *Heartbreak House*, 1943; Stogumber, *St. Joan*, 1943; Agrippa, *Antony and Cleopatra*, 1943; Prince, *Trouble in Troy*, 1944; Mortimer, *Arsenic and Old Lace*, Dublin, 1944; Ben, *Uncle Harry*, 1944; Rosen, *Tsar Paul*, 1944; Kreon, *Oedipus*, 1944; John Worthing, *The Importance of Being Earnest*, 1945; Monk, *Oliver Twist*, 1945; Manningham, *Gaslight*, 1945; Dr. Schumacher, *The Doctor's Dilemma*, 1945; Cassio, *Othello*, 1945; Pastor Manders, *Ghosts*, 1946; Police Sgt, *Winterset*, 1946; Stephen,

Murder Without Crime, 1946; Drinkwater, *Captain Brassbound's Conversion*, 1946; Gratiano, *The Merchant of Venice*, 1946; Warwick, *Biography*, 1947; Rabbi Sender, *The Dybbuk*, 1947; Hastings, *She Stoops to Conquer*, 1947; Brunton, *Where Stars Walk*, 1948; Radfern, *Laburnum Grove*, 1948; Sir Hugo Const, *Suspect*, 1948; *The Old Lady Says No*, Mansfield, 1948.

Now I Lay Me Down to Sleep, 1950; *The King of Friday's Men*, 48th Street Playhouse, 1951; Beverly Carlton, *The Man Who Came to Dinner*, 1952; Tybalt, *Romeo and Juliet*, 1952; Albert Feather, *Ladies in Retirement*, 1953; Simon, *Family Album*, 1954; George Pepper, *Red Peppers*, 1954; Jim, *Quiet Wedding*, 1954; Tony, *Heaven Can Wait*, 1954; Bob Cratchit, *A Christmas Carol*, 1954; Henri, *Sailor's Delight*, 1954; Green, *Richard II*, 1954; Cassius, *Julius Caesar*, 1954; Burgess, *Candida*, 1955; King Magnus, *The Apple Cart*, 1955; *My Three Angels*, 1955; *The Little Glass Clock*, 1956; Sampson, *A Pound in Your Pocket*, 1957; Jamie, *Maggie*, 1958; Percy, *Epitaph for George Dillon*, 1959; Mr. Secondborn, *Buoyant Billions*, and Reverend Soames, *Getting Married*, Provincetown Playhouse, New York, 1959; Mr. Dabble, *Lock up Your Daughters*, 1960; Inspector, *Not in the Book*, 1960; Sgt. Reynolds, *Little Moon of Alban*, 1960; Gaev, *The Cherry Orchard*, Washington Arena, 1960; Blair, *Kwamina*, 1960; Alick, *Maggie*, 1962; Herbert Getliffe, *Time of Hope*, 1963; Polonius, *Hamlet*, 1963; Jesuit/Philippe, *Poor Bitos*, Cort, New York, 1964; Tommy, *The Zulu and the Zayda*, 1965; *The Queen and the Rebels*, Theatre Four, New York, 1965; Milburn, *Hostile Witness*, 1966; Meadows/Truscott (stand-by), *Loot*, Biltmore, New York, 1968; *Little Boxes*, New Theatre, New York, 1969; *Saved*, Cherry Lane, New York, 1970; Sam, *The Homecoming*, 48th Street Theatre, New York, 1971; Captain Lesgate, *Dial M for Murder*, 1972; *The Jockey Club Stakes*, 1973; Robertson, *Lloyd George Knew My Father*, 1974; Cunningham, *Ulysses in Nighttown*, Winter Garden, New York, 1974; William, *You Never Can Tell*, Roundabout, New York, 1978; Alex, *The Hiding Place*, 1982. MAJOR TOURS—Repertory seasons in England, Ireland, Scotland, Germany, and Canada, 1937–40; Dublin Gate Theatre Co., ENSA tours, 1940–47; King Magnus, *The Apple Cart*, National Tour, 1957; Lindsay Woolsey, *Auntie Mame*, 1958; *Hostile Witness*, 1966–7; *The Jockey Club Stakes*, 1975.

PRINCIPAL FILMS—*The Colonial Naturalist; Hostile Witness*, 1967; *F. Scott Fitzgerald and the Last of the Belles*, 1973. RADIO APPEARANCES—heard on NBC Theatre Guild on the Air; WOR Sherlock Holmes series; U.N. Radio, BBC, CBS, and Radio Eireann. TELEVISION APPEARANCES—since 1949, seen on over one hundred major shows, including: *Hallmark Hall of Fame; Camera Three; Ed Sullivan Show; Omnibus; Kraft, Television Theatre;* also commercials.

SIDELIGHTS: MEMBERSHIPS—AFTRA, A.E.A., SAG.

Mr. Barrs has made a specialty of British dialect roles. For seven years he was a permanent member of the Dublin Gate Theatre (1941–48) and has taught at the American Academy of Dramatic Art, Stella Adler Studio, AMDA, and the New York Academy of Theatrical Arts. He has also stage-managed several shows (three on Broadway, four at the Blackfriars Theatre) and directed shows for Equity Library Theatre, Equity Community Plays and the MacArthur Summer Theatre in Vermont. Between 1940 and 1941 he had his own "fitup" touring company in Ireland. He records books for the American Foundation for the Blind. For ten years he was a professional, practicing astrologer. At the beginning of his career he was a practicing magician, did a single and a double musical act in British Vaudeville and performed straight man stand-up comedy for Dublin comedians Jimmy O'Dea, Noel Purcell and Cecil Sheridan. He was also seen in many musical revues in Dublin between 1941 and 1948.

ADDRESS: Home—55 E. 78th Street, New York, NY 10021.

* * *

BARRY, B. Constance (nee Barbara D.), actress

PERSONAL: Born April 29, 1913, in New York, NY; daughter of Richard Henry and Ebba (Bohm) Duffy; married Raymond John Barry, April 24, 1938; children: Raymond John, Sharon Joan, Barbara. EDUCATION: Attended Hofstra and Pratt universities; trained for the stage with Raymond John Barry. POLITICS: Independent.

CAREER: NEW YORK DEBUT—Mother, *Blue Heaven*, Theater for the New City, New York, 1975. PRINCIPAL STAGE APPEARANCES—*Strange Beast, Silver Bee, Nine to Five*, Theater for the New City, NY, 1975–79; Irma, *Lucky Star*, America Theater of Actors, NY; Helen, *Passing Time*, Quaigh, NY; Howardina, *Concerning the Effects of Trimethylchloride*, Theater for the New City, NY; Mrs. Dalton, *Native Son*, Perry Street, NY; Mrs. Allen, *Dark of the Moon*, Theater of the Open Eye, NY; Grandma, *Asylum*, Ensemble Studio Theater, NY; Sally Dugan, *Naomi Court*, Players, NY; Ella Taske, *Life Boat Drill*, Ensemble Studio, NY;

Halie, *Buried Child*, Repertory Theater of St. Louis, MO, 1981; Elder, *The Antigone*, New York Shakespeare Festival, 1982.

PRINCIPAL FILM APPEARANCES—Nettie Dedham, *Ghost Story*, 1981; wedding guest, *Arthur*, 1982; Ethel, *Fat Chance*, 1982; shopper, *Without a Trace*, 1983; browser, *Easy Money*, 1983; cook, *Trading Places*, 1983. PRINCIPAL TELEVISION APPEARANCES—Mrs. Hooper, *Bloodhound Gang*, 1983; *David Letterman Late Night; Saturday Night Live*.

SIDELIGHTS: MEMBERSHIPS—AEA, SAG, AFTRA.

ADDRESS:Agent—c/o The Starkman Agency, 1501 Broadway, New York, NY 10036.

* * *

BARRY, B. H. (ne Barry Halliday), actor, fight director, choreographer, director

PERSONAL: Born February 19, 1940; son of Ronald (an architect) and Dorothy (Mansell) Halliday. EDUCATION: Corona Academy, England.

CAREER: U.S. DEBUT—Fight Director, *Hamlet*, Arena Stage, Washington, DC, 1978. NEW YORK DEBUT—Fight Director, *Hot Grog*, Phoenix, 1978. LONDON DEBUT—Bell Boy, *Oh Dad, Poor Dad, Mama's Hung You in the Closet and I'm Feeling So Sad*, Piccadilly, 48 performances, 1962. PRINCI-

B. CONSTANCE BARRY **B. H. BARRY**

PAL STAGE WORK—Directed—*Toad of Toad Hall,* Pittsburgh, PA, 1975; *Cyrano de Bergerac,* Alley, Houston, TX, 1981.

Fight Director—*King Lear,* Acting Company, NY; *Troilus and Cressida,* Yale Repertory, New Haven, CT; *Mahagonny,* Metropolitan Opera, NY; *Passione,* Playwrights Horizons, NY; *Cyrano de Bergerac:* Long Warf, New Haven, CT, Center Stage, Baltimore, MD, Williamstown Theatre Festival, Williamstown, MA, Santa Fe Stage Festival, Santa Fe, NM; *Mary Stuart, Hamlet,* Circle Repertory Company, NY; *True West,* Public Theatre, NY; *Holeville,* Dodger, NY; *Mass Appeal,* Booth, NY; *Frankenstein,* Palace, NY; *Romeo and Juliet:* Alley, Houston, TX, Long Wharf, New Haven, CT, La Jolla Playhouse, La Jolla, CA; *Henry IV,* Public Theatre, NY; *Macbeth,* Vivian Beaumont, NY., Toronto Arts, Canada; *Hamlet,* Players State Theatre, Coconut Grove, FL; *A View from the Bridge,* Ambassador, NY;

Hamlet, New York Shakespeare Festival; *Mary Stuart,* New York Shakespeare Festival; *Some Men Need Help,* 47th Street Theatre, NY; *Geniuses,* Playwrights Horizons, NY; *Othello,* Winter Garden, NY; *The Woods,* Second Stage, NY; *After the Prize,* Phoenix, NY; *Extremities,* West Side Arts, NY; *Three Musketeers,* Hartman, Stamford, CT; *As You Like It,* Arena Stage, Washington, DC; *Macbeth,* Metropolitan Opera, NY; *Heartbreak House,* Circle in the Square, NY; *Noises Off,* Brooks Atkinson, New York; *Friends,* Manhattan Theatre Club, New York; *Full Hook Up,* Circle Repertory, NY; Royal Shakespeare Company, London, England: *Island of the Mights, Titus Andronicus, Anthony and Cleopatra, Romeo and Juliet, Othello, As You Like It, Women Pirates, Too True to Be Good, Bewitched, Taming of the Shrew, Julius Caesar.*

FILM DEBUT—Prefect, *French Mistress,* 1960. PRINCIPAL FILM WORK—Fight Director—*Crossed Swords; Pirates of Penzance; Macbeth.* TELEVISION DEBUT—*Billy Bunter, Dixon of Dock Green,* England. PRINCIPAL TELEVISION APPEARANCES—*Mike Douglas Show; David Letterman; Morning Show.*

TELEVISION WORK—BBC, London—*Twelfth Night, Hamlet, Macbeth, Anthony and Cleopatra, Tales of Hoffman, Legend of King Arthur.*

THEATRE-RELATED CAREER: Faculty member: Julliard, New York University, Circle in the Square. Master teacher, Shakespeare & Co.

SIDELIGHTS: MEMBERSHIPS—Founding member, Society of British Fight Directors, AEA, Stunt Man's Association.

In addition to his professional stage work, Mr. Barry has staged combat and taught master classes at Southern Methodist University, Temple University, Yale School of Drama, and Carnegie-Mellon University. In England, he has taught at the Royal Academy of Dramatic Arts, Central School of Speech and Drama, London School of Music, Guildhall School of Music and Dramatic Arts, and the Corona Academy.

ADDRESS: Home—58 W. 89th Street, New York, NY 10024. Agent/Lawyer—Jerold Couture, 270 Madison Avenue, New York, NY 10016.

PAUL BARRY

BARRY, Paul, director, manager, actor, fencing choreographer

PERSONAL: Born August 29, 1931, in Waterford, MI; son of Clement Stanley (an operatic tenor) and Doris (an actress; maiden name, Manier) Barry; married Ellen Francis Reiss (an actress), February 22, 1969; children: Kevin Michael, Timothy Brian, Shannon Elizabeth. EDUCATION: Wayne State University, B.A.; U.C.L.A., M.A.; studied for the theatre with Michael Chekhov and Peter Ballbusch.

CAREER: PRINCIPAL STAGE APPEARANCES—Mr. Keres, *Tiger Tiger Burning Bright,* off-Broadway; with the New York Shakespeare Festival, American Savoyards, and other companies played such roles as: Quixote/Cervantes, *Man of La Mancha;* Littlechap, *Stop the World, etc.;* Og, *Finian's Rainbow;* George, *Of Mice and Men;* Frank Elgin, *The Country Girl;* Shannon, *Night of the Iguana;* Berrenger, *Rhinoceros;* Bill Maitland, *Inadmissible Evidence;* Archie Rice, *The Entertainer;* and the title roles in *Hamlet, Richard III, Luther, Macbeth,* and *Cyrano de Bergerac.* MAJOR TOURS—*Macbeth* and *Spoon River Anthology,* title I–III tours through New Jersey.

DIRECTED: PLAYS—New Jersey Shakespeare Festival (1963–83): *Taming of the Shrew, Richard III, Antony and Cleopatra, Luther, Merry Wives of Windsor, The Devils, The Comedy of Errors, Marat/Sade, Much Ado About Nothing, Julius Caesar, Desire Under the Elms, Othello, A Midsummer Night's Dream, Hamlet, The Tempest, Rosencrantz and Guildenstern Are Dead, Troilus and Cressida, The Bourgeois Gentleman, Coriolanus, Summer and Smoke, As You*

Like It, Measure for Measure, Under Milk Wood, J.B., Steambath, Richard II, Henry IV—Parts I & II, Henry V, The Devil's Disciple, The Best Man, The Playboy of the Western World, Of Mice and Men, Cyrano de Bergerac, An Enemy of the People, The Glass Menagerie, Love's Labours Lost, The Country Girl, King Lear, A Streetcar Named Desire, Travesties, Two for the Seesaw, Who's Afraid of Virginia Woolf?, Macbeth, Volpone, Romeo and Juliet, The Caretaker, A Christmas Carol, Cymbeline, Tartuffe, Da, That Championship Season, Sweet Bird of Youth, The Lady's Not for Burning, New Jersey Shakespeare Festival, 1963–83; *Call a Spade a Shovel,* Princeton University 81st Annual Triangle Show; *Rashomon, The Hostage, South Pacific, Anna Christie, A Taste of Honey, My Fair Lady, The Rose Tattoo, The King and I, Incident at Vichy, How to Succeed, Carnival, The Birthday Party, The Apple Tree, Beyond the Fringe,* others, Cape May Playhouse; *Kismet,* Equity Library Theatre; *The Rainmaker, Teahouse of the August Moon, Diary of Anne Frank, Cat on a Hot Tin Roof, The Matchmaker, The Emperor Jones, Look Back, The Rainmaker, Teahouse of the August Moon, Diary of Anne Frank, Cat on a Hot Tin Roof, The Matchmaker, The Emperor Jones, Look Back in Anger, The Music Man, West Side Story, The Merry Widow, Paint Your Wagon,* others, Keweenaw Playhouse, Calument Michigan; *Twelfth Night, The Rivals,* others, Boston Herald-Traveler Repertory; *Romeo and Juliet, West Side Story,* Bucks County Playhouse; *The Rose Tattoo, The Tavern,* Repertory Theatre, New Orleans; *Richard III,* Asolo State Theatre, 1978; *Transfiguration in Precinct 12,* Kennedy Center, 1979.

TELEVISION SHOW—*Hamlet,* WHDH-Boston. FENCING CHOREOGRAPHER: Plays—staged duels, battles, military movements, murders, and other violence for over one hundred classics. TELEVISION SHOW—*Cyrano de Bergerac, Hallmark Hall of Fame* production. THEATRE-RELATED CAREER: Director, guest artist, lecturer at University of California at Riverside; Marymount College, New York; SUNY, New Paltz; Drew, Madison, NJ; Rutgers, New Brunswick, NJ; Fairleigh-Dickinson, Madison, NJ; University of Toledo, OH; Pennsylvania State, University Park, PA; taught acting, direction, movement, voice and weaponry at New Jersey Shakespeare Festival since 1963.

WRITINGS: Books—*The Care and Feeding of Dinosaurs: A Treatise on Acting.*

AWARDS: Holder of three State Titles (A.F.L.A.) in sabre and epee.

SIDELIGHTS: Proficient in rapier and dagger, broadsword and shield, Roman short sword, kendo (Samurai), net and trident, mace, battle-axe, quarterstaff, karate, and judo. Artistic director of the New Jersey Shakespeare Festival.

ADDRESS: Home—34 Hillcrest Ave., Morristown, NJ 07960. Office—N.J. Shakespeare Festival, Madison, NJ 07940.

* * *

BARRY, Raymond J., actor, director, and writer

PERSONAL: Born March 14, 1939, in Hempstead, New York; son of Raymond (a salesman) and Barbara (an actress;

RAYMOND J. BARRY

maiden name Duffy) Barry; married Regine Stock (a dental hygienist); children: Dona. EDUCATION: Attended Yale University, School of Drama; Brown University, B.A. (philosophy). Studied with Bill Hickey. RELIGION: Catholic.

CAREER: NEW YORK DEBUT—Prisoner #2, *The Brig,* Living Theatre, 1962. PRINCIPAL STAGE APPEARANCES (New York)— Sheriff, *Zoot Suit,* Martin Beck, 1979; Baby Face, *Happy End,* Martin Beck, 1978; Gitaucho, *The Leaf People,* Booth, 1975; *Egyptology,* Public Theatre, 1983; Leading Role, *Hot Lunch Apostles,* LaMama; Messenger, *Antigone,* Public Theatre; Volker, *Hunting Scenes from Lower Bavaria,* Public Theatre; Transvestite Agent, *Tourists and Refugees,* LaMama Winter Project; Mike, *Soft Targets,* LaMama; Dangerous Man, *Penguin Touquet,* Dope King, *Landscape of the Body,* Miller, *Curse of the Starving Class,* Drum Major/Grandmother, *Woyzek,* Rory, *Fishing,* Marlon Brando, *A Movie Star Has to Star in Black or White,* Amerind, *The Last Days of British Honduras,* all at the Public Theatre; Clown, *Nightwalk,* Man Who Hits Himself, *Mutation Show,* Executed Man, *Terminal,* Cain, *The Serpent,* all at the Open Theatre. MAJOR TOURS—*The Serpent, Terminal, Nightwalk,* Open Theatre Tour of United States, Canada, Europe, Near East.

FILM DEBUT—Conceptual artist, *Between The Lines,* 1975. PRINCIPAL FILM APPEARANCES—Edward Thoreau, *An Unmarried Woman,* 1977; Shakespearean Actor, *The Goodbye Girl,* 1977; Detective, *Santa;* Leading Role, *Tar Gardens.* TELEVISION DEBUT—Ed Emschwiller, *Surfaces,* WNET. PRINCIPAL TELEVISION APPEARANCES—Jenks, *As The World Turns;* Sonny Lundstrom, *One Life to Live;* Stavros, *The*

Hamptons; Sid, Convicted Rapist, *The Face of Rage,* ABC Movie of the Week; Gangster, *The Doctors;* Factory Worker, *Daddy, I Don't Like It This Way Anymore;* Leading Role, *Cat in the Ghetto;* Camera Three, *Works of the Open Theatre;* Cain, *The Serpent;* Sergeant Spinoli, *All My Children;* Sutar, *Texas.*

WRITINGS: Play—*Once in Doubt,* performed at La Mama Theatre Company, 1983.

SIDELIGHTS: Mr. Barry worked as an actor with Joseph Chaikin's Open Theatre 1967–73 and with The Living Theatre in 1964; he served as director for Quena Company 1973–83,

ADDRESS: Home—339 E. Tenth Street, New York, NY 10010. Agent—Robert Kass.

* * *

BARTENIEFF, George, producer, manager, actor

PERSONAL: Accent on second syllable: bar-TEN-yeff; born January 24, 1935 in Berlin, Germany; son of Michael (a dance teacher and physiotherapist) and Irmgard (a dance teacher, author, and physiotherapist; maiden name, Dombois) Bartenieff; married Crystal Field (director, producer, playwright, actress) on January 27, 1963; children: Alexander. EDUCATION: Studied at the Professional Children's School, Royal Academy of Dramatic Arts, London, England, two years; Guildhall School of Music and Drama, two years; American School of Ballet; studied with Morris Carnovsky and Paul Mann; Katherine Dunham School of Dance. POLITICS: Democrat. RELIGION: "Several."

CAREER: STAGE APPEARANCES—*Pinocchio,* Rooftop Theatre, NY, 1946; Vanya Shopolyanski, *The Whole World Over,* Plymouth for 100 performances, 1947.

President and Co-Artistic Director with wife, of Theatre for the New City, 1970–present.

ADDRESS: Office—c/o Theatre for the New City, 162 Second Avenue, New York, NY 10003. Agent—Monty Silver, 200 W. 57th Street, New York, NY 10019.

* * *

BARTLETT, Hall, director, producer, writer

PERSONAL: Born November 27, 1925, in Kansas City, MO; son of Paul Dana and Alice (Hiestand) Bartlett; children: Cathy, Laurie. EDUCATION: Yale University, 1942. RELIGION: Presbyterian. MILITARY: U.S. Navy Reserve, 1942–46.

CAREER: PRINCIPAL FILM WORK—Writer/producer, *Navajo* (documentary), *Crazylegs;* writer/producer/director, *Unchained,* 1955, *Drango,* 1957; writer/producer, *Zero Hour,* 1957; writer/producer/director, *All the Young Men,* 1960; producer/director, *The Caretakers,* 1963; producer, *A Global Affair,* 1964; writer/producer/director, *Changes,* 1969, *The Sandpit Generals;* producer/director, *Jonathan Living-*

ston Seagull, 1973; co-author/producer/director, *The Children of Sanchez,* 1978, *Comeback,* 1983. FILMS IN PRODUCTION—Burnout, Flangan's Run, The Third Angel.

PRINCIPAL TELEVISION WORK—Writer/director/producer, *The Search for Zubin Mehta, The Cleo Laine Show—The Greatest Superstar in the World.*

AWARDS: *The Children of Sanchez:* Academy Award Nomination for music, nominated Best Picture, Best Director, Moscow Film Festival, official representative of the American Film industry Moscow Film Festival, Grammy winner for Best Film Score by Chuck Mangione; chosen for the Honored Night and Grand Reception at the Deauville Film Festival, Latin American Academy of Cinema Art winner for Best Film Score, Best Director, Best Picture, Best Actor, Best Actress, Best Photography, 1979; *Jonathan Livingston Seagull:* 2 Academy Award Nominations; Foreign Press Golden Globe for Best Film and Best Musical Score, Spanish Film Festival Award for Best Director, Motion Picture Council of America—Best Picture, American Freedom Award, Best Picture, National Conference of Christians and Jews, Best Picture, Motion Picture Society of America, Best Picture; Grammy, Best Motion Picture Score, 1973; *The Sandpit Generals:* Grand Prize, International Moscow Film Festival; *Changes:* Two awards from the Spanish Film Festival, 1969; *A Global Affair:* Foreign Press Golden Globe Nomination, *Parents* Magazine Gold Medal Award, Honorable Mention, Cannes Film Festival, special award, *Box Office* Magazine; *The Caretakers:* Academy Award Nomination, Golden Globe Nominations of Best Director and Best Actress, special citation in Congressional Record as first film to be shown before a Joint Session of Congress, Special Merit Award from National Institute of Mental Health, *Parents* Magazine Gold Medal Award, Venice Festival Medallion; *All the Young Men:* Movie of the Year, National Conference of Christians and Jews, special award, Protestant Motion Picture Council, Movie of the Year, Chicago Urban League, Movie of the Year, New York Urban League, citation from Venice Film Festival for Special Achievement in the Field of International Relations; *Zero Hour:* Academy Award Nomination, Motion Picture of the Year of the Association of American Editors, *Redbook* Gold Medal Award, Protestant Motion Picture Council; *Drango:* Valley Forge Freedom Medal, Golden Globe, *Photoplay* Gold Medal, First Prize Edinburgh Film Festival; *Unchained:* 2 Academy Award Nominations, Movie of the Year, National Conference of Christians and Jews, Freedom Foundation Award, United Nations Award for Contribution to International Understanding, *Parents* Magazine Gold Medal Award; *Redbook* Picture of the Year; *Crazylegs:* Academy Award Nomination, Golden Globe, *Parents* Magazine Gold Medal Award, *Sporting News* Award—Best Football Film Ever Made, Football Writers of America Award; Football Coaches of America Award, America Editors Award; *Box Office* Magazine Award, *Photoplay* Gold Medal Award; *Navajo:* 3 Academy Award Nominations, Golden Globe Award, top prize, Edinburgh Film Festival, top prize, Venice Film Festival, Picture of Year, the National Conference of Christians and Jews, special award, Protestant Motion Picture Council, *Parents* Magazine Gold Medal Award and 27 other national and international awards.

SIDELIGHTS: MEMBERSHIPS—Academy of Motion Picture Arts and Sciences; Academy of Television Arts and Sciences; Friends of the Library; board of directors, Producers

Guild; Cinema Circulus; Phi Beta Kappa; Bel Air Country Club; board of directors, Hollywood Greek Theatre.

"From the start, Bartlett has mastered his craft, dedicating himself to making films that center upon the dignity of the human spirit and man's aspirations for a better world. His conviction has been and remains, that the work of a filmaker should be committed to people and the ideas in which he believes, but at the same time must be entertaining and commercially successful."

ADDRESS: Office—Hall Bartlett Films, 9200 Sunset Blvd., LA, CA 90069.

* * *

BASS, George Houston, playwright, educator, director, producer

PERSONAL: Born April 23, 1938 in Murfreesboro, TN; son of Clarence Cornelius (a minister) and Mable Augustus (a teacher and educational administrator; maiden name, Dixon) Bass; married Ramona Gwendolyn Wilkins (a storyteller and writer) on January 15, 1972; children: Kwame Noel, Khari Takeo, Ayana Vernice. EDUCATION: Fisk University, B.A. 1959; New York University Film School, M.A. 1964; Yale University School of Drama, 1966–68.

WRITINGS: PLAYS, PRODUCED—Roots, narrative, Alvin Ailey Dance Company, 1963; Kaleidoscope in Black, Strait Gate Pentecostal Church, Mamaroneck, NY, 1966; Games, Youth Street Theatre Company, NY, 1966; one-act plays performed at Yale School of Drama, 1966–67—Twelve Mortal Men, Due Day, The Booby, Mourners at the Bier, Twelve Noon at the Lido; A Trio for the Living, Yale University Chapel, 1968; Black Blues, Black Arts Theatre, New Haven, CT, 1968; The Funhouse, Long Wharf, New Haven, CT, 1968; Portraits of a People, Carnegie Hall, NY, 1967; Soul Convention, Carnegie Hall, 1968; How Long Suite, Blacks Arts Theatre, Onyx Arts Conference, NY, 1968; Oh, Lord, This World (Get It Together) a musical, Queen of Angels Players, Newark, NJ, 1969; The Knee-High Man/Babu's Ju-Ju, one acts for children, Country Day School, NY, 1974–75; One into the Other, Wastepaper Theatre, Providence, RI, 1974; Providence Garden Blues, Rites and Reason, Brown University, 1975; Mama Do Blew, with music by Thomas Riggsbee and Kambon Obayani, Rites and Reason, Brown University, Lincoln Center, 1975; The Articulate Sound of an Articulate Tale, Rites and Reason, Brown University, 1977; De Day of No Mo', Rites and Reason, Brown University, 1980; Malacoff Blue, Rites and Reason, Brown University, 1981.

TELEPLAYS—One More Mile to Go, 1965. DIRECTED—Rites and Reason, Brown University: Black Masque, 1971; El Hajj Malik, 1971; Oh, Lord, This World, 1972; Garvey Lives, 1972; Ti-Jean and His Brothers, 1973; Voice in the Wilderness, 1973; Chile Woman, 1973; Dream Dust, 1974; One into the Other, 1974; Providence Garden Blues, 1975; Mama Do Forms, 1975; Mama Do Blew, 1975; Mama Easter, 1975; Providence Festival (an eight-day ritual drama), 1976; John Willie McGee, 1977; Malacoff Blue, 1976; My Mark, My Name, 1978; Be-Bop Blue, 1979; The Blacker the Berry, (a forty-day ritual drama), 1980; Black

Children's Day, 1980; DIRECTED, TELEVISION—Wine in the Wilderness, 1969; 1741, 1969.

THEATRE-RELATED CAREER—Secretary and literary assistant to Langston Hughes, Harlem, NY, 1959–64; free-lance writer/director, NY, 1964–66; Artistic Director, Jacob Riis Amphitheatre, NY, 1966; Artistic Director, Third Party, Long Wharf, 1968; Associate Producer and Story Editor, On Being Black, WGBH-TV Boston, MA, 1968–69; Associate to the Director and Resident Playwright, Urban Arts Corps, NY, 1969–70; Artistic Director, Rites and Reason, the research theatre of the Afro-American Studies Program at Brown University, Providence, RI, 1970–present; Associate Professor of English and Theatre Arts, Brown University, 1973–76; Associate Professor of Theatre Arts and Afro-American Studies, Brown University, 1976–present.

AWARDS: Delta Sigma Theta Community Award for the Arts, 1980; Ford Foundation Travel and Study Grant, 1978; Howard Foundation Fellowship, 1977–78; Fulbright Research Scholar (India), 1977; Harlem Cultural Council Award, 1969; George Bass Day, a festival of one-act plays by George H. Bass produced by the Directing Program, Yale School of Drama, 1967; John Golden Playwriting Fellow, Yale School of Drama, 1966–68; American Society of Cinematologists' Rosenthal Award, 1964; John Hay Whitney Fellowship, 1963–64; University Scholarship, Fisk University, 1955–59.

SIDELIGHTS: MEMBERSHIPS—Board of Directors, Arts Rhode Island and United Arts Rhode Island, 1972–76; Expansion Arts Panel, National Endowment for the Arts, 1973–75; Member of Policy and Planning Committee, Chairman of Arts in Education Panel, Vice-Chairman of the Council, Rhode Island State Council on the Arts, 1976–82; Board of Directors, Afro-Arts Center, Providence, RI, 1972–73; Professional Advisory Board for Theatre, Department of Public Schools, 1978; Educational Theatre Association, RI, High School Drama Festival Judge, 1980; Dramatists Guild; American Theatre Association; Langston Hughes Society.

ADDRESS: Home—11 Poplar Street, Providence, RI 02906. Office—Box 1904, Brown University, Providence, RI 02912.

* * *

BATES, Kathy (nee Kathleen Doyle Bates), actress

PERSONAL: Born June 28, 1948, in Memphis TN; daughter of Langdon Doyle (a mechanical engineer) and Bertye Kathleen (Talbot) Bates. EDUCATION: Southern Methodist University, B.F.A., 1969.

CAREER: DEBUT—Duck and others, Virginia Folk Tales, Wayside Children's Theatre, Middletown, VA, 1973. NEW YORK DEBUT—Joanne, Vanities, Chelsea Westside Theatre, 1976. PRINCIPAL STAGE APPEARANCES—New York: Goodbye Fidel; Fifth of July; Jessie Cates, 'night, Mother, Golden, 1983; Come Back to the Five and Dime, Jimmy Dean, Jimmy Dean; The Art of Dining, New York Public Theatre. REGIONAL—Lenny MaGrath, Crimes of the Heart, Extremities, Actor's Theatre of Louisville; also appeared with Hartman Theatre Company, Stamford, CT, Buffalo Studio Arena Theatre, NY, Folger Theatre Group, Washington, D.C., and spent two summers with the O'Neill National

Playwrights Conference, Waterford, CT. New York—member of Circle Repertory Company, Playwrights Horizons, and Lion Theatre Company.

FILM DEBUT—BoBo, *Taking Off,* 1971. PRINCIPAL FILM APPEARANCES—Selma, *Straight Time,* 1977; Stella Mae, *Come Back to the Five and Dime Jimmy Dean, Jimmy Dean,* 1982. TELEVISION DEBUT—*The Loveboat,* ABC, 1977. PRINCIPAL TELEVISION APPEARANCES—Belle Bodeker, *All My Children.*

WRITINGS: Song, ''And Even the Horses Had Wings,'' for film, *Taking Off,* 1971.

AWARDS: Antoinette Perry Award Nomination, Jessie Cates, *'night, Mother,* 1983; Outer Critics Circle Award, Jessie Cates, *'night, Mother,* 1983.

SIDELIGHTS: MEMBERSHIPS—Actors Fund of America (new life member), ASCAP.

Miss Bates created the role of Jessie Cates for Robert Brustein's American Repertory Theatre production of Marsha Norman's Pulitzer Prize winning *'night, Mother.*

* * *

BAUMANN, K. T. (nee Kathryn Silliman), actress, singer, dancer

PERSONAL: Born August 13, in Bronx, NY; daughter of Russell James (an airlines sales manager) and Eleanor Matilda (a secretary; maiden name, Manzitti) Silliman. EDUCATION: Neighborhood Playhouse, NY; studied with Sanford Meisner, graduate, 2 years. POLITICS: Democrat. RELIGION: Catholic.

CAREER: DEBUT—Pippa, *The Spider's Web,* stock tour, 1967. NEW YORK DEBUT—Mary Macgregor, *The Prime of Miss Jean Brodie,* Helen Hayes, 300 performances, 1968. PRINCIPAL STAGE APPEARANCES—Ermengarde, *Hello Dolly,* Lunt-Fontanne, NY, 1977–78; Janice Vickery, *The Effect of Gamma Rays on Man-in-the-Moon Marigolds,* New Theatre, NY, 1972; Lois, *The Penny Wars,* NY; Sarah, *Trelawny of the "Wells",* NY; Penny, *Lemon Sky,* NY; Popeye, *The Miss Firecracker Contest,* Studio Arena Theatre, Buffalo, NY; Ensemble, *Rhino Fat from Red Dog Notes,* Studio Arena Theatre, Buffalo, NY; Tillie, *The Effect of Gamma Rays on Man-in-the-Moon Marigolds,* Studio Arena, Buffalo, NY; Susie, *Boy Meets Girl,* Center Stage, Baltimore; Sheba, *Dandy Dick,* Center Stage, Baltimore.

Jackie, *Hay Fever,* Center Stage, Baltimore; Tillie, . . . *Man-in-the-Moon Marigolds,* American Conservatory Theatre, San Francisco; Patricia, *A Memory of Two Mondays,* Cincinnati Playhouse in the Park, OH; Julie, *A Bird in the Hand,* Indiana Repertory Company; Juliet, *Romeo and Juliet,* Alliance Theatre, Atlanta; Tanglewood Barn Theatre, Clemmons, NC: Josefa, *A Shot in the Dark,* Edith, *Blithe Spirit,* Kitty, *Charley's Aunt,* Elaine, *Arsenic and Old Lace;* Phebe, *As You Like It,* Equity Library Theatre, NY; Jean, *The Lark,* Riverside Theatre Workshop, NY; Jean, *Kid's Games,* WPA, NY; *The Housewives Cantata,* Theatre-at-Noon, NY; Mrs. Forbes, *Dulcy,* Quaigh Theatre, NY.

K. T. BAUMANN

MAJOR TOURS—Tillie, . . . *Man-in-the-Moon Marigolds,* Boston, Detroit, Baltimore, San Francisco; *The Prime of Miss Jean Brodie,* summer tour; *The House of Blue Leaves; The Spider's Web; Hello Dolly.*

FILM DEBUT—Maxie, *Maxie,* 1972. TELEVISION DEBUT—Nurse, *The Guiding Light,* 1968. PRINCIPAL TELEVISION APPEARANCES—*The Edge of Night; Search for Tomorrow.*

WRITINGS: Play—*Rhino Fat from Red Dog Notes* (contributing), 1982.

AWARDS: Buffalo Evening News, Best Supporting Actress, Tillie, *The Effect of Gamma Rays on Man-in-the-Moon Marigolds,* 1971.

SIDELIGHTS: MEMBERSHIPS—Board of Directors, Actors Federal Credit Union; Actors Fund; Catholic Actors Guild; Auxiliary Police Officer, New York City; Rape Intervention Progam, Roosevelt Hospital, NY.

ADDRESS: Agent—Jerry Kahn, 853 Seventh Avenue, New York, NY 10019.

* * *

BAUMGARTEN, Craig, executive, producer

PERSONAL: Born August 27, 1949; married Vicki Frederick (an actress), April 18, 1981.

CAREER: Executive Vice President, Columbia Pictures; former president of Keith Barish Productions. PRINCIPAL FILM WORK—Co-executive producer, *Misunderstood,* 1983; executive producer, *Prisoners,* 1983.

ADDRESS: Office—Columbia Pictures, Columbia Plaza East, Burbank, CA 91505.

* * *

BEACH, Gary, actor

PERSONAL: Born October 10, 1947, in Alexandria, VA; son of Vernon Lester (a painter contractor) and Ellen Elena (Lipscomb) Beach. EDUCATION: North Carolina School of the Arts, B.F.A.

CAREER: DEBUT—Rutledge, *1776,* Majestic, NY, 1971. PRINCIPAL STAGE APPEARANCES—Nigel Rancour, *Something's Afoot,* Lyceum, NY, 1976; Rooster Hannigan, *Annie,* Alvin, NY, 1980–81; Duke, *Doonesbury,* Biltmore, NY, 1983. MAJOR TOURS—Rooster Hannigan, *Annie,* Toronto, Miami, Washington D.C., Chicago, 1978–79.

AWARDS: New Jersey Drama Critics Award: *Something's Afoot.*

SIDELIGHTS: MEMBERSHIPS—Player's Club. MAJOR INTEREST—American History.

ADDRESS: Agent—c/o Charles Kerin, 25 Central Park West, New York, 10023.

* * *

BEARDSLEY, Alice, actress

PERSONAL: Born March 28, 1925 in Richmond, VA; daughter of Grant Lindley (in advertising) and Virginia (a teacher; maiden name Driver) Beardsley; married James William Carroll (in publishing) on June 8, 1968; children: Matthew (Chip) Beardsley. EDUCATION: Agnes Scott College, B.A., 1947; University of Iowa, graduate study in the School of Fine Arts, 1949–50. POLITICS: Independent. RELIGION: Protestant.

CAREER: DEBUT—The Witch, *Hansel and Gretel,* Dunedin Junior High School, Dunedin, FL, 1937. NEW YORK DEBUT—Maggie, *Eastward in Eden,* Actors Playhouse, 1955–56. PRINCIPAL STAGE APPEARANCES—Flora, *Leave It to Jane,* Sheridan Square Playhouse, NY, 1957–58; Mrs. Basham, *In Good King Charles' Golden Day,* NY; Birdcage Lady, *The Wall,* Billy Rose, NY, 1960; Nursie, *Camino Real,* Circle in the Square, NY, 1960–61; Della, *Cindy,* NY, 1965; Mrs. Peachum, *Threepenny Opera,* Buffalo Studio Arena, 1967; Della, *Boy on the Straight Backed Chair,* American Place, NY, 1969; Belle, *The Kid,* American Place, NY, 1972; Marta Bolle, *The Physicists,* McCarter, Princeton, NJ, 1977; Mrs. Schlosser, *The Front Page,* Long Wharf, New Haven, CT, 1982.

FILM DEBUT—Landlady, *The Tiger Makes Out.* PRINCIPAL

ALICE BEARDSLEY

FILM APPEARANCES—Goldie Pease, *Where the Lilies Bloom,* 1972; Mrs. Kepos, *Promises in the Dark,* 1978; Betty Boo, *Honky Tonk Freeway,* 1981; Telephone Operator, *Zelig,* 1983. TELEVISION DEBUT—*Car 54 Where Are You?* PRINCIPAL TELEVISION APPEARANCES—*Naked City; U.S. Steel Hour; Sid Caesar Show; CBS Repertoire Workshop; Trio; Too Far to Go; Keeping On, American Playhouse;* Rose, *Search for Tomorrow.*

SIDELIGHTS: "My debut as the Witch in *Hansel & Gretel* was so memorable an experience, and so heady, that I'm sure it was the seed that settled in my heart to make me an actress forever. While filming *Where the Lilies Bloom,* in Boone, N.C., I was introduced to quilting by a lady in the hills with a still in the backyard and my life has been enriched by that hobby. I have made many quilts and never seem to tire of starting another. I also enjoy braiding rugs as our early Americans did. These crafts seem to suit my 100-year-old house in Westchester and my cottage by the sea in the Hamptons."

ADDRESS: Home—24 Locust Road, Pleasantville, NY 10570. Agent—Harry Abrams Associates, 575 Lexington Avenue, New York, NY 10019.

* * *

BEAUMONT, Gabrielle (nee Toyne), producer, director

PERSONAL: Born July 4, 1942, in London, England; daughter of Gabriel (an actor and director) and Diana (an actress; maiden name, Beaumont) Toyne; married Olaf Pooley (an actor and writer); children: Amanda. EDUCATION: Educated in England and Europe; special training in film and television at the BBC.

CAREER: THEATRICAL DEBUT—Michael, *Peter Pan*, 1948 (toured U.S., Australia, New Zealand, South Africa, India, and Brazil in role from 1948–53). PRINCIPAL STAGE APPEARANCES—Juvenile leads with the Foldstone Repertory: *Taste of Honey, Roots, Billy Liar, Romeo and Juliet, The Three Sisters, Saint Joan, Five Finger Exercise, The Cherry Orchard, Hamlet, Blitz,* all West End productions. PRINCIPAL STAGE WORK: Director—*Billy Liar; A Taste of Honey; The Chalk Circle; The Norman Conquests; The Rainmaker; Bingo; The Sea; Cat on a Hot Tin Roof; Black Comedy; Teahouse of the August Moon.*

PRINCIPAL FILM WORK: Producer/director—*Velvet House,* 1969; *The Johnstown Monster,* 1971; *The Godsend,* 1979.

PRINCIPAL TELEVISION WORK: Producer/director/writer—*The Playwright,* BBC; *Dame Sybil Thorndike,* BBC; *Treasures of Britain,* BBC; *The Osmond's First Tour of Britain,* BBC; *Britain's Source of Arts,* BBC. Director—*M*A*S*H; Private Benjamin; Archie Bunker's Place; Zorro and Son; After M*A*S*H; Greatest American Hero; Dukes of Hazard; Hart to Hart; Vega\$; Trauma Center; Dynasty; The Waltons; Knots Landing; Secrets of Midland Heights; Flamingo Road; Hill Street Blues; The Dorothy Stratten Story,* 1981; *Secrets of a Mother and Daughter,* 1983; *Gone Are the Days,* 1983; *The Corvini Inheritance,* 1984.

SIDELIGHTS: MEMBERSHIPS—Directors Guild of America, Academy of Television Arts and Sciences.

ADDRESS: Agent—William Morris Agency, 151 El Camino Drive, Beverly Hills, CA 90212.

* * *

BEERS, Francine, actress

PERSONAL: Born November 26, in New York City; daughter of Harry and Sylvie Beers. EDUCATION: City College, New York; studied for the theatre with Bill Hickey at Herbert Berghof and with Wynn Handman. NON-THEATRICAL CAREER—worked in the Radio-TV department of the advertising firm of Young and Rubicam, 1944–64.

CAREER: DEBUT—Hannah Klein, *King of the Whole Damn World,* Jan Hus Playhouse, New York, 1962. PRINCIPAL STAGE APPEARANCES—Celia Perlman, *Cafe Crown,* 1964; *Kiss Mama,* 1964–65; *Monopoly,* Establishment Theatre, New York, 1966; Lady in 4A and Trixie's "Mother," *6 Rms Riv Vu,* 1972–73; Fanny Margulies, *The American Clock,* 1980–81; *Curse of an Aching Heart,* Little, New York, 1982; also: New Theatre Workshop Monday Evening Series; BMI Workshop appearances. MAJOR TOURS—Mrs. Hatch, *On a Clear Day, etc.,* national company, 1967; Clara, *Midnight Ride of Alvin Blum,* pre-Broadway, 1966.

FILM DEBUT—*Made for Each Other,* 1971. PRINCIPAL FILMS—*A New Leaf,* 1971; Ruth, *Over the Brooklyn Bridge,* 1983. TELEVISION DEBUT—*The Nurses,* 1965. TELEVISION APPEAR-

FRANCINE BEERS

ANCES—Mrs. Goodman, *The Edge of Night; Another World; Search for Tomorrow; The Doctors; The Carol Burnett Show;* Sybil Gooley-Baby Predictor, *All in the Family;* Lady in 4A/Trixie's Mother, *6 Rms Riv Vu* (TV film); *One of the Boys,* 1981; *All My Children,* 1983; *It's Only Money* (TV film), 1983; *Starstruck* (TV film). RECORDINGS—Jenny, *Death of a Salesman.*

SIDELIGHTS: MEMBERSHIPS—Actors Equity, SAG, AFTRA.

Ms. Beers can be seen in a multitude of television commercials and her voice can be heard on radio, also in commercials.

ADDRESS: Agent—DHKPR, 165 W. 46th Street, New York, NY 10036.

* * *

BEIM, Norman, actor, director, playwright

PERSONAL: Surname rhymes with "time"; born October 2, 1923, in Newark, NJ; son of Herman (a tavern owner) and Frieda (Tall) Beim; married Virginia Rapkin (divorced). EDUCATION: Ohio State University, 1941–42; Hedgerow Theatre School, 1946–47; Institute of Contemporary Art, Washington, DC, 1949; studied for the theatre with Jasper Deeter and Rose Shulman. POLITICS: Democrat. RELIGION: Jewish background. MILITARY: U.S. Army, Field Artillery, 1942–45. NON-THEATRICAL CAREER: English Teacher, Fisher School of Languages, New York.

CAREER: DEBUT—Nat, *Gold,* Provincetown Playhouse, Provincetown, MA. NEW YORK DEBUT—Bill Snellings, *In-*

NORMAN BEIM

herit the Wind, National, 1955. PRINCIPAL STAGE APPEARANCES—White Detective, *Black Visions*, NY Shakespeare Festival Public Theatre; Senator/Soldier, *Coriolanus*, Phoenix, NY. MAJOR TOURS—Prisoner 402, *Darkness at Noon*, National (Civic Drama Guild); standby for Van Johnson, *Tribute*, National.

FILM DEBUT—Police Officer, *Supercops*. PRINCIPAL FILMS—Policeman, *Alone in the Dark; Hot Rock*. TELEVISION DEBUT—Intern, *Search for Tomorrow*. TELEVISION APPEARANCES—*Guiding Light, The Doctors, One Life to Live, All My Children, Another World, As the World Turns, Ryan's Hope, The Edge of Night, Playhouse 90, Andros Targets*. RADIO APPEARANCES—for WNYC and WEVD: *The Emperor's New Clothes, Hedda Gabler, Rip Wan Winkle, Uncle Tom's Cabin, The Rivals, Macbeth, Volpone, The School for Scandal*.

WRITINGS: PLAYS, PUBLISHED—*The Deserter* (One Act), 1979. PLAYS, PRODUCED—*Inside*, Provincetown Playhouse, NY, 1951; *The Battle of Valor*, Ansonia, NY, 1967; *David and Jonathan*, Assembly, NY, 1967; *Guess Who's Not Coming to Dinner*, 1968; *The World of Dracula*, Troupe, NY, 1978; *The Failure*, Troupe, 1978; *A Queen's Revenge*, Troupe, 1978; *Marvelous Party*, Troupe, 1978; *A Marriage of Convenience*, Troupe, 1978; *The Professor Graduates*, Troupe, 1979; *The Lively Art*, Studio, NY.

AWARDS: National Theatre Conference, Second Prize, *Inside*, 1944; Samuel French Competition, First Prize, *The Deserter*, 1978.

SIDELIGHTS: MEMBERSHIPS—AEA; SAG; AFTRA; Dramatists Guild. "Theatre is my vocation and my hobby."

ADDRESS: Home—425 W. 57th Street, New York, NY 10019.

* * *

BELAFONTE, Harry, singer, actor, producer

PERSONAL: Born March 1, 1927 in New York City; son of Harold George and Melvine (Love) Belafonte; married Marguerite Mazique (divorced); married Julie Robinson, on March 8, 1957; children: Adrienne, Shari, David, Gina. EDUCATION: Attended public school in New York City; studied at the Actors Studio and the New School for Social Research as well as the American Negro Theatre. MILITARY: U.S. Navy, 1943–45.

CAREER: DEBUT—*Juno and the Paycock*, American Negro Theatre. NEW YORK DEBUT—*Almanac*, 1953. PRINCIPAL STAGE APPEARANCES—*Three for Tonight*, NY, 1955. MAJOR TOURS—Concert tours of Europe, United States, Japan, Australia, Canada.

FILM DEBUT—*Bright Road*, 1952. PRINCIPAL FILM APPEARANCES—*Carmen Jones*, 1954; *Island in the Sun*, 1957; *The World, the Flesh and the Devil*, 1958; *Odds Against Tomorrow*, 1959; *The Angel Levine*, 1969; *Buck and the Preacher*, 1971; *Uptown Saturday Night*, 1974. PRINCIPAL TELEVISION APPEARANCES—*Tonight with Belafonte*, 1960; *Strolling 20's* (producer), 1965; *A Time for Laughter*, 1967; *Harry and Lena*, 1970; *Grambling's White Tiger* (TV movie), 1981.

WRITINGS: Songs—*Island in the Sun*, with Irving Burgie; *Jump Down, Spin Around*, with William Attaway, Norman Luboff.

THEATRE-RELATED CAREER: President, Belafonte Enterprises Inc.

AWARDS: Honorary Doctorate of the Arts, New School for Social Research, 1968; Honorary Doctor of Humane Letters, Park College, Parkville, MO, 1968; Emmy, *Tonight with Belafonte*, 1960; Antoinette Perry Award, *Almanac*, 1953.

SIDELIGHTS: MEMBERSHIPS—TransAfrica; Martin Luther King Center for Non-violent Social Change. RECREATION—Photography.

ADDRESS: Office—157 W. 57th Street, New York, NY 10019.

* * *

BELKIN, Jeanna, stage manager

PERSONAL: Born April 13, 1924, in New York City; daughter of Sam (a dental technician) and Ida (a children's underwear worker; maiden name, Lukin) Belkin; married Sidney Klein (in postoperative drains), April 16, 1950; children: Karen (a doctor). EDUCATION: Attended New York area schools including Roosevelt College and Brooklyn College; Antioch, B.A., 1981; studied dance at the School of American Ballet with Hanya Holm (modern), Emily Frankel (ballet), also Matt Mattox, Frank Wagner, and Luigi's American Dance Center (jazz).

CAREER: DEBUT—dancer, New York City Ballet Company, Carnegie Hall, New York, 1945. PRINCIPAL STAGE APPEARANCES—dancer, *A Flag Is Born,* Alvin, New York, 1946; dancer *Down in the Valley* and *Man in the Moon,* Lemonade Opera Company, New York, 1948; dancer, *Two's Company,* Alvin, New York, 1952; dancer, *The Girl in Pink Tights,* Mark Hellinger, New York, 1954; lead dancer, *One Touch of Venus,* Cape Cod Melody Tent, Hyannis, Massachusetts, 1953; *Sandhog,* Phoenix, 1954; *Hit the Trail,* Mark Hellinger, New York, 1954; *Guys and Dolls,* New York City Center, 1955; *Reuben, Reuben* (closed in Boston), 1955; dancer, *The Body Beautiful,* Broadway, New York, 1958; dancer, *Whoop-Up,* Shubert, New York, 1958; dancer, *Fiorello!,* Broadhurst, New York, 1959; dancer, *Fiorello!,* New York City Center, 1962; second girl, *The Dragon,* Phoenix, New York, 1963; dancer, *Can-Can,* Meadowbrook Dinner Theatre, New York, 1964; dancer and assistant to the choreographer, *The Most Happy Fella,* Paper Mill Playhouse, Milburn, NJ, 1965; assistant to the choreographer, *Brigadoon,* Pabst, Milwaukee, 1965; assistant to the choreographer, *The Tenth Man,* Mineola, NY, 1966; assistant stage manager, *Annie Get Your Gun,* Broadway, New York, 1966; assistant choreographer, *On a Clear Day, etc.,* Paper Mill, Milburn, 1967; assistant stage manager, *Love Match,* Ahmanson, Los Angeles, 1969; assistant stage manager, *Jimmy,* Winter Garden, New York, 1969; assistant stage manager, Philadelphia Drama Guild productions of *The Imaginary Invalid, Born Yesterday, The Rivals,* 1971–72; *Volpone, Tartuffe, The Waltz of the Toreadors, Ceremonies in Dark Old Men,* 1972–73; *Juno and the Paycock, Death of a Salesman,* and *The Little Foxes,* 1974. MAJOR TOURS—dancer, *One Touch of Venus,* First National Company, 1945–46; dancer, *Call Me Mister,* National Company, 1946; dancer, *Make Mine Manhattan,* 1949; dancer, *The Chevrolet Show,* 1956, dance-captain, *The Chevrolet Show,* 1961 and 1962; Maggie, *Brigadoon,* Stock tour, 1963; stage manager, *Camelot,* 1977; stage manager, *Timbuktu,* 1978–79.

TELEVISION DEBUT—*The Dragon (DuPont Show of the Week),* 1963. CONCERT WORK—Assistant to the choreographer, *Sophie Maslow Dance Co.,* Brooklyn College, 1966; dancer, with Betty Lind; assistant to Sophie Maslow, YMHA, New York, 1967; choreographer, *Chanukah Festival,* Madison Square Garden, New York, 1967–71.

SIDELIGHTS: MEMBERSHIPS—Actors Equity Association (former second Vice-President, former third Vice-President, Councilor at present); Chair, Equity portion of Equity-League Pension and Welfare Trust Funds; AGMA, AFTRA, SAG, Association of American Dance Companies.

Ms. Belkin has taught jazz dance at the Matt Mattox School of Dance and the International School of Dance and is currently working toward a Masters Degree in Industrial and Labor Relations at Cornell/Baruch in New York City.

ADDRESS: Home—245 E. 19th Street, New York, NY 10003.

LYNNE BELL

BELL, Lynne (nee Lynette Maria Bell), actress

PERSONAL: Born May 9, 1944 in Newark, NJ; daughter of Frank Richards (a funeral director) and Doris Louise (a funeral director and former educator; maiden name, Dunn) Bell; married Ely A. Dorsey Jr. on July 23, 1966 (divorced 1972); children: Ely, III. EDUCATION: Attended public schools in Brooklyn and Elizabeth, NJ; studied at the Herbert Berghof Studios and with acting teacher Michael Holmes as well as with the Negro Ensemble Company in New York City. POLITICS: Democrat. RELIGION: Religious Science. NON-RELATED THEATRICAL CAREER—Publisher/Editor, *The Bell Tolls,* a community newspaper in Brooklyn, 1970–71; executive and legal secretary for several agencies of the City of New York, 1980–83.

CAREER: NEW YORK DEBUT—Creole Lil/Lil Bits, *Fat Tuesday,* N. Heritage Repertory Theatre, NY, 1976. PRINCIPAL STAGE APPEARANCES—One Woman Show, *An Evening with Lynne,* La Martinique Supper Club, NY, 1975; *One-Woman Tribute to Black Theatre,* American Place Theatre, NY, 1976; Lula White, *One Midnight, Friday the 13th,* N. Heritage Repertory Theatre, NY, 1977; lead role, *Vonetta Sweetwater Carries On,* NY, 1982.

PRINCIPAL FILM APPEARANCES—Policewoman, *Fort Apache, the Bronx,* 1981; Irma Preston, *They Don't Come by Ones,* 1983; Gloria, *The Sistuhs,* 1983.

TELEVISION DEBUT—Hooker, *All My Children,* 1977;

PRINCIPAL TELEVISION APPEARANCES—Teacher, *Can You Hear the Laughter: The Freddie Prinz Story,* 1977; Nurse,

One Life to Live, 1978; Mrs. Waters, *All My Children*, 1983.

THEATRE-RELATED CAREER: Executive producer and host, *Bridging the Gap with Lynne Bell*, WHBI-FM, New York, 1976–79

SIDELIGHTS: MEMBERSHIPS—AFTRA, SAG.

Ms. Bell was a protégé of Frederick Bried, piano master teacher from 4½ years of age to 14. She has performed recitals at Carnegie Hall Recital Hall and at the George Gershwin Theatre in Brooklyn, NY. "My first love is theatre—love and talent being shared with live audiences. Life is made up of challenges and it is those who overcome those challenges who make life a success. My motto since I was 5 years old is 'Always Keep Smiling.'"

ADDRESS: Agent—Jack Rose Agency, 6430 Sunset Blvd., 1203, Hollywood, CA 90028; FWA, 3518 Cahuenga Blvd. West, Hollywood, CA 90068.

* * *

BELLA, Joseph F., designer, writer, teacher

PERSONAL: Born August 12, 1940, in Greensburg, PA; son of Joseph A. (a cost clerk) and Frances M. (Dengg) Bella. EDUCATION: Carnegie Mellon, B.F.A., 1962; Catholic University of America, M.F.A., 1976. NON-THEATRICAL CAREER: Pattern maker, Sportswear and Children's Wear for Spartan Industries, 1973; designed clothes for Carol Burnett and Julie Andrews for the Inaugural Gala, Washington, DC, 1965.

CAREER: DEBUT—Costume designer, *Philosophy in the Boudoir*, Off-Broadway, 1969. BROADWAY DEBUT—Costume designer, *The Waltz of the Toreadors*, Circle in the Square, 1973. PRINCIPAL STAGE WORK—Costume designer, Olney Theatre productions, including *Plays from Bleecker Street, The Visit, Poor Richard, Romulus, Tartuffe, Mother Courage* (22 productions in all), Olney, MD, 1963–65, 1967; costume designer, Great Lakes Shakespeare Festival productions: *Twelfth Night, The Winter's Tale, Love's Labours Lost, She Stoops to Conquer, Romeo and Juliet, The Importance of Being Earnest, King Lear,* 1966–67; assistant costume designer (to Rouben Ter-Arutunian), *The Devels of Loudon,* Santa Fe Opera, 1969; costume designer, Baltimore Opera Company productions: *Manon Lescaut, Tosca, Don Pasquale, Faust, Otello, Manon, The Barber of Seville, Madama Butterfly, Rigoletto,* 1969–72; costume designer, Opera Society of Washington productions: *La Boheme, Koanga* (American premiere), *Falstaff* (Kennedy Center), 1970–71; costume designer, *Fly Blackbird,* Workshops for Careers in the Arts, 1970; costume designer, The Philadelphia Drama Guild productions: *The Imaginary Invalid, Born Yesterday, The Rivals, Volpone, Tartuffe, Waltz of the Toreadors, Ceremonies in Dark Old Men, Juno and the Paycock, The Rose Tattoo, The Taming of the Shrew,* 1971–74; costume designer, *The Fourposter,* Windmill Theater, Dallas, 1972; costume designer, Lake George Opera Festival productions: *La Boheme, Carmen, Man of Mancha, Abduction From the Seraglio, Tartuffe, Gianni Schicchi, I Pagliacci, The Tales of Hoffman, La Cenerentola,* 1970–82; costume designer, *Kiss Me, Kate,* Minnesota Opera, 1983.

MAJOR TOURS—Costume, scenery, and lighting designer, *King Lear, The Lady's Not for Burning,* National Players, 1969. Built and executed costumes for the following: National Players, 1962–64 tours, including *Othello, School for Wives, Oedipus Rex, The Taming of the Shrew, Hamlet, Twelfth Night;* The Opera Society of Washington, 1964–67 productions: *The Marriage of Figaro, Madama Butterfly, Natalia Petrovna, Faust, Werther; The Nutcracker,* The National Ballet, Washington, 1964; Santa Fe Opera productions: *The Elixir of Love, Der Rosenkavalier, The Bassarids, Jacob's Ladder,* 1968; Barbara Matera, Ltd., twelve productions including *Promises, Promises, Dear World, Mame, The Fig Leaves are Falling, Zorba, Last of the Mobile Hotshots,* all New York productions, 1968–69.

FILM DEBUT—Costume designer, *The Bride,* 1972. TELEVISION—Executed costumes for *The Shepherd's Play,* 1967; *The Play of Herod,* 1969; Pearl Bailey, television special.

AWARDS: Boettcher Scholarship, Carnegie-Mellon University, 1961–62; American College Theatre Festival Citation for Excellence in Costume Design, 1980.

SIDELIGHTS: MEMBERSHIPS—The Costume Society of America; United Scenic Artists, Local 829.

In university theatre, Mr. Bella has designed costumes at Pennsylvania State University, Summer 1962, Catholic University of America, 1962–65, Carnegie-Mellon University, 1965–68, Hunter College, 1970–71, and Montclair State College since 1973. He has taught at Carnegie-Mellon and Hunter and is currently assistant professor in Costume Design at Montclair State College, Upper Montclair, New Jersey.

ADDRESS: Home—305 W. 18th Street, New York, NY 10011; Office—Montclair State College, Upper Montclair, NJ 07043.

* * *

BELLAMY, Ralph, actor

PERSONAL: Born June 17, 1904, in Chicago, IL; son of Charles Rexford (an advertising executive) and Lilla Louise (Smith) Bellamy; married Alice Delbridge, 1922 (divorced 1930); married Catherine Willard, 1931 (divorced 1945); married Ethel Smith, 1945 (divorced 1947); married Alice Murphy, November 27, 1949; children: Lynn, Willard (2nd marriage). EDUCATION: Graduated New Trier High School, Winnetka, IL. POLITICS: Democrat.

CAREER: DEBUT—with William Owen's Shakespearean Troupe, 1921. NEW YORK DEBUT—*Townboy,* 1929. PRINCIPAL STAGE APPEARANCES—*Roadside,* 1930; *Tomorrow the World,* 1943–44; *State of the Union,* 1945–46; *Detective Story,* 1949–50; *Sunrise at Campobello,* 1958.

FILM DEBUT—*The Secret Six,* 1930. PRINCIPAL FILM APPEARANCES—*Surrender, Rebecca of Sunnybrook Farm, Young America, Disorderly Conduct, The Virginian,* 1932–34; *Forbidden, The Awful Truth, His Girl Friday, Carefree, Wedding Night, Trade Winds, Boy Meets Girl, Hands Across the Table,* 1934–37; *Sunrise at Campobello, The Profession-*

RALPH BELLAMY

als, *Rosemary's Baby, Doctor's Wives, Cancel My Reservation, Oh God!,* 1960–79.

TELEVISION DEBUT—*Man Against Crime,* 1949–54. PRINCIPAL TELEVISION APPEARANCES—(live) *Playhouse 90; Theatre Guild U.S. Steel Hour; Climax; Philco; Kraft; Telephone Hour; Hallmark; Perry Como Show; Studio One; Armstrong Theatre of the Air; Sid Caesar Show; Donald O'Connor Show; Dinah Shore Show; G.E. Theatre; To Tell the Truth; What's My Line; CBS Special,* "My Father and My Mother"; *Defenders* (film) *Bob Hope Chrysler; Run for Your Life; F.B.I.; Gunsmoke; Rawhide; Four Star Theatre; 12 O'clock High; Dick Powell Theatre; Zane Grey Theatre; Ford Theatre; Owen Marshall; The Log of the Black Pearl; Missiles of October; Moneychangers; Once an Eagle; Search for the Gods; Boy in the Plastic Bubble; Medical Center; McNaughton's Daughter; Flight 502; Canon; Nightmare in Badham County; Westside Medical; Hunter; Charlie Cobb; Julie Farr; MD; Testimony of Two Men; Bob Newhart Show; Wheels; The Millionaire; Adventure; Clone Master; Power; Condominium; The Memory of Eva Ryker; The Winds of War.*

RADIO—*Theatre of Romance; U.S. Steel Hour; Gertrude Lawrence Show; Armstrong Theatre of the Air; Kate Smith Show; Philip Morris Show; Suspense; Helen Hayes Show; Stage Door Canteen; Rudy Vallee Fleishman Hour; Route 66; Lux Radio Theatre; Philco Playhouse; Cresta Blanca Show.*

PRODUCED/DIRECTED: PLAYS—*Pretty Little Parlor,* New York, 1944.

AWARDS: Antoinette Perry Award, Critics Circle Award, Delia Austrian Award, 1958: *Sunrise at Campobello;* Emmy Award Nomination, 1974: *Missiles of October;* Award of Merit, State of Israel, 1968; Emmy Award, 1969: *One Reach One;* Emmy Award Nomination, 1955: *Fearful Decision;* Academy of Radio and TV Arts and Sciences Award, Best Dramatic Actor, 1950: *Man Against Crime;* Academy Award Nomination, 1937: *The Awful Truth.*

SIDELIGHTS: MEMBERSHIPS—AEA (president, 1952–64); SAG (a founder, first board of directors, 1933); American Arbitration Association (director, 1962–64); Players Club (board, 1958–64); Dutch Treat, Lambs Club (council 1952–56).

Mr. Bellamy donated career memorabilia to the Center for Film and Theater Research, University of Wisconsin.

ADDRESS: Office—116 E. 27th Street, New York, NY 10016. Agent—c/o Grossman-Stalmaster Agency, 10100 Santa Monica Blvd., Suite 310, Los Angeles, CA 90067.

* * *

BELLAVER, Harry, actor

PERSONAL: Born February 12, 1905 in Hillsboro, IL; son of Matteo (a coalminer) and Maria (Copa) Bellaver; married G. Dudley Smith, January 7, 1932; children: Vaughan Bianca, Dudley Maria. EDUCATION: Attended Brookwood Labor College; trained for the stage at the Hedgerow Theatre with Jasper Deeter. POLITICS: Democrat. MILITARY: U.S. Army special services, 1944.

CAREER: DEBUT—Yank, *The Hairy Ape,* Hedgerow Theatre, Media, PA, 1928. NEW YORK DEBUT—*House of Connley,* Martin Beck, 1931. PRINCIPAL STAGE APPEARANCES—Major Petkoff, *Arms and the Man,* Idiot Brother, *The Devil's Disciple,* Robert de Boudricourt, *Saint Joan,* Jackson, *He Who Gets Slapped,* James Mayo, *Beyond the Horizon,* Liliom, *Liliom,* Sam, *Lucky Sam McCarver,* Hedgerow Theatre Repertory Company, Media, PA, 1928; Broadway—Landlord, *Carrie Nation;* Mike Ramsey, *We the People;* Muggi, *She Loves Me Not;* Ham, *Noah;* Ruby Herter, *How Beautiful with Shoes;* Pablo, *Russet Mantle;* Abbe Vignall, *St. Helena;* Pablo Sanchez, *Tortilla Flat;* Sergeant Snyder, *The World's Full of Girls;* Sitting Bull, *Annie Get Your Gun; That Championship Season;* Stock—Eddie Carbone, *A View from the Bridge.*

FILM DEBUT—*The Thin Man,* 1939. PRINCIPAL FILM APPEARANCES—Creeps, *Another Thin Man;* Max Coburg, *The House on 92nd Street;* Larry Giff, *Side Street;* Bailiff, *Perfect Strangers;* George Biddle, *No Way Out;* Billy, *Something to Live For;* Mazzioli, *From Here to Eternity;* Joe Horner, *Miss Sadie Thompson;* Marty Kennedy, *The Birds and the Bees;* Manager, *Serenade;* Martin, *The Old Man and the Sea;* Judge, *One Potato Two Potato;* Madrigan, *Hot Rock; Hero at Large.* PRINCIPAL TELEVISION APPEARANCES—Detective Frank Acaro, *Naked City* (four seasons); *Studio One; Omnibus; Philco Television Playhouse; Kraft Television Theatre; Climax; Alfred Hitchcock Presents; Danger; Robert Montgomery Presents; Somerset Maugham Theatre; You Are There; Wanted, Dead or Alive; Twilight Zone;* Ernie

HARRY BELLAVER

DIRK BENEDICT

Downs, *Another World; Knots Landing.*

SIDELIGHTS: MEMBERSHIPS—Actors Equity, SAG, AFTRA, Tappan Town Historical Society.

"Did so much, I can't remember them all."

ADDRESS: Agent—c/o Fifi Oscard, 19 W. 44th Street, New York, NY 10036.

* * *

BENEDICT, Dirk (nee Dirk Niewoehner), actor

PERSONAL: Born March 1, 1945, in Helena, MT; son of George Edward (a lawyer) and Priscilla Mella (an accountant) Niewoehner. EDUCATION: Whitman College, B.F.A., 1967; trained for the stage at the John Fernald Academy of Dramatic Art at Oakland University.

CAREER: DEBUT—Young Man, *Summertree*, Seattle Repertory, Seattle, WA, 1970. NEW YORK DEBUT—*Abelard and Heloise*, Brooks Atkinson, 1971, 48 performances. PRINCIPAL STAGE APPEARANCES—Company, Meadow Brook Rochester, NY, 1968–69; Don Baker, *Butterflies Are Free*, Booth, NY, 1972. MAJOR TOURS—Li'l Abner, *Li'l Abner*, Ohio and Michigan cities, 1977; Curly, *Oklahoma*, Ohio and Michigan cities, 1979.

FILM DEBUT—Michael, *Georgia, Georgia*, 1971. PRINCIPAL FILM APPEARANCES—lead, *SSSSS*, 1973; lead, *W*, 1974; *Scavenger Hunt*, 1979; *Underground Aces*, 1979; lead, *Ruckus*, 1980. TELEVISION DEBUT—guest star, *Hawaii Five-*

O, 1972. PRINCIPAL TELEVISION APPEARANCES—lead, *Chopper One* (series), 1973–74; lead, *Battlestar Galactica* (series), 1978–79; *Scruples*, 1980; co-star, *The A-Team*, 1982.

ADDRESS: Agent—c/o IBM, Suite 1132, 1801 Century Park East, Los Angeles, CA 90062. Agent—c/o Michael Greenfield, Suite 1112, 9000 Sunset Blvd., Los Angeles, CA 90069.

* * *

BENJAMIN, P. J. (ne Paul Brozowski), actor

PERSONAL: Born September 2, 1951; son of Michael (a tavern owner) and Helen (Marciniak) Brozowski. EDUCATION: Attended Loyola University; trained for the stage with Ted Liss, David LeGrant, and Richard Edelman. RELIGION: Roman Catholic.

CAREER: DEBUT—juggler, *Carousel*, Lourdes High School, Chicago, IL, 1966. NEW YORK DEBUT—chorus, *The Pajama Game*, Lunt-Fontanne, 1972, 103 performances. PRINCIPAL STAGE APPEARANCES—standby for narrator, *Pippin*, Imperial, NY, 1976; Vadinho, *Sarava*, Mark Hellinger, NY, 1979; Charlie Gordon, *Charlie and Algernon*, Helen Hayes, NY, 1981; co-star, *Sophisticated Ladies*, Lunt-Fontanne, NY, 1981; (regional) *Wind in the Willows; Tea and Sympathy; Street Car Named Desire; Mary of Scotland.* MAJOR TOURS—leading player, *Pippin*, U.S. cities, 1976; Charlie, *Bubbling Brown Sugar*, FL, 1976.

FILM DEBUT—Warren Livergans, *Muggable Mary*, 1981. PRINCIPAL FILM APPEARANCES—Riccardo, *Born Beautiful*, 1982; featured player, *Serpico*. TELEVISION DEBUT—*Eight Is Enough*, "8 Days in February."

P. J. BENJAMIN

WRITINGS: How I Trained Algernon, 1981; *Scout* (with Stephen Rosenfield).

AWARDS: Los Angeles Weekly Award, Drama-Logue Award, Robbie Award, Best Actor in a Musical, 1981: *Charlie and Algernon.*

SIDELIGHTS: MEMBERSHIPS—Players Club.

"I love training exotic animals. I have owned a monkey, a raccoon, an oppossum, a ferret, a skunk, ducks, chickens, a myna bird and I'd love to own a fox."

ADDRESS: Agent—c/o Lionel Larner, William Morris Agency, 1350 Avenue of the Americas, New York, NY 10019.

* * *

BENJAMIN, Richard, actor, director

PERSONAL: Born May 22, 1938, in New York City; married Paula Prentiss.

CAREER: NEW YORK DEBUT—*Star Spangled Girl*, 1966. PRINCIPAL STAGE APPEARANCES—*The Taming of the Shrew*, Central Park Production, NY; *As You Like It*, Central Park Production, NY; *The Little Black Book*, NY, 1972; *The Norman Conquest*, NY, 1976. MAJOR TOURS—*Tchin, Tchin; A Thousand Clowns; Barefoot in the Park; The Odd Couple.* PRINCIPAL STAGE WORK—Director, *Barefoot in the Park*, London.

PRINCIPAL FILM APPEARANCES—*Goodbye Columbus*, 1968; *Catch-22*, 1970; *Diary of a Mad Housewife*, 1970; *The Marriage of a Young Stockbroker*, 1971; *The Steagle*, 1971;

Portnoy's Complaint, 1972; *Westworld*, 1973; *The Last of Sheila*, 1973; *The Sunshine Boys*, 1975; *House Calls*, 1977; *Love at First Bite;* 1978; *Scavenger Hunt*, 1979; *The Last Married Couple of America*, 1980; *How to Beat the High Cost of Living*, 1980; *First Family*, 1980. PRINCIPAL FILM WORK—Director: *My Favorite Year*, 1982; *Racing with the Moon*, 1983.

PRINCIPAL TELEVISION APPEARANCES—*He and She*, 1967; *Quark*, 1977; *Hallmark of Fame Production* of Arthur Miller's *Fame*, 1978.

ADDRESS: The Gersh Agency, 222 N. Canon Drive, Beverly Hills, CA 90210.*

* * *

BENNETT, Fran, actress, voice and movement teacher

PERSONAL: Born August 14, 1937; daughter of Isom (a lay Baptist Minister) and Virginia (a math and English teacher and union worker; maiden name, Smith) Bennett. EDUCATION: University of Wisconsin, B.S., 1951, M.S., 1952, one year and two summers towards Ph.D.; studied with Osceola Archer at the American Theatre Wing and Paul Mann and Lloyd Richards at the Paul Mann Actors Workshop in New York.

FRAN BENNETT

CAREER: NEW YORK DEBUT—School Clerk, *Me, Candido,* Greenwich Mews. PRINCIPAL STAGE APPEARANCES—*In White America,* NY; *The Cantilevered Terrace,* NY; *Mandigo,* Lyceum, NY; Guthrie, Minneapolis, MN—*Request Concert, House of Atreus, Oedipus, The Crucible, The National Health, Dr. Faustus, The White Devil, Pantagleize; Mahalia,* Hartman Theatre, Stamford, CT; *Comedy of Errors,* Shakespeare and Co., Lenox, MA; Ruby, *A Land Beyond the River,* Greenwich Mews, NY.

FILM DEBUT—*Woman without Shadow,* 1957. PRINCIPAL FILM APPEARANCES—*Promises in the Dark; That Night.* TELEVISION DEBUT—*Robert Montgomery Presents.* PRINCIPAL TELEVISION APPEARANCES—*Lou Grant; Righteous Apples; Here's Boomer; One Day at a Time; Family; Knot's Landing; Roots; Diff'rent Strokes; The Guiding Light; The Tonight Show; Matt Houston; Romantic Comedy; The Woman Who Willed a Miracle; General Hospital.*

THEATRE-RELATED CAREER: Instructor of Speech and Technical Director of Theatre, Fisk University, Nashville, TN, 1954–55; Voice and Movement Director, Guthrie, Minneapolis, MN, 1966–78; Voice and Movement teacher, California Institute of the Arts, Valencia, CA, 1978–present; Director of Training, Shakespeare and Co., Lenox, MA, 1983.

AWARDS: Ford Foundation Study Grant, to study movement with Litz Pisk, 1969–70; Rockefeller Foundation Study Grant, for study with Litz Pisk and to form training program at the Guthrie Theatre and in New York, 1966–67; Paul Mann's Actors Workshop Scholarship, 1955–56; winner of combined Acting/Dance Scholarship, American Theatre Wing, 1955–57; Delta Sigma Theta Outstanding Student Award, 1947; IBPOEW (Negro Elks) Wisconsin Winner of State, Regional, and National Oratorical contest, 1947.

ADDRESS: Office—24700 McBean Parkway, Valencia, CA 91355. Agent—The Gage Group, 9229 Sunset Blvd., Los Angeles, CA 90069.

* * *

BERG, Barry, writer

PERSONAL: Born March 22, 1942; son of David (a writer and businessman) and Suki (an artist; maiden name, Mantell) Berg; married Alice Becker, September 10, 1977 (divorced 1981). EDUCATION: Brandeis, B.A., 1962; Yale Drama School, M.F.A., 1966; studied writing with John Matthews at Brandeis and John Gassner at Yale. NON-THEATRICAL CAREER: Speech and Communications professor, Borough of Manhattan Community College, 1973–75; professor of Theatre, Fairleigh Dickinson University, 1971–73; professor of Prose Writing, New York University, 1983–.

CAREER: PLAYS, PUBLISHED—*Kindly Observe the People,* 1973; *Musical Chairs* (with Tom Savage and Ken Donnelly), 1981. PLAYS, UNPUBLISHED—The Horror Show, 1969; I'd Rather Sit Alone on a Pumpkin, 1972; Toussaint, 1972; Hello, I Love You, 1974; Nightlight, 1975; The Man Who Drew Circles, 1977. FILMS—*The Kentuck,* 1977; *The Adversary,* 1979; *Husky,* 1983. TELEVISION SHOWS—*Your Daily Horoscope,* 1969; *The Kokomo Jr. Show,* 1970; *The*

Who What or Where Game, 1971; *Another World,* 1975–77. ARTICLES—''Who Really Wrote Neil Simon's Plays?,'' *New York Times,* 1973.

AWARDS: Emmy Nomination, Writer, 1976, *Another World;* C. Brooks Frye Award, Best Play of season, Theatre Americana, 1972–73, *I'd Rather Sit Alone on a Pumpkin;* State University of New York Playwrighting competition, First Prize, 1975, *Kindly Observe the People.*

SIDELIGHTS: MEMBERSHIPS—Dramatists' Guild, Writer's Guild of America, East.

Mr. Berg is currently working on his second novel.

ADDRESS: Home—28 W. 70th Street, New York, NY 10023. Agent—Al Zuckerman, Writers House, 21 W. 26th Street, New York, NY 10010.

* * *

BERGER, Robert, producer

PERSONAL: Born February 9, 1914; married Janet Nelson; children: James Casey.

CAREER: PRINCIPAL TELEVISION WORK—Producer: *The Defenders; The Nurses; For the People; Coronet Blue and Shane; The Classic Ghosts; Light Out,* ''When Windows Weep,'' 1972; *RX for the Defense,* ''The Prisoner of Plattsville,'' 1973; *ABC Theatre,* ''Pueblo,'' 1973; *ABC Theatre,* ''F. Scott Fitzgerald and the Last of the Belles,'' 1973; *ABC Theatre,* ''The Missiles of October,'' 1974; *ABC Theatre,* ''F. Scott Fitzgerald in Hollywood,'' 1975; *Land of Hope,* 1975; *The Four of Us,* 1976; *The Deadliest Season,* 1977; *Siege,* 1978; *Holocaust,* 1978; *The Last Tenant,* 1978; *Hollow Image,* 1979; *Death Penalty,* 1980; *Dr. Franken,* 1980; *The Henderson Monster,* 1980; *F.D.R. The Last Year,* 1980; *King Crab,* 1980; *Skokie,* 1980–81; *My Body, My Child,* 1981; *Benny's Place,* 1982; *The Firm,* 1982; *Ghost Dancing,* 1983; *Sakharov,* 1984. FILMS—*Sebastian,* 1967.

AWARDS: Emmy Award (8), American Jewish Committee Award, Anti-Defamation League Award, Golden Gate Award, Peabody Award, 1978: *Holocaust;* Emmy Award Nominations (8), Edward L. Bernays Foundation Award, Golden Hugo Award, 1974: *The Missiles of October;* Silver Phoenix Award, Best Movie for Television, 1973: *F. Scott Fitzgerald and the Last of the Belles;* Emmy Awards (5), Peabody Award, Golden Hugo Award, 1973: *Pueblo;* Emmy Award (3), 1969: *The People Next Door.*

ADDRESS: Titus Productions, 211 E. 51st Street, New York, NY 10022.

* * *

BERGER, Senta, actress, producer, writer, dancer

PERSONAL: Born May 13, 1947, in Vienna, Austria; daughter of Josef (a composer) and Therese Berger; married Dr. Michael Verhoeven (a director, writer, producer, and doctor of medicine) on September 26, 1966; children: Simon, Luca. EDUCATION: Lyceum, Academy for Art and Classic Ballet, Vienna, Austria.

CAREER: DEBUT—Frieda, *Henry IV* (Pirandello), Vienna, Austria. PRINCIPAL STAGE APPEARANCES—Buhlschaft, *Jedermann,* Salzburg Festival, 1979–82; Hedda, *Hedda Gabler,* Salzburg Festival, 1979–80; Elmire, *Tartuffe,* Burgtheatre, Vienna, 1979–81; Marion, *Danton,* Salzburg Festival 1980; Actress, *La Ronde,* Berlin, Germany, 1980–83.

FILM DEBUT—In an Austrian film by Willi Forst, 1956. PRINCIPAL FILM APPEARANCES—*The Journey,* 1956; *Major Dundee,* 1969; *Cast a Giant Shadow,* 1965; *The Quiller Memorandum,* 1966; Julien Duvivier, *Diabolically Yours,* 1967; *Operation San Gennaro,* 1966; *Marquis de Sade.*

PRINCIPAL TELEVISION APPEARANCES—*The Danny Kaye Show, The Magic Hour,* with Orson Welles. PRODUCER: Owns film-producing company, Sentana; produced *The White Rose,* 1982.

AWARDS: Best Actress Award in Italy, 1970, 1971, 1972; Best Actress Award in Germany, 1967.

SIDELIGHTS; "I have no hobbies, thank God, because I have a profession which fulfills me completely. I want to grow old with it and in it, trying to stay true to myself and open to others."

* * *

BERGER, Sidney L., writer, director, producer

PERSONAL: Born January 25, 1936; son of Sam and Pauline Berger; married Sandra Hopkins (a psychotherapist), March 2, 1963; children: Jennifer, Erik. EDUCATION: Brooklyn College, B.A., 1957; University of Kansas, M.A., 1960; University of Kansas, Ph.D., 1964. NON-THEATRICAL CAREER: Assistant instructor, University of Kansas, 1958–63; assistant/associate professor, Michigan State University, 1964–69; professor, chairman of Department of Drama, University of Houston, 1964–.

CAREER: Directed over one hundred productions including *Hamlet, West Side Story, Marat/Sade, Macbeth, Shadow Box, The Homecoming, Richard III, Equus, Romeo and Juliet, Jacques Brel Is Alive and Well and Living in Paris, Diary of Anne Frank, The Taming of the Shrew, The Threepenny Opera, Man of La Mancha, Candide, The Robber Bridegroom.*

WRITINGS: PLAYS, UNPUBLISHED—That Caveman Touch (book), Gershwin, New York, 1956; Hell of an Angel, Gershwin, New York, 1957; The Mudlark (book and lyrics), 1970; Birdboy (book and lyrics), Jones Hall, Houston, 1972; The Fall and Rise of Bertholt Brecht (adapted book), Attic, Houston, 1977; The Last Temptation of Christ (book and lyrics), 1980; The Little Match Girl (book and lyrics), 1982. ARTICLES—"Show Stopping: The Musical Play," *Bulletin of Education,* April 1962; "The Musical Theatre Before 1850" (book review), *Players Magazine,* May 1963; "An Annotated Listing of Full-Length Plays," *Speech and Drama Service Center Bulletin;* "The Yiddish Theatre in America"

(book review), *Players Magazine,* January 1966; "The Jew in Contemporary Drama," *Jewish Book Annual,* vol. 28, October 1970; "Contradictory Characters" (book review), *American Theatre Journal,* March 1974; "A Look at Trovatore," *Opera Cues,* Fall 1974; "Showboating," *Opera Cues,* 1983; served as senior staff editor, *Speech and Drama Service Center Bulletin,* 1959–64.

SIDELIGHTS: MEMBERSHIPS—American Theatre Association; Board of Directors, Texas Opera Theatre; Miller Theatre Advisory Council; Advisory Board, World Center for Shakespeare Studies; elected member, National Theatre Conference; Texas Commission on the Arts in Education, 1977; Screening Committee on International Exchange of Persons (Fulbright-Hayes), Washington, DC; National USO Shows Committee, 1978–79; Theatre Panel, Cultural Arts Council of Houston, 1978–.

Mr. Berger has served on numerous councils and commissions on the arts. He traveled to Germany and Poland as an American specialist in drama, sponsored by the U.S. State Department in 1963–64, and made four trips to Asia, Greenland, Iceland, and Europe sponsored by the AETA, the USO, and the Department of Defense with productions of *Brigadoon,* 1960, *The Boy Friend,* 1963, *The Boys from Syracuse,* 1968, and *Sweet Charity,* 1972. He has been a judge for many state and regional theatre festivals, produced children's theatre and has been the producing director of the Houston Shakespeare Festival since 1975.

ADDRESS: Home—4711 Imogene, Houston, TX 77035.

* * *

BERGER, Stephen, actor

PERSONAL: Born May 16, 1954, in Philadelphia; son of Marvin E. (a shoe importer) and Gwen (Wapner) Berger. EDUCATION: Graduate, Oakland University's Academy of Dramatic Art, 1976; University of Cincinnati, Conservatory of Music, 1972–74. Studied fencing with Istvan Danosi.

CAREER: DEBUT—Colonel Howard, *Yankee Ingenuity,* Meadowbrook Theatre, Oakland, MI, 1976. NEW YORK DEBUT—Sarge, Doctor, *Little Me,* Eugene O'Neill, 1982. PRINCIPAL STAGE APPEARANCES—Celebrant, *Mass* (Leonard Bernstein), Detroit Music Hall, 1975; Charlie, *Tintypes,* Seattle Repertory, 1981; Buck Holden, *Nite Club Confidential,* Riverwest Theatre, New York, 1983. MAJOR TOURS—Bert Healy, *Annie,* 3rd National Company, 1979–80.

AWARDS: Orpheus Club Award, Detroit, 1974; Michigan Music Educators Award, Battle Creek, 1975.

ADDRESS: Home—642 Amsterdam Avenue, New York, NY 10025.

* * *

BERGMAN, Ingrid, actress

PERSONAL: Born August 29, 1915, in Stockholm, Sweden,

died August 29, 1982; daughter of Justus and Friedel (Adler) Bergman; married Dr. Peter Lindstrom, 1937 (divorced); Roberto Rossellini (divorced); Lars Schmidt, 1958; children: (first marriage) Pia; (second marriage) Roberto, Isabella, Ingrid. EDUCATION: Lyceum, Flickor; studied for the stage at the Royal Dramatic Theatre School, Stockholm.

CAREER: FILM DEBUT—*Munkbrogreven*, 1934. PRINCIPAL FILM APPEARANCES—*Swedenhielms*, 1935; *Pa Solsidan; Intermezzo*, 1936; *Dollar*, 1937; *Die Vier Gesellen*, 1937; *En Enda Natt*, 1938; *En Kvinnas Ansikte*, 1938; *Intermezzo: A Love Story*, 1939; *Adam Had Four Sons*, 1941; *Rage in Heaven*, 1941; *Dr. Jekyll and Mr. Hyde*, 1941; *Casablanca*, 1943; *For Whom the Bell Tolls*, 1943; *Gaslight*, 1944; *Spellbound*, 1945; *Bells of St. Mary's*, 1945; *Saratoga Trunk*, 1946; *Notorious*, 1946; *Arch of Triumph*, 1948; *Joan of Arc*, 1948; *Under Capricorn*, 1949; *Stromboli*, 1950; *Greatest Love; Siamo Donne, Viaggio in Italia*, "*Europa '51*," 1953; *Giovanna d'Arco al Rogo*, 1954; *Angst*, 1954; *Elena et les Hommes*, 1956; *Strangers Fear; Anastasia*, 1956; *Paris Does Strange Things*, 1957; *Indiscreet*, 1957; *Inn of the Sixth Happiness*, 1958; *Goodbye Again*, 1961; *The Visit*, 1963; *The Yellow Rolls-Royce*, 1964; *Stimulanti*, 1967; *Cactus Flower*, 1969; *Walk in the Spring Rain*, 1969; *Mixed Up Files of Mrs. Basil Frankweiler*, 1973; *Murder on the Orient Express*, 1974; *A Matter of Time*, 1976; *Autumn Sonata*, 1978.

PRINCIPAL STAGE APPEARANCES—Julie, *Liliom*, 44th Street Theatre, NY, 1940; Anna Christopherson, *Anna Christie*, Santa Barbara, CA, 1941; Mary Grey (Joan), *Joan of Lorraine*, Alvin, NY, 1946; Joan, *Joan of Arc at the Stake*, San Carlo Opera House, Naples, Italy, 1953, Stoll, London, 1954, Opera House, Stockholm, 1955; Laura, *Tea and Sympathy*, Theatre de Paris, 1956; lead, *Hedda Gabler*, Theatre Gaston Baty-Montparnasse, Paris, 1962; Natalia Petrovna, *A Month in the Country*, Yvonne Arnaud Theatre, Guildford, UK, Cambridge Theatre, London, 1965; Deborah, *More Stately Mansions*, Broadhurst, NY, 1965; Lady Cicely Wayneflete, *Captain Brassbound's Conversion*, Cambridge Theatre, London, 1971, U.S. tour, 1971–72, Ethel Barrymore, NY, 1972; Constance Middleton, *The Constant Wife*, Albery, London, 1973, U.S. tour, 1973–74, Shubert, NY, 1975; Helen Lancaster, *Waters of the Moon*, Chichester Festival, 1977, Haymarket, London, 1978.

PRINCIPAL TELEVISION APPEARANCES—*Turn of the Screw*, 1960; lead, *Hedda Gabler*, 1963; lead, *A Woman Called Golda*, 1982.

AWARDS: Emmy Awards, Best Actress, 1983: *A Woman Called Golda*, 1960: *Turn of the Screw;* Academy Awards, Best Actress, 1956: *Anastasia*, 1944: *Gaslight;* New York Film Critics, 1956: *Anastasia.**

* * *

BERGMAN, J. Peter (ne Jay Peter Bergman), actor, composer, sound designer, director, writer, teacher

PERSONAL: Surname pronounced "Berriman;" born April 29, 1946 in New York City; son of William (an accountant and drummer) and Ruth (a dancer and electrolysist; maiden name, Percival) Bergman. EDUCATION: Attended Queens

J. PETER BERGMAN

College in Flushing, NY, and the Juilliard School of Music in New York City; studied film/music at the New School for Social Research in New York; also studied acting, singing, and dancing with his grandfather, Harry Percival, an English music hall performer; music with Luciano Berio and theatre with Jean-Claude van Italie. POLITICS: Democrat. RELIGION: "Lapsed Jew." NON-THEATRICAL CAREER: File clerk, Liberty Mutual Insurance Company, 1963; various positions, The Port Authority of New York, 1964–68.

CAREER: PRINCIPAL STAGE WORK, ACTING—DEBUT: Neighborhood kid, *Street Scene*, summer stock package, 1951. PRINCIPAL STAGE APPEARANCES, ACTING—Timothy, *A Girl Called Kilmeny*, West Side Theatre for Children, NY, 1970; *The Man Who Ate People Raw*, NY Theatre Ensemble, 1974; Buck's Mother, *By Which We Play*, Berkshire Theatre Festival, 1982.

PRINCIPAL STAGE WORK, DIRECTED—*Tosca*, Monteverdi Repertory Singers, 1972; *The Whole Megillah*, Amas Repertory, NY, 1971; *Caesar and Cleopatra*, Amas Repertory, 1972; *Widower's Houses*, Cyrano Repertory, 1974; *The Man Who Ate People Raw, I Want to Be with You, The Holy Cross, Triple Threat*, NY Theatre Ensemble, 1974; *By Which We Play*, Berkshire Theatre Festival, MA, 1982.

PRINCIPAL STAGE WORK, SOUND DESIGN—*A Tide of Voices*, South Street Seaport, 1976; *How He Did It*, Sharon Playhouse, CT, 1979; *Monsieur Ribadier's System*, Hartman, Stamford, CT, 1979; *A Safe Place*, Berkshire Theatre Festival, 1982; *Q.E.D.*, 78th Street Theatre Lab, 1983; *The Palace of Amateurs, Vamps and Rideouts, A Thousand*

Clowns, The Animal Kingdom, Sunrise at Campobello, Berkshire Theatre Festival, 1983.

WRITINGS: PLAYS, PRODUCED—*The Whole Megillah,* Amas Repertory, NY, 1971; *Family Circle,* Neuestheatre, Munich, Germany, 1974; *Ragtime and Romance Review,* Library for the Performing Arts, 1978; *The Final Word,* Playwrights Ink (reading) at Wonderhorse, NY, 1980. PLAYS, UNPRODUCED—Jane Eyre (musical); The Italian Caprice; I Never Come to These Places; Wedding A.M.; The Goodbyes Again (musical libretto). COMPOSITIONS—SONGS, "Chip, Chip Chipermonkey" for production of *A Thousand Clowns,* Berkshire Theatre Festival; "The Hypochondriacs." SCREENPLAY—Sara; Lullabye. BOOKS—co-author, *The Films of Jeannette Macdonald and Nelson Eddy,* 1975. ARTICLES—*Gay News: New York Notes; ARSC Journal; Library Journal; M.L.A. Notes; Washington Market Review; The Dictionary of American Biography; Encore Magazine.*

THEATRE-RELATED CAREER: Researcher, Rodgers & Hammerstein Archives of Recorded Sound, New York, 1968–78; editorial director, *Ticket Connection* Magazine, 1981–83; teacher, Acting/Playwriting, Amas Repertory, NY; producer, WOR-Radio, *Night Talk* program on the first 50 years of Film Music; coordinator-key speaker, "Musical Theatre on Record," Musical Theatre in America Conference, C. W. Post College, NY, 1982.

AWARDS: Obie Award Nomination, 1969: *A Girl Called Kilmeny.*

SIDELIGHTS: MEMBERSHIPS—President, Southwest Soho Preservation Association; Dramatists Guild; vice-president, 1981–83, Association for Recorded Sound Collections; American Society for Theatre Research.

Mr. Bergman has worked as a house manager (*Jacques Brel, Peg O' My Heart*), a producer (performing arts festivals at the Library at Lincoln Center), a music consultant to the Lincoln Center Repertory Company; he built the breakable props for *The Royal Family* on Broadway and on its tour.

ADDRESS: Office—18 Thompson Street, New York, NY 10013. Agent—Sheldon Lubliner, c/o News & Entertainment Agency, 230 W. 55th Street, New York, NY 10019.

* * *

BERLIND, Roger, producer

PERSONAL: Born June 27, 1930 in New York City; son of Peter S. (a hospital administrator) and Mae (Miller) Berlind; married Helen Polk Clark in July, 1962 (died 1975); married Brook Wheeler May 19, 1979; children: (first marriage) Helen Carroll (deceased), Peter Stuart (deceased), Richard Clark (deceased), William Polk. EDUCATION: Princeton University, B.A., 1952; studied at New York University Graduate Business School, 1956–58. MILITARY: U.S. Army Counter-Intelligence Corps, 1954–55. NON-THEATRICAL CAREER: Chairman of executive committee, vice chairman, chief executive officer, Shearson American Express, 1965–75.

PRINCIPAL STAGE WORK, PRODUCER AND CO-PRODUCER, BROADWAY PRODUCTIONS—*Rex,* 1976; *Music Is,* 1977; *The*

Merchant, 1978; *Diversions & Delights,* 1978; *The Lady from Dubuque,* 1979; *Passione,* 1979; *The 1940's Radio Hour,* 1980; *Amadeus,* 1980; *Sophisticated Ladies,* 1981; *Nine,* 1982; *All's Well That Ends Well,* 1983; *The Rink,* 1983; *The Real Thing,* 1983.

PRODUCER, FILM—*Aaron Loves Angela,* 1975.

SIDELIGHTS: MEMBERSHIPS—Trustee, Eugene O'Neill Theatre Center, MacDowell Colony, American Academy of Dramatic Arts, Fresh Air Fund; League of New York Theatres and Producers; Princeton Club.

ADDRESS: Home—120 East End Avenue, New York, NY 10028. Office—54 E. 64th Street, New York, NY 10021.

* * *

BERMEL, Albert, critic, playwright

PERSONAL: Surname rhymes with "farewell"; born December 20, 1927, in London, England; son of Harry (a shoe stall holder) and Rae (her husband's partner; maiden name Sanders) Bermel; married: Joyce Hartman (a magazine editor/writer), 1956; children: Neil, Derek. EDUCATION: London School of Economics and Political Science, B.Sc. 1952. POLITICS: Non-partisan egalitarian. RELIGION: Non-sectarian Jewish. MILITARY: British Army, 1946–48. NON-THEATRICAL CAREER: Advertising and publicity copywriter, London, Montreal, Toronto, New York, 1951–56; freelance writer, New York, 1956–58; magazine and book editor, New York, 1958–60, 1961–63; freelance writer, New York, 1963–66; associate professor of theatre, Columbia University, 1966–72; associate professor, Herbert H. Lehman College, C.U.N.Y., 1972–75, professor of theatre, 1972–date; visiting professor, Rutgers, 1966–67, Juilliard School, 1972–73, S.U.N.Y., Purchase, 1974; Columbia seminars, 1981–84.

WRITINGS: PLAYS, PUBLISHED—*Six One-Act Farces (The Workout,* 1963, *The Adjustment,* 1963, *The Recovery,* 1965; *The Mountain Chorus, The Imp or Imps,* 1970, *The Seizure,* 1970); *One-Act Comedies of Molière* (translations of *The Jealous Husband, The Flying Doctor, Two Precious Maidens Ridiculed, Sganarelle, or The Imaginary Cuckold, The Rehearsal at Versailles, The Forced Marriage, The Seductive Countess*); *Three Popular French Comedies* (translations of Beaumarchais, *The Barber of Seville,* Labiche, *Pots of Money,* Courteline, *The Commissioner Has a Big Heart*); *The Plays of Courteline* (including: *Boubouroche, Hold On, Hortense, Afraid to Fight, Badin the Bold*).

PLAYS, PRODUCED—*One Leg Over the Wall,* Royal Court, London, 1960; *Herod First,* Saville, London, 1965; *Thrombo,* Columbia Summer Theatre, NY, 1968; *Family Weather (The Terror of Suspension),* House Theatre, NY, 1975; *Thank Harry Miner; Backyard Utopias; Up and Up; Thirty Million Dollars* (musical); translator, *Ubu Cocu* (by Jarry), *Horatius* (by Corneille).

BOOKS, PUBLISHED—*The Genius of the French Theatre; Contradictory Characters: An Interpretation of the Modern Theatre; Artaud's Theatre of Cruelty; Farce: A History from Aristophanes to Woody Allen; August Strindberg.* ARTICLES—

130 essays for *The New Leader,* 1964–68, 1973–74; major periodicals including: *Harpers, The Nation, The New Republic, Shaw Review, Columbia Forum, N.Y. Times Book Review* and *Arts & Leisure Section,* many others.

FILM DEBUT—Screenplay, *Run.* TELEVISION: Scenes and narrative, *Shakespeare's Italy.*

AWARDS: Guggenheim Fellowship for Playwriting, 1965–66; George Jean Nathan Award for Dramatic Criticism, 1973–74.

SIDELIGHTS: MEMBERSHIPS—Dramatists Guild; Glenwood Lake Association (president). Obie Awards Judge, 1966; Tony Awards Judge, 1974.

Mr. Bermel came to the United States in 1955 and became a naturalized citizen in 1962.

''Every playwright yearns to be a critic. Every critic yearns to be a playwright. Every theatre teacher yearns to be a director. I am not a director, but have otherwise tried to satisfy my yearnings—without having quite succeeded.''

ADDRESS: Office—Department of Speech and Theatre, Herbert H. Lehman College, Bronx, NY, 10468. Agent—Elaine Markson, 44 Greenwich Avenue, New York, NY 10011.

* * *

BERNARD, Kenneth, playwright

PERSONAL: Born May 7, 1930, in Brooklyn, NY; son of Otis (a businessman) and Mary (Travaglini) Bernard; married Elaine C. Reiss (a teacher), September 2, 1952; children: Lucas, Judd, Kate. EDUCATION: City College of New York, B.A., 1953; Columbia, M.A., 1956, Ph.D., 1962. MILITARY: U.S. army, 1953–55. NON-THEATRICAL CAREER: Teacher, fiction writer, poet, lecturer, literary critic.

WRITINGS: PLAYS, PUBLISHED—*The Monkeys of the Organ Grinder,* 1969; *The Lovers,* 1969; *Marko's: A Vegetarian Fantasy,* 1969; *Mary Jane,* 1970; *Goodbye, Dan Bailey,* 1971; *Night Club and Other Plays,* 1971; *La Fin de Cirque,* 1972; *The Unknown Chinaman,* 1973; *The Sensuous Ape,* 1975; *The Magic Show of Dr. Ma-Gico,* 1979; *The Baboon in the Night Club,* 1982; *Dirty Old Man* (radio play), 1982. PLAYS, UNPUBLISHED—The Moke Eater, 1968; Kong Monolog, 1972; The Adjustment, 1973; How We Danced While We Burned, 1973; King Humpy, 1975; The Sixty Minute Queer Show, 1977; La Justice, or The Cock That Crew, 1979. Other writings in many journals, including *Paris Review; Harpers; New York Herald Tribune; Antioch Review; Mutiny; Discourse: A Review of the Liberal Arts; Prairie Schooner; Grand Street; Margins; Confrontation; Yale/Theater.*

AWARDS: Rockefeller Grant, Playwriting, 1975; New York State Creative Arts Public Service Grant, Playwriting, 1973, Fiction, 1976; Guggenheim Fellowship, Playwriting, 1972–73; Office for Advanced Drama Research, University of Minnesota Grant, 1971; NEA Grant, Fiction, 1978; Arvon Poetry Prize, 1980; Long Island University Trustees' Award, 1982. Artist in Residence—Genesee Community College,

Batavia, NY, 1974; Mineola High School, Long Island, NY, 1974; Oswego College, Oswego, NY, 1974; West Winfield, NY, Free Public Library, 1976.

SIDELIGHTS: MEMBERSHIPS—PEN.

In addition to his other activities, Mr. Bernard has served as a consultant in the following capacities: in playwriting, New York Creative Artist Public Service Program for 1974 and 1975 awards; Massachusetts Arts and Humanities Foundation, for 1975 awards; in playwriting, fiction, poetry, nonfiction, Wisconsin Arts Board, for 1975 awards; in fiction, Maryland Arts Council, for 1978 awards; coordinating Council of Literary Magazines, awards to magazines in the arts, 1974.

ADDRESS: Home—800 Riverside Drive, New York, NY 10032. Office—Long Island University, Brooklyn, NY 11201.

* * *

BERNSTEIN, Walter, writer, director

PERSONAL: Born August 20, 1919, in New York, NY; son of Louis (a teacher) and Hannah (Bistrong) Bernstein; married Judith Braun, October, 1961 (divorced 1984); children: Joan, Peter, Nicholas, Andrew, Jacob. EDUCATION: Dartmouth College, B.A., 1940. POLITICS: Socialist. RELIGION: Jewish. MILITARY: U.S. Army, 1941–45.

WRITINGS: SCREENPLAYS—*Heller in Pink Tights; Paris Blues,* 1961; *Fail Safe,* 1964; *The Molly Maguires,* 1970; *The Front,* 1976; *Semi-Tough,* 1977; *Yanks,* 1979; *Little Miss Marker,* 1980.

AWARDS: Academy Award Nomination, Best Original Screenplay, 1976: *The Front.*

SIDELIGHTS: MEMBERSHIPS—Writers Guild, Directors Guild, PEN.

ADDRESS: Home—320 Central Park West, New York, NY 10025. Agent—Sam Cohn, ICM, 40 W. 57th Street, New York, NY 10019.

* * *

BERTRAND, Sandra (nee Sandra Deutshmaur), playwright

PERSONAL: Born March 19, 1943, in Bakersfield, CA; daughter of Joseph J. and Marjorie D. (Bertrand) Deutschmaur. EDUCATION: Attended Bakersfield Junior College.

CAREER: FIRST STAGE WORK—Princess, *Sweet Bird of Youth,* Pan Players, San Francisco, CA, 1962. THEATRE-RELATED CAREER: Contributing editor, *Places: A Journal of Theatre,* 1973; book reviewer, *West Scene;* book reviewer, *Our Town.*

WRITINGS: PLAYS—*Manikin*, finalist O'Neill National Playwrights Conference; *The Transformation of Aura Rhanes*, finalist, O'Neill Playwrights Conference; *Days and Nights of an Ice Cream Princess; Something About the Albatross*, selected by the Office of Advanced Drama Research, 1973; *The Sentry and the Laughing Ladies*, 1974; *Death in the Robe Arbor*, 1976; *Snow White*, book and lyrics for Project Educational Theatre. TELEVISION PLAYS—*Chameoleon*, produced at the O'Neill Playwrights Conference in the Television category; *Coming Attractions; The Big Blue Marble*.

AWARDS: Electee, Eugene O'Neill National Playwrights Conference, 1978.

SIDELIGHTS: MEMBERSHIPS—Associate member, Dramatists Guild.

Sandra Bertrand's work has received staged readings or production at The Viridian Gallery in New York, The Manhattan Theatre Club, The Direct Theatre, LaMama Theatre Company in Hollywood as well as the O'Neill Playwrights Conference. She was an original member of the New York Theatre Strategy Workshop with Maria Irene Fornes. Her current projects include 'Nostradamus,' a contemporary full-length rock opera, writing both book and lyrics, and 'The Santorini Journal,' an autobiographical novel based on the Aegean island of Lost Atlantis fame.

ADDRESS: 220 E. 85th Street, New York, NY 10028.

*   *   *

BESCH, Bibi, actress

PERSONAL: Surname sounds like "fresh;" born February 1, 1940, in Vienna, Austria; daughter of Joseph G. (an entrepreneur) and Gusti (an actress; maiden name, Huber) Besch; children: Samantha. EDUCATION: Attended Connecticut College for Women, for two years; studied for the stage at the HB Studios with Bill Hickey and Herbert Berghof in New York and with Milton Katselas in California.

CAREER: DEBUT— NEW YORK DEBUT—*An Evening of Frost Poetry*, HB Theatre, 1962. PRINCIPAL STAGE APPEARANCES—(New York) Eliza Doolittle, *Pygmalion*, Mt. Kisco Summer Theatre, 1964; *Fame; The Chinese Prime Minister; Here Lies Jeremy Troy; Once for the Asking; Macbeth; The Cherry Orchard; Primitives;* (Regional) *Medea; Up Your Curtain; Life with Father; Come Back Little Sheba; Light up the Sky; Come Blow Your Horn; Take Her, She's Mine; Invitation to a March; Philadelphia Story; Poor Murderer.*

FILM DEBUT—Joanne, *Distance*, 1975. PRINCIPAL FILM APPEARANCES—*Black Harvest; The Pack; The Promise*, 1979; *Meteor*, 1979; *Hardcore*, 1979; *The Beast Within*, 1982; *Star Trek II*, 1982; *Lonely Lady*, 1984.

TELEVISION DEBUT—*Russians: Self Expressions*, 1965. PRINCIPAL TELEVISION APPEARANCES—(episodes), *Trapper John, M.D., McClain's Law, Insight, ABC After School Special, Hart to Hart, Secrets of Midland Heights, Skag, Eischeid, Mrs. Columbo, Police Woman, Rockford Files, Charlie's Angels, Six Million Dollar Man, Police Story, Executive Suite, The Quest, First Ladies Diaries, Ellery Queen, Camera Three, Somerset*, for two years, *Love Is a Many Splen-*

dored Thing, for three years, *Secret Storm*, for two years, *The Edge of Night*, for one year; (movies of the week) *The Hamptons, Mother and Daughter, The Day After, Skyward II, Centerfold: The Dorothy Stratton Story, Midland Corners, An Element of Risk, Sophisticated Gents, Steeltown, Victory at Entebbe, Transplant, Backstairs at the White House, How the West Was Won, Betrayal, Tom and Joann, Peter Lundy and the Medicine Hat Stallion, Three Times Daily;* talk shows *Merv Griffin Show; John Davidson Show*.

SIDELIGHTS: MEMBERSHIPS—Academy of Motion Picture Arts and Sciences.

"I am currently involved in the anti-nuclear movement."

When not performing, Miss Besch attends acting class with Milton Katselas, enjoys gardening, exercising, reading, and bicycling.

ADDRESS: Agent—Abrams, Harris & Goldberg, 9201, Sunset Blvd., Los Angeles, CA 90069.

*   *   *

BETTGER, Lyle, actor

PERSONAL: Born February 13, 1915; son of Franklin L. (a baseball player, life insurance salesman, and author) and Mertie (a teacher; maiden name Stathem) Bettger; married Mary Rolfe (an actress), April 8, 1941; children: Frank, Lyle, Paula. EDUCATION: Haverford School, Haverford, PA; trained for the stage at the American Academy of Dramatic Arts, New York. RELIGION: Protestant.

CAREER: DEBUT—*Brother Rat*, Biltmore, New York, 1936. PRINCIPAL STAGE APPEARANCES—*The Eve of St. Mark*, 1942; *The Moon Is Down*, 1942; *John Loves Mary*, 1947; *Love Life*, 1948.

FILM DEBUT—The villain, *No Man of Her Own*, 1949. PRINCIPAL FILM APPEARANCES—*Union Station*, 1950; *The First Legion*, 1951; *The Denver and Rio Grande*, 1952; *The Unvanquished*, 1952; *All I Desire*, 1953; *The Greatest Show on Earth*, 1953; *The Great Sioux Uprising*, 1953; *Forbidden*, 1953; *Carnival Story*, 1954; *Drums Across the River*, 1954; *Destry*, 1954; *Gunfight at the O.K. Corral*, 1954; *Guns of the Timberland*, 1960; *Nevada Smith*, 1966; *Return of the Gunfighter*, 1967; others. TELEVISION DEBUT—Closed-circuit television for NBC, 1938. TELEVISION APPEARANCES—Sam Larsen, *Court of Last Resort*, 1957–60; *Bonanza; Gunsmoke; Wells-Fargo; Laramie; The Rifleman; Pursuit; Hawaii Five-O; Grand Jury; Ironside;* others.

SIDELIGHTS: MEMBERSHIPS—SAG, board of directors, 1963–73.

"My best parts were in *No Man of Her Own, Union Station, Carnival Story*, and *Return of the Gunfighter*—all three-dimensional characters with balls."

ADDRESS: Agent—Lew Sherrell Agency, Ltd., 7060 Hollywood Blvd. Hollywood, CA 90028.

BILLIG, Robert, musicial director, arranger, conductor

PERSONAL: Born February 26, 1947 in New York City; son of Lewis Sherwin (an electrical engineer) and Sally Carol (a school psychologist; maiden name, Neuwifth) Billig. EDUCATION: New York University, College of Arts and Sciences, B.A. (Music), 1969.

CAREER: FIRST STAGE WORK—Musical Director, *Annie Get Your Gun*, Wayland High School, MA, 1964. NEW YORK DEBUT—Assistant Conductor, *Dames at Sea*, Theatre de Lys, 376 performances, 1969. LONDON DEBUT—Musicial Supervisor/Arranger, *The Best Little Whorehouse in Texas*, Theatre Royal, Drury Lane, 208 performances, 1981; PRINCIPAL STAGE WORK—Assistant Conductor, *Annie*, Alvin Theatre, NY, 1977; Musical Director/Supervisor/Arranger, *The Best Little Whorehouse in Texas*, Entermedia Theatre, 46th Street Theatre, NY, 1978; Musical Director/Supervisor/Vocal Arranger, *Little Shop of Horrors*, WPA Theatre/Orpheum Theatre, NY, 1982; MAJOR TOURS—Assistant Conductor, *George M*, Bus & Truck Tour, 1971; Assistant Conductor, *Promises, Promises*, 2nd National Tour, 1971–72; Assistant Conductor, *Applause*, National Tour, 1972; Musical Conductor, *No, No Nanette*, Bus & Truck Tour, 1973–74; Musical Director, *Seesaw*, National Tour, 1974; Musical Director, *The Baker's Wife*, pre-Broadway Tour, 1976; Musical Conductor, *Neferiti*, pre-Broadway Tour, 1977; Musical Director/Supervisor/Arranger, *The Best Little Whorehouse in Texas*, 1st National Tour, 1981 and 2nd National Tour, 1982; Musical Director, *Barnum*, National Tour, 1981; Musical Supervisor/Vocal Arranger, *Little Shop of Horrors*, Los Angeles, London, 1983.

PRINCIPAL TELEVISION WORK—Conducted for Luci Arnaz, *The Tonight Show*, 1975, and *The Mike Douglas Show*, 1974; *The Merv Griffin Show*, appeared conducting for *Best Little Whorehouse in Texas* sequence; *Good Morning America*, accompanied Andrea McArdle, 1977.

THEATRE-RELATED CAREER: Music Teacher, Director of Concert Choir and Madrigal Singers, John F. Kennedy Memorial High School, Iselin, NJ, 1969–70.

ADDRESS: Home—170 W. 73rd Street, New York, NY, 10023. Agent—Larry Weiss, The Shukat Company Ltd., 340 W. 55th, New York, NY, 10019.

* * *

BILLINGTON, Ken, lighting designer

PERSONAL: Born December 29, 1946, in White Plains, NY; son of Kenneth Arthur (an automobile dealer) and Ruth (Roane) Billington. EDUCATION: Studied at the Lester Polakov Studio and Form of Stage Design. RELIGION: Presbyterian.

CAREER: FIRST STAGE WORK—Lighting designer, *Carnival*, Berkshire Playhouse, Stockbridge, MA, 1965. NEW YORK DEBUT—Lighting designer, *Fortune and Men's Eyes*, Stage 73, 1969. LONDON DEBUT—Lighting designer, *Sweeney Todd*, Drury Lane, 1980. PRINCIPAL STAGE WORK (lighting design)—(Broadway) *Don't Bother Me I Can't Cope*, Playhouse, 1972; *The Visit*, Barrymore, 1973; *Chemin de Fer*, Barrymore, 1973; *Holiday*, Barrymore, 1973; *Bad Habits*, Booth, 1974; *Hosanna*, Bijou, 1974; *Love for Love*, Helen

KEN BILLINGTON

Hayes, 1974; *The Rules of the Game*, Helen Hayes, 1974; *The Hashish Club*, Bijou, 1974; *The Member of the Wedding*, Helen Hayes, 1975; *Rodgers and Hart*, Helen Hayes, 1975; *The Skin of Our Teeth*, Mark Hellinger, 1975; *Sweet Bird of Youth*, Harkness, 1975; *Wheelbarrow Closers*, Bijou, 1976; *Checking Out*, Longacre, 1976; *Fiddler on the Roof*, Winter Garden, 1976; *She Loves Me*, Town Hall, 1977; *Side by Side by Sondheim*, Music Box, 1977; *Knickerbocker Holiday*, Town Hall, 1977; *Ethel Merman and Mary Martin Together on Broadway*, Winter Garden, 1977; *Some of My Best Friends*, Longacre, 1977; *Do You Turn Somesaults?*, 46th Street Theater, 1978; *On the Twentieth Century*, St. James, 1978; *Working*, 46th Street Theater, 1978; *Sweeney Todd*, Uris, 1979; *Lerner and Loewe, a Very Special Evening*, Winter Garden, 1979; *The Madwoman of Central Park West*, Princess, 1979; *But Never Jam Today*, Longacre, 1979; *Happy New Year*, Morosco, 1980; *Perfectly Frank*, Helen Hayes, 1980; *Copperfield*, ANTA, 1981; *Wally's Cafe*, Brooks Atkinson, 1981; *Fiddler on the Roof*, New York State, 1981; *My Fair Lady*, Uris, 1981; *A Talent for Murder*, Biltmore, 1981; *Blues in the Night*, Rialto, 1982; *A Doll's Life*, Mark Hellinger, 1982; *Foxfire*, Barrymore, 1982; *Shirley Maclaine on Broadway*, Gershwin, 1984; *Play Memory*, Longacre, 1984; *End of the World*, Music Box, 1984.

(Pre-Broadway) *Step Lively Boy*, Locust, Philadelphia, PA, 1973; *$600 and a Mule*, Huntington Hartford, Los Angeles, CA, 1973; *Snoopy!!!*, Forest, Philadelphia, PA, 1975; *The Philanthropist*, National, Washington, DC, 1975; *Long Days Journey into Night*, Eisenhower, Washington, DC,

1976; *Seven Brides for Seven Brothers,* Bob Carr Auditorium, Orlando, FL, 1979; *Noel,* Goodspeed Opera House, East Haddam, CT, 1981; *Chaplin,* Dorothy Chandler Pavilion, Los Angeles, CA, 1984.

(Off-Broadway) *The Dream on Monkey Mountain,* St. Marks, 1971; *Heloise,* Equity Library, 1971; *Nightride,* Van Dam, 1971; *A Meeting by the River,* Edison, 1972; *Strike Heaven on the Face,* Playhouse, 1973; *Games and After Liverpool,* Playhouse, 1973; *The Government Inspector,* Playhouse, 1973; *Thoughts,* Theatre de Lys, 1973; *A Breeze from the Gulf,* Eastside Playhouse, 1973; *The Great Mac-Daddy,* St. Marks, 1974; *Pretzels,* Theatre Four, 1974; *When Hell Freezes Over I'll Skate,* Mitzi Newhouse, 1979; *People in Show Business Make Long Goodbye's,* Orpheum, 1979; *Styne after Styne,* Manhattan Theatre Club, 1980; *Snoopy,* Lambs, 1982; *Talullah,* Westside Arts, 1984; *Get Happy,* Westwood Playhouse, 1984.

(Regional) *Journey of the Fifth Horse,* Milwaukee Repertory, WI, 1972; *The Play's the Thing, Two Gentlemen of Verona,* Milwaukee Repertory, WI, 1973; *Doctor Faustus,* Milwaukee Repertory, 1974; *The Philanthropist,* Goodman, Chicago, IL, 1975; *King Lear, Our Town, The Winter's Tale,* American Shakespeare Festival, Stratford, CT, 1975; *Kiss Me Kate,* Wolf Trap Farm, 1979; *Play Memory,* McCarter, 1983.

(Opera) *Simon Boccanegra,* Philadelphia Lyric, PA, 1973; *Le Coq D'Or,* Dallas Civic, TX, 1973; *Il Tabarro/Gianni Schicchi,* Philadelphia Lyric, PA, 974; *Anna Bolena,* Dallas Civic, TX, 1975; *Ashmedai,* New York City, NY, 1976; *L'Histoire Soldat, The Voice of Ariadne,* New York City, NY, 1977; *The Merry Widow, Naughty Marietta,* New York City, NY, 1978; *La Fanciulla del West,* Lyric of Chicago, IL, 1978; *Un Ballo in Maschera,* Dallas Civic, TX, 1978; *La Fanciulla del West,* San Francisco, CA, 1979; *The Pearl Fishers,* Dallas Civic, TX, 1979; *Silverlake,* New York City, NY, 1980; *The Merry Widow,* Greater Miami, FL, 1981; *Willie Stark,* Houston Grand, TX, 1981; *Ernani,* Dallas Civic, TX, 1981; *Candide,* New York City, NY, 1982; *Madama Butterfly,* Lyric of Chicago, IL, 1982; *Lucia di Lammermoor,* Dallas Civic, TX, 1982; *Faust,* Greater Miami, FL, 1983; *Turandot,* Vienna State, 1983; *Candide,* Houston Grand, TX, 1983; *Cosi Fan Tutte,* Greater Miami, FL, 1984; *Sweeney Todd,* Houston Grand, TX, 1984.

MAJOR TOURS—*Mame,* Los Angeles, CA, 1970; *International Ice Review,* Brooklyn, NY, 1971; *Fiddler on the Roof,* Los Angeles, CA, 1976; *Equus,* Burlington, VT, 1976; *My Fair Lady,* St. Louis, MO, 1977; *On the Twentieth Century,* Detroit, MI, 1979; *Da,* Amherst, MA, 1979; *Snow White and the Seven Dwarfs,* Washington, D.C., 1979; *Fiddler on the Roof,* Baltimore, MD, 1980; *Da,* Portland, OR, 1980; *My Fair Lady,* New Orleans, LA, 1980; *Sweeney Todd,* Washington, DC, 1980.

AWARDS: Antoinette Perry Award Nomination, Best Lighting Design, 1984: *End of the World;* Antoinette Perry Award Nomination, Drama Desk Award Nomination, Boston Drama Critics Award, Maharam Award Nomination, Best Lighting Design, 1982: *Foxfire;* Antoinette Perry Award Nomination, Drama Desk Award Nomination, Los Angeles Drama Critics Award, Best Lighting Design, 1979: *Sweeney Todd;* Antoinette Perry Award Nomination, Best Lighting Design, 1978: *Working;* Antoinette Perry Award Nomina-

tion, Best Lighting Design, 1973: *The Visit;* Ace Award, Monitor Award Nomination, Best Lighting Design, 1982: *Broadway;* Lumen Award, Illuminating Engineering Society of North America Edwin F. Guth Memorial Lighting Design Award of Merit: *The Red Parrot.*

SIDELIGHTS: MEMBERSHIPS—United Scenic Artists.

ADDRESS: Office—200 W. 70th Street, New York, NY 10023.

* * *

BILOWIT, Ira J., critic, writer, producer

PERSONAL: Born September 12, 1925, in New York City; son of Isidor William (a restaurateur) and Fanny (Goodinsky) Bilowit; married Alice Spivak (an actress), March 11, 1956 (divorced, 1970); married Debbi Wasserman (a writer/television programmer), May 23, 1976; children: (first marriage) William (a filmmaker) and Michael. EDUCATION: City College–C.U.N.Y., B.S.S., 1946. NON-THEATRICAL CAREER: Graduate Fellow, City College, 1947–50; Tutor, City College, 1950–51.

CAREER: WRITER: PLAYS—*Of Mice and Men* (adaptation and lyrics), 1958; *For Love of Candy,* 1971. BOOKS—ANTA publication on Off-Broadway Theatre. PERIODICALS—Editor and reviewer for *Show Business,* 1953–58, and managing editor, *Show Business,* 1961–63 and 1972–75; contributing editor, *Back Stage* (also responsible for Annual Legit Section of Anniversary Issues) 1980–83; editor-publisher, *New York Theatre Review,* 1976–80; articles in *American Way Magazine, Theatre Crafts, Other Stages.*

AWARDS: Second Prize, *Inter-Collegiate Play Contest,* 1947.

SIDELIGHTS: MEMBERSHIPS—Dramatists Guild, American Theatre Critics Association (editor, Newsletter), Drama Desk (former vice-president), New Drama Forum (secretary).

Mr. Bilowit has worked in various fields within the theatre including work as stage manager, production manager, general manager for dance presentations, children's theatre, and Off-Broadway, community, and summer stock productions. He produced, with Unicorn Productions, his musical, *Of Mice and Men;* with Terese Hayden and Elaine Aiken, *The Secret Concubine,* Carnegie Hall Playhouse, New York, 1960; and directed his play, *For Love of Candy* at the Forestburgh Summer Theatre, Monticello, NY, 1971. For Pancosmas Productions he has produced films for television and commercial release.

ADDRESS: Home—240 W. 10th Street, New York, NY 10014; Office—41 W. 72nd Street, New York, NY 10023.

* * *

BINDER, Steve, producer, director, and writer

PERSONAL: Born in Los Angeles, CA. EDUCATION: Attended University of Southern California.

CAREER: PRINCIPAL TELEVISION WORK—Producer, *Petula Clark Special,* 1967; producer/director, *The First Elvis Presley Special;* director, *The Big Show;* producer/director, *The Olivia Newton-John Special;* producer/director, *Holiday Star Wars Special;* producer/director, *Christmas at Disney World;* producer/director, *Shields and Yarnell;* director, *Don Kirschner's Rock Concerts;* director, *Hullaballoo;* producer/director, *The Diana Ross Special,* 1981; producer, *An Innocent Love;* producer, *Stanley; Annual Emmy Awards Show,* 1981, 1982, 1983; director, *Diana Ross in Central Park,* 1983; *Jane Fonda's Celebrity Comedy Fashion Show,* 1983; producer/director, *One Step Closer,* producer/director, *The Ringling Brothers, Barnum and Bailey Circus,* 1983, 1984; producer/director, *Blondes vs. Brunettes,* 1984.

PRINCIPAL FILM WORK—Director, *Give 'Em Hell, Harry,* 1976; director, *T.A.M.I.*

AWARDS: Emmy Award, Best Special: *The First Barry Manilow Special.*

SIDELIGHTS: MEMBERSHIPS—National Academy of Recording Arts and Sciences (board of governors), Directors Guild, Producers Guild, Writers Guild of America.

ADDRESS: Office—c/o Freeman, Heinecke and Sutton, 8961 Sunset Blvd., Los Angeles, CA 90069.

* * *

BINGHAM, Sallie, playwright

PERSONAL: Born January 21, 1937 in Louisville, KY; daughter of George Barry (a journalist) and Mary (Caperton) Bingham; married Timothy C. Peters (a contractor), June 21, 1983; children: Barry, Chris, Timothy, Will, Doug. EDUCATION: Radcliffe, B.A., 1958. POLITICS: Democrat. RELIGION: Episcopalian. NON-THEATRICAL CAREER: Instructor of creative writing, University of Louisville, 1977–83.

WRITINGS: PLAYS, UNPUBLISHED—Milk of Paradise, American Place Theatre, New York, 1980; The Country Boy, University of Louisville, 1980; The Wall Between, St. Edward's University, Austin, Texas, 1982; Couvade, Actors Theatre, Louisville, 1983.

SIDELIGHTS: MEMBERSHIPS—Authors Guild, PEN.

ADDRESS: Business—525 West Broadway, Louisville, KY 40202.

* * *

BIRNEY, David E., actor, director

PERSONAL: Born April 23, in Washington, DC; son of Edwin B. (a special agent for the F.B.I.) and Jeanne (McGee) Birney; married Meredith Baxter (an actress) April 10, 1974; children: Kathleen Jeanne (from wife's previous marriage), Theodore, Eva. EDUCATION: Dartmouth College, A.B. English Literature, 1961; UCLA, M.A. Theatre. MILITARY: U.S. Army, Second U.S. Army Showmobilie, an

DAVID BIRNEY

entertainment unit, toured the Eastern, Southern and Midwestern United States.

CAREER: DEBUT—Simon, *Hay Fever,* Barter Theatre, Abingdon, VA, 1965. NEW YORK DEBUT—Antipholus of Syracuse, *Comedy of Errors,* New York Shakespeare Festival, 1967. PRINCIPAL STAGE APPEARANCES—Streetsinger, *Threepenny Opera,* Algernon, *The Importance of Being Earnest,* Orsino, *Twelfth Night,* Barter Theatre, 1965–66; resident actor at Hartford Stage Company roles included: Fedotik, *Three Sisters,* Clov, *Endgame,* 1966–67; 1967 season at the New York Shakespeare Festival, Delacorte Theatre: Dauphin, *King John,* Chiron, *Titus Andronicus;* Chorus and Egg of Head, *MacBird,* Village Gate, 1967; Edmund, *Ceremony of Innocence,* American Place, 1968; Young Man, *Summertree,* Forum, Lincoln Center, 1968; Cleante, *The Miser,* Vivian Beaumont, 1969; Andocides, *The Long War,* Triangle, 1969; Wilson, *The Ruffian on the Stair* and Kenny, *The Erpingham Camp,* University of Pennsylvania, 1969; title role, *Hamlet,* University of Pennsylvania, 1970; Yang Sun, *The Good Woman of Setzuan,* Vivian Beaumont, 1970; Christy Mahon, *The Playboy of the Western World,* Vivian Beaumont, 1970; Jan, Hovstad, *An Enemy of the People,* Vivian Beaumont, 1970; Mar/Haemon, *Antigone,* Vivian Beaumont, 1970; Adolphus Cusins, *Major Barbara,* Mark Taper Forum, 1971; Mercutio, *Romeo and Juliet,* Arena Stage, Buffalo, 1972; Valentine, *You Never Can Tell,* Arlington Park, Chicago, 1973; Romeo, *Romeo and Juliet,* American Shakespeare Festival, Stratford, CT, 1974; King Arthur, *Camelot,* St. Louis Municipal Opera, 1975; Kentridge, *The Biko Inquest,* Mark Taper Forum, 1979.

MAJOR TOURS—*Brecht and Strindberg,* an anthology, Strolling Players, 1967; Sky Masterson, *Guys and Dolls,* 1973; Higgins, *My Fair Lady,* St. Louis production, 1979; Matt Friedman, *Talley's Folly,* 1981.

PRINCIPAL STAGE WORK: Director—*The Zoo Story,* Barter Theatre, 1965; *Yanks 3, Detroit 0, Top of the Seventh,* Stratford, CT, 1974; *A Life in the Theatre,* Matrix, Los Angeles, CA, 1980; *The Sorrow of Stephen,* Dartmouth Repertory, 1980.

PRINCIPAL FILM APPEARANCES—Neil Bowman, *Caravan to Vaccares,* 1976; *Oh God, Book II,* 1980; Frank, *Good Bye . . . See You Monday;* John, *Trial By Combat.*

PRINCIPAL TELEVISION APPEARANCES—Dr. Ben Samuels, *St. Elsewhere;* Lyon Burke, *The Valley of the Dolls;* Dr. Jonathan Ferrier, *Testimony of Two Men;* Daniel, "Daniel in the Lions Den", *The Bible;* Frank Serpico, *Serpico;* John Quincy Adams, *The Adams Chronicles;* Bernie Steinberg, *Bridget Loves Bernie; Glitter.* FILMS FOR TELEVISION—David, *The Master of the Game;* Henry Hawksworth, *The Five of Me; Mom, the Wolfman and Me;* Tony Gianetti, *High Midnight,* 1979; Jan, *Ohms,* 1980; Paul Winkless, *High Rise; The Deadly Game* (pilot for *Serpico*); *Only with Married Men; The Champions;* Willie Harvey, *Bronc.*

THEATRE-RELATED CAREER: Visiting professor of Drama, Dartmouth College, 1980.

AWARDS: L.A. Weekly Award, Best Director, 1980: *A Life in the Theatre; Photoplay* Magazine Award, most promising newcomer, 1973; *Sixteen* Magazine Award, performance, *Bridget Loves Bernie,* 1973; Buffalo Courier Express Award, Mercutio, *Romeo and Juliet,* 1972; Theatre World, Clarence Derwent Award, Best Performance, 1968: the dying soldier, *Summertree;* Barter Theatre Award, 1965.

SIDELIGHTS: MEMBERSHIPS—AEA, SAG, AFTRA, Players Club, Academy of Motion Picture Arts and Sciences; large theatre panel, National Endowment for the Arts, 1979.

RECREATIONS—Skiing, sailing, poetry, literature, music, running.

ADDRESS: Agent—c/o Myrna Post Assoc., 145 E. 49th Street, New York, NY 10017.

* * *

BIRNEY, Reed, actor

PERSONAL: Born September 11, 1954, in Alexandria, VA; son of James Gillespie II (a minister) and Marion Elizabeth (Marsh) Birney. EDUCATION: Boston University School of Fine Arts, 1972–74.

CAREER: DEBUT—Juvenile lead in a traveling children's theater company, December 1974. NEW YORK DEBUT—Randy Hastings, *Gemini,* Little Theater, 1977, 669 performances. PRINCIPAL STAGE APPEARANCES—Ivan Homeless, *The Master and Margarita,* New York Shakespeare Festival, 1978; Simon, *Hay Fever,* Kenyon Festival Theater, 1982; Sam, *In a Northern Landscape,* Actor's Theater of Louisville, 1983;

REED BIRNEY

Jonathan, *Winterplay,* Second Stage, New York, 1983. MAJOR TOURS—*The Dining Room,* Cape Cod, Westport, Ogunquit, 1983.

FILM DEBUT—Louis Carnahan, *Four Friends,* 1981. PRINCIPAL FILMS—Vic, *The XYZ Murders,* 1984. TELEVISION DEBUT—James Thurber, "The Greatest Man in the World," *American Short Story* (PBS).

SIDELIGHTS: "Arthur Penn's *Four Friends* has been the most important experience in my career, both professionally and personally."

ADDRESS: Agents—c/o Monty Silver, 200 W. 57th Street, New York, NY 10019; c/o Scott Harris, 9220 Sunset Blvd., Suite B, Los Angeles, CA 90069.

* * *

BISHOP, Andre, producer, director

PERSONAL: Born November 9, 1948, in New York City; son of Andre V. (an investment banker) and Felice H. (Francis) Smelianinoff. EDUCATION: Harvard College, 1970.

CAREER: PRINCIPAL STAGE WORK—Producer, Playwrights Horizons: *Table Settings; Coming Attractions; March of the Falsettos; The Dining Room; The Transfiguration of Benno Blimpie; Sister Mary Ignatius Explains It All for You; Geniuses; Isn't It Romantic; Sunday in the Park with George.*

THEATRE-RELATED CAREER—Worked with the New York Shakespeare Festival and the American Place Theatre, New York City; consultant to the CAPS Playwriting Program; teacher, NYU, Hunter College; artistic director, Playwrights Horizons, 1978–present.

SIDELIGHTS: MEMBERSHIPS—Board of Overseers, Loeb Drama Center; Theatre Panel, NEA.

ADDRESS: Office—Playwrights Horizons, 416 W. 42nd Street, New York, NY 10036.

* * *

BISHOP, Conrad J., playwright, director, actor

PERSONAL: Born October 8, 1941, in Denver, CO; son of Conrad W. (a construction worker) and Margaret L. (a bookkeeper; maiden name, Pitzer) Bishop; married Elizabeth Fuller (an actress/writer), November 27, 1961; children: Eli R., Johanna M. EDUCATION: Northwestern, B.S., 1962, M.A. 1963; Stanford, Ph.D., 1967.

CAREER: PRINCIPAL STAGE APPEARANCES—Since 1969, a full-time ensemble performer for The Independent Eye and Theatre X with over two thousand performances in thirty-three states and abroad. DIRECTED: PLAYS—Seventy productions for The Independent Eye, Theatre X, Penninsula Drama Guild, University of Delaware, University of Wisconsin/Milwaukee, University of South Carolina, Yellow Springs Fellowship of the Arts, KPIX-TV, WHA-TV, WUHY-FM, others; U.S. premiere of D. H. Lawrence's *David;* first U.S. production with complete score of Brecht/Eisler, *The Measures Taken; Medea/Sacrament,* CSC Repertory, New York, 1983; *Macbeth,* Performing Garage, New York.

THEATRE-RELATED CAREER: Associate professor of English/associate director of Theatre, University of South Carolina, 1966–68; associate professor of Theatre Arts, University of Wisconsin/Milwaukee, 1968–71.

WRITINGS: PLAYS, UNPUBLISHED—(all written in collaboration with Elizabeth Fuller) The Silk Block, 1965; The Bitch of Kynossema, 1968; (for Theatre X, 1969–74) Meet, Monday Morning, Comedying, Mister Punch, The Wizard of Spring, Alice in Wonder, Alice Wake Up, My Wife Dies at Stonehenge, The Whiteskin Game, The People vs. The People, Giveaway, X Communication, 1969–74; Halfway to Somewhere, 1973; Songs of Passersby, 1973; Knock Knock, 1975; I Wanna Go Home, 1977; Who's There, 1979; (for the Independent Eye, 1974–83) Le Cabaret de Camille, Marvels, Families, Lifesaver, Black Dog, Dreambelly, Dessie, The Money Show, Goners, Song Stories, Sunshine Blues, Action News, 1974–83; Wanna, 1980; Families, 1980; Full Hookup, 1982; Medea/Sacrament, 1983. Dramatic sketches and articles published in *Theatrework, Arts in Society, Theatre News, Other Stages, The Hyde Parkers, Theatre in Pennsylvania,* and *Dramatics Magazine.*

AWARDS: Silver Gavel Award, American Bar Association, for TV production, *Halfway to Somewhere,* 1975; invited presenter, First World Workshop on Social Action Theatre, Jerusalem, 1979; Best of Festival Award, American Personnel and Guidance Association, television production of *Dessie,* 1980; playwriting fellowship, Pennsylvania Council on the Arts, 1980; O'Neill Playwright, National Playwrights conference, 1980; Ohio State Award for public radio performance of *Families,* 1982; Co-Winner, Great American Play Contest, Actors Theatre of Louisville, *Full Hookup,* 1982.

SIDELIGHTS: MEMBERSHIPS—Dramatists Guild; UNIMA; Theatre Panel, Pennsylvania Council on the Arts, 1980–84.

Mr. Bishop co-founded two professional TCG-affiliate theatres, The Independent Eye and Theatre X.

* * *

BIVENS, Diane E., actress, choreographer, singer

PERSONAL: Born June 19, in New York City; daughter of Fred D. and Frances R. (a retired union leader; maiden name Horne) Bivens; married Marvin Jones, June 27, 1970 (divorced 1977); children: Themba. EDUCATION: New York University School of the Arts, B.F.A., 1973; studied speech with Nora Dunfee. NON-THEATRICAL CAREER: Graduate teaching assistant, NYU-School of the Arts, 1974–75; consultant/teacher, Frederick Douglass Creative Arts Center, 1975; teacher/coordinator, Afro-American Studio for Acting and Speech, 1975–76; consultant/teacher, The Family Ex-Inmate Theatre Co., 1976; consultant/teacher, New York Foundation for the Arts, 1977; consultant/teacher, Theatre for the Forgotten, 1978; consultant/teacher, New Jersey Department of Education, 1980; teacher, Mind Builders

DIANE E. BIVENS

Creative Arts Center, 1981; workshop instructor, New York Department of Parks and Recreation, 1983.

CAREER: NEW YORK DEBUT—The Bird, *Ti-Jean and His Brothers,* New York Shakespeare Festival, Delacorte, July 1972, approximately 64 performances. PRINCIPAL STAGE APPEARANCES—Understudy, *My Sister, My Sister,* Little Theatre, New York, 1974; Rita, *The Mighty Gents,* Urban Arts Corps, New York, 1977; Woman of Bath, *Canterbury Tales,* New York Renaissance Festival, Sterling Forest, NY, 1979; Lady in Red, *For Colored Girls Who Have Considered Suicide When the Rainbow Is Enuf,* ACT, Seattle, 1980.

FILM DEBUT—Minnie Gaston, *A.G. Gaston—A Light in the Darkness,* 1976. PRINCIPAL FILMS—Revolutionary woman, *Wolfen,* 1981. TELEVISION DEBUT—*All My Children.*

AWARDS: American Legion Award, 1960.

SIDELIGHTS: MEMBERSHIPS—Ethnic Minorities Committee–Actors Equity Association; Treasurer, building tenants committee.

ADDRESS: Home—788 Riverside Drive, New York, NY 10032. Agent—Robert Kass, 156 Fifth Ave., New York, NY 10011.

* * *

BLACK, Malcolm, director, producer, writer

PERSONAL: Born May 13, 1928, in Liverpool, England; citizen of the United States; son of Kenneth L. (a businessman) and Althea V. (Hanks) Black; married Diane Forhan, August, 1958 (divorced 1967); children: Duncan, Trevor. EDUCATION: Bryanston School, Blandford, England; trained for the theatre at the Old Vic School. MILITARY: Second Lieutenant, British Army, 1946–48.

CAREER: DIRECTED: Plays—*Ghosts,* Hart House Theatre, Toronto; *The Pillars of Society,* Crest Theatre, Toronto; *The Pleasure of His Company,* Hunterdon Hills, NJ; *The Thracian Horses,* New York; *The Curate's Play,* New York; *Critics Choice,* Playhouse in the Park, Philadelphia; *A Thousand Clowns,* Palm Beach; *Julius Caesar,* Beverly, MA; *Lord Pengo,* Pocono Playhouse; *The Hostage,* Playhouse Theatre Company of Vancouver, BC; *The Sound of Music, Anything Goes, Finian's Rainbow, Gypsy,* Rainbow Stage, Winnipeg, Manitoba; *Come Live with Me* (world premiere), Westport, CT; *Like Father Like Fun* (world premiere), Playhouse Theatre Company of Vancouver, BC; *Big Soft Nellie* (North American premiere), Vancouver International Festival; *Count Down to Armageddon* (world premiere), Playhouse Theatre Company of Vancouver, BC; *The Marriage of Mr. Mississippi,* Center Theatre Group, Los Angeles; *Enrico IV,* North Carolina school of the Arts; *A Midsummer Night's Dream,* Inner City Repertory, Los Angeles; *Oedipus Rex,* National Shakespeare Company; *The Fourth Monkey* (world premiere) Playhouse Theatre Company of Vancouver, BC; *Shelley,* University of Washington, Seattle; *Tosca,* Seattle Opera Association; *Crabdance* (world premiere), ACT Seattle; *Hobson's Choice,* Manitoba Theatre Centre, Winnipeg; *The Way of the World,* Long Wharf, New Haven, CT; *House of Blue Leaves,* Juilliard Drama Division; *A Taste of Honey,*

MALCOLM BLACK

Queen's College, New York; *The Taming of the Shrew,* Walnut Street, Philadelphia; *Bittersweet,* St. Louis Municipal Opera; *Hunting Stuart,* Festival Lenoxville, Quebec; *The Speckled Band,* St. Lawrence Center, Toronto; *Waltz of the Toreadors,* Theatre Plus, Toronto; *The Taming of the Shrew,* Alliance, Atlanta; *Hansel & Gretel,* The Guelph Spring Festival, Ontario; *The Return of A. J. Raffles* (North American premiere), Theatre New Brunswick/The Neptune Theatre, Halifax, NS; *Arms and the Man,* National Theatre School, Montreal; *Murder Game* (world premiere), Theatre New Brunswick, Fredericton, NB; many others. THEATRE-RELATED CAREER: Professor of Drama/Theatre: University of Washington, 1968–70; City University of New York, 1970–74; York University, 1974–78.

WRITINGS: BOOKS—*From First Reading to First Night,* University of Washington Press.

AWARDS: Canadian Drama Award, 1967; Silver Jubilee Medal, 1978; Canada Council Senior Arts Grant, 1978; trained at Old Vic on full scholarship.

SIDELIGHTS: MEMBERSHIPS—Canadian Equity; Society of Stage Directors and Choreographers; Directors Guild of America.

From 1957 to 1959 Mr. Black served as production manager for the Crest Theatre, Toronto; he was administrator, 1959–61, of the American Shakespeare Festival Academy; he served as artistic director, 1964–67, of the Vancouver Playhouse; since 1978 he has been artistic director of Theatre New Brunswick.

ADDRESS: Office—The Playhouse, PO Box 566, Fredericton, NB, E3B 5A6 Canada.

* * *

BLACKMAN, Eugene Joseph, director, writer, educator

PERSONAL: Born November 8, 1922; son of Jacob (a shoeworker) and Lillian (Orloff) Blackman; married Edna Ruth Feldman, July 5, 1945; children: Debra Ann, Lawrence Mark. EDUCATION: Boston University, BS in Education, 1944, MA, 1947. MILITARY: Battalion sergeant major, U.S. Infantry.

CAREER: DIRECTED: Plays—*My Sister Eileen, Night of January 16, Finian's Rainbow, The Browning Version, If Men Played Cards as Women Do,* 1952–53; *The Philadelphia Story, Joan of Lorraine, Allegro, Born Yesterday,* 1953–54; *The Barretts of Wimpole Street, The Male Animal, Paint Your Wagon, My Three Angels,* 1954–55; *Ah! Wilderness, All My Sons, South Pacific, Dial "M" for Murder,* 1955–56; *You Can't Take it With You, Our Town, Kiss Me, Kate, John Loves Mary,* 1956–57; *The Man Who Came to Dinner, Dark of the Moon, Oklahoma!, The Caine Mutiny Court Martial,* 1957–58; *Pygmalion, The Great Sebastians, Carousel, A View from the Bridge,* 1958–59; *Teahouse of the August Moon, Tea and Sympathy, Fanny, The Mousetrap,* 1959–60; *Life with Father, Anastasia, South Pacific, Good News,* 1960–61; *The Diary of Anne Frank, George Washington Slept Here, Once Upon a Mattress, The Fantasticks,* 1961–62; *The Skin of Our Teeth, Picnic, Finian's Rainbow, The Gazebo,* 1962–63; *Dark of the Moon, The Pursuit of Happiness, A View from the Bridge, Take Me Along,* 1963–64; *Twelfth Night, The World of Carl Sandburg, Carnival,* 1964–65; *The Imaginary Invalid, Born Yesterday, A Funny Thing Happened on the Way to the Forum, Angel Street,* 1965–66; *A Streetcar Named Desire, How to Succeed in Business Without Really Trying,* 1966–67; *The Boys from Syracuse, Come Back Little Sheba,* 1967–68; *Detective Story, Lysistrata, Once Upon a Mattress, The Reluctant Dragon, Tom Sawyer, Androcles and His Pal,* 1968–69; *Rashomon, Mandragola, Celebration,* 1969–70; *Dark of the Moon, Antigone, Canterbury Tales,* 1970–71; *A Flea in Her Ear, The Adding Machine, Anyone Can Whistle,* 1971–72; *Tartuffe, Kiss Me, Kate,* 1972–73; *A Streetcar Named Desire, Two Gentlemen of Verona,* 1973–74; *A View from the Bridge, Guys and Dolls,* 1974–75; *You Can't Take it with You, Paint Your Wagon,* 1975–76; *Scapino!, A Funny Thing, etc.,* 1976–77; *My Sister Eileen, Damn Yankees,* 1977–78; *Pygmalion, Promises, Promises,* 1978–79; *The Mousetrap, The Fantasticks,* 1979–80; *Marriage Is . . .* (an adaptation of *School for Wives*), *Carnival,* 1980–81; *Androcles and the Lion* (a children's play), *Grease,* 1981–82, *The Princess and the Swineherd* (a children's play), *Pippin,* 1982–83.

THEATRE-RELATED CAREER: Professor of drama, chairperson, Northeastern University, 1960–82; professor of drama, Northeastern University, 1982–present.

WRITINGS: PLAYS, UNPUBLISHED—The Imaginary Invalid (adaptation), Phaedra (adaptation with Mort Kaplan), Lysistrata (adaptation), Tartuffe (adaptation), Marriage Is . . . (adaptation of Molière's *School for Wives*). BOOKS—co-editor with Eliot Norton, *The Actor in America: The Problem and the Promise,* 1965; co-editor with Mort Kaplan, *The Playwright in America,* 1966; contributor, *International Encyclopedia of Higher Education,* 1977.

AWARDS: Distinguished Service Awards, Northeastern University College, 1962, 1967, 1972, 1977, 1982; Distinguished Service Award, Northeastern University, 1973; Alpha Psi Omega (International Drama Fraternity) 1952; New England Theatre Conference, Special Recognition Award—elected into College of Fellows, 1982 .

SIDELIGHTS: MEMBERSHIPS—American Theatre Association; National Theatre Conference; Society of Stage Directors and Choreographers; Speech Community Association; Massachusetts Metropolitan Cultural Alliance; New England Theatre Conference (secretary, 1957–60, president, 1960–63, 1967–68, advisory council, incorporator). HOBBIES—Theatregoing, music, rug weaving, gardening. Proficient in French and Spanish.

ADDRESS: Home—51 Sumner Street, Milton, MA 02186. Office—Northeastern University, Department of Drama, 360 Huntington Ave., Boston, MA 02115.

* * *

BLAKE, Betty (nee Gibbs), publisher-editor

PERSONAL: Born August 16, 1920 in New York City; daughter of Frederick (an actor) and Violet (an actress; maiden name Fisher) Gibbs; married Glyn Lewis (an artist), May 31, 1947; NON-THEATRICAL CAREER—Editorial staff of *Newsweek.*

CAREER: Since 1944 Miss Blake, with her partner, Joan Marlowe, has been co-editor and publisher of *Theatre Information Bulletin,* and since 1964, of *Theatre Critics Review.*

WRITINGS: BOOKS, PUBLISHED—*The Keys to Broadway* (with Joan Marlowe), 1951; *Broadway—The Last Decade* (with Joan Marlowe), 1954.

SIDELIGHTS: MEMBERSHIPS—Drama Desk; Outer Circle, treasurer 1961–75; New Drama Forum, Inc. (association of theatre professionals), co-President with Joan Marlowe, 1980–83.

Miss Blake comes from a theatrical family—her grandfather was Charles E. Fisher, an actor and her great-grandfather was Alexander Fisher, also an actor, Ms. Blake is among the women profiled in the first edition of *Who's Who of American Women,* 1958.

ADDRESS: Business—Proscenium Publications, 4 Park Ave., New York, NY 10016.

* * *

BLAKE, Charles H., actor, choreographer, producer, and dancer

PERSONAL: Born June 9, 1916; son of Joseph Woods (a businessman) and Blanche Messick (an artist; maiden name,

Hibbitt) Blake. EDUCATION: Washington and Lee University, A.B.; Chalif School, Dance Diploma; trained for the stage with Reb Groupe, Benno and Batame Schneider. POLITICS: Independent. RELIGION: Episcopalian.

CAREER: DEBUT—The Magician, *Aska the Magician,* Rialto, Louisville, KY, 1930. NEW YORK DEBUT—understudy (the Kids), *Dead End,* Belasco, 1936. LONDON DEBUT—corps, Ballet Russe, Convent Garden, 1938. PRINCIPAL STAGE APPEARANCES—dancer, *New Faces,* Court, New York, 1937; dancer/magician, *Crazy with the Heat,* 44th Street Theater, 1939; singer, *This Is the Army,* Broadway, 1942. MAJOR TOURS—singer, *Right This Way* and *This Is the Army,* Cleveland, Cincinnati, Columbus, OH, Pittsburgh, PA; Groucho Marx Touring Revue, 1946.

FILM DEBUT—singer, *This Is the Army,* 1944. PRINCIPAL FILM APPEARANCES—dancer, *Her Sister's Secret,* 1946; lead, *The Red Wagons,* 1946; pilot, *The Master Key,* 1945. PRINCIPAL TELEVISION APPEARANCES—dancing magician, *Rainbow Grill Room Broadcast* and *Trianon Room Broadcast,* 1939.

DIRECTED: Films—*The Eighth Lively Art.* Ballet—*International Ballet.*

CHOREOGRAPHED: Plays—*Showboat,* Germany, 1972. Film—*The Eighth Lively Art.* Television—*Pee Wee King Show.*

THEATRE-RELATED CAREER: Consultant—San Juan Ballet; Buffalo Ballet. Coached/Staged—*Emmett Kelly Circus;* Musical Revue (Spain); *Palmer the Magician,* European Magic Festival.

WRITINGS: PLAYS, UNPUBLISHED—The Mago (musical). BOOKS—*Inner Dancing,* 1980; *A Dancer's Handbook,* 1981.

AWARDS: Hollywood Writer's Club Award, Contributions to Community Theaters; Canadian Société de Bonne Homme, 1967: *Expo '67.*

SIDELIGHTS: "I have enjoyed diversity at the cost of celebrity. All theater is within each of us to give to others—always with joy."

ADDRESS: Home—484 W. 43rd Street #460, New York, NY 10036; 3325 N. Knoll Drive, Hollywood, CA 90068.

* * *

BLAXILL, Peter, actor

PERSONAL: Surname is pronounced "Blacksill"; born September 27, 1931, in Cambridge, MA; son of Francis Harold and Alice (Arnold) Blaxill. EDUCATION: Bard College, Annandale-on-Hudson, New York, B.A. (drama); studied at the American Theatre Wing and with the Paul Mann Actors Workshop. MILITARY: U.S. army, 1953–55.

CAREER: DEBUT—Og, *Finian's Rainbow,* Brandywine Music Box, PA, 1956. NEW YORK DEBUT—Dr. Schoenfeld, *Scuba Duba,* New Theatre. PRINCIPAL STAGE APPEARANCES—*Marat/Sade,* Majestic, New York; *Semmelweiss,* Kennedy Center for the Performing Arts, Washington, DC, 1978;

FILM DEBUT—Economist, *The Groove Tube,* 1977.

SIDELIGHTS: Peter Blaxill has appeared in many productions in regional theatre companies; he also writes poetry.

ADDRESS: Home—321 W. 22nd Street, New York, NY 10011.

* * *

BLOCH, Scotty, actress

PERSONAL: Daughter of U. S. Grant (a salesman) and Edith Grace (Crowley) Scott; married Daniel J. Bloch (a coffee broker); children: Anthony Grant, Andrew Leonard. EDUCATION: Studied at the American Academy of Dramatic Art, New York, with Michael Howard and Allan Miller. POLITICS: Democrat. RELIGION: Raised a Catholic.

CAREER: DEBUT—Eileen, *My Sister Eileen,* Opera House, Wiesbaden, Germany, 1946. NEW YORK DEBUT—*Craigs Wife,* 78th Street Theatre, 1945. PRINCIPAL STAGE APPEARANCES—Esther, *The Price,* The Playhouse, New York, 1979; Mother, *Children of a Lesser God,* Longacre, New York, 1980; Blanche, *An Act of Kindness,* Harold Clurman, New York, 1980; Grace, *Grace,* American Place, New York, 1981.

PRINCIPAL TELEVISION APPEARANCES—*Search for Tomorrow, The Doctors, All My Children, Another World, Love Sidney;* Made-for-Television Movies—*A Knock on the Door,* NBC, *Nurse,* NBC, *Gentleman Bandit,* CBS, *Puddin' Head Wilson,* PBS. FILM DEBUT—Secretary, *King of Comedy,* 1982.

AWARDS: Theatre World Award, Outstanding Performer,

SCOTTY BLOCH

1981. Military Service Awards—Honorary Captain, while working as a Civilian Actress/Technician in Europe after WWII.

SIDELIGHTS: RECREATION: Travel, gardening, cooking, and wine culture. ''I was cast in a Halloween play in kindergarten, chosen from 30 other little 5-year-old girls. Thus began my interest in the theatre. My career was chosen for me in this way. My favorite roles: Eleanor, *The Lion in Winter*, Mary, *Long Day's Journey into Night*, Beatrice, *Gamma Rays on Man in the Moon Marigolds*, Billie, *Born Yesterday*. . . . in Mexico City, 1959–60, I helped run a theatre workshop, did a radio series and performed in two plays in English, *Love's Labours Lost*, and *Angel Street*. I learned to speak Spanish and travelled around Mexico with my husband and little sons, who learned Spanish better than I. I lived with my family in Geneva, Switzerland 1961–65 and learned to speak French . . . and had the good fortune to appear at the famous Théâtre Corps St. Pierre in *Miss Julie, The Stronger, Private Lives* and *Born Yesterday*. I am interested and vitally concerned with saving our wonderful old theatres, and of course our wonderful 'old world.' ''

ADDRESS: Home—311 W. 83rd Street, New York, NY 10024; Agent—Monty Silver, 200 W. 57th Street, New York, NY 10019.

* * *

BOGART, Paul, director

PERSONAL: Born November 21, 1919, in New York City; son of Benjamin and Molly (Glass) Bogart; married Jane (a set decorator), March 22, 1941; children: Peter, Tracy, Jennifer. EDUCATION: Attended public schools in New York City. MILITARY: U.S. Army Air Force, 1944–46.

CAREER: FIRST FILM WORK—Director, *Marlowe*, 1968. PRINCIPAL FILM WORK—Director, *The Skin Game*, 1971; *Class of '44*, 1973; *Oh, God! You Devil*, 1984.

FIRST TELEVISION WORK—Director, *One Man's Family*, 1952. PRINCIPAL TELEVISION WORK—Director, *CBS Playhouse; The Defenders; Goodyear Playhouse; Armstrong Circle Theatre; Kraft Theatre; US Steel Hour; All in the Family*.

AWARDS: Emmy Awards, *The Defenders*, 1964–65, *CBS Playhouse*, 1967–68 and 1969–70, *All in the Family*, 1977–78; Christopher Awards, 1955, 1973, 1975; Golden Globe, 1977.

SIDELIGHTS: MEMBERSHIPS—DGA, AMPAS (Governor 1980–81), ATAS, American Society of Directors and Choreographers, American Film Institute.

Mr. Bogart has spoken and lectured at the University of Tennesee, University of California at Irvine and UCLA.

ADDRESS: Office—760 N. La Cienega Blvd., Los Angeles, CA 90069. Agent—Contemporary Artists Agency, 1888 Century Park E., Los Angeles, CA 90067.

BOGDANOVICH, Peter, director, writer, and actor

PERSONAL: Born July 30, 1939, in Kingston, NY; son of Borislav and Herma (Robinson) Bogdanovich; married Polly Platt, 1962 (divorced 1970); married Cybill Shepherd, 1971 (divorced 1978); children: Antonia, Alexandra (first marriage). EDUCATION: Trained for the stage with Stella Adler.

CAREER: PRINCIPAL STAGE APPEARANCES—American Shakespeare Festival, Stratford, CT, 1956; New York Shakespeare Festival, 1958. DIRECTED/PRODUCED: Plays—(Off-Broadway) *The Big Knife*, 1959; *Camino Real*, 1961; *Ten Little Indians*, 1961; *Rocket to the Moon*, 1961; *Once in a Lifetime*, 1964.

FILM CAREER: 2nd-unit director, co-writer, actor, *The Wild Angels*, 1966; director, co-writer, producer, actor, *Targets*, 1968; director, co-writer, *The Last Picture Show*, 1971; director, writer, producer, *Directed by John Ford*, 1974; director, writer, producer, *What's Up, Doc?*, 1972; director, producer, co-writer, *Paper Moon*, 1973; director, co-writer, producer, *Daisy Miller*, 1974; director, writer, producer, *At Long Last Love*, 1975; director, co-writer, *Nickelodeon*, 1976; director, co-writer, actor, *Saint Jack*, 1979; director, writer, *They All Laughed*, 1981. THEATRE-RELATED CAREER: Film Feature Writer—*Esquire, New York Times, Village Voice, Cahiers du Cinéma, Los Angeles Times, New York Magazine, Vogue, Variety*, 1961–present; owner, Saticoy Productions Inc., Los Angeles, 1968–present; co-founder, Directors Company, 1972; Copa de Oro Productions, Los Angeles, 1973; owner, Moon Pictures, 1981–present; general partner, Bogdanovich Film Partners, 1982.

WRITINGS: Books—*The Cinema of Orson Wells*, 1961; *The Cinema of Howard Hawks*, 1962; *The Cinema of Alfred Hitchcock*, 1963; *John Ford*, 1968; *Fritz Lang in America*, 1969; *Allan Dwan: The Last Pioneer*, 1971; *Pieces of Time (Picture Shows in U.K.): Peter Bogdanovich on the Movies*, 1973–74; *The Killing of the Unicorn: Dorothy Ruth Stratten (1960–1980): A Memoir*, 1984.

AWARDS: Pasinetti Award, Critics Prize, Venice Film Festival, 1979: *Saint Jack*; Brussels Festival Award, Best Director, 1974: *Daisy Miller*; Silver Shell Award (Spain), 1973: *Paper Moon*; Writers Guild of America Award, Best Screenplay, 1972: *What's Up Doc?*; British Academy Award and New York Film Critics' Award, Best Screenplay, 1971: *The Last Picture Show*.

SIDELIGHTS: MEMBERSHIPS—Directors Guild of America, Writers Guild of America, Academy of Motion Picture Arts and Sciences.

ADDRESS: Agent—c/o CPK, 2040 Avenue of the Stars, Century City, CA 90067.

* * *

BOGIN, Abba, musical director and arranger

PERSONAL: Born November 24, 1925 in New York City; son of Morris (a postal clerk) and Anna (a poet; maiden name, Pinson) Bogin; married Silvana Casti, 1952 (divorced 1965); married Suzanne Cogan, 1965 (divorced 1970); married Masako Yanagito (a concert violinist), December 5,

ABBA BOGIN

1971; children: (first marriage) Nina, David. EDUCATION: Curtis Institute of Music, Philadelphia, B.Mus., 1949 (piano—Isabella Vengerova; conducting—Alexander Hilsberg; orchestration—Samuel Barber and Gian-Carlo Menotti); additional music training—conducting and chamber music at Berkshire Music Center, Tanglewood, Lenox, MA, 1946; conducting student of Pierre Monteux, L'école Monteux, Hancock, ME, 1947–52. MILITARY: U.S. Army, 1944–46 (staff sergeant). NON-THEATRICAL CAREER: Teaching—faculty of the Curtis Institute of Music, Philadelphia, piano, 1948–52; faculty of the Music School of the Henry Street Settlement, New York, piano, 1955–57; private students: piano, vocal coaching, opera repertoire, arranging, New York; faculty of Greenwood Music Camp, Cummington, MA, 1981–present.

CAREER: DEBUT—Musical director of GI Symphony Orchestra, Germany, 1945. NEW YORK DEBUT—(as pianist) Town Hall, 1947. PRINCIPAL STAGE WORK, Musical Director/Conductor—*Greenwillow*, Alvin, New York, 1960; *How to Succeed in Business Without Really Trying*, 46th Street Theatre, New York, 1961; *New Faces of 1962*, New York, 1962; *The Beauty Part*, New York, 1962; *Riverwind*, New York, 1962; *The Megillah of Itzahk Manger*, New York, 1968; *The Fig Leaves Are Falling*, New York, 1969; musical director for the New York City Light Opera Company at the City Center for revivals of: *The Most Happy Fella, Guys and Dolls, Where's Charley?, How to Succeed, etc., Finian's Rainbow, Oklahoma!,* and *Wonderful Town;* musical director for more than fifty shows—Broadway, Off-Broadway, and stock between 1950 and 1970; musical

director—*The Threepenny Opera,* Theatre de Lys, New York, 1957–58; *Beggar on Horseback,* Repertory Theatre of Lincoln Center, New York, 1970; musical director and arranger—*Another Evening with Harry Stoones,* 1964; arranger—small orchestra version of *How to Succeed in Business Without Really Trying,* 1962; *Riverwind,* 1965; dance music for City Light Opera production of *Where's Charley?,* 1966; *By Jupiter,* 1967; *Blood Red Roses,* 1970; opera, musical director—associate, *Koanga* (U.S. Premiere), Opera Society of Washington, DC, 1970; musical director, Young Artists Opera Company, New York, 1970–72; After Dinner Opera Company, New York, 1970–72; *La Boheme,* Queens Opera Company, Summer, 1971; Lyric Opera Theatre of New York, 1972; also musical staff of New York City Ballet, 1953–55, and New York City Opera, 1955. MAJOR TOURS—Associate musical director, *Peter Pan,* national tour, 1950; musical director, *Finian's Rainbow,* national tour, 1952; musical director, *Guys & Dolls,* USO tour of Vietnam and Far East, 1967.

PRINCIPAL FILMS—Musical director/producer (with Mark Bucci), *A Time to Play,* 1967; musical director and arranger, *The Flying Matchmaker,* 1970; musical director and arranger, *Memorial Day.* TELEVISION WORK—Assistant conductor, *Omnibus* and *Producers' Showcase,* 1950's; musical director, *American Musical Theatre,* 1963–65; associate musical director, *The Hero,* 1966; musical director and arranger, *The Beggar's Opera,* 1967; musical director, arranger, and composer, numerous commercial spots, including Mercury, Nesquick, Country Corn Flakes, Esso, and Blue Coal. INDUSTRIAL SHOWS—Musical director for Oldsmobile, Ford, Westinghouse, Armstrong Cork, Coca-Cola, and others.

RECORDINGS: Musical director—*Mrs. Patterson,* 1954; *Greenwillow,* 1960; *Riverwind,* 1962; musical director and arranger—*Politics and Poker;* conductor—*Songs of Perfect Propriety;* pianist—complete Beethoven *Sonatas for Cello and Piano* (with Janos Starker); Complete Brahms *Sonatas for Cello and Piano* (with Janos Starker); Mozart and Beethoven, *Trios* (The Boston Trio); Swanson, *Sonata for Cello and Piano* (with Carl Stern); *Petrouchka* (with New York Philharmonic, Dimitri Mitropoulos, conducting); Copland, *Clarinet Concerto* (with Benny Goodman and New York Philharmonic, Aaron Copland conducting); Bax *Sonata for Viola and Piano* (with Emanuel Vardi).

AWARDS: Walter W. Naumberg Award, 1947; Philadelphia Orchestra Award, 1948; Chamber Music Guild Award, 1948; YMHA-YWHA Recital Award, 1948; Premio Prix Italia (First Prize for TV opera in Italy), *The Hero,* 1968.

SIDELIGHTS: MEMBERSHIPS—AGMA (permanent trustee since 1958; treasurer, 1954–60); consultant to New York State Council on the Arts since 1970; Panel of Arbitrators, American Arbitration Association since 1960; Boston Trio (Ruth Posselt, violin, Samuel Mayes, cello, Abba Borgin, piano).

Abba Bogin has appeared as guest conductor and/or soloist with various orchestras throughout his career. He was pianist for the New York Philharmonic from 1956 to 1962, music editor for Frank Music Corporation from 1958–60, and has conducted many orchestras on tour in Japan and Romania since 1974. His career began in Wiesbaden, Germany in 1946, moved to the United States in the same year, and became international in the mid-1950's. He has worked in virtually every form of music. In the course of his career he has made several appearances at the White House. In 1967 he conducted two performances of *Salute to American Musical Theatre* for President Lyndon Johnson and in 1968 he was the musical director for a special performance of *Fiorello!*, also for President Johnson.

ADDRESS: Home—838 W. End Ave., New York, NY 10025. Agent—Raymond Weiss Concert Management, 200 W. 55 Street, New York, NY 10019.

* * *

BOLASNI, Saul, costume designer

PERSONAL: Born in Cleveland, OH; son of Bernard (a businessman) and Bertha (a nurse and professional swimmer; maiden name, Bodner) Bolasni. EDUCATION: Attended public schools in Cleveland, OH. NON-THEATRICAL CAREER—Commercial Artist: *Town and Country, Mademoiselle, Ladies' Home Journal, New Yorker;* advertising art work for Columbia Records, Ponds, Hattie Carnegie, Vanguard Press, Lentheric, Moore-McCormack Lones, Kayser Hosiery, Stendahl Cosmetics, Lippincott Press, Rosemarie De Paris, Galey & Lord; portrait artist.

CAREER: COSTUME DESIGN, THEATRE—*Courtin' Time*, National, NY, 1951; *The Rainmaker*, Cort, NY, 1954; *The Threepenny Opera*, Theatre de Lys, NY, 1954; *The Duchess of Malfi*, Phoenix, NY, 1957; *A Minor Adjustment*, Brooks Atkinson, NY, 1967; *Of Love Remembered*, ANTA, NY, 1967.

COSTUME DESIGN, BALLET—*Nimbus Rodeo, Pas de Deux Tropicale*, American Ballet Theatre; solo and group concert pieces, Valerie Bettis Dance Company; *Italian Concerto, Les Preludes*, American Negro Theatre of Dance; *The Silent Screen*, Mata & Hari's; *Streetcar Named Desire*, Franklin-Shavenska Company; *Les Ballets Ho*, A.B.C. Theatre; Tamaris-Nagrin Company; National Ballet Company; *Streetcar Named Desire*, Dance Theatre of Harlem (3rd revival), 1981.

COSTUME DESIGN, TELEVISION—*Hallmark Hall of Fame*, 1951–52; *Chesterfield Suspense Dramas*, 1952; *Salute to Baseball*, 1956; *The Martha Raye Show*, 1956; *La Boheme*, 1956; *Omnibus*, 1956–61; *Crescendo*, 1957; *The Polly Bergen Show*, 1957–58; *Leonard Bernstein's Christmas Special*, 1959 and all of Mr. Bernstein's Philharmonic broadcasts 1959–62; *Dow Mystery Series*, 1960; *Bell Telephone Hour*, 1960–61; *Thanksgiving Specials*, 1961, 1963; *The Nurses*, 1963; *Love of Life*, 1966–70; *Another World*, 1973; *All My Children*, 1976–80; *The Doctors*, 1980–82; *Ryan's Hope*, 1983–present.

SIDELIGHTS: MEMBERSHIPS—Scenic Artists Local 829, President, Costume Designer Membership.

Mr. Bolasni was a dancer and performed with the Valerie Bettis Dance Company, most notably, in *Up in Central Park* in 1945. He has also performed in Italy, in 1949 and in the Compagnia Salvini Festival of Antique Classics. His portrait of Lotte Lenya as Pirate Jenny from *The Threepenny Opera* is

on permanent display at the National Portrait Gallery in Washington, DC.

ADDRESS: Home—57 W. 69th Street, New York, NY 10023.

* * *

BOND, Derek, actor and writer

PERSONAL: Born January 26, 1920, in Glasgow, Scotland; son of Frank Herbert (a sales executive) and Dorothy Blanche (a beautician) Bond; married Grace Ann, January 28, 1942 (divorced 1970); married Gail Warner, July 24, 1970 (divorced 1977); married Margaret Ann Glover (a personal assistant and secretary), November 11, 1977; children: Anthony (first marriage), Belinda (second marriage). EDUCATION: H.A.H. School, 1930–36; Royal Military College, Sandhurst, 1939–40. POLITICS: Pragmatist. RELIGION: Church of England. MILITARY: Grenadier Guards, 1940–45.

CAREER: DEBUT—Joe, *As Husbands Go*, Garrick, London, 1938, 200 performances. PRINCIPAL STAGE APPEARANCES—Colchester Repertory, 1938–39; Etienne, *From the French*, Duchess, London, 1949; *To Dorothy a Son*, Gaiety, Dublin, 1950's; *Dial M for Murder, Gaslight, Tunnel of Love, Gracious Living*, Olympia, Dublin, 1950's; David, *A Scent of Flowers*, Duke of York's, London, 1964; The Vicar, *Murder at the Vicarage*, Savoy, 1976–77, Fortune, 1977–78; the Commander, *Not Now Darling*, Savoy, London, 1981; the Major, *The Mousetrap*, St. Martin's, London,

DEREK BOND

1982; Bromhead, *No Sex Please, We're British*, Garrick, 1983.

MAJOR TOURS—Sir Robert Chiltern, *The Ideal Husband*, South African cities, 1969; Uncle Edward, *Roar Like a Dove*, U.K. cities, 1970; the Butler, *The Grass Is Greener*, U.K. cities, 1971; the M.P., *Getting On*, U.K. cities, 1972; Robert, *How the Other Half Loves*, U.K. cities, 1973; Major, *End of Conflict*, U.K. cities, 1974; the Vicar, *Murder at the Vicarage*, U.K. cities, 1974–75; the Judge, *Deep Blue Sea*, U.K. cities, 1977; Northbrook, *The Sleeping Prince*, U.K. cities, 1977.

FILM DEBUT—Lt. Harley, *The Captive Heart*, 1945. PRINCIPAL FILM APPEARANCES—Nicholas, *Nicholas Nickleby*, 1946; Martin Trevor, *The Loves of Joanna Godden*, 1946; Lord Ilbury, *Uncle Silas*, 1947; Faber, *Broken Journey*, 1947; Captain Oates, *Scott of the Antarctic*, 1948; Peter, *The Weaker Sex*, 1948; Diego de Arana, *Christopher Columbus*, 1949; the Poet, *Poet's Pub*, 1949; Tim Shields, *Tony Draws a Horse*, 1949; Sir John, *Hour of Thirteen*, 1951; Sandy, *Svengali*, 1952; Sergeant, *Gideon's Day*, 1957; Stanley, *Wonderful Life*, 1965; the Boss, *Press for Time*, 1967; Lord Charnley, *When Eight Bells Toll*, 1969; Bank Manager, *Intimate Reflections*, 1974.

TELEVISION DEBUT—Robot, *R.U.R.*, 1937. PRINCIPAL TELEVISION APPEARANCES—one of John Brown's men, *Gallows Glorious*, 1938; David, *The Silver Cord*, 1949; His Lordship, *199 Park Lane*, 1965; Straight Man, *Cooperama*, 1966; Hunter, *Callan*, 1968; General, *Vanishing Army*, 1978.

WRITINGS: PLAYS, PRODUCED—*Akin to Death*, U.K. cities, 1954. SCREENPLAYS—*Unscheduled Stop*, 1966.

SIDELIGHTS: MEMBERSHIPS—British Actors' Equity (vice-president, 1976–79).

''After early ambitions to become a playwright or journalist when I was at school, a few appearances on stage with my mother's amateur dramatic company convinced me that I had to be an actor. . . I very much enjoy gardening, walking, swimming, sun-bathing, the company of attractive people, good dinner-table conversation and heated political debate. . . I dislike being unemployed, cocktail parties, official receptions, smoking at the dinner table and political extremism. . . I am very British and intensely patriotic but not a jingoist. I love London.''

ADDRESS: Agent—c/o Plunket Greene Ltd., 91 Regent Street, London W1R 8RU.

* * *

BOND, Sheila (Sheila Phylis Berman), actress, dancer, singer

PERSONAL: Born March 16, 1928, in New York City; daughter of Samuel (a painter) and Yetta (Krantz) Berman; married Leo Peter Coff, March 19, 1947 (divorced, 1953); married Barton Lawrence Goldberg, March 15, 1957; children: Brad J. Goldberg, Lori Gene Goldberg. EDUCATION: Attended Children's Professional School, New York; New Utrecht High School, Brooklyn; studied ballet with Anthony

Tudor and Frances Cole, tap dancing with Ernest Carlos. RELIGION: Jewish.

CAREER: DEBUT—chorus, *Let Freedom Sing*, Longacre, New York 1942. PRINCIPAL STAGE APPEARANCES—chorus, *Artists and Models*, Broadway, New York, 1943; clerk/dancer, *Allah, Be Praised*, Adelphi, New York, 1944; Mae Jones, *Street Scene*, Adelphi, New York, 1947; comedienne, *Make Mine Manhattan*, Broadhurst, New York, 1948; Ursula Poe, *The Live Wire*, Playhouse, New York, 1950; Fay Fromkin, *Wish You Were Here*, Imperial, New York, 1952; Sable Wellington, *Lunatics and Lovers*, Broadhurst, New York, 1954; Lola, *Damn Yankees* (for two weeks), 46th Street Theatre, New York, 1955; Billy Devine, *Deadfall*, Holiday, New York, 1955; Gladys, *Pal Joey*, City Center, New York, 1961. MAJOR TOURS—Fay, *Wish You Were Here*, Chicago, Shubert, 1953.

FILM DEBUT—Joan, *The Marrying Kind*, 1952. TELEVISION DEBUT—as Ronson Lighter Girl (age 9) broadcast from Radio City Music Hall. TELEVISION APPEARANCES—*Ed Sullivan Show*, appearances 1947–55; *Inside U.S.A. with Chevrolet*, 1949–50; *Playhouse 90; Perry Como Show;* others.

AWARDS: Antoinette Perry Award, Supporting Actress in a Musical, *Wish You Were Here*, 1953; Clarence Derwent Award, *Street Scene*, 1947.

SIDELIGHTS: MEMBERSHIPS—SAG, TVA, AEA. HOBBIES—Golf (won club championship at Bonaventure, 1980); bridge. Ms. Bond has also been a nightclub performer appearing at the Versailles, New York (1943), Belmont Plaza, New York (1944), La Martinique, New York (1945), the Latin Quarter, New York, (1946).

ADDRESS: Home—5 Tudor City Place, New York, NY 10017; Agent—Jeff Hunter, D.H.K.P.R., 165 W. 46th Street, New York, NY 10036.

* * *

BOND, Sudie, actress, singer and dancer

PERSONAL: Born July 13, 1928, in Louisville, KY; daughter of James Roy and Carrie (Showers) Bond; married Massen Cornelius Noland (divorced). EDUCATION: Rollins College, B.A., 1950; trained for the stage at the Herbert Berghof Studio with Uta Hagen and Herbert Berghof; studied dance with José Limon, Martha Graham, and Merce Cunningham.

CAREER: NEW YORK DEBUT—Mrs. Winemiller, *Summer and Smoke*, Circle in the Square, 1952. PRINCIPAL STAGE APPEARANCES—Olga, *Tovarich*, City Center, NY, 1952; Estelle, *Waltz of the Toreadors*, Coronet, NY, 1957; Agnes Gooch, *Auntie Mame*, City Center, NY, 1958; Grandma, *American Dream*, York, NY, 1961; Justine, *The Egg*, Cort, NY, 1962; Grandma, *The American Dream*, Grandma, *The Sandbox*, Nell, *Endgame*, Bertha, *Bertha*, Cherry Lane, NY, 1962; Miss Prose, *Harold*, Cort, NY, 1962; Mrs. Lazar, *My Mother, My Father, and Me*, Plymouth, NY, 1963; Grandma, *The American Dream*, Cherry Lane, NY, 1964; Vivienne, *Home Movies*, Provincetown Playhouse, NY, 1964; Nona, *Softly and Consider the Nearness*, Provincetown Playhouse, NY, 1964; matron, *The Great Western Union*, Bouwerie Lane, NY, 1965; Miss Hammer, *The*

Impossible Years, Playhouse, NY, 1965; Betsy Jane, *Keep It in the Family*, Plymouth, NY, 1967; Hana, *The Memorandum*, Anspacher, NY, 1968; Old Woman, *Quotations from Chairman Mao-tse Tung*, Billy Rose, NY, Spoleto Festival, Italy, 1968; Grandma, *The American Dream*, Billy Rose, NY, 1968; various roles, *Sketches*, Actors Playhouse, NY, 1969;

Mrs. Margolin, *Forty Carats*, Morosco, NY, 1970; Clara, *Hay Fever*, Helen Hayes, NY, 1970; *Grease*, Plymouth, NY; *Over Here*, Shubert, NY; *Thieves*, Broadhurst, NY; *Come Back to the Five and Dime, Jimmy Dean, Jimmy Dean*, Martin Beck, NY; Felicity, *The Shadow Box*, Center Stage, Baltimore, MD; *Carbona*, Arena, Washington, DC; Charlotta, *The Cherry Orchard*, Roundabout, NY; Alma, *The Mind with the Dirty Man*, Bucks County Playhouse, New Hope, PA; Lucy, *Nobody's Home*, Landmark Alliance. MAJOR TOURS—Agnes Gooch, *Auntie Mame*, U.S. cities, 1958; Lily, *A Piece of Blue Sky*, U.S. cities, 1959; *Albee One Acts*, East Asian cities.

PRINCIPAL FILM APPEARANCES—*Andy; A Thousand Clowns; Love Story; Where the Lilies Bloom;* Mrs. Hulsey, *Tomorrow; Cold Turkey; Come Back to the Five and Dime, Jimmy Dean, Jimmy Dean; The Cheese Stands Alone;* Thelma Rice, *Silkwood;* Annie, *Swing Shift;* Mary Margaret, *Johnny Dangerously.* PRINCIPAL TELEVISION APPEARANCES—*Mary Hartman, Mary Hartman; Rag Business; Love of Life; Barnaby Jones; The New Temperature's Rising; Benson; Mama Malone; Come Back to the Five and Dime, Jimmy Dean, Jimmy Dean; American Short Story; Four of Us; All in the Family; Guiding Light; Maude; Masquerade; Father Brown; Landon vs. Landon; Flo.*

AWARDS: Village Voice Award, Obie Award, 1962: *Theatre of the Absurd.*

SIDELIGHTS: RECREATION: Swimming, painting.

ADDRESS: Agent—c/o Smith-Freedman, 850 Seventh Avenue, New York, NY 10019. Agent—c/o Smith-Freedman, 9869 Santa Monica Blvd., Beverly Hills, CA 90212.

*　*　*

BONDOR, Rebecca, actress

PERSONAL: Born June 27, in Youngstown, OH; daughter of Ladeslaus Frank (an engineer) and Evelyn Ruth (Tulip) Bondor. EDUCATION: Miami University, B.F.A.; studied acting with Bill Esper.

CAREER: DEBUT—Miranda, *Davey Jones' Locker*, Bil Baird Theatre, New York, 1976. PRINCIPAL STAGE APPEARANCES—Estelle/ensemble, *The Haggadah*, New York Shakespeare Festival, 1981; Authea, *Masquerade*, Loretto Hilton Theatre (now Repertory Theatre of St. Louis), Long Wharf Theatre, New Haven, CT, 1978–79; Alice, *Alice in Wonderland*, Bil Baird Theatre, New York, 1977. MAJOR TOURS—Authea, *Masquerade*, Edinburgh Fringe Festival, 1979.

SIDELIGHTS: "The highest motivational factor for me pursuing a life in the theatre is the process of developing new works in an ensemble situation. . . . I believe totally in the immeasurable value of ongoing acting ensembles. These

groups seem to create a higher standard of acting and clearer communication with the audiences. . . . The greatest influence on my acting has been my teacher William Esper, who taught me the two-year technique that is taught at the Neighborhood Playhouse. One of the greatest influences on my feelings about acting and the theatre was the late director Stuart White. Stuart understood better than any director I've ever worked with the importance of the spirit and fun that must be created in any cast in order for the play to truly come to life."

ADDRESS: Agent—c/o Diane Commius, DMI Talent, 250 W. 57th Street, New York, NY 10019.

*　*　*

BONERZ, Peter, actor

PERSONAL: Born August 6, 1938, in Portsmouth, NH; son of Christopher Andrew (a military intelligence officer) and Elfrieda (Kern) Bonerz; married Rosalind DiTrapani, December 13, 1963; children: Eric, Eli. EDUCATION: Marquette University, B.S. MILITARY: U.S. Army (2 years).

CAREER: DEBUT—Chorus, *Agamemnon*, Columbia University, New York, 1961. NEW YORK DEBUT—Improvisatory actor, *The Premise*, The Premise, 1962, thirty weeks, approximately. PRINCIPAL STAGE APPEARANCES—Improvisatory actor, *The Committee*, The Committee, San Francisco, 1963–69; President, *The White House Murder Case*, Circle in the Square, New York, 1970; Actor, *Story Theatre*, Ambassador, New York, 1970.

FILM DEBUT—Perry, *Funnyman*, 1967. PRINCIPAL FILMS—*A Session with the Committee*, 1969; *The Serial*, 1969; *Medium Cool*, 1969; *Catch-22*, 1970. TELEVISION DEBUT—*The Addams Family*, 1963. TELEVISION APPEARANCES—*U.S.A.*, Hollywood Television Theatre; *Storm in Summer*, Hallmark Hall of Fame; *The Bob Newhart Show*, 1972–78. DIRECTED: Plays—*The Committee; Story Theatre.* Film—*Nobody's Perfekt.* Television—Episodes of *The Bob Newhart Show, Two of Us*, others.

WRITINGS: Films—co-author, *Funnyman*, 1967.

ADDRESS: Agent—Creative Artists Agency, Inc., 132 Lasky Drive, Beverly Hills, CA 90212.

*　*　*

BOOCKVOR, Steve, actor, choreographer, dancer

PERSONAL: Born November 8, 1945; son of Joseph (in manufacturing) and Betty (a salesperson; maiden name, Orenstein) Boockvor; married Denise Penee (an actress) on February 24, 1973; children: Jolan, Brette. EDUCATION: High School for the Performing Arts; Queens College, B.A., 1969; studied acting with Bill Esper and Wynn Handman, in New York. POLITICS: Independent. RELIGION: Jewish. MILITARY: U.S. Army (Military Police).

CAREER: DEBUT—featured dancer, José Limon Dance Company, Bogota, Colombia. NEW YORK DEBUT—dancer, *Anya*, Ziefield, 1965, 16 performances. PRINCIPAL STAGE APPEARANCES—*A Chorus Line*, Shubert, 1982–83; *The*

First, Martin Beck, 1981–83; *One Night Stand,* Nederlander, 1981; Eric Nesterenko, *Working,* Broadway, 1978; Rust, *Billy,* New York. FILM DEBUT—Jesus's Tormentor, *Jesus Christ Superstar,* 1973. TELEVISION DEBUT—*Ed Sullivan Show,* 1965. PRINCIPAL TELEVISION APPEARANCES—*Shirley MacLaine Special.* CHOREOGRAPHY—assistant to Grover Dale, *Billy,* New York; *Follies, Lady Be Good, Carousel,* summer stock. TELEVISION—*Singing in The Rain, Ed Sullivan Show, Shirley MacLaine Special.*

THEATRE-RELATED CAREER—Teacher, SUNY at Purchase, New York; teacher, Queens College, New York.

AWARDS: Antoinette Perry Award Nomination best supporting actor in a musical, Eric Nesterenko, *Working,* 1978.

SIDELIGHTS: MEMBERSHIPS—AEA, AFTRA, SAG. Favorite roles—Eric Nesterenko in *Working,* Rust in *Billy.*

ADDRESS: Agent—Hesseltine/Baker Associates Ltd., 165 W. 46th Street, New York, NY 10036.

* * *

BOONE, Debby (Deborah Ann Boone Ferrer), actress, vocalist, writer, and dancer

PERSONAL: Born September 22, 1956, in Hackensack, NJ; daughter of Charles Eugene (Pat) (an entertainer) and Shirley Lee (Foley) Boone; married Gabriel Ferrer (a manager), September 1, 1979; children: Jordan Alexander, Gabrielle Monserrate, Dustin Boone. EDUCATION: Graduated Marymount High School, Los Angeles, CA, 1974. RELIGION: Christian.

CAREER: DEBUT—Millie, *Seven Brides for Seven Brothers,* E. J. Thomas Hall, Akron, OH, 1981. NEW YORK DEBUT—Millie, *Seven Brides for Seven Brothers,* Alvin, 1982, 23 performances. MAJOR TOURS—Millie, *Seven Brides for Seven Brothers,* U.S. cities, 1981–82.

TELEVISION DEBUT—singer, *Pat Boone's Chevy Showroom.* PRINCIPAL TELEVISION APPEARANCES—*Same Old, Brand New Me; One Step Closer,* numerous appearances on talk and variety shows.

WRITINGS: BOOKS—*Debby Boone—So Far* (autobiography), 1980.

AWARDS: NARAS Award, Best Inspirational Performance, 1980: *With My Song* (album); Dove Award, 1980: *With My Song;* Golden Plate Award, 1978; Grammy Award, Best New Artist, 1977.

ADDRESS: Agent—c/o ICM, 8899 Beverly Blvd., Los Angeles, CA 90048.

* * *

BOOTHBY, Victoria, actress

PERSONAL: Born February 1, in Chicago, IL; daughter of James E. (a businessman) and Victoria L. (a dancer; maiden

VICTORIA BOOTHBY

name, Van Engers) Boothby; married Harry S. Ross (an Episcopal priest) on February 1, 1954, (divorced 1968); children: Sarah, Deborah, Harry, James. EDUCATION: Barnard College, B.A., 1949; attended the Old Vic School in London, England, studying with Michel St. Denis and George Devine. POLITICS: Democrat. RELIGION: Episcopal.

CAREER: DEBUT—Witch, *Dark of the Moon,* Surrey Playhouse, Surrey, ME, 1948. NEW YORK DEBUT—Leocadia Begbick, *A Man's a Man,* WPA Theatre, for 12 performances, 1971. PRINCIPAL STAGE APPEARANCES—Amanda, *The Glass Menagerie,* Syracuse Stage, NY, 1979; Miss Havisham, *Great Expectations,* Pennsylvania Stage Company, 1980; Professor George, *Professor George,* Playwrights Horizons, NY, 1976. MAJOR TOURS—Helga, *Passion of Dracula,* Boston, Montreal, Ottawa, 1978; Mrs. Prynne, *Da,* Boston, Washington, DC, Philadelphia, San Francisco, L.A., Detroit, Chicago, 1979–80.

FILM DEBUT—Mrs. Bodine, *The Goodbye Girl,* 1977; PRINCIPAL FILM APPEARANCES—Lucille Farmer, *Committed,* 1982. TELEVISION DEBUT—Helen Cooper, *All My Children,* 1980–82.

AWARDS: Fulbright Scholarship, 1951, for study at the Old Vic School.

SIDELIGHTS: "Major pre-occupation: PEACE. Went to Russia in 1982 with a group from Trinity Parish, NY, to promote peace."

ADDRESS: Agent—Gerry Bloomberg, c/o Thomas-Baldwin Agency, 260 Fifth Avenue, New York, NY 10001.

* * *

BOOTHE, Power, designer

PERSONAL: Born March 12, 1945, in Dallas, TX; son of Tom Wheeler (an engineer) and Shirlee Virginia (Barth) Boothe; married Sarah Schoentsen 1969 (divorced 1974); Elizabeth Rheem Rectanus (Director of Development, City Center Theatre) August 17, 1980. EDUCATION: San Francisco Art Institute, 1963, Colorado College, B.A. 1967, Whitney Museum independent study program, 1967–68.

CAREER: FIRST STAGE WORK—Art director, *Elephant Steps*, Tanglewood, MA, 1968. FIRST NEW YORK STAGE WORK—Set designer, *Southern Exposure*, Performing Garage, 1978. PRINCIPAL STAGE WORK—Set design: *Red Horse Animation*, Mabou Mines, Guggenheim Museum, 1970; *Step Wise Motion*, Dance Theatre Workshop, NY, 1982; *Trying Times*, Dance Theatre Workshop, NY, 1982; *The Mother of Us All*, (opera), Music Theater Group/Lenox Arts Center at St. Clements Theatre, NY, Lenox Arts Center, MA, Wolftrap Farm Park, VA, 1983; *Phantom Limbs*, Theatre of the Open Eye, NY, 1983; *Bill Loman*, Kitchen, NY, 1983; *Formal Abandon*, (dance), University of California, Berkeley, 1984; *Variety Show*, (dance), Dance Theatre Workshop, NY, New Performance Gallery, San Francisco, CA, 1984; *Framework*, (dance), Dance Theatre Workshop, NY, Loeb Theatre, Cambridge, MA, 1984.

PRINCIPAL FILM AND VIDEO WORK—Producer/director, Out of Line Series: *Match*, (3 minute film), Los Angeles, CA, 1973; producer/director, Portrait Series: *Jim*, (3 minute film) NY, 1973; producer/director, Out of Line Series: *Glass Curtains*, (5 minute film), Los Angeles, CA, 1974; producer/director, Portrait Series: *Victor*, (3 minute film), Denver, Co, 1974; set design, *A Peculiar Turn of Events*, (15 minute film), NY, 1980; set design, *The Cold Eye*, (30 minute film), NY, 1980; set design, *It Starts at Home*, (30 minute video), Whitney Museum, NY, 1982; production design, *Lies*, (4 minute video), 1983; production design, *Far from the Beaten Path*, (4 minute video), 1983; production design, *Girls Just Want to Have Fun*, (4 minute video), 1983; producer/director, Portrait Series: *Brook*, (3 minute film), Collective for Living Cinema, 1983.

AWARDS: NEA Inter Arts Grant, 1983, 1984; New York State Council Grant, 1982; NEA Grant, 1975; Theodoron Award, Guggenheim Museum, 1971.

SIDELIGHTS: MEMBERSHIPS—Secretary to the Abstract Artists Association, 1979–82.

In addition to his dance and theatre designs, Mr. Boothe's work has been exhibited in galleries and museums throughout the country from 1968 to the present.

ADDRESS: Home—49 Crosby Street, New York, NY 10012.

BOSCO, Philip, actor

PERSONAL: Born September 26, 1930, Jersey City, NJ; son of Philip Lupo and Margaret Raymond (Thek) Bosco; married Nancy Ann Dunkle (formerly a carnival worker and truck driver). EDUCATION: Attended Catholic University, Washington, DC; studied for the stage with James Marr, Josephine Callan and Leo Brady.

CAREER: DEBUT—Machiavelli the Cat, *The Fairy Cobbler*, St. John's School, Jersey City, NJ, 1944. NEW YORK DEBUT—Brian O'Bannion, *Auntie Mame*, City Center, 1958. PRINCIPAL STAGE APPEARANCES—Title roles, *Hamlet* and *Richard III*, Malvolio, *Twelfth Night*, Catholic University; resident actor with Arena Stage, Washington, DC, appearing in some twenty plays, 1957–60; Angelo, *Measure for Measure*, Belvedere Lake Amphitheatre, Central Park, NY, 1960; Heracles, *The Rape of the Belt*, Martin Beck, NY, 1960; Will Danaher, *Donnybrook*, 46th Street Theatre, NY, 1961; Hawkshaw, *The Ticket-of-Leave Man*, Mayfair, NY, 1961; at the Shakespeare Festival, Stratford, CT: Henry Bolingbroke, *Richard II*, title role, *Henry IV, Part I*, 1962, Kent, *King Lear*, Rufio, *Anthony and Cleopatra*, Pistol, *Henry V*, Aegeon, *Comedy of Erros*, 1963, Benedick, *Much Ado about Nothing*, Claudius, *Hamlet*, 1964, title role, *Coriolanus*, 1965; Duke of Buckingham, *Richard III*, Delacorte, NY, 1966; resident actor, Lincoln Center Repertory at the Vivian Beaumont, NY: Lovewit, *The Alchemist*, 1966, Jack, *The East Wind*, 1967, Sagredo, *Galileo*, 1967, Bastard of Orleans, *Saint Joan*, 1968, Hector, *Tiger at the Gates*, 1968, Comte de Guiche, *Cyrano de Bergerac*, 1968, Kent, *King Lear*, 1968; at the Forum, NY, for the same company, Zelda and Mr. Gray, *An Evening for Merlin Finch*, 1968; Curtis Moffat Jr., *In The Matter of J. Robert Oppenheimer*, Vivian Beaumont, NY, 1968 and 1969, Anselme, *The Miser*, Nick, *The Time of Your Life*, 1970, Baron de Charlus, *Camino Real*, 1970, Captain Bovine, *Operation Sidewinder;* Jupiter, *Amphitryon*, Forum, NY, 1970; First God, *The Good Woman of Setzuan*, Vivian Beaumont, NY, 1971; Jimmy Farrell, *The Playboy of the Western World*, 1971; Peter Stockman, *An Enemy of the People*, 1971; Creon, *Antigone*, 1971; Earl of Leicester, *Mary Stuart*, 1972; Prime Minister, *Narrow Road to the Deep North*, 1972; Antonio, *Twelfth Night*, 1972; Reverend John Hale, *The Crucible*, 1972; Mikhail Sktobotov, *Enemies*, 1973; Gratiano, *The Merchant of Venice*, 1973; Harold Mitchell, *A Streetcar Named Desire*, 1973; Crofts, *Mrs. Warren's Profession*, Vivian Beaumont, NY, 1976; Pistol, *Henry V*, Delacorte, NY, 1976, Mack the Knife, *Threepenny Opera*, 1976; Sgt. Cokes, *Streamers*, Newhouse, NY, 1977; Warwick, *Saint Joan*, Circle of the Square, NY, 1977; *Stages*, Belasco, NY, 1978; Goosen, *The Biko Inquest*, Theatre Four, NY, 1978; Mendoza, *Man and Superman*, Circle in the Square, NY, 1978; Dr. Emerson, *Whose Life Is It, Anyway?*, Trafalgar, NY, 1979; Dr. Spigelsky, *A Month in the Country*, Roundabout Stage One, NY, 1979; Andrew Undershaft, *Major Barbara*, Circle in the Square, NY, 1980; at the Roundabout Stage One: *Inadmissible Evidence*, 1981, *Hedda Gabler*, 1982, *Learned Ladies*, 1982; *Some Men Need Help*, off-Broadway, 1982; *Eminent Domain*, Circle in the Square, NY, 1982; *Caine Mutiny*, Circle in the Square, NY, 1983; *Misalliance*, Roundabout Stage One, 1983; *Ah! Wilderness*, Roundabout Stage One, 1983; *Come Back Little Sheba*, Roundabout Stage One, 1984; *Heartbreak House*, Circle in the Square, NY, 1984.

FILM DEBUT—*Requiem for a Heavyweight*, 1961. PRINCIPAL FILM APPEARANCES—*A Lovely Way to Die*, 1968. TELEVISION DEBUT—*The Prisoner of Zenda*, 1960. PRINCIPAL TELEVISION APPEARANCES—*The Nurses; O'Brien; Hawk; The NET Play of the Month*.

AWARDS: Antoinette Perry Award Nomination, Best Featured Actor, 1984: *Heartbreak House;* Clarence Derwent Award, General Excellence, 1966–67; Antoinette Perry Award Nomination, Best Featured Actor, 1960: *The Rape of the Belt;* Drama Critics Award, 1960: *The Rape of the Belt;* Shakespeare Society Award, 1957.

SIDELIGHTS: FAVORITE ROLES—*Richard III*, Pistol, *Henry V*, Thomas Mendip, *The Lady's Not for Burning, Hamlet*, Malvolio, Benedick, *Cyrano de Bergerac*. RECREATIONS—Horses.

* * *

BOULÉ, Kathryn (nee Kathryn Wood), actress

PERSONAL: Born December 27, 1949; daughter of Fergus J. (a geophysical scientist) and Doris M. (a pianist; maiden name Hack) Wood; married Ronald Madden (an opera singer) on February 11, 1984. EDUCATION: University of Maryland, B.A. (Theatre Education), 1972; studied acting with Wynn Handman and Ada Brown Mather.

CAREER: DEBUT—Marie, *Fiorello!*, Equity Library Thea-

KATHRYN BOULÉ

tre, New York, 1977. BROADWAY DEBUT—Grace Farrell, *Annie*, Alvin, 1980–81. PRINCIPAL STAGE APPEARANCES—(New York) Betsy, *Stars and Stripes*, Town Hall; Vera Claythorne, *Ten Little Indians*, Equity Library Theatre; Eve, *Viva Reviva*, Open Space Theatre; *Morse Data*, Manhattan Theatre Club; REGIONAL THEATRE—*A Midsummer Night's Dream; Joe Egg*. MAJOR TOURS—Grace Farrell, *Annie*, First and Second National Companies, 1978.

PRINCIPAL FILM APPEARANCES—Sarah, *Summer Dreams*. TELEVISION DEBUT—Elaine, *Working Stiffs*, with Jim Belushi and Michael Keaton. PRINCIPAL TELEVISION APPEARANCES—*All My Children; Super Night at Forest Hills*. THEATRE-RELATED CAREER: Taught Drama, Speech, and English for the Montgomery County Public Schools, 1973–75.

AWARDS: Outstanding Citizenship Award, Kansas City Fire Department, for evacuating a theatre of 2000 people from a fire during a performance of *Annie*.

SIDELIGHTS: Miss Boulé appeared in twelve hundred performances of *Annie*. She is a published poet, interested in psychology, religion, social services, and human development and has traveled in Europe extensively.

ADDRESS: Home—56 W. 75th Street, New York, NY 10023. Agent—c/o Bruce Savan, Agency for the Performing Arts, 888 Seventh Avenue, New York, NY 10106.

* * *

BOWES, Janet Elizabeth, actress, director

PERSONAL: Born January 22, 1944; daughter of Alfred L. (a school principal) and Irma Renee (a translator; maiden name, Bontempo) Bowes; married William E. McKinney, 1971 (divorced 1978). EDUCATION: Ohio Weslyan, B.A. (English), 1966; Boston University School of Fine Arts, M.F.A. (Acting), 1968. RELIGION: Protestant. NON-THEATRICAL CAREER: Assistant to president, Vietnam Veteran's Relief Fund.

CAREER: PRINCIPAL STAGE APPEARANCES—Maybelle, *Albino Kind of Logic*, White Barn, Westport, CT, 1966; Anna Livia Plurabelle, *Finnegan's Wake*, New Poet's Cambridge, MA, 1968; Gloria, *You Never Can Tell*, Ghislaine, *The Waltz of the Torreadors*, Carmen, *The Balcony*, Andromache, *Troilus and Cressida*, Loeb, Cambridge, MA, 1968; Ann Sullivan, *The Miracle Worker*, Weathervane, OH, 1970; Maureen, *The Minstrel Boy*, Cooperative, NY, 1972; Regan, *King Lear*, Roundabout, NY; *Private Life of the Master Race*, Nighthouse, NY, 1975; Lula, *The Dutchman*, Actor's Playhouse, NY, 1975; standby for Joanne and Shirley, *Ladies at the Almo*, Martin Beck, 1977; Eleanor, *Welded*, A.A.T.C., NY, 1978. DIRECTED—*Dustoff*, Westside Mainstage, NY, 1982.

PRINCIPAL TELEVISION APPEARANCES—*Guiding Light; As the World Turns*.

RELATED CAREER—Manager and booking agent for the Westside Mainstage, NY, 1981–83.

AWARDS: Theta Alpha Phi (dramatic honorary), 1966.

SIDELIGHTS: MEMBERSHIPS—AEA, AFTRA, SAG, UN-ICEF, Vietnam Veteran's Relief Fund, Agent Orange Victims International.

"I had the opportunity to travel to England and Ireland in 1968 to observe theatre there. I was able to observe the Royal Shakespeare Company during rehearsals, and many regional repertory groups as well. While in Dublin, I assisted the American director in a production of *Indian Wants the Bronx* at the Abbey Theatre's experimental space, the Peacock. In 1982 I directed *Dustoff,* at the Westside Mainstage, New York City. The play is about a medical evacuation unit in Vietnam towards the end of the war. In working on this project, I discovered a lot about this experience, showing its terrifying, humorous, and painful reality with an audience who until recently could neither understand nor cope with the Vietnam veterans' unique experience. Having our audience respond to this play with compassion and a new understanding of the vets, and having veterans themselves say that this play helped 'to bring them home' was a highly motivating and moving experience for me. Further involvement in Vietnam veterans' issues followed, in particular with agent orange/dioxin, and the Vietnam Veteran's Relief Fund has kept me searching for more opportunities to explore these and other issues on the stage."

ADDRESS: Home—42 W. 13th Street, New York, NY 10011.

*　*　*

BOWLES, Paul, composer, writer

PERSONAL: Born December 30, 1910 in Jamaica, NY; son of Dr. Claude Dietz (a dentist) and Rena (Winnewisser) Bowles; married Jane Sidney Auer (a playwright and novelist) on February 21, 1938 (deceased). EDUCATION: Attended School of Design and Liberal Arts, NY, 1928; University of Virginia, 1928–30; studied with Aaron Copland and Virgil Thompson.

WRITINGS: INCIDENTAL MUSIC, THEATRE—Debut—*Horse Eats Hat,* Federal Theatre Project, Maxine Elliott's Theatre, NY, 1936; *Dr. Faustus,* FTP, Maxine Elliott's, 1937; *My Heart's in the Highlands,* Guild, NY, 1939; *Love's Old Sweet Song,* Plymouth, NY, 1940; *Twelfth Night,* St. James, NY, 1940; *Liberty Jones,* Shubert, NY, 1941; *Watch on the Rhine,* Martin Beck, NY, 1941; *South Pacific* (a play) Cort, NY, 1943; *Jacobowsky and the Colonel,* Martin Beck, NY, 1944; *The Glass Menagerie,* Playhouse, NY, 1945; *Twilight Bar,* Ford's, Baltimore, MD, 1946; *On Whitman Avenue,* Cort, NY, 1946; *Land's End,* Playhouse, NY, 1946; *Summer and Smoke,* Playhouse, NY, 1948; *Cyrano de Bergerac,* City Center, NY, *In the Summer House,* Playhouse, NY, 1953; *The Glass Menagerie,* (revival), City Center, NY, 1956; the song "Heavenly Grass," *Orpheus Descending,* Martin Beck, NY, 1957; *Edwin Booth,* 46th Street, NY, 1958; *Sweet Bird of Youth,* Martin Beck, NY, 1959; *The Milk Train Doesn't Stop Here Anymore,* Morosco, NY, 1963.

BALLETS—*Yankee Clipper,* 1937; *Pastorelela,* 1941; *Sentimental Colloquy,* 1944; *Blue Roses,* 1957. OPERAS—*Denmark Vesey,* 1937; *The Wind Remains,* Museum of Modern Art, 1943. FILMS—*Roots in the Soil,* U.S. Department of Agriculture, 1940; *Congo,* Belgian Government in exile, 1944.

BOOKS—*The Sheltering Sky,* 1949; *The Delicate Prey and Other Stories,* 1950; *Let It Come Down,* 1952; *The Spider's House,* 1955; *Their Heads Are Green and Their Hands Are Blue,* 1963; *The Time of Friendship,* 1967; *Without Stopping,* 1972. PLAYS, TRANSLATIONS—*No Exit,* and adaptation, produced at the Biltmore, NY 1946.

AWARDS: Guggenheim Fellowship, 1941; Rockefeller Grant, 1959.

SIDELIGHTS: MEMBERSHIPS—ASCAP, American Academy and Institute of Arts and Letters.

ADDRESS: Home—2117 Tanger Socco, Tangier, Morocco. Agent—Ned Leavitt, c/o William Morris Agency, 1350 Avenue of the Americas, New York, NY 10019.

*　*　*

BOYLE, Katie (nee Caterina Imperiali di Francavilla), columnist, actress, producer

PERSONAL: Born May 29, 1926 in Florence, Italy; daughter of Marquis Demetrio Imperiali and Dorothy Kate (Ramsden) di Francavilla; married Richard Boyle, Earl of Shannon (divorced); married Greville Baylis (deceased); married Sir Peter Saunders. EDUCATION: in Switzerland and Italy.

CAREER: DEBUT—at the Theatre Royal, Windsor, England. PRINCIPAL STAGE APPEARANCES—*Pardon My Claws,* 1955; Stella Manners, *Silver Wedding,* Cambridge, 1957.

PRINCIPAL FILM APPEARANCES—*Old Mother Riley Goes to School,* 1956; *Not Wanted on Voyage,* 1957; *Intent to Kill,* 1958. PRINCIPAL TELEVISION APPEARANCES—Panelist, *The Name's the Same, I've Got a Secret, To Tell the Truth* and others; *Pop Over Europe,* 1960–78; starred in two series of the *Golden Girl.*

WRITINGS: BOOKS—*What This Katie Did, Boyle's Lore.* COLUMNS—the problem page in *TV Times, The Evening Standard, The Sun, The Sunday Mirror,* regular page in *Here's Health.*

AWARDS: Europremio Award in Venice, for the Radio and Television Personality of Europe, 1964.

SIDELIGHTS: RECREATIONS—gardening, embroidery, jigsaw puzzles, animals in general and rescuing dogs in particular.

ADDRESS: Office—c/o Vaudeville Theatre Office, 10 Maiden Lane, London WC2E 7NA England.

*　*　*

BRADY, Leo, playwright, director

PERSONAL: Born January 23, 1917, in Wheeling, WVA; son of Joseph T. (a bookbinder) and Nannie B. (Beans) Brady; married Eleanor Buchroeder, April 17, 1945; children: Brigid, Paula, Peter, Monica, Ann, Martin, Elizabeth, Daniel, Stephen. EDUCATION: Catholic University, B.A.,

English, 1941, M.A. Drama, 1942; studied for the theatre with Walter Kerr, Alan Schneider, and Josephine Callan. RELIGION: Roman Catholic. MILITARY: Master Sergeant, U.S. Army (recruiting—radio scripts and production).

CAREER: Director, Olney Theatre, Olney, Maryland, 1954–present. THEATRE-RELATED CAREER: professor of Drama, Catholic University, 1946–83.

WRITINGS: PLAYS, PUBLISHED—*Brother Orchid,* 1939 (with Walter Kerr); *Count Me In,* 1941 (with Walter Kerr). PLAYS, UNPUBLISHED—Yankee Doodle Boy (with Walter Kerr), The Bum's Rush, Father Time, The Coldest War of All. TELEVISION SHOWS—*Oresteia* (for *Omnibus*).

AWARDS: Golden Book Award—Catholic Writers Guild, 1949, novel—*The Edge of Doom;* graduated Phi Beta Kappa.

ADDRESS: Office—Drama Department, Catholic University, Washington, DC 20064.

* * *

BRAND, Oscar, actor, composer, lyricist, critic, director, producer, writer

PERSONAL: Born February 7, 1920, in Winnipeg, Manitoba, Canada; son of I. Z. (a salesperson and Indian interpreter for Hudson's Bay Co.) and Beatrice (a salesperson; maiden name Shulman) Brand; married Rubyan Antonia Schwaeber, May 10, 1955 (divorced); married Karen Lynn Grossman (a lawyer), June 14, 1970; children: (first marriage) Jeannie, Eric, James; (second marriage) Jordan. EDUCATION: Brooklyn College, B.S., 1942. POLITICS: Liberal. RELIGION: Jewish. MILITARY: Sergeant, U.S. Army, 1942–45 (unit citation; special merit). NON-THEATRICAL CAREER: Teacher—New School for Social Research since 1968; Hofstra University since 1969.

CAREER: DEBUT—Will, *Oklahoma,* Mr. Snow, *Carousel,* Schroon Crest Playhouse, Schroon Lake, NY, 1956. NEW YORK DEBUT—Jim, *How to Steal an Election,* Gem, 1968 for 68 performances. PRINCIPAL STAGE APPEARANCES—Wanderer, *It's a Jungle Out There,* 78th Street Playhouse, New York, 1982.

FILM DEBUT—The Farmer, *The Farmer Goes to Town* (Encyclopedia Britannica), 1950. PRINCIPAL FILMS—over one hundred documentaries as principal actor, host, or narrator. TELEVISION DEBUT—with Herb Shriner on CBS, 1946. TELEVISION APPEARANCES—The Editor, *Whistlestop,* 1947; *Kate Smith Hour,* 1948; *Americana,* 1948; panelist, *Draw Me a Laugh,* 1949; *Presidential Timber,* 1952; *The Longines Hour,* 1955; host, *The Bell Telephone Hour,* 1963; music director, *Exploring,* 1964; *The Right Man,* 1964; *Sunday,* 1965; star and host, *Let's Sing Out,* 1966; *Brand New Scene,* 1967; *American Odyssey,* 1970; host, *Touch the Earth;* critic-reviewer, *Arts in Review* (CBC). RADIO APPEARANCES—Host, *Folk Song Festival,* 1945–74; lead, *Dr. Christian,* 1948; soloist, *Citizen of the World,* 1949. CONCERTS: Debut—Narrator, *Peter and the Wolf,* Midwood Auditorium, New York, 1938.

WRITINGS: PLAYS—score, *In White America,* 1967; score, *A Joyful Noise,* 1967; score, *Education of H*Y*M*A*N K*A*P*-

*L*A*N,* 1968; score, *How to Steal an Election,* 1968; book and score, *Sing America Sing,* 1975; score, *It's a Jungle Out There,* 1982; also unproduced shows: *Thunder Bay,* 1972; *Fun and Games,* 1977; *Second Scroll,* 1982. SONG BOOKS, PUBLISHED—*Singing Holidays,* 1957; *Bawdy Songs,* 1958; *Folk Songs for Fun,* 1962; *Courting's a Pleasure,* 1963; *The Ballad Mongers,* 1964; *Songs of '76,* 1972; *When I First Came to This Land,* 1974; also ten song folios.

AWARDS: Among Mr. Brand's awards are two Emmys, three Peabodys, the Golden Reel, the Golden Lion, the Thomas Alva Edison Award, the Freedoms Foundation Award, the *Scholastic* Award, an Ohio State Award, prizes from Cannes, Venice, and Edinburgh Festivals as well as a Laureate from Fairfield University in 1972.

SIDELIGHTS: MEMBERSHIPS—AFM; AFTRA; ACTRA; Dramatists Guild; SAG. Mr. Brand has been the curator for the Songwriters' Hall of Fame in New York City. RECREATION: Sailing, carpentry.

ADDRESS: Home—141 Baker Hill, Great Neck, NY 11023. Office—One Times Square, New York, NY 10026. Agent—Vince Cirincione, 300 W. 55 Street, New York, NY 10019.

* * *

BRANDON, Johnny, composer, lyricist, playwright, dancer, actor, choreographer

PERSONAL: Born pre–World War II, in London, England; son of Edgar (an artist and engraver) and Florence (a schoolteacher; maiden name Brown) Brandon; EDUCATION: Lawrence House (Prep), Southgate, London, England; Brentwood College, London, England; studied for the theatre with Buddy Bradley at the Buddy Bradley School of Dance and with Kate Rourke, Guildhall School of Drama. POLITICS—Independent Progressive. MILITARY—Royal Signals/Combined Operations, British Army (Sgt., Broadcaster with British Forces Network).

CAREER: PRINCIPAL STAGE APPEARANCES—as a song-and-dance man in British Vaudeville from age 11, also in Revue; Harry, *The Time of Your Life,* Old Vic, London; lead, *Love from Judy,* Saville, London, 1954; tap choreography, *Ace of Clubs,* London, 1950. PRINCIPAL FILMS—*The Day Will Dawn,* 1940; *The Young Mr. Pitt,* 1942. PRINCIPAL TELEVISION WORK—choreography, *Jill Darling;* series, *Dreamer's Highway.* Lyrics, music, *A Piece of the Action;* lyrics, music, *Hey, Jennie,* 1956–60; themes for *Kraft Television Theatre.*

WRITINGS: PLAYS, PUBLISHED—Lyrics, music, sketches, *Maid to Measure;* lyrics, music, *Cindy;* lyrics, music, *Billy NoName;* lyrics, music, concept, *Love! Love! Love!.* PLAYS, UNPUBLISHED—lyrics, music, sketches, Party; lyrics, music, Who's Who, Baby?; lyrics, music, Peg; lyrics, music, concept, Ain't Doin' Nothin' but Singin' My Song; lyrics, music, Helen; lyrics, music, Sparrow in Flight; lyrics, music, concept, Suddenly the Music Starts; lyrics, Eubie!; lyrics, music, concept, Touch!; lyrics, music, book, Vonetta Sweetwater Carries On; lyrics, music, The More You Get the More You Want; lyrics, music, Shim Sham; SPECIAL MATERIAL—Dialogue, lyrics, music, staging, choreography for night club acts for Cab Calloway, Vivian Reed, Chris

Calloway, Alexis Smith, Lynnie Godfrey, Terry Burrell, others. SONGS—over 600 published songs including *Once Upon a Wintertime, Opportunity, Tomorrow, Hang up the Phone, Let's, The Years Between, Venetian Sunset, A Love to Last a Lifetime, A Screamin' Ball at Dracula Hall.*

AWARDS: Ivor Novello Award, Lyrics and Music, *Your Love Is My Love,* 1957; Antoinette Perry Award Nomination, Lyrics, *Eubie!,* 1979; Audelco Award Nomination, Revue—*Suddenly the Music Starts,* 1979; Audelco Award Nomination, *The More You Get,* 1980.

SIDELIGHTS: MEMBERSHIPS—Broadcast Music, Inc.; Dramatists Guild; AGAC/Songwriters' Guild (at present a member of AGAC Council).

"In my formative years (10–20) Buddy Bradley was the single most important influence on my professional life and to some extent on my social development. Not only did he teach me to be a very good dancer (tap) but he introduced me to the writings of Langston Hughes, jazz music (we danced to Dizzy Gillespie records), *The Chicago Defender* and *Ebony* (what other English kid knew of the Black American Press?), the ballet (I was strictly show biz and had at that time little interest in ballet), Wimbledon Tennis, the legit theatre. He also encouraged me to write songs and the exposure he gave me to jazz music still stands me in good stead today with lyrical rhythms and meter.

"I love America and live here because it is the only truly multi-racial society today. I feel strongly that American writers in the theatre should reflect this multi-racial, multi-ethnic society. There are times, of course, when for dramatic purposes roles have to be cast ethnically, but in the vast majority of cases, when a play or musical is *not* concerned with specific ethnic groups, I feel strongly that roles should be cast across the board. In this respect, strangely enough, the theatre seems to be lagging far behind national television, due, it seems, to the indifference of the successful Broadway writers and dramatists.

"I love class! Lena Horne has it (in abundance), so does Johnny Carson, Reggie Jackson, Julius Irving, Carl Rowan, the Kennedys, Elizabeth Drew, Mayor Andy Young.

"Friendships are the most important human relationships—friends are the 'family one chooses.'"

ADDRESS: Home—200 E. 17th Street, New York, NY 10003. Agent—Robert Youdelman (attorney), 3 E. 54th Street, New York, NY 10022.

* * *

BREGMAN, Martin, film producer, writer

PERSONAL: Born May 18, 1926 in New York City; son of Leon and Ida (Granwski) Bregan; married Elizabeth Driscoll (divorced); married Cornelia Sharpe; children: Michael, Christopher, Marissa. EDUCATION: Attended Indiana University and New York University.

CAREER: PRODUCED, FILMS—*Serpico,* 1974; *Dog Day Afternoon,* 1975; *The Next Man,* 1977; *The Seduction of Joe Tynan,* 1979; *SHE,* 1980; *The Four Seasons,* 1980; *Venom,* 1982.

SIDELIGHTS: Chairman of the Mayor's Office of Motion Pictures and TV, City of New York.

ADDRESS: Office—Martin Bregman Productions, 641 Lexington Avenue, New York, NY 10022. Agent—William Morris Agency, 1350 Avenue of the Americas, New York, NY 10019.

* * *

BRENNAN, Eileen, actress

PERSONAL: Born September 3, 1935, in Los Angeles, CA; daughter of John Gerald (an M.D.) and Jeanne (Menehan) Brennan; married David Lampson, December 28, 1968 (divorced 1974); children: Samuel, Patrick. EDUCATION: Attended public schools in Los Angeles; studied at the American Academy of Dramatic Arts in New York City.

CAREER: DEBUT—Little Mary Sunshine, *Little Mary Sunshine,* Orpheum, NY, 1959. PRINCIPAL STAGE APPEARANCES—Irene Malloy, *Hello Dolly,* St. James, NY, 1964; *The Student Gypsy,* off-Broadway; *A Couple White Chicks Sitting Around Talking,* Public, NY, 1982. MAJOR TOURS—Annie Sullivan, *The Miracle Worker,* national tour, 1961–62.

FILM DEBUT—Eunice, *Divorce: American Style,* 1966. PRINCIPAL FILM APPEARANCES—*The Last Picture Show,* 1971; *Genevieve,* 1971; Billie, *The String,* 1973; *Scarecrow,* 1973; *Daisy Miller,* 1974; *At Long Last Love,* 1975; *Hustle,* 1975;

EILEEN BRENNAN

Murder by Death, 1976; *The Cheap Detective,* 1978; *FM,* 1978; Capt. Lewis, *Private Benjamin,* 1979; *Richie.*

TELEVISION DEBUT—*13 Queens Boulevard.* PRINCIPAL TELEVISION APPEARANCES—movies for television, *My Old Man, And When She Was Bad. . . , Black Beauty, Incident at Crestridge, Working,* PBS; guest star, *Lily for President;* series, *A New Kind of Family, Private Benjamin;* play for television, *Answers.*

AWARDS: Emmy Award and 5 Emmy Nominations; Golden Globe Award; Academy Award Nomination, *Private Benjamin;* Theatre World Award; Obie Award, Best Actress, *Little Mary Sunshine;* Newspaper Guild Award.

ADDRESS: Agent—Ron Meyer, Creative Artists, 1888 Century Park East, Los Angeles, CA 90212.

* * *

BREWSTER, Townsend Tyler, playwright, translator

PERSONAL: Born July 23, 1924 in Glen Cove, Long Island, NY; son of Townsend (a postal clerk) and Sara Frances (a teacher; maiden name, Tyler) Brewster. EDUCATION: Queens College, Flushing NY, B.A. (Classical languages) 1947; Columbia University, M.A. (French) 1962; studied playwriting with Edward Mabley at the American Theatre Wing. MILITARY: U.S. Army, 1943–45. NON-THEATRICAL CAREER: Copywriter, Hicks & Greist Advertising Agency, 1959–61; Librarian, Lennen & Newell Advertising Agency, 1962–67; editor/critic, *Harlem Cultural Review,* present.

WRITINGS: PLAYS PRODUCED—*Little Girl/Big Town,* 1953; *Singapore Sling,* Queens Community Theatre, 1955; *Please Don't Cry and Say No,* Circle-in-the Square (downtown), 1972; *Though It's Been Said Many Times, Many Ways,* Harlem Performance Center, 1976; *The Girl Beneath the Tulip Tree,* Harlem Performance Center, 1977; *Black-Belt Bertram,* Double Image Theatre, 1979; *Arthur Ashe and I,* Theatre of Riverside Church, 1979.

LIBRETTOS—*The Choreography of Love,* WNYC radio, 1946; *The Tower,* Santa Fe Opera, 1957; "Squaw Winter" in Pinter's *Revue Sketches,* Weathervane Theatre, Akron OH, 1970; Interlude's *Harlequinades for Mourners,* New Theatre, NY, 1970; *Of Angels and Donkeys,* Israeli Music Publication; *Lady Plum Blossom,* Oregon State University, 1973.

TRANSLATIONS—*Rudens,* Plautus, 1958; *How the West Was Fun; Chief Rathebe; Mowgli; The Bougival Vampire,* University of Denver, 1968; *The Brown Overcoat* (Victor Séjour), Circle-in-the-Square (downtown), NY, 1972; *The Botany Lesson,* (Joaquim Maria Machado de Assis), Circle-in-the-Square (downtown), 1972; *Fiancailles pour rire* (Poulenc), 1976; *L'Amant anonyme* (18th-century black composer Joseph Boulogne, the Chevalier de Saint Georges), 1976; *Cid,* papers in the anthology *Dramatic Theory and Criticism Greeks to Grotowski,* 1974; *The Cocktail Sip,* 1982; *The Liar* (Corneille) Apollo Drama Company, 1984.

SHORT STORIES—"The Widows Mite"; "An Evening with Josephine Baker," 1977.

POETRY—in *Pioneer, Counterpoint, Classical Outlook, Commonweal, Dasein, Other Stages, Foothills,* published in *Today's Negro Voices,* 1970.

THEATRE-RELATED CAREER: Lecturer in Theatre Department, City College of New York, 1969–73.

AWARDS: Performing Arts Repertory Theatre Foundation Grant for *Lady Plum Blossom,* 1983; *Mascara and Confetti,* selected ASCAP Musical Comedy Workshop, 1980; Finalist, Writers Guild of America East, Foundation Fellowship for teleplay, *Amator, Amator,* 1980; Jonathan Swift Award for Satire, *The Ecologists,* Virginia Commonwealth University, 1979; National Endowment for the Arts Grant, 1977; Louise Bogan Memorial Prize in Poetry, *Dos Sueños,* New York Poetry Forum, 1975; Award from *Story Magazine* for *Please Don't Cry and Say No,* 1969; Ford Foundation Grant, Librettists, 1959; William Morris Scholarship in Playwriting, American Theatre Wing, 1955.

SIDELIGHTS: MEMBERSHIPS—Vice President, Harlem Performance Center; Board of Directors Frank Silvera's Writers Workshop; Board of Directors, Harlem Cultural Council; Dramatists Guild; Maple Leaf Society; Ragtime Society; New Dramatists (alumnus); International Brecht Society; Outer Critic's Circle.

"Wisely or unwisely, instead of capitalizing on my reported gifts as a scholar and critic, I have kept them ancillary to my creative writing. Eric Bentley has stated that in the American theatre, one finds whimsy rather than comedy. . . . For one who believes the greatest living dramatist to be Wole Soyinka and whose favorite playwrights are Marivaux, Brecht, Euripides, Corneille, and Anouilh, whimsy is not likely to be the strong suit. In music my favorites are Mozart, Donizetti, Offenbach, and Joplin, in painting, Fragonard, and in poetry, Gautier."

ADDRESS: Home—171-29 103rd Road, Jamaica, NY 11433; Office—Harlem Cultural Council, One West 125th Street, New York, NY 10027; Agent—Ronelad Roberts, 9214 Ridge Blvd., Brooklyn, NY 11209.

* * *

BRILL, Fran (Frances Joan), actress

PERSONAL: Born September 30, 1946, in Chester, PA; daughter of Joseph M. (M.D.) and Linette Brill; married Clint Ramsden, July 14, 1979 (divorced 1983); EDUCATION: Boston University of Fine Arts, B.F.A., 1968. RELIGION: Methodist.

CAREER: DEBUT—Theatre Atlanta, 1968. NEW YORK DEBUT—Student Leader, *Red, White and Maddox,* Cort, New York, 1969. PRINCIPAL STAGE APPEARANCES—Maggie, *What Every Woman Knows,* Roundabout, New York, 1975; Ersilia, *To Clothe the Naked,* Roundabout, New York, 1977; Lorraine, *Scribes,* Phoenix, New York, 1977; Helena, *Look Back in Anger,* Roundabout, New York, 1980; Jennie, *Knuckle,* Hudson Guild, New York, 1981; Rita, *Skirmishes,* Manhattan Theater Club, New York, 1983; Helen, *Baby with the Bathwater,* Playwright's Horizons, New York, 1983; *Fish,*

Dusa, Fish, Stas and VI, Mark Taper Forum, Los Angeles, 1978.

PRINCIPAL FILMS—Sally Hayes, *Being There,* 1979. TELEVISION DEBUT—Fran, *How to Survive a Marriage.* TELEVISION APPEARANCES—*Nurse; Today's FBI; Look Back in Anger; Amber Waves; Family; Barnaby Jones;* one of the Muppets, *Sesame Street.*

AWARDS: Drama Desk Award Nomination, 1981: *Knuckle.* Drama Desk Award Nomination, 1975: *What Every Woman Knows.* Emmy, 1974: *Sesame Street.*

ADDRESS: Agent—c/o Writers and Artists Agency, 162 W. 56th Street, New York, NY 10019.

* * *

BROGGER, Ivar, actor

PERSONAL: Pronounced "*EEvar*"; son of Arne W. (an attorney) and Helga (a librarian, Bjornson) Brogger; EDUCATION: University of Minnesota, B.A., M.F.A..

CAREER: PRINCIPAL STAGE APPEARANCES—Murderer/Caithness, *Macbeth,* Broadway, New York; Rivers, *Richard III,* New York Shakespeare Festival; Clive/Edward, *Cloud 9,* Lucille Lortel, New York; Scott, *Magic Time,* Actors and Directors Lab, New York; Salvation Army Preacher, *In the Jungle of Cities,* Colonnades, New York; Pat Garret, *Collected Works of Billy the Kid,* Brooklyn Academy of Music, Brooklyn, NY; Cusins, *Major Barbara,* Yale Repertory, New Haven, CT; Philinte, *Misanthrope,* Hartford Stage Company, Hartford, CT; Hildy, *The Front Page,* Playmakers Repertory; Hank, *History of the American Film,* Alliance, Atlanta, GA; Marlow, *She Stoops to Conquer,* Syracuse Stage Company, Syracuse, NY; Joe, *Animal Kingdom,* Hartman, Stamford, CT; Roderigo, *Othello,* Hartman; Valentine, *You Never Can Tell,* Pittsburgh Public, Pittsburgh, PA; Harold, *Father's Day,* Pittsburgh Public; Dennis, *Loot,* Pittsburgh Public; Snake, *School for Scandal,* Guthrie, Minneapolis; Longaville, *Love's Labors Lost,* Guthrie; Postmaster, *Inspector General,* Guthrie; Elder, *Oedipus the King,* Guthrie; Reverend Parris, *The Crucible,* Guthrie; Young Monk, *Beckett,* Guthrie; Jerry Devine, *Juno and the Paycock,* Guthrie; Lysander, *Midsummer Night's Dream,* Guthrie.

ADDRESS: Agent—c/o J. Michael Bloom, Ltd., 400 Madison Ave., New York, NY 10017.

* * *

BROMKA, Elaine, actress

PERSONAL: Born January 6, 1950; daughter of Bernie A. (a building inspector) and Genevieve A. (a teacher; maiden name Costello) Bromka; married Peter Phillips (an actor), November 27, 1976. EDUCATION: Smith College, A.B.,

ELAINE BROMKA

1972, M.A.T. 1973; trained for the theatre at the National Theatre Institute.

CAREER: DEBUT—National Theatre of the Deaf, 1973. PRINCIPAL STAGE APPEARANCES—Carol, *Split* (Premiere), Ensemble Studio, New York, 1978; Mildred, *The Good Parts,* Actors Studio, New York, 1980; Shirley, *Inadmissible Evidence,* Roundabout, New York, 1981; First Witch, *Macbeth,* Circle in the Square, New York, 1982; Edward/Victoria, *Cloud Nine,* Lucille Lortel, New York, 1983; regional theatre appearances at Long Wharf, Hartford Stage, Berkshire Theatre Festival, Actors Theatre of Louisville, O'Neill Playwrights Center, McCarter, Syracuse Stage, Folger Theatre Group, ACT/Seattle, American Stage Festival, 1975–83. MAJOR TOURS—National Theatre of the Deaf, cross country and Australia, 1973–75. FILM DEBUT—Eda, *Without a Trace,* 1983. TELEVISION DEBUT—*Flashback: Hindenburg, Ship of Doom,* HBO. TELEVISION APPEARANCES—*Playing for Time,* 1981; Tanya, *All My Children.*

AWARDS: New England Emmy, *Catch a Rainbow,* 1978; graduated from Smith Magna cum laude, Phi Beta Kappa.

SIDELIGHTS: MEMBERSHIPS—Actors Studio; Ensemble Studio Theatre; Circle Repertory Lab.

Miss Bromka is a specialist in deaf sign language.

ADDRESS: Home—214 Lincoln Road, Brooklyn, NY 11225. Agent—Peter Strain, Bauman Hiller, 250 W. 57 Street, New York, NY 10019.

BROOKS, David, actor, director, producer, and singer

PERSONAL: Born September 24, 1920, in Portland, OR; son of Henry (a photographer) and Grace (Gruenwald) Berger. EDUCATION: Attended University of Washington and Columbia University; trained for the stage by Lee Strasberg and Robert Lewis.

CAREER: DEBUT—Octavian, *Der Rosenkavalier,* Academy of Music, Philadelphia, PA, 1942. NEW YORK DEBUT—Jeff Calhoun, *Bloomer Girl,* Shubert, 1944. PRINCIPAL STAGE APPEARANCES—(Broadway) Tommy, *Brigadoon;* Captain, *Rosalie;* Clyde, *Pink Tights;* Man, *Sunday Man;* President, *Mr. President;* Prince, *Girl Who Came to Supper;* Father, *Park;* Judge, *Can Can;* (Off-Broadway) Suitor, *The Boar;* Mac Heath, *Threepenny Opera;* Narrator, *Ulysses in Nighttown;* Himmelman, *Last Analysis;* Fam, *Fam and Yam;* Grandpa, *Jack or the Submission;* Ghost, *Hamlet;* Cop, *Nightshift;* Father, *Memory of Whiteness;* (Regional) Robert Burns, *Comin' Thro' the Rye,* Olney, MD, 1952; Clyde, *The Girl in Pink Tights,* New Haven, CT, 1954.

PRINCIPAL FILM APPEARANCES—*A Stranger Is Watching.* PRINCIPAL TELEVISION APPEARANCES—*Search for Tomorrow; Go Away Kid.*

DIRECTED: PLAYS—*Trouble in Tahiti,* 1955; *The Bald Soprano; Jack,* Sullivan Street Playhouse, 1958; *Sally, George and Martha,* Theatre de Lys, 1971. PRODUCED: PLAYS—*Endgame,* Cherry Lane, 1958; *Ulysses in Nighttown,* Rooftop, 1958.

SIDELIGHTS: MEMBERSHIPS—AEA, AFTRA, SAG. RECREATION—farming, horses.

ADDRESS: Home—400 W. 43rd Street, #30 E, New York, NY 10036.

* * *

BROOKS, Jeff, actor

PERSONAL: Born April 7, 1950, in Vancouver, B.C., Canada; son of Fred H. (a salesman) and Eileen M. (an Oregon State social worker; maiden name Russell) Brooks. EDUCATION: Portland State University, 1969–72;

CAREER: DEBUT—Howie, *Mrs. McThing,* Grover Cleveland High School, Portland, Oregon, 1966. NEW YORK DEBUT—The Captain, *Titanic,* Vandam Theatre, 1976, for 16 performances. PRINCIPAL STAGE APPEARANCES—Aloysius/George, *Sister Mary Ignatius Explains It All for You/The Actor's Nightmare,* Westside Arts, New York, 1981–83; Phil, *Loose Ends,* Circle in the Square (uptown) 1979–80; Mickey, *A History of the American Film,* ANTA, New York, 1978. MAJOR TOURS—Dr. Stuart Framingham, *Beyond Therapy,* Westport, CT, St. Louis, MO, Falmouth, MA, 1983; Bobby Randall, *Good News,* Milburn, NJ, Hyannis, MA, 1976. Served as actor/teacher at the Oregon Shakespeare Festival, Ashland, OR, 1972–75.

TELEVISION DEBUT—Dwayne Miller, *One More Try.*

SIDELIGHTS: MEMBERSHIPS—AEA.

Originated the role of George Spelvin in *The Actor's Nightmare,* the companion piece to *Sister Mary Ignatius,* and played it in New York for 707 performances. Played in six different plays by Christopher Durang, originating five of them.

ADDRESS: Home—411 Park Ave. S., New York, NY 10016. Agent—c/o Joe Ohla, Writers and Artists Agency, 162 W. 56th Street, New York, NY 10019.

* * *

BROOKS, Mel, director, writer, actor

PERSONAL: Born 1926, in Brooklyn, NY married Anne Bancroft.

CAREER: STAGE DEBUT—*Golden Boy,* Redbank, NJ.

PRINCIPAL FILM WORK—Narrator, *The Critic* (short); director: *The Twelve Chairs,* 1970, *Blazing Saddles,* 1973, *Young Frankenstein,* 1974, *Silent Movie,* 1976; director/producer: *High Anxiety,* 1977, *History of the World, Part I,* 1981, *To Be or Not to Be,* 1983.

PRINCIPAL FILM APPEARANCES—*Silent Movie,* 1976; *High Anxiety,* 1977; *History of the World, Part I,* 1981; *To Be or Not to Be,* 1983. PRINCIPAL TELEVISION WORK—Co-creator, *Get Smart;* creator, *When Things Were Rotten.*

WRITINGS: SCREEPLAYS—*The Critic* (short); *The Twelve Chairs,* 1970; *History of the World, Part I,* 1981; *Blazing Saddles* (co-writer), 1973; *Young Frankenstein,* 1974; *Silent Movie,* 1976; *High Anxiety,* 1977; *History of the World, Part I,* 1981; *To Be or Not to Be,* 1983. TELEVISION—writer for Sid Caesar's *Broadway Review,* Sid Caesar's *Your Show of Shows; Caesar's Hour;* writer, *Get Smart.* RECORDINGS—Comedy albums, *2000 Year Old Man, The 2000 and 13 Year Old Man.*

ADDRESS: Office—Brooksfilms Ltd., c/o 20th Century Fox Studios, P.O. Box 900, Beverly Hills, CA 90213.*

* * *

BROUGH, Colin, manager, producer

PERSONAL: Born 1945 in London, England; son of K. David and F. Elizabeth (Davies) Brough; married Helen Gilman; children: two daughters.

CAREER: PRINCIPAL STAGE WORK, PRODUCER—*Fat Harold,* Shaw, London, 1977; *Breezeblock Park,* Whitehall, London, 1977; *The Dark Horse,* Comedy, London, 1978; *Rose,* Duke of York's, London, Cort, NY, 1980–81; *Harvest,* Ambassadors, London, 1981; *Summit Conference,* Lyric, London, 1982; *When the Wind Blows,* Whitehall, London, 1983.

THEATRE-RELATED CAREER: Chairman and Managing Director, Lupton Theatre Company, Ltd.

SIDELIGHTS: MEMBERSHIPS—Society of West End Theatre;

Theatrical Management Association; Association of British Theatre Technicians (Vice-Chairman, 1982–82); Fellow of the Institute of Chartered Accountants in England and Wales.

ADDRESS: c/o The Lupton Theatre Company Ltd., 39 Stormont Road, London N64NR, England.

* * *

BROUN, Heywood Hale, announcer, actor, author

PERSONAL: Born March 10, 1918, in New York City; son of Heywood Campbell (a journalist, critic, and actor) and Ruth (a journalist; maiden name, Hale) Broun; married Jane Lloyd-Jones, 1949; children: Heywood Orren. EDUCATION: Swarthmore College, B.A., 1940; trained for the stage with Joseph Leon. MILITARY: U.S. Army, World War II.

CAREER: DEBUT—Mr. Thorkelson, *I Remember Mama*, Woodstock Playhouse, NY, 1949. BROADWAY DEBUT—Phone man, *Love Me Long*, 48th Street Theatre, 1949. PRINCIPAL STAGE APPEARANCES—Mr. Hawkes, *Peg O' My Heart*, Vicar, *Yes and No*, Lakeside, CT, 1949; Mr. Ripley, *The Bird Cage*, Coronet, NY, 1950; Harry Holland, *The Live Wire*, Playhouse, NY, 1950; the Great Chesterton, *The Small Hours*, National, NY, 1951; bank clerk, *Point of No Return*, Alvin, NY, 1951; Bluntschli, *Idiot's Delight*, Westport Country Playhouse, CT, 1952; Ed Glennon, *The Pink Elephant*, Playhouse, NY, 1953; her lawyer, *His and Hers*, 48th Street Playhouse, NY, 1954; *Anna Lucasta, Joy to the World, A Sound of Hunting, The Live Wire, The Enchanted, Mr. Roberts, Finian's Rainbow, Picnic, Sabrina Fair, My Three Angels, Look Homeward, Angel, The Disenchanted, The Solid Gold Cadillac, The Bad Seed, Tovarich, The Rainmaker*, Woodstock Playhouse, NY, 1950–58; inspector, *Dial "M" for Murder*, Westchester County Playhouse, Mt. Kisco, NY, 1954; psychiatrist, *The Seven Year Itch*, Leroy, *The Bad Seed*, insurance man, *Affair of Murder*, Westchester County Playhouse, Mt. Kisco, NY, 1955;

Postman, *The Gimmick*, Westport Country Playhouse, CT, 1956; Francis, *The Bells Are Ringing*, Shubert, NY, 1956; *Janus*, Bucks County Playhouse, New Hope, PA, 1958; clerk, *The Andersonville Trial*, Henry Miller's, NY, 1959; Mr. Akins, *Send Me No Flowers*, Brooks Atkinson, NY, 1960, Pocono Playhouse, Mountainhouse, PA, Falmouth Playhouse, MA, Cape Playhouse, Dennis, MA, Ogunquit Playhouse, ME, Lakewood Theater, Skowhegan, ME, Playhouse-on-the-Mall, Paramus, NJ, Clinton, NJ, Royal Poinciana Playhouse, Palm Beach, FL; Mr. Whitmyer, *Take Her, She's Mine*, Biltmore, NY, 1961; *Love Among the Platypi*, Bucks County Playhouse, New Hope, PA, 1962; Mr. Kelly, *My Mother, My Father, and Me*, Plymouth, NY, 1963; man in periwig, *My Kinsman, Major Molineaux, The Old Glory*, American Place, NY, 1964; Dr. Franklin Dugmore, *The Man with the Perfect Wife*, Royal Poinciana, Palm Beach, FL, 1965, Coconut Grove Playhouse, Miami, FL, 1965; Michael Wellspot, *Xmas in Las Vegas*, Ethel Barrymore, NY, 1965; William Tracy, *The Philadelphia Story*, Royal Poinciana, Palm Beach, FL, 1966; Carol Newquist, *Little Murders*, Broadhurst, NY, 1967.

PRINCIPAL FILM APPEARANCES—*It Should Happen to You*, 1952; *All the Way Home*, 1963; *Black Like Me*, 1964; *The*

Odd Couple, 1968; *For Pete's Sake*, 1974.

TELEVISION DEBUT—*Phil Silver's Arrow Television Theatre*, 1949. PRINCIPAL TELEVISION APPEARANCES—*Bloomer Girl*, 1956; *Ethan Frome*, 1960; moderator, *Under Discussion*, "Poet Looks at the 20th Century," 1964; *The Nurses*, 1964; *Car 54, Where Are You?*, 1965; *The Defenders*, 1965, 1966; *The Today Show*, 1965; *The Quote Unquote Panel Series*, 1966–67; *The Patty Duke Show; The U.S. Steel Hour; All My Children*, 1979; *The Doctors*, 1980. RADIO—*The Eternal Light Series; Invitation to Learning*, 1960–62.

WRITINGS: BOOKS—editor, *The Collected Edition of Heywood Broun*, 1940; *A Studied Madness*, 1965; *A Tumultous Merriment*, 1977; *Whose Little Boy Are You?*, 1982.

SIDELIGHTS: MEMBERSHIPS—AEA, SAG, AFTRA, American Newspaper Guild, the Coffee House.

ADDRESS: Office—c/o CBS News, 51 W. 52nd Street, New York, NY 10019. Agent—c/o Bill Cooper Associates, 224 W. 49th Street, New York, NY 10036.

* * *

BROWN, Barry, producer

PERSONAL: Born August 28, 1942; son of Irving R. (a music publisher) and Hannah (Streicher) Brown. EDUCATION: University of Michigan, B.A., 1964.

CAREER: PRODUCED: Plays—*Gypsy*, London and United States, 1973–74 (with Fritz Holt); *Saturday Sunday Monday*, 1974 (with Fritz Holt); *Summer Brave*, 1975 (with Fritz Holt); *The Royal Family*, 1975 (with Fritz Holt); *Platinum*, 1978 (with Fritz Holt); *The Mad Woman of Central Park West*, 1979 (with Fritz Holt); *Wally's Cafe*, 1981 (with Fritz Holt); *La Cage aux Folles*, Palace, 1983 (with Fritz Holt).

AWARDS: Drama Desk Award, Best Revival, 1975: *The Royal Family*.

SIDELIGHTS: MEMBERSHIPS—Leage of New York Theatres and Producers. Mr. Brown was also the Producing Director and Manager of the Berkshire Theatre Festival in Stockbridge, MA in 1976.

ADDRESS: Office—250 W. 52nd Street, New York, NY 10019.

* * *

BROWN, Kermit (ne Kermit E. Brown Jr.), actor

PERSONAL: Born February 3, 1939, in Asheville, NC; son of Kermit English (a doctor) and Rosalind (Read) Brown. EDUCATION: Duke University, B.A. (Business Administration); Christ School for Boys, college preparation, Arden, NC. MILITARY: U.S. Army.

CAREER: DEBUT—Henderson, *You Can't Take It with You*, with Cliff Arquette, Tour. NEW YORK DEBUT—Bank Manager,

KERMIT BROWN

Pantagleize, APA Phoenix Repertory Company, Lyceum Theatre, New York. PRINCIPAL STAGE APPEARANCES—APA Phoenix Repertory Company, Lyceum, New York—Mr. Rogers, *The Show Off*, Postmaster, *The Cherry Orchard*, Understudy, *War and Peace*. Off-Broadway, New York—Tony, *Arcata Promise*, No Smoking Playhouse; Randall, *Heartbreak House*, Equity Library Theatre; Mr. Gallagher, *Shadow of a Gunman*, and Sweatshop Owner, *Millionairess*, Sheridan Square Playhouse. Off-Off Broadway, New York—The York Theatre Company—Peter Quince, *A Midsummer Night's Dream*, Mayor, *The Enchanted*, Cromwell, *A Man for All Seasons*, Sant, *Hadrian VII*, Detmold, *Anyone Can Whistle*, *Façade*. Regional Theatre—Alabama Shakespeare Festival/Great Lakes Shakespeare Festival—Orgon, *Tartuffe*, Mr. Ford, *Merry Wives of Windsor*, Leonato, *Much Ado About Nothing*, Player King, *Hamlet*, Oswald, *King Lear*, Nicola, *Arms and the Man*, Nonancourt, *Italian Straw Hat*, Hastings, *Richard III*, Sir Andrew, *Twelfth Night*, Father Tim, *Mass Appeal*, Tranio, *Taming of the Shrew*, Casca, *Julius Caesar*, Roderigo, *Othello*, Teleygin, *Uncle Vanya*. Other Geoffrey Thornton, *The Dresser*, Cincinnati Playhouse in the Park; Godalming, *Passion of Dracula*, GeVa Theatre, Rochester, NY; Carr Gomm, *The Elephant Man*, Alaska Repertory Theatre; Praed, *Mrs. Warren's Profession*, Virginia Stage Company, Norfolk, VA; Harry, *Home*, Carnegie-Mellon Theatre Company; Cecil, *Elizabeth the Queen* and Harry Dalton, *Equus*, Buffalo Studio Arena; Diamond Louis, *The Front Page*, Cleveland Playhouse; Joshua, *Ring Round the Moon*, Hartford Stage Company; Sebastian, *The Tempest*, Center Stage, Baltimore. MAJOR TOURS—Lawyer Craven, *Sly Fox*, with Jackie Gleason; Fred, *Present Laughter*, with Louis Jourdon. Summer Stock—The

Court Theatre, Beloit College—Peter, *The Zoo Story*, Player, *Rosencrantz and Guildenstern Are Dead*, Peterbono, *Thieves Carnival*, George, *That Championship Season*, Jimmy, *The Gingerbread Lady*, Bensinger, *The Front Page;* Father Tim, *Mass Appeal*, Allenberry Playhouse. Dinner Theatre—Charles, *Blithe Spirit*, Limestone Valley Dinner Theatre; Jacques, *Pajama Tops*, Beef'n Boards, Dinner Theatre. PRINCIPAL FILM APPEARANCES—*Without a Trace, Daniel, Nighthawks*. PRINCIPAL TELEVISION APPEARANCES—*Edge of Night, Kojak, After the Fall*.

SIDELIGHTS: MEMBERSHIPS—AEA, SAG, AFTRA.

''Mr. Brown's father was a doctor in Asheville, and everyone expected his only son to choose the same career. 'It's very difficult for a youngster to grow up with that,' says Brown, who didn't fully realize 'that it was my life' until he started working in theatre as an undergraduate at Duke University. He switched majors—to business administration, not theatre—and received his degree, went into the Army and 'acted on every base I was stationed on,' then 'went back to Asheville and worked in a glass factory while I decided whether I could make a living as an actor.' He went to New York and studied . . . his most valuable acting lesson came during three years with the APA Phoenix Repertory Company which he joined as a journeyman apprentice. 'I spent three seasons doing lots of carrying flags and doing walk-ons and watching people like Rosemary Harris, Ellis Rabb, Keene Curtis, at work.' ''

ADDRESS: Agent—Roxy Horen Management, 1650 Broadway, New York, NY 10019.

* * *

BROWN, William F., writer

PERSONAL: Born April 16, 1928, in Jersey City, NJ; son of Douglas (a pharmaceuticals salesman) and Dorothy (a cosmetics salesperson; maiden name Ferrett) Brown; married Ann Distler, June 21, 1950 (divorced 1980); married Christinia Tippit (a writer) October 3, 1981; children: Debra Susan, William Todd. EDUCATION: Princeton University, A.B., 1950. MILITARY: U.S. Army, 1950–52.

WRITINGS: PLAYS, PUBLISHED—*The Girl in the Freudian Slip*, 1967; *A Single Thing in Common*, 1978; *The Wiz*, 1979 (with Charlie Smalls). TELEVISION SHOWS—*Silents Please*, 1960; Max Liebman Specials (1960–61); *The Jackie Gleason Show*, 1962; *That Was the Week That Was*, 1964–65; *Love American Style; The David Frost Revue*, 1968; *World War II: G.I. Diary*, 1980. BOOKS—*Tiger Tiger*, 1950; *Beat Beat Beat*, 1959; *The Girl in the Freudian Slip*, 1959; *The Abominable Showmen*, 1960; *The World Is My Yo-Yo*, 1963.

AWARDS: Antoinette Perry Award Nomination, Best Musical, 1975: *The Wiz;* Drama Desk Award, Best Musical, 1975: *The Wiz*.

SIDELIGHTS: MEMBERSHIPS—Dramatists Guild, Writers Guild, A.S.C.A.P., National Cartoonists Society, Artists and Writers.

''The turning point came in 1961, when I decided to quit my

full-time job in an advertising agency and see if I could make it as a free-lance writer. That first year, 1962, I wrote everything I could . . . a book, night club acts, television, magazine articles, cabaret, the works. And the works worked. Year two I began writing my first play, *The Girl in the Freudian Slip,* and after many rejections and many rewrites, it found a producer (Wally Perner and Mike Ellis) and eventually, after a successful tour, found its way to Broadway. Nothing will ever be such a kick as that first opening night in the Big Apple, not even the success, eight years later, of *The Wiz.* (Although it sure makes a big difference whether a show runs four performances or four years). But no matter what it is, theatre, television industrial shows, writing is a joy. Mostly, I feel lucky I'm doing what I want to do and am fairly successful at it. I have a wonderful wife who also writes, Tina Tippit; two great children; and if I could ask for more, it would be a little extra time off to get my golf game in shape.''

ADDRESS: Agent—c/o Charles Hunt, Fifi Oscard Associates, 19 W. 44th Street, New York, NY 10036.

* * *

BROWN, Zack, designer

PERSONAL: Born July 10, 1949 in Honolulu, HI; son of Zack F. and Yvette C. (Bilodeau) Brown, Jr. EDUCATION: University of Notre Dame; Yale University, School of Drama.

CAREER: FIRST STAGE WORK, DESIGNED—*Threepenny Opera,* Loeb Drama Center, Harvard University, 1974. PRINCIPAL STAGE WORK, DESIGNED—*The Importance of Being Earnest,* Circle in the Square, NY, 1977; sets and costumes for *On Your Toes,* Palace, London, England, 1984; Circle in the Square, NY: *Tartuffe, Man and Superman, The Man Who Came to Dinner, Major Barbara, #13 Rue de L'Amour, St. Joan.* MAJOR TOURS—*On Your Toes,* Miami, New Orleans, San Francisco, Los Angeles, San Diego.

PRINCIPAL TELEVISION WORK, Costume Design—*Mourning Becomes Electra;* sets and costumes, *La Gioconda.*

AWARDS: Two Emmy Awards for Sets and Costumes for telecast of San Francisco Opera's *La Gioconda.*

ADDRESS: 308 W. 91st Street, New York, NY 10024.

* * *

BRUCE, Shelley (nee Michele Merklinghaus), actress

PERSONAL: Born May 5, 1965, in Passaic, NJ; daughter of Bruce Harry (a sales manager) and Margaret Ann (Pollina) Merklinghaus. EDUCATION: Attended New Jersey public schools.

CAREER: DEBUT—*The Children's Mass,* Theater de Lys, New York, 1973. PRINCIPAL STAGE APPEARANCES—Annie, *Annie,* Alvin, 1978–79; Sandy, *Broadway Scandals of 1928,* O'Neal's 43rd Street, New York, 1982.

SHELLEY BRUCE

FILM DEBUT—Tiger, *The Burning,* 1980. TELEVISION DEBUT— *The Mike Douglas Show.* TELEVISION APPEARANCES—*1977 Tony Awards; The Merv Griffin Show; The Today Show; CBS Sports Spectacular* (co-host); *The Annie Christmas Show; Kids Are People, Too; The Tomorrow Show; Midday Live, Broadway Plays Washington.*

WRITINGS: Tomorrow Is Today (autobiography), 1983.

AWARDS: National Cancer Courage Award, presented by Nancy Reagan on behalf of the American Cancer Society, 1983.

SIDELIGHTS: MEMBERSHIPS—Actors Equity Association, AFTRA, SAG, American Cancer Society, Make-a-Wish Foundation, Annie Fan Club (president).

TELETHONS—Arthritis, Easter Seals, UJA/F, Cerebral Palsy, Buffalo Children's Hospital; BENEFIT SHOWS—Fight for Sight, The Floating Hospital, Girl Scouts of America, Felician School for Exceptional Children; WHITE HOUSE—COMMAND PERFORMANCE for President Carter, March 1977; Christmas Show for President Carter, December 1977; Easter Show, April 1981; Command Performance for Nancy Reagan.

FAVORITE PART—''Annie was my favorite role because it trained me in theater. Working with Martin Charnin was a very rewarding learning experience. I enjoy all aspects of show business as they are all unique.''

ADDRESS: Office—P.O. Box 261, East Rutherford, NJ 07073.

* * *

BRUCKHEIMER, Jerry, producer

CAREER: PRINCIPAL FILM WORK: Producer—*Farewell, My Lovely,* 1975; *American Gigolo,* 1980; *Thief,* 1981; *Cat People,* 1982; *Young Doctors in Love,* 1982; *Flashdance,* 1983; *Thief of Hearts* (forthcoming); *Beverly Hills Cop* (forthcoming).

ADDRESS: Office—Paramount Studios, 5555 Melrose Avenue, Los Angeles, CA 90046.

* * *

BUCHHOLZ, Horst, actor

PERSONAL: Born December 4, 1933, in Berlin, Germany; married Myriam Bru (an actress and manager), December 7, 1958; children: Christophe, Beatrice. EDUCATION: Studied for the theatre with Marliese Ludwig in Berlin.

CAREER: DEBUT—Supernumary, Metropol Theatre, Berlin, 1946. NEW YORK DEBUT—Title role, *Cherie,* Majestic, 1959. PRINCIPAL STAGE APPEARANCES—Young actor, *Emil und die Detektive* (Emil and the Detective), Metrolpol, Berlin, 1947; *Das Floss der Medussa* (Medussa's Hair), Hebbeltheatre, Berlin, 1948; *Das Dunkel Ist Licht Genug* (The Dark Is Light Enough), Schillertheatre, Berlin; *Willst Du Nicht Das Lammelen Hüten,* Renaissancetheatre, Berlin; *Peter Pan,* Schillertheatre, Berlin; The Young Count, *Schule der Vater* (School for Fathers), Berlin; Kosinski, *Die Räuber* (The Thieves), Schillertheatre, Berlin; *Andorra,* NY, 1963; title role, *Ein Tag in Sterben des Joe Egg* (A Day in the Death of Joe Egg), Tournee Schweiz and BRD, Switzerland, 1977; Master of Ceremonies, *Cabaret,* Theatre des Westerns, Berlin, 1981.

FILM DEBUT—*Die Spur Fuhrt Nach Berlin,* 1952. PRINCIPAL FILMS—*Warum* (Why?), 1952; *Marianne,* 1954; *Himmel Ohne Sterne,* 1955; Harald Braun, *Regine,* 1955; *Die Halbstarken,* 1956; King Christian, *Herrscher Ohne Krone,* 1956; title role, *Die Bekenntnisse des Hochstaplers Felix Krull (The Confessions of Felix Krull),* 1957; *Robinson Dark Nicht Sterben,* 1957; *Monpti,* 1957; *Endstation Liebe,* 1957; *Nasser Asphalt,* 1958; *Auferstehung* (Resurrection), 1958; *Tiger Bay,* 1958; *Das Totenschiff,* 1959; *The Magnificent Seven,* 1960; Marcel, *Fanny,* 1960; *One-Two-Three,* 1961; *Nine Hours to Rama,* 1962; *La Noia (The Empty Canvas),* 1963; *Our Man in Istanbul,* 1964; title role, *The Fabulous Adventure of Marco Polo,* 1964; *Johnny Banco,* 1966; *Cervantes,* 1966; *Aber Johnny* (But Johnny. . .), 1967; *L'Astragale,* 1968; *Come, Quando, Perche,* 1968; *La Colombo non deve Volare,* 1970; *Le Saveur,* 1971; Johann Strauss, the Younger, *The Great Waltz,* 1972; *Frauenstation* (House of Women), 1975; *Raid on Entebbe,* 1977; *Logan's Run,* 1977; *How the West Was Won,* 1978; *The Cat and the Canary,* 1978; *The Amazing Captain Nemo,* 1978; *From Hell to Victory,* 1978; *Aphrodite,* 1982; *Sahara,* 1982; *Der Blick vom Turm,* 1983.

TELEVISION DEBUT—*Longhelder fur Pittsville,* 1973; *No Such Thing as a Vampire,* 1974; *Das Superding,* 1976; *The Savage Bees,* 1976; *Return to Fantasy Island,* 1977; *The Return of Captain Nemo,* 1978; *Solo fur Margarethe,* 1978; *Angel Come Home,* 1978; *Avalanche Express,* 1978; *The French-Atlantic Affair,* 1979; *Auf Einem Gutshof,* 1980; *Berlin Tunnel 21,* 1981; *Liebe Hat Ihren Preis* (Love Has Its Price), 1983; *H. Weis—Special,* 1983.

AWARDS: Deutscher FilmPreis, *Himmel ohne Sterne,* 1956; . . . *Felix Krull,* 1957; Bambi Award, 1957 and 1958.

SIDELIGHTS: Mr. Buchholz's career has spotlighted him as a star in Germany, Great Britain, the United States, France and Italy. He has made films, or television films, in all of these countries for their own consumption, as well as for international release.

ADDRESS: Agent—Toni Mackeben, Douglousstrasse 2-4, D-1000, Berlin 33, West Germany.

* * *

BUCKLEY, Betty Lynn, actress

PERSONAL: Born July 3, 1947, in Fort Worth, TX; daughter of Ernest (dean of engineering; lieutenant colonel, U.S. Air Force) and Betty Bob (a dancer and journalist; maiden name, Diltz) Buckley; married Peter Flood 1972 (divorced 1974). EDUCATION: Texas Christian, B.A., Journalism; studied voice with Paul Gavert, acting with Stella Adler.

CAREER: NEW YORK DEBUT—Martha Jefferson, *1776,* 1969. LONDON DEBUT—Fran Kubelik, *Promises, Promises.* PRINCIPAL STAGE APPEARANCES—*Johnny Pott,* Off-Broadway; *What's a Nice Country Like You Doing in a State Like This?,* Upstairs at Jimmy's, NY, 1972; *Pippin,* Imperial, NY, 1973–75; Heather, *I'm Getting My Act Together and Taking It on the Road,* Circle in the Square, Downtown, NY, 1981; Grizabella, *Cats,* Winter Garden, NY, 1982.

PRINCIPAL FILM WORK—Miss Collins, *Carrie,* 1976; *Tender Mercies,* 1983. PRINCIPAL TELEVISION WORK—*The Devil's Work,* PBS; Abby Bradford, *Eight Is Enough,* 1977.

AWARDS: Antoinette Perry Award, Best Featured Actress in a Musical, 1983: Grizabella, *Cats.*

ADDRESS: Office—Amy Lanier Vall, Vall Associates, (212) 834-9283. Agent—John Kimble, DHKPR, 7319 Beverly Blvd., Los Angeles, CA 90036.

* * *

BUDRIES, David, sound designer

PERSONAL: Born September 12, 1953 in Port Chester, NY; son of Charles (a salesman) and Catherine (a horticulturalist; maiden name, Paladino) Budries. EDUCATION: University of Hartford (Communications/Theatre and Biology), two years.

CAREER: PRINCIPAL STAGE WORK, SOUND DESIGN—*Is There*

Life After High School?, Hartford Stage Company, CT, 1981; *Aida*, Hartford Civic Center, CT, 1981; *The Greeks*, Hartford Stage Company, CT, 1982; *Turandot*, Hartford Civic Center, CT, 1982; *Portage to San Cristobal*, Hartford Stage Company, CT, 1982; *And a Nightingale Sang . . .*, Newhouse, Lincoln Center, NY, 1983; *As You Like It*, Hartford Stage Company, CT, 1983; *The Three Sisters*, Hartford Stage Company, CT, 1984.

THEATRE-RELATED CAREER: Director, Hartt Recording Studio, University of Hartford, 1979–84; instructor, Sound Technology Program, University of Hartford, 1980–84; instructor, Advanced Sound Design, Yale University, School of Drama.

SIDELIGHTS: MEMBERSHIPS—Technical Director; Peace Train Foundation, 1973–80; Audio Engineering Society. RECREATION—Piano, guitar, gourmet cooking.

ADDRESS: Home—130 Griswold Street, Glastonbury, CT 06033. Office—c/o University of Hartford, 200 Bloomfield Avenue, Hartford, CT 06117.

* * *

BUELL, Bill, actor

PERSONAL: Born September 21, 1952, in Taipai, Taiwan; son of William Ackerman (a diplomat) Buell. EDUCATION: East 15 Acting School, London, England; studied with Nikos Psachorapolous and Sue Seton in New York.

CAREER: NEW YORK DEBUT—Derek, *Once a Catholic*, Helen Hayes, 1979. PRINCIPAL STAGE APPEARANCES—Jimmy Johnson/Louis Howe, *Annie*, New York; Patsy/Brian Waterhouse/Dodger, *The First*, New York; *Apollo's Night Out*, Playwrights Horizons, New York; Harry, *Declasse*, Lion Theatre, New York; Verges, *Much Ado About Nothing*, Yale Repertory; Philadelphia Drama Guild: Perry, *The Royal Family*, Jim, *The Glass Menagerie*, Bernardo/Second Grave Digger, *Hamlet*, Poulengey/D'Estivet, *St. Joan*, Albert Proesser, *Hobson's Choice;* Alaska Repertory: Tom Snout, *A Midsummer Night's Dream*, Slovitch, *Fools;* Christopher Wren, *The Mousetrap*, Birmingham Theatre. MAJOR TOURS—Judas/Herbie, *Godspell;* Jameson, *Passion of Dracula*.

PRINCIPAL FILM APPEARANCES—*Wet Exit* (shown at the Museum of Modern Art, New York.) PRINCIPAL TELEVISION APPEARANCES—*Ryan's Hope*.

ADDRESS: Home—400 W. 43rd Street, New York, NY 10036. Agent—Dorothy Scott, c/o Marje Fields, 165 W. 46th Street, New York, NY 10036.

* * *

BULL, Peter, actor, producer, and writer

PERSONAL: Born March 21, 1912 in London; died May 27, 1984 in London, of a heart attack; son of Sir William James (a lawyer and Member of Parliament) and Lilian Hester (Roandon) Bull. EDUCATION: Attended Winchester College (England) and Tours University (France); trained for the

PETER BULL

stage at the Central School of Drama (England). POLITICS: Conservative. RELIGION: Church of England. MILITARY: Royal Navy.

CAREER: DEBUT—small parts, *If I Were You*, Shaftesbury, London, 1933. NEW YORK DEBUT—three roles, *Escape Me Never*, Shubert, 1935. PRINCIPAL STAGE APPEARANCES—*Lady's Not for Burning*, London, 1948 and New York, 1950; Pozzo, *Waiting for Godot*, London, 1953; Tetzel, *Luther*, London, 1961; Sergeant Buzfuz, *Pickwick*.

FILM DEBUT—Russian officer, *Knight without Armour*, 1937. PRINCIPAL FILMS—Saraband, *George I*, 1947; German Captain, *The African Queen*, 1951; Russian Ambassador, *Dr. Strangelove*, 1963; Thwackum, *Tom Jones*, 1963; Duchess, *Alice's Adventures in Wonderland*. TELEVISION APPEARANCES—*Steve Allen Show; Jack Paar Show; Dick Cavett Show; Tonight Show; Merv Griffin Show*.

WRITINGS: BOOKS—*The Teddy Bear Book*, 1970 (reprinted as *The House of Nisbet*, 1983); *Life is a Cucumber* (autobiography); *I Say Look Here* (autobiography); *It Isn't All Greek to Me* (autobiography); *Bulls in the Meadows* (autobiography); *I Know the Face But . . .* (autobiography); *Not on Your Telly* (autobiography); *Bear with Me; Bully Bear and The Teddy Bear Rally; Bully Bear Goes to a Wedding*.

AWARDS: MEMBERSHIPS—Theatre Managers Association, Screen Actor's Guild, A.F.T.R.A., British Equity.

"I have a small house on the Greek Island of Paxos. I speak French, German and Greek. I attend Teddy Bear Conventions all over the world."

ADDRESS: Agent—c/o Milton Goldman, International Creative Management, 40 W. 57th Street, New York, NY 10019.

* * *

BULLARD, Thomas, director

PERSONAL: Born November 14, 1944 in Oakland, CA; son of Allan Fleming (an attorney) and Carolyn Culver (Oliver) Bullard; married Susan V. Smyly (a sculptor) on January 12, 1984. EDUCATION: Middlebury College, B.A. 1966; Yale University School of Drama, M.F.A. (Directing) 1969.

CAREER: NEW YORK DEBUT—Director—*Strings Snapping,* Manhattan Theatre Club, 1972. PRINCIPAL STAGE WORK, Director—*Marouf,* Manhattan Theatre Club (MTC), NY, 1973; *Blessing,* MTC, NY, 1974; *Staircase,* MTC, 1975; *The Blood Knot,* MTC, 1976; *La Voix Humaine,* MTC, 1976; *Boesman and Lena,* MTC, 1977; *The Last Street Play,* MTC, 1977; *Krapp's Last Tape,* Lincoln Center Institute, NY, 1977; *Scenes from Soweto,* MTC, 1978; *Statements. . . ,* MTC, 1978; *Unfinished Women,* Public Theatre, NY, 1978; *Sizwe Bansi Is Dead,* GeVa, Rochester, NY, 1978; *The Blood Knot,* Philadelphia Drama Guild, Syracuse Stage, 1979; *Henry IV, Part I,* Dallas Shakespeare Festival, 1979; *Willie Callendar,* Philadelphia Drama Guild, 1979; *One Wedding,* MTC, 1980; *One Tiger to a Hill,* MTC, 1980; *Playboy of the Western World,* University of Washington, 1981; *Miss Julie,* Lincoln Center Institute, NY, 1981; *Strange Snow,* MTC, 1982; *A Lesson from Aloes,* Cincinnati Playhouse, OH, 1982; *Misalliance,* Actors Theatre of Louisville, 1982–83; *Elba,* MTC, 1983; *A Raisin in the Sun* (25th Anniversary Production) Goodman, Chicago, IL, 1983; *Extremities,* Actors Theatre of Louisville, toured to Okinawa and Japan, 1984.

THEATRE-RELATED CAREER—Artistic Director, Penn Players, University of Pennsylvania, 1969–70; Associate Director, Annenberg Center, Philadelphia, 1970–71; Teaching Artist, Lincoln Center Institute, 1972–present; Artistic Associate, Manhattan Theatre Club, 1972–78; Guest Lecturer, Brooklyn College, 1977–79; Adjunct Associate Professor, Brooklyn College, 1979–80; Adjunct Associate Professor, S.U.N.Y. at Stony Brook, 1980–81; Associate Director, Manhattan Theatre Club, 1983–84.

AWARDS: Village Voice Obie Award for Outstanding Directorial Achievement, *Statements After an Arrest Under the Immorality Act,* 1978; Audelco Award, Best Dramatic Production, *The Last Street Play,* 1977; Phi Beta Kappa, 1966.

ADDRESS: Office—P.O. Box 197, New York, NY 10038.

* * *

BURNETT, Carol, actress, commedienne, singer

PERSONAL: Born April 26 in San Antonio, TX; married Joe Hamilton (a producer; separated); children: Erin Kate, Jody, Carrie. EDUCATION: Attended UCLA.

CAREER: DEBUT—UCLA Theatre department. NEW YORK DEBUT—Princess Winifred Woebegone, *Once Upon a Mattress,* off-Broadway, later transferred to a Broadway theatre for one year, 1959. PRINCIPAL STAGE APPEARANCES—*Fade Out, Fade In,* Broadway, 1964; *Plaza Suite,* Huntington Hartford, Los Angeles, CA, 1970; *I Do!, I Do!,* Huntington Hartford, 1973; *Same Time Next Year,* Huntington Hartford, Burt Reynolds Dinner Theatre, FL, 1977–80.

PRINCIPAL FILM APPEARANCES—*Who's Been Sleeping in My Bed,* 1963; *Pete 'n Tillie,* 1972; *The Front Page,* 1974; *A Wedding,* 1978; *Health,* 1980; *The Four Seasons,* 1980; *Chu Chu and the Philly Flash,* 1981; *Annie,* 1982.

TELEVISION DEBUT—Paul Winchell's progam. PRINCIPAL TELEVISION APPEARANCES—*The Garry Moore Show,* 1959–62; *Julie* (Andrews) *& Carol at Carnegie Hall,* 1963; *Carol & Company,* 1963; *Calamity Jane,* 1963; *Once Upon a Mattress,* 1964; *Carol & Company,* 1966; *Carol + 2,* 1966; *The Carol Burnett Show,* 1966–77; *Julie & Carol at Lincoln Center,* 1972; *Once Upon a Mattress,* 1972; *6 Rms Riv Vu,* 1974; *Twigs,* 1975; *Sills & Burnett at the Met,* 1976; *Dolly* (Parton) *& Carol in Nashville,* 1978; *The Grass Is Always Greener Over the Septic Tank,* 1979; *Friendly Fire,* 1979; *The Tenth Month,* 1979; *Carol Burnett & Friends,* syndicated, 1977–present; *Life of the Party: The Story of Beatrice,* 1982; *Between Friends,* 1983; *Burnett 'Discovers' Domingo* (Placido), 1984.

PRINCIPAL CLUB APPEARANCES—The Blue Angel; Ceasar's Palace.

AWARDS: Gold Medal Award of the International Radio and Television Society, 1984; named One of the World's Ten Most Admired Women, *Good Housekeeping* magazine, 1983; Humanitarian of the Year, Variety Clubs International, 1983; People's Choice Award, Favorite Female Television Star, 1981–82; honored by the fourth annual Women in Film Crystal Awards, 1980; Honorary Doctorate of Humane Letters, Emerson College, Boston, 1980; The Jack Benny Humanitarian of the Year from the March of Dimes, 1983; Best Actress, San Sebastian Film Festival, 1978: *A Wedding;* winner, the First Annual National Television Critics Circle Award for Outstanding Performance, 1977–78; named one of the World's 20 Most Admired Women in a poll conducted by George Gallup; Favorite All-Around Female Entertainer, voted by the public in a poll conducted by A. C. Neilson Company, 1977–78–79, co-winner, 1976; winner, People's Choice Award for the Best Variety Show, 1975; Entertainer of the Year, Friars Club; Most Popular Television Star as voted by the Newspaper Enterprise Association; Top Female Star, Variety Club Award; four successive Entertainer of the Year Awards as Best Female Comedienne, AGVA; five Photoplay Gold Medals as the Most Popular Television Star; Fame Award as Best Comedienne for six seasons; six consecutive Hollywood Foreign Press Association Golden Globe Awards; The Los Angeles *Times* Woman of the Year Award; Carol Burnett and *The Carol Burnett Show* were nominated for Emmy Awards in 1967–68, 1968–69, 1969–70, 1970–71, 1971–72, 1972–73, 1973–74, 1974–75, 1975–76, 1976–77; Carol and the *Carol Burnett Show* won Emmy Awards for 1971–72, 1973–74, and 1974–75; Emmy Award for *Julie & Carol at Carnegie*

Hall, 1962–63; Emmy Award Nominations for *Julie and Carol at Lincoln Center,* 1972–73, *6 Rms Riv Vu,* 1973–74, *Sills and Burnett at the Met,* 1976–77.

SIDELIGHTS: "While attending UCLA as a theatre arts student, hoping to go into playwriting or journalism, Miss Burnett had to take acting courses and wound up getting A's in her performances classes, and, although she was not catapulted from campus actress to professional comedienne, a strange incident occured which was to change the course of her life. With other members of the UCLA drama school, she was invited to perform at a society party in San Diego. There Carol met a wealthy businessman who encouraged her to go to New York. When she explained she did not have the necessary funds, the stranger staked her to a thousand dollars, to be paid back when she became successful. She has also abided by two additional conditions of the loan—never to reveal her benefactor's name and to help others if she did become successful. Five years later she settled the debt. Toward the latter condition, she has established scholarships at Emerson College in Boston and at UCLA, her alma mater, where she has been named a Franklin D. Murphy Associate and is a member of the Board of Trustees. She has also established 'The Carol Burnett Musical Theater Competition,' among UCLA Theatre Arts students to encourage the study and practice of musical comedy in the theatre."

ADDRESS: c/o ICPR Public Relations, 1900 Avenue of the Stars, Suite 300, Los Angeles, CA 90067.

* * *

BURNS-BISOGNO, Louisa, writer

PERSONAL: Born September 23, 1936, in Brooklyn, NY; daughter of Philip J. (an auditor) and Johanna C. (Hansen) Burns; married Thomas Bisogno (a writer), 1955; children: Meg, Tom, Glenn, Lisa, Keith. EDUCATION: Lehmann College, B.A., 1969; New School, New York, M.A., 1983.

WRITINGS: PLAYS, UNPUBLISHED—Emma; The Lilac Season. SCREENPLAYS—*Oaxacan Gold; Return to Wounded Knee; Boardwalk Blue; Love Signs* (with Thomas Bisogno), 1981; *My Body, My Child,* 1982; *The Golden Rivet,* 1983; *Thin Ice,* 1983; *Shadows,* 1984.

TELEVISION—*One Day in the Life of Ivan Denisovich* (adaptation), 1974; *Lilac Season,* 1979; *The Firm,* "Against Her Will" (pilot), 1982; *The Veil and the Ring* (treatment), 1982; *Meine Liebe Cousin* (treatment), *Klanwatch* (treatment), *The Last Act of Love* (treatment), 1983.

THEATRE-RELATED CAREER—Instructor, Communications and Theatre Arts, Western Connecticut State University, 1982–present.

AWARDS: Channel 13 Award, Best Use of Television in the Classroom, 1974: *One Day in the Life of Ivan Denisovich* (adaptation); Maxine Heller Award, Outstanding Woman Graduate in Political Science, 1969; grants—Bicentennial, 1975–76; National Science Foundation, 1968; fellowships—Urban Research Center, Hunter College, NY, 1970.

ADDRESS: Home—Ice Pond Farm, Brewster, NY 10509.

Agent—c/o Leo Bookman, William Morris Agency, 1350 Avenue of the Americas, New York, NY 10019.

* * *

BURSTYN, Ellen (nee Edna Rae Gillooly), actress

PERSONAL: Born December 7, 1932, in Detroit, MI; daughter of John Austin (a building contractor) and Correine (Hammel) Gillooly; children: Jefferson.

CAREER: NEW YORK DEBUT—*Fair Game,* 1957. PRINCIPAL STAGE APPEARANCES—*Same Time Next Year,* NY, 1974; *84 Charing Cross Road,* NY, 1983.

PRINCIPAL FILM APPEARANCES—*Goodbye, Charlie,* 1964; *For Those Who Think Young,* 1965; *Tropic of Cancer,* 1970; *The Last Picture Show,* 1971; *The King of Marvin Gardens,* 1972; *The Exorcist,* 1973; *Thursday's Game,* 1973; *Harry and Tonto,* 1974; *Alice Doesn't Live Here Anymore,* 1974; *Providence,* 1977; *A Dream of Passion,* 1978; *Same Time Next Year,* 1978; *Resurrection,* 1980; *Silence of the North,* 1980.

AWARDS: Doctor of Humane Letters, Dowling College, 1983; Doctor of Fine Arts, School of Visual Arts, New York, 1983; Academy Award Nomination, Best Actress, 1978: *Same Time Next Year;* Golden Globe Award, Best Actress, 1978: *Same Time Next Year;* Antoinette Perry Award, Drama Desk Award, Outer Critics Circle Award, Best Actress,

ELLEN BURSTYN

1974: *Same Time Next Year;* Academy Award, British Academy Award, Golden Globe Award, Best Actress, 1974: *Alice Doesn't Live Here Anymore;* Academy Award Nomination, Best Actress, 1973: *The Exorcist;* New York Film Critics Award, Golden Globe Award, National Film Critics Award, Academy Award Nomination, Best Supporting Actress, 1971: *The Last Picture Show.*

SIDELIGHTS: MEMBERSHIPS—AEA (President, 1982–present), Actors Studio (co-director, 1982–present).

Ms. Burstyn's first job as a performer was pointing out automotive parts in a cutaway section of a Ford truck at the Michigan State Fair.

ADDRESS: Agent—c/o Todd Smith, Creative Artists, 1888 Century Park E., Suite 1400, Los Angeles, CA 90067.

* * *

BUSEY, Gary, actor

PERSONAL: Born June 29, 1944; son of Delmer Lloyd (a construction design manager) and Virginia (Arnett) Busey; married Judy Lynn Hakenberg (a photographer) December 30, 1968; children: William Jacob. EDUCATION: Coffeyville Junior College A.A., 1963; and attended Kansas State College and Oklahoma State University; trained for the theatre in the educational institutions he attended. RELIGION: Protestant.

CAREER: PRINCIPAL FILM APPEARANCES—*A Star Is Born,* 1978; *Straight Time,* 1978; *The Buddy Holly Story,* 1979; *Carny,* 1980; *Barbarosa,* 1981; *D.C. Cab,* 1983; *The Bear,* 1983. TELEVISION DEBUT—*High Chapparal,* 1970. PRINCIPAL TELEVISION APPEARANCES—*Bloodsport; The Law; Texas Wheelers; Gunsmoke; Education of Private Slovik; The Jerry Lee Lewis Special.*

AWARDS: Academy Award Nominee, Best Actor, 1979: *The Buddy Holly Story;* National Film Critics' Award, Best Actor, 1979: *The Buddy Holly Story;* Golden Globe Award Nominee, Best Actor, 1979: *The Buddy Holly Story.*

SIDELIGHTS: MEMBERSHIPS—Screen Actors' Guild, A.F.T.R.A., Kiwanis.

''I was the last actor to die on *Gunsmoke.*''

ADDRESS: c/o Creative Artists Agency, Inc., 1888 Century Park East, Suite 1400, Los Angeles, CA 90067.

* * *

BUSSERT, Meg, actress and singer

PERSONAL: Born December 21, 1949 in Chicago, IL; daughter of Martin Joseph (computers) and Rosemary (Daly) Bussert; married Steve Cochrane (a production electrician and lighting designer), February 5, 1977; children: Rachel Kelly Cochrane. EDUCATION: Attended University of Illinois; trained for the stage at Herbert Berghof Studios.

CAREER: DEBUT—Chorus/understudy, *Lolita My Love.*

MEG BUSSERT

NEW YORK DEBUT—Marian Paroo, *The Music Man,* City Center, New York, 1980. PRINCIPAL STAGE APPEARANCES— Fiona, *Brigadoon,* Majestic, New York, 1980; Guenevere, *Camelot,* Winter Garden, New York, 1981; *Irene* (Broadway); *Gorey Stories* (Broadway); *Lorelei* (Broadway); *Something's Afoot* (Broadway); *The Most Happy Fella* (regional); *Promises, Promises* (regional); *The Boy Friend* (regional); *Cabaret* (regional); *She Loves Me* (regional); *Kiss Me Kate* (regional); *Jacques Brel . . .* (regional); *Oklahoma* (regional). MAJOR TOURS—*Irene,* U.S. cities; *Applause,* U.S. cities.

TELEVISION DEBUT—Guenevere, *Camelot.*

AWARDS: Antoinette Perry Award Nomination, Outstanding Actress in a Musical, 1981: *Brigadoon;* Theatre World Award, 1981: *Brigadoon,* 1981: *Music Man.*

SIDELIGHTS: RECREATION—sailing.

''I'm into motherhood and song.''

ADDRESS: Agent—c/o Katy Rothacker, William Morris Agency, 1350 Ave. of Americas, New York, NY 10019.

* * *

BUTLER, Robert, director

CAREER: PRINCIPAL TELEVISION WORK: Director—*The Blue Knight; James Dean: Portrait of a Friend; Dark Victory; In the Glitter Palace,* 1977; *Death Takes a Holiday; Columbo; Hill Street Blues.*

AWARDS: Three Emmy Awards: *Hill Street Blues* (1); *The Blue Knight* (2).

ADDRESS: Agent—James Wiatt, ICM, 8899 Beverly Blvd., Los Angeles, CA 90048.

* * *

BYERS, (Bobbie) Catherine, actress, narrator, announcer

PERSONAL: Born October 7, in Sioux City, IA; daughter of Robert Earl (a salesman and investor) and Pauline Katherine (Rudbeck) Byers; married Lee Tombs (an actor) on December 20, 1976; children: Alexander McMillan. EDUCATION: University of Iowa, Iowa City, B.A.; studied at Studio '68 in London and with Wynn Handman in New York. POLITICS: Republican. RELIGION: Christian Science.

CAREER: DEBUT—Reenie, *The Dark at the Top of the Stairs,* Barn Theatre, Augusta, MI, 1960; NEW YORK DEBUT—Araminta, *The Philanthropist,* Barrymore, March to mid May, 1971. LONDON DEBUT—She, *The Creatures of the Chase,* Charles Marowitz Open Space Theatre, for three weeks, 1970. PRINCIPAL STAGE APPEARANCES—Ann, *All My Sons,* Roundabout, NY, 1974; Mrs. Chisholm, *The Petrified Forest,* St. Clements, NY, 1974; Claire, *Don't Call Back,* Helen Hayes, NY, 1975; Nurse/Dora Strang, *Equus,* Plymouth, NY, 1976; Carrie, *Toys in the Attic,* McCarter, Princeton, NJ, 1978; Magda Doebbels, *The Fuehrer Bunker,* American Place, NY, 1981; Mae, *Grace,* American Place, NY, 1981; *Passion,* Longacre, NY, 1983; Ensemble, *Great Days,* American Place, NY, 1983; has performed for four seasons with the New Jersey Shakespeare Festival, 1972, 1974, 1978, 1980. MAJOR TOURS—Dora Strang, *Equus,* Washington, DC, Philadelphia, Baltimore, Toronto, Detroit, Cleveland; Lady Macduff, *Macbeth,* Southeastern states, 1975.

TELEVISION DEBUT—*The Doctors.*

AWARDS: Best Actress Nomination New Jersey Critics

CATHERINE BYERS

Award, 1978: Martha, *Who's Afraid of Virginia Woolf?;* Best Actress, New Jersey Critics Award, 1974: Sarah, *JB.*

SIDELIGHTS: Miss Byers has narrated several hundred books for the American Foundation for the Blind Talking Books and has done extensive work in TV commercial voiceovers.

ADDRESS: Home—65 W. 95th Street, New York, NY 10025. Agent—Monty Silver, 200 W. 57th Street, New York, NY 10019.

C

CACOYANNIS, Michael, director and writer

PERSONAL: Born in Limassol, Cyprus; son of Panayotis (a lawyer) and Angeliki (Efthyvnlou) Cacoyannis. EDUCATION: Gray's Inn (London), Barrister-at-Law, 1942; attended Central School of Dramatic Art (London), 1946 and Old Vic School, 1946.

CAREER: DEBUT—Herod, *Salome*, Rudolf Steiner, London, 1946. NEW YORK DEBUT—DIRECTOR, *The Trojan Women*, Circle in the Square, 1963–64.

DIRECTED: PLAYS—*The Rainmaker* (Greece), 1957; *Gigi* (Greece), 1958; *The Devils*, Broadway Theatre, New York, 1965; *Iphigenia in Aulis*, Circle in the Square, New York; 1967; *Les Troyennes*, TNP (France), 1967; *Romeo and Juliet*, TNP (France), 1968; *King Oedipus*, Abbey, (Ireland), 1973; *Miss Margarita* (Greece), 1974; *Les Bacchantes*, Comédie Française (France), 1979; *The Glass Menagerie* (Greece), 1979; *The Bacchae*, Circle in the Square (New York), 1980; *Antony and Cleopatra* (Greece), 1981; *The Three Sisters* (Greece), 1982; *Electra* (Greece), 1983; *Zorba*, Broadway Theatre, New York, 1983.

FILMS—*Windfall in Athens*, 1954; *Stella*, 1955; *A Girl in Black*, 1956; *A Matter of Dignity*, 1957; *Electra* 1961; *Zorba the Greek*, 1964; *The Day the Fish Came Out*, 1967; *The Trojan Women*, 1971; *Iphigenia*, 1977. TELEVISION SHOWS—*The Story of Jacob and Joseph*, 1974. OPERAS—*Mourning Becomes Electra*, Metropolitan Opera Theatre, New York, 1967; *La Bohème*, Julliard Theatre, New York, 1971; *La Traviata*, (Greece), 1982.

WRITINGS: FILMS—*Windfall in Athens*, 1954; *Stella*, 1955; *A Girl in Black*, 1956; *A Matter of Dignity*, 1957; *Electra*, 1961; *Zorba the Greek*, 1964; *The Day the Fish Came Out*, 1967; *The Trojan Women*, 1971; *Iphigenia*, 1977.

AWARDS: Honorary Doctor of Arts, Columbia College, 1981; Officer des Arts et des Lettres, 1980; Golden Phoenix Medal (Greece), 1964; Grand Jury Prize, Cannes Film Festival, 1961.

SIDELIGHTS: MEMBERSHIPS—Society of Stage Directors and Choreographers.

ADDRESS: Home—15 Mouson Street, Athens 401, Greece; Agent—c/o John Planco, William Morris Agency, 1350 Ave. of the Americas, New York, NY 10019.

CAESAR, Sid, actor

PERSONAL: Born September 8, 1922, in Yonkers, NY; son of Max and Ida (Raffel) Caesar; married Florence Levy, June 17, 1943; children: Michele, Richard, Karen. EDUCATION: Attended public schools in Yonkers, NY; studied the saxophone and clarinet. MILITARY: US Coast Guard, orchestra and writer of sketches for the USCG revue *Six On, Twelve Off*, 1942–44.

CAREER: NEW YORK DEBUT—*Tars and Spars*, Strand, 1944. PRINCIPAL STAGE APPEARANCES—*Make Mine Manhattan*, Broadhurst, NY, 1948; *Little Me*, Lunt-Fontanne, NY, 1962; *Four on a Garden*, Broadhurst, NY, 1971; Barney Cashman, *Last of the Red Hot Lovers*, Westport Country Playhouse, CT, 1972; Mel Edison, *The Prisoner of Second Avenue*, Arlington Park, Chicago, 1973; cabaret, Rainbow Grill, NY, 1974; *Double Take*, Arlington Park, Chicago, 1974; Barney Cashman, *The Last of the Red Hot Lovers*, Crystal Palace, Dallas, TX, 1975; *Night of 100 Stars*, NY, 1982.

FILM DEBUT—*Tars and Spars*, 1946. PRINCIPAL FILM APPEARANCES—*Guilt of Janet Ames; It's a Mad, Mad, Mad, Mad, World*, 1963; *The Spirit is Willing*, 1967; *Ten from Your Show of Shows*, 1973; *Silent Movie*, 1976; *Fire Sales*, 1977; *The Cheap Detective*, 1978; *Grease*, 1978; *History of the World, Part I*, 1981.

TELEVISION DEBUT—*Broadway Revue*, 1949. PRINCIPAL TELEVISION APPEARANCES—*Your Show of Shows*, 1950–54; *Caesar's Hour*, 1954–57; *Sid Caesar Invites You*, 1958; *As Caesar Sees It*, 1962–63; guest appearances—*Jackie Gleason Show*, *Carol Burnett Show*, *Robert Morse Show*, etc.

RELATED CAREER: Saxophonist and clarinetist with the Charlie Spivak, Claude Thornhill and Shep Fields dance bands.

WRITINGS: AUTOBIOGRAPHY—*Where Have I Been?* (with Bill Davidson), 1982.

AWARDS: Named to US Hall of Fame, 1967; Sylvania Award, Best Comedy-Variety show of 1958; Emmy Award, Best Comedian, 1956; *Look* Magazine, Best Comedian on TV, 1951.

SIDELIGHTS: MEMBERSHIPS—Old Falls Rod and Gun Club, Fallsburgh, NY.

ADDRESS: Agent—c/o Contemporary-Korman Artists Ltd, 132 Lasky Drive, Beverly Hills, CA 90212.*

CAIN, William, actor, director

PERSONAL: Born May 27, 1931, in Tuscaloosa, AL; son of John Calhoun (a machinist) and Minnie Lee (Smith) Cain; married Leta Henderson (an actress). EDUCATION: George Washington University, Washington DC, A.A., 1951; Catholic University, Washington DC, B.A., 1953. MILITARY: U.S. Army, 1953–55 (corporal).

CAREER: DEBUT—Shand, *What Every Woman Knows,* Patchwork Players, Roanoke, VA, 1949. NEW YORK DEBUT— Ayamonn Braydon, *Red Roses for Me,* Greenwich Mews, 1959, six-month run. PRINCIPAL STAGE APPEARANCES—President Wilson, *Wilson in The Promised Land,* New York; understudy to Jason Robards, *You Can't Take It with You,* New York; Jake, *Of the Fields Lately,* New York; Jeffery, *Night and Day,* Boston; Arthur Kirk, *Nuts,* Birmingham, MI. OFF-BROADWAY, NEW YORK—President Harding, *The Gang's All Here;* Creon, *Antigone;* Jim Crow, *Jericho Jim Crow.* REGIONAL THEATRE—Andrew, *Sleuth;* Coach, *That Championship Season;* F.D.R., *Sunrise at Campobello;* Elwood P. Dowd, *Harvey;* Stockman, *Enemy of the People;* Dysart, *Equus;* Marcus, *Another Part of the Forest;* Horace, *The Little Foxes;* Russell, *The Best Man;* Proctor, *The Crucible;* Walter, *The Price;* Miller, *Ah! Wilderness;* Jamie, *A Moon for the Misbegotten;* Hero, *The Rehearsal;* Philip, *Relatively Speaking;* Scott, *Terra Nova;* Dobbs, *Childs Play;* Devil, *Don Juan in Hell.* THEATRES WORKED—Trinity Square Repertory Theatre, Providence, RI, 1964–73; Actor's Theatre of Louisville, Louisville, KY, 1974–78; Milwaukee Repertory Theatre, Milwaukee, WI; A Contemporary Theatre, Seattle, WA; Buffalo Studio Arena, Buffalo, NY. MAJOR TOURS—Steve, *Broadway,* summer tour and West Coast, 1964; Dr. Seward, *Dracula,* East Coast tour, 1979; *Year of the Locusts,* Edinburgh Festival; *School for Wives,* Phoenix Festival.

WILLIAM CAIN

FILM DEBUTS—Butler, *The Betsy,* 1978. PRINCIPAL FILM APPEARANCES—George Quigley, *The Ultimate Solution of Grace Quigley,* 1983; General Lemnitzer, *Kennedy,* 1983; Joe, *The Hamptons,* 1983; *The Dogs of War; Sessions; Lowlife* (PBS). TELEVISION DEBUT—Hughes, *All My Children.* PRINCIPAL TELEVISION APPEARANCES—*Omnibus; Hallmark Hall of Fame; Kraft Mystery Theatre; The Sergeant Bilko Show; The Guiding Light; One Life to Live; As the World Turns; Another World; The Edge of Night.*

AWARDS: Nominated for Best New Actor on Broadway, for Wilson in *Wilson and the Promised Land,* 1969.

SIDELIGHTS: "I am principally interested in acting but I direct when I find the time and also used to choreograph."

ADDRESS: Home—484 W. 43rd Street, Apt. 40n, New York, NY 10036.

* * *

CALDWELL, Zoe, actress, director

PERSONAL: Born September 14, 1933, in Hawthorn, Victoria, Australia; married Robert Whitehead (producer). EDUCATION: Methodist Ladies College, Melbourne. THEATRE-RELATED CAREER: Teacher (Shakespeare), Neighborhood Playhouse, NY, 1970.

CAREER: DEBUT—Original member, *Union Theatre Repertory Company,* Melbourne, Australia, 1953. NEW YORK DEBUT—Prioress, *The Devil's,* December 1965. LONDON DEBUT—Ismene, *Antigone,* Royal Cort, November 1960. PRINCIPAL ENGAGEMENTS—*Elizabethan Theatre Trust,* including Bubba in *Summer of the Seventeenth Doll,* Australia, 1954–57; daughter of Antiochus, *Pericles,* Margaret, *Much Ado about Nothing,* Shakespeare Memorial Theatre Company, Stratford-on-Avon, England, 1958–59; Bianca, *Othello,* Helena, *All's Well That Ends Well,* a Fairy, *A Midsummer Night's Dream,* Cordelia, *King Lear,* Memorial Theatre, Stratford-on-Avon, England, 1959; whore, *Cob and Leach* in the double bill *Trials by Logue,* Royal Court, London, 1961; Isabella, *The Changeling,* Royal Court, 1961; Jacqueline, *Jacques,* Royal Court, 1961; Rosaline, *Love's Labour's Lost,* Sonja Downfahl, *The Canvas Bridge,* Stratford Shakespeare Festival, Stratford, Ontario, Canada, 1961; Pegeen Mike, *Playboy of the Western World,* Manitoba Theatre Centre, Manitoba, Canada, 1961; Joan, *St. Joan,* Adelaide Festival of the Arts, Australia; *The Ham Funeral,* Elizabethan Theatre Trust, Sydney, Australia, 1962; Nola Boyle, *The Season at Sarsparilla,* Union, Melbourne, Australia, 1962; Frosine, *The Miser,* Natasha, *The Three Sisters,* opening season of the Minnesota Theatre Company, Tyrone Guthrie, Minneapolis, 1963; title role, *Mother Courage,* Manitoba Theatre Centre, Canada, 1964; Countess Aurelia, *The Madwoman of Chaillot,* Goodman, Chicago, IL, 1964; Millament, *The Way of the World,* Grusha, *The Caucasian Chalk Circle,* Frosine, *The Miser,* Guthrie, Minneapolis, 1965; Polly, *Gnadiges Fraulein (Slapstick Tragedy),* Longacre, NY, 1966; Orinthia, *The Apple Cart,* Shaw Festival, Niagra-on-the-Lake, 1966; Lena Szezepanowska, *Misalliance,* Shaw Festival, 1966; Cleopatra, *Anthony and Cleopatra,* Lady Anne, *Richard III,* Mrs. Page, *The Merry Wives of Windsor,* Stratford Festival,

ZOE CALDWELL

Ontario, 1967; Jean, *The Prime of Miss Jean Brodie*, Helen Hayes, NY, 1968; title role, *Colette*, Ellen Stewart, NY, 1970; Emma Hamilton, *A Bequest to the Nation*, Haymarket, London, 1970; Eve, *The Creation of the World and other Business*, Shubert, NY, 1972; *Love and Master Will*, Kennedy Center, Washington, DC, 1973; Alice, *The Dance of Death*, Vivian Beaumont, Lincoln Center, NY, 1974; Mary Tyrone, *Long Day's Journey into Night*, Eisenhower, Washington, DC, Brooklyn Academy, NY, 1976; title role, *Medea*, Cort, NY, 1982. MAJOR TOURS—*Hamlet, Twelfth Night, Romeo and Juliet*, Shakespeare Memorial Theatre Company, tour of Russia, 1959; *St. Joan*, Elizabethan Theatre Trust, Australia, 1962.

DIRECTRED: Plays—*An Almost Perfect Person*, Belasco, NY, 1977; *Richard II*, Stratford, ON, 1979; *These Men*, NY, (off-Broadway), 1980; (unbilled co-director), *Othello*, Winter Garden, NY, 1981.

TELEVISION APPEARANCES—*Witness to Yesterday*, WNET, 1974; Madame Arkadina, *The Seagull*, BBC-TV; Sarah Bernhardt, *Sarah*, CBC-TV; *The Lady's Not for Burning, Macbeth, The Apple Cart*.

*AWARDS:*Antoinette Perry Award: *Slapstick Tragedy, The Prime of Miss Jean Brodie, Medea*; OBE, New Year's Honours, 1970.

ADDRESS: Office—Whitehead-Stevens, 1501 Broadway, New York, NY 10036.

* * *

CALLAN, K (nee Kay Borman), actress

PERSONAL: Born January 9, in Dallas, TX; daughter of James Elias (a grocer) and Catherine Amanda (a musician, O'Connor) Borman; married James R. Callan June 4, 1957 (divorced 1968); children: James Patrick, Kelly Linn, Kristi Ann. EDUCATION: North Texas State University, B.A., 1964; trained for the stage at the Pasadena Playhouse and the Herbert Berghof Studio with Herbert Berghof and Stella Adler.

CAREER: DEBUT—Hawker, *Inherit the Wind*, Margo Jones Theatre, Dallas, TX, 1955. NEW YORK DEBUT—Hooker, *The Broofer*, Herbert Berghof Playwrights Theater, 1969, 24 performances. PRINCIPAL STAGE APPEARANCES—*Blessing*, Manhattan Theater Club, New York, 1975; Vic, *Red Rover, Red Rover*, Melrose, Los Angeles; Grady, *April Snow*, South Coast Repertory, Costa Mesa, CA, 1983.

FILM DEBUT—Mary Lou, *Joe*, 1970. PRINCIPAL FILMS—Patty, *A Touch of Class*, 1972; Mrs. Powell, *The Onion Field*, 1979; Ms. Tidwell, *Fast Break*, 1979; Lisa, *An American Gigolo*, 1980; Alice, *A Change of Season*, 1981. TELEVISION DEBUT—*Route 66*, 1962. TELEVISION APPEARANCES—*All in the Family; One Day at a Time, Barney Miller; Ike, the War*

K CALLAN

Years; Cutter to Houston; Newhart; Visions: Ladies in Waiting.

THEATRE-RELATED CAREER—Teacher of Drama, Our Lady of Good Counsel Academy, Dallas, TX, 1955–64; Teacher and Director, Oak Cliff Civic Theatre, Dallas, TX, 1957–64; Director, Lancaster Little Theatre, Lancaster, TX, 1960–63.

SIDELIGHTS: MEMBERSHIPS—Academy of Motion Picture Arts and Sciences.

"Because of my mother's health and the general family structure, I grew up feeling pretty invisible. I'm sure that is the thing that led me to acting . . . because I am in every sense of the word, living my fantasy, I am a real believer in 'You can do anything you really want to do.'"

ADDRESS: Agent—c/o The Gage Group, 8732 Sunset Blvd., Los Angeles, CA 90069.

* * *

CAMPBELL, Glen, singer, entertainer

PERSONAL: Born April 22, 1938, in Delight, AR; son of Wesley and Carrie (Stone) Campbell; married Billie Jean Nunley, September 20, 1959 (divorced 1976); Kim Woollen, October 25, 1982; children: (first marriage) Debby, Kelli, Travis, Kane; (second marriage) Dillon, Cal. EDUCATION: Attended public schools in Arkansas and New Mexico.

CAREER: PRINCIPAL FILM APPEARANCES—*True Grit,* 1969; *Norwood,* 1970. PRINCIPAL TELEVISION APPEARANCES—*Hollywood Champs,* 1960, 1963–64; *Shindig,* 1964; host, *Smothers Brothers Summer Show,* 1968; host, *The Glen Campbell Good Time Hour,* 1969–71; movie for television, *Strange Homecoming;* guest performer on many variety and talk shows; HBO cable music special, 1984.

AWARDS: 5 Grammy awards, 5 Country Music Association awards; Television Personality of the Year, 1969; Best Male Vocalist, 1968–69; Entertainer of the Year, Great Britain Country Music Association, 1969; Entertainer of the Year, U.S., 1968.

SIDELIGHTS: MEMBERSHIPS—National Reading Council; co-sponsor, Glen Campbell-Los Angeles Open Golf Tournament.

ADDRESS: Agent—Regency Artists, Ltd., 9200 Sunset Blvd., Suite 823, Los Angeles, CA 90069.

* * *

CANDLER, Peter, manager, producer, and writer

PERSONAL: Born March 21, 1926 in New York City; son of Fred B. (a salesman) and Caroline K. (fashion) Candler; EDUCATION: Williams College, B.A., 1949; trained for the stage at Columbia University with Louis Kronenberger, Milton Smith, and Stanley McCandlish. MILITARY: U.S. Army Air Force, 1944–45.

CAREER: FIRST STAGE WORK—Director/Publicity, Monomoy Theatre, Chatham, MA, 1948. FIRST NEW YORK STAGE WORK—Playreader, Holtzmann and Holtzmann, 1952–64. PRINCIPAL STAGE WORK—General manager, Cape Playhouse, Dennis, MA, 1953–59; general manager, Cape Cod Melody Tent, Hyannis, MA, 1960–64.

THEATRE-RELATED CAREER—director of drama, Lawrenceville School, Lawrenceville, NJ, 1960–present; director, Kirby Arts Center, Lawrenceville, NJ, 1960–present; board of directors, Ocean County Center for the Arts, Lakewood, NJ, 1980–present; board of directors, June Opera Festival, Princeton, NJ, 1983–present.

AWARDS: Ford Foundation Project in Drama, 1965–68;

SIDELIGHTS: MEMBERSHIPS—American Theatre Association, American Film Institute, New Jersey Speech Association, MATA, ETA, Kappa Alpha, Phi Alphs Delta.

ADDRESS: Office—Box 6039, Lawrenceville, NJ 08648.

* * *

CANOVA, Diana (nee Rivero), actress, singer

PERSONAL: Born June 1, 1953; daughter of Filberto (a radio talk show host) and Judy (an actress; maiden name, Canova) Rivero; married Elliot R. Scheiner (a record producer) July 24, 1982; children: Matthew Philip. EDUCATION: Los Angeles City College, 1971–74; studied singing with Seth and Florence Riggs.

CAREER: DEBUT—One act plays, Porterville Playhouse, Porterville, CA, 1974. NEW YORK DEBUT—Sonia, *They're Playing Our Song,* Imperial, 1981. PRINCIPAL STAGE APPEARANCES—Daisy, *On a Clear Day, You Can See Forever,* Bucks County Playhouse, PA, Falmouth Playhouse, MA, 1984. MAJOR TOUR—Lady Larkin, *Once upon a Mattress,* USO tour, 1973.

FILM DEBUT—Juanita Juanita, *The First Nudie Musical,* 1973. TELEVISION DEBUT—*Ozzie's Girls.* PRINCIPAL TELEVISION APPEARANCES—*Happy Days; Love Boat; Fantasy Island; Hotel; Chico and the Man; Barney Miller; Soap; I'm a Big Girl Now;* movies—*Peking Encounter; Night Partners; With This Ring; Death of Ocean View Park.*

AWARDS: People's Choice award, Favorite Female Performer, 1981.

SIDELIGHTS: MEMBERSHIPS—AFTRA, SAG, AEA.

Miss Canova served as the second puppeteer on *Dusty's Treehouse,* 1972–75.

ADDRESS: Office—c/o Borod & Co., 515 Madision Avenue, New York, NY 10022. Agent—DHKPR, 7319 Beverly Blvd., Los Angeles, CA 90036.

CAPALBO, Carmen, director, producer, writer, theater operator

PERSONAL: Born November 1, 1925, in Harrisburg, PA; son of Joseph (a merchant) and Concetta (Riggio) Capalbo; married Patricia McBride (a ballet dancer), July 9, 1950 (divorced 1961); children: Carla, Marc. EDUCATION: Attended Yale School of Drama. MILITARY: U.S. Army, 1944–45.

CAREER: DEBUT—Jester, *The Forest Prince,* William Penn High School, Harrisburg, PA. PRINCIPAL STAGE WORK—Producer (with Leo Lieberman)/director, *Juno and the Paycock,* Cherry Lane, NY, 1946; producer/actor, *Awake and Sing,* Cherry Lane, NY, 1946; producer, *Dear Brutus,* Cherry Lane, NY, 1946; producer/director, *Shadow and Substance,* Cherry Lane, NY, 1946; stage manager, *Emlyn Williams as Charles Dickens,* John Golden, NY, 1952, Bijou, NY, 1953; production stage manager, *Jean-Louis Barrault-Madeleine Renaud Company,* Ziegfeld, NY, 1952; producer (with Stanley Chase), *The Threepenny Opera,* Theater de Lys, NY, 1954, 1955, Marines Memorial, San Francisco, CA, 1960, Music Box, Los Angeles, CA, 1960, Royal Alexandra, Toronto, Canada, 1961; producer (with Stanley Chase)/director, *The Potting Shed,* Bijou, NY, 1957, *A Moon for the Misbegotten, The Cave Dwellers,* Bijou, NY, 1957; director, *The Good Soldier Schweik,* City Center, NY, 1958; director/co-producer, *The Threepenny Opera,* Paper Mill Playhouse, Milburn, NJ, 1961; director, *Seidman and Son,* Belasco, NY, 1962; director, *The Strangers,* Westport Country Playhouse, CT, 1963; director, *Enter Solly Gold,* Paramus Playhouse, NJ, 1965; director/co-producer, *The Rise and Fall of the City of Mahagonny,* Anderson, NY, 1970; director, *Slowly, by Thy Hand Unfurled,* ESIPA, Albany, NY, 1984. MAJOR TOURS—Director, *A Connecticut Yankee,* 1951; stage manager, *Emlyn Williams as Charles Dickens,* 1952.

PRINCIPAL TELEVISION AND RADIO WORK—Writer/director/producer, WKBO, Harrisburg, PA, 1941–45; story editor, *Studio One,* 1951–52; director, *Play of the Week,* "The Power and the Glory," 1959.

RELATED CAREERS: Theater Operator—Cherry Lane, NY, 1946; Theater de Lys, NY, 1955–62; Bijou, NY, 1956–57; Music Box, Los Angeles, CA, 1960; Anderson, NY, 1969–70. Television Consultant—Central Independent Television, United Kingdom, 1983.

AWARDS: Antoinette Perry Award, Obie Award, 1956: *The Threepenny Opera.* Military—Bronze Star, Purple Heart.

SIDELIGHTS: MEMBERSHIPS—Leauge of Off-Broadway Theatres (co-founder), League of New York Theatres, SSD&C (contract negotiating committee), Dramatists Guild, Screen Directors Guild, Royal Philatelic Society (London). RECREATION—piano, reading, baseball, painting, philately.

ADDRESS: Office—c/o Floria Lasky, Fitelson, Lasky, Aslan and Couture, 551 Fifth Avenue, New York, NY 10176. Agent—c/o Bruce Savan, Agency for the Performing Arts, 888 Seventh Avenue, New York, NY 10106.

CARAMBÓ, Cristóbal, actor, dancer, director, and teacher

PERSONAL: Born November 17, 1950; son of Orlando and Eloisa (Scull) Carambó. EDUCATION: Attended Brandeis University and Harvard College; trained for the stage at Herbert Berghof Studio and Clark Center with Ed Morgithouse and Thelma Hill.

CAREER: DEBUT—*Boxes,* Theatre Project, Baltimore, MD, 1971. NEW YORK DEBUT—Calibash, *Drinkwater,* New Federal Theatre, New York, 30 performances. PRINCIPAL STAGE APPEARANCES—*Trespassing,* LaMama Theater, 1982; *Specimen Days,* Public Theatre, 1982–83; *Tibetan Book of the Dead,* LaMama, 1983. MAJOR TOURS—Charles Dyer, *Staircase,* New England Repertory Theatre, Worcester, MA, 1979–80; *Salford Road/Night City Diaries,* Edinburgh Theatre Festival, Scotland, 1979; *Specimen Days,* Paris, Strasbourg, Parma, 1982.

FILM DEBUT—*Apartment 6-D,* Film Festival, Mexico City, 1976. TELEVISION DEBUT—American Folk Theatre's Children's Theatre Workshop, 1982.

THEATRE-RELATED CAREER—Teaching—Bard College, New York, 1980–81; Teachers and Writers Collaborative, New York, 1980–83; City College of New York, , 1983–present; associate artistic director, American Folk Theatre, New York, 1980–83.

WRITINGS: BOOKS—*Curriculum Guide for "Mummenschantz,"* 1979; *The Search for Self-Confidence,* 1981; *Bustin out the Box,* 1982.

SIDELIGHTS: Mr. Carambo worked extensively in the field of children's theatre in public and private schools. He has received several State Education Department grants, and has been an Artist in Residence for New York Foundation for the Arts and Manhattan Laboratory Museum, The Roundabout Theatre and Playwrights Horizons. Spanish by birth, Mr. Carambo speaks his native tongue, as well as French and Italian; he is currently studying medieval Italian and Latin. His primary avocations are foreign cuisines—Italian, French and Indian—and medieval and classical studies.

ADDRESS: Home—671 Ninth Avenue, New York, NY 10036. Office—10 Leonard Street, New York, NY 10013.

* * *

CAREY, Harry, Jr., actor

PERSONAL: Born May 16, 1921 in Saugus, CA; son of Harry (an actor) and Olive (Fuller) Carey; married Marilyn Frances Fix, August 12, 1944; children: Steven, Melinda, Thomas, Cary, Patricia. EDUCATION: Attended public schools in California and the Black Fox Military Academy in Hollywood, CA. MILITARY: U.S. Navy, 1941–46. NON-THEATRICAL CAREER: Page boy at NBC, NY.

CAREER: FILM DEBUT—*Pursued.* PRINCIPAL FILM APPEARANCES—*Red River; Moonrise; Three Godfathers; She Wore a Yellow Ribbon; Wagonmaster; Rio Grande; Copper Canyon; Warpath; Wild Blue Yonder; Monkey Business; San*

Antone; Island in the Sky; Gentlemen Prefer Blondes; Beneath the 12 Mile Reef; Silver Lode; The Outcast; The Long Grey Line; Mister Roberts; House of Bamboo; The Great Locomotive Chase; The Undefeated Big Jake; Something Big; One More Train to Rob.

THEATRICAL DEBUT—Summer Stock, Lakewood, Skowhegan, ME, 1940.

SIDELIGHTS: ''I am what you call an old western character actor. I have enjoyed making all of those horse operas and other movies but if I had it to do over again I would start on the New York stage.''

ADDRESS: 4513 Vista Del Monte, Sherman Oaks, CA 91403.

* * *

CARIOU, Len (ne Leonard), actor, singer, director, administrator

PERSONAL: Born September 30, 1939, in St. Boniface, Manitoba, Canada; son of George Marius and Mary Estelle (Moore) Caribou. EDUCATION: Holy Cross School, St. Paul's College, Winnipeg, Canada; studied for the theatre with Kristin Linklater, Fran Bennett, and Judith Liebowitz and at Stratford, Ontario and the Guthrie in Minneapolis. NON-THEATRICAL CAREER—Salesman for farm machinery and men's clothing.

CAREER: DEBUT—Chorus, *Damn Yankees*, Rainbow, Winnipeg, Canada, 1959. NEW YORK DEBUT—Orestes, *The House of Atreus*, Billy Rose, 1968. PRINCIPAL ENGAGEMENTS—Walter Sugarsop, *The Taming of the Shrew*, Stratford Shakespearean Festival of Canada, also parts in *The Tempest, Macbeth, Cyrano de Bergerac*, 1962; Margarelon, *Troilus and Cressida*, Servilius, *Timon of Athens*, Stratford Festival, also parts in *Cyrano de Bergerac*, and *The Comedy of Errors*, 1963; Longaville, *Love's Labour's Lost*, Chichester, England, 1964; Sir John Bushy, *Richard II*, Cleonte, *Le Bourgeois Gentilhomme*, Stratford Festival, ON, also parts in *The Country Wife*, 1964; Orlando, *As You Like It*, Minnesota Theatre Company, Tyrone Guthrie, Minneapolis, also parts in *The Skin of Our Teeth, S.S. Glencairn*, 1966; Orestes, *The House of Atreus*, Feste, *Twelfth Night*, Musgrave, *Serjeant Musgrave's Dance*, Minnesota Theatre Company, Guthrie, Minneapolis, 1968; Henry, *Henry V*, American Shakespeare Festival, Stratford, CT, also roles in *Much Ado about Nothing* and *The Three Sisters*, 1969; Henry, *Henry V*, ANTA, New York, 1969; Bill Sampson, *Applause*, Palace, NY, 1970; Christian, *Cyrano de Bergerac*, Guthrie, Minneapolis, also in *The Taming of the Shrew*, 1971; John Wheeler, *Night Watch*, Morosco, NY, 1972; Oberon, *A Midsummer Night's Dream*, Guthrie, 1972; Oedipus, *Oedipus the King*, Guthrie, 1973; Frederick Egerman, *A Little Night Music*, Shubert, NY, 1973; *Sondheim: A Musical Tribute*, Shubert, NY, 1973; Lear, *King Lear*, Guthrie, 1974; appeared in *Equus* and *Cyrano . . .*, Manitoba Theatre Centre, Winnipeg, 1975; Monodrama, *A Sorrow Beyond Dreams*, Marymount Manhattan, NY, and Guthrie, 1977; Richard Landau, *Cold Storage*, Lyceum, 1977; Todd, *Sweeney Todd*, Uris, 1979; Harry, *Dance a Little Closer*, Minskoff, NY, 1983. DIRECTED, PLAYS—*Of Mice and Men*, Guthrie, 1972; *The Petrified Forest*, Guthrie,

1974; *The Crucible*, Guthrie, 1974; *Don't Call Back*, 1979.

MANAGED, THEATRES/THEATRE COMPANIES—Associate director, Tyrone Guthrie Theatre, 1972; artistic director, Manitoba Theatre Centre, 1975.

PRINCIPAL FILMS—*A Little Night Music; One Man; The Four Seasons.* TELEVISION DEBUT—Ragnar Brovik, *The Master Builder*, November 1965. TELEVISION APPEARANCES—*Juno and the Paycock; Applause.*

AWARDS: Antoinette Perry Award, Best Actor, 1979: *Sweeney Todd;* Antoinette Perry nominations, 1972: *A Little Night Music*, 1970: *Applause.*

SIDELIGHTS: RECREATION—Baseball, golf, tennis, gymnastics.

ADDRESS: Agent—c/o STE Representation, 888 Seventh Avenue, New York, NY 10019.*

* * *

CARLE, Cynthia, actress, singer

PERSONAL: Last name, ''e'' is silent. Born March 4, in Hollywood, CA; daughter of Walter R. (a newsman) and Louise Adele (writer; maiden name Doty) Carle; married Curtis Armstrong (an actor) on July 10, 1980. EDUCATION: Carnegie-Mellon University, B.F.A. (drama) 1974; studied at Los Angeles City College with Jerry Blunt.

CAREER: DEBUT—Petra, *A Little Night Music*, Chanhassen Dinner Theatre, Minneapolis, MN, 1975. NEW YORK DEBUT—Irene St. Claire (understudy), *The Crucifier of Blood*, Helen Hayes Theatre, 1 performance, November 20, 1978. PRINCIPAL STAGE APPEARANCES—Nurse, *Piaf*, 1981; *Is There Life After High School?*, Barrymore, New York, 1982; Baker's Wife, *The Baker's Wife*, Woodfest, 1983; Eva Jackson, *Absurd Person Singular*, Buffalo Studio Arena, 1983; Anne Protheroe, *Murder at the Vicarage*, Actor's Theatre of Louisville, KY, 1982–83; Simone, *L'Atelier*, Trinity Square Repertory, 1981; Constance Neville, *She Stoops to Conquer*, Guthrie Theatre, Minneapolis, MN, 1978; Sweet Young Miss, *La Ronde*, Guthrie Theatre, 1977; Lisa Belmondo, *The Conversion of Aaron Weiss*, Guthrie Theatre, 1977; Clara Morris, Charlotte Cushman, Lola Montez, Junius Brutus Booth, *Stark Mad in White Satin*, Milwaukee Repertory, 1980. MAJOR TOURS—Irene St. Claire, *The Crucifer of Blood*, 1979; the Yellow Peril, *Da*, 1979–80.

FILM DEBUT—Betsy Nicolas, *Decades of Decision*, 1976. TELEVISION DEBUT—Ophelia, *Hamlet*, PBS, 1976.

THEATRE-RELATED CAREER—Visiting instructor in acting, University of Minnesota, 1977.

AWARDS: Bush Foundation Fellowship.

SIDELIGHTS: MEMBERSHIPS—AEA, SAG, AFTRA, NOW, ACLU.

''I chucked the fellowship and started working professionally.''

ADDRESS: Agent—c/o Monty Silver, 200 W. 57th Street, New York, NY. 10019.

* * *

CARLIN, Lynn, actress

PERSONAL: Born January 31, 1938 in Los Angeles, CA; daughter of Laurence Kramer (a business manager) and Muriel Elizabeth (Ansley) Reynolds; married John Wolfe (a restaurateur), July 12, 1983; children: Daniel, Ansley. EDUCATION: Attended Orange Coast College and Immaculata College; trained for the stage at the Stanislavsky Studio in London. RELIGION: Roman Catholic.

CAREER: DEBUT—*The Women,* Laguna Beach Playhouse. FILM DEBUT—*Faces,* 1968.

AWARDS: Academy Award Nomination, Best Supporting Actress, 1968: *Faces;* New York Drama Critics Award, Best Supporting Actress, 1968: *Faces.*

ADDRESS: Office—12601 Ventura Blvd., Studio City, CA; Agent—David Shapira and Associates, Inc., 15301 Ventura Blvd., Sherman Oaks, CA 91403.

* * *

CARNEY, Kay, actress, director, and teacher

PERSONAL: Born August 3, 1933; daughter of Rexford Hugh and Margot (Haanstad) Carney. EDUCATION: University of Wisconsin, B.S., 1955; Mount Holyoke College, M.A., 1958; Case Western Reserve, Columbia University, University of Colorado, graduate work in theatre, drama; Centre du Theatre National de Sud-Est, 1970. Attended seminar with Jerzy Grotowski; studies with Lee Grant, Bill Hickey, Irene Daily, Mira Rostova, Bill Ball.

CAREER: FIRST STAGE WORK—Directed, *King of Hearts,* Circle Players, Northampton, MA, 1955. NEW YORK DEBUT—Wife/Mother, *The Coach with Six Insides,* Village South (now the Van Dam Theatre), 1962–63. LONDON DEBUT—one-woman show, *Off Off-Broadway,* New Arts Lab, 8 performances, 1970. PRINCIPAL STAGE APPEARANCES—Joan, *St. Joan/Joan of Lorraine,* Henry Street Playhouse, New York, 1962; Gittel Mosca, *Two for the Seesaw,* Asheville, NC, 1965; workshop ensemble, Spring Street Loft, NY 1965–67; ensemble, *Viet Rock,* Martinique, NY, 1966; Sue, *The Next Thing,* La Mama, E.T.C., NY, 1966; *Angry Arts Agst War,* Negro Ensemble Company, NY, 1966–67; Miss Prism, *Earnest in Love,* Penn State Festival, PA, 1967; La Mama Plexus, La Mama E.T.C., NY, 1968–69; Mrs. Ortega, *Calling in Crazy,* Fortune (now E. 4th Street Theatre), NY, 1969; Mary, *Life with Father,* Walnut Street Theatre, Philadelphia, 1972; one-woman show, *New Roots,* Interart Theatre, NY, 1977; Californi' Kate, *El Bandido,* El Teatro Campesino, San Juan Bautista, CA, 1979; Esther Johnson, *Captive Rites,* Bay Area Playwrights Festival, San Francisco, 1980; Cora Groves, *Rimers of Eldritch,* La Mama E.T.C., NY, 1981; Sonya, *The Wedding,* Theatre-in-Works, Amherst, MA, 1981; lead, *Behind a Mask,* Theatre of the

KAY CARNEY

Open Eye, NY, 1982; one-woman show, *Off Off-Broadway,* St. Clements, NY, 1982. MAJOR TOURS—Wife/Mother, *Coach with the Six Insides,* U.S. and Canada, 1964–65; Daisy, *Rhinoceros,* APA-Phoenix Theatre tour, 1967–68; Mariane, *Dr. in Spite of Himself,* APA-Phoenix tour, 1967–68; Edie, *Lullaby,* 1968; one-woman show, *Off Off-Broadway,* U.S. major cities and universities and internationally, 1970–present.

DIRECTED—Thomas Wolfe Playhouse, Asheville, NC: *Thurber Carnival, Typist and the Tiger, An Evening with Thomas Wolfe; Christophe Colombe,* Hunter Playhouse, NY, 1972; *A Difficult Borning,* Cubiculo, NY, 1973; *Mourning Pictures,* Lyceum, NY, 1974; *Ordinances,* 78th Street Theatre Lab, NY, 1977; Interart Theatre, NY: *A Pretty Passion, A Roomful of Salamanders* (staged reading), *Reflections in a Window* (staged reading), 1982; *Quilt Pieces,* Theatre of the Open Eye, NY, 1983.

TELEVISION DEBUT—*U.S. Steel Hour.* PRINCIPAL TELEVISION APPEARANCES—*All My Children; Search for Tomorrow; As the World Turns; Look Up and Live; ABC-Scope; The Nurses; Secret Storm.*

THEATRE-RELATED CAREER: Instructor, adjunct lecturer, Hunter College, 1961–72; associate professor, State University of New York at Purchase, 1972–77; visiting professor, University of California at Santa Cruz, 1977–80; associate professor, Smith College, 1980–83; associate professor, Brooklyn College, 1983–present.

WRITINGS: ARTICLES—"Exodus," *Theatre Journal,* 1977;

''Plastiques,'' *Theatre News*, 1976; ''Wroclaw/Paratheatrical Experiment,'' *Alternative Theatre*, 1976.

AWARDS: Theatre and Film Study Tour of Poland, 1979; Grant to work with El Teatro Campesino, SUNY Research Foundation, 1976; Shakespeare/Creative Artist's Grant, University of Colorado, 1963; Musicarnival Fellow, Case-Western Reserve, 1957; National Collegiate Players, Most Valuable Player, University of Wisconsin, 1955.

SIDELIGHTS: MEMBERSHIPS—Performing Artists for Nuclear Disarmament, donated benefit performance at St. Clement's Church; AEA, SSD&C, AFTRA, Founding member, Steering Committee, League of Professional Theatre Woman, 1981; Women's Project, American Place Theatre, American Theatre Association, Women's Program Executive Committee, East Central Theatre Conference. ·

''Ever since my La Mama work, my interests have lain with alternative theatre and new plays. When I do classics, I like to work with them as springboards, responses to the plays, so that they are about our artistic responses to today. I like to set aside the traditional in order to see old truths in light of our times. I'm interested in psycho-physical work, yoga, and tai-chi, healing and breaking through our self-imposed barriers.''

ADDRESS: Home—396 Bleecker Street, New York, NY, 10014. Office—c/o Theatre Department, Brooklyn College, Brooklyn, NY, 11210.

* * *

CARPENTER, John, director, screenwriter

PERSONAL: Born January 16, 1948, in Carthage, NY; son of Howard Ralph and Milton Jean (Carter) Carpenter; married Adrienne Barbeau, January 1, 1979; EDUCATION: University of Southern California.

CAREER: PRINCIPAL FILM WORK—Editor/composer, *The Resurrection of Broncho Billy*, 1970; director, *Dark Star*, 1974; director, *Assault on Precinct 13*, 1976; director, *Halloween*, 1978; director, *The Thing*, 1982; director/composer, *The Fog*, 1980; director/co-producer, *Escape from New York*, 1981; co-producer, *Halloween II*, 1981. PRINCIPAL TELEVISION WORK—Director: *Someone's Watching Me*, 1978, *Elvis*, 1979.

WRITINGS: SCREENPLAYS—*The Resurrection of Broncho Billy* (co-writer), 1970; *Halloween*, 1978; *The Eyes of Laura Mars*, 1978; *The Fog*, 1979; *Escape from New York*, 1981; *Halloween II*, 1981.

SIDELIGHTS: MEMBERSHIPS—Directors Guild of America, West; Writers Guild of America, West.

ADDRESS: Office—9454 Wilshire Blvd., Beverly Hills, CA 90212. Agent—c/o The Gersh Agency, 222 N. Canon Drive, Beverly Hills, CA 90210.*

CARRADINE, Keith, actor, writer, singer, composer, and musician

PERSONAL: Born August 8, 1949, in San Mateo, CA; son of John Richmond Reed (an actor) and Sonia Sorel (an actress and artist; maiden name, Henius) Carradine; married Sandra Will (an actress), February 2, 1982; children: Martha Campbell Plimpton, Cade Richmond. EDUCATION: Colorado State University, B.A., 1971.

CAREER: DEBUT—Claude, *Hair*, Biltmore, NY, 1969–70. PRINCIPAL STAGE APPEARANCES—Dude, *Tobacco Road*, Alhambra, Jacksonville, FL, 1970; Benjamin Hubbard, *Another Part of the Forest*, Seattle Repertory, 1981; Dillard Nations, *Foxfire*, Ethel Barrymore, NY, 1982–83.

FILM DEBUT—Cowboy, *A Gunfight*, 1970. PRINCIPAL FILM APPEARANCES—Cowboy, *McCabe and Mrs. Miller*, 1971; Cigarette, *Emperor of the North*, 1972; Bowie, *Thieves Like Us*, 1973; Tom Frank, *Nashville*, 1975; Carroll Barber, *Welcome to L.A.*, 1976; D'Hubert, *The Duellists*, 1977; Bellocq, *Pretty Baby*, 1978; Jim Younger, *The Long Riders*, 1979; Spencer, *Southern Comfort*, 1980; Mickey, *Choose Me*, 1983; Clarence, *Maria's Lovers*, 1983. TELEVISION DEBUT—*Bonanza*, 1971. PRINCIPAL TELEVISION APPEARANCES—*A Rumour of War*, 1980; *Chiefs*, 1983.

AWARDS: Academy Award, Best Song, 1975: ''*I'm Easy;*'' Golden Globe Award, Best Song, 1975: ''*I'm Easy;*'' Outer Critics Circle Award, Outstanding Debut, 1982–83.

SIDELIGHTS: MEMBERSHIPS—Sierra Club, Player's Club.

ADDRESS: Agent—c/o Ed Limato, William Morris Agency, 1350 Avenue of the Americas, New York, NY 10019.

* * *

CARRERA, Barbara, actress, model

PERSONAL: NON-THEATRICAL CAREER: Modeling in *Vogue*, *Paris Match*, *Harper's Bazaar*, *Playboy*.

CAREER: FILM DEBUT—*The Master Gunfighter*, 1976. PRINCIPAL FILM APPEARANCES—Victoria, *Embryo*, 1976; *The Island of Dr. Moreau*, 1977; *When Time Ran Out*, 1980; *Condorman*, 1981; *I, the Jury*, 1982; *Lone Wolf McQuade*, 1983; Fatima Blush, *Never Say Never Again*, 1983. TELEVISION DEBUT—Indian Clay Basket, *Centennial*, 1979. PRINCIPAL TELEVISION APPEARANCES—*Matt Houston* (pilot); *Masada*.

ADDRESS: Agent—Gloria Luchenbill, c/o Rogers & Cowan, Inc., 9665 Wilshire Blvd., Beverly Hills, CA 90212.

* * *

CARROLL, David-James, actor

PERSONAL: Born July 30, 1950 in Rockville Centre, NY; son of Derek Joseph (Vice President, Thomas J. Lipton Inc.)

and Joan Theresa (Breitenberger) Carroll. EDUCATION: Dartmouth College, B.A., 1972.

CAREER: DEBUT—Tom, *No, No Nanette,* Shady Grove Playhouse, Gaithersburg, MD, 1974. NEW YORK DEBUT—*Rodgers and Hart,* Helen Hayes, 108 performances, 1975. PRINCIPAL STAGE APPEARANCES—Next, *A Matter of Time,* Playhouse, NY, 1975; Joseph, *Joseph and the Amazing Technicolor Dreamcoat,* BAM, 1977; Chip Beaumont, *Spotlight,* National Theatre, Washington, DC, 1977; MAJOR TOURS—Clifford, *Death Trap,* Chicago, L.A., St. Louis, San Diego, 1978–79; Adam, *Seven Brides for Seven Brothers,* San Diego, Seattle, Detroit, 1981.

FILM DEBUT—Actor #1, *Hero at Large,* 1980. TELEVISION DEBUT—*Ball Four.* PRINCIPAL TELEVISION APPEARANCES—*Rockford Files; Knots Landing; CHiPS; To Race the Wind; The Promise of Love; Splendor in the Grass.*

ADDRESS: Agent—DHKPR, 165 W. 46th Street, New York, NY, 10036.

* * *

CARROLL, Helena, actress, writer

PERSONAL: Born in Glasgow, Scotland; daughter of Paul Vincent (a playwright) and Helena (Reilly) Carroll. EDUCATION: Attended Notre Dame de Namur in Scotland and studied at the Webber Douglas School, London, England.

CAREER: DEBUT—*A Babble of Greenfields,* Citizens Theatre, Glasgow, Scotland, 1949. NEW YORK DEBUT—Doreen, *Separate Tables,* Music Box, NY, 1956, 365 performances. PRINCIPAL STAGE APPEARANCES—Broadway—*Private Lives,* with Elizabeth Taylor and Richard Burton; *Georgie Girl; Oliver; Pickwick; Borstal Boy; Something Different; Separate Tables; The Wayward Saint; Pictures in the Hallway.* Off-Broadway—*Small Craft Warnings; Three Hand Reel; The Effect of Gamma Rays on Man-in-the-Moon Marigolds; Shadow and Substance; Playboy of the Western World; The Slab Boys;* MAJOR TOURS—*The Hostage; The Effect of Gamma Rays on Man-in-the-Moon Marigolds.* REGIONAL THEATRE—*Nicholas Nickleby,* Great Lakes Shakespeare Festival; *The 13th Chair; The Recruiting Officer,* Long Wharf Theatre; *A Man's a Man,* Goodman Theatre, Chicago; *Plaza Suite,* Hampton Playhouse, NH; *Juno and the Paycock,* Syracuse Stage, Syracuse NY; *Philadelphia Here I Come,* Olney Theatre, MD. LONDON DEBUT—Ingenue, *The Monkey Puzzle,* The New Lindsay Theatre, 1950.

FILM DEBUT—Nurse Hora, *Midnight Episode,* 1949. PRINCIPAL FILM APPEARANCES—*The Killing Hour; Ghost Story; Ordinary Madness; The Jerk; The Loving Couples; The Friends of Eddie Coyle; The Molly Maguires; Midnight Episode.* PRINCIPAL TELEVISION APPEARANCES—*Ryan's Four; Flame Is Love; Backstairs at the White House; Mrs. Colombo; Little Women; Hizzoner;* Molly O'Connor, *The Edge of Night; General Hospital; Mannix; Kojak; Starsky and Hutch; Matt Helm; Kiss Me Deadly; WRKP Cincinnati; BJ and The Bear; Laverne and Shirley.*

THEATRE-RELATED CAREER: Co-producer with Dermot McNamara, The Irish Players, New York, 1956–68. Produced

plays by Irish authors, including plays by her father, *Shadow and Substance* and *The White Seed.*

WRITINGS: PLAY—*Daughter of Ireland* (one woman show).

AWARDS: Best Actress, Dublin, *The Effect of Gamma Rays on Man-in-the-Moon Marigolds;* Best Character Actress, Dublin, *Prelude in Kasbeck St.*

ADDRESS: Home—325 W. 45th Street, New York, NY 10036. Agent—Stone and Masser, 1052 Carol Drive, Los Angeles, CA 90069.

* * *

CARTER, Lonnie, writer

PERSONAL: Born December 25, 1942, in Chicago, IL; son of Harold Walter (a real estate broker) and Evelyn V. (Lipsey) Carter; married Marilyn Smutko, November 26, 1966 (divorced 1972); Julia L. Devlin (a writer), December 25, 1980; EDUCATION: Marquette University, B.A., 1964, M.A., 1966; Yale University, M.F.A., 1969. POLITICS: Democrat. RELIGION: Roman Catholic.

WRITINGS: PLAYS, PUBLISHED—*Iz She Izzy or Iz He Ain'tzy or Iz They Both,* 1970; *The Big House,* 1971; *Watergate Classics* (sketches), 1973–74; *Cream Cheese,* 1974; *Bleach,* 1977; *Victoria Fellows,* 1978. PLAYS, UNPUBLISHED—*Smokey Links,* 1972; *Trade-Offs,* 1976; *Bicicletta,* 1978; *Sirens,* 1979; *Certain Things About the Trombone,* 1982; *Tarara-Boom-Dee-Ay,* 1982; *The Girl in the Shiny Black Helmet; The Northwest Corner; Planning & Zoning.* PLAYS, PUBLISHED IN PERIODICALS—*Iz She Izzy or Iz He Ain'tzy or Iz They Both,* 1972; *Agamilhous Rebound, High Shame, Waiting for G.,* (sketches), 1974; *Trade-Offs,* 1976; *Off-off-Obits,* 1977.

AWARDS: PEN Grant, 1978; Connecticut Commission on the Arts Grant, 1976; CBS Foundation Grant in Creative Writing, 1974–75; National Endowment for the Arts Grant, 1974; John Simon Guggenheim Fellowship in Playwriting, 1971; Yale Repertory Theatre Grant, 1970, 1971, and 1973; Shubert Fellowships, 1967–68 and 1968–69.

SIDELIGHTS: "I have taught writing at Marquette, Yale, Rockland Community College, the University of Connecticut at Storrs, and since 1979 in the new Dramatic Writing Program at New York University."

ADDRESS: Home—Cream Hill Road, West Cornwall, CT 06796.

* * *

CARVER, Mary, actress and director

PERSONAL: Born May 3; daughter of Carmen (an artist, Delman) Carver; married Joseph Sargent (a director; divorced, 1969); children: Athena, Lia. EDUCATION: University of Southern California, B.A.; trained for the stage with Stella Adler, Paul Mann, Lee Strasberg and Joe Anthony.

CAREER: DEBUT—Mariane, *Tartuffe,* Miss Prism, *Importance of Being Earnest,* Midwife, *Duchess of Malfi,* National Repertory Theatre, tour of U.S. cities, 1945. NEW YORK DEBUT—Honeychile Wainright, *Lo and Behold,* Booth, New York, 1950. PRINCIPAL STAGE APPEARANCES—Felicity, *Shadow Box,* Morosco, New York, 1977; Aunt Sally, *Fifth of July,* Apollo, New York, 1981. MAJOR TOURS—Daisy, *Rhinoceros,* eastern U.S. cities, 1966–67.

FILM DEBUT—Jo, *Goodbye My Fancy,* 1952. PRINCIPAL FILM APPEARANCES—Eugenia, *I Never Promised You a Rose Garden; 3 Women; Nurse; Golden Girl; Frances.* TELEVISION DEBUT—*Danger.* PRINCIPAL TELEVISION APPEARANCES—Celia Simon, *Simon and Simon,* current; *Gunsmoke; McCloud; Wide World of Entertainment; Lou Grant; Quincy.*

AWARDS: TV Mother of the Year, Role of Celia Simon on *Simon and Simon,* 1983; Dramalogue Award, Best Actress, 1981: *Fifth of July.*

SIDELIGHTS: MEMBERSHIPS—All theatrical unions.

ADDRESS: Agent—Helen Barkan, Aimee Entertainment Association, 14241 Ventura Blvd., Sherman Oaks, CA 91423.

* * *

CARVER, Steven, director

PERSONAL: Born April 5, 1945 in New York City; son of Murray Leonard and France (Gross) Carver. EDUCATION: High School of Music and Art, NY, Regents Diploma; University of Buffalo, B.F.A. (Art and Photography); Washington University, St. Louis, MO, M.F.A. (Art, Filmmaking, Photography); American Film Institute, Center for Advanced Studies, Beverly Hills, CA (Film-making, Directing, Writing), two years.

CAREER: PRINCIPAL FILM WORK—Assistant director, *Johnny Got His Gun,* 1971; director, producer, writer, cinematographer, *More Than One Thing,* documentary, St. Louis, MO; director, producer, writer, *Patent,* American Film Institute; director, producer, writer, cinematographer, *The Tell-Tale Heart,* American Film Institute; director, *The Arena;* director, *Big Bad Mama;* director, *Capone,* 1975; director, *Drum,* 1976; director of cinematography, *World's Greatest Lover,* 1977; director, *Moonbeam Rider;* director, *Steel;* director, *An Eye for an Eye,* 1981; director, *Lone Wolf McQuade,* 1983.

PRINCIPAL TELEVISION WORK—Trailers, radio and TV spots for *The Woman Hunt, Night Call Nurses, Cobra Woman, Hot Box, Lady Frankenstein, The Arena;* cinematographer, *Wide World of Sports,* National Football League, St. Louis Cardinals Club; second unit, cinematographer, *Zodiac Couples;* director of cinematography, *Censorship USA;* director, cinematography, *Hot Connections.*

RELATED CAREER: Professional photographer, *Constructivism,* Rickey, St. Louis, MO, Art Publications for Ernest Trova, St. Louis Post-Dispatch, Magazine section, United Press International News Service, St. Louis, MO; teacher, Film-making, Art and Photography, Florissant Valley College, MO, Film-making and Photography, Metropolitan Educational Council in the Arts, St. Louis, MO.

AWARDS: Cine Golden Eagle Award, Cork Film Festival Winner: *The Tell-Tale Heart;* New York Festival Bronze Award, Best Film in Documentary Category, National Educational Television, Honorable Mention: *More Than One Thing;* San Francisco Festival Bronze Medal, Chicago Film Festival Gold Medal: *Syndrome.*

SIDELIGHTS: Scholarship, Buffalo Art Department; Fellowship, Washington University, St. Louis, MO; two year Fellowship, American Film Institute. HOBBIES—Semi-pro football with the Los Angeles Eagles, tennis, baseball, basketball, swimming, scuba diving, skiing, canoeing, judo.

ADDRESS: Home/Office—1010 Pacific Avenue, Venice, CA 90291.

* * *

CASTANG, Veronica, actress, director

PERSONAL: Surname CASTang, accent on first syllable; born April 22, in Uxbridge, Middlesex, England; daughter of Philip (a businessman) and Kathleen (a writer; maiden name, Webb) Castang; married Richard Herr on December 24, 1964 (divorced 1968); married David Leary on June 26, 1972 (divorced 1978). EDUCATION: Institute Francais De Londres, Graduate, 1956; Sorbonne, Paris France, Cours De Civilisation Francaise, 1958; studied at the Questors Theatre in London and with Alfred Emmet, Anthony Mannino Studio in New York. POLITICS: Liberal.

VERONICA CASTANG

CAREER: DEBUT—Gabrielle, *The Madwoman of Chaillot*, InterPlayers, San Francisco, CA, 1962. NEW YORK DEBUT—Understudy, *How's The World Treating You*, Morosco, 40 performances, 1964. LONDON DEBUT—*All My Own Work*, Questors, 1960.

PRINCIPAL STAGE APPEARANCES—Mabel, *The Trigon*, Stage '73, NY, 1965; Annie, *Sargeant Musgrave's Dance*, Theatre DeLys, NY, 1966; Nancy, *The Knack*, Red Barn, Northport L.I., NY, 1966; Pam, *Saved*, Chelsea Theatre Center, NY, 1970; *Self Accusation*, Chelsea Theatre Center, NY, 1971; Diane, *Rooted*, Hartford Stage Company, CT, 1972; *Kaspar*, Chelsea Theatre Center, NY, 1973; Laura, *The Widowing of Mrs. Holroyd*, Long Wharf, New Haven, CT, 1973; Petronella, *A Pagan Place*, Long Wharf, 1973; *Ionescopade*, Theatre Four, NY, 1974; Sister McPhee, *The National Health*, Circle in the Square, NY, 1974; Araminta, *The Philanthropist*, Goodman Theatre, Chicago, IL, 1975; Timothea, *Sea Marks*, Manhattan Theatre Club, NY, 1975; Stella, *Life Class*, Manhattan Theatre Club, NY, 1976; Sonya, *Uncle Vanya*, Pittsburgh Public Theatre, 1976; Mistress Quickly/Princess Katherine, *Henry V*, Pittsburgh Public, 1977; Clara, *A History of the American Film*, Hartford Stage Company, CT, 1977; Valrie, *Ashes*, New York Public, 1977; Nurse Sweet, *The National Health*, Arena Stage, Washington, DC, 1977; Ludowicka, *The Caucasian Chalk Circle*, Arena Stage, Washington, DC, 1978; Frieda Joubert, *Statements after an Arrest under the Immorality Act*, Manhattan Theatre Club, 1978; Jane Hopcroft, *Absurd Person Singular*, Players State Theatre, Coconut Grove, FL, 1978; Lucienne, *Bonjour La, Bonjour*, Guthrie, Minneapolis, 1978; Fanny, *Ride a Cock Horse*, Hudson Guild, NY, 1979; Mrs. Boyle, *Whose Life Is It Anyway?*, Trafalgar, NY, 1979; Ruth, *The Banana Box*, Hudson Guild, NY, 1979; Olga, *Summerfolk*, Long Wharf, CT, 1979; Lucienne, *Bonjour La, Bonjour*, Phoenix, NY, 1980; Brenda, *Mary Barnes*, Long Wharf, 1980; Marianne, *Close of Play*, Manhattan Theatre Club, 1981; Florence, *A Call from the East*, Manhattan Theatre Club, 1981; Maude/Lin, *Cloud 9*, Theatre DeLys, NY, 1981; Wasp, *After the Prize*, Phoenix, NY, 1981; Performed at the Eugene O'Neill Theatre Center, Playwright's Conference, 1982; Paula, *David and Paula*, American Jewish Theatre, NY, 1983; Mrs. Rogers, *Make and Break*, Seattle Repertory, 1983. MAJOR TOURS—Margaret, *Life with Father*, New England.

TELEVISION DEBUT—Timothea, *Sea Marks*, PBS. PRINCIPAL TELEVISION APPEARANCES—*The Widowing of Mrs. Holroyd*; *The Elephant Man*; Evelyn Lincoln, *Kennedy*; *Ryan's Hope*; *As The World Turns*; *A Doctor's Story*.

SIDELIGHTS: MEMBERSHIPS—AEA, Women's Committee, Alien Committee, Performers with Disabilities Committee; Rape Intervention Program, Roosevelt Hospital, New York. FAVORITE ROLES—Sonya, *Uncle Vanya*, Lin, *Cloud 9*, Timothea, *Sea Marks*. Listed in *Performers and Performances*, Jack B. Kamermaw/ Interviews in *Praeger Special Studies*, Rosanne Martorella.

"I was born in England and educated at the Lycee Francais de Londres and at the Sorbonne. I was trained in Art History and worked at an art gallery in London and at the San Francisco Art Institute when I first came to America. Only my complete ignorance of "show business" enabled me to finally take the plunge and attempt to be an actress. I must have had a strong motivation as I stuck it out during long periods of unemployment and not much encouragement, except that the people I auditioned for did say that I was good, they just didn't know what to do with me. Some times I longed for them to tell me that I was terrible, so that I would have an excuse to give it up. Anyway, ultimately acting is what I do and I seem to be able to make a living and sometimes be good and I do have an awfully good time. One has to have a good time, otherwise why bother with the madness one has to go through in order to act? I travelled a lot when I was very young: Yugoslavia, France, Belgium, Italy, Spain, Switzerland, Austria, Germany. I lived in Morocco for a while, ostensibly to teach English to a couple of French children. I wasn't very successful. I worked in a Chinese restaurant in London. I am fluent in French. My hobbies are swimming, bycycling, photography and old houses. I have just bought a late Georgian early Federal house in upstate New York. I am starting to be a director and have directed several one-person shows in the New York area. I am a Foster Parent. I love Ameria and am very grateful to her for giving me the opportunites that I have had here. There is something strange and special about being an immigrant, because one is in a country one has chosen to be in, rather than the one in which one was born. However, I still feel strong allegiance to England, which gave me the backbone and the strength to carry on, when I needed it."

ADDRESS: Agent—Bret Adams, 448 W. 44th Street, New York, NY   10036.

* * *

CAVETT, Dick, entertainer, writer

PERSONAL: Born November 19, 1936, in Gibbon, NE; son of A.B. Cavett; married Carrie Nye (an actress). EDUCATION: Yale University, 1958.

CAREER: PRINCIPAL STAGE APPEARANCES—Acted in plays and musicals at Yale University. PRINCIPAL FILM APPEARANCES—Acted in U.S. Army training films.

PRINCIPAL TELEVISION APPEARANCES—*Where It's At*, (special), 1967; *What's In*, (special); began daytime series for ABC-TV in 1968, three-weekly series summer of 1969; guest host, *The Tonight Show*; *The Dick Cavett Show*, Public Broadcasting Service; occasional host, *ABC Wide World of Entertainment*; *This Morning*, (host).

WRITINGS: Television comedy writer for Jack Paar, and his successors on *The Tonight Show*; Johnny Carson; Merv Griffin; Jerry Lewis; in 1967, wrote for self and appeared in night clubs. BOOKS—*Cavett*, (with Christopher Porterfield).

ADDRESS: Office—228 W. 55th Street, New York, NY 10019. Agent—Jerry Hogan, Henderson/Hogan Associates, 200 W. 57th Street, New York, NY 10019.

* * *

CHAIKIN, Shami, actress, singer, playwright

PERSONAL: Born April 21, 1931; daughter of Abraham (a teacher) and Leah (maiden name, Tirochinsky) Chaikin.

SHAMI CHAIKIN

EDUCATION: Studied for 10 years with The Open Theatre, Joseph Chaikin, New York.

CAREER: PRINCIPAL STAGE APPEARANCES—*Uncle Vanya*, La Mama Theatre, NY; *Bag Lady*, Theatre for the New City and Manhattan Theatre Club, NY; *Loving Reno*, New York Theatre Studio; *The Antigone*, New York Public Theatre; *Specimen Days*, New York Public Theatre; *The Haggadah*, New York Public Theatre; *America Hurrah*, Pocket Theatre; *Mystery Play*, Cherry Lane Theatre; *A Fable*, Lenox Arts Center; *Electra*, New York Public Theatre; *Endgame*, Princeton, NJ; *The Dybbuk*, New York Public Theatre. MAJOR TOURS (New York, U.S., Canada, Europe, Middle East)—*Viet Rock*, Open Theatre Productions; *The Serpent*, Open Theatre Productions; *Terminal*, Open Theatre Productions; *Mutation Show*, Open Theatre Productions; *Nightwalk*, Open Theatre Productions.

PRINCIPAL FILM APPEARANCES—*Zabriskie Point; Surfaces*. PRINCIPAL TELEVISION APPEARANCES—*One Life to Live*, ABC. CABARET APPEARANCES—*Love Songs*, La Mama.

WRITINGS: Play—*Selma*, produced at The Theatre for the New City, 1981.

AWARDS: Obie, *Mutation Show;* Downtown Villager Award, Solo Performance, *Bag Lady*.

SIDELIGHTS: MEMBERSHIPS—AEA, AFTRA, Dramatists Guild.

Miss Chaikin worked with following directors: Andrei Serban, Elinor Renfield, Dorothy Lyman, Joseph Chaikin, Meredith Monk, Elizabeth Swados, Jacques Levy, Michelangelo Antonioni, Ed Emshwiller.

ADDRESS: Home—463 West Street, New York, NY 10014.

* * *

CHAMBERLAIN, (George) Richard, actor

PERSONAL: Born March 31, 1935, Los Angeles, CA; son of Charles and Elsa Chamberlain; EDUCATION: Attended Pomona College, studied voice at the Los Angeles Conservatory of Music and acting with Jeff Corey. MILITARY: U.S. Army, 1956–58.

CAREER: DEBUT—in college productions, including *King Lear.* NEW YORK DEBUT—Jeff Claypool, *Breakfast at Tiffany's* (a musical which never officially opened), 1966. BRITISH DEBUT—title role, *Hamlet*, Birmingham Repertory Theatre, 1969. PRINCIPAL STAGE APPEARANCES—*Richard II*, Seattle Repertory, 1971; Ahmanson, Los Angeles, 1972; Eisenhower, Washington, DC, 1972; Thomas Mendip, *The Lady's Not for Burning*, Chichester Festival, 1972; *The Fantasticks*, Arlington Park, IL, 1973; title-role, *Cyrano de Bergerac*, Ahmanson, Los Angeles, 1973; Reverend Shannon, *The Night of the Iguana*, Ahmanson, 1975, Circle in the Square, NY, 1976; Wild Bill Hickock, *Fathers and Sons*, Public/Other Stage, 1978; *Born Every Minute*, NY (forthcoming); also, director *The Shadow Box*.

FILM DEBUT—*Secret of Purple Reef*, 1960. PRINCIPAL FILM APPEARANCES—*A Thunder of Drums*, 1961; *Twilight of Honor*, 1963; *Joy in the Morning*, 1965; *Petulia*, 1968; *The Madwoman of Chaillot*, 1969; *The Music Lovers*, 1971; *Julius Caesar*, 1971; *Lady Caroline Lamb*, 1972; *The Three Musketeers*, 1974; *Towering Inferno*, 1974; *The Four Musketeers*, 1975; *The Slipper and the Rose: The Story of Cinderella*, 1977; *The Swarm*, 1978; *The Last Wave*, 1979; *Murder by Phone*.

PRINCIPAL TELEVISION APPEARANCES—*Gunsmoke; Bourbon Street Beat; Thriller; Mr. Lucky; Alfred Hitchcock Presents; Dr. Kildare*, 1961–65; *Portrait of a Lady*, 1968; *Hamlet*, 1970; *The Woman I Love*, 1973; *F. Scott Fitzgerald and the Last of the Belles*, 1974; *The Lady's Not for Burning*, 1974; *The Count of Monte Cristo*, 1975; *The Man in the Iron Mask*, 1978; *Centennial*, 1979; *Shogun*, 1980; *The Thorn Birds*, 1983; Raol Wallenberg, *Lost Hero* (forthcoming); *King Solomon's Mines* (forthcoming); *John C. Fremont* (forthcoming).

AWARDS: Golden Globe Award, 1980: *Shogun;* Named favorite male performer, TV Guide Poll, 1963.

ADDRESS: Agent—c/o Chasin-Park-Citron Agency, 9255 Sunset Blvd., Los Angeles, CA 90069.*

* * *

CHAMPION, Marge (nee Marjorie Belcher), actress, choreographer, dancer, director

PERSONAL: Born September 2, 1919, in Hollywood, CA; daughter of Ernest (a dance master and choreographer) and Gladys (Rosenberg) Belcher; married Gower Champion,

October 5, 1947 (divorced 1973); married Boris Sagal (a director), January 1, 1977 (died May 22, 1981); children: Gregg, Blake (first marriage). EDUCATION: Graduated Hollywood High School; trained for the stage with Ernest Belcher, Sandy Meisner, Harriet Lee and Clytie Mundy. POLITICS: Democrat. RELIGION: Presbyterian.

CAREER: DEBUT—Dancer, *Gower and Bell*, Montreal, Canada, 1947. NEW YORK DEBUT—Dancer, *Marge and Gower Champion*, Hotel Plaza. PRINCIPAL STAGE APPEARANCES—(Broadway) Dancer, *Dark of the Moon;* dancer, *Beggar's Holiday;* choreographer (with Gower Champion), *Lend an Ear, Make a Wish;* choreographer, *Whose Life Is It, Anyway,* NY, 1981. MAJOR TOURS—*Three for Tonight,* U.S. cities.

PRINCIPAL FILM WORK—Dancer/actress, *Hemingway and All Those People, The Swimmer, The Party, The Cockeyed Cowboy of Calico County, The Great Sebastians, Invitation to a March, The Women, High Button Shoes, Sabrina Fair;* dancer/choreographer (with Gower Champion), *Mr. Music, Show Boat, Lovely to Look At, Everything I Have Is Yours, Give a Girl a Break, Three for the Show, Jupiter's Darling, That's Entertainment!, Part II, That's Dancing.*

PRINCIPAL TELEVISION WORK—Dancer/choreographer, *Admiral Broadway Revue, Toast of the Town, Three for Tonight, Shower of Stars, GE Theatre, Dinah Shore Show, Bell Telephone Hour, Accent on Love, Marge and Gower Champion Show;* choreographer/dialogue coach, *The Awakening Land, Masada, Diary of Anne Frank, When the Circus Comes to Town;* choreographer, *Day of the Locust, Queen of the Stardust Ballroom, FAME,* 1982.

WRITINGS: BOOKS—*Catch the New Wind* (with Marilee Zdenek); *God Is a Verb* (with Marilee Zdenek).

AWARDS: Emmy Award, Best Choreography, 1975: *Queen of the Stardust Ballroom; Los Angeles Times* Woman of the Year Award.

SIDELIGHTS: MEMBERSHIPS—Center Theatre Group (board of directors), Jacobs Pillow, Academy of Motion Picture Arts and Sciences, American Women for International Understanding.

ADDRESS: Office—c/o Singer, 2001 S. Barrington, Los Angeles, CA 90069. Agent—c/o William Morris, 1350 Avenue of the Americas, New York, NY 10019.

* * *

CHANG, Tisa (nee Yu Chang), actress, dancer, producer, and director

PERSONAL: First name rhymes with ''Lisa''; born April 5, 1941 in Chungking, China; daughter of P.H. (a Chinese diplomat) and Teresa (Kang) Chang; married Ernest Abuba (an actor), January 25, 1976; children: a son, Auric. EDUCATION: Barnard College, 1960; City College of New York, 1961–62; trained for the stage with Uta Hagen and studied dance at Martha Graham School of Dance. POLITICS: Liberal.

CAREER: DEBUT—Lilli, *The World of Susie Wong*, Melody

TISA CHANG

Tent Theater, Buffalo, NY, 1962. NEW YORK DEBUT—Mother, *Lovely Ladies, Kind Gentlemen,* Majestic, 1970. PRINCIPAL STAGE APPEARANCES—Vietnamese nurse, *Brothers,* Theatre Four, New York, 1972; Yen, *The Basic Training of Pavlo Hummel,* Boston, 1972; *The Basic Training of Pavlo Hummel,* Longacre, New York, 1977; *The King and I; Sweet Charity; Flower Drum Song.*MAJOR TOURS—Tintinabula, *A Funny Thing Happened on the Way to the Forum,* 1963–64; *Pacific Overtures.*

FILM DEBUT—Miyazaki, *Ambush Bay,* 1966. PRINCIPAL FILMS—Vietnamese Girl, *Greetings,* 1968. TELEVISION DEBUT—Nurse, *NBC Catholic Hour,* 1967. TELEVISION APPEARANCES—Pat Taylor, *Escape from Iran;* various soap operas.

DIRECTED: Bilingual production of *The Return of the Phoenix* at LaMama, E.T.C.; resident director at LaMama, E.T.C.; twelve productions for the Pan Asian Repertory Theatre; several productions at Equity Library Theatre, Lincoln Center Library and Museum of the Performing Arts, the women's Project at American Place Theatre, and Studio Arena of Buffalo.

WRITINGS: Adapted *Return of the Phoenix* from the original Chinese for bilingual production at LaMama, E.T.C., which was later adapted for Festival of Lively Arts for Young Audiences on CBS-TV. Developed bi-lingual version of *A Midsummer Night's Dream* for the Pan Asian Repertory Theatre and LaMama, E.T.C., 1973.

AWARDS: Chinatown YMCA award for Excellence in the Arts, 1982; Chinese American Arts Council award for Outstanding Achievement in the Arts, 1979.

SIDELIGHTS: MEMBERSHIPS—AEA; AFTRA; SAG; ASCAP; Society of Stage Directors and Choreographers; Professional Women in Theatre; Off Broadway Producers League.

''I arrived in New York in 1947 at the age of six, and I have been attending theater since then. I have been a professional in the American theater since 1962, and in 1977 I formed the Pan Asian Repertory Theatre to promote Asian and Asian-American works and artists. The commercial theater is no longer a representative yardstick of American theater. The impact of American theatre is now more far-reaching and meaningful.''

ADDRESS: Office—c/o Pan Asian Repertory Theatre, 74A E. Fourth Street, New York, NY 10003.

* * *

CHANNING, Stockard (nee Susan Stockard), actress, singer

PERSONAL: Born February 13, 1944, in New York City; daughter of Lester Napier and Mary Alice (English) Stockard; married Walter Channing Jr. (divorced); Paul Schmidt, (divorced); David Debin. EDUCATION: Radcliffe College, B.A. 1965.

CAREER: DEBUT—Candy Coke, *The Investigation,* Theatre Company of Boston, 1966. NEW YORK DEBUT—Chorus, *Two Gentlemen of Verona,* St. James, 1971. PRINCIPAL STAGE APPEARANCES—Female player, *Adaptation,* Boston Company, 1969, Greenwich Mews, NY, 1969; Alice, *Play Strindberg,* Theatre Company of Boston, 1972; Joanna Wilkins, *No Hard Feelings,* Martin Beck, NY, 1973; Julia, *Two Gentlemen of Verona,* Ahmanson, Los Angeles, 1973; Mary, *Vanities,* Mark Taper Forum, Los Angeles, 1976; Jane, *Absurd Person Singular,* Ahmanson, Los Angeles, 1978; Rosalind, *As You Like It,* Long Beach, CA, 1979; Sonia Walsk, *They're Playing Our Song,* Imperial, NY, 1980; *A Day in the Death of Joe Egg,* Long Wharf, New Haven, CT, 1982; *The Lady and the Clarinet,* Long Wharf, 1983; Angel, *The Rink,* Martin Beck, NY, 1984.

PRINCIPAL FILM APPEARANCES—*Comforts of Home,* 1970; *Hospital,* 1971; *The Fortune,* 1975; *Sweet Revenge,* 1975; *The Big Bus,* 1976; *Grease,* 1978; *The Cheap Detective,* 1978; *The Fish That Saved Pittsburgh,* 1979.

PRINCIPAL TELEVISION APPEARANCES—*The Girl Most Likely To,* 1973; *Silent Victory: The Kitty O'Neil Story,* 1979; *Just Friends,* retitled *The Stockard Channing Show,* 1979–80.*

* * *

CHANSKY, Dorothy, actress, writer

PERSONAL: Born February 16, 1951 in Beverly, MA; daughter of George H. (a lawyer) and Edna (a teacher: maiden name Agranovitch) Chansky; EDUCATION: Smith College, A.B., 1973; Catholic University, 1973–74; studied

DOROTHY CHANSKY

at the Herbert Berghof Studios and with Austin Pendleton and Stella Adler, in New York.

CAREER: An actress for eight years, appearing on Broadway, in stock, regional dinner theatre, and numerous television commercials.

WRITINGS: ARTICLES—in *Stagebill* and *New York Womensweek;* PLAYS—*The Brooklyn Bridge* (a musical), 1983. PRODUCED: *The Brooklyn Bridge,* Quaigh Theatre, off-Broadway, New York, 1983.

ADDRESS: Home—107 W. 70th Street, #5R New York, NY 10023. Agent—Sharon Ambrose, 1466 Broadway, New York, NY 10036.

* * *

CHAPIN, Miles, actor

PERSONAL: Born December 6th, 1954; son of Schuyler Garrison (an impresario) and Elizabeth (an arts advocate; maiden name Steinway) Chapin. EDUCATION: Trained for the stage at Herbert Berghof Studio and the National Theatre Institute. POLITICS: Independent. RELIGION: Unitarian.

CAREER: DEBUT—chorus, *Street Scene,* New York City Opera, New York, 1962. PRINCIPAL THEATRE APPEARANCES—Wallace Magruder, *In the Clap Shack,* Yale Repertory, New Haven, CT, 1973; Beano, *Summer Brave,* ANTA, New York, 1975; Jean d'Arc, *Joan of Lorraine,* Good Shepherd Faith Church, 1976; Jack Hayes, *Poor Little Lambs,* Theatre at St. Peters, 1982.

FILM DEBUT—Joel, *Ladybug, Ladybug,* 1964. PRINCIPAL FILM APPEARANCES—Sammy Shecker, *Bless the Beasts and Children,* 1970; Steve Wright, *Hair,* 1977; Joel Weber, *French Postcards,* 1978; Johnny the Bellhop, *Buddy, Buddy,* 1980; Mark Champlain, *The Funny Farm,* 1980; Sammy Fox, *Get Crazy,* 1982. TELEVISION DEBUT—*The Patty Duke Show.* PRINCIPAL TELEVISION APPEARANCES—*PBS' Ourstory; Bulba; Tomorrow's Families.*

ADDRESS: Agent—c/o Creative Artists Agency, Inc., 1888 Century Park East, Suite 1400, Los Angeles, CA 90067; Abrams Artists and Associates, Inc., 575 Lexington Avenue, New York, NY 10022.

* * *

CHARLES, Walter (Jacobsen), actor

PERSONAL: Born April 4, 1945, in Stroudsburg, PA; son of Theodore Edmund (a manufacturer's representative) and Catherine Alexandra (an executive secretary; maiden name Carstensen) Jacobsen; EDUCATION: Boston University, Bachelor of Music, 1968; studied for the stage with Mary Tarcai.

CAREER: DEBUT—Frank Butler, *Show Boat,* Kenley Star Theatre, Wichita, KS, 1969. NEW YORK DEBUT—Vince Fontaine, *Grease,* Royale, New York, 1974, 650+ performances. PRINCIPAL STAGE APPEARANCES—Sweeney Todd (understudy),

WALTER CHARLES

Sweeney Todd, Uris, New York, 1979; understudy, *Cats,* Winter Garden, 1982; Renaud, *La Cage aux Folles,* Palace, New York, 1983; Walt Whitman, *Song of Myself,* Pennsylvannia Stage Company, 1982; Prince, *Operetta, My Dear Watson,* Indiana Repertory Company, Indianapolis, IN, 1982; Cooley, *Anyone Can Whistle,* Berkshire Theatre Festival, 1980; Dr. Carrasco, *Man of La Mancha,* 1978; Aristide, *Can-Can,* 1976; *I Do, I Do,* 1971.

TELEVISION DEBUT—*The Doctors,* 1973. PRINCIPAL TELEVISION APPEARANCES—District Attorney Levene, *All My Children,* 1978; *Antoinette Perry Awards Show,* 1981.

SIDELIGHTS: FAVORITE PARTS—Dickenson, *1776;* Sweeney Todd; Albin, *La Cage Aux Folles.*

"The other great love of my life is classical music. I started out as a pianist, and still play for my own amusement—and the amusement of my friends, I might add. I support several musical organizations, especially Carnegie Hall. Great music goes directly to the emotions, more than any other art, in my view. I still remember being thrilled when I read that John Gielgud orchestrated his great readings of Shakespeare. . . . Having recently purchased a country house, I've become increasingly concerned with environmental issues, and I'm passionately supportive of all attempts to clean up the water, air, and protect as much of our wildlife as possible."

ADDRESS: Agent—Baldwin-Scully, Inc., 501 Fifth Ave., New York, NY 10017.

* * *

CHARLESON, IAN, actor

PERSONAL: Born August 11, 1949, in Edinburgh, Scotland; son of John and Jane Charleson. EDUCATION: Royal HS, Edinburgh; Edinburgh University, MA, 1970; trained for the stage at the London Academy of Music and Dramatic Art.

CAREER: DEBUT—(at age 8) *Kith and Kin,* Edinburgh. LONDON DEBUT—Jimmy Porter, *Look Back in Anger,* Young Vic, 1972. NEW YORK DEBUT—Lucentio, *The Taming of the Shrew,* Young Vic, Brooklyn Academy of Music, 1974 (in repertory with Ottavio, *Scapino,* Brian Curtis, *French Without Tears*). PRINCIPAL ENGAGEMENTS—Guildenstern, *Rosencrantz and Guildenstern Are Dead,* Young Vic, London, 1974; Hamlet, *Hamlet,* Cambridge Theatre Company, England, 1975; Dave, *Otherwise Engaged,* Queens, London, 1975; Octavius, *Julius Caesar,* Peregrine, *Volpone,* National Theatre Company, London, 1977; Ariel, *The Tempest,* Tranio, *The Taming of the Shrew,* Longaville, *Love's Labour's Lost,* Royal Shakespeare Company, Stratford, England, 1978; *Piaf,* Other Place, London, 1978; Tranio, *The Taming of the Shrew,* Longaville, *Love's Labour's Lost,* Aldwych, London, 1979; Lawrence Vail, *Once in a Lifetime,* Aldwych, London, 1979; Joe Maguire, *The Innocent,* Warehouse, London, 1979; *Piaf,* Warehouse, Aldwych, Wyndham's, London, 1979; Sky Masterson, *Guys and Dolls,* National, London, 1982–83. MAJOR TOURS—Gad, *Joseph and the Amazing Technicolor Dreamcoat,* Young Vic, Edinburgh Festival (professional debut), 1972.

PRINCIPAL FILMS—*Jubilee*, 1978; Eric Liddell, *Chariots of Fire*, 1981; *Ghandi*, 1982; *Ascendancy*, 1983; *Greystoke*, 1984. TELEVISION APPEARANCES—*Rock Follies; Churchill's People; The Paradise Run; Antony and Cleopatra; Something's Got to Give*, Scot TV, 1982; *All's Well That Ends Well; Louisianna; Master of the Game; Oxbridge Blues; A Month in the Country; The Devil's Lieutenant.*

SIDELIGHTS: RECREATION—Collecting jigsaws, reading, painting.

ADDRESS: c/o Jeremy Conway, Eight Cavendish Place, London W1M 9DJ, England.

* * *

CHARTOFF, Melanie, actress, singer

PERSONAL: Born December 15 in New Haven, CT; daughter of Harold (a stockbroker) and Frances (a secretary; maiden name, Olenik) Chartoff. EDUCATION: Adelphi University, B.A. (Acting and Directing); studied acting and pantomime with Mary Tarcai, Stella Adler, and Jacques Burdick.

CAREER: DEBUT—young prostitute, *Threepenny Opera*, Yale University Theatre, New Haven, CT, 1966. BROADWAY DEBUT—Giacinta, (Young Vic's) *Scapino*, Circle-in-the-Square (uptown), 1975. PRINCIPAL STAGE APPEARANCES—Improvisational Comedienne, *The Propostion*, Mercer Arts Center, NY, 1974; Jenny, *Do I Hear a Waltz*, Equity Library, NY, 1975; Lead, *Tuscaloosa's Calling Me . . .* , Chelsea Westside, NY, 1976; *Lovesong*, Village Gate, NY, 1976; Mandala, *Via Galactica*, NY.

MAJOR TOURS—Prudence, *Beyond Therapy*, Westport Country Playhouse, Falmouth Playhouse, St. Louis, 1983.

FILM DEBUT—Prudence, *American Hot Wax*, 1977. PRINCIPAL FILM APPEARANCES—Linda Libel, *The Big House*, 1983.

TELEVISION DEBUT—Nancy, *Search for Tomorrow*. PRINCIPAL TELEVISION APPEARANCES—*Having It All; Can You Hear the Laughter—The Freddie Prinz Story; Fridays; The Everyday Show;* Ronnie Bernstein, *Richie Brockelman, Private Eye;* Nadia Samara, *Wonder Woman;* Ginny, *Tony Randall Show;* Guest and Mighty Carson Art Players as Nancy Reagan, *The Tonight Show Starring Johnny Carson; Merv Griffin Show; Good Morning America; Tom Cottle: Up Close; Allan Thicke Show; What Ever Happened to . . . .*

THEATRE-RELATED CAREER: Teacher, improvisational workshops, various studios in Los Angeles, 1979–present; Indian Children's Conference, Spokane, WA, 1983; The Real Stage, NY, 1983.

AWARDS: Dramalogue Award for Outstanding Achievement in the Theatre for Huntington Hartford production of *March of the Falsettos*, 1982; Outstanding Contribution to the Theatre, Adelphi University.

SIDELIGHTS: MEMBERSHIPS—Save the Children; Women in Film; Academy of Television Arts and Sciences; AFTRA; AEA; AGVA; SAG.

Ms. Chartoff has recorded a comedy album on which she portrays Nancy Reagan in *The First Family Rides Again*, with Rich Little; she has also recorded *Lovesongs*, which is a collection of famous love poems sung in all styles. She has performed her stand-up comedy and singing act in night clubs in New York and Los Angeles. ''I was pretty fortunate to be on a show like *Fridays;* we strove to enlighten and educate, as well as entertain a broad spectrum of viewers. Comedy is a pretty painless way to preach. Hopefully we left them laughing and thinking. . . . I want my work to project a positive attitude toward people and the planet and this seems best done with a sense of humor.''

ADDRESS: Agent—Fred Weistheimer, William Morris Agency, 151 El Camino Drive, Beverly Hills, CA 90212.

* * *

CHAYEFSKY, Paddy, writer

PERSONAL: Born January 29, 1923, in New York City; died August 1, 1981; son of Harry and Gussie (Stuchevsky) Chayefsky; married Susan Sackler, February 24, 1949; children: Dan. EDUCATION: City College of New York, B.S., 1943. MILITARY: U.S. Army, World War II. NON-FILM CAREER: Printer.

WRITINGS: PLAYS—*Middle of the Night*, 1956; *The Tenth Man*, 1959; *Gideon*, 1961; *The Passion of Josef D*, 1964; *The Latent Heterosexual*, Dallas, TX, Aldwych, London, 1968. SCREENPLAYS—*Marty* (also associate producer), 1955; *Bachelor Party*, 1957; *The Goddess*, 1958; *Middle of the Night*, 1959; *The Americanization of Emily*, 1964; *The Hospital*, 1971; *Network*, 1975; *Altered States*, 1979. TELEPLAYS—*Holiday Song; Marty; Bachelor Party; The Mother; Catered Affair; Printer's Measure; The Big Deal; The Sixth Year; Middle of the Night.* BOOKS—*Television Plays by Paddy Chayefsky* (anthology), 1955; *The Goddess*, 1958; *Middle of the Night*, 1958; *The Tenth Man*, 1960; *Gideon*, 1961; *The Passion of Josef D*, 1964; *The Latent Heterosexual*, 1968; *Altered States*, 1978.

RELATED CAREER—President, Carnegie Productions, 1957; S.P.D. Corporation, 1959; Sudan Corporation, 1956; Sidney Productions, 1967; Simcha Productions, 1971.

AWARDS: Academy Awards, Best Screenplay, 1976: *Network*, 1971: *The Hospital*, 1955: *Marty;* Purple Heart medal, U.S. Army.*

* * *

CHINOY, Helen Krich, writer, theatre historian, and teacher

PERSONAL: Born September 25, 1922, in Newark, NJ; daughter of Benjamin (an automobile dealer) and Anne (a community worker and writer; maiden name, Kalen) Krich; married Ely Chinoy (a sociologist and college professor), June 4, 1948; children: Michael, Claire Nicole. EDUCATION: New York University, B.A., 1943; M.A., 1945; University of Birmingham, Shakespeare Institute, University Fellowship in English Certificate, 1947; Columbia University, Ph.D., 1963.

WRITINGS: BOOKS—*Actors on Acting* (edited with Toby Cole) 1949, 1970, paperback edition, 1980; *Directors on Directing* (edited with Toby Cole), 1953, 1963; *The Impact of the Drector on American Plays,* Playwrights and Theatres, 1963; *The American Theatre: A Sum of Its Parts,* 1972; *Women in American Theatre* (edited with Linda Walsh Jenkins), 1981. ARTICLES IN PERIODICALS—"The Director as Mythagog: Jonathan Miller Talks about Directing Shakespeare," *Educational Theatre Journal,* 1976; "Reunion: A Self-Portrait of the Group Theatre," *Educational Theatre Journal,* 1977; "Art Versus Business: The Role of Women in American Theatre" *The Drama Review,* 1980; "The Poetics of Politics," *Theatre Journal,* 1983. CONTRIBUTIONS TO BOOKS OF COLLECTED ARTICLES—"Hallie Flanagan Davis" in *Notable American Women,* 1980; "The Founding of the Group Theatre" in *Theatrical Touring and Founding,* 1981; "Women in Theatre in the 1920's" in *Women, the Arts, and the 1920's in Paris and New York,* 1982.

THEATRE-RELATED CAREER: Teaching—New York University, Queens College, Rutgers University, 1944–48; Smith College, 1953–60; University of Leicester (England), 1963–64; Smith College, 1965–present. Articles and Reviews—*Encyclopedia Britannica; Enciclopedia dello Spettacolo; Dictionary of American Biography; Theatre Arts Magazine; Players Magazine; Modern Drama.* Associate Editor—*Educational Theatre Journal.*

AWARDS: FELLOWSHIPS—National Endowment for the Humanities, 1979–80; American Association of University Women, 1962–63: New York University, 1945.

SIDELIGHTS: MEMBERSHIPS—American Society for Theatre Research (executive committee, program chair, research committee chair, representative to American Council of Learned Societies); American Theatre Association; National Theatre Conference.

"I feel that I was marked for life by the idea of theatre as culture, community and commitment."

ADDRESS: Office—Theatre Department, Smith College, Northampton, MA 06010.

* * *

CHOATE, Tim, actor

PERSONAL: Born October 11, 1954; son of Ben Tom (in building and construction) and Betty Nell (commercial artist; maiden name, Strong) Choate; married Pari Stave (an art consultant) on June 25, 1982. EDUCATION: University of Texas at Austin, B.F.A., 1977. RELIGION: Christian.

CAREER: DEBUT—Mio, *Winterset,* Loeb Drama Center, Cambridge, MA, 1977. NEW YORK DEBUT—Young Charlie, *Da,* Morosco, for 196 performances, 1978. PRINCIPAL STAGE APPEARANCES—Barnette Lloyd, *Crimes of the Heart,* Golden, NY, 1982; Gethin Price, *Comedians,* Manhattan Punch Line, NY, 1983.

FILM DEBUT—Clifford Wentworth, *The Europeans,* 1977. PRINCIPAL FILM APPEARANCES—Eastman, *Times Square,* 1978; Jamie, *Jane Austen in Manhattan,* 1979; Charlie Lichenstein, *The First Time,* 1979; Harry, *Blow Out,* 1979; Young Ricky, *Ghost Story,* 1980; Howe, *Dark Eye,* 1983.

ADDRESS: Agent—Gage Group, 1650 Broadway, New York, NY 10036.

* * *

CHRISTINE, Virginia, actress

PERSONAL: Born March 5, 1920, in IA; daughter of George Allen (a musician) and Helga Judith Naomi (a musician; maiden name, Ossian) Ricketts; married Fritz Feld (an actor, writer, director), November 1940; children: Steven, Danny. EDUCATION: Attended UCLA; studied with her husband Fritz Feld for two years.

VIRGINIA CHRISTINE

CAREER: DEBUT—Hedda, *Hedda Gabler.*

FILM DEBUT—*The Edge of Darkness.* PRINCIPAL FILM APPEARANCES—*Mission to Moscow; Counter Attack; The Killers; Cyrano de Bergerac; High Noon; Not as a Stranger; Three Brave Men; Judgement at Nuremberg; The Prize; Four for Texas; A Rage to Live; Hail Hero; Daughter of the Mind; Woman of the Year; Kojak; Guess Who's Coming to Dinner?* PRINCIPAL TELEVISION APPEARANCES—Spokeswoman for Folger's Coffee as "Mrs. Olson," 1960–present.

AWARDS: First Place, National Forensic League, piano solo, Iowa; Hollywood Golden Mask Award; Harlequin Award; Honorary Mayor, Brentwood, CA.

SIDELIGHTS: MEMBERSHIPS—Family Planning and Planned Parenthood.

"Mrs. Feld is most frequently recognized as Mrs. Olson in the Folger Coffee commercials as the likeable Swedish woman who brings happiness to young married couples."

ADDRESS: Agent—Chris Shiffrin, Robert-Shiffrin Artists, Ltd., 7466 Beverly Blvd., Los Angeles, CA 90036.

* * *

CIZMAR, Paula, writer

PERSONAL: Born August 30, 1949 in Youngstown, OH; daughter of Paul (a civil servant) and Lena Frances (Abrutz) Cizmar; married Douglas Gower (a playwright) November 3, 1979. EDUCATION: Ohio University, A.B., 1971; attended San Francisco State University; trained for the stage with Jean Shelton and Bob Ernst.

WRITINGS: PLAYS, PUBLISHED—*The Girl Room,* 1978; *Madonna of the Powder Room,* 1981; *The Death of a Miner,* 1982. PLAYS, UNPUBLISHED—Apocryphal Stories, Exceptional Friends; Candy and Shelley Go to the Desert; Cupcakes; Escape from the 44th Floor. SCREENPLAYS—*M.U.T.H.R.* (with Douglas Gower); Tough Girls (with Douglas Gower); The Voyage of the Mimi (with Douglas Gower, John Griesemer, and Dick Hendrick).

THEATRE-RELATED CAREER: Playwright-in-residence, Portland Stage Company, Portland, ME, 1981; member playwright, Women's Project, American Place Theatre, New York, NY, 1981–present; Dramaturg, Capital Rep, Albany, NY, 1982.

AWARDS: FELLOWSHIPS—National Endowment for the Arts, 1982. GRANTS—Rockefeller Foundation, 1983.

SIDELIGHTS: MEMBERSHIPS—Dramatists Guild, League of Professional Theatre Women.

"Though some of my work deals with social issues, I am primarily concerned simply with people—particularly their emotional lives. I love to explore rhythms in language and expressionistic aspects of behavior in an effort to illuminate who we are as modern people."

ADDRESS: Agent—c/o Peter Franklin, William Morris Agency,

1350 Ave. of the Americas, New York, NY 10019.

* * *

CLAIRE, Ludi, actress and writer

PERSONAL: Born April 15, 1927; daughter of Georges Laurent (a concert pianist) and Lyssa Edith (a singer, Nickell) Bailhé; married Laurence Victor Hugo (an actor) March 13, 1975. EDUCATION: Attended École Internationale de Geneve, Switzerland; prepared for the stage with Lee Strasberg.

CAREER: DEBUT—Rosalind, *As You Like It,* Civic Theatre, Fort Wayne, IN. NEW YORK DEBUT—Slave, *Medea,* 1947. PRINCIPAL STAGE APPEARANCES—(Broadway) *The Small Hours; Tower Beyond Tragedy; Venus Observed; Legend of Lovers; Silk Stockings; Seventh Heaven; Goodbye Again; Someone Waiting; Holiday for Lovers; The First Gentlemen; The Country Wife; Duel of Angels; The Prisoner of Second Avenue; The Bed Before Yesterday;* (Repertory) Alice, *Tiny Alice,* ACT, San Francisco, CA; Gertrude, *Hamlet,* Old Globe Shakespeare Festival, San Diego, CA; *Phaedre, The Price, Life with Father,* Old Globe Shakespeare Festival, San Diego, CA; *Peter Pan,* Atlanta Alliance, Atlanta, GA; Birdie, *The Little Foxes,* Hartman Theatre, Stamford, CT; Mama, *The Diary of Anne Frank,* Manitoba Theatre Centre; (Stock) *Biography; Blithe Spirit; Rain, The Fourposter; Ring Round the Moon; Goodbye My Fancy; Clutterbuck; A Streetcar Named Desire; Charley's Aunt; Springtime for Henry; The Happy Time; The Potting Shed; Once More with Feeling.*

LUDI CLAIRE

PRINCIPAL TELEVISION APPEARANCES—Liz McGrath, *The Edge of Night; Three's Company; Hidden Faces; The Today Show; Medical Story.*

WRITINGS: PLAYS, UNPUBLISHED—Draw Black. MUSICAL BOOK—Major Barbara. TELEVISION SHOWS—*The 28th of June* (screenplay); *Family; ABC Afterschool Specials; Cleopatra* (screenplay).

AWARDS: Sylvania Award: *The Bridge of San Luis Rey* (adaptation). Christopher Award: *The Bridge of San Luis Rey* (adaptation), *Bernadette of Lourdes.*

SIDELIGHTS: MEMBERSHIPS—Actors' Equity Association (council), Screen Actors' Guild, A.F.T.R.A., Writers Guild.

"Vital influences in development have been my associations with many great talents—Sir Tyrone Guthrie, Dame Judith Anderson, Lord Olivier, Vivien Leigh, Katherine Hepburn, Dorothy Stickney. They are great ladies and gentlemen of the theatre, a vanishing breed, who taught much by their own behavior. Hume Cronyn and Jessica Tandy were Best Man and Maid of Honor at my marriage to Laurence Hugo."

* * *

CLAMAN, Barbara S. (nee Sherman), casting director

PERSONAL: Born June 28, 1939, in Brooklyn, NY; daughter of Benjamin Zion (a real estate broker) and Hannah (Goldstein) Sherman; married Allyn Claman, November 29, 1959 (divorced 1968); children: Eric Barnett. EDUCATION: Mills College, Nursery School Education, 1962; studied with Renee Valente and Rose Tobins, David Susskind's *Talent Associates.* POLITICS: Radical Democrat. RELIGION: Jewish.

CAREER: PRINCIPAL FILMS AND TELEVISION WORK—Casting director: Formed Barbara Claman Inc., NY, 1972, later a service of IDC for casting television commercials and features; films—*The Marvel of Haunted Castle, The Oasis, XYZ Murders, Lost in America, Predator, Nickel Mountain, Purple Hearts, Summer Lovers, Flicks, The Entity, Long Shot, Liars Moon, Modern Romance, The Hand, House of God, Times Square, G.O.R.P., Boardwalk, Gwendoline, Up the Pentagon, Never–ending Story, Traces, On Golden Pond, Tribute, Changling, Oh God Book II, Wise Blood, The Awakening, The Butter Boys, Days of Heaven.*

Movies for television—*He's Not Your Son, Intent to Kill, Mail Order Bride, Games Mother Never Taught You, Cry for the Strangers, Dropout Father, The Gift of Life, Side by Side, The Ordeal of Bill Carney, Dial M for Murder, Summer Solstice, A Gun in the House, 300 Miles for Stephanie, When the Circus Came to Town, The Day the Women Got Even, Father Figure, Nurse* (pilot), *Orphan Train, The Freddie Prinze Story, Mom, the Wolfman & Me.* Television series 1981–82—*Today's FBI, Nurse, Counterattack-Crime in America;* 1982–83—*Sunday's Child, Seven Brides for Seven Brothers, For Love and Honor;* 1984—*His & Hers;* PBS casting—*King of America, Guest of the Nation, The American Short Story Series, Bloodhound Gang, 3–2–1 Contact;* children's television—*Sometimes I Don't Love My Mother,*

Tell Me No Lies, Dirkham Detective Agency, Secret Agent Boy; theatre—*Homesteaders,* Los Angeles Theatre.

ADDRESS: Office—6565 Sunset Blvd., Los Angeles, CA 90028.

* * *

CLARK, Candy, actress

PERSONAL: Born June 20, in Norman, OK; daughter of Thomas Prest (a chef) and Ella Lee (Padberg) Clark.

CAREER: FIRST STAGE WORK—*Coupla' White Chicks Sitting Around Talking,* Astor Place Theatre, New York, NY. FILM DEBUT—*Fat City,* 1972. PRINCIPAL FILMS—Debbie, *American Graffiti,* 1973; Mary Lou, *The Man Who Fell to Earth,* 1976; *The Big Sleep,* 1977; *Citizens Band,* 1977; *More American Graffiti,* 1978; *Blue Thunder,* 1983; *Amityville 3-D,* 1983. PRINCIPAL TELEVISION APPEARANCES—*Rodeo Girl,* 1980; *Amateur Night at the Dixie Bar and Grill,* 1980; *Johnny Belinda,* 1982.

AWARDS: Academy Award Nomination, Best Supporting Actress, 1974: *American Graffiti.*

ADDRESS: c/o Pat McQueeney, 146 N. Almont Drive, Apt. 8, Los Angeles, CA 90048.

CANDY CLARK

CLARKE, David, actor, writer

PERSONAL: Born August 30, 1908; son of Charles M. (a minister) and Nora E. (Coakley) Clarke; married Nora Dunfee (an actress and teacher); children: Katharine, Susan. EDUCATION: Attended Butler College in Indianapolis; studied at the Actors Lab in Hollywood with Hume Cronyn. POLITICS: Independent. RELIGION: Christian. MILITARY: U.S. Naval Reserve, 1942–45.

CAREER: DEBUT—American version of the *Passion Play*, tour of California and Washington State, 1929. NEW YORK DEBUT—Stage Manager, *Roadside*, Longacre, 1930. PRINCIPAL STAGE APPEARANCES—*Abe Lincoln in Illinois*, Plymouth, NY, 1938–40; *The Visit*, Lunt Fontanne, NY, 1958–60. MAJOR TOURS—*Abe Lincoln in Illinois, The Visit.*

FILM DEBUT—*The Knockout*, 1940. PRINCIPAL FILM APPEARANCES—*The Set Up; The Gunfighter;* and 50 others. TELEVISION DEBUT—*Somerset Maugham Show*, 1951. PRINCIPAL TELEVISION APPEARANCES—*Ryan's Hope*, 1979–80.

WRITINGS: PLAYS, PRODUCED—*Never a Snug Harbour*, Milwaukee Repertory, 1976.

AWARDS: National Endowment Grant for Creative Writing, 1978.

SIDELIGHTS: MEMBERSHIPS—New Dramatists.

ADDRESS: Home—225 Central Park West, New York, NY 10024. Office—New Dramatists, 424 W. 44th Street, New York, NY 10036.

* * *

CLARY, Robert, actor

PERSONAL: Born March 1, 1926, in Paris; son of Maurice (a tailor) and Berthe (Stulman) Widerman; married Natalie Cantor, May 18, 1965; children: Michael Metzger (stepson). EDUCATION: Attended public schools in France. RELIGION: Jewish.

CAREER: DEBUT—nightclub singer, France, 1938. NEW YORK DEBUT—*New Faces of 1952*, New York, 1952. PRINCIPAL STAGE APPEARANCES—*Seventh Heaven; La Plume de Ma Tante; Around the World in Eighty Days; Sugar.* FILM DEBUT—*Ten Tall Men.* PRINCIPAL FILMS—*Thief of Damascus, New Faces; A New Kind of Love; The Hindenburg.* PRINCIPAL TELEVISION APPEARANCES—Louis LeBeau, *Hogan's Heroes; The Young and the Restless; Days of Our Lives; The Colgate Comedy Hour; The Merv Griffin Show.*

SIDELIGHTS: Mr. Clary is a volunteer in the outreach program of the Simon Wiesenthal Center, which teaches high school students about the Nazi extermination of European Jewry.

ADDRESS: Office—9015 Cynthia, Los Angeles, CA 90069.

CLAVELL, James, writer, producer, director

PERSONAL: Son of R. C. (a career soldier, OBE) and Eileen (Ross) Clavell; married April 1949; children; Michaela Fleur, Holly Jane. EDUCATION: University of Maryland, Ph.D., 1980. MILITARY: Royal Artillery, World War II.

CAREER: DIRECTED: Films—*Where's Jack*, 1968. PRODUCED: Television shows—*Shogun*, 1980. WRITER-DIRECTOR-PRODUCER: Films—*Five Gates to Hell*, 1959; *Walk Like a Dragon*, 1963; *To Sir with Love*, 1966; *Last Valley*, 1969; *The Children's Story But Not for Children*, 1982.

WRITINGS: FILMS—*The Fly*, 1958; *Watussi*, 1958; *The Great Escape*, 1960; *Satan Bug*, 1962; *633 Squadron*, 1963. NOVELS—*King Rat*, 1962; *Taipan*, 1966; *Shogun*, 1976; *Noble House*, 1980; *The Children's Story But Not for Children*.

AWARDS: Emmy Award, Peabody Award, Critics Award, Golden Globe Award.

SIDELIGHTS: MEMBERSHIPS—Caledonia Club, Royal Overseas League. Mr. Clavell was a prisoner of war in the Far East, 1941–45.

ADDRESS: Office—c/o Hodder-Stoughton, 47 Bedford Square, London WC1, England.

* * *

COBURN, D(onald) L., playwright

PERSONAL: Born August 4, 1938, in Baltimore, MD; son of Guy Dabney (a salesman) and Ruth Margaret (a secretary; maiden name, Sommers) Coburn; married Nazlee Joyce French, October 24, 1964 (divorced 1971); married Marsha Woodruff Maher (a writer), February 22, 1975; children: (first marriage) Donn Christopher, Kimberly. EDUCATION: Attended Baltimore public schools. MILITARY: U.S. Navy (Seaman), 1958–60. NON-THEATRICAL CAREER: Advertising salesman, Baltimore *Sun* papers, 1961; radio times salesman, Baltimore, 1962–66; Coburn and Associates Advertising Agency, 1966–70; Donald L. Coburn Corporate Consultant, 1973–75.

WRITINGS: PLAYS, PRODUCED—*The Gin Game*, 1976; *Bluewater Cottage*, 1979; *The Corporation Man*, 1981; *Currents Turned Awry*, 1982; *Guy*, 1983.

AWARDS: Antoinette Perry Award Nomination, 1978: *The Gin Game*; Pulitzer Prize for Drama, 1978: *The Gin Game*; Golden Apple, 1977: *The Gin Game.*

SIDELIGHTS: MEMBERSHIPS—Dramatists Guild, Author's League, Texas Institute of Letters, Soaring Society of America.

ADDRESS: Agent—c/o Flora Roberts, 157 W. 57th Street, Penthouse A, New York, NY 10019.

COCO, James, actor

PERSONAL: Born March 21, 1929, in New York City; son of Feliche and Ida (Detestes) Coco. EDUCATION: Graduated from Evander Childs High School; trained for the stage at the Herbert Berghoff Studio with Uta Hagen.

CAREER: THEATER DEBUT—Old King Cole, Clare Tree Majors Theater. NEW YORK DEBUT—Tabu, Hotel Paradiso, Henry Miller's, 1957. PRINCIPAL STAGE APPEARANCES—Darwin's Theories, Madison Avenue Playhouse, NY, 1960; Tausch, The Moon in the Yellow River, East End, NY, 1961; Doctor, Everybody Loves Opal, Longacre, NY, 1961; Mr. Hammidullah, A Passage to India, Ambassador, NY, 1962; O'Casey, Arturo Ui, Lunt-Fontanne, NY, 1963; Leslie Edwards, The Sponge Room, Stanley Mintey, Squat Betty, East End, NY, 1964; The First, That 5 AM Jazz, Astor Place, NY, 1964; Roger Varnum, Lovey, Cherry Lane, NY, 1965; A Sewerman, The Devils, Broadway Theatre, NY, 1965; Barber, Man of La Mancha, Washington Square, NY, 1966; Inspector Rogers, The Astrakhan Coat, Helen Hayes, NY, 1967; Leo, Basement, Max, Fragments, Cherry Lane, NY, 1967; Lee, Here's Where I Belong, Billy Rose, NY, 1968; Window Washer, Witness, Gramercy Arts, NY, 1968; Marion Cheever, Next, Greenwich Mews, NY, Mark Taper, Los Angeles, CA, 1969; Barney Cashman, Last of the Red Hot Lovers, Eugene O'Neill, NY, 1969; Benno Blimpie, The Transfiguration of Benno Blimpie, Astor Place, NY, 1977.

FILM DEBUT—Ensign Pulver, 1963. PRINCIPAL FILM APPEARANCES—Generation, 1969; End of the Road, 1970; The Strawberry Statement, 1970; Tell Me That You Love Me Junie Moon, 1970; A New Leaf, 1971; Such Good Friends, 1971; Man of La Mancha, 1972; The Wild Party, 1975; Murder by Death; Charlestown; Bye Bye Monkey; The Cheap Detective, 1978; Scavenger Hunt, 1979; Wholly Moses, 1980; Only When I Laugh, 1981; The Muppets Take Manhattan, 1984.

PRINCIPAL TELEVISION APPEARANCES—Johnny Carson Show; Calucci's Department, 1974; The Dumplings, 1976; Diary of Anne Frank; Raquel Welch Special; The French Atlantic Affair, 1979; St. Elsewhere, 1983.

AWARDS: Emmy, 1984: St. Elsewhere.

WRITINGS: BOOKS—The James Coco Diet Book, 1984.

SIDELIGHTS: FAVORITE ROLES—Marion Cheever, Barney Cashman.

ADDRESS: Agent—c/o Paul H. Wolfowitz, 59 E. 54th Street, New York, NY 10022.*

*　*　*

CODY, Iron Eyes, actor

PERSONAL: Born April 3, 1915, in OK; son of Thomas and Frances (Salpet) Long Plume; married Bertha Parker, September 15, 1936; children: Robert Francis, Arthur William. EDUCATION: Attended Los Angeles City College, 1940–41.

CAREER: PRINCIPAL STAGE APPEARANCES—The American,

1930; My Blossom Bride, 1931; White God and Red God, 1932.

PRINCIPAL FILM APPEARANCES—Crazy Horse, Sitting Bull, 1954; Sun Dance Priest, A Man Called Horse, 1970; Crazy Foot, The Cockeyed Cowboys of Calico County, 1970; Santana, El Condor, 1970; Standing Bear, Grey Eagle, 1977; Wilderness Trail; narration, educational films: The American Indian—Before the White Man, The American Indian—After the White Man, Indian Culture, LAPD.

PRINCIPAL TELEVISION APPEARANCES—Indian in the Canoe/Crying Indian, Keep America Beautiful series of commercials, 1970–; The Donny and Marie Show; Quest; Walt Disney Studios and others.

WRITINGS: BOOKS—Indian Sign Talk in Pictures, 1952; Little White Chieftain, 1963; Indian Talk, 1970; Indian Legends; My Life as a Hollywood Indian. Has contributed articles to many newspapers on the American Indian.

SIDELIGHTS: MEMBERSHIPS—Honorary representative, Shakespeare Archery Corp.; master of ceremonies, Little Big Horn Indian Association; Grand Council American Indians, Confederated Tribes of American Indians; American Indian Week; president, Little Big Horn Indian Charitable Association; chairman, National American Indian Drug Prevention Program; national honorary chairman, We Turn in Pushers; honorary member, American Indian Free Clinic; active in Boy Scouts of America; board of directors, Los Angles City–County Native American Indian Commission; board of directors, Southwest Museum; life member, Los Angeles Indian Center; director of photography, Los Angeles Library Association; official photographer, board of directors, Los Angeles, Corral of the Westerners; SAG, AFTRA, Los Angeles Karate Association.

ADDRESS: Agent—c/o Dade/Rosen Associates, 999 N. Doheny Drive, Los Angeles, CA 90069.

*　*　*

COE, Richard L., critic, lecturer

PERSONAL: Born November 8, 1914 in New York City; son of Elmer James Secor (a banker) and Lillie Isabelle (a writer; maiden name, Musgrave) Coe; married Christine Sadler (a writer) on May 4, 1946 (died 1983). EDUCATION: George Washington University, 1934–38.

CAREER: Theatre/Film Critic-Editor, Washington Post, 1938–78; Critic Emeritus, Washington Post, 1979–present; lecturer, George Washington University, American University, 1955–present; lecturer, Smithsonian Institute, 1980.

WRITINGS: Contributing author—New York Herald Tribune, The New York Times, The Nation, Theatre Arts, Show, The Washingtonian, Beau, Good Life Magazine, The Smithsonian, Amerika, and other newspapers in Egypt and England.

AWARDS: American College Theatre Festival instituted the Richard L. Coe Award in 1980; ODK; Women's Club of America; Washingtonian of the Year, 1980; Directors Guild of America, 1962; Washington Board of Trade, 1957.

SIDELIGHTS: MEMBERSHIPS—Antoinette Perry Award Nominating Committee; Pulitzer Prize in Drama Jury; Public Committee for Integration in the Capital's Theaters; Margo Jones Awards Committee; National Press Club; Overseas Press Club; The Players Club. RECREATION: Travel.

"Beliefs: that the audience is half the play; the universal appeal and influence of the performing arts always will transcend professional union's astronomical costs." Mr. Coe served as a commentator on NBC, WRC from 1969 to 1975 and has been a panelist on radio and television programs.

ADDRESS: Home—2101 Connecticut Avenue, Washington, DC 20008. Agent—Potomac Speakers, 3001 Veazy Terrace N.W. Washington, DC 20008.

* * *

COFFIN, Frederick (D.), actor, composer, and playwright

PERSONAL: Born January 16, 1943; son of Dean F. (a writer) and Winnifred (an actress; maiden name, DeForest) Coffin; married Barbara Monte-Britton (an actress) on September 25, 1977. EDUCATION: Western Reserve Academy, 1957–61; University of Michigan, B.A., M.A., 1961–67; Wayne State University, 1967–69; studied movement, speech and stage combat.

CAREER: DEBUT—Member of Touring and Resident Company, Center Stage in Baltimore, MD, 1969–71. NEW YORK DEBUT—Mickey, *The Basic Training of Pavlo Hummel*, New York Shakespeare Festival, for five months of performances followed by two additional months, 1972. PRINCIPAL STAGE APPEARANCES—Eliot Rosewater, *God Bless You Mr. Rosewater*, Entermedia, NY, 1979; Borachio, *Much Ado About Nothing*, Winter Garden, NY, 1974; Ralphie, *In the Boom Boom Room*, Lincoln Center, NY, 1975; MAJOR TOURS—Football Player, *Wonderful Town*, 1978; *Room Service*, 1979.

FILM DEBUT—Teacher, *King of the Gypsies*. PRINCIPAL FILM APPEARANCES—*Concealed Enemies; Without a Trace*. TELEVISION DEBUT—*Much Ado About Nothing*. PRINCIPAL TELEVISION APPEARANCES—*Kojak; Andros Targets; One of the Boys; Love Sydney; Edge of Night; Ryan's Hope; Search for Tomorrow; Another World; The Dain Curse; Invasion of Privacy; Death Penalty*.

THEATRE-RELATED CAREER: Teacher of Speech and Acting, Wayne State University, 1968–69; teacher of Children's Drama, Oakland University, 1963–.

WRITINGS: PLAY, UNPUBLISHED—Moving. SONGS—"The Roach Motel," published, 1983.

ADDRESS: 820 West End Avenue, New York, NY, 10025. Agent—STE Representation, 888 Seventh Avenue, New York, NY, 10019.

COGAN, David J., producer, theatre owner, artists representative

PERSONAL: Born July 24, 1923, in Rumania; brought to U.S., 1923; naturalized 1928; son of Morris (a manufacturer) and Helen (Meyers) Cogan; married Ferne, 1946. EDUCATION: St. John's University, B.B.S., 1945. MILITARY: U.S. Army.

CAREER: PRODUCED: PLAYS—*A Raisin in the Sun* (with Philip Rose), Barrymore, NY, 1959; *The Midnight Sun* (with Howard Erskine and Joseph Hayes), Shubert, New Haven, CT, Wilbur, Boston, MA, 1959; *In the Counting House*, Biltmore, NY, 1962. PRODUCED: FILMS—*Run Across the River*, 1954.

RELATED CAREERS—Owner, Biltmore and Plaza Theaters, NY; owner, Viking Theater, Philadelphia, PA; instructor, theater production and management, New School for Social Research, NY, 1971–present; partner, Cogan and Bell and Company, NY, 1955–present; president, David J. Cogan Agency, NY, 1955–present; president, Cogan Management, Inc., NY, 1968–present.

AWARDS: New York Drama Critics Circle Award, Best American Play, 1959: *A Raisin in the Sun;* Emmy Award, 1970.

SIDELIGHTS: MEMBERSHIPS—National Society of Public Accountants, Actors Studio (board of directors), League of New York Theatre Owners Association, New York Chapter of the American Red Cross, Young Children's Music School and Dance (director), Berkshire Theatre Festival, Eugene O'Neill Foundation.

ADDRESS: Office—350 Fifth Avenue, New York, NY 10001.

* * *

COHEN, Alexander H., producer

PERSONAL: Born July 24, 1920, in New York City; son of Alexander H. and Laura (Tarantous) Cohen; married Jocelyn Newmark (divorced); Hildy Parks. EDUCATION: New York University; Columbia University.

CAREER: FIRST STAGE WORK—Producer, *Ghost for Sale*, Daly's, NY, 1941. PRINCIPAL STAGE WORK—Produced or co-produced: *Bright Lights*, 1943; *The Duke in Darkness*, 1944; *Jenny Kissed Me*, 1948; *King Lear*, 1950; *Make a Wish, Courtin' Time*, 1951; *Be Your Age*, 1953; *The Magic and The Loss*, 1954; *The First Gentleman*, 1957; *Love Me Little*, 1958; *At the Drop of a Hat*, 1959; *An Evening with Mike Nichols and Elaine May*, 1960; *An Evening with Yves Montand*, Lena Horne in her *Nine O'Clock Revue*, 1961; *Beyond the Fringe*, 1962; *The School for Scandal, An Evening with Maurice Chevalier, Lorenzo, Ages of Man* (with Sir Gielgud), *Karmon Israeli Dancers, Man and Boy*, 1963; *Rugantino, Hamlet* (Richard Burton), *Comedy in Music* (Victor Borge), 1964; *Baker Street, Maurice Chevalier at 77, The Devils*, 1965; *Ivanov, A Time for Singing, At the Drop of Another Hat*, 1966; *The Homecoming, White Lies, Black Comedy, Little Murders, The Unknown Soldier and His Wife, Marlene Dietrich, Halfway Up the Tree, Hellzapoppin'* at Montreal Expo, '67, *Marlene Dietrich,* 1968; *Dear World,* 1970; *Fun City, 6 Rms Riv Vu,* 1972; *Good Evening,* 1973; *Ulysses in Nighttown, Words and Music, Who's Who in Hell,* 1974; *Comedians,* 1976; *Anna Christie,* 1977; *I Remember Mama,* 1979; *A Day in Hollywood/A Night in the Ukraine,* 1980; *84 Charing Cross Road,* 1982; Ben Kingsley as *Edmund Kean,* Peter Brook's *La Tragedie de Carmen,* 1983; *Play Memory,* 1984.

London productions—*The Doctor's Dilemma, Man and Boy,* 1963; *The Roses Are Real, Season of Goodwill,* 1964; *Ivanov,* 1965; *You Never Can Tell, The Importance of Being Oscar, The Rivals,* 1966; *Halfway Up the Tree, The Merchant of Venice,* 1967; *Plaza Suite, The Price, Mixed Doubles, His, Hers, Theirs,* 1969; *Come As You Are, The Happy Apple, Who Killed Santa Claus?, 1776,* 1970; *Applause,* 1972; *Harvey,* 1975; *Overheard,* 1981; *Beethoven's Tenth,* 1983, NY, 1984.

PRINCIPAL TELEVISION WORK—Producer: since 1967 has produced the annual television coverage of the *Antoinette Perry Awards,* presented live from a New York theatre; *A World of Love,* for UNICEF; *CBS: On the Air (A Celebration of 50 Years); Emmy Awards Show,* 1978; The Centennial Celebration of the Actors Fund of America: *Night of 100 Stars; Parade of Stars; The Best of Everything.*

THEATRE-RELATED CAREER: Founder of the Nine O'Clock Theatre.

AWARDS: Sam S. Shubert Award, 1962–63.

SIDELIGHTS: MEMBERSHIPS—Vice-President and member of board of governors, League of New York Theatres and Producers; director, Independent Booking Office; vice-president and trustee, Actor's Fund of America; Society of West End Theatre; Players Club; City Athletic Club; Friars Club.

ADDRESS: Office—Shubert Theatre, 225 W. 44th Street, New York, NY, 10036; London Office—Eight Sloane Street, London, SW1, England.

* * *

COHEN, Edward M., director, playwright

PERSONAL: Born April 15, 1936 in New York, NY; son of Harry M. (an attorney) and Betty (Mendell) Cohen; married Sheila Miller in 1955 (divorced 1959); married Susan Simon (a psychoanalyst) on June 22, 1969; children: Noel, Joy.

CAREER: PRINCIPAL STAGE WORK, DIRECTED—Jewish Repertory, NY—*The Cold Wind and the Warm,* 1977, *Unlikely Heroes,* 1979, *Liliom,* 1979, *Me and Molly,* 1980, *Elephants,* 1981, *Taking Steam,* 1983 also at Leah Posluns, Toronto, Canada, 1983; *Night Thoughts,* Theatre at St. Clements, 1973; *Urlicht,* Playwrights Horizons, 1974; *Typhoid Mary,* Theatre Genesis, NY, 1974; *Zero Sum,* Cubiculo, NY, 1975; *Apple Pie,* (workshop) New York Shakespeare Festival, 1975; *Cakes with Wine,* Playwrights Horizons, Queens Festival Playhouse, 1976; *Dances with Words,* Cubiculo, NY, 1976; *Once and For All,* Cubiculo, 1976; *Pop-a-Few,* Playwrights Horizons, 1977; *Benny Leonard*

and the Brooklyn Bridge, Open Space, NY, 1977; *Beethoven/Karl,* Green Gate Summer Theatre, 1977, Queens Festival Playhouse, 1975, Playwrights Horizons, 1975; *Candida,* Green Gate Summer Theatre, 1977; *The Hot L Baltimore,* Sarah Lawrence College, 1978; *When Petulia Comes,* Playwrights Horizons, 1976, Theatre Genesis, 1978; *Old Times,* Green Gate Summer Theatre, 1978; *Canzada and the Boys,* Hudson Guild, NY, 1978; *Any Wednesday,* Little Theatre of Winston-Salem, NC, 1979; *La Musica/The Square,* White Barn, 1979; *The Childrens Hour,* Sarah Lawrence College, 1980; *Home Bodies,* Playwrights Horizons, 1980; *The Loves of Shirley Abramowitz,* International Festival of Jewish Theatre, Tel Aviv University, 1982, Jewish Repertory, NY, 1982, Ensemble Studio Theatre, 1981.

WRITINGS: PLAYS, PRODUCED—*Breeding Ground,* Albee-Barr Playwrights Unit, 1971; *The Complaint Department Closes At Five,* O'Neill Theatre Center, Playwrights Conference, 1971, Mercer Arts Center, 1972, Manhattan Theatre Club, 1973, NY Cultural Center, 1973; *A Gorgeous Piece,* actors Studio Playwrights Unit, 1972; *Two Girls and a Sailor,* Theatre at St. Clements, 1973; *Cakes With Wine,* Albee-Barr Playwrights Unit, 1971, New Dramatists Committee, 1975, Queens Festival Playhouse, 1976, Playwrights Horizons, 1976; *The Last Stage of Labor,* New Dramatists Committee, 1978, Playwrights Horizons, 1979.

THEATRE-RELATED CAREER: Script reader, Playwrights Horizons, 1977–80; CETA Panel Review Board Member, Hospital Audiences, Inc., 1979; Consultant on Playwriting Projects, National Foundation for Jewish Culture, 1980–present; Literary Advisor, Jewish Repertory Theatre, NY, 1979–present.

AWARDS: Directing Fellowship, National Endowment for the Arts, 1982–83; John Golden Award, *Cakes With Wine,* 1976; Playwright in Residence, Playwrights Horizons, 1975–76; Fellow, Edward Albee Foundation, 1972–75; Fellow, National Playwrights Conference, O'Neill Theatre Center, 1971.

SIDELIGHTS: MEMBERSHIPS—New Dramatists Committee, 1973–80; Actors Studio, 1972; O'Neill Playwrights, Chairman, 1972; Dramatists Guild; SSD&C.

Mr. Cohen has served as guest lecturer at Hebrew University College, Hunter College, New York University, Manhattan Marymount College and Fairleigh Dickinson University.

ADDRESS: Home—949 West End Avenue, New York, NY 10025.

* * *

COLEMAN, Nancy, actress

PERSONAL: Born December 30, 1917 in Everett, WA; daughter of Charles Sumner (a newspaper editor) and Grace (a violinist; maiden name Sharpless) Coleman; married Whitney Bolton (a newscaster, columnist, and critic), August 16, 1943 (died 1969); children: Charle, Grania (twins). EDUCATION: trained for the stage with Reginald Trevers, Harold Clurman, and Stella Adler.

NANCY COLEMAN

CAREER: NEW YORK DEBUT—Blossom, *Susan and God*, Plymouth, New York, 1938. PRINCIPAL STAGE APPEARANCES—Liberty, *Liberty Jones*, Shubert, New York, 1941; Ellen, *The Male Animal*, Music Box, New York, 1953; Eleanor Hilliard, *The Desperate Hours*, Music Box, New York, 1955. MAJOR TOURS—Blossom, *Susan and God*, U.S. cities and Canada, 1938–39; Laura, *The Glass Menagerie*, Europe and Latin America, 1961; Kate Keller, *The Miracle Worker*, Latin America, 1961; Edith, *Never Too Late*, South Africa, 1964; Cora, *Morning's at Seven*, Florida and Atlanta, 1981.

FILM DEBUT—Louise Gordon, *King's Row*, 1941. PRINCIPAL FILM APPEARANCES—Jane, *Dangerously They Live*, 1941; Susanna, *The Gay Sisters*, 1942; Kaethe Brahms, *Desperate Journey*, 1942; Katia, *The Edge of Darkness*, 1943; Janina, *In Our Time*; 1944; Anne Brontë, *Devotion*, 1946; Toni Dubois, *Her Sister's Secret*, 1947; Ann Mason, *Violence*, 1947; Hazel Niles, *Mourning Becomes Electra*, 1947; Mary Ellen Saunders, *That Man from Tangier*, 1953; Mrs. Stillwell, *Slaves*, 1969. PRINCIPAL RADIO APPEARANCES—*Hawthorne House; Winning the West; Death Valley Days; Tales of California; Grand Central Station; Young Doctor Malone*. TELEVISION DEBUT—*Kraft Theatre*, 1949. PRINCIPAL TELEVISION APPEARANCES—*The Edge of Night*, 1966; *You Are There*, 1972; *The Adams Chronicles*, 1976; *Colgate Theatre; Studio One; Lux Theatre; Theatre Guild Playhouse; Producer's Showcase; Philco Playhouse; Kraft Theatre; Robert Montgomery Presents; Alcoa; Valiant Lady; Play of the Week*.

SIDELIGHTS: MEMBERSHIPS—Actors Equity Association,

Screen Actors Guild, AFTRA, National Academy of Television Arts and Sciences, American Film Institute.

ADDRESS: Agent—c/o D.M.I. Talent Associates, Ltd., 250 W. 57th Street, New York, NY 10107.

* * *

COLLAMORE, Jerome, actor, writer

PERSONAL: Born September 25, 1891 in Somerville, MA; son of Joshua Thomas (in real estate) and Margaret Fuller (Collamore) Butler; married Helena Claire Benedict (an actress) on January 16, 1917. EDUCATION: Attended public schools. Studied with S. M. Munro (a former actor) for two years. RELIGION: Mormon.

CAREER: DEBUT—Jimmy Valentine, *Alais*, Rand's Opera House, Troy, NY, 1912. NEW YORK DEBUT—*Salome*, Washington Square Players, Comedy Theatre, 1917. PRINCIPAL STAGE APPEARANCES—*Mr. Barnum*, with Tom Wise, Criterion, New York, 1918; *Her Honor the Mayor*, Fulton, New York; *The Good Men Do*, Fulton, New York, 1918; *The Awakening*, Criterion, New York, 1918; *Potiphar's Wife; Freddy; Jacob Slovak; Would-Be Gentleman; Hamlet*, with Walter Hampden; *Hamlet* with E. H. Sothern and Julia Marlowe; *Taming of the Shrew*, with Sothern and Marlowe; *Twelfth Night*, with Sothern and Marlowe; *The Merchant of Venice*, with Sothern and Marlowe; *Abraham Cochran; Cheri; Romeo and Juliet*, with Walter Hampden. MAJOR TOURS—*That Other Woman*, international circuit, 1916–17; Madam Bertha Kalich in *Magda, Riddle Woman*, 1926–27; *George Washington Slept Here*, with Ernest Truex; *Androcles and the Lion; Twelve Pound Look*, with Sylvia Field; *Witness for the Prosecution*, with Basil Rathbone; *Little Foxes*, with Ruth Chatterton; *Kind Lady*, with Sylvia Sydney; *Christopher Bean*, with Zasu Pitts; *Pleasure of His Company*, with Joan Bennett and Don Cook; *Golden Rainbow*. REGIONAL—California, *Romance*, with Doris Keane; *Czarina; Starlight;* Greek Theatre Berkley, CA with Margaret Anglin—*Hippolytus;* San Francisco—*Woman of No Importance; Charming Conscience; Great Lady Dedlock;* Missouri Repertory Theatre, 1981—Nonno, *Night of the Iguana;* Williamstown Theatre Festival, Williamstown, MA—Firs, *Cherry Orchard;* Brooklyn Academy of Music, *The New York Idea;* New York—*That Hat*, with Pierre Olaf.

PRINCIPAL FILM APPEARANCES—*Arthur; Annie; Klute; Funny Girl; To Find a Man; Grace Quigley*. TELEVISION DEBUT—Brand, *The Ivory Door*, NBC. PRINCIPAL TELEVISION APPEARANCES—*Cinderella; Meyerling; Little Moon of Alban; Mrs. Miniver; Arsenic and Old Lace; Saturday Night Live*. DIRECTED—*Woman of No Importance; Charming Conscience; Romance; Czarina; Starlight; Magda; Riddle Woman; Kreutzer Sonata*.

WRITINGS: Plays (one act)—*Those Dennett Girls; Family Reunion; Mazie from Carolina; Subversive*.

SIDELIGHTS: "Directed at the following schools: Marta Oatman's (L.A.), Alvenie (N.Y.). Helped found the Hilda Spong Dramatic School and directed there. (N.Y.C.)"

ADDRESS: Home—147-05 Sanford Ave., Flushing NY 11355.

Agent—Marje Fields, 165 W. 46th Street, New York, NY 10036.

* * *

COLLINS, Robert, director, writer, designer

PERSONAL: Born June 1, 1930; son of Bert (a businessman) and Ethel Lillian (Pink) Collins. EDUCATION: University of California, Los Angeles, 1953, B.A.

CAREER: PRINCIPAL TELEVISION WORK: Director—*Quality of Mercy*, 1974; *Huey Long*, 1975; *Serpico*, 1976; *Gideon's Trumpet*, 1980. PRINCIPAL FILM WORK—Director—*Walk Proud*, 1978; *Savage Harvest*, 1981.

WRITINGS: TELEVISION PILOTS—*Police Woman; Moving On; Serpico.* EPISODES OF A SERIES—*Police Story.* TELEVISION MOVIES—*Quality of Mercy; Huey Long.*

AWARDS: Christopher, 1980: *Gideon's Trumpet;* Writers Guild of America, 1975: *Quality of Mercy;* Image from the NAACP, 1975; Edgar from Mystery Writers of America, 1974; Emmy Nominations, *Quality of Mercy, Huey Long.*

SIDELIGHTS: MEMBERSHIPS—Directors Guild, Writers Guild, IATSE, ACMPS, ATVS.

ADDRESS: Office—760 W. La Cienega Blvd., Los Angeles, CA 90069. Agent—Bill Haber, Creative Artists Agency, 1888 Century Park E., Suite 1400, Los Angeles, CA 90067.

* * *

COMMIRE, Anne, writer, director

PERSONAL: Born August 11; daughter of Robert (in U.S. Navy) and Shirley (Moore) Commire. EDUCATION: Eastern Michigan University, B.S., 1961; attended New York University and Wayne State University. NON-THEATRICAL CAREER: Editor, *Something About the Author*, Gale Research Company, 1973–present.

WRITINGS: PLAYS, PRODUCED—*Shay*, O'Neill Theatre Center's Playwright's Conference, CT, 1973, Westport Country Playhouse, CT, 1974, Playwrights Horizons, NY, 1978, London and Edinburgh, UK, 1979; *Put Them All Together*, O'Neill Center's Playwright's Conference, CT, 1978, Mc-Carter, Princeton, NJ, 1978, WPA Theatre, NY, 1979, broadcast on *Earplay*, 1979; *Melody Sisters*, O'Neill Theatre Center's Playwright's Conference, CT, 1983, Public Theatre, Los Angeles, 1984, presented on ABC Television, 1984. PLAYS, PUBLISHED—*Shay*, 1979; *Put Them All Together*, 1982.

AWARDS: ABC Television Theatre Award, *Melody Sisters*, 1984; Rockefeller Grant in Playwriting, 1979; New York State Council on the Arts CAPS Grant for the play *Shay*, 1974.

SIDELIGHTS: MEMBERSHIPS—Writer's Guild of America, East; Dramatists Guild.

"As Dorothy Parker once said: 'Hate writing; love having written.'"

ADDRESS: Home—81R Oswegatchie Rd. Waterford, CT 06385 and 274 W. 95th Street, New York, NY 10025. Office—#306, 345 W. 86th Street, New York, NY 10024. Agent—Esther Sherman, William Morris Agency, 1350 Avenue of the Americas, New York, NY 10019.

* * *

CONCANNON, John N., stage manager

PERSONAL: Born May 28, 1946; son of John M. and Mildred M. (Barrett) Concannon. EDUCATION: Marquette University, B.A. (Speech-Theatre) 1968; University of Connecticut, M.A. (Dramatic Arts) 1974.

MILITARY: U.S. Army Infantry, Specialist 4th Class.

CAREER: STAGE MANAGEMENT—*Plain and Fancy*, Equity Library, NY, 1980; *Bishop Street*, White Barn, Westport, CT, 1980; *Jane Avril*, White Barn, 1980; *Sittin*, Ensemble Studio, NY, 1980; *The Freak*, WPA, NY, 1981; *Broadway Salutes Off-Broadway*, Theatre de Lys, NY, 1981; *The Waltz of the Stork*, INTAR, NY, 1981; *Life Is a Dream*, INTAR, 1981; *Bodybags*, INTAR, 1981; *The Waltz of the Stork*, Century, NY, 1982; *The Learned Ladies*, Roundabout, NY, 1982; *Bugles at Dawn*, American Theatre of Actors, NY, 1983; *Marat/Sade*, NYU School of the Arts, 1983; *Talley's Folly*, Greeley St. Theatre, Chappaqua, NY, 1983; *Star-blast*, 1983; *Hurray for Hollywood*, St. Regis Hotel, NY, 1983; *It's Hard to Be a Jew*, American Jewish Theatre, 1984. MAJOR TOURS—*The High-Heeled Woman* (comedy troupe), 1983–84. Others—Production Assistant, *Alice in Wonderland*, Virginia, NY, 1982; assistant Stage Manager, *A Christmas Carol*, Ford's, Washington, DC, 1979–80; Stage Manager/Lighting Designer, Timothy Gray and The Sound (Nightclub group), 1981.

AWARDS: U.S. Army Bronze Star and Army Commendation Medal with Oak Leaf Cluster.

SIDELIGHTS: MEMBERSHIPS—Stage Managers' Association.

ADDRESS: Home—127 W. 82nd Street, New York, NY 10024.

* * *

CONNOLLY, Michael (ne James M. Connolly, Jr.), actor

PERSONAL: Born September 22, 1947; son of James Michael (an engineer and writer) and Mary Louise (a writer; maiden name Ross) Connolly. EDUCATION: Fordham College, Fordham University, Bronx, NY. RELIGION: Catholic.

CAREER: DEBUT—Jim Warrington, *Little Mary Sunshine*, Bonner Playhouse, Redding, CT, 1967. NEW YORK DEBUT—Steven Hench, *Otherwise Engaged*, Plymouth, 1977. PRINCIPAL STAGE APPEARANCES—Pepe Lubauer, *Break a Leg*, Palace, New York, 1979; Gerald Murphy, *Clothes for a*

Summer Hotel, Cort, New York, 1980; Mr. Murdstone, *Copperfield*, ANTA, New York, 1981; Venticello #1, *Amadeus*, Broadhurst, New York, 1982–83. MAJOR TOURS—Dr. Watson, *Sherlock Holmes*, U.S. and Canada, 1976; Bert Healy and Drake, *Annie*, U.S. and Canada, 1978; Max Jacobs, *On the Twentieth Century*, U.S., 1979.

FILM DEBUT—Maître d'hôtel, *Hanky Panky*, 1982. PRINCIPAL FILM APPEARANCES—Maître d'hôtel, *The Muppets Take Manhattan*, 1984. TELEVISION DEBUT—Mr. Klemp, *Another World*. PRINCIPAL TELEVISION APPEARANCES—Designer to Mrs. Kennedy, *Kennedy*, 1983; Kurt (kidnapper), *Search for Tomorrow*.

SIDELIGHTS: MEMBERSHIPS—The Players Club. FAVORITE ROLES: Elwood P. Dowd, *Harvey*, Elyot in *Private Lives*, Thomas More, *A Man for All Seasons*, Scrooge, *A Christmas Carol;* Operatic: Germont in *La Traviata*, Barnaba in *La Gioconda*, Scarpia in *Tosca*, Rodrigo, *Don Carlo*, Bartolo in *Barber of Seville*, Marcello, *Le Boheme*. RECREATION—gardening and music, especially 19th-century Italian opera. Foreign languages: Italian, French. Recital repertoire includes songs and arias in nine languages. Operatic repertoire (baritone and bass), 57 roles. Gilbert and Sullivan repertoire (comic and lead baritone) includes 22 roles.

ADDRESS: Home—300 W. 49th Street, New York, NY 10019. Agent—Monty Silver, 200 W. 57th Street, New York, NY 10019.

* * *

CONNOR, Whitfield, actor

PERSONAL: Born December 3, 1916, in Rathdowney, Ireland; son of James (an engineer) and Eleanor (Wilde) Connor; married Haila Stoddard (an actress and producer), in 1956. EDUCATION: Wayne State University, B.A., 1940; University of Michigan, M.A., 1941. MILITARY: U.S. Coast Guard Reserve, 1942–46.

CAREER: DEBUT—Horatio, *Hamlet*, Columbus Circle Theater, New York, 1935. PRINCIPAL STAGE APPEARANCES—Antonio Bologna, *The Duchess of Malfi*, Ethel Barrymore, 1946; Lt. Aengus Macogue, *Kathleen*, Mansfield, 1948, Macduff, *Macbeth*, National, 1948; David Browning, *The Winner*, Playhouse, 1954; Will Harrison, *Lunatics and Lovers*, Broadhurst, 1954; Father, *Six Characters in Search of an Author*, Phoenix, 1955; Suitor, *The Makropolous Secret*, Phoenix, 1957; Victor Milgrim, *The Disenchanted*, Coronet, 1958; Mr. Newton, *There Was a Little Girl*, Cort, 1960; Chuck, *Everything in the Garden*, Plymouth, 1967; Thomas A. Morgan, *In the Matter of J. Robert Oppenheimer*, Vivian Beaumont, 1969; (Stock) six seasons, Elitch Gardens, Denver, CO. MAJOR TOURS—*Janus and the Complaisant Lover*, summer theaters.

PRINCIPAL FILM APPEARANCES—*Tap Roots*, 1948; *The Scarlet Angel*, 1952; *The President's Lady*, 1953; *Prince of Pirates*, 1953; *City of Bad Men*, 1953; *The Saracen Blade*, 1954; *Butterfield 8*, 1960. PRINCIPAL TELEVISION APPEARANCES—*Willy*, 1953; *Omnibus; Studio One; The Guiding Light*.

AWARDS: Theatre World Award, 1948: *Macbeth*.

SIDELIGHTS: MEMBERSHIPS—AEA, SAG, AFTRA, Council of Stock Theatres (President, 1968–72). RECREATION—Tennis, swimming, reading, Irish poetry.

ADDRESS: Home—5 Ladder Hill Road South, Weston, CT 06880.

* * *

CONROY, Kevin, actor

PERSONAL: Born November 30, 1955; son of Thomas F. and Patricia A. O'Connor. EDUCATION: graduate of the Juilliard Theatre Centre.

CAREER: PRINCIPAL STAGE APPEARANCES—(Broadway) Dick, *Lolita;* (Off-Broadway) Laertes, *Hamlet*, and Lysander, *A Midsummer Night's Dream*, New York Shakespeare Festival Theatre; Donald, *Accounts*, Hudson Guild; (Regional) Achilles/Orestes, *The Greeks*, Hartford Stage; Edmund, *King Lear*, and Claudio, *Much Ado About Nothing*, San Diego Shakespeare Festival. MAJOR TOURS—Edgar, *King Lear*, Eilif, *Mother Courage*, Florizel, *Chapeau*, Lord Mulligan, *Camino Real*, U.S. cities; Oberon, *A Midsummer Night's Dream*, Bermuda Festival. PRINCIPAL TELEVISION APPEARANCES—Jerry Grove, *Another World;* Husband, *Born Beautiful;* Phil, *A Find Romance;* Ted Kennedy, *Kennedy;* John Laurens, *George Washington*.

ADDRESS: Agent—c/o Milton Goldman, International Creative Management, 40 W. 57th Street, New York NY 10019.

KEVIN CONROY

CONTI, Tom, actor, director

PERSONAL: Born November 22, 1941; son of Alfonso and Mary Conti; married Kara Wilson (an actress). EDUCATION: Hamilton Park School, Glasgow, Scotland; trained for the stage at the RSAMD, Glasgow.

CAREER: DEBUT—*The Roving Boy,* Citizens', Glasgow, January 1959. LONDON DEBUT—Carlos, *Savages,* Royal Court (then the Comedy), 1973. NEW YORK DEBUT—Ken Harrison, *Whose Life Is it, Anyway?,* Trafalgar, April, 1979. PRINCIPAL ENGAGEMENT—Harry Vine, *The Black and White Minstrels,* Edinburgh Festival, 1972; Ben, *Let's Murder Vivaldi,* King's Head, Islington, 1972; Harry Vine, *The Black and White Minstrels,* Hampstead, London, 1974; Enrico Zamati, *Other People,* Hampstead, London, 1974; title role, *Don Juan,* Hampstead, London, 1976; Dick Dudgeon, *The Devil's Disciple,* Royal Shakespeare, London, 1978; Ken Harrison, *Whose Life Is It, Anyway?,* Mermaid, then the Savoy, London, 1978.

DIRECTED: PLAYS—*Last Licks,* Longacre, NY, 1979; *Before the Party,* Oxford Playhouse and Queens, London, 1980.

FILM DEBUT—*Galileo,* 1974. FILM APPEARANCES—*Full Circle; The Duellists,* 1978; *Merry Christmas, Mr. Lawrence,* 1983; *Reuben, Reuben,* 1983.

TELEVISION DEBUT—*Mother of Men,* 1959. TELEVISION APPEARANCES—*The Glittering Prizes; Madame Bovary,* Norman, *The Norman Conquests.*

AWARDS: Antoinette Perry Award, Best Actor, 1979: *Whose Life Is It, Anyway?;* Bronze Bust, Theatre Museum—Victoria and Albert Museum of London; Academy Award Nomination, Best Actor, 1983: *Reuben, Reuben.*

SIDELIGHTS: RECREATION—Flamenco guitar.

ADDRESS: Agent—c/o Chatto and Linnit, Globe Theatre, Shaftesbury Avenue, London W1, England.*

* * *

CONVY, Bert, actor

PERSONAL: Born July 23, 1934, in St. Louis, MO; son of Bert Fleming and Monica (Whalen) Convy; married Anne Anderson; children: Jennifer, Joshua, Jonah. EDUCATION: North Hollywood High School; University of California at Los Angeles, BA, 1955; studied for the stage with Jeff Corey in Hollywood. NON-THEATRICAL CAREER—Played baseball with the Philadelphia Phillies farm team, 1951.

CAREER: DEBUT—Barnaby, *The Matchmaker,* Players Ring, Hollywood, CA, 1957. NEW YORK DEBUT—*The Billy Barnes Revue,* Golden, August 1959. PRINCIPAL STAGE APPEARANCES—Johnny, *A Tree Grows in Brooklyn,* Billy Bigelow, *Liliom,* Players Ring, Hollywood; *Vintage '60,* NY, 1960; *Nowhere to Go But up,* Winter Garden, NY, 1962; *The Beast in Me,* Plymouth, 1963; El Gallo, *The Fantasticks,* Sullivan Street Playhouse, NY, 1963; Rome, *Morning' Sun,* Phoenix, NY, 1963; Freddy Winters, *Love and Kisses,* Music Box, NY, 1963; Perchik, *Fiddler on the Roof,* Imperial, NY,

1964; Richard Merrick, *The Impossible Years,* Playhouse, NY, 1965; Clifford Bradshaw, *Cabaret,* Broadhurst, NY, 1966; Peter, *Shoot Anything with Hair That Moves,* Provincetown Playhouse, NY, 1969; Hildy Johnson, *The Front Page,* Ethel Barrymore, NY, May 1969 and October 1969; Guido Contini, *Nine,* 46th Street, NY, 1983. CONCEIVED AND DIRECTED—*Do It Again!,* Promenade, NY, 1971.

FILM DEBUT—*Gunman's Walk,* 1958. PRINCIPAL FILMS—*Susan Slade,* 1962; *Act One,* 1963; *Giver Her the Moon,* 1969; *John Goldfarb, Please Come Home,* 1964.

TELEVISION APPEARANCES—*Alfred Hitchcock Presents; Perry Mason; The Untouchables; The Nurses; East Side/West Side; Navy Log; Love of Life; To Tell the Truth; What's My Line?;* host, *The Late Fall, Early Summer Bert Convy Show,* 1976; Lt. Ostrowski, *The Snoop Sisters* 1973–74; host, *Tattletales,* 1974; *ABC After School Specials; The Man in the Santa Claus Suit* (TV film), 1979; *It's Not Easy,* 1983.

THEATRE-RELATED CAREER—Part of singing group, The Cheers, 1960.

AWARDS: Emmy, Game Show Host, 1976–77: *Tattletales;* Emmy Nomination, Best Actor, 1974–75: *Oh, Baby, Baby* (ABC Afternoon Playbreak).*

* * *

COOGAN, Jackie (ne John Leslie Coogan), actor

PERSONAL: Born October 26, 1914; died March 1, 1984; son of John (a vaudeville performer and Jackie's manager) and Lillian (a child star; maiden name Dolliver) Coogan; married Betty Grable in 1937 (divorced 1939); Dorothy (Dodi) Lahphere (a dancer and actress) on May 27, 1950; children: (first marriage) Anthony, Joan; (second marriage) Leslie, Christopher. EDUCATION: Attended Santa Clara University and University of Southern California; was tutored from an early age by his father, John Coogan, Sr. MILITARY: U.S. Army, Medical Corps, 1940; U.S. Air Force (glider pilot), 1940–44.

CAREER: DEBUT—Appeared with his father (dancing) at the Orpheum, Los Angeles, 1919. LONDON DEBUT—Vaudeville act with John Coogan, Sr., performed special material plus solo, Near East tour, 1924. PRINCIPAL STAGE APPEARANCES—*Make a Million,* 1968; *Sweet Bird of Youth,* 1968; *The Odd Couple,* 1969; *Come Blow Your Horn,* 1969; *The Music Man,* 1971.

MAJOR TOURS—Vaudeville show with father, 1928–29; vaudeville shows, 30 weeks, 1935; tour with Jackie Coogan Orchestra, Betty Grable vocalist, nine months, 1937; night club show, *What a Life,* 21 weeks, 1940; European vaudeville tour, 1938; summer tours with Ted Cassidey, 1963–65; *Blue Denim,* Canada, 1967; U.S. and Europe with Donald O'Connor, 1950; *Brother Rat,* NY; *Take Me Along,* Buffalo, NY.

FILM DEBUT—*Skinner's Baby,* 1916. PRINCIPAL FILM APPEARANCES—*The Kid,* 1919–20; *Peck's Bad Boy,* 1920; *My Boy,* 1921; *Trouble,* 1921; *Daddy,* 1922; *Circus Days,* 1922; *Oliver Twist,* 1923; *Long Live the King,* 1924; *Boy of*

Flanders, 1924; *Little Robinson Crusoe*, 1925; *Ragman*, 1925; *Old Clothes*, 1925; *Johnny Get Your Hair Cut*, 1925; *Bugle Call*, 1927; *Buttons et Lou*, 1926; *Tom Sawyer*, 1930; *Huckleberry Finn*, 1931; *Home on the Range*, 1933; *College Swing*, 1938; *Million Dollar Legs*, 1939; *The Joker Is Wild*, 1957; *The Actress*, 1958; *A Fine Madness*, 1965; *The Shakiest Gun in the West*, 1967; *Roques Gallery*, 1967; *Shakiest Gun in the World*, 1969. TELEVISION DEBUT—*Irwin Allen Show*, 1947. PRINCIPAL TELEVISION APPEARANCES—Series: *Pantomine Quiz*, 1948–56; *McKeever and the Colonel*, 1960s; *Cowboy G-Men*, 1951–53; *The Addams Family*, 1963–65. Guest Appearances—*Playhouse 90*, 1955; *Frank Sinatra Special*, *Milton Berle Show*, *Bob Hope Show*, *Suspense*, *Red Skelton Show*, 1956–59, *Joey Bishop Show*, 1967; *U Don't Say*, 1967; *Truth or Consequences*, 1967; *Woody Woodbury Show*, 1967; *The Name of the Game*, 1969; *The Interns*, 1970; *Jeanie*, 1970; *Partridge Family*, 1970; *Stump the Stars*, 1970; *Barefoot in the Park*, 1970; *Matt Lincoln*, 1970.

AWARDS: Emmy Nomination, *Forbidden Area, Playhouse 90*, 1955; Distinguished Flying Cross; Unit Citation; Presidential Citation; The Order of King George, The Greek Orthodox Cross, The Papal Medal, and the Phi-Philippine Order in Rome along with a locket containing a piece of the "true cross" for collecting clothes and food for the starving children of Greece, 1924.

SIDELIGHTS: "At the age of six, Jackie Coogan was a millionaire with Jackie Coogan Productions, under the directions of his father, doing a multimillion dollar business. His childhood was sheltered in a tinsel world of mansions, swimming pools, 10 custom built Rolls Royces, with a special chair built-in for "The Kid" that was really a stationary upholstered swivel rocker. He lived in a world of adults and at a very early age learned to hunt and fish under the able tutelage of his dad, who was his constant companion. His love of the outdoors, developed a such an early age, remained one of the most important aspects of his life. He did a great deal of flying, golfing, fishing and hunting. His favorite indoor hobby was cooking. Jackie was considered one of the finest gourmets in the non-pro field. He was the only theatrical personality to have a law named for him—the 'Jackie Coogan Law' also known as the child labor law."

* * *

COOK, Roderick, actor, director

PERSONAL: Born 1932, in London, England; EDUCATION: Cambridge University, B.A., 1953.

CAREER: DEBUT—Feste, *Twelfth Night*, directed by Peter Hall. NEW YORK DEBUT (BROADWAY)—*Kean* (with Alfred Drake). PRINCIPAL STAGE APPEARANCES—London, *Listen to the Wind*, *Waiting for Godot*, *Waltz of the Toreadors*, *Zuleika*, *Share My Lettuce* (revue); New York, *The Girl Who Came to Supper*, *Roar Like a Dove*, *Hadrian VII*, *A Scent of Flowers*, *The Man Who Came to Dinner*, *Woman of the Year*; REGIONAL THEATRE ENGAGEMENTS—The Devil, *Don Juan in Hell*, Alley Theatre, Houston, TX; Ernest, *Design for Living*, with Maggie Smith, Music Center, Los Angeles, CA, and The Kennedy Center for the Performing Arts, Washington, D.C.

PRINCIPAL FILM APPEARANCES—*The Great Waldo Pepper*, *Girl Friends*, *Silent Madness*, *Amadeus*. PRINCIPAL TELEVISION APPEARANCES—*The Guiding Light*, *Search for Tomorrow*, *One Life to Live* (as twins).

DIRECTED: *Present Laughter*, with Peter O'Toole; *Uncle Vanya* (also played Vanya in production). OFF-BROADWAY—devised, produced, directed, and starred in *Oh Coward!*, which moved to London, Los Angeles, Washington, D.C. San Francisco, and many regional companies over the past few years.

SIDELIGHTS: RECREATION—needlepoint and serendipity.

ADDRESS: Agent—Monty Silver, 200 W. 57th St. New York, NY 10019.

* * *

COOPER, Hal, director, writer, producer

PERSONAL: Born February 23, 1923, in New York City; son of Benjamin (a merchant) and Adeline (Rachimov) Cooper; married Pat Meikle, 1945 (divorced 1970; died 1972); Marta Lucille Salcido (an artist), June 26, 1971; children: (first marriage) Bethami, Pamela; (second marriage) James Benjamin. EDUCATION: University of Michigan, B.A., 1946 (attended 1940–43, 1946). MILITARY: U.S. Navy, 1943–46.

CAREER: DEBUT—Child actor in radio programs from 1932. TELEVISION DEBUT—Child actor, *Bob Emery's Rainbow House*, Mutual, 1936–46. PRINCIPAL TELEVISION WORK—Writer/producer, *Your School Reporter*, *TV Baby Sitter*, DuMont, 1948–52, *The Magic Cottage*, 1950–56; director, *Valiant Lady*, *Search for Tomorrow*, *Portia Faces Life*, CBS-TV; director/associate producer, *Kitty Foyle*, NBC-TV, 1950–57; producer/director, *Indictment*, Paramount TV; associate producer/director, *The Happy Time*, Paramount TV; producer/director, *For Better or Worse*, CBS-TV; director, *The Clear Horizon*, CBS-TV; associate producer/director, *Surprise Package*, CBS-TV; director, *The Dick Van Dyke Show*; producer/director, *The Art Linkletter Show;* producer/director, *The Object Is;* directed episodes of *Death Valley Days*, *I Dream of Jeannie*, *That Girl*, *I Spy*, *Hazel*, *Gidget*, *Gilligan's Island*, *NYPD*, *Mayberry RFD*, *Courtship of Eddie's Father*, *It's My World and Welcome to It*, *Odd Couple*, *Mary Tyler Moore Show*, *All in the Family;* executive producer/director: *Maude*, 1972–78, *Phyl and Mikky*, 1980, *Love, Sidney*, 1982–83, *Gimme a Break*, 1983–84.

PRINCIPAL STAGE WORK—Assistant director, Dock Street Theatre, Charleston, SC, 1946–48; Butler, *First Lady*, City Center, 1951; producer, *The Troublemakers*, Strand, London, 1951.

WRITINGS: TELEVISION—*The Magic Cottage*, 1950–56; *TV Baby Sitter*, 1948–50.

AWARDS: Three Emmy Nominations, four Directors Guild Nominations, Best Comedy Director: *Maude*.

SIDELIGHTS: MEMBERSHIPS—National board member since

1960, various offices including secretary, Directors Guild; AFTRA; SAG; AEA; Writers Guild; ASCAP.

ADDRESS: Home—2651 Hutton Drive, Beverly Hills, CA 90210. Agent—Major Talent Agency, 11812 San Vicente Blvd., Suite 510, Los Angeles, CA 90049.

* * *

COPELAND, MAURICE D., actor

PERSONAL: Born June 13, 1911; son of William Gentry (a contractor and farmer) Copeland; married Vera Myrtle Ammons; children: Michael, Maureen, Claudia. EDUCATION: Pasadena Playhouse, graduated 1938. POLITICS: Republican. RELIGION: Methodist.

CAREER: DEBUT—*The Thirteenth Chair*, Chicago. NEW YORK DEBUT—Judge, *Freedom of the City*, Alvin, 1974. PRINCIPAL STAGE APPEARANCES—*The Misanthrope*, Ravinia Festival, IL, 1968; *The Recruiting Officer*, Goodman, Chicago, 1969; Mr. Barrett, *The Barretts of Wimpole Street*, Goodman, Chicago; *Hogan's Goat, Rhinoceros, The Front Page*, Academy Playhouse, Wilmette, IL; also: *The Little Foxes, Papa Is All, Happy Birthday, The Solid Gold Cadillac, King Lear, Galileo; The Sugar Bowl*, New Dramatists, NY, 1978; *Henry V*, Off-Broadway; Associate Justice Waldo Thompson, *First Monday in October*, Majestic, NY, 1978; Theodore Swanson, *Mornings at Seven*, Lyceum, 1980.

MAJOR TOURS—Oscar, *The Royal Family; The Pleasure of His Company;* Theodore, *Mornings at Seven*, national, 1982.

PRINCIPAL FILM APPEARANCES—*The Seduction of Joe Tynan*, 1979; *Being There*, 1979; *Blow Out*, 1981; *Arthur*, 1981. TELEVISION APPEARANCES—Ralph Charm, *Those Endearing Young Charms*, (live series originating out of Chicago), 1951–52.

ADDRESS: Home—47 Rockwood Drive, Larchmont, NY 10538. Agent—Michael Thomas, 22 E. 60th Street, New York, NY 10022.

* * *

COPPOLA, Francis Ford, film writer, producer, director

PERSONAL: Born April 7, 1939, in Detroit, MI; son of Carmine (an arranger and composer) and Italia (Pennino) Coppola; married Eleanor Neil; children: three. EDUCATION: Hofstra University, B.A., 1958; UCLA, Master of Cinema, 1968.

CAREER: PRINCIPAL FILM WORK—Director, *Dementia 13*, 1964; writer, *This Property Is Condemned*, 1966; writer, *Is Paris Burning?*, 1966; director, *You're a Big Boy Now*, 1967; writer, *Reflections in a Golden Eye*, 1967; director, *Finian's Rainbow*, 1968; writer/director, *The Rain People*, 1969; writer, *Patton*, 1970; producer, *TXH 1138*, 1971; writer/producer/director, *The Godfather*, 1972; producer,

American Graffiti, 1973; writer/producer/director, *The Godfather, Part II*, 1974; writer/producer/director, *The Conversation*, 1974; writer, *The Great Gatsby*, 1974; writer/producer/director, *Apocalypse Now*, 1979; executive producer, *The Black Stallion*, 1979; executive producer, *Hammett;* co-writer/producer/director, *One from the Heart*, 1981; executive producer, *The Escape Artist*, 1982; producer/director, *The Outsiders*, 1983; executive producer, *The Black Stallion Returns*, 1983; co-writer/director/producer, *Rumble Fish*, 1983.

PRINCIPAL TELEVISION WORK—Director, *The People*.

AWARDS: Academy Awards, Best Screenplay, Best Director, Best Picture, 1974: *The Godfather, Part II;* Academy Awards, Best Screenplay, Best Picture, 1972: *The Godfather;* Academy Award Nomination, Best Director, 1972: *The Godfather;* Director Guild of America, Film Directors Award, 1972: *The Godfather.*

SIDELIGHTS: MEMBERSHIPS—Directors Guild of America.*

* * *

CORD, Alex (ne Viespi), actor, writer

PERSONAL: Born August 3, 1931, in Floral Park, NY; son of Alexander (in the construction business) and Marie (Paladino) Viespi; married Joanna Pettet (an actress); children: Wayne, Toni, Damien. EDUCATION: New York University; studied with Lee Strasberg, Walt Witcover, Herbert Berghof, Morris Cornovsky. NON-THEATRICAL CAREER: Professional rodeo rider.

CAREER: PRINCIPAL STAGE APPEARANCES—Laertes, *Hamlet*, American Shakespeare Festival, Stratford, CT; six months with the Compass Players, Crystal Palace, St. Louis, MO; lead, *Play with a Tiger*, London; *Midsummer Night's Dream; The Umbrella*, London.

PRINCIPAL TELEVISION APPEARANCES—*U.S. Steel Hour; Playhouse 90; Kraft Theatre; Naked City; Eastside-Westside; The Rose Tatoo*, BBC; *The Joker*, ITV; *Chrysler Theatre; Fire!; Web; Beggarman, Thief; Airwolf.*

PRINCIPAL FILM APPEARANCES—Lead, *Synanon*, 1965; *Stagecoach*, 1966; *The Scorpio Letters; The Prodigal Gun; The Brotherhood*, 1968; *Stiletto*, 1969; *The Last Grenade;* 1970; *The Dead Are Alive; Chosen Survivors*, 1974; *Sidewinder one*, 1977; *Grayeagle*, 1977; *Inn of the Damned.*

WRITINGS: Novels—*Sandsong, The Harbinger.*

AWARDS: London Critics, Best Actor: *Play with a Tiger.*

SIDELIGHTS: "Mr. Cord is an accomplished and dedicated horse trainer and polo player."

ADDRESS: Agent—David Shapira and Assoc., 15301 Ventura Blvd., Sherman Oaks, CA 91403.

CARIS CORFMAN

CORFMAN, Caris, actress

PERSONAL: Born May 18, 1955, in Boston, MA; daughter of Philip A. (a doctor) and Eunice (a writer; maiden name, Luccock) Corfman. EDUCATION: Florida State University, B.A., 1977; Yale School of Drama, M.F.A., 1980.

CAREER: DEBUT—Minnie Fay, *Hello, Dolly!,* St. John's Academy, Washington, DC, 1971. NEW YORK DEBUT—Katherina Cavalieri, *Amadeus,* Broadhurst, 1980, 400 performances. PRINCIPAL STAGE APPEARANCES—(Off-Broadway) Nurse, *Wings; Stops and Virgins;* Jonquil, *Fish Riding Bikes;* (Regional) Gummersinda, *The Sleep of Reason,* Center Stage, Baltimore, MD; Imogene, *Cymbeline,* Arena Stage, Washington, DC; Esmeralda, *Camino Real,* Williamstown Theatre Festival; Company, *Jacques Brel . . . ,* Nurse, *Wings,* Connie Miller, *The 1940's Radio Hour,* Nina, *The Sea Gull,* Emma, *Curse of the Starving Class,* Yale Repertory Theatre. MAJOR TOURS—Miranda, *The Tempest,* Shakespeare and Company, U.S. cities.

PRINCIPAL FILM APPEARANCES—Eve, *Nesto Izmedu,* 1983. TELEVISION DEBUT—*Nurse.*

AWARDS: Carol Dye Award (Yale School of Drama), 1980.

SIDELIGHTS: MAJOR INTERESTS—dance, swimming, traveling.

ADDRESS: Agent—c/o Leaverton Sames Association, 1650 Broadway, New York, NY 10036.

CORMAN, Gene, motion picture/television producer

PERSONAL: Born September 24, 1927 in Detroit, MI; son of William (an engineer) and Anne (a housewife; maiden name Hugh) Corman; married Nan Chandler Morris on September 4, 1955; children: Todd William, Craig Allan. EDUCATION: Stanford University, graduate. POLITICS: Republican.

CAREER: PRODUCED—*Tobruk,* Universal Studios; *You Can't Win Them All,* Columbia Pictures; *Vigilante Force,* United Artists; *F.I.S.T.,* United Artists; *Avalanche Express,* Lorimar/20th Century–Fox; *The Big Red One,* Lorimar/United Artists. PRODUCED TELEVISION—*A Woman Called Golda,* with Ingrid Bergman; *Emerald Point,* series for CBS/20th Century-Fox Television.

THEATRE-RELATED CAREER: Talent executive with MCA with clients Joan Crawford, Fred MacMurray, Ray Milland, among others; left MCA to form own independent production company specializing in science fiction/youth-oriented features.

AWARDS: Emmy, *A Woman Called Golda,* 1982; U.S. entry to Cannes Film Festival and *Time* magazine ten best films, *The Big Red One,* 1980.

SIDELIGHTS: MEMBERSHIPS—Theta Delta Chi; patron, Los Angeles County Museum; Membership Board of the Academy of Motion Picture Arts and Sciences; Television Academy, Beverly Hills Tennis Club.

"[Corman] was at the front of the black-oriented films starring such celebrities as Jim Brown, Bernie Casey and Pam Grier while heading his own independent unit for MGM. Gene Corman has been a consistent participant at film symposiums and festivals both here and abroad, talking on all facets of motion picture production."

ADDRESS: 9255 Sunset Blvd., Los Angeles, CA 90069.

* * *

CORNTHWAITE, Robert, actor, director, scriptwriter

PERSONAL: Born April 28, 1917, in Stephens, OR; son of Henry (a storekeeper) and Bessie Eva (Graham) Cornthwaite. EDUCATION: University of Southern California, B.A., 1947. MILITARY: US Army Air Force (Sergeant).

CAREER: DEBUT—Fabian, *Twelfth Night,* Portland Civic, Portland, Oregon, July 1935. NEW YORK DEBUT—Andie, *And a Nightingale Sang,* Newhouse, Lincoln Center, November, 1983. PRINCIPAL STAGE APPEARANCES—*Cymbeline,* Hartford Stage, CT, 1981; *Mary Stuart,* Ahmanson, Los Angeles, 1981; *The Visions of Simone Machard,* La Jolla Playhouse, La Jolla, CA, 1983.

FILM DEBUT—Ambulance Driver, *Union Station,* 1950. PRINCIPAL FILMS—Dr. Carrington, *The Thing,* 1951; Doctor, *Whatever Happened to Baby Jane,* 1962. TELEVISION DEBUT—*I'm the Law.* TELEVISION APPEARANCES—John James Audubon, *The Adventures of Jim Bowie,* 1956–58; *Lux Video Theatre; Climax; Gunsmoke; The Untouchables; Wagon Train; The Twilight Zone; Burns & Allen.*

WRITINGS: The Blue, 1980.

AWARDS: Phi Beta Kappa, USC, 1947; Military—Bronze Star.

SIDELIGHTS: Mr. Cornthwaite speaks French, German, and Italian.

ADDRESS: Home—11656 Jacaranda Avenue, Hesperia, CA 92345.

* * *

CORT, Bud (ne Walter E. Cox), actor

PERSONAL: Born March 29, 1950 in New Rochelle, NY; son of Joseph Parker (a pianist and merchant) and Alma Mary (a reporter and merchant; maiden name, Court) Cox. EDUCATION: New York University School of the Arts, 1967–69; studied with Bill Hickey, George Griffin, David Craig, Joan Darling, Groucho Marx, and at the HB Studios in New York. RELIGION: Catholic.

CAREER: DEBUT—*Wise Child,* Helen Hayes, NY. PRINCIPAL STAGE APPEARANCES—Young Frank, *Forget Me Not Lane,* Mark Taper Forum, L.A., CA; Spirit, *August 6, 1945,* Mark Taper Forum, L.A., CA. MAJOR TOURS—*Gershwin Tribute,* cabaret act throughout U.S. and Europe.

FILM DEBUT—Private Boone, *M.A.S.H.* PRINCIPAL FILM APPEARANCES—Brewster, *Brewster McCloud;* Harold, *Harold and Maude;* Max Brown, *Why Shoot the Teacher?;* Freud, *The Secret Diary of Sigmund Freud.*

TELEVISION DEBUT—Delivery boy, *The Doctors.* PRINCIPAL TELEVISION APPEARANCES—*Brave New World; Bernice Bobs Her Hair; Faerie Tale Theatre.*

AWARDS: Crystal Star (Academy of Cinema, Paris, France), Best Actor, *Harold and Maude.*

SIDELIGHTS: MEMBERSHIPS—Academy of Motion Picture Arts and Sciences; Cinémathèque; Directors Unit of the Actors Studio.

"I am active in a lot of charitable work, most notably, American Indian rights, abused children, end to hunger and anti-nuclear efforts."

ADDRESS: Agent—c/o Silverman and Co., 9021 Melrose Avenue, Los Angeles, CA 90069.

* * *

CORWIN, Norman, playwright, director, producer

PERSONAL: Born May 3, 1910 in Boston, MA; son of Samuel H. (a printer) and Rose (an artist; maiden name Ober) Corwin; married Katherine Locke (an actress) on March 17, 1947; children: a son and a daughter. EDUCATION: Attended public schools in Boston and Winthrop, MA. NON-THEATRICAL CAREER—Journalist, radio writer.

WRITINGS: OPERA (libretto), *Warriors,* Metropolitan Opera House, NY, 1947. PLAYS, PRODUCED (also Directed)—*The Golden Door* (cantata), Music Hall, Cleveland, OH, 1955; *The Rivalry,* Bijou, NY, 1959; *The World of Carl Sandburg,* Henry Miller's Theatre, NY, 1960; *Overkill and Megalove,* Festival, San Anselmo, CA, 1967; *The Odyssey of Runyon Jones,* Valley Music, Los Angeles, CA, 1972; *Cervantes,* American Theatre, Washington, DC, 1973. FILMS—*The Blue Veil,* 1951; *Scandal at Scourie,* 1953; *Lust for Life,* 1956; *The Story of Ruth,* 1961. RADIO—*Words Without Music,* 1938; *They Fly Through the Air,* 1939; *Ballad for Americans,* 1939; *Pursuit of Happiness,* 1939; *Showcase,* 1940; *26 by Corwin,* 1941; *We Hold These Truths,* 1941; *This Is War,* 1942; *An American in England,* 1942; *Transatlantic Call,* 1943; *Passport for Adams,* 1943; *Columbia Presents Corwin,* 1944–45; *On a Note of Triumph,* 1945; *Word from the People,* 1945; *Stars in the Afternoon,* 1945; *Citizen of the World,* 1949; *Six Holidays,* 1983. TELEVISION—series, episodes #1 and #26, *F.D.R.,* 1963; *Inside the Movie Kingdom,* 1964; *Guest of Honor* (26 programs), 1971; *Norman Corwin Presents,* 1971–72; *The Last GI's,* 1971; *The Plot to Overthrow Christmas,* 1974; *The Trial of Yamashita,* 1974; culminating Ode, *CBS 60th Anniversary,* 1978; *Academy Leaders,* 1979. BOOKS—*Thirteen by Corwin,* 1942; *More by Corwin,* 1944; *Untitled and Other Plays,* 1947; *Dog in the Sky,* 1952; *Prayer for the Seventies,* 1969; *Gettysburg and the Few Appropriate Remarks,* 1971; *Corwin on Media; Jerusalem Printout,* 1972; *Holes in a Stained Glass Window,* 1978; *Trivializing America,* 1983;

PERFORMANCES—narration, *Oedipus Rex,* New York City Center, 1946; *Joshua,* Royce Hall, UCLA, 1961. DIRECTED—*The Chinese Wall,* Theatre Group, UCLA, 1962.

THEATRE-RELATED CAREER—Lecturer, UCLA, 1967–69; Telecommunications, University of Southern California, 1970; judge, Norman Corwin One-Act Play Contest, San Diego State College, 1968–70; lecturer, documentary film, University of North Carolina, 1972; distinguished visiting lecturer, San Diego State University, 1977–78; Patten Memorial Lecturer, Indiana University, 1980; visiting professor, University of Southern California, present.

AWARDS: Preceptor Award, San Francisco State University, 1979; Valentine Davies Award, Writers Guild of America, 1972; Artist of the Year Award, University of Judaism, 1972; inducted, Radio Hall of Fame (first writer), 1962; elected fellow, American College of Radio Arts, Crafts and Sciences, 1962; Women's American ORT Award, screenplay *The Story of Ruth,* 1960.

Academy Award Nomination, screenplay, *Lust for Life,* 1957; Film Critics Circle of the Foreign Language Press Award, screenplay, *Lust for Life,* 1957; National Conference of Christians and Jews Documentary Award, *A/777,* 1951; honor medal, Freedom Foundation, *Between Americans,* 1950; American Jewish Committee Citation, for contributions to better human understanding, 1950; Radio Award of the Speakers Research Committee of the United Nations, for distinguished service in presenting the U.N. to the people of the world, 1950.

Metropolitan Opera Award for libretto, *Warriors,* 1946; Wendell Wilkie One World Award, for his writing in radio and other media, 1946; American Schools and College Association Award, for distinguished radio writing, 1946;

First Place, *Billboard's* National Poll of Radio Editors, 1946; National Council of Teachers of English Citation, *On a Note of Triumph*, 1945; Inter-Racial Film and Radio Guild Unity Award, for contributions to universal understanding through the medium of radio, 1945; Distinguished Merit Award, National Conference of Christians and Jews, *Untitled*, 1945; Page One Award, for using his journalistic talents to create a unique literature of the air, 1944; American Acadey of Arts and Letters Award, for the high standards of his work, 1942; Peabody Medal, *We Hold These Truths*, 1942; Bok Medal, for distinguished service to radio, 1942; American Writers Congress Award, *26 by Corwin*, 1941; Institute for Education by Radio Award: *Pursuit of Happiness*, 1940; *Words Without Music*, 1939, *They Fly Through the Air*, 1939.

SIDELIGHTS: MEMBERSHIPS—Board of Directors, Writers Guild of America; Board of Governors, Motion Picture Academy of Arts and Sciences; Secretary, Foundation of the Motion Picture Academy; Dramatists Guild; Filmex. Mr. Corwin has directed, produced, and acted as host/narrator for many of his unique radio and television productions, spanning a career of over 40 years.

ADDRESS: 10401 Wellworth Ave., Los Angeles, CA 90024.

* * *

COSTIGAN, Ken, actor, director

PERSONAL: Born April 4, 1934 in New York City; son of Thomas Joseph (a doctor) and Kathleen (McCrann) Costigan; married Barbara Sue Ellenberger in July 1972 (divorced February 1983); children: Kevin T. EDUCATION: Fordham University, B.S., 1956; Yale University, School of Drama, M.F.A. (Directing), 1960. MILITARY: U.S. Army Reserves, 1st Lieutenant, Signal Corps, 1956–64.

CAREER: NEW YORK DEBUT—Purah, *Gideon*, Plymouth, New York, 1962. PRINCIPAL STAGE APPEARANCES—*The Seagull*, New York Shakespeare Festival; *Big Apple Messenger*, WPA Theatre, New York; *Diary of Anne Frank*, Theatre Four, New York; *The Show-Off*, Roundabout, New York; *Peg O' My Heart*, Lion, New York; *The Runner Stumbles*, Manhattan Theatre Club, New York; *The Hostage*, One Sheridan Square, New York; *Curley McDimple*, Bert Wheeler Theatre, New York; *The Browning Version*, Roundabout, New York. SELECTED ROLES—W. O. Gant, *Look Homeward Angel*; Mayor Quinn, *Hogan's Goat*; Mayor Shinn, *Music Man;* George, *Who's Afraid of Virginia Woolf*; Harry Berlin, *Luv;* Hank, *Boys in the Bank;* Brian, *Joe Egg;* Rossetti, *Boy Meets Girl;* Old Man Mahon, *Playboy of the Western World*. REGIONAL THEATRE COMPANIES—Asolo State Theatre, Sarasota, FL; Pittsburgh Playhouse, Pittsburgh, PA; Guthrie Theatre, Minneapolis, MN; McCarter Theatre, Princeton, NJ; Barter Theatre, Abingdon, VA. MAJOR TOURS—*The Matchmaker*, Phoenix Theatre, New York; *A Short Happy Life*, national tour; Heartland Productions. Artistic Director, Pittsburgh Playhouse, Pittsburgh PA., 1969–74.

TELEVISION DEBUT—Deacon Billson, *The Man That Corrupted Hadleyburg*, American Short Story Series, PBS. PRINCIPAL TELEVISION APPEARANCES—John Adams and Patrick Henry, *Decades of Decision; One Life to Live;*

Ryan's Hope; Love of Life; Guiding Light; All My Children; Search for Tomorrow.

SIDELIGHTS: MEMBERSHIPS—AEA, SAG, AFTRA, SSD&C, IATSE Local B-183.

ADDRESS: Home—305 W. 45th Street, New York, NY 10036. Agent—Ambrose Company, 1466 Broadway, Suite 1610, New York, NY 10036.

* * *

COTSIRILOS, Stephanie, actress, composer, writer, singer

PERSONAL: Born February 24, 1947 in Chicago, IL; daughter of George John (a criminal defense attorney) and Theresa (Latto) Cotsirilos. EDUCATION: Brown University, B.A. (Comparative Literature), 1968; Yale University School of Music, M.M.A. (Voice), 1971; studied acting with Michael Howard. NON-THEATRICAL CAREER: Patron and contributor to *Letters*, a literary magazine and forum.

CAREER: DEBUT—Anna, *The Seven Deadly Sins*, Yale Repertory Theatre, New Haven, CT, 1971. NEW YORK DEBUT—Jessie, *The Little Mahagonny*, Manhattan Theatre Club, for 20 performances, 1972. PRINCIPAL STAGE APPEARANCES—Yale Repertory Theatre, 1971–74—Jessie, *The Little Mahagonny*, Lillian, *Happy End*, Vittoria, *I Married You for the Fun of It*, *Life Is a Dream*, *The Big House*, *Watergate Classics*, *The Rise and Fall of the City of Mahagonny*, Googie, *The Ritz; An Evening of Cole Porter*, Manhattan Theatre Club, 1973; Clara, *Signor Deluso*, Manhattan Theatre Club, 1974; Adrienne, *In the Voodoo Parlor of Marie Laveau*, Phoenix, NY, 1974; Daisy, *The Animal Kingdom*, Phoenix, NY, 1975; Lisa, *Apple Pie*, New York Shakespeare Festival, 1976; Liz, *Green Pond*, Chelsea Theatre, NY, 1977; Bianca, *Othello*, Hartman Theatre Company, 1978; Franc, *The Animal Kingdom*, Cincinnati Playhouse in the Park, 1978; *A Kurt Weill Cabaret*, NY, 1980; Carmen, and understudy, *Goodbye Fidel*, NY, 1980; Stephanie Necrophorus, *Nine*, 46th Street, NY, 1982–83. MAJOR TOURS—*Side by Side by Sondheim*, national tour, 1978–79.

FILM DEBUT—Marta, *Beyond the Limit*, 1983. PRINCIPAL FILM APPEARANCES—Veronica Cohen, *Moscow on the Hudson*, 1984.

TELEVISION DEBUT—*Rachel, NET Opera Theatre*, 1973. PRINCIPAL TELEVISION APPEARANCES—*Hardhat & Legs*, 1980; *The Guiding Light*, 1983.

WRITINGS: MUSICAL PLAYS—*Summer Friends*, with Mel Marvin, songs performed at Playwrights Horizons, Colonnades Theatre Lab, 1980; *About Face*, with Cheryl Hardwick, Manhattan Theatre Club, Writers Theatre, NY, 1983. POETRY—published in *Poets On*, 1980.

THEATRE-RELATED CAREER: Performer in clubs and concerts at Carnegie Recital Hall, Williamstown Theatre Festival, Colorado Music Festival, Midwest and East Coast tours as well as night clubs in New York City.

AWARDS: ASCAP Special Awards for cabaret/authorship, 1980–81.

STEPHANIE COTSIRILOS

SIDELIGHTS: MEMBERSHIPS—AEA; SAG; AFTRA; ASCAP; ACLU; UNICEF.

Ms. Cotsirilos has performed benefit performances for Hospital Audiences, Inc.

ADDRESS: Agent—Dulcina Eisen Associates, 154 E. 61st Street, New York, NY 10021.

* * *

COURTENAY, Tom, actor

PERSONAL: Born February 25, 1937, in Hull, Yorkshire, England; son of Thomas Henry and Annie (Quest) Courtnay; married Cheryl Kennedy (November 12, 1973). EDUCATION: Kingston High School, Hull; University College, London; trained for the theatre at the Royal Academy of Dramatic Art.

CAREER: DEBUT—Konstantin Treplyef, *The Seagull,* Old Vic Company, Lyceum, Edinburgh, August, 1960. LONDON DEBUT—Treplyef, *The Seagull,* Old Vic, 1960. NEW YORK DEBUT—Simon, *Otherwise Engaged,* Plymouth, February, 1977. PRINCIPAL STAGE APPEARANCES—Poins, *Henry V, Part I,* Feste, *Twelfth Night,* Old Vic, London, 1961; took over the role of Bill Fisher, *Billy Liar,* Cambridge, London, 1961; Andri, *Andorra,* National Theatre Company, Old Vic, London, 1964; Trofimov, *The Cherry Orchard,* Malcolm, *Macbeth,* Chichester Festival, 1966; Lord Fancourt Babberly, *Charley's Aunt,* 69 Theatre Company, Manchester, Eng-

land, 1966; *Playboy of the Western World,* Manchester, 1967; *Hamlet,* Young Marlow, *She Stoops to Conquer,* Garrick, London, 1969; *Peer Gynt,* University Theatre, Manchester, 1970; Lord Fancourt Babberly, *Charley's Aunt,* Apollo, London, 1971; Leonard, *Time and Time Again,* Comedy, London, 1972; Capt. Bluntschli, *Arms and the Man,* Manchester, 1973; Norman, *The Norman Conquests,* Greenwich, May 1974, Globe, London, August 1974; John Clare, *The Fool,* Royal Court, London, 1975; *The Prince of Homburg,* Faulkland, *The Rivals,* Royal Exchange, Manchester, 1976; Raskolnikov, *Crime and Punishment,* Royal Exchange, Manchester, 1978; Owen, *Clouds,* Duke of York's, London, 1978; Norman, *The Dresser,* Royal Exchange, Manchester, March, 1980, Queens, London, April, 1980, Brooks Atkinson, NY, November, 1981; *Andy Capp,* London, 1983.

FILM DEBUT—*The Loneliness of the Long Distance Runner,* 1962. FILM APPEARANCES—*Private Potter,* 1962; Billy, *Billy Liar,* 1963; *King and Country,* 1964; *Operation Crossbow,* 1965; *King Rat,* 1965; *Doctor Zhivago,* 1965; *The Night of the Generals,* 1965; *The Day the Fish Came Out,* 1967; *A Dandy in Aspic,* 1968; *Otley,* 1969; *Catch Me a Spy,* 1971; *One Day in the Life of Ivan Denisovitch,* 1971; *The Dresser,* 1983.

TELEVISION APPEARANCES—*Private Potter;* Dobley, *The Lads; Ghosts,* 1967; *I Heard the Owl Call My Name,* (TV film), 1973; Jesus, *Zeffirelli's Life of Christ* (TV film), 1975.

AWARDS: French Academie du Cinema, Best Actor, 1967: *Billy Liar,* 1967; Antoinette Perry Award Nominations, Best Actor, 1977: *Otherwise Engaged,* 1981: *The Dresser,* 1981; Academy Award Nominations, Best Supporting Actor, 1965: *Doctor Zhivago,* Best Actor, 1983: *The Dresser.*

SIDELIGHTS: RECREATION—Listening to music, playing golf.

ADDRESS: Agent—c/o CMA, Ltd., 22 Grafton Street, London W1, England.*

* * *

COWAN, Edie, actress, choreographer

PERSONAL: Born April 14 in New York City; daughter of Pincus (a businessman) and Stephanie (Mandula) Cohen. EDUCATION: Butler University, Indianapolis, IN, B.A.

CAREER: NEW YORK DEBUT—Maude, *Funny Girl,* Winter Garden, for 1,200 performances, 1964. PRINCIPAL STAGE APPEARANCES—Chorus, *Sherry,* Alvin, NY, 1967; Essie Whimple, *Redhead,* Mt. Gretna, PA, 1969; Ruby, *Dames at Sea,* Tampa, FL, 1970; Jill Tanner, *Butterflies Are Free,* Allenberry Playhouse, PA, 1973; various roles, *Annie,* Goodspeed Opera House, CT, Alvin, NY, 1976–80; Daisy, *Bloomer Girl,* Goodspeed Opera House, CT, 1981.

MAJOR TOURS—Josie Cohan, *George M,* National Tour, 1969–70; Young Phyllis, *Follies,* 1973–74; Lily St. Regis, *Annie,* Second National Tour, 1980.

PRINCIPAL TELEVISION APPEARANCE—*Annie Christmas Spe-*

EDIE COWAN

cial. PRINCIPAL CHOREOGRAPHY—*Little Shop of Horrors*, WPA, NY, Orpheum, NY, Westwood Playhouse, CA, Comedy Theatre, London, England, 1982–83; *Good News; Cabaret; Kiss Me Kate; Once Upon a Mattress; Brigadoon; Man of La Mancha; Dames at Sea; Princess Ida*, Hunter College Playhouse, NY; *Erotic Tale of a Tall Girl*, Theatre at St. Clements, NY; *Battle of Bunker Hill*, American Theatre Company, NY; *You're a Good Man, Charlie Brown*, Bert Wheeler; *Knickerbocker Holiday*, Bert Wheeler.

TELEVISION CHOREOGRAPHY—Promo for *Dick Cavett Show*.

THEATRE-RELATED CAREER: Faculty, American Dance Machine; faculty, Theatre Department, Indiana University.

SIDELIGHTS: MEMBERSHIPS—AEA; AFTRA; SAG; SSD&C.

Ms. Cowan re-created Carol Haney's original choreography of *Funny Girl* for the American Dance Machine.

ADDRESS: Agent—Shukat Company, Ltd. 340 W. 55th Street, New York, NY 10019.

* * *

COX, Ronny, actor, producer, writer

PERSONAL: Born July 23, 1938; son of Bob P. (a carpenter) and Lounette (a housewife, maiden name, Rucker) Cox; married Mary Griffith (a writer) on September 10, 1960; children: Brian, John, EDUCATION: Eastern New Mexico University, B.A., 1963.

CAREER: DEBUT—Bruz, *King KoKo,* Portales NM, 1951. NEW YORK DEBUT—Jesse James, *Indians,* Brooks Atkinson, New York, 1969, 130 performances. PRINCIPAL STAGE APPEARANCES—Miles, *Happiness Cage,* New York Shakespeare Festival, Public Theatre, New York, 1970, also performed in Delacorte Theatre in Central Park, 1970. MAJOR TOURS—Johnny Buccannon, *Summer and Smoke,* "Straw Hat Circuit" ending in the Huntington-Hartford Theatre, Los Angeles.

FILM DEBUT—Drew Ballinger, *Deliverance,* 1971. PRINCIPAL FILMS—Ozark, *Bound for Glory,* 1975; Pierce Brooks, *The Onion Field,* 1978; Colonel Kerby, *Taps,* 1980; Colonel Powers, *Some Kind of Hero,* 1980; Pete Caufield, *Courage,* 1983. TELEVISION DEBUT—Jerry Rubin, *Chicago 7 Trial,* BBC, 1970. PRINCIPAL TELEVISION APPEARANCES—George Apple, *Apple's Way; A Case of Rape;* Editor Webb, *Our Town; Hatter Fox; Alcatraz; Fallen Angel.*

WRITINGS: Film—*Courage* (with Mary Cox.)

AWARDS: Straw Hat Award, Best Supporting Actor, *Summer and Smoke;* Distinguished Alumnus Award, Eastern New Mexico University.

SIDELIGHTS: MEMBERSHIPS—AEA, AFTRA, ASCAP, SAG, SWG, Academy of Motion Picture Arts and Sciences, Academy of Television Arts and Sciences.

ADDRESS: Agent—Merritt Blake, Blake-Glenn Agency, 409 N. Camden Drive, Beverly Hills, CA 90210.

* * *

COYLE, J. J., writer

PERSONAL: Born May 27, 1928 in Gloucester, MA; son of John J. (a police chief) and Alice (Walters) Coyle. EDUCATION: Tufts College, B.A., 1950; Hunter College, M.A., 1981. POLITICS: "Liberal" MILITARY: U.S. Army, Korean War, 1950–52.

CAREER: NEW YORK DEBUT—Dancer, *Bye Bye Birdie,* Martin Beck, New York, 1960. LONDON DEBUT—Assistant Choreographer, *Bye Bye Birdie,* Her Majesty's Theatre, 1961.

WRITINGS: PLAYS PUBLISHED—*The Ninety Day Mistress,* 1967.

SIDELIGHTS: MEMBERSHIPS—Dramatists Guild, AEA.

ADDRESS: Home—437 W. 44th St. New York, NY 10036.

* * *

CRIST, Judith, critic

PERSONAL: Born May 22, 1922, in New York City; daughter of Solomon (a businessman) and Helen (a librarian;

maiden name, Schoenberg) Klein; married William B. Crist (an educational planner) July 3, 1947; children: Steven. EDUCATION: Hunter College, B.A., 1941; Columbia University, M.S., 1945. POLITICS: Democrat. RELIGION: Jewish.

WRITINGS: BOOKS—*The Private Eye, the Cowboy & the Very Naked Girl,* 1968; *Judith Crist's TV Guide to the Movies,* 1974; *Take 22: Moviemakers on Moviemaking,* 1984; has contributed numerous articles in various magazines.

PRINCIPAL FILM/STAGE WORK—Critic–reporter, NY *Herald Tribune,* 1945–60, editor arts, 1960–63, theater critic, 1958–63, film critic, 1963–66; film, theatre critic, NBC-TV, *Today Show,* 1963–73; film critic, *World Journal Tribune,* 1966–67; critic-at-large, *Ladies Home Journal,* 1966–67; film critic, *TV Guide,* 1965–present; film critic, *New York* Magazine, 1968–75; film critic, *The Washingtonian,* 1970–72; film critic, *Palm Springs Life,* 1971–75; contributing editor, film critic, *Saturday Review,* 1975–77, 1980–present; film critic, New York *Post,* 1977–78, *MD/Mrs.,* 1977–present; film critic, *50 Plus,* 1978–present. RELATED CAREER: Instructor, journalism, Hunter College, 1947, Sarah Lawrence College, 1958–59; associate journalism Columbia Graduate School Journalism, 1959–62, adjunct professor, 1964–present.

AWARDS: Named to Hunter Alumni Hall of Fame, 1973; Centennial President's Medal, Hunter College, 1970; Columbia Graduate School Journalism Alumni Award 1961, named to 50th Anniversary Honors Lits, 1963; Educational Writers Association Award, 1952; New York Newspaper Women's Club Award, 1955, 59, 63, 65, 67; George Polk Award, 1951; Page One Award, New York Newspaper Guild, 1955.

SIDELIGHTS: MEMBERSHIPS—Trustee, Anne O'Hara McCormick Scholarship Fund; president, Columbia Journalism Alumni, 1967–70; New York Film Critics; National Society of Film Critics; Sigma Tau Delta.

Mrs. Crist made her film debut as an actress as a night club onlooker in *Stardust Memories* in 1980.

ADDRESS: Office—180 Riverside Drive, New York, NY 10024.

* * *

CRITT, C. J. (nee Carol Jane Crittenden), actress, playwright

PERSONAL: Born April 6, 1954 in Portland, OR; daughter of Charles Jay (a roofing contractor) and Manellen J. (an educator; maiden name, Wilbur) Crittenden. EDUCATION: American Academy of Dramatic Arts, Graduate, 1976. RELIGION: Roman Catholic.

CAREER: DEBUT—Miss Jones, *How to Succeed in Business without Really Trying,* Fir Acres Summer Theatre, Portland, OR, 1970. NEW YORK DEBUT—Ghost, *Death & Devil,* Perry Street, 1976. PRINCIPAL STAGE APPEARANCES—Dottore, Mercenary, Bell Hop, *Crisp,* Intar, 1981; Phantom, *Waltz of the Stork,* Century, NY, 1982; Marge MacDougall, *Promises,* Equity Library, 1983.

MAJOR TOURS—Sonja, *Godspell,* East Coast, 1977; *The Rocky Horror Show,* International, 1980–81.

FILM DEBUT—Vicki Redding, *The Circle,* 1972. PRINCIPAL FILM APPEARANCES—Doris, *Stardust Memories,* 1980. TELEVISION DEBUT—*Consumer Reports.* PRINCIPAL TELEVISION APPEARANCES—*P.M. Magazine,* Boston, Chicago, Toronto, San Francisco.

WRITINGS: PLAYS, UNPRODUCED—Rockbound (under development at Ensemble Studio Theatre). Commissioned by New York Shakespeare Festival to write a mini-musical for 1984.

AWARDS: Lawrence Langner Award, Excellence in Speech, 1976; Clio Award, Weight Watchers commercial as Jessica.

SIDELIGHTS: MEMBERSHIPS—Dramatists Guild.

Interested in night club and cabaret work with special emphasis on pop music development. Comedy and improvisation is a special interest.

ADDRESS: Home—221 W. 28th Street, New York, NY 10001. Agent—C.E.D. 919 Third Avenue, New York, NY 10022.

* * *

CROFOOT, Leonard John, actor, dancer

PERSONAL: Born in Utica, NY; son of Leonard Vernon and Nancy (Roberts) Crofoot; married Diane Abrams (an actress, singer, dancer) on June 26, 1978. EDUCATION: Attended Lawndale public schools in California; studied ballet with George Zoritch.

CAREER: DEBUT—Grasshopper, *The Nutcracker,* Kirov Ballet Tour, Shrine Auditorium, Los Angeles, CA 1963. NEW YORK DEBUT—Bibi (understudy), *The Happy Time,* Broadway Theatre, 1968. PRINCIPAL STAGE APPEARANCES—(Broadway) General Tom Thumb, *Barnum,* St. James, 1980–82; Rudolph, *The Happy Time,* Broadway Theatre; Noah, *Come Summer;* waiter, bellhop, installer, law clerk, *Gigi;* (Off Broadway) Benjamin, *Joseph and His Amazing Technicolored Dream Coat,* Brooklyn Academy of Music; soloist, *The American Dance Machine;* country singer, *Circus;* (Summer Stock) *Barnum,* Kenley Players, Ohio; student jogger, *A Long Way to Boston,* Goodspeed Opera House, East Haddam, CT; (Regional Theatre) Theatre Group, CA—Corydon, *Aria Da Capo,* Frankie, *Mrs. Dally Has a Lover,* Buddy, *Come Blow Your Horn,* Don, *Butterflies Are Free;* (Dinner Theatre) Baby John, *West Side Story,* Chateau de Ville.

MAJOR TOURS—Barnaby Tucker, *Hello Dolly; Tony Martin and Cyd Charisse Act; Ten Stout-Hearted Men Review,* Theatre Royal, Drury Lane, London, England, and a Command Performance for the Duke of Edinburgh (H.R.H. Prince Philip) at the Talk of the Town; *Barnum.*

PRINCIPAL FILM APPEARANCES—Danny, *Echo's;* Arron,

LEONARD JOHN CROFOOT

Laybrinth; Three Days of the Condor, 1975; *Goodbye Girl,* 1977; *Warriors,* 1979.

PRINCIPAL TELEVISION APPEARANCES—*The Man in the Middle; The Day Before Sunday; Once Upon a Mattress; Of Thee I Sing; Carol Channing's TV Special; 50th Academy Awards Show; Pinocchio; Tony Martin and Cyd Charisse TV Special; 1980 Tony Awards Show.*

SIDELIGHTS: MEMBERSHIPS—AEA, AFTRA, SAG.

RECREATION—Painting, writing, snow skiing, and family.

ADDRESS: Agent—Honey Sanders, 229 W. 42nd Street, New York, NY 10036.

* * *

CRONYN, Hume, actor, director, writer

PERSONAL: Born July 18, 1911, London, ON, Canada; son of Hume Blake and Frances Amelia (Labatt) Cronyn; married Jessica Tandy (an actress), September 27, 1942; children: Susan, Christopher, Tandy. EDUCATION: Ridley College, 1930; attended McGill University, 1930–31; graduate, American Academy of Dramatic Arts, 1934; studied at the Mozarteum, Salzburg, Austria, summers, 1932–33.

CAREER: DEBUT—*The Adding Machine, Dr. Faustus, From Morn to Midnight, The Road to Rome, Alice in Wonderland,* with Montreal Repertory Theatre and McGill Player's Club, 1930–31. NEW YORK DEBUT—Janitor, *Hipper's Holiday,*

Maxine Elliott's, 1934. PRINCIPAL STAGE APPEARANCES—Paper Boy, *Up Pops the Devil,* National Theatre Stock Company, Washington, DC, 1931; joined Robert Porterfield's Barter Theatre, Abingdon, VA: Austin Lowe, *The Second Man,* Dr. Haggett, *The Late Christopher Bean,* Jim Hipper, *He Knew Dillinger,* Dole Odum, *Mountain Ivy,* 1934; Erwin Trowbridge, *Three Men on a Horse,* Cort, NY, 1936; Green, *Boy Meets Girl,* Cort, NY, 1936; Leo Davis, *Room Service,* Cort, NY, 1937; Elkus, *High Tor,* Cort, NY, 1937; Steve, *Escape This Night,* Cort, NY, 1938; Abe Sherman, *There's Always a Breeze,* Windsor, 1938; Harry Quill, *Off to Buffalo,* Barrymore, NY, 1939; Andrei, *The Three Sisters,* Longacre, NY, 1939; at the Lakewood Theatre, Skowhegan, ME: Hutchens Stubbs, *Susan and God,* Toby Cartwright, *Ways and Means,* George Davies, *We Were Dancing,* Francis O'Connor, *Shadow and Substance,* Christy Dudgeon, *The Devils Disciple,* Lloyd Lloyd, *Kiss the Boys Goodbye,* Judas, *Family Portrait,* Stage Manager, *Our Town,* Denis Dillon, *The White Seed,* Karl Baumer, *Margin for Error,* Joe Bonaparte, *Golden Boy,* 1939–40; Peter Mason, *The Weak Link,* Golden, NY, 1940; Lee Tatnall, *Retreat to Pleasure,* Belasco, NY, 1940; Harley L. Miller, *Mr. Big,* Lyceum, NY, 1941; Jodine Decker, *The Survivors,* Plymouth, NY, 1948; Gandersheim, *The Little Blue Light,* Brattle, Cambridge, MA, 1950; Michael, *The Fourposter,* Barrymore, NY, 1951; Dr. Brightlee, *Madame, Will You Walk,* Phoenix, NY, 1953; Curtis/Bennett Honey, *The Honeys,* Longacre, NY, 1955; Julian Anson, *A Day by the Sea,* ANTA, NY, 1955;

Mr. Tule, *I Spy,* John J. Mulligan, *Bedtime Story,* Professor

HUME CRONYN

Nyukhin, *The Harmful Effects of Tobacco*, Jerry, *Pound on Demand* with the overall title, *Triple Play*, Palm Beach Playhouse, FL, 1959; *Triple Play* (with the Doctor in *Portrait of a Madonna* substituted for *I Spy*), Playhouse NY, 1959; Jimmie Luton, *Big Fish, Little Fish*, ANTA, NY, 1961, Duke of York's, London, 1962; at the Tyrone Guthrie Theatre, Minneapolis, MN: Harpagon, *The Miser*, Dr. Tchebutykin, *The Three Sisters*, Willy Loman, *Death of a Salesman*, 1963; Polonius, *Hamlet*, Lunt-Fontanne, NY, 1964; Herbert Georg Beutler, *The Physicists*, Martin Beck, NY, 1964; appeared at the White House at the request of President Johnson in *Hear America Speaking*, 1965; at the Tyrone Guthrie, Minneapolis, MN: Duke of Glouster, *Richard III*, Yepihodov, *The Cherry Orchard*, Harpagon, *The Miser*, 1965; Tobias, *A Delicate Balance*, Martin Beck, NY, 1966; Harpagon, *The Miser*, Mark Taper Forum, Los Angeles, CA, 1968; Fr. Rolfe, *Hadrian VII*, Stratford Ontario Shakespeare Festival, Canada, 1969; Lt. Commander Queeg, *The Caine Mutiny Court Martial*, Ahmanson, Los Angeles, CA, 1971; Grandfather/Willie, *Promenade All!*, Alvin, NY, 1972; Willie, *Happy Days*, the Player, *Act without Words I*, Krapp, *Krapp's Last Tape*, Forum, NY, 1972; Krapp, *Krapp's Last Tape*, St. Lawrence Theatre Centre, Toronto, Canada, 1972, Arena Stage, Washington, DC, 1973; Verner Conklin, *Come into the Garden*, Barrymore, NY, 1974; Maude/Hugo Latymer, *A Song at Twilight*, double bill *Noel Coward in Two Keys*, Barrymore, NY, 1974; Shylock, *Merchant of Venice*, Bottom, *A Midsummer Night's Dream*, Stratford Ontario Shakespeare Festival, Canada, 1976; Weller Martin, *The Gin Game*, Golden, NY, 1977; *Foxfire*, Stratford Ontario Shakespeare Festival, 1980, Guthrie, Minneapolis, 1981–82, Barrymore, NY, 1982–83; *Traveler in the Dark*, American Repertory, Cambridge, MA, 1984.

MAJOR TOURS—Sir Charles Marlowe, *She Stoops to Conquer*, Gideon Bloodgood, *The Streets of New York*, with the Jitney Players, Plymouth, Boston, Garrick, Philadelphia, 1935; produced, directed and appeared in revue for Canadian Active Service Canteen, 1941 and for USO Camp Shows, 1942–43; produced *Junior Miss* and produced and appeared in the revue, *It's All Yours;* toured U.S. military installations as Tommy Tarner, *The Male Animal*, and in Canada in a vaudeville sketch for Loan Victory program, 1944; *Face to Face*, 1954–55; *The Egghead* and Oliver Walling, *The Man in the Dog Suit*, 1958, ending at the Coronet, NY; Fr. Rolfe, *Hadrian VII*, national tour, 1970; Grandfather/Wille, *Promenade All!*, 1971, 1973; Maude/Hugo Latymer *A Song at Twilight, Noel Coward in Two Keys*, 1974; *The Many Faces of Love* (a dramatic reading), 1974–75; Weller Martin, *The Gin Game*, U.S. and Canada, Lyric, London, and tour of Russia, 1979.

PRINCIPAL STAGE WORK—Director: *Portrait of a Madonna*, LA, 1946; *Now I Lay Me Down to Sleep*, 1949–50; *Hilda Crane*, 1950; *The Egghead*, 1957, Brattle Theatre, Cambridge, MA. produced—*Slow Dance on a Killing Ground*, Plymouth, 1964.

PRINCIPAL FILM APPEARANCES—*Shadow of a Doubt*, 1943; *Life Boat*, 1944; *The Seventh Cross*, 1944; *The Postman Always Rings Twice*, 1946; *The Green Years*, 1946; *A Letter for Evie*, 1945; *Brute Force*, 1947; *Top O' the Morning*, 1949; *People Will Talk*, 1951; *Sunrise at Campobello*, 1960; *Cleopatra*, 1963; *Gaily Gaily*, 1968; *The Arrangement*, 1968; *There Was a Crooked Man*, 1969; *Conrack*, 1974;

Parallax View, 1974; *Honky Tonk Freeway*, 1980; *Garp*, 1981; *Roll Over*, 1981, *Impulse*, 1983.

PRINCIPAL TELEVISION APPEARANCES—Ned Ferrar, *Her Master's Voice*, 1939; *The Marriage* (also produced), 1953–54; *Omnibus; Ed Sullivan;* Michael, *The Fourposter*, 1955; *The Great Adventure*, 1956; *The Confidence Man*, 1956; *The Big Wave*, 1956; *The Five Dollar Bill*, 1957; *Member of the Wedding*, 1957; *The Bridge of San Luis Rey*, 1958; *The Moon and Sixpence*, 1959; *A Doll's House*, 1959; *Juno and the Paycock*, 1960; *John F. Kennedy Memorial Broadcast*, 1963; Polonius, *Hamlet*, 1964; *Many Faces of Love*, 1977; *The Gin Game*, 1979; also, produced and directed *Portrait of a Madonna*, 1948.

THEATRE-RELATED CAREER: Lecturer, drama, American Academy of Dramatic Arts.

WRITINGS: SCREENPLAYS—*Rope*, 1947; *Under Capricorn*, 1948. PLAYS—*Foxfire* (with Susan Cooper). TELEPLAYS—*The Dollmaker* (with Susan Cooper), 1983. Short stories and articles contributed to periodicals.

AWARDS: Common Wealth, 1983; named to Theatre Hall of Fame, 1979; Los Angeles Critics Award, 1979: *The Gin Game;* Antoinette Perry Award Nomination, 1979: *The Gin Game;* Brandeis University Creative Arts Award, 1978; Hon. LLD, University of Western Ontario, London, Canada, 1974; Obie Award for outstanding achievement, distinguished performance, 1973: *Krapp's Last Tape;* Straw Hat Award directing, 1972: *Promenade All!*, Los Angeles Drama Critics Award, 1972: *The Caine Mutiny Court Martial;* Award for Achievement by Alumni, American Academy of Dramatic Arts, 1964; Antoinette Perry Award, 1964: *Polonius, Hamlet;* Variety-New York Drama critics poll, 1964: Polonius, *Hamlet;* Delia Austria medal, NY Drama League 1961: *Big Fish, Little Fish;* Barter Theatre award for outstanding contribution to theatre, 1961; Comodedia Matinee Club award, 1952: *The Fourposter.*

SIDELIGHTS: MEMBERSHIPS—AFTRA; SAG; Screen Writers Guild; AEA; SSD&C; Dramatists Guild; board of governors, Stratford Festival, Canada. RECREATIONS—Skin diving, fishing.

ADDRESS: Office—63–23 Carlton Street, Rego Park, NY 11374.

* * *

CRONYN, Tandy, actress

PERSONAL: Born November 26, 1945; daughter of Hume (an actor, writer, producer, director) and Jessica (an actress; maiden name, Tandy) Cronyn. EDUCATION: Central School of Speech and Drama, London, England, 1965–67.

CAREER: DEBUT—Doreen, *The Private Ear*, Instant Theatre, Montreal, Canada, 1965. NEW YORK DEBUT—Sally Bowles, *Cabaret*, Broadway Theatre, for 32 performances, July, 1969. BRITISH DEBUT—Sibyl, *Private Lives;* Regina, *Ghosts;* Uncle Ted, *A Resounding Tinkle*, Theatre Royal, Bury-St.-Edmonds, summer repertory season, 1967. PRINCIPAL STAGE APPEARANCES—Denver Center Theatre Company,

TANDY CRONYN

CO: Natella, *The Caucasian Chalk Circle,* Armande, *The Learned Ladies,* Lady Percy, *Henry IV, Pt. 1,* Hypatia, *Misalliance,* Chorus, *Medea;* The Old Globe Theatre, San Diego, CA: Lady Capulet, *Romeo and Juliet,* Silvia, *Two Gentlemen of Verona,* Princess of France, *Love's Labour's Lost,* Mrs. Patrick Campbell, *Dear Liar,* Lina Szczepanowska, *Misalliance; Poets from Inside,* New York Public Theatre; Childe, *The Killing of Sister George,* Roundabout, New York; Helen, *Bodies,* South Coast Repertory, Costa Mesa, CA; Grace, *The Philanderer,* Yale Repertory, New Haven, CT; Celimene, *The Misanthrope,* Hartford Stage Company, Hartford, CT; Petra, *An Enemy of the People,* Lincoln Center Repertory; Ismene, *Antigone,* Lincoln Center Repertory. MAJOR TOURS—Sally Bowles, *Cabaret,* second National Tour, 1969–70; Myrtle Mae, *Harvey,* Central City, Los Angeles, San Francisco, Chicago; Amy, *Company,* National Tour. Eugene O'Neill Theatre Center, National Playwrights Conference, 1970, 1972, 1983.

TELEVISION DEBUT—*Seaway* (pilot episode, Montreal) *A Medal for Mirko,* 1965. PRINCIPAL TELEVISION APPEARANCES—*Murder: An Even Chance,* Manchester, 1968; *Star Quality,* London, 1968; *The Crazy Kill,* London, 1975; *The Guardian.*

THEATRE-RELATED CAREER: Trustee, Colonnades Theatre Lab, New York, 1974–77; assistant to director, National Theatre of the Deaf, 1974–76; business manager, National Theatre of the Deaf, 1976–77.

SIDELIGHTS: ''I spent the summer of 1963 hanging around the newly formed Guthrie Theatre in Minneapolis. I had not yet finished high school, but this first glimpse of what classical repertory could and should be made a permanent impression.'' Biographical articles appeared in New York *Post,* November 24, 1983 and in the Hollywood *DramaLogue,* September 18–24, 1980.

ADDRESS: Home—810 Broadway, 7th floor, New York, NY 10003.

* * *

CROSWELL, Anne (nee Anne Pearson Croswell), playwright, lyricist

PERSONAL: Born December 12; daughter of John Hale (a Methodist minister) and Eudora Maxwell (a drama teacher; maiden name, Yerby) Pearson; married Volney R. Crosswell (an artist) on September 4, 1954 (separated 1971). EDUCATION: Randolph-Macon Women's College, B.A.; studied TV and radio script writing with Gilbert Seldes. POLITICS: Founder of Village Independent Democrats and lyricist of National Democratic Party official campaign song for Adlai Stevenson; New York County Committeewoman.

WRITINGS: PLAYS, PRODUCED—*Ernest in Love* (book and lyrics), Grammercy Arts, NY, Cherry Lane, NY, and has been performed throughout the United States and abroad; *Tovarich* (lyrics), received Broadway production, NY; *I'm Solomon* (co-book, lyrics), received Broadway production, NY; *Chips 'n Ale* (co-book, lyrics), Actors Theatre of Louisville, KY; *Bodo* (lyrics), Goodspeed Opera House, East Haddam, CT, 1983.

PRINCIPAL TELEVISION WORK—Theme song and special material, *Washington Square,* hourly bi-weekly series; ''Huck Finn'' (book), *U.S. Steel Hour;* ''Who's Earnest'' (book and lyrics), *U.S. Steel Hour;* lyrics for *Sesame Street,* 1980–82.

BOOKS, PUBLISHED—*Some of My Best Friends Are Runners,* 1979; *Sidekicks or A Merger of Marvelous Magnitude,* 1983. ARTICLES, PUBLISHED in *U.S.A. Today; Financial World; Detroit Free Press; Institutional Investor; Directors Publications, Inc.*

SIDELIGHTS: MEMBERSHIPS—ASCAP; Authors Guild; The Dramatists Guild.

ADDRESS: Agent—Scott Shukat, c/o The Shukat Company, Ltd., 340 W. 55th Street, New York, NY 10019.

* * *

CROUCH, J. H., actor, critic, director, producer, writer, teacher

PERSONAL: Born August 13, 1918 in Montpelier, ID; son of James Herbert (a railroad engineer) and Georgia Ruth (a teacher; maiden name, Bathe) Crouch; married Shirley Crouch on October 23, 1939 (divorced; died, 1982); Linda Johnson, (a nurse) on December 22, 1978; children: (first marriage) Shirley Anne Kessler, Michael, Stephen. EDUCATION: U.C.L.A., B.A., 1939; Cornell University, M.A.,

1941, Ph.D., 1951. MILITARY: U.S. Navy Reserve, 1943–45.

CAREER: DIRECTED: *Coriolanus,* Oregon Shakespeare Festival, 1960; *Cymbeline,* Oregon Shakespeare Festival, 1983; FOUNDER—Colorado Shakespeare Festival, 1958; directed about 70 plays in academic and professional theatre.

THEATRE-RELATED CAREER—instructor in drama, Mills College, Oakland, CA, 1941–42; professor of English, University of Colorado, Boulder, CO, 1946–present; visiting professor of Drama, University of Saskatchewan, Saskatoon, Canada, 1961–62; visiting lecturer in English and American Studies, University of Sussex, England, 1981–82.

AWARDS: Tajiri Award for Outstanding Contribution to the Performing Arts in Colorado, 1975.

SIDELIGHTS: MEMBERSHIPS—International Shakespeare Association.

ADDRESS: Home—6175 Habitat Drive, #1077, Boulder, CO 80302 Office—c/o University of Colorado, Boulder, CO 80302

* * *

CUKOR, George Dewey, film director

PERSONAL: Born July 7, 1899, in New York City; died January 24, 1983; son of Victor F. and Helen (Gross) Cukor. MILITARY: U.S. Army.

CAREER: PRINCIPAL STAGE WORK—Director: *The Constant Wife, The Cardboard Lover, The Furies, The Great Gatsby;* director and manager for Charles Frohman Co., 1920–28 at the Lyceum in Rochester, NY, Empire, New York City, 1926–29.

PRINCIPAL FILM WORK—Wrote dialogue for *All Quiet on the Western Front,* 1929; Director: *River of Romance,* 1930; *Grumpy,* 1930; *The Virtuous Sin,* 1930; *The Royal Family of Broadway,* 1931; *Bill of Divorcement,* 1932; *One Hour with You,* 1932; *What Price Hollywood?,* 1932; *Rockabye,* 1932; *Our Betters,* 1932; *Dinner at Eight,* 1933; *Little Women,* 1933; *Tarnished Lady,* 1933; *Girls About Town,* 1933; *David Copperfield,* 1934; *Sylvia Scarlett,* 1935; *Romeo and Juliet,* 1936; *Camille,* 1936; *Holiday,* 1938; *Zaza,* 1938; *Gone with the Wind* (first director), 1939; *The Women,* 1939; *Susan and God,* 1940; *The Philadelphia Story,* 1940; *A Woman's Face,* 1941; *Two-Faced Woman,* 1941; *Her Cardboard Lover,* 1942; *Keeper of the Flame,* 1942; *Resistance and Ohm's Law,* 1943; *Gaslight,* 1944; *Winged Victory,* 1944; *Desire Me,* 1947; *A Double Life,* 1948; *Edward, My Son,* 1948; *Adam's Rib,* 1949; *A Life of Her Own,* 1950; *Born Yesterday,* 1950; *The Model and the Marriage Broker,* 1951; *The Marrying Kind,* 1952; *Pat and Mike,* 1952; *The Actress,* 1953; *It Should Happen to You,* 1954; *A Star Is Born,* 1954; *Bhowani Junction,* 1956; *Les Girls,* 1957; *Wild Is the Wind,* 1957; *Heller in Pink Tights,* 1959; *Song without End* (completed after death of Charles Vidor), 1959; *Let's Make Love,* 1960; *The Chapman Report,* 1962; *Something's Got to Give,* (uncompleted), 1963; *My Fair Lady,* 1964; *Justine,* 1969; *Travels with My Aunt,* 1972; *The Blue Bird,* 1976; *Rich and*

Famous, 1981; Mr. Cukor became a staff director at MGM in 1933.

PRINCIPAL TELEVISION WORK—Director: *Love Among the Ruins; The Corn Is Green.*

AWARDS: Emmy Award, 1974: *Love Among the Ruins;* Academy Award, 1964: *My Fair Lady.* *

* * *

CUMMINGS, Bob (ne Charles Clarence Robert Orville Cummings), actor, director

PERSONAL: Born June 9, 1910 in Joplin, MO; son of Charles Clarence (an M.D. physician and surgeon) and Ruth Annabelle (an ordained minister, Science of Mind; maiden name Kraft) Cummings; married Mary Elliot Daniels; married fourth wife, Regina Maria Helena deAssise Young, March 27; children: Robert, Melinda, Patricia, Laurel, Tony, Charles. EDUCATION: Drury College, Springfield, MO, one year; Carnegie Institute of Technology, Pittsburgh, PA, one year; American Academy of Dramatic Arts, New York, one year. POLITICS: Conservative. RELIGION: Science of Mind. MILITARY: Civilian flight instructor, WWII.

CAREER: NEW YORK DEBUT—The Hon. Reggie Fanning, *The Roof,* 49th Street Theatre, New York, 1931. PRINCIPAL STAGE APPEARANCES—Leading man, *Earl Carroll's Vanities,* Broadway Theatre, New York, 1932; young leading man, *Ziegfeld Follies,* Winter Garden, New York, 1933–34. MAJOR TOURS—*Ziegfeld Follies,* with Fanny Brice and Willie and Eugene Howard, coast to coast and return through Toronto, Montreal, and Quebec, 1934–35.

FILM DEBUT—Archie Pendleton, *So Red the Rose,* Paramount, 1935. PRINCIPAL FILM APPEARANCES—*The Virginia Judge,* 1936; Captain Sanford, *The Texans,* 1936; *Souls at Sea,* 1936; *Hollywood Boulevard,* 1937; *Wells Fargo,* 1937; *I Stand Accused,* 1938; *Touch Down Army,* 1938; *Smart Girls Grow Up,* 1938; *The Underpup,* 1939; *Rio,* 1939; *Spring Parade,* 1940; *Flesh and Fantasy,* 1941; *It Started With Eve,* 1941; *Love and Kisses Caroline,* 1942; *Sabateur,* 1942; *Free for All,* 1942; *Forever and a Day,* 1942; *The Devil and Miss Jones,* 1941; *Everything Happens at Night,* 1939; *Moon over Miami,* 1940; *Kings Row,* 1942; *Princess O'Rouke,* 1942; *One Was Beautiful,* 1941; *You Came Along,* 1944; *The Accused,* 1945; *Paid in Full,* 1944; *The Chase,* 1945; *Sleep My Love,* 1946; *For Heavens Sake,* 1946; *Montana Mike,* 1947; *The First Time,* 1947; *The Petti Girl,* 1947; *Tell It to the Judge,* 1948; *The Barefoot Mailman,* 1948; *The Black Box,* 1948; *Let's Live a Little,* 1949; *The Lost Moment,* 1950; *Marry Me Again,* 1949; *How to Be Very Very Popular,* 1955; *What a Way to Go,* 1955; *Stage Coach,* 1963; *Dial M for Murder,* 1964; *Lucky Me!* 1964; *Promise Her Anything,* 1963; *Carpet Baggers,* 1965; *My Geisha,* 1960; *Gidget Grows Up,* 1970; *The Great American Beauty Contest,* 1972. TELEVISION DEBUT—*Robert Montgomery Presents* (live) NBC, New York, 1951. PRINCIPAL TELEVISION APPEARANCES—*My Hero,* 1952; *The Bob Cummings Show,* NBC, 1954; *12 Angry Men,* CBS Studio I, 1954; *My Living Doll.*

BOB CUMMINGS

WRITINGS: Books published—*Stay Young and Vital*, 1960.

AWARDS: Emmy, Best Actor in a Single Performance, *12 Angry Men*, 1954; Golden Mike Award from Western Pioneer Broadcasters, for 50 years in show business, 1982; honorary colonel, U.S. Air Force Reserve.

SIDELIGHTS: "Because of enormous demand for English plays and actors in the thirties, Cummings travelled to the British Isles 1931 and returned after one month as an English actor "Blade Stanhope Conway". He was signed three days later for his first professional role in John Galsworthy's *The Roof*. His flying career spans 50 years as a commercial pilot for single, and multi-engine airplanes, and is instrument rated. Cummings received 1st Civilian Flight Instructors Rating, 1937. His father was Orville Wright's physician, and Orville Wright became Bob's Godfather, hence the given name Orville. Bob Cummings has been much criticized and castigated for years by segments of the medical profession for his views on natural, organic foods, vitamins and food supplements. His views now vindicated, medics have reluctantly adopted use of food supplements for themselves, their families and patients. Cummings is openly recognized as forty years ahead of his time in the field of nutrition."

* * *

CURRIE, Glenne, critic

PERSONAL: Born March 1, 1926; son of Donald (a farmer) and Winifred Amenia (in retailing; maiden name, Spaul) Currie; married Irene Ramsey (ne Wilson) on January 10, 1953 (divorced, 1978). EDUCATION: University of Toronto, 1943–46.

WRITINGS: United Press International, Lively Arts Editor, 1975–present.

SIDELIGHTS: MEMBERSHIPS—New York Drama Critics Circle; American Theatre Critics Association, Treasurer, 1979–present; Association Internationale des Critiques du Théâtre; Dance Critics Association.

ADDRESS: Home—174 E. 90th Street, New York, NY 10128. Office—c/o UPI, 220 E. 42nd Street, New York, NY 10017.

* * *

CUTHBERT, Neil, playwright

PERSONAL: Born May 5, 1951 in Montclair, NJ; son of Herman Girvin and Ruth Janet (McNeilly) Cuthbert; married Wende Dasteel (an actress), September 6, 1980. EDUCATION: Rutgers University, B.A. 1973; Mason Gross School of the Arts, Rutgers, M.F.A. 1978.

WRITINGS: PLAYS, PUBLISHED—*The Soft Touch*, 1973. PLAYS, PRODUCED—*Snapping People*, Rutgers University, 1975; *Buddy Pals* (one-act) Ensemble Studio, NY, 1978; *First Thirty*, Ensemble Studio, 1979; *The Perfect Stranger*, Ensemble Studio, 1980; *The Smash*, Ensemble Studio, 1981; *Strange Behavior*, Ensemble Studio, 1983. PLAYS, UNPRODUCED—The Home Planet.

SCREENPLAYS—*Saucer*, 1982; *Pluto Nash*, 1983. TELEPLAYS—"Cora", *St. Elsewhere*; *When in Rome*.

AWARDS: Best New Play, American College Theatre Festival, *The Soft Touch*, 1974.

SIDELIGHTS: MEMBERSHIPS—Dramatists Guild; Writers Guild of America; Ensemble Studio Theatre.

In addition to his plays produced at the Ensemble Studio Theatre, Mr. Cuthbert has served the company as its Literary Manager, 1979–81.

ADDRESS: Agent—George Lane, William Morris Agency, 1350 Avenue of the Americas, New York, NY, 10019.

D

DABNEY, Augusta, actress

PERSONAL: Born October 23 in Berkeley, CA; daughter of Thomas Gregory (a doctor) and Jessie F. (Keith) Dabney; married Kevin McCarthy on September 12, 1941 (divorced 1965); married William Prince (an actor) on March 27, 1965; children: (first marriage) James, Lillah, Mary. EDUCATION: University of California, Berkeley, B.A.; studied at the American Academy of Dramatic Arts in New York. POLITICS: Democrat.

CAREER: NEW YORK DEBUT—Maid, *Abe Lincoln in Illinois*, Plymouth, 1939. PRINCIPAL STAGE APPEARANCES—Mrs. Norman, *Children of a Lesser God*, NY; *Another Love Story*, NY; *Dear Ruth*, NY, Chicago; *The Playroom; Who's Afraid of Virginia Woolf?*, NY; *Return Engagement*, NY; *Everything in the Garden; Seascape.*

PRINCIPAL FILM APPEARANCES—*Plaza Suite; Fire Scale; The Heartbreak Kid; That Night; Cold River.*

PRINCIPAL TELEVISION APPEARANCES—*Young Doctor Malone; A World Apart; The Guiding Light; As the World Turns; Another World; One Life to Live; General Hospital; The Doctors; Loving; Love Is a Many Splendored Thing; Most Wanted; Quincy; Policewoman; Lou Grant Show; The Best of Families; Nurse; F.D.R. The Last Year.*

SIDELIGHTS: "In daytime television, Ms. Dabney is known to audiences for many memorable roles, starting with Tracey Malone, the wife of *Young Doctor Malone*. The young doctor was played by William Prince and after the serial ended, Ms. Dabney and Mr. Prince married. They now live in New York's Westchester County and commute to the West Coast when roles demand. They also played a husband and wife team in *Another World*. Ms. Dabney recalled that the serial writer, Irna Phillips, decided one day to move Ms. Dabney and Mr. Prince from *Another World* to *As The World Turns*. 'She gave us new characters with new names in a new town, but we were still a married couple on the show.' They were also featured as a couple in *A World Apart*."

ADDRESS: Home—2 N. Mountain Dr., Dobbs Ferry, NY 10522. Agent—Dulcina Eisen, & Associates, 154 E. 61st Street, New York, NY 10021.

* * *

DALE, Jim (ne Smith), actor

PERSONAL: Born August 15, 1935, in Rothwell, North-amptonshire, England; son of William Henry (a foundry worker) and Miriam (a shoe factory worker; maiden name, Wells) Smith; married Patricia Gardiner (died 1970); married Julie Schafler (a crafts shop owner), March 24, 1981; children: (first marriage) Belinda, Murray, Adam, Toby. EDUCATION: Kettering and District Grammar Schools; studied for the theater by taking ballet, tap and "eccentric" dance lessons for six years as a child. MILITARY: Royal Air Force (discharged 1956). NON-THEATRICAL CAREER: Worked in a shoe factory.

CAREER: DEBUT—Solo comedian, Savoy, Kettering, 1951. LONDON DEBUT—William Dowton, *The Wayward Way*, Lyric, Hammersmith, 1964. NEW YORK DEBUT—Petruchio, *The Taming of the Shrew*, Old Vic, Brooklyn Academy of Music, 1974. PRINCIPAL STAGE APPEARANCES—Autolycus, *The Winter's Tale*, National Theatre, Edinburgh Festival, then Cambridge, London, 1966; Burglar, *The Burglar*, Vaudeville, U.K. 1967; Bottom, *A Midsummer Night's Dream*, Edinburgh Festival, then Saville, 1967; Barnet, *The National Health*, National Theatre, Old Vic, 1969; Nicholas, *The Travails of Sancho Panza*, National, Old Vic, 1969; Costard, *Love's Labours Lost*, National, Old Vic, 1969; Launcelot Gobbo, *The Merchant of Venice*, National, Old Vic, 1970; Scapino, *The Cheats of Scapino*, Young Vic, 1970; Petruchio, *The Taming of the Shrew*, Young Vic, 1970; the Architect, *The Architect and the Emperor of Assyria*, Mr. Lofty, *The Good-Natured Man*, Kalle, *The Captain of Kopenick*, Old Vic, 1971; Denry Machin, *The Card*, Queens, London, 1973; title role, *Scapino*, Brooklyn Academy of Music, then Circle in the Square, then Ambassador, NY, 1974; Gethin Price, *Comedians*, Mark Taper Forum, Los Angeles, 1977; Terri Dennis, *Privates on Parade*, Long Wharf, New Haven, CT, 1979; P.T. Barnum, *Barnum*, St. James, NY, 1980.

MAJOR TOURS—with *Carroll Levis and his Discovers*, Vaudeville, England, 1951–52; Young Vic European tour, 1972.

PRINCIPAL FILMS—*Carry On, Cabby*, 1963; *Carry On, Cleo*, 1964; *Carry On Spying*, 1964; *The Big Job*, 1965; *Carry On, Cowboy*, 1965; *Carry On Screaming*, 1969; *Lock Up Your Daughters*, 1969; *Adolf Hitler–My Part in His Downfall*, 1972; *The National Health or Nurse Norton's Affair*, 1973; *Digby–The Biggest Dog in the World*, 1974; *Pete's Dragon*, 1977; *Joseph Andrews*, 1977; *Hot Lead and Cold Feet*, 1979; *Bloodshy; Comedians; Unidentified Flying Oddball*, 1980.

TELEVISION DEBUT—Warmup comedy act for Tommy Steele, *6:05 Special*, 1957. TELEVISION APPEARANCES—*Lunchtime Show*, 1959; others.

RELATED CAREER—Pop singer; BBC disc jockey; TV comedy writer.

WRITING: SONG LYRICS—Theme, *Georgy Girl,* 1966. MUSIC, FILM—*Shalako,* 1968; *Lola,* 1970.

AWARDS: Antoinette Perry Award, 1980: *Barnum;* Drama Desk Award, Outer Critics Circle Award, Antoinette Perry Award nomination, 1974: *Scapino;* Academy Award nomination, Best Song, 1966: *Georgy Girl.*

SIDELIGHTS: RECREATION—Collecting puppets, dolls in bell-jars and antique toys; loves fishing. FAVORITE ROLES—Petruchio, Scapino.

ADDRESS: Office—c/o David Powers, 1501 Broadway, New York, 10036. Agent—I.C.M., 22 Grafton Street, London, W1, England.*

*   *   *

DALLAS, Meredith Eugene, teacher, actor, director

PERSONAL: Born December 3, 1916 in Detroit, MI; son of William Roderick (a factory foreman) and Ethel Maude (Mcqueen) Dallas; married Willa Louise Winter (a social worker) on October 12, 1940; children: Barbara, Patricia, Wendy, Anthony. EDUCATION: Albion College, B.A., 1939; Western Reserve University, M.A., 1949; Union Graduate School, Ph.D., 1975; studied with Basil Langton.

CAREER: DEBUT—Strepsiades, *The Clouds,* Yellow Springs Summer Theatre. NEW YORK DEBUT—Malvolio, *Twelfth Night,* New York Shakespeare Festival in the Park, 1958. PRINCIPAL STAGE APPEARANCES—Antioch Shakespeare Festival—Citizen of Angiers, *King John; Richard II;* Hotspur, *Henry VI, Pt. 1;* Snare and Silence, *Henry VI, Pt. 2;* Exeter, *Henry V;* Warwick, *Henry VI;* Buckingham, *Richard III;* Cranmer, *Henry VIII;* Poet, *Timon of Athens;* Aaron, *Titus Andronicus;* Marc Anthony, *Julius Caesar;* Host, *Merry Wives of Windsor;* Malvolio, *Twelfth Night;* Macduff, *Macbeth;* New York—Sergeant Winchell, *Family Reunion,* Phoenix Theatre, 1958; Governor's Cousin, *The Power and the Glory,* Phoenix Theatre, 1958; Gibbet, *The Beau Strategem,* Phoenix Theatre, 1959; Caliban, *The Tempest,* Bermuda, 1959. Performed a the following theatres—Cain Park Playhouse, Cleveland; Shaw Festival, Martha's Vineyard, MA; Springfield Civic Theatre, Springfield, OH; Hyde Park Playhouse, Hyde Park, NY; Group 20, Wellesley, MA. DIRECTED—Founder/artistic director, Antioch Shakespeare Festival, 1953–55—*Richard II, Henry V, Henry VII, Coriolanus, Pericles, As You Like It, Cymbeline.* Artistic director, Antioch Amphetheatre, 1961–62; artistic director, Shakespeare at Antioch program, 1964; director, Trotwood Circle Theatre, OH, 1957–60. Guest director—Long Wharf Theatre, New Haven CT; Bear Republic Theatre, Santa Cruz CA. CONCERT—Caliban, premiere, *The Tempest* by Sibelius, Cincinnati Symphony Orchestra, Cincinnati, 1955.

THEATRE RELATED CAREER—Chairman, Department of Drama and Speech, Antioch College, 1963–; research assistant, Fels Research Institute, Yellow Springs, OH; at Antioch College—assistant to the dean, 1946–47; instructor, 1946; assistant professor, 1950, associate professor, 1954.

AWARDS: G.L.C.A. Fellow, theatre study in Japan and Greece, 1967.

SIDELIGHTS: Since 1945, Dr. Dallas has acted in more than 50 productions and directed approximately 50 others at the Antioch Area Theatre and Amphiteatre. "In 1975 I received a PhD in Psychotherapy and Theatre. Subsequently I have formulated the Theatre for Personal Awareness and Theatre of Dreams. I continue to direct in legitimate theatre."

ADDRESS: Home—110 E. Whiteman Street, Yellow Springs, OH 45387.

*   *   *

DALVA, Robert, film editor, director

PERSONAL: Born April 14, 1942, in New York City; son of Leon (an art dealer) and Jean (an art dealer; maiden name, Casewell) Dalva; married Marcia Smith (an artist), December 29, 1965; children: Matthew, Cory, Marshall. EDUCATION: Colgate University, B.A., 1964; University of Southern California, 1964–67.

CAREER: FIRST FILM WORK—Editor, *Lions Love,* 1969. PRINCIPAL FILM WORK—Editor, *Forever,* 1977; editor, *The Black Stallion,* 1979; director, *The Black Stallion Returns,* 1983.

AWARDS: Academy Award Nomination, editor, 1979: *The Black Stallion;* 2 Clio Nominations for public service; Gold Medal, Atlanta Film Festival, political commercials, 1972.

SIDELIGHTS: MEMBERSHIPS—Directors Guild of America, Writers Guild of America, IATSE local 659 and 776; board, Public Media Center, San Francisco, CA. INTERESTS—Sailing, Bonsai trees, disarmament, nuclear disengagement.

ADDRESS: Office—33 Walnut Avenue, Larkspur, CA, 94939. Agent—Jim Berkus, Leading Artists, 445 N. Bedford Street, Beverly Hills, CA 90210.

*   *   *

DANIEL, T. (ne T. Daniel Heagstedt), performer, creator, producer of mime

PERSONAL: Born August 23, 1945 in Evergreen Park, IL; son of Theodore Charles (a businessman) and Thelma L. (an artist; maiden name, Soderlind) Heagstedt; married Laurie J. Willets (a mime artist) on July 14, 1976. EDUCATION: Illinois State University, B.S. (Speech/Theatre), 1967, M.S. (Directing), 1969; Ecole Internationale de Mime: Marcel Marceau, Certificate 1970; Ecole de Mime: Etienne Decroux, Paris, 1974.

CAREER: FIRST STAGE WORK—As a magician, age 7. DEBUT—Mime, *A World of Mime,* Festival Playhouse, Wilmette, IL, 1971. PRINCIPAL WORKS PRODUCED: Mimes—*Collage of Mime, The Body, Sawing a Woman in Half, Death, Listen to Your Heartbeat, Bureaucrats, Wait, 1812 Overture, Sun's Day, The Magician, The Date, White Bird,*

Public Speaker, The Plant, The Bike, Photo Album, The Clown, Haunted House, The Museum, Wandering thru a Forest, Treasure Hunt, Ex Machina, Circus of Mime, The Ball, The Trap, Starlight, Morning, Mysteries of the Orb, Shadows of a Mind, Between the Hand and the Self, A World of Mime, Smiles, Fantasmia.

PRINCIPAL WORKS CREATED OR CHOREOGRAPHED—*The Bike,* 1966; *Sawing a Woman in Half,* 1968; *The Body, 1812 Overture, White Bird, Public Speaker,* 1970; *Sun's Day, Wait, The Date,* 1972; *Photo Album, The Clown, The Museum,* 1973; *Wandering thru a Forest, Ex Machina, Bull on the Roof, Four Seasons, History of a Soldier, The Ball,* 1974; *Peter and the Wolf,* 1976; *Sorcerer's Apprentice, Musicians of Bremen,* 1977; *The Magic Medal (The Comedians), Nightrides and Sunrise, Legend of Sleepy Hollow (Night on Bald Mountain),* 1978; *Between the Hand and the Self, Morning, Starlight, Mysteries of the Orb,* 1980; *Shadows of a Mind,* 1982; *Carnival of the Animals,* 1983.

PRINCIPAL PERFORMANCES: Chicago Symphony Orchestra, Chicago; Indiana Chamber Orchestra, Fort Wayne, IN; Milwaukee Summerfest, Milwaukee; Columbia Museum of Art, Columbus, SC; Art Institute of Chicago; University of Puerto Rico, San Juan, PR; Universidad Catolica de Puerto Rico, Ponce, PR; Quincy Fine Arts Society, Quincy, IL; University of New Brunswick, Fredrickton, NB, Canada; University of Wisconsin–River Falls, WI; University of Minnesota, Morris; University of Minnesota, Duluth; Quincy Symphony Orchestra, Quincy, IL; Culver-Stockton College, Canton, MO; College of Holy Cross, Worcester, MA; Mountain View College, Dallas, TX; Lamar University, Beaumont, TX; Stephen F. Austin State University, Nacogdoches, TX; West Texas University, Canyon, TX; Eastern Michigan University, Ypsilanti, MI; Theatre am Hechtplatz, Zurich; Iowa State University, Ames, IA; State University of New York, NYC; Art Park, Lewiston, NY; Niavaran Cultural Center, Tehran, Iran; Mary Washington College, Fredricksburg, VA; Centro Cultural de la Ville, Madrid, Spain; Instituto de Estudios Norte Americanos, Barcelona, Spain; Ljubljana Festival, Ljubljana, Austria; Spectrum Theatre Festival, Villach, Austria; Vienna Festival, Vienna, Austria; Minnesota Symphony Orchestra, Minneapolis; Atlanta Symphony Orchestra, Atlanta; Omaha Symphony Orchestra, Omaha, NE; Grand Brown Opera House, Concordia, KS; Occidental College, Los Angeles; Eastern Illinois University, Charleston, IL; Drake Theatre, Barat College, Lake Forest, IL; Ravinia Festival, Highland Park, IL; Bemdji State University, Bemdji, MN; St. Cloud University, St. Cloud, MN; Istanbul Festival, Istanbul, Turkey; Eastern New Mexico University, Portales, NM.

THEATRE-RELATED CAREER: Instructor of mime, Kendall College, Evanston, IL, 1972; special instructor, Ruth Page Foundation for the Dance and School of the Chicago Ballet, 1974; instructor and creator of program in mime, South High School, Park Ridge IL, 1974–76; instructor of movement, Art Institute of Chicago, 1975–76; T. Daniels studio of Mime, Winnetka, IL, 1976–80;

AWARDS: Barat College Performance Award, 1982; Urban Gateways Artistic and Dedication Award, 1981; grants, Illinois Arts Council, 1981, 1979; nominated, Illinois Governor's Award for the Arts, 1979; grants, National Endowment for the Arts, 1978 and 1976.

SIDELIGHTS: MEMBERSHIPS—board of directors, Illinois Arts Alliance and Illinois Arts Coalition, 1982; steering committee and program director, Kennedy Center Imagination Celebration Festival, Chicago, 1979.

Mr. Daniel served as special consultant on movement for animated film for Don Bluth Productions, Los Angeles, 1981; he has toured United States and Europe for 11 years in *A World of Mime,* and has written two unpublished works for children, Smiles and Fantasmia.

ADDRESS: Home—1047 Gage St., Winnetka, IL 60093.

* * *

DANNER, Blythe, actress

PERSONAL: Born in Philadelphia, PA; daughter of Harry Earle (a bank executive and singer) and Katharine Danner; married Bruce Paltrow, December 14, 1969; children: Gwyneth Kate, Jake, Laura. EDUCATION: Bard College, 1965.

CAREER: DEBUT—*The Service of Joseph Axminster, The Way Out of the Way In,* Theatre Company of Boston, 1966. NEW YORK DEBUT—Girl, *The Infantry,* 81st Street Theatre, 1966. PRINCIPAL STAGE APPEARANCES—Helena, *A Midsummer Night's Dream,* Irene, *The Three Sisters,* Trinity Square Players, Providence, RI, 1967; Michele, *Mata Hari,* National, Washington, DC, 1967; the Girl, *Summertree,* Forum, NY, 1968; Sister Martha, *Cyrano de Bergerac,* Vivian Beaumont, NY, 1968; Violet Bean, *Up Eden,* Jan Hus, NY, 1968; Connie Odum, *Someone's Comin' Hungry,* Pocket, NY, 1969; Elsie, *The Miser,* Vivian Beaumont, NY, 1969; Jill Tanner, *Butterflies Are Free,* Booth, NY, 1969; Barbara, *Major Barbara,* Mark Taper Forum, Los Angeles, 1971; Viola, *Twelfth Night,* Vivian Beaumont, NY, 1972; Cynthia Karslake, *The New York Idea,* Brooklyn Academy of Music, NY, 1977; Emma, *Betrayal,* Trafalgar, NY, 1980; Tracy Lord, *The Philadelphia Story,* Vivian Beaumont, NY, 1980; also is often a company member of the Williamstown Theatre Festival where her roles include: Nina, *The Seagull,* 1974, Isabel, *Ring Round the Moon,* 1975, Lisa, *Children of the Sun,* 1979, many others.

FILM DEBUT—*To Kill a Clown,* (unreleased), 1972. PRINCIPAL FILMS—*Lovin' Molly,* 1974; *Futureworld,* 1976; Martha Jefferson, *1776,* 1976; *Hearts of the West,* 1976; *The Great Santini,* 1980.

TELEVISION APPEARANCES—*N.Y.P.D.,* 1968; *To Confuse an Angel,* 1970; *George M!,* 1970; *Dr. Cook's Garden,* 1971; *The Scarecrow,* 1972; *To Be Young, Gifted and Black,* 1972; Amanda, *Adam's Rib,* 1973; Nina, *The Seagull,* PBS; Alma, *Eccentricities of a Nightingale,* PBS, 1976; Joan Maple, *Too Far to Go,* PBS, 1979; Alice, *You Can't Take It With You,* PBS, 1979; Zelda, *F. Scott Fitzgerald and the Last of the Belles,* 1981.

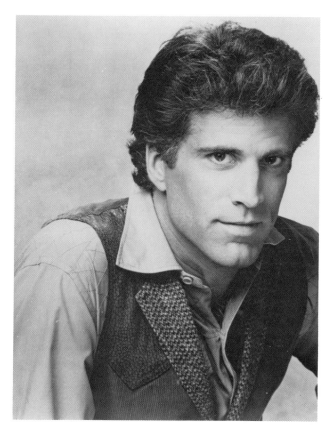

TED DANSON

DANSON, Ted, actor

PERSONAL: Born December 29, 1947; son of Edward B. (an archeologist) and Jessica (MacMaster) Danson; married Randall Lee Gosch in August of 1970 (divorced 1977); married Cassandra Coates (a designer) on July 30, 1977; children: Kate. EDUCATION: Attended the Kent School, 1961–66, Stanford University 1966–68 and Carnegie-Mellon University 1968–72; studied at the Actors Institute with Dan Fauci.

CAREER: NEW YORK DEBUT—Reginald, *The Real Inspector Hound,* Theatre Four, 1972. PRINCIPAL STAGE APPEARANCES—*Comedy of Errors,* New York Shakespeare Festival, NY; *Comedians,* NY; *Status Quo Vadis,* NY.

FILM DEBUT—Cop, *The Onion Field.* PRINCIPAL FILM APPEARANCES—Lawyer, *Body Heat; Creepshow; A Little Treasure.*

TELEVISION DEBUT—*The Doctors.* PRINCIPAL TELEVISION APPEARANCES—*Somerset; The Women's Room; The Good Witch at Laurel Canyon; Cowboy; Something About Amelia;* currently starring lead on *Cheers.*

THEATRE-RELATED CAREER: Acting Teacher, Actors Institute, Los Angeles, CA, 1978–80.

AWARDS: Emmy Award Nomination for comedy male Lead; Discovery of the Year, Women's Press Assocation, 1983.

ADDRESS: Office—c/o Paramount Studios, Bldg D Rm. 201, 5555 Melrose, Los Angeles, CA 90038. Agent—Richard Bauman, c/o Bauman & Hiller, 9220 Sunset Blvd., Los Angeles, CA 90069.

* * *

DARLOW, Cynthia, actress

PERSONAL: Born June 13, 1949, in Detroit, MI; daughter of Frank R. and Harriet N. (an office manager; maiden name, Sears) Darlow. EDUCATION: North Carolina School of the Arts, 1967–70; Pennsylvania State University, 1969; Rose Bruford Training School of Speech and Drama, Bromley-Kent, England, 1970.

CAREER: DEBUT—Jo, *A Taste of Honey,* North Carolina Festival Theatre, Winston-Salem, NC, 1968. NEW YORK DEBUT—Willie, *This Property Condemned,* Manhattan Theatre Club, 1973. PRINCIPAL STAGE APPEARANCES—Rebecca Gibbs, *Our Town,* Penn State Festival Theatre, 1969; Mrs. Hardcastle, *She Stoops to Conquer,* Ford's Theatre, Washington, DC, 1969; Electra, *Clytemnestra,* Cubiculo, NY, 1974; Jan, *Grease,* Imperial, NY, 1978–80; Keystone Cop, *VIP Night on Broadway,* NY, 1979; American Repertory Theatre, 1980: Phoebe, *As You Like It,* Hermia, *Midsummer Night's Dream,* Magalone, Countess Geschwitz, *Lulu,* ensemble, *Seven Deadly Sins;* Arlie, *Getting Out,* A Contemporary Theatre, Seattle, WA, 1981; Lisette, Dorimene,

CYNTHIA DARLOW

Lucinde, *Sganerelle,* Goodman, Chicago, 1982; Ellen, Terry, Philomena, *The Actor's Nightmare,* and *Sister Mary Ignatius Explains It All for You,* Westside Arts, NY, 1982; understudy Jackie, Sorel, *Hayfever,* Ahamson, Los Angeles, 1983; Penny, *That's It Folks,* Playwrights Horizons, NY, 1983; Nanny, Kate, Principal, *Baby with the Bathwater,* Playwrights Horizons, 1984; Libby, Jill, Dierdre, Peggy, Ginny, *Fables for Friends,* Playwrights Horizons, 1984; Isabel, Doris, Harriet, Lucy, *American Clock,* Mark Taper Forum, Los Angeles, 1984; Jane, *Wild Oats,* Mark Taper Forum, 1984.

MAJOR TOURS—Fool (understudy), *King Lear,* Ophelia, *Hamlet,* Ismene, *Antigone,* National Shakespeare Company, 1972; Jan, *Grease,* national tour, 1974; Charwoman, *A Christmas Carol,* national tour, 1983.

PRINCIPAL FILM APPEARANCES—Hermia, *A Midsummer Night's Dream,* PBS, 1980.

SIDELIGHTS: MEMBERSHIPS—Board of Directors, National Theatre Workshop of the Handicapped, AEA, SAG, AFTRA.

ADDRESS: Home—125 W. 96th Street, New York, NY 10025. Agent—Gage Group, 1650 Broadway, New York, NY 10036.

* * *

DAVIS, Allen III, director, manager, writer

PERSONAL: Born March 9, 1929; son of Allen Jr. (a manufacturer) and Rose (Gershon) Davis. EDUCATION: Syracuse University, B.A. (cum laude), 1950; Yale University, School of Drama, M.F.A., 1956; studied acting technique with Paul Mann and Lloyd Richards, 1957–59. MILITARY: U.S. Marine Corps, 1951–53.

CAREER: FIRST STAGE WORK—Assistant stage manager, *A Midsummer Night's Dream,* Cain Park Theatre, Cleveland Heights, OH, 1950. NEW YORK DEBUT: Directed—*The Prodigal,* Riverside Church, 1960. DIRECTED: Director, off-Broadway and community theatres, stage manager and light designer in summer stock, 1950–70.

THEATRE-RELATED CAREER: Administrator, Puerto Rican Traveling Theatre, New York, 1970–78; administrator/leader, The Imagination Workshop, Department of Psychiatry, Mount Sinai Hospital, New York, 1972–74; general manager, Santa Fe Theatre Company, Santa Fe, NM, 1967–68; general manager, Cincinnati Playhouse in the Park, Cincinnati, OH, 1966; executive director, North Shore Community Arts Center, Great Neck, NY; director, Playwrights Unit, Puerto Rican Traveling Theatre, New York, 1981–82; writing instructor, Project Find, Senior Citizen Center, New York, 1980–82; writer-in-residence, University of Alaska, Anchorage, 1975; instructor, acting technique, Senior Dramatic Workshop, New York, 1962.

WRITINGS: PLAYS PRODUCED—*Montezuma's Revenge,* produced at St. Clement's Theatre, New York, 1979; *Bull Fight Cow,* produced at The New Dramatists, New York, 1976; *The Rag Doll,* produced at New Dramatists, and University of Texas, Austin, 1974; *Where the Green Bananas Grow,*

produced at the HB Foundation and New Dramatists, New York, 1972; *The Head of Hair,* produced at New Theatre Workshop, New York, 1970, and at the Milwaukee Repertory Theatre, Milwaukee, 1967. PLAYS PUBLISHED—*Rocco the Rolling Stone* (children's play) and *Leroy and the Ark* (children's play), 1970.

AWARDS: CAPS Grant, New York State Council on the Arts, 1980; National Endowment for the Arts, grant, 1978.

SIDELIGHTS: MEMBERSHIPS—board of directors, American Repertory Stage Company; AEA; SSD&C; The Dramatists Guild; The New Dramatists.

''I have a special interest in developing new plays by Third World writers.''

ADDRESS: Office—c/o Puerto Rican Traveling Theatre, 276 W. 43rd Street, New York, NY 10036.

* * *

DAVIS, Ariel, designer and manufacturer of theatre lighting equipment

PERSONAL: Born February 14, 1912; son of Rual Dennis (a millwright) and Mary Louise (a schoolteacher; maiden name, Kitchen) Davis; married Dorothy Jean Harding; children: Ronald, Steven. EDUCATION: Brigham Young University, B.S. (physics), 1946. MILITARY: U.S. Navy, Chief Petty Officer, 1943–46 (South Pacific).

AWARDS: Outstanding Engineer of the Year Award, state of Utah, by the combined Engineering Councils of Utah, 1961; Franklin S. Harris Fine Arts Award, Brigham Young University, 1970.

SIDELIGHTS: MEMBERSHIPS—Theta Alpha Phi; Illumination Engineering Society; National Committee on Stage Lighting.

THEATRE-RELATED CAREER: President, Davis Enterprises, Provo, UT; president, Ariel Davis Manufacturing Company, Salt Lake City, UT; Inventor—Davis Dimmer Switch; has 58 patents on other lighting control and stage lighting equipment.

ADDRESS: Home—134 E. 4380 N. Street, Provo, UT.

* * *

DAVIS, Bette (nee Ruth Elizabeth), actress

PERSONAL: Born April 5, 1908, in Lowell, MA; daughter of Harlow Morell and Ruth Elizabeth (Favor) Davis; married Harmon Oscar Nelson, Jr., August 18, 1932 (divorced); Arthur Farnsworth, December, 1940 (died August 25, 1943); William Grant Sherry, November 30, 1945 (divorced); Gary Merrill, August 1950 (divorced); children: (third marriage) Barbara; (fourth marriage) adopted Margot, Michael. EDUCATION: Attended public schools in New York City and Newton, MA; studied dance with Roshanara and Martha

BETTE DAVIS

Graham; studied for the stage with Michael Mordkin, Robert Bell, George Currie and attended the John Murray Anderson School of the Theatre.

CAREER: DEBUT—*Broadway*, Temple, Rochester, NY, 1928. NEW YORK DEBUT—Floy Jennings, *The Earth Between*, Provincetown Playhouse, 1929. LONDON DEBUT—*An Informal Evening with Bette Davis*, Palladium, 1975. PRINCIPAL STAGE APPEARANCES—*Excess Baggage, Yellow, The Squall*, Temple, Rochester, NY, 1928; Elaine Bumpstead, *The Broken Dish*, Ritz, NY, 1929; Dinah, *Mr. Pim*, Cape Dennis Playhouse, MA, 1930; Bam, *Solid South*, Lyceum, NY, 1930; *Two Company*, Alvin, NY, 1952; *The World of Carl Sandburg*, Henry Miller's, 1959; Maxine Faulk, *The Night of the Iguana*, Royale, NY, 1961; title-role, *Miss Moffat*, Shubert, Philadelphia, 1974; *An Informal Evening with Bette Davis*, Opera House, Sydney, Australia, 1975.

FILM DEBUT—Laura, *Bad Sister*, 1931. PRINCIPAL FILM APPEARANCES—*The Man Who Played God*, 1932; *Of Human Bondage*, 1934; *Dangerous*, 1935; *The Petrified Forest*, 1936; *Jezebel*, 1938; *Dark Victory*, 1939; *The Private Lives of Elizabeth and Essex*, 1939; *The Letter*, 1940; *The Little Foxes*, 1941; *The Man Who Came to Dinner*, 1941; *Watch on the Rhine*, 1943; *Mr. Skeffington*, 1944; *The Corn Is Green*, 1945; *The Great Lie; The Bride Came; All About Eve*, 1950; *Payment on Demand*, 1951; *Phone Call from a Stranger*,

1952; *The Star*, 1953; *The Virgin Queen*, 1955; *Storm Center; The Catered Affair*, 1956; *John Paul Jones*, 1959; *The Scapegoat*, 1959; *What Ever Happened to Baby Jane*, 1962; *Dead Ringer; Painted Canvas; Where Love Has Gone; Hush, Hush, Sweet Charlotte*, 1964; *The Nanny*, 1965; *The Anniversary*, 1967; *Connecting Rooms*, 1969; *Bunny O'Hare*, 1970; *Madam Sin*, 1971; *The Game*, 1972; *Burnt Offerings*, 1977; *Death on the Nile*, 1979; *Watcher in the Woods*, 1979.

PRINCIPAL TELEVISION APPEARANCES—Television movies: *Sister Aimee*, 1977; *The Dark Secret of Harvest Home*, 1978; *Strangers*, 1979; *White Momma*, 1980; *Skyward*, 1980; *Family Reunion*, 1981; *A Piano for Mrs. Cimino*, 1982; *Little Gloria—Happy At Last*, 1982; *Right of Way*, 1983. Series appearances—*General Electric Theatre, Wagon Train, Alfred Hitchcock Presents, Hotel*.

WRITINGS: BOOKS—*The Lonely Life*, 1962; co-author, *Mother Goddam*, 1974.

AWARDS: Women in Films Crystal Award, 1983; Department of Defense Medal for Distinguished Public Service, 1983; American Academy of Arts Award, 1983; Rudolph Valentino Life Achievement Award, 1982; Emmy Award, 1979: *Strangers;* American Film Institute Life Achievement Award, 1977; Academy Award, Best Actress, 1938: *Jezebel.*

ADDRESS: Office—c/o Gottlieb Schiff Ticktin Sternklar & Harris, P.C., 555 Fifth Avenue, New York, NY 10017.

* * *

DAVIS, Jeff, designer

PERSONAL: Born April 14, 1950, in Philadelphia, PA; son of John Wallace (a surgeon) and Gail (Gardner) Davis. EDUCATION: Northwestern University, B.A., 1972.

CAREER: FIRST STAGE WORK—Lighting designer/scenic designer, *Death of a Salesman*, Walnut Street Theatre, Philadelphia, PA, 1974. NEW YORK DEBUT—Lighting designer, *Ride the Winds*, Bijou Theatre, New York, 1975. PRINCIPAL LIGHTING DESIGNER WORK—New York: *The Man Who Had Three Arms*, Lyceum; *The Man Who Came to Dinner*, Circle in the Square; *Ride the Winds*, Bijou; associate designer, *Foxfire*, Barrymore; associate designer, *Blues in the Night*, Rialto; associate designer, *Fiddler on the Roof*, New York State Theatre; associate designer, *Oh Brother!*, ANTA; *Becoming Memories*, South Street Theatre; *Portrait of Jennie*, Henry Street Theatre; *Album*, Cherry Lane Theatre, *Judgement*, St. Peter's Church; *The Slab Boys*, Hudson Guild; *I Paid My Dues*, Astor Place Theatre; Regional companies: Goodspeed Opera House, East Haddam, CT; Cincinnati Playhouse, Cincinnati; American Shakespeare Festival, Stratford, CT; Indiana Repertory Company, Indianapolis, IN; Hartman Theatre Company, Stamford CT; Huntington Theatre Company, Boston; Philadelphia Drama Guild, Philadelphia; Berkshire Theatre Festival, Stockbridge, MA.

MAJOR TOURS, Lighting Design—*Fiddler on the Roof*, national company; *The River Niger*, national company. LIGHTING SUPERVISION—*Annie*, Shubert, Los Angeles, and three national companies; *The Oldest Living Graduate*, Wilshire

Theatre, Los Angeles; *Morning's At Seven,* national company. PRE-BROADWAY, LIGHTING DESIGN—*Dancin' in the Streets,* Ford's Theatre, Washington, DC; *Death of a Salesman,* Walnut Street Theatre, Philadelphia. CONCERT LIGHTING DESIGN—Marvin Hamlisch, Maxine Andrews. DANCE LIGHTING DESIGN—José Limon Dance Company; Annabelle Gamson. INDUSTRIAL PRODUCTION LIGHTING DESIGN—Johnson & Johnson Company, Care Bears, Strawberry Shortcake. Associate Designer to Jo Mielziner. Lighting Assistant to Tharon Musser, Ken Billington, Richard Nelson, John McLain.

SIDELIGHTS: MEMBERSHIPS—United Scenic Artists, Local 829.

"Most important to my development and education was my training by Delbert Unruh and my association with Jo Mielziner."

ADDRESS: Home—114 W. 76th Street, New York, NY 10023.

* * *

DAWBER, Pam, actress

PERSONAL: Born October 18, 1954 in Detroit, MI; daughter of Eugene E. (a commercial artist) and Thelma M. (Fisher) Dawber. EDUCATION: Attended Oakland Community College, Farmington Hills, MI, for one year; studied voice with Jack Woltzer and Nate Lam in Los Angeles, CA, and with Pappy Earnhart in New York City.

CAREER: DEBUT—Jennie, *Sweet Adeline,* Goodspeed Opera House, East Haddam, CT, 1977. NEW YORK DEBUT—Mabel, *Pirates of Penzance,* Minskoff, 1982. PRINCIPAL STAGE APPEARANCES—Mabel, *Pirates of Penzance,* Ahmanson, Los Angeles, 1981.

MAJOR TOURS—Eliza Doolittle, *My Fair Lady,* Kenley Theatres, Columbus, Dayton, Akron, OH, 1980.

FILM DEBUT—Tracy, *A Wedding,* 1977.

TELEVISION DEBUT—Mindy, *Mork and Mindy,* 1978–82. PRINCIPAL TELEVISION APPEARANCES—*The Girl, the Gold Watch and Everything,* 1980; *Tony Award Show,* 1982; *Texaco Star Theatre—A Salute to the American Musical,* 1982; *Remembrance of Love,* 1982; *Last of the Great Survivors,* 1983; *Thru Naked Eyes,* 1983; *Parade of Stars,* 1983; *Voyeurs.*

THEATRE-RELATED CAREER: Teacher, tv commercial class, Wilhemina Modeling Agency, 1977–78.

AWARDS: People's Choice Award, Favorite Newcomer, 1978; Photoplay Award, Favorite Actress in a new series, 1978.

SIDELIGHTS: MEMBERSHIPS—SAG; AFTRA; AEA; Board of Directors, Solar Lobby, Washington, DC. RECREATIONS—canoeing, cooking, horseback riding, reading, listening to classical music and swimming.

PAM DAWBER

"When I was a child, I would pantomime records and the radio . . . when my parents would go out and leave me at home, I'd take out all the Broadway musical albums, acting and singing with them, but, because we lived in Detroit, I never imagined I would ever do anything with it when I grew up . . ." Ms. Dawber eventually ended up in New York working as a successful model when she set her sights on acting and singing, winning a role at the Goodspeed Opera House in East Haddam Connecticut. During the run of the show, she received a call from the West Coast to audition for a new television series, while out there auditioning, she was offered a screen test which led to a one-year contract with ABC. One day she picked up one of the trade papers to discover she was announced to star in a new series, *Mork and Mindy,* with Robin Williams. The news left her flattered but dismayed, knowing nothing about either the show or her co-star.

ADDRESS: Office—Rabbit Productions-Paramount Studies, 5555 Melrose Avenue, Los Angeles, CA 90038. Personal Manager—Mimi Weber, 9200 Sunset Blvd., Los Angeles, CA 90069.

* * *

de BANZIE, Lois, actress

PERSONAL: Born May 4, in Glasgow, Scotland; daughter of Eric (a journalist) and Stella (Wood-Sims) de Banzie. EDUCATION: Attended schools in Scotland; studied with David Craig, Phillip Burton, Eve Collyer.

CAREER: PRINCIPAL STAGE APPEARANCES—*The Boyfriend*, Golden Hind, San Francisco, CA, Mexico City, 1959–60; Festival, San Francisco, CA: *Toys in the Attic, The Flowering Peach, The Skin of Our Teeth, Plays for Bleecker Street*, 1961–64; *The Macaroni Show*, Spaghetti Factory, San Francisco, 1962; *San Francisco's Burning*, San Francisco Playhouse, 1963; *Elizabeth the Queen*, City Center, NY, 1966; *Miaow*, Theatre at Noon, NY, 1971; Lincoln Center Repertory, NY: *Mary Stuart, People Are Living There, Ride Across Lake Constance*, 1971–72; *Blithe Spirit*, Hartford Stage Company, CT, 1971; *The Divorce of Judy and Jane*, Bijou, NY, 1972; *The Last Days of Mrs. Lincoln*, ANTA, NY, 1972–73; *Man and Superman*, APA/Phoenix, NY; *The Paisley Convertible*, Alhambra Dinner Theatre, 1973; *The Three Sisters*, AMAS Repertory, NY, 1973; *The Judas Applause*, Chelsea Theatre Center, NY; *The Misanthrope*, Asolo State, Sarasota, FL; *Arms and the Man*, Asolo State; *Any Wednesday*, Alhambra Dinner Theatre, 1974; *The Royal Family*, Philadelphia Drama Guild, 1975; *Move Over Mrs. Markham*, Showboat Dinner Theatre, 1976; *Hamlet*, Philadelphia Drama Guild, 1977; *The Utter Glory of Morrissey Hall*, McCarter, Princeton, NJ, 1977; *Da*, Morosco, NY, 1978–79; *Morning's At Seven*, Lyceum, NY, 1980–81; *The Dining Room*, Playwrights' Horizons, Astor Place Theatre, NY, 1982. MAJOR TOURS—*Lloyd George Knew My Father*, Kennedy Center, Ottawa Arts Center, Canada, 1974; *The Mousetrap*, Royal Poinciana Playhouse, Parker Playhouse, Peachtree Playhouse, 1976; *Blithe Spirit* (same theatres), 1978.

PRINCIPAL FILM APPEARANCES—*So Fine*, 1981; *Annie*, 1981; *Sudden Impact*, 1983; *Mass Appeal*, 1983. PRINCIPAL TELEVISION APPEARANCES—*AfterM*A*S*H*; Lottery; Mr. Smith; The Bob Newhart Show; Remington Steele; Cheers; Gimme a Break; Taxi; The Return of the Man From U.N.C.L.E.; One of the Boys; The Witches of Salem.*

AWARDS: Antoinette Perry Nomination, Myrtle Brown, 1980: *Mornings at Seven*; Drama Desk Award, Outer Critics Circle Award, Myrtle Brown, 1980: *Morning's At Seven*.

SIDELIGHTS: MEMBERSHIPS—AEA, AFTRA, SAG.

ADDRESS: Agent—STE Representation, Ltd. 211 S. Beverly Drive, Beverly Hills, CA 90212; STE, 888 Seventh Avenue, New York, NY 10019.

* * *

DE CORDOVA, Frederick, producer, director

PERSONAL: Born October 27, 1910, in New York City; son of George (in the theatre) and Margaret (Timmins) de Cordova; married Janet Thomas, September 27, 1963. EDUCATION: Northwestern, 1931, B.A.

CAREER: THEATRICAL DEBUT—Assistant to John Shubert, Shubert Office, 1932. PRINCIPAL STAGE WORK—Stage manager, director, producer, Shubert productions, 1932–42. PRINCIPAL FILM WORK—Director, Warner Brothers, 1943–48; director, Universal, International, 1948–53.

PRINCIPAL TELEVISION WORK: Producer, director—*Burns*

and Allen Show; Jack Benny Program; December Bride; Mr. Adams and Eve; My Three Sons; The Tonight Show, 1970–

AWARDS: Six Emmys, eleven Emmy Nominations.

ADDRESS: Office—*The Tonight Show*, 3000 W. Alameda Avenue, Burbank, CA 91505.

* * *

DEE, Ruby (nee Ruby Ann Wallace), actress

PERSONAL: Born October 27, 1924, in Cleveland, OH; daughter of Marshall Edward and Emma (Benson), Wallace; married Ossie Davis (an actor and writer), December 9, 1948; children: Nora, La Verne, Guy. EDUCATION: Hunter College, B.A., 1945; worked as an apprentice at the American Negro Theatre, 1941–44; studied with Morris Carnovsky, 1958–60 and at the Actors Workshop with Paul Mann and Lloyd Richards.

CAREER: DEBUT—A native, *South Pacific* (drama), Cort, NY, 1943. PRINCIPAL STAGE APPEARANCES—Ruth, *Walk Hard*, Library (for the American Negro Theatre), NY, 1944; Libby George, *Jeb*, Martin Beck, NY, 1946; title role, *Anna Lucasta*, Mansfield, 1946; Marcy, *A Long Way from Home*, Maxine Elliot's, 1948; Mrs. Ellen McClellan, *The Washington Years*, American Negro Theatre Playhouse, 1948; Evelyn, *The Smile of the World*, Lyceum, NY, 1949; Defending Angel, *The World of Sholom Aleichem*, Barbizon Plaza, NY, 1959; Ruth Younger, *A Raisin in the Sun*, Barrymore, NY, 1959; Luttiebelle Gussie Mae Jenkins, *Purlie Victorius*, Cort, NY, 1961; Cordelia, *King Lear*, Kate, *The Taming of the Shrew*, American Shakespeare Festival, Stratford, CT, 1965; Cassandra, *The Oresteia*, Ypsilanti Greek Theatre, MI, 1966; Julia Augustine, *Wedding Band*, Ann Arbor, MI, 1966; Lena, *Boesman and Lena*, Circle in the Square, NY, 1970; *The Imaginary Invalid*, Walnut, Philadelphia, 1971; Julia Augustine, *Wedding Band*, Newman, 1972; Gertrude, *Hamlet*, Delcorte, NY, 1975. FILM DEBUT—*No Way Out*, 1950. PRINCIPAL FILM APPEARANCES—*The Jackie Robinson Story*, 1950; *Tall Target*, 1951; *Go Man Go*, 1953; *Edge of the City*, 1959; *St. Louis Blues; A Raisin in the Sun*, 1961; *Gone Are the Days*, 1963; *The Balcony*, 1963; *Purlie Victorious; To Be Young, Gifted and Black; Uptight*, 1968; *Buck and the Preacher*, 1972; *Black Girl*, 1972; *Countdown at Kusini*, 1976.

PRINCIPAL TELEVISION APPEARANCES—*Actor's Choice*, 1960; *Seven Times Monday*, 1961; *Go Down Moses*, 1963; *It's Good to Be Alive*, 1974; *Today Is Ours*, 1974; *Twin-Bit Gardens*, 1975; *The Defenders; Police Woman; Peyton Place; All God's Children; Roots: The Next Generation; I Know Why the Caged Bird Sings; Wedding Band; To Be Young, Gifted and Black; With Ossie and Ruby*, 1981.

RELATED CAREER: Co-producer of television program, *Today Is Ours; Ossie Davis and Ruby Dee Story Hour* (radio), 1974–78; recorded poems and stories.

WRITINGS: PLAYS PRODUCED—*Twin-Bit Gardens*, revised as *Take It from the Top*, 1979; SCREENPLAY—co-author, *Uptight;* POETRY—*Glowchild*, 1972; columnist, NY Amsterdam News; associate editor, Freedomways magazine.

AWARDS: Drama Desk Award, 1974; Anniversary Martin Luther King Jr., Operation PUSH, 1972; Obie Award, 1971: Lena, *Boseman and Lena;* with husband, Frederick Douglass Award, NY Urban League, 1970.

SIDELIGHTS: MEMBERSHIPS—NAACP; CORE; Students for Non-Violence, (co-ordinating committee); Southern Christian Leadership Conference.*

* * *

DE LAURENTIIS, Dino, producer

PERSONAL: Born August 8, 1919, in Torre Annunziata, Italy; son of Rosario Aurelio and Giuseppina (Salvatore) de Laurentiis; married Silvana Magnano (an actress), July 17, 1949; children: Veronica, Rafaella, Federico, Francesca. EDUCATION: Attended high school and commercial school in Naples; Centro Sperimentale di Cinematografia in Rome, 1937–39.

CAREER: Organized first production company in 1941; PRODUCER: *Bitter Rice,* 1952; *Ulysses,* 1955; *War and Peace,* 1956; *La Strada,* 1956; *Nights of Cabiria,* 1957; *This Angry Age,* 1958; *The Tempest,* 1959; *Under Ten Flags,* 1960; *The Best Enemies,* 1962; *Barabbas,* 1962; *Three Faces of a Woman (Soraya),* 1964; *The Bible,* 1966; *Barbarella,* 1968; *Anzio,* 1968; *Waterloo,* 1971; *The Valachi Papers,* 1972; *The Stone Killer,* 1973; *Serpico,* 1974; *Death Wish,* 1974; *Mandingo,* 1975; *Three Days of the Condor,* 1975; *Lipstick,* 1976; *Face to Face,* 1976; *Buffalo Bill and the Indians,* 1976; *The Shootist,* 1976; *King Kong,* 1976; *Orca,* 1977; *The Serpent's Egg,* 1978; *King of Gypsies,* 1978; *The Brink's Job,* 1978; *The Great Train Robbery,* 1978; *Hurricane,* 1979; *Flash Gordon,* 1980; *Halloween II,* 1981; *Ragtime,* 1981; *Striking Back,* 1982; *Conan the Barbarian,* 1982; *Amityville II: The Possession,* 1982; *Amityville-3D,* 1983; *The Dead Zone,* 1983; *Dune,* 1984.

AWARDS: Academy Awards: 1957: *Nights of Cabiria,* 1956: *La Strada.*

ADDRESS: Dino de Laurentiis Corp., One Gulf + Western Plaza, New York, NY 10023.*

* * *

DE NIRO, Robert, actor

PERSONAL: Born August 17, 1943 in New York; son of Robert (an artist) and Virgina (Admiral) De Niro; married Diahnne Abbott (an actress); children: Drena, Raphael. EDUCATION: Studied with Stella Adler and Lee Strasberg at the Actors Studio.

CAREER: PRINCIPAL STAGE APPEARANCE—*One Night Stand of a Noisy Passenger,* NY.

PRINCIPAL FILM APPEARANCES—*Greetings,* 1968; *The Wedding Party,* 1969; *Bloody Mama,* 1970; *Hi, Mom,* 1970; ·*Jennifer on My Mind,* 1971; *Born to Win,* 1971; *The Gang*

That Couldn't Shoot Straight, 1971; *Bang the Drum Slowly,* 1973; *Mean Streets,* 1973; Vito Corleone, *The Godfather, Part II,* 1974; *1900,* 1975; Travis Bickle, *Taxi Driver,* 1976; *The Last Tycoon,* 1977; Jimmy Doyle, *New York, New York,* 1977; *The Deer Hunter,* 1979; Jake la Motta, *Raging Bull,* 1980; *True Confessions,* 1982; *King of Comedy,* 1983; *Once upon a Time in America,* 1984.

AWARDS: Academy Award, Best Actor, 1981: *Raging Bull;* Hasty Pudding Award, Harvard University, 1979; Academy Award, Best Supporting Actor, 1974: *The Godfather Part II.*

SIDELIGHTS: MEMBERSHIPS—AEA; SAG.

ADDRESS: c/o Julien, 1501 Broadway, New York, NY 10036.

* * *

DENNIS, Sandy, actress

PERSONAL: Born April 27, 1937, in Hastings, NE; daughter of Jack and Yvonne Dennis; married Gerry Mulligan (a jazz musician), June, 1975. EDUCATION: Attended Nebraska Wesleyan University, University of Nebraska; studied acting at the Herbert Berghof Studios in New York City.

CAREER: DEBUT—Elma Duckworth, *Bus Stop,* Royal Poinciana Playhouse, Palm Beach, FL, 1956. NEW YORK DEBUT—Millicent Bishop, *Face of a Hero,* O'Neill, 1960. PRINCIPAL STAGE APPEARANCES—understudy, Flirt Conroy and Reenie Flood, *The Dark at the Top of the Stairs,* Music Box, NY, 1957; Nancy, *Motel,* Wilbur, Boston, MA, 1960; Ann Howard, *The Complaisant Lover,* Barrymore, NY, 1961; Sandra Markowitz, *A Thousand Clowns,* O'Neill, NY, 1962; Ellen Gordon, *Any Wednesday,* Music Box, NY, 1964; Daphne, *Daphne in Cottage D,* Longacre, NY, 1967; Cherry, *Bus Stop,* Ivanhoe, Chicago, 1970; Teresa Phillips, *How the Other Half Loves,* Royale, NY, 1971; Hannah Heywood, *Let Me Hear You Smile,* Biltmore, NY, 1973; Blanche, *A Streetcar Named Desire,* Ivanhoe, Chicago, 1973; Billie Dawn, *Born Yesterday,* Westport Country Playhouse, CT, 1974; Eva, *Absurd Person Singular,* Music Box, NY, 1974, 1975, 1976; Maggie, *Cat on a Hot Tin Roof,* Playhouse in the Park, Philadelphia, 1975; Doris, *Same Time Next Year,* Brooks Atkinson, NY, 1976; Sally, *The Supporting Cast,* Biltmore, NY, 1981; Mona, *Come Back to the 5 & Dime, Jimmy Dean, Jimmy Dean,* Martin Beck, NY, 1982; Sophia Bowsky, *Buried Inside Extra,* Public, NY, 1983.

MAJOR TOURS—Reenie Flood, *The Dark at the Top of the Stairs,* 1959; Anna Reardon, *And Miss Reardon Drinks a Little,* 1971–72; Billie Dawn, *Born Yesterday,* 1974; Maggie, *Cat on a Hot Tin Roof,* 1975.

FILM DEBUT—*Splendor in the Grass,* 1961. PRINCIPAL FILM APPEARANCES—Honey, *Who's Afraid of Virginia Woolf?,* 1965; *Up the Down Staircase,* 1967; *The Fox,* 1967; *Sweet November,* 1968; *Daphne in Cottage D; The Millstone; Thank You All Very Much,* 1969; *That Cold Day in the Park,* 1969; *The Out of Towners,* 1970; *Same Time Next Year,* 1979; *The Four Seasons,* 1981; *Nasty Habits,* 1981.

AWARDS: Moscow Film Festival Award, Best Actress, 1967: *Up the Down Staircase;* Academy Award, Best Supporting Actress, 1965: *Who's Afraid of Virginia Woolf?*; Antoinette Perry Award, 1964: *Any Wednesday;* Antoinette Perry Award, Variety's New York Critics Poll, 1963: *A Thousand Clowns.**

* * *

DEPALMA, Brian Russell, director

PERSONAL: Born September 11, 1940, in Newark, NJ; son of Anthony Frederick and Vivenne (Muti) DePalma; married Nancy Allen, January 12, 1979. EDUCATION: Columbia College, B.A., 1962; Sarah Lawrence College, M.A., 1964.

CAREER: FILM DEBUT—Director/writer, *Woton's Wake,* 1963. PRINCIPAL FILM WORK—Director: *The Responsive Eye,* 1966 (documentary); *Dionysus in '69,* 1970 (documentary); *Murder a la Mod,* 1966; *Greetings,* 1968; *The Wedding Party,* 1969; *Hi Mom,* 1970; *Get to Know Your Rabbit,* 1972; *Sisters,* 1973; *Phantom of the Paradise,* 1974; *Obession,* 1976; *Carrie,* 1976; *The Fury,* 1978; *Home Movies,* 1979; *Dressed to Kill,* 1980; *Blow Out,* 1981; *Scarface,* 1983.

AWARDS: Avoriaz Prize, 1977: *Carrie;* Grand Prize, 1975: *Phantom of the Paradise;* Silver Bear, Berlin Film Festival, 1969: *Greetings;* Rosenthal Foundation, 1963: *Woton's Wake.*

ADDRESS: Office Fetch Productions, 1600 Broadway, New York, NY 10036.*

* * *

DE SANTIS, Joe (ne Joseph V. De Santis), actor, teacher, sculptor

PERSONAL: Born June 15, 1909 in New York City; son of Pasquale (a tailor) and Maria (Paoli) de Santis; married Miriam Moss (an actress) on October 19, 1935 (divorced); married Margaret Draper (an actress) on May 23, 1949 (divorced); married Wanda June Slye on November 23, 1959 (died 1977); children (first marriage) one son, (second marriage) one son. EDUCATION: Attended public schools in New York City and the City College of New York. Studied at the Leonardo da Vinci Art School and was apprenticed to Onorio Ruotolo at the Beaux Arts Institute of Design, 1927–29. NON-THEATRICAL CAREER—Worked in his own sculptor studio and taught sculpting at the Henry Street Settlement and the YMHA at 92nd St. in New York City, 1936–40.

CAREER: DEBUT—Giulio Bernini, *Scampolo,* Columbia University, 1929. NEW YORK DEBUT—Leone, *Sirena,* Waldorf Theatre, 1931. PRINCIPAL STAGE APPEARANCES—Mr. Tevenson, *Gl' Incoscienti,* Brooklyn Academy of Music, 1931; Abner, *Saul,* Willis, 1932; Cuigy, *Cyrano de Bergerac,* Albany, NY, New Amsterdam Theatre, NY, 1932; member, La Compagnia del Teatro d'Arte—Beauchamp, *The Count of Monte Cristo,* Longacre, NY, 1934, Dr. Servou, *Il Padrone delle Ferriere,* Longacre, 1934, Borniche, *Il Colonello Bridau,* Longacre, 1934, Brabantio, *Othello,* Playhouse, NY, 1934, Giovanni Ansperti, *Romanticismo,* Longacre, NY, 1934, Generico, *Fantasma,* Fleisher

Auditorium, Philadelphia, PA, 1934. Chenildieu/Basco, *Les Miserables,* Longacre, 1934; St. Gaudens, *Camille,* Longacre, 1934; Dr. Antommarachi, *St. Helena,* Lyceum, 1936; Caifas, *La Passione,* Teatro Cine-Roma, 1937; Joe, *Bangtails,* Atlantic City, NJ, 1940; Soothsayer, *Journey to Jerusalem,* National, NY, 1940; Luigi, *Walk into My Parlour,* Glen Rock, NJ, 1941; Ricci, *Keep Covered,* Baltimore, MD, 1941; Officer Klein, *Arsenic and Old Lace,* Fulton, NY, 1941; Moy, *Men in Shadow,* Morosco, NY, 1943; Arabian Bread Seller, *Storm Operation,* Belasco, NY, 1944; Young Italian Waiter, *The Searching Wind,* Fulton, 1944; Diamond Louie, *The Front Page,* Royale, NY, 1946; Eddie Fuselli, *Golden Boy,* ANTA, NY, 1952.

Lead role, *Liliom,* Brattle, Cambridge, MA, 1952; Carminelli, *In Any Language,* Cort, NY, 1952; Herbie Milton, *A Certain Joy,* Playhouse, Wilmington, DE, 1953; Renato, *The Time of the Cuckoo,* Clinton Playhouse, CT, 1954; Gus, *Strictly Dishonorable,* Somerset Theatre, Somerset, MA, 1954; Sam Gordon, *A Stone for Danny Fisher,* downtown National, NY, 1954; Bronislau Partos, *The Highest Tree,* Longacre, 1959; Police Chief, *The Balcony,* Civic Playhouse, Los Angeles, CA, 1961; Emilio Galuzzi, *Daughter of Silence,* Music Box, NY, 1961; Brabantio, *Othello,* Mark Taper Forum, Los Angeles, CA, 1971; Bank Manager, *How to Rob a Bank,* PAF Playhouse, Long Island, NY, 1977; standby, *Cold Storage,* Lyceum, NY, 1978; Doctor Tannenbaum, *Horowitz and Mrs. Washington,* Golden, NY, 1980; Isaac, *Goodnight Grandpa,* Syracuse, NY, 1981.

MAJOR TOURS—Member Walter Hampden Repertory Company, 1933—Giotti, *Caponsacchi,* Francisco, *Hamlet,* Doctor, *It Happened,* Marquis de Priego, *Ruy Blas;* Brutus, *Julius Caesar,* C.W.A. E.R.B. Theatre (forerunner of WPA Theatre).

FILM DEBUT—Gregory, *Slattery's Hurricane,* 1949. PRINCIPAL FILM APPEARANCES—*Man with a Cloak,* 1951; *The Last Hunt,* 1956; *Full of Life,* 1957; *Case Against Brooklyn,* 1958; *I Want to Live,* 1958; *Buchanan Rides Alone,* 1958; *Dino,* 1958; *Cry Tough,* 1959; *Al Capone,* 1959; *The George Raft Story,* 1961; *Cold Wind in August,* 1961; *And Now Miguel,* 1966; *An American Dream,* 1966; *The Professionals,* 1966; *Madame X,* 1966; *The Venetian Affair,* 1967; *Chubasco,* 1968; *The Brotherhood,* 1968; *Blue,* 1968; *Little Cigars,* 1973. TELEVISION DEBUT—*See! Hear!,* 1940. PRINCIPAL TELEVISION APPEARANCES—*Danger; Theatre Guild of the Air; Playhouse 90; Studio One; Robert Montgomery Presents; The Red Buttons Show; The Martha Raye Show; Colgate Comedy Hour; Texaco Star Theatre; Caesar's Hour;* Lotito, *The Untouchables;* Father, *Golden Windows;* Morelli, *Don't Grow Old, East Side/West Side; 77 Sunset Strip; Bonanza; Desilu Playhouse; Gunsmoke; Rawhide; Perry Mason; Dr. Kildare; Sam Benedict; The Virginian; The Name of the Game; Cheyenne; Mission: Impossible; Route 66; Naked City; General Electric Theatre; Ben Casey; Wagon Train; Hawaii Five-O; The New Dick Van Dyke Show.* RADIO DEBUT—*Pepper Young's Family,* 1940. PRINCIPAL RADIO APPEARANCES—*They Live in Brooklyn; The Goldbergs; Kitty Foyle; Light of the World; Stand by for Adventure; The Clock; Dick Tracy; Tennessee Jed; The Sparrow and the Hawk; Brighter Day; The Greatest Story Ever Told; Eternal Light;* Narrator, *This is War, On a Note of Triumph; So Proudly We Hail.*

THEATRE-RELATED CAREER—Acting teacher, ANTA, 1964–68; dialect teacher, American Theatre Wing.

WRITINGS: Articles published in *Progresso Italo-American; Remember Radio,* column in *The Studio* magazine.

SIDELIGHTS: MEMBERSHIPS—AEA, AFTRA, Los Angeles Board, National Board, Convention Delegate, SAG, ANTA Board of Directors of Los Angeles Chapter; The Masquers; Players Club.

Mr. De Santis's sculpting has been exhibited at the Robinson and Feragil Galleries at the 1939 World's Fair, and in a group show at the A.C.A. Gallery. His portrait of Walter Hampden as *Cyrano de Bergerac* is in the Walter Hampden Memorial Library. RECREATION—Flying, photography, gardening, gourmet cooking, directing plays for The Masquers and sculpting in wood and stone.

ADDRESS: Home—P.O. Box 1513, Provo, UT 84603.

* * *

DeVINE, Lawrence (ne Joseph Lawrence DeVine), critic

PERSONAL: Born September 21, 1935, in New York City; son of John Justin (an advertising executive) and Hazel (Tippit) DeVine; married Jane Christian on September 29, 1959 (divorced April 8, 1968); married Lucy Memory Williamson (a teacher) on July 26, 1968; children: (first marriage) John Justin, Ellen Morse. EDUCATION: Georgetown University, Washington, D.C., 1953–54; Northwestern University, Evanston, IL, B.S. (Journalism), 1957. RELIGION: Roman Catholic. MILITARY: U.S. Army Counter-Intelligence, 1958–62.

LAWRENCE DeVINE

CAREER: Herald, Miami, FL, architectural writer and arts columnist, 1962–65; theatre critic, 1965–67; *Herald-Examiner,* Los Angeles, entertainment editor and theatre critic, 1967–68; *Free Press,* Detroit, theatre critic, 1968–present.

AWARDS: Professional Journalism Fellowship, National Endowment for the Humanities, at University of Michigan, Ann Arbor, MI 1975–76.

SIDELIGHTS: MEMBERSHIPS—Pulitzer Prize jury for drama, 1981–82; National New Playwrights jury, American College Theatre Festival, critic-in-residence, ATCA festivals, 1978–83; fellow, National Endowment for the Humanities seminar on the arts; U.S. delegate, biennial congresses, International Association of Theatre Critics—Tel Aviv, Israel, 1981, Mexico City, 1983; on the faculty of the National Critics Institute, Eugene O'Neill Theatre Center, Waterford, CT, 1973–present, Critic Fellow, 1971; Beta Theta Pi, Sigma Delta Chi, professional journalism society; Advisory Committee, American Theatre Critics Association; former chairman, ATCA Executive Committee, 1978–80.

ADDRESS: Home—17315 E. Jefferson Ave., Grosse Pointe, MI 48230. Office—c/o Detroit *Free Press,* 321 W. Lafayette Blvd., Detroit, MI 48226.

* * *

DEVLIN, Jay, actor, dancer, and writer

PERSONAL: Born May 8, 1929, in Fort Dodge, IA; son of Joseph John (a railroad engineer) and Clara Marie (Korth) Devlin; married Carol Marie Butler, August 19, 1957 (divorced 1972); children: Julie Ann. EDUCATION: Attended Sacred Heart School, Fort Dodge, IA; trained for the stage at the American Theatre Wing. MILITARY: U.S. Air Force, 1950–54.

CAREER: DEBUT—Dancer—*Wonderful Town,* Camden Music Fair, Camden, NJ, 1958. NEW YORK DEBUT—Ringmaster/Clown, *The Littlest Circus,* Golden, 1960, 19 performances. PRINCIPAL THEATER APPEARANCES—Alfred, *Little Murders,* Circle in the Square, NY, 1969; Bill, *Hot L Baltimore,* Circle in the Square, NY, 1975; Lt. McNeil, *King of Hearts,* Minskoff, NY, 1979. MAJOR TOURS—Dancer, *Wonderful Town,* East Coast cities, 1958; Dancer, *Carnival,* East Coast cities, 1963.

FILM DEBUT—District Attorney, *Cross and the Switchblade,* 1969. PRINCIPAL FILM APPEARANCES—Tall thin man, *Three Days of the Condor,* 1978. PRINCIPAL TELEVISION APPEARANCES—Hank Ferguson, *All My Children.*

AWARDS: Andy Award (television advertising), 1970.

SIDELIGHTS: MEMBERSHIPS—AEA, SAG, AFTRA. FAVORITE ROLES—Senex, *Funny Thing Happened on the Way to the Forum;* Alfred, *Little Murders;* Charley, *Where's Charley;* Walter Burns, *Front Page.*

JAY DEVLIN

DE VRIES, Peter, playwright, novelist, editor

PERSONAL: Born February 27, 1910 in Chicago, IL; son of Joost and Henrietta (Eldersveld) De Vries; married Katinka Loeser on October 16, 1943; children: Jan, Peter, Jon, Emily, Derek. EDUCATION: Calvin College, B.A. 1931. NON-THEATRICAL CAREER: Editor, community newspaper, Chicago, 1931–32; associate editor/co-editor, *Poetry* magazine, 1938–44; member editorial staff, *The New Yorker*, 1944–present.

WRITINGS: PLAYS, PUBLISHED—*The Tunnel of Love,* with Joseph Fields, Royale, NY, 1957, Her Majesty's Theatre, London, 1957; a dramatization of his novel *Reuben, Reuben* by Herman Shumlin, *Spofford*, ANTA, NY, 1967.

FILMS (made from Mr. De Vries' books)—*The Tunnel of Love,* 1958; *How Do I Love Thee,* 1970; *Pete 'n' Tillie,* 1973; *Reuben, Reuben,* 1983.

BOOKS—*No, But I Saw the Movie,* 1952; *The Tunnel of Love,* 1954; *Comfort Me with Apples,* 1956; *The Mackerel Plaza,* 1958; *The Tents of Wickedness,* 1959; *Through the Fields of Clover,* 1961; *The Blood of the Lamb,* 1961; *Reuben, Reuben,* 1964; *Let Me Count the Ways,* 1965; *The Vale of Laughter,* 1967; *The Cat's Pajamas and Witch's Milk,* 1968; *Mrs. Wallop,* 1970; *Into Your Tent I'll Creep,* 1971; *Without a Stitch in Time,* 1972; *Forever Panting,* 1973; *The Glory of the Hummingbird,* 1974; *I Hear America Swinging,* 1976; *Madder Music,* 1977; *Consenting Adults or The Duchess Will Be Furious,* 1980; *Sauce for the Goose,* 1981.

SIDELIGHTS: MEMBERSHIPS—National Institute of Arts and Letters.

ADDRESS: Office—c/o The New Yorker, 25 W. 43rd Street, New York, NY 10036.

* * *

DIAMOND, I. A. L. (Isidore), writer

PERSONAL: Born June 27, 1920, in Rumania; son of David and Elca (Waldman) Diamond; married Barbara Bentley (a writer), July 21, 1945; children: Ann, Paul. EDUCATION: Columbia College, B.A., 1941.

WRITINGS: FILMS—(with Billy Wilder) *Love in the Afternoon,* 1957; *Some Like It Hot,* 1959; *The Apartment,* 1960; *One Two Three,* 1961; *Irma La Douce,* 1963; *The Fortune Cookie,* 1966; *The Private Life of Sherlock Holmes,* 1970; *Avanti,* 1972; *The Front Page,* 1974.

AWARDS: Laurel Award, 1980; Academy Award, 1960, New York Film Critics Award, 1960: *The Apartment;* Writers Guild Award, 1957, 1959, 1960.

SIDELIGHTS: MEMBERSHIPS—ASCAP.

ADDRESS: Agent—c/o Irving Lazar, 211 S. Beverly Drive, Beverly Hills, CA 90212.

* * *

DIETRICH, Dena, actress, director

PERSONAL: Born in Pittsburgh, PA; daughter of Mahlon Lloyd (an actor) and Helen Frances (an actress) Dietrich. EDUCATION: Westminster College, B.A.; American Academy of Dramatic Arts, New York, 2 years; studied with Uta Hagen at the H.B. Studios in New York City.

CAREER: DEBUT—Olive, *Voice of the Turtle,* Boothbay Playhouse, Boothbay, ME, 1950. NEW YORK DEBUT—*Out of This World,* 1962. PRINCIPAL STAGE APPEARANCES—Lucy Brown, *Threepenny Opera,* Charles Playhouse, Boston, MA, 1963; Della, *Cindy,* Gate, NY, 1963; Mildred, *The Freaking Out of Stephanie Blake,* O'Neill, NY; Wilma, *The Rimers of Eldritch,* Cherry Lane, NY, 1967; Olive, *Here's Where I Belong,* Billy Rose, NY, 1968; Pauline, *Prisoner of Second Avenue,* O'Neill, NY, 1971; *Sunset, Sunrise,* Public Theatre, Los Angeles; *Shea,* Coronet, Los Angeles. MAJOR TOURS—Mrs. Strakosh/Mrs. Brice, *Funny Girl,* National Company, 1965–66.

DIRECTED—*Dulcy,* Equity Waiver Theatre, Los Angeles; *Mrs. January and Mr. Ex; Two,* Actor's Playhouse, Los Angeles, 1982–83.

FILM DEBUT—Mrs. Vrooder, *The Crazy World of Julius Vrooder,* 1973–74. PRINCIPAL FILM APPEARANCES—*History of the World, Part I; The Wild Party; North Avenue Irregulars; Captain Midnight.*

TELEVISION DEBUT—Grace, *Adams Rib.* PRINCIPAL TELEVISION APPEARANCES—*Karen; The Practice; Friends and Lov-*

ers; *The Ropers; But Mother; The American Bag; Four in Love; Night Visit; Trouble with People; And Baby Comes Home; Fay; Getting Married; Dean Martin Roast; Trapper John, M.D.; Dinah Shore Show; Merv Griffin Show; Mike Douglas Show; Gary Collins Show; Kelley Lange Show; Square Pegs; Scamps.*

THEATRE-RELATED CAREER: Acting Teacher, N. Hollywood Theatre, 1978–79; Acting Teacher, performing Arts Co-operative, Los Angeles, 1980; Hostess/Co-producer, ''Keys to the City,'' Video Magazine Tour of Los Angeles, Cable TV, 1983.

AWARDS: Clio Award, ''Mother Nature'' commercial, 1971–72; Best Supporting Actress, Miami Herald Award, *Spofford,* 1969.

SIDELIGHTS: MEMBERSHIPS—AEA, SAG, AFTRA.

''Although Miss Dietrich's career has spanned every area of show business, it was through a well-loved commercial on television that she gained national prominence; 'Mother Nature' was seen for over nine years, 1972–81.''

ADDRESS: Agent—J. Michael Bloom, 9200 Sunset Blvd., Hollywood, CA 90069.

* * *

DILLER, Phyllis (nee Phyllis Ada Driver), stand-up comedienne

PERSONAL: Born July 17, 1917, in Lima, Ohio; daughter of Perry M. (in insurance) and Frances Ada (Romshe) Driver; married Sherwood Diller (divorced); married Warde Donovan Iatum (divorced); children: (first marriage) Peter, Sally, Suzanne, Stephanie, Perry. EDUCATION: Studied music for three years at Sherwood Music School, Chicago, and at Bluffton College, Bluffton, OH.

CAREER: DEBUT—Purple Onion, night club, San Francisco. PRINCIPAL STAGE APPEARANCES—Dolly Levi, *Hello Dolly,* New York; *Happy Birthday; Dark at the Top of the Stairs; Everybody Loves Opal; What Are We Going to Do with Jenny?; Subject to Change.* TELEVISION DEBUT—*The Jack Paar Show,* New York. PRINCIPAL TELEVISION APPEARANCES—Her own shows include *The Phyllis Diller Special,* ABC, 1963; *Show Street,* ABC, 1965; *An Evening With Phyllis Diller,* WGN, Chicago, 1966; *The Pruits of South Hampton,* ABC, 1966; *The Beautiful Phyllis Diller Show,* NBC, 1968; *Phyllis Diller Special,* NBC, 1968; *Phyllis Diller's 102nd Birthday Party,* ABC, 1974; guestings and appearances—*Academy Awards, All Nonsense News Network, America 2-Night, Julie Andrews Show, Annual Rock n' Roll Sports Classic, Chuck Barris Rah Rah Hour, Jack Benny Show, The Bonkers, Carol Burnett Show, Dick Cavett Show, Celebrity Battle Stars, Celebrity Bullseye, CHiPS, Comedy Tonight, Norm Crosby's Comedy Shop, Crosswits, Dance Fever, John Davidson Show, Daytime, Do or Diet Show, Phil Donahue Show, Mike Douglas Show, Epcot Magazine, Fantasy, David Frost Show, Jackie Gleason Show, Gong Show, Good Morning America, Grammy Awards, Merv Griffin Show, Heavenly Bodies, Hollywood*

PHYLLIS DILLER

Squares, Bob Hope Show (21 shows), *Hour Magazine, How Hollywood Stays in Shape, Phyllis Diller Hosts an Evening at The Improv, Jack Jones Show, Joys of Aging and How to Avoid Them, Laugh-In, Liberace Show, The Love Boat, Macy's Thanksgiving Day Parade, Madame's Place, Made in Hollywood, Barbara Mandrell Show, Dean Martin Roasts, Dean Martin Show, Match Game, Mindreaders, Minsky's Burlesque, Monte Carlo Show, The Muppets, Jim Nabors Show, Over Easy, Jack Paar Show, Password +, Regis Philbin Show, Salute to Gordon Sinclair, Vidal Sassoon, Dinah Shore Show, Richard Simmons Show, Red Skelton Show, Soap World, Ed Sullivan Show, Take Off, Take One, Tattletales, Toni Tennille Show, Alan Thicke Show, This Is Your Life, Today Show, The Tonight Show, The Twenty-four Days of Christmas, Bobby Vinton Show, John Wayne Special, Whatever Happened to . . . , Andy Williams Show, Flip Wilson Show, Women Who Rate a 10.*

PRINCIPAL FILM APPEARANCES—Texas Guinan, *Splendor in the Grass,* 1961; *The Fat Spy,* 1966; *Boy, Did I Get a Wrong Number,* 1966; *Eight on the Lam,* 1967; voice of Mrs. Frankenstein, cartoon *Mad Monster Party,* 1967; *Did You Hear the One About the Traveling Saleslady?,* 1967; *Private Navy of Sgt. O'Farrell,* 1967; *The Adding Machine,* 1969; *The Sunshine Boys,* 1975; *A Pleasure Doing Business,* 1978; *Motel,* 1982. RECORDINGS—*Phyllis Diller Laughs,* Verve; *Are You Ready for Phyllis Diller?,* Verve; *Great Moments of Comedy with Phyllis Diller,* Verve; *Born to Sing,* Columbia; *Harold Arlen Revisited,* Crewe Records. NIGHT CLUBS—''Every major nitery here and abroad.'' CONCERTS—Appeared as piano soloist with 100 symphony orchestras across the country; her piano virtuoso name was Dame Illya Dillya.

WRITINGS: BOOKS PUBLISHED—*Phyllis Diller's Housekeeping Hints; Phyllis Diller's Marriage Manual; The Complete Mother by Phyllis Diller; The Joys of Aging and How to Avoid Them*—all Doubleday.

AWARDS: AMC Cancer Research Center Humanitarian Award; USO Liberty Bell Award, Philadelphia; Governor's Award, Ohio; Distinguished Service Citation, Ladies Auxiliary of Veterans of Foreign Wars; Woman of the Year Award, Variety Club Women of Baltimore; TV Radio Mirror Award; Golden Apple, Hollywood Women's Press Club; Minutemen Award, U.S. Treasury Department; Honorary Mayor, Brentwood California, Honorary Ph.D., National Christian University, Dallas, TX; Honorary Doctorate, Kent State University, Kent, OH.

SIDELIGHTS: "Phyllis Diller has starred on television, in movies and the stage, and has headlined in six countries for over a quarter of a century as a professional comic. A 'late bloomer,' she started her show business career at the age of 37. At the time, she was a working housewife and mother of five children employed at radio station KSFO, San Francisco as a publicist. Urged on by her husband, Sherwood Diller, she prepared a night club act and was booked into San Francisco's Purple Onion. She slithered around the piano, lampooned current celebrities, brandished a cigarette holder, and made fun of high fashion and life in general. Booked for two weeks, she stayed for 89! She followed this with a tour, polishing her act and developing the housewife and daily-life routines that have made her the high priestess of the ridiculous. She played the Blue Angel in New York and appeared on the *Jack Paar Show*. From that point her career rocketed. Miss Diller has starred in three television series, countless specials and has made guest appearances on hundreds of top-rated shows. 'I love TV,' she says, 'It's not my fault if the tubes blow out when I laugh.' Miss Diller's approach to comedy is unique. She writes most of her own material, editing her words so tightly that she can deliver as many as 12 punchlines per minute. And she strictly avoids off-color jokes and situations, even in today's permissive atmosphere. The butt of many of her jokes is her husband 'Fang.' As she notes, 'Fang is purely a figment and bears no resemblance to either of my former husbands.' . . . In private life, she is a devoted mother, a fine cook, and uncommonly well-dressed—a far cry from the harridan she portrays so convincingly. In spite of her youthful appearance, she continues to kid herself about ugliness, skinniness, ineptness and just about every defect a woman can have."

ADDRESS: c/o Frank Liberman & Associates, Inc., 9021 Melrose Ave., Suite 308, Los Angeles, CA 90069.

* * *

DILLON, John, artistic director

PERSONAL: Born October 23, 1945; son of Louis M. and Vaiborg A. (Anderson) Dillon. EDUCATION: Northwestern University, B.A., M.A.; Columbia University, M.F.A. studied with the National Theatre of the Deaf, New York.

CAREER: Artistic Director of the Milwaukee Repertory Theatre since 1977. Directed at more than a dozen not-for-profit theatres from coast to coast. Began as a member of Joseph Chaikin's Open Theatre, New York; directed major productions in Japan and England and has directed two television productions.

SIDELIGHTS: MEMBERSHIPS—S.S.D. and C.

ADDRESS: Office—929 N. Water Street, Milwaukee, WI 53202.

* * *

DILLON, Mia, actress

PERSONAL: Mia is pronounced with a long ''i.'' Born in Colorado Spring, CO.

CAREER: DEBUT—Virginia, *The Canterville Ghost*, Des Moines Community Theatre, IA. NEW YORK DEBUT—Mary Tate (The Yellow Peril), *Da*, Hudson Guild, Morosco, for 560 performances, 1978–79. PRINCIPAL STAGE APPEARANCES—Mary Mooney, *Once a Catholic*, Helen Hayes, NY, 1979; Babe Botrell, *Crimes of the Heart*, Golden, NY, 1981–82.

TELEVISION DEBUT—*The Jilting of Granny Weatherall*, PBS American Short Story.

AWARDS: Antoinette Perry Award Nomination, 1982: *Crimes of the Heart;* Clarence Derwent Award, 1981; Drama Desk Award Nomination, 1979: *Once a Catholic.*

ADDRESS: Agent—Milton Goldman, c/o International Creative Management, 40 W. 57th Street, New York, NY 10019.

* * *

DODDS, William, stage manager

PERSONAL: Son of Horace (a farmer) and Florence (Hillgartner) Dodds; married Marian Hatfield, May 1, 1950; children: Christopher, Laurie. EDUCATION: Cornell College, IA, B.A., 1943; graduate study at University of Washington, Seattle.

CAREER: PRINCIPAL STAGE MANAGEMENT—NEW YORK: *Five Finger Exercise*, 1959–60; *Write Me a Murder*, 1961–62; *Little Me*, 1962–63; *Dylan*, 1963–64; *Ben Franklin in Paris*, 1964–65; *Pickwick*, 1965; *The Star-Spangled Girl*, 1966–67; *Henry Sweet Henry*, 1967; *The Great White Hope*, 1968–70; *No No Nanette*, 1971–72; *Night Watch*, 1972; *Via Galactica*, 1972; *Full Circle*, 1974; *Saturday, Sunday, Monday*, 1974; *The Magic Show*, 1975; *A Musical Jubilee*, 1975–76; *1600 Pennsylvania Avenue*, 1976; *A Texas Trilogy*, 1976; *Caesar and Cleopatra*, 1977; *Carmelina*, 1979; *Night and Day*, 1979–80; *Betrayal*, 1980; *The Elephant Man*, 1980–81; *Mass Appeal*, 1981–82; *On Your Toes*, 1983. PRE-BROADWAY STAGE MANAGEMENT—*Semmelweiss*, 1978; *The Prince of Grand Street*, 1978. MAJOR TOURS—*Shenandoah*, national company, 1977–78; *Dracula*, national company, 1978; *Sophisticated Ladies*, national company, 1982.

ADDRESS: Home—711 Amsterdam Avenue, New York, NY 10025

* * *

DODSON, Jack, actor

PERSONAL: Born May 16, 1931, in Pittsburgh, PA; son of John M. and Margaret S. Dodson; married Mary Weaver (a motion picture and television production designer), August 28, 1959; children: Cristina, Amy. EDUCATION: Carnegie-Mellon University, B.F.A., 1953. MILITARY: U.S. Army, 1953–56.

CAREER: PRINCIPAL STAGE APPEARANCES—The Country Wife, New York, 1957; The Trial of Dimitri Karamazov, New York, 1957; The Italian Straw Hat, New York, 1957; The Quare Fellow, New York, 1958; Our Town, New York, 1959; The Golem, New York, 1959; The Balcony, New York, 1960; The Torchbearers, New York, 1960; Under Milkwood, New York, 1961; Follies of Scapin, New York, 1962; Pullman Car Hiawatha, New York, 1962; Plays for Bleecker Street, New York, 1962; Six Characters in Search of an Author, New York, 1963; Chemin de Fer, Mark Taper Forum, 1968; Who's Happy Now, Mark Taper Forum, 1976; You Can't Take It With You, New York, 1983; A Penny for a Song, New York; American premiere of Hughie, and three revivals from 1964–76.

FILM DEBUT—Angel in My Pocket, 1968. PRINCIPAL FILMS—The Getaway, 1972; Pat Garrett and Billy the Kid, 1973; Thunderbolt and Lightfoot, 1974; Something Wicked This Way Comes, 1983. Narrated Why Man Creates. TELEVISION APPEARANCES—The Andy Griffith Show, 1965–68; Mayberry R.F.D., 1968–71; All's Fair, 1976; In the Beginning, 1977; Phyl and Mikhy, 1978; Million Dollar Infield; MOW; Newhart; Benson; Lou Grant; Mork and Mindy; Barney Miller; Quincy; 13 Queens Blvd.; One Day at a Time; Welcome Back Kotter; Carter Country; Police Story; A.E.S. Hudson Street; CPO Sharkey; Maude; Manhunter; Room 222; Happy Days.

ADDRESS: Office—MJD Enterprises, Inc., c/o Equitable Investment Corp., Suite 1122, 6253 Hollywood Blvd., Hollywood, CA 90028.

* * *

DONAT, Peter (ne Pierre Collingwood Donat), actor, writer

PERSONAL: Born January 20, 1928 in Kentville NS, Canada; son of Philip Ernst (an agriculturalist) and Marie (Bardet) Donat; married Michael Learned, on September 8, 1956 (divorced 1974); married Maria C. DeJong (a writer) on February 9, 1983; children: (first marriage) Caleb, Christopher, Lucas. EDUCATION: Acadia University, Wolfeville, B.A., B.S., 1946; post-graduate study at Yale University, School of Drama, 1950–51; studied with Curt Conway, scene study in New York and further studies at Shakespeare Festival of Canada, Stratford, Canada, and American Conservatory Theatre, San Francisco.

CAREER: DEBUT—Prince Charming, Cinderella, Kings County Academy, Kentville, NS, Canada, 1938. NEW YORK DEBUT—Arthur, Highlights of the Empire, Empire Theatre, New York, 1953. LONDON DEBUT—A Touch of Spring, Comedy Theatre. PRINCIPAL STAGE APPEARANCES—Cyrano, Cyrano De Bergerac, ACT, San Francisco, 1973; Hadrian VII, ACT, 1971; Piet, A Lesson from Aloes, Mark Taper Forum, Los Angeles, 1980. MAJOR TOURS—The Son, Jane; My Three Angels. FILM DEBUT—Hamlet, Scenes from Hamlet, Shakespeare Festival, Stratford, Ont., Canada.

PRINCIPAL FILM APPEARANCES—Senator, Godfather II; Conductor, A Different Story; News Chief, China Syndrome. TELEVISION DEBUT—Camera Three, New York, 1957. PRINCIPAL TELEVISION APPEARANCES—The editor, Flamingo Road, NBC, 1980–82.

WRITINGS: Adaptations—The Master Builder, CBC-TV, 1963; Traveller Without Luggage, CBC-TV, 1981; Dr. Chekhov, with Marijke De Jong.

AWARDS: Radiant American Artist Award, American Conservatory Theatre, San Francisco, 1983; Theatre World Award, Best Featured Actor, The First Gentleman, 1957.

ADDRESS: Office—c/o American Conservatory Theatre, 450 Geary Street, San Francisco, CA 94102; Agent—Bob Gersh, 222 N. Canyon Drive, Beverly Hills, CA 90210.

* * *

DONNELL, Jeff (nee Jean Marie Donnell), actress

PERSONAL: Born July 10, 1921 in S. Windham, ME; daughter of Harold Eugene (Head of Prisons, Baltimore, MD) and Mildred Ayer (a teacher) Donnell; married Aldo Ray (an actor, divorced); married William R. Anderson on December 21, 1940; children: M. Phineas, Sarah Jane. EDUCATION: Leland Powers School of Drama, 1940; Yale School of Drama, 1940–41. POLITICS: Democrat. RELIGION: Church of Religious Science.

CAREER: DEBUT—Performed lead roles in summer stock on the East Coast, in California and Arizona.

FILM DEBUT—Helen, My Sister Eileen, 1942. PRINCIPAL FILM APPEARANCES—In a Lonely Place; Over 21; The Sweet Smell of Success; Tora, Tora, Tora. TELEVISION DEBUT—Wife, Alan Young Show, 1950's. PRINCIPAL TELEVISION APPEARANCES—Hallmark Hall of Fame; Jimmy Stewart Show; The George Gobel Show; Playhouse 90; U.S. Steel Hour; Julia; Stella, General Hospital.

THEATRE-RELATED CAREER—Actress, Columbia Pictures, Burbank, CA, 1942–48; Actress, RKO Studios, Hollywood, CA, 1948–49; Theatre Guild, New York, 1958–62.

SIDELIGHTS: MEMBERSHIPS—SAG, AFTRA, AEA, Academy of Motion Picture Arts and Sciences, Academy of Television Arts and Sciences.

Miss Donnell has appeared in over 100 television shows and 56 motion pictures.

JEFF DONNELL

ADDRESS: Agent—20th Century Artists, 13273 Ventura Boulevard, Studio City, CA 91604.

* * *

DOOLEY, Ray, actor

PERSONAL: Born December 20, 1952; son of Lawrence (a field engineer) and Dorothy Evelyn (a tape librarian; maiden name Theisinger) Dooley; married Diana Claire Stagner (an actress) on May 20, 1978. EDUCATION: Hamilton College, B.A. (English Literature and Theatre), 1975; Advanced Training Program, American Conservatory Theatre, San Francisco, CA, 1975–77.

CAREER: Max Halliday, *Dial M for Murder*, Playhouse on the Hill, Clinton, 1977. PRINCIPAL STAGE APPEARANCES— Malcolm, *Macbeth;* John Wilkes Booth, *The Stitch in Time;* CSC Repertory, NY—Peer, *Peer Gynt*, Prince Hal, *Henry IV, Parts 1 & 2*, Harry Thunder, *Wild Oats*, Inspector Raspe, *The Marquis of Keith;* Owen, *Translations*, Hungtington Theatre, Boston; Ariel, *The Tempest*, American Shakespeare Theatre, Stratford, CT; Octavius, *Julius Caesar*, American Shakespeare Theatre, Stratford, CT; Adolphus Cusins, *Ma-*

jor Barbara, Seattle Repertory, WA; The Dauphin, *The Lark*, Citadel, Edmonton, AB; John Worthing, *The Importance of Being Earnest*, Cincinnati Playhouse in the Park, OH; Little Monk, *Galileo*, Pittsburgh Public Theatre, PA; Endicott, *The Front Page*, Center Stage, Baltimore, MD; Cuigy, *Cyrano de Bergerac*, Center Stage.

TELEVISION DEBUT—Paxton Villeque, *One Life to Live*, 1982. PRINCIPAL TELEVISION APPEARANCES—*The Edge of Night, Search for Tomorrow*.

AWARDS: Obie, Distinguished Performance, *Peer Gynt*, 1982.

ADDRESS: Agent—c/o DMI Talent, 250 W. 57th Street, New York, NY 10019.

* * *

DORN, Dolores, actress, teacher

PERSONAL: Born on March 3; daughter of Edward (an insurance executive) and Alice (a medical office manager; maiden name Eaomin) Heft; married Franchot Tone (actor); Ben Piazza (actor). EDUCATION: Goodman Theatre, B.F.A., 1954; studied with Lee Strasberg, Uta Hagen, and Harold Clurman.

CAREER: DEBUT—Lead ingenue, Neil Schaffner Repertory Company, toured Midwest, 1954. NEW YORK DEBUT—Ylena, *Uncle Vanya*, Fourth Street Theatre, 1956, 100 performances. PRINCIPAL STAGE APPEARANCES—*Hide and Seek*, Broadway, 1957; *Plays for Bleecker Street*, Circle in the Square, 1963; *To Damascus*, Eastside Theatre, 1964; *The Pinter Plays*, Cherry Lane Theatre, 1965; *Lime Green Khaki Blue*, Provincetown Playhouse, 1969; *The Midnight Sun*, New York; *Starward Ark*, New York; *Between Two Thieves*, New York; *Catch as Catch Can*, Los Angeles. MAJOR TOURS—*A Mighty Man Is He*, New England Summer Circuit, 1955.

FILM DEBUT—*The Bounty Hunter*, Warner Brothers, 1958. PRINCIPAL FILM APPEARANCES—*Phantom of the Rue Morgue*, Warner Brothers, 1958; *Underworld U.S.A.*, 1961; *13 West Street*, 1961; *The Stronger*, 1979; *Uncle Vanya; The Candy Snatchers, Tell Me a Riddle*, 1981. TELEVISION DEBUT—*The Untouchables*. PRINCIPAL TELEVISION APPEARANCES—*Night Cries*, ABC; *Intimate Strangers*, ABC; *Charlie's Angels; Jigsaw John; Girls of Huntington House*, ABC; *Run for Your Life; Strawberry Blond*.

THEATRE-RELATED CAREER—Teacher, film, American Film Institute, 1977; teacher, acting, Lee Strasberg Institute, 1983; acting coach on *Star Search*, Metromedia TV, 1983.

AWARDS: Best Actress, San Francisco International Film Festival, *Uncle Vanya*, 1957.

SIDELIGHTS: MEMBERSHIPS—Actor's Studio (life member); see *From Reverence to Rape* (a treatment of women in film), Molly Haskell; *Dames*, I. and E. Cameron.

ADDRESS: Office—c/o American Film Institute, 2021 North Western Avenue, P.O. Box 27999, Los Angeles, CA 90027.

DOLORES DORN

Agent—Henderson/Hogan 247 S. Beverly Drive, Beverly Hills, CA 10019.

* * *

DOUGLAS, Diana (nee Dill), actress

PERSONAL: Born January 22, 1923, in Bermuda; daughter of Thomas Neville (an attorney) and Ruth Rapalje (Neilson) Dill; married Kirk Douglas, November 2, 1943 (divorced 1950); married William Darrid (a writer) December 14, 1956; children: (first marriage) Michael, Joel. EDUCATION: Upper Chine, Shanklin, Low, England, Cambridge School Certificate, 1939; studied for the theatre at the American Academy of Dramatic Art (graduate 1941); studied Poetic Drama; studied with Sanford Meisner. POLITICS: Democrat. RELIGION: Anglican.

CAREER: DEBUT—Sister, *The Hasty Heart,* Lobero, Santa Barbara, 1948. NEW YORK DEBUT—Deb (and understudy for Margaret Sullavan), *Sabrina Fair,* National, 1953, for six months. PRINCIPAL STAGE APPEARANCES—Mary, *The Highest Tree,* Longacre, NY, 1959; Hermione, *A Winter's Tale,* Stratford, CT, 1960; Hecuba, *The Trojan Women,* L.A.A.T, Los Angeles, 1980.

FILM DEBUT—Catherine, *Sign of the Ram,* 1947. FILM APPEARANCES—*Whistle at Eaton Falls,* 1950; *Storm over Tibet,* 1951; *Monsoon,* 1952; *Indian Fighter,* 1955; *Loving,*

1970; *Another Man, Another Chance,* 1978; *Star Chamber,* 1983.

TELEVISION DEBUT—Commentator, *1944 Fasion Show,* Dumont. TELEVISION APPEARANCES—Mrs. Anderson, *The Cowboys,* 1974; *Arrowsmith; The Rivals; The Web;* others.

AWARDS: Los Angeles Dramalogue Award for performance in Harold Pinter's *Old Times.*

SIDELIGHTS: MEMBERSHIPS—Red Cross, Westport, CT.

ADDRESS: Agent—Bauman Hiller, 9220 Sunset Blvd., Los Angeles, CA 90069.

* * *

DOUGLAS, Kirk, (ne Issur Danielovich Demsky), actor, producer, director

PERSONAL: Born December 9, 1916, in Amsterdam, NY; son of Harry and Bryna (Sanglel) Danielovich; married Diana Dill (an actress; divorced 1950); Anne Buydens, May 29, 1954; children: (first marriage) Michael, Joel; (second marriage) Peter, Eric Anthony. EDUCATION: St. Lawrence University, A.B., 1938; American Academy of Dramatic Arts, 1939–41. MILITARY: U.S. Navy, World War II.

CAREER: NEW YORK STAGE DEBUT—*Spring Again.* PRINCIPAL STAGE APPEARANCES—*The Sisters; Kiss and Tell; The Wind is Ninety,* 1945; *Alice in Arms; Man Bites Dog; One Flew over the Cuckoo's Nest* (also produced).

FILM DEBUT—*The Strange Love of Martha Ivers,* 1946. PRINCIPAL FILM APPEARANCES—*Out of the Past; Build My Gallows High,* 1947; *I Walk Alone,* 1947; *Mourning Becomes Electra,* 1947; *Walls of Jericho,* 1948; *Letter to Three Wives,* 1949; *The Champion,* 1949; *Young Man with a Horn; The Glass Menagerie,* 1950; *Big Carnival; Ace in the Hole,* 1951; *Along the Great Divide,* 1951; *Detective Story,* 1951; *Big Trees, Big Sky,* 1952; Jonathan Shields, *The Bad and the Beautiful,* 1952; *The Story of Three Loves; The Juggler,* 1953; *Act of Love,* 1953; *20,000 Leagues under the Sea,* 1954; *Man without a Star,* 1955; *The Racer,* 1955; *Ulysses,* 1955; *Indian Fighters* (also produced), 1955; *Lust for Life,* 1956; *Top Secret Affair,* 1957; *Lizzie,* 1957; Doc Holliday, *Gunfight at the O.K. Corral,* 1957; *Paths of Glory* (also produced), 1958; *Vikings* (also produced), 1958; *Last Train from Gunhill,* 1959; *The Devil's Disciple,* 1959;

Spartacus (also produced), 1961; *Town without Pity,* 1961; *Lonely Are the Brave* (also produced), 1962; *Two Weeks in Another Town,* 1962; *List of Adrian Messenger* (also produced), 1963; *For Love or Money,* 1963; *Seven Days in May* (also produced), 1964; *In Harm's Way,* 1965; *Heroes of Telemark,* 1966; *Cast a Giant Shadow,* 1966; *The Way West,* 1967; *The War Wagon,* 1967; *A Lovely Way to Die,* 1968; *The Brotherhood* (also produced), 1968; *The Arrangement,* 1969; *There Was a Crooked Man,* 1970; *A Gunfight* (also produced), 1971; *The Light at the Edge of the World,* 1971; *Catch Me a Spy; Scalawag* (also produced and directed), 1973; *Once Is Not Enough,* 1975; *A Man to Respect; Posse* (also produced and directed); *Holocaust 2000; The Fury,*

1978; *Villian* (also produced), 1979; *Home Movies* (also produced), 1979; *Final Countdown*, 1980; *Man from Snowy River* (also produced), 1983; *Eddie Macon's Run* (also produced), 1983; also co-produced *One Flew over the Cuckoo's Nest*, 1975.

PRINCIPAL TELEVISION APPEARANCES—*Mousey*, 1974; *The Money Changers*, 1976; Harry Holland, *Draw!*, 1984.

AWARDS: New York Critics Award, 1956: *Lust for Life;* Cecil B. deMille Award, 1968; Academy Award Nominations: *The Champion, The Bad and the Beautiful, Lust for Life;* U.S. Freedom Medal, 1981; honorary doctorate, 1958 from St. Laurence University.

SIDELIGHTS: Mr. Douglas was cited in the Congressional Record of 1964 for service as goodwill ambassador. He is a member of the U.N. Association, Los Angeles chapter.

ADDRESS: The Bryna Company, 141 El Camino Drive, Beverly Hills, CA 90212.*

* * *

DOUGLAS, Melvyn (ne Hesselberg), actor, producer, director

PERSONAL: Born April 5, 1901, in Macon, GA; died August 4, 1981; son of Edouard (a concert pianist) and Lena (Shackelford) Hesselberg; married Helen Gahagan, April 5, 1931; children: Gregory, Peter, Mary Helen. MILITARY: U.S. Army as a private, transferred to special service with the rank of Captain, served overseas in India, China, Burma, 1942–45.

CAREER: DEBUT—with Jessie Bonstelle's stock company, Chicago, IL, 1919. NEW YORK DEBUT—Ace Wilfong, *A Free Soul,* Playhouse, 1928. PRINCIPAL STAGE APPEARANCES—Sergeant Terry O'Brien, *Back Here,* Klaw Theatre, 1928; Boyd Butler, *Now-a-Days,* Forrest, 1929; Henry C. Martin, *Recapture,* Eltinge, 1930; Josef, *Candle Light,* Shubert-Riviera, 1930; Unknown Gentleman, *To-night or Never,* Belasco, NY, 1930; Sheridan Warren, *No More Ladies,* Booth, NY, 1934; Carey Reed, *Mother Lode,* Cort, NY, 1934; Pat Dantry, *De Luxe,* Booth, NY, 1935; Erik Nordgren, *Tapestry in Gray,* Shubert, NY, 1935; Tommy Thurston, *Two Blind Mice,* Cort, NY, 1949; Wally Williams, *The Bird Cage,* Coronet, NY, 1950; Sayre Nolan, *Let Me Hear the Melody,* Playhouse, Wilmington, DE, 1951; Steve Whitney, *Glad Tidings,* Lyceum, NY, 1951; Howard Carol, *Time Our for Ginger,* Lyceum, NY, 1952; Henry Drummond, *Inherit the Wind,* National, NY, 1956; Zeus, *Maiden Voyage,* Forrest, Philadelphia, 1957; General St. Pe, *The Waltz of the Toreadors,* Coronet, NY, 1958; Captain Jack Boyle, *Juno,* Winter Garden, NY, 1959; Griffith P. Hastings, *The Gang's All Here,* Ambassador, NY, 1959; William Russell, *The Best Man,* Morosco, NY, 1960; title-role, *Spofford,* ANTA, NY, 1967; *The Great American Fourth of July Parade,* Carnegie Music Hall, Pittsburgh, PA, 1975; Justice Daniel Snow, *First Monday in October,* Cleveland Playhouse, OH, 1975.

MAJOR TOURS—Josef, *Candle Light,* 1930; Tommy Thurston, *Two Blind Mice,* 1950; Howard Carol, *Time Out for Ginger,*

national tour, 1953–55, Australia, 1955; Henry Drummon, *Inherit the Wind,* national tour, 1956; General St. Pe, *The Waltz of the Toreadors,* 1958; William Russell, *The Best Man,* 1960.

PRODUCED—*Call Me Mister,* National, NY, 1946; *The 49th Cousin,* Ambassador, NY, 1960; DIRECTED—*Moor Born,* Playhouse, 1934; *Within the Gates,* National, NY, 1934; *Mother Lode,* Cort, NY, 1934; *Glad Tidings,* Lyceum, NY, 1951; *The Man in the Dog Suit,* Hinsdale, IL, 1957.

FILM DEBUT—*Tonight or Never,* 1931. PRINCIPAL FILM APPEARANCES—*As You Desire Me,* 1932; *The Old Dark House,* 1932; *Annie Oakley; Arsene Lupin Returns; She Married Her Boss,* 1935; *Theodora Grows Wild,* 1936; *The Gorgeous Hussy,* 1936; *Angel,* 1937; *I'll Take Romance,* 1937; *Women of Romance,* 1937; *There's Always a Woman,* 1938; *The Shining Hour,* 1938; *There's That Woman Again,* 1939; *Good Girls Go to Paris,* 1939; *Ninotchka,* 1939; *Too Many Husbands,* 1940; *He Stayed for Breakfast,* 1940; *That Uncertain Feeling,* 1941; *A Woman's Face,* 1941; *They All Kissed the Bride,* 1942; *Two-Faced Woman,* 1942; *Three Hearts for Julia; Sea of Grass,* 1947; *The Guilt of Janet Ames,* 1947; *Mr. Blandings Builds His Dream House,* 1948; *A Woman's Secret,* 1948; *The Great Sinner,* 1949; *My Forbidden Past,* 1949; *Carriage Entrance,* 1949; *Billy Budd,* 1962; *Hud,* 1962; *Advance to the Rear,* 1963; *The Americanization of Emily,* 1964; *Rapture,* 1965; *Hotel,* 1967; *I Never Sang for My Father,* 1970; *The Candidate,* 1972; *One Is a Lonely Number,* 1972; *The Tenant,* 1976; *That's Entertainment, Part 2,* 1976; *Twilight's Last Gleaming,* 1977; *The Seduction of Joe Tynan,* 1979; *Ghost Story,* 1981.

PRINCIPAL TELEVISION APPEARANCES—*The Plot to Kill Stalin,* 1958; *Do Not Go Gentle into That Good Night,* 1968.

AWARDS: Emmy Award, Outstanding Performance, 1968: *Do Not Go Gentle into That Good Night;* Academy Award, Best Supporting Actor, 1964: *Hud;* Antoinette Perry Award, 1960: *The Best Man.**

* * *

DOUGLAS, Michael, actor, producer

PERSONAL: Born September 25, 1944, in New Brunswick, NJ; son of Kirk (an actor) and Diana (an actress; maiden name, Dill) Douglas; married Diandra Luker, March 20, 1977; children: Cameron Morrell. EDUCATION: University of California, Santa Barbara, (Drama); three summers in residence at the O'Neill Center's National Playwrights Conference; studied with Wynn Handman at the American Place Theatre in New York.

CAREER: PRINCIPAL STAGE APPEARANCES—Appeared in half-dozen off-Broadway plays in New York.

PRINCIPAL TELEVISION APPEARANCES—Actor, *The Experiment,* CBS Playhouse; *The FBI; Medical Center;* co-star, *Streets of San Francisco.*

PRINCIPAL FILM APPEARANCES—*Hail Hero,* 1969; *Adam at 6:00 A.M.,* 1970; *Summertree,* 1971; *Napoleon and Sa-*

mantha, 1972; *Coma,* 1978; *The China Syndrome,* 1979; *Running,* 1979; *It's My Turn,* 1980; *Star Chamber,* 1983; *Romancing the Stone,* 1984. PRODUCED—*One Flew Over the Cuckoo's Nest,* 1975; *The China Syndrome,* 1979; *Romancing the Stone,* 1984.

CURRENT PROJECTS—Film production, *Starman,* 1984, *Zoo Plane,* 1984; television mini-series, *Conquistador, the Conquest of Mexico.*

AWARDS: Academy Award, Best Picture, Best Actor, Best Actress, Best Director, Best Screenplay, 1975: *One Flew Over the Cuckoo's Nest.*

SIDELIGHTS: MEMBERSHIPS—Trustee, University of California Santa Barbara; Trustee, Eugene O'Neill Memorial Theatre Foundation.

ADDRESS: Office—20th Century Fox, 10201 W. Pico Blvd., Los Angeles, CA 90035. Agent—Ron Meyer, Creative Artists Agency, 1888 Century Park East, Suite 1400, Los Angeles, CA 90067.

* * *

DRAGOTI, Stan(ley G.), director, producer

PERSONAL: Born October 4, 1932, in New York City; married Cheryl Tiegs (the model; divorced). EDUCATION:

STAN DRAGOTI

Attended Cooper Union and the School of Visual Arts, NY.

CAREER: PRINCIPAL FILM WORK—Director: *Dirty Little Billy,* 1973; *Love at First Bite,* 1979; *Mr. Mom,* 1983; *Tall Blond Man with One Red Shoe* (upcoming); *Slammer* (upcoming).

RELATED CAREER—Associate creative director, Young & Rubicam Advertising Agency; art director/supervisor, Compton Advertising; vice president/head of art department/member, board of directors, Wells, Rich, Green Advertising Agency; producer/director, over 150 television commercials.

SIDELIGHTS: MEMBERSHIPS—Director's Guild of America; Writers Guild of America, West.

"Mr. Dragoti is the recipient of every top award in the field of television advertising, including a special Tony Award and a Golden Apple for his adaption of the 'I Love New York' campaign for the Broadway theatre scene. In recognition of his contributions to the television field, the Museum of Modern Art has included Dragoti's commercial reel in its permanent collection."

ADDRESS: Agent—Fred Specktor, Creative Artists Agency, 1888 Century Park E., Suite 1400, Los Angeles, CA 90067.

* * *

DREXLER, Rosalyn, playwright

WRITINGS: PLAYS PUBLISHED—*The Line of Least Existence and Other Plays,* 1967; *Theatre Experiment,* 1967; *Collision Course,* 1967–68; *Methuen Playscripts,* 1969; *The Off-Off Broadway Book,* 1972; *Fiction,* 1972. PLAYS PRODUCED—*Home Movies,* Judson Church, Provincetown Playhouse, NYC, 1964; *The Investigation,* Miami University, Ohio, 1979, Theatre Company of Boston, 1966, New Dramatist's Committee, NYC, 1966, Milwaukee Repertory, 1966, Open Space, London, England, 1969; *The Line of Least Existence,* Judson Poets' Theatre, NYC, 1969, Theatre of the Living Arts, Philadelphia, 1970, Traverse, Edinburgh, Scotland, 1968, New York, Network Theatre, New York, 1980; *Hot Buttered Roll,* New Dramatist's Committee, New York, 1968, Milwaukee Repertory, 1966, Open Space Theatre, London, England, 1969; *Skywriting,* Cafe Au GoGo, New York, 1968, Dowling College, 1973; *The Ice Queen,* The Proposition, Boston, 1973, Kornblee Gallery (with puppets), 1965; *Softly and Consider the Nearness,* Manhattan Theatre Club, 1973, West Carolina University, Cullowee, NC, 1973; *The Bed Was Full,* New Dramatist's Committee, 1972; *She Who Was He,* Virginia Commonwealth University, Richmond, 1974; New York Theatre Strategy, New York, 1974; *Travesty Parade,* Center Theatre Group, Los Angeles, 1974; *The Writer's Opera,* Theatre for the New City, New York, 1979; *Graven Image,* Theatre for the New City, 1980, Oberlin College, Ohio, 1980; *Vulgar Lives,* La Mama, New York, 1979; *The Tree Artist,* Gateway, Long Island, New York, 1981; *Starburn,* Theatre for the New City, New York, 1983; *The Mandrake,* Center Stage, Baltimore, 1983; *Dear,* SoHo Repertory, New York, 1983; *Room 17C,* Omaha Magic, Omaha, NE, 1983; *Delicate Feelings,* Theatre for the New City, New York, 1984.

BOOKS—*I Am the Beautiful Stranger* (novel), 1965; *One or Another* (novel), 1970; *To Smithereens* (novel), 1972; *The Cosmopolitan Girl* (novel), 1975; *Starburn: The Story of Jenny Love* (novel), 1979; *Bad Guy* (novel), 1982; books written under pseudonym of Julia Sorel, (novelizations of movies)—*Rocky*, 1976; *Dawn, Story of a Teenage Runaway*, 1976; *Alex, The Other Side of Dawn*, 1977; *See How She Runs*, 1978; *Unwed Widow* (novel), 1975. ANTHOLOGIES—*The Bold New Women*, 1966; *New American Review*, 1969. REVIEWS, ARTICLES, CRITICISM—*Vogue*, movie reviews; *New York Times*, Sunday Arts and Leisure section, movies, theatre and art; *Sports Illustrated, Esquire, The Village Voice, Viva, Madamoiselle, Harper's Bazaar, Craft Horizons, Paris Review, MS, New York Magazine.*

PRINCIPAL FILM APPEARANCE—*Who Does She Think She Is?*, an hour film about Rosalyn Drexler, distributed by New Yorker Films. PRINCIPAL TELEVISION APPEARANCES—*Sunday Morning*, CBS, 1980; *David Frost Show; Dick Cavett Show.* THEATRE-RELATED CAREER—Teacher, creative writing, University of Iowa Writers Workshop, 1976–77; teacher, playwriting, Miami University Center for the Performing Arts, OH, 1979; teacher, playwriting, and directed a new play, Oberlin College, OH, 1980; teacher, playwriting, Arizona State University, Tempe, 1981–82; teacher, playwriting, Hofstra, NY, 1980; teacher, playwriting, Rhode Island University, 1982; distringuished visiting writer and teacher, creative writing and dream literature, Eastern Washington University, Cheney, WA, 1983; New York University's Writers Conference, Vermont, 1983; teacher, creative writing, Western Washington University, Bellingham, WA, 1983–84.

AWARDS: Yaddo (Saratoga Springs) Fellow, 1980; Obie, *The Writer's Opera*, 1979; Emmy (for writing excellence), *The Lily Show*, a Lily Tomlin Special, 1974; Guggenheim Fellow, 1970–71; Rockefeller Grants in Playwriting, 1965, 1968, 1974; *Paris Review* Humor Prize, short story, "Dear," 1966; Obie, *Home Movies*, 1964; Mac Dowell Fellow, 1965.

SIDELIGHTS: Vocalist with jazz group Écoutez at S.n.a.f.u. in New York City.

ADDRESS: Home—400 W. 43rd Street, New York, N.Y. 10036.

* * *

DREYFUSS, Richard, actor

PERSONAL: Born October 29, 1947, in Brooklyn, NY; married Jeramie Rain (a.k.a. Susan Davis; an actress and writer), March 20, 1983. EDUCATION: Beverly Hills High School; spent one year at San Fernando Valley State College.

CAREER: DEBUT—(as a child) *In Mama's House*, Gallery, Los Angeles. NEW YORK DEBUT—Stanely, *But Seriously. . .*, Henry Miller's, 1969. PRINCIPAL STAGE APPEARANCES—Stephen, *Line*, Theatre de Lys, NY, 1971; *And Whose Little Boy Are You?*, McAlpin Rooftop, NY, 1971; Adolphus Cusins, *Major Barbara*, Mark Taper Forum, Los Angeles, 1972; Harry, *The Time of Your Life*, Los Angeles; Jean, *Miss Julie* and Napoleon, *A Man of Destiny*, Arlington Park, Chicago, 1976; *The Tenth Man*, Solari Ensemble, Los

Angeles, 1977; Cassius, *Julius Ceasar*, Brooklyn Academy of Music, NY, 1978; Iago, *Othello*, New York Shakespeare Festival, Delacorte, NY, 1979, Alliance Theatre Company, Atlanta, GA, 1979; Ken Harrison, *Whose Life Is It, Anyway?*, Williamstown Festival, MA, 1980; (reading) *The Don Juan and the Non-Don Juan*, Loeb Center, NY, 1981; Joe, *A Day in the Death of Joe Egg*, Long Wharf, New Haven, CT, 1981; *Total Abandon*, Golden, NY, 1983; also: *Journey to the Day, People Need People, Incident at Vichy, Enemy, Enemy*, all at the Mark Taper Forum; *Aesop in Central Park*, Los Angeles.

FILM DEBUT—*Hello, Down There*, 1968. PRINCIPAL FILM APPEARANCES—*The Graduate*, 1968; *Valley of the Dolls*, 1968; *American Graffiti*, 1973; *Dillinger*, 1973; *Jaws*, 1973; *The Apprenticeship of Duddy Kravitz*, 1974; *Inserts*, 1976; *Close Encounters of the Third Kind*, 1977; Elliott Garfield, *The Goodbye Girl*, 1977; *The Competition*, 1980; *Whose Life Is It, Anyway?*, 1981; *The Second Coming of Suzanne*, (unreleased), 1982; *The Buddy System*, 1983; also: *Sub-a-Dub-Dub* and *The Young Runaways*.

TELEVISION APPEARANCES—*Love on a Rooftop*, 1966–67; *Judd for the Defense*, 1968; *The Mod Squad; Room 222*, 1975; *Victory at Entebbe*, 1977; *Saturday Night Live.*

AWARDS: Academy Award, 1977: *The Goodbye Girl*; L.A. Drama Critics Award Nomination: *The Time of Your Life*, *Aesop in Central Park*.

SIDELIGHTS: Mr. Dreyfuss also co-produced his film, *The Big Fix* in 1979.*

* * *

DRULIE, Sylvia, producer

PERSONAL: Born January 28, in Boston MA; daughter of Elias A. (in retail sales) and Ethel R. Drulie; married John W. Mazzola (president, Lincoln Center for the Performing Arts) on March 7, 1959; children: Alison, Amy. EDUCATION: Tufts University, A.B. (cum laude), 1948.

CAREER: PRODUCED—Associate Producer, *West Side Story*, New York, 1957; *Music Man*, New York, 1957; Producer, *Auntie Mame*, road company, with Sylvia Sidney, Claudette Colbert (produced three companies).

SIDELIGHTS: MEMBERSHIPS—Board of Directors, Byrd Hoffman Foundation (Robert Wilson), Dance Theatre Foundation (Alvin Ailey), Trisha Brown Dance Company.

ADDRESS: Office—Bryd Hoffman Foundation, 147 Spring Street, New York, NY 10012.

* * *

DRUMMOND, Alice (nee Ruyter), actress

PERSONAL: Born May 21, 1928 in Providence, RI; daughter of Arthur (an automobile mechanic) and Sarah Irene (a secretary; maiden name, Alker) Ruyter; married Paul Drummond on March 3, 1951 (divorced 1975). EDUCATION: Brown University, Providence, RI, B.A., 1950.

CAREER: DEBUT—Carole Arden, *Personal Appearances,* Wickford Players, Wickford, RI, 1950. NEW YORK DEBUT—Anne of Cleves, *The Royal Gambit,* Sullivan Street Playhouse, New York, 1959. PRINCIPAL STAGE APPEARANCES—New York—*Ballad of the Sad Café,* Martin Beck, 1963; Eloisa Brace, *Malcolm,* Shubert, 1966; Mrs. Lee, *The Chinese and Dr. Fish,* Barrymore, 1970; Bag Lady, *Thieves,* Broadway, 1974; Christine Shoewalter, *Summer Brave,* ANTA, 1975; Dorothy, *Some of My Best Friends,* Longacre, 1977; Gay Wellington, *You Can't Take It With You,* Plymouth, 1983; Miss Crewes, *Boy Meets Girl,* Phoenix, 1975, Mrs. Varney, *Secret Service,* Phoenix, 1975; Off-Broadway—*Go Show Me a Dragon; Sweet of You to Say So; Gallows Humor,* Cherry Lane Theatre; *The American Dream,* Cherry Lane; *The Giant's Dance,* Cherry Lane; *The Carpenters,* American Place; *Charles Abbott and Son,* Roundabout; *God Says There is No Peter Ott,* McAlpin Rooftop Theatre; *Enter a Free Man,* St. Clement's; *Savages,* Hudson Guild; *Killings on the Last Line,* American Place; *Knuckle,* Hudson Guild; *Wonderland,* Hudson Guild.

FILM DEBUT—extra, *Face in the Crowd.* PRINCIPAL FILM APPEARANCES—*Where's Poppa; Man on a Swing; Thieves; King of the Gypsies; Eyewitness; Hide in Plain Sight; The Best Little Whorehouse in Texas.* TELEVISION DEBUT—a nurse, *Dark Shadows.* PRINCIPAL TELEVISION APPAEARANCES—Loretta Jardin, *Where the Heart Is; The Guiding Light; Search for Tomorrow; Love of Life; As the World Turns; Another World; Ryan's Hope; One Life to Live;* Mrs. Baldwin, *The Best of Families,* PBS; Frances, *Park Place,* CBS; Mommy, *The Sandbox,* PBS; Mrs. Ewing, *Particular Men;* Mrs. Mulligan, *The Mulligan Case;* Mrs. Varney, *Secret Service,* PBS; *Father Brown, Detective; Love Sidney.* THEATRE-RELATED CAREER: English teacher, Brown University, 1951–52; acting teacher, Princeton University, 1973.

AWARDS: Antoinette Perry Award Nomination, *The Chinese and Dr. Fish,* 1970; Phi Beta Kappa, Brown University, 1949; Math Entrance Premium, Brown University, First Prize, 1946.

SIDELIGHTS: "I am a better actress each year of my life, and yet I work less because there are very few parts for older women—this is true of all middle aged actresses."

ADDRESS: Home—242 E. 26th Street New York, NY 10010. Agent—c/o STE Representation, 888 7th Ave., New York, NY 10019.

* * *

DUBERMAN, Martin Bauml, playwright, writer

PERSONAL: Born August 6, 1930; son of Joseph (a clothing manufacturer) and Josephine Bauml. EDUCATION: Yale University, New Haven, CT, B.A., 1952; Harvard University, Cambridge, MA, M.A., 1953, Ph.D., 1957. THEATRE-RELATED CAREER: Professor of history, Harvard University, Yale University, Princeton University, 1956–71; professor of history, Lehman College, City University of

MARTIN DUBERMAN

New York, 1971–. POLITICS: Active in civil rights, anti–Vietnam war, and gay liberation movements.

CAREER: FIRST STAGE WORK—George, *Our Town,* MacArthur Summer Theatre, Vermont/New Hampshire, 1948.

WRITINGS: PLAYS PUBLISHED—*In White America,* 1963, produced at the Sheridan Square Playhouse, over 500 performances; *The Memory Bank,* Tambellini's Gate, 1970; *The Colonial Dudes,* Manhattan Theatre Club, 1973, John Drew Theatre, Easthampton, NY, 1972; *Payments,* The New Dramatists, New York, 1971–72; *Visions of Kerouac,* Lion Theatre, New York, 1976, Odyssey Theatre, Los Angeles, 1977; *Metaphors,* 1968; *The Guttman Ordinary Scale,* 1975; *The Recorder,* 1969; *Male Armor,* 1968; BOOKS—author of nine books. CRITICISM—*Show,* 1965; *Partisan Review,* 1966–67; *Harper's,* 1976–77.

AWARDS: Special award from National Academy of Arts and Letters for Contributions to Literature, 1971; finalist, National Book Award, Biography, *James Russell Lowell,* 1966; Vernon Rice Drama Desk Award, *In White America,* 1964; Bancroft Prize, Biography, *Charles Francis Adams,* 1962.

SIDELIGHTS: MEMBERSHIPS—board of directors, New York Civil Liberties Union, Glines Theatre Company, Lambda

Legal Defense Fund, Gay Task Force, SIGNS; Member, The New Dramatists. Written about in Livesey, 1975, *The Professors,* and in *Gay Sunshine Interviews,* 1982.

ADDRESS: Home—475 W. 22nd Street, New York, NY 10011. Agent—Frances Goldin, 305 E. 11th Street, New York, NY 10003. Office—c/o History Department, Lehman College, CUNY, Bedford Park Blvd. W. Bronx, New York, NY 10468.

* * *

DUCHIN, Peter, musician, composer, actor

PERSONAL: Born July 28, 1937, New York City; son of Edwin Frank (a pianist) and Marjorie (Oelrichs) Duchin; married Cheray Zauderer, June 22, 1964; children: Jason, Courtnay, Colin, Malcolm. EDUCATION: Yale University, B.A., 1958; studied for the stage privately with Wynn Handman. RELIGION: Episcopalian. MILITARY: U.S. Army, 1958–60.

CAREER: Concert pianist, conductor, entertainer; president, Peter Duchin Orchestras, 1963–present.

SIDELIGHTS: MEMBERSHIPS—Board of Directors, New York council, Boy Scouts of America, Boys Harbor, Dance Theatre of Harlem, International Medical Research Foundation, American Council on the Arts, American Jazz Alliance, council, Yale University, New York State Council on the Arts, 1976–present, National Symphony Advisory Board, Yale Club, NYC, Bedford Golf and Tennis Club, Stanley Rod and Gun.

ADDRESS: Office—400 Madison Avenue, New York, NY 10017.

* * *

DUFOUR, Val (ne Albert Valery DuFour), actor, director

PERSONAL: Born February 5, 1927; son of Albert Valery (a doctor) and Cleotild (Brouillette) Dufour. EDUCATION: Louisiana State University, B.A.; Catholic University, Washington, DC, M.A.; studied with Uta Hagen and at Actors Studio in New York. RELIGION: Catholic

CAREER: DEBUT—Song and dance man, *Minstrel Show,* Sanger Theatre, New Orleans, LA, 1934. NEW YORK DEBUT—Johnnie, *Frankie and Johnnie,* Theatre DeLys, 1952. PRINCIPAL STAGE APPEARANCES—*High Button Shoes; Mister Roberts; Electra; South Pacific; The Grass Harp; Abie's Irish Rose.* MAJOR TOURS—*Mister Roberts; Stalag 17; Personal Appearance; Hamlet; A Steetcar Named Desire; Wondeful Town; No Hard Feelings.*

FILM DEBUT—Quentus, *The Undead,* 1962. PRINCIPAL FILM APPEARANCES—*The Lonely Night; Ben Hur; King of Kings; Watchtower; L.A. Confidential; She-God; Land of Plenty.* TELEVISION DEBUT—*First Love,* 1952. PRINCIPAL TELEVISION APPEARANCES—Appeared in over 3,000 shows in Hol-

VAL DUFOUR

lywood and New York—*Edge of Night, Another World, Search for Tomorrow.*

AWARDS: Emmy Best Actor in a Dramatic Series, 1977; Emmy Nominations: *Gunsmoke,* 1959, *Matinee Theatre,* 1958.

ADDRESS: Home—40 W. 22nd Street, New York, NY 10010.

* * *

DUKAKIS, Olympia, actress, director, producer

PERSONAL: Surname pronounced Du/ka'/kis; born on June 20, 1931 in Lowell, MA; daughter of Constantine S. (a manager) and Alexandra (Christos) Dukakis; married Louis Zorich (an actor); children: Christina, Peter, Stefan. EDUCATION: Boston University, B.A., M.F.A. POLITICS: Democrat.

CAREER: DEBUT—Mrs. Cleveden-Banks, *Outward Bound,* Rangeley, Maine. NEW YORK DEBUT—Italian peasant, *The Breaking Wall,* St. Mark's. Professional actress since 1960, appearing on Broadway, Off-Broadway, regional and summer theatres, with American Place Theatre, New York Shakespeare Festival, Phoenix Theatre, Second City, Circle Repertory Theatre, The Whole Theatre Company, and over 110 productions in various summer theatres. RECENT PRINCIPAL STAGE APPEARANCES—*Curse of the Starving Class,* New

York Public Theatre, 1981; *Snow Orchid*, Circle Repertory, 1982.

FILM DEBUT—Madomi, *Twice a Man*. PRINCIPAL FILM APPEARANCES—*The Idolmaker; Lilith; King of America; The Wanderers; FDR—The Last Days; National Lampoon Goes to Hollywood; Deathwish.* TELEVISION DEBUT—*CBS Workshop.* PRINCIPAL TELEVISION APPEARANCES—*Made for Each Other; The Rehearsal; Sisters; Nicky's World; Search for Tomorrow.*

DIRECTED—*U.S.A.; Orpheus Descending; House of Bernarda Alba; Arms and the Man; Uncle Vanya;* The Whole Theatre Company, Upper Montclair, NJ; *Six Characters in Search of an Author; A Touch of the Poet,* Williamstown Theatre Festival (associate director—three years) Williamstown, MA; *One Flew over the Cuckoo's Nest,* Delaware Summer Festival; *Kennedy's Children,* Commonwealth Stage.

THEATRE–RELATED CAREER: Instructor in acting, 1967–70, master teacher, 1974–83, New York University School of the Arts; teacher, undergraduate department, Yale University, New Haven, CT, 1976.

WRITINGS: ADAPTATIONS—*Mother Courage; House of Bernarda Alba; Edith Stein,; Trojan Women; Uncle Vanya,* for The Whole Theatre Company.

SIDELIGHTS: MEMBERSHIPS—AEA, SAG, AFTRA. Founding Member/Artistic Director, The Whole Theatre Company, Upper Montclair, NJ, 1970–present. FAVORITE ROLES—*Mother Courage;* Luba in *The Cherry Orchard;* Mary Tyrone in *Long Day's Journey into Night;* Tamara in *Titus Andronicus;* Serafina in *The Rose Tattoo.*

Conceived of The Whole Theatre Company with husband, Louis Zorich and guided the artistic development during the formative years. Has served as artistic director since 1977, developing the artistic identity and supervising all elements of production. Active in the development of The New Jersey Theatre Foundation, the organization responsible for the fiscal and property needs of the Whole Theatre Company, she worked with architects and designers in planning renovation of a bank building into a 200-seat totally flexible theatre. She helped negotiate with Actor's Equity Association, a special letter of agreement, now a national model for developing theatres, that permitted WTC to gradually grow towards a LORT contract realized in the 1982 season. She also developed a New Play Series and workshops at WTC. She was a founding member of The Charles Playhouse in Boston, MA (known initially as Actors Company) for three seasons in Boston and two seasons in Edgartown, MA, establishing a summer theatre, 1957–60.

ADDRESS: Office—c/o The Whole Theatre Company, 544 Bloomfield Avenue Upper Montclair, NJ 07042.

* * *

DUNAWAY, Faye, actress

PERSONAL: Born January 14, 1941, in Tallahasee, FL; married Peter Wolf (divorced); Terry O'Neill; children: (second marriage) Liam. EDUCATION: University of Florida; Boston University.

CAREER: NEW YORK DEBUT—Succeeded Olga Bellin as Margaret More, *A Man for All Seasons,* ANTA, 1962. PRINCIPAL STAGE APPEARANCES—Nurse, *After the Fall,* 1964, Faith Prosper, *But for Whom Charlie,* 1964, Elsie, *After the Fall,* 1964, maid to Beatrice, *The Changeling,* 1965, understudy, *Tartuffe,* ANTA Washington Square, NY, 1965; Kathleen Stanton, *Hogan's Goat,* American Place Theatre, NY, 1965; *Old Times,* Mark Taper Forum, Los Angeles, 1972; Blanche du Bois, *A Streetcar Named Desire,* Ahmanson, Los Angeles, 1973; lead, *The Curse of an Aching Heart,* Little, NY, 1982.

FILM DEBUT—*The Happening,* 1967. PRINCIPAL FILMS—*Hurry, Sundown,* 1967; Bonnie Parker, *Bonnie and Clyde,* 1967; *The Thomas Crown Affair,* 1968; *The Extraordinary Seaman,* 1969; *A Place for Lovers,* 1968; *The Arrangement,* 1969; *Puzzle of a Downfall Child,* 1970; *Little Big Man,* 1970; *Doc,* 1971; *Oklahoma Crude,* 1973; M'Lady, *The Three Musketeers,* 1973; *The Towering Inferno,* 1974; *Chinatown,* 1974; M'Lady, *The Four Musketeers* (made at the same time as "The Three Musketeers" but released later), 1975; *The Voyage,* 1975; *Three Days of the Condor,* 1975; *Network,* 1976; *Voyage of the Damned,* 1976; *The Eyes of Laura Mars,* 1977; *The Champ,* 1978; *The First Deadly Sin,* 1980; Joan Crawford, *Mommie Dearest,* 1982; more.

TELEVISION APPEARANCES—Aimee Semple McPherson, *The Disappearance of Aimee,* 1976; Eva Peron, *Evita,* 1983.

AWARDS: Theatre World Award, 1965–66: *Hogan's Goat;* Academy Award, 1976: *Network;* Academy Award Nominations, 1967: *Bonnie and Clyde,* 1974: *Chinatown.*

ADDRESS: c/o Screen Actors Guild, 7750 Sunset Blvd., Los Angeles, CA 90046.

* * *

DUNN, Thomas G., playwright, director, manager

PERSONAL: Born December 17, 1950; married Marellen Johnson on August 16, 1976 (divorced, 1983). EDUCATION: University of Minnesota, B.A. (Theatre and Biology).

CAREER: Artistic director, Playwrights' Center, Minneapolis, MN, 1971–81; executive director, New Dramatists, New York, NY, 1981–present.

WRITINGS: BOOKS—*Playwriting: A Workshop Approach,* with Frank Pike, 1984. Over sixty plays written, including works for adults and young people.

AWARDS: Humboldt State University New Play Festival Winner, 1983: *In Pursuit of the Song of Hydrogen;* Lakeshore Players One-Act Play Award, 1981: *Wedding Day Tragedy;* Center Stage Playwriting Award, 1980: *The King of Lodz.*

SIDELIGHTS: MEMBERSHIPS—PEN, Dramatists Guild.

RECREATIONS—Interested in travel, nonfiction and fiction writing, numismatology, and tennis.

ADDRESS: Office—c/o The New Dramatists, 424 W. 44th Street, New York, NY 10036. Agent—Susan Shulman, 165 West End Avenue, New York, NY 10023.

* * *

DURAND, Charles (ne Charles E. Springmeyer Jr.), stage manager, actor, director

PERSONAL: Born April 27, 1912; son of Charles E. (a high school principal) and Sarah A. (a teacher) Springmeyer; married Virginia Mattis on September 10, 1948 (an actress); children: Sarah E. EDUCATION: Columbia University, B.A., 1933; studied acting, stage management, etc. at The American Theatre Wing. POLITICS: Liberal Democrat. RELIGION: Episcopalian. MILITARY: U.S. Army, 1940–45.

CAREER: NEW YORK DEBUT—Malinov, *Judgement Day*, Belasco, New York, 1934, 93 performances. PRINCIPAL STAGE WORK (stage manager, New York)—*Season in the Sun*, Cort, 1950; *The Seven Year Itch*, Fulton, 1952; *Cactus Flower*, Royale, 1965. MAJOR TOURS (stage manager)—*My Fair Lady*, national company, 1962; *How to Succeed in Business Without Really Trying*, national company, 1963–64; *1776*, Chicago, Washington, and Boston, 1971–72.

SIDELIGHTS: MEMBERSHIPS—Phi Kappa Psi.

ADDRESS: Home—310 W. 72nd Street, New York, NY 10023.

* * *

du RAND, le Clanché, actress, writer, and teacher

PERSONAL: First name pronounced luh/clah'ng/shay; born August 12, 1941 in Mafeking, South Africa; EDUCATION: Rhodes University, South Africa, B.A.; University of California at Berkeley, M.A. (Dramatic Arts).

CAREER: DEBUT—Alison, *Look Back in Anger*, University Theatre, Rhodes University, Grahamstown, South Africa, 1960. NEW YORK DEBUT—Maria, *Twelfth Night*, Perry Street Theatre, for 22 performances, 1976. PRINCIPAL STAGE APPEARANCES—Mrs. Boyle, *Whose Life Is It Anyway*, NY, 1979; understudy/Helen Bullins, *Einstein and the Polar Bear*, NY; the Woman, *Invitation to the Dance*, A.T.A., NY; Mrs. Prentice, *What the Butler Saw*, Westside Arts, NY; Millamant, *The Way of the World*, East 91st Street, NY; Pasha, *Unfinished Women*, NY Shakespeare Festival; Marion, *Absurd Person Singular*, Buffalo Studio Arena, NY; Yvette, *Impromptu of Outremont*, Syracuse Stage, NY; Myra Arundel, *Hay Fever*, Kenyon Festival Theatre, OH; Molly, *Paradise Is Closing Down*, Syracuse Stage; Cissy, *Loved*, Syracuse Stage; Cecily, *The Importance of Being Earnest*, Indiana Repertory Company; Alcestis, *The Alcestiad*, PCPA, California; Mag, *The Sea Plays*, Long Wharf Theatre, New Haven, CT; Anna Tot, *The Tot Family*, Arena Stage, Washington, DC; Anna Christie, *Anna Christie*,

Theatre-by-the-Sea, NH; Elvira, *Blithe Spirit*, Cohoes Music Hall; Oregon Shakespeare Festival, Ashland, OR—Hermione, *The Winter's Tale*, Helena, *All's Well That Ends Well*, Julia, *Two Gentlemen of Verona*, Maria, *Twelfth Night*, Tintinabula, *A Funny Thing Happened on the Way to the Forum*, Thea, *Hedda Gabler*; Irene, *Idiots Delight*, Berkeley Repertory Theatre; Nora, *The Plough and the Stars*, Berkeley Repertory Theatre; Colorado Shakespeare Festival—Mrs. Ford, *The Merry Wives of Windsor*, Portia, *The Merchant of Venice*, Margaret, *Henry VI*, pt. 2, Elizabeth, *Richard III*.

MAJOR TOURS—Mrs. Boyle, *Whose Life Is It Anyway*, Parker Playhouse, Ft. Lauderdale, FL, 1979–80.

THEATRE-RELATED CAREER: Faculty (Acting, Playwriting), Lincoln Center Institute, 1982–83.

WRITINGS: ADAPTATION—C. S. Lewis's *The Lion, the Witch and the Wardrobe*, for the Lincoln Center Institute (published) 1983.

AWARDS: Eisner Award, University of California at Berkeley, for Outstanding Creative Achievement, 1967–68.

SIDELIGHTS: MEMBERSHIPS—AEA.

''To have come from the African bush to Berkeley in the Sixties, was an education in itself and one that changed my life forever. I have acted in many of the regional theatres in America as well as Broadway and off and off-off Broadway. . . . I studied Balinese dance and drama in Indonesia which caused a radical change in my viewpoint towards theatre which I have since considered as a holy art . . . of personal transformation. . . . I view my basic training as an actor to have taken place as an actor in the theatre and through observing the best actors of our time. Except for vocal speech and physical training, I don't think there is much one can teach in an acting class. I believe that besides talent and soul, an actor needs a keen sense of aesthetic discrimination.''

ADDRESS: Agent—Bruce Savin, c/o Agency for the Performing Arts, 888 Seventh Avenue, New York, NY 10106.

* * *

DURANG, Christopher, playwright, actor

PERSONAL: Born January 2, 1949, in Montclair, NJ; son of Francis Ferdinand and Patricia Durang. EDUCATION: Harvard University, B.A. (English), 1971; Yale University, School of Drama, M.F.A. (Playwriting), 1974.

WRITINGS: PLAYS PUBLISHED/PRODUCED—*The Nature of the Universe*, Northampton, MA, 1971, NY, 1975; *'dentity Crisis*, Cambridge, MA, 1971, New Haven, CT, 1975; *Better Dead Than Sorry* (musical), New Haven, CT, 1972, NY, 1975; *I Don't Generally Like Poetry But Have You Read "Trees?"* (with Albert Innaurato), New Haven, CT, 1972, Manhattan Theatre Club, 1973; *The Life Story of Mitzi Gaynor, or Gyp* (with Albert Innaurato), New Haven, CT, 1973; *The Marriage of Bette and Boo*, New Haven, CT, Yale Theatre, 1973, revised NY, 1979; *The Idiots Karamazov* (with Albert Innaurato), New Haven, CT, Yale Theatre, 1974; *Titanic*, New Haven, CT, 1974, NY, 1976; *Death Comes to Us All, Mary Agnes*, New Haven, CT, 1975; *When Dinah Shore Ruled the Earth* (with Wendy Wasserstein), New Haven, CT, 1975; *Das Lusitania Songspiel*, (musical) NY, 1976, 1980; *A History of the American Film*, Hartford Stage Company, CT, 1976, NY, 1978; *The Vietnamization of New Jersey*, New Haven, CT, 1977, NY, 1978; *Sister Mary Ignatius Explains It All for You*, and *The Actor's Nightmare*, Westside Arts, 1982; *Beyond Therapy*, Brooks Atkinson, NY, 1982; *Baby with the Bath Water*, American Repertory Theatre, Cambridge, MA, 1983–84.

PRINCIPAL STAGE APPEARANCES—Yale School of Drama: Gustaf, *Urlicht*, 1971; Darryl, *Better Dead Than Sorry*, 1972; performer, *The Life Story of Mitzi Gaynor, or Gyp*, 1973; Bruce, *Happy Birthday, Montpelier Pizz-zazz*, 1974; Emcee, *When Dinah Shore Ruled the Earth*, 1975; Yale Repertory Theatre: chorus, *The Frogs*, 1974; student, *The Possessed*, 1974; Alyosha, *The Idiots Karamazov*, 1974; performer, *I Don't Generally Like Poetry But Have You Read "Trees?"*, NY, 1973; performer, *Das Lusitania Songspiel*, 1976, 1980; young cashier, *Hotel Play*, NY, 1981; Wallace, *The Birthday Present*, Circle Rep., NY, 1983.

AWARDS: Obie Award, 1980: *Sister Mary Ignatius Explains It All For You;* Guggenheim playwriting fellowship, 1979; Rockefeller grant, 1976; CBS Fellowship, 1975.*

* * *

DUVALL, Robert, actor, director, screenwriter

PERSONAL: Born 1931, in San Diego, CA; son of William Howard Duvall. EDUCATION: Principia College, IL; trained at the Neighborhood Playhouse, NY. MILITARY: U.S. Army.

CAREER: PRINCIPAL STAGE APPEARANCES—*A View from the Bridge*, Off-Broadway, 1955; *Wait Until Dark*, 1966; *American Buffalo*, 1977.

FILM DEBUT—Boo Radley, *To Kill a Mockingbird*, 1963. PRINCIPAL FILM APPEARANCES—*Captain Newman, M.D.*, 1964; *The Chase*, 1966; *Countdown*, 1968; *The Detective*, 1968; *Bullitt*, 1968; *True Grit*, 1969; *The Rain People*, 1969; *M*A*S*H*, 1970; *The Revolutionary*, 1970; *THX-1138*, 1971; *Lawman*, 1971; Tom Hagen, *The Godfather*, 1972; *Tomorrow*, 1971; Jesse James, *The Great Northfield Minnesota Raid*, 1972; *Joe Kidd*, 1972; *Lady Ice*, 1973; *Badge 373*, 1973; *The Outfit*, 1974; *The Conversation*, 1974; Tom Hagen, *The Godfather, Part II*, 1974; *Breakout*, 1975; *The Killer Elite*, 1975; *Network*, 1976; Dr. Watson, *The Seven Per-Cent Solution*, 1976; *The Eagle Has Landed*, 1977; *The Greatest*, 1977; *The Betsy*, 1978; *Apocalypse Now*, 1979; *The Great Santini*, 1979; *True Confessions*, 1981; *The Pursuit of D.B. Cooper*, 1981; *Tender Mercies*, 1983; *The Stone Boy*, 1984; *The Natural*, 1984; also director, *We're Not the Jet Set*, 1977; writer/director, *Angelo, My Love*, 1983.

PRINCIPAL TELEVISION APPEARANCES—*Ike*, 1979.

AWARDS: Academy Award, Best Actor, 1983: *Tender Mercies;* New York Film Critics, Best Supporting Actor, 1972: *The Godfather;* Academy Award Nominations, Best Actor, 1981: *The Great Santini*, Best Supporting Actor, 1972: *The Godfather;* Golden Globe; British Academy Award; National Association of Theatre Owners Award; Obie: *A View from the Bridge*.

ADDRESS: Office—c/o John H. Duvall, Old Towne Ltd., 510 King Street, Suite 311, Alexandria, VA 22314.*

E

EAKER, Ira, publisher

PERSONAL: Born January 14, 1922; son of Samuel and Hannah Eaker; married Lee on November 24, 1946; children: Sherry Ellen, Dean Ross. EDUCATION: City College of New York, Certificate of Achievement (Advertising and Marketing). MILITARY: U.S. Army, 1943–46 (four major battle campaigns).

CAREER: Publisher—*BackStage* (weekly trade paper).

SIDELIGHTS: MEMBERSHIPS—Friars Club, Woodcrest Club, Knights of Pythias.

ADDRESS: Home—15-72 216 Street, Bayside, NY 11360. Office—330 West 42nd Street, New York, NY 10036.

* * *

EASTWOOD, Clint, actor, director, producer

PERSONAL: Born May 31, 1930, in San Francisco, CA. EDUCATION: Oakland Tech High School; Los Angeles City College. NON-FILM CAREER: Worked as a lumberjack in Oregon. MILITARY: U.S. Army.

CAREER: PRINCIPAL FILM APPEARANCES—*Francis in the Navy*, 1951; *The First Travelling Saleslady*, 1955; *Lafayette Escadrille*, 1958; *A Fistful of Dollars*, 1967; *For a Few Dollars More*, 1967; *The Witches; The Good, the Bad, and the Ugly*, 1967; *Hang 'Em High*, 1968; *Coogan's Bluff*, 1968; *Where Eagles Dare*, 1969; *Two Mules for Sister Sara*, 1970; *Kelly's Heroes*, 1970; *The Beguiled*, 1971; *Play Misty for Me* (also directed), 1971; *Dirty Harry*, 1972; *Joe Kidd*, 1972; *High Plains Drifter*, 1973; *Magnum Force*, 1973; *Thunderbolt and Lightfoot*, 1974; *The Eiger Sanction*, 1975; *The Outlaw Josey Wales*, 1976; *The Enforcer*, 1976; *The Gauntlet*, 1977; *Every Which Way But Loose*, 1978; *Escape from Alcatraz*, 1979; *Bronco Billy* (also directed), 1980; *Any Which Way You Can*, 1980; *Foxfire* (also produced and directed), 1982; *Honkytonk Man* (also produced and directed), 1982; *Sudden Impact* (also produced and directed), 1983; also director, *Breezy*, 1973.

SIDELIGHTS: MEMBERSHIPS—National Council on the Arts.

Mr. Eastwood formed Malpaso Productions in 1969.

ADDRESS: Office—Malpaso Productions, 4000 Warner Blvd., Burbank, CA 91522.*

EDE, George, actor

PERSONAL: Born December 22, 1931; son of Edward and Louise (Goepel) Ede; married Leona Arciszewski, in May 1951 (divorced); children: Thomas, Jan, Foley. EDUCATION: Attended public schools in San Francisco, California; Special Theatre Training: Bown Adams Studio, New York, with Bown Adams and Virginia Daly. MILITARY: U.S. Army, 1949–53.

CAREER: DEBUT—Antonio, *The Merchant of Venice*, Gate Theatre, Sausalito, CA, 1964. NEW YORK DEBUT—Ferapont, *The Three Sisters*, ANTA, 1969. PRINCIPAL STAGE APPEARANCES—Toby Belch, *Twelfth Night*, King Lear, *King Lear*, Marin Shakespeare Festival, San Rafael, CA, 1967; Mjr Swindon, *Devil's Disciple*, Spettigue, *Charley's Aunt*, Corey, *The Crucible*, American Conservatory Theatre, San Francisco, 1967–69; Polonius/Gravedigger, *Hamlet*, Leo Herman, *A Thousand Clowns*, Dr. Gibbs, *Our Town*, Baptista, *Taming of the Shrew*, Foreman, *The Tenth Man*, Actors Theatre of Louisville, Louisville, KY, 1969–71; Pozzo, *Waiting for Godot*, Uncle Sid, *Ah, Wilderness*, Morton Kiil, *Enemy of the People*, Loeb Drama Center, Cambridge, MA, 1970; Old Dogsborough, *Arturo Ui*, Williamstown Theatre Festival, N. Adams, MA, 1972; Wetjen, *Iceman Cometh*, Tappercoom, *The Lady's Not for Burning*, Ferguson, *What Price Glory?*, Dr. Boyd, *The National Health*, Danny Crosby, *The Changing Room*, Long Wharf, New Haven, CT, 1972–73; Major, *The Visit*, Hubertin, *Chemin de Fer*, Father, *Holiday*, Sir Sampson, *Love for Love*, Fillipo, *Rules of the Game*, Father, *Member of the Wedding*, Phoenix Repertory, New York and touring, 1973–74; Shamrayev, *The Seagull*, Sir Lucius, *The Rivals*, Williamstown Theatre Festival, N. Adams, MA, 1975; Orgon, *Tartuffe*, Center Stage, Baltimore, 1975; Ballestad, *Lady from the Sea*, Circle-in-the-Square, New York, 1976; Wagner, *Room Service*, Kenley Players, OH, 1976; Craven, *The Philanderer*, Roundabout, New York, 1976; Sir Rowland, *Spider's Web*, Peachtree Playhouse, Atlanta, GA, 1977; Gadsby, *Touch of the Poet*, New York and touring, 1977; Amos Hart, *Chicago*, Starlight Theatre, Atlanta and touring, 1978; Sir Charles Gurney, *Ruling Class*, SUNY-Purchase, NY, 1980; Uncle Willie, *The Philadelphia Story*, Vivian Beaumont Theatre, New York, 1980; Pastor Manders, *Ghosts*, Virginia Museum Theatre, Richmond, VA, 1981; Pellinore, *Camelot*, Starlight Theatre, Kansas City, KS, 1981; Mr. Driver, *No End of Blame*, Manhattan Theatre Club, New York, 1981; Bellamy/Achille, *The Magistrate*, Hartman Theatre Company, Stamford, CT, 1982; Loyal, *Tartuffe*, Kennedy Center, Washington, DC, 1982; Max, *The Sound of Music*, Cincinnati Opera, Cincinnati, OH, 1982; W.S. Gilbert, *Sullivan and Gilbert*, American Stage

Festival, Milford, NH, 1982; Pellinore, *Camelot*, Artpark, Lewiston, NY, 1982; Father Farley, *Mass Appeal*, Midland Theatre, Kansas City, KS, 1983. MAJOR TOURS: Plays—Porter Milgrim, *DeathTrap*, 1978; Major General Stanley, *Pirates of Penzance*, 1982.

FILM DEBUT—Mr. Wagner. *Funnyman*, 1966. PRINCIPAL FILMS—Inspector Flynn, *Serpico*, 1973; Dean Bodger, *The World According to Garp*, 1981. TELEVISION DEBUT—Uncle Willie, *Glory Hallelujia*, 1969. TELEVISION APPEARANCES—Shamrayev, *The Seagull* (Theatre in America Series), 1974; Fillipo, *Rules of the Game* (Theatre in America Series); Father Tom, *Beacon Hill*, 1974; Reverend Baldwin, *Best of Families*.

SIDELIGHTS: MEMBERSHIPS—AEA, SAG, AFTRA.

"Favorite Roles: *Dracula*, Pellinore, *Camelot*, Toby Belch, Pastor Manders in *Ghosts*, and W. S. Gilbert in a new play *Sullivan & Gilbert*, which I did at American Stage Festival, NH. . . . Theatre, that particular confluence of energy and attention between actor and audience, is my first and continuing love. Nothing equals performing before that live presence. . . . I've vacationed in Europe only twice—both times, a superbly rewarding experience. Capri and Salzburg, for different reasons, have got to be the very few 'special places' on earth. I was born and raised in San Francisco, and the great and ancient Sequoias fill me with an indescribable awe and veneration. I must see and touch them every few years to renew myself in some mysterious way. I am possessed by an impulsive, eclectic and insatiable curiosity, especially but not exclusively in the field of human history, which I hope will never diminish."

ADDRESS: Agent—c/o Jeff Hunter, c/o DHKPR Agency, 165 W. 46th Street, New York, NY 10036.

* * *

EDELMAN, Herbert, actor, producer

PERSONAL: Born November 5, 1933, in Brooklyn, NY; son of Mayer and Jennie (Greenberg) Edelman; married Louise Sorel, December 1964; married Merrilyn Crosgrove; children: Briana, Jack. EDUCATION: Brooklyn College, three years; Cornell, Pre-Veterinary (one year). MILITARY: U.S. Army, Corporal.

CAREER: NEW YORK DEBUT—Harry Pepper (Telephone Man), *Barefoot in the Park*, Biltmore, 1963. PRINCIPAL STAGE APPEARANCES—King of Newark Gypsies, *Bajour*, Shubert, NY, 1965. MAJOR TOURS—Harry Berlin, *Luv*, National, 1967–68; Leo, *Chapter Two*, National, 1979–80.

FILM DEBUT—Russian Premier, *In Like Flint*, 1966. PRINCIPAL FILMS—*Barefoot in the Park*, 1967; *The Odd Couple*, 1968; *I Love You, Alice B. Toklas*, 1968; *The War Between Men and Women*, 1972; *The Way We Were*, 1973; *The Front Page*, 1974; *The Yakuza*, 1975; *California Suite*, 1980; *Tora's Dream of Spring*.

TELEVISION DEBUT—*East Side, West Side*, 1964. TELEVISION APPEARANCES—*The Good Guys*, 1968–70; *Ladies Man; Strike Force*, 1981–82; *9 to 5*, 1983–84; *Steambath;* various guest appearances and TV movies.

SIDELIGHTS: "Acting is still the most rewarding, exciting experience imagineable. Only equalled by life itself (I am a rancher, a father and a husband). I am intent on the constant commitment of fulfilling my abilities and my obligation to those who like my work."

ADDRESS: Agent—Bauman & Hiller, 9220 Sunset Boulevard, Beverly Hills, CA 90069.

* * *

EDMEAD, Wendy, actress, dancer, singer

PERSONAL: Born July 6; granddaughter of George and Inez (a postal worker) Hicks. EDUCATION: Attended the High School for the Performing Arts, New York; City College, Davis Center; studied at the Herbert Berghof Studio, New York.

CAREER: NEW YORK DEBUT—Eye of the Tornado, *The Wiz*, Majestic, 1974. PRINCIPAL STAGE APPEARANCES—Susan, *Stop the World, I Want to Get Off*, New York; *Dancin'*, Broadhurst, New York, 1979; Demeter, *Cats*, Winter Garden, New York, 1981; *Encore*, Radio City Music Hall, *America*, Radio City Music Hall. MAJOR TOURS—*The Wiz*, Baltimore, MD, Detroit, MI, Philadelphia; *Stop the World, I Want to Get Off*, Chicago, Los Angeles, San Diego, CA.

FILM DEBUT—Poppie, *The Wiz*, 1977. PRINCIPAL FILM APPEARANCES—LuLu, *The Cotton Club; Stop the World I Want to Get Off*. TELEVISION DEBUT—*The Doctors*. PRINCIPAL TELEVISION APPEARANCES—*One Life to Live; The Joe Franklin Show; Bob Hope Special; Jerry Lewis Telethon; Entertainment Tonight; People's TV Tonight*.

SIDELIGHTS: MEMBERSHIPS—AEA, SAG, AFTRA, AGUA.

ADDRESS: Agent—Michael Hartig, 527 Madison Ave. New York, NY 10022.

* * *

EDWARDS, Blake, director, producer, screenwriter

PERSONAL: Born July 26, 1922, in Tulsa OK; married Julie Andrews, November 12, 1969. EDUCATION: Beverly Hills High School. MILITARY: U.S. Coast Guard, World War II.

CAREER: PRINCIPAL FILM WORK—Actor, *Ten Gentlemen from West Point*, 1942; actor, *Strangler of the Swamp*, 1945; actor, *Leather Glove*, 1948; actor/writer/co-producer, *Panhandle*, 1948; actor/writer/co-producer, *Stampede*, 1949; writer, *Rainbow Round My Shoulder*, 1952; writer, *Sound Off; writer, All Ashore*, 1953; writer, *Cruisin' Down the River*, 1953; writer, *Drive a Crooked Road*, 1954; writer, *My Sister Eileen*, 1955; writer/director, *Bring Your Smile Along*, 1955; writer/director, *He Laughed Last*, 1956; writer, *Operation Madball*, 1957; writer/director, *Mr. Cory*, 1957; writer/director, *This Happy Feeling*, 1958; writer/director,

The Perfect Furlough, 1959; director, *Operation Petticoat,* 1959; director, *High Time,* 1960; director, *Breakfast at Tiffany's,* 1961; writer, *The Notorious Landlady,* 1962; director, *The Days of Wine and Roses,* 1963; writer, *Soldier in the Rain,* 1963; producer/director/co-writer, *The Pink Panther,* 1964; producer/director/co-writer, *Shot in the Dark,* 1964; director/co-writer, *The Great Race,* 1966; producer/director/co-writer, *What Did You Do in the War, Daddy?,* 1966; producer/director/co-writer, *Gunn,* 1967; producer/director/co-writer, *The Party,* 1968; writer, *Inspector Clouseau,* 1968; producer/director/co-writer, *Darling Lili,* 1970; producer/director/co-writer, *The Wild Rovers,* 1971; director, *The Carey Treatment,* 1972; producer/director, *Experiment in Terror,* 1973; producer/director/writer, *The Tamarind Seed,* 1974; producer/director/co-writer, *The Return of the Pink Panther,* 1975; producer/director/co-writer, *The Pink Panther Strikes Again,* 1976; producer/director/co-writer, *Revenge of the Pink Panther,* 1978; director/writer/co-producer, *"10,"* 1979; director/co-producer, *S.O.B.,* 1981; director/writer/co-producer, *Victor/Victoria,* 1982; producer/director/co-writer, *The Man Who Loved Women,* 1983.

PRINCIPAL RADIO WORK—Writer, *Johnny Dollar;* writer, *Line-Up;* creator/writer, *Richard Diamond.* PRINCIPAL TELEVISION WORK—Creator: *Dante's Inferno, Peter Gunn, Mr. Lucky.*

AWARDS: Academy Award, Best Screenplay, 1983: *The Man Who Loved Women* (with Geoffrey Edwards), 1982: *Victor/Victoria.*

ADDRESS: Office—Blake Edwards Entertainment, 1888 Century Park E., Suite 1616, Los Angeles, CA 90067.*

* * *

EDWARDS, Maurice, actor, director, producer, playwright

PERSONAL: Born December 7, 1922; son of Henry Samson (a merchant) and Sophia (Manhoff) Levine; married Ann Alpert (an actress and dancer) on July 8, 1955; children: Jacob Lee. EDUCATION: New York University, B.A., 1948; Columbia University, M.A., 1955; received additional training at the Dramatic Workshop and the Stella Adler Studio, also with Erwin Piscator and Harold Clurman. MILITARY: U.S. Army, Infantry, Sergeant, 1943–46. NON-THEATRICAL CAREER: Managing director, Brooklyn Philharmonic Orchestra, Brooklyn, NY, 1971–present.

CAREER: DEBUT—played roles in high school in New London, WI, and later at the University of Wisconsin at Madison, where he appeared as Mr. Dangle in *The Critic.* NEW YORK DEBUT—Major, *The Silver Tassie,* Interplayers, Carnegie Recital Hall, 24 performances, 1950. PRINCIPAL STAGE APPEARANCES—Mr. Peachum, *Threepenny Opera,* Theatre de Lys, NY, 1959–60; Reb Nahum, *Fiddler on the Roof,* Imperial, NY, 1963–66; the Bachelor, *The Bachelor,* Classic Theatre, 16 performances, 1980.

DIRECTED—(first performances in New York), Pirandello's *The Life I Gave You,* Lord Byron's *Cain,* Olyesha's *The Conspiracy of Feelings,* Dannie Abse's *The Dogs of Pavlov,*

Witkiewicz's *Tropical Madness,* Buchner's *Danton's Death,* Pirandello's *Each in His Own Way,* Euripides' *Alcestis,* Ben Jonson's *Epicoene,* Massinger's *A New Way to Pay Old Debts.*

WRITINGS: PLAYS, TRANSLATIONS PUBLISHED—*Jest, Satire, Irony and Deeper Significance,* by Christian Dietrich Grabbe; *The Strongbox,* by Carl Sternheim; *Cry of the Streets,* by Rolf Lauckner. BOOK—with Winthrop Palmer and Jean Reavey, *The Place for Chance: An American Chronicle.* PLAYS, TRANSLATIONS, UNPUBLISHED—*Purgatory in Ingolstadt,* by Marieluise Fleisser.

THEATRE-RELATED CAREER: Program Coordinator, Cubiculo Theatre, 1969–74.

AWARDS: Bronze Star Medal, U.S. Army, 1945.

SIDELIGHTS: MEMBERSHIPS—AEA, AGMA, AFTRA. "Was early active in the Off Off-Broadway scene; served as co-founder and co-director of The Cubiculo Theatre, an experimental center doing new plays, new dance, new music. Similarly, produced and directed new operas for Actors Opera, the Brooklyn Philharmonic at the Brooklyn Academy of Music."

ADDRESS: Home—534½ Pacific Street, Brooklyn, NY 11217. Office—c/o Brooklyn Philharmonic, 30 Lafayette Avenue, Brooklyn, NY 11217. Agent—Barna Ostertag, 501 Fifth Avenue, New York, NY 10017.

* * *

EGGAR, Samantha, actress

PERSONAL: Born March 5, 1939, in London, England; daughter of Ralph Alfred James (Brigadier General, British Army) and Muriel (Palache-Bouman) Eggar; married Tom Stern (an actor, producer, and concert promoter) October 24, 1964; children: Nicolas, Jenna Louise. EDUCATION: Graduated, Holy Cross Convent, Assumption Convent, England; studied at Thanet School of Art and at the Webber-Douglas Drama School in London. RELIGION: Roman Catholic.

CAREER: PRINCIPAL STAGE APPEARANCES—Two seasons with the Oxford Playhouse, England; appeared at the Royal Court Theatre, London, England; *Midsummer Night's Dream; Twelfth Night; The Taming of the Shrew, Hamlet,* England, 1960's.

FILM DEBUT—*The Wild and the Willing,* 1961. PRINCIPAL FILM APPEARANCES—*Dr. Crippen,* 1964; *Doctor in Distress,* 1964; *Psyche 59,* 1964; *The Collector,* 1965; *Walk Don't Run,* 1966; *Return from the Ashes,* 1965; *Doctor Doolittle,* 1967; *The Molly Maguires,* 1969; *The Lady in the Car,* 1970; *Walking Stick,* 1969; *Light at the Edge of the World,* 1971; *The Seven Per Cent Solution,* 1976; *Why Shoot the Teacher; Blood City; The Brood; The Uncanny; Curtains; French Kiss; Macabre; The Exterminator; Mareth Line.*

PRINCIPAL TELEVISION APPEARANCES—*Anna and the King; Man of Destiny; Double Indemnity; The Hope Diamond; Ziegfeld; McMillan and Wife; Streets of San Francisco; Starsky and Hutch; Baretta; Columbo; The Hemingway*

Play; Love Boat; Kojak; The Killer Who Wouldn't Die.

AWARDS: Golden Globe Award, 1966; Cannes Film Festival Acting Award, 1965: *The Collector;* Academy Award Nomination, 1965: *The Collector.*

SIDELIGHTS: MEMBERSHIPS—Screen Actors Guild, AFTRA, ACTRA, AEA, AMPAS, Daughters of the British Empire, Cousteau Society, Greenpeace, Centre for Environmental Education, Special Olympics, British Olympics, Kidney Foundation, Young Musicians Foundation.

Miss Eggar works for charities in Los Angeles, where she resides with her family, combining her professional life with that of a parent, which she says is "the largest and most exquisite role in life."

ADDRESS: Office—c/o Tucker, Morgan and Martindale, 9200 Sunset Blvd., Los Angeles, CA 90069. Agent—Tom Korman, Contemporary Korman Artists, 132 Lasky Drive, Beverly Hills, CA 90212.

* * *

EGGERTH, Marta, actress, singer

PERSONAL: Born April 17, 1916, in Hungary; daughter of Paul and Tilly (Herczeg) Eggerth; married Jan Kiepura, October 31, 1936 (died August 15, 1966); children: John, Marjan. EDUCATION: Studied voice with Elisabeth Gerbay of Budapest. RELIGION: Lutheran.

CAREER: DEBUT—child's part, *Mannequin* (French Musical), Magyar Szinhas, April 1925. NEW YORK DEBUT—Lead female, *Higher and Higher,* Shubert, April 4, 1940, 104 performances. LONDON DEBUT—Concert, 1930s through 1950s. PRINCIPAL STAGE APPEARANCES—Sonja, *The Merry Widow,* Majestic, New York, 1943; female lead, *Polonaise,* Alwyn, New York, 1945. MAJOR TOURS—Sonja, *The Merry Widow,* Chicago, Los Angeles, San Francisco, England, Europe, 1945–47. FILM DEBUT—*The Bridegroom's Widow* (German film), 1931. PRINCIPAL FILMS—*Unfinished Symphony, My Heart Is Calling You, Charm of La Boheme* (over forty films in four languages); *For Me and My Gal,* 1942; *Presenting Lily Mars,* 1943.

SIDELIGHTS: Miss Eggerth often appeared with her husband, Jan Kiepura, the internationally acclaimed operatic tenor. Their son John is also a singer.

ADDRESS: Home—Park Drive North, Rye, NY 10580.

* * *

EISNER, Michael D., executive producer

PERSONAL: Born March 7, 1942; son of Lester Jr. and Margaret (Damman) Eisner; married Jane Breckenridge; children: Michael, Eric, Anders. EDUCATION: Denison University, Granville, OH, B.A. (English Literature and Theatre). THEATRE-RELATED CAREER: Programming Department, CBS; manager of Talent and Specials, ABC, 1966; director

of Program Development, ABC; director of Program Planning and executive assistant to the vice president in Charge of Programming, ABC; vice-president, Daytime Television Programming, ABC; vice-president, Program Development and Children's Programs, ABC; vice-president Prime Time Program Development/Production, ABC; vice-president, Prime Time Series Television and senior vice president, Prime Time Production and Development, ABC; president and chief operating officer, Paramount Pictures Corporation, with creative responsibilities for all divisions of Paramount, 1976–present.

CAREER: PRINCIPAL FILMS PRODUCED, at Paramount—*Saturday Night Fever; Grease; Raiders of the Lost Ark; Heaven Can Wait; Star Trek: The Motion Picture; Foul Play; Urban Cowboy; Airplane; Ordinary People; The Elephant Man; Star Trek: The Wrath of Khan; An Officer and a Gentleman.*

PRINCIPAL TELEVISION PRODUCTION, at Paramount—*Solid Gold; Entertainment Tonight; Madame's Place; Happy Days; Laverne and Shirley; Taxi; Golda; The Winds of War; Miss Universe Pageant; Miss USA Pageant;* at ABC—*Afternoon Playbreak; Scholastic Rock; Happy Days; Barney Miller; The Six Million Dollar Man; The Rookies; Welcome Back Kotter; Starsky and Hutch; Baretta; Laverne and Shirley; Charlie's Angels; Donny and Marie; Rich Man, Poor Man; Roots; What's Happening; Family; The Bionic Woman.*

SIDELIGHTS: MEMBERSHIPS—Board of directors, Dennison University: California Institute of the Arts, American Film Institute, and the Performing Arts Council of the Los Angeles Music Center.

"During the five years since Eisner came to Paramount, the company's Motion Picture Division has enjoyed a period of unprecedented success with a series of nonstop box office hits led by three films which became entertainment icons for the past decade, *Saturday Night Fever, Grease,* and *Raiders of the Lost Ark.* Most recently Mr. Eisner was named to the Board of Directors of Sega Enterprises, Inc. a leading designer manufacturer, distributor, and operator of commercial amusement games. Paramount and Sega have a common bond in their affiliation as they are committed to producing high-quality entertainment products. In television, Paramount has enjoyed equal success with an increase from two shows on national television when Mr. Eisner came to Paramount, to nine shows for the 1981–82 season. While at ABC, Mr. Eisner as vice-president for Daytime Television Programming took that network from #3 in the ratings to #1; he created the After-School Specials and Afternoon Playbreak, as Vice President of Childrens Program's; he also placed ABC #1 in that area. Mr. Eisner is a native New Yorker who lives with his wife Jane and their three sons, Michael, Eric, and Anders in Los Angeles, California."

ADDRESS: c/o Paramount Motion Picture Corporation, 1 Gulf + Western Plaza, New York, NY 10023.

* * *

ELG, Taina, actress, dancer

PERSONAL: First name rhymes with China; born March 3, 1930, in Helsinki, Finland; daughter of Ake Ludvig (a pianist) and Helena (a singer; maiden name Dobroumova) Elg; married Carl-Gustav Gorkenheim (divorced, 1961); married Rocco Caporale (a professor), May 2, 1982; children: (first marriage) Raoul. EDUCATION: Studied voice with Leone Cepparo and Bob Tucker, prior to 1960; with Bill Russel from 1962–77; with Sam Sakarian since 1976.

CAREER: PRINCIPAL STAGE APPEARANCES—Second female lead, *Paul and Constantine*, La Jolla Playhouse, 1957; Essie, *Redhead*, Dallas State Fair, 1960; female lead, *The Tender Trap*, Paper Mill, New Jersey, 1963; Claudine, *Can-Can*, Kenley Players, Columbus, OH, 1964; Nonotchka, *Silk Stockings*, Melodyland, CA, 1964; Maria, *West Side Story*, Finnish National Opera, Helsinki, 1966; Elsa, *The Sound of Music* (three different productions), 1966–71; stand-by for Julie Christie, *Uncle Vanya*, Circle in the Square Uptown, New York, 1974; Charley's Aunt, *Where's Charley*, Circle in the Square Uptown, 1976; *The Utter Glory of Morrisey Hall*, New York, 1980; female lead, *Strider*, 1980; Mamma, *Nine*, 46th Street Theatre, New York, 1982. MAJOR TOURS— Irma, *Irma la Douce*, national, 1962; second female lead, *There's a Girl in My Soup*, national, 1968; Esther, *Two by Two*, national, 1968; Angel, *I Married an Angel*, summer tour, 1970; Desiree, *A Little Night Music*, Australia, 1975; Madame Hortense, *Zorba*, summer tour, 1976; female lead, *13 Rue de l'Amour*, summer tour, 1978.

PRINCIPAL FILMS—*The Prodigal*, 1955; *Diane*, 1956; *Gaby*, 1956; *Les Girls*, 1957; *Imitation General*, 1958; *The 39 Steps*, 1958; *Watusi*, 1959; *The Bacchae*, 1959. TELEVISION APPEARANCES—*The Great Wallendas*, 1978; Dr. Fisher, *The Guiding Light*, 1980; Nicole/Olympia, *One Life to Live*, 1980–81; narrator, *Blood and Honor, Youth Under Hitler*, 1981; also *Andros Target; It Takes a Thief; The Doctors; Hong Kong; Northwest Passage; Wagon Train*, others. Guest appearances on *Ed Sullivan Show, Perry Como Show, Bell Telephone Hour, Chevrolet Special*, talk shows.

SIDELIGHTS: MEMBERSHIPS—AEA, SAG, AFTRA.

Ms. Elg has appeared with the Finnish National Radio, the Monte Carlo Ballet of the Marquis de Cuevas, Swedish Dance Theatre, and the Finnish Opera Ballet. She is fluent in English, French, Italian, German, Finnish, Swedish, and Russian. She enjoys swimming, skiing and tennis and is an American citizen.

ADDRESS: c/o Hartig-Josephson Agency, 527 Madison Avenue, NY, NY 10022

* * *

ELIASBERG, Jan, director, producer, writer

PERSONAL: Born January 6, 1954; daughter of Jay (director of research, Warner Communications) and Ann Pringle (a copywriter for Lavey, Wolff, Swift) Eliasberg. EDUCATION: Wesleyan University, Middletown, CT, B.A. (magna cum laude); Yale University, School of Drama, New Haven, CT, M.F.A.

CAREER: DIRECTED: Plays, New York—*Autumn Ladies and Their Lover's Lovers, Lenz*, Manhattan Theatre Club; *Spring Awakening*, Circle Repertory; *Money*, Ensemble Studio; *St.*

Joan of the Stockyards, Encompass Theatre/Epic Construction Company; Regional—*Sore Throats, Hedda Gabler, A Christmas Tapestry, Brecht on Brecht, A Lesson from Aloes*, Repertory Theatre of St. Louis, MO; *A History of the American Film, A Midsummer Night's Dream, Threepenny Opera, Street Songs, The Cote D'Azur Triangle, The Importance of Being Earnest*, Atlantic Theatre Company, Barnstable, MA; *Through the Leaves*, Los Angeles Theatre Works, Odyssey; *Request for "L"*, Central Casting, Ithaca, NY.

FILMS—*The Doctor*, starring Richard Masur, for American Film Institute; *Sore Throats*, American Film Institute, served as co-screenwriter for both films. OPERA—*I Due Timidi*, C.A.S.A./Opera Theatre of St. Louis, MO. THEATRE-RELATED CAREER: Resident director, Sundance Film and Theatre Conference, Sundance, UT, 1983; assistant to the head writer, *The Best of Families*, WNET/CTW, 1975–76; assistant to producer, *Beacon Hill*, CBS, 1974–75; associate artistic director, Repertory Theatre of St. Louis, 1980–83; artistic director/founder, Atlantic Theatre Company, Barnstable, MA.

WRITINGS: ARTICLES—"On the Need for an Ibsen Theatre," 1982; "Uncharted Territory," 1982. PLAYS PRODUCED— *Second Chances*, Repertory Theatre of St. Louis; *Blow Up*, Yale School of Drama. Five original radio dramas for WESU, Middletown, CT. Criticism for New York State Council for the Arts, Theatre Program, 1975–78.

AWARDS: Directing Fellow in the American Film Institute's Directing Workshop for Women, 1983–85; National Endowment for the Arts Fellowship, 1981; Theatre Communications Group Travel Grant 1981; Production of *A Lesson From Aloes*, selected to represent America at the Dublin International Theatre Festival, 1982.

SIDELIGHTS: MEMBERSHIPS—National Endowment for the Arts Consultant; Ibsen Society of America; Trustee, New York State Council on the Arts; Society of Stage Directors and Choreographers; American Film Institute, (fellow).

ADDRESS: Home—4607 Ambrose Ave., Los Angeles, CA 90027. Agent—c/o Peter Franklin or Gil Parker, William Morris Agency, 1350 Ave. of the Americas, New York, NY 10019.

* * *

ELLENSTEIN, Robert, actor, director, singer, teacher

PERSONAL: Born June 18, 1923; son of Meyer Charles (a politican, lawyer, dentist) and Hilda (Hausher) Ellenstein; married Lois Sylvia Stang (a bookseller, caterer) on May 30, 1952; children: Jan, David, Peter. EDUCATION: University of Iowa, B.A., 1947.

CAREER: PRINCIPAL STAGE APPEARANCES—Parmigian, *Cold Storage*; Scrooge, *A Christmas Carol*; Rabbi Azrielke, *The Dybbuk*; Glas, *Slow Dance on the Killing Ground*; Martin, *The Royal Hunt of the Sun*; Vladimir, *Waiting for Godot*; Don Juan, *Don Juan in Hell*; Ham, *Endgame*; Inquisitor, *St. Joan*; Adam, *Back to Methuselah*; Cris, *All My Sons*; Cassius, *Julius Caesar*; C. F., *Boy Meets Girl*; David, *Hay*

Fever; Professor, *Bus Stop;* Orgon, *Tartuffe;* Doolittle, *Pygmalion;* Joe, *Shadow Box;* Spettigue, *Charley's Aunt;* Marcus, *Titus Andronicus;* Weller, *The Gin Game;* Walter, *Don't Drink the Water;* Patsy, *Three Men on a Horse;* Carroll, *The Two Mrs. Carrolls;* Tom, *The Glass Menagerie;* Faustus, *Dr. Faustus;* Ragpicker, *The Madwoman of Chaillot;* Coney, *Home of the Brave;* Merlin, *Thor, with Angels; Fiddler on the Roof; The Red Mill; On the Town; Bittersweet: The Desert Song; Tarantara! Tarantara!; Oliver; Upholstered Pieces.* MAJOR TOURS—Bob le Hotu, *Irma La Douce,* with Juliet Prowse, national company.

PRINCIPAL FILM APPEARANCES—*North by Northwest; Rogue Cop; The Young Lions; Too Much Too Soon; Gazebo; 3:10 to Yuma; Pay or Die; Love at First Bite;* and others. PRINCIPAL TELEVISION APPEARANCES—over 50 featured or starring roles—from Albert Einstein to Quasimodo—Philco, Montgomery, *Omnibus,* Kraft, Armstrong, Theatre Guild, etc.

DIRECTED, PLAYS—*The Comedy of Errors,* Great Lakes Shakespeare Festival; *Hamlet,* Arizona Theatre Company; *Hope Is a Thing with Feathers, Three by Tennessee Williams, Back to Methuseleh, Part 1,* Cleveland Playhouse; *My Aunt Daisey,* Westport Country Playhouse, CT; *Montserrat, The Lower Depths, Tonight We Improvise,* Company of Angels, Los Angeles; *Yerma, The Heavenly Express,* Karamu Playhouse, Cleveland, OH; *Misalliance, Tiger at the Gates, The Great God Brown, Gallows Humor, Chronicles of Hell,* Los Angeles Repertory Company; *Irma La Douce,* Valley Music Theatre, Los Angeles; *Don Juan in Hell,* Lindy Opera House, Los Angeles; *Endgame,* Vanguard Theatre, Los Angeles; *The Girls in 509; Romeo and Juliet; Oedipus; Legend of Lovers; The Drunkard; Three Cuckholds; The Threepenny Opera; As You Like It.* TELEVISION—*Robert Montgomery Presents,* NBC; *Love on a Rooftop,* Screen Gems.

THEATRE-RELATED CAREER: Professional coach and teacher (30 years), Cleveland, OH, New York, and Los Angeles; guest professor and director—California State University, Northridge (3 years), and at Los Angeles; Otterbein College, Case-Western Reserve University, University of Iowa. Co-founder and director, Ellenstein-Palter Studio, Los Angeles, CA; co-founder/managing director, Academy of Stage and Cinema Arts, Los Angeles. Contract talent coach, Screen Gems, Los Angeles.

AWARDS: Best Direction, Cleveland Critics Circle Award, 1979–80.

SIDELIGHTS: MEMBERSHIPS—DGA, AEA, SAG, AFTRA.

Mr. Ellenstein's resume and credits do not include his 40 years of extensive acting experience in a wide variety of stage, feature film, and television work: In film and television, he has performed in over 100 featured or starring roles, including 14 feature-length films, and over 100 roles on stage. His early training came from the Dramatic Workshop of the New School for Social Research and the University of Iowa, as well as the Actors Studio and The American Theatre Wing in New York.

ADDRESS: Home—5215 Sepulveda Blvd., Culver City, CA 90203.

ELLERBE, Harry, actor, director

PERSONAL: Born January 13, 1906; son of Alexander Washington (a publisher) and Marie Louise (De Treville) Ellerbe. EDUCATION: Attended Georgia Tech; studied with the Stuart Walker Company, in Cincinnati, OH. RELIGION: Episcopalian.

CAREER: NEW YORK DEBUT—Philip, *Philip Goes Forth,* Biltmore Theatre, 1932. PRINCIPAL STAGE APPEARANCES—*The Man on Stilts; The Tadpole; Strange Orchestra; Junior Miss; The Mad Hopes; Outward Bound* (revival); *Thoroughbred; The Desk Set; Whiteoaks; Feathers in a Gale; Ghosts; Hedda Gabler; The Ghost Sonata; The Rivals.* MAJOR TOURS—*Whiteoaks,* with Ethel Barrymore; *Outward Bound; Junior Miss; The Cocktail Party; Ghosts; Hedda Gabler; Summer and Smoke;* PRINCIPAL FILM APPEARANCES—*The Desk Set; So Red the Rose; The Young Lions; He Understood Women; The House of Usher.* DIRECTED: *For Love or Money,* Broadway (plus three other shows), New York.

SIDELIGHTS: MEMBERSHIPS—Sigma Phi Epsilon; Masquers Club, Hollywood, CA.

ADDRESS: Home—1896 Wycliff Road N.W., Atlanta, GA 30309.

* * *

ELLIOTT, Michael (Alwyn), administrator

PERSONAL: (assumed stepfather's name) Born: July 15, 1936 in Haverfordwest, Wales; son of W. A. Edwards and J. B. Elliot; married Caroline McCarthy; children: Gregory, Dominic, Sophie. EDUCATION: Raynes Park Grammar School, Middlesex, England. NON-THEATRICAL CAREER: Journalist, 1955–59; public relations, Avon Rubber Company, Ltd., 1959–63; marketing executive/assistant corporate planning manager, CPC International, 1963–68; product manager, 1968, marketing manager, 1969, marketing and development manager, 1975, general manager, 1976, director, 1977–79, Kimberly-Clark, Ltd.

CAREER: General administrator, National Theatre of Great Britain.

SIDELIGHTS: MEMBERSHIPS—Executive Council, Society of West End Theatres, 1980.

RECREATION: Acting, golf.

ADDRESS: Office—The National Theatre, South Bank, SE1, London, England.

* * *

ELLIOTT, Sumner Locke, playwright, actor

PERSONAL: Born October 17, 1917, in Australia; son of Henry Logan (a journalist) and Helena Sumner (a writer; maiden name Locke) Elliott. EDUCATION: Graduate high school, New South Wales, Australia; trained for the theatre with Doris Fitton of the Independent Theatre.

CAREER: DEBUT—Morgan Evans, *The Corn Is Green*, Independent Theatre, Sydney, Australia, 1940. NEW YORK DEBUT—Author, *Buy Me Blue Ribbons*, Empire, October 17, 1951 for thirteen performances. PRINCIPAL STAGE APPEARANCES—Constantin, *The Seagull*, Independent Theatre, Sydney, 1943; *Sweetest and Lowest Revue*, Minerva, Sydney, 1947; Leo, *The Little Foxes*, Independent Theatre, Sydney, 1947.

TELEVISION DEBUT—Author, *Studio One*, 1949. TELEVISION WORK: Wrote for *Philco Playhouse, Playhouse 90*, others.

WRITINGS: Books—*Careful, He Might Hear You*, 1963 (filmed 1983); *Eders Lost*, 1969; *Going*, 1972; *Water Under the Bridge*, 1976; *Signs of Life*, 1979; *About Tilly Beamis.*

AWARDS: Patrick White Prize (Australia), 1978; Miles Franklyn Award, best novel, 1964.

SIDELIGHTS: MEMBERSHIPS—PEN; Writers Guild; Authors Guild.

After being one of Australia's foremost playwrights and radio writers, Mr. Elliott emigrated to the United States in 1948, where he became one of the first well-known television playwrights in the days of live television under the direction of Fred Coe.

ADDRESS: Agent—Gloria Safier, 667 Madison Ave., New York, NY 10021.

* * *

ELSTON, Robert, actor, director, producer, playwright

PERSONAL: Born May 29, 1934. MILITARY: U.S. Army, Corporal, 1953–55.

CAREER: PRINCIPAL STAGE APPEARANCES—*Memo*, NY; Sherman, *Maybe Tuesday*, NY; Jake Eldridge, *Golden Fleecing*, NY; Ray Blent, *Tall Story*, NY; *Spoon River Anthology*, NY; Playwright/Salesman/Old Man, *You Know I Can't Hear You When the Water's Running*, NY; Robert Dudley, *Vivat, Vivat, Regina*, NY; One-Man Show, *Portrait of a Man*, NY; One-Man Show, *Notes from the Underground*, NY; *Undercover Man*, NY; *After Many a Summer*, NY; Trigorin, *The Seagull*, NY; Teacher, *Andorra*, Jewish Repertory, NY; Tyrone T. Tattersall, *Archy and Mehitabel*, NY; MAJOR TOURS—Jefferson, *1776*, national tour; *You Know I Can't Hear You When the Water's Running*, national tour; *The World of Susie Wong*, national tour.

DIRECTED—*Phyllis Rice and Marcia Brushingham in Concert*, American Renaissance Theatre (ART), 1977; *Romeo and Juliet*, North Shore Music Theatre, 1978; *Molly Bloom and the Women of Ireland*, ART, 1978; *Act of Kindness*, ART, 1978; *The Owl and the Pussycat*, Club Benet Dinner Theatre, NJ, 1979; *Sweethearts*, ART, 1979; *Equals, Silences, Curses*, ART, 1979; *Do You Still Believe the Rumor*, ART, 1980; *Archy and Mehitabel*, ART, 1980; *After Many a Summer*, ART, 1982; *Pas de Deux*, ART, 1983.

PRINCIPAL FILM APPEARANCES—Charles Schwab, *The Rise of America; Mark of the Witch; Garp*, 1981; *A Private Matter*, 1981. PRINCIPAL TELEVISION APPEARANCES—*The Steve Allen Show; Saints and Sinners; NET Christmas Special; CBS Repertoire; The Lloyd Bridges Show; Hennessey; Camera 3; The Edge of Night; Love Is a Many Splendored Thing; Love of Life;* Dr. Howell, *As the World Turns*, 1981–82; Peyton Randolph, *George Washington*, 1983.

THEATRE-RELATED CAREER—Founding Member, Theatre West, Los Angeles, CA, 1960–64; Teacher, Herbert Berghof Studios, New York, 1964–75; Co-Founder/Teacher, American Renaissance Theatre, New York, 1975–present.

WRITINGS: PLAYS, PRODUCED—*Murder at the Gaiety*, music by Murray Grand; *Run Children Run*, with Harvey Keith, Karamu House, Cleveland, OH, 1974–75, Henry Street Settlement, NY; *After Many a Summer*, ART, 1982.

SIDELIGHTS: Mr. Elston is a familiar face to television audiences, having appeared in hundreds of commercials, three of which have garnered Clio awards.

ADDRESS: Home—112 Charlton Street, New York, NY 10014.

* * *

EMONTS, Ann, costume designer

PERSONAL: Born June 23, 1952; daughter of Robert J. and Janet (French) Emonts. EDUCATION: University of California at Santa Barbara, B.A. 1974; New York University School of the Arts, M.F.A. 1978.

CAREER: PRINCIPAL COSTUME DESIGN WORK—*The Tap Dance Kid*, Broadhurst, NY; *Oh Brother*, ANTA, NY; *Comin Uptown*, Winter Garden, NY; *Isn't It Romantic*, Playwrights Horizons, NY; *Geniuses*, Playwrights Horizons, NY; *The Rise and Rise of Daniel Rocket*, Playwrights Horizons, NY; *Tom Foolery*, Village Gate, NY; *Coming Attractions*, Playwrights Horizons, NY; *The Brides*, Music Theatre Group/Lenox Arts Center; *Colombine String Quartet*, Cubiculo, NY; *Bone Songs*, NY; *Fat Chances*, Circle Repertory Company at the Westbeth Theatre Center, NY; *Potholes*, Cherry Lane, NY; *Twelfth Night*, Cherry Lane, NY; *The Shaft of Love*, New York University; *Camino Real*, New York University; *The Dragon*, New York University; *Terra Nova*, Old Globe, San Diego, CA; *Alone Together*, Whole Theatre Company, Montclair, NJ; *Richard III*, American Shakespeare Festival, Stratford, CT; *One Mo' Time*, bus and truck tour; *A Flea in Her Ear*, Pennsylvania Stage Company; *Volpone*, New Jersey Shakespeare Festival; *King Lear*, New Jersey Shakespeare Festival; *A Midsummer Night's Dream*, New Jersey Shakespeare Festival; *A Streetcar Named Desire*, New Jersey Shakespeare Festival; *Same Time Next Year*, North Shore Music Theatre; *Bye Bye Birdie*, North Shore Music Theatre; *Loves Labour Lost*, Santa Barbara, CA; *The Tempest*, Santa Barbara, CA; Assistant costume designer, *Cats*, Winter Garden, NY.

ADDRESS: Office—11 Charles Street, New York, NY 10014.

ERMAN, John, film and television director

PERSONAL: Born August 3, 1935 in Chicago; son of Milton G. (a salesman) and Lucille Arlie (Straus) Erman. EDUCATION: University of California, Los Angeles, B.A., 1957. POLITICS: Democrat. RELIGION: Jewish.

CAREER: TELEVISION DEBUT—Director—*Stoney Burke,* 1962. PRINCIPAL TELEVISION WORK—Director—*Green Eyes,* 1977; *Alexander, the Other Side of Dawn,* 1977; *Child of Glass,* 1978; *Just Me and You,* 1978; *My Old Man,* 1979; *Roots: The Next Generation,* 1979; *Family, Moviola,* 1980; *The Letter,* 1981; *Eleanor, First Lady of the World; Who Will Love My Children,* 1983; *A Streetcar Named Desire,* 1984.

PRINCIPAL FILM WORK—Director—*Making It,* 1970; *Ace Eli and Rodger of the Skies,* 1972.

AWARDS: Emmy Award, 1983: *Who Will Love My Children;* Directors Guild of America Award and Christopher Award, 1977: *Roots: The Next Generation;* Humanitas Prize, 1977: *Green Eyes.*

RELATED CAREER: Founder, Faculty Acting School, Los Angeles, CA; casting director, 20th Century Fox, 1959–63; head, TV Casting, 20th Century Fox, 1960–61.

SIDELIGHTS: MEMBERSHIPS—Directors Guild of America.

''I always try to find a positive statement in the material I'm directing and then endeavor to decide how I can best express that statement and help my fellow creators to do the same.''

ADDRESS: Office—9777 Wilshire Blvd., Suite 900, Beverly Hills, CA 90210.

* * *

ERNOTTE, André, director, writer, adaptor, French/English

PERSONAL: Born June 3, 1943, in Liège, Belgium; son of Jules Gilbert and Fanny Ernotte. EDUCATION: Athenée Royale de Liège, 1961; INSAS/National Institute of Performing Arts (Drama), 1966. MILITARY: Belgian Armed Services.

CAREER: DIRECTED: PLAYS, NEW YORK—*Brecht & Feydeau & Emigrés,* Brooklyn Academy of Music; *Coming Attractions, Company, Vienna Notes & Jungle Coup,* Playwrights Horizons; *Crossing Niagara,* Manhattan Theatre Club. REGIONAL—*A House Not Meant to Stand, Betrayal,* Goodman Theatre, Chicago; *Servant of Two Masters,* Philadelphia Drama Guild; *Richard III,* Stratford Shakespeare Theatre, Stratford, CT, and the Kennedy Center, Washington, DC. National Theatre of Belgium—*Miss Margarida's Way, Kennedy's Children, Comedians, The Day They Kidnapped the Pope, Attention Fragile, Reveillon;* TRM Royal Opera House—*Die Walküre;* Improv Theatre—*Last Sweet Days of Issac, Fiddler on the Roof, Tartuffe, Glass Menagerie, All My Sons, Hamlet, Pas Op Breekbaar, Uncle Vanya, Medea.*

FILMS—*High Street; Low Tides.* TELEVISION—*Attention Fragile; Last Sweet Days of Issac; Sketch Up.*

WRITINGS: *Rue Haute* (novel).

AWARDS: Obie, *Vienna Notes & Jungle Coup,* at Playwrights Horizons; Drama Critics Circle—Best Director, Belgium; Liège Film Critics, Grand Prix Best Director, Scenarist; New Orleans Film Festival—Grand Prix—Best Director, Scenarist; Harkness Fellow, Salzburg American Theatre Fellow, Berliner Ensemble Fellow. Best Director, Humanitarian Motion Picture Award, 1981.

SIDELIGHTS: Mr. Ernotte has staged over 80 productions in Europe and the United States as well as directing for films and TV. He has been collaborating with Elliot Tiber since 1971. His current credits include: *The Music Keeper,* starring Jan Miner at the South Street Theatre and *Christmas On Mars* at Playwrights Horizons as well as *The Philanthropist* with David McCallum at the Manhattan Theatre Club. His current projects are *Alyce thru the Computer Glass* and *Attention Fragile* for French TV.

ADDRESS: Office—484 W. 43rd Street, New York, NY 10036. Agent—c/o Bruce Savan, Agency for the Performing Arts, 888 Seventh Ave., New York, NY 10019.

* * *

ERSKINE, Howard (Weir), producer, actor, director

PERSONAL: Born June 29, 1926 in Bronxville, NY; son of Howard Major (a public utilities financier) and Agnes (Weir) Erskine; married Lou Prentis (an actress) on March 3, 1955; children: one daughter. EDUCATION: Williams College, B.A. 1949. MILITARY: U.S. Navy, OM-2, WWII.

CAREER: DEBUT—Berkshire Playhouse, Stockbridge, MA, summer, 1949. PRINCIPAL STAGE APPEARANCES—Played three seasons at the Berkshire Playhouse, Stockbridge MA; Bermudiana Theatre, Hamilton, Bermuda, 1950; Atterbury Playhouse, Albany, NY, 1952; Quentin Armstone, *Calculated Risk,* Ambassador, NY, 1962; Victor Prynne, *Private Lives,* Theatre de Lys, NY, 1968.

DIRECTED—*The Happiest Millionaire,* Lyceum, NY, 1956 and subsequent tour; *Calculated Risk,* two stock tours; *Any Wednesday,* Royal Poinciana Playhouse, Coconut Grove Playhouse, 1965; *Minor Miracle,* Henry Miller Theatre, NY, 1965. CO-PRODUCED—*The Desperate Hours,* Barrymore, 1955, Hippodrome, London, England, 1955, West Coast Tour, 1956; *The Midnight Sun,* Shubert, New Haven, CT, 1959; *Calculated Risk,* Ambassador, NY, 1963; *Any Wednesday,* Music Box, NY, 1964;

PRINCIPAL FILM WORK—actor, *Seminole,* 1953.

PRINCIPAL TELEVISION WORK—Produced, *Rendezvous* series, CBS, 1959; *Portofino,* 1961.

THEATRE-RELATED CAREER: Eastern Regional Manager, Ticketron, 1970–present.

AWARDS: Antoinette Perry Award with Joseph Hayes, Best Production, *The Desperate Hours,* 1955.

SIDELIGHTS: MEMBERSHIPS—AEA; SAG; AFTRA; Chi Psi.

ADDRESS: Home—Cushman Rd. R.D. 2, Patterson, NY 12463.

* * *

ESTERMAN, Laura, actress

PERSONAL: Born April 12, in New York; daughter of Benjamin (a doctor) and Sophie (Milgram) Esterman. EDUCATION: Radcliffe College, B.A.; trained for the stage at the London Academy of Music and Dramatic Art.

CAREER: DEBUT—Masha, *Three Sisters*, Mummers Theater, Oklahoma City, OK. NEW YORK DEBUT—Essie, *The Time of Your Life*, Vivian Beaumont. PRINCIPAL STAGE APPEARANCES—(Broadway) *Waltz of the Toreadors; God's Favorite; Teibele, Teibele and Her Demon;* Cleopatra, *The Suicide*. (Off-Broadway) Masha, *The Seagull*, Roundabout; Regina, *Ghosts*, Roundabout; *The Carpenters*, American Place; Mrs. Brimmins, *Rubbers*, American Place; Melinda, *The Recruiting Officer*, BAM Theatre Company; Helena, *A Midsummer Night's Dream*, BAM Theatre Company; Mimi, *Chinchilla*, Phoenix; Dusa, *Dusa, Fish, Stas, and VI*, Manhattan Theatre Club; *The Bridge at Belharbor*, Manhattan Theatre Club; *Golden Boy*, Manhattan Theatre Club; *The Pokey*, Manhattan Theatre Club; Margarita, *The Master and Margarita*, New York Shakespeare Festival; Lady Macbeth, *Macbeth*, New York Shakespeare Festival; Irene, *Two Fish in the Sky*, New York Shakespeare Festival; Mary Barnes, *Mary Barnes*, AMDA Theater. (Regional) Giulianella, *Saturday, Sunday, Monday*, Arena Stage, Washington, DC; Beatrice, *Much Ado About Nothing*, McCarter; Lavinia, *Mourning Becomes Electra*, Goodman Theatre, Chicago; Nicole, *Bonjour la Bonjour*, Guthrie, Minneapolis; Kathleeen, *Terra Nova*, Mark Taper Forum, Los Angeles; *Rip Van Winkle*, Yale Repertory; *Animal Kingdom, Sunrise at Campobello*, Berkshire Theatre Festival.

PRINCIPAL FILM APPEARANCES—*Alone in the Dark*. PRINCIPAL TELEVISION APPEARANCES—*Another World*.

ADDRESS: Agent—c/o Writers and Artists, 162 W. 56th Street, New York, NY 10019.

* * *

EVANS, Don, playwright, educator

PERSONAL: Born April 27, 1938 in Philadelphia, PA; son of Mary A. Evans; married Frances Gooding in November, 1962; children: Todd, Rachel, Orrin. EDUCATION: Cheyney State College, B.S. (Secondary English) 1962; Temple University, M.A., M.F.A. 1968–72; studied with Herbert Berghof at the H.B. Studios in New York City. MILITARY: U.S. Marine Corps. NON-THEATRICAL CAREER: Associate Professor of Afro-American Studies, Princeton University and Trenton State College, 1971–present.

WRITINGS: PLAYS, PUBLISHED—*Sugarmouth Sam Don't*

Dance No More, 1973; *Showdown*, 1976; *The Prodigals*, 1977; *One Monkey Don't Stop No Show*, 1982.

PLAYS, PRODUCED—*Orrin* and *Sugarmouth Sam Don't Dance No More*, H.B. Playwrights Foundation, NY, 1972, Dashiki Theatre, New Orleans, LA, 1972, ANTA Matinee Series, NY, 1972, Concept East Theatre, Detroit, MI, 1974, Freedom Theatre, Philadelphia, PA, 1975, Negro Ensemble Company, NY, 1976, Kuumba Playhouse, Chicago, IL, 1977 (published under the title *The Prodigals*); *Matters of Choice*, H.B. Playwrights Foundation, NY, 1974, Karamby Theatre, Cleveland, OH, 1974, Players' Company, Trenton, NJ, 1975, Afro-American Cultural Center, Buffalo, NY, 1976, Smith College, Amherst, MA, 1977, *Matters of Choice*, Morris Brown College, Atlanta, GA, 1977; *It's Showdown Time*, New Federal, NY, National Tour, 1977; *Miss Lydia*, Southwest Comminity Theatre, San Diego, CA, Crossroads, New Brunswick, NJ, H.B. Playwrights Foundation, Negro Ensemble Company, NY, Public Television in New Jersey, 1979; *Louis* (musical based on the life of Louis Armstrong), Henry Street Playhouse, NY, 1981; *Mahalia* (musical biography of Mahalia Jackson), Hartman Theatre Company, Stamford, CT, Harry de Jur Playhouse, NY, 1978; *One Monkey Don't Stop No Show*, Public Television, New Jersey, 1983, Billie Holiday Theatre Company, NY, 1981, Crossroads Theatre Company, New Brunswick, NJ, 1980.

PLAYS, UNPUBLISHED—What Harriet Did, 1982; Honky Tonk, music by Michael Renzi, 1982. ARTICLES, CRITICISM, FICTION—"The Dead-Assed Mules, A Response," *Pride* Magazine, 1973; "Bloods Ain't Into That," *Player's* Magazine, 1974; "Youngblood," *Essence* Magazine, 1975; "The Theatre of Confrontation," *Black World* Magazine, 1974; "Up Against the Wall, Ed Bullins," *Contemporary Literary Criticism*, 1976; "Notes of a Theatre Hustler," *American Arts* Magazine, 1982.

THEATRE-RELATED CAREER: Director of College Theatre, Cheyney State College, 1968–72; Founder/Executive Director, Lorraine Hansberry Arts Center, Princeton, NJ; Artistic Director, Players Company of Trenton, Trenton, NJ–present.

AWARDS: National Endowment for the Arts Fellowship in Playwriting, 1982; Citation of Merit, City of Trenton, New Jersey, 1977; Alumnae Citation Cheyney State College, 1977; Nominated Best Production, Audience Development Corporation, *Showdown*, New York City, 1976; Fai-Ho-Chi Award for Service to the Arts, 1976; Outstanding Contributions to the Development of Black Theatre, Arena, Baltimore, 1974; Eugene O'Neill Playwrights Foundation first alternate play, *Orrin*, 1972.

SIDELIGHTS: MEMBERSHIPS—Commissioner of Arts, City of Trenton, New Jersey; Board of Directors, Mercer Country School for the Performing Arts; American Theatre Association; ASCAP; AGAC; AAUP.

ADDRESS: Office—c/o Trenton State College, Hillwood Lakes, Trenton, NJ 08625. Agent—Lucy Kroll, 390 W. End Avenue, New York, NY 10024.

EVANS, Ray (ne Raymond G. Evans), lyricist

PERSONAL: Born February 4, 1915, in Salamanca, NY; son of Philip (a waste materials worker) and Frances (Lipsitz) Evans; married Wyn Ritchie, on April 19, 1947. EDUCATION: Wharton School, University of Pennsylvania, B.S. (Economics), 1936. POLITICS: Democrat. RELIGION: Jewish.

CAREER: FIRST STAGE WORK—Lyricist, *I Love Lydia*, Players Ring of Hollywood, 1950. NEW YORK DEBUT—Lyricist, *Oh Captain!*, Alvin, 1958, six months of performances. LONDON DEBUT—Lyricist, *Six of a Kind*, 1962. PRINCIPAL STAGE WORK—Lyricist, *Let It Ride*, Eugene O'Neill, New York, 1961; lyricist, *Sugar Babies*, Mark Hellinger, New York, 1979.

FILM DEBUT—Lyricist, *Monsieur Beaucaire*, 1945. PRINCIPAL FILM WORK—Lyricist, *To Each His Own, Golden Earrings, The Paleface, My Friend Irma, My Friend Irma Goes West, Aaron Slick from Punkin' Crick, Houseboat, Red Garters, This Property Condemned, Dear Heart, What Did You do in the War, Daddy?, The Man Who Knew Too Much.* PRINCIPAL TELEVISION WORK—Lyricist, *Satins 'n Spurs* (first color TV musical).

AWARDS: Academy Awards (3) for songs: "Buttons and Bows," "Mona Lisa," 'Que Sera Sera," Songwriters' Hall of Fame.

SIDELIGHTS: MEMBERSHIPS—Board, Southern California Chapter Myasthenia Gravis Foundation; ASCAP-West Coast Advisory Board; AGAC-West Coast Executive Board; Academy of Motion Picture Arts and Sciences. RECREATION: Sports, world affairs.

"Have traveled to almost 100 countries on all continents." Listed: *Great Songwriters of Hollywood, ASCAP Biography,* etc.

ADDRESS: Home—1255 Angelo Drive, Beverly Hills, CA 90210.

* * *

EYEN, Tom, playwright and director

PERSONAL: Born August 14, 1941, in Cambridge, OH; son of Abraham and Julia (Farhat) Eyen; married Liza Giraudoux. EDUCATION: Ohio State University.

CAREER: DIRECTED: Plays—Theatre of the Eye, 1964–present (see plays, produced); *Rachel Lily Rosenbloom (And Don't You Forget It),* (replaced Ron Link), Broadhurst, Y, 1973.

WRITINGS: PLAYS, PRODUCED—*(When) The Clock Strikes Thirteen,* also wrote it, in his garage at age eight, Cambridge, OH, 1950; *Frustrata, the Dirty Little Girl with the Red Paper Rose Stuck in Her Head, Is Demented,* La Mama Experimental Theatre Club, NY, 1964; *Tour de Four,* Writers Stage, NY, 1963; since then, has written many avant garde and experimental plays and musicals for Cafe La Mama, Playwright's Workshop, and the commercial theatre, most of which were performed by his troupe, the Theatre of the Eye, and directed by him: *The White Whore and Bit Player, My Next Husband Will Be a Beauty,* 1964; *Can You See a Prince?* (children's musical), *The Demented World of Tom Eyen, Why Hanna's Skirt Won't Stay Down, Miss Nefertiti Regrets,* 1965; *Cinderella Revisited* (children's musical), *Sinderella Revisted* (adult musical), *Eyen on Eyen, Give My Regards to Off-Off-Broadway,* 1966; *Court, Sarah B. Divine!* (Part 1), *Grand Tenement,* November 22, 1967; *Why Johnny Comes Dancing Home, The Kama Sutra (An Organic Happening), Who Killed My Bald Sister Sophie?, A Vanity Happening, Alice through the Looking Glass Lightly,* 1968; *The Four No Plays, Caution: A Love Story, Eye in New York,* 1969; *Areatha in the Ice Palace, What Is Making Gilda So Gray, Gertrude Stein and Other Great Men, The Dirtiest Show in Town,* 1970; *2008½: A Space Oddity,* 1973; *Women Behind Bars,* 1974; *The Dirtiest Musical,* 1975; *The Neon Woman,* 1978; *Dreamgirls,* Majestic, NY, 1981. London first saw Mr. Eyen's work in 1970 with *The White Whore and the Bit Player,* at the Mercury; *The Dirtiest Show in Town,* Duchess, 1971; *Women Behind Bars,* 1977. PLAYS, UNPRODUCED—Kicks, 1984. SCREENPLAYS—*The White Whore and the Bit Player,* 1969; *Ava,* 1982. TELEVISION SHOWS—*Mary Hartman, Mary Hartman,* 1976–77; *The Bette Midler Special,* 1977.

AWARDS: Antoinette Perry Award, 1982: *Dreamgirls.*

SIDELIGHTS: MEMBERSHIPS—Harvard Club; Knights of Columbus. RECREATION—Scuba diving, sky-diving.

ADDRESS: Agent—Bridget Aschenberg, I.C.M., 40 W. 57th Street, New York, NY 10019.*

F

FALK, Peter, actor

PERSONAL: Born September 16, 1927, in New York City; son of Michael and Madeline (Hockhauser) Falk; married Alice Mayo, 1960; married Shera Lynn Danese (an actress), 1977; children: (first marriage) Catherine, Jacqueline. EDUCATION: Hamilton College; New School for Social Research, B.A.; Syracuse University, MPA. MILITARY: U.S. Merchant Marines.

CAREER: NEW YORK DEBUT—Bartender, *The Iceman Cometh,* Circle-in-the-Square, 1956, 95 performances. PRINCIPAL STAGE APPEARANCES—*Saint Joan,* Phoenix, NY, 1956; *Purple Dust,* Cherry Lane, NY, 1957; *The Lady's Not for Burning,* Little Carnegie, NY, 1958; *Bonds of Interest,* Sheridan Square Playhouse, NY, 1958; Mel Edison, *The Prisoner of Second Avenue,* O'Neill, NY, 1971.

FILM DEBUT—*Wind Across the Everglades,* 1958. PRINCIPAL FILMS—Abe Reles, *Murder, Inc.,* 1960; *A Pocketful of Miracles,* 1961; *Pressure Point,* 1962; *It's a Mad, Mad, Mad, Mad World,* 1963; *The Balcony,* 1964; *Robin and the Seven Hoods,* 1964; Max, *The Great Race,* 1965; *Penelope,* 1966; *Luv,* 1967; *Anzio,* 1968; *Castle Keep,* 1969; *Husbands,* 1970; *A Woman Under the Influence,* 1974; *Murder by Death,* 1976; *Mikey and Nickey; The Cheap Detective,* 1978; *The In-Laws,* 1979.

TELEVISION DEBUT—*Law and Mr. Jones,* 1960. TELEVISION APPEARANCES—"The Price of Tomatoes,"—*The Dick Powell Show,* 1961; Daniel J. O'Brien, *The Trials of O'Brien,* 1965–66; Lieutenant Columbo, *Columbo,* 1971–77; *Sacco & Vanzetti; Roots; Montgomery; The Dupont Show of the Week; Omnibus; Bob Hope Presents the Chrysler Theatre; Studio One; Kraft Theatre; Philco Theatre.*

AWARDS: Academy Award Nomination, Best Supporting Actor 1960: *Murder, Inc.;* 1961: *Pocketful of Miracles;* Emmy Award, Best Dramatic Performance, 1961: *The Price of Tomatoes,* Best Actor in a Series, 1970, 1971, 1972: *Columbo;* Emmy Award Nomination, Best Dramatic Performance, 1960: *The Law and Mr. Jones;* Obie Award, Best Performance, 1956: *The Iceman Cometh.*

ADDRESS: Agent—ICM, 8899 Beverly Blvd., Los Angeles, CA 90048.

* * *

FALLON, Richard G., educator, director, producer, manager, writer, actor

PERSONAL: Born September 19, 1923, in New York; son of Perlie Peter (an attorney) and Margaret Elizabeth (Julia) Fallon; married Suzanne Constance Bowkett, on January 7, 1946; children: Diane, Richard.

EDUCATION: Brown University, 1940–42; Old Vic Theatre School, London, Certificate of "Excellent," 1945; Columbia College, B.A. (Theatre), 1948; Columbia University, M.A. (Theatre), 1951; Columbia University, all work completed toward Ph.D. in theatre under supervision of Joseph Wood Krutch, which was abandoned upon his retirement. MILITARY: U.S. Army, WWII.

CAREER: NEW YORK DEBUT, ACTOR—Jim, *The World We Make,* Equity Library, 1946. LONDON DEBUT, ACTOR—*Dear Ruth,* Scala Theatre, 1945. PRINCIPAL FILM APPEARANCES—*The True Glory; Naked in the Sun.* PRINCIPAL RADIO APPEARANCES—*Young Doctor Malone; Mr. District Attorney; Jack Armstrong.* DIRECTED—*The Last Days of Lincoln; Never, Never Ask His Name; The Long Night; My Mother, My Father and Me; Eleonora Duse; Cyrano de Bergerac; Trog; Assignment in Judea; Morgan Rock;* directed at the Asolo State Theatre, Sarasota, FL—*The Barber of Seville; Cyrano de Bergerac; The Lady's Not for Burning; Tiger at the Gates; A Man for All Seasons; Eleonora Duse; Othello.*

AWARDS: Ross Oglesby Award, Florida State University, 1982; ODK Man of the Year Award, 1981; Suzanne Davis Award for Distinguished Service to Southern Theatre, 1981; American Theatre Association College of Fellows, 1980; Robert O. Lawton Distinguished Professor of the Year, Florida State University, 1975; elected to the Players, 1974; Governor's Award for the Arts, 1974; Alumni Professor of the Year, 1971; Outstanding Educator of America, 1971–72; E. Harris Harbison Award for Gifted Teaching, 1970; listed in *Who's Who in South and Southwest, Who's Who in American Theatre, American Scholar;* elected to Lambs, 1965; elected to ODK at Florida State University, 1965; Best Director of Off-Broadway Production, National Conference of Christians and Jews, 1962; certificate of appreciation from student government, Florida State University, 1961–62; Ambassador for the Arts in Florida; Eminent Scholar Chair, Florida State University.

SIDELIGHTS: MEMBERSHIPS—American Theatre Association, University/Resident Theatre Association, National Theatre Conference, The Players, The Lambs, Southeastern Theatre Conference, American Speech Association, American National Theatre and Academy, American Association of University Professors, Florida Theatre Conference, Theatre Library Association, Florida Speech Association, Florida

League of the Arts. PRINCIPAL PROFESSIONAL AFFILIATIONS: Dean emeritus and director of Professional Programs, School of Theatre, Florida State University; Burt Reynolds Eminent Scholar Chair, School of Theatre, Florida State University; executive director, Asolo State Theatre, Sarasota; director, Charles MacArthur Center for American Theatre; president, Jekyll Island Music Theatre, Inc.; director, Burt Reynolds Foundation for Theatre Training; president, American Theatre Association, 1982–83; founder, Eddie Dowling University Theatre Foundation; executive director, Jacksonville Little Theatre, 1955–57; professor of theatre, chairman of theatre, Maryland State University, 1950–54; professor of theatre, chairman of speech and theatre, Hartwick College, Oneonta, NY, 1946–50; director, Scala Theatre, London, England (U.S. Army post theatre) 1943–45; president, University/Resident Theatre Association 1973–75; vice president, Florida Arts Council, 1964; president, AAUP Chapter at Florida State University, 1963; state representative, International Theatre Month, ANTA, 1960–64; vice-president, Florida Speech Association, 1960–61; president, Florida Theatre Conference, 1958–61; chairman, State Theatre Board; chairman, Committee to Establish American Research Council in Theatre; president, Florida League of the Arts; vice-president, Eddie Dowling University Theatre Foundation; Founder of the Asolo State Theatre in Sarasota Florida. Major Work in Preparation: With Burt Reynolds, planning a new theatre with video facility in Jupiter, Florida. Development of Charles MacArthur Center for American Theatre.

ADDRESS: Home—2302 Delgado Drive, Tallahassee, FL 32304. Office—School of Theatre, Florida State University, Tallahassee, Fl 32304.

* * *

FALLS, Gregory A., director, producer

PERSONAL: Born April 4, 1922; EDUCATION: Park College, B.A., 1943; Northwestern University, M.A., 1949, Ph.D., 1953; Fulbright Scholar, Central School of Speech and Drama, London, England, 1950. MILITARY: U.S. Army 1943–46 (combat infantry), WWII.

CAREER: Founder/Artistic Director—A Contemporary Theatre (ACT), Seattle, WA, 1965. Directed more than 50 productions at ACT including *The Greeks, Catholics, Getting Out, Fanshen, Henry IV, Ballymurphy, Echoes, The Odyssey, The Forgotton Door, A Christmas Carol.* Off-Broadway—*The Indian Experience.* Founder, Champlain Shakespeare Festival, 1958, directed—*Hamlet, Richard III, Julius Caesar, A Midsummer Night's Dream, Henry IV, Pt 1.* Seattle Center Playhouse—*The Dybbuk.* Directed at Mad Anthony Players, Toledo, OH, and The Stowe Playhouse, VT.

THEATRE-RELATED CAREER: Executive Director, University of Washington, School of Drama, 10 years.

WRITINGS: PLAYS—*A Wrinkle in Time; The Forgotten Door.* ADAPTATION—The Odyssey.

AWARDS: Phi Beta Kappa (honorary); Gold Medal for Contribution to American Theatre, American College Thea-

tre Festival at the John F. Kennedy Center for the Performing Arts, 1973; Fulbright Scholarship.

SIDELIGHTS: MEMBERSHIPS—The Players; University Club, Seattle, WA. PRINCIPAL PROFESSIONAL AFFILIATIONS—President, National Theatre Conference; president, Washington Association of Theatre Artists; founding board member, United Arts Council of Puget Sound, reorganized as the Corporate Council for the Arts; served on boards for American Council for Arts in Education, American Theatre Association, Bush School, Henry Art Gallery.

In September of 1979, Mr. Falls was selected by the International Theatre Institute to represent the United States at the prestigious Belgrade International Theatre Festival in Yugoslavia. In service to his community, he has been actively involved in the United Way Campaign, including a stint as head of the Campaigns Community Division.

ADDRESS: Office—c/o A Contemporary Theatre, 100 W. Roy Street, Seattle, WA 98119.

* * *

FARGAS, Antonio, actor

PERSONAL: Born August 14, 1946, in New York City; son of Manuel and Mildred (Bailey) Fargas; married Taylor Hustie (a fashion designer), July 13, 1979; children: Matthew, Justin. EDUCATION: Fashion Industry High School, New York, 1965; studied for the stage at the Negro Ensemble Company, New York. POLITICS: Liberal. RELIGION: Christian. MILITARY: Conscientious objector.

CAREER: DEBUT—George Davis, *The Toilet*, St. Mark's, New York, 1963. LONDON DEBUT—David, *The Amen Corner*, Saville, 1965. PRINCIPAL STAGE APPEARANCES—Scipio, *The Great White Hope*, Alvin, New York, 1968; *Ceremonies in Dark Old Men*, Negro Ensemble Company, New York, 1969–70; *Isle Is Full of Noises*, Hartford Theatre, Hartford, CT, 1982; *Ain't Supposed to Die a Natural Death*, Theatre of Universal Images, 1983. MAJOR TOURS—*The Amen Corner*, world tour, 1965; *Dream on Monkey Mountain.* FILM DEBUT—Coolie, *The Cool World*, 1961. PRINCIPAL FILMS—Arab, *Putney Swope*, 1968; *Next Stop Greenwich Village*, 1976; *Across 110th Street*, 1973; *Pretty Baby*, 1978; *Carwash.* TELEVISION DEBUT—Huggy Bear, *Starsky and Hutch*, 1974–78.

SIDELIGHTS: MEMBERSHIPS—California Volunteers of America; Family Services of Westchester Big Brothers. RECREATION—restoration of colonial houses; travel abroad.

ADDRESS: Agent—Fred Amsel & Associates, 215 S. La Cienega, Suite 200 Beverly Hills, CA 90211.

* * *

FARR, Jamie (ne Jameel Joseph Farah), actor and director

PERSONAL: Born July 1, in Toledo, OH; son of Samuel (a grocer) and Jamelia (a seamstress; Abodeely) Farah; married

JAMIE FARR

Joy Richards (a clothing manufacturer), February 16, 1963; children: Jonas, Yvonne. EDUCATION: Columbia College, B.A.; trained for the stage at the Pasadena Playhouse.

CAREER: FILM DEBUT—Santini, *Blackboard Jungle,* 1955. PRINCIPAL FILM APPEARANCES—*The Cannonball Run,* 1981; *Murder Can Hurt You; Return of the Rebels; The Cannonball Run II,* 1984. TELEVISION DEBUT—*Dear Phoebe.* PRINCIPAL TELEVISION APPEARANCES—*The Red Skelton Show; The Danny Kaye Show; Dick Van Dyke Show; Chicago Teddy Bears;* Klinger, *M*A*S*H;* Klinger, *After M*A*S*H.* DIRECTED—*M*A*S*H ; After M*A*S*H.*

THEATRE DEBUT—Shore patrolman/understudy Ensigna, *Mr. Roberts,* Las Palmas, Los Angeles, CA. PRINCIPAL STAGE APPEARANCES—Ali Haim, *Oklahoma!,* Pantages, 1979; *Murder at the Howard Johnsons,* dinner theatre.

AWARDS: Jamie Farr Day-and-a-Half, Toledo, OH; Governor's Award, Entertainment, State of Ohio; Honorary Doctorate, University of Ohio, 1983.

SIDELIGHTS: MEMBERSHIPS—SAG, Dramatists Guild of America, Writers Guild of America, AFTRA, Academy of Television, Academy of Motion Pictures, Arts and Sciences.

ADDRESS: Office—20th Century Fox, Box 900, Beverly Hills, CA 90213. Agent—c/o Sylvia Gold, I.C.M., 8899 Beverly Blvd., Los Angeles, CA 90048.

FARRELL, Mike, actor, director

PERSONAL: Born February 6, 1939, in St. Paul, MN; son of Michael Farrell (a film scenic carpenter); married Judy Hayden (an actress), 1963; children: Michael Joshua, Erin. EDUCATION: Attended Los Angeles City College and University of California at Los Angeles; trained for the stage with Jeff Corey, and David Alexander. MILITARY: U.S. Marine Corps.

CAREER: PRINCIPAL TELEVISION APPEARANCES—Scott Banning, *Days of Our Lives;* B. J. Hunnicutt, *M*A*S*H; The Interns; The Man and the City; Mannix; The Bold Ones; Marcus Welby, M.D.; Owen Marshall; Harry O;* (television movies) *The Longest Night; The Questor Tapes; Battered; Sex and the Single Parent; Damien, the Leper Priest; Prime Suspect; Memorial Day; Choices of the Heart.*

FILM DEBUT—*Captain Newman, M.D.,* 1964. PRINCIPAL FILM APPEARANCES—*The Americanization of Emily,* 1964; *The Graduate,* 1967; *Targets,* 1968. PRINCIPAL STAGE APPEARANCES—*Rain,* Los Angeles Civic Stage, CA; *A Thousand Clowns, Mary, Mary, Under the Yum-Yum Tree, The Skin of Our Teeth,* Laguna Beach Playhouse, CA.

SIDELIGHTS: RECREATION—Chess, reading (politics and psychology), motorcycling.

ADDRESS: Agent—Arcara, Bauman and Hiller, 9220 Sunset Blvd., Suite 202, Los Angeles, CA 90069.

MIKE FARRELL

FARROW, Mia, actress

PERSONAL: Born February 9, 1946, in CA; daughter of John Villiers (a film director) and Maureen (an actress; maiden name, Sullivan) Farrow; married Frank Sinatra, 1966 (divorced 1968); married Andre Previn, 1970 (divorced 1979).

CAREER: NEW YORK DEBUT—Cecily Cardew, *The Importance of Being Earnest*, Madison Avenue Playhouse, 1966. LONDON DEBUT—Title role, *Mary Rose*, Shaw, 1972. PRINCIPAL STAGE APPEARANCES—Irina, *The Three Sisters*, Greenwich, 1973; Jan and Adela, *The House of Bernarda Alba*, Greenwich, 1973; Ann Leete, *The Marrying of Ann Leete*, Royal Shakespeare Company, Aldwych, London, 1975; Pavla Tselovnyeva, *The Zykovs*, RSC, Aldwych, 1976; Sasha, *Ivanov*, RSC, Aldwych, 1976; Phoebe Craddock, *Romantic Comedy*, Barrymore, 1979.

FILM APPEARANCES—*Guns at Batasi*, 1964; Rosemary, *Rosemary's Baby*, 1968; *A Dandy in Aspic*, 1968; *Secret Ceremony*, 1968; *John and Mary*, 1969; *Blind Terror/See No Evil*, 1971; *Follow Me/The Public Eye*, 1972; *Docteur Popaul/Scoundrel in White*, 1972; *The Great Gatsby*, 1974; *Trikimia/The Tempest*, 1975; *Full Circle*, 1977; *Avalanche*, 1978; *A Wedding*, 1978; *Death on the Nile*, 1978; *Hurricane*, 1979; *A Midsummer Night's Sex Comedy*, 1982; *Zelig*, 1983; *Broadway Danny Rose*, 1983.

TELEVISION APPEARANCES—Allison Mackenzie/Harrington, *Peyton Place*, 1964–66; *Johnny Belinda; Peter Pan; Goodbye, Raggedy Ann*.

SIDELIGHTS: RECREATION—Reading, riding, listening to music and certain people.

ADDRESS: Agent—Lionel Larner, 850 Seventh Avenue, New York, NY 10019.*

*   *   *

FASSBINDER, Rainer Werner, writer, film director

PERSONAL: Born May 31, 1946, Bad Worrishofen, Germany; died, June 10, 1982; son of Helmut and Liselotte Pempeit (Eder) Fassbinder. EDUCATION: Attended public schools in Germany and Fridl-Leonhard Studio in Munich, West Germany.

CAREER: PRINCIPAL FILM WORK—Director, *Der Stadtstreicher*, 1966; *Das Kleine Chaos*, 1966; *Love Is Colder than Death*, 1969; *Katzelmacher*, 1969; *Gotter der Pest*, 1970; *Why Does Herr R. Run Amok?*, 1970; *The American Soldier*, 1970; *Die Niklashauser Fahrt*, 1970; *Rio das Mortes*, 1971; *Pioniere in Ingolstadt*, 1971; *Whity*, 1971; *Beware of a Holy Whore*, 1971; *The Merchant of Four Seasons*, 1972; *The Bitter Tears of Petra Von Kant*, 1972; *Eight Hours Don't Make a Day*, 1972; *Wildwechsel*, 1973; *Welt am Draht*, 1973; *Fear Eats the Soul/Ali*, 1974; *Martha*, 1974; *Effi Briest*, 1974; *Faustrecht der Freiheit*, 1975; *Mother Kuster's Trip to Heaven*, 1975; *Fear of Fear*, 1975; *Satan's Brew*, 1976; *Chinese Roulette*, 1976; *Germany in Autumn*, 1977; *Despair*, 1977; *Die Ehe der Maria Braun*, 1978; *In einem Jahr mit 13 Monden*, 1978; *The Third Generation*, 1979.

RELATED CAREER: Actor, Munich Action Theater, 1967; founder, Munich Antitheater, 1968; author, producer avant-garde adaptations of classical plays, 1968–70; director, Theater am Turm, Frankfurt, W. Germany, 1974–75.

PRINCIPAL TELEVISION WORK—Director/writer, *Love Is Colder than Death*, 1969; *The Bitter Tears of Petra von Kant*, 1972; *Fox and His Friends*, 1974.

AWARDS: Patron award, Gerhard-Hauptmann prize; TV award German Academy of Producing Arts; Critics award, Cannes Film Festival, 1974: *Fear Eats the Soul/Ali*; Federal Film Prize, 1970: *Why Did Herr R. Run Amok?*; West German Film Critics prize and the Federal Film prize, 1969: *Katzelmacher*.*

*   *   *

FAWCETT, Farrah, actress

PERSONAL: Born February 2, 1947; daughter of James (an oil field contractor) and Pauline Fawcett. married Lee Majors (divorced 1982). EDUCATION: Attended University of Texas.

CAREER: DEBUT—Jill, *Butterflies Are Free*, Burt Reynolds Dinner Theatre, Jupiter, FL. NEW YORK DEBUT—Marjorie, *Extremities*, West End, 1983.

PRINCIPAL TELEVISION APPEARANCES—*Harry O, McCloud,*

FARRAH FAWCETT

Apple's Way, The Six-Million Dollar Man, Marcus Welby, M.D., 1976; *Charley's Angels,* 1976; *Murder in Texas,* 1981; *The Red-Light Sting,* 1984; *The Burning Bed,* 1984. PRINCIPAL FILM APPEARANCES—*Somebody Killed Her Husband,* 1978; *Sunburn,* 1979; *Saturn III,* 1979; *Cannonball Run,* 1981.

AWARDS: People's Choice Award; *Bravo* Magazine Award.

SIDELIGHTS: RECREATION—sculpture, painting, drawing, tennis, racquetball, golf.

ADDRESS: Agent—c/o Sue Mengers, ICM, 8899 Beverly Blvd., Los Angeles, CA 90048.

* * *

FEARL, Clifford, actor, singer

PERSONAL: Surname rhymes with "pearl"; son of James Silas and Helen (Baynes) Fearl; married Patricia Downward, December 16, 1943. EDUCATION: Columbia University; studied for the theatre at the American Theatre Wing and with Barbara Bulghakov. RELIGION: Episcopalian. MILITARY: Artillery, World War II (captain)

CAREER: PRINCIPAL STAGE APPEARANCES—Buyer, *Flahooley,* Broadhurst, New York, 1951; Patrick, *Three Wishes for Jamie,* New York, 1952; Hillary, *Two's Company,* Alvin,

CLIFFORD FEARL

New York, 1952; HassanBen, *Kismet,* New York, 1953; Harry Watson, *Happy Hunting,* New York, 1956; Bos'n, *Oh, Captain,* New York, 1958; Gus, *Redhead,* 46th Street Theatre, New York, 1959; Florestan, *La Plume de ma Tante,* New York, 1960; Al, *Let It Ride,* New York, 1961; Clem, *110 in the Shade,* Broadhurst, New York, 1963; Turgot, *Ben Franklin in Paris,* Lunt-Fontanne, New York, 1964; Uncle Jeff, Babcock, Upson, Woolsey, *Mame,* Winter Garden, New York, 1966; Director, *Dear World,* Mark Hellinger, New York, 1969; Warrington Brock, *Jimmy,* Winter Garden, New York, 1969; Butler, *My Fair Lady,* New York, 1976; Le Duc, *King of Hearts,* Minskoff, New York, 1978; Olin Britt, *The Music Man,* Jones Beach, New York; The King, *Snow White and the Seven Dwarfs,* New York; Jamie, Pickering, *My Fair Lady,* New York, 1980–81; also stock in Lambertville, Paper Mill, Highland Park, Oakdale.

SIDELIGHTS: MEMBERSHIPS—SAG, AEA, AFTRA.

ADDRESS: Home—36 W. 56th Street, New York, NY 10019.

* * *

FEARNLEY, John (ne Johannes Schiott), director and writer

PERSONAL: Born April 8, 1914, in Westport, CT; son of Johannes (an executive) and Kitta (Knudsen) Schiott. EDUCATION: Attended Yale University and RADA, London. MILITARY: AFS, World War II.

CAREER: NEW YORK DEBUT—Chorus, *Thumbs Up,* St. James. 1934. PRINCIPAL STAGE WORK—First Man Tourist, *Key Largo,* Ethel Barrymore, NY, 1939. Assistant stage manager, *Tovarich,* Plymouth, NY, 1936; assistant stage manager, *Oscar Wilde,* Fulton, NY, 1938; technical director of the Westport (CT) Country Playhouse, 1941; production assistant for the Theatre Guild, 1941–42; stage manager, *Lifeline,* Belasco, NY, 1942; stage manager, *Harriet,* Henry Miller's Theatre, 1943. Casting director and production assistant for Richard Rodgers and Oscar Hammerstein, worked on *Carousel,* Majestic, 1945; *Annie Get Your Gun,* Imperial, 1946; *Allegro,* Majestic, 1947; *Happy Birthday,* Broadhurst, 1946; *John Loves Mary,* Booth, 1947; *South Pacific,* Majestic, 1949; *Burning Bright,* Broadhurst, 1950; *The King and I,* St. James, 1951; *Pipe Dream,* Shubert, 1955.

DIRECTED: New York City Center—*Oklahoma!,* 1958, 1963, *Carousel,* 1957, *South Pacific,* 1957, 1961, *The King and I,* 1959, 1960, 1963, 1968, *Brigadoon,* 1962, 1963, *Porgy and Bess,* 1964; *Carousel,* Brussels World's Fair, 1958; *The Music Man,* Melbourne, 1959; *Eddie Fisher at the Winter Garden,* 1962; Jones Beach Theatre, Wantaugh, NY—*Sound of Music,* 1970–71, 1980, *The King and I,* 1972, *Carousel,* 1973, *Fiddler on the Roof,* 1974, *Oklahoma!,* 1975, *Show Boat,* 1976, *Finian's Rainbow,* 1977, *The Music Man,* 1979; Japanese-language production, *South Pacific,* Takarazuka Theatre, Tokyo, 1979; guest director, Pioneer Memorial Theatre, Utah, 1975–83. Co-director, co-adapter (with James Hammerstein), *South Pacific,* Thunderbird Hotel, Las Vegas, 1962; conceived (with Richard Lewine) *Rodgers and Hart,* Helen Hayes, NY, 1975. Adaptor, *Hans Christian*

Andersen, Pioneer Memorial Theatre, Salt Lake City, 1977. PRINCIPAL FILMS—Production aide, *Oklahoma!,* 1955.

AWARDS: Florida Theatre Critics Award Nomination, Best Direction of a Musical, 1976: *The King and I;* Antoinette Perry Award Nomination, Best Director, 1963: *Brigadoon.*

SIDELIGHTS: MEMBERSHIPS—AEA, SSD&C, Dramatist's Guild.

ADDRESS: 484 W. 43rd Street, No. 36C, New York, NY 10036.

* * *

FEIFFER, Jules, playwright, cartoonist, satirist

PERSONAL: Born January 26, 1929, in New York City; son of David (a salesman and dental technician) and Rhoda (a fashion designer; maiden name, Davis) Feiffer; married Judith Sheftel (a film story editor; died 1983); married Jennifer Allen (a reporter) September 11, 1983; children: (first marriage) Kate. MILITARY: Signal Corps, 1951–53. NON-THEATRICAL CAREER—Illustrator, 1954; advertising layout man, 1954 (Mr. Feiffer's theatrical career has been coincidental with his career as cartoonist and author of satirical material).

WRITINGS: PLAYS, PRODUCED—*The Explainers* (adapted from his cartoons), the playwrights at Second City, Chicago, 1961; *Crawling Arnold,* Spoleto Festival, 1961; *Feiffer's People,* (adapted from cartoons), first seen at Loeb Center, NY, 1962; *Passionella/The Apple Tree,* (cartoon adapted as one of three acts of a musical), Shubert, NY, 1966; *Little Murders,* NY, 1967 (also RSC production in London, 1967); *God Bless,* Yale Drama School, 1968 (also RSC in London, 1968); *The White House Murder Case,* NY, 1970; *Feiffer's People,* Theatre Eight, 1972; *The Unexplained Memoirs of Bernard Mergendeiler,* Kings Head, Islington, London, 1972; (sketches) *The Watergate Classics,* Yale Repertory, 1973–74; *Knock, Knock,* Circle Repertory, NY, then Biltmore, NY, 1976; *Hold Me!* (based on cartoons), American Place, NY, 1977; *Grownups,* Lyceum, NY, 1981; *A Think Place,* Circle Repertory, NY, 1982; also sketches for revues *Collision Course* and *Oh, Calcutta!.* SCREENPLAYS—*Little Murders,* 1971; *Carnal Knowledge,* 1971; *Popeye,* 1980. NOVELS—*Harry, the Rat with Women; Little Murders; Ackroyd,* 1977. CARTOON COLLECTIONS—*Passionella,* 1953; *Sick, Sick, Sick,* 1956; *Boy, Girl, Boy, Girl,* 1961. TELEVISION WRITING—Cartoon-drama, *Steve Allen Show,* WPIX, 1964; *Crawling Arnold,* WEAV-TV, 1963; *V.D. Blues* (skit), 1972; *Happy Endings,* (with Neil Simon, Herb Gardner and Peter Stone), ABC, 1975; documentary subject, *Artists in Residence: Jules Feiffer,* PBS, 1971. NON-FICTION—*The Great Comic Book Heroes,* 1965; *Feiffery; Jules Feiffer's America from Eisenhower to Reagan,* 1982.

AWARDS: London Drama Critics Award, Best Foreign Play, *Little Murders;* Obie Award, *Little Murders;* Outer Critics Circle Award, *Little Murders, The White House Murder Case;* Antoinette Perry Award, *Grownups.*

SIDELIGHTS: MEMBERSHIPS—MacDowell Colony, Dramatists Guild Council.

"I agree with Ken Tynan who said there can't be satire unless at least part of the audience gets up and walks out."

ADDRESS: Agent—Field Newspaper Syndicate, 30 E. 42nd Street, New York, NY 10017.*

* * *

FELDMAN, Marty, actor, writer, director

PERSONAL: Born July 8, 1934, in London, England; died December 2, 1982, in Mexico City, of a massive heart attack; son of Cecillia Feldman; married Lauretta Sullivan, January 14, 1959.

CAREER: PRINCIPAL STAGE APPEARANCES—*Waiting for Godot,* National Theatre, London.

PRINCIPAL FILM WORK—*Every Home Should Have One, (Think Dirty),* 1969; *Flying Nurse; The Bed Sitting Room,* 1969; Igor, *Young Frankstein,* 1974; *Slapstick;* Sgt. Orville Sacker, *The Adventures of Sherlock Holmes' Smarter Brother,* 1976; Marty Eggs, *Silent Movie,* 1976; co-writer/co-director, *The Last Remake of Beau Geste,* 1977; director/co-writer, Brother Ambrose, *In God We Trust,* 1980; *Yellowbeard,* 1983.

PRINCIPAL TELEVISION WORK—series, *England,* Marty, *Marty;* writer, *Round the Horne,* BBC Radio, 1965–69; writer, *The Frost Report,* 1967; *Marty Feldman Comedy Machine,* 1971–72; *Insight: The Sixth Day; Bonjour Monsieur Lewis,* French TV; *Dean Martin Presents the Goldiggers,* 1970; specials—*Marty Amok; Marty Abroad; Marty—Back Together Again;* plays for television—*The Compartment; Playmates.*

AWARDS: City of Montreux Trophy, world's top comedy show, *The Best of the Comedy Machine,* 1971; Golden Rose of Montreux, *The Best of the Comedy Machine,* 1971; Montreux Silver Rose, *Marty, Marty,* 1970; Personality of the Year Award, Royal Television Society, 1970; BBC TV Personality of the Year Award, Variety Club of Great Britain, 1970; Writers Guild Award, Best Comedy series scripts, *Round the Horne,* 1967; Daily Mirror Award (with Barry Took) for *Bootsie & Snudge* and *The Army Game,* 1961.*

* * *

FELDSHUH, Tovah, actress

PERSONAL: Surname pronounced "felt-shoe;" born December 27, in New York City; daughter of Sidney and Lillian (Kaplan) Feldshuh; married Andrew Harris Levy (a lawyer), March 20, 1977. EDUCATION: Sarah Lawrence College; University of Minnesota; studied for the theatre with Uta Hagen and Jacques Lecoq.

CAREER: DEBUT—Bit parts, *Cyrano de Bergerac,* Guthrie, Minneapolis, MN, 1971. NEW YORK DEBUT—Foodseller/ Nun, *Cyrano* (musical) Palace, 1973. PRINCIPAL STAGE

APPEARANCES—Over twenty roles with the Guthrie Company between 1971 and 1973; Myriam, *Dreyfuss in Rehearsal*, Ethel Barrymore, NY, 1974; title role, *Yentl*, Brooklyn Academy of Music, NY, 1974; *Rodgers and Hart*, Helen Hayes, NY, 1975; *Yentl*, Eugene O'Neill, NY, 1975; Abigail Williams, *The Crucible*, Celia, *As You Like It*, Stratford, CT, 1976; Irina, *The Three Sisters*, BAM Company, NY, 1977; *The Torchbearers*, McCarter, Princeton, NJ, 1978; Dona Flor, *Sarava*, Broadway Theatre, NY, 1979; Juliet, *Romeo and Juliet*, Old Globe, San Diego, 1980; Isabella, *Measure for Measure*, Margery Pinchwife, *The Country Wife*, Festival, Old Globe, San Diego, 1981; *A Touch of Tovah*, Old Globe, San Diego, 1981; Regina, *Another Part of the Forest*, 1982. MAJOR TOURS—title role, *Peter Pan*, summer stock, 1978.

FILM DEBUT—*Nunzio*, 1978. FILM APPEARANCES—*Cheaper to Keep Her*, 1980; *The Idolmaker*, 1981; *Daniel*, 1983; *Brewster's Millions*, 1984.

TELEVISION APPPEARANCES—Katharine Hepburn, *The Amazing Howard Hughes*, 1977; *Holocaust*, 1978; *The Women's Room*, 1982; *The Triangle Factory Fire*, 1983.

AWARDS: Drama Logue for Outstanding Achievement in the Theatre, 1981, 1980; Antoinette Perry Award Nominations, 1979: *Sarava!*, 1976; *Yentl*; Emmy Nomination, 1978: *Holocaust*; Obie, Drama Desk, Theatre World, Outer Critics Circle, 1976: *Yentl*; Israel Friendship Award; Israel Peace Medal; Israel Humanitarian Award.

SIDELIGHTS: FAVORITE ROLES—St. Joan, Viola, Rosalind, Juliet.

ADDRESS: Agent—c/o Hildy Gottlieb, ICM, 8899 Beverly Boulevard, Los Angeles, CA 90048; Milton Goldman, ICM, 40 W. 57th Street, New York, NY 10019.

* * *

FELLINI, Federico, director, screenwriter

PERSONAL: Born January 20, 1920, in Rimini, Italy; son of Urbano (a salesman) and Ida (Barbiani) Fellini; married Giulietta Masina (an actress), October, 1943. EDUCATION: Attended University of Rome.

CAREER: FILM DEBUT—Director, *The White Sheik*, 1952. PRINCIPAL FILM WORK: Director—*I Vitellone*, 1953; *La Strada*, 1954; *Il Bidone*, 1955; *Nights of Cabiria*, 1957; *La Dolce Vita*, 1959; *8½*, 1963; *Juliet of the Spirits*, 1965; *Never Bet the Devil Your Head*, 1968; *Histoires Extraordinaires*, 1968; *Satyricon*, 1969; *The Clowns*, 1970; *Fellini's Roma*, 1972; *Amarcord*, 1974; *Cassanova*, 1977; *City of Women*, 1981.

WRITINGS: SCREENPLAYS—*Open City, Paisan, Ways of Love, Senza Pieta*; BOOKS—*Amarcord*, 1974, *Quattro Film*, 1975, *Fellini on Fellini*, 1977.

AWARDS: Academy Awards, Best Foreign Films, 1975: *Amarcord*, 1964: *8½*, 1960: *La Dolce Vita*, 1958: *Nights of Cabiria*, 1957: *La Strada*; numerous other international awards.

ADDRESS: Office—Cinecitta Studios, Rome, Italy.

* * *

FERRIS, Monk, playwright

See SHARKEY, Jack

* * *

FIEDLER, John, actor

PERSONAL: Born February 3, 1925, in Plateville, WI; son of Donald and Margaret (Phelan) Fiedler. EDUCATION: Attended Wisconsin public schools; trained for the stage at the Neighborhood Playhouse with Sanford Meisner. MILITARY: U.S. Navy.

CAREER: FILM DEBUT—2nd juror, *Twelve Angry Men*, 1956. PRINCIPAL FILM APPEARANCES—*Touch of Mink*; Mr. Lindner, *Raisin in the Sun*, 1961; Vinnie, *The Odd Couple*, 1968; *True Grit*, 1969; *Sharkey's Machine*, 1981.

TELEVISION DEBUT—*The Aldrich Family*, 1949. PRINCIPAL TELEVISION APPEARANCES—*Gunsmoke; Buffalo Bill; Star Trek; Fantasy Island;* Mr. Petersen, *Bob Newhart Show*.

THEATRE DEBUT—*The Seagull*, Phoenix, 1954. PRINCIPAL STAGE APPEARANCES—Mr. Lindner, *A Raisin in the Sun*, 1954; Vinnie, *The Odd Couple*, New York, 1964.

SIDELIGHTS—John Fielder has appeared in 37 films.

ADDRESS: Agent—c/o Blake Agency, 409 N. Camden Drive, #202, Beverly Hills, CA 90210.

* * *

FIELD, Barbara, playwright

PERSONAL: Born February 25, 1935, in Buffalo, NY; daughter of Harry (a salesman) and Esther Edith (a teacher and actress; maiden name, Siegel) Field; married Lewis H. Nosanow, February 6, 1955 (divorced 1973); children: Maria Nicole, James Harry. EDUCATION: University of Pennsylvania, B.A., 1955; University of Minnesota, M.A., 1971.

WRITINGS: PLAYS, PRODUCED—*Sleight-of-Hand*, Pittsburgh Public Theatre, 1980, Harbor Front Theatre, Toronto, 1980; *Coming of Age*, Indiana Repertory, 1981; *Matrix*, Metro Theatre, Pittsburgh, 1983; *Neutral Countries*, Actors Theatre of Louisville, KY, 1983. PLAYS, ADAPTIONS/TRANSLATIONS—*A Christmas Carol*, Guthrie, Minneapolis, MN, 1975–83, also performed annually at Actors Theatre of Louisville, Goodman Theatre, Chicago, Missouri Repertory Theatre, Kansas City, Virginia Stage Company, Norfolk; *Pantagleize* (from de Ghelderode's play), Guthrie, Minneapolis, 1977; *Marriage* (from Gogol's play), Guthrie,

1978; *Monsieur de Moliere* (from Bulgakov's play), Guthrie, 1979; *Camille* (adapted from the novel), Guthrie, 1980; *Great Expectations,* Seattle Children's Theatre, 1983. Plays, Readings—Winds of Change, National Playwrights' Conference, O'Neill Theatre Center, Waterford, CT, 1976; Pen, National Playwrights' Conference, CT, 1979; Education of Paul Bunyan, New Dramatists, NY, 1983. ORIGINAL LIBRETTO—*Rosina* (with composer Hiram Titus), for the Minnesota Opera Company, 1980, Midwestern Opera Company, 1981, Arizona State Opera Company, 1982.

THEATRE-RELATED CAREER—Literary Manager, Guthrie Theatre, Minneapolis, MN, 1974–81; Playwright-in-Residence, Playwright's Center, Minneapolis, MN, 1971–83.

AWARDS: Individual Artist's Award, Minnesota State Arts Board, 1983–84; McKnight Fellowship in Playwriting, 1983; Co-Winner, Great American Play Contest, Actors Theatre of Louisville, 1983; Jerome Fellowship, Playwrights' Center, Minneapolis, MN, 1982; Kudos Award, Best Play, *Camille,* Twin Cities Drama Critics Circle, 1980; Grant, Work-in-Progress, Minnesota Opera Company, 1979–80; Grant, National Playwright's Conference, Eugene O'Neill Theatre Center, 1976, 1979; Individual Artist's Award, Minnesota State Arts Board, 1973–74.

SIDELIGHTS: MEMBERSHIPS—Dramatists Guild.

ADDRESS: Home—2719 Raleigh Avenue, Minneapolis, MN, 55416. Agent—Lois Berman, Little Theatre Building, 240 W. 44th Street, New York, NY 10036.

* * *

FIELD, Crystal, director, actress, choreographer, playwright, artistic director

PERSONAL: Born December 10, 1940; daughter of Frederick (a writer-journalist and teacher) and Fanny, (an M.D.; maiden name Stoll) Field; married George Bartenieff (an artistic director) on January 27, 1963; children: Alexander. EDUCATION: Hunter College, B.A., 1968; Julliard Drama School, two years; studied acting with Paul Mann and Lloyd Richards; dance, with Martha Graham and the New Dance Group in New York.

CAREER: DEBUT—Puss, *Puss n' Boots,* Free Acres Summer Theatre, 1945. NEW YORK DEBUT—Aunt March, *Little Women,* P.S. 69, 1947. PRINCIPAL STAGE APPEARANCES—Suzanne, *Writers Opera,* Theatre for the New City, 1979; Felece, *After the Fall,* Lincoln Center Repertory Company, 1964; Marya, *Platonov,* Greenwich Mews Theatre; Donata, *Marco Millions,* Lincoln Center Repertory Company; member—Living Theatre, New York; member—Philadelphia Theatre of the Living Arts; member, Lincoln Center Repertory Company, two years; writer-director, artistic director, Theatre for the New City, 14 years.

FILM DEBUT—Hazel, *Splendor in the Grass,* 1963. PRINCIPAL FILM APPEARANCES—Has "dubbed" extensively in America. TELEVISION DEBUT—Babysitter, *We the People.*

WRITINGS: 12 Street Theatre Plays, Theatre for the New

City. PLAYS PRODUCED—Plays for the Damned; Desire; Loco Loco; The Red Kinevo.

AWARDS: Obie, Lead Role, *Day Old Bread; Village Voice* Award for Street Play, *Keep Touchin.*

SIDELIGHTS: MEMBERSHIPS—AEA, SAG, League of Professional Women in Theatre.

ADDRESS: Home—190 Riverside Drive, New York, NY 10024. Office—162 Second Avenue, New York, NY 10003. Agent—c/o Tommy McCarthy, Zali Agency, 146 E. 56th Street, New York, NY 10022.

* * *

FIERSTEIN, Harvey, actor, producer, and writer

PERSONAL: Born June 6, 1954 son of Irving (a manufacturer) and Jacqueline Harriet (a teacher; maiden name Gilbert) Fierstein. EDUCATION: Pratt Institute, B.F.A., 1973; studied acting technique with Barbara Bulgokova. POLITICS: Gay and human rights activist.

CAREER: DEBUT—Amelia, Andy Warhol's *Pork,* LaMama, E.T.C., New York, 1971. PRINCIPAL STAGE APPEARANCES—*Torch Song Trilogy,* Helen Hayes, New York, 1981. MAJOR TOURS—*Haunted Host,* Boston, Provincetown.

WRITINGS: PLAYS, PUBLISHED—*Torch Song Trilogy; La Cage Aux Folles; SPOOKHOUSE.*

AWARDS: Two Antoinette Perry Awards and two Drama Desk Awards for *Torch Song Trilogy;* Theatre World Award; Fund for Human Dignity Award; four Villager Awards; Obie Award; Association of Comedy Artists Award; Rockefeller Grant; CAPS Grant; Ford Foundation Grant; P.B.S. Grant.

SIDELIGHTS: MEMBERSHIPS—Ibsen Society of America; Masons. Founding member, Gallery Players Community Theatre, 1965.

ADDRESS: Agent—c/o William Morris Agency, 1350 Ave. of the Americas, New York, NY 10019.

* * *

FINNEGAN, Bill, producer

PERSONAL: Born June 29, 1928.

CAREER: PRINCIPAL TELEVISION WORK: Produced—*Hawaii Five-O,* 1971–75; *Hec Ramsey; Big Hawaii; Danger in Paradise; King; Stranger in Our House; The Ordeal of Patty Hearst; Vacation in Hell,* 1978; *The $5.20 an Hour Dream,* 1980; *The Choice,* 1981; *Inmates: A Love Story,* 1981; *Between Two Brothers,* 1982; *Dangerous Company,* 1982; *World War III,* 1982; *Father Figure; Summer Girl,* 1983; *Your Place . . . or Mine; The Dollmaker,* 1984; *Flight 90: Disaster on the Potomac,* 1984; *Death of a Salesman* (forthcoming).

ADDRESS: Office—Finnegan Associates, 4225 Coldwater Canyon, Studio City, CA 91604.

* * *

FINNEY, Albert, actor

PERSONAL: Born May 9, 1936, in Salsford, Lancaster, England; son of Albert (a bookmaker) and Alice (Hobson) Finney; married Jane Wenham, 1957 (divorced 1961); married Anouk Aimee, 1970 (divorced 1975). children: (first marriage) Simon. EDUCATION: Salsford Grammar School; studied for the theatre at the Royal Academy of Dramatic Art.

CAREER: DEBUT—Decius Brutus, *Julius Caesar,* Birmingham Repertory, 1956. LONDON DEBUT—Belzanor, *Caesar and Cleopatra,* Birmingham Rep, Old Vic, 1956. NEW YORK DEBUT—Martin Luther, *Luther,* St. James, 1963. PRINCIPAL STAGE APPEARANCES—*Macbeth, Henry V,* Francis Archer, *The Beaux Strategem,* Face, *The Alchemist,* Malcolm, *The Lizard on the Rock,* Birmingham Rep, 1956–58; Soya Marshall, *The Party,* New, London, 1958; Edgar, *King Lear,* Cassio, *Othello,* Lysander, *A Midsummer Night's Dream,* Shakespeare Memorial Theatre Company, Stratford-on-Avon, 1959; Ted, *The Lilly-White Boys,* Royal Court, London, 1960; title role, *Billy Liar,* Cambridge, London, 1960; Martin Luther, *Luther,* Paris International Festival, Theatre des Nations, France, 1961, the Holland Festival, then Royal Court, London, 1961; Feste, *Twelfth Night,* Royal Court, London, 1962; title role, *Pirandello's Henry IV,* Glasgow Citizens, Scotland, 1963; Don Pedro, *Much Ado About Nothing,* National Theatre Company, Old Vic, 1965; John Armstrong, *Armstrong's Last Goodnight,* Jean, *Miss Julie,* Harold Gorringe, *Black Comedy,* Chichester Festival, 1966; Bri, *A Day in the Death of Joe Egg,* Brooks Atkinson, NY, 1968; Mr. Elliot, *Alpha Beta,* Royal Court, then Apollo, 1972; Krapp, *Krapp's Last Tape,* Royal Court, 1973; O'Halloran, *Cromwell,* Royal Court, 1973; Phil, *Chez Nous,* Globe, London, 1974; *Hamlet,* National Theatre, Old Vic and opening production of Lyttleton, 1975, 1976; title role, *Tamburlaine the Great,* Olivier, 1976; Mr. Horner, *The Country Wife,* Olivier, 1977; Lopakhin, *The Cherry Orchard,* Olivier, 1978; *Macbeth,* 1978; title role, *Uncle Vanya,* Gary Essendine, *Present Laughter,* Royal Exchange, Birmingham; John Bean, *Has 'Washington' Legs?,* Cottsloe, 1978.

PRODUCED—Plays: *A Day in the Death of Joe Egg,* Comedy, London, 1967; was associate artistic director of the Royal Court Theatre, 1972–75; in June 1965, formed Memorial Enterprises Ltd, an independent production company for the presentation of television programs, films, and stage plays. DIRECTED—plays: *The Birthday Party, A School for Scandal,* Glasgow Citizens, Scotland, 1963; *Armstrong's Last Goodnight,* Old Vic, 1965; *The Freedom of the City,* Royal Court, 1973; *Loot,* Royal Court, 1975. PRINCIPAL FILMS—*The Entertainer,* 1959; *Saturday Night and Sunday Morning,* 1960; *Tom Jones,* 1963; *The Victors,* 1963; *Night Must Fall,* 1963; *Two for the Road,* 1967; *Charlie Bubbles* (also produced and directed), 1968; Poirot, *Murder on the Orient Express,* 1968; *The Picasso Summer,* 1969; *Alpha Beta; Gumshoe,* 1971; *Bleak Moment* (also produced), 1972; *O, Lucky Man* (produced only), 1973; *If* (produced only); *The Adventures of Sherlock Holmes Smarter Brother,* (unbilled cameo), 1976;

Scrooge, 1977; *Loophole,* 1980; *Wolfen,* 1980; *Looker,* 1980; *Shoot the Moon,* 1981; Daddy Warbucks, *Annie,* 1982; *The Dresser,* 1983; *Under the Volcano,* 1984.

TELEVISION DEBUT—British television, 1956. TELEVISION APPEARANCES—*View Friendship and Marriage, The Claverdon Road Job, The Miser, Forget-Me-Not-Lane,* others; Karel Wojtyla, *Pope John Paul II,* 1983. RECORDINGS—(lyrics and vocals) *Albert Finney's Album,* Motown, 1977.

AWARDS: Academy Award, 1968: *Murder on the Orient Express;* Academy Award Nominations, 1984: *The Dresser,* 1963: *Tom Jones;* British Film Academy Award, 1960: *Saturday Night and Sunday Morning.*

ADDRESS: Office—c/o Memorial Films, 74 Campden Hill Court, Campden Hill Road, London W8, England.*

* * *

FISHER, Douglas, actor

PERSONAL: Born July 9, 1934, in Brooklyn, NY; son of Patrick (an engineer) and Margaret (Healy) Fisher. EDUCATION: St. John's University, B.A., 1956; American Academy

DOUGLAS FISHER

of Dramatic Arts, 1960–61. MILITARY: U.S. Army, 1957–59.

CAREER: DEBUT—Tarleton, *Misalliance,* Garrett County Playhouse, MD. NEW YORK DEBUT—*My Beginning,* Blackfriars Theatre, 1960. PRINCIPAL STAGE APPEARANCES—Convener, *The Skin of Our Teeth,* ANTA, New York; Major Metcalf, *The Mousetrap,* Buffalo Studio Arena, Buffalo, NY; Bellomy, *The Fantasticks,* Hartman Theatre, Stamford, CT; Major Metcalf, *The Mousetrap,* Stage West, West Springfield, MA; Olin Potts, *The Last Meeting of the White Knights of the Magnolia,* Goodman Theatre, Chicago, IL; Sgt. Match, *What the Butler Saw,* Syracuse Stage, NY; Gilhooley, *Of Thee I Sing,* Berkshire Theatre Festival, Stockbridge, MA; Mazzini Dunn, *Heartbreak House,* Cincinnati Playhouse in the Park, OH; Dr. Zubritsky, *Fools,* Alaska Repertory, Anchorage, AK. MAJOR TOURS—Understudy Norman, *On Golden Pond;* Hubert Laurie, *Night Must Fall;* Canon Throbbing, *Habeas Corpus;* Purser, Sir Evelyn, *Anything Goes;* Eichelberger, Dobitch, *Promises, Promises;* Colonel Pickering, *My Fair Lady;* Daddy Ellis, *My Daughter, Your Son;* Cucurucu, *Marat/Sade,* national company; Hortensio, *Taming of the Shrew,* National Shakespeare Company; Colonel Pickering, *My Fair Lady,* Burt Reynolds Dinner Theatre.

OFF-BROADWAY—Mr. Gilfain, *Florodora;* Mr. Roche, *Death and Resurrection of Mr. Roche;* Congressman Wilkins, *Call Me Madam;* Van Fleet, *Penthouse Legend;* Richard Hackett, *Say Darling;* Professor Lloyd, *Best Foot Forward;* Christy, *Devil's Disciple;* Melville, *My Beginning;* Burton, *Lost in the Stars;* Johnson, *Frere Jacques;* Flogdell, *Accent on Youth; Shoestring Revue;* Tienhoven, *Knickerbocker Holiday;* Claughton, *A Mad World, My Masters;* SUMMER STOCK—Aubrey Piper, *The Show-Off;* Wiley, *Mr. Roberts;* Henry, *The Fantasticks;* Savage, *The Pleasure of His Company;* Ted/Julian Christoforou, *The Private Ear and the Public Eye;* Gravedigger, *Hamlet;* Peter, *A Taste of Honey;* Paul, *The Marriage-Go-Round;* Witherspoon, *1776;* Dr. Seward, *Dracula.*

PRINCIPAL TELEVISION APPEARANCES—*Ryan's Hope; One Life to Live; For Richer, for Poorer; Another World.*

ADDRESS: Home—1431 York Avenue, New York, NY 10021.

* * *

FISHER, Linda, costume designer

PERSONAL: Born September 30, 1943, in Lindsay, CA; daughter of James Howard (an Air Force pilot) and Doris (Lundgren) Fisher; married Richard Paul Cressen (a psychologist), November 1976. EDUCATION: University of Texas, B.F.A., 1966; Yale University, M.F.A., 1969.

CAREER: FIRST STAGE WORK—*Little Malcolm and His Struggle Against the Eunuchs,* Yale Drama School, New Haven, CT, 1968. FIRST NEW YORK STAGE WORK—*The Brass Butterfly,* Chelsea Theatre Centre, 1970. PRINCIPAL STAGE WORK—*Morning's at Seven,* Lyceum, New York, 1980; *Rose,* Cort, New York, 1981; *Foxfire,* Barrymore, New York, 1982.

FIRST FILM WORK—*A Sunday Dinner,* 1974. PRINCIPAL TELEVISION WORK—Two Mark Twain stories for PBS; *Private History of a Campaign That Failed,* 1981; *Pudd'nhead Wilson,* 1984.

ADDRESS: Home—139 W. 82nd Street, New York, NY 10024

* * *

FITZGERALD, Geraldine, actress, director

PERSONAL: Born November 24, 1914, in Dublin, Ireland; daughter of Edward (an attorney) and Edith Fitzgerald; married Edward Lindsay Hogg (songwriter) 1936 (divorced 1946); married Stuart Scheftel (president, Museum of Famous People; co-founder Pan-Am Building; member, New York City Youth Board), 1946; children: (first marriage) Michael; (second marriage) Susan. EDUCATION: Dublin Art School.

CAREER: DEBUT—Gate, Dublin, 1932. NEW YORK DEBUT—Ellie Dunn, *Heartbreak House,* Mercury, 1938. PRINCIPAL STAGE APPEARANCES—Rebecca, *Sons and Soldiers,* Morosco, NY, 1943; Tanis Talbot, *Portrait in Black,* Shubert, New Haven, CT, 1945; Jennifer Dubedat, *The Doctor's Dilemma,* Phoenix, NY, 1955; Goneril, *King Lear,* City Center, NY, 1956; Ann Richards, *Hide and Seek,* Ethel Barrymore, NY, 1957; Gertrude, *Hamlet,* American Shakespeare Festival, Stratford, CT, 1958; the Queen, *The Cave Dwellers,* Greenwich Mews, NY, 1961; Third Woman, *Pigeons,* Cherry Lane, NY, 1965; the Mother, *Ah, Wilderness!,* Ford's Washington, DC, 1969; Mary Tyrone, *Long Day's Journey into Night,* Promenade, NY, 1971; *Everyman and Roach,* (also co-author with Brother Jonathan OSF), Society for Ethical Culture Auditorium, NY, 1971; Jenny, *The Threepenny Opera,* WPA, NY, 1972; Juno Boyle, *Juno and the Paycock,* Long Wharf, New Haven, CT, 1973; Amy, *Forget-Me-Not Lane,* Long Wharf, 1973; Aline Solness, *The Master Builder,* Grandmother, *The Widowing of Mrs. Holroyd,* (U.S. premiere), Long Wharf, 1973–74; *Cabaret in the Sky,* New York Cultural Center, 1974; Essie Miller, *Ah, Wilderness!,* Circle in the Square, NY, 1974; Mary Tyrone, *Long Day's Journey into Night,* Walnut, Philadelphia, 1975; Mrs. Webb, *Our Town,* Stratford, CT, 1975; Essie, *Ah, Wilderness!,* Circle in the Square, NY, 1975; Amanda Wingfield, *The Glass Menagerie,* Walnut, Philadelphia, 1975; Felicity, *The Shadow Box,* Long Wharf, then Morosco, NY, 1977; Nora Melody, *A Touch of the Poet,* Helen Hayes, NY, 1978; *Out of My Father's House,* White House, Washington, DC, 1978; has appeared in New York and elsewhere since 1976 in one-woman show *Songs of the Streets; O'Neill and Carlotta,* Public, NY, 1979; in 1976 Ms. Fitzgerald made theatrical history appearing as the first woman ever to play the Stage Manager in *Our Town* at the Williamstown Festival in Massachusetts.

PRODUCED—Plays: In 1968, with Brother Jonathan Ringkamp, Ms. Fitzgerald founded the Everyman Street Theatre; co-produced the Lincoln Center Community Street Festival, Aug–Sept. 1972, and 1973. DIRECTED—Plays: *Mass Appeal,* Manhattan Theatre Club, then Booth, NY, 1980; *The Lunch Girls,* Theatre Row, NY, 1981.

FILM DEBUT—*The Turn of the Tide,* 1935. PRINCIPAL FILMS—

Three Witnesses, 1935; *Blind Justice*, 1935; *Radio Parade of 1935*; 1935; *Department Store*, 1935; *The Mill on the Floss*, 1936; *Dark Victory*, 1939; *Wuthering Heights*, 1939; *A Child Is Born*, 1939; *Till We Meet Again*, 1940; *Flight from Destiny*, 1941; *Shining Victory*, 1941; *The Gay Sisters*, 1942; *Watch on the Rhine*, 1943; *Ladies Courageous*, 1944; *Wilson*, 1944; *(The Strange Affair of) Uncle Harry*, 1945; *Three Strangers*, 1946; *O.S.S.*, 1946; *Nobody Lives Forever*, 1946; *So Evil, My Love*, 1948; *The Late Edwina Black* (*"The Obsessed"*), 1951; *10 North Frederick*, 1958; *The Fiercest Heart*, 1961; *The Pawnbroker*, 1965; *Rachel, Rachel*, 1968; *Believe in Me*, 1971; *The Last American Hero*, 1973; *Harry and Tonto*, 1974; *Echos of a Summer*, 1976; *The Mango Tree*, 1977; *Arthur*, 1981; *Easy Money*, 1983; *Pope of Greenwich Village*, 1984.

TELEVISION APPEARANCES—Violet Jordan, *The Best of Everything*, 1970; *Yesterday's Child*, 1976; Orgon's Mother, *Tartuffe*, 1977; *Street Songs*, 1979; also: *Our Private World, The Moon and Sixpence, Dodsworth, The Jilting of Granny Weatherall*.

AWARDS: Academy Award Nomination, 1939: *Wuthering Heights;* first Handel Medallion, New York City's special award, for the Everyman Street Theatre.

SIDELIGHTS: MEMBERSHIPS—New York State Council on the Arts, 1977, AEA, SAG, AFTRA. RECREATION—painting.

ADDRESS: Office—655 Madison Avenue, New York, NY 10021.*

* * *

FJELDE, Rolf, playwright, educator, poet

PERSONAL: Surname pronounced F(yell)-dee; born March 15, 1926; son of Paul (a sculptor and teacher) and Amy (Nordstrom) Fjelde; married Christel Mueller (a teacher) on September 1, 1964; children: Michele, Eric, Christopher. EDUCATION: Yale University, B.A. 1946; Columbia University, M.A. 1947; post-graduate study at the Universities of Copenhagen, Heidelberg and Oslo. Studied at the Yale School of Drama and the Neighborhood Playhouse. POLITICS: Independent. RELIGION: Protestant.

WRITINGS: PLAYS, PRODUCED—*One Simple Flower*, 1956; *Port Harmony*, 1957; *Switzerland*, 1967; *The Rope Walk*, 1968; *Rafferty One by One*, 1970; *The Bernini Look*, 1981. BOOKS, PUBLISHED—*Washington*, 1955; *The Imaged Word*, 1963; *Ibsen: Four Major Plays*, 1965–70; *Ibsen: A Collection of Critical Essays*, 1965; *Ibsen: The Complete Major Prose Plays*, 1978; *Peer Gynt* (Ibsen works, translations with interpretive introductions). POETRY, ARTICLES, SHORT STORIES, REVIEWS—*Hudson Review; Paris Review; Poetry; Voices; Epoch; Western Review; New Republic; New York Times Book Review; The Drama Review; Modern Drama; Ibsen Yearbook; Scandinavian Review; Columbia Forum*.

THEATRE-RELATED CAREER: Editor, *Yale Poetry Review*, 1945–49; editor, *Poetry New York*, 1949–51; editor, *Ibsen News and Comment*, 1979–present; lecturer in Drama History, Julliard School, NY, 1973–83; professor of English and Drama, Pratt Institute, NY, 1954–present; guest lec-turer on Drama at Harvard University, Yale University, the College of William and Mary, Cambridge College, Columbia University, New York University and the Universities of Minnesota, Wisconsin, Ohio, South Carolina, Missouri, Temple University, and PBS Television.

AWARDS: A. W. Mellon Foundation Grant for Studies in Film and Myth, 1974–75; National Translation Center Ford Foundation Fellowship, 1967–68; American Scandinavian Foundation Fellowship, 1952–53; Yaddo Fellowship in Creative Writing, 1952–54.

SIDELIGHTS: MEMBERSHIPS—President, Ibsen Society of America, 1978–present; Chairman, Board of Advisors and Member of Board of Directors American Ibsen Theatre Center; American Theatre Association.

"I began as a poet, writing, publishing and reviewing poetry and editing two 'little magazines.' My first work . . . a poem-suite titled *Washington*, was composed in response to Ezra Pound's injunction to make my work 'a barometer of the times.' Having always loved the theatre, I was drawn to the translation of Ibsen, because I sensed . . . a sensitive barometer of our entire civilization—of the immense shift of consciousness in the nineteenth century that broke from what he termed the preceeding First and Second Empires, of the deepest tendencies of our own age. My life since engaging with Ibsen's achievement has been a constantly renewed attempt to follow out those implications, to understand them better, and thereby keep ultimate faith with a central vision that is evolving through seeming chaos and unremitting struggle toward a future of unprecedented promise."

ADDRESS: Home—261 Chatterton Parkway, White Plains, NY 10606. Office—DeKalb Hall 3, Pratt Institute, Brooklyn, NY 11205. Agent—Samuel French Inc., 25 W. 45th Street, New York, NY 10036.

* * *

FLAGG, Fannie, actress, writer

PERSONAL: Born September 21, 1944, in Birmingham, AL; daughter of William Hurbert, Jr. (an artist) and Marion Leona Neal. EDUCATION: University of Alabama, drama major; studied for the theatre at the Pittsburgh Playhouse and with James Hatcher at the Town & Gown Theatre.

CAREER: DEBUT—Maid, *Cat on a Hot Tin Roof*, Town and Gown Theatre, Birmingham, AL. NEW YORK DEBUT—Player, *Just for Openers*, Upstairs at the Downstairs, 1966. PRINCIPAL STAGE APPEARANCES—*Patio/Porch*, New York, 1977; *Come Back to the Five and Dime, Jimmy Dean, Jimmy Dean*, Martin Beck, New York, 1979; *The Best Little Whorehouse in Texas*, 46th Street, New York, 1980. MAJOR TOURS—*Private Lives; Annie; Mary Mary; Finishing Touches; Once More with Feeling;* all United States.

PRINCIPAL FILMS—*Five Easy Pieces*, 1972; *Stay Hungry*, 1978; *Grease*, 1979; *Rabbit Test*, 1979. TELEVISION APPEARANCES—*Tonight Show; The Merv Griffin Show; The Mike Douglas Show; Candid Camera; Dick Van Dyke; Harper Valley, PTA; Love Boat; The Match Game*.

WRITINGS: Material for revues at Upstairs at the Downstairs; four comedy albums; material for *Candid Camera*. Books—*Coming Attractions*.

AWARDS: Two first-place awards in fiction at the Santa Barbara Writers Conference; six talent awards in the Miss Alabama Contest.

ADDRESS: Home—390 Ortega Road, Monticito, CA 93108. Agent—William Morris, 151 El Camino, Beverly Hills, CA 90212.

* * *

FLANAGAN, Pauline, actress

PERSONAL: Born June 29, 1925, in Sligo, Ireland; daughter of Patrick Joseph (a merchant) and Elizabeth Frances (Mulligan) Flanagan; married George F. Vogel (an actor), June 18, 1958; children: Jane, Melissa. EDUCATION: Graduated from Ursuline Convent in Sligo.

CAREER: PRINCIPAL STAGE APPEARANCES—(Broadway) *God and Kate Murphey; Step on a Crack; Under Milkwood; The Innocents; The Father; Medea; Steaming.* (Off-Broadway) Lincoln Center: *The Crucible, Antigone, The Plough and the Stars; Drums under the Window; Ulysses in Nighttown; Later,* Phoenix Theater; *Summer,* Hudson Guild; *Close of Play,* Manhattan Theatre Club. (Repertory) Buffalo Arena; Seattle Repertory; Arena Stage; Guthrie; Houston Alley; Goodman; Loretto Hilton; Antioch Shakespeare Festival. (Stock) Spoleto Festival; Ivanhoe; Berkshire Playhouse; Olney; Pocono Playhouse; Playhouse in the Park; Corning Summer Theatre.

SIDELIGHTS: MEMBERSHIPS—AEA, AFTRA, SAG.

ADDRESS: Agent—c/o D.H.K.P.R., 165 W. 46th Street, New York, NY 10036.

* * *

FLEISCHER, Richard, director

PERSONAL: Born December 8; son of Max (an animator cartoonist and producer) and Essie (Goldstein) Fleischer; married Mary Dickson, June 26, 1943; children: Bruce, Mark, Jane. EDUCATION: Brown, B.A., 1939; Yale, M.F.A., 1942. POLITICS: Democrat. RELIGION: Jewish. MILITARY: U.S. Air Force, 1941.

CAREER: FILM DEBUT—Director, *Child of Divorce,* 1947. PRINCIPAL FILM WORK: Director—*20,000 Leagues under the Sea,* 1954; *Compulsion,* 1959; *Fantastic Voyage,* 1966; *The Boston Strangler,* 1968; *Tora! Tora! Tora!,* 1970; *The New Centurians,* 1972; *Soylent Green,* 1973; *Mandingo,* 1975; *The Jazz Singer,* 1982; *Conan, the Destroyer,* 1984.

AWARDS: Cinematheque Francais Retrospective, 1975.

SIDELIGHTS: MEMBERSHIPS—Directors Guild of America,

American Film Institute, Cinema Circulus.

ADDRESS: Agent—Gersh Agency, 222 N. Canon Drive, Beverly Hills, CA 90210.

* * *

FLICKER, Ted (Theodore Jonas), actor, script writer, director, and producer

PERSONAL: Born June 6, 1930, in Freehold, NJ; son of Sidney and Rebecca (Lopatin) Flicker; married Barbara Perkins (model, actress, writer), September 30, 1966; EDUCATION: Attended Bard College; studied for theatre at Royal Academy of Dramatic Arts, London, England, 1952. MILITARY: U.S. Army, 1952–54 (corporal).

CAREER: NEW YORK DEBUT—Actor, *Once Around the Block* (world premiere), Cherry Lane, 1954. LONDON DEBUT—Actor, director, producer, *The Premise,* Comedy Theatre, 1962. PRINCIPAL STAGE WORK—Actor, director, producer, *The Compass Theatre,* Chicago, 1955; actor, director, producer, *The Compass Players,* Crystal Palace, St. Louis, MO, 1956–58; founder, actor, producer, director, writer, *Winter Monthly Repertory: Waiting for Godot, Love Success, Friend of the Family, Clerambard, Endgame, The Nervous Set,* Crystal Palace, St. Louis, 1958–59; actor, director, producer, *The Premise,* New York, 1960–64; director (with Joan Darling), producer *The Living Premise,* New York, 1963; author, director, *The Nervous Set,* Henry Miller's Theatre, New York, 1959; producer, director, *I Want You,* Maidman, New York, 1961. PRINCIPAL TOURS—Actor, *Macbeth, Thirteen Clocks, My Three Angels,* Barter Theatre Winter Tour, 1954–55; actor, director, producer, *The Premise,* Washington, DC, 1963, Ivar Theatre, Los Angeles, 1964.

FILM DEBUT—Actor, writer (with Buck Henry), director, producer, *The Troublemaker,* 1963. PRINCIPAL FILMS—Writer, *Spinout,* 1966; writer, director, *The President's Analyst,* 1968; writer, director, *Three in the Cellar,* 1970; writer, director, *Jacob Two-Two Meets the Hooded Fang,* 1976. TELEVISION DEBUT—Actor, *Studio One,* 1954. TELEVISION WORK—Directed, *The Bill Dana Show, The Dick Van Dyke Show, The Andy Griffith Show, The Man from U.N.C.L.E., The Rogues;* writer, director, episodes of *Night Gallery, Mod-Squad, Banacek, Columbo, McMillan and Wife;* created and wrote (with Danny Arnold) and directed pilot, *Barney Miller;* co-author, director, *Just a Little Inconvenience,* 1977; co-author, director, *Last of the Good Guys,* 1978; director, *Where the Ladies Go,* 1980.

AWARDS: Obie, *The Premise,* 1960; Vernon Rice Award, *The Premise,* 1960; W.G.A. Nomination, Best Original Screenplay for a Musical, *Spinout,* 1966; W.G.A. Nomination, Best Original Screenplay, *The President's Analyst,* 1967; Christopher Award, *Just a Little Inconvenience,* 1977.

SIDELIGHTS: MEMBERSHIPS—Actors Equity, SAG, Writers Guild of America (Board of Directors, 1973–75), DGA (council, 1970–73); Academy of Motion Picture Arts and Sciences (Executive Committee, Writers Branch, 1973–76), Caucus for Writers, Producers, and Directors.

With *The Compass Theatre,* Mr. Flicker was one of the

founders of Improvisational Theatre in America. As of 1981, he has retired from "Hollywood" and is planning a return to the theatre as an actor and playwright.

ADDRESS: Agent—Friedman, Kinzelberg and Broder, 1801 Avenue of the Stars, Los Angeles, CA 90067.

* * *

FLYNN, Don, playwright, writer

PERSONAL: Born November 18, 1928 in St. Louis, MO; son of George J. (a teamster) and Mary (Filey) Flynn; married Charlotte J. Bayton (a free-lance writer) on October 26, 1957; children: Kevin, Christopher, Colin. EDUCATION: University of Missouri, School of Journalism, Bachelors of Journalism, 1952. NON-THEATRICAL CAREER: Newspaper reporter: *Kansas City Star*, 1956–57; *Chicago Daily News*, 1957–58; *New York Herald Tribune*, 1966; *New York Daily News*, 1966–present.

WRITINGS: PLAYS, PRODUCED—*Pull the Covers Over My Head*, The Actor's Place, NY; *The Petition*, O'Neill National Playwrights Conference, Manhattan Theatre Club, NY; *Something That Matters*, ANTA, Hollywood, CA, American Theatre Company, NY; *The Man Who Raped Kansas*, under title: *Keep Krap Out of Kansas*, Arena Players, 1982, Gilford Playhouse, Gilford, NH; *The Pilgrims Just Landed Down the Road*, Arena Players Repertory Theatre, 1982, Quaigh, NY; *Around the Corner from the White House*, No Smoking Playhouse, NY, 1983, The Phoenix Festival Baltimore, 1983. PRINCIPAL TELEVISION SCRIPTS—*Room Nine; One of the Boys: Too Young of Too Old, His Old Flame; Street Cop.* BOOKS—(novel) *Murder Isn't Enough*, 1983.

SIDELIGHTS: MEMBERSHIPS—Dramatists Guild; Writers Guild of America; Newspaper Guild.

ADDRESS: Office—New York Daily News, 220 E. 42nd Street, New York, NY 10017.

* * *

FOLSEY, George Jr., film producer, editor

PERSONAL: Born January 17, 1939, in Los Angeles, CA; son of George Sr. (a cameraman) and Angele Folsey; married Belinda Comer. EDUCATION: Pomona College, B.A. (English Literature), 1961.

CAREER: PRINCIPAL FILM WORK—Film editor, *Animal House*, 1978; film editor, *Blues Brothers*, 1980; producer, *An American Werewolf in London*, 1981; associate producer, *Twilight Zone—The Movie*, 1982; executive producer, *Trading Places*, 1983; co-producer, editor, *Michael Jackson's Thriller*, 1983; co-producer, *Into the Night*, 1984.

ADDRESS: Agent—Mike Marcus, Creative Artists Agency, 1888 Century Park E., Los Angeles, CA 90067.

GEORGE FOLSEY, JR.

FONDA, Henry, actor

PERSONAL: Born May 16, 1905, in Grand Island, NE; died August 12, 1982; son of William Brace and Herberta (Jaynes) Fonda; married Margaret Sullavan (divorced); Frances Seymour Brokaw (deceased); Susan Blanchard (divorced); Afdera Franchetti (divorced); Shirlee Mae Adams; children: (second marriage) Jane, Peter; Amy (adopted). EDUCATION: Attended University of Minnesota, 1922–25. MILITARY: U.S. Navy, served in the South Pacific, World War II.

CAREER: DEBUT—Ricky, *You and I*, Omaha Community Playhouse, NE, 1925. NEW YORK DEBUT—Walk-on, *The Game of Life and Death*, Guild, 1929. LONDON DEBUT—Title-role, *Clarence Darrow*, Piccadilly, 1975. PRINCIPAL STAGE APPEARANCES—Stock seasons with the University Players, West Falmouth, Cape Cod, MA, 1928; stock seasons in Washington, DC, Philadelphia, Baltimore, 1929; Eustace, *I Love You Wednesday*, Harris, NY, 1932; Gentleman, *Forsaking All Others*, Times Square, NY, 1933; *New Faces of 1934*, Fulton, NY, 1934; Dan Harrow, *The Farmer Takes a Wife*, 46th Street, NY, 1934; Hayden Chase, *Blow Ye Winds*, 46th Street, NY, 1937; Lieutenant Roberts, *Mister Roberts*, Alvin, NY, 1948; Charles Gray, *Point of No Return*, Alvin, NY, 1951; Lieutenant Barney Greenwald, *The Caine Mutiny Court Martial*, Plymouth, NY, 1954; Jerry Ryan, *Two for the Seesaw*, Booth, NY, 1958; John, *Silent Night, Lonely Night*, Morosco, NY, 1959; Parker

Ballantyne, *Critic's Choice*, Barrymore, NY, 1960; Charles Wertenbaker, *A Gift of Time*, Barrymore, NY, 1962; Jim Bolton, *Generation*, Morosco, NY, 1965; Stage Manager, *Our Town*, ANTA, NY, 1969; Abraham Lincoln, *The Trial of Abraham Lincoln*, Mark Taper Forum, Los Angeles, 1971; Joe, *The Time of Your Life*, Eisenhower, Washington, DC, 1972; title-role, *Clarence Darrow*, Helen Hayes, NY, 1974, Minskoff, NY, 1975, Royal Alexandra, Toronto, Canada, 1975; Justice Daniel Snow, *First Monday in October*, Eisenhower, Washington, DC, 1977, Majestic, NY, 1978. MAJOR TOURS—Abraham Lincoln, *The Trial of Abraham Lincoln*, 1971; Joe, *The Time of Your Life*, 1972; title-role, *Clarence Darrow*, 1974–75; Justice Daniel Snow, *First Monday in October*, 1979. Directed—*Caine Mutiny Court Martial*, Ahmanson, Los Angeles, 1971.

FILM DEBUT—*The Farmer Takes a Wife*, 1935. PRINCIPAL FILM APPEARANCES—*Way Down East*, 1935; *I Dream Too Much*, 1935; *The Trail of the Lonesome Pine*, 1936; *Spendthrift*, 1936; *You Only Live Once*, 1937; *That Certain Woman*, 1937; *Wings of the Morning*, 1937; *I Met My Love Again*, 1938; *Jezebel*, 1938; *Blockade*, 1938; *Spawn of the North*, 1938; *Jesse James*, 1939; *Young Mr. Lincoln*, 1939; *The Story of Alexander Graham Bell*, 1939; *Drums Along the Mohawk*, 1939; *Grapes of Wrath*, 1940; *Lillian Russell*, 1940; *The Return of Frank James*, 1940; *Chad Hannah*, 1940; *The Lady Eve*, 1941; *Wild Geese Calling*, 1941; *The Male Animal*, 1942; *The Big Street*, 1942; *Rings on Her Fingers*, 1942; *Tales of Manhattan*, 1942; *The Immortal Sergeant*, 1942; *The Magnificent Dope*, 1942; *The Ox-Bow Incident*, 1943; *My Darling Clementine*, 1946; *Daisy Kenyon*, 1947; *The Long Night*, 1947; *The Fugitive*, 1947; *A Miracle Can Happen*, 1947; *On Our Merry Way*, 1948; *Fort Apache*, 1948; *Mister Roberts*, 1955; *War and Peace*, 1956; *Twelve Angry Men*, 1957; *The Wrong Man*, 1957; *Tin Star*, 1957; *Stage Struck*, 1958; *Warlock*, 1959; *The Man Who Understood Women*, 1959; *Advise and Consent*, 1962; *The Longest Day*, 1962; *How the West Was Won*, 1962; *Fail Safe*, 1964; *The Best Man*, 1964; *Sex and the Single Girl*, 1965; *In Harm's Way*, 1965; *The Rounders*, 1965; *Battle of the Bulge*, 1966; *The Dirty Game*, 1966; *A Big Hand for the Little Lady*, 1966; *Welcome to Hard Times*, 1967; *Firecreek*, 1968; *Yours, Mine, and Ours*, 1968; *The Boston Strangler*, 1968; *Madigan*, 1968; *Once Upon a Time in the West*, 1969; *Too Late the Hero*, 1970; *Cheyenne Social Club*, 1970; *There Was a Crooked Man*, 1970; *Sometimes a Great Notion*, 1971; *The Serpent*, 1973; *Ash Wednesday*, 1973; *My Name Is Nobody*, 1974; *Midway*, 1976; *Tentacles*, 1977; *Rollercoaster*, 1977; *The Swarm*, 1978; *The Great Smokey Roadblock*, 1978; *Fedora*, 1979; *Meteor*, 1979; *The Journey of Simon McKeever*, 1979; *Wanda Nevada*, 1979; *City on Fire*, 1979; *Battle of Mareth*, 1980; *On Golden Pond*, 1981.

PRINCIPAL TELEVISION APPEARANCES—movies for television, *The Red Pony*, 1970; *Clarence Darrow*; *Home to Stay*; *Roots II*; *Gideon's Trumpet*; *Oldest Living Graduate*; *Summer Solstice*; series—star, *The Deputy*; *The Smith Family*; *The Alpha Caper*, 1973; *Collision Cours.*

AWARDS: Academy Award, Best Actor, 1981: *On Golden Pond*; American Film Institute Life Achievement Award, 1979; Achievement Award, Kennedy Center for the Performing Arts, 1979; Antoinette Perry Award, 1979: *First Monday in October*; Bronze Star Medal and a Presidential Citation, World War II.*

FONDA, Jane, actress

PERSONAL: Born December 21, 1937, in New York City; daughter of Henry (an actor) and Frances Seymour (Brokaw) Fonda; married Roger Vadim (divorced); Tom Hayden (a political activist), January 20, 1973; children: (first marriage) Vanessa; (second marriage) Troy. EDUCATION: Attended Emma Willard's School and Vassar College; trained for the stage at the Actors Studio with Lee Strasberg.

CAREER: THEATRE DEBUT—Nancy Stoddard, *The Country Girl*, Omaha Playhouse, NE, 1954. NEW YORK DEBUT—Toni Newton, *There Was a Little Girl*, Cort, 1960. PRINCIPAL STAGE APPEARANCES—Patricia Stanley, *The Male Animal*, 1956; Patty O'Neill, *The Moon Is Blue*, 1959; Jacky Durrant, *No Concern of Mine*, Westport Country Playhouse, CT, 1960; Tish Stanford, *The Fun Couple*, Lyceum, NY, 1962; Madeline Arnold, *Strange Interlude*, Hudson, NY, 1963. MAJOR TOURS—*Free the Army* (revue), U.S. Army bases, foreign cities, 1970–71.

TELEVISION DEBUT—*A String of Beads*, 1961.

FILM DEBUT—*Tall Story*, 1960. PRINCIPAL FILM APPEARANCES—*Chapman Report*, 1962; *Walk on the Wild Side*, 1962; *Period of Adjustment*, 1962; *In the Cool of the Day*, 1963; *Les Felins*, 1963; *The Love Cage*, 1963; *Sunday in New York*, 1964; *La Ronde*, 1964; *Cat Ballou*, 1965; *The Chase*, 1966; *La Curee*, 1966; *Any Wednesday*, 1966; *The Game Is Over*, 1967; *Hurry Sundown*, 1967; *Barefoot in the Park*, 1967; *Barbarella*, 1968; *Spirits of the Dead*, 1969; *They Shoot Horses, Don't They?*, 1969; *Klute*, 1971; *F.T.A.*, 1972; *Steelyard Blues*, 1973; *A Doll's House*, 1973; *Blue Bird*, 1976; *Julia*, 1977; *Fun with Dick and Jane*, 1977; *California Suite*, 1978; *Coming Home*, 1978; *Comes a Horseman*, 1978; *China Syndrome*, 1979; *Electric Horseman*, 1979; *Nine to Five*, 1980; *Rollover*, 1981; *On Golden Pond*, 1981.

AWARDS: Academy Awards, Best Actress, 1978: *Coming Home*, 1970: *Klute*; Golden Globe, Best Actress, 1978: *Coming Home*; Golden Apple, Hollywood Women's Press Club, 1977.

WRITINGS: BOOKS—*Jane Fonda's Workout Book*, 1981.

ADDRESS: Office—Twentieth Century Fox, P.O. Box 900, Beverly Hills, CA 90213.*

* * *

FORD, Constance, actress

PERSONAL: Born July 1, in New York City; daughter of Edwin (a stockbroker) and Cornelia (a teacher) Ford; married Shelley Hull, 1946 (divorced 1956). EDUCATION: Hunter College and Marymount Manhattan; studied for the theatre with Betty Cashman, Robert Lewis, and Herbert Berghof.

CAREER: DEBUT—Katrin, *I Remember Mama*, Ivoryton Playhouse, Ivoryton, CT, August 1946. NEW YORK DEBUT—Miss Forsyth, *Death of a Salesman*, Morosco, February 1949, for two years. PRINCIPAL STAGE APPEARANCES—*Say Darling*, ANTA, NY, 1958; *The Golden Fleecing*, Henry

CONSTANCE FORD

Miller's, NY; *Nobody Loves an Albatross*, Lyceum, NY, 1963; Elaine, *The Last of the Red Hot Lovers*, Papermill Playhouse, 1973. MAJOR TOURS—Understudy, *John Loves Mary*, National, 1948; Lorna Moon, *Golden Boy*, Eastern Summer tour.

FILM DEBUT—Saloon Woman, *The Last Hunt*, 1956. FILM APPEARANCES—Helen, *A Summer Place*, 1960; Opal, *Home from the Hills*, 1960; *House of Women*, 1961; Nurse Bracken, *The Caretakers*, 1962.

TELEVISION DEBUT—*Hollywood Screen Test*, 1951. TELEVISION APPEARANCES—*Philip Morris Playhouse—A Journey to Nowhere*, October 8, 1953 (premiere); *Philco Playhouse; Studio One; Kraft Theatre; Danger; Suspense; Lux Video; Chrysler Playhouse;* Connie, *Playhouse 90—The Comedian*, 1957; Ada, *Another World*, 1968–present.

AWARDS: Emmy Award, Certificate of Merit, Outstanding Contribution to Daytime Drama, 1983; Afternoon T.V. Best Supporting Actress, 1973, 1974, 1975.

SIDELIGHTS: "It's hard to believe that (this) represents a thirty-seven year career . . . it has been, nonetheless, interesting."

ADDRESS: Agent—Gloria Safier, 667 Madison Avenue, New York, 10021.

*   *   *

FORD, Frances (nee Fuller), actress, director, singer

PERSONAL: Born November 10, 1939, in Appleton, WI; daughter of Harold Elmer (a businessman) and Bertha (an accountant; maiden name, Furminger) Fuller; married Victor Seymour, November 1967 (divorced, 1971); married Walter Ford-Altenburg (a sugar chemist), May 1, 1977; children: (first marriage) Nathaniel Fuller. EDUCATION: Northwestern University, 1957–59; University of Wisconsin, 1959–61; trained for the theatre at the Neighborhood Playhouse, 1961–63. RELIGION: Society of Friends. NON-THEATRICAL CAREER: Artist-in-Residence, PACE, Huntington, NY School System, 1968; Artist-in-Residence (Director), Friends Seminary, 1974–82; Teacher-Director, Brooklyn Friends School, 1978–79.

CAREER: DEBUT—Betty Price, *Middle of the Night*, Green Ram Baraboo, WI. NEW YORK DEBUT—Baby, *The Fairhaired Boy*, Amateur Comedy Club, October 29–November 9, 1963, ten performances. PRINCIPAL STAGE APPEARANCES—Barbara Allen, *Dark of the Moon*, Calumet Playhouse, MI, 1966; Mary McKellway, *Mary, Mary*, Calumet Playhouse, MI, 1966; Miep, *Diary of Anne Frank*, PACE, Huntington, NY, 1968; Mary Cratchitt, *The Stingiest Man in Town*, Town Hall, NY/Shubert, Cincinnati, OH, 1972; Liza Elliott, *Lady in the Dark*, Queensboro Community College, 1977; Katrin Rommel, *Howling in the Night*, Edinburgh Festival Fringe, 1979; also: Mrs. Pearce/Mrs. Higgins, *Pygmalion*, Classic Theatre, NY; Lady Bracknell, *The Importance of Being Earnest*, Meat and Potatoes, NY; Edith Piaf, others, *The Paris of Jean Cocteau*, Classic, NY; Mrs. Hardcastle, *She Stoops to Conquer*, Meat and Potatoes, NY; Mariette, *Medusa in the Suburbs*, ELT Informal at Lincoln Center, NY; Madame, *The Maids*, Entermedia Marquee, NY.

MAJOR TOURS: Understudy to The Woman, *The Coach with Six Insides*, upstate New York, Indiana, and Pennsylvania, 1965–66; ensemble and understudy, *The Pirates of Penzance*, *H.M.S. Pinafore*, *The Mikado*, Gloriana Productions, New York, Ohio, Indiana, Iowa, Minnesota, Florida, N. Carolina, S. Carolina, Mississippi, Tennessee, 1980–83.

PRINCIPAL FILMS—Mrs. Kaufman, *Darkness at Night*; Simon. TELEVISION DEBUT—Miss Ophelia, *Uncle Tom's Cabin*, Brooklyn College Cable TV, 1982. CABARET APPEARANCES—singer, The Bushes of Central Park West, Tramps, The Art of the Accompanist, at the Ballroom.

AWARDS: Scholarship for second year of study at Neighborhood Playhouse; University of Wisconsin, awards for Best Student Director/Best Supporting Actress, 1961.

SIDELIGHTS: MEMBERSHIPS—SAG (SAG Conservatory Woman's Committee, SAG Support Group); AEA; Newgate Child Care Center (supervisor—downtown Brooklyn); vice-president, Local Block Association.

RECREATION—Plasterer, painter, yoga, bread-baker, backpacking.

"My favorite role in my early years was Annie Sullivan in *The Miracle Worker*, played in non-Equity stock in Weston, Vermont. Annie is so well written and so real that her strength and determination became mine. My most important role recently was Madame in *The Maids* . . . being a sensual bitchy type pointed a direction for future roles. I have in the

FRANCES FORD

past been a speaker for American Friends Service Committee to raise money for the starving in the Horn of Africa, Ethiopia in particular. I spend time with several Ethiopian refugees as a friend to help them get used to the hectic pace of our life. I have taught and practice Yoga every day . . . a great way to get your head back together. I enjoy being a mother . . . my son acted with me for a while and belongs to both SAG and AEA; now he'll use the money he made in commercials to learn to fly. My politics are liberal, I suppose, and all seems to center on my firm belief that we all must learn to share and take care of the good things of this earth.''

* * *

FORD, Nancy, composer

PERSONAL: Born October 1, 1935; daughter of Henry III (an attorney) and Mildred (a teacher; maiden name Wotring) Ford; married Robert D. Currie, June 7, 1957 (divorced 1962); married Keith Charles (an actor), May 23, 1964. EDUCATION: DePauw University, A.B., 1957.

CAREER: DEBUT—Chorus, Iroquois Ampitheatre, Louisville, KY, 1955. NEW YORK DEBUT—Pianist for *Brecht on Brecht,* Theatre de Lys, 1962. PRINCIPAL STAGE APPEARANCES—*I'm Getting My Act Together and Taking It on the Road,* Circle-in-the-Square, New York, 1980.

TELEVISION APPEARANCES—*Dinah Shore Show; Today Show; Dick Cavett Show; Good Morning America.*

WRITINGS: Composer of *Now Is the Time for All Good Men,* 1967; *Last Sweet Days of Isaac,* 1970; *Shelter,* 1972; and *I'm Getting My Act Together and Taking It on the Road,* 1978 (all with book and lyrics by Gretchen Cryer). Scriptwriter for daytime television dramas: *Love of Life; Ryan's Hope; As the World Turns; The Guiding Light;* and *Search for Tomorrow,* 1970–84.

AWARDS: Drama Desk Award, Obie Award, and New York Outer Critics' Circle Award, 1970: *The Last Sweet Days of Isaac;* Writers Guild Award, 1972: *Love of Life;* Emmy, 1983: *Ryan's Hope.*

SIDELIGHTS: MEMBERSHIPS—Dramatists Guild; Writers Guild; AEA, AFTRA: League of Professional Theatre Women; American Federation of Musicians. Miss Ford occasionally appears in concert and cabaret with Gretchen Cryer, performing their own material.

* * *

FORDIN, Hugh, writer and producer

PERSONAL: Born December 17, 1935 in New York, NY; son of Lee (a luggage manufacturer and distributor) and Annette (Bernstein) Fordin. EDUCATION: Syracuse University, B.S., 1957.

CAREER: PRODUCED: Plays—Northport Country Playhouse, Long Island, NY, 1954; Mount Tom Playhouse, Holyoke, MA, 1965, 1966. MAJOR TOURS—*Critic's Choice,* U.S. cities, 1962. FILMS—production executive, *M.A.S.H.,* 1968; executive assistant, *Hello Dolly,* 1969.

WRITINGS: BOOKS—*The World of Entertainment: Hollywood's Greatest Musicals,* 1976; *Getting to Know Him: The Biography of Oscar Hammerstein II,* 1978; *Jerome Kern: The Man and His Music,* 1979.

THEATRE-RELATED CAREER: Producer, Edith Piaf's Final Concert Tour, 1962–63; head of casting, David Merrick Productions, 1965–68; executive director, 20th-Century-Fox Film Corporation, 1968–71.

AWARDS: All American Press Association Special Award, 1975.

SIDELIGHTS: MEMBERSHIPS—Writers Guild, B'nai Brith/Music and Performing Arts Lodge, NARAS.

ADDRESS: Office—157 W. 57th Street, New York, NY 10019. Agent—c/o Perry Knowlton, Curtis Brown Ltd., 575 Madison Ave., New York, NY 10022.

* * *

FORMAN, Milos, director

PERSONAL: Born February 18, 1932, in Czechoslovakia. EDUCATION: Academy of Music and Dramatic Art, Prague and Laterna Magika, Prague 1958–62.

CAREER: FILM DEBUT—Director, *Black Peter*, 1963. PRIN-CIPAL FILM WORK—Director: *Peter and Pavla*, 1963; *Talent Competition; Loves of a Blonde*, 1965; *Fireman's Ball*, 1967; *Taking Off*, 1971; *Visions of Eight*, "The Deathlon", 1973; *One Flew over the Cuckoo's Nest*, 1975; *Hair*, 1979; *Ragtime*, 1981; *Amadeus*, 1984.

AWARDS: Academy Award, Best Director, 1975: *One Flew Over the Cuckoo's Nest;* Grand Prix, 17th International Film Festival, Locarno, 1964, Czechoslovak Film Critics Award, 1963: *Peter and Pavla*.

SIDELIGHTS: Mr. Forman teaches film at New York University.

ADDRESS: Agent—Robert Lantz, 888 Seventh Avenue, New York, NY 10016.*

* * *

FORNES, Maria Irene, writer and director

PERSONAL: Born May 14, 1930, in Havana, Cuba; daugh-

MARIA IRENE FORNES

ter of Carlos Luis (a public servant) and Carmen Hismenia (Collado) Fornes. EDUCATION: Attended Havana public schools. POLITICS: Democrat. RELIGION: Catholic.

WRITINGS: PLAYS—*Tango Palace*, 1963; *The Widow*, 1963; *The Successful Life of B*, 1965; *Promenade*, 1965; *The Office*, 1966; *A Vietnamese Wedding*, 1967; *The Annunciation*, 1967; *Dr. Kheal*, 1968; *The Red Burning Light*, 1968; *Molly's Dream*, 1968; *The Curse of the Langstons House*, 1972; *Aurora*, 1974; *Cap-a-Pie*, 1975; *Fefu and Her Friends*, 1977; *Lolita in the Garden*, 1977; *In Service*, 1978; *Eyes on the Harem*, 1979; *Evelyn Brown*, 1980; *Life Is a Dream*, 1981; *A Visit*, 1981; *Danube*, 1982; *Mud*, 1983.

THEATRE-RELATED CAREER—Teacher (playwriting)—Theatre for the New City, New York, 1972–73; Padua Hills Festival, Claremont, CA, 1978–present; INTAR, New York, NY 1981–present.

AWARDS: Obie, Sustained Achievement, 1982; Obies, 1979: *Eyes on the Harem;* Obie, 1977: *Fefu and Her Friends;* Obie, 1965: *Successful Life of B;* Obie, 1965: *Promenade;* National Endowment for the Arts Grant, 1974; CAPS Grant, 1972; Rockefeller Foundation Grant, 1971; Yale University Grant, 1967; Centro Mexicano de Escervitores, Mexico Grant, 1962; John Hay Whitney Foundation Grant, 1961.

SIDELIGHTS: MEMBERSHIPS—Dramatists Guild, ASCAP, League of Professional Theatre Women.

"I teach playwriting and develop methods and techniques for writing that apply to both students and professionals."

ADDRESS: Office—One Sheridan Square, New York, NY 10014. Agent—c/o Berttia Case, 345 W. 58th Street, New York, NY 10019.

FORSYTHE, Charles (ne Lambros Charles Vocalis), producer, actor, and director

PERSONAL: Born in West Palm Beach, FL; son of Charles D. (a real estate owner) and Helen (Gerakitis) Vocalis; EDUCATION: University of Georgia, B.F.A.; trained for the stage with Robert Lewis. MILITARY: U.S. Army.

CAREER: DEBUT—Tom, *The Glass Menagerie*, University of Georgia, Athens, GA, 1947. NEW YORK DEBUT—Marc Antony's servant, *Julius Caesar*, Arena, Edison Hotel, 1950. PRINCIPAL STAGE APPEARANCES—Sebastian, *Twelfth Night*, Lorenzo, *The Merchant of Venice*, Paris, *Romeo and Juliet*, Shakespearewrights, New York, 1954–56.

PRINCIPAL FILM APPEARANCES—*Feeling Right*, 1949. PRINCIPAL TELEVISION APPEARANCES—Charles, *Barretts of Wimpole Street*, 1956.

DIRECTED, PLAYS—*Under the Yum Yum Tree*, Coconut Grove Playhouse, Miami, FL, 1961, Bucks County Playhouse, New Hope, PA, 1962; *Oh Dad, Poor Dad . . .*, Brown, Louisville, KY, Sombrero Playhouse, Phoenix, AZ, Playhouse-in-the-Park, Philadelphia, Ivoryton Playhouse, CT, 1964, Piccadilly, London, 1965; *Beekman Place*, Elitch Gardens, Denver, CO, Westport Country Playhouse, CT,

Photograph by Rena Hansen

Royal Poinciana Playhouse, Palm Beach, FL, 1965; *A Remedy for Winter,* Westport Country Playhouse, Mt. Tom Playhouse, Holyoke, MA, 1965; *The Time of the Cuckoo,* Cape Playhouse, Dennis, MA, Corning Summer Theater, NY, 1966; *Generation,* Playhouse-in-the-Park, Philadelphia, Ogunquit Playhouse, ME, 1967–68; *The Impossible Years,* Royal Poinciana Playhouse, Palm Beach, FL, 1967–68; *Boeing, Boeing,* Ivoryton Playhouse, CT, Westport Country Playhouse, Westport, CT, 1970–71; *Here Today* and *You Know I Can't Hear You When the Water's Running,* Royal Poinciana Playhouse, Palm Beach, FL, 1971; *The Owl and the Pussycat,* Pellman, Milwaukee, WI, 1973; *Barefoot in the Park,* Carillon, Miami Beach, FL, 1973; *Arsenic and Old Lace,* Corning Summer Theater, NY, Town and Country Playhouse, Rochester, NY, 1974; *Lovers and Other Strangers,* Chateau de Ville, Dinner Theater, MA, 1974.

PRODUCED: PLAYS—Has produced many plays, most recently *Send Me No Flowers,* Westchester Playhouse, Yonkers, NY, Corning Summer Theatre, Corning, NY, *The Best Man,* Corning Summer Theatre, Corning, NY, Elitch Gardens, Denver, CO, *Habeas Corpus,* Chateau DeVille, Saugus, MA, *Grass Widows,* Manhattan Theatre Club, 1976; *Night Must Fall,* Playhouse-in-the-Park, Philadelphia, Cape Playhouse, Dennis, MA; *Come Blow Your Horn,* Cape Playhouse, Dennis, MA, Pocono Playhouse, Mountainhome, PA; *The Voice of the Turtle,* Cape Playhouse, Dennis, MA, Ogunquit Playhouse, Ogunquit, ME, 1977; *Come Blow Your Horn,* Candlewood, New Fairfield, CT, North Shore Music Theater, Beverly, MA, *Vanities,* North Shore Music Theater, Beverly, MA, *Vanities,* North Shore Music Theatre, Beverly, MA, Falmouth, MA, 1978; *Same Time, Next Year,* Playhouse-in-the-Park, Philadelphia, Ogunquit Playhouse, Ogunquit, ME; *The Impossible Years,* Pocono Playhouse, Mountainhome, PA, Cape Playhouse, Dennis, MA, 1979.

Deathtrap, Elitch Gardens, Denver, CO, Falmouth Playhouse, Falmouth, MA; *I Love My Wife,* Corning Summer Theatre, Corning, NY, Westport Playhouse, St. Louis, MO, 1980; *The Gin Game,* Cherry County Playhouse, Traverse City, MI, Elitch, Denver, CO; *I Ought to Be in Pictures,* Elitch, Denver, CO, 1981; *Mass Appeal,* Pocono Playhouse, Mountainhome, PA, Theatre-on-the-Square, Sullivan, IL, 1982; *Mass Appeal,* Ogunquit Playhouse, Ogunquit, ME, Elitch, Denver, CO, 1983.

AWARDS: Faberge's Straw Hat Award, Council of Stock Theatres, Best Director, 1971: *Boeing, Boeing.*

SIDELIGHTS: MEMBERSHIPS—AEA; AGTRA; AGMA; SSD&C.

ADDRESS: Office—Forsythe Productions, 1841 Broadway, New York, NY 10023.

* * *

FORSYTHE, John (ne John Lincoln Freund), actor

PERSONAL: Born January 29, 1918, in Carney's Point, NJ; son of Samuel Jeremiah and Blanche Materson (Blohm) Freund; married Parker McCormick (divorced); married Julie Warren (a radio baseball commentator); children: Dall,

Page, Brooke. EDUCATION: Attended University of North Carolina.

CAREER: THEATRE DEBUT—Captain, *Dick Whittington and His Cat,* Clare Tree Major's Children's Theatre, Chappaqua, NY, 1939. NEW YORK DEBUT—Private Cootes, *Vickie,* Plymouth, 1942. PRINCIPAL STAGE APPEARANCES—Coast Guardsman, *Yankee Point,* Longacre, NY, 1942; *Winged Victory* (revue), 44th Street Theater, NY, 1943; *Yellowjack,* 44th Street Theater, NY, 1945; *Woman Bites Dog,* Belasco, NY, 1946; Chris Keller, *All My Sons,* Coronet, NY, 1947; Bill Renault, *It Takes Two,* Biltmore, NY, 1947; Mr. Roberts, *Mr. Roberts,* Alvin, NY, 1950; Captain Fisby, *The Teahouse of the August Moon,* Martin Beck, NY, 1953; Detective McLeod, *Detective Story,* Westport Country Playhouse, CT, 1955; Senator MacGruder, *Weekend,* Broadhurst, NY, 1956; Lt. Greenwald, *The Caine Mutiny Court Martial,* Ahmanson, Los Angeles, CA, 1971.

FILM DEBUT—*Destination, Tokyo,* 1942. PRINCIPAL FILM APPEARANCES—*The Captive City; It Happens Every Time; The Glass Web; Escape from Fort Bravo,* 1953; *Ambassador's Daughter,* 1956; *The Trouble with Harry,* 1956; *Everything but the Truth,* 1956; *Kitten with a Whip,* 1964; *Madame X,* 1966; *In Cold Blood,* 1968; *The Happy Ending,* 1969; *Topaz,* 1969; *And Justice for All,* 1979.

PRINCIPAL TELEVISION APPEARANCES—*Studio One; Kraft Theatre; Robert Montgomery Presents; Bachelor Father,* 1957; *Wuthering Heights; Teahouse of the August Moon; Miracle in the Rain; To Rome with Love,* 1969–71; *World of Survival; Terror on the 40th Floor,* 1974; *The Deadly Tower,* 1975; *Charlie's Angels; Cruise into Terror,* 1978; *Dynasty,* 1981–present.

SIDELIGHTS: RECREATIONS—Sailing, music, painting.

ADDRESS: Office—11560 Bellagio Road, Los Angeles, CA 90049.*

* * *

FOSSE, Bob (Robert Louis), director, choreographer

PERSONAL: Born June 23, 1927, in Chicago, IL; son of Cyril K. and Sarah (Stanton) Fosse; married Mary Ann Miles (divorced); married Joan McCracken (divorced); married Gwen Verdon (divorced). EDUCATION: Attended Amundsen High School, Chicago, IL; trained for the stage at the American Theatre Wing.

CAREER: STAGE DEBUT—Vaudeville, 1941. NEW YORK DEBUT—*Dance Me a Song* (revue), St. James, 1950. LONDON DEBUT—Choreographer, *Little Me,* Cambridge, 1964. PRINCIPAL STAGE WORK—Choreographer, *The Pajama Game,* St. James, NY, 1954; choreographer, *Damn Yankees,* NY, 1955; choreographer (with Jerome Robbins), *Bells Are Ringing,* NY, 1956; choreographer, *New Girl in Town,* NY, 1957; director, *Redhead,* 1959; choreographer, *How to Succeed in Business without Really Trying,* NY, 1961; director, *Little Me,* 1962;1 director/choreographer, *Sweet Charity,* Palace, NY, 1966; director/choreographer, *Pippin,* NY, 1972; director/choreographer, *Liza,* NY, 1974; director/choreographer, *Chicago,* NY, 1975; director/choreographer,

Dancin', NY, 1977. MAJOR TOURS—*Make Mine Manhattan*, U.S. cities, 1948–49.

PRINCIPAL FILM WORK—Actor, *The Affairs of Dobie Gillis;* actor, *Kiss Me, Kate;* choreographer, *The Pajama Game,* 1957; choreographer, *Damn Yankees,* 1958; choreographer, *Sweet Charity,* 1969; director/choreographer, *Cabaret,* 1972; director, *Lenny,* 1974; Snake, also choreographer, *The Little Prince,* 1974; director/choreographer, *All That Jazz,* 1979; director, *Star 80,* 1983. TELEVISION—*Liza with a Z,* 1973.

WRITINGS: PLAYS, PRODUCED—*Chicago* (with Fred Ebb), NY, 1975.

AWARDS: Antoinette Perry Award, Best Director, Best Choreographer, 1972: *Pippin;* Antoinette Perry Awards, 1955, 1956, 1959, 1963, 1966; Emmy Award, 1973: *Liza with a Z.*

SIDELIGHTS: MEMBERSHIPS—Stage Directors and Choreographers (treasurer).

ADDRESS: Office—c/o Society of Stage Directors and Choreographers, 1501 Broadway, New York, NY 10019.*

* * *

FOWLER, Clement, actor

PERSONAL: Born December 27, 1924; son of Morris (a

CLEMENT FOWLER

businessman) and Lillian Fowler; married Edith Samuel (a book designer), April 7, 1951. EDUCATION: Wayne State University, 1941–43, 1946–48, B.A.; studied for the theatre with Sanford Meisner and Harold Clurman. MILITARY: Army Air Corps., 1943–45 (Staff Sergeant).

CAREER: DEBUT—Jack, *The Importance of Being Earnest,* Actors Company of Detroit, 1947. NEW YORK DEBUT—Exton, *Richard II,* City Center, 1951, for 24 performances. PRINCIPAL STAGE APPEARANCES—Pfc. Bernstein, *Fragile Fox,* NY, 1954; *Legend of Lovers; Salt of the Earth;* Bibinski, *Silk Stockings,* Van Buren, *Damn Yankees,* M. Broun, *Fanny,* Rye Music Theatre, NY, 1957; Sosia, *A God Slept Here,* Provincetown Playhouse, NY, 1957; Starkeeper, *Carousel,* Rye Music Theatre, NY, 1958; Rosencrantz, *Hamlet,* Lunt-Fontanne, NY, 1964; Grandfather, *Transfiguration of Benno Blimpie,* Playwright's Horizons, NY, 1983; Governor of Harfleur, *Henry V,* Delacourt, NY, 1984; also regional and Off-Broadway shows.

TELEVISION DEBUT—*I Cover Times Square,* 1950. TELEVISION APPEARANCES—*Studio One; Robert Montgomery Presents; Danger; Omnibus; The Web; Hallmark Hall of Fame; Suspense; Decoy; The Big Story.*

SIDELIGHTS: Since his debut in 1947, Mr. Fowler has never missed a single performance.

ADDRESS: Home—422 E. 58th Street, New York, NY 10022. Agent—Beverly Chase Management, 162 W. 54th Street, New York, NY 10019.

* * *

FOX, Terry Curtis, writer and critic

PERSONAL: Born May 22, 1948 in Brooklyn, NY; son of Sidney (an attorney) and Jean (Berman) Fox; married Susan Lerner (an attorney), August 26, 1973; children: Avra Beth. EDUCATION: University of Chicago, A.B., 1970. POLITICS: Democrat. RELIGION: Jewish.

CAREER: NEW YORK DEBUT—Playwright, *Cops,* Performing Garage, 1978.

WRITINGS: PLAYS, PRODUCED—*Cops,* Organic Theatre, Chicago, 1976, Performing Garage, New York, 1978; *Justice,* Playwrights' Horizons, NY, 1979; *The Summer Garden,* O'Neill Theatre Center, CT, 1980; *The Pornographer's Daughter,* Chicago Theatre Project, 1984. PLAYS, PUBLISHED—*Cops,* 1978; *Justice,* 1979. SCREENPLAYS—*Byline; Sunstroke.*

RELATED THEATRICAL CAREER—Drama Critic, *Village Voice,* New York, 1975–81.

AWARDS: CAPS Grant, 1979. Fellowship, O'Neill Theatre Center, CT, 1980.

SIDELIGHTS: MEMBERSHIPS—Dramatists Guild, Writers Guild, Bloodhounds.

''I am not sure whether I became devoted to the theatre when I was six and saw Mary Martin in *Peter Pan* or when I was three and witnessed an actor make an entrance through the house at the 92nd Street Y in *The Emperor's New Clothes*. In any event, by the time I was sixteen and understood that I would never play the piano as well as Artur Schnabel, there were only three things I wanted to do with my life: work on a newspaper, work in the theatre, and make movies. I have abandoned each any number of times but have inevitably been drawn back.

"When I began writing theatrical criticism, I was a dogmatic exponent of ritualistic theatre. When I began writing plays, they turned out to be realistic. I am no longer dogmatic. I like to think of my writing as musical, as much influenced by Beethoven as Chekhov. I am not sure this matters to anyone but me. My plays seem to be about the specifics of American professional life and about the difficulty of acting morally in a time without moral standards. I collect American hard-boiled fiction, spend as much time in the kitchen as possible, and tell stories to six-year olds."

ADDRESS: Agents—c/o Elaine Markson, 44 Greenwich Avenue, New York, NY 10011; c/o Nancy Blaylock, The Gersh Agency, 222 N. Canon Drive, Beverly Hills, CA 90210.

* * *

FOXWORTH, Robert, actor

PERSONAL: Born November 1, 1941, in Houston, TX; son of John Howard (a roofing contractor) and Erna Beth (a writer; maiden name, Seamman) Foxworth; married Marilyn McCormick, September 24, 1964 (divorced 1974); children: Brendon, Kristyn. EDUCATION: Carnegie Tech (now Carnegie-Mellon), B.F.A.; studied for the theatre at Arena Stage in Washington, DC. POLITICS: Democrat.

CAREER: DEBUT—The Leading Child, *The Indian Captive*, Little Red School House, Houston, TX, 1950. NEW YORK DEBUT—Chorus, *Henry V*, ANTA, NY, 1969, for 30 performances. PRINCIPAL STAGE APPEARANCES—10 roles in repertory, Alley, Houston, TX, 1958–61; 18 roles in repertory, Arena Stage, Washington, DC, 1965–68; 3 roles in repertory, American Shakespeare Festival, Stratford, CT, 1969; John Proctor, *The Crucible*, Vivian Beaumont, Lincoln Center, NY, 1972; McMurphy, *One Flew Over the Cuckoo's Nest*, Huntington Hartford, Los Angeles, 1975; Earl of Leicester, *Mary Stuart*, Ahmanson, Los Angeles, 1980.

FILM DEBUT—Leading Man, *The Treasure of Matecumbe*, 1973. FILM APPEARANCES—*Damien—Omen II*, 1977; *Prophecy*, 1978; Valnikov, *The Black Marble*, 1979.

TELEVISION DEBUT—*C.B.S. Playhouse—Sadbird*, 1969. TELEVISION APPEARANCES—David Hansen, *Storefront Lawyers (Men at Law)*, 1970–71; Karpis, *F.B.I. vs. Alvin Karpis*; Jack Maddock, *Mrs. Sundance*; Peter, *Peter and Paul*; Questor, *The Questor Tapes*.

AWARDS: Theatre World Award, John Proctor, *The Crucible*, 1972.

SIDELIGHTS: MEMBERSHIPS—Environmental concern organizations; antinuclear/nuclear freeze, etc. FAVORITE ROLES—

ROBERT FOXWORTH

Valnikov (*The Black Marble*) and McMurphy (*One Flew Over the Cuckoo's Nest*).

"Vital: that the world move back from the nuclear precipice."

ADDRESS: Office—c/o BKM, 9076 St. Ives Drive, Los Angeles, CA 90069.

* * *

FRANK, Mary K., producer

PERSONAL: Daughter of Frederick Guy (a career army officer) and Maud Helen (Hill) Knabenshue; married William Klee Frank (an engineer), July 14, 1945; children: Maud Ellen. EDUCATION: Attended Miss Beard's School; trained for the stage at the Royal Academy of Dramatic Art and Columbia University. MILITARY: Navigation instructor for the Army and the Navy during World War II.

CAREER: FIRST STAGE WORK—co-producer, *Tea and Sympathy*, Barrymore, New York, 1953. PRODUCED: PLAYS—*Too Late the Phalarope*, New York, 1956; *One More River*, New York, 1960; *Sponono*, New York, 1964; *K2* (co-produced), 1983.

SIDELIGHTS: MEMBERSHIPS—Cosmopolitan Club, Colony Club, Turf and Field Club, New Dramatists (president 20 years, now president emeritus).

Mary Frank has been the owner of the Abacus Ranch, a thoroughbred breeding and racing stable, since 1965.

ADDRESS: Office—745 Fifth Avenue, New York, NY 10151.

* * *

FRANKEL, Kenneth, director

PERSONAL: Born December 10, 1941 in Cleveland, OH; son of Elmer M. and Doris (Folph) Frankel. EDUCATION: Northwestern University, B.S. 1963; served as assistant director to Sir Tyrone Guthrie.

CAREER: FIRST STAGE WORK, DIRECTED—*In White America,* Karamu, Cleveland, OH. NEW YORK DEBUT, DIRECTED—*When You Comin' Back Red Ryder,* Circle Repertory Company, East Side Playhouse. PRINCIPAL STAGE WORK, DIRECTING—*Spokesong,* Circle in the Square (Uptown), 1981; *Quartermain's Terms,* 91st Playhouse, NY, 1983–84; *Old Times,* Roundabout, NY, 1984. MAJOR TOURS—*The Lion in Winter; A Christmas Carol,* 1982–83.

THEATRE-RELATED CAREER: Associate Artistic Director, Long Wharf Theatre, New Haven, CT, 1981–present.

AWARDS: Obie Award, *Quartermain's Terms,* 1983.

SIDELIGHTS: MEMBERSHIPS—Society of Stage Directors and Choreographers; Affiliate Artists.

ADDRESS: Office—222 Sargent Drive, New Haven, CT, 06511.

* * *

FRANKLIN, Bonnie, actress

PERSONAL: Born January 6, 1944; daughter of Samuel B. (an investment banker) and Claire (Hersch) Franklin; married Ron Sossi, March 1967 (divorced 1970); married Marvin Minoff (a producer), August 31, 1980. EDUCATION: Smith College, 1961–63; UCLA, B.A., 1966.

CAREER: DEBUT—Viola, *Your Own Thing,* Marines Memorial Theatre, San Francisco, 1968. NEW YORK DEBUT—Viola, *Your Own Thing,* Orpheum, 1968. PRINCIPAL STAGE APPEARANCES—Ruby, *Dames at Sea,* Theatre de Lys, New York, 1969; Bonnie, *Applause,* Palace, New York, 1970; Peter Pan, *Peter Pan,* Studio Arena, Buffalo, 1972.

TELEVISION DEBUT—*The Law,* TV-film, 1974 (Emmy award–winning film). TELEVISION APPEARANCES—Ann Romano, *One Day at a Time,* 1975–84.

AWARDS: Antoinette Perry Award Nomination, Bonnie, *Applause,* 1970; Outer Critics Circle Award; Theatre World Award; Emmy Nomination, *One Day at a Time;* "Torch of Liberty" from Antidefamation League.

ADDRESS: Agent—Creative Artists Agency, 1888 Century Park East, Century City, CA 90064.

LAURIE FRANKS

FRANKS, Laurie, actress and singer

PERSONAL: Born August 14, 1929, in Lucasville, OH; daughter of Guy (a teacher) and Nell (a writer; maiden name Yeager) Bumgarner; married Dobbs Franks (a conductor), June 4, 1953 (divorced, 1961). EDUCATION: Cincinnati College of Music, Bachelor of Music and Master of Music; trained for the stage at the Actors Studio with Stella Adler and David LeGrant. POLITICS: Democrat. RELIGION: Methodist.

CAREER: DEBUT—chorus, Lousiville Amphitheatre, Iroquois Park, Louisville, KY, 1951. NEW YORK DEBUT—*Christmas Show,* Radio City Music Hall, 1956. AUSTRALIAN DEBUT—Marion, *The Music Man,* Sydney, 1960. PRINCIPAL STAGE APPEARANCES—Jane, *Leave It to Jane,* Sheridan Square Playhouse, NY, 1959; Gaby, *Around the World in 80 Days,* Jones Beach, NY, 1961; Agnes Gooch, *Mame,* Winter Garden, NY, 1966–69. Mrs. Carter, *Oh Boy,* Goodspeed, East Haddam, CT, 1983; Miss Hicks, *The Human Comedy,* New York Shakespeare Festival, 1984;

Broadway—Marchese Crespi, *Something More;* Olga, *Anya;* Winkle, *Utter Glory of Morrissey Hall;* Karen, *Applause;* Off-Broadway—Ruth Carter Stapleton, *Jimmy and Billy;* Repertory—Madame Yepanchin, *Subject to Fits,* Soho Rep, NY; Madame Aigreville, *In Fashion,* Actors Theatre of Louisville, KY; Teacake Magee, *The Ponder Heart,* New Stage; Stock—Bianca, *Kiss Me Kate;* Kathy, *The Student Prince;* Mrs. Darling, *Peter Pan;* Marietta, *Naughty Marietta;* Mrs. Sowerberry/Old Sally, *Oliver;* Lady Catherine, *Vagabond King;* Fermina, *Man of La Mancha;* Laurey, *Oklahoma;* Erikson/Lady Saltburn, *Present Laughter;* Rosabella, *Most Happy Fella;* Desiree, *A Little Night Music;*

Dinner Theatre—Donna Lucia, *Where's Charley;* Marion, *Don't Drink the Water;* Phyllis, *Ninety-Day Mistress;* Laura, *Tenderloin;* Maud, *Oh Captain;* Mrs. Harcourt, *Anything Goes;* Polly, *Boy Friend;* Madame Hortense, *Zorba;* Countess, *Song of Norway;* Vera Charles, *Mame;* Eleanor, *A Lion in Winter.*

TELEVISION DEBUT—pianist, local Cincinnati station, 1949. PRINCIPAL TELEVISION APPEARANCES—*American Musical Theater Series,* 1960; Miss Kaye, *Ryan's Hope;* Mrs. Dodd, *One Life to Live;* Mrs. Heller, *Faith for Today;* Molly O'Keefe, *Another World.*

AWARDS: Gypsy Robe Award, 1970: *Applause;* Teller of the Year Award, Actors' Federal Credit Union.

SIDELIGHTS: MEMBERSHIPS—Sigma Alpha Iota (musical fraternity), Actors' Federal Credit Union, Board of Directors.

"I used to get bowling trophies when I bowled on the Broadway Show League teams for *Mame* and *Applause.* I am now on a dart team in the New York City Raven Division."

ADDRESS: Home—74 Riverside Drive, New York, NY 10024.

* * *

FRANZ, Joy (nee Maybelle Gordon), actress

PERSONAL: Born June 13, 1945; daughter of Harold H. (an engineer) and Doroty B. (Haitt) Gordon. EDUCATION: University of Missouri at Kansas City, B.M. 1968.

CAREER: NEW YORK DEBUT—*Jacques Brel Is Alive and Well and Living in Paris,* Village Gate, 1969. LONDON DEBUT—Susan, *Company,* Her Majesty's, 1972, for three months. PRINCIPAL STAGE APPEARANCES—Mary Turner, *Of Thee I Sing,* Equity Library, then Anderson, NY, 1970; Bernstein's *Mass,* Kennedy Center, Washington, DC, 1970; Susan, *Company,* Alvin, NY, 1971–72; *Out of This World,* Equity Library, NY, 1974; Mrs. Nordstrom, *A Little Night Music,* Shubert, then Majestic, NY, 1975; Catherine, *Pippin,* Imperial, then Minskoff, 1976–78; *Tomfoolery,* Village Gate, NY, 1980; *I Can't Keep Running in Place,* Westside Arts, NY, 1981; Janet, *Musical Chairs,* Rialto, NY, 1981; *High Button Shoes,* Goodspeed Opera House, East Haddam, CT, 1982; title role, *Penelope,* Perry Street, NY, 1982. MAJOR TOURS—Susan, *Company,* National, 1972; Mrs. Molloy, *Hello, Dolly,* 1979–80; Aldonza, *Man of La Mancha,* 1981.

FILM DEBUT—Susan Campbell, *No Picnic for Penny,* 1978. TELEVISION DEBUT—Mrs. Betty Heywood, *Search for Tomorrow,* 1977–78. TELEVISION APPEARANCES—Mrs. Goodrich, *One Life to Live,* 1982; Mrs. Kimball, *Texas,* 1982.

ADDRESS: Agent—Peggy Hadley Enterprises, 250 W. 57th Street, New York, NY 10107.

* * *

FRAZIER, Ronald, actor

PERSONAL: Born February 18, 1942; son of Cavilla and

RONALD FRAZIER

Virginia (Thompson) Frazier; children: Christopher. EDUCATION: Georgetown University, B.A. (cum laude); Carnegie-Mellon, M.F.A., Theatre. MILITARY: US Infantry (First Lieutenant). NON-THEATRICAL CAREER: Director/teacher, American Academy of Dramatic Art.

CAREER: DEBUT—*Caesar and Cleopatra,* Center Stage, Baltimore, 1965. NEW YORK DEBUT—Franklin Roosevelt, *Wilson in the Promised Land,* ANTA, 1970. PRINCIPAL STAGE APPEARANCES—*The Subject Was Roses,* St. Louis Company; *Years of the Locust,* Edinburgh Festival; *Measure for Measure, Macbeth,* Kennedy Center, Washington, DC; *An Enemy of the People,* Alaska Repertory; *What Every Woman Knows,* Roundabout, NY; *Sunrise at Campobello, The Animal Kingdom, A Thousand Clowns,* Berkshire Theatre Festival, MA, 1982; others. MAJOR TOURS—*Tartuffe,* Philadelphia; *The Trial of the Catonsville Nine,* National (Boston).

FILM DEBUT—Bookkeeper, *Brubaker,* 1979. PRINCIPAL FILMS—*Rollover, Honky Tonk Freeway, It's My Turn, The World According to Garp.*

TELEVISION DEBUT—*The Adams Chronicles,* 1975. TELEVISION APPEARANCES—*Max and Sam; Kennedy; Remington Steele; As the World Turns; Kent State; Special Bulletin; Rita Hayworth, Love Goddess; An Evening with Pirandello; Our Story—Yorktown.*

RADIO: *The Empire Strikes Back* (NPR series).

ADDRESS: Agent—Schumer-Oubre Management, 1697 Broadway, New York, NY 10019; Smith-Friedman, 850 Seventh Avenue, New York, NY 10019.

* * *

FREEK, George, playwright

PERSONAL: Born November 8, 1945, in Champaign, IL; son of William S. (a lawyer) and Marguerite Lorraine (a court reporter; maiden name Oakley) Freek; EDUCATION: University of Illinois (Champaign), B.A., 1967; Southern Illinois University (Carbondale), M.A., A.B.D., 1975. NON-THEATRICAL CAREER: Graduate teaching assistant (English), Southern Illinois University (Carbondale), 1970–75.

CAREER: DEBUT—Playwright, *For Left-Handed Piano with Obbligato*, Midwest Playwrights Program, Madison, WI, August 1979. NEW YORK DEBUT—Playwright, *Filial Pieties*, Second Stage, March 1983.

WRITINGS: PLAYS, UNPUBLISHED—The Cellar, Changing Scene, Denver, CO, 1981; Tarantella on a High Wire, Academy Theatre, Atlanta, GA, 1981; Getting Together, Corner Theatre, Baltimore, MD, 1982; The Sweet Land, New American Theatre, Rockford, IL, 1983.

AWARDS: Southeastern Theatre Conference New Play Contest, first prize, *Filial Pieties*, 1982; playwriting residencies: Southern Methodist University, 1981, New American Theatre, Rockford, IL, 1982, Southern Illinois University, 1983; playwriting grant, Illinois Arts Council, 1980.

SIDELIGHTS: MEMBERSHIPS—Dramatists Guild.

ADDRESS: Home—516 E. Menomonie Street, Belvedere, IL.

* * *

FRIDELL, Squire, actor, writer

PERSONAL: Born February 9, 1943, in Oakland, CA; son of Squire (a salesman) and Harriet (Harper) Fridell, Jr.; married Suzanne Mildermaid (an actress and dancer), August 13, 1977; children: Alexandra. EDUCATION: University of the Pacific, B.A., 1965; Occidental, M.A., 1975; special theatrical training in acting and directing. MILITARY: Marine Corps.

CAREER: PRINCIPAL STAGE APPEARANCES—South Coast Repertory, 1969–75: Kent, *La Turista*, Mike, *Saved*, Geronimo, *Indians*, Kress, *The Basic Training of Pavlo Hummel*, Son, *We Bombed in New Haven*, Ensemble, *Mother Earth*, Hero, *A Funny Thing Happened on the Way to the Forum*, Harold Hill, *The Music Man*, Speed, *The Odd Couple*, Nickles, *J.B.*; M.C., *Doug Henning's World of Magic*, Pantages, Los Angeles, CA.

TELEVISION APPEARANCES—Alvin Rice, *MASH—Identity Crisis;* George, *Motel;* host, *American Pie;* Frank, *Between the Lines;* Dr. Pete Berkus, *Eight Is Enough—Mary, He's Married;* My Boy Bill, *The Ropers—Rosie and Beer;* Ryan,

Rosetti and Ryan; Scooter Jackson, *The Waverly Wonders;* Phil, *Human Feelings;* Lieutenant Meadows, *Operation Petticoat—Tostin times Two;* also on *Vegas, Holmes and Yoyo, The Heist, Strangers in 7A, Love Story, Police Story, Adam-12, Ironside, The Young Lawyers, The Bold Ones, The Toni Tenille Show, Good Morning, America, A.M. Los Angeles, A.M. San Francisco, A.M. San Diego, Merv Griffin Show, Mike Douglas Show;* telethon host, *KSCI Christmas Telethon.*

THEATRE-RELATED CAREER—Director of dramatics, El Rancho High School, 1966–75; acting and film instructor, Rio Hondo College, 1975–77, 1980, Cerritos College and L.B. City College, 1976–77, 1980.

WRITINGS: BOOKS—*Acting in Television Commercials.*

SIDELIGHTS: MEMBERSHIPS—SAG, Equity, AFTRA.

Mr. Fridell was dubbed by *Newsweek* magazine the "uncrowned king of commercials," when he racked up a total of 110 thirty and sixty second spots during 1981.

ADDRESS: J. Michael Bloom, Ltd., 400 Madison Ave., New York, NY 10017.

* * *

FRIEDMAN, Bruce Jay, playwright, novelist

PERSONAL: Born April 26, 1930, The Bronx, New York; married Ginger Howard (an interior designer), 1954 (divorced); married Pat O'Donahue, July 2, 1983. EDUCATION: University of Missouri, 1951. MILITARY: Air Force (two years).

WRITINGS: PLAYS, PRODUCED—*23 Pat O'Brien Movies*, American Place, NY, 1966; *Scuba Duba*, Truck and Warehouse, NY, 1968; *A Mother's Kisses*, 1968; *The Car Lover*, 1968; *Steambath*, Truck and Warehouse, NY, 1970; *First Offenders*, (with Jacques Levey; also co-directed), 1973; *Turtlenecks* (aka *One Night Stand*), Philadelphia, 1973; *A Foot in the Door*, American Place Theatre, NY, 1979. THEATRE SKETCHES, PRODUCED—in revue, *Oh, Calcutta*, 1969. SCREENPLAYS—Story only, *The Heartbreak Kid*, 1972; *Stir Crazy*, 1981; (with Lowell Ganz and Babaloo Mandel) *Splash*, 1983. NOVELS—*Stern*, 1962; *A Mother's Kisses*, 1964; *The Dick*, 1970; *About Harry Townes*, 1974; *The Lonely Guy's Book of Life*, 1982 (basis for the movie, *The Lonely Guy*), 1983. SHORT STORIES—*From the City of Class*, 1963; *Black Angels*, 1966.

ADDRESS: Agent—The Lantz Office, 888 Seventh Avenue, New York, NY 10019.*

* * *

FRIEDMAN, Phil, stage manager

PERSONAL: Born October 31, 1921. RELIGION: Jewish. MILITARY: U.S. Army, Warrant Officer, WWII (4 years).

CAREER: FIRST STAGE WORK, STAGE MANAGER—*Louisiana Purchase*, San Francisco, CA, 1947. NEW YORK DEBUT, STAGE MANAGER—*Kismet*, NY, 1953; *The Boy Friend*, NY, 1955 and 1970 revival, NY; *How to Succeed in Business without Really Trying*, 46th Street Theatre, NY, 1961; *Little Me*, Lunt-Fontanne, NY, 1962; *Pippin*, Imperial, 1971; *Chicago*, 46th Street, 1975; *The Act*, Majestic, 1977; *Dancin'*, Broadhurst, 1978. MAJOR TOURS—*Kismet*, National Tour, 1954; *The Boy Friend*, National Tour, 1957; *Auntie Mame*, National Tour, 1958; *Dancin'*, National Tour, 1979.

FILM WORK—Actor, Stage Manager, *All That Jazz*, 1978. TELEVISION WORK: Stage Manager, *Liza with a Z*, 1972.

AWARDS: U.S. Army, Bronze Star.

SIDELIGHTS: MEMBERSHIPS—AEA; Stage Managers Association.

ADDRESS: Home—347 E. 53rd Street, New York, NY 10022.

* * *

FRIESEN, Rick (ne Stanley Richardson Friesen II), actor

PERSONAL: Born November 29, 1943; son of Stanley R. (a medical doctor) and Beth (Hatton) Friesen; married Stephanie Satie (an actress). EDUCATION: University of Kansas, B.A., 1966; trained for the stage with Wynn Handman and Bella Itkin.

RICK FRIESEN

CAREER: DEBUT—Arrow Rock Repertory, Arrow Rock, MO, 1964. NEW YORK DEBUT—Edward, *Mystery Play*, Cherry Lane Theater, 1973. PRINCIPAL STAGE APPEARANCES—Fyedka/Russian Tenor Soloist, *Fiddler on the Roof*, Winter Garden, New York, 1976–77; *UBU Cocu*, The Open Theater, New York, 1969; Antipholus, *Comedy of Errors*, Ensemble Studio, New York; *Brecht on War;* Brecht, *St. Joan of the Stockyards*, Encompass Theater, New York; *Edward II*, Westbeth Theater, New York; *East of Kansas*, Harold Clurman, New York; *Medicine Show*, St. Clements, New York; *Chantecler*, 47th Street Theater, New York; (Regional) Shawn Keogh, *Playboy of the Western World;* Ariel, *The Tempest;* Cleante, *The Imaginary Invalid;* Diggory, *She Stoops to Conquer;* (Stock) Eugene, *Look Homeward Angel;* Romanoff, *Romanoff and Juliet;* Eisenring/Biedermann, *The Firebugs;* Albert Amundson, *A Thousand Clowns;* Oglethorpe, *Blood, Sweat and Stanley Poole*.

MAJOR TOURS—Fyedka, *Fiddler on the Roof*, U.S. cities, 1976; Lomov, *A Marriage Proposal*, World Cruise, Holland America Line; *The Good Doctor*, Herbert, *I'm Herbert*, Adam, *The Apple Tree*, Norwegian America Cruise Line, Russia, Baltic, Panama, Alaska; Peter, *Zoo Story*, Wilder, *Childhood*, Improvisational Review, State Department Tour, Poland, Yugoslavia, Romania; *Medicine Show*, European cities; Johnny, *Johnny Moonbeam*, International Children's Theater Conference, London.

PRINCIPAL TELEVISION APPEARANCES—*Ryan's Hope, As the World Turns*.

SIDELIGHTS: MEMBERSHIPS—AEA, SAG, AFTRA. FAVORITE PARTS—Lomov, *The Marriage Proposal;* Ariel, *The Tempest*. RECREATION—birdwatching, backpacking.

ADDRESS: Home—412 E. 89th Street, New York, NY 10128.

* * *

FRUCHTMAN, Milton Allen, producer and director

PERSONAL: Born in New York City; son of Benjamin M. and Fanny F. (Ryan) Fruchtman; married Eva Sternbert; children: Eleanor, Jordan. EDUCATION: Columbia University, B.S.; M.S.

CAREER: PRINCIPAL TELEVISION WORK—Producer/director: *High Adventure*, 1957; *Verdict for Tomorrow*, 1961; *The Secret of Michaelangelo—Every Man's Dream*, 1968; *Dance Theater of Harlem*, 1973; *Those Who Sing Together*, 1979.

AWARDS: New York Film Festival Award, 1974, 1977; American Film Festival Award, 1974; Martin Luther King Festival Award, 1974; Gold Hugo Award, Chicago Film and Television Festival, 1973; Emmy Award, 1962; Peabody Award, 1962, 1969.

SIDELIGHTS: MEMBERSHIPS—Media Institute (president), Directors Guild of America, Columbia University Alumni Association.

ADDRESS: Office—P.O. Box 1979, Banff, AB, Canada T0L 030.

FUGARD, Athol, playwright, actor, director

PERSONAL: Born June 11, 1932 in Middleburg, Cape Province, South Africa; son of Harold David and Elizabeth Madalena (Potgeiter) Fugard; married Sheila Mering (poet, novelist, actress); children: Lisa, Maria. EDUCATION: University of Cape Town.

CAREER: PRINCIPAL STAGE APPEARANCES—Morris, *The Blood Knot*, South Africa, 1961, Hapstead, England, 1966. FILM APPEARANCES—General Jan Christian Smuts, *Ghandi*, 1982; Eugene Marais, *The Guest*, 1984 (filmed in 1976; U.S. release, 1984).

DIRECTED—*Blood Knot*, Hampstead, England, 1966; *The Trials of Brother Jero*, Hampstead, 1966; *The Island, Sizwe Bansi Is Dead, Statements After an Arrest Under the Immorality Act*, Royal Court, London, 1974; *Dimetos*, Edinburgh Festival, 1975, then the Comedy, London, 1976; *Hello and Goodbye*, Riverside, NY, 1978; also *Sizwe Bansi* and *The Island*, in NY.

WRITINGS: PLAYS, PRODUCED—*The Cell*, Cape Town, 1957; *Klaas and the Devil*, Cape Town, 1957; *No-Good Friday*, Bantu Mews Social Center, Johannesburg, South Africa, 1958; *Nongogo*, South Africa, 1959; *A Place for the Pigs*, South Africa, 1959; (adaptation of "Mandragola"), *The Cure*, South Africa, 1962–63; *People are Living There*, 1968; *Hello and Goodbye*, 1969; *Friday's Bread on Monday*, 1970; *Boesman and Lena*, 1970; (adaptation) *Orestes*, 1971; *People Arriving There*, Forum, NY, 1971; (co-deviser) *Siswe Bansi Is Dead*, (co-deviser) *The Island*, 1973; *Statements After an Arrest Under the Immorality Act*, Royal Court, London, 1974; *Dimetos*, Comedy, London, 1976; *A Lesson from Aloes*, 1979; *Master Harold . . . and the Boys*, Lyceum, NY, 1982; *The Road to Mecca*, Yale Repertory, New Haven, CT, 1984. TELEVISION SCRIPT—*Millie Miglia*, 1968; also adaptations of his stage works. FILM SCRIPTS—*The Guest*, 1976; *Boesman and Lena, Marigolds in August*. (Most of Mr. Fugard's plays have been published.) NOVELS—*Tostsi*, 1960–80. NON-FICTION—*Notebooks, 1960–77*, 1984.

AWARDS: Antoinette Perry Award, 1982: *Master Harold . . . and the Boys;* Drama Critics Circle, Best Play, Best Director, 1982: *Master Harold . . . and the Boys;* Drama Desk, 1982: *Master Harold . . . and the Boys;* Antoinette Perry Award Nominations, *A Lesson from Aloes*, Best Director, 1980: *Sizwe Bansi Is Dead/The Island*.

SIDELIGHTS: Helped create the Serpent Players in Port Elizabeth, South Africa, with whom he has worked and for whom he created *Sizwe Bansi* and *The Island*.

ADDRESS: Box 5090, Walmer, Port Elizabeth, South Africa.*

FULLER, John G., writer, director, and producer

PERSONAL: Born November 30, 1913; son of John G. and Alice Carey (Jenkins) Fuller; married Elizabeth Braucae (a writer), November 17, 1977; children: John G. III, Geoffrey T., Judd W., Christofer L. EDUCATION: Lafayette College, B.A., 1936. POLITICS: Democrat. RELIGION: Quaker.

CAREER: PRODUCED/DIRECTED/WRITTEN: FILMS (documentary)—*Light Across the Shadow; American Welcome; The Handyman; The People Speak; Independence Day, U.S.A.; Miracle in the Desert; Labor of Love; The Making of a Champion; Drug Abuse: A Call to Action; Problem Drinking: A Call to Action; VD: A Call to Action; New Big Game in Africa: Basketball*. DIRECTED/WRITTEN: FILMS (documentary)—*Re-Entry from Space; Fire Rescue*. DIRECTED/PRODUCED: FILMS (documentary)—*Countdown to 2001*. DIRECTED: FILMS (documentary)—*The Crowded Air*.

WRITINGS: PLAYS, PRODUCED—*The Pink Elephant*, Playhouse Theatre, NY, 1952; *Love Me Little*, Helen Hayes, NY, 1958. FILMS (documentary)—*The Last of the Battlewagons*. TELEVISION SHOWS—*Gary Moore Show; Candid Camera; Home Show*. BOOKS—*The Gentlemen Conspirators*, 1962; *The Money Changers*, 1962; *Games for Insomniacs*, 1965; *Incident at Exeter*, 1966; *The Interrupted Journey*, 1966; *The Great Soul Trial*, 1969; *The Day of St. Anthony's Fire; 200,000,000 Guinea Pigs*, 1972; *Arigo: Surgeon of the Rusty Knife*, 1974; *Fever: The Hunt for a New Killer Virus*, 1974; *We Almost Lost Detroit; The Ghost of Flight 401*, 1976; *The Poison that Fell from the Sky*, 1978; *The Airmen Who Would Not Die*, 1979; *Are the Kids All Right?*, 1981; *Passport to Anywhere* (with Lars Lindblad), 1983; *The Day We Bombed Utah*, 1984.

AWARDS: Young Adult Award, American Library Association, 1978: *The Poison That Fell from the Sky;* Golden Eagle Award, Belgrade Film Festival, 1977: *Century III: The Oceans;* New York Academy of Sciences Award for Young Adults, 1974: *Fever: The Hunt for a New Killer Virus;* Emmy Award, Outstanding Achievement in Magazine-Type Programming, 1971: *The Great American Dream Machine;* National Association of Teachers Award, 1966: *Incident at Exeter;* Sigma Delta Chi Journalism Award, Best Documentary, 1965: *Light Across the Shadow*.

SIDELIGHTS: MEMBERSHIPS—Dramatist's Guild, Author's League, WGA East.

ADDRESS: Agent—c/o Roberto Pryor, ICM, 40 W. 57th Street, New York, NY 10019.

G

GABLE, June, actress, dancer, director, singer and writer

PERSONAL: Born June 5, in Brooklyn; daughter of Joseph and Shirl Galup. EDUCATION: Carnegie-Mellon University, B.F.A., 1968. NON-THEATRICAL CAREER: Certified teacher of Yoga.

CAREER: DEBUT—Beatnik Witch, *MacBird!*, Circle in the Square, NY, 1969. NEW YORK DEBUT—*Jacques Brel Is Alive and Well . . .*, Duchess, 1969. PRINCIPAL STAGE APPEARANCES—Old Woman, *Candide*, Broadway Theatre, 1973–74; Lucy, *Beggars Opera*, Chelsea Theatre Center, Brooklyn, 1974–75; *Wanted; Lady Audley's Secret; The Madonna; A Comedy of Errors*, New York Shakespeare Festival, 1976; Googie Gomez, *The Ritz*, Longacre, 1976; Snooks, *Moose Murders*, O'Neill, 1983; Bette, *A History of the American Film*, Mark Taper Forum, Los Angeles, 1981–82. MAJOR TOURS—Sonia, *They're Playing Our Song*, U.S. cities; Retta, *Pump Boys and Dinettes*, U.S. cities, 1983–84.

PRINCIPAL TELEVISION APPEARANCES—Lucy, *Beggars Opera*, 1976; Detective Battista, *Barney Miller*, 1977; *Newmans Drug Store* (pilot), 1977; *Bay City Amusement* (pilot), 1978; *Laugh-In*, 1978; *Sha-Na-Na*, 1979; *Tonight Show*, 1980, *Merv Griffin*, 1980.

AWARDS: Obie Award, 1976: *Comedy of Errors;* Antoinette Perry Award nomination, 1973–74: *Candide*.

SIDELIGHTS: MEMBERSHIPS—AEA, SAG, AFTRA, Himalayan Institute. "I've traveled through India, the Himalayan Mountains, Europe, China and Tibet."

ADDRESS: Agency for the Performing Arts, 888 Seventh Avenue, New York, NY 10019.

* * *

GABOR, Eva, actress, comedienne

PERSONAL: Pronounced, Ayva, born February 11; daughter of Jolie and Vilmos Gabor; married Frank Gard Jameson (an industrialist). EDUCATION: Attended Forstner Girls Institute, Budapest, Hungary and Notre Dame de Sion in Lausanne, Switzerland.

CAREER: NEW YORK DEBUT—*The Happy Time*. PRINCIPAL STAGE APPEARANCES—*Present Laughter*, with Noel Coward; *You Can't Take It With You*, New York, 1983; NA-

TIONAL TOURS—*Blithe Spirit; Strike a Match; Oh Men, Oh Women; Her Cardboard Lover; Uncle Vanya; A Shot in the Dark; Private Lives; A Little Night Music; Applause;* replaced Vivien Liegh in *Tovarich* on Broadway.

PRINCIPAL FILM APPEARANCES—*Gigi; Don't Go Near the Water; The Trouble with Women; New Kind of Love; It Started with a Kiss; Artists and Models; The Last Time I Saw Paris; My Man Godfrey; The Aristocrats; The Rescuers.* PRINCIPAL TELEVISION APPEARANCES—*Green Acres* (six years); *The Eva Gabor Show;* GUEST APPEARANCES—*Tonight Show, Merv Griffin, Dean Martin Bob Hope, Liberace.*

THEATRE-RELATED CAREER: Chairman of the Board, Eva Gabor International, "the world's largest wig company."

WRITINGS: Book—*Orchids and Salami* (autobiography).

SIDELIGHTS: Chairwoman, "I Quit" branch of the American Cancer Society. "Eva was the first of the Gabor sisters to arrive in the United States, followed by Magda and Zsa Zsa. Eva is currently touring the country as a featured speaker at various women's conventions, where she expounds on her three lives: an actress, a wife and a businesswoman. Miss Gabor, who speaks English, French, German and Hungarian, lives in West Los Angeles with her husband, and has three dogs, three cats, 20 chickens, and 36 rabbits—at last count. She is an enthusiastic tennis player, as well as an avid collector of art and antiques. She also has a "green thumb," having planted a complete vegetable garden, and has one of the outstanding non-commercial orchid greenhouses in Southern California."

ADDRESS: Office—c/o Katz-Gallin-Makey, 9255 Sunset Blvd., Los Angeles, CA 90069. Agent—Jack Fielns & Associations Inc., 9255 Sunset Blvd., Los Angeles, CA 90069.

* * *

GALLAGHER, Mary, actress, director, writer

PERSONAL: Born July 7, 1947; daughter of Thomas L. (a C.P.A.) and Berenice (a teacher; maiden name, Hanrahan) Gallagher; married Michael Swift (a carpenter and writer), July 21, 1979; children: Leslie, Sarah. EDUCATION: Bowling Green University, B.S. in English, 1969.

WRITINGS: PLAYS, PRODUCED—*Fly Away Home*, American Conservatory Theatre (Plays in Progress Series), San Francisco, 1977; *Father Dreams*, American Conservatory Theatre (Plays in Progress Series), 1978, University of Wisconsin, La Crosse, 1978, Loretto-Hilton Repertory, 1980, Ensemble Studio, NY, 1981, Theatre Three, Dallas, 1981; *Little Bird,* Berkshire Theatre Festival, Stockbridge, MA, 1980, 78th Street Theatre Lab, NY, 1980, Syracuse University, 1981, Bates College, Lewiston, ME, 1983; *Chocolate Cake,* Actors Theatre of Louisville (Festival of New American Plays), 1981, Toronto International Theatre Festival, 1981, Provincetown Playhouse (as part of bill called *Win/Lose/Draw*), NY, 1983, Abbey Theatre, Dublin, 1983; *Buddies,* Ensemble Studio, 1982, Victory Gardens Theatre, 1983; *Dog Eat Dog,* Hartford Stage Company, CT, 1983. PLAYS, PUBLISHED—*Father Dreams,* 1982; *Chocolate Cake,* 1982; *Buddies,* 1983; *Little Bird,* 1984; *Dog Eat Dog,* 1984.

BOOKS—*Spend It Foolishly* (novel), 1978; *Quicksilver* (novel), 1982. STORIES—''The Sublet,'' *Cosmopolitan,* July 1975; ''Leaving the City,'' *Cosmopolitan,* July 1976; ''Let Me Buy You Lunch,'' *Cosmopolitan,* November 1978; ''The Midget Bride,'' *Redbook,* March 1980.

AWARDS: Guggenheim Fellowship, 1983; Heideman Award, Best One-Act Play of Festival, Actors Theatre of Louisville, 1981: *Chocolate Cake;* Alaska State Council on the Arts Grant to direct *The Radio Show* in Sitka, AK; National Endowment for the Humanities/University of Wisconsin Grant, 1978: *Father Dreams;* Production and Residency Grant, Office for Advanced Drama Research, 1976: *Fly Away Home.*

SIDELIGHTS: MEMBERSHIPS—Dramatists Guild, Writers Guild of America, New Dramatists, AEA, SAG, Ensemble Studio Theatre.

''I began work in the theatre as an actress in 1969, I began writing stories in 1970 and novels in 1971. I first directed a play in 1970 and wrote my first play in 1970, a one-act called *Trees.* Since 1978, I have been writing only, mostly plays.''

ADDRESS: Agent—Mary Harden, Bret Adams, Ltd., 448 W. 44th Street, New York, NY 10036.

* * *

GALLOWAY, Jane, actress

PERSONAL: Born February 27, 1950, in St. Louis, MO; daughter of Edward Miller (a singer/radio director/salesmen) and Marjorie Jane (a singer; maiden name, Stormont) Galloway. EDUCATION: Webster College, St. Louis, MO (three years of theater arts studies); studied with Uta Hagen and Anna Sokolow. NON-THEATRICAL CAREER: Taught music and theater to preschool children (1972–76).

CAREER: DEBUT—*Not Enough Rope,* New Kensington High School, 1966. NEW YORK DEBUT—Kathy, *Vanities,* Chelsea Westside Theater. PRINCIPAL STAGE APPEARANCES—Florabelle Fly, *Little Johnny Jones,* Alvin, New York, 1982; Ronnie, *Domino Courts/Comanche Cafe,* American Place Theatre, New York; Amy, *Company,* Playwrights Horizons, New York; *Music Hall Sidelights,* Lion Theatre Co., New York; Martine, *A Doctor in Spite of Himself,* Lion Theatre Co.; The Dybbuk, *Shekina,* La Mama E.T.C., New York; Mary, *Kitty Hawk,* Lion Theatre Co.; Iris, *The Tempest,*

Lion Theatre Co.; Chick, *Crimes of the Heart,* Center Stage, New York; Susie, *Jitters,* Longwharf Theatre; *Night Riders,* Berkshire Theatre Festival; Karen, *Laughing on the Outside,* Greeley St. Theatre. Children's Theater—City Center Young People's Theater, City Center, New York; Guest Artist, Brighton Festival, Brighton, Eng. MAJOR TOURS—Florabelle Fly, *Little Johnny Jones,* Los Angeles, Denver, Seattle, Chicago, Dallas, Washington, DC, Detroit, Boston, New York, May 1981–March 1982.

TELEVISION APPEARANCES—Florabelle Fly, *Little Johnny Jones; The Dain Curse;* Jane Robbins, *As the World Turns.*

SIDELIGHTS: MEMBERSHIPS—Actors Equity Association, SAG, AFTRA.

ADDRESS: Agent—c/o Don Buchwald & Associates, 10 E. 44th Street, New York, NY 10017.

* * *

GAM, Rita, actress, writer

PERSONAL: Born April 2, 1928; daughter of Milton and Belle (Fately) Mackey; married Sidney Lumet (a director), 1949 (divorced 1954); married Thomas Guinzburg (a publisher) 1955 (divorced 1964); children: (second marriage) Kate, Michael. EDUCATION: Ethical Culture—Fieldston; Columbia University; studied for the theatre with Harold Clurman and Lee Strasberg at the Actor's Studio. POLITICS: Democrat.

CAREER: NEW YORK DEBUT—*A Flag Is Born,* 1946. PRINCIPAL STAGE APPEARANCES—*The Insect Comedy,* NY; *The Young and the Fair,* NY; *Temporary Island,* NY; *Montserrat,* NY, 1949; *There's a Girl in My Soup,* NY, 1967; Masha, *The Three Sisters,* Minnesota Theatre Company; *The Sea Gull,* Syracuse Stage, NY; Elise, *The Miser,* Minnesota Theatre Company; *The Apple Cart,* Actors Studio, NY; *The Importance of Being Earnest,* Fort Lee, NJ; *The Taming of the Shrew,* Nantucket, MA; *Macbeth,* Straight Wharf Theatre, Nantucket, MA; *Anthony and Cleopatra,* Memphis, TN; *Camino Real,* Seattle Repertory, Seattle, WA; *Idiot's Delight,* Actor's Studio, Los Angeles; *Born Yesterday,* Fort Lee, NJ; *Will Success Spoil Rock Hunter?,* Fort Lee, NJ; *The Marriage-Go-Round,* Stockbridge, MA; Kate & Ann, *Old Times,* L.A. Actors Theatre, Los Angeles; Gertrude, *Hamlet,* The Old Globe. MAJOR TOURS—*Suddenly, Last Summer, I Am a Camera,* New York State Repertory Co., South America; Gillian, *Bell, Book and Candle,* Southern U.S.

FILM DEBUT—*The Thief,* 1952. FILM APPEARANCES—*Saadia,* 1953; *Sign of the Pagan,* 1954; *Night People,* 1954; *Magic Fire,* 1955; *Mohawk,* 1956; *Atilla, the Hun,* 1958; *Hannibal,* 1960; *King of Kings,* 1961; *Costa Azzura; No Exit; Law and Disorder; Klute,* 1971; *Shootout,* 1971; *Such Good Friends,* 1971; wrote and produced, *Woman to Woman* (Israeli Film).

TELEVISION APPEARANCES—*Romance Theatre,* 1949; *A Family Affair; Mannix; Voyage to the Bottom of the Sea; McMillan and Wife; The Jackie Gleason Show; Heroes of the Bible; The Rockford Files; Hidden Faces; Love of Life; The Edge of Night; Tucker's Witch; Tales of the Unexpected,*

RITA GAM

1977; Newscaster, WNEW, New York; *Uncle Vanya*, (CBC).

WRITINGS: DOCUMENTARY FILMS—*Woman to Woman*. BOOKS—*The Beautiful Woman; My Actresses*. ARTICLES—''Princess Grace: A Tribute,'' *McCalls;* ''Russia'' (and other travel pieces), *Los Angeles Herald Examiner*.

AWARDS: Berlin Silver Bear, Best Actress, *No Exit;* L.A. Dramalogue, Best Actress, *Hamlet*.

SIDELIGHTS: MEMBERSHIPS—I.F.A.; Actor's Studio; Women in Film; Academy of Motion Picture Arts and Sciences.

ADDRESS: Agent—Milton Goldman, ICM, 40 W. 57th Street, New York, 10019.

* * *

GARFIELD, Julie, actress

PERSONAL: Born in Los Angeles, CA; daughter of John Garfield (an actor) and Roberta Garfield Cohn. EDUCATION: University of Wisconsin; trained for the stage at the Neighborhood Playhouse and studied with Sanford Meisner.

CAREER: NEW YORK DEBUT—Sonya, *Uncle Vanya*, Roundabout, 1971, 40 performances. PRINCIPAL STAGE APPEARANCES—*Love for Love*, Neighborhood Playhouse, New York. *The Good Doctor*, Eugene O'Neill, New York; *Death of a Salesman*, Circle in the Square, New York; *Poor*

JULIE GARFIELD

Murderer, Shubert, New York; *The Merchant*, Kennedy Center, Washington, and Plymouth Theatre, New York; *The Chekhov Sketchbook*, Harold Clurman Theatre, New York; Molly Goldberg, *Me and Molly*, Jewish Repertory Theatre, New York; *The Sea*, Manhattan Theater Club, New York; *The Voice of the Turtle*, Manhattan Theater Club, New York; *East Lynne*, Manhattan Theatre Club, New York; *The Honest-to-God Schnozzola; The Modern Ladies of Guanabacoa*, Ensemble Studio Theatre, New York; *Rosario and the Gypsies*, New York; *Coming of Age*, Indiana Repertory; *The Workroom*, Milwaukee Repertory.

FILM DEBUT—*The Hospital*. PRINCIPAL FILMS—*Goodbye, Columbus; Love Story; John and Mary; The Front; King of the Gypsies*. TELEVISION DEBUT—Mrs. Cooper, *Edge of Night*. TELEVISION APPEARANCES—*Kojak; Family Reunion; The Nativity; Your Place or Mine; Psychodrama; Plaza Suite*.

AWARDS: Theater World Award and Variety Drama Critics Award, 1970–71: *Uncle Vanya*.

SIDELIGHTS: MEMBERSHIPS—The Actors Studio; Ensemble Studio Theatre.

''My work in regional theaters has been most important to my development as an actress.''

ADDRESS: Agent—c/o Bob Barry, The Barry Agency, 165 W. 46th Street, New York, NY 10036.

GARLAND, Beverly (nee Beverly Fessenden), actress

PERSONAL: Born October 17, in Santa Cruz, CA; daughter of James Atkins (a salesman and singer) and Amelia Rose (a housewife/business woman; maiden name, Scherer) Fessenden; married Bob Campbell (divorced); married Richard Garland, 1952 (an actor, divorced, 1956); married Fillmore Paseau Crank (a land developer) on May 23, 1960; children: (third marriage) a daughter, Carrington Kendall and son, James, (third marriage) step-daughter, Cathy and step-son Fill Jr. EDUCATION: Attended public schools in Phoenix, AZ, and Glendale, CA; studied voice with Anita Arliss, apprenticed with professional stock company, Laguna Beach, CA. NON-THEATRICAL CAREER: Worked as a waitress, office nurse, an I. Magnin's model, elevator operator, mailgirl for a mortuary; Hotel Owner/Developer, with husband Fillmore, Beverly Garland's Howard Johnson Resort Lodge, North Hollywood, CA, The Beverly Garland Motor Lodge in Sacramento, CA.

CAREER: DEBUT—Acted with a professional stock company in Tustin, CA, 1949. PRINCIPAL STAGE APPEARANCES—*The Dark of the Moon*, Player's Ring Theatre, Hollywood, CA; MAJOR TOUR—*Happy Birthday.*

FILM DEBUT—*D.O.A.*, with Edmond O'Brien, 1950. PRINCIPAL FILM APPEARANCES—*It's My Turn; Roller Boogie; Sixth and Main; Where the Red Fern Grows; Airport 1975; The Mad Room; Pretty Poison; Twice Told Tales; Stark Fear; The Alligator People; The Sage of Hemp Brown; Chicago Confidential; The Joker Is Wild; Badlands of Montana; Naked Paradise; Not of This Earth; Gunslinger; The Steel Jungle; Curucu, Beast of the Amazon; It Conquered the World; New Orleans Uncensored; Swamp Women; Sudden Danger; The Desperado; The Desperate House; Bitter Creek; The Maimi Story; The Go-Getter; Two Guns and a Badge; The Rocket Man; Killer Leopard; The Glass Web; The Neanderthal Man; Problem Girls; Fearless Fagan; Strictly Dishonorable; A Life of Her Own.*

TELEVISION DEBUT—Acting out songs in pantomime, *Al Jarvis Show.* PRINCIPAL TELEVISION APPEARANCES—Pregnant leukemia victim, *Medic—White Is The Color*, 1954; Fred McMurray's wife, *My Three Sons; Scarecrow and Mrs. King; The Bing Crosby Show; Stump the Stars;* Casey Jones, *Decoy;* Daughter, *Mama Rosa;* GUEST APPEARANCES—*Remington Steele; Magnum P.I.; Matt Houston; Trapper John M.D.; Hart to Hart; The Young and the Restless; Flamingo Road; Charlie's Angels; How the West Was Won; The Six Million Dollar Man; The Mary Tyler Moore Show; Marcus Welby, M.D.; Kung Fu; Ironsides; The Rookies; Love American Style; The Mod Squad; Cannon; Gunsmoke; The Wild Wild West; Mary Hartman, Mary Hartman; Mannix; Insight; Then Came Bronson; Laredo; The Nurses; Going My Way; Dr. Kildare; Wanted Dead or Alive; Riverboat; Perry Mason; Twilight Zone; Walt Disney's World; Trackdown; Rawhide; Playhouse 90; Bell Telephone Hour; Lux Video Theatre; Climax; Science Fiction Theatre; The Millionaire; Zane Grey Theatre; Four Star Playhouse; The Lone Ranger; O. Henry Playhouse; The Hollywood Palace; The Tonight Show; The Merv Griffin Show; The Match Game; Truth or Consequences; The Newlywed Show;* and many more.

AWARDS: Emmy nomination, *Medic;* Angel of Distinction Award, Los Angeles Central Civic Center; Torch Award,

City of Hope; Star placed on the Walk of Fame, Hollywood Boulevard, Hollywood Chamber Commerce; Honorary Mayor of North Hollywood for the past nine years.

SIDELIGHTS: MEMBERSHIPS—Spokeswoman for Citizens for Decency (an anti-pornography organization); Director and Corporate Secretary of the Greater Los Angeles Visitors and Convention Bureau; Actors and Others for Animals; Spokeswoman for Children's Village, U.S.A.; YMCA Support Programs; National Tour Association; Howard Johnson National Operators Council. "Upon graduating from high school, Miss Garland's initial idea was to become a nurse. She even went so far as to send in her tuition fee to Stephens College in Columbus, Missouri—yet, she wavered. Her mother finally brought the truth out of her—the acting profession was what Beverly really wanted to try her hand at. While acting in a stock company in Tustin, California, in 1949, agent Ray Cooper noticed her and was sufficiently impressed with her work to sign her up. Shortly thereafter Beverly made her motion picture debut in *D.O.A.* with Edmond O'Brien. In 1954, her performance in the initial epidsode of *Medic* on television gave her career a big push forward with an Emmy nomination, scores of television shows and dozens of movies followed. Thus far, she has starred in 46 motion pictures and literally hundreds of television programs. Her hobbies include flower beading and crewel work. She is also an excellent cook and a self-taught interior decorator."

ADDRESS: Agent—Dick Berman, T.N.I. 638 Wilshire Blvd., Los Angeles, CA.

* * *

GARLAND, Geoff (ne William Henry Beesley), actor, director, and writer

PERSONAL: First name sounds like "Jeff"; born June 10, 1926 in Warrington, England; son of Major Percy Robert, MBE (career officer, British Army) and Jenny Maud (Towler) Beesley.

EDUCATION: Attended schools on army bases and Liverpool public schools; trained for the stage at Questor's Theatre, London, 1948–52. POLITICS: Liberal. MILITARY: Royal Air Force, 1943; British Army, 1944–48.

CAREER: DEBUT—Micky, *Pick Up Girl*, Opera House, St. Helens, England, 1952. NEW YORK DEBUT—Leslie, *The Hostage*, One Sheridan Square, 1961, over 400 performances. LONDON DEBUT—Voice of Hans, *Hans the Bellringer* (puppet show), Lyric Hammersmith, 1952. PRINCIPAL STAGE APPEARANCES—(New York)—Lucianus, *Hamlet;* Mickey, *A Touch of the Poet;* Henry Gow, *Tonight at Eight Thirty;* Dr. Purgon, *The Imaginary Invalid;* Earl Williams, *The Front Page;* Capucine, *Cyrano* (musical); Drinkwater, *Captain Brassbound's Conversion;* Henry, *My Fat Friend;* Sid Prince, *Sherlock Holmes;* Truckle, *Sly Fox;* Two of Spades, *Alice in Wonderland;* Poet, *Timon of Athens;* Estragon, *Waiting for Godot;* Billy, *Billy Liar;* Father Farley, *Mass Appeal.* REGIONAL THEATRE—*A Christmas Carol; Cyrno de Bergerac; The Taming of the Shrew; Saint Joan; Macbeth; A Man for All Seasons; The Lion in Winter; Too Much John-*

GEOFF GARLAND

son. MAJOR TOURS—*A Comedy of Errors; She Stoops to Conquer; John Brown's Body; The Boy Friend; Beyond the Fringe; Time of the Barracudas; See How They Run; Dracula.*

FILM DEBUT—*A King in New York,* 1958. PRINCIPAL FILMS—Mr. Robinson, *The Killing of Sister George,* 1968; *The Prince and the Showgirl; House of Secrets; Teddy Boy.* TELEVISION DEBUT—Bartender, *Sixpenny Corner* (BBC). TELEVISION APPEARANCES—Bob Cratchit, *A Christmas Carol;* Frankie, *Love of Life;* Jock, *The Old Lady Shows Her Medals; A Parable for Fools; The Joey.*

DIRECTED: Plays—*The Hostage,* Cincinnati Playhouse.

WRITINGS: PLAYS, PUBLISHED—*Home on the Range.*

AWARDS: Obie, 1962: *The Hostage;* New York Drama Desk (Vernon Rice Award), 1962: *The Hostage;* 39/45 medal and SEDC medal for service with the Royal Artillery.

SIDELIGHTS: MEMBERSHIPS—AEA, SAG, AFTRA. REC-REATION—Gardening, photography, home movies. FAVORITE PARTS—Leslie, *The Hostage;* Truckle, *Sly Fox;* Sid Prince, *Sherlock Holmes;* Tony, *She Stoops to Conquer;* Henry Fow, *Tonight at Eight Thirty.*

"As an 'army brat,' I have traveled and served all over the Middle and Far East."

ADDRESS: Home—340 W. 11th Street, New York, NY 10014.

GARNETT, Gale (ne Galina), actress and writer

PERSONAL: Born July 23, in Auckland, New Zealand; daughter of Nicholas Phillip and Luba (Seranova) Garnett. EDUCATION: Attended public schools through grade 10. POLITICS: Mixed economy—left. RELIGION: Christian-born pantheist.

CAREER: DEBUT—*This Property Is Condemned,* One Ring Stage, London, 1959. NEW YORK DEBUT—Jacqueline, *Jack,* 1962. PRINCIPAL STAGE APPEARANCES—*Hair,* Royal Alexandra, Canada, 1970; *Effect of Gamma Rays,* St. Lawrence Centre Theatre, Toronto, Canada, 1971; Anne/Suzanne/Jane, *Sisters of Merry,* Theatre De Lys, NY, 1973; Kitty, *Ulysses in Nighttown,* Winter Garden, NY, 1974; Abigail, *The Crucible,* Stratford (ON) Shakespeare Festival, 1975; *Cracks,* Theatre De Lys, NY, 1976; *The Groundlings,* Los Angeles, CA, 1977; Maggie, *Teeth n' Smiles,* Folger, Washington, DC, 1977; Terry, *Lady House Blues,* Phoenix, NY, 1977; Vera, *Duck Hunting,* Arena Stage, Washington, DC, 1978; *Gale Garnett and Company,* Orpheum, NY 1979; Belle Starr, *Jesse and the Bandit Queen,* IRT Theater, NY 1980; Tran/Kim/Nurse Traumond, *Short Timers,* Theatre for the New City, NY, 1981; Josephine, *Josephine the Mouse Singer,* WPA, NY, 1981; Sarah, *My Sister's Keeper,* Hudson Guild, NY, 1981; *Gale Garnett and Company,* Toronto Theatre Festival International, Canada, 1981; Lorraine, *Goose and Tom Tom,* Public Theatre, NY, 1982; Meg, *Crimes of the Heart,* Citadel Theatre, Edmonton, Canada, 1983; Rita, *Educating Rita,* A.C.T., Seattle, WA, 1983.

FILM DEBUT—Morgan, *The Journey,* 1971. PRINCIPAL FILM APPEARANCES—Libby, *Run Stranger Run,* 1974; Kathy, *The Children,* 1979; Hilary, *Tribute,* 1980. TELEVISION DEBUT—*Hawaiian Eye,* 1961. PRINCIPAL TELEVISION APPEARANCES—*Norman Corwin Presents; Bonanza; Kojak; King of Kensington; Hangin' In.*

AWARDS: Genie (Canadian Academy Award) nomination, 1981: *Tribute;* Villager Award, Excellence in Solo Performance, 1979: *Gale Garnett and Company;* Grammy Award, Best Folk Album, 1965; Country Music Association Award: *We'll Sing in the Sunshine.*

SIDELIGHTS: MEMBERSHIPS—AEA, SAG, AFTRA, CAA, ACTRA, ASCAP, Canadian Equity Council, 1970–74, Performing Artists for Nuclear Disarmament, Actors and Artists Against Apartheid, Amnesty International.

"I love the lateral longevity of living lots of lives through creating characters. I am proud of my one-woman show because I created all the characters myself. I own it and can do it anywhere and at any time, which makes me feel slightly less at the mercy of outside forces. I think all artists (and all people) must be involved in working for a nuclear-free, just and sane world before the fools in charge get us all killed!"

ADDRESS: Agent—c/o J. Michael Bloom, 400 Madison Avenue, New York, NY 10021.

* * *

GARRETT, Joy, actress

PERSONAL: Daughter of Clarence Alford (a building contractor) and Kathleen (a building contractor; maiden name, Davis) Garrett. EDUCATION: Texas Wesleyan College, B.A., 1967; American Academy of Dramatic Arts, New York, 1969; postgraduate work in theatre at California State; studied theatre with Jim Gregory.

CAREER: DEBUT—Janie, *Wildcat,* Casa Manana, Fort Worth, TX, 1963. NEW YORK DEBUT—Joy, *Gertrude Stein's First Reader,* Astor Place Theatre, 1969. PRINCIPAL STAGE APPEARANCES—Betty Rizzo, *Grease;* the hooker, *Inner City;* Connie, *The Candy Apple;* Marie Claire, *Silver Queen;* Agnes, *The Drunkard;* Review, *One for the Money;* *24-Hours—An Evening of One-Act Plays;* Adelaide, *Guys and Dolls;* Nancy, *Oliver!;* Christine, *Room Service;* Elaine, *Arsenic and Old Lace;* Sybil, *Private Lives;* Daisy Gamble, *On a Clear Day You Can See Forever;* Sugar, *Sugar;* Julie, *Showboat.* MAJOR TOURS—Mary Magdalen, *Jesus Christ, Superstar,* eastern tour (Boston, Chicago, etc.), 1976.

FILM DEBUT—Donna, *Who,* 1976. TELEVISION DEBUT—*Callie and Son,* 1981. TELEVISION APPEARANCES—*The Young and the Restless; Three's Company; Too Close for Comfort; Cassie and Co.; Sanford; Benson; The Incredible Hulk; The Stockard Channing Show; 13 Queens Boulevard; The Dukes of Hazzard; Baby Brokers; Steve Martin Special; Operation Petticoat; Quincy; Charlie's Angels; Having Babies; Ball Four; General Hospital; Hotline; Alice; The Hoyt Axton Show.*

SIDELIGHTS: MEMBERSHIPS—Actors Equity Association, AFTRA, SAG, Fund for Animals. RECREATION—Making stained-glass windows, roller skating, watching Dallas Cowboys football games.

"I am deeply involved in saving animals from laboratory experimentation. Also, I love to play the harp. I just purchased the harp that Harpo Marx played on the *I Love Lucy* show."

ADDRESS: Agent—c/o Gage Group, 9229 Sunset Blvd., Suite 306, Los Angeles, CA 90069.

* * *

GARSON, Barbara, playwright

PERSONAL: Born July 7, 1941, in New York City; daughter of Harry (an office manager) and Frances (a bookkeeper) Kilstein; children: Juliet Garson. EDUCATION: University of California, Berkeley, B.A. (Classical History).

WRITINGS: PLAYS, PRODUCED—*MacBird,* Village Gate, NY, 1967; *The Co-op* (*Going Co-op;* with Fred Gardner), Theatre for the New City, NY, 1972; *A Winner's Tale,* Village Gate, 1974; *Dinosaur Door,* Theatre for the New City, 1976; *The Department,* Theatre for the New City, 1983. PLAYS, PUBLISHED—*MacBird,* 1967.

BOOKS—*All the Livelong Day,* 1975. Over 150 magazine articles, stories, reviews.

AWARDS: Obie, *The Dinosaur Door,* 1977; Guggenheim Fellowship, 1977; NEA Fellowship, 1977; ABC Writings for Cameras Grant, the New School, 1967.

ADDRESS: 463 West Street, New York, NY 10014.

* * *

GASPARD, Raymond L., actor, producer, writer

PERSONAL: Born July 9, 1949, in Chicago, IL; son of Joseph Henry (a postal worker) and Charlie Etta (a registered nurse; maiden name, Taylor) Gaspard; children: Charlotte. EDUCATION: Columbia University.

CAREER: FIRST STAGE WORK—Producer, *We Won't Pay, We Won't Pay,* Chelsea Westside, NY, 1980. PRINCIPAL STAGE WORK—Producer, *I Can't Keep Running in Place,* Westside Arts, NY, for 233 performances, 1981; associate producer, *Woza Albert,* Criterion, London, England, for 214 performances, 1983; co-producer, *Woza Albert,* Empty Space Theatre, Seattle, WA, Annenberg Center, Philadelphia, PA. Producer-Director, Westside Arts Theatre, NY, 1980–present.

SIDELIGHTS: MEMBERSHIPS—Off-Broadway League.

ADDRESS: Home—77 Hudson Avenue, Brooklyn, NY 11201. Office—Westside Arts Theatre, 407 W. 43rd Street, New York, NY 10036.

* * *

GAZZO, Michael V(incente), actor, director, playwright

PERSONAL: Born April 5, 1923, in Hillside, NJ; son of Michael B. (a bartender) and Elvira (Lunga) Gazzo; married Grace Benn, July 8, 1944; children: Peppi, Michael, Christopher. EDUCATION: Attended New Jersey public schools; studied at Dramatic Workshop, New School for Social Research; trained for the stage at the Actors Studio, New York. MILITARY: U.S. Army Air Force, 1942–44.

CAREER: PRINCIPAL STAGE APPEARANCES—Tripe Face, *The Aristocrats,* President Theatre, New York, 1946; Dr. Einstein, *Arsenic and Old Lace,* Great Neck Playhouse, NY, 1946; dramatic workshop productions, 1946–49: Ben Hubbard, *The Little Foxes,* Shields, *The Shadow of a Gunman,* Captain Boyle, *Juno and the Paycock, The Petrified Forest, The Trial;* Destructive Desmond, *The Dog Beneath the Skin,* Cherry Lane, 1947; Beggar, *Night Music,* ANTA, New York, 1951; A. Ratt, *Camino Real,* National Theatre, 1953.

PRINCIPAL FILMS—*On the Waterfront,* 1954; *The Pride and the Passion,* 1957; *Godfather II,* 1975; *Black Sunday; Fingers; Love and Bullets; King of the Gypsies; The Fish That Saved Pittsburgh; Blood Barrier; Cuba Crossing; Alligator; Backroads; Hoodlums; Body and Soul; Fear City; Sudden Impact; Cannonball Run II.* TELEVISION DEBUT—Russian Officer, *Philco Television Playhouse,* 1950. TELEVISION APPEARANCES—*The Clock; Crime Syndicated; Goodyear Television Playhouse; Danger; Casey; Crime Photographer; Robert Montgomery Lucky Strike Theatre; Celebrity Time; Suspense; Assignment Manhunt; The Defenders; Kojak; Ellery Queen; Medical Center; Crime of the Century; Baretta; Alice; Welcome Back Kotter; Switch; Starsky and Hutch; Future Cop; Feather and Father Gang; Serpico; Columbo;*

Barnaby Jones; Sweepstakes; Supertrain; Bad Cats; Beggerman Thief; Vegas; Beach Patrol; Fantasy Island; Taxi; Magnum P.I.; Dark Room; The Fall Guy; Cagney and Lacey; Small and Frye; Quest; Brinks: Crime of the Century; Sizzle; Blood Feud.

DIRECTED: Plays—*Androcles and the Lion,* Great Neck Playhouse, NY, 1946; *Alfred* (associate director), Great Neck Playhouse, NY, 1946; *The Imbecile,* Dramatic Workshop production, late 1940s; On Stage production of *Dog Beneath the Skin* (associate director with Alexis Solomas); *Within the Gates,* Provincetown Playhouse, 1947; *Yes Is for a Very Young Man,* for Off-Broadway, Inc., New York, 1949.

THEATRE-RELATED CAREER: Began teaching acting privately in 1950, in addition to teaching classes at Studio Six, the Actor's Cine Lab, and the Dramatic Workshop of the New School for Social Research. Formerly conducted an actors, directors, and writers workshop in New York (1972–75), and continues to conduct the Gazzo Theatre Workshop in Westwood, CT.

WRITINGS: PLAYS, PUBLISHED—*A Hatful of Rain,* 1955; *Night Circus,* 1958. FILMS—*A Hatful of Rain,* 1957; *King Creole,* 1958; *The World of Johnny Cool,* 1964.

AWARDS: Tied with Paddy Chayefsky as Promising Playwright of 1955–56: *A Hatful of Rain; A Hatful of Rain* included in Film Daily's "Filmdom's Famous Five" as one of the best screenplays of 1957; Academy Award Nomination, *Godfather II:* 1975.

SIDELIGHTS: MEMBERSHIPS—AEA, AFTRA, Dramatists Guild, SWG, SAG.

ADDRESS: Agent—c/o Charter Management, Mike Greenfield, 9000 Sunset Blvd., Los Angeles, CA 90069.

GEER, Ellen, actress, director, producer, and writer

PERSONAL: Born August 29, 1941, in New York City; daughter of Will Auge (an actor and horticulturist) and Herta (an actress; maiden name Ware) Geer; children: Ian, Megan, Willow. EDUCATION: Attended public schools; trained for the stage at the American Shakespeare Academy, New York; studied acting with John Houseman, Morris Charnovsky, Phoebe Brand, and others.

CAREER: DEBUT—First Fairy, *A Midsummer Night's Dream,* American Shakespeare Festival, 1956. NEW YORK DEBUT— Alice, *Alice in Wonderland,* 1956. PRINCIPAL STAGE APPEARANCES—Tyrone Guthrie Theatre, Minneapolis, MN, 1963–66: Joan, *Saint Joan,* Rosalinde, *As You Like It,* Laura, *The Glass Menagerie,* Irina, *Three Sisters,* Lady Anne, *Richard III,* Marianne, *The Miser,* Dunyasha, *The Cherry Orchard,* Mrs. Fainall, *Way of the World,* Gladys, *The Skin of Our Teeth;* American Conservatory Theatre, San Francisco, CA, 1967–69: Nina, *The Seagull,* Masha, *Long Live Life,* Julia, *A Delicate Balance,* Kitty, *Charley's Aunt,* Viola, *Twelfth Night,* Elaine, *Arsenic and Old Lace,* Emily, *Our Town,* Minnie Faye, *The Matchmaker;* Association of Producing Artists (APA), New York, 1959–63: Maria, *School for Scandal,* Nina, *The Seagull,* First Fairy, *A Mid-*

ELLEN GEER

summer Night's Dream, Gertrude, *Fashion,* Jessica, *Merchant of Venice,* Queen, *Richard II;* Old Globe Shakespeare Festival, 1961: Desdemona, *Othello,* Lady Percy, *Henry IV,* 1972: Imogen, *Cymbeline,* Hero, *Much Ado About Nothing,* Bianca, *The Taming of the Shrew;* The Will Geer Theatricum Botanicum, from 1973: Ariel, *The Tempest,* Hermione, *A Winter's Tale,* Lady Capulet, *Romeo and Juliet,* Titania, *A Midsummer Night's Dream,* Mistress Ford, *Merry Wives of Windsor,* Kate, *The Taming of the Shrew,* Rosalinde, *As You Like It,* Olga, *The Three Sisters,* Madame Arkadina, *The Seagull; Women and Other People,* 1976; Estelle, *Father's Day,* Mark Taper Forum, Los Angeles.

MAJOR TOURS—American Shakespeare Festival, 1958: Dorcas, *A Winter's Tale;* First Fairy, *A Midsummer Night's Dream.* DIRECTED: Plays—*Twelfth Night; Merry Wives of Windsor; The Tempest; A Midsummer Night's Dream; Romeo and Juliet; Cymbeline; As You Like It; The Taming of the Shrew; A Winter's Tale; Three Sisters; The Seagull; The Skin of Our Teeth; Lysistrata; House of Atreus; Glass Menagerie; Voices; Americana.* PRINCIPAL FILMS—*Memory of Us,* 1973; *Harold and Maude,* 1974; *On the Edge,* 1978; *On the Nickle; Something Wicked This Way Comes; The Reivers; Kotch; Abraham and Isaac; Silence; Petulia.* TELEVISION DEBUT—Daughter-in-law, *Jimmy Stewart Show,* 1971; *Quincy; Night Cries; Code Red; The Lindbergh Kidnapping; Babe Didrikson Story; A Shining Season; Heart Like a Wheel; Dark Side of Love; Dallas; Trial of Lee Harvey Oswald; Fantasy Island; The Car; Strike Force; The Waltons; Ghost Story; Name of the Game.*

WRITINGS: PLAYS, PUBLISHED—*Women and Other People* (co-writer), 1979; *Americana—The Labor Story,* 1980. FILMS—*Abraham and Isaac* (co-wrote with Kaye Dyal), 1970; *Silence* (co-writer), 1972; *Memory of Us,* 1973.

AWARDS: Atlanta Film Festival Gold Medal, 1973: *Memory of Us.*

SIDELIGHTS: Since 1973, Miss Geer has been artistic

director of the Will Geer Theatricum Botanicum, an outdoor summer theater that performs free Shakespeare on Sundays.

ADDRESS: Office—c/o Will Geer Theatricum Botanicum, P.O. Box 1222, Topanga, CA. Agent—c/o Dade/Rosen Associates, 9172 Sunset Blvd., Suite 2, Los Angeles, CA 90069.

* * *

GELB, Arthur, writer

PERSONAL: Born February 3, 1924, in New York; son of Daniel and Fanny Gelb; married Barbara Stone (a writer) on June 2, 1946; children: Michael, Peter. EDUCATION: New York University, B.A., 1946. NON-THEATRICAL CAREER— Chief cultural correspondent, *The New York Times*, 1961–63; metropolitan editor, *The New York Times*, 1967–76; deputy managing editor, *The New York Times*, 1976–present.

WRITINGS: BIOGRAPHY—*O'Neill*, with (wife) Barbara Gelb, 1962; *Bellevue Is My Home*, with Barbara Gelb, 1973. OTHER BOOKS—*One More Victim*, with A. M. Rosenthal, 1967. AS EDITOR—*The Pope's Journey to the United States*, with A. M. Rosenthal, 1965; *The Night the Lights Went Out*, 1965.

THEATRE-RELATED CAREER—Assistant drama critic (under Brooks Atkinson) *New York Times*, 1956–61; lecturer on Drama and Eugene O'Neill at institutions around the country.

SIDELIGHTS: MEMBERSHIPS—American Society of Newspaper Editors; The Century Club.

ADDRESS: c/o The New York Times, 229 W. 43rd Street, New York, NY 10036.

* * *

GELB, Barbara, writer

PERSONAL: Born in New York; daughter of Harold (a businessman) and Elza (Heifetz) Stone; married Arthur Gelb (deputy managing editor, *New York Times*) June 2, 1946; children: Michael, Peter. EDUCATION: Swarthmore College, 1946.

CAREER: WRITINGS: BIOGRAPHY—*O'Neill*, with (husband) Arthur Gelb, 1962; BOOKS—*So Short a Time: A Biography of John Reed and Louise Bryant*, 1973; *Bellevue Is My Home*, with Arthur Gelb, 1973; *On The Tracks of Murder*, 1975; *Varnished Brass: The Decade after Serpico*, 1983.

SIDELIGHTS: MEMBERSHIPS—PEN; American Society of Historians; Co-chairman, Theatre Committee for Eugene O'Neill.

ADDRESS: Agent—Robert Lantz, The Lantz Office, 888 Seventh Avenue, New York, NY 10106.

GELBART, Larry, writer, producer

PERSONAL: Born February 25, 1923, in Chicago, IL; son of Harry and Frieda Gelbart; married Pat Marshall (an actress and singer), November 25, 1956; children: Cathy, Gary, Paul, Adam, Becky. EDUCATION: Attended Chicago and Los Angeles public schools. MILITARY: U.S. Army, 1945–46.

WRITINGS: RADIO—*Duffy's Tavern*, 1945–48; *Jack Parr Show*, 1947; *Jack Carson*, 1947–48; *Bob Hope Show*, 1947–51. PLAYS, PRODUCED—*My L.A.*, 1950; *The Conquering Hero*, 1960; *A Funny Thing Happened on the Way to the Forum*, 1961; *Jump*, London, 1972; *Sly Fox*, 1976. SCREENPLAYS—*The Notorious Landlady*, 1962; *The Wrong Box* (also producer), 1966; *Not with My Wife, You Don't*, 1966; *Little Me*, 1968; *The Ecstacy Business*, 1968; *Sly Fox*, 1976; *Oh, God*, 1977; *Movie, Movie*, 1979; *Tootsie* (with Murray Schisgal), 1982; *Rio* (with Charlie Peters), 1983. TELEVISION—*Bob Hope*, 1949–51; *Red Buttons*, 1951–52; *Sid Caesar*, 1953–55; *Art Carney*, 1960; *M*A*S*H* (also producer), 1972; *Karen* (also producer), 1975; *AfterM*A*S*H* (also producer), 1983–present. BOOKS—*The Conquering Hero*, 1961.

AWARDS: Academy Award Nomination, Best Screenplay, 1983: *Tootsie;* Emmy Awards, 1974, 1960; Writers Guild Awards, 1974, 1972; Antoinette Perry Award, 1962: *A Funny Thing Happened on the Way to the Forum;* Sylvania, 1960.

SIDELIGHTS: MEMBERSHIPS—Dramatists Guild, Writers Guild of America, ASCAP, Writers Guild of Great Britain, Directors Guild of America.

ADDRESS: Agent—Howard Rothberg, 9255 Sunset Blvd., Suite 609, Los Angeles, CA 90069.*

* * *

GELLER, Marc, actor

PERSONAL: Born July 5, 1959 in Providence, RI; son of Jerome A. (a businessman) and Gertrude R. (Fasulo) Geller.

CAREER: NEW YORK DEBUT—Don Baker, *Butterflies Are Free*, Wonderhorse, 1980. PRINCIPAL STAGE APPEARANCES— Young Man, *Summertree*, Vandam, NY, 1980; Stacy Colt, *The Street in the Kid*, Theatre 22, NY, 1981; John Leeds, *The Wager*, Cubiculo, NY, 1983.

PRINCIPAL FILM APPEARANCES—*The UFO Follower; Stardust Memories*, 1980.

SIDELIGHTS: MEMBERSHIPS—AEA; AFTRA; SAG.

* * *

GERBER, Ella, director, actress, playwright, teacher

PERSONAL: Born August 25, 1916, in New York, NY; daughter of Isadore (a linguist) and Esther (a seamstress; maiden name, Treisman) Gerber; married Sam Kasakoff (an actor and photographer) May 29, 1943. EDUCATION: Studied directing and acting in New York City with Lee Strasberg, Sanford Meisner, Morris Carnovsky, Lewis Leverett, Mary Virginia Farmer, Margaret Barker, Benno Schneider, 1934–38; received a scholarship to study with Michael Chekhov 1942; directing classes at Columbia University, 1943; acting classes at American Theatre Wing, 1948; special studies at the Shakespeare Institute, University of Birmingham, Stratford-upon-Avon, England, 1955; International Theatre Research Tour studying theatre productions and techniques in Russia, Poland, Czechoslovakia, Austria, France, Germany, and England, 1956; member of the Robert Lewis Theatre Workshop and the director's unit of Actors Studio, NY, 1960–61; Television and Film Workshop, New York University, 1963; Directors and Playwrights Workshop, Actors Studio, NY 1975–76; Robert Lewis's Westchester Laboratory Theatre, NY, 1977; College at Sixty Fordham University, 1979–80. MILITARY: Served as a civilian actress-technician with the U.S. Army Special Services, 1945–47.

CAREER: DEBUT—appeared in Off-Broadway productions with the Knickerbocker Players, Playmart, Davenport Theatre, Theatre Collective, 1933–36. PRINCIPAL STAGE APPEARANCES—Appeared in *Just Married, Up Pops the Devil, Hardy Family,* and *The Ferguson Family,* Lippitt Players, Cumberland Hills, RI, 1936; lead, *Pins and Needles,* Labor Stage Theatre, NY, and U.S. and Canadian tour, 1938–41; Marguerite, *The End of the World,* Geary, San Francisco, CA, 1945; Mother, *Psalm for Fat Tuesdays,* New Dramatists, NY, 1957; Emily, *Inside Emily Payne,* Erie Playhouse, Erie, PA, 1959; Yvonne, *The Laundry,* Gate, NY, 1962.

MAJOR TOURS—*Theatre Brief* (collection of scenes), *Michael and Mary, Winterset, Private Lives, Dead End, Idiot's Delight, Our Town, Craig's Wife,* New York, Chicago and Hollywood, 1941; *Lunch Hour Follies,* American Theatre Wing tour to war plants in the East, 1943; Violet, *My Sister Eileen,* U.S. Army Special Services tour, Japan, 1946; Martha, *Dear Ruth,* U.S.O. tour, Korea, 1946; Laura, *The Glass Menagerie,* U.S. Army Special Services tour, University of Hawaii, Honolulu, Hawaii, 1946; Julia, *Goodbye Again,* U.S. Army Special Services tour, Japan, 1947.

PRINCIPAL FILM APPEARANCES—*Barabbas,* 1961; *Beat Street,* 1984. PRINCIPAL TELEVISION APPEARANCES—*Divorce Court,* 1969.

PRINCIPAL STAGE WORK, DIRECTOR—Productions at Los Angeles Community Centers, Actors Community Theatre, Hollywood, CA, and for U.S. Army Special Servies production of the *Lunch Hour Follies,* 1943–45; *Blind Alley,* Hollywood, CA, 1945; *Goodbye Again, Room Service, Dear Ruth, My Sister Eileen,* U.S. Army Special Services, Hawaii, Japan, Korea, 1946–47; stock productions at Fairhaven, MA, 1949; *Dark of the Moon,* Equity Library Theatre, NY, 1949; *My Sister Eileen, Summer and Smoke,* La Petite Théâtre du Vieux Carré, New Orleans, LA, 1950; stock productions, Watkins Glen, NY, 1950; *Homecoming,* Theatre 108, NY, 1950; *Primrose Path,* Equity Library Theatre, NY, 1950; *Design for a Stained Glass Window,* Wilbur Theatre, Boston, MA, Brooks Atkinson, NY, 1950; *Dark of the Moon, The Glass Menagerie,* Youngstown Playhouse, Youngstown, OH, 1951; stock productions at Corning Summer Theatre, Corning, NY, 1951; *All God's Chillun Got*

Wings, O Distant Land, Equity Library Theatre, NY, Lenox Hill Playhouse, NY, 1952; *Porgy and Bess,* Ziegfeld Theatre and international tour, 1952–55; stock productions at Lakewood Summer Playhouse, Barnesville, PA, 1956; *The Reluctant Debutante, Rain, Janus, Picnic, Anniversary Waltz,* Peabody Summer Theatre, Daytona Beach, FL, 1957; *Candida, Harvey, Ah! Wilderness, They Came to a City,* American Academy of Dramatic Arts, NY, 1958; *Flight into Egypt, Dial M for Murder,* Equity Library Theatre, 1958; *Showboat,* Oakdale Music Theatre, Wallingford, CT, 1958; *Oh Captain,* Oakdale Music Theatre, Warwick Music Theatre, RI, 1958; *Porgy and Bess,* Musicarnival, Cleveland, OH, 1958; *Porgy and Bess,* Warwick Music Theatre, RI, Oakdale Music Theatre, CT, Carousel Theatre, Framingham, MA, Music Fair, Toronto, Ontario, Canada, Melody Fair, Buffalo, NY, Westbury Music Fair, Westbury, LI, Camden County Music Fair, Haddonfield, NJ, Valley Forge Music Fair, Devon, PA, Civic Light Opera Co., Pittsburgh, PA, 1958; *Most Happy Fella,* Carousel, MA, 1959; stock productions at Oakdale Music, Warwick Music, Colonie Music, RI, CT, NY, 1959; *Dark of the Moon,* Acorn Civic, Miami Beach, FL, 1960; *Look Homeward, Angel,* Youngstown Playhouse, OH, 1960; *Blue Island,* New Dramatists, NY, 1960; stock productions at Oakdale Music, CT, and Warwick Music, RI, 1960; *Skylark,* Drury Lane, Chicago, IL, 1961;

Dark of the Moon, Teatro dei Servi, Rome, Italy, 1961; *Tiger Rag,* Cherry Lane, NY, 1961; *Come Blow Your Horn,* Golonka Gladiators Arena, Totowa, NJ, 1962; *Gypsy,* East Coast tour, 1962; *Come Blow Your Horn,* Coconut Grove Playhouse, Miami, FL, 1962; *Guys and Dolls,* Gladiators Arena, Totowa, NJ, 1963; *Kiss Me Kate,* East Coast tour, 1963; *Porgy and Bess,* St. Louis Municipal Opera, MO, Starlight Opera, Kansas City, MO, 1964; *Clowns, The Desperate Hours,* Youngstown Playhouse, OH, 1964; *Gypsy,* Coconut Grove Playhouse, Miami, FL, 1965–66; *Porgy and Bess,* International tour and U.S. tour, 1965–66; *Clearing in the Woods,* American Academy of Dramatic Arts, NY, 1966; *Camelot,* East Coast tour, 1966; *Porgy and Bess,* Habimah National, Tel Aviv, Israel and tour throughout country, 1966; *The Little Foxes,* American Academy of Dramatic Arts, 1967; *Porgy and Bess,* U.S. college tour and Canadian tour, 1967; *Holy Hang-Up,* Spencer Memorial Church, NY, 1968; *Peer Gynt,* American Musical and Dramatic Academy, 1968; *Lost in the Stars,* Equity Library Theatre, NY, 1968;

Carousel, Johannesburg Operatic and Dramatic Society, South Africa, 1968; excerpts from *The Consul, The Telephone, Porgy and Bess,* London Opera Centre, London, England, 1968; *The Miser,* Theatre Nashville, Vanderbilt University, TN, 1969; *You Can't Take It with You, See How They Run,* Youngstown Playhouse, OH, 1969; *Muzeeka, The Private Ear, Used Car for Sale, The Boor, The Man with the Flower in His Mouth, The Marriage Proposal,* an Arts/Six–Title III Project, Brookline, Waltham and Belmont, MA, 1969; *Hallelujah Train,* U.S. university and college tour, 1969; *Porgy and Bess,* South Carolina Tricentennial Celebration Production, Charleston, SC, 1970; *School for Wives, Summertree,* Wayside Theatre, Middletown, VA, 1971; *Porgy and Bess,* Memphis Opera Company, Casa Manana, Fort Worth TX, 1971; *Madwoman of Chaillot,* Duke University, NC, 1972; *Porgy and Bess,* Teatro Nacional de San Carlos, Lisbon, Portugal, 1973; *The Flying*

Doctor, The Marriage Proposal, The Lovers, Chinamen, South Carolina Open Road Ensemble, Columbia, SC and tour throughout SC, 1973; *Porgy and Bess,* Los Angeles Civic Light Opera Company, Los Angeles, CA, Theatre of the Stars, Atlanta, GA, 1974;

Bicycle Riders, Directors/Playwrights Workshop, Actors Studio, NY, 1975; *Porgy and Bess,* Michigan Opera Theatre, Detroit, MI, University of Michigan, Ann Arbor, MI, 1975; *Teach Me How to Cry, Charley's Aunt, The Richest Woman in Town,* American Academy of Dramatic Arts, 1976; *The Crucible,* St. Lawrence University, Canton, NY, 1976; *The Skin of Our Teeth, Gnadiges Fraulein, I Can't Imagine Tomorrow, The Unsatisfactory Supper, At Liberty,* East Carolina University, Greenville, NC, 1977; *The Children's Hour,* Harvard University, Cambridge, MA, 1978; *A Thread of Scarlet,* Encompass, NY, 1978; *The Lady from the Sea,* Hollins College, Hollins, VA, 1979; *An Evening of One Acts,* Lynn Canal Community Players, Haines, AK, 1980; *The Three Sisters,* Valley Performing Arts, Colony Theatre, Palmer, AK, 1980; *A Doll's House,* Fairbanks Drama Association, Fairbanks, AK, 1980; *Porgy and Bess,* University of Utah, Salt Lake City, 1981; adjudicator, Festival of American Community Theatres, Haines, AK, 1983.

WRITINGS: PLAYS, PRODUCED—Co-author, co-adaptor with Howard Richardson, *Thread of Scarlet,* Juneau-Douglas Little Theatre, Juneau, AK, 1977, Theatre Tulsa, OK, 1978, Encompass, NY, 1978; *Glory for Me,* Durham Theatre Guild and City Acting Company, NC, 1977.

PLAYS, UNPRODUCED—Alexandra, Idols and the Prey, Desire and Disarray.

TELEPLAYS—Aftermath of a Conviction.

THEATRE-RELATED CAREER: Lecturer: "Acting Technique," Spelman College, Atlanta, GA; "Theatre Techniques: Theory and Practice," London Opera Centre, London, England, Stage Studio, Washington, DC, Hamline University, St. Paul, MN; "Theatre in Iron Curtain Countries," Columbia University, Quota Club, Youngstown, OH, Youngstown Playhouse, OH; "The Arts in Education: Confrontation of the Arts," Smoky Mountain Cultural Arts Foundation, Western Carolina University, Cullowhee, NC; "Women in the Arts," Goucher College, Baltimore, MD; conducted acting classes for private schools, community theatres, summer camps, settlement houses, NY, ME, and PA, 1935–43; private class work, Studio of the Theatre, Hollywood, CA, 1947–48; acting/directing seminars, Acorn Civic Theatre, Miami Beach, FL, 1962; acting/directing seminars, Youngstown Playhouse, OH, 1963; faculty, American Academy of Dramatic Arts, NY, 1957–59 and 1966–67; faculty, American Musical and Dramatic Academy, NY, 1967–68; guest faculty, London Opera Centre, 1968; Arts/Six, Title III project, MA, 1969–72; acting seminars, S.C.O.R.E., South Carolina and Washington, DC, 1973; acting seminars, Waltham, MA, 1972–76; faculty, East Carolina University, Greenville, NC, 1977; acting and directing seminars, Fairbanks, Palmer, Skagway and Haines, AK, 1980; acting and directing seminars, Women-in-Theatre, NY, 1984; private acting coach, NY, and CA, presently.

AWARDS: Resident Fellowships from MacDowell Colony, Peterborough, NH, 1966 and 1967.

SIDELIGHTS: MEMBERSHIPS—AEA, AFTRA, SSD&C, Board of Directors, Foundation for the Extension and Development of American professional Theatre, 1968, Dramatists Guild.

ADDRESS: 329 E. 58th Street, New York, NY 10022.

* * *

GERROLL, Daniel, actor and director

PERSONAL: Surname rhymes with "peril"; born October 16, 1951; son of Harry (a clothing manufacturer) and Kathleen Cordelia (Norman) Gerroll. EDUCATION: Attended Nottingham University; trained for the stage at the Central School of Speech and Drama, London.

CAREER: DEBUT—*A Public Mischief,* Southwold Summer Theatre, Southwold, England, 1974. NEW YORK DEBUT—Bruno, *Marching Song,* Greenwich Theatre, 1974. PRINCIPAL STAGE APPEARANCES—Derek, *Once a Catholic,* Royal Court, London, 1977; Friend, *A Respectable Wedding,* Open Space, London, 1978; Prince of Wales, *Love of a Good Man,* Royal Court, London, 1980; Mick, *Plenty,* Public Theatre and Broadway, New York, 1983. MAJOR TOURS—Unexpected Guest, *Harrogate,* Richmond, Bath, England, 1976; *Murder with Love,* Harrogate, England and Cork, Ireland, 1977.

FILM DEBUT—Rafe, *Sir Henry at Rawlinson End,* 1979. PRINCIPAL FILMS—Henry Stallard, *Chariots of Fire,* 1980.

DANIEL GERROLL

TELEVISION DEBUT—*The Glums* (London Weekend TV), 1977. TELEVISION APPEARANCES—Walter Hartwright, *Woman in White*, 1981.

THEATRE-RELATED CAREER: Works as a dialect coach.

WRITINGS: Film criticism for *Films in Review* since 1982 (under pseudonym); feature articles for same publication under real name.

AWARDS: Theatre World Award, 1981: *The Slab Boys;* Outer Critics Circle Award, 1981: *Knuckle.*

SIDELIGHTS: MEMBERSHIPS—AEA, SAG, AFTRA.

* * *

GIELGUD, Sir John (Arthur) (CH, 1977; Kt, 1953), actor and director

PERSONAL: Born April 14, 1904, in London; son of Frank and Kate (Terry-Lewis) Gielgud. EDUCATION: Attended Westminster School; trained for the stage at the Royal Academy of Dramatic Arts and at Lady Benson's School.

CAREER: STAGE DEBUT—Herald, *Henry the Fifth,* Old Vic, London, 1921. NEW YORK DEBUT—Grand Duke Alexander, *The Patriot,* Majestic, 1928. PRINCIPAL STAGE APPEARANCES—*King Lear, Wat Tyler, Peer Gynt,* Old Vic, London, 1921; Felix, *The Insect Play,* Regent, London, 1923; Aide-de-Camp to General Lee, *Robert E. Lee,* London, 1923; Charles Wykeham, *Charley's Aunt,* Comedy, London, 1923; J.B. Fagan's Repertory, Oxford Playhouse, UK, 1924; Romeo, *Romeo and Juliet,* Regent, London, 1924; Oxford Playhouse Repertory, UK, 1924; Castalio, *The Orphan,* Aldwych, London, 1925; Nicky Lancaster, *The Vortex,* Little, London, 1925; Peter Trophimoff, *The Cherry Orchard,* Lyric, Hammersmith, UK, 1925; Konstantin Treplev, *The Sea Gull,* Little, London, 1925; Sir John Harrington, *Gloriana,* UK, 1925; Robert, *L'Ecole des Cocottes,* Princes, London, 1925; Ferdinand, *The Tempest,* Savoy, London, 1926; Baron Nikolay, *The Three Sisters,* George Stibelev, *Katerina,* Barnes, UK, 1926; Lewis Dodd, *The Constant Nymph,* New, London, 1926; Dion Anthony, *The Great God Brown,* Strand, London, 1927; Oswald, *Ghosts,* Wyndhams, London, 1928; Dr. Gerald Marlowe, *Holding Out the Apple,* Globe, London, 1928; Captain Allenby, *The Skull,* Shaftesbury, London, 1928; Felipe Rivas, *The Lady from Albuqueque,* Court, London, 1928; Alberto, *Fortunato,* Court, London, 1928; John Marstin, *Out of the Sea,* Strand, London, 1928; Fedor, *Red Rust,* Little, London, 1929; Henry Tremayne, *The Lady with a Lamp,* Garrick, London, 1929; Bronstein, *Red Sunday,* Arts, London, 1929; Romeo, *Romeo and Juliet,* Antonio, *The Merchant of Venice,* Cleante, *The Imaginary Invalid,* Richard II, *Richard II,* Oberon, *Midsummer Night's Dream,* Mark Antony, *Julius Caesar,* Emperor, *Androcles and the Lion,* Macbeth, *Macbeth,* Hamlet, *Hamlet,* Old Vic, London, 1929;

Hamlet, *Hamlet,* Queen's, London, 1930; John Worthing, *The Importance of Being Earnest,* Lyric, Hammersmith, UK, 1930; Hotspur, *Henry IV, Part I,* Prospero, *The Tempest,* Lord Trinket, *The Jealous Wife,* Antony, *Antony*

and *Cleopatra,* Old Vic, London, 1930; Malvolio, *Twelfth Night,* Sadler's Wells, UK, 1931; Sergius Saranoff, *Arms and the Man,* Benedick, *Much Ado About Nothing,* King Lear, *King Lear,* Sadler's Wells, UK, 1931; Inigo Jollifant, *The Good Companions,* His Majesty's, London, 1931; Joseph Schindler, *Musical,* Arts, London, 1931, Criterion, London, 1932; Richard II, *Richard of Bordeaux,* New, London, 1932; Roger Maitland, *The Maitlands,* Wyndham's, London, 1934; Hamlet, *Hamlet,* New, London, 1934; Noah, *Noah,* New, London, 1935; Mercutio, *Romeo and Juliet,* New, London, 1935; Romeo, *Romeo and Juliet,* New, London, 1935; Boris Trigorin, *The Seagull,* New, London, 1936; Hamlet, *Hamlet,* Empire, St. James, NY, 1936; Mason, *He Was Born Gay,* Queen's, London, 1937; King Richard, *Richard II,* Joseph Surface, *The School for Scandal,* Vershinin, *The Three Sisters,* Shylock, *The Merchant of Venice,* Queen's, London, 1937–38; Nicholas Randolph, *Dear Octopus,* Queen's, London, 1938; John Worthing, *The Importance of Being Earnest,* Globe, London, 1939; Hamlet, *Hamlet,* Lyceum, London, Elsinore, Kronberg Castle, 1939; MacHeath, *The Beggar's Opera,* Haymarket, 1940; King Lear, *King Lear,* Prospero, *The Tempest,* Old Vic, London, 1940; *Fumed Oak, Hands Across the Sea, Swan Song,* Globe, London, 1940; Will Dearth, *Dear Brutus,* Globe, London, 1941; Macbeth, *Macbeth,* Piccadilly, London, 1942; John Worthing, *The Importance of Being Earnest,* Phoenix, London, 1942; Louis, *The Doctor's Dilemma,* Haymarket, London, 1943; Valentine, *Love for Love,* Phoenix, London, 1943; Arnold Champion-Cheney, *The Circle,* Valentine, *Love for Love,* Hamlet, *Hamlet,* Oberon, *A Midsummer Night's Dream,* Ferdinand, *The Duchess of Malfi,* Haymarket, London, 1944–45; Raskolnikoff, *Crime and Punishment,* New, London, 1946; John Worthing, *The Importance of Being Earnest,* Royale, NY, 1947; Valentine, *Love for Love,* National, NY, 1947; Jason, *Medea,* 1947; Eustace Jackson, *The Return of the Prodigal,* Globe, London, 1948; Thomas Mendip, *The Lady's Not for Burning,* Globe, London, 1949;

Angelo, *Measure for Measure,* Benedick, *Much Ado About Nothing,* Cassius, *Julius Caesar,* King Lear, *King Lear,* Memorial, Stratford-on-Avon, UK, 1950; Thomas Mendip, *The Lady's Not for Burning,* Royale, NY, 1950; Leontes, *The Winter's Tale,* Phoenix, London, 1951; Benedick, *Much Ado About Nothing,* Phoenix, London, 1952; Mirabell, *The Way of the World,* Lyric, Hammersmith, UK, 1953; Jaffier, *Venice Preserv'd,* Lyric, Hammersmith, UK, 1953; Julian Anson, *A Day by the Sea,* Haymarket, London, 1953; Benedick, *Much Ado About Nothing,* King Lear, *King Lear,* Palace, London, 1955; Sebastien, *Nude with Violin,* Globe, London, 1956; Prospero, *The Tempest,* Memorial, Stratford-on-Avon, Drury Lane, London, 1957; James Callifer, *The Potting Shed,* Globe, London, 1958; Cardinal Wolsey, *Henry VIII,* Old Vic, London, 1958; *Ages of Man,* 46th Street Theater, NY, 1958; *Ages of Man,* Queen's, London, 1959; Benedick, *Much Ado About Nothing,* Cambridge Drama Festival, Boston, MA, Lunt-Fontanne, NY, 1959; *Ages of Man,* Haymarket, London, 1959; Prince Ferdinand Cavanati, *The Last Joke,* Phoenix, London, 1960; Othello, *Othello,* Royal Shakespeare, London, 1961; Gaev, *The Cherry Orchard,* Aldwych, London, 1961; Joseph Surface, *The School for Scandal,* Haymarket, London, 1962, Majestic, NY, 1963; *Ages of Man,* Lyceum, NY, 1963; Caesar, *Ides of March,* Haymarket, London, 1963; *Homage to Shakespeare,* Philharmonic Hall, NY, 1964; Julian, *Tiny Alice,* Billy Rose, NY, 1964; Nikolai Ivanov, *Ivanov,*

Yvonne Arnaud, Guildford, UK, Phoenix, London, 1965, Shubert, NY, 1966; Orgon, *Tartuffe*, National, London, 1967; Oedipus, *Oedipus*, Old Vic, London, 1968; Headmaster, *Forty Years On*, Apollo, London, 1968;

Gideon, *The Battle of Shrivings*, Lyric, London, 1970; Harry, *Home*, Royal Court, London, Morosco, NY, 1970; Julius Caesar, *Caesar and Cleopatra*, Chichester Festival, UK, 1971; Sir Geoffrey Kendle, *Veterans*, Royal Court, London, 1972; Prospero, *The Tempest*, National, London, 1974; Shakespeare, *Bingo*, Royal Court, London, 1974; Milton, *Paradise Lost*, Royal, York, Old Vic, London, 1974; Spooner, *No Man's Land*, Old Vic, Wyndham's, 1975, Lyttelton, London, Longacre, NY, 1976, Lyttelton, London, 1977; *Tribute to a Lady*, Old Vic, London, 1976; Julius Caesar, *Julius Caesar*, Olivier, London, 1977; Sir Politic Wouldbe, *Volpone*, Olivier, London, 1977; Sir Noel Cunliffe, *Half-Life*, Cottesloe, 1977, Duke of York's, London, 1978.

MAJOR TOURS—Understudy/stage manager, *The Wheel*, UK cities, 1922; *The Constant Nymph*, UK cities, 1927; Worthing, *The Importance of Being Earnest*, UK cities, 1939; *Fumed Oak, Hands Across the Sea, Swan Song*, Army and RAF theaters, UK, 1940; Charles Condamine, *Blithe Spirit*, SEAC theatres, 1945; Benedick, *Much Ado About Nothing*, European and UK cities, 1955; *Ages of Man*, Haifa, Jerusalem, Tel Aviv, 1962; *Ages of Man*, Australian and New Zealand cities, 1963; *Ages of Man*, Scandinavia, Finland, Poland, USSR, 1964; *Men and Women of Shakespeare*, South America, U.S. universities, 1966.

PRINCIPAL FILM APPEARANCES—*Who Is the Man?*, 1924; *The Clue of the New Pin*, 1929; *The Insult*, 1932; *The Good Companions*, 1933; *Secret Agent*, 1936; *Diary for Timothy*, (documentary), 1937; *The Prime Minister*, 1942; *Julius Caesar*, 1953; *Richard III*, 1955; *Around the World in 80 Days*, 1956; *Barretts of Wimpole Street*, 1957; *St. Joan*, 1957; *Becket*, 1964; *The Loved One*, 1965; *Chimes at Midnight*, 1966; *Sebastian*, 1967; *Assignment to Kill*, 1968; *Shoes of the Fisherman*, 1968; *Charge of the Light Brigade*, 1968; *Oh! What a Lovely War*, 1969; *Eagle in a Cage*, 1972; *Lost Horizon*, 1972; *11 Harrowhouse*, 1974; *Murder on the Orient Express*, 1974; *Galileo*, 1974; *Gold*, 1974; *Joseph Andrews*, 1976; *Aces High*, 1976; *Providence*, 1977; *Portrait of the Artist as a Young Man*, 1977; *Caligula*, 1977; *Murder by Decree*, 1978; *The Director*, 1979; *The Formula*, 1980; *The Conductor; The Human Factor*, 1980; *Elephant Man*, 1980; *Lion of the Desert*, 1981; *Arthur*, 1981; *Priest of Love*, 1981; *Chariots of Fire*, 1981; *Gandhi*, 1982; *Wicked Lady*.

PRINCIPAL TELEVISION APPEARANCES—*Ivanov; Cherry Orchard; Mayfly and the Frog; Heartbreak House; Good King Charles;* QBV II, 1973; *Golden Days; Richard II*, 1979; *Brideshead Revisited; English Gardens; Neck; Parson's Pleasure; Why Didn't They Ask Evans?; Seven Dials Mystery; A Day by the Sea; The Browning Version; The Rehearsal; Great Acting; Ages of Man; From Chekhov with Love; Conversation at Night; Hassan; Deliver Us From Evil.*

DIRECTED—Plays: *Richard of Bordeaux*, New London, 1932; *Strange Orchestra*, St. Martin's, London, 1932; *Sheppey*, Wyndham's, London, 1933; *Spring 1600* (also produced), Shaftesbury, London, 1934; *Queen of Scots*, New London, 1934; *Hamlet*, New, London, 1934; *The Old

Ladies, New, London, 1935; *Romeo and Juliet*, New, London, 1935; *He Was Born*, Queen's, London, 1937; *Richard II, The Merchant of Venice*, Queen's, London, 1938; *Spring Meeting*, Ambassadors', London, 1938; *Scandal in Assyria*, Globe, London, 1939; *The Beggar's Opera*, Haymarket, London, 1940; *Ducks and Drakes*, Apollo, London, 1941; *Love for Love*, Phoenix, London, 1943; *Landslide*, Westminster, London, 1943; *The Cradle Song*, Apollo, London, 1944; *Crisis in Heaven*, Lyric, London, 1944; *The Last of Summer*, Phoenix, London, 1944; *Lady Windermere's Fan*, Haymarket, London, 1945; *Medea*, National, London, 1947; *The Glass Menagerie*, Haymarket, London, 1948; *Medea*, Globe, London, 1948; *The Heiress*, Haymarket, London, 1949; *The Lady's Not for Burning*, Globe, London, 1949; *Much Ado About Nothing*, Stratford-on-Avon, UK, 1949; *Treasure Hunt*, Apollo, London, 1949;

Shall We Join the Ladies?, Lyric, Hammersmith, UK, 1950; *Indian Summer*, Criterion, London, 1951; *Much Ado About Nothing*, Phoenix, London, 1952; *Macbeth*, Memorial, Stratford-on-Avon, UK, 1952; *Richard II*, Lyric, Hammersmith, UK, 1952; *A Day by the Sea*, Haymarket, London, 1953; *Charley's Aunt*, New, London, 1954; *The Cherry Orchard*, Lyric, Hammersmith, UK, 1954; *Twelfth Night*, Memorial, Stratford-on-Avon, UK, 1955; *Much Ado About Nothing*, European and UK cities, 1955; *The Chalk Garden*, Haymarket, London, 1956; *Nude with Violin*, Globe, London, 1956; *The Trojans* (opera), Covent Garden, London, 1957; *Variations on a Theme*, Globe, London, 1958; *Five Finger Exercise*, Comedy, London, 1958; *The Complaisant Lover*, Globe, London, 1959; *Much Ado About Nothing*, Lunt-Fontanne, NY, 1959; *Five Finger Exercise*, Music Box, NY, 1959; *Big Fish, Little Fish*, ANTA, NY, 1961; *Dazzling Prospect*, Globe, London, 1961; *The School for Scandal*, Haymarket, London, 1962; *Hamlet*, Lunt-Fontanne, NY, 1963; *Ivanov*, Phoenix, London, Shubert, NY, 1965; *Halfway Up the Tree*, Queen's, London, 1967; *Don Giovanni* (opera) Coliseum, London, 1968; *Private Lives*, Queen's, London, 1972; *The Constant Wife*, Albery, London, 1973; *Private Lives, The Constant Wife*, US cities, 1975; *The Gay Lord Quex*, Albery, London, 1975.

WRITINGS: BOOKS—*Early Stages* (autobiography), 1939; *Stage Directions*, 1963; *Distinguished Company*, 1972; *An Actor and His Times*, 1979.

AWARDS: Evening Standard Award, Best Actor, 1970: *Home;* Companion of Honour, 1977; Chevalier of the Legion d'Honneur. Honorary Degrees—Doctor of Laws, St. Andrews University, 1950; Hon DLitt, Oxford University, 1953.

SIDELIGHTS: RECREATION —stage designing, music.

ADDRESS: Agent—c/o ICM, 22 Grafton Street, London, W1.*

* * *

GILBERT, Bruce, producer

PERSONAL: Born March 29, 1947 in Los Angeles; son of Ross and Laurie Gilbert; married Ellen, April 15, 1979;

children: Jordan Robert. EDUCATION: Boston University, 1965–67; University of California, Berkeley, 1967–69.

CAREER: PRINCIPAL FILM WORK—Associate producer, *Coming Home*, 1978; executive producer, *The China Syndrome*, 1979; producer, *Nine to Five*, 1980; producer, *On Golden Pond*, 1981.

PRINCIPAL TELEVISION WORK—Co-executive producer, *Nine to Five* (first thirteen episodes); executive producer, *The Dollmaker*, 1984.

WRITINGS: SCREENPLAYS—*The Grand Tour* (based on the novel *Trinity's Child*); *Coming Home* (co-writer).

AWARDS: Golden Globe, Best Film, 1981: *On Golden Pond;* Academy Award Nomination, Best Film, 1981: *On Golden Pond.*

SIDELIGHTS: MEMBERSHIPS—Academy of Motion Picture Arts and Sciences.

ADDRESS: Office—9336 W. Washington Blvd., Culver City, CA 90230. Agent—Creative Artists Agency, 1888 Century Park E., Suite 1400, Los Angeles, CA 90067.

* * *

GILHOOLEY, Jack (ne John Charles, Jr.) playwright/screenwriter

PERSONAL: Born June 26, 1940; son of John Charles (a life insurance broker) and Margaret (Cotter) Gilhooley. EDUCATION: Syracuse, B.A. (Drama); Villanova, M.A. (Theatre); University of Pennsylvania, M.A. (American Civics).

NON-THEATRICAL CAREER—Teacher, department chairman, Jersey City State College, New Jersey as well as seven years teaching Theatre and English; guest artist/lecturer, U. of Kansas, Vassar, Williams, Syracuse, U. of New Hampshire, Keuka College.

WRITINGS: PLAYS, PRODUCED—*The Last Act & The Entrepreneurs of Avenue B*, 1973; *Homefront Blues*, 1973; *The Last Christians*, 1974; *The Comeback*, 1974; *The Time Trial*, 1974; *The Competitors*, 1975; *Mummers End*, 1975; *The Elusive Angel*, 1976 *Afternoons in Vegas*, 1976; *Descendents*, 1978; *Bankers Hours*, 1979; *Relations*, 1980; *Shirley Basin*, 1982.

PLAYS, PUBLISHED—*The Brixton Recovery*, Samuel French, 1982.

PLAYS, UNPRODUCED—Avenue B, 1974; Dancin' to Calliope, 1979; Winterfire, 1982; Faraway Places . . . Strangesounding Names, The Kiss, Cookie's Dream, The Checkered Flag, 1983. TELEVISION SCRIPTS—*The Brothers*, 1977; *The Brixton Recovery*, 1981. RADIO SCRIPTS—*Dancin' to Calliope, Earplay*, 1980.

AWARDS: Shubert Playwriting Fellowship, 1973; Fenimore Playwriting Award, 1974; Jane L. Gilmore Award (playwriting), 1976; MacDowell Colony Residency, 1976; Eugene O'Neill Conference Guest Playwright, 1977; National En-

dowment for the Arts Grant, 1978; Millay Colony Residency, 1979; Actors Theatre of Louisville Commissions, 1979, 1980; Guest Playwright, Dorset Colony, 1980, 81, 82, 83; Guest Playwright, Minnesota Playwrights Lab, 1980; Guest Playwright, Cricket Theatre, Minneapolis, 1980; Corp. for Public Broadcasting Commission (American Playhouse), 1981; Guest Playwright (North Light Repertory (Chicago), 1982; Winner, Hutchison Rep. Co, Playwrighting Award, 1982; Guest Playwright, Johnson State College, Vermont, 1982; Guest Playwright, Empire State Institute for the Performing Arts, 1983; Yaddo Residency, 1983; Guest Playwright, Sundance Institute (Utah), 1983; Tyrone Guthrie Institute (Ireland) Residency, 1983–84.

SIDELIGHTS: MEMBERSHIPS—New Dramatists (1975–82); Dramatists Guild; American Federation of Teachers; AEA; SAG; Actors Studio—Playwrights Unit.

ADDRESS:Home—639 West End Avenue, New York, NY 10025.

* * *

GILLIATT, Penelope Ann Douglass, critic, playwright, novelist

PERSONAL: Born London, England; daughter of Cyril and Mary (Douglass) Conner; married R. W. Gilliatt (divorced); married John Osborne (divorced); children: daughter, Nolan. EDUCATION: Attended Queens College, London, England; Bennington College, VT.

WRITINGS: PLAYS, PRODUCED—*Property* and *Nobody's Business*, American Place Theatre, NY. PLAYS, UNPRODUCED—*But When All's Said and Done.* SCREENPLAYS—*Sunday Bloody Sunday*, 1971. BOOKS—*One by One*, 1965; *A State of Change*, 1968; *The Cutting Edge*, 1979; *Jacques Tati*, 1976; *Three-Quarter Face*, 1979. SHORT STORIES—*Come Back If It Doesn't Get Better*, 1970; *Nobody's Business*, 1972; *Splendid Lives*, 1979. ESSAYS—*Unholy Fools*, 1973; *Jean Renoir: Essays, Conversations, Reviews*, 1975.

THEATRE-RELATED CAREER: Film critic, *Observer* (London), 1961–67; theatre critic, *Observer* (London), 1965; guest film critic, *The New Yorker*, 1967; regular film critic, *The New Yorker*, 1968; writer feature film scripts and plays filmed for BBC-TV.

AWARDS: Award for Creative Work in Literature, American Academy, National Institute of Arts and Letters Society, 1972; Fellow, Royal Society of Literature; Academy Award Nomination, Best Screenplay, 1971: *Sunday Bloody Sunday;* Best Original Screenplay, Writers Guild of America, Writers Guild of England, National Society of Film Critics, New York Film Critics, 1971: *Sunday Bloody Sunday.*

SIDELIGHTS: MEMBERSHIPS—British Labour Party.

ADDRESS: Office—c/o The New Yorker Magazine, 25 W. 43rd Street, New York, NY 10036.

GILPIN, Jack, actor

PERSONAL: Born May 31, 1951, in Boyce, VA; son of Kenneth Newcomer (a businessman) and Lucy Trumbull (Mitchell) Gilpin. EDUCATION: Harvard University, B.A., 1973; studied acting with Michael Howard. RELIGION: Episcopalian.

CAREER: DEBUT—Easter Bunny, *Visit of the Easter Bunny,* Christ Church, Millwood, VA, 1956. NEW YORK DEBUT—Victor Vargo, *Goodbye and Keep Cold,* Ensemble Studio Theatre, 1976, 16 performances. LONDON DEBUT—Eli, *Honey,* Square One, 1976, 16 performances. PRINCIPAL STAGE APPEARANCES—Bob, *Beyond Therapy,* Brooks Atkinson, New York, 1982; Barney, *The Middle Ages,* St. Peter's Church, New York, 1983; extensive work in regional theatre throughout the United States.

TELEVISION DEBUT—*For Ladies Only.* TELEVISION APPEARANCES—*It's Only Money.*

SIDELIGHTS: MEMBERSHIPS—Ensemble Studio Theatre (Vice President; Board of Directors).

* * *

GLASS, Joanna McClelland, playwright

PERSONAL: Born October 7, 1936 in Saskatoon, Canada; daughter of Morrill MacKenzie and Kate (Switzer); married Alexander Glass on December 18, 1959 (divorced 1976); children: Jennifer, Mavis, Lawrence. EDUCATION: Attended public schools in Saskatoon, Canada.

WRITINGS: PLAYS, PRODUCED—*Canadian Gothic* (one-act), Manhattan Theatre Club, Phoenix, NY, CBC Radio Canada, Earplay, Public Radio, U.S.A., BBC, Radio, London, England, 1972–82; *American Modern* (one-act), Manhattan Theatre Club, Phoenix, NY, CBC Radio, Earplay, National Public Radio (U.S.), 1972–79; *Artichoke,* Long Wharf, New Haven, CT, 1975, Manhattan Theatre Club, 1979, Tricycle, London England, 1982, CBC-TV, Toronto, Canada, 1979, has been produced in most major American and Candian cities; *To Grandmother's House We Go,* Alley, Houston, TX, 1980, Biltmore, NY, 1980, Kammerspiele, Hamburg, Germany, 1982; *Play Memory,* McCarter, Princeton, NJ, Zellerbach, Philadelphia, PA, Longacre, NY, 1983.

PLAYS, PUBLISHED—*Canadian Gothic,* 1977; *American Modern,* 1977; *Artichoke,* 1979; *To Grandmother's House We Go,* 1980.

NOVELS—*Reflections on a Mountain Summer,* 1974; *Woman Wanted,* 1983.

SHORT STORIES—"At the King Edward Hotel," in *Winter's Tales 22,* 1976.

AWARDS: Guggenheim Fellowship, 1981; National Endowment for the Arts Grant, 1979.

SIDELIGHTS: MEMBERSHIPS—Dramatists Guild; Writers Guild of America East.

Ms. Glass's novel *Reflections on a Mountain Summer* was read in ten segments on the BBC, in 1976.

ADDRESS: Agent—Lucy Kroll Agency, 390 West End Avenue, New York, NY 10024.

* * *

GLINES, John, producer, playwright, actor

PERSONAL: Born October 11, 1933, in Santa Maria, CA; son of Denzil Cassius (a cowboy) and Ellen (Lanza) Glines. EDUCATION: Yale, B.A. in Drama, 1955. POLITICS: Democrat. RELIGION: Protestant. NON-THEATRICAL CAREER: Contract Supervisor, CBS News, 1959–60.

CAREER: DEBUT—Actor/Producer, *The Comedy Theatre,* Oakland, CA, 1956. NEW YORK DEBUT—Richard Hare & Lord Mount Severin, *East Lynne,* Theatre East, 1959. PRODUCED: PLAYS—(also composed) *Gulp!,* NY, 1977; *Last Summer at Bluefish Cove,* Actors Playhouse, NY, 1980–81; Executive Producer/Artistic Director, The Glines, Inc., productions including: *Torch Song Trilogy, A Loss of Memory, Last Summer at Bluefish Cove, My Blue Heaven, A Perfect Relationship, Forever After, T-Shirts, Niagra Falls, Newsboy, If This Isn't Love, Iolanthe, Pines '79,* 1976–present; *Torch Song Trilogy,* Helen Hayes (Little), 1982.

WRITINGS: PLAYS, PUBLISHED—*In the Desert of My Soul,* Best Short Plays of 1976, Dramatist Play Service; PLAYS, PRODUCED—author/composer/lyricist, *God Bless Coney,* Orpheum, New York, 1972; composer, *Gulp!,* 1977. TELEVISION SHOWS—Staff Writer, *Captain Kangaroo,* 1965–71; staff writer, *Sesame Street,* 1978–81.

AWARDS: Antoinette Perry Award, Best Play, *Torch Song Trilogy,* 1983; Two Emmy Nominations for Sesame Street programs, 1980–81, 1981–82.

SIDELIGHTS: MEMBERSHIPS—AEA, SAG; National Association of TV Arts and Sciences; ASCAP; The League of New York Theatres and Producers; Dramatists Guild; Writers Guild of America, East.

Creator/writer, *Sesame Street Cassette* for Omni Game, Milton Bradley.

"*Torch Song Trilogy* teaches indirectly; *Sesame Street* directly; and both entertain in a highly original way. I believe that when you can combine enlightenment and entertainment in a daring and original way, you have something worth devoting your heart and soul to."

ADDRESS: Home and Office—28 Willow Street, Brooklyn, NY 11201.

* * *

GLYNN, Carlin, actress

PERSONAL: Born February 19, 1940; daughter of Guilford Cresse Jr. (an accountant) and Lois Carlin (a psychiatric

CARLIN GLYNN

social worker; maiden name, Wilks) Glynn; married Peter Masterson (actor, writer, director, producer) on December 29, 1960; children: Carlin Alexandra, Mary Stuart, Peter C. B. EDUCATION: Attended Texas Public Schools and Sophie Newcomb College, 1957–58; studied acting with Stella Adler, Wynn Handman and Lee Strasberg in New York City.

CAREER: DEBUT—Gigi, *Gigi,* Alley, Houston, TX, 1959. NEW YORK DEBUT—*Waltz of the Toreadors,* Sheridan Square Playhouse, 1960. LONDON DEBUT—Mona (the madam) *The Best Little Whorehouse in Texas,* Theatre Royal, Drury Lane, for six months, 1981. PRINCIPAL STAGE APPEARANCES—Mona (the madam), *The Best Little Whorehouse in Texas,* 46th Street Theatre, NY, for three years, 1979; Louise, *Winterplay,* Second Stage, South Street, NY, 1983; Erica, *Alterations,* Whole Theatre Company, Montclair, NJ, 1984.

FILM DEBUT—May, *Three Days of the Condor,* 1976. PRINCIPAL FILM APPEARANCES—Sylvia, *Continental Divide,* 1980; Brenda, *Sixteen Candles,* 1984.

TELEVISION DEBUT—Host, *Today's Health.*

THEATRE-RELATED CAREER: Acting Teacher, The Real Stage, New York City.

AWARDS: Society of West End Theatre, Best Actress in a Musical Award, 1981; The Eleanora Duse Award, 1980; Antoinette Perry Award, Mona, *The Best Little Whorehouse*

in Texas, 1979; Drama Desk Award Nomination, Mona, *The Best Little Whorehouse in Texas,* 1979; Theatre World Award, *The Best Little Whorehouse in Texas,* 1978.

SIDELIGHTS: MEMBERSHIPS—Board of Directors, Consumer Action Now.

ADDRESS: Office—Tejas Productions, Inc., 1165 Fifth Avenue, New York, NY 10029; Agent—Eric Schepard, c/o ICM, 40 W. 57th Street, New York, NY 10019.

* * *

GOING, John, director

PERSONAL: Born November 28, 1936 in Lancaster, PA; son of John J. (a credit manager) and Marion C (Morton) Going. EDUCATION: Catholic University, Washington, DC, B.A. (Cum Laude), 1958; University of Minnesota, M.A., 1964; Served as assistant to Sir Tyrone Guthrie during the inaugural season of the Guthrie Threatre in Minneapolis, MN, 1963. MILITARY: U.S. Army, Honor Guard Company, Washington, DC, Specialist 4th Class, 1960–62.

CAREER: NEW YORK DEBUT, DIRECTED—*A Breeze from the Gulf,* Eastside Playhouse, 1973. PRINCIPAL STAGE WORK, DIRECTED—Cleveland Playhouse, 1969–71: *Harvey, The Country Wife, Red's My Color, What's Yours? The Taming of the Shrew, The Threepenny Opera, Summer and Smoke, Lysistrata, You Know I Can't Hear You When the Water's Running, The Devil's Disciple, Plaza Suite; The Man Who Came to Dinner,* Mummers, Oklahoma City, 1971; *The Odd Couple,* Meadow Brook, MI, 1971; *A Breeze from the Gulf,* Bucks County Playhouse, PA, 1973; *Dear Liar,* Homestead Theatre, Hot Springs, VA, 1973; *The Imaginary Invalid,* Repertory Theatre of St. Louis, MO, 1973; *Plain and Fancy,* American Heritage Festival, Lancaster, PA, 1974; *Candida,* Hartford Stage Company, 1977; *The Show Off,* Seattle Repertory, 1977; *Peter Pan,* Alliance, Atlanta GA, 1978; *The Animal Kingdom,* Hartman Theatre Company, Stamford, CT, 1978; *Period of Adjustment,* Advent, Nashville, TN, 1979; *Biography,* Barter, Abingdon, VA, 1975; *The Threepenny Opera,* Barter, 1976; *Misalliance,* Barter, 1979; *One Flew Over the Cuckoo's Nest,* Pittsburgh Public, PA, 1975; *You Never Can Tell,* Pittsburgh Public, 1977; *Mister Roberts,* Pittsburgh Public, 1979; *The Sea Gull,* Pittsburgh Public, 1979; Indiana Repertory, Indianapolis, IN: *The Servant of Two Masters,* 1974, *The Little Foxes,* 1975, *The Tavern,* 1976, *The Last Meeting of the White Knights of the Magnolia,* 1976, *The Importance of Being Earnest,* 1979, *Toys in the Attic,* 1980; *Philadelphia Here I Come,* Philadelphia Drama Guild, 1981; *Mirandolina,* Michigan Ensemble, MI, 1981; Syracuse Stage Company, Syracuse, NY; *The Little Foxes,* 1975, *Blithe Spirit,* 1976, *A Streetcar Named Desire,* 1977, *Tartuffe,* 1977, *Vanities,* 1978, *She Stoops to Conquer,* 1978, *Cat on a Hot Tin Roof,* 1982;

Cincinnatti Playhouse in the Park, OH: *Harvey,* 1973; *Relatively Speaking,* 1975, *Oliver,* 1976, *Vanities,* 1977, *The Royal Family,* 1978, *Hedda Gabler,* 1979, *Man of La Mancha,* 1979, *The Cherry Orchard,* 1980, *Tintypes,* 1981, *Inherit the Wind,* 1982; *You Can't Take It With You,* Empire State Institute of Performing Arts, Albany, NY, 1983; *The Man Who Came to Dinner,* Alaska Repertory, 1981; *Major*

JOHN GOING

Barbara, Alaska Repertory, 1982; *The Philadelphia Story,* Alaska Repertory, 1983; *The Rivals,* Alley, Houston, TX, 1982;' *Uncle Vanya,* Alley, 1984; *Juno's Swans,* Ensemble Studio, NY, 1978; *Lola,* York Theatre Company, NY, 1982; *The Sunshine Boy's,* Manitoba Theatre Centre, Winnipeg, Canada, 1974; *Vanities,* Barnato Theatre, Johannesburg, South Africa, 1977.

MAJOR TOURS—*My Daughter, Your Son,* 1971; *Butterflies Are Free,* 1973; *Send Me No Flowers,* 1975–76; *The Best Man,* 1976; *Come Blow Your Horn,* 1977–78; *Vanities,* 1978; *Children,* 1980. MAJOR STOCK PRODUCTIONS—DIRECTED—*Private Lives,* Little Theatre-on-the-Square, 1971; *Champagne Complex,* Little Theatre-on-the-Square, 1971; *I Do, I Do,* Little Theatre-on-the-Square, 1972; *Forty Carats,* Little Theatre-on-the-Square, 1972; *Butterflies Are Free,* Elitch Gardens, 1972; *The Play's the Thing,* Academy Festival, 1974; *Come Blow Your Horn,* Showplace, 1975; *The Mousetrap,* Olney, 1973; *Tonight at 8:30,* Olney, 1974; *Uncle Vanya,* Olney, 1976; *Peg O' My Heart,* American Stage Festival, 1978; *Life with Father,* Royal Poinciana Playhouse, 1975; *Send Me No Flowers,* Royal Poinciana Playhouse, 1976; *Lunch Hour,* Cherry County Playhouse, 1982.

THEATRE-RELATED CAREER: Associate Professor of Drama, Edgecliff College, 1964–69; Drama Department Head, Edgecliff College, 1968–69; Associate Artistic Director, Edgecliff Theatre, 1964–68; Acting Artistic Director, Edgecliff Theatre, 1968–69; Resident Director, Cleveland Playhouse, 1969–71; Resident Director, Cherry County Playhouse, 1969–72; Associate Artistic Director, Alaska Rep-

ertory Theatre, 1982–83; Acting Artistic Director, Alaska Repertory Theatre, 1983–84.

AWARDS: Phi Beta Kappa.

SIDELIGHTS: MEMBERSHIPS—Society of Stage Directors and Choreographers; AEA.

ADDRESS: Agent—Bret Adams, 448 W. 44th Street, New York, NY 10036.

* * *

GOLDEMBERG, Rose Leiman, writer

PERSONAL: Born in New York; daughter of Louis I. and Esther (Friedman) Leiman; married Raymond Schiller (divorced 1968); married Robert L. Goldemberg (a cosmetic chemist), August 25, 1969; children: (first marriage) Lee J., Lisa. EDUCATION: Brooklyn College, B.A. (magna cum laude); Ohio State University, M.A.; studied at the American Theatre Wing in New York.

WRITINGS: PLAYS, PRODUCED—*Gandhiji,* O'Neill Playwrights' Conference, 1970, Fairleigh Dickinson University, NJ, 1970, Back Alley Theatre, Washington, DC, 1977, Actors Theatre, Los Angeles, 1982; *The Merry War,* Fairleigh Dickinson, 1973, New Dramatists, 1973; *The Rabinowitz Gambit,* Cleveland Playhouse, 1973, Whole Theatre Company of Montclair, NJ, 1975, 18th Street Playhouse, NY, 1977; *Love One Another,* New Dramatists, NY, 1974; *Letters Home,* American Place, NY, 1979, Theatre at New End, London, 1980, Playbox Theatre, Melbourne, 1981, Dublin Festival, 1982, Century City Playhouse, Los Angeles, 1983. PLAYS, UNPRODUCED—*Sophie.*

FILM SCREENPLAYS—*Doubles.* TELEVISION SCRIPTS—*Out of Wedlock; Classified Love; Born Beautiful; Victory of the Heart; The Burning Bed; Mother and Daughter: The Loving War, Memoirs of an Ex-Prom Queen; Death at Dinner (The Booth); Life in the Fast Lane; Growing Pains; The Medicine Men; Land of Hope; A Celebration of Women.*

BOOKS, PUBLISHED—*Here's Egg on Your Face,* 1969; *The Complete Book of Natural Cosmetics,* 1974; *Antique Jewelry: A Practical and Passionate Guide,* 1976; *All About Jewelry,* 1983. ARTICLES, PUBLISHED—*Woman Writer, Man's World, New York Times* Sunday drama section, 1970.

AWARDS: Heritage Poetry Award; Atlantic Monthly, College Poetry Award; American Theatre Wing Playwriting Scholarship; Ford Foundation Award for one hour television drama, *The Pencil Box War;* Winner, National Visual Presentation Association, Sales Executives Club of New York, *You're It;* Certificate of Merit, American Film Festival, *You're It;* Humanitas Award Nomination: *Born Beautiful, Mother and Daughter: The Loving War* and *Land of Hope;* WGA Best Drama Nomination, American Women in Radio and Television Award, *Mother and Daughter: The Loving War;* Concord Bicentennial Contest, *Apples in Eden,* 1975; Earplay Purchase Award, *Voices in My Head,* 1975; Armstrong Award for Best Radio Drama, *Voices in My Head,* 1975; Armstrong Award for Best Radio Drama, *Voices in My Head,* 1975; Grant, New Jersey State Council on the Arts,

The Merry War, 1973; Research Grant, Fairleigh Dickinson University for *Women in Theatre,* 1973–74; OADR honors, *Rites of Passage,* 1972; Research Grant, Fairleigh Dickinson University, for *Rites of Passage,* 1972; Dramatists Guild Fund Grant, for *Marching As To War,* 1971; First Prize, Sullivan County Dramatic Workshop, *The Rabinowitz Gambit,* 1975.

SIDELIGHTS: MEMBERSHIPS—The Dramatists Guild, Board of Directors, Writers Guild of America; Playwright in Residence, Eugene O'Neill Theatre Center, 1970.

ADDRESS: Office—61 Jane Street, 15M, New York, NY 10014. Agent—Lee Rosenberg, Adams, Ray & Rosenberg, 9200 Sunset Blvd., Los Angeles, CA 90069.

* * *

GOLDSTONE, James, director

PERSONAL: Born June 8, 1931, in Los Angeles, CA; son of Jules C. (an attorney) and Anita M. (Rosenberg) Goldstone; married Ruth Liebling, June 21, 1953; children: Peter, Jeffrey, Barbara. EDUCATION: Dartmouth College, B.A., 1953; Bennington College, M.A., 1957; studied film editing with Merrill White. MILITARY: U.S. Army, Pvt. 1st Class, 1953–55.

CAREER: FILM DEBUT—Director, *Jigsaw,* 1967. PRINCIPAL FILM WORK—Director: *Winning,* 1969; *Red Sky at Morning,* 1970; *The Gang That Couldn't Shoot Straight,* 1971; *Swashbuckler,* 1975; *Rollercoaster,* 1977.

TELEVISION DEBUT—Director, *Court of Last Resort,* 1957. PRINCIPAL TELEVISION WORK—Director: *Kent State; Calamity Jane; A Clear and Present Danger; Studs Lonigan Trilogy; Journey from Darkness; Eric; Star Trek,* (pilot); currently shooting, *The Sun Also Rises.*

AWARDS: Emmy Award, *Kent State;* Emmy Nomination, *A Clear and Present Danger;* International Film Festival Award, *Eric;* Christopher Award, *Journey from Darkness.*

SIDELIGHTS: MEMBERSHIPS—Academy of Motion Picture Arts and Sciences, Academy of Television Arts and Sciences, Writers Guild of America: directors council and National Board, creative rights negotiating committee.

ADDRESS: Office—James Goldstone Productions Inc., 6420 Wilshire Blvd. 19th floor, Los Angeles, CA 90048. Agent—John Gaines, APA, 9000 Sunset Blvd., Los Angeles, CA 90069.

* * *

GORDON, Hannah, actress

PERSONAL: Born April 9, 1941, Edinburgh, Scotland; married Norman Warwick (film cameraman), February 5, 1970; children: Ben. EDUCATION: St. Denis School, 7 years; attended College of Dramatic Art, Glasgow.

CAREER: DEBUT—with Dundee Repertory, 1959. LONDON

HANNAH GORDON

DEBUT—Helen, *Baggage,* Vaudeville Theatre, 1976, four months. PRINCIPAL STAGE APPEARANCES—Appeared with the Belgrade Theatre, Coventry, the Citizens Theatre, Glasgow, Yvonne Arnaud Theatre in Guildford; Marguerite Duras, *Suzannah Andler;* Desdemona, *Othello,* Chichester Festival and Hong Kong Festival, 1975; *Can You Hear Me at the Back,* Piccadilly, London, 1979–80; *The Killing Game,* Apollo, London, 1981; *The Jewellers Shop,* Westminster, London, 1982; Georgie, *The Country Girl,* Apollo, London, 1983–84,

FILM DEBUT—*Spring & Port Wine,* 1969. PRINCIPAL FILM APPEARANCES—*The Elephant Man,* 1979. TELEVISION DEBUT—*Johnson over Jordan,* 1965. PRINCIPAL TELEVISION APPEARANCES—*Great Expectations; Middlemarch; David Copperfield; Abelard & Heloise; When the Bow Breaks;* Celia, *Three Stories of Orkney; Dear Octopus; What Every Woman Knows; Waste; Miss Morison's Ghosts,* 1982; *Good Behaviour,* 1983; *Upstairs, Downstairs; My Wife Next Door; Telfords Change;* guest appearances with *Morecombe & Wise* and *Cilla Black.* PRINCIPAL RADIO SHOW—*Hedda Gabler, Candida, Paradise Lost, Everything in the Garden, Macbeth.*

AWARDS: Fellow of the Royal Scottish Academy of Music
and Dramatic Art, 1980; Gold Medallist, Royal Scottish
Academy of Music and Dramatic Art, 1962.

ADDRESS: Agent—David White Associates, 31 Kings Road,
London, SW 3.

* * *

GORDON, Michael, director, teacher

PERSONAL: Born September 6, 1909 in Baltimore, MD;
son of Paul (a manufacturer) and Eva (Kunen) Gordon;
married Elizabeth Cane on November 25, 1939 (died 1971).
EDUCATION: Johns Hopkins University, B.A. 1929; Yale
University, School of Drama, M.F.A. 1932.

CAREER: PRINCIPAL STAGE WORK—DIRECTED—New York
Productions, 1932–40: *Black Pit, Sailors of Cattaro;* 1943–
46: *Storm Operation, Rebecca, Sophie, Home of The Brave,
Laura;* 1951–59: *Anna Christie, One Bright Day, The Male
Animal, See the Jaguar, Maggie, The Magic and the Loss,
The Tender Trap, His and Hers, Champagne Complex,
Deadfall, The Lovers;* UCLA Resident Theatre: *Rhinoceros,*
1978, *Triptych,* 1979, *Forest Murmurs,* 1980.

PRINCIPAL FILM WORK—DIRECTED—1940–43: *Boston Blackie
Goes Hollywood, Underground Agent, One Dangerous
Night, The Crime Doctor;* 1946–51: *The Web, Another Part
of the Forest, An Act of Murder, The Lady Gambles, Woman
in Hiding, Cyrano de Bergerac, I Can Get It For You
Wholesale, The Secret of Convict Lake;* 1960–70: *Pillow
Talk, Portrait in Black, Boys Night Out, Move Over Darling,
For Love or Money, A Very Special Favor, Texas Across the
River, The Impossible Years, How Do I Love Thee.*

PRINCIPAL TELEVISION WORK—DIRECTED—*Decoy* (Series).

THEATRE-RELATED CAREER: Teacher, Acting, Neighborhood
Playhouse, 1938–40; lecturer, Theatre Arts, UCLA, 1971–
73; Professor of Theatre Arts, UCLA, 1973–present (Emeritus, on re-call since 1977).

AWARDS: Best Direction, *Home of The Brave,* Variety's
Annual New York Critics Poll, 1946.

SIDELIGHTS: MEMBERSHIPS—Directors Guild of America;
Academy of Motion Picture Arts and Sciences; The Group
Theatre, 1935–40.

Mr. Gordon directed José Ferrer in his film performance of
Cyrano de Bergerac for which he won the Academy Award
for Best Actor in 1950. "On my third sojourn to Hollywood,
1959–70, I directed nine features, the first of which, *Pillow
Talk,* did so well at the box office that I found myself almost
instantaneously and ridgidly type-cast as a director of feather-
weight comedies—a box out of which I was never wholly
able to extricate myself. In the summer of 1970, I accepted an
invitation to conduct a class in acting in the Department of
Theatre Arts at UCLA. This belated return to teaching
proved as rewarding to me as it appeared to be to the students
under my instruction. Subsequently, I accepted a one-year
appointment as a lecturer and began on a full-time basis in
1971."

ADDRESS: Home—259 N. Layton Drive, Los Angeles, CA
90049. Office—c/o UCLA, 405 Hilgard, Los Angeles, CA
90024.

* * *

GORDON, Ruth, actress and writer

PERSONAL: Born October 30, 1896, in Wollaston, MA;
daughter of Clinton and Annie (Ziegler) Jones; married
Gregory Kelly (died); married Garson Kanin. EDUCATION:
Attended Massachusetts public schools.

CAREER: PRINCIPAL STAGE APPEARANCES—Nibs, *Peter
Pan,* Empire, NY, 1915; *The Little Mininister,* 1915; Lola
Pratt, *Seventeen,* NY, 1917; *Nothing But the Truth,* Murat,
Indianapolis, IN, 1918; *Piccadilly Jim,* 1919; Cora Wheeler,
Clarence, Blackstone, Chicago, IL, 1920; Grace, *The First
Year,* Little, NY, 1922; Winsora Tweedles, *Bristol Glass,*
Blackstone, Chicago, IL, 1923; *Tweedles,* Frazee, NY,
1923; *The Phantom Ship,* 1925; Collision, Rochester, NY,
1925; Helen, *Holding Helen,* Copley, Boston, MA, 1925;
Katie Everett, *Mrs. Partridge Presents,* Belmont, NY, 1925;
Eva Hutton, *The Fall of Eve,* Booth, NY, 1925; *Lovely Lady,*
1927; Bobby, *Saturday's Children,* Booth, NY, 1928; Ses-
saly, *King's,* Asbury Park, Atlantic City, NJ, 1928; Serena,
Serena Blandish, Morosco, NY, 1929; Lily Malone, *Hotel
Universe,* Martin Beck, NY, 1930; Ilona Stobri, *The Violet,*

RUTH GORDON

Henry Miller, NY, 1930; Susie Sachs, *A Church Mouse*, Playhouse, NY, 1930–31; Trixie Ingram, *The Wiser They Are*, Plymouth, NY, 1930–31; Mary Hilliard, *Here Today*, Ethel Barrymore, NY, 1932; Elizabeth Rumplegar, *Three-Cornered Moon*, Cort, NY, 1933; Lucy Wells, *They Shall Not Die*, Royale, NY, 1933; Harriet Marshall/Hope Cameron/Wilhemina Cameron, *The Sleeping Clergyman*, Guild, NY, 1934; Mary Hilliard, *Here Today*, Boston, MA, Chicago, IL, 1935; Epiphania, *The Millionairess*, Berkshire Playhouse Stockbridge, MA, 1935; Lady Cicely, *Captain Brassbound's Conversion*, White Plains, NY, 1935; Mattie Silver, *Ethan Frome*, National, NY, 1935; Mrs. Pinchwife, *The Country Wife*, Henry Miller, NY, 1936–37; Nora Helmer, *A Doll's House*, Morosco, Broadhurst, NY, 1937; Linda Marsh, *The Birds Stop Singing*, NY, 1939;

Sheila Munson, *Portrait of a Lady*, NY, 1941; Iris Ryan, *The Strings, My Lord, Are False*, Royale, NY, 1942; Natasha, *The Three Sisters*, Ethel Barrymore, NY, 1942–43; Paula Wharton, *Over Twenty-One*, Music Box, NY, 1943–45; Gay Marriot, *The Leading Lady*, National, NY, 1948; Sara Boulting, *The Smile of the World*, Lyceum, NY, 1949; Adele, *The Amazing Adele*, Westport Country Playhouse, CT, 1950; Natalia, *Month in the Country*, Westport Country Playhouse, CT, 1950; Mrs. Levi, *The Matchmaker*, London, Berlin, 1954; Mrs. Levi, *The Matchmaker*, Royale, Booth, NY, 1955–57; Marie-Paule, *The Good Soup*, Plymouth, NY, 1960; Ron Halperin, *My Mother, My Father and Me*, Boston, NY, 1963; Mrs. Goforth, *The Milk Train Doesn't Stop Here Anymore*, London, 1963; Mrs. Lord, *A Very Rich Woman*, Belasco, NY, 1966; Cass, *The Loves of Cass McGuire*, Helen Hayes, NY, 1966; Zina, *Dreyfus in Rehearsal*, Ethel Barrymore, NY, 1974; Mrs. Warren, *Mrs. Warren's Profession*, Vivian Beaumont, NY, 1976; Gladys Bassett, *HO! HO! HO!*, Berkshire Theatre Festival, Cape Playhouse, 1976.

MAJOR TOURS—Blanny, *Fair and Warmer*, U.S. cities, 1916; Lola Pratt, *Seventeen*, U.S. cities, 1919; Cora Wheeler, *Clarence*, U.S. cities, 1920; Grace, *The First Year*, U.S. cities, 1923; Bobby, *Saturday's Children*, U.S. cities, 1928.

PRINCIPAL FILM APPEARANCES—Mary Todd, *Abe Lincoln in Illinois*, 1939; Mrs. Ehrlich, *Dr. Ehrlich's Magic Bullet*, 1939; *Information, Please*, 1939; *Edge of Darkness*, 1942; *Action on the North Atlantic*, 1942; the Dealer, *Inside Daisy Clover*, 1965; *Lord Love a Duck*, 1966; Minnie Castevet, *Rosemary's Baby*, 1967; Aunt Alice, *Whatever Happened to Aunt Alice*, 1968; Momma, *Where's Poppa*, 1970; Maude, *Harold and Maude*, 1971; *The Big Bus*, 1976; *Every Which Way but Loose*, 1978; *Boardwalk*, 1979; *Scaveger Hunt*, 1979; *Any Which Way You Can*, 1980; *Jimmy the Kid*; Sheriff, *Attack of the Rock and Roll Alien*, 1984; Mugsy, *Mugsy's Girls*, 1984.

PRINCIPAL TELEVISION APPEARANCES—(movies) Marge, *Isn't It Shocking?*, 1973; Mrs. Miller, *The Prince of Central Park*, 1975; Minnie Castevet, *Rosemary's Baby II*, 1976; Mrs. Houdini, *The Great Houdini*, 1976; Mama Cavagnaro, *The Perfect Gentlemen*, 1977; *Don't Go to Sleep*, 1982; (others) Madam Arcati, *Hallmark Hall of Fame*, ''Blithe Spirit,'' 1966; *The Flip Wilson Show*, 1970; Mrs. Eudora Temple, *Kojak*, 1975; Carlton's Mother, *Rhoda*, 1975; Mrs. Emily Dobson, *Medical Story*, 1975; Abigail Mitchell, *Columbo*, ''Try and Catch Me,'' 1977; *Love Boat*, 1977; Sugar Mama,

Taxi, 1979; *The Bob Newhart Show*, 1983; Blanche, *The Bob Newhart Show*, 1984.

WRITINGS: PLAYS, PRODUCED—*Over Twenty-One*, Music Box, NY, 1944; *Years Ago*, 1946; *The Leading Lady*, National, NY, 1948; *A Very Rich Woman*, Belasco, NY, 1965; SCREENPLAYS—(with Garson Kanin) *A Double Life*, 1948; *Adam's Rib*, 1949; *The Marrying Kind*, 1952; *Pat and Mike*, 1952; *Hardhat and Legs*, 1978. BOOKS—*Myself Among Others* (autobiography), 1971; *My Side* (autobiography), 1976; *An Open Book* (autobiography), 1980; *Shady Lady* (novel), 1984.

AWARDS: Academy Award, Best Supporting Actress, 1967: *Rosemary's Baby;* Emmy Award, 1979: *Taxi.*

ADDRESS: Office—200 W. 57th Street, Suite 1203, New York, NY 10019.

* * *

GORNEY, Karen Lynn, actress and dancer

PERSONAL: Born January 28 in Hollywood, CA; daughter of Jay (a composer) and Sondra (a writer) Gorney. EDUCATION: Carnegie-Mellon University, B.F.A.; Brandeis University, M.F.A.; studied acting with Morris Charnovsky, Bill Ball, and Allen Fletcher; studied dance with Alvin Ailey and Madam Mordkin; scholarship student, Stratford Shakespeare Festival; fellowship, Helen Tamiris Dance Company. THEATRE-RELATED CAREER: Acting teacher, Jo-Jo's Dance Company, 1980–82.

KAREN GORNEY

CAREER: DEBUT—Annabelle, *Dylan,* Mercer Arts Theatre, New York. PRINCIPAL STAGE APPEARANCES—Berkshire Regional Theatre: Lavinia, *Androcles and the Lion;* Jocasta, *Oedipus Rex;* Woman-Wife-Girl, *Thurber Carnival.* Springold Theatre, Waltham, MA: Nina, *The Seagull;* Claire, *The Maids;* Ceres, *The Tempest;* Ana, *Schweyk in the Second World War;* Wellesley, *Workhouse Donkey;* Fran/Mercedes, *Only When I Laugh.* Loeb Drama Center, Cambridge, MA: Pentinent/Mistress, *The Balcony;* Estelle, *Waltz of the Toreadors.* Tufts Arena Theatre, Medford, MA: Rosie, *Live Like Pigs;* Marie Jeanne, *The Cavern.* Torches Repertory Theatre, Canada: Rosa, *Summer and Smoke;* Miss Gilchrist, *The Hostage;* Lucinde, *The Doctor in Spite of Himself.* Trotwood Circle Theatre, Ohio: The Girl, *The Cavedwellers;* Gertrude, *Fashion.* Birmingham Theatre: Nora, *Lunch Hour.* MAJOR TOURS—Lavinia, *Androcles and the Lion,* 1969; Mina, *Dracula,* 1978.

FILM DEBUT—Josette, *David and Lisa,* 1963. PRINCIPAL FILMS—Stephanie Mangano, *Saturday Night Fever,* 1977; Alicia, *Magic Garden of Stanley Sweetheart.* TELEVISION DEBUT—Tara, *All My Children.* TELEVISION APPEARANCES—Sally Seiple, *Harry O;* Anne, *The Doctors;* Mary, *Secret Night Caller.*

SIDELIGHTS: MEMBERSHIPS—Actors Equity, ASCAP, AGAC, SAG, AFTRA, P.A. Stage Company (honorary advisory board, 1980–82).

"In addition to being an actress and a dancer, I am also a composer, having recorded in London for EMI. I am also a painter for Cicle Fine Arts."

ADDRESS: Agent—c/o ICM, Doris Mantz, 40 W. 57th Street, New York, NY 10019.

* * *

GORSHIN, Frank, comic, actor

PERSONAL: Born April 5, 1934; son of Frank Sr. and Frances Gorshin; married Christina Randazzo, April 8, 1960; children: Mitchell. EDUCATION: Attended Carnegie Tech School of Drama, Pittsburgh, PA; trained for the stage while in the special services division of the U.S. Army, 1953–55. RELIGION: Catholic. MILITARY: U.S. Army, 1953–55.

CAREER: NEW YORK DEBUT—James J. Walker, *Jimmy,* Winter Garden, 1969. PRINCIPAL STAGE APPEARANCES—Capidistrion, *Whodunnit,* Biltmore, New York, 1983; Sidney Bruhl, *Deathtrap,* Westport County Playhouse, Westport, CT, 1983; Sammy, *What Makes Sammy Run?,* Valley Music Theater, Los Angeles.

FILM DEBUT—Blake Barton, *Bells Are Ringing,* 1959. PRINCIPAL FILMS—*Where the Boys Are,* 1961; *The Upper Crust,* 1981. TELEVISION DEBUT—*The Riddler,* Batman. TELEVISION APPEARANCES—*Hennesy; The Edge of Night; Goliath Awaits.*

SIDELIGHTS: MEMBERSHIPS—AEA, AFTRA, SAG, AGVA.

FRANK GORSHIN

ADDRESS: Office—c/o The Shefrin Company, 800 South Robertson Blvd., Los Angeles, CA 90035.

* * *

GOTLIEB, Ben, actor

PERSONAL: Born June 27, 1954; son of Abram and Ita (Grosman) Gotlieb. EDUCATION: CUNY, Brooklyn College, NY, 1970–74; graduate, Royal Academy of Dramatic Art, London, 1977.

CAREER: DEBUT—Giles Corey, *The Crucible,* Abraham Lincoln HS, Brooklyn, NY, 1969. NEW YORK DEBUT—Hamlet, *Dogg's Hamlet, Cahoot's Macbeth,* 22 Steps, 1979. LONDON DEBUT—Hamlet, *Dogg's Hamlet, Cahoot's Macbeth,* Collegiate, 1979. PRINCIPAL STAGE APPEARANCES—Billing, *An Enemy of the People,* Alaska Repertory, 1982; Edgar Linton, *Wuthering Heights,* Actors Theatre of Louisville, KY, 1983. MAJOR TOURS—Member of British American Repertory Company: Chamberlain, *Dirty Linen,* Arthur, *New-Found-Land,* Warwick, England, Sterling, Scotland, Nottingham, England, Theatre Royal, Brighton, England, the Wilbur, Boston, MA, Marine's Memorial, San Francisco, CA, 1979; Hamlet, *Dogg's Hamlet, Cahoot's Macbeth,* Warwick, Sterling, Nottingham, Brighton, Collegiate Theatre, London, John F. Kennedy Center, Washington, DC, Wilbur, Boston, MA, Marine's Memorial Theatre, San Francisco, CA, 1979.

AWARDS: Elizabeth P. Casey Award in Theatre, CUNY, Brooklyn College, 1974.

BEN GOTLIEB

ADDRESS: Home—2522 W. Second Street, Brooklyn, NY 11232.

* * *

GOTTLIEB, Carl, writer, director, and actor

PERSONAL: EDUCATION: Syracuse University, B.S., 1960.

CAREER: FILM DEBUT—Ugly John, *M*A*S*H*, 1969. PRINCIPAL FILM APPEARANCES—Meadows, *Jaws;* Iron Balls McGinty, *The Jerk.* TELEVISION DEBUT—*Hey Landlord.* DIRECTED: Films—*Absent Minded Waiter*, 1978; *Caveman*, 1981.

WRITINGS: SCREENPLAYS—*Jaws* (with Peter Benchley), 1974; *Which Way Is Up?* (with Cecil Brown), 1977; *Jaws II* (with Howard Sackler), 1978; *The Jerk* (with Steve Martin), 1979; *Caveman* (with Bruce Jay Friedman), 1981; *Jaws 3D* (with Richard Matheson), 1983.

AWARDS: Academy Award Nomination, Best Director, 1978: *Absent Minded Waiter.*

SIDELIGHTS: MEMBERSHIPS—Writers Guild of America West (board of directors), Academy of Motion Picture Arts and Sciences.

ADDRESS: Agent—c/o Larry Grossman, 211 S. Beverly Drive, #206, Beverly Hills, CA 90212.

GOULD, Harold (ne Harold V. Goldstein), actor

PERSONAL: Born December 10, 1923, in Schenectady, NY; son of Louis Glen (a post office clerk) and Lillian (a NY State Department of Health clerk) Goldstein; married Lea Shampanier (an actress; professional name, Lea Vernon), August 20, 1950; children: Deborah, Joshua, Lowell. EDUCATION: NY State College for Teachers, Albany (now State University of NY, Albany), B.A., 1947; Cornell University, M.A., 1948, Ph.D., 1953. MILITARY: U.S. Army, 1943–45.

CAREER: DEBUT—Thomas Jefferson, *The Common Glory*, Amphitheatre, Williamsburg, VA, 1955. NEW YORK DEBUT—Dr. Huml, *The Increased Difficulty of Concentration*, Forum, 1969. PRINCIPAL STAGE APPEARANCES—Edmund, *King Lear*, Ashland, OR, Shakespeare Festival, 1958; Benedick, *Much Ado About Nothing*, Ashland, OR, Shakespeare Festival, 1958; Old Man, *World of Ray Bradbury*, Coronet, Los Angeles, 1964; Goldberg, *The Birthday Party*, UCLA Theatre Group, Los Angeles, 1966; Anselme, Harpagon, *The Miser*, Mark Taper Forum, Los Angeles, 1968; Artie Shaughnessy, *The House of Blue Leaves*, Truck and Warehouse, NY, 1971; Glogauer, *Once in a Lifetime*, Mark Taper Forum, Los Angeles, 1975; Dr. Zubritsky, *Fools*, Eugene O'Neill, NY, 1981; Jack, *Grown Ups*, Lyceum, NY, 1981; Mr. Antrobus, *Skin of Our Teeth*, Old Globe, San Diego, 1983.

FILM DEBUT—*The Couch*, 1960. PRINCIPAL FILMS—Sheriff, *Harper*, 1965; Policeman, *Inside Daisy Clover*, 1965; Lawyer, *An American Dream*, 1966; Psychiatrist, *The Ar-*

HAROLD GOULD

rangement, 1969; Eric Scott, *The Lawyer,* 1969; Col. Nexhet, *Mrs. Pollifax: Spy,* 1971; Dr. Zerny, *Where Does It Hurt?,* 1972; Kid Twist, *The Sting,* 1973; Mayor, *The Front Page,* 1974; *Love and Death,* 1975; Prof. Baxter, *The Big Bus,* 1976; Chairman of the Board, *Silent Movie,* 1976; Judge, *Seems Like Old Times,* 1980.

TELEVISION DEBUT—Hong Kong, *To Catch a Star,* 1960. TELEVISION APPEARANCES—*Feather and Father Gang; Park Place; Foot in the Door; Rhoda; Moviola; Washington Behind Closed Doors; Aunt Mary; Better Late Than Never; King Crab; Have I Got a Christmas for Your; Man in the Santa Claus Suit; Hawaii Five-O; Gunsmoke; Soap; Mary Tyler Moore Show; Lou Grant; Dick Van Dyke; Police Story; Medical Story; Big Valley; Wild, Wild West; Jack Benny Show; Danny Kaye Show; Red Skelton Show.*

THEATRE-RELATED CAREER: Instructor of theatre and speech (1953–56), assistant professor of drama and speech (1956–60).

AWARDS: Emmy Nominations, 1979: *Moviola,* 1977: *Rhoda,* 1974: *Police Story;* Obie, 1969: *The Increased Difficulty of Concentration.*

SIDELIGHTS: MEMBERSHIPS—Academy of Motion Picture Arts and Sciences. RECREATION—Reading, jogging, swimming.

ADDRESS: Agent—c/o Sylvia Gold, ICM, 8899 Beverly Blvd., Los Angeles, CA 90048.

* * *

GOULD, Morton, composer

PERSONAL: Born December 10, 1913, in Richmond Hill, New York; son of James H. (a manager) and Frances (Arkin) Gould; married Shirley Uzin; Shirley Bank (a teacher); children: Eric, David, Abby, Deborah. EDUCATION: attended Richmond Hill High School; studied music with Abby Whiteside (piano) and Dr. Vincent Jones (composition).

CAREER: FIRST STAGE WORK—*Billion Dollar Baby,* New York, 1945, 219 performances. PRINCIPAL STAGE WORK—*Arms and the Girl,* 1950.

PRINCIPAL FILM WORK—*Delightfully Dangerous,* 1945; *Cinerama Holiday, Windjammer.* PRINCIPAL TELEVISION WORK—*World War I Documentary Series,* CBS, 1964–65; *F. Scott Fitzgerald in Hollywood,* ABC; *Holocaust,* 1978; hosted *The World of Music with Morton Gould,* NET.

PRINCIPAL BALLET WORK—Jerome Robbins' *Interplay;* Agnes de Mille's *Fall River Legend;* George Balanchine's *Clarinade;* Eliot Feld's *Santa Fe Saga* and *Halftime.*

OTHER COMPOSITIONS—*Piano Concerto,* 1938; *Pavanne,* 1938; *Stephen Foster Gallery,* 1940; *Latin-American Symphonette,* 1941; *Spirituals for Orchestra,* 1941; *Lincoln Legend,* 1942; *Symphony for Band,* 1952; *Tap Dance Concerto,* 1952; *Showpiece for Orchestra,* 1954; *Derivations for Clarinet and Band,* 1956; *Jekyll and Hyde Variations,* 1957; *American Ballads,* 1976; *Something to Do (Cantata-Musi-*

MORTON GOULD

cal); 1976; *Cheers (Celebration March);* 1979; *Housewarming,* 1982; also several symphonies, orchestral and instrumental works.

AWARDS: Grammy, Best Classical Recording of the year, *Charles Ives with the Chicago Symphony,* 1966.

SIDELIGHTS: MEMBERSHIPS—ASCAP (Board of Directors), American Symphony Orchestra League (Board of Directors).

Mr. Gould is also a well-respected conductor, guesting with such orchestras as the New York Philharmonic, Cleveland, Chicago, London, Pittsburgh Symphonies, and the London Philharmonic. He has recorded extensively and has toured with the above as well as with his own orchestra.

ADDRESS: Home—327 Melbourne Road, Great Neck, NY 11021; Agent—Walter Gould, 866 Third Avenue, New York, NY 10022.

* * *

GRANGER, Percy, actor, writer

PERSONAL: Born August 8, 1945, in Ithaca, NY; son of Bruce Ingham (a professor of American Literature) and Rosemary (an artist) Granger; married Helen Wright (a floral designer) on July 11, 1975; children: Andrew, Jamie. EDU-

CATION: Attended public schools in Norman, OK; Harvard College, B.A., (cum laude, English Literature) 1967.

CAREER: DEBUT—Teddy, *The Homecoming*, Provincetown Playhouse, MA, 1968. NEW YORK DEBUT—David, *The Dog Ran Away*, Ensemble Studio Theatre, 8 performances, 1974. PRINCIPAL STAGE APPEARANCES—Provincetown Playhouse: Yank, *The Hairy Ape*, 1968; Kilroy, *Camino Real*, 1968; Guildenstern, *Rozencrantz and Guildenstern Are Dead*, 1969; Bottom, *A Midsummer Night's Dream*, 1969; MAJOR TOUR—Rimbaud, *Total Eclipse*, Centaur Theatre, Montreal, 1971.

FILM DEBUT—Richard, *Golden Apples of the Sun*, 1971. TELEVISION DEBUT—Lawyer, *The Silence*, 1974.

WRITINGS: PLAYS, PRODUCED—*Studs Edsel*, Folger, Washington, DC, 1971; *Enchanted Cottage* (musical adaptation, with John McKinney), St. Nicholas, NY, 1980; *Vivien*, Lincoln Center, NY; *Eminent Domain*, McCarter, Princeton, NY, Circle-in-the-Square, NY. PLAYS, PUBLISHED—*Vivien*, 1982, *Leaving Cheyenne, Working Her Way Down* and *Forbidden Copy*, 1982; *Eminent Domain*, 1983; *Dolphin Position*, 1983.

FILM SCREENPLAYS—*Blind Love*. TELEVISION SCREENPLAYS—*The Scarlet Thread; Solitude Forty; Loving; Where the Air Is Clean.*

AWARDS: Honorable Mention, Radio Drama, Writers Guild, 1978–79; Eugene O'Neill Theatre Center, National Playwrights' Conference, *Eminent Domain*, 1977.

SIDELIGHTS: MEMBERSHIPS—Writers Guild, Dramatists Guild, ASCAP. RECREATION—rugby, squash.

Mr. Granger has written sixty-five radio dramas for Radio Mystery Theatre and other shows, a street theatre musical, and cabaret sketches.

ADDRESS: Agent—c/o Rick Leed, Hesseltine/Baker Ltd., 165 W. 46th Street, Suite 409, New York, NY 10036.

* * *

GRANT, Lee, actress, director

PERSONAL: Born October 31, 1931, in New York City; daughter of A.W. and Witia (Haskell) Rosenthal; married Arnold Manoff (a playwright; deceased); Joseph Feury (a producer), 1962; children: (first marriage) Dinah; (second marriage) Belinda. EDUCATION: Juilliard School of Music for voice, violin, and dance, Metropolitan Opera Ballet School, Neighborhood Playhouse.

CAREER: STAGE DEBUT—At age 4 as a princess, *L'Orocolo*, Metropolitan Opera. PRINCIPAL STAGE APPEARANCES—American Ballet; series of one-acters with Henry Fonda, ANTA, 1949; *Detective Story*, 1949; *Arms and the Man; All You Need Is One Good Break; Lo and Behold; Wedding Breakfast; Hole in the Head; Two for the See-Saw; Captains and Kings; The Prisoner of Second Avenue*, 1972; *The Maids; Electra.*

PRINCIPAL FILM APPEARANCES—*Detective Story*, 1952; *Terror in the Streets; The Balcony*, 1963; *Affair of the Skin*, 1964; *Divorce American Style*, 1967; *Valley of the Dolls*, 1967; *In the Heat of the Night*, 1968; *Buona Sera Mrs. Campbell*, 1969; *The Big Bounce*, 1969; *Marooned*, 1970; *The Landlord*, 1970; *There Was a Crooked Man*, 1970; *Plaza Suite*, 1971; *Portnoy's Complaint*, 1972; *Shampoo*, 1975; *Voyage of the Damned*, 1976; *Airport 77*, 1977; *The Swarm*, 1978; *The Mafu Cage*, 1978; *Damien: Omen II*, 1978; *When You Comin' Back, Red Ryder*, 1979; *Little Miss Marker*, 1980; *Charlie Chan and the Curse of the Dragon Queen*. PRINCIPAL TELEVISION APPEARANCES—*Studio One; The Kraft Theatre; Slattery's People; The Respectful Prostitute* (BBC); *The Fugitive; Ben Casey; The Nurses; The Defenders; East Side/West Side; Peyton Place; Bob Hope Show; The Love Song of Bernard Kempenski; The Neon Ceilings; The Spell; Laugh-In; Lieutenant Shuster's Wife*, 1972; *Partners in Crime*, 1973; *Fay*, 1975.

PRINCIPAL DIRECTING WORK—Film: *Tell Me a Riddle*, 1980, *The Willmar Eight, A Private View;* television: *Shape of Things*, 1973, *A Matter of Sex, When Women Kill.*

AWARDS: Academy Award, Best Supporting Actress, 1975: *Shampoo;* Academy Award Nominations: *Voyage of the Damned, The Landlord;* Cannes Film Festival, Best Actress, 1952: *Detective Story;* Emmy Awards, Best Actress, 1971: *The Neon Ceilings*, Best Supporting Actress, 1966: *Peyton Place;* Emmy Nomination: *The Bob Hope Show;* Outer Critics Circle Award: *Detective Story;* Obie: *The Maids.*

SIDELIGHTS: Miss Grant was honored by the Congressional Arts Caucus in 1983 for Oustanding Achievement in Acting and Independent Filmmaking for her film, *Tell Me a Riddle.*

ADDRESS: Agent—William Morris Agency, 151 El Camino Drive, Beverly Hills, CA 90212.

* * *

GRAVES, Peter (ne Peter Aurness), actor

PERSONAL: Born March 8, 1926, in Minneapolis, MN; son of Rolf C. (a businessman) and Ruth O. (a journalist; maiden name, Duesler) Aurness; married Joan Endress (community activist), December 16, 1950; children: Kelly Jean, Claudia, Amanda. EDUCATION: Attended University of Minnesota for three years. MILITARY: U.S. Army Air Force, 1944–45.

CAREER: FILM DEBUT—*Rogue River*, 1950. PRINCIPAL FILM APPEARANCES—*Fort Defiance; Stalag 17; Court Martial of Billy Mitchell; The Long Gray Line; Rage to Live; East of Sumatra; Beneath the 12-Mile Reef; The Raid; Black Tuesday; Wichita; Night of the Hunter; Naked Street; Fort Yuma; The Ballad of Josie; Sergeant Ryker; The Five Man Army; Sidecar Racers; Airplane; Airplane II.*

TELEVISION DEBUT—Fireside Theatre, 1951. PRINCIPAL TELEVISION APPEARANCES—*Fury*, 1955–59, *Mission Impossible*, 1967–73, two additional series and many single performances.

SIDELIGHTS: MEMBERSHIPS—SAG, AFTRA, AEA.

PETER GRAVES

ADDRESS: Office—415 N. Cresent Drive, Suite 210, Beverly Hills, CA 90210. Agent—The Artists Group, 10100 Santa Monica Blvd., Suite 310, Los Angeles, CA 90067.

* * *

GRAY, Amlin, playwright

PERSONAL: Born April 19, 1946, in New York; son of Ernest Amlin (a business man and teacher) and Marguerite (a social worker; maiden name, Tietjer) Gray; married Sharon Ott (divorced 1984). EDUCATION: Attended public schools in Bedford, NY; studied at the American Academy of Music and Dramatic Arts, New York City. MILITARY: U.S. Army, Specialist 4th Class, 1966–68.

WRITINGS: PLAYS, PRODUCED—*Founding Father,* O'Neill Theatre Center's National Playwrights Conference, CT, Cubiculo Theatre, NY; *Pirates, or Rackham in Love,* O'Neill Playwrights Conference, CT; *Namesake,* Milwaukee Repertory, WI; *Bo,* Milwaukee Repertory, Intiman Theatre, Seattle, WA; *How I Got That Story,* Milwaukee Repertory, Theatre Three, TX; *The Fantod,* Theatre X,

Milwaukee, Actors Theatre of St. Paul, MN; *Sixties,* Milwaukee Repertory; *Outlanders,* Actors Theatre of St. Paul, Milwaukee Repertory. PLAYS, PUBLISHED—*The Fantod,* 1982; *How I Got That Story,* 1982; *Kingdom Come,* 1983.

THEATRE-RELATED CAREER—Instructor of Theatre, University of Wisconsin, Milwaukee, 1978–80.

AWARDS: Guggenheim Fellowship, 1983; Rockefeller Foundation Award, 1982; Obie, *How I Got That Story,* 1981; National Endowment for the Arts Award, 1980.

SIDELIGHTS: MEMBERSHIPS—New Dramatists, Dramatists Guild.

ADDRESS: Home—2925 Stowell Avenue, Milwaukee, WI, 53211. Office—c/o Milwaukee Repertory Theatre, 929 N. Water Street, Milwaukee, WI, 53202. Agent—Lois Berman, 240 W. 44th Street, New York, NY 10036.

* * *

GRAY, Sam, actor

PERSONAL: Born July 18, 1923, in New York City; married Phyllis Coretz, August 24, 1946; children: Marsha, Sharon. EDUCATION: B.F.A. degree; studied for the theatre at Columbia College (Radio and Drama); with the Actors Company in Chicago; acting with Lee Strasberg and the American Theatre Wing, NY. MILITARY: U.S. Army Colonel, 334 Infantry, 84th Division, 1943–46.

CAREER: NEW YORK DEBUT—Dr. Paul Stone, *Deadfall,* Broadway, 1954. PRINCIPAL STAGE APPEARANCES—*Shadow of Heroes,* NY, 1961; Dr. Lefencola, *Saturday, Sunday, Monday,* Martin Beck, NY, 1974; Willie Loman, *Death of a Salesman,* Cincinnati Playhouse in the Park, 1975; Andrew Wyke, *Sleuth,* Syracuse Stage, NY, 1976; Sandor, *The Play's the Thing,* Counterpoint, NY, 1977; King Abdullah/Ben Gurion/Religious Minister/D.P., *Golda,* Morosco, NY, 1977; *The Royal Family,* Cincinnati Playhouse in the Park, 1978; *Conversation-Sinfonietta (Diversions),* Counterpoint, NY, 1978; *Semmelweis,* Kennedy Center, 1978; Alfieri, *A View from the Bridge,* Ambassador, NY, 1983.

MAJOR TOURS—Captain Henry Wirz, *The Andersonville Trial,* national company, 1959–60; Barney Greenwald, *The Caine Mutiny Court-Martial,* 1954; Mark Water, *In Praise of Love,* summer stock.

TELEVISION DEBUT—in Chicago, 1948. TELEVISION APPEARANCES—*Naked City; U.S. Steel Hour; Robert Montgomery Presents;* soap operas and over 850 appearances in other shows.

AWARDS: MILITARY—Bronze Star for Heroic Distinction, three Battle Stars; Combat Badge; Presidential Citation and Battalion Citation.

SIDELIGHTS: MEMBERSHIPS—The Players Club, AEA, AFTRA, SAG.

Mr. Gray has appeared in over one hundred plays on the legitimate stage.

ADDRESS: Agent—Dulcina Eisen Associates, 154 E. 61st Street, New York, NY 10021.

* * *

GRAYSON, Kathryn (nee Zelma Kathryn Elizabeth Hedrick), actress, singer

PERSONAL: Born February 9, 1924, in Winston-Salem, NC; daughter of Clarence Evans (a real estate broker builder) and Lillian Florence (Gray) Hedrick; married John Shelton, 1941 (divorced); married Johnny Johnston (a singer/actor), August 22, 1947; children: (second marriage) Patricia Kathryn (Patti-Kate). EDUCATION: St. Louis, and Los Angeles, public schools; MGM's "Little Red School House"; studied voice with Frances Marshall, Chicago Civic Opera. RELIGION: Episcopalian.

CAREER: NEW YORK DEBUT—Guinevere, *Camelot*, Majestic, October, 1962. PRINCIPAL STAGE APPEARANCES—Cio-Cio-San, *Madame Butterfly*, Mimi, *La Boheme*, Violetta, *La Traviata*, 1960; Sonja, *The Merry Widow*, Marietta, *Naughty Marietta*, 1961; Rosalinda, *Rosalinda*, 1962; Magnolia *Show Boat*; Lilly, *Kiss me, Kate*; *Night Watch*, Gateway, St. Petersburg, 1982. MAJOR TOURS—Guinevere, *Camelot*, National Tour, 1962.

KATHRYN GRAYSON

FILM DEBUT—*Andy Hardy's Private Secretary*, 1940. FILM APPEARANCES—*The Vanishing Virginian*, 1941; Rita, *Rio Rita*, 1941; *Seven Sweethearts*, 1942; *Thousands Cheer*, 1943; Susan Abbott, *Anchors Aweigh*, 1945; *Ziegfeld Follies*, 1945; *Till the Clouds Roll By*, 1945; *Two Sisters from Boston*, 1946; *It Happened in Brooklyn*, 1947; *The Kissing Bandit*, 1948; *That Midnight Kiss*, 1949; *The Toast of New Orleans*, 1950; *Grounds for Marriage*, 1950; Magnolia, *Show Boat*, 1951; Stephanie, *Lovely to Look At*, 1952; Margo, *The Desert Song*, 1952; Grace, *The Grace Moore Story*, 1953; Lilly, *Kiss Me, Kate*, 1954; Katherine de Vaucelles, *The Vagabond King*, 1955.

TELEVISION DEBUT—*General Electric Theatre—Shadow on the Heart*. TELEVISION APPEARANCES—*The Ed Sullivan Show, The Perry Como Show, The Jackie Gleason Show, The Pat Boone Show; Playhouse 90—Lone Women; General Electric Theatre—The Invitation, The Game of Hate;* others.

AWARDS: Emmy Nomination, Best Actress, *Shadows on the Heart*.

SIDELIGHTS: MEMBERSHIPS—SAG; AFTRA; AEA; Musicians Union Local 47.

Ms. Grayson has appeared in concerts all over the world, in opera houses, concert halls, the London Palladium. As a night club personality she has appeared at New York's Latin Quarter, the Sahara, Riviera and Harrah's Reno and Tahoe; her 1968 club act brought her together with her MGM co-star, Howard Keel, and they toured, world-wide. Ms. Grayson also appeared extensively on radio during her years as a movie star and prior to her arrival at MGM in 1938.

ADDRESS: Agent—Ruth Webb, 7500 DeVista Drive, Los Angeles, CA 90046.

* * *

GREEN, Guy, director, writer, director of photography

PERSONAL: Son of Charles Frederick and Anne Green; married Celia Josephine, April 24, 1948; children: Michael, Marilyn.

CAREER: FIRST FILM WORK—Projectionist at school, 1933. PRINCIPAL FILM WORK—Director of photography, *Great Expectations*, 1946; director, *Sea of Sand*, 1958; director, *The Angry Silence*, 1960; director, *The Mark*, 1961; director, *Light in the Piazza*, 1962; director/screenwriter, *A Patch of Blue*, 1965; director, *The Magus*, 1968; director, *Luther*, 1972; director, *Once Is not Enough*, 1974; director, *Devil's Advocate*, 1976.

TELEVISION DEBUT—*The Incredible Adventures of Dr. Meg Laurel*, 1978. PRINCIPAL TELEVISION WORK—Director: *Jennifer*, 1978; *Jimmy B & Andre*, 1980; *Inmates: A Love Story*, 1981; *Isobel's Choice*, 1982.

WRITINGS: SCREENPLAY—*A Patch of Blue*, 1965; *Infinity of Mirrors* (with Stewart Stern), 1966.

AWARDS: Samuel Goldwyn International Award, 1961: *The Mark*, 1961; Writers Guild Nomination, 1965: *A Patch of*

GUY GREEN

Blue; Academy Award, Black and White Photography, *Great Expectations,* 1947.

SIDELIGHTS: MEMBERSHIPS—DGA, WGA, British Society of Cinematographers.

ADDRESS: Agent—Phil Gersh, 222 N. Canon Drive, Beverly Hills, CA 90210.

* * *

GREEN, Hilton A., producer

PERSONAL: Born March 3, 1929, in Hollywood, CA; son of Alfred E. (a director) and Vivian (a silent film actress; maiden name, Reed) Green; married Helen Harker, June 6, 1952; children: Wendy, Bradley, Pamela. EDUCATION: University of California, B.S., 1952. MILITARY: U.S. Army.

CAREER: PRINCIPAL FILM WORK—Producer, *Psycho II,* 1983.

ADDRESS:Office—Universal Studios, 100 Universal City Plaza, Universal City, CA 91608.

* * *

GREEN, Joanne, puppet designer, milliner, costume designer

PERSONAL: Born June 16, 1955 in Philadelphia, PA; daughter of Byron L. (a steamfitter) and Dorothy E. (a secretary; maiden name, Miller) Green; married Anthony Galzarano (a chiropractor) on June 16, 1983. EDUCATION: University of Pennsylvania, 1972–73; Pennsylvania State University, B.F.A., 1976.

CAREER: PRINCIPAL STAGE WORK, millinery and costume crafts—*Annie,* NY; *Sugar Babies,* NY; *Evita,* NY; *A Chorus Line,* NY; *On the Twentieth Century,* NY; *Spotlight,* NY; *Sweeney Todd,* NY; *The Little Prince and the Aviator,* NY; *Grand Magic,* Manhattan Theatre Club, NY; *Eccentricities of a Nightingale,* Playwrights Horizons, NY; *Othello,* Juilliard School, NY; *A Midsummer Night's Dream,* Folger Theatre, Washington, DC; Center Stage, Baltimore, MD, 1976–77 season; Santa Fe Opera, ten operas, 1977–78; Opera Theatre of St. Louis, five operas, 1978; Spoleto Festival, USA, three operas, 1979; ballet—*Half Time,* Eliot Feld Ballet; Munich Ballet, 1978.

PRINCIPAL FILM WORK—(Puppet design, millinery and costume crafts) *The Great Muppet Caper,* Henson Associates, 1980; *The Dark Crystal,* Henson Associates, 1980–81; (specialty design) *The Wiz,* millinery, 1977; *All That Jazz,* 1979. PRINCIPAL TELEVISION WORK, puppet design, millinery, costume crafts—*The Muppet Show,* Henson Associates, 1979–80; *Sesame Street,* Henson Associates, 1979–82; *Fraggle Rock,* Henson Associates, 1982; *Bartleby the Scrivener,* millinery/costume crafts, 1977; *La Gioconda,* millinery, 1979.

THEATRE-RELATED CAREER: Costume and millinery work, Brooks Van Horn and Eaves Costumes; assistant to Woody Shelp at Barbara Matera Ltd., two years; staff designer, Henson Associates, 1979–present.

SIDELIGHTS: MEMBERSHIPS—United Scenic Artists; Association of Theatrical Artists and Craftpeople.

Joanne Green has served as millinery assistant through Brooks Van Horn to the Ringling Brothers, Barnum and Bailey Circus, and with Eaves Costume Company she worked on the Reno Floorshow at the MGM Grand Hotel and did the millinery work for Blackstone the Magician's national tour. For Henson Associates, she has designed the displays and served as a stylist for *The Art of the Muppets* touring museum show.

ADDRESS: Home—39 Charles Street, New York, NY 10014. Office—117 E. 69th Street, New York, NY 10021.

GREEN, Stanley, historian

PERSONAL: Born May 29, 1923, in New York City; son of Rudy Francis (a businessman) and Frances (Kuschner) Green; married Catherine Hunt (1954); children: Susan, Rudy. EDUCATION: Union College, Schenectady, NY; University of Nebraska; ASTP.

WRITINGS: BOOKS, PUBLISHED—*Encyclopedia of the Musical Theatre*, 1980; *The World of Musical Comedy*, 1981; *Encyclopedia of the Musical Film*, 1981; *Broadway Musicals of the 30's*, 1982; *Starring Fred Astaire*, 1973.

SIDELIGHTS: MEMBERSHIPS—The Players Club.

ADDRESS: Home—169 State Street, Brooklyn, NY 11201

* * *

GREEN, William, theatre historian, educator

PERSONAL: Born July 10, 1926, in New York City; son of Louis (a musician) and Hanna (Bernstein) Green; married Marguerite Joan Mayer (a teacher), August 14, 1960; children: Jonathan, Natalie. EDUCATION: Queens College, NY, A.B. 1949; Columbia University, M.A. 1950; Ph.D. 1959; studied for the theatre with Milton Smith at Columbia University. MILITARY—U.S. Navy, 1944–46 (musician 1/c). NON-THEATRICAL CAREER: Lecturer, Upsala College, Department of English, 1953–56; tutor, 1957–59/instructor, 1959–63/assistant professor, 1963–67/associate professor, 1967–72/professor, 1972–present, Queens College, Department of English.

CAREER: Lighting director, Woodstock Playhouse, Woodstock, NY; tech staff, *Lady in the Dark*, ELT, New York, 1952; play reader, theatre service department, ANTA, New York, 1952–53; finance department staff, Play Series: *Desire Under the Elms, Mrs. McThing, Golden Boy, Four Saints in Three Acts, Sunday Breakfast,* ANTA, New York, 1952; production assistant, *Evening with Will Shakespeare,* American Shakespeare Festival Theatre and Academy, 1953; business manager, Salt Creek Summer Theatre, Hinsdale, IL, 1953; stage manager, special entertainment unit, General Electric Company, Henderson Harbor, NY, 1956; host, CBS—Camera Three, *A Peek at Burlesque,* 1978.

WRITINGS: BOOKS, PUBLISHED—*Shakespeare's Merry Wives of Windsor,* 1962; editor, *The Merry Wives of Windsor,* 1965; co-editor with John Gassner, *Elizabethan Drama,* 1967; editor (with others), *A Style Manual for College Students,* 1973.

ARTICLES, PUBLISHED—"Eastward Ho! Theatrical Renaissance on New York's Lower East Side," *The Manchester Review,* Spring, 1957; "Fifty Years of Development in Musical Theater," in "Reestablishing the Speech Profession: The First Fifty Years," Speech Association of America, 1959; "Hendez Ballester's 'The Miracle' in New York," *Island Times* (Puerto Rico), December 1960; "Broadway Book Musicals: 1900–1969," *The American Theatre: A Sum of Its Parts,* Samuel French, 1971; "Humorous Characters and Attributive Names in Shakespeare's Plays," *Names,* September 1972; "The Audiences of the American Bur-

lesque Show of the Minsky Era (ca. 1920–1940) in New York," *Das Theatre und sein Publikum,* Vienna, 1977; "Oscar Wilde and the Bunburys," *Modern Drama,* March 1978; others.

AWARDS: Scholarship in Elizabethan and Shakespearean Drama, University of Birmingham, Post-Graduate Summer School, Stratford-Upon-Avon, 1950; Research Fellowship, Department of English, University of Manchester (England), 1956–57; A.B. Cum Laude; Phi Beta Kappa; U.S. Delegate to the University Commission of the International Federation for Theatre Research, 1973; National Chairman for the Conference on the History of American Popular Entertainment, Lincoln Center, NY, November, 1977; National Treasurer and member of the program committee for the Musical Theatre in America Conference, C. W. Post College, April, 1981; Queens College Andrew W. Mellon Foundation Fellowship for research on New York City Theatre, 1700–1900, awarded 1982–83–84; City University of New York Research Award for work on William Hallam, awarded 1982–83 (renewed 1983–84); Fulbright lecturer in American Theater, University of Vienna, spring, 1983.

SIDELIGHTS: MEMBERSHIPS—Renaissance Society of America; College English Association; Modern Language Association; Malone Society; Shakespeare Association of America; Theatre Library Association; American Society for Theatre Research (Secretary/Treasurer, 1966–73; Executive Committee, 1973–76, 1978–81); International Federation for Theatre Research (President, 1983–87); Local 802, AFM (clarinet). RECREATION—Music, photography, philately, travel.

ADDRESS: Home—50-10 199th Street, Fresh Meadows, NY 11365; Office—Department of English, Queens College, Flushing, NY 11367.

* * *

GREENBERG, Edward M., director, producer, writer

PERSONAL: Born July 22, 1924, in New York City; son of Herman M. (a salesman) and Bess (a legal secretary; maiden name, Levy) Greenberg; married Sara Dillon (an actress and singer), April 30, 1957; children: Elizabeth, David. EDUCATION: City College of New York, B.S.S., 1948; University of Wisconsin, M.A., 1949; studied with Erwin Piscator at the New School Dramatic Workshop. MILITARY: U.S. Army, PFC, Signal Corps, Pacific Theatre Operation, 1942–46.

CAREER: FIRST STAGE WORK—Assistant Stage Manager, Music Circus, Hyannis, MA, 1950. PRINCIPAL THEATRE WORK—Director, Warwick, Oakdale, Milwaukee, Jacksonville, Miami, and other Summer Theatres, 1951–55; Director, Municipal Opera of St. Louis, 1957–59; Director, Jones Beach Marine Theatre, NY, 1960; Director, Richard Rogers Music Theatre of Lincoln Center, NY, 1960; Resident Director/Associate Producer, Civil Light Opera Associations, Los Angeles and San Francisco, 1969–70; Director, White House Conference on Children—Stage and Television Production, 1970; Executive Producer, Municipal Opera of St. Louis, St. Louis, MO, 1971–present.

TELEVISION DEBUT—Director, *Roberta,* 1958. PRINCIPAL

TELEVISION WORK—Director, *Archy and Mehitabel*, Play of the Week, 1959.

THEATRE-RELATED CAREER—Instructor, Department of Drama and Theatre, Queens College, 1951–57; Instructor, Department of Speech, City College of New York, 1953–55; Founder/Director, Musical Theatre Workshop of Los Angeles Civic Light Opera, 1963–70; Director, Colden Center for the Performing Arts, Queens College, 1975–80; Professor of Theatre, Department of Drama, Theatre, and Dance, Queens College, 1971–present.

WRITINGS: ADAPTATIONS—*The Merry Widow, The Student Prince.*

SIDELIGHTS: MEMBERSHIPS—SSDC, AEA, ISPAA, Players Club.

"As a director and teacher, I believe in the primacy of the word—the full understanding of the playwrights intention and the theatrical visual, aural, and kinetic communication of that intention."

ADDRESS: Home—161 E. 79th Street, New York, NY 10021. Office—c/o Municipal Theatre Association, St. Louis, Forest Park, St. Louis, MO, 63112; Department of Drama, Theatre, and Dance, Queens College, CUNY, Flushing, NY 11360.

* * *

GREENE, David, director, writer, actor

PERSONAL: Born February 22, 1921, in Manchester, England; married Lauren Rickey (an historian and researcher of Native American arts and crafts); children: Lindy, Nicolas, Laurence, Linsel. POLITICS: "One World or None." MILITARY: Conscientious Objector.

CAREER: PRINCIPAL TELEVISION WORK: Director—*Hamlet, Othello, Macbeth,* CBC, Toronto; *Hallmark Hall of Fame; Playhouse 90; Studio One; Omnibus; Defenders; Leonard Bernstein and the New York Philharmonic; People Next Door,* 1970; *Vacation in Hell; Trial of Lee Harvey Oswald; World War III; The Choice; Rehearsal for Murder; Count of Monte Cristo; Take Your Best Shot; Ghost Dancing; Rich Man, Poor Man,* 1976; *Roots,* 1977; *Prototype; The Guardian; For Love of a Soldier; Friendly Fire,* 1979; *Future Vision* (forthcoming).

PRINCIPAL FILM WORK: Director—*The Shuttered Room,* 1968; *Sebastian,* 1968; *The Strange Affair,* 1968; *I Start Counting; Godspell,* 1973; *Gray Lady Down,* 1978; *Hard Country.*

PRINCIPAL THEATRE APPEARANCES—Actor, *Anthony and Cleopatra,* Ziegfeld, NY, 1952.

WRITINGS: SCREENPLAYS—*Godspell.*

AWARDS: Emmy Awards, 1979: *Friendly Fire,* 1977: *Roots,* 1976: *Rich Man, Poor Man,* 1970: *The People Next Door,*: Writers Guild Nomination, 1973: *Godspell.*

SIDELIGHTS: MEMBERSHIPS—Native American Rights Fund, Campaign for Economic Democracy, South Poverty Law Center, Amnesty International, ACLU, Union of Concerned Scientists, "and every other group warning the world about the imminence of nuclear war."

ADDRESS: Agent—Bill Haber, Creative Artists Agency, 1888 Century Park E., Suite 1400, Los Angeles, CA 90067.

* * *

GREENE, James (ne James Nolan), actor

PERSONAL: Born December 1, 1926, in Lawrence, MA; son of Timothy (a policeman) and Martha (Greene) Nolan; married Betty Miller, December 5, 1955. EDUCATION: Emerson College, Boston, B.A., 1950. MILITARY: U.S. Navy Air Force, 1943–45.

CAREER: DEBUT—Capulet Servant, *Romeo and Juliet,* Broadhurst, New York, 1951. PRINCIPAL STAGE APPEARANCES—(Broadway)—*Foxfire, School for Wives, Ring Around the Bathtub, The Andersonville Trial, Compulsion, Inherit the Wind, Night Life, Shadow of a Gunman, Girl of the Via Flaminia, Romeo and Juliet, You Can't Take It with You, War and Peace, School for Scandal, Pantagleize, The Wild Duck, The Showoff, Right You Are If You Think You Are;* (Off-Broadway)—*One Crack Out, Down River, Nourish the Beast, The Iceman Cometh, In White America, Misalliance, The Hostage, Desire under the Elms, Plays for Bleecker Street, American Gothic, Moon in the Yellow River, Danton's Death, Incident at Vichy, The Changeling, Marco Millions, After the Fall, Fathers and Sons, The Arbor, Artichoke, Othello, Salt Lake City Skyline, Summer, Bella Figura, The Freak, Great Days; Play Memory,* McCarter Theatre, Princeton, NJ; *Ragged Mountain Elegies,* Petersborough Playhouse, NH; *The Elephant Man,* Westport Country Playhouse, CT; *The Rope Dancers,* New York; *The Carnival of Glorie,* New York; *Man Is Man,* State University of New York production.

FILM DEBUT—Pool player, *The Hustler.* PRINCIPAL FILMS—*The Lincoln Conspiracy; The Missouri Breaks; Crazy Joe; The Bug; Doc; The Traveling Executioner; Pound; Mad Dog Coll; Soup for One; Ghost Story; A Little Sex; Hanky Panky; Some Sunny Day; Trust Me.* TELEVISION DEBUT—*You Are There.* TELEVISION APPEARANCES—*Rage of Angels; All in the Family; The Tony Randall Show; The Spell; My Luke and I; Good Times; Hollywood Television Theatre; Love of Life; Stubby Pringle's Christmas; Blind Ambition; As We with Candles Do; Attica; Thin Ice; Short Stories, Tall Tales; The Cop and the Anthem; The Hand-Me-Down Kid; Another World; Edge of Night; Puddinhead Wilson.*

ADDRESS: Home—128 W. 70th Street, New York, NY 10023.

* * *

GREENE, Richard, actor

PERSONAL: Born January 8, 1946, in Cornwall-on-the-Hudson, New York; son of Morris E. (a pharmacist) and

RICHARD GREENE

Leona (Hoffman) Greene; married Lynne Milgrim, June 30, 1980; children: Jocelyn. EDUCATION: University of Florida, 1963; University of Miami and Florida Atlantic University (1965–66), B.A.; Wayne State University (Detroit), (1966–68), in Hillberry Classic Repertory Theatre, M.A. program.

CAREER: DEBUT—The Professor, *The Lesson,* Ring, Miami, Florida, 1966. NEW YORK DEBUT—Macduff, *Macbeth,* Mercer O'Casey Theatre, January 1971, 112 performances. PRINCIPAL STAGE APPEARANCES—Gentleman Caller, *The Glass Managerie,* Center Stage, Baltimore, 1970; Stage Manager, *Play Strindberg,* O'Kelly, *Mary Stuart,* Repertory Theatre of Lincoln Center, NY, 1971; Gunner Tar, *Narrow Road to the Deep North,* Sea Captain, *Twelfth Night,* Ezekiel Cheever, *The Crucible,* Repertory Theatre of Lincoln Center, NY, 1972; Mitch, *A Streetcar Named Desire,* Hartford, CT, 1972; Petruchio, *The Taming of the Shrew,* Studio Arena, Buffalo, NY, 1973; Antonio, *The Merchant of Venice,* Panthino, *Two Gentlemen of Verona,* Gloucester, *King Lear,* Old Globe, San Diego, 1973;

James Daley, *That Championship Season,* Studio Arena, Buffalo, 1973; Dan King, *Plain and Fancy,* John Proctor, *The Crucible,* Love, *Tobacco Road,* Fulton Opera House, Lancaster, PA, 1974; Cleante, *Tartuffe,* Playhouse-in-the-Park, Cincinnati, OH, 1974; John Chisum, *The Collected Works of Billy the Kid,* Folger, Washington, DC, 1975; Smirnov, *The Bear,* 1975; Alan, *Endangered Species,* Peachtree Playhouse, Atlanta, GA, Poinciana Playhouse, Palm Beach, FL, 1976; Biff, *Death of a Salesman,* Studio Arena, Buffalo, 1976; Astrov, *Uncle Vanya,* Olney, MD, 1976; Prince Escalus, *Romeo and Juliet,* Circle-in-the-Square, NY, 1977; George, *Same Time, Next Year,* Studio Arena,

Buffalo, NY, 1977; Bobby Stein, *Family Business,* Astor Place, Roundabout, NY, 1978–79;

Arthur, *The Tenth Man,* Performing Arts Foundation of Long Island, NY, 1980; Alcibiades, *Timon of Athens,* Yale Rep, New Haven, CT, 1980; LeBret, *Cyrano de Bergerac,* Williamstown Theatre Festival, MA, 1980; Markowsky, *The Survivor,* Morosco, NY, 1981; Tyrone, *A Moon for the Misbegotten,* Victory, Dayton, OH, 1981; Jerry, *Betrayal,* Syracuse Stage, NY, 1981; Marshall, *Alms for the Middle Class,* Pittsburgh Public, PA, 1983; Catesby, *Richard III,* NY Shakespeare Festival, 1983.

MAJOR TOURS—Bill Ray, *On Golden Pond,* Ogunquit, Maine, Corning, New York, Falmouth, MA, Cape Playhouse, Dennis, MA 1981; Peter, *Lunch Hour,* Birmingham, MS, Elitch Theatre, Denver, CO, Pocono Playhouse, Mountain Home, PA, Corning, NY, 1982.

TELEVISION DEBUT—Bobby Stein, *Family Business,* PBS American Playhouse, 1983.

AWARD: Focus Stage Award (Buffalo Courier-Express), *That Championship Season,* 1973, *Death of a Salesman,* 1976.

ADDRESS: Agent—Bret Adams, Ltd., 448 W. 44th Street, New York, NY 10036.

* * *

GREENWALD, Robert Mark, director, teacher

PERSONAL: Born August 8, 1943; son of Harold (a psychologist) and Ruth Greenwald; married Nancy; children: Rachel, Leah. EDUCATION: Antioch College, New School for Social Research.

CAREER: PRINCIPAL STAGE WORK: Director—*I Have a Dream; Me and Bessie; A Sense of Humor.*

PRINCIPAL TELEVISION WORK: Director—*The Burning Bed; In the Custody of Strangers; The Mistress; Centerfold.*

RELATED CAREER: Teacher of theatre, New York University; teacher, California Institute of the Arts.

ADDRESS: Office—2217 S. Purdue, Los Angeles, CA 90064. Agent—Lenny Hershaun, William Morris Agency, 151 El Camino Drive, Beverly Hills, CA 90212.

* * *

GRETH, Roma, playwright

PERSONAL: Born December 18, 1935 in Philadelphia, PA; daughter of Walter Leeser (a book dealer) and Helen Linton Eshbach. NON-THEATRICAL CAREER: Freelance writer, advertising, short stories, religious writing and articles.

WRITINGS: PLAYS, PRODUCED—*Narcissus,* Plaza Players,

Oxnard, CA; *Worms*, Omni Theatre Club, NY, Brookdale Community College, NJ; *The American War Women*, WPA, NY, Washington Area Feminist Theatre, DC; *Cassiopea*, Lincoln Center Showcase, NY, George Washington University, Washington, DC; *Curtain Call*, WPA, NY, Expressionist, NY; *The Greatest Day of the Century*, Aspen Playwrights Conference, CO, American Place, NY; *Halfway*, WPA, NY, Women's Prison, Claymont, CA; *The Heaven Mother*, Academy, GA, NY Shakespeare Festival; *November People*, Actors Place, NY; *The Pottstown Carnival*, Atlantic City Playhouse, NJ; *Quality of Mercy*, Playwrights Horizons, NY, Syracuse Stage, NY; *Windfall Apples*, O'Neill Theatre Center's Playwrights Conference, Impossible Ragtime, NY; *Four Lanes to Jersey*, St. Clements, NY. PLAYS, UNPRODUCED—A Second Summer; On Summer Days; The Believers.

AWARDS: Pennsylvania Council for the Arts Grant, 1981; University of Miami, Playwrights Award, 1978; Bicentennial Playwriting Award, Washington Area Feminist Theatre; Winner, Scene Award, New York City.

SIDELIGHTS: MEMBERSHIPS—Writers Guild of America, East; associate member, Dramatists Guild; Women's Project, American Place, NY;

ADDRESS: Home—148 Clymer Street, Reading, PA 19602. Agent—Ivy Stone and Charles Hunt, c/o Fifi Oscard Associates, 19 W. 44th Street, New York, NY 10036.

* * *

GRIFASI, Joe (Joseph G.), actor

PERSONAL: Born June 14, 1944, in Buffalo, NY; son of Joseph J. (a skilled laborer) and Patricia T. (Gaglione) Grifasi; married Jane Ira Bloom (a musician). EDUCATION: Yale School of Drama, M.F.A., 1975. MILITARY: U.S. Army, 1963–66 (Specialist fourth class).

CAREER: DEBUT—*The Bourgeois Gentleman*, Yale Repertory, New Haven, CT, 1972. NEW YORK DEBUT—Frank, *Memory of Two Mondays*, Phoenix, 1975, 50 performances. PRINCIPAL STAGE APPEARANCES—Flute/Thisbe, *A Midsummer Night's Dream*, Yale Repertory, New Haven, CT, 1975; Mic Phelan, *Says I Says He*, Phoenix, NY, 1979; Semyon, *The Suicide*, Yale Repertory, 1981; *Non Pasquale*, New York Shakespeare Festival, 1983.

FILM DEBUT—Bandleader, *The Deerhunter*, 1977. PRINCIPAL FILMS—Morris, *On the Yard*, 1977; Manny, *Hide in Plain Sight*, 1978; Osvaldo, *Honky Tonk Freeway*, 1980; Detective Vitucci, *Still of the Night*, 1981; Mario, *Sweet Ginger Brown*, 1983.

TELEVISION DEBUT—*Police Surgeon*, 1974. TELEVISION APPEARANCES—*The Elephant Man; The Gentleman Bandit; Search for Tomorrow*.

SIDELIGHTS: MEMBERSHIPS—AEA; SAG; AFTRA; ACTRA (Canada).

ADDRESS: Agent—Bruce Savan, Agency for the Performing Arts, 1650 Broadway, New York, NY 10019.

GRIFFIN, Tom, actor, playwright

PERSONAL: Born February 14, 1946 in Providence, RI; son of Thomas E., Sr. (a hospital maintenance supervisor) and Violet (Drumm) Griffin; married Martha McGowan (a teacher) in 1981; children: Jamie Thomas. EDUCATION: University of Rhode Island, B.A., 1969.

CAREER: PRINCIPAL STAGE WORK, ACTOR—Member of the company, Trinity Square Repertory Company, Providence, RI, 1974–83, and has performed with Theatre Company of Boston.

WRITINGS: PLAYS, PRODUCED—*Will The Gentlemen in Cabin Six Please Rise to the Occasion* (one-act), Joanne Meredith Repertory Theatre, Los Angeles, CA, 1968; *Workers*, St. Clement's, NY, 1975; *The Taking Away of Little Willie*, Mark Taper Forum Lab, 1978, Mark Taper Forum, 1979; *Einstein and the Polar Bear*, Hartford Stage Company, CT, 1980, Cort, NY, 1981, published, 1982; *Pasta*, Long Wharf, New Haven, CT, 1982; *Amateurs*, Alley, Houston, TX, 1984. PLAYS, UNPRODUCED—Damaged Hearts, Broken Flowers, 1983. SCREENPLAYS—*Einstein and the Polar Bear*, 1984.

AWARDS: Foundation for the Dramatists Guild/CBS Award, *Amateurs;* National Endowment for the Arts Playwriting Fellowship, 1981; selected for National Playwrights Conference, Eugene O'Neill Theatre Center, 1980: *Einstein and the Polar Bear;* LA Drama Critics Cricle Award Nomination, Oustanding Achievement in Playwriting, 1979: *The Taking Away of Little Willie;* Editorial Award, *Playboy* Magazine, short story, 1973: "Flies, Snakes, Fat Benny."

ADDRESS: Agent—Gilbert Parker, c/o William Morris Agency, 1350 Avenue of the Americas, New York, NY 10019.

* * *

GRIMES, Tammy (Lee), actress, director, writer

PERSONAL: Born January 30, 1934, in Lynn, MA; daughter of Nicholas Luther (farmer, innkeeper, and country club manager) and Eola Willard (a spiritualist and naturalist; maiden name, Niles) Grimes; married: Christopher Plummer (actor), August, 1956 (divorced 1960); Jeremy Brett (actor); married and divorced, 1964; Richard Jameson Bell (composer, arranger, and writer), December 25, 1982 (Miss Grimes announced that this was a mock marriage on June 8, 1983, but her current biography refers to him as her "sometimes husband"); children: (first marriage) Amanda. EDUCATION: Beaver Day School, Chestnut Hill, MA; Stephens College, Columbia, MO; studied for the theatre with Sanford Meisner at the Neighborhood Playhouse and voice with Marjorie Schloss. RELIGION: Protestant.

CAREER: DEBUT—Lady-in-waiting, *Victoria Regina*, Beaver Day School, 1949. NEW YORK DEBUT—Replacement for Kim Stanley as Cherie, *Bus Stop*, Music Box, 1955, for eight weeks. LONDON DEBUT—singing "Melancholy Baby", *Actors Benefit*, Palladium, 1960. PRINCIPAL STAGE APPEARANCES—Sabrina, *The Skin of Our Teeth*, 1950; *Three Men on a Horse*, Falmouth Playhouse, MA, 1952; Apprentice, Westport Country Playhouse, including role of Cockney

Juror, *The Verdict*, 1954; Eshtemoa, *Jonah and the Whale*, Neighborhood Playhouse, NY, 1955; *The Littlest Revue*, Phoenix, NY, 1956; the Flounder, *Clerembard*, Rooftop, NY, 1957; Mistress Quickly, *Henry IV, Part I*, Mopsa, *The Winter's Tale*, Shakespeare Festival Theatre, Stratford, Ontario, Canada, 1958; Lulu D'Arville, *Look after Lulu*, Henry Miller's, NY, 1959; Moll, *The Cradle Will Rock*, City Center, NY, 1960; Molly Tobin, *The Unsinkable Molly Brown*, Winter Garden, NY, 1960; Cyrenne, *Rattle of a Simple Man*, Booth, NY, 1963; Elvira, *High Spirits*, Alvin, NY, 1964; Sharon McLonergan, *Finian's Rainbow*, Burlingame, CA, 1965;

The Decline and Fall of the Entire World as Seen Through the Eyes of Cole Porter, Huntington Hartford, Los Angeles, 1967; Fran Walker, *The Only Game in Town*, Broadhurst, NY, 1968; Amanda Prynne, *Private Lives*, Billy Rose, NY, 1969; *The Imaginary Invalid*, Walnut Street, Philadelphia, 1971; Kate, *The Taming of the Shrew*, Walnut Street, Philadelphia, 1974; Pamela Fox, *Perfect Pitch*, Eisenhower, Washington, DC, 1974; title role, *Gabrielle*, Studio Arena, Buffalo, NY, 1974; Vicky, *My Fat Friend*, Royal Poinciana Playhouse, Palm Beach, FL, 1975; Lydia Cruttwell, *In Praise of Love*, Westport Country Playhouse, Westport, CT, 1975; *A Musical Jubilee*, St. James, NY, 1975; Hannah Warren, Diana Nichols, Gert Franklin, *California Suite*, Ahmanson, Los Angeles, then O'Neill, NY, 1976; title role, *Molly*, Hudson Guild, NY, 1978; Elmire, *Tartuffe*, Circle in the Square, NY, 1978; Paula Cramer, *Trick*, Playhouse, NY, 1979; Marian, *Father's Day*, American Play, NY, 1979; Natalya Petrovna, *A Month in the Country*, Roundabout Stage One, NY, 1979; Dorothy Brock, *42nd Street*, Winter Garden, then Majestic, NY, 1981; *Actors & Actresses*, pre-Broadway, 1983; also: Madame Arcati, *Blithe Spirit*, Stratford, Ontario; Maria, *Twelfth Night*, Cambridge Festival Theatre.

MAJOR TOURS—Adele, *The Amazing Adele*, national, 1955–56; Agnes Sorel, *The Lark*, national, 1956; *The Unsinkable Molly Brown*, national, 1962; *The Private Ear and the Public Eye*, 1965; *The Warm Peninsula*, Summer, 1971; . . . *Molly Brown*, Summer, 1973; Amanda, *Private Lives*, Spring, 1974; Vicky, *My Fat Friend*, 1974; *Molly*, 1975.

FILM APPEARANCES—*Three Bites of the Apple*, 1967; *Play It as It Lays*, 1972; Erna, *The Runner Stumbles*, 1977; *Somebody Killed Her Husband*, 1978; *Can't Stop the Music*, 1980.

TELEVISION APPEARANCES—*U.S. Steel Hour*, "The Bride Cried," 1955; *Holiday Special*, 1956; *Studio One*, "Babe in the Woods," 1957; *Heaven Will Protect the Working Girl*, 1957; Mary, *Omnibus*, "Forty Five Minutes from Broadway," 1959; Mehitabel, *Archie and Mehitabel*, 1960; *Four for Tonight*, 1960; *Hollywood Sings*, 1960; *The Datchet Diamonds*, 1960; She, *The Four Poster*, 1962; *The Virginian*, "The Exiles," 1963; *Route 66*, "Come Home Greta Inger Gruenschaffen," 1963; *Burke's Law*, "Who Killed Jason Shaw," 1964; *Destry*, "The Solid Gold Girl," 1964; *Trials of O'Brien*, 1964; Tammy Ward, *The Tammy Grimes Show*, 1966; *Tarzan*, 1967; *The Smothers Brothers Comedy Hour*, 1967; *The Outcasts*, 1969; *The Other Man*, 1970; *Love, American Style*, 1971; *The Horror at 37,000 Feet*, 1973; *The Borrowers*, 1973; *The Spy Who Returned from the Dead*, 1974; *The Snoop Sisters*, 1974; *'Twas the Night Before Christmas*, 1974; *You Can't Go Home Again*, 1978.

RECORDINGS: In addition to the original cast recordings of *The Littlest Revue, The Unsinkable Molly Brown, High Spirits* and *42nd Street*, Miss Grimes recorded two solo albums for Columbia records, *Tammy Grimes* and *The Unsinkable Tammy Grimes* as well as the following for Caedmon: *A.A. Milne's The Rabbit, Higglety-Pigglety-Pop, Kenny's Window, Where the Wild Things Are, William Faulkner's "Wash" and "A Rose for Emily"*, the complete works of Tomie de Paole and *Othello Bachs' "Lilly, Willy and the Mail Order Witch"*. She can also be heard on many of the Ben Bagley "Revisited" series.

NIGHT CLUBS: Miss Grimes has appeared at the *Downstairs at the Upstairs*, 1958, *The Hollywood Palace*, in Las Vegas, 1967, *Freddy's* and *Les Mouche*, both in New York, 1981, among others.

AWARDS: Antoinette Perry Award and Drama Critics Circle Award, 1970: *Private Lives*, 1961: *The Unsinkable Molly Brown;* NYC Mayor's Award of Honor, 1977; two "Mother of the Year" awards by the Talbot Foster Children's Services Association for creatively combining a career in the performing arts and parenting; Order of St. Joan, Knights of Malta Ecumenical award, 1984; she was a recipient of a 1981 National Endowment Award; the Boston Botannical Society named a flower after her in 1969.

SIDELIGHTS: MEMBERSHIPS—ASPCA, Landmarks Preservation Society, Whale Protection Society, Save the Seals Foundation, Save the Theatres, East 74th Street Association (board member), Whitney Museum. RECREATION—Drawing, baking bread.

Miss Grimes has also written poetry for the Olympics. "To be an original . . . to be you . . . to act is to be . . . to be is to merely seem, the truth." quote from Hans Eckhardt.

ADDRESS: Agent—Don Buchwald Ten E. 44th Street, New York, NY 10017.

*   *   *

GROENENDAAL, Cris, actor, singer

PERSONAL: Born February 17, 1948, in Erie, PA. EDUCATION: Allegheny College, BA 1970. NON-THEATRICAL CAREER—Peace Corps, 1971–72.

CAREER: NEW YORK DEBUT—Anthony Hope, *Sweeney Todd*, Uris, July 31, 1979. PRINCIPAL STAGE APPEARANCES—Dinny Doyle, *Eileen*, Town Hall, NY, 1981; *A Stephen Sondheim Evening*, Whitney Museum, NY, 1983; Danilo, *The Merry Widow*, New York City Opera, 1983; Candide, *Candide*, New York City Opera, 1983. MAJOR TOURS—Anthony Hope, *Sweeney Todd*, Washington, DC, Philadelphia, Boston, Chicago, San Francisco, Los Angeles, October 1980–September 1981.

TELEVISION DEBUT—Dr. Harrow, *The Doctors*. TELEVISION APPEARANCES—Anthony Hope, *Sweeney Todd;* Merv Griffin Show.

ADDRESS: Agent—Baldwin-Scully, Inc., 501 Fifth Avenue, New York, NY 10017.

GROSSVOGEL, David, I., critic, writer, educator

PERSONAL: Born June 19, 1925, in San Francisco, CA; son of Roula Gur and Ada (Bloom) Grossvogel; married Anita Vidossoni in 1953 (divorced 1973); married Jill E. Jacobs, June 22, 1974; children: (first marriage) Steven, Deborah. EDUCATION: University of California at Berkley, B.A., 1949; Certificat d'Université (Grenoble, France), 1950; Columbia University, M.A., 1951, Ph.D., 1954. MILITARY: U.S. Air Force, 1943–45.

CAREER: EDUCATIONAL—Instructor, Columbia University, 1954–56; Assistant Professor, Harvard University, 1956–60; Associate Professor, Cornell University, 1960–64; Professor, Cornell University, 1964; First Goldwin Smith Professor of Comparative Literature and Romance Studies, Cornell University, 1970–present.

WRITINGS: EDITORIAL—Managing Editor, *Romantic Review*, 1954–56; Founder/Editor, *Diacritics*, 1971–76; BOOKS, PUBLISHED—*The Self Conscious Stage*, 1958, reprinted as *Twentieth-Century French Drama*, 1961; *Four Playwrights and a Postscript*, 1962, reprinted as *The Blasphemers*, 1964; *Limits of the Novel: Evolutions of a Form from Chaucer to Robbe-Grillet*, 1968 and 1971; *Divided We Stand: Reflections on the Crisis at Cornell*, with C. Strout, 1970 and 1971; *Mystery and Its Fictions: From Oedipus to Agatha Christie*, 1979. ARTICLES—"A Belgian Notebook," *Alumni*, (Brussels), 1953; "New Departures in Contemporary Comedy," *RR*, 1954; "The Play of Light and Shadow," *YFS*, 1956–57; "Pierre Reverdy: The Fabric of Reality," *YFS*, 1958; "The French Dramatist," *The Saturday Review*, 1958; "The Depths of Laughter," *YFS*, 1959; "Ritual and Circumstance in Modern French Drama," *L'Esprit Créateur*, 1962; "Jean Genet: The Difficulty of Defining," *YFS*, 1962; "Claudel," *Encyclopedia of World Literature*, 1967; "Perception as a Form of Phenomenological Criticism, "*Hartford Studies in Literature*, 1970; "Fellini's Satyricon," *Diacritics*, 1971; "Visconti and the Too, Too Solid Flesh," *Diacritics*, 1971; "Some Reasons for the Phenomenon of the New," *KRO*, 1971; "Bunuel's Obssessed Camera," *Diacritics*, 1972; "When the Stain Won't Wash: Polanski's Macbeth," *Diacritics*, 1972; "Blow-up: The Forms of an Esthetic Itinerary," *Diacritics*, 1972; "Truffaut and Roché," *Diacritics*, 1973; "Show and Tell: Movies, Movie Making," *Diacritics*, 1973; "Conversation with A. R. Ammons," *Diacritics*, 1973; "Ionesco et l'absurde," Chapter III in *Ionesco*, Garnier: *Les Critiques de notre temps*, 1973; "Sinews of Revolution: The Revolutionary, the Artist, and Death," *Diacritics*, 1974; "Desnoes and Gutiérrez Alea," *Diacritics*, 1974; "Recuperating the Political Film," *Diacritics*, 1975; "Heads or Tails: Women in American Movies and Society," *Diacritics*, 1975; "Signs of Our Times," *Diacritics*, 1976; "Lina Wertmüller and the Failure of Criticism," *YIS*, 1977; "Semi-optics: Lotman and Cinema," *Journal of the University Film Association*, 1980; "Avant que l'escés n'excéde," *Michel de Ghelderode et le théatre contemporain*, Brussels: *S.I.D.E.M.D.G.*, 1980; "The Wake of Daedalus: Further Discontents of an Ever More Pervasive Civilization," *Diacritics*, 1980; "Ionesco: Symptom and Victim," *The Dream and the Play*, 1982; "The Long Life and Surprising Afterdeath of Agatha Christie," (forthcoming). REVIEWS—Entries on Cammaerts, Crommelynck, Ghelderode, Lemonnier, Mallet-Joris, Rodenbach, Verhaeren, Belgian literature, for *Arete's Encyclopedia*, 1978; "Adam's *AfterJoyce*," *Georgia Review*, 1978;

"Girard's *Critique dans un souterrain*," *MLN*, 1978; "Bombert's *The Romantic Prison*," *MLN*, 1979; "Vais: *L'Ecrivain scenique*," *Canadian Review of Comparative Literature*, 1981; "Porter's *Pursuit of Crime*," *CL*, 1983.

AWARDS: Departmental Nominee: Clark Distinguished Teaching Award, 1982; Grant, Centre for Postgraduate Hebrew Studies (Oxford), 1981; Grant, Camargo Foundation (Cassis), 1972; Guggenheim Fellowship (Paris), 1964–65; Fulbright Scholar, postdoctoral (Paris), 1959–60; Clark Research Award, (Harvard), 1959; CRB Fellow (Brussels), 1952–53; Columbia University Fellow, 1951–52; Fulbright (Grenoble), 1949–50; Honors in French (Berkley), 1949; Phi Beta Kappa (Berkley), 1949.

ADDRESS: Office—282 Goldwin Smith Hall, Cornell University, Ithaca, NY, 14853.

* * *

GRUENEWALD, Thomas, director

PERSONAL: Born July 20, 1935, in Potsdam, Germany; son of Ludwig (a physician) and Lisbeth (Feldstein) Gruenewald; married Valerie von Volz, (an actress), December 19, 1980. EDUCATION: University of Wisconsin, B.A., 1955; Columbia, M.F.A., 1958; studies acting with Uta Hagen and Robert Lewis.

NON-THEATRICAL CAREER: Teacher, acting, directing, University of Montana, 1963–65; teacher, acting, directing, University of Missouri, 1973–74; teacher, directing, SUNY Albany, 1979.

CAREER: DEBUT, DIRECTOR—*Hotel Paradiso*, New Hilltop Theatre, Owings Mills, MD, 1959. NEW YORK DEBUT—Stage Manager, New York Shakespeare Festival, Central Park, 1957–59. DIRECTED: *Androcles and the Lion*, Phoenix, NY, 1961; *Man with a Load of Mischief*, Jan Hus, NY, 1966; *Oh, Boy*, Goodspeed Opera House, East Haddam, CT, 1983.

SIDELIGHTS: MEMBERSHIPS—AEA; SSCD&C.

ADDRESS: Dale Davis & Co., 1650 Broadway, New York, NY 10019.

* * *

GUARE, John, playwright

PERSONAL: Born February 5, 1938, in New York City; son of John and Helen Clare (Grady) Guare. EDUCATION: Georgetown University; Yale University, M.A.

WRITINGS: PLAYS—*Muzeeka*, 1968; *Cop-out*, 1969; *House of Blue Leaves*, 1970; *Rich and Famous*, 1977; (musicals) co-adapter/lyricist, *Two Gentlemen of Verona*, 1971, *Marco Polo Sings a Solo*, 1973; *Rich and Famous*, 1974; *Landscape of the Body*, 1977. SCREENPLAYS—*Taking-Off* (co-author), 1970.

AWARDS: Jefferson Award in Playwriting, 1977; Antoinette

Perry Award, Best Libretto, Best Musical, New York Drama Critics Award, Best Musical, 1972: *Two Gentlemen of Verona;* Outer Critics Circle Award for Playwriting, 1971; Obie Award, Best American Play, New York Drama Critics Award, Best American Play, 1971: *House of Blue Leaves;* Variety Poll Award New York Drama Critics Most Promising Playwright, 1968–69; Obie Award, 1968: *Muzeeka.*

SIDELIGHTS: MEMBERSHIPS—Dramatist Guild (council), Authors League.

ADDRESS: Office—c/o Dramatists Play Service, Inc., 440 Park Avenue S., New York, NY 10016.*

* * *

GUETTEL, Henry A., producer, manager, arts executive

PERSONAL: Surname rhymes with "metal." Born: January 8, 1928 in Kansas City, MO; son of Arthur Abraham and Sylvia (Hershfield) Guettel; married (second marriage) Mary Rodgers (an author and composer) on October 14, 1961; chidren: (first marriage) Laurie, (second marriage) Matthew (deceased), Adam, Alexander. EDUCATION: Attended Wharton School of Business, University of Pennsylvania, 1944–47; University of Kansas City, 1947–48; studied at the Actor's Lab in Los Angeles, CA. MILITARY: U.S. Army, 1954–56.

CAREER: PRINCIPAL STAGE WORK—Producer, National Touring Companies—*The Best Man, Sound of Music, Camelot, Oliver;* General Manager, Theatre of Lincoln Center, Touring Companies, 1964–67—*The Merry Widow, Kismet, Carousel, Annie Get Your Gun, Show Boat.*

THEATRE-RELATED CAREER: Managing Director/Vice President, American National Opera Company, 1967–68; Production Supervisor, exploratory music theatre productions forum, Vivian Beaumont Theatre and theatre concerts, Lincoln Center NY, 1966–69; Lecturer, Kaplan Veidt Associates Ltd., 1970–72; Vice President, Production Associates, Cinema 5, Ltd., 1972–78; Vice President, Creative Affairs, Columbia Pictures, 1978–80; Senior Vice President, East Coast Production, Twentieth Century Fox, 1980–present; Executive Director, Theatre Development Fund, New York–present.

SIDELIGHTS: MEMBERSHIPS—Theatre Advisory Panel, New York State Council of the Arts, 1965–70; Theatre Consultant to the State University of New York, 1969–70; Board of Directors, Chelsea Theatre Center, 1966–72, Performing Arts Repertory Theatre, 1971–present. The Century Association; League of New York Theatres; International Association of Concert Managers.

ADDRESS: Home—115 Central Park West, New York, NY 10023; Office—c/o Theatre Development Fund, 1501 Broadway, New York, NY 10036.

* * *

GUINNESS, Sir Alec (created 1959); CBE, actor

PERSONAL: Born April 2, 1914, in London; married:

Merula Salaman. EDUCATION: Attended Pembroke Lodge, Southbourne and Roborough, Eastbourne; trained for the state at the Fay Compton Studio of Dramatic Art.

CAREER: STAGE DEBUT—*Libel!,* Playhouse, U.K., 1934. PRINCIPAL STAGE APPEARANCES—*Queer Cargo,* Cambridge, U.K., 1934; Osric/Third Player, *Hamlet,* New, London, 1934; Wolf, *Noah,* U.K., 1935; Sampson/Apothecary, *Romeo and Juliet,* U.K., 1935; Workman/Yakov, *The Sea Gull,* U.S., 1936; Boyet, *Love's Labour's Lost,* Le Beau/William, *As You Like It,* Old Thorney, *The Witch of Edmonton,* Reynaldo/Osric, *Hamlet,* Aguecheek, *Twelfth Night,* Exeter, *Henry V,* Old Vic, London, 1936–37; Osric/Reynaldo/Player Queen, *Hamlet,* Elsinore, 1937; Aumerle/Groom, *Richard II,* Snake, *The School for Scandal,* Feodotik, *The Three Sisters,* Lorenzo, *The Merchant of Venice,* Queen's, London, 1937; Louis Debedat, *The Doctor's Dilemma,* Richmond, 1938; Arthur Gower, *Trelawny of the "Wells",* Hamlet, *Hamlet,* Bob Acres, *The Rivals,* Old Vic, London, 1938; Michael Ransom, *The Ascent of F6,* Old Vic, London, 1939; Romeo, *Romeo and Juliet,* Perth, Scotland, 1939; Herbert Poskett, *Great Expectations,* Rudolf Steiner Hall, London, 1939; Richard Meilhac, *Cousin Muriel,* Globe, London, 1940; Ferdinand, *The Tempest,* Old Vic, London, 1940; Flight Lieutenant Graham, *Flare Path,* Henry Miller's, NY, 1942; Mitya, *The Brothers Karamazov,* Lyric, Hammersmith, 1946; Garcin, *Vicious Circle,* Arts, London, 1946; Fool, *King Lear,* Eric Birling, *An Inspector Calls,* Comte de Guiche, *Cyrano de Bergerac,* Abel Drugger, *The Alchemist,* Richard II, Dauphin, *St. Joan,* Klestakov, *The Government Inspector,* Menenius Agrippa, *Coriolanus,* Old Vic, New, 1946–48; Dr. James Y. Simpson, *The Human Touch,* Savoy, London, 1949;

Unidentified Guest, *The Cocktail Party,* Lyceum, Edinburgh, Scotland, Henry Miller's, NY, 1950; Hamlet, *Hamlet,* New London, 1951; Scientist, *Under the Sycamore Tree,* Aldwych, London, 1952; Richard III, *Richard III,* King, *All's Well That Ends Well,* Stratford Festival, Ontario, Canada, 1953; Prisoner, *The Prisoner,* Globe, London, 1954; Boniface, *Hotel Paradiso,* Winter Garden, London, 1956; Ross, *Ross,* Haymarket, London, 1960; Berenger the First, *Exit the King,* Edinburgh Festival, Scotland, Royal Court, London, 1963; Dylan Thomas, *Dylan,* Plymouth, NY, 1964; Von Berg, *Incident at Vichy,* Phoenix, London, 1966; Macbeth, *Macbeth,* Royal Court, London, 1966; Mrs. Artminster, *Wise Child,* Wyndham's, London, 1967; Harcourt-Reilly, *The Cocktail Party,* Chichester Festival, UK, Wyndham's, London, 1968, Haymarket, London, 1969; John, *Time Out of Mind,* Arnaud, Guildford, U.K., 1970; Father, *A Voyage Round My Father,* Haymarket, London, 1971; Dr. Wicksteed, *Habeau Corpus,* Lyric, London, 1973; Dudley, *A Family and a Fortune,* Apollo, London, 1975; Jonathan Swift, *Yahoo,* Queen's, London, 1976; Hilary, *The Old Country,* Queen's, London, 1977; *The Merchant of Venice,* Chichester Festival, U.K., 1984.

FILM DEBUT—*Great Expectations,* 1947. PRINCIPAL FILM APPEARANCES—*Oliver Twist; Kind Hearts and Coronets; The Man in the White Suit; The Lavender Hill Mob; The Bridge on the River Kwai,* 1957; *The Horse's Mouth,* 1959; *Tunes of Glory,* 1960; *Lawrence of Arabia,* 1962; *Dr. Zhivago,* 1965; *Cromwell,* 1970; *Murder by Death; Star Wars,* 1977; *A Passage to India,* 1984.

PRINCIPAL TELEVISION APPEARANCES—*Conversation at Night; Tinker, Tailor, Soldier, Spy; Smiley's People; Edwin.*

DIRECTED—Plays: *Hamlet,* New, London, 1951. PRODUCED—Plays: *Twelfth Night,* Old Vic, London, 1948.

AWARDS: Antoinette Perry Award, Best Actor, 1964: *Dylan;* Evening Standard Award, 1961: *Ross;* Honorary Doctor of Literature, Oxford, 1978.

ADDRESS: Agent—c/o London Management, 235–241 Regent Street, London W1.

* * *

GUNTON, Bob, actor

PERSONAL: Born November 15, 1945; son of Robert Patrick (a labor union executive) and Rose Marie (Banouetz) Gunton, Sr.; married Annie McGreevey (an actress), July 6, 1980. EDUCATION: St. Peter's College (Paulist Fathers Junio Seminary), Baltimore, MD, A.A.; University of California, Irvine. RELIGION: Roman Catholic. MILITARY: U.S. Army, 1969–71 (Sgt. E-5).

CAREER: DEBUT—Johnny Timberlake, *Tennesee, U.S.A.,* Cumberland Co. Playhouse, Crossville, TN, 1965. NEW YORK DEBUT—Bill Cracker, *Happy End,* Brooklyn Academy of Music, then Martin Beck, July, 1976 for 56 performances. PRINCIPAL STAGE APPEARANCES—Juan Peron, *Evita!,* Broadway Theatre, NY, 1980; The Event, *How I Got That Story,* Westside Arts, NY, 1982; James Croxley, *Passion,* Longacre, NY, 1983.

FILM DEBUT—Sal Naftari, *Rollover,* 1982. TELEVISION DEBUT— Lead, *Lois Gibbs and the Love Canal,* 1982.

AWARDS: Drama Desk Award, 1980, *Evita!;* Los Angeles Dramalogue Award, 1980, *Evita!;* Antoinette Perry Nomination, Best Actor, 1980: *Evita!;* Obie, 1981: *How I Got That Story;* Clarence Derwent Award, 1981: *How I Got That Story;* CIB, Viet Service Medal, Arcom Medal, Bronze Star for Valor.

SIDELIGHTS: MEMBERSHIPS—AEA; SAG; AFTRA.

ADDRESS: Home—317 W. 54th Street, New York, NY 10019; Agent—Sheila Robinson, ICM, 40 W. 57th Street, New York, NY 10019.

* * *

GUSTAFSON, Carol (nee Elsie Carol), actress

PERSONAL: Born December 25, 1925, in New York City; daughter of Herman (a hairdresser) and Ida Christina (a hairdresser; maiden name Johanson) Gustafson; married Larry M. Ward, September 1949; children: Christine Helene, Matthew McCormick. EDUCATION: Attended New York City public schools; trained for the stage at the Dramatic Work-

shop of the New School and studied with Erwin Piscator. POLITICS: Conservative.

CAREER: PRINCIPAL STAGE APPEARANCES—Guthrie Theatre, Minneapolis—*Arturo Ui, House of Atreus, Merton of the Movies;* Arena Stage, Washington, DC—*The Cherry Orchard, You Can't Take It with You; The House of Bernarda Alba,* Pennsylvania State University; Indiana Repertory *The Real Inspector Hound, Black Comedy, The Tavern; Awake and Sing,* Harvard's Loeb Theatre, Cambridge, MA; *She Stoops to Conquer,* Center Stage, Baltimore, MD; *Waltz of the Toreadors,* Geva on Stage, Rochester, NY; *The Odd Couple,* New York; *Becket,* New York; *Dylan,* New York; Big Mama, *Cat on a Hot Tin Roof,* Kennedy Center, Washington, DC; Yenta, *Fiddler on the Roof,* Elmsford, NY; Mme. Vauclain/Mme. Manzoni/the Aunt, *The Grand Tour,* Chicago. MAJOR TOURS—*Separate Tables; Time of the Cuckoo; Twigs;* Parthy, *Showboat,* Miami Beach, Fort Lauderdale.

PRINCIPAL FILMS—*The Group; Bye Bye Braverman; Going Home; Such Good Friends; Three Days of the Condor; The First Deadly Sin.* TELEVISION APPEARANCES—*The Prince of Central Park; Ryan's Hope; One Life to Live; All My Children.*

ADDRESS: Office—c/o Pittsburgh Public Theatre, Pittsburgh, PA 15212. Agent—c/o Michael Hartig Agency, 527 Madison Ave., New York, NY 10022.

* * *

GUTIERREZ, Gerald, director

PERSONAL: Born February 3, 1950 in Brooklyn, NY; son of Andrew (a New York City detective) and Obdulia (a flamenco dancer; maiden name, Concheiro) Gutierrez. EDUCATION: State University of New York at Stony Brook, 1967–68; Juilliard School, New York City, B.S. (Theatre Arts); studied Musical Theatre with Lehman Engel.

CAREER: PRINCIPAL STAGE WORK, DIRECTED—*The Apple Tree,* Juilliard School, NY, 1970; *A Life in the Theatre,* Theatre de Lys, NY, 1977; *Elegy for Young Lovers,* San Francisco Opera, CA; 1978; *No Time for Comedy,* McCarter, Princeton, NJ, 1978; *You Can't Take It with You,* 1978; *Broadway,* Acting Company, national tour, 1979; *She Loves Me,* Playwrights Horizons, NY, 1980; *Meetings,* Phoenix, NY, 1981; *The Curse of an Aching Heart,* Little Theatre, NY, 1982; *Geniuses,* Playwrights Horizons, Douglas Fairbanks, NY, 1982; *The Rise and Rise of Daniel Rocket,* Playwrights Horizons, NY, 1982; *Isn't It Romantic,* Playwrights Horizons, NY, 1983–84; *Terra Nova,* American Place, NY, 1984.

PRINCIPAL FILM WORK, DIRECTED—*A Bag of Shells,* 1981. PRINCIPAL TELEVISION WORK, DIRECTED—*A Life in the Theatre,* PBS, 1979.

WRITINGS: TELEPLAY—*A Bag of Shells.*

THEATRE-RELATED CAREER: Directing instructor, New York University; instructor, Comedy Technique, Juilliard School, NY.

AWARDS: Joseph Jefferson Award Nominations: *The Curse of an Aching Heart, The Primary English Class;* Winner, Joseph Jefferson Award, Best Director, *You Can't Take with You,* 1978.

SIDELIGHTS: MEMBERSHIPS—AEA; Society of Stage Directors and Choreographers, Directors Guild, The Players Club.

As an actor, Mr. Gutierrez has performed with the Acting Company in *The Three Sisters, Beggars Opera, The Time of Your Life* and *The Cradle Will Rock.* He is fluent in Spanish.

ADDRESS: Agent—Flora Roberts, 157 W. 57th Street, New York, NY 10019.

H

HACKETT, Joan, actress

PERSONAL: Born March 1, 1942, in New York City; died October 8, 1983; daughter of John and Mary (Esposito) Hackett; married Richard Mulligan, January 3, 1966 (divorced 1973). EDUCATION: Attended public schools in New York City and studied with Mary Welch, 1958; studied with Lee Strasberg, 1958–63.

CAREER: NEW YORK DEBUT—A Clearing in the Woods, 1959. PRINCIPAL STAGE APPEARANCES—The Play's the Thing; Call Me by My Rightful Name; Two Queens of Love and Beauty; Journey to the Day; Peterpat; Park; Night Watch; She Didn't Say Yes.

FILM DEBUT—The Group, 1966. PRINCIPAL FILM APPEARANCES—Will Penny, 1968; Support Your Local Sheriff, 1969; Assignment to Kill, 1969; The Rivals, 1972; The Last of Sheila, 1973; The Terminal Man, 1974; Mackintosh and T.J., 1976; Treasure of Matecumbe, 1976; Mr. Mike's Mondo Video, 1979; The North Avenue Irregulars, 1979; One Trick Pony, 1980; Only When I Laugh, 1981; The Escape Artist, 1982.

PRINCIPAL TELEVISION APPEARANCES—Ellery Queen; Alcoa Premiere; Alfred Hitchcock Theatre; Bob Hope Chrysler Theatre; Bonanza; Mission: Impossible; The American Woman: Portraits of Courage; Another Day; movies for television—How Awful About Allan; The Other Man; Five Desperate Women; Reflections of Murder; The Young Country; Dead of Night; Possessed; Stonestreet; series—Young Doctor Malone, 1959–60; The Defenders, 1961–62.

AWARDS: Theatre World, Vernon Rice, Obie, 1961.*

* * *

HACKMAN, Gene, actor

PERSONAL: Born January 30, 1930, in San Bernardino, CA; son of Eugene Ezra Hackman; married Fay Maltese, 1956; children: Christopher, Elizabeth, Leslie.

CAREER: PRINCIPAL FILM APPEARANCES—Lilith, 1964; Hawaii, 1966; A Covenant with Death, 1967; Bonnie and Clyde, 1967; Banning, 1967; First to Fight, 1967; The Split, 1968; Riot!, 1969; The Gypsy Moths, 1969; Downhill Racer, 1969; Marooned, 1969; I Never Sang for My Father, 1970; Doctors' Wives, 1971; The Hunting Party, 1971; The French Connection, 1971; Cisco Pike, 1971; The Poseiden Ad-

venture, 1972; Scarecrow, 1973; The Conversation, 1974; Young Frankenstein, 1974; Zandy's Bride, 1974; The French Connection II, 1975; Bite the Bullet, 1975; Night Moves, 1975; Lucky Lady, 1975; A Bridge Too Far, 1977; The Domino Principle, 1977; March or Die, 1977; Superman, 1978; All Night Long, 1981; Superman II, 1981; Eureka; Under Fire, 1983.

PRINCIPAL TELEVISION APPEARANCES—My Father, My Mother; The FBI; The Invaders; The Iron Horse; Rowan and Martin's Laugh In, others.

PRINCIPAL STAGE APPEARANCES—Any Wednesday; Poor Richard; Children from Their Games; A Rainy Day in Newark; The Natural Look.

AWARDS: Cannes Film Festival Award: Scarecrow; British Academy Award: The Poseidon Adventure; Academy Award, British Academy Award, Golden Globe, New York Film Critics, Best Actor, 1971: The French Connection; Academy Award Nomination, 1967: Bonnie and Clyde; named Star of the Year by the National Association of Theatre Owners, 1974.

SIDELIGHTS: Mr. Hackman formed his own production company, Chelly Ltd.*

* * *

HAINES, Larry, actor

PERSONAL: Born August 3, in Mt. Vernon, NY; married (second marriage) Jean Pearlman; children: (first marriage) Debbie. EDUCATION: Attended public schools in Mt. Vernon, NY, and Yonkers Collegiate Center.

CAREER: PRINCIPAL STAGE APPEARANCES—A Thousand Clowns, NY; Generation, NY; Promises, Promises, NY; Twigs, NY; Tribute, NY; Last of the Red Hot Lovers, NY; Paris Is Out, Philadelphia Playhouse in the Park; God's Country, Coconut Grove Playhouse, Coconut Grove, FL.

PRINCIPAL FILM APPEARANCES—The Odd Couple; The Seven Ups.

PRINCIPAL TELEVISION APPEARANCES—The First Hundred Years; The Big Story; Robert Montgomery Presents; The Defenders; Maude; Doc; Kojak; The Country Girl; Phyl and Mikhy; Stu Bergman, Search for Tomorrow.

AWARDS: Emmy Award, Outstanding Performances by an Actor in a Supporting Role for a Daytime Drama Series, 1980: *Search for Tomorrow;* Emmy Award, Outstanding Actor in a Daytime Drama Series, 1976: *Search for Tomorrow;* Antoinette Perry Award Nomination, *Generation;* Antoinette Perry Award Nomination, *Promises, Promises.*

SIDELIGHTS: "Following graduation, Mr. Haines began a career in radio in which he achieved more than 15,000 acting performances, including roles on *The Columbia Workshop, Inner Sanctum, Gangbusters, The FBI in Peace and War, Suspense,* and in the title role of *Mike Hammer.* . . . He has been featured on *Search for Tomorrow,* almost since it made its debut in September 1951."

ADDRESS: One Hidden Meadow Rd., Weston, CT. 06883 Agent—Stark Hesseltine, 165 W. 46th Street, New York, NY 10036.

* * *

HAIRSTON, William (William, Jr.), actor, writer, director

PERSONAL: Born April 1, 1928, in Goldsboro, NC; married Enid Carey (a psychiatric social worker), June 2, 1957; children: Ann Marie. EDUCATION: New York University, B.S. in Public Administration; studied for the theatre with Robert Lewis, Harry Gribble, and Betty Cashman; also attended University of Northern Colorado and Columbia University.

CAREER: PRINCIPAL STAGE APPEARANCES—roles in such plays as *The Hasty Heart, No Time for Sergeants, Rain, The Petrified Forest, Louisiana Purchase, The Respectful Prostitute* in New York, Summer Stock, and on tour, 1950–57. DIRECTED: *Curtain Call, Mr. Aldredge, Sir!,* New York, 1963; *Jericho-Jim Crow,* New York, 1964.

FILM APPEARANCES—*Take the High Ground,* 1953. TELEVISION APPEARANCES—Live TV dramas in New York, 1950–55; lead, *Harlem Detective,* 1953.

WRITINGS: PLAYS, UNPUBLISHED—Swan Song of the 11th Dawn, 1962; Curtain Call, Mr. Aldredge, Sir!, 1963; Walk in Darkness, 1963; Black Antigone, 1966 (all produced). Film/TV scripts—various documentary scripts for the U.S. Information Agency. BOOKS—*The World of Carlos,* 1968.

AWARDS: Ford Foundation Grant, work with Arena Stage in Washington, DC, 1965–66; National Endowment for the Arts, grant to assist the NEA in its search for young, talented writers, 1967.

SIDELIGHTS: MEMBERSHIPS—Dramatists Guild, Authors League, AEA, SAG, AFTRA, Boy Scouts of America (executive board), National Capital Council.

In the area of theatre administration, Mr. Hairston was production coordinator for the Greenwich Mews Theatre, New York, in 1963 as well as its coproducer from 1963 to 1964. Under the Ford Grant, he served as assistant to the executive director of Arena Stage in Washington, DC, from September 1965 to September 1966. At the New York

Shakespeare Festival he was theatre manager of the Delacorte Theatre in Central Park from May 1963 to September 1964 and also co-director of community relations for its mobile theatre unit during the 1965 season.

ADDRESS: Home—9909 Conestoga Way, Potomac, MD 20854. Office—Government of District of Columbia. Agent—Ilse Kahn, Paul Kohner, Inc., 9169 Sunset Blvd., Hollywood, CA 90069.

* * *

HALE, Fiona (nee Campbell-Shields), actress

PERSONAL: Born February 7, 1926; daughter of Albert Bequith (a clergyman and artist) and Elizabeth Bancroft (an actress; maiden name, Campbell) Shields; married Richard Hale (an actor, singer, and narrator), November 3, 1951 (died, 1982); children: Melissa, Elizabeth, Patrick. EDUCATION: University of California at Los Angeles, B.A. (Linguistics), 1973; trained for the stage at the Guy Bates Post Academy; studied movement with Lotte Goslar.

CAREER: DEBUT—Malvina, *The Higher Glory,* Pelican, Hollywood, CA, 1942. NEW YORK DEBUT—Lady Friend, *Walk Hard.* PRINCIPAL STAGE APPEARANCES—Maria, *The Heiress,* Biltmore, NY, 1948; Housekeeper, *Drinks Before Dinner,* Public; Aaronetta, *Morning's at Seven,* Lyceum, NY; (Off-Broadway) Glenda, *The Seduction of Peewee;* Mrs. Railton-Bell, *Separate Tables;* Mrs. Perpetua, *The Cantilevered Terrace;* (Regional) Mrs. Kirby, *You Can't Take It with You,* Guthrie, Minneapolis, MN; Mrs. Webb, *Our Town,* Meadowbrook, MI; Mme. Spritzer, *13 Rue de L'Amour,* Alhambra, Jacksonville, FL; Claudine, *Lu Ann Hampton Laverty Oberlander,* Halie, *Buried Child,* Mrs. Hudson/Mother Midnight, *The Incredible Murder of Cardinal Tosca,* Rebecca Nurse, *The Crucible,* Mrs. Fezziwig/Charwoman, Virginia Stage Company, Norfolk, VA; Mrs. Frayne, *The Second Man,* Los Angeles.

FILM DEBUT—Mrs. Fraser, *Harriet Craig,* 1949. PRINCIPAL FILM APPEARANCES—Redhead, *Westward the Women,* 1950; Eileen Lawrence, *Interrupted Melody,* 1953; Oma, *Resurrection,* 1980.

PRINCIPAL TELEVISION APPEARANCES—Title role, *The Woman of Ballybunion; Gunsmoke; Dennis the Menace; Wagon Train; Police Story; Cavalcade of America; Highway Patrol; Playhouse 90; Divorce Court; Day in Court; Black Saddle; Zane Grey Theatre; Fireside Theatre; G.E. Theatre; Family Theatre; Lock Up; Dr. Kildare;* Mrs. Cooper, *Guiding Light.*

SIDELIGHTS: MEMBERSHIPS—AEA; SAG; AFTRA; SAG Conservatory; Twelfth Night Club.

"I started my professional career with Miss Eva Le Gallienne. This lovely lady was a wonderful teacher and inspiration. And through acting I have continued to learn about myself and about human nature. I have always been interested in psychology and human potential. Now Drama Therapy brings it all together. I like swimming and dancing. I speak Spanish and a little French. I studied Mandarin Chinese at UCLA for a year."

ADDRESS: Office—c/o Actors Equity Association, 165 W. 46th Street, New York, NY 10036. Telephone Service—(212) 840-1234.

* * *

HALL, Davis, actor, director

PERSONAL: Born April 10, 1946, in Atlanta, GA; son of William Davis (consultant to process industries) and Harriet Elizabeth (Hartwell) Hall, Jr.; married Ingrid Price (film and stage costumer), October 31, 1983. EDUCATION: Northwestern University, B.S. in speech; studied for the stage at Studio '68, London for three years and also with Wynn Handman.

CAREER: DEBUT—Prince de Conde, *The Devils*, Cape May Playhouse, NJ, 1966. NEW YORK DEBUT—Mr. Gardner, *Butley*, Morosco, February 21, 1973. LONDON DEBUT—Cootie, *Cancer (a.k.a. Moonchildren)*, Royal Court, September 14, 1970, five weeks. PRINCIPAL STAGE APPEARANCES—Tom, *The Glass Menagerie*, Indiana Repertory, Indianapolis, 1972; Young Charlie, *Da*, Olney Theatre, MD, 1973; Leonidik, *The Promise*, Roundabout, New York, 1977; Mauer, *Undiscovered Country*, Hartford Stage, CT, 1981; Paul, *The Team*, Corner Loft, New York, 1982; title role, *Henry VI*, New Jersey Shakespeare Festival, 1983. MAJOR TOURS—Charlie/Ophelia, Inspector/MacDuff, *Dogg's Hamlet, Cahoot's Macbeth*, world premiere tour of England

DAVIS HALL

and America of the British American Repertory Company, April-December, 1979.

TELEVISION APPEARANCES—Cliff Adams, *Another Life*, 1982.

SIDELIGHTS: MEMBERSHIPS—AEA, SAG, AFTRA.

FAVORITE ROLES—"Hamlet and Marchbanks in *Candida* at the Roundabout, in New York. Very special were the world premiere of *Da* (with the late, wonderful John McGiver) and *Summer* (with my sister Harriet Hall) at the Olney Theatre."

ADDRESS: Home—20 W. 95th Street, New York, NY 10025. Agents—free lance through ICM, 40 W. 57th Street, New York, NY 10019 and Ann Wright Representatives, Inc., 136 E. 57th Street, New York, NY 10022.

* * *

HALL, Delores, actress, singer

PERSONAL: Born February 26; daughter of Isaac H. and Vernice Estrella (Leadbetter) Addison; married (first marriage) Sylvester Hall; (second marriage) Michael Goodstone (owns an iron shop); children: (first marriage) Deadra, (second marriage) Aaron. EDUCATION: Attended public schools and 1½ years of college.

CAREER: DEBUT—daughter (singer) *Portraits in Bronze*, Cabaret Concert Theatre, Los Angeles, CA 1959. NEW YORK DEBUT—chorus/Sheila, *Hair*, Biltmore, 1970–71. PRINCIPAL STAGE APPEARANCES—*The Delores Hall Singers with Harry Belafonte*, National Tour and Canada, 1968; April, *Godspell*, 1975; *Your Arms Too Short to Box with God*, 1970–76.

PRINCIPAL TELEVISION APPEARANCES—*The Dinah Shore Show; The Smothers Brothers Show;*

AWARDS: Joesph Jefferson Award Nomination, 1983; Antoinette Perry Award Nomination, 1977; Woman of Distinction Award from the National Association of Negro Business and Professional Women, 1977.

ADDRESS: Home—484 W. 43rd Street, New York, NY 10036. Agent—Peggy Grant, 1650 Broadway, New York, NY 10019.

* * *

HAMILTON, Kelly, playwright, composer

PERSONAL: Born July 5, 1945 in San Francisco, CA; son of Francis Kennedy (a journalist) and Doris Lillian (Carlson) Hamilton. EDUCATION: College of San Mateo, CA, 1963–65; UCLA, 1967–69; studied Musical Theatre Writing with Lehman Engel. RELIGION: Christian.

WRITINGS: PLAYS, PRODUCED (musicals)—*Dance on a Country Grave*, Arlington Park, Chicago, 1973; *Surprise*, Alcazar, San Francisco, 1977; *Saga*, Wonderhorse, NY, 1979; *Trixie True, Teen Detective*, Theatre de Lys, NY, 1980.

AWARDS: David B. Marshall Award, *Saga,* 1978; Joseph Jefferson Award, Chicago Critics, *Dance on a Country Grave,* 1974.

SIDELIGHTS: MEMBERSHIPS—Dramatists Guild; B.M.I.

"Musical Theatre has the power to uplift and inspire during these perilous times. My every contribution will be toward that end."

ADDRESS: Home—19 Christopher Street, New York, NY 10014. Agent—Gilbert Parker, c/o William Morris Agency, 1350 Avenue of the Americas, New York, NY 10019.

* * *

HAMILTON, Lynn, actress

PERSONAL: Born April 25, 1930; daughter of Louis (a blue-collar worker) and Nancy (Tate) Hamilton; married Frank S. Jenkins (a poet and writer) on November 15, 1973. EDUCATION: Goodman Theatre, Chicago, IL, four years.

CAREER: NEW YORK DEBUT—*The Face of a Hero.* PRINCIPAL STAGE APPEARANCES—*Only in America; The Cool World; Tambourines to Glory.* MAJOR TOURS—*The Miracle Worker, The Skin of Our Teeth,* President Kennedy's Cultural Exchange Program to Europe, Near East, Central and South America.

PRINCIPAL FILM APPEARANCES—*Lead Belly; Buck and the Preacher; Lady Sings the Blues; Hang Up; The Seven Minutes; Brother John; The Learning Tree; Shadows.* PRINCIPAL TELEVISION APPEARANCES—*Roots—The Next Generation; A Dream for Christmas; Sanford and Son; The Marcus Nelson Murders; Longstreet; Gunsmoke; Room 222; Then Came Bronson; The Waltons; The Rockford Files; Good Times; Barnaby Jones; The Psychiatrist; Mannix; Insight; Ironside; Hawaii Five-O; Knight Rider; The Power of Matthew Star; Quincy; Afternoon Special.*

SIDELIGHTS: MEMBERSHIPS—NAACP. Miss Hamilton was a resident member of the New York Shakespeare Festival for four years. A highlight of her stage career was being selected to perform in President Kennedy's Cultural Exchange Program.

ADDRESS: Office—P.O. Box 36012, Los Angeles, CA 90036. Agent—Alex Brewis Agency, 8800 Sunset Blvd., Los Angeles, CA 90012.

* * *

HAMMOND, David, director

PERSONAL: Born June 3, 1948 in New York, NY; son of Jack (a physician) and Elizabeth Alida (a nurse; maiden name, Furno) Hammond. EDUCATION: Harvard University, B.A. (Magna Cum Laude), 1970; Carnegie-Mellon University, M.F.A., 1972.

CAREER: First Stage Work, Associate Director, *Pillars of the Community,* American Conservatory, San Francisco, CA, 1974. NEW YORK DEBUT—Director, *The Master Builder,* Roundabout, 1983. PRINCIPAL STAGE WORK, Directed—*The Penitentes,* Aspen Music Festival, CO, 1974; *La Traviata,* Aspen Music Festival, 1975; *The Barber of Seville,* Aspen Music Festival, 1975; *Candide,* Pacific Conservatory of the Performing Arts, Santa Maria, CA, 1976; *The Italian Girl in Algiers,* San Francisco Opera, Spring Opera Theatre, 1978; *The Magic Flute,* Carmel Bach Festival, CA, 1979; *The Crucifer of Blood,* American Conservatory Theatre, San Francisco, 1980; *The Marriage of Figaro,* Carmel Bach Festival, CA, 1980; *The Rivals,* American Conservatory, San Francisco, 1981; *A Midsummer Night's Dream,* Sherwood Shakespeare Festival, CA, 1981; *Macbeth,* Sherwood Shakespeare Festival, 1981; *The Man Who Could See Through Time,* Yale Repertory, New Haven, CT, 1982; *The Philanderer,* Yale Repertory, 1982; *Richard II,* Yale Repertory, 1983.

THEATRE-RELATED CAREER: Faculty, Juillard School, Drama Division, New York, NY, 1972–74; Assistant Conservatory Director, American Conservatory Theatre, San Francisco, CA, 1974–81; Associate Professor of Acting and Directing, Yale University, School of Drama, 1981–present.

AWARDS: Dramalogue Critics' Award, Sherwood Shakespeare Festival, CA, 1981: *Macbeth;* Dramalogue Critics' Award, American Conservatory Theatre, 1980: *The Crucifer of Blood;* Bay Area Critics' Award Nomination, 1980.

SIDELIGHTS: MEMBERSHIPS—Society of Stage Directors and Choreographers; American Guild of Musical Artists; AEA.

ADDRESS: Office—c/o Yale School of Drama, 222 York Avenue, New Haven, CT 06520.

* * *

HANCOCK, John, director, writer

PERSONAL: Born February 12, 1939, in Kansas City, MO; son of Ralph (a musician and farmer) and Ella Mae (a teacher and farmer; maiden name Rosenthall) Hancock; married Ann Arensberg, 1966 (divorced 1974); married Dorothy Tristan (an actress and writer), on December 29, 1975. EDUCATION: Harvard University, B.A., studied at Actors Studio, director unit, with Lee Strasberg, in New York.

CAREER: ARTISTIC DIRECTOR—San Francisco Actors Workshop, 1965–66; Pittsburgh Playhouse, 1966–67. DIRECTED—*Midsummer Night's Dream; The Last Analysis; Edward II; The Father; Milk Train; Galileo; As You Like It; Antigone; A Man's a Man; The Plough and the Stars; The Glass Menagerie; The Caucasian Chalk Circle; Dream Play; The Respectful Prostitute; Christmas Party and Healing Spring; The Judge of the Divorce Court; The Two-Character Play; Bedtime Story;* DIRECTED, NEW YORK—*Midsummer Night's Dream; Endecott and the Red Cross; The Storm.*

PRINCIPAL FILMS DIRECTED—*Bang the Drum Slowly; Let's Scare Jessica To Death; Baby Blue Marine; California Dreaming; Sticky My Fingers, Fleet My Feet.*

THEATRE-RELATED CAREER: Associate professor, University of California, Berkeley; teacher, Hunter and Richmond Colleges, New York.

AWARDS, HONORS, AND PRIZES: Academy Award Nomination, *Sticky My Fingers, Fleet My Feet;* Obie, *A Midsummer Night's Dream;* Brandeis Citation in Film, Christopher Award.

SIDELIGHTS: MEMBERSHIPS—Society of Stage Directors and Choreographers; Trustee, American Film Institute. RECREATION —gardening, beekeeping, fishing, cooking; he is an accomplished violinist.

ADDRESS: Home—21531 Deerpath Lane, Malibu, CA 90265.

* * *

HANDLER, Evan, actor

PERSONAL: Born January 10, 1961; son of Murray Raymond (an advertising designer) and Enid Irene (a mental health administrator; maiden name, Ostrov) Handler. EDUCATION: Attended the Julliard School, 1979–81.

CAREER: DEBUT—Thomas/Waiter, *Biography: A Game,* Chelsea Theatre Center, New York, 1978. PRINCIPAL STAGE APPEARANCES—Groom, *Strider,* Chelsea Theater Center, New York, 1979; Tom the Cabin Boy, *Derelict* (now *Final*

EVAN HANDLER

Passages), Studio Arena, Buffalo, NY, 1982; Shelley Solomon, *Solomon's Child,* Little Theater, New York, 1982; Billy, *Weapons of Happiness,* Studio Arena, Buffalo, NY, 1983; "Final Orders" Mike, *Early Warnings,* Manhattan Theater Club, New York, 1983; Eugene, *Brighton Beach Memoirs,* Neil Simon, New York, 1983. MAJOR TOURS—Hally, *Master Harold . . . and the Boys,* Boston, Baltimore, Philadelphia, Austin, Dallas, Houston, Los Angeles, 1983–84.

FILM DEBUT—Goldberg, *The Chosen,* 1980. PRINCIPAL FILMS—Eddy West, *Taps,* 1981; Ray, *Dear Mr. Wonderful,* 1982; Eli, *The Children's War,* 1983.

SIDELIGHTS: MEMBERSHIPS—AEA, SAG. FAVORITE PARTS—Tom the Cabin Boy in *Derelict* (now *Final Passages*).

"I'm happy to be doing *Master Harold.* The role of Hally was withheld from me for two years due to bizarre circumstances."

ADDRESS: Agent—c/o Monty Silver Agency, 200 W. 57th Street, #1303, New York, NY 10019.

* * *

HANNING, Geraldine, actress, singer

PERSONAL: Born August 31, 1923 in Cleveland, OH; daughter of Maurice F. (an attorney) and Mary M. (a nurse; maiden name, Miller) Hanning. EDUCATION: Connecticut College, B.A. (English Literature), 1945; Western Reserve University, M.A. (Drama), 1947; American Theatre Wing, NY.

CAREER: DEBUT—Cowgirl, *Green Grow the Lilacs,* Cain Park, Cleveland, OH, 1944. NEW YORK DEBUT—Barbara, *In Good King Charles' Golden Days,* Downtown Theatre, for over 100 performances, 1957. PRINCIPAL STAGE APPEARANCES—Liza Elliot, *Lady in the Dark,* Cain Park, Cleveland, OH, 1948; Ruth, *Blithe Spirit,* Cain Park, OH, 1949; Olive, *Voice of the Turtle,* Cleveland Playhouse, 1950; Lady India, *Ring Round the Moon,* Cleveland Playhouse, 1951; Natalie, *The Merry Widow,* Finger Lakes Lyric Circus, 1952; Princess Margaret, *The Student Prince,* Pittsburgh Civic Light Opera, 1954; Gussi, *Bittersweet,* Pittsburgh Civic Light Opera, 1954; Grace, *The Philanderer,* Downtown Theatre, NY, 1958; Kalonika, *Lysistrata,* E. 74th Street Theatre, NY, 1959; Mrs. Baker, *Butterflies Are Free,* 1973, Louise, *The Five Finger Exercise,* 1974, Fiona, *How the Other Half Loves,* 1974, Jane, *Absurd Person Singular,* 1978, Mrs. Tarleton, *Misalliance,* 1978, Older Woman, *The Good Doctor,* 1979, Sharon Playhouse, CT; Queen, *Jubilee,* in Michigan, 1975; Socialite, *Let's Face It,* AMDA, NY, 1977; Lillian, *Oh Brother,* ANTA, NY, 1981. MAJOR TOURS—Ivy London, *Critic's Choice,* national tour, 1962; Wife, *The Impossible Years,* national tour, 1966.

FILM DEBUT—Macy's Clerk, *The Thief,* 1950. TELEVISION DEBUT—Strange Lady, *Man of Destiny,* 1948. PRINCIPAL TELEVISION APPEARANCES—*All My Children; Edge of Night; Love of Life; One Life to Live; Search for Tomorrow; Calucci's Department.*

SIDELIGHTS: MEMBERSHIPS—National Academy of Television Arts and Sciences; Metropolitan Museum of Art. RECREATION—''A Franz Liszt aficionada,'' collector of miniatures and antique Chinese embroidery.

ADDRESS: Answering Service—(212) 753-2310.

* * *

HANSON, Curtis, director, writer

PERSONAL: Born March 24, 1945.

CAREER: PRINCIPAL FILM WORK—screenwriter/director, *Sweet Kill,* 1972; co-producer/director, *The Little Dragons,* 1977; director, *Losin' It,* 1983.

WRITINGS: SCREENPLAYS—*The Dunwich Horror,* 1970; *Sweet Kill,* 1972; *The Silent Partner,* 1978; *White Dog* (with Sam Fuller), 1982; *Never Cry Wolf* (with Sam Hamm and Richard Cletter), 1983.

ADDRESS: Agent—c/o Leading Artists Agency Inc., 445 N. Bedford Drive, Beverly Hills, CA 90210.

* * *

HARMON, Charlotte (nee Buchwald), critic, producer, director, writer, editor

PERSONAL: Born May 26, in New York City; daughter of Ephraim (in real estate) and Jennie (Heyman) Buchwald; married Lewis Harmon (a press agent), June 27, 1938; children: Jill. EDUCATION: Columbia University; studied playwriting with Minor Latham. POLITICS: Independent.

CAREER: DEBUT—Producer/director, Chapel Playhouse, Guilford, CT, 1946–50. PRINCIPAL STAGE WORK—producer/director, Clinton Playhouse, 1950–58. Produced over one hundred plays between 1946 and 1958.

THEATRE-RELATED CAREER: Radio commentator, WMCA, WNEW; also appeared on CBS-TV, NBC-TV, WNHC, New Haven, 1937–58.

WRITINGS: PLAYS, PUBLISHED—*Strawberries in January,* 1946; *You Have to Be Crazy,* 1949; *That Foolish Age,* 1956. Editor—legit section, *Back Stage,* 1961–76. BOOKS—*Broadway in a Barn,* 1957 (with Rosemary Taylor); *How to Break into the Theatre,* 1961. ARTICLES—*Theatre Arts, New York Times Magazine,* others.

SIDELIGHTS: MEMBERSHIPS—Twelfth Night Club. HOBBIES—travel.

Writes on antiques, antique jewelry, flea markets, thrift shops. Lectures on theatre at High School of Performing Arts, etc.

ADDRESS: Office—205 West 57 Street, New York, NY 10019.

HARMON, Lewis, producer, press representative

PERSONAL: Born February 14, 1911 in Newark, NY; son of Charles (a cotton broker) and Amelia (Yokel) Harmon; married Charlotte Buchwald (a writer, director, producer) on June 27, 1938; children: Jill. EDUCATION: Attended public schools in New Jersey. POLITICS: Independent.

CAREER: FIRST STAGE WORK—Assistant Press Representative for Florenz Ziegfeld, *Rio Rita, Sunny, Showboat, Ziegfeld Follies,* 1928. COMPANY MANAGER—*Three Men on a Horse,* Playhouse, NY, 1935; *Love from a Stranger,* Fulton, NY, 1936; *Young Mr. Disraeli,* Fulton, 1937, also served as casting director and playreader. PRESS AGENT—*Mexican Hayride; Pickup Girl; Catherine Was Great; Teahouse of the August Moon; Fiddler on the Roof; West Side Story.* MAJOR TOURS—*Pygmalion,* national tour, 1941; *Death of a Salesman,* 1951–52.

PRODUCER—with Charlotte Harmon, Chapel Playhouse, Guilford, CT, 1946–50; Clinton Playhouse, Clinton, CT, 1950–58, produced over 100 shows. PRESS AGENT—Film—Warner Brothers, Vitaphone Campaign, 1929–33; *The Jazz Singer; Bambi; The Magnificent Ambersons; The Pride of the Yankees,* 1941–42.

SIDELIGHTS: MEMBERSHIPS—Association of Theatrical Press Agents and Managers, Chairman, New York Press Agents Chapter, 1955–56; Players Club.

ADDRESS: Office—205 W. 57th Street, New York, NY 10019.

* * *

HARNICK, Sheldon, composer, producer

PERSONAL: Born April 30, 1924, in Chicago, IL; son of Harry Michael (a dentist) and Esther Dorothea (Kanter) Harnick; married Mary Boatner, August 29, 1950 (annulled 1957); married Elaine May, March 25, 1962 (divorced May 1963); married Margery Gray (an artist), October 8, 1965; children: Beth, Matthew. EDUCATION: Northwestern, BA, Music, 1950. POLITICS: Independent. RELIGION: Jewish. MILITARY: Signal Corps, attached to Air Corps, 1943–46 (T-4).

CAREER: DEBUT—Musician, Harry Brandon's Dance Orchestra, Chicago, 1950. NEW YORK DEBUT—Songwriter (''The Boston Beguine''), *New Faces of 1952.* PRINCIPAL STAGE WORK—Songwriter, *Two's Company,* New York, 1952; songwriter, *John Murray Anderson's Almanac,* 1953; lyricist, *Horatio,* Margo Jones Theatre, Dallas, TX, 1954; songwriter, *Shoestring Revue,* 1955; songwriter, *Kaleidoscope;* songwriter, *The Littlest Revue,* 1956; lyricist (anonymous), *Shangri-La,* New York, 1956; songwriter, *Shoestring '57,* New York, 1957; lyricist, *Portofino,* New York, 1958; lyricist (music by Jerry Bock), *The Body Beautiful,* Broadway Theatre, New York, 1958; lyricist *Fiorello!,* Broadhurst, New York, 1959; lyricist, *Tenderloin,* 46th Street, New York, 1960; lyricist, *Smiling the Boy Fell Dead,* Cherry Lane, New York, 1961; lyricist, *She Loves Me,* Eugene O'Neill, New York, 1963; lyricist, *To Broadway with Love,* New York World's Fair, 1964–65; lyricist, *Fid-*

dler on the Roof, Imperial, New York, 1964; lyricist (anonymous) *Baker Street,* Broadway Theatre, New York, 1965; lyricist, *The Apple Tree,* Shubert, New York, 1966; English translation, *L'Histoire du Soldat,* Chamber Symphony of Philadelphia, also: Bil Baird Marionettes, 1967; lyricist, *The Rothschilds,* Lunt-Fontanne, New York, 1970; English translation/adaptation: *L'Enfant et les Sortilèges,* Manhattan School of Music, New York, 1971; lyricist, *Pinocchio,* Bil Baird Marionettes, New York, 1973; lyricist, *Alice in Wonderland,* Bil Baird Marionettes, New York, 1975; librettist, *Captain Jinks of the Horse Marines,* Kansas City, MO, 1975; lyricist, *Rex,* Majestic, New York, 1976; English translation/adaptation, *The Merry Widow,* San Diego Opera, 1977; librettist, *Dr. Heidigger's Fountain of Youth,* National Arts Club, New York, 1978; librettist, *The Umbrellas of Cherbourg,* New York Shakespeare Festival, New York, 1979; music/text, *Frustration—A Mini-Opera,* Encompass Theatre, New York, 1979; texts, *Sutter's Gold—A Cantata,* Boston Symphony, Boston, 1980; English translation/adaptation, *Carmen,* Houston Opera, Houston, TX, 1981, Vivian Beaumont, NY, 1984; English translation/adaptation, *L'Oca del Cairo,* Lyric Opera of Kansas City, 1982; English translation/adaptation, *Songs of the Auvergne,* concert, New York, 1982. MAJOR TOURS—Lyricist, *A Christmas Carol,* 1981 Christmas tour.

PRINCIPAL FILMS—Lyricist, *The Heartbreak Kid,* 1972. TELEVISION WORK—Lyricist, ''William's Doll,'' *Free to Be You and Me,* 1974; lyricist, theme, *We'll Get By,* 1974; lyricist, theme, *Marriage Is Alive and Well,* 1980; lyricist, theme, *The Way They Were,* 1981; lyricist—vocal version of ''Stars and Stripes Forever'' called 'The Man with the Sign,'' *I Love Liberty,* 1982.

AWARDS: Antoinette Perry Award, lyricist, *Fiorello!,* 1959, *Fiddler on the Roof,* 1964; New York Drama Critics Circle Award, *Fiorello!,* 1959, *Fiddler on the Roof, 1964; Newspaper Guild of New York Page One Award,* Fiddler on the Roof, 1964; Grammy, *She Loves Me,* 1963, Best New Opera Recording, *The Merry Widow,* 1978–79; gold records for original cast album of *Fiddler on the Roof,* the soundtrack album of *Fiddler on the Roof, Free to Be You and Me* (contributed song: ''William's Doll,'' music by Mary Rodgers and poem ''Housework'').

SIDELIGHTS: MEMBERSHIPS—Dramatists Guild—Secretary; American Guild of Authors and Composers/The Songwriters Guild—Executive Vice-President; BMI Affiliate; National Institute for Music Theatre—Trustee.

Mr. Harnick began writing parodies and sketches while still in high school with his first collaborator, Stanley Orzey. Since that time he has written with David Baker, Lloyd Norlin, Jerry Bock (his principal collaborator), Mary Rodgers, Michel Legrand, Joe Raposo, Jack Beeson, Cy Coleman, Richard Rodgers, Fred Karlin, Larry Grossman, and, without their knowledge, Igor Stravinsky, Maurice Ravel, Wolfgang Mozart, Franz Lehar, Georges Bizet, and Emmanuel Chabrier. He has also created English texts for Jean-Michel Damase's opera, *The Heiress,* which has not yet been produced in English. During the 1950s Mr. Harnick worked at Green Mansions, the summer resort–training ground for many Broadway writers. He also played violin with Xavier Cugat's Orchestra on a theatre date in Minneapolis, and wrote industrial shows for such clients as

Buick, Esso, Nabisco, Columbia phonograph, Milliken and did, with Jerry Bock, a Ballantine beer commercial for television in 1965. Between 1966 and 1973, Mr. Harnick wrote special material for John V. Lindsay, then mayor of New York, for his appearances before the Inner Circle (Press Club show).

ADDRESS: Business manager—David J. Cogan, 350 Fifth Avenue, New York, NY 10118.

* * *

HARRELL, Gordon Lowry, arranger, orchestrator, conductor

PERSONAL: Born September 19, 1940. EDUCATION: Baylor University, Waco, TX, B.B.A. (Accounting/Taxation and Finance), B.M. (Theory & Composition) 1958–64. Was a scholarship student in the School of Music, and studied privately with the dean.

CAREER: PRINCIPAL STAGE WORK—Arranger/Orchestrator, *Sergeant Pepper's Lonely Hearts Club Band,* NY; *Rockabye Hamlet,* NY; *Inner City,* NY; *Mary C. Brown,* NY; Musical Direction—*Dancin',* NY; *Jesus Christ Superstar,* NY and Hollywood; *Rocky Horror Show; Six Flags Over Texas;* Dance/Vocal Arranger—*Hellzapoppin; Georgy;* Dance Music—*La Cage aux Folles,* NY; Assistant Conductor—*Canterbury Tales,* NY; *Georgy,* St. Louis Municipal Opera, MO; Indianapolis Starlight Musicals, IN; Dallas Summer Musicals, TX; Casa Manana, Fort Worth, TX; Houston Music Theatre, TX.

PRINCIPAL TELEVISION WORK—Composer, *Harlequin; Dance of the Athletes;* Arranger—*Antoinette Perry Awards, Silver Anniversary; Miss Teenage America Pageant.* PRINCIPAL ARRANGER—Liza Minnelli; Ann Reinking; Betty Buckley; Leata Galloway.

SIDELIGHTS: Memberships—ASCAP: NATAS; NARAS.

ADDRESS: c/o Sherman Square Studios, 160 W. 73rd Street, New York, NY, 10023.

* * *

HART, Harvey, director, producer

PERSONAL: Born March 19, 1928, in Toronto, ON; married Helena Esther Postell, October 28, 1951; children: Edana Anne, Bethelene Ellen, David Harris. EDUCATION: University of Toronto, 1945–48; Dramatic Workshop, New York City, 1949–50.

CAREER: PRINCIPAL FILM WORK—Producer/director, Canadian Broadcasting Corporation, Toronto, 1952–64: *Double Cure; The Littlest of Kings; Panic at Parth Bay; Strike; The Dybbuk; The Crucible; Enemy of the People; The Lark; The Wild Duck; Ondine; Home of the Brave; The Luck of Ginger Coffey; The Blue Hotel; The Gambler; Queen and the Rebels; A Very Close Family; Mrs. Dally Has a Lover/Today Is Independence Day; Ward Six; Gallows Humor; Roots* (by Arnold Wesker); *David Chapter II; David Chapter III; The*

Morning after Mr. Roberts; The Quare Fellow; The Police; Eli The Fanatic; Man on My Back; The Hostage; Sun In My Eyes; Flipside. NEW YORK VIDEO-TAPE PRODUCTION—*He Who Gets Slapped.* PILOTS FOR TELEVISION FILM—*Judd for the Defense; The Young Lawyers; W.E.B.; The Yellow Rose; Dan August; Courtmartial; Laredo.* MINI-SERIES FOR TELEVISION—*Master of the Game; East of Eden.* SPECIALS AND MOVIES FOR TELEVISION—*Born Beautiful; Murder or Mercy; The Prince of Central Park; Standing Tall; The City; Street Killing; Woman Running;* four episodes of *Columbo, By Dawn's Early Light, Now You See It, Now You Don't, A Deadly State of Mind; Can Ellen Be Saved; Panic on the 5:22; Like Normal People; Captains Courageous; The Aliens; This Is Kate Bennett; Shipwrecked;* three episodes of *Alfred Hitchcock Presents;* two episodes of *The Name of the Game.* OTHER FILMS: *Fortune and Men's Eyes; Goldenrod; Bus Riley's Back In Town; The Dark Intruder; Sullivan's Empire; The Sweet Ride; The PYX; Shoot; The High Country.*

AWARDS: Best Director, Canadian Film Award, 1976: *Goldenrod;* Emmy Awards, *Columbo, By Dawn's Early Light;* Venice Film Award, 1971: *Fortune and Men's Eyes.*

SIDELIGHTS: MEMBERSHIPS—Directors Guild of America, Directors Guild of Canada, Academy of Motion Picture Arts and Sciences, Academy of Television Arts and Sciences.

ADDRESS: Office—c/o Rohar Productions Limited, Five Sultan Street, Toronto, ON, Canada M5S 1L6.

* * *

HARTLEY, Mariette, actress

PERSONAL: Born June 21, 1940; daughter of Paul Hembree (an account executive) and Mary Ickes (a saleswoman and manager; maiden name Watson) Hartley; married Patrick François Boyriven (a producer), August 13, 1978; children: Sean Paul, Justine Emelia. EDUCATION: attended Carnegie Tech (Mellon) in Pittsburgh; studied for the theatre with Eva LeGallienne at the American Shakespeare Festival. RELIGION: Methodist.

CAREER: DEBUT—Perdita, *A Winter's Tale,* American Shakespeare Festival, Stratford, CT, 1956–57. NEW YORK DEBUT—Isabella, *Measure for Measure,* Shakespeare-in-the-Park 1958–59, three weeks. PRINCIPAL STAGE APPEARANCES—Portia, *The Merchant of Venice,* Goodman, Chicago, 1959; Antigone, *Antigone,* UCLA Theatre Group, Los Angeles, 1961–62; Marianna, *The Miser,* Mark Taper Forum, Los Angeles, 1968; Maggie, *Put Them All Together,* McCarter, Princeton, NJ, 1978 and Coronet, Los Angeles, 1982. MAJOR TOURS—Helena, *A Midsummer Night's Dream* and Perdita, *A Winter's Tale,* American Shakespeare Festival tour, 1959–60.

FILM DEBUT—*Ride the High Country,* 1962. FILM APPEARANCES—*Marooned,* 1969; *Skyjacked,* 1972; *Improper Channels,* 1979. TELEVISION DEBUT—*Gunsmoke,* 1962. TELEVISION APPEARANCES—Candy Lightner, *M.A.D.D. Mothers Against Drunk Drivers,* 1982; *Goodnight, Beantown,* 1983; numerous commercials, including running role as James Garner's wife for Polaroid cameras.

MARIETTE HARTLEY

AWARDS: One Emmy, six Emmy nominations; three Cleo awards.

SIDELIGHTS: "Trying to balance a career and a marriage with chilren has been utmost. The Polaroid commercials were invaluable to me at a time when both children were infants and I could really pick and choose what I wanted. Now, with my series *Goodnight, Beantown,* we all feel more pressure. . . . I loved doing 'Maggie' in Anne Commier's play *Put Them All Together.* The reviews in Princeton were glowing . . . and in Los Angeles, too. The play opened my eyes to the tragedy of hyperkinetic children. Since then, I've been involved with an organization specializing in its treatment. I'm also involved with M.A.D.D., Save the Children and various other organizations. . . . But my main priority is my two children and a beloved and patient husband. . . . I am now co-producing, along with *Reader's Digest,* the story of Pat Hope, due to be filmed in Long Island in June, 1984. My company's name is Maraday."

* * *

HARVEY, Anthony, film director, editor

PERSONAL: Born June 3, 1931 in London, England; son of Morris (an actor) and Dorothy (Leon) Harvey. EDUCATION: Royal Academy of Dramatic Art.

CAREER: PRINCIPAL FILM WORK—Directed—*Dutchman, The Lion in Winter, They Might Be Giants, The Abduction,*

The Glass Menagerie, The Disappearance of Aimee, The Pat Neal Story, Eagles Wing, Richard's Things, Playin; for Television—*The Ultimate Solution of Grace Quigley.* PRINCIPAL FILM WORK—Editing—*I'm All Right Jack, The Spy Who Came in from the Cold, The L-Shaped Room, Dr. Strangelove, Lolita.*

AWARDS: Academy Award Nomination, *The Lion in Winter;* Golden Globe Award Nomination, *The Lion in Winter;* Directors Guild of America Award, *The Lion in Winter;* Directors Guild of American Award Nominations, *The Glass Menagerie, The Pat Neal Story.*

SIDELIGHTS: MEMBERSHIPS—Academy of Motion Picture Arts and Sciences; Directors Guild of America.

Played Ptolemy in Gabriel Pascal's film of Shaw's *Caesar and Cleopatra,* 1944.

ADDRESS: Office—c/o Anthony Greene, 666 Fifth Avenue, New York, NY 10014; Agent—Fred Milstein, William Morris Agency, 1350 Avenue of the Americas, New York, NY 10019.

* * *

HASKELL, Peter, actor

PERSONAL: Born October 15, 1934 in Boston, MA; son of Norman A. (a geophysicist) and Rose V. (a blood technician; maiden name, Golden) Haskell; married Anne E. Crompton on February 27, 1960 (divorced 1974); married Dianne Tolmich (a theatrical agent) on October 26, 1974; children: (second marriage) Audra Rosemary, Jason Abraham. EDUCATION: Harvard University, B.A. 1962; studied with Peter Kass at the Peter Kass Workshop. POLITICS: Democrat. MILITARY: U.S. Army, private first class, 1954–56.

CAREER: NEW YORK DEBUT—The son, *The Love Nest,* Writer's Stage, East Fourth Street, for 13 performances, 1963. PRINCIPAL STAGE APPEARANCES—Flamineo, *The White Devil,* Loeb Drama Center, 1961; Alceste, *Misanthrope,* Loeb Drama Center, 1962; Trigorin, *The Seagull,* UCLA, CA, 1979; MAJOR TOURS—Hal, *Henry IV, Pt. I,* United States and Canada, 1963.

FILM DEBUT—Shem, *Passages from Finnegans Wake,* 1963. PRINCIPAL FILM APPEARANCES—Paul, *Christina,* 1974; Durand, *Durand;* Maris, *Forty Days of MusaDaugh,* 1981.

TELEVISION DEBUT—*Bracken's World,* 1969–71. PRINCIPAL TELEVISION APPEARANCES—Charles Estep, *Rich Man, Poor Man, Book II; Shirley; The Cracker Factory; Love, Hate, Love; The Ballad of Andy Crocker;* Hollis Kirkland III, *Ryan's Hope,* 1982; *Search for Tomorrow,* 1983–present.

SIDELIGHTS: MEMBERSHIPS—AEA; AFTRA; SAG, National Treasurer, 1981–82, Board of Directors, 1978–83; AFI; Harvard Club of S.C. and Harvard Club of NY.

"After serving in the U.S. Army paratroopers, Mr. Haskell returned to Harvard and graduated as an English Major. He

was accepted at Columbia University Law School when a Harvard professor recommended him to playwright Derek Washburn for the off-Broadway play, *The Love Nest.* The play led to the film *Passages from Finnegans Wake* and to the National Tour of *Henry IV, Pt. I* as Prince Hal—then on to Hollywood. Peter continues to be a commuter to California where his wife, Dianne, nicknamed Crickett, had just established the Crickett Company theatrical agency.''

ADDRESS: Agent—Jack Fields Agency, 9255 Sunset Blvd., Los Angeles, CA 90069.

* * *

HAWKINS, Trish, actress

PERSONAL: Born October 30, 1945 in Hartford, CT; daughter of Lester George (professor of political science) and Elizabeth (works for New York State environmental agency; maiden name, Duffy) Hawkins. EDUCATION: Radcliffe College, B.A. 1967; studied at the Neighborhood Playhouse.

CAREER: NEW YORK DEBUT—*Oh! Calcutta!,* 1970. PRINCIPAL STAGE APPEARANCES—New York—*Iphigenia;* Girl, *The Hot l Baltimore,* Him, *Come Back Little Sheba; Battle of Angels; Mound Builders; The Farm; Ulysses in Traction; Lulu; Hogan's Folly; Twelfth Night; A Tale Told; Some of My Best Friends,* 1977; Sally, *Talley's Folly,* 1979.

AWARDS: Villager Award, 1980; Drama Desk Award, 1973; Theatre World Award, 1973.

* * *

HAWN, Goldie, actress, producer

PERSONAL: Born November 21, 1945, in Washington, DC; daughter of Edward Rutledge and Laura (Steinhoff) Hawn; married Gus Trinkonis, 1969 (divorced); Bill Hudson (divorced); children: Oliver, Kate, Garry. EDUCATION: American University.

CAREER: PRINCIPAL TELEVISION WORK—Dancer, *Andy Griffith Special; Good Morning World,* 1967–68; *Laugh-In,* 1968–70; *Pure Goldie,* 1971.

FILM DEBUT—*Cactus Flower,* 1969. PRINCIPAL FILM APPEARANCES—*There's a Girl in My Soup,* 1970; *Dollars,* 1971; *Butterflies Are Free,* 1972; *The Sugarland Express,* 1974; *The Girl from Petrovka* (also produced), 1974; *Shampoo,* 1975; *The Duchess and the Dirtwater Fox,* 1976; *Foul Play,* 1978; *Travels with Anita,* 1979; *Seems Like Old Times,* 1980; *Private Benjamin* (also producer), 1980; *Best Friends,* 1982; *Swing Shift* (also producer), 1984.

AWARDS: Academy Award, Best Supporting Actress, 1969: *Cactus Flower.*

ADDRESS: Agent—William Morris Agency, 151 El Camino Drive, Beverly Hills, CA 90212.*

HAYDON, Julie (nee Donella Lightfoot Donaldson), actress

PERSONAL: Born June 10, 1910, in Oak Park, IL; daughter of Orren Madison (a publisher, editor, founder of weekly newspapers and magazines) and Ella Marguerite (a musician and music critic; maiden name Horton) Donaldson; married: George Jean Nathan (a drama critic), June 19, 1955. EDUCATION: Studied for theatre with coach Josephine Dillon. POLITICS: "Equality for All." RELIGION: Catholic. NON-THEATRICAL CAREER—Sketch artist for a costumer.

CAREER: DEBUT—Olivia, *Twelfth Night* (with the California Traveling Shakespearean Company), Lobero Theatre, Santa Barbara, 1927. NEW YORK DEBUT—Hope Blake, *Bright Star,* Empire, 1935. PRINCIPAL STAGE APPEARANCES—Maid, *Mrs. Bumpstead-Leigh,* Los Angeles, Santa Barbara, San Francisco, 1929; Ophelia, *Hamlet,* Hollywood Playhouse, 1931; Lady in Spectacles, *Autumn Crocus,* El Capitan, Hollywood and Alcazar, San Francisco, 1934; Titania, *A Midsummer Night's Dream,* Hollywood Bowl, 1934; *A Family Affair,* Cape Playhouse, Dennis, MA, 1937; Brigid, *Shadow and Substance,* John Golden, New York, 1938; Maggie, *What Every Woman Knows,* Bucks County Playhouse, New Hope, PA, 1939; Kitty Duval, *The Time of Your Life,* Booth, New York, 1939; Patricia Carleon, *Magic,* and Ethel, *Hello, Out There,* Belasco, New York, 1942; Patsy Jefferson, *The Patriots,* City Center, New York, 1943; Laura, *The Glass Menagerie,* Civic, Chicago, 1944, Playhouse, New York, 1945; Cicely, *Miracle in the Mountains,* Playhouse, New York, 1947; Libeth Arbarbanel, *Our Lan',* Royale, New York, 1947;

Stella, *Springboard to Nowhere,* Selwyn, Chicago, 1950; Catherine, *The Intruder,* Locust Street Theatre, Philadelphia, 1952; *The Great Debate,* Pasadena Playhouse, CA, 1961; *Mr. Broadway,* John Drew, East Hampton, NY, 1962; Amanda, *The Glass Menagerie,* Victoria Texas Community Theatre, 1964; *Never Ask His Name,* Florida State University, 1965; *Long Day's Journey into Night,* Studio M, Miami, FL, 1965; Amanda, *The Glass Menagerie,* Eastern New Mexico University, Studio M, Miami, Jacksonville Community Theatre, Orlando Community Theatre, Troy State University, Alabama, 1965–66; *The Skin of Our Teeth,* Sister Marie Carol Catholic Girls College, Miami, FL, 1966; *Arsenic and Old Lace,* Ocala, FL, 1966; *Madwoman of Chaillot,* College of Saint Teresa, Winona, MN, 1967; Madame Arcati, *Blithe Spirit,* Wisconsin State University, Eau Claire, 1968; Mother, *Boy with Cart,* Oklahoma City University; seven roles, *Spoon River Anthology,* Langston University, OK, 1977; Amanda, *The Glass Menagerie,* Scranton University, PA, 1980, Lion Theatre, New York, 1980; also appeared in productions of *Uncle Vanya* (as Masha), *The Lower Depths* (Nastya), *The Seagull* (Masha), *Major Barbara, Man and Superman, Joan of Lorraine, The Barretts of Wimpole Street, Serena Blandish, Birds without Wings, Guest in the House, Uncle Harry, Nine Pine Street, Little Women, Peg O' My Heart, Mrs. Moonlight, The Enchanted, A Streetcar Named Desire, There's Always Juliet, Happy Birthday, The Silver Whistle, Angel Street, Twelfth Night,* and *Mrs. McThing;* for ten years she was "actress-in-residence" at College of St. Teresa, Winona, MN. MAJOR TOURS—*Springtime for Henry,* 1939; Kitty, *The Time of Your Life,* 1940–41; Patsy Jefferson, *The Patriots,* 1942; Celia Copplestone, *The Cocktail Party,* national company, 1951; university tours of three shows: *Encore for*

George Jean Nathan, Realm of a Critic, and Profiles of a Critic, all based on the writings of her husband.

FILM DEBUT—*The Great Meadow,* 1931. FILM APPEARANCES—Two Tom Keene westerns, 1932; short subject on bridge, 1932; *The Conquerors,* 1932; was Fay Wray's scream in *King Kong,* 1933; Farm Girl, *From Dawn 'til Dawn,* 1933; *Golden Harvest,* 1933; Cora Moore, *The Scoundrel,* 1935; *A Son Comes Home,* 1936; *The Longest Night,* 1936; Eldest Sister, *Andy Hardy Gets Spring Fever,* 1939. TELEVISION APPEARANCES—Fanny Gray, *Autumn Crocus,* 1952; *Grand Tour.*

WRITINGS: BOOKS—*Every Dog Has Its Day.* ARTICLES—"Still Shining Star" (about Laurette Taylor), *Town and Country.*

AWARDS: Miami *Tribune* Award, Best Performance by an Actress (shared with Eve Arden), 1966.

SIDELIGHTS: MEMBERSHIPS—AEA, SAG, AFTRA.

Ms. Haydon has toured with her three shows about her husband George Jean Nathan in almost every state in the union. She is currently at work on two books, one about Mr. Nathan and the other about the actors she has worked with over the years.

* * *

HAYERS, Sidney, director, writer, and film editor

PERSONAL: Born August 24, 1922, in Edinburgh, Scotland; son of Thomas (a naval officer) and Isabella Benn (a hotel manager; maiden name, Watson) Hayers; married Patricia Arnold, 1947 (divorced 1980); married Ellen Stolenwork Clark (an actress); children: Susan Margaret, Robert Michael. EDUCATION: Trinity College, Cambridge, Bsc. MILITARY: Royal Air Force, World War II.

CAREER: FIRST FILM WORK—Assistant editor, *Brief Encounter,* 1944. PRINCIPAL FILM WORK—Editor: *Warning to Wantons; Stop Press Girl; Prelude to Fame; Never Take No for an Answer; While the Sun Shines; Romeo and Juliet,* 1954; *The One That Got Away,* 1958; *A Town Like Alice; A Night to Remember,* 1959; *White Corridors; High Tide at Noon; Tiger Bay; Canterbury Tale; Edge of the World; Something Money Cannot Buy; Night and the City; House of Secrets; Passage Home; Blanche Fury; A Matter of Life and Death.* second unit director/editor: *A Night to Remember,* 1958; *Operation Amsterdam,* 1959; director, *Circus of Horror,* 1960; director, *Payroll,* 1961; director, *Night of the Eagle,* 1962; director, *This is My Street,* 1963; director, *Three Hats for Liza,* 1964; director, *The Trap,* 1965; director, *Finders Keepers,* 1966; director, *Southern Star,* 1967–68; director, *Mr. Jericho,* 1969; director, *Revenge,* 1973; co-producer/director, *Deadly Strangers,* 1974; co-producer/director, *What Changed Charlie Farthing,* 1975; co-producer/director, *Diagnosis Murder,* 1975; co-producer/director, *One Away,* 1976; action sequence director, *A Bridge Too Far.*

PRINCIPAL TELEVISION APPEARANCES—Director: *6 One Hour Films,* 1960–61; *The Human Jungle,* 1962–63; *The Avengers,* 1964–65; *The Persuaders,* 1971; *Arthur of the Britons,*

1972; *The Zoo Gang,* 1974; *The New Avengers,* 1976; *The Professionals,* 1977; *Famous Five,* 1978; *The Seekers, The Last Convertible, Condominium, Battlestar Galactica, Jack Flash, Fitz and Bones, Magnum P.I., Fall Guy, Knight Rider, Remington Steele, Marlow PI,* 1979–83.

SIDELIGHTS: MEMBERSHIPS—American Film Institute, Directors Guild of America.

ADDRESS: Office—c/o Susan Grode, 2029 Century Park E., Suite 1260, Los Angeles, CA 90067. Agent—c/o Shapiro-Lichtman, 1800 Avenue of the Stars, Los Angeles, CA 90067.

* * *

HAYES, Joseph, writer, director, manager

PERSONAL: Born August 2, 1918; son of Harold Joseph (a businessman) and Pearl Margaret (Arnold) Hayes; married Marrijane Johnstone (a writer); children: Gregory, Jason, Daniel. EDUCATION: Indiana University, B.A., 1941.

CAREER: PRODUCED—*The Desperate Hours,* 1955. CO-PRODUCED—*The Happiest Millionaire, Calculated Risk.*

WRITINGS: PLAYS—Debut—*Leaf and Bough,* produced at The Margo Jones Theatre, Dallas, Texas, 1947. NEW YORK DEBUT—*Leaf and Bough,* Cort Theatre, 1949, for 9 performances. LONDON DEBUT—*The Desperate Hours,* Hippodrome Theatre, 1955, for 217 performances. NOVELS—*The Desperate Hours,* 1955; *The Hours After Midnight,* 1957; *Bon Voyage* (with Marrijane Hayes), 1958; *The Third Day,* 1960; *Like Any Other Fugitive,* 1971; *Missing and Presumed Dead,* 1973; *Don't Go Away Mad,* 1963; *The Deep End,* 1965; *The Long Dark Night,* 1975; *Island on Fire,* 1980; *Winner's Circle,* 1981; *No Escape,* 1982. SCREENWRITING—*The Desperate Hours,* 1955; *The Young Doctors; Bon Voyage; Stolen Hours; The Third Day.* TELEVISION SCRIPTS—*Suspense, Philco, Playhouse 90.*

AWARDS: Antoinette Perry Award, Author and Producer, *The Desperate Hours,* 1955; Edgar Allan Poe Award, Best Screenplay, *The Desperate Hours;* Honorary Master of Humane Letters, Indiana University 1974.

SIDELIGHTS: MEMBERSHIPS—Dramatists Guild, Authors League, Writers Guild of America, West. Joseph Hayes remains the only writer who has ever done the original novel, the Broadway play, and the screenplay, single-handedly, of a single work, (*The Desperate Hours*). "Have traveled around world; still loving as often as possible. Once lived in Florida part-time, same home, have now sold Conecticut home and live in Florida full-time when not traveling. Still writing full-time."

ADDRESS: Home—1168 Westway, Sarasota, FL 33577. Agent—James Oliver Brown, Curtis Brown Ltd. 575 Madison Ave., New York, NY 10022.

HAYES, Patricia, actress

PERSONAL: Born December 22, 1909 in London, England;

PATRICIA HAYES

daughter of George Frederick (a civil servant) and Florence Alice (a schoolteacher; maiden name, Lawler) Hayes; married Valentine Brooke (an actor), June 8, 1939 (divorced 1951); children: Richard, Teresa, Gemma. EDUCATION: Sacred Heart Convent, Hammersmith, England; studied at the Royal Academy of Dramatic Art. POLITICS: Liberal. RELIGION: Roman Catholic.

CAREER: DEBUT—Molly & Mark, *The Great Big World,* Court, London, 1921. PRINCIPAL STAGE APPEARANCES—Archie, *Eileen,* Globe, London, 1922; young Giovanni, *The White Devil,* Scala, London, 1925; Kitty, *The Glory of the Sun,* Fortune, London, 1931; Mara Vercos, *The Tidings Brought to Mary,* Chelsea Place, London, 1934; Dora Parker, *Night Must Fall,* Cambridge Theatre, 1936; Dimple, *Family Hold Back,* Aldwych, London, 1936; Frankie, *George & Margaret,* Strand, London, 1937; Mary Ellen, *Lady Sarah's Bailiff,* and Lizzie, *Little Earthquake,* Players, London, 1937–38; Kathie, *Old Heidelberg,* and others for Jevan Brandon Thomas' repertory season at the Kings Theatre, Hammesmith, 1938; Ruby, *Getting Married,* St. Martin's, London, 1938; Brenda Gee, *Goodnight Children,* New Theatre, London, 1942; Mrs. Swabb, *Habeas Corpus,* Lyric, London, 1973; Maria, *Twelfth Night,* Royal Shakespeare Company at the Aldwych in London and the Stratford Memorial Theatre, 1974; *Liza of Lambeth,* Shaftesbury, London, 1976; Rosalia, *Filumena,* Lyric, London, 1977–78; *True West,* National Theatre of Great Britain, 1982; Rummy, *Major Barbara,* National Theatre of Great Britain, 1982–83.

PRINCIPAL FILM APPEARANCES—Jacqueline, *Epitaph for a Spy;* Mrs. Beale, *Great Day;* Phoebe, *Nicholas Nickelby,* 1946; Postmistress, *To The Public Danger;* Mrs. Litt, *Poet's Pub;* Emma Binns, *The Love Match;* Woman Prisoner, *The Deep Blue Sea,* 1955; Waitress, *Kill or Cure,* 1962; Mrs. Freeman, *Reach for Glory,* 1963; Victim's Mother, *A Hard Day's Night,* 1964; Mrs. Jones, *The Terrornauts,* 1969; Mother, *Heironymous Merkin;* Mrs. Honeybun, *Goodbye Mr. Chips,* 1969; Mrs. Beasley, *Carry on Again Doctor;* Mrs. Baird, *Fragment of Fear,* 1971; Mama the Turk, *Escort Service;* Anna, *Love Thy Neighbor; Danger on Dartmoor;* Urgl, *The Never Ending Story,* 1984.

PRINCIPAL TELEVISION APPEARANCES—*The Benny Hill Show; Eric Sykes Show; Ken Dodd Show; Citizens James; Van Parnell Saturday Spectacular; Jo Stafford Show; Hugh & I; Maigret; Bootsie & Snudge; Boyd Q.C.; Crime and Punishment; Doddy's Music Box; According to Dora;* Millicent Martin series, *Up She Goes;* Mrs. Telfer, *Master & Man,* 1970; Mrs. Skinner, *Catweazle,* 1970; Mrs. Patric, *Doomwatch,* 1970; Mrs. Batchelor, *Haven of Rest; Two D's and a Dog,* 1970; *Grasshopper Island,* 1970; *The Trouble with You Lillian,* 1971; *The Last of the Baskets,* 1971; Edna, *Edna the Inebriate Woman,* 1972; *Comedy Playhouse,* 1974; *Les Dawson Show,* 1974; *Till Death Do Us Part,* 1975; *A Choice of Friends,* 1975; *Softly, Softly,* 1975; *Centre Play,* 1975; Annie Druce, *The Victorians,* 1976; Mother, *Galton & Simpson Playhouse, "I Tell You It's Burt Reynolds,"* 1977; *Bruce & More Girls,* 1977; Connie, *London Belongs to Me,* 1977; *The Corn Is Green,* 1978; *Crown Court,* 1979; *Storm in a Teacup,* 1980; *Spooners Patch,* 1981; Soothsayer, *Cymbeline,* 1982; *Lady Is a Tramp,* 1982; Miss Bendybones, *Witches & Grinnygogs,* 1983; *Winter Sunlight,* 1984.

AWARDS: Television Actress of the Year Award, 1972: Edna, *Edna the Inebriate Woman,* also voted Television Actress of the Year by the *Sun* newspaper readers for the same role, 1972; Bancroft Gold Medal, Royal Academy of Dramatic Art, 1928.

ADDRESS: Agent—Hazel de Leon, 122 the Colonnades, Porchester Square, London W2, England.

* * *

HAYES, Peter Lind, actor, composer, critic, writer

PERSONAL: Born June 25, 1915, in San Francisco; son of Joseph and Grace (Hayes) Lind; married Mary Healy (an entertainer), December 19, 1940; children: Michael, Cathy. EDUCATION: Vaudeville training with Grace Hayes. POLITICS: Republican. RELIGION: Catholic. MILITARY: U.S. Air Corps.

CAREER: DEBUT—Office Boy, *Merton of the Movies,* Alcazar, San Francisco, 1924. NEW YORK DEBUT—*Winged Victory,* 1943. LONDON DEBUT—Entertainer, *Review,* Palladium, 1952, for 42 performances. PRINCIPAL STAGE APPEARANCES—Lead, *Heaven On Earth,* Century, NY, 1947; David, *Who Was That Lady I Saw You With?,* Martin Beck, NY, 1958; Lead, *Lovers.* MAJOR TOURS—*Who Was That Lady I Saw You With?,* MA, NY, PA, MD, 1961.

FILM DEBUT—*Million Dollar Legs,* 1939. FILM APPEARANCES—

PETER LIND HAYES

The Five Thousand Fingers of Dr. T, 1953; *Once You Kiss A Stranger,* 1969; *The Ying and Yang of Dr. Go.*

TELEVISION DEBUT—*Inside U.S.A. with Chevrolet,* 1949–50. TELEVISION APPEARANCES—*The Peter Lind Hayes Show,* 1950–51; *The Stork Club,* 1950; *Star of the Family,* 1951–52; Peter Lindsey, *Peter Loves Mary,* 1960–61; Narrator, *The Dupont Show of the Week—Regards to George M. Cohan,* 1961; Host, *The Tonight Show,* 1962; *The Perry Como Show; The Ed Sullivan Show; The Dinah Shore Show;* others; *All About Faces,* 1972. RADIO—*The Peter Lind Hayes–Mary Healy Show.*

WRITINGS: SONG, PUBLISHED—*Come to Me* (with Robert Allen). TELEVISION SHOWS—*Come to Me—Kraft Theatre.* NEWSPAPER COLUMN—*Hayseed.*

AWARDS: Entertainer of the Year, Las Vegas (with wife Mary Healy), 1979; American Cancer Award, 1981; Military: Bronze Star; two battle stars.

SIDELIGHTS: MEMBERSHIPS—SAG, AFTRA, AEA, ASCAP; Authors Guild.

Mr. Hayes and his wife have played every top nightclub in America. He also lectures on "The Anatomy of Humor" at colleges and women's clubs. In its heyday, their radio show, broadcast from their New York home, was heard by an estimated six million listeners five days a week.

ADDRESS: Home—3538 Pueblo Way, Las Vegas, NV 89109. Agent—Lester Lewis Associates, 110 W. 40th Street, New York, NY 10018.

MARY HEALY

HEALY, Mary, actress, critic, dancer, singer

PERSONAL: Born April 14, 1920, in New Orleans, LA; daughter of John George and Viola (Armbruster) Healy; married Peter Lind Hayes (an entertainer), December 19, 1940; children: Michael, Cathy. EDUCATION: Studied for the theatre at the New Orleans Vieux Carre Theatre. POLITICS: Republican. RELIGION: Catholic.

CAREER: NEW YORK DEBUT—Lead, *Count Me In,* Barrymore, 1942. LONDON DEBUT—Entertainer, *Review,* Palladium, 1952. PRINCIPAL STAGE APPEARANCES—*Common Ground,* Golden, NY, 1943; Mrs. Aouda, *Around the World in Eighty Days,* Adelphi, NY, 1946; Ann, *Who Was That Lady I Saw You With?,* Martin Beck, NY, 1958. MAJOR TOURS—*Who Was That Lady I Saw You With?,* MA, NY, PA, MD, 1961.

FILM DEBUT—Lead, *Second Fiddle,* 1939. PRINCIPAL FILMS— *Star Dust,* 1940; *Hotel for Women,* 1940; *The Five Thousand Fingers of Dr. T,* 1953.

TELEVISION DEBUT—*Inside U.S.A. with Chevrolet,* 1949– 50. TELEVISION APPEARANCES—*The Peter Lind Hayes Show,* 1950–51; *The Stork Club,* 1950; *Star of the Family,* 1951– 52; Mary Lindsey, *Peter Loves Mary,* 1960–61; Panelist, *Masquerade Party,* 1955–56; *The Ed Sullivan Show; The Perry Como Show; The Arthur Godfrey Show; The Dinah Shore Show;* others. RADIO—*The Peter Lind Hayes–Mary Healy Show.*

WRITINGS: Shows—*25 Minutes from Broadway.*

AWARDS: Doctor of Humane Letters, St. Bonaventure, 1978; Entertainer of the Year, Las Vegas (with husband Peter Lind Hayes), 1979; American Cancer Award, 1981.

SIDELIGHTS: MEMBERSHIPS—SAG; AFTRA; AEA.

With her husband, Miss Healy has performed in many community benefits. They have played every top nightclub in America, and she often works on her own. In its heyday, their radio show, broadcast from their New York home, was heard by an estimated six million listeners five days a week.

ADDRESS: Home—3538 Pueblo Way, Las Vegas, NV 89109. Agent—Lester Lewis Associates, 110 W. 40th Street, New York, NY 10018.

* * *

HECHT, Paul, actor

PERSONAL: Born August 16, 1941, in London, England. EDUCATION: National Theatre School of Canada, 1963 (first graduating class).

CAREER: DEBUT—Member of the Canadian Players Touring Company, which toured the United States and Canada, 1963–64, played in *Henry IV, Part I* and Ibsen's *An Enemy of the People.* NEW YORK DEBUT—The Player, *Rosencrantz and*

PAUL HECHT

Guildenstern Are Dead, 1967. PRINCIPAL ENGAGEMENTS—
(Broadway) John Dickenson, *1776;* Nathan, *The Rothschilds;*
Herzl, *Herzl;* Don Juan, *Don Juan,* Phoenix, NY; Belcredi,
Henry IV; Ruffio, *Ceasar and Cleopatra;* (Off-Broadway)
Macduff, *Macbeth,* Voltore, *Volpone,* New York Shake-
speare Festival; Rakityin, *A Month in the Country; Serjeant
Musgrave's Dance; MacBird; Ride Across Lake Constance;
Night and Day;* (Regional) *Cyrano de Bergerac,* Guthrie,
Minneapolis, MN; Marc Antony, *Julius Ceasar, Antony and
Cleopatra,* American Shakespeare Festival, Stratford, CT;
Dick Dudgeon, *The Devil's Disciple,* Shaw Festival, Canada.

FILM APPEARANCES—*Rollover, The Tempest.* TELEVISION
APPEARANCES—*All My Children; The Guiding Light; Another
World; Starsky and Hutch; Mary and Joseph; Family
Reunion.*

AWARDS: Antoinette Perry Award Nomination, 1967:
Rosencrantz and Guildenstern Are Dead; Academy Award
Nomination, Animated Film Short narration, 1968; *Selfish
Giant.*

SIDELIGHTS: Mr. Hecht has done voices for Bil Baird's
puppets and is a regular on Hi Brown's Radio Mystery
Theatre.

ADDRESS: Office: Schumer-Oubre Management, Ltd., 1697
Broadway, Suite 1102, New York, NY 10019. Agent—
Susan Smith, 850 Seventh Avenue, New York, NY 10036.

* * *

HEFLIN, Frances, actress

PERSONAL: Born September 20, 1924; daughter of Emmett
Evan (a dentist) and Fanny Bleeker (Shippey) Heflin; married Sol Kaplan (a composer), December 29, 1945; children:
Jonathan, Nora, Mady. EDUCATION: University of Oklahoma
(for one year); Barnard College (for one semester); studied
for the theatre for two years with Benno Schneider (while
working in the theatre).

CAREER: DEBUT—Understudy, *Charley's Aunt,* Cort, NY,
1940. LONDON DEBUT—Laura, *The Glass Menagerie,* Haymarket, August 1948, for approximately six months. PRINCI-
PAL STAGE APPEARANCES—Bicky, *The Walrus and the Carpenter,* Cort, NY, 1941; Cynthia, *All in Favor,* Henry
Miller's, NY, 1941; Gladys, *The Skin of Our Teeth,* Plymouth, NY, 1942; *The World's Full of Girls,* Royale, NY,
1944; *Sheppey,* 48th Steet, NY, 1944; Christina, *I Remember Mama,* Music Box, NY, 1945; Miranda, *The Tempest,*
Alvin, NY, 1945; Katrin, *I Remember Mama,* Music Box,
NY, 1946; Virginia, *Galileo,* Coronet, Los Angeles, 1947;
Frau, *The Physicists,* Martin Beck, NY, 1964; Wife of a
"Mollie," *The Mollie Maguires,* 1969.

MAJOR TOURS—*Punch and Julia,* Baltimore and Washington, DC, 1941; Gladys, *The Skin of Our Teeth,* five cities,
1942; *The Hasty Heart,* Summer tour; Lizzie, *The Rainmaker,* Summer Tour.

TELEVISION APPEARANCES—*Philco TV Playhouse, U.S. Steel
Hour, Omnibus, Studio One; All My Children,* since 1970.

FRANCES HEFLIN

SIDELIGHTS: MEMBERSHIPS—AEA; SAG; AFTRA.

"The flops I listed—only because they were distinguished. I
had lead roles and played with the likes of Pauline Lord,
Edmund Gwenn, Jane Cowl, Greg Peck . . . and was directed by Guthrie McClintock, Jed Harris, Sir Cedric Hard-
wicke and Alfred de Liagre, Jr. The hits, I reckon, speak for
themselves."

* * *

HEIFNER, Jack, writer

PERSONAL: Surname is pronounced "Hefner"; born March
31, 1946; son of Lee B. (an automobile dealer) and Naomi C.
(a salesperson; maiden name, Norris) Heifner. EDUCATION:
Southern Methodist University, Dallas, TX, B.F.A., 1968.

WRITINGS: PLAYS, PUBLISHED—*Casserole,* 1975; *Vanities,*
1976; *Porch,* 1977; *Music-Hall Sidelights,* 1978; *Star Treatment,* 1980; *America Was,* 1982; *Tornado,* 1983; *Smile,*
1983. FILMS—*A Wide Place in the Road* (unproduced),
1964. TELEVISION SHOWS—pilot for *Vanities* (1977); pilot for
Loveland (1979).

SIDELIGHTS: MEMBERSHIPS—The Dramatists Guild, AS-
CAP, Actors Equity Association, New Dramatists. Founding member of the Lion Theatre Company, New York.

Mr. Heifner has worked with the technical and design

departments of the New York Shakespeare Festival, The Julliard School, and the American Opera Theatre. He has acted in summer stock, Off-Off Broadway, American Shakespeare Festival productions, and appeared on Broadway in *Othello* in 1970. He was coproducer of the Off-Broadway revue *Das Luistania Songspiel,* 1979.

ADDRESS: Home—77 W. 85th Street, 5A, New York, NY 10024; Agent—c/o Bret Adams, Ltd., 448 W. 44th Street, New York, NY 10036.

* * *

HELLER, Paul M., producer and director

PERSONAL: Born September 25, 1927; son of Alex Gordon (an inventor) and Anna (an activist; maiden name, Rapapport) Heller; married: Georganne Aldrich (divorced 1981); children: Michael. EDUCATION: Columbia University, B.A., 1951. MILITARY: U.S. Army.

CAREER: PRINCIPAL FILM WORK—Producer: *David and Lisa,* 1963; *The Eavesdropper; Secret Ceremony,* 1969; *The Skin Game,* 1971; *Dirty Harry,* 1972; *Enter the Dragon,* 1973; *Outlaw Blues,* 1977; *The Promise,* 1979; *First Monday in October,* 1981.

PRINCIPAL TELEVISION WORK—Producer: *Wait Until Dark; Falcon's Gold.* THEATRE WORK—Stage manager, *Angel in the Pornshop,* NY. MULTI-MEDIA—*The New York Experience; South Street Seaport Museum.*

RELATED CAREERS: Instructor, New York University, American Film Institute, Columbia University.

AWARDS: Academy Award Nomination (2), 1962: *David and Lisa;* Venice Film Festival Award, Best First Work, Mar Del Plata Festival Award, Best Film, French Film Award Nomination, 1964: *The Eavesdropper;* French Film Award, Best Foreign Film: *Secret Ceremony.*

SIDELIGHTS: MEMBERSHIPS—SAG, Directors Guild of America, American Film Institute, Community Film Workshop Council (chairman of the board), Human-Dolphin Foundation, United Scenic Artists, Lotos Club.

ADDRESS: Office—Paul Heller Productions, 1666 N. Beverly Drive, Beverly Hills, CA 90210.

* * *

HENLEY, Beth, playwright

PERSONAL: Born May 8, 1952 in Mississippi; daughter of Charles Boyce (an attorney) and Elizabeth Josephen (an actress; maiden name, Becker) Henley. EDUCATION: Southern Methodist University, B.F.A. 1974; University of Illinois, 1975–76.

WRITINGS: PLAYS, PRODUCED—*Am I Blue,* Margo Jones, Dallas, TX, 1974, Circle Repertory, NY, 1982; *Crimes of the Heart,* Manhattan Theatre Club, NY, 1980–81, Golden, NY, 1981–82; *The Wake of Jamey Foster,* O'Neill, NY,

1982; *The Miss Firecracker Contest,* Bush, London, England, 1982.

PLAYS, PUBLISHED—*The Debutante Ball, Hymn in the Attic.* TELEPLAYS—Coauthor with Budge Threldkeld, first episode of *Survival Guide.*

THEATRE-RELATED CAREER: Graduate Teacher, Beginning Acting/Voice, University of Illinois, 1975–76.

AWARDS: Pulitzer Prize for Drama and New York Drama Critics Circle Award, 1981: *Crimes of the Heart;* Co-Winner, Great American Play Contest, Actors Theatre of Louisville, 1979.

SIDELIGHTS: MEMBERSHIPS—Dramatists Guild; Writer's Guild of America, AEA; SAG.

Ms. Henley's plays have been widely produced by such American regional theatre companies as Actors Theatre, Louisville, KY, Steppenwolf Theatre Company, Chicago, Studio Arena Theatre, Buffalo, NY, Hartford Stage Company, CT.

ADDRESS: c/o Gilbert Parker, William Morris Agency, 1350 Avenue of the Americas, New York, NY 10019.

* * *

HENRY, Buck (ne Henry Zuckerman), writer, director, actor

PERSONAL: Born in New York City; son of Paul (Air Force General) and Ruth (former Mack Sennett bathing beauty; maiden name, White) Zuckerman. EDUCATION: Darthmouth College. MILITARY: U.S. Army, Transportation Corps.

CAREER: DEBUT—a Day son, *Life with Father,* national tour, 1948. PRINCIPAL STAGE APPEARANCES—*Fortress of Glass,* Circle in the Square, NY, *Bernardine,* NY, 1952; *The Premise* (Improvisational Theatre Company), Off–Broadway, NY, 1961–62. MAJOR TOURS—*No Time for Sergeants,* national, 1956.

FILM DEBUT—*The Troublemaker,* 1962. FILM APPEARANCES—*The Graduate,* 1967; Colonel Korn, *Catch-22,* 1970; *The Man Who Fell to Earth,* 1976; *Heaven Can Wait,* 1978; *Old Boyfriends,* 1979; *Gloria,* 1979; *The First Family,* 1980. DIRECTED—(co-director) *Heaven Can Wait,* 1978; *The First Family,* 1980.

TELEVISION APPEARANCES—Panelist, *Who Said That?,* 1952–53; *The Steve Allen Show,* 1961; *That Was the Week That Was,* 1964–65; Felix, *The Owl and the Pussycat,* series pilot, 1970; guest host, *The Dick Cavett Show,* 1970; guest host, *Saturday Night Live.*

WRITINGS: SCREENPLAYS—*The Troublemaker* (for the Premise Company), 1962; *The Graduate,* 1967; *Candy,* 1968; *Catch-22,* 1970; *The Owl and the Pussycat,* 1970; *Taking Off,* 1971; *What's Up, Doc?,* 1972; *The Day of the Dolphin,* 1973; *Heaven Can Wait,* 1978; *The First Family,* 1980. TELEVISION—*The Steve Allen Show,* 1961; co-creator with Mel Brooks, *Get Smart,* 1965–70; *That Was the Week That*

Was, 1964–65; *Captain Nice*, 1967; *The Garry Moore Show*, 1958–67; *Quark*, 1978.

AWARDS: Academy Award Nomination, 1967: *The Graduate*.

SIDELIGHTS: MEMBERSHIPS—Writers Guild of America; Directors Guild; AMPAS.

ADDRESS: Office—760 N. La Cienega Blvd., Los Angeles, CA 90069.

* * *

HENSON, Jim (James Maury), puppeteer, producer, director

PERSONAL: Born September 24, 1936, in Greenville, MS; son of Paul R. (an agronomist) and Elizabeth (Brown) Henson; married Jane Nebel (an executive), May 28, 1959; children: Lisa, Cheryl, Brian, John, Heather. EDUCATION: University of Maryland, B.A., 1960.

CAREER: PRINCIPAL TELEVISION WORK—Producer, *Sam and Friends*, WRC-TV, Washington, DC, 1954; puppeteer, *Jimmy Dean Show*, 1963–66; creator, puppeteer, *Sesame Street*, 1969–present; creator, producer, puppeteer, *The Muppet Show*, 1976–82; executive producer, *Fraggle Rock*, 1982–present.

PRINCIPAL FILM WORK—Producer, *The Muppet Movie*, 1979; director, *The Great Muppet Caper*, 1981; co-director, co-producer, *The Dark Crystal*, 1982; executive producer, *The Muppets Take Manhattan*, 1984.

RELATED-CAREER—President, Henson Associates.

AWARDS: Emmy Awards, 1958, 1973–74, 1975–76; Writers Guild, 1979, 1980; Grammy, 1979: *The Muppet Show* album; Peabody, 1979: *The Muppet Show;* Film Advisory Board citation, 1979: *The Muppet Movie;* Television Academy Award, 1978: *The Muppet Show;* Entertainer of the Year, 1976.

SIDELIGHTS: MEMBERSHIPS—Directors Guild, AFTRA, SAG, Writers Guild, Puppeteers of America (past President), president emeritus, UNIMA (International Puppetry).

ADDRESS: Henson Associates, 117 E. 69th Street, New York, NY 10021.

* * *

HEPBURN, Katharine Houghton, actress

PERSONAL: Born November 9, 1909, in Hartford, CT; daughter of Dr. Thomas N. (a surgeon) and Katharine (a feminist; maiden name, Houghton) Hepburn; married Ludlow Ogden Smith, 1928 (divorced 1934). EDUCATION: Hartford School for Girls; Bryn Mawr College.

CAREER: THEATRICAL DEBUT—*The Czarina*, Baltimore,

1928. NEW YORK DEBUT—Hostess, *Night Hostess*, Martin Beck, 1928. LONDON DEBUT—The Lady, *The Millionairess*, New, 1952. PRINCIPAL STAGE APPEARANCES—Veronica Sims, *These Days*, Cort, NY, 1928; understudies Hope Williams, *Holiday*, Plymouth, NY, 1928; Katia, *A Month in the Country*, Guild, NY, 1930; Judy Bottle, *Art and Mrs. Bottle*, Maxine Elliott, NY, 1930; summer stock, Ivoryton, CT, 1931; Antiope, *The Warrior's Husband*, Morosco, NY, 1932; Stella Surrege, *The Lake*, Martin Beck, NY, 1933; title role, *Jane Eyre*, New Haven, CT, 1936; Tracy Lord, *The Philadelphia Story*, Shubert, NY, 1939; Jamie Cow Rowan, *Without Love*, St. James (for the Guild), NY, 1942; Rosalind, *As You Like It*, Cort, NY, 1950; The Lady, *The Millionaress*, Shubert, NY, 1952; Portia, *The Merchant of Venice*, Beatrice, *Much Ado About Nothing*, Shakespeare Festival, Stratford, CT, 1957; Viola, *Twelfth Night*, Cleopatra, *Anthony and Cleopatra*, Shakespeare Festival, Stratford, CT, 1960; Coco Chanel, *Coco*, Mark Hellinger, NY, 1969; Mrs. Basil, *A Matter of Gravity*, Broadhurst, NY, 1976; *The West Side Waltz*, NY, 1980.

MAJOR TOURS—Grazia, *Death Takes a Holiday*, 1929; *Jane Eyre*, 1937; Rosalind, *As You Like It*, 1950; Portia, *The Merchant of Venice*, Katherine, *The Taming of the Shrew*, Isabella, *Measure for Measure*, Old Vic, Australian tour, 1955; Beatrice, *Much Ado About Nothing*, national, 1958; *Coco*, 1971; also toured her last two Broadway plays.

FILM DEBUT—Sydney, *A Bill of Divorcement*, 1932; title role, *Christopher Strong*, 1933; *Morning Glory*, 1933; Jo, *Little Women*, 1934; *Spitfire*, 1934; Lady Babbie, *The Little Minister*, 1934; *Break of Hearts*, 1935; title role, *Alice Adams*, 1935; title role, *Sylvia Scarlett*, 1935; Queen Mary, *Mary of Scotland*, 1936; *A Woman Rebels*, 1936; *Quality Street*, 1937; *Stage Door*, 1937; *Bringing Up Baby*, 1938; *Holiday*, 1938; Tracy Lord, *The Philadelphia Story*, 1940; *Woman of the Year*, 1942; *Keeper of the Flame*, 1942; herself, *Stage Door Canteen*, 1943; *Dragon Seed*, 1944; *Without Love*, 1945; *Undercurrent*, 1946; *The Sea of Grass*, 1947; Clara Wieck Schumann, *Song of Love*, 1947; *State of the Union*, 1948; Amanda, *Adam's Rib*, 1949; *The African Queen*, 1951; *Pat and Mike*, 1952; *Summertime/Summer Madness*, 1955; Lizzie, *The Rainmaker*, 1956; *The Iron Petticoat*, 1956; *The Desk Set*, 1957; Mrs. Vail, *Suddenly, Last Summer*, 1959; Mary Tyrone, *Long Day's Journey Into Night*, 1962; *Guess Who's Coming to Dinner*, 1968; Eleanor, *The Lion in Winter*, 1968; title role, *The Madwoman of Chaillot*, 1969; Hecuba, *The Trojan Women*, 1971; *A Delicate Balance*, 1975; *Rooster Cogburn*, 1975; Ethel Thayer, *On Golden Pond*, 1981; *Olly, Olly Oxenfree*, 1983.

TELEVISION APPEARANCES—Amanda Wingfield, *The Glass Menagerie*, 1973; *Love Among the Ruins*, 1978; Miss Moffatt, *The Corn Is Green*, 1979; (documentary, NET), *Starring Katharine Hepburn*, 1981.

AWARDS: Academy Award, *Morning Glory*, 1932/33, *Guess Who's Coming to Dinner*, 1967, *The Lion in Winter*, 1968; *On Golden Pond*, 1981; other Academy Award Nominations: *Alice Adams*, 1935, *The Philadelphia Story*, 1940, *Woman of the Year*, 1942, *The African Queen*, 1951, *Summertime*, 1955, *The Rainmaker*, 1956, *Suddenly, Last Summer*, 1959, *Long Day's Journey Into Night*, 1962; Cannes Film Festival Award, Best Actress, 1962: *Long Day's Journey Into Night;* British Film Academy Award, 1967: *The Lion in Winter/Guess Who's Coming to Dinner.*

SIDELIGHTS: RECREATION—Tennis, swimming, riding, golf, cycling, loves the sea.

Miss Hepburn once said that she "preferred being comfortable to being beautiful" and also "I only want to go on being a star; it's all I know how to be."*

* * *

HERLIHY, James Leo, playwright, actor, writer

PERSONAL: Born February 27, 1927, in Detroit, MI; son of William Francis (an engineer) and Grace (Oberer) Herlihy. EDUCATION: Attended Black Mountain College, 1947–48; Yale University, School of Drama, 1956–57; studied at the Pasadena Playhouse in California, and with the Playwrights Unit of Actors Studio in New York City. MILITARY: U.S. Navy 1945–46 (Yeoman 3rd Class).

CAREER: PRINCIPAL STAGE APPEARANCES—Jerry, *The Zoo Story*, Rockport Playhouse, MA, 1962, Théâtre Charles-de-Rochefort, Paris, France, 1963, Boston Playhouse, MA, 1963; Aston, *The Caretaker*, Boston Playhouse, 1963. DIRECTED—*Crazy October.*

THEATRE-RELATED CAREER: Distinguished visiting professor, University of Arkansas, J. William Fulbright College of Fine Arts and Sciences, 1983; teacher, playwriting, narrative writing, City College of New York, Colorado College, Colorado Springs, University of Southern California, Los Angeles. Taught acting workshops at the Milton Katselas workshops in Hollywood, CA.

WRITINGS: PLAYS—*Moon in Capricorn*, produced at Theatre de Lys, New York, 1953; *Blue Denim*, with William Noble, produced at the Pasadena Playhouse, CA, 1958; *Crazy October*, produced at the Shubert Theatre, New Haven, CT, 1958; *Streetlight Sonata*, produced at the Pasedena Playhouse, 1950; *Stop, You're Killing Me*, an evening of one-act plays, Boston, 1968. NOVELS—*All Fall Down*, 1960; *Midnight Cowboy*, 1965. SHORT FICTION—*The Sleep of Baby Filbertson; A Story That Ends with a Scream.* PRINCIPAL FILMS MADE FROM WRITINGS—*Blue Denim*, 1959; *All Fall Down*, 1962; *Midnight Cowboy*, 1969.

SIDELIGHTS: MEMBERSHIPS—Dramatists Guild, AEA, SAG, ALA.

Mr. Herlihy's novel *Midnight Cowboy* was a Literary Guild selection and met with international acclaim. Four years after it was published, John Schlesinger's screen adaptation won Academy Awards for Best Picture and Best Screenplay and virtually all foreign best film awards. Recently Mr. Herlihy returned to acting, playing a featured role in Arthur Penn's *Four Friends*. His latest novel, *The Season of the Witch*, 1971, is a study of the Woodstock generation.

ADDRESS: 3527 Landa Street, Los Angeles, CA 90039.

* * *

HERMAN, Jerry, songwriter

PERSONAL: Born July 10, 1933, in New York City; son of Harry (a summer camp operator) and Ruth (a piano teacher; maiden name, Sachs) Herman; EDUCATION: Parsons School of Design; University of Miami, A.B. 1954. RELIGION: Jewish. MILITARY: U.S. Army, 1954–55.

CAREER: DEBUT—(actor) Og, *Finian's Rainbow*, University of Miami, Florida, 1954. NEW YORK DEBUT—Songwriter, *I Feel Wonderful*, Theatre de Lys, 1954. LONDON DEBUT—Songwriter, *Hello, Dolly!*, Drury Lane, 1965. PRINCIPAL WORKS: *Nightcap*, 1958; *Parade*, 1960; *A to Z*, 1960; *Milk and Honey*, Martin Beck, NY, 1961; *Madame Aphrodite*, Phoenix, NY, 1961; *Hello, Dolly!*, St. James, NY, 1964; *Mame*, Winter Garden, NY, 1966; *Dear World*, Mark Hellinger, NY, 1966; *Mack and Mabel*, Palace, NY, 1974; *The Grand Tour*, Palace, NY, 1978; *Mother of Burlesque* (unproduced), 1979; Songwriter/Doctor, *A Day in Hollywood/A Night in the Ukraine*, NY, 1981; *La Cage Aux Folles*, Palace, NY, 1983. Mr. Herman's work also provided the material for *Jerry's Girls*, a revue of Herman material, first presented 1981.

RECORDINGS—*Hello, Jerry!*, 1965. PUBLICATIONS—Sheet music, 1960–83; *Jerry Herman Songbook*, E. H. Morris, 1975.

AWARDS: Antoinette Perry Award, 1964: *Hello, Dolly!*, 1984; *La Cage Aux Folles;* Antoinette Perry Award Nomination, 1966: *Mame;* two Grammy Awards, *Hello, Dolly!;* two Solid Gold Records, *Hello, Dolly!;* Variety Poll Best Lyricist Award, 1967; Iron Arrow, University of Miami's Honor Society; Zeta Beta Tau Award, 1968.

SIDELIGHTS: MEMBERSHIPS—Zeta Beta Tau Fraternity.

"Mr. Herman has also appeared in concert at Kaufmann Concert Hall, NY, in *An Evening with Jerry Herman*, 1974, and more recently has toured with productions of *Jerry's Girls.* Mr. Herman, reportedly, cannot read or write music and plays by ear into a tape recorder."

ADDRESS: Home—55 Central Park West, New York, NY 10023.

* * *

HERRMANN, Edward Kirk, actor

PERSONAL: Born July 21, 1943, in Washington, DC; son of John Anthony and Jean Eleanor (O'Connor) Herrmann. EDUCATION: Bucknell University, B.A., 1965; Fulbright Scholar, London Academy of Music and Dramatic Art, 1968–69.

CAREER: PRINCIPAL STAGE APPEARANCES—Four years with the Dallas Theatre Center; in New York: *The Basic Training of Pavlo Hummel*, NY, 1970; *Midsummer Night's Dream*, NY; *Gardenia*, NY; *Moonchildren*, NY, 1972; *Mrs. Warren's Profession*, 1976; *Journey's End*, NY, 1978; *The Beach House*, 1979; *Whose Life Is It Anyway?; Hedda Gabler; Candida; The Philadelphia Story*, NY; *The Front Page*, NY, 1981; *Plenty*, NY, 1982; *Uncle Vanya*, Williamstown Festival, MA, 1984.

PRINCIPAL FILM APPEARANCES—*The Paper Chase*, 1973; *The Great Gatsby*, 1974; *Day of the Dolphin*, 1973; *The*

Great Waldo Pepper, 1975; *The Betsy*, 1978; *The North Avenue Irregulars*, 1979; *The Brass Target*, 1979; *Take Down*, 1979.

PRINCIPAL TELEVISION APPEARANCES — *Beacon Hill; M*A*S*H;* movies: *Valley Forge; Eleanor and Franklin: The White House Years*, 1977; *A Love Affair: The Eleanor and Lou Gehrig Story*, 1978; *Portrait of a Stripper*, 1979; *The Sorrows of Gin*, 1979; *Harry's War*, 1979; *The Private History of a Campaign That Failed*, 1980; *The John Reed and Louise Bryant Story*, 1981; *A Little Set*, 1982; *The Alger Hiss Story*, 1984.

AWARDS: TV Critics Circle, Best Actor, 1977: *Eleanor and Franklin: The White House Years;* Antoinette Perry Award, Best Supporting Actor, 1976: *Mrs. Warren's Profession.*

ADDRESS: Agent—Blake Agency, 409 N. Camden Drive, Beverly Hills, CA 90210; Lantz Agency, 888 Seventh Avenue, New York, NY 10016.*

* * *

HERRMANN, Keith, composer, producer, and pianist

PERSONAL: Born March 4, 1952, in Brooklyn, NY; son of John Bucher (a salesman) and Marilyn Jean (a church music director; maiden name Kuhlman) Herrmann. EDUCATION: Wittenberg School of Music, Springfield, OH, Bachelor of Music, 1973. RELIGION: Presbyterian.

CAREER: FIRST STAGE WORK—musical director, *Godspell* national tour, 1974–75. FIRST NEW YORK STAGE WORK—keyboardist, *The Magic Show*, Cort Theatre, 1975. PRINCI-PAL STAGE WORK—conductor, *Whoopee!*, ANTA Theatre, 1979; musical director, *St. Regis Revues*, St. Regis Hotel, New York, 1980–82; conductor, *Cats*, Winter Garden, New York. MAJOR TOURS—musical director for *Godspell; The Magic Show; Starting Here, Starting Now;* and *Grease.* FILM DEBUT—Mummy, *Climbin' to the Top*, 1983. TELEVISION DEBUT—*The Jolly Jack Show*, 1956. TELEVISION APPEAR-ANCES—*Kennedy Center Honors; CBS: The People (Economics of the Theatre).*

WRITINGS: PLAYS—composer, *Onward Victoria;* composer, *The Little Comedy.*

SIDELIGHTS: MEMBERSHIPS—Dramatists Guild; American Federation of Musicians; ASCAP.

ADDRESS: Office—850 Seventh Avenue, Suite 1200, New York, NY 10019.

* * *

HESTON, Charlton (ne Carter), actor

PERSONAL: Born October 6, 1922, in Evanston, IL; son of Russell Whitford and Lilla (Charlton) Carter; married Lydia Clarke, March 17, 1944; children: Fraser Clarke, Holly Ann.

EDUCATION: Attended Northwestern University. MILITARY: U.S. Air Force, World War II.

CAREER: NEW YORK DEBUT—Proculeuis, *Antony and Cleopatra*, Martin Beck, 1947.

FILM DEBUT—*Dark City*, 1950. PRINCIPAL FILM APPEAR-ANCES—*Greatest Show on Earth; The Savage; Ruby Gentry; President's Lady; Pony Express; Arrowhead; Bad for Each Other; Naked Jungle; Secret of the Incas; Far Horizons*, 1955; *Lucy Galland*, 1955; *Private War of Major Benson*, 1955; *The Ten Commandments*, 1957; *The Maverick; The Big Country*, 1958; *The Buccaneers*, 1959; *Ben Hur*, 1959; *Wreck of the Mary Deare*, 1959; *El Cid; The Pigeon That Took Rome*, 1962; *55 Days at Peking*, 1963; *Major Dundee*, 1965; *The Agony and the Ecstacy*, 1965; *The War Lord*, 1965; *The Greatest Story Ever Told*, 1966; *Khartoum*, 1966; *The Battle Horns; Will Penny*, 1968; *Planet of the Apes*, 1968; *Number One*, 1969; *Julius Caesar; Beneath the Planet of the Apes*, 1970; *The Hawaiians*, 1970; *The Omega Man*, 1971; *Anthony and Cleopatra* (also directed); *Skyjacked*, 1972; *Soylent Green*, 1973; *The Three Musketeers*, 1975; *The Last Hard Men*, 1976; *Midway*, 1976; *Two-Minute Warning*, 1976; *Crossed Swords*, 1978; *Gray Lady Down*, 1978; *The Awakening*, 1980; *Mother Lode* (also directed).

TELEVISION DEBUT—*Julius Caesar*, 1949. TELEVISION AP-PEARANCES—*Macbeth; The Taming of the Shrew; Jane Eyre; Wuthering Heights; Of Human Bondage.*

PRINCIPAL STAGE APPEARANCES—*State of the Union, The Glass Menagerie*, Thomas Wolfe Memorial Theatre, Ashe-ville, NC, 1947; Glenn Campbell, *Leaf and Bough*, Cort, NY, 1949; A2, *Cock-a-Doodle-Doo*, Lenox Hill Playhouse, NY, 1949; John Clitherow, *Design for a Stained Glass Window*, Mansfield, NY, 1950; *The Traitor*, 1952; Roberts, *Mister Roberts*, City Center, NY, 1956; Kell, *The Tumbler*, Helen Hayes, NY, 1960; Sir Thomas More, *A Man for All Seasons*, Mill Run Playhouse, Skokie, IL, 1965; John Proc-tor, *The Crucible*, Ahmanson, Los Angeles, CA, 1972; Macbeth, *Macbeth*, Ahmanson, Los Angeles, CA, 1975; *Long Day's Journey into Night*, Ahmanson, Los Angeles, CA, 1977; More, *A Man for All Seasons*, Ahmanson, Los Angeles, CA, 1979.

WRITINGS: AUTOBIOGRAPHY—*An Actor's Life.*

AWARDS: American Academy of Motion Picture Arts & Sciences, Jean Hersholt Humanitarian of the Year Award, 1978; Academy Award, Best Actor, 1959: *Ben Hur.*

SIDELIGHTS: MEMBERSHIPS—SAG (president, 1966–71), American Film Institute (chairman), Los Angeles Theatre Group (trustee), National Council on the Arts, 1967–72; President's Task Force on Arts and Humanities, 1981–present. RECREATION —Tennis, horseback riding.*

* * *

HEWITT, Alan, actor, director

PERSONAL: Born January 21, 1915, in New York City; son of William M. (an advertiser/publisher) and Hortense J. (a manufacturer; maiden name Baum) Hewitt. EDUCATION:

Dartmouth College, B.A., 1934; studied acting with Benno Schneider, 1937 and at the American Theatre Wing, 1946–51; studied voice with Clytie Hine Mundy, 1947–51. MILITARY: U.S. Army, 1943–46 (staff sergeant with Armed Forces Radio).

CAREER: DEBUT—*The Death of Bad Grammar,* 1925, P.S. 6, New York. PROFESSIONAL DEBUT—Mose, *The Pursuit of Happiness,* Cohasset, MA, 1934. NEW YORK DEBUT—Lucentio, *The Taming of the Shrew,* Guild, 1935. PRINCIPAL STAGE APPEARANCES—Cohasset, 1934—Douglas Helder, *Interference,* Tom Crosby, *Song and Dance Man,* Philip, *You Never Can Tell,* Al Diamond, *Minick,* Lord Clinton, *Mary Tudor;* Westport Country Playhouse, 1935—Dorilant, *The Country Wife,* Sgt. Duval, *Ode to Liberty,* interned officer, *The Coward;* first officer, *Idiot's Delight,* Shubert, New York, 1936; Westport, 1936—Jeremy, *Love for Love,* Pat, *Dr. Knock,* Juggins, *Fanny's First Play,* music master, *The Would-Be Gentleman;* Clayton Herrick, *The Golden Journey,* Booth, New York, 1936; Fritzi, *The Masque of Kings,* Shubert, New York, 1937; Warrior, *Amphitryon 38,* Shubert, New York, 1937; Yacov, *The Seagull,* Shubert, New York, 1938; Lydia Mendelsohn, Ann Arbor, MI, 1938—Martin Holme, *The Ghost of Yankee Doodle,* Wolf Beifeld, *Liliom,* Hon. Alan Howard, *French without Tears,* Clendon Wyatt, *Rain, From Heaven;* Bill Chapman, *Away from It All,* Rockridge, Carmel, NY, 1938; David Kingsley, *Stage Door,* Suffern, NY 1938; Casino, Newport, RI, 1938—Toby Cartwright, *Ways and Means,* Alec Harvey, *Still Life,* Homer Sampson, *Grandpa,* Hon. Alan Howard, *French without Tears,* Corbier, *Cognac; One for the Money,* Suffern, New York, 1938; Mago, *The Road to Rome,* Maplewood, NJ, Albany, NY, 1938; Alex Hewitt, *The American Way,* Center, New York, 1939; Philip Graves, *Here Today,* Berkshire Playhouse, Stockbridge, MA, 1939;

David F. Winmore, *Love's Old Sweet Song,* Plymouth, New York, 1940; Lawrence Vail, *Once in a Lifetime,* Suffern, New York, 1941; Wilfred Marks, *The Walrus and the Carpenter,* Cort, New York, 1941; Captain Loft, *The Moon is Down,* Martin Beck, New York, 1942; Tony Kenyon, *Skylark,* Stock, 1947; Captain Jensen, *The Skull Beneath,* stock, 1947; Morgan Kilpatrick, *The Gentleman from Athens,* Mansfield, New York, 1947; Howard Wagner, *Death of a Salesman,* Morosco, 1949; Pemberton Maxwell, *Call Me Madam,* Imperial, New York, 1950; Valentine, *You Never Can Tell,* Lord Allan Frobisher, *Jane,* Berkshire Playhouse, Stockbridge, MA, 1953; Lord Chamberlain/First Judge, *Ondine,* 46th Street Theatre, New York, 1954; Cardinal Richelieu, *The Three Musketeeers,* St. Louis Municipal Opera, 1956; E. K. Hornbeck, *Inherit the Wind,* National, New York, 1955; Angelo, *Measure for Measure,* Library of Congress, Washington, DC, 1958; Judge Michael Lengel, *Outrage,* Eisenhower, Kennedy Center, Washington, DC, 1982. MAJOR TOURS—Delivery boy, *Bring on the Girls,* 1934; third huntsman/Philip, *The Taming of the Shrew,* 1935; Sir James Fenton, *Petticoat Fever;* Mr. Dermott, *At Mrs. Beam's;* Frederick Ogden, *The Virginian;* Boze Hertzlinger, *The Petrified Forest,* 1937; Lucentio, *The Taming of the Shrew,* 1939–40 (subsequently played it at the Alvin, New York, 1940); Warwick Wilson, *Biography;* Brooks, *The Bat;* Alastair Fitzfassenden, *The Millionairess;* Philip Graves, *Here Today,* 1940; Rudd Kendall, *Old Acquaintance,* 1942.

FILM DEBUT—Matt Helmsley, *Career,* 1959. PRINCIPAL

FILMS—*A Private's Affairs,* 1959; *The Absent-Minded Professor,* 1961; *Bachelor in Paradise,* 1961; *Follow That Dream,* 1962; Dr. Gruber, *That Touch of Mink,* 1962; *Days of Wine and Roses,* 1962; *Son of Flubber,* 1963; *The Misadventures of Merlin Jones,* 1964; *How to Murder Your Wife,* 1964; *The Monkey's Uncle,* 1965; *The Horse in the Grey Flannel Suit,* 1968; *The Brotherhood,* 1969; *Sweet Charity,* 1969; *The Computer Wore Tennis Shoes,* 1970; *R.P.M.,* 1970; *The Barefoot Executive,* 1971; *Now You See Him, Now You Don't,* 1972; *Seniors,* 1978. RADIO AND TELEVISION APPEARANCES—*Theatre Guild on the Air; NBC Cavalcade; The Greatest Story Ever Told; Famous Jury Trials; Radio Reader's Digest; Alfred Hitchcock Presents; The Defenders; Dr. Kildare; Perry Mason; U.S. Steel Hour; Omnibus; Bewitched; Gomer Pyle; I Dream of Jeannie; Lost in Space; Love, American Style; Daktari; The Bob Newhart Show; Slattery's People; Hec Ramsay; Wild, Wild West; Felony Squad;* Lieutenant Brennan, *My Favorite Martian,* 1964–66; *ABC Movie of the Week; NBC World Premiere; Pueblo; The Adams Chronicles;* various radio and television commercials and voiceovers.

DIRECTED—*Bus Stop,* Berkshire Playhouse, Stockbridge, MA, 1957; *Inherit the Wind,* Grist Mill Playhouse, Andover, NJ, 1957; *Who Was That Lady I Saw You With?,* Bucks County Playhouse, New Hope, PA, 1959.

WRITINGS: Essay on American acting in the twentieth century in *The American Theatre: A Sum of Its Parts,* Samuel French; shorter pieces in *The New Republic, Theatre Arts, Equity Magazine, Equity News, Screen Actor, The New York Times.*

SIDELIGHTS: MEMBERSHIPS—AEA (Council, 1940-51; House Affairs Committee, 1963–81; Life Member); SAG; AFTRA; Actors Fund (Board of Trustees since 1971, Executive Committee since 1977, named chairman in 1981); Drama League (Advisory Committee, 1972–82); Friends of the Dartmouth Library (Executive Committee, 1970–80). RECREATION—Swimming, timetables and road maps, transportation in general. Mr. Hewitt has recorded more than 225 books for the blind and physically handicapped at American Foundation for the Blind, Talking Books Program of the Library of Congress. He prepared the chronology of the careers of Alfred Lunt and Lynn Fontanne printed in the program book for the ANTA/West tribute to the Lunts, June 11, 1972; also for Helen Hayes ANTA/West program-book, July 6, 1976.

ADDRESS: Home—400 East 52nd Street, New York, NY 10022. Agent—Hesseltine-Baker Associates, Inc., 165 W. 46th Street, New York, 10036.

* * *

HEYMAN, Barton, actor

PERSONAL: Born January 24, 1937; son of Henry (an attorney) and Phyllis Selma (Block) Heyman; married Mary Pat Preciado (divorced 1964); children: Sean Thomas. EDUCATION: Attended University of California at Los Angeles; trained for the stage with Warren Robertson and Lee Strasberg. POLITICS: Democrat. RELIGION: Zen. MILITARY: U.S. Army, 1960–65.

Maude, 1971; *Foul Play,* 1978; *Nine to Five,* 1980; *The Best Little Whorehouse in Texas,* 1982 (also directed the last three films noted).

AWARDS: Playwright-in-residence, Théâtre de National, Paris, France, under the direction of Peter Brook.

SIDELIGHTS: MEMBERSHIPS—Writers Guild of America, West; Dramatists Guild.

ADDRESS: Agent—Michael Ovitz, Creative Artists Agency, 1888 Century Park East, Los Angeles, CA 90067.

* * *

HIGGINS, James, actor and director

PERSONAL: Born June 1, 1932, in Worksop, UK; son of Joseph and Molly (Bealby) Higgins; married Isabel Grandin (an actress), June 27, 1977. EDUCATION: Cambridge University, B.A., 1956; M.A. 1958; trained for the stage with Mira Rostova. POLITICS: Radical Independent. MILITARY: Royal Navy.

CAREER: DEBUT—King Henry, *Henry V,* Vermont Shakespeare Festival, Burlington, VT. NEW YORK DEBUT—Wicke, *The Magistrate,* Equity Library, 1962–63, 12 performances. LONDON DEBUT—Interlocutor, *Ain't We Got a Right?,*

BARTON HEYMAN

CAREER: DEBUT—lead, *Hello Out There,* Los Alamos, NM, 1952. NEW YORK DEBUT—Puck, *Midsummer Night's Dream,* Theatre de Lys. PRINCIPAL THEATRE APPEARANCES—Wild Bill Hickok, *Indians,* NY, 1969; Icrogstadt, *Doll's House,* Lincoln Center, NY, 1974; John Hogan, *Trial of the Catonsville Nine,* NY.

FILM DEBUT—El Segundo, *Valdez Is Coming,* 1970. PRINCIPAL FILM APPEARANCES—Red, *Bang the Drum Slowly;* Dr. Klein, *The Exorcist; Let's Scare Jessica to Death.*

TELEVISION DEBUT—*Simas Kadurka.* PRINCIPAL TELEVISION APPEARANCES—*Tracking the Goodbar Killer; Question of Honor; Living Proof; It's Only Money.*

ADDRESS: Agent—c/o Hesseltine-Baker, 165 W. 46th Street, New York, NY 10036; c/o Don Buchwald, 10 E. 44th Street, New York, NY 10017.

* * *

HIGGINS, Colin, scriptwriter, playwright, director

PERSONAL: Born July 28, 1941, in Noumea, New Caledonia; son of John Edward and Joy (Kelly) Higgins. EDUCATION: Stanford, B.A., 1967; U.C.L.A., M.A., 1969.

WRITINGS: PLAYS, PUBLISHED—*Harold and Maude,* 1981 (Samuel French, 1983); PLAYS, UNPUBLISHED—The Ik, written with Denis Cannan, 1974. SCREENPLAYS—*Harold and*

JAMES HIGGINS

Greenwich, 1969, 45 performances. PRINCIPAL THEATER APPEARANCES—man, *Stevie*, Manhattan Theater Club, New York, 1979; Judge, *Who's Life Is It Anyway?*, Trafalgar, Royale, NY, 1979–80; Desmond Curry, *The Winslow Boy*, Roundabout, NY, 1980–81; Von Strack, *Amadeus*, Broadhurst, NY, 1982–83. DIRECTED: Plays—*Charley's Aunt*, U.S. cities, 1976. THEATRE-RELATED CAREER—Artist-in-Residence, Stephens College, Columbia, MO, 1966–69; 1970–74.

SIDELIGHTS: RECREATION—bicycling, fishing, gardening.

ADDRESS: Home—97 Barrow Street, New York, NY 10014; Agent—c/o Michael Thomas, 22 E. 60th Street, New York, 10022.

* * *

HIGGINS, Michael, actor, director

PERSONAL: Born January 20, 1925, in Brooklyn, NY; son of Michael Peter (a poet and grocer, and in the insurance business) and Mary Katherine (McGowan) Higgins; married Elizabeth Lee Goodwin on March 2, 1946; children: Swen, Christopher, Deirdre. EDUCATION: American Theatre Wing, 1946–52. MILITARY: U.S. Army, 1st Lieutenant, Infantry, 1942–45.

CAREER: DEBUT—Lucentio, *The Taming of the Shrew*, Shakespeare Fellowship of America, New York City area, 1936. NEW YORK DEBUT—Third Guard, *Antigone*, Cort, 1946. PRINCIPAL STAGE APPEARANCES—Understudy, Marchbanks, *Candida*, Cort, NY, 1946; Tommy Tucker, *The First Year*, Greenwich Mews, NY, 1947; Michael Barnes, *The Male Animal* and Geoffery Cole, *The Vinegar Tree*, Chapel, Great Neck, LI, NY, 1947; Second Rebel Soldier, *Our Lan'*, Royale, NY, 1947; played many roles for the Equity Library, at Lenox Hill, NY, 1948–53; member of the acting company at Theatre-on-the-Green in Wellesley, MA, for 1953–57; Daniele, *Sky Is Red*, University Place, NY, 1949; Benvolio, *Romeo and Juliet*, Broadhurst, NY, 1951; Billy, *Billy the Kid*, Carnegie Recital Hall, NY, 1951; University of Puerto Rico, Rio Piedras; Poulengey, *Saint Joan*, Hortensio, *Taming of the Shrew*, Captain, *Androcles and the Lion*, 1954; John Proctor, *The Crucible*, Arena Stage, Washington, DC, 1954; Starbuck, *Moby Dick*, Kaufmann Auditorium, NY, 1955; Duke of Brachiano, *The White Devil*, Phoenix, NY, 1955; Fifth Son, *The Carefree Tree*, Phoenix, NY, 1955; Ladvenu, *The Lark*, Longacre, NY, 1955; Ninian Edwards, *Abe Lincoln in Illinois*, Boston Arts Festival, MA, 1956; Hamlet, *Hamlet*, Antioch Arena, Yellow Springs, OH, Toledo Ampitheatre, OH, 1956; Eddie Carbone, *A View from the Bridge*, Arena Stage, Washington, DC, 1956; Elis, *Easter*, Fourth Street, NY, 1957; Herod, *For the Time Being*, Theatre de Lys, NY, 1957; John Proctor, *The Crucible*, Martinique, NY, 1958; title role, *J.B.*, ANTA, NY, 1959; Hector, *Tiger at the Gates*, Arena Stage, Washington, DC, 1961; Kent, *King Lear*, NY Shakespeare Festival, 1962; Antony, *Antony and Cleopatra*, NY Shakespeare Festival, 1963; Segismund, *Life Is a Dream*, Astor Place, NY, 1964; Boston Arts Festival: Cauchon/Beaudricourt, *Saint Joan*, Eddie Carbone, *A View from the Bridge*, Lord Byron, *Camino Real*, 1964; Amos, *The Queen and the Rebels*, Theatre Four, NY, 1965;

MICHAEL HIGGINS

James Sr., *Long Day's Journey into Night*, Arena Stage, Washington, DC, 1965; Jason, *Medea*, Martinique, NY, 1965; Karl, *Break-Up*, Renata, NY, 1966; James Sr., *Long Day's Journey into Night*, Long Wharf, New Haven, CT, 1966; David Wylie, *What Every Woman Knows*, Goodspeed Opera House, East Haddam, CT, 1966; Macbeth, *Macbeth*, Arena Stage, Washington, DC, 1966; Inspector Messiter, *The Magistrate*, Arena Stage, Washington, DC, 1967; John Proctor, *The Crucible*, Arena Stage, Washington, DC, 1967; Cabot, *Desire Under the Elms*, Theatre Company of Boston at University of Rhode Island, 1967; Alfred Allmens, *Little Eyolf*, Artists Theatre Festival, Southhampton College, LI, NY, 1968; Tom Paine, *Tom Paine*, Goodman, Chicago, 1969; Uncle Vanya, *Uncle Vanya*, Buffalo Studio Arena, Buffalo, NY, 1970; John Adams, *John and Abigail*, Circle in the Square, NY, 1971; James, Sr., *Long Day's Journey into Night*, Hartke, Catholic University, Washington, DC, 1971; George Washington, *Sally, George and Martha*, Theatre de Lys, NY, 1971; The President, *Conflict of Interest*, Arena Stage, Washington, DC, 1972; Herman, *Wedding Band*, Ivanhoe, Chicago, IL, 1972; The Father, *Canadian Gothic*, Manhattan Theatre Club, NY, 1972; Half-cherry, *L'été*, Cherry Lane, NY, 1973; Astrov, *Uncle Vanya*, Circle in the Square, NY, 1973; Larry Slade, *The Iceman Cometh*, Circle in the Square, NY, 1973;

Tom Giordano, *Dear Mr. Giordano*, H.B. Playwright's Foundation, NY, 1974; H. R. Haldeman, *Expletive Deleted*, Theatre of Riverside Church, NY, 1974; Frank Strang, *Equus*, Plymouth, NY, 1974; Ralph Michaelson, *The Day Mr. and Mrs. Michaelson Ran Away from Home*, Actors Studio, NY, 1976; Roberto Da Fralizi, *Statues, Exhibitions* and the Bridge of Belharbour, Manhattan Theatre Club, NY, 1976; Lieutenant Lonegan, *The Dream*, Forrest, Philadelphia, 1977; Teddy, *Molly*, Dock Street, Spoleto Festival, Charleston, SC, 1977; Frank Strang, *Equus*, Playhouse in the Park, Philadelphia, 1977; Butch Carey, *Reunion*, Yale Repertory, New Haven, CT, 1977; Amundsen, *Terra Nova*, Yale Repertory, 1977; Teddy, *Molly*, Hudson Guild, NY, 1978; Gramps, *Artichoke*, Manhattan Theatre Club, NY, 1979; Mr. Justice Millhouse, *Whose Life Is It Anyway?*, Trafalgar, NY, 1979; Alden, *Slightly Delayed*, Ogunquit Playhouse, Ogunquit, ME, Falmouth Playhouse, MA, Star, Flint, MI, Westport Country Playhouse, CT, 1979; Butch Carey, *Reunion*, Circle in the Square, NY, 1979; Edward, *Chieftains*, Theatre at St. Clements, NY, 1979; Alden, *Mixed Couples*, Kennedy Center, Washington, DC, Brooks Atkinson, NY, 1980; Eldon, *A Tale Told*, Circle Repertory Company, NY, 1981; Abbot Thomas, *Catholics*, Citadel, Edmonton Alberta, Canada, Hartman Theatre, Stamford, CT, 1981; John of Gaunt, *Richard II*, Circle Repertory Company, NY, 1982; Dennis Riordan, *Outrage*, Kennedy Center, Washington, DC, 1983; Sorin, *The Sea Gull*, Little, Saratoga, NY, Circle Repertory Company, NY, American Place, NY, 1983; Arthur, *Levitation*, Circle Repertory Company, NY, 1984.

MAJOR TOURS: Burleigh, *The Milky Way*, and Bud, *Personal Appearance*, toured veteran and army hospitals with the American Theatre Wing, 1947; Jeff Douglas, *Brigadoon*, toured veterans and Army hospitals with the American Wing, 1949; toured colleges in a two-character drama program for Equity Library Theatre, 1952; Ephraim Cabot, *Desire Under the Elms*, Circle in the Square tour, 1964; Betencourt, *The Only Game In Town*, Boston, Baltimore and New Haven, 1968;

FILM DEBUT—*The Edge of Fury*, 1958. PRINCIPAL FILM APPEARANCES—*The Arrangement*, 1969; *Wanda*, 1971; *Desperate Characters*, 1971; *Deathplay*, 1971; *The Conversation*, 1974; *The Godfather Part II*, 1974; *The Stepford Wives*, 1975; *King of the Gypsies*, 1978; *The Black Stallion*, 1979; *The Seduction of Joe Tynan*, 1979; *Fort Apache—The Bronx*, 1981; *Enemy of the People*, 1982; *Midsummer Night's Sex Comedy*, 1982; *Rumble Fish*, 1983; *Nineteen Eighteen*, 1984.

TELEVISION DEBUT—*A Strange Christmas Dinner*, 1945. PRINCIPAL TELEVISION APPEARANCES—Johnny Roberts, *One Man's Family*, 1949–50; Hector, *The Iliad, Omnibus*, 1955; newspaperman, *The Secret Storm*, 1959; psychiatrist, *As the World Turns*, 1960; Ed Lawson, *Our Five Daughters*, 1962; *The Patriots, Hallmark Hall of Fame*, 1963; Herb, *The Secret Storm*, 1964; *Pulitzer Prize Theatre; Studio One; You Are There; Ethel and Albert; Camera Three; US Steel Hour; Lamp Unto My Feet; GE Theatre; Playhouse 90; The Verdict Is Yours; Armstrong Circle Theatre; Look Up and Live; Best of the Post; Alcoa Presents; The Jackie Gleason Show; Great Ghost Tales; The Eternal Light; The Defenders; The Nurses; Ben Casey; Outer Limits; Gunsmoke; The Doctors; The Virginian; Andy Griffith Show; Paul's Case; Mother Seton; Kent State; Carl Sandburg; The Hamptons; Gift of Love; Reunion.*

AWARDS: Obie Award, Butch Carey, *Reunion*, 1980; Drama Desk Award Nomination, Best Actor, *Molly*, 1978; NY Film Critics Award Nomination, *Wanda*, 1971; National Society of Film Critics Best Actor and Best Supporting Actor

Nomination, *Wanda*, 1971; Best Actor of the Year, Buffalo, *Uncle Vanya*, 1970; Obie Award, John Proctor, *The Crucible*, 1958; Purple Heart Medal, Bronze Star Medal for Heroic Achievement in Action, World War II.

SIDELIGHTS: MEMBERSHIPS—AEA; SAG; AFTRA.

ADDRESS: Agent—Milton Goldman, c/o ICM, 40 W. 57th Street, New York, NY 10019.

* * *

HILL, George Roy, director and writer

PERSONAL: Born December 20, 1922, in Minneapolis, MN; son of George Roy and Helen Frances (Owens) Hill; married Louisa Horton. EDUCATION: Attended Yale University and Trinity College (Dublin).

CAREER: DIRECTED: Films—*Period of Adjustment*, 1962; *Toys in the Attic*, 1963; *The World of Henry Orient*, 1964; *Hawaii*, 1966; *Thoroughly Modern Millie*, 1967; *Butch Cassidy and the Sundance Kid*, 1969; *Slaughterhouse-Five*, 1972; *The Sting*, 1973; *The Great Waldo Pepper*, 1975; *Slap Shot*, 1977; *A Little Romance*, 1979; *The World According to Garp*, 1982; *The Little Drummer Girl*, 1984.

Plays—*Biography at the Gate*, Dublin, Eire, 1948; *Look Homeward, Angel*, NY, 1957; *The Gang's All Here*, NY, 1959; *Greenwillow*, NY, 1960; *Period of Adjustment*, NY, 1960; *Moon on a Rainbow Shawl*, NY, 1962; *Henry, Sweet Henry*, NY, 1967.

Television—*A Night to Remember; Helen Morgan; Child of Our Time; Judgment at Nuremberg.*

ADDRESS: Office—Pan Arts Productions, 75 Rockefeller Plaza, New York, NY 10019.

* * *

HILL, Leonard F., producer, writer

PERSONAL: Born October 11, 1947; son of Herbert (a banker) and Edith (a psychologist; maiden name, Steinhardt) Hill. EDUCATION: Yale University, B.A., 1969 (Phi Beta Kappa); Stanford University, M.A., 1970 (summa cum laude).

CAREER: PRINCIPAL FILM WORK: All co-produced with Philip Mandelker—*Dream House*, 1981; *Mae West*, 1982; *Having It All*, 1983; *Parade* (forthcoming).

SIDELIGHTS: MEMBERSHIPS—Writers Guild of America, Caucus for Writers, Producers, and Directors.

ADDRESS: Office—Hill/Mandelker Films, c/o Twentieth Century Fox, 10201 W. Pico Blvd., Los Angeles, CA 90035. Agent—Bill Haber, Creative Artists Agency, 1888 Century Park E., Suite 1400, Los Angeles, CA 90067.

HILL, Mars Andrew III, playwright, educator, director

PERSONAL: Born November 18, 1927; in Pine Bluff, AR; son of Mars Andrew (a merchant) and Kattie (Temple) Hill; married Alvania Fraizer (a teacher) on May 2, 1956; children: Joffrey Haymen. EDUCATION: University of Illinois, B.S. (Architectural Engineering), 1954; State University of New York at Albany, M.A., 1974. Studied with Ernie McGlintuck at the Afro-American Studio in New York City. POLITICS: Progressive. MILITARY: U.S. Army, Sharpshooter. NON-THEATRICAL CAREER: Math Instructor, Adult Education Program, Albany Public Schools, 1966–67; Lecturer/Teacher, Black History, the Albany Academy, Albany, NY, 1976.

WRITINGS: PLAYS, PRODUCED—*The Man in the Family; Occupation; The Street Walkers; Eclipse; Huzzy; Celebration; House & Field; First in War; The Militant Preacher; Slaveship; The Visitors; Improvisations; Monkey Motions; Malice in Wonderland; Cavorting with the Whartons; Sugar Mouth Sam, Sezwe Bansi;* PLAYS, UNPRODUCED—*Two Ten; The Cage; The Trader; A Very Special Occasion; You Ain't Got No Place to Put Yo Show; Peck; To Have and to Have Not; Hide and Go Seek; Sodalbany & Machinemora; Ghostwriters Legacy; On the Winsome.*

THEATRE-RELATED CAREER: Teacher, Black Theatre, State University of New York at Albany, 1970; Coordinator, the Abor Hill Community Center, 1970–72; Coordinator, the Community Black Arts Festival, 1970–73; founder, The Black Experience Ensemble, 1968–present; Director, Theatre Program, Kenwood Academy, 1969. Consultant, Congress of African People, 1970.

AWARDS: New York State Creative Artists Public Service Award, 1980; Survival Award, New Heritage Theatre, 1980; Capitol District Business and Professional Association Certificate of Appreciation, 1973; Community Achievement Award, Neighborhood Playhouse, 1972.

SIDELIGHTS: MEMBERSHIPS—Writers Guild; President CORE; Ex Director The Black Experience Ensemble.

In addition to his writings and teaching, Mr. Hill has performed as an actor in over 30 roles with the various groups he has organized and worked with, including The Contemporary Player in Seattle, WA.

ADDRESS: Home—Five Homestead Avenue, Albany, NY 12203.

* * *

HILLER, Arthur, director

PERSONAL: Born November 22, 1923, in Edmonton, AB; son of Harry and Rose (Garfin) Hiller; married Gwen Pechet, February 14, 1948; children: Henryk, Erica. EDUCATION: University of Toronto, B.A., 1947, M.A., 1950; University of British Columbia, 1948 (one year of law studies). MILITARY: Royal Canadian Air Force (Flying Officer), 1942–45.

CAREER: DIRECTED: FILMS—*The Americanization of Emily,*

1965; *Poppi,* 1968; *The Out-of-Towners,* 1969; *Love Story,* 1970; *Hospital,* 1971; *Man of La Mancha,* 1972; *Man in the Glass Booth,* 1974; *Silver Streak,* 1976; *The In-Laws,* 1979; *Making Love,* 1981; *Author, Author,* 1982. TELEVISION SHOWS—Canadian Broadcasting Corp. *Dramatic Series,* 1953–55; *Naked City; Playhouse 90; Climax; Gunsmoke; Alfred Hitchcock Presents; Route 66.*

FIRST STAGE WORK—Director, *Blithe Spirit,* Niagara-on-the-Lake Summer Theatre, 1953.

AWARDS: Yugoslav Film Festival Award, 1974: *Hospital;* Golden Globe, 1970: *Love Story;* New York Foreign Critics Award, 1970: *Love Story;* Academy Award Nomination, 1970: *Love Story;* Emmy Nomination, 1962: *Naked City;* Institute for Education, Radio and Television Award, 1952–53; Canadian Radio Award, 1951–52.

SIDELIGHTS: MEMBERSHIPS—Academy of Motion Picture Arts and Sciences (Board of Governors), Directors Guild of America (National Board), Anti-Defamation League (Regional Board), Commission on Soviet Jewery (Board).

''I prefer to direct works that are 'vastly entertaining and have something to say.' Though admittedly sometimes I've missed on both counts—and often on one or the other. It worked in my favorite films, namely *The Americanization of Emily* and *Hospital,* both of which, by the way, were written by Paddy Chayefsky (the only genius I've ever worked with). That does bring me to one of my strong feelings. I drop to my knees in front of the good writers. I don't mean to belittle what the rest of us contribute creatively, but we start from a 'floor plan' (the play or screenplay), while the writer starts with a blank page. Mind you, once we have the written word, eighty percent of my work is to find the right actors, because when you do they sure make you, the director, look good.

''My work has taken me to Europe, to the Mideast, to Canada, and Australia, and as the family loves to travel, to see the wonders of nature and of man, and to mix with peoples of different cultures and tastes, we couldn't be happier with this aspect of 'theatre.' When work didn't take me, the financial rewards permitted further visits to these areas and to the Soviet Union, China, Japan, the Far East, and to parts of South America.

''I'm involved in community activities and have directed play readings for a number of fund raisers. I particularly am involved with areas of freedom and individual rights, domestic and international, and am happiest when my work and my life are aimed to forwarding an affirmation of the human spirit and freedom of thought and travel for each person, so that we can look to the future with a maximum of sanity and hope.''

ADDRESS: Agent—c/o Phil Gersh Agency, 222 N. Canon Drive, Beverly Hills, CA 90212.

* * *

HINKLE, Vernon, playwright, director

PERSONAL: Born June 23, 1935 in Amsterdam, NY; son of Vernon M. (a carpenter) and Lovina M. (Lawrence) Hinkle;

married Sally Applegate on June 3, 1956 (divorced 1975); married Mary Sanders Shartle; children: Lawrence. EDUCATION: Ithaca College, B.A. 1956; Yale University, School of Drama, M.F.A. 1961; studied with Herbert Berghoff at the H.B. Studios in New York. NON-THEATRICAL CAREER: Writer, J.C. Penney Company, 1971–77.

CAREER: FIRST STAGE WORK—Playwright, *Before Gabriel Blew*, Ithaca College, 1954. NEW YORK DEBUT—Playwright, *Characters in a Play,* LaMama E.T.C., six performances, 1965. PRINCIPAL STAGE WORK—Directed: Polka Dot Playhouse, Bridgeport, CT—*A Streetcar Named Desire, The Male Animal, Middle of the Night, Born Yesterday,* 1978 season. PRINCIPAL STAGE APPEARANCES—Actor, *After Maigret,* Quaigh Theatre, NY, 1983.

WRITINGS: PLAYS, PRODUCED—*Before Gabriel Blew,* Ithaca College, 1954; *Musicians of Bremen,* Bradford College, 1963; *Characters in a Play,* LaMama E.T.C., NY, 1965; *The Concept (The Showcase),* O'Neill Theatre Center, 1969; *Edna,* Kansas Wesleyan University, 1973; *If I'm Dead, Start without Me,* Polka Dot Playhouse, Bridgeport, CT, 1982. BOOKS—(novels) *Music to Murder By,* 1978; under pseudonym, H. V. Elkin: *Eagle Man,* 1978; *Playground,* 1979; *Yellowstone,* 1980; *Mustang,* 1980; *Tiger's Chance,* 1980. THEATRE-RELATED CAREER: Drama Instructor, Bradford College, Bradford, MA, 1961–66; Chairman Drama Department, Bradford College, Bradford, MA, 1966–71.

AWARDS: O'Neill Theatre Center Playwrights Conference, 1969; Bradford College Faculty Grant, 1966; Ithaca College Playwriting Award, 1953.

SIDELIGHTS: MEMBERSHIPS—Dramatists Guild.

"Plays became private fantasies on the farm where I was brought up, isolated from friends my own age. Sometimes in later years, it became difficult to collaborate on a fantasy, as in theatre work. After some unhappy experiences trying, I started my first novel and enjoyed the privacy and control. Finally restless, I emerged from the novelist's cocoon with a new readiness to collaborate in theatre, even with some entrepreneuring spirit—a necessary quality for most playwrights who want to work in, not out of, the theatre. If my work is any one thing besides eclectic, it is mystery, in the sense that each piece (novel or play) is a puzzle or a quest for unknown answers. In this respect, I regard most fiction as mystery."

ADDRESS: Home—470 W. 24th Street, New York, NY 10011. Office—437 W. 22nd Street, New York, NY 10011.

* * *

HIRSCH, Judd, actor

PERSONAL: Born March 15, 1935, in New York City; son of Joseph Sidney (an electrician) and Sally (Kitzis) Hirsch; children: Alexander. EDUCATION: City College of New York, B.S. (Physics), 1960, studied Architecture at Cooper Union, NY, 1957; studied for the theatre at the American Academy of Dramatic Arts, the HB Studio, and the Gene Frankel Studio; with Bill Hickey and Viveca Lindfors. RELIGION: Jewish. MILITARY: U.S. Army, 1958. NON-THEATRI-

JUDD HIRSCH

CAL CAREER: Worked as a busboy, hospital bill collector, summer camp driver, library page, and law office clerk.

CAREER: STAGE DEBUT—Villain, *Crisis in the Old Sawmill,* Back Room, Estes Park, CO, 1962. NEW YORK DEBUT—Lead, *On the Necessity of Being Polygamous,* Gramercy Arts, 1964. PRINCIPAL STAGE APPEARANCES—*Diary of a Madman, The Fantasticks, The Threepenny Opera, My Fair Lady,* Woodstock, NY, 1964; telephone man, *Barefoot in the Park,* Biltmore, NY, 1966–67; Harold Wonder, *Scuba Duba,* New, NY, 1967–69; Theatre of the Living Arts, Philadelphia, 1969–70; Senator, *King of the United States,* Westbeth, NY, 1972; Senator, *Mystery Play,* Cherry Lane, NY, 1972; Bill, *Hot L Baltimore,* Circle Rep., NY, 1972, Circle in the Square, NY, 1973; Wiseman, *Knock, Knock,* Circle Rep., NY, 1975, Biltmore, NY, 1976; George Schneider, *Chapter Two,* Ahmanson, Los Angeles, 1977, Imperial, NY, 1978; Matt Friedman, *Talley's Folly,* Circle Rep., NY, 1979, Mark Taper Forum, Los Angeles, 1979, Brooks Atkinson, NY, 1980; Trigorin, *The Sea Gull,* Circle Rep., 1983.

MAJOR TOURS—Peter, *Peterpat,* Houston, Fort Worth, TX dinner theater, 1970; Wilson, *Harvey,* Chicago, 1971.

DIRECTED—Plays: *Not Enough Rope,* Circle Rep., NY, 1974; *Twist, Name of a Soup/Baby Elephant,* Actors Studio Directors Unit.

FILM DEBUT—*King of the Gypsies,* 1978. FILM APPEARANCES—Dr. Berger, *Ordinary People,* 1980; Det. Al Minetti, *With-*

out a Trace, 1983; Arthur Korman, *The Goodbye People*, 1984; Roger Reubel, *Teachers*, 1984.

TELEVISION DEBUT—Murray Stone, *The Law*, 1974. PRINCIPAL TELEVISION APPEARANCES—*The Keegans*, 1975; *Two Brothers*, 1975; *The Legend of Valentino*, 1975; *Medical Story*, 1975; Dominic DelVecchio, *DelVecchio*, 1976; *Fear on Trial; Rhoda*, 1977; Alex Rieger, *Taxi*, 1978–83; *Sooner or Later;* Dracula, *The Halloween That Almost Wasn't;* Pontius Pilate, *The Resurrection; Marriage Is Alive and Well in the U.S.A.;* Dr. Petrofsky, *First Steps*, 1984.

WRITINGS: ARTICLES—"Andy Kaufman, 1949–84," *Rolling Stone*, July 5, 1984.

AWARDS: Emmy Awards, 1983, 1981: *Taxi;* Obie, 1979: *Talley's Folly;* Drama Desk, 1976: *Knock, Knock;* Academy Award Nomination, Best Supporting Actor, 1980: *Ordinary People;* Antoinette Perry Nomination, Best Actor, 1979: *Talley's Folly;* five Emmy Nominations: *Taxi.*

SIDELIGHTS: MEMBERSHIPS—Circle Rep. since 1972.

ADDRESS: Agent—Sandy Bresler, 15760 Ventura Blvd., Encino, CA 91436.

* * *

HIRSCHFELD, Albert, theatre caricaturist

PERSONAL: Born June 21, 1903, in St. Louis, MO; son of Isaac and Rebecca (Rothberg) Hirschfeld; married Dolly Haas (an actress) on September 9, 1943; children: Nina. EDUCATION: Art Students League, 1920; National Academy, 1922; Julians, Paris, 1924; London County Council, 1927.

CAREER: FIRST STAGE WORK—co-author with S. J. Perelman and Ogden Nash, a musical, *Sweet Bye and Bye*, closed in Philadelphia at Forrest Theatre, 1947.

WRITINGS: *Manhattan Oases*, 1932; *Harlem*, 1941; *Show Business is No Business*, 1951; *The American Theatre*, 1961; *The World of Hirschfeld*, 1971; *The Entertainers*, 1977; *Hirschfeld by Hirschfeld*, 1979; *Hirschfeld's World*, 1981.

AWARDS: Doctor of Fine Arts, University of Hartford, 1982.

SIDELIGHTS: MEMBERSHIPS—Players Club. Biographies published in St. Louis *Dispatch*, October 29, 1961, and June 15, 1983, St Louis *Globe Democrat* on April 10, 1977, and in *New York Times*, September 3, 1983.

ADDRESS: Home—122 E. 95th Street, New York, NY 10028. Agent—Robert Lantz, 880 Seventh Ave. New York, NY 10106.

* * *

HITCHCOCK, Alfred (Joseph), film writer, director

PERSONAL: Born August 13, 1899, in England; died April 29, 1980; son of William and Emma Hitchcock; married

Alma Reville (a writer); children: one daughter. EDUCATION: Attended St. Ignatius College, London, England.

CAREER: FIRST FILM WORK—Junior technician, Famous Players Lasky British Studios, 1920; scenario writer, production manager, art director, Gainsborough Studios, Islington, England, 1923.

PRINCIPAL FILM WORK—Director: *The Pleasure Garden*, 1925; *The Mountain Eagle*, 1926; *The Lodger*, 1926; *Downhill*, 1927; *Easy Virtue*, 1927; *The Ring*, 1927; *The Farmer's Wife*, 1928; *Champagne*, 1928; *The Manxman*, 1928; *Blackmail*, 1929; *Elstree Calling* (co-director), 1930; *Juno and the Paycock*, 1930; *Murder*, 1930; *The Skin Game*, 1931; *Rich and Strange*, 1932; *Number Seventeen*, 1932; *Waltzes from Vienna*, 1933; *The Man Who Knew Too Much*, 1934; *The Thirty-Nine Steps*, 1935; *The Secret Agent*, 1936; *Sabotage*, 1936; *Young and Innocent*, 1937; *The Lady Vanishes*, 1937; *Jamaica Inn*, 1939; *Rebecca*, 1940; *Foreign Correspondent*, 1940; *Mr. and Mrs. Smith*, 1941; *Suspicion*, 1941; *Saboteur*, 1942; *Shadow of a Doubt*, 1943; *Lifeboat*, 1943; *Bon Voyage*, 1944; *Adventure Malgache*, 1944; *Spellbound*, 1945; *Notorious*, 1946; *The Paradine Case*, 1947; *Rope*, 1948; *Under Capricorn*, 1949; *Stage Fright*, 1950; *Strangers on a Train*, 1951; *I Confess*, 1952; *Dial M for Murder*, 1954; *Rear Window*, 1954; *To Catch a Thief*, 1955; *The Man Who Knew Too Much*, 1955; *The Trouble with Harry*, 1956; *The Wrong Man*, 1957; *Vertigo*, 1958; *North by Northwest*, 1959; *Psycho*, 1960; *The Birds*, 1963; *Marnie*, 1964; *Torn Curtain*, 1966; *Topaz*, 1969; *Frenzy*, 1971; *Family Plot*, 1976.

PRINCIPAL TELEVISION WORK—presented series: *Alfred Hitchcock Presents*, 1955–61; *Alfred Hitchcock Hour*, 1961–65.

WRITINGS: BOOKS—*My Favorite in Suspense*, 1959; *Alfred Hitchcock's Ghostly Gallery*, 1962; *Stories My Mother Never Told Me*, 1963.

AWARDS: American Film Institute Life Achievement Award; Irving Thalberg Memorial Award, Academy of Motion Picture Arts and Sciences, 1968; created Knight of the British Empire; decorated chevalier French National Order Legion of Honor; Honorary Doctor of Fine Arts, University of California, Santa Cruz, 1968; Doctor of Humane Letters, Columbia University, 1972.

* * *

HOFFMAN, Dustin (Lee), actor and director

PERSONAL: Born August 8, 1937, in Los Angeles, CA; son of Harry (a set decorator) and Lillia (a jazz pianist; maiden name, Gold) Hoffman; married Anne Byrne, (a ballerina), May 4, 1969 (divorced 1980); married Lisa Gottsegen (a lawyer), September 1980; children: (first mariage) Karina, Jenna; (second marriage) Jake, Rebecca. EDUCATION: Santa Monica City College; studied for the theatre at the Pasadena Playhouse and with Barney Brown, Lonny Chapman, and Lee Strasberg.

CAREER: DEBUT—Tiny Tim, *A Christmas Carol*, John Burroghs Junior High School, Los Angeles, California. NEW

YORK DEBUT—Young Man, *Gertrude Stein's Yes Is for a Very Young Man*, Sarah Lawrence College, 1960. PRINCIPAL STAGE APPEARANCES—Ridzinski, *A Cook for Mr. General*, Playhouse, NY, 1961; Clov, *Endgame*, Dunlavin, *The Quare Fellow*, C Couch (Babboon), *In the Jungle of Cities*, Nicholas Trilestski, *A Country Scandal*, Ben, *The Dumbwaiter*, Bert Hudd, *The Room*, Pozzo, *Waiting for Godot*, Zapo, *Picnic on the Battlefield*, Hugo, *Dirty Hands*, Peter, *The Cocktail Party*, all for Theatre Company of Boston, 1964; Frankie, *Three Men on a Horse*, McCarter, Princeton, NJ, 1964; Immanuel, *Harry, Noon and Night*, American Place, NY, 1965; Zoditch, *The Journey of the Fifth Horse*, American Place, NY, 1966; title role, *The Old Jew*, Max, *Reverberations*, Jax, *Fragments*, all in a program entitled *Fragments*, Berkshire Theatre Festival, Stockbridge, MA, 1966; Valentine Bross, *Eh?*, Circle in the Square, NY, 1966; title role, *Jimmy Shine*, Brooks Atkinson, NY, 1968; Willy Loman, *Death of a Salesman*, Broadhurst, NY, 1984.

DIRECTED—Plays: Assistant to Ulu Grosbard, *A View from the Bridge*, NY, 1964; *All Over Town*, Booth, NY, 1974; *Jimmy Shine*,

FILM DEBUT—*The Tiger Makes Out*, 1967. PRINCIPAL FILMS—*The Graduate*, 1967; *Midnight Cowboy*, 1969; *John and Mary*, 1969; *Little Big Man*, 1971; *Who Is Harry Kellerman and Why Is He Saying Those Terrible Things About Me?*, 1971; *Straw Dogs*, 1972; *Alfredo, Alfredo*, 1972; *Papillon*, 1973; *Lenny*, 1974; *All the President's Men*, 1975; *Marathon Man*, 1976; *Straight Time*, 1976; *Agatha*, 1978; *Kramer vs. Kramer*, 1979; *Tootsie*, 1983.

TELEVISION DEBUT—*Naked City*, 1961. TELEVISION APPEARANCES—*The Star Wagon*, 1975; *The Trap of Solid Gold; The Journey of the Fifth Horse*.

RECORDINGS: Young Ben, *Death of a Salesman*, Caedmon, 1968.

AWARDS: Academy Award, Best Actor, 1979: *Kramer vs. Kramer;* Academy Award Nominations, Best Actor, 1982: *Tootsie*, 1974: *Lenny*, 1969: *Midnight Cowboy*, 1967: *The Graduate;* Theatre World, Drama Desk, Vernon Rice, 1966: *Eh?;* Obie, 1965: *Harry, Noon, and Night*.

SIDELIGHTS: RECREATION: Tennis, jazz piano playing, photography.

ADDRESS: Office—Punch Productions Inc., 711 Fifth Avenue, New York, NY 10022.

* * *

HOFFMAN, William M., playwright, director, producer, editor

PERSONAL: Born April 12, 1939, in New York City; son of Morton (a caterer) and Johanna (a jeweler; maiden name Papiermeister) Hoffman. EDUCATION: City College of New York, B.A. (Latin, cum laude) 1960.

THEATRE-RELATED CAREER: Editor, High and Wang, 1961–68; literary advisor, *Scripts*, magazine, 1971–74; artist-in-residence, Lincoln Center Student Program, 1971–72; visit-

WILLIAM M. HOFFMAN

Photograph by Jerry Vezzuso

ing lecturer, Theatre Arts, University of Massachusetts, 1973; playwriting consultant, CAPS Program, New York State Council on the Arts, 1975–77; playwriting consultant, Massachusetts Arts and Humanities Foundation, 1978; playwright-in-residence, American Conservatory Theatre, San Francisco, CA, 1978; playwright-in-residence, LaMama Theatre, New York, 1978–79; star adjunct professor in Playwriting, Hofstra University, 1980–83.

WRITINGS: PLAYS PUBLISHED—*Cornbury*, with Anthony Holland, 1979; *The Last Days of Stephen Foster*, 1978; *A Quick Nut Bread to Make Your Mouth Water (Spontaneous Combustion)*, 1973; *Saturday Night at the Movies*, 1973; *From Fool to Hanged Man*, 1970; *Thank You Miss Victoria*, 1970. PLAYS PRODUCED—*A Book of Etiquette*, s.n.a.f.u. Theatre, New York, 1983, LaMama Theatre, New York, 1978–79; *X's*, LaMama Theatre, New York, 1981; *Gulliver's Travels*, LaMama Theatre, New York, 1978; *Shoe Palace Murray*, American Conservatory Theatre, San Francisco, CA, 1978; *Cornbury*, staged reading, Public Theatre, New York, 1976; *Gilles de Rais*, Gate Theatre, New York, 1975; *A Nut Bread to Make Your Mouth Water*, Manhattan Theatre Club, 1973; *From Fool to Hanged Man*, Playwrights Horizons, New York, 1972; *The Children's Crusade*, Playwrights Horizons, New York, 1972. TELEVISION WORKS—*Whistler, 5 Portraits, Camera 3*, CBS, 1978; *The Last Days of Stephen Foster, Camera 3*, CBS, 1977; *Pink Panther's Magic Music Hall* (a pilot), 1977; scripts for WNET, Channel 13, 1976–77; *Notes from the New World: Louis Moreau Gottschalk, Camera 3*, CBS, 1976. POETRY AND LYRICS—*The Cloisters*, song cycle, 1968, included in anthology, *31 New American Poets* and *Fine Frenzy*, 1972; *Wedding Song*, 1979.

AWARDS: Metropolitan Opera, commission for libretto for 100th anniversary opera, *A Figaro for Antonia*, 1983; Creative Writing Fellowship, National Endowment for the Arts, 1976–77; librettists grant, National Endowment for the Arts, 1975–76; Guggenheim Fellowship, 1974–75; MacDowell Fellowship, 1971;

SIDELIGHTS: MEMBERSHIPS—Phi Betta Kappa, ASCAP, PEN, Circle Repertory Theatre's Playwrights Workshop, Dramatists Guild, New York Theatre Strategy.

ADDRESS: Agent—c/o Luis SanJuro, International Creative Management, 40 W. 57th Street, New York, 10019.

* * *

HOLBROOK, Hal, actor

PERSONAL: Born February 17, 1925, in Cleveland, OH; son of Harold Rowe, Sr. and Aileen (a dancer in vaudeville; maiden name Davenport) Holbrook; married Ruby Elaine Johnston (divorced); Carol Rossen, (divorced); Dixie Carter; children: three. EDUCATION: Attended Denison University and Culver Military Academy; studied with Uta Hagen at the HB Studios in New York City. MILITARY: U.S. Army Engineers, WWII.

CAREER: DEBUT—Richard, *The Man Who Came to Dinner,* Cain Park, Cleveland, OH, 1942. NEW YORK DEBUT—One-man show, *Mark Twain Tonight!,* 41st Street, 1959. PRINCIPAL STAGE APPEARANCES—*The Vagabond King, Time to Come,* Cain Park, Cleveland, 1942; four seasons of stock at Granville, OH, Denison University: *The Male Animal, Three Men On a Horse, Our Town, George Washington Slept Here, The Guardsman, The Constant Wife,* 1947–50; first solo appearances as *Mark Twain,* Lock Haven State Teachers College, PA, 1954; one-man show, *Mark Twain Tonight!,* Purple Onion, Upstairs at the Duplex, NY, 1955; *The Doctor in Spite of Himself,* Westport Country Playhouse, CT, 1958; Young Man, *Do You Know the Milky Way?,* Billy Rose, NY, 1961; with the American Shakespeare Festival, Stratford, CT: John of Gaunt, *Richard II,* Hotspur, *Henry IV, Pt. 1,* 1962; title-role, *Abe Lincoln in Illinois,* Phoenix, NY, 1963; with Lincoln Center Repertory Company, ANTA Washington Square, NY: Harley Barnes/Quentin, *After the Fall,* Marco Polo, *Marco Millions,* 1964, A Major, *Incident at Vichy,* 1964, Prologue/M. Loyal, *Tartuffe,* 1965; Jim (the gentleman caller), *The Glass Menagerie,* Brooks Atkinson, NY, 1965; *Mark Twain Tonight!,* Longacre, NY, 1966; Adam/Captain Sanjur/Flip/Prince Charming, *The Apple Tree,* Shubert, NY, 1967; Gene Garrison, *I Never Sang for My Father,* Longacre, NY, 1968; Cervantes/Don Quixote, *Man of La Mancha,* Martin Beck, NY, 1968; Mr. Winters, *Does a Tiger Wear a Necktie?,* Belasco, NY, 1969; Winnebago, *Lake of the Woods,* American Place, NY, 1971; *Mark Twain Tonight!,* Ford's Theatre, Washington, DC, 1972; Jake Bowsky, *Buried Inside Extra,* Public, NY, and London, 1983.

MAJOR TOURS—with Ruby Johnston in scenes from the classics, 1948–53; one-man show, *Mark Twain Tonight!,* U.S., Europe, Saudi Arabia, 1959–61, U.S. 1963, 1975–77; Andrew Mackerel, *The Mackerel Plaza,* 1963; King Arthur, *Camelot,* 1962.

FILM DEBUT—Gus Leroy, *The Group,* 1966. PRINCIPAL FILM

HAL HOLBROOK

APPEARANCES—*Wild in the Streets,* 1968; *The People Next Door,* 1970; *The Great White Hope,* 1970; *They Only Kill Their Masters,* 1972; *Magnum Force,* 1973; *The Girl from Petrovka,* 1974; *Midway,* 1975; *All the Presidents Men,* 1976; *Rituals; Julia,* 1977; *Capricorn One,* 1978; *Natural Enemies,* 1979; *The Fog,* 1980; *The Kidnapping of the President; Star Chamber,* 1983; *Creep Show,* 1983; *Final Clue.*

TELEVISION DEBUT—*Hollywood Screen Test,* 1953. PRINCIPAL TELEVISION APPEARANCES—*The Brighter Day,* 1954–59; movies/plays for television—*The Glass Menagerie; Mark Twain Tonight!; The Whole World Is Watching; A Clear and Present Danger; The Senator,* 1970–71; *Travis Logan; Suddenly Single; Goodbye, Raggedy Ann; That Certain Summer,* 1972; *Pueblo,* 1974; *Sandburg's Lincoln,* 1975–76; *Our Town,* 1977; *The Awakening Land,* 1977; *Murder by Natural Causes,* 1978; *Legend of John Hammer,* 1979; *When Hell Was in Session,* 1979; *Off the Minnesota Strip,* 1980; *Omnibus,* 1980; *The Killing of Randy Webster,* 1981; *Celebrity,* 1984; *George Washington,* 1984; host and narrator, *Portrait of America,* 1983–88.

AWARDS: Honorary Doctor of Arts from Kenyon College and Denison University, 1979; Honorary Doctor of Humane Letters, Ohio State University, 1979; Emmy Award Nominations, 1977: Stage Manager, *Our Town, The Awakening Land;* Emmy Award, 1976: *Sandburg's Lincoln;* Emmy

Award, Best Actor, 1974: Commander Boucher, *Pueblo;*
Emmy Award Nomination, 1972: *That Certain Summer.*

SIDELIGHTS: MEMBERSHIPS—AEA, AFTRA, SAG, The
Players Club.

''In 1959, after five years of researching his character and
material and honing it in front of audiences in small towns all
over America, Mr. Holbrook opened *Mark Twain Tonight!*
in a tiny theatre Off–Broadway in New York. . . . He was
able to quit his soap-opera job and toured the country twice
appearing in major cities and played for President Eisenhower and at the Edinburgh Festival. The State Department
sent him on a tour of Europe. He was a star who had never
appeared in a Broadway play, a major television show, or a
movie. At this point he tried to quit his bonanza. He was 36
years old and the only offers he was getting were for roles
over 70. But he has never been able to quit Mark Twain and
probably never will. He has toured the show in some part of
every year since 1954, thus making 1984 the 30th anniversary
for this one-man show. . . . When he is not acting, Mr.
Holbrook can usually be found sailing his 40-foot sailboat,
'Yankee Tar.' ''

ADDRESS: Agent—Don Wolff, Artists Agency, 10,000 Santa
Monica Blvd., Los Angeles, CA 90067.

* * *

HOLM, Celeste, actress

PERSONAL: Born April 29, 1919, in New York City;
daughter of Theodor (director of Lloyd's Agency) and Jean
(a painter and writer; maiden name, Parke) Holm; married
Ralph Nelson, 1938 (divorced); Francis Davis, 1940; A.
Schuyler Dunning, 1946 (divorced 1952); Robert Wesley
Addy (an actor) May, 22, 1966. children: (first marriage)
Theodore Nelson; (third marriage) Daniel Dunning. EDUCA-
TION: University School for Girls, Chicago, IL; Lycee Victor
Duryui, Paris, France; studied ballet for ten years with
Adolph Bolm, Chicago, acting (1938–40) with Benno
Schneider, NY; also studied with Francis W. Parker in
Chicago. RELIGION: Christian.

CAREER: DEBUT—Mary L., *The Time of Your Life,* Booth,
NY, 1939. PRINCIPAL STAGE APPEARANCES—Emma, *Papa
Is All,* Guild, NY, 1941; Calla, *The Damask Cheek,* Play-
house, NY, 1942; Ado Annie, *Oklahoma!,* St. James, NY,
1943; Evelina, *Bloomer Girl,* Shubert, NY, 1944; Kate, *She
Stoops to Conquer,* City Center, NY, 1949; Irene Eliot,
Affairs of State, Music Box, NY, 1950; Anna, *The King and
I,* St. James, NY, 1952; Helen, *Third Best Sport,* Ambas-
sador, NY, 1958; Camilla, *Invitation to a March,* Music
Box, NY, 1960; Natalya, *A Month in the Country,* NY,
1963; title role, *Candida,* New York and Great Lakes Shake-
speare Festival, 1970; Lady Rumpers, *Habeas Corpus,*
Martin Beck, NY, 1975; Headmistress, *The Utter Glory of
Morrisey Hall,* Mark Hellinger, NY, 1979; Judith, *Hay
Fever,* Williamstown Theatre Festial, MA, 1980 and again at
the Ahmanson, Los Angeles, 1983; Liza Elliot, *Lady in the
Dark,* London, 1983.

MAJOR TOURS—Title role, *Mame,* Winter Garden, NY, then
National Tour, 1967–69; Lady Cicely, *Captain Brassbound's*

CELESTE HOLM

Conversion, California State Tour, 1968; Judith, *Hay Fever,*
tour, 1980; also stock tours of *Butterflies Are Free, A Very
Private Affair, Not Even in Spring, The Irregular Verb to
Love, Finishing Touches, Light Up the Sky,* and her one-
woman show, *Janet Flanner's ''Paris Was Yesterday''.*
With her husband, Wesley Addy, she has appeared in a
theatre-in-concert program, *Interplay,* on tour in this country
an in eight counties as part of the United States State
Department Cultural Presentations Program.

FILM DEBUT—*Three Little Girls in Blue,* 1946. PRINCIPAL
FILMS—*Gentlemen's Agreement,* 1947; *Chicken Every Sunday,* 1948; *The Snake Pit,* 1948; *Road House,* 1948; *Come to
the Stable,* 1949; *Everybody Does It,* 1949; *All About Eve,*
1950; *Champagne for Caesar,* 1951; *The Tender Trap,* 1954;
A Letter To Three Wives (voice only), 1955; *High Society,*
1956; *Bachelor Flat,* 1961; *Doctor, You've Got to Be
Kidding,* 1967; *Tom Sawyer,* 1973.

TELEVISION APPEARANCES—*Jack and the Beanstalk; A Clearing in the Woods; The Yeoman of the Guard; The FBI;
Disney's Wonderful World of Color; Medical Center; Columbo; Captains and Kings; The Streets of San Francisco;
Fantasy Island; Love Boat II;* NBC special, *The Underground Man;* Fairy Godmother, *Rodgers and Hammerstein's
''Cinderella'';* Mrs. Warren Harding, *Backstairs at the
White House; Trapper John, MD,* 1982; *The Shady Hill Kidnapping,* 1983; Stephanie's Grandmother, *Archie Bunker's*

Place, 1982–83; reading of Phyllis McGinley's poetry on PBS.

RECORDINGS—Original cast albums of *Oklahoma!*, *Bloomer Girl*, and *The Utter Glory of Morrisey Hall*.

AWARDS: Academy Award, Best Supporting Actress, 1947: *Gentlemen's Agreement;* Academy Award Nominations, Best Supporting Actress, 1949: *Come to the Stable*, 1950: *All About Eve;* Emmy Award Nomination, *Backstairs at the White House;* Sarah Siddons Award, 1968: *Mame;* French equivalent of the Academy Award from the Alliance Francaise, *Come to the Stable;* Northwood Institute's Distinguished Woman Award, 1977; Anti-Defamation League, Woman of the Year, 1972; Performer of the Year Award by Variety Clubs of America, 1973; Knighthood (Dame Celeste Holm) by King Olav of Norway, 1979; Zonta International Award, Australia, 1984; many others including several honorary doctorates and many citations for outstanding contributions to the Mental Health movement.

SIDELIGHTS: MEMBERSHIPS—Actor's Studio; Save the Theatres (board member since 1982); Creative Arts Rehabilitation Center (president since 1977); New York City Arts and Business Council (vice-president); Mental Health Association (permanent member, governing board); National Arts Council (appointed by President Reagan in 1982); New Jersey Motion Picture and Television Development Commission (appointed chairman by Governor Kean, 1983). RECREATION—Restoring an early eighteenth century farm house with her husband.

As an active member of the Save the Theatres committee, Miss Holm was among those people arrested for vigorously protesting the demolition of several New York Theatres. As an ardent supporter of UNICEF she has raised $14,000 for them by charging 50¢ apiece for autographs.

ADDRESS—Agent—Lionel Larner, 850 Seventh Avenue, New York, NY; Meyer Mishkin, 9255 Sunset Blvd., Los Angeles, CA 90069.

* * *

HOLT, Fritz (ne George William, III), producer, director, and manager

PERSONAL: Born October 9, 1940, in San Francisco, CA; son of George William (a real estate broker) and Leah Beryl (an accountant; maiden name Lester) Holt, Jr. EDUCATION: University of Oregon, BS in Business Administration (minor in drama), 1962. POLITICS: Republican. RELIGION: Episcopalian. MILITARY: U.S. Air Force, 1962–65 (first lieutenant).

CAREER: DEBUT—Producer/Director, *Mister Roberts, John Loves Mary,* six others, U.S.O. Korea tour of Far East, 1962–63. NEW YORK DEBUT—Associate Producer/Production Stage Manager, *By Jupiter*, Theatre Four, 1967, 160 performances. LONDON DEBUT—Producer, *Gypsy*, Piccadilly, 1973, 350 performances. PRINCIPAL STAGE WORK—Producer, *Platinum*, Mark Hellinger, New York; *Summer Brave*, New York; *Saturday Sunday Monday*, Martin Beck, New York; *The Royal Family*, Helen Hayes, New York, 1975; *The Madwoman of Central Park West*, New York; *Wally's Café,*

FRITZ HOLT

New York; *Your Own Thing*, National Tour; *Gypsy*, National Tour and subsequent Broadway; *La Cage aux Folles*, Palace, New York, 1983.

DIRECTED—regional or touring companies of *Cabaret, Company, Gypsy, The Gingerbread Lady, George Washington Slept Here*, Bette Midler's 1976 concert tour; *Styne After Styne; Perfectly Frank*, Helen Hayes, New York; *Wally's Café*, New York; the gala opening of ARTPARK in Niagara Falls and tributes to Jule Styne at the Palace, New York and Ira Geshwin, Lincoln Center, New York. STAGE MANAGED/PRODUCTION SUPERVISED—*Company*, New York; *Follies*, New York; *Cabaret*, National tour; Bette Midler's *Clams on the Half Shell Revue; Indians; The Goodbye People; Teibele and Her Demon;* numerous industrial shows and tours.

TELEVISION WORK—HBO Cable TV Bette Midler Concert; Texaco Star Theatre, *Opening Night*, 1982; director, *Perfectly Frank*, 1980.

AWARDS: Drama Desk Award, Best Revival, *The Royal Family*, 1975.

SIDELIGHTS: MEMBERSHIPS—League of New York Theatres and Producers (Board of Governors), Society of Stage Directors and Choreographers, AEA, Writers Guild of America.

ADDRESS: Home—8600 Appian Way, Los Angeles, CA 90046; Office—250 W. 52nd Street, New York, NY 10019. Agent—Loren Plotkin, 485 Madison Ave., New York, NY 10022.

HOPKINS, Anthony, actor

PERSONAL: "H" in Anthony is silent; born December 31, 1937, in Port Talbot, Wales; son of Richard Arthur (a baker) and Muriel Annie (Yeats) Hopkins; married Petronella Barker, 1967 (divorced 1972); married Jennifer Lynton, January 13, 1973; children: Abigail. EDUCATION: Cowbridge Grammar School, Wales, 1951–55; studied for the theatre at RADA, 1961–62. MILITARY: Royal Artillery, 1958–60.

CAREER: DEBUT—Mickser, *The Quare Fellow*, Library Theatre, Manchester, England, 1960. LONDON DEBUT—Metellus Cimber, *Julius Caesar*, Royal Court, 1964. NEW YORK DEBUT—Martin Dysart, *Equus*, Plymouth, 1974. PRINCIPAL STAGE APPEARANCES—Undershaft, *Major Barbara*, Phoenix, Leicester, England, 1963; repertory, Leicester, Liverpool, Hornchurch, 1963–64; Irregular Mobiliser, *Juno and the Paycock*, Etienne Plucheaux, *A Flea in Her Ear*, National Theatre Company, 1966; Blagovo, *A Provincial Life*, Royal Court (Sunday-Night Production), Edgar, *The Dance of Death*, Andrei Prosorov, *The Three Sisters*, Audrey, all-male cast, *As You Like It*, NTC, Old Vic, 1966–67; Emperor, *The Architect and the Emperor of Assyria*, John Frankford, *A Woman Killed with Kindness*, title role, *Coriolanus*, 1971, NTC, Old Vic, 1971; title role, *Macbeth*, NTC, Old Vic, 1972; Petruchio, *The Taming of the Shrew*, Chichester Festival, 1972; Martin Dysart, *Equus*, Huntington Hartford, Los Angeles, 1977; Prospero, *The Tempest*, Mark Taper Forum, 1979; Deeley, *Old Times*, Roundabout, NY, 1983.

FILM DEBUT—Richard, *The Lion in Winter*, 1967. FILM APPEARANCES—*The White Bus* (Short), 1967; *The Looking Glass War*, 1968; *When Eight Bells Toll*, 1969; Claudius, *Hamlet*, 1969; *Young Winston*, 1971; Torvald, *A Doll's House*, 1972; *The Girl from Petrovka*, 1973; *Juggernaut*, 1974; *A Bridge too Far*, 1976; *Audrey Rose*, 1976; *Victory at Entebbe*, 1976; Capt. Johnson, *International Velvet*, 1977; Corky Withers, *Magic*, 1978; Dr. Treves, *The Elephant Man*, 1979; *A Change of Seasons/Consenting Adults*, 1980; *The Hunchback of Notre Dame*, 1982; Capt. Bligh, *The Bounty*, 1984.

TELEVISION DEBUT—*A Heritage and Its History*, 1968. TELEVISION APPEARANCES—*A Walk Through the Forrest*, 1968; *The Three Sisters*, 1968; title role, *Danton*, 1970; *Dickens*, 1970; *Hearts and Flowers*, 1971; *The Poet Game*, 1971; *Uncle Vanya*, 1971; Pierre, *War and Peace*, 1971–72; title role, *Lloyd George*, 1972; Lloyd George, *The Edwardians*, 1972; Adam Kelno, *QB VII*, 1973; *Posessions*, 1974; Marek, *(Omnibus) Find Me*, 1974; *All Creatures Great and Small*, 1974; *The Arcata Promise*, 1974; Bruno Hauptmann, *The Lindberg Kidnapping Case*, 1975; *Dark Victory*, 1975; *Kean*, 1978; Capt. Christopher Jones, *The Mayflower*, 1979; Hitler, *The Bunker*, 1980; title role, *Othello*, 1980; *Acts of Peter and Paul*, 1980; *Little Eyolf*, 1981; *A Married Man*, 1983; *The Arch of Triumph*, 1984.

AWARDS: B.A.F.T.A., Best Actor, 1973: *War and Peace;* Emmy Awards, Best Actor, 1976: *The Lindbergh Kidnapping Case*, Best Actor, 1981: *The Bunker;* Outstanding Actor of the Year Award, Authors and Celebrities Forum, 1975.

SIDELIGHTS: MEMBERSHIPS—Motion Picture Academy; American Film Institute. RECREATION—Astronomy and the piano.

On March 21, 1982, Mr. Hopkins made his debut as a conductor with the New Symphony Orchestra, at Royal Albert Hall.

ADDRESS: Agent—Creative Artists Agency, 1888 Century Park East, Los Angeles, CA 90067; I.C.M., 338–396 Oxford Street, London, W1N 9HE, England.

* * *

HORSFORD, Anna Maria, actress, producer

PERSONAL: Born in New York City; daughter of Victor A. (an investment real estate broker) and Lillian Agatha (Richardson) Horsford. EDUCATION: High School of Performing Arts, drama major, 1964; spent two years at the Inter-American University of Puerto Rico (1966–67). NONTHEATRICAL CAREER—Teacher, College of New Rochelle, DC 37 Extension, 1978–79 and 1981.

CAREER: DEBUT—Maiden Lady, *Coriolanus*, New York Shakespearean Theatre, Delacorte, Central Park, July 1965. PRINCIPAL STAGE APPEARANCES—Secretary, *In the Well of the House*, Public Theatre, New York, 1972; Perfection, *Perfection in Black*, Negro Ensemble Company, New York, 1973; *Les Femmes Noires*, Public, New York, 1974; Rita, *Sweet Talk*, Public Theatre, New York, 1975; Red, Blue, Purple, *For Colored Girls Who Have Considered Suicide/ When the Rainbow Is Enuf*, Booth, New York, 1978; Amazon, *Peep*, South Street Theatre, New York, 1981; Women, *Not*, Lion, New York, 1981. MAJOR TOURS—Voice, *The Time Is Now*, 1964.

FILM DEBUT—Amy Zon, *An Almost Perfect Affair*, 1978. FILM APPEARANCES—Rose Washington, *Times Square*, 1979; Smily Stolz, *The Fan*, 1980; Mara, *Love Child*, 1981; Maggie, *Class*, 1982; Slam Dunk, *Crackers*, 1982. TELEVISION DEBUT—*The Doctors*. TELEVISION APPEARANCES—Mother, *The Tap Dance Kid*, 1978; Monica, *Hollow Image*, 1978; Clara Jones, *The Guiding Light*, 1979; Hilly, *Murder, Inc.*, 1981; Jessica, *Star Struck*, 1982; Marge Keating, *Bill*, 1981; Officer Thomas, *Muggable Mary*, 1981; Charmaine, *Benny's Place*, 1982; Leigh Williams, *A Doctor's Story*, 1984; Stephanie Marshak, *Summer Switch*, 1984.

PRODUCED—for WNET-13, National Educational Television, New York, 1970–81; talent coordinator, *Soul at the Center*, Concert Series at Lincoln Center, 1972–73; coordinator, *Minority Writers Conference on T.V. Production*, 1979–81.

AWARDS: NY-Brooklyn Links, Best Comedy Actress, 1963; NAACP Award, Outstanding Leadership, Gary, IN, 1973.

SIDELIGHTS: MEMBERSHIPS—Variety Club of America; Black Women in Theatre (president, 1983–84).

"I feel that acting is the greatest teaching/learning experience I could have. I have been in so many different lifestyles and situations from the stories and characters I have re-enacted. . . . I was encouraged to travel as a child, first throughout the United States and later Europe and North Africa. At nineteen I moved from Harlem to Stockholm, Sweden where I remained for one year. . . . My greatest motivation has been never to accept a limiting idea or concept

ANNA MARIA HORSFORD

about me or my world without question. I have used every lesson I have learned or experienced in my acting roles. My studies in Science of the Mind has supported those feelings and expanded my horizons in pursuing my goals.''

For more information see: *Outstanding American Women, 1983–84.*

ADDRESS: Agent—Monty Silver, 200 W. 57th Street, New York, NY 10019

* * *

HOSKINS, Bob, actor

PERSONAL: Born October 26, 1942, in Bury St. Edmonds, Suffolk, England; son of Robert and Elsie (Hopkins) Hoskins; married Jane Livesey (divorced). EDUCATION: Stroud Green School, Finsbury Park.

CAREER: DEBUT—Peter, *Romeo and Juliet,* Victoria, Stoke-on-Trent, 1969. PRINCIPAL STAGE APPEARANCES—Pinchwife, *The Country Wife,* Century, 1970; *The Baby Elephant* (Pantomime), Theatre Upstairs, 1971; Uriah Shelley, *Man Is Man,* Royal Court, 1971; Lenny, *The Homecoming,* title role, *Richard III,* Hull Arts Center, 1971; Azdak, *The Caucasian Chalk Circle,* Northcott, Exeter, 1971; soldiers, *Edward Bond's Lear,* Royal Court, 1971; Butcher Brunt, *Cato Street,* Young Vic, 1971; Bernie the Volt, *Veterans,* Royal Court, 1971; title role, *Edward Bond's Lear,* Dartington Hall, 1972; Sextus Pompeius, *Antony and Cleopatra,*

Bankside Globe, 1973; *Geography of a Horse Dreamer,* Royal Court, 1974; Doolittle, *Pygmalion,* Albert, 1974; Touchstone, *As You Like It,* Oxford Playhouse, 1974; Bill Cracker, *Happy End,* Oxford Playhouse, then Lyric, London, 1974–75; Rocky, *The Iceman Cometh,* Borkin, *Ivanov,* Sergeant, *The Devil's Disciple,* Royal Shakespeare Company, Aldwych, 1976; Jake, *England, England,* Jeannetta Cochrane, 1977; *The World Turned Upside Down,* Joe Veriatio, *Has Washington Legs?,* Cottesloe, 1978; Nathan Detroit, *Guys and Dolls,* National, 1982.

FILM APPEARANCES—*The National Health,* 1974; *Royal Flash,* 1975; *Inserts,* 1976; *Zulu Dawn,* 1980; *The Wall,* 1982; *The Long Good Friday,* 1982; *The Honorary Consul,* 1983.

TELEVISION APPEARANCES—*Her Majesty's Pleasure,* 1972; *Villians on the High Road,* 1972; *If There Weren't Any Black. . . ,* 1973; *Softly, Softly,* 1973; *Thick as Thieves,* 1973; *Schmoedipus,* 1974; *The Gentle Rebellion,* 1974; *On the Move,* 1975; Arthur Parker, *Pennies from Heaven,* 1977–78; title role, *Sheppey,* 1980; Arnie Cole, *Flickers,* 1980; Iago, *Othello,* 1981; *You Don't Have to Walk to Fly,* 1982; also: *Thriller, Omnibus, The Crezz, Three Piece Suit, Rock Follies, In the Looking Glass, Napoleon.*

SIDELIGHTS: FAVORITE PARTS—Bernie the Volt, *Richard III,* Lear. RECREATION—Writing, listening to music, his children.

ADDRESS: Agent—c/o Hope and Lyne, Five Milner Place, London N1, England.*

* * *

HOUGHTON, Katharine, actress and playwright

PERSONAL: Surname rhymes with ''trough''; daughter of Ellsworth S. (a writer and filmmaker) and Marion Houghton (a writer and historian; maiden name, Hepburn) Grant. EDUCATION: Sarah Lawrence, B.A.; studied with Lynn Masters.

CAREER: DEBUT—Pearl, *A Very Rich Woman,* Belasco, NY, 1965. PRINCIPAL STAGE APPEARANCES—*Where's Daddy;* Peggy, *The Front Page;* Zoe, *A Scent of Flowers; To Heaven in a Swing;* Deborah, *A Touch of the Poet,* Yale Repertory, New Haven, CT; Portia, *Merchant of Venice,* South Coast Repertory, CA; Hypatia, *Misalliance,* Hartford Stage, CT; Isabel, *Ring Round the Moon,* Hartford Stage; Actors Theatre of Louisville: Kate, *Taming of the Shrew,* Barbara, *Major Barbara,* Laura, *The Glass Menagerie,* Louka, *Arms and the Man,* Kathleen, *Terra Nova;* Catherine, *Suddenly Last Summer,* Ivanhoe, Chicago; Patient, *Too True to Be Good,* Academy Festival Theatre of Lake Forest, IL; Yelena, *Uncle Vanya,* Academy Festival Theatre of Lake Forest; Christina, *Prodigal Daughter,* Kennedy Center, Washington, DC; Sabrina, *Sabrina Fair,* National Theatre, Washington, DC; Nina, *The Sea Gull,* Pittsburgh Public Theatre, PA. MAJOR TOURS—Mollie Ralston, *The Mousetrap,* Palm Beach, Ft. Lauderdale, Arlington Park, 1975; Sabrina, *Sabrina Fair,* Indianapolis, Wilmington, Arlington Park, Royal Alex, Pittsburgh, 1976; Patient, *Too True to Be Good,* Lake Forest, Brandeis, Annenberg, 1977.

KATHARINE HOUGHTON

FILM DEBUT—Joey, *Guess Who's Coming to Dinner*, 1968.
PRINCIPAL FILMS—Isabel, *Eyes of the Amaryllis; The Gar-
dener*. TELEVISION DEBUT—Ingenue, *The Confession*, 1970.
TELEVISION APPEARANCES—*The Hawk; Judd for the Defense; Adams Chronicles; Color of Friendship*.

WRITINGS: PLAYS, PUBLISHED—*Two Beastly Tales*, 1975
(with J. B. Grant); *To Heaven in a Swing*, 1983.

AWARDS: Theatre World Award, 1969–70: *A Scent of
Flowers*.

SIDELIGHTS: Co-founder of the Pilgrim Repertory Co.

ADDRESS: Agent—c/o Leaverton-Somes, 1650 Broadway,
New York, NY 10019.

* * *

HOWARD, Ron, actor and director

PERSONAL: Born March 1, 1954; son of Rance (an actor/
writer) and Jean (Speegle) Howard; married Cheryl Alley (a

writer), June 7, 1975; children: Bryce Dallas. EDUCATION:
Attended University of Southern California.

CAREER: FILM DEBUT—Billy, *The Journey*, 1958. PRINCI-
PAL FILM APPEARANCES—Winthrop, *The Music Man*, 1962;
Courtship of Eddie's Father, 1963; *The Village of the
Giants*, 1965; *American Graffitti*, 1973; *Happy Mother's
Day . . . Love George*, 1973; *The Spikes Gang*, 1974; *Eat
My Dust*, 1976; *The Shootist*, 1976; *Grand Theft Auto*,
1973. TELEVISION DEBUT—*Police Station*, 1958. PRINCIPAL
TELEVISION APPEARANCES—*Red Skelton Show; Dennis the
Menace; Dobie Gillis; G.E. Theatre; Playhouse 90; Dinah
Shore Show; Five Fingers; Johnny Ringo; Danny Thomas
Show; Hennessey; Twilight Zone; Cheyenne; June Allison
Show; New Bread; Eleventh Hour; Dr. Kildare; Route 66;
Great Adventure; Fugitive; Big Valley; Gomer Pyle Show;
Danny Kaye Show; I Spy; The Monroes;* "A Boy Called
Nothing", *Disney;* Opie, *The Andy Griffith Show; Mayberry
RFD; Gentle Ben; Land of the Giants; Lancers; Daniel
Boone; Judd for the Defense; F.B.I.; Gunsmoke;* "Smoke",
Disney; Partner for Lassie; Bob, *The Smith Family; Love
American Style;* Richie Cunningham, *Happy Days;* Bob
Hope Special; Television Movies: *The Migrants; The Lo-
custs; Huck Finn; Act of Love; Bitter Harvest; Fire on the
Mountain*.

DIRECTED: *Night Shift*, 1982; *Splash*, 1984.

THEATRICAL DEBUT—Rickie Sherman, *Seven Year Itch*, Hill
Top Summer Theatre, Baltimore, MD, 1956. PRINCIPAL
STAGE APPEARANCES—Ally, *Hole in the Head*, Bridge Bay
Summer Theater, Redding, PA, 1963.

SIDELIGHTS: MEMBERSHIPS—SAG, AFTRA, Writer's Guild.

RON HOWARD

ADDRESS: Agent—c/o Larry Becsey, Talent Management International, 6380 Wilshire Blvd., Suite, 910, Los Angeles, CA 90048.

* * *

HUGHES, Barnard, actor

PERSONAL: First name pronounced Baar-nid; born July 16, 1915, in Bedford Hills, NY; son of Owen and Madge (Kiernan) Hughes; married Helen Stenborg; children: Douglas, Laura. EDUCATION: Manhattan College. MILITARY: U.S. Army, WW Two (four years in Italy and Africa).

CAREER: DEBUT—Haberdasher, *The Taming of the Shrew*, Shakespeare Fellowship Company, NY, 1934. PRINCIPAL STAGE APPEARANCES—Son, *Please, Mrs. Garibaldi*, Belmont, NY, 1936; Martin, *The Ivy Green*, Lyceum, NY, 1949; Clancy, *Dinosaur Wharf*, National, NY, 1951; Captain MacLean, *The Teahouse of the August Moon*, City Center, NY, 1956; Lanty, *The Will and the Way*, Theatre East, NY, 1957; Doctor Genoni, *Enrico IV*, Erlanger, Philadelphia, 1958; Captain Norcross, *A Majority of One*, Shubert, NY, 1959; August, *Advise and Consent*, Cort, NY, 1960; Peter Mortensagaard, *Rosmersholm*, Fourth Street, NY, 1962; Nils Krogstad, *A Doll's House*, Theatre Four, NY, 1963; The Governor, *The Advocate*, ANTA, NY, 1963; Bert Howell, *Nobody Loves an Albatross*, Lyceum, NY, 1963; Marcellus, Priest, *John Gielgud's Hamlet*, Lunt-Fontanne, NY, 1964; Father Frank Feeley, *I Was Dancing*, Lyceum, NY, 1964;

Father Stanislas Coyne, *Hogan's Goat*, American Place, NY, 1965; Senator McFetridge, *How Now, Dow Jones*, Lunt-Fontanne, NY, 1967; Judge Belknap, *The Wrong Way Light Bulb*, John Golden, NY, 1969; General Fitzhugh, *Sheep on the Runway*, Helen Hayes, NY, 1970; Arnall, *Line*, Theatre de Lys, NY, 1970; Fulbert, *Abelard and Heloise*, Brooks Atkinson, NY, 1971; *Older People*, Anspacher, Philadelphia, 1972; Polonius, *Hamlet*, Dogbury, *Much Ado About Nothing*, Delacorte, New York Shakespeare Festival, 1972 (repeated Dogberry at Winter Garden, NY, 1972); Alexander Serebryakov, *Uncle Vanya*, Circle in the Square—Joseph E. Levine, NY, 1973; various roles, *The Good Doctor*, Eugene O'Neill, NY, 1973; Gower, *Pericles*, Sir John Falstaff, *The Merry Wives of Windsor*, Delcorte, New York Shakespeare Festival, 1974; Dr. Lionel Morris, *All Over Town*, Booth, NY, 1974; *The Devil's Disciple*, Brooklyn Academy of Music, NY, 1976; *The Three Sisters*, Brooklyn Academy of Music, NY, 1977; title role, *Da*, Morosco, NY, 1978; *Translations*, Manhattan Theatre Club, NY, 1980; Orgon, *Tartuffe*, Kennedy Center, Washington, DC, 1982; *Angels Fall*, Circle Repertory, then Broadway, NY, 1983; Philip Stone, *End of the World*, Music Box, NY, 1984.

MAJOR TOURS—Captain MacLean, *The Teahouse of the August Moon*, national tour, ending at the City Center, NY, 1954–56; Jim Bolton (replacing Robert Young), *Generation*, national tour, 1966; *Da*, national, 1979–80.

FILM APPEARANCES—*Midnight Cowboy*, 1969; *Cold Turkey*, 1970; *Where's Papa?*, 1970; *Hospital*, 1971; *Rage*, 1972; *Oh, God!*, 1977; *Best Friends*, 1981; *Tron*, 1982; others.

BARNARD HUGHES

TELEVISION DEBUT—Bob Cratchit, *A Christmas Carol*, 1946. TELEVISION APPEARANCES—''Doc'' Joe Bogert, *Doc*, 1975–76; title role, *Mr. Merlin*, 1981; also *Pueblo*, *Much Ado About Nothing*, *Look Homeward, Angel*, *The Judge*, *Lou Grant*, others.

AWARDS: Antoinette Perry Award, Drama Desk and Outer Critics Circle Awards, 1978: *Da;* Antoinette Perry Award Nomination, 1972: *Much Ado About Nothing;* Emmy Awards, *The Judge, Lou Grant;* Theatre Father of the Year, 1983, Eire Society of Boston.

SIDELIGHTS: MEMBERSHIPS—Circle Repertory Theatre; Players Club. FAVORITE PARTS—Dogberry, Polonius, Serebryakov, Da.

ADDRESS: Agent—Milton Goldman, I.C.M., 40 W. 57th Street, New York, NY 10019.

* * *

HUGHES, Del (ne Delbert Charles Hughes), actor, director, stage manager

PERSONAL: Born September 4, 1909, in Detroit, MI; son of Albert J. (a shipping clerk and farmer) and Lena Sophia (Meilstrup) Hughes; married Julia Johnston (an actress) on September 12, 1937 (died July 31, 1979); children: Julie. EDUCATION: Attended public schools in Detroit MI; I.B.M.

Service School, Endicott, NY, 1928; American Theatre Wing, New York, 1946. MILITARY: U.S. Army, Special Services, 1944–46, (P.T.O. Sergeant).

CAREER: DEBUT—Justin Stock, *Oliver, Oliver,* Brattleboro Theatre, VT, 1935. NEW YORK DEBUT—Captain Tim, *Tobacco Road,* Forrest Theatre, 1936 until closing, 1941. PRINCIPAL STAGE WORK—Assistant Director to Elia Kazan, *Death of a Salesman,* Phoenix Theatre, 1949.

TELEVISION DEBUT—Directed, *A Face in the Crowd,* 1957. PRINCIPAL TELEVISION WORK—Actor, Larry Knox, *The Brighter Day,* 1953; Director, *The Brighter Day,* 1954–59; *All My Children,* 1969–78.

SIDELIGHTS: MEMBERSHIPS—AEA, Member of Council; AFTRA; SAG; Directors Guild, 1954, Member of Council; Society of Stage Directors and Choreographers; Lambs Club; Players Club.

ADDRESS: 30 Norman Avenue, Amityville, New York, 11701.

* * *

HUGHES, Laura, actress

PERSONAL: Born January 28, 1959, in New York City; daughter of Barnard (an actor) and Helen (an actress; maiden name Stenborg) Hughes. EDUCATION: Neighborhood Playhouse.

CAREER: DEBUT—Mary Tate, *Da,* National Tour, 1979–80. NEW YORK DEBUT—Darlene, *The Diviners,* Circle Repertory Company, 1980. PRINCIPAL STAGE APPEARANCES—Avalaine, *A Tale Told,* Circle Repertory Company, 1981; Laura, *The Glass Menagerie,* Hartford Stage Company, CT, 1983; Phoebe, *As You Like It,* Hartford Stage Company, 1983.

* * *

HUGO, Laurence (ne Laurence Victor Hugo), actor and director

PERSONAL: Born December 22, 1927, in Berkeley, CA; son of Mathias (an accountant) and Margaret (a teacher and housewife; maiden name, O'Toole) Hugo; married Ludi Bailhe (an actress), March 13, 1975; children: Victoria; Laurence, Jr. EDUCATION: University of California, A.B., 1939; studied theatre at the Neighborhood Playhouse and the Royal Academy of Dramatic Art. MILITARY: U.S. Army, European theatre, World War II.

CAREER: DEBUT—*The Distant City,* 1941. NEW YORK DEBUT—*Skin of Our Teeth,* 1943. PRINCIPAL STAGE APPEARANCES—*Decision,* New York, 1944; Paul Verrall, *Born Yesterday,* New York, 1944–49; *The Bird Cage,* New York, 1950; *Stalag 17,* New York, 1950–51; *Double in Hearts,* 1955; *Tiger at the Gates,* 1956; Larry Larkin, *King of Hearts,* Olney, MD, 1959; *U.S.A.,* Martinique Theatre, New York, 1960; Polixenes, *Winter's Tale,* Stratford Shakespeare Theatre, CT, 1960; *Antony and Cleopatra,* Olney,

LAURENCE HUGO

MD, 1960; *Life with Father,* 1960; The Alchemist, *San Francisco,* 1961; *Misalliance,* San Francisco, 1961; Kent, *King Lear,* San Francisco, 1961; *There's a Girl in My Soup,* New York, 1969; *The Price,* Halifax, NS, 1972; *The Enclave,* Theatre-Four, New York, 1976; *Prisoner of Second Avenue,* Palm Beach Playhouse, 1977; *The Seagull,* Winnipeg, 1979; *Old World,* Syracuse, NY, 1980; *The Vinegar Tree,* Seattle Repertory Company, 1983. MAJOR TOURS—Claudius/Ghost, *Hamlet,* 1970–71; *Morning's at Seven,* 1981–82.

TELEVISION APPEARANCES—Mike Karr, *Edge of Night,* 1961–69; *City of Angels; Rossetti and Ryan; Trial of General George Armstrong Custer.*

SIDELIGHTS: MEMBERSHIPS—The Players.

ADDRESS: 244 E. 23rd St., New York, NY 10010.

* * *

HUNKINS, Lee (nee Leecynth Hunkins), playwright

PERSONAL: Born January 8, 1930; daughter of Joseph K. (a porter) and Iona (Wyatt) Hunkins; divorced. RELIGION: Religious Science. NON-THEATRICAL CAREER: Federal employee, Department of Health, Education, and Welfare, claims authorizer, 1948–82.

WRITINGS: PLAYS, PUBLISHED—*Revival,* Sea Urchin Press, 1981. PLAYS, PRODUCED—*The Square Peg,* American Community Theatre; *Another Side of Tomorrow*, American Community Theatre; *The Cage*, American Community Theatre; *26501*, American Community Theatre; *Fading Hours*, American Community Theatre; *The Dolls*, Old Reliable Theatre; *Revival*, Old Reliable Theatre; *Maggie*, Negro Ensemble Company (summer festival). TELEVISION PLAYS—*Hollow Image*.

AWARDS: One of sixteen teleplays chosen by the Eugene O'Neill Theatre Center, Playwrights Conference, 1978, and winner of ABC Theatre Award for *Hollow Image*, 1978; Best Play, 1964, American Community Theatre Award, *Another Side of Tomorrow;* Countee Cullen Award (short stories), "A Testimonial to Henry Bannister," 1958.

SIDELIGHTS: MEMBERSHIPS—Writers Guild of America—East, Dramatists Guild, Authors League of America.

"As a Black woman writer, I think it's important for me to write plays in which my characters can be used as role models for the black children of today. We have no heroes, no Wonder Woman . . . no Superman . . . no presidents or kings. Well, our heroes exist, and it is my hope to help bring the heroes out of the shadows and into the light."

* * *

HUNT, Peter, director

PERSONAL: Born December 16, 1938, in Pasadena, CA; son of George S. (an industrial designer) and Gertrude (an opera singer; maiden name, Ophüls) Hunt; married Virginia Osborn, January 19, 1965 (divorced, 1971); Barbette Tweed (an actress) February 6, 1972; children: Max, Daisy, Amy. EDUCATION: Yale University, B.A., School of Drama, M.F.A. POLITICS: "Varied." RELIGION: "Any and all."

CAREER: DEBUT—Child actor, *Chicken Every Sunday*, Pasadena Playhouse, 1947. FIRST STAGE WORK—Lighting designer, *Merry Mount*, Hotchkiss. NEW YORK DEBUT—Lighting designer, *The Sap of Life*, One Sheridan Square Theatre, 1961. PRINCIPAL STAGE WORK—Lighting design: *Cracks*, 1963; *Tambourines to Glory, Color of Darkness*, 1964; *Dynamite Tonight, The Wayward Stork*, 1966; *Have I Got One for You, Noel Coward's Sweet Potato, The Firebugs*, 1968; for Richard Rodgers at Lincoln Center, and at the New York State Theatre, *Kismet, Carousel, Annie Get Your Gun, West Side Story* and tours of *Oliver, Sound of Music, Camelot*, 1964–68. DEBUT—Director, *The Fantasticks*, Williamstown Theatre Festival, MA. NEW YORK DEBUT—Director, *Booth*, Lincoln Center, 1968. LONDON DEBUT—Director, *1776*, New Theatre, 1970. PRINCIPAL STAGE WORK—Director: *1776*, 46th Street, NY, 1969; *Threepenny Opera*, Williamstown, MA, 1969; *Gregory*, Winter Garden, 1970; *Scratch*, St. James, NY, 1972; *Arturo Ui*, Williamstown, 1972; *Goodtime Charley*, Winter Garden, NY, 1974; *Savages*, Williamstown, 1975.

MAJOR TOURS—*Give 'em Hell Harry*, 1975; *The Magnificent Yankee*, Washington, DC, 1977; *Bully*, NY, 1977; *S Miles Is Me*, San Francisco, CA, 1978.

FILM DEBUT—Director, *1776*, 1972. PRINCIPAL FILM WORK—Director: *Gold*, 1974; *Give 'em Hell Harry*, 1975; *Bully*,

1977; TELEVISION DEBUT—Producer/director, *Adams Rib*, 1973. PRINCIPAL TELEVISION WORK—Director: *Life on the Mississippi*, 1979; *A Private History of a Campaign that Failed*, 1980; *Skeezer*, 1981; *Sherlock Holmes*, 1982; *Bus Stop*, 1982; *The Parade*, 1983; *It Came Upon a Midnight Clear*, 1984.

THEATRE-RELATED CAREER: Associate director, Williamstown Theatre Festival, MA, 1964–84.

AWARDS: Antoinette Perry Award, Best Director, 1972: *1776;* New York Drama Critics Award; Christopher Award; Ace Award; Peabody Award (two); Edgar Allen Poe Award.

SIDELIGHTS: Actor, 1947–67, lighting designer, 1957–67, director 1967–. HOBBIES: Flying his own plane.

"Divide time between LA/NY and will do anything to keep 'Bio' separate from the English Peter Hunt."

ADDRESS: Home—1799 Westridge Road, Los Angeles, CA 90049. Agent—Robert Lantz, 888 Seventh Avenue, New York, NY 10106.

* * *

HURLEY, Kathy, actress and writer

PERSONAL: Born April 1, 1947, in Plainfield, NJ; daughter of James Francis (an actor) and Gertrude Marie (an actress/director/producer, Fawcette) Hurley. EDUCATION: Arizona State University, B.A., 1969; Illinois State University, B.A., 1971; trained for the stage with Lee Strasburg. POLITICS: Democrat. RELIGION: Christian Mystic.

CAREER: DEBUT—The Letter H, *The Christmas Pagaent*, St. Francis P.T.A., Phoenix, AZ, 1952. NEW YORK DEBUT—Mrs. Chestnut, *Malcolm X*, Double Image Theatre, 1974. PRINCIPAL STAGE APPEARANCES—Jocasta, *Oedipus Rex*, Illinois State Repertory Company, 1969; Hermia, *A Midsummer Night's Dream*, Illinois State University Repertory Company, Normal, IL, 1970; Emilia, *Othello*, Colorado Shakespeare Festival, Boulder, 1970; Sarah, *Trail of Tears*, TSA-La-Gi Theater, Tahlequah, OK, 1973; Alison, *Canterbury Tales*, Theatre Three, Dallas, TX, 1973.

MAJOR TOURS—Mollie, *Take Her She's Mine*, Southern cities, Anne, *40 Carats*, Southern cities, Marie Louise, *My Three Angels*, Southern cities, 1971–72.

FILM DEBUT—extra, *People Trap*, 1968.

WRITINGS: PLAYS, PRODUCED—*For an Eggshell*, Scottsdale Stagebrush Theatre, Glendale Colle, Stone Soup Players; *The Alchemist's Book*, Henry Street Settlement; *The Black Princess*, Lincoln Center Library, Double Image Theatre, New York Ethical Culture Society, American Theatre of Actors, Pierre's Playhouse; *The Forgotten Treasure*, New York Cultural Council on the Arts' Free Programs in the Park, West Side YMCA, New York Ethical Culture Society, Chappaquah Camp Theatre, American Theatre of Actors, Double Image Theatre; *Beauty Like the Night*, Octagon/Burt Wheeler Theatre, Actors' Alliance; *Duet at a Bus Stop*, Double Image Theatre, Actors' Alliance, Pierre's Playhouse,

Glendale Little Theatre; *The Fading of Miss Dru*, Double Image Theatre, Actors' Alliance; *Yes, But What Do You Do for a Living?*, Actors' Alliance, Kathryn Engles Center; *From Our Point of View*, Double Image Theatre, Long Island Community Center; *A Poet Against the World*, Actor's Alliance. PLAYS, PUBLISHED—*The Alchemist's Book*.

AWARDS: National Society of Arts and Letters Playwriting Award. Grants—National Endowment for the Arts Playwright in Residency, New York; Heckshire Grant for Children's Theatre.

SIDELIGHTS: MEMBERSHIPS—AEA; AFTRA; Dramatists' Guild, B.M.I. Musical Theatre Workshop; ASCAP Libretto Workshop; Authors' League of America.

ADDRESS: Office—597 Fifth Aveue, New York NY 10017. Agent—c/o Gloria Safier, 667 Madison Avenue, New York, NY 10021.

* * *

HURT, John, actor

PERSONAL: Born January 22, 1940, in Chesterfield, Derby's, England; son of Reverend Arnould Herbert (an Anglican minister) and Phyllis (an engineer; maiden name, Massey) Hurt; married Annette Robertson (an actress; divorced); Marie-Lise Volpeliere-Pierrot (a composer), died January 26, 1983. EDUCATION: The Lincoln School, Lincoln; studied for the theatre with a full scholarship at RADA. NON-THEATRICAL CAREER—painter.

CAREER: DEBUT—Mytyl, *The Blue Bird*, 1953. LONDON DEBUT—Knocker White, *Infanticide in the House of Fred Ginger* Arts, 1962. PRINCIPAL STAGE APPEARANCES—Lady Bracknell, *The Importance of Being Earnest*, 1954; *Chips with Everything*, Vaudeville, 1962; Len, *The Dwarfs*, Arts, 1963; title role, *Hamp*, Edinburgh Festival, 1964; Jones, *Inadmissable Evidence*, Wyndham's, 1965; Malcolm Scrawdyke, *Little Malcolm and His Struggle Against the Eunuchs*, Garrick, 1966; Victor, *Belcher's Luck*, Royal Shakespeare Company, Aldwych, 1966; Malcolm, *Macbeth*, 1967; Octavious, *Man and Superman*, Gaiety, Dublin, 1969; Peter, *Ride a Cocked Horse*, Hampstead, 1972; Mick, *The Caretaker*, Mermaid, 1972; Martin, *The Only Street*, Eblana, Edinburgh Festival, then King's Head, Islington, 1973; Ruffian, *The Ruffian on the Stair*, SoHo Poly, 1973; Ben, *The Dumb Waiter*, SoHo Poly, 1973; Tristan Tzara, *Travesties*, RSC, Aldwych, 1974; Young Man, *The Arrest*, Bristol Old Vic, 1974; Romeo, *Romeo and Juliet*, Coventry, 1973; Donal, *Shadow of a Gunman*, 1978.

FILM DEBUT—Phil, *The Wild and the Willing*, 1962. FILM APPEARANCES—Richard Rich, *A Man for All Seasons*, 1966; *Sinful Davey*, 1969; *Before Winter Comes*, 1969; *In Search of Gregory*, 1970; Timothy Evans, *10 Rillington Place*, 1970; *Mr. Forbush and the Penguins*, 1971; *The Ghoul*, 1975; *East of Elephant Rock*, 1977; Kane, *Alien*, 1977; Max, *Midnight Express*, 1978; *The Shout*, 1978; Hazel, *Watership Down*, 1978; Strider, *Lord of the Rings*, 1978; John Merrick, *The Elephant Man*, 1980; *Heaven's Gate*, 1980; *The Disappearance*, 1981; Jesus, *A History of the World, Part I*,

1981; *Night Crossing*, 1982; *Partners*, 1982; *The Oestermann Weekend*, 1983.

TELEVISION APPEARANCES—*Mourtzanos*, 1961; *The Waste Places*, 1967; Quentin Crisp, *The Naked Civil Servant*, 1975; *The Playboy of the Western World*, 1976; Caligula, *I, Claudius*, 1977–78; Raskolnikov, *Crime and Punishment*, 1980; also: *The Hard Case, Acquit and Hang, Watch Me, I'm a Bird, Menace, The Stone Dance, The Spectre*.

AWARDS: British Academy Award, Emmy Award, *The Naked Civil Servant;* Academy Award Nominations, 1978: *Midnight Express*, 1980: *The Elephant Man*.

SIDELIGHTS: "I consider Chekhov the greatest playwright who ever lived, including Shakespeare."

ADDRESS: Agent—c/o Leading Artists, 60 St. James Street, London W1, England.*

* * *

HURT, Mary Beth (nee Supinger), actress

PERSONAL: Born September 26, in Marshalltown, IA; daughter of Forrest Clayton and Delores Lenore (Andre) Supinger; married William Hurt (divorced 1982); married Paul Schrader (director, screenwriter) August 6, 1983; children: (second marriage) Molly. EDUCATION: University of Iowa; studied for the theater at New York University's School of the Arts.

CAREER: DEBUT—Lily, *New Girl in Town*, Equity Library Theatre, NY, 1963. PRINCIPAL STAGE APPEARANCES—Lucy Schmieler, *On the Town*, lead, *The Drunkard*, Gatlinburg, TN; Tirsa, *Three Wishes for Jamie*, Off-Broadway Concert; Celia, *As You Like It*, New York Shakespeare Festival, Delacorte, 1973; Nurse and Uncle Remus, *More Than You Deserve*, Public, NY, 1974; Marina, *Pericles*, Delacorte, NY, 1974; Miss Prue, *Love for Love*, New Phoenix, Helen Hayes, NY, 1974; Frankie Addams, *The Member of the Wedding*, New Phoenix, Helen Hayes, NY, 1975; Rose Trelawney, *Trelawney of the Wells*, Vivian Beaumont, NY, 1976; Caroline Mitford, *Secret Service*, Vivian Beaumont, NY, 1977; Susie, *Boy Meets Girl*, Vivian Beaumont, NY, 1977; Anya, *The Cherry Orchard*, Vivian Beaumont, NY, 1977; Vi, *Dusa, Fish, Stas and Vi*, Mark Taper Forum, Los Angeles, 1978; *All-Shakespeare Concert*, Alice Tully Hall, NY, 1978; Estelle, *Father's Day*, American Place, NY, 1979; Meg McGrath, *Crimes of the Heart*, Manhattan Theatre Club, then Golden, NY, 1981; Cymbeline, *The Misanthrope*, Circle in the Square, NY, 1982; Lizzie, *The Rainmaker*, Berkshire Theatre Festival, MA, 1981; *Crimes of the Heart*, Los Angeles, 1983; *The Nest of the Woodgrouse*, Public, NY, 1984. MAJOR TOURS—Mazeppa, *Gypsy*.

FILM DEBUT—*Interiors*, 1978. FILM APPEARANCES—*Head Over Heels*, 1979 (re-released in 1982 as *Chilly Scenes of Winter*); *Change of Seasons*, 1980; Helen Garp, *The World According to Garp*, 1982.

TELEVISION DEBUT—*The Bette Lee Show*, Birmingham, Alabama. TELEVISION APPEARANCES—*The Five Forty Eight*, NET.

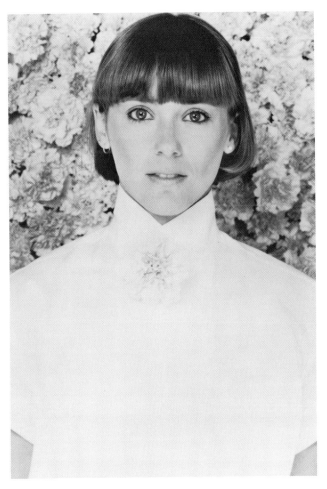

MARY BETH HURT

AWARDS: Clarence Derwent Award, 1974–75; Obie, 1981: *Crimes of the Heart;* Antoinette Perry Award Nominations, 1975: *Trelawney of the Wells,* 1981: *Crimes of the Heart;* Drama Desk Nomination, 1981: *Crimes of the Heart.*

SIDELIGHTS: FAVORITE PARTS—Susie, *Boy Meets Girl,* Lizzie, *The Rainmaker.*

ADDRESS: Agent—Paul Martino, ICM, 40 W. 57th Street, New York, NY 10019.

* * *

HURT, William, actor

PERSONAL: Born March 20, 1950, in Washington, DC; married Mary Beth Hurt (divorced). EDUCATION: Tufts University; trained at the Julliard School.

CAREER: PRINCIPAL STAGE APPEARANCES—*Henry V,* New York Shakespeare Festival, 1976; *Long Day's Journey into Night,* Oregon Shakespeare Festival; *My Life; Ulysses in Traction; Lulu; The Fifth of July; The Runner Stumbles; Hamlet; Childe Byron; The Diviners; Richard II; The Great Grandson of Jedediah Kohler; Mary Stuart; A Midsummer*

Night's Dream, 1982; *Hurlyburly,* Promenade, then Barrymore, NY, 1984.

PRINCIPAL FILM APPEARANCES—*Altered States,* 1980; *Eyewitness,* 1981; *Body Heat,* 1981; *The Big Chill,* 1983; *Gorky Park,* 1983. PRINCIPAL TELEVISION APPEARANCES—*Verna: USO Girl.*

AWARDS: Theatre World, 1978.

ADDRESS: Agent—DHKPR, 7319 Beverly Blvd., Los Angeles, CA 90036.*

* * *

HUSTON, John, director, actor, writer

PERSONAL: Born August 5, 1909, in Nevada, MO; son of Walter (an actor) and Rhea (Gore) Huston; married Evelyn Keyes, 1946; Enrica Soma, 1949 (died 1969); Celeste Shane, 1972 (divorced 1975); children: Walter Anthony, Anjelica, Daniel, Allegra. EDUCATION: Attended art school. MILITARY: U.S. Army, Signal Corps, 1942–45 (Legion of Merit). NON-RELATED CAREER: Reporter, editor, painter.

CAREER: PRINCIPAL FILM WORK: Director—*The Maltese Falcon,* 1941; *In This Our Life,* 1942; *Across the Pacific,* 1942; *Key Largo,* 1948; *The Treasure of Sierra Madre,* 1949; *We Were Strangers; The Asphalt Jungle,* 1950; *The Red Badge of Courage; The African Queen; Moulin Rouge; Beat the Devil; Moby Dick,* 1956; *Heaven Knows, Mr. Allison,* 1957; *Roots of Heaven,* 1958; *The Barbarian and the Geisha,* 1958; *The Unforgiven,* 1960; *The Misfits,* 1961; *Freud,* 1962; *The List of Adrian Messenger,* 1963; *Night of the Iguana,* 1964; *The Bible,* 1966; *Reflections in a Golden Eye,* 1967; *Casino Royale,* 1967; *Sinful Davey,* 1969; *A Walk with Love and Death,* 1969; *The Kremlin Letter,* 1970; *Fat City,* 1972; *The Life and Times of Judge Roy Bean,* 1972; *The Mckintosh Man,* 1973; *The Man Who Would Be King,* 1975; *Wise Blood,* 1980; *Escape to Victory,* 1981; *Annie,* 1982; directed World War Two Documentaries—*Report from the Aleutians; Let There Be Light; The Battle of San Peitro.*

PRINCIPAL FILM APPEARANCES—*The Cardinal Man in the Wilderness; The Bible,* 1966; *Battle for the Planet of the Apes,* 1973; *Chinatown,* 1974; *The Wind and the Lion,* 1975; *Hollywood on Trial,* 1977; *Winter Kills,* 1979; *Lovesick,* 1983.

PRINCIPAL STAGE WORK—Director—*A Passenger to Bali,* 1939; *In Time to Come; No Exit,* 1945; *The Mines of Sulpher* (opera), La Scala, 1966.

WRITINGS: SCREENPLAYS—*Amazing Dr. Clitterhouse,* 1938; *Juarez,* 1939; *Dr. Ehrlich's Magic Bullet,* 1940; *High Sierra,* 1941; *Sergeant York,* 1941; *The Maltese Falcon,* 1941; *Three Strangers,* 1945; *The African Queen; Moulin Rouge; Moby Dick,* 1956; *Freud,* 1962; *Night of the Iguana,* 1964; *Reflecting in a Golden Eye,* 1967; *Fat City,* 1972; *The Man Who Would Be King,* 1975; *Wise Blood,* 1980; *Annie,* 1982; *Under the Volcano,* 1984. PLAYS—*In Time to Come* (collaborator). BOOKS—*John Huston: An Open Book* (autobiography).

AWARDS: Motion Pictures Exhibitor's International Laurel, 1968: *Reflections in a Golden Eye;* Martin Buber, David di Donatello, 1966: *The Bible;* Silver Directors Guild, 1964: *Night of the Iguana;* Screen Writers Guild, Silver Laurel, 1963; National Board of Review of Motion Pictures, 1956; New York Film Critics, Best Director, 1956: *Moby Dick;* Screen Directors Guild, 1950: *The Asphalt Jungle;* One World, 1949; Academy Award, New York Film Critics, Best Director, Best Screenplay, 1949: *The Treasure of Sierre Madre;* New York Drama Critics Circle: *In Time to Come;* honorary degrees from Trinity College, Dublin and Monmouth College, NJ.

SIDELIGHTS: MEMBERSHIPS—Writers Guild, Directors Guild, SAG.

ADDRESS: Office—c/o Jess Morgan, 6420 Wilshire Blvd., Los Angeles, CA 90048. Agent—Paul Kohner, 9169 Sunset Blvd., Los Angeles, CA 90069.

I

IMMERMAN, William J., executive producer and business affairs manager

PERSONAL: Born December 29, 1937, in New York City; son of Nathan (an attorney) and Sadye (a teacher) Immerman; children: Scott, Eric, Lara. EDUCATION: University of Wisconsin, 1959; Stanford Law School. MILITARY: U.S. Army Reserve, 1959–68.

CAREER: PRINCIPAL FILM ASSOCIATIONS—Associate counsel, American International Pictures, 1965 (also director of business affairs, executive assistant to the chairman of the board, vice-president in charge of business affairs, production committee), production executive, *Wild in the Streets, Three in the Attic;* vice-president in charge of business affairs, Twentieth Century Fox, 1972 (also chief negotiator for talent, production and distribution; board of directors, Motion Picture Association of America, Association of Motion Picture and Television Producers); senior vice-president of feature film division, Twentieth Century Fox, 1975–77; founder, Scoric Productions, Inc., 1977 (executive producer), *Highpoint;* founder, Cinama Group, 1979; executive producer, *Take This Job and Shove it,* 1981; *Southern Comfort,* 1981; *Hysterical,* 1981; president, Salem Productions, 1982.

PRINCIPAL TELEVISION ASSOCIATIONS—Production executive, *An Evening of Edgar Allan Poe;* financing and distribution arranger, *That's Entertainment;* financial arranger, *Likely Stories.*

SIDELIGHTS: MEMBERSHIPS—The Thalians (executive vice-president).

ADDRESS: Office—Salem Productions, Inc., 2029 Century Park East, #2050, Los Angeles, CA 90067.

* * *

INGHAM, Robert E., writer, actor

PERSONAL: Born January 27, 1934, in Bedford County, VA; son of Gordon Carlyle (a farmer and post office employee) and Pattie Virginia (Dickerson) Ingham; married Rosemary Gleason (a writer and costume designer) on September 14, 1958; children: Richard, James, Robert Jr., Stephen. EDUCATION: University of Virginia, B.S. (History), 1960 (graduate study for one year in History); Yale University, School of Drama, M.F.A. (Playwriting), 1965. MILITARY: U.S. Army, 1945–46 (corporal).

CAREER: Resident actor—Milwaukee Repertory Theatre,

1974–76. Actor—Goodman Theatre, Chicago, IL; Arlington Park Theatre, Chicago, IL; Lincolnshire Theatre, Chicago, IL; Williamstown Theatre Festival, Williamstown, MA; Dallas Shakespeare Festival, Dallas, TX.

THEATRE-RELATED CAREER: Professor of playwriting, University of Virginia, Charlottesville, VA, 1981–present; assistant professor of acting and directing, University of Montana, Missoula, 1970–73; assistant professor, acting and directing, Grinnell College, IA, 1967–70.

WRITINGS: PLAYS—*A Simple Life,* produced at the Yale School of Drama, 1964; *No Better,* produced at Grinnell College, IA, 1968; *Custer,* produced at Milwaukee Repertory Theatre 1976 and 1978, O'Neill Theatre Center, 1977, Kennedy Center for the Performing Arts, 1979, Hartman Theatre, Stamford, CT, 1980, Cleveland Playhouse, A Contemporary Theatre, Seattle, WA, Arizona Repertory Theatre, Stage One, Dallas, TX, all 1980, McCarter Theatre, Princeton, NJ, 1981, Heritage Theatre, Charlottesville, VA, 1981. TELEVISION—*The High-Priced Men of Homestead.*

AWARDS: Best Play Done Outside New York City, *Custer,* American Theatre Critics Association, 1979–80 season; Kazan Prize for Playscripts, *A Simple Life,* 1964.

SIDELIGHTS: MEMBERSHIPS—Dramatists Guild, AEA, SAG.

ADDRESS: Home—143 Mimosa Drive, Charlottesville, VA 22903. Office—Drama Department, University of Virginia, Charlottesville, VA 22903. Agent—Helen Harvey, 410 W. 24th Street, New York, NY 10011.

* * *

IRELAND, John (ne John Benjamin Ireland), actor, director, writer

PERSONAL: Born January 30, 1916 in Victoria, B.C. Canada; son of John (a rancher) and Katherine (an educator; maiden name, Ferguson) Ireland; married Elaine Gudman in 1940 (divorced 1949); married Joanne Dru (an actress) in 1949 (divorced 1956); married Daphne Myrick in 1962; children: (first marriage) two sons. EDUCATION: Attended public schools in New York City; studied theatre at the Davenport Free Theatre. NON-THEATRICAL CAREER: Professional swimmer.

CAREER: DEBUT—apprenticed at Robin Hood, Arden, DE, 1939. NEW YORK DEBUT—Sergeant/First Murderer, *Macbeth,*

National, 1941. PRINCIPAL STAGE APPEARANCES—Reporter, *Native Son*, Majestic, 1942; Krafft, *Counterattack*, Windsor, 1943; First Murderer, *Richard III*, Forrest, 1943; Gustave Jensen, *A New Life*, Royale, 1943; Mr. Deane, *Doctors Disagree*, Bijou, 1943; Sir Archibald Mackenzie, *A Highland Fling*, Plymouth, 1944; Buck Carpenter, *Deadfall*, Holiday, 1955; Brutos, *Infidel Caesar*, Music Box, 1962; *Macbeth*, Ahmanson, Los Angeles, CA, 1975; *An Evening of Samuel Beckett*, Dublin Theatre Festival. MAJOR TOURS—Shakespearean Repertory Company: Horatio, *Hamlet*, Lorenzo, *The Merchant of Venice*, Macduff, *Macbeth*, Iago, *Othello*, 1940; *Peter Pan*, national tour, 1940; the Miner, *The Moon Is Down*, national tour, 1942; Dr. John Buchanan, *Summer and Smoke*, national tour, 1950; Murray Burns, *A Thousand Clowns*, national tour, 1963–64; *Outward Bound*, national tour, 1983.

FILM DEBUT—*A Walk in the Sun*, 1945. PRINCIPAL FILM APPEARANCES—*Wake up and Dream*, 1946; *My Darling Clementine*, 1946; *The Gangster*, 1947; *Red River*, 1948; *Roughshod*, 1949; *All the King's Men*, 1949; *The Return of Jesse James*, 1950; *The Scarf*, 1951; *Vengeance Valley*, 1951; *Red Mountain*, 1951; *The Basketball Fix*, 1951; *The Bushwackers*, 1952; *Hurricane Smith*, 1952; *The 49th Man*, 1953; *Combat Squad*, 1953; *Outlaw Territory*, 1953; *The Fast and the Furious*, 1954; *Southwest Passage*, 1954; *Security Risk*, 1954; *Steel Cage*, 1954; *Queen Bee*, 1955; *Hell's Horizon*, 1955; *The Good Die Young*, 1955; *Gunfight at OK Corral*, 1957; *Spartacus*, 1960; *55 Days at Peking*, 1963; *Ceremony*, 1963; *The Fall of the Roman Empire*, 1964; *Faces in the Dark*, 1964; *I Saw What You Did*, 1965; *Fort Utah*, 1967; *Once Upon a Time in the West*, 1969; *The Adventurers*, 1970; *Escape to the Sun*, 1972; *Farewell My Lovely*, 1980; *Martin's Day*, 1983.

TELEVISION DEBUT—"Confession," *Philco Playhouse*, 1951. PRINCIPAL TELEVISION APPEARANCES—"Time Bomb," *Philco Playhouse*, 1954; *Schlitz Playhouse of the Stars*, 1952–56; *Prologue to Glory*, 1956; *This Land Is Mine*, 1956; "Without Incident," *Playhouse 90*, 1957; "A Sound of Different Drummers," *Playhouse 90*, 1957; "Obituary for Mr. 'X'," *Dick Powell Theatre*, 1962; "The Matched Pearl," *Alfred Hitchcock Presents*, 1962; *Asphalt Jungle*, 1961; *Rawhide*, 1962; *Burke's Law*, 1963; *Branded*, 1965–66; *Gunsmoke*, 1966–67; *Bonanza*, 1967; *Daniel Boone*, 1967; *Name of the Game*, 1969; *Men from Shiloh*, 1970; *Mission Impossible*, 1972; *Marilyn: The Real Story*; *Crossbar*; *The Cheaters* (BBC); *The Last Tycoon* (BBC).

WRITINGS: LYRICS—"No Head on My Pillow."

AWARDS: Academy Award Nomination, *All the King's Men*, 1950.

SIDELIGHTS: MEMBERSHIPS—SAG; AEA; SDG; Writers Guild of America.

"Mr. Ireland has enjoyed an enduring and distinguished career in film, T.V. and theatre. He achieved renown for his performance in the film *All the King's Men*. Beginning in the sixties, Ireland alternated between film, television and the stage and has worked all over the globe. Aside from his home in Santa Barbara, CA, Ireland's time is devoted to his daughter Daphne, to tennis and to the pursuit of his culinary tastes. His plans include a more active role in the theatre as well as T.V. and films."

ADDRESS: Agent—c/o The Characters Talent Agency Ltd., 107 Queen Street East, Toronto, Ontario, M5C 1S1.

* * *

IRVING, Amy, actress

PERSONAL: Born September 10, 1953, in Palo Alto, CA; daughter of Jules (a director and cofounder of Actors Workshop, San Francisco) and Priscilla Pointer (an actress) Irving. EDUCATION: American Conservatory Theatre, San Francisco, 1971–72; London Academy of Music and Dramatic Art, 1972–75.

CAREER: DEBUT—nine-month-old baby, *Rumpelstiltskin*, Actor's Workshop, San Francisco, 1954. NEW YORK DEBUT—Constanza Weber, *Amadeus*, Broadhurst Theatre, 1981, 8 months of performances. PRINCIPAL STAGE APPEARANCES—Juliet, *Romeo and Juliet*, Seattle Repertory Theatre, 1982, and Los Angeles Free Shakespeare Theatre, 1975; Elvira, *Blythe Spirit*, Santa Fe Festival Theatre, 1983; Ellie Dunn, *Heartbreak House*, Circle in the Square, New York, 1983.

FILM DEBUT—Sue Snell, *Carrie*, 1976. PRINCIPAL FILM APPEARANCES—Gillian, *The Fury*, 1977; Rosemary, *Voices*, 1978; Lily Ramsey, *Honeysuckle Rose*, 1979; Heidi, *The Competition*, 1980; Hadass, *Yentl*, 1983. TELEVISION DEBUT—*The Rookies*. PRINCIPAL TELEVISION APPEARANCES—*I'm a Fool*; *Once an Eagle*; *Panache*; Anjuli, *The Far Pavilions*, 1984.

SIDELIGHTS: Miss Irving keeps a quarter horse called Buddy in Santa Fe, NM, where she lives.

ADDRESS: Agent—DHKPR, 165 W. 46th Street, New York, NY 10036.

* * *

IVEY, Judith, actress

PERSONAL: Born September 4, 1951, in El Paso, TX; daughter of Nathan Aldean (a college president) and Dorothy Lee (a teacher; maiden name Lewis) Ivey. EDUCATION: Illinois State University, B.S., 1973. RELIGION: Catholic.

CAREER: DEBUT—Jilly, *The Sea*, Goodman, Chicago, 1974. NEW YORK DEBUT—Kate, *Bedroom Farce*, Brooks Atkinson, 1979, 140 performances. PRINCIPAL STAGE APPEARANCES—Shirley, *The Goodbye People*, Jean, *The Moundbuilders*, various, *Oh, Coward!*, Evanston Theatre Company, 1977–78; Gilda, *Design for Living*, Arena Stage, Washington, D.C., 1979; Fish, *Dusa, Fish, Stas, and VI*, Manhattan Theatre Club, NY, 1980; Piaf/Madeleine, *Piaf*, Broadway, 1980–81; *The Dumping Ground*, Ensemble Studio, 1981; Evelyn, *The Rimers of Eldritch*, La Mama, NY, 1981; Melanie, *Pastorale*, Second Stage, NY, 1982; Eileen, *Two Small Bodies*, Production Company, 1982, Matrix Theatre, Los Angeles, 1982; Josie, *Steaming*, Broadway, 1982–83; Kathy, *Second Lady*, Production Company, NY, 1983. MAJOR TOURS—Margaret, *Much Ado About Nothing*, American Shakespeare Festival, Philadelphia, PA, 1978.

FILM DEBUT—Sally, *Harry and Son,* 1984. PRINCIPAL FILM APPEARANCES—Iris, *The Lonely Guy,* 1984; Didi, *The Woman in Red,* 1984. TELEVISION DEBUT—Louise, *The Shady Hill Kidnapping.* PRINCIPAL TELEVISION APPEARANCES—Sister Margaret, *Dixie: Changing Habits.*

AWARDS: Antoinette Perry Award, 1983: *Steaming;* Drama Critics Award, 1983: *Steaming;* Dramalogue Award, 1983: *Steaming;* Dramalogue Award, 1982: *Two Small Bodies;* Joseph Jefferson Award nomination, 1978: *The Goodbye People.*

SIDELIGHTS: MEMBERSHIPS—AEA, SAG, AFTRA, National Organization of Women, A.S.P.C.A.

"I am involved with the Actors' Equity Alien Committee. I feel that far too many American actors go unemployed or have the growth of their careers delayed or retarded because of the 'open door' policy extended to British actors. *Steaming* is an example of an American actress capable of performing a British role with credibility and style. Had the British actress been allowed to come, my career possibly would not have blossomed as it did. Therefore, I am very involved in helping the American audience understand that they need to encourage and support their artists first, as England supports theirs."

ADDRESS: Agent—c/o D.H.K.P.R., 165 W. 46th Street, New York, NY 10036.

* * *

IVORY, James, producer, director

PERSONAL: Born 1928, in Berkeley, CA. EDUCATION: University of Oregon; University of Southern California, MA. MILITARY: U.S. Army.

CAREER: FIRST FILM WORK—*Venice: Theme and Variations,* USC. PRINCIPAL FILM WORK—Director/photographer/editor, *The Sword and the Flute;* formed Merchant Ivory Productions, 1961, produced: *The Householder,* 1962; *The Delhi Way,* 1963; *Shakespeare Wallah,* 1965; *The Guru,* 1969; *Bombay Talkie,* 1970; *Savages,* 1972; *Autobiography of a Princess,* 1975; *The Wild Party,* 1975; *Roseland,* 1977; *Hullabaloo Over Georgie and Bonnie's Pictures,* 1975; *The Europeans,* 1979; *Jane Austen in Manhattan,* 1980; *Quartet,* 1981; *Heat and Dust,* 1982; *The Bostonians,* 1984.

ADDRESS: Office—Merchant Ivory Productions, Ltd., 250 W. 57th Street, Suite 1913A, New York, NY 10107.

J

JACKSON, Anne, actress

PERSONAL: Born September 3, 1926, in Allegheney, PA; daughter of John Ivan and Stella Germaine (Murray) Jackson; married Eli Wallach (an actor), March 5, 1948; children: Peter, Roberta, Katherine. EDUCATION: Attended public schools in Brooklyn, NY; studied at the Neighborhood Playhouse with Sanford Meisner, also with Herbert Berghof and Lee Strasberg at the Actors Studio in New York City.

CAREER: DEBUT—Anya, *The Cherry Orchard*, Wilmington, DE, 1944. NEW YORK DEBUT—a guest, *The Cherry Orchard*, City Center, 1945. LONDON DEBUT—*The Tiger* and *The Typists*, Globe, 1964. PRINCIPAL STAGE APPEARANCES—Alice Stewart, *Signature*, Forrest, NY, 1945; with the American Repertory Company at the International Theatre: minor roles in *What Every Woman Knows*, *Henry VIII*, *Androcles and the Lion*, Frida Foldal, *John Gabriel Borkman*, Miss Blake, *Yellow Jack*, 1947; Judith, *The Last Dance*, Belasco, NY, 1948; Nellie Ewell, *Summer and Smoke*, Music Box, NY, 1948; Nita, *Magnolia Alley*, Mansfield, NY, 1949; Margaret Anderson, *Love Me Long*, 48th Street, NY, 1949; Hilda, *The Lady from the Sea*, Fulton, NY, 1950; Louka, *Arms and the Man*, Hotel Edison, NY, 1950; Coralie Jones, *Never Say Never*, Booth, NY, 1951; Mildred Turner, *Oh, Men! Oh, Women!*, Henry Miller's, NY, 1953; Daughter, *The Middle of the Night*, ANTA, NY, 1956; title role, *Major Barbara*, Martin Beck, NY, 1957; Daisy, *Rhinoceros*, Longacre, NY, 1961; reading of *Brecht on Brecht*, Theatre de Lys, NY, 1962; appeared with her husband in *The Tiger* and *The Typists* (double bill), Orpheum, NY, 1963; Ellen Manville, *Luv*, 1964; the actress, *The Exercise*, Golden, NY, 1968; Ethel Rosenberg, *The Inquest*, Music Box, NY, 1970; Mother H, Doris, Joan J, *Promenade All!*, Alvin, NY, 1972; Madame St. Pe, *Waltz of the Toreadors*, Eisenhower, Washington, DC, Circle in the Square, NY, 1973; Madame Ranevskaya, *The Cherry Orchard*, Hartford Stage Company, CT, 1974; Mrs. McBride, *Marco Polo Sings a Solo*, Public, NY, 1977; Diana, *Absent Friends*, Long Wharf, New Haven, CT, 1977; Mrs. Frank, *The Diary of Anne Frank*, Theatre Four, NY, 1978; *Twice Around the Park*, Cort, NY, 1982–83; Natalya, *The Nest of the Woodgrouse*, Public, NY, 1984; *Twice Around the Park*, Edinburgh Festival, Scotland, 1984.

MAJOR TOURS—Zelda Rainier, *Dunnigan's Daughter*, 1945; Bella, *The Barretts of Wimpole Street*, 1947; *The Tiger* and *The Typists*, 1966; *Promenade All!*, 1971; Diana, *Absent Friends*, 1977; also has played stock seasons at Bucks County, in Clinton, NJ, and with Equity Library Theatre and Actors Studio in New York City.

ANNE JACKSON

FILM DEBUT—*So Young, So Bad*, 1950. PRINCIPAL FILM APPEARANCES—*The Secret Life of an American Wife*, 1968; *Zig Zag*, 1970; *Lovers and Other Strangers*, 1970; *Dirty Dingus Magee*, 1970.

SIDELIGHTS: FAVORITE ROLES—Hilde, *The Master Builder*, Anya, *The Cherry Orchard*. RECREATION—Dancing.

ADDRESS: Agent—c/o Creative Artists Agency, 1888 Century Park E., Los Angeles, CA 90067.

* * *

JACKSON, Nagle, director, writer

PERSONAL: Born April 28, 1936 in Seattle, WA; son of

Paul J. (professor, English Literature, Whitman College) and Gertrude J. (Dunn) Jackson; married Sandra S. Suter (former actress and singer) on September 15, 1963; children: Rebecca, Hillary. EDUCATION: Portsmouth Priory School, Diploma Cum Laude, 1954; Whitman College, A.B. 1958; studied mime with Etienne Decroux in Paris, France.

CAREER: FIRST STAGE WORK, Actor—Speed, *Two Gentlemen of Verona,* Oregon Shakespeare Festival, Ashland, 1957. NEW YORK DEBUT, ACTOR-SINGER—*Julius Monk's Plaza 9 Revue,* Plaza Hotel for three years, 1963. NEW YORK DEBUT, DIRECTOR—*The Utter Glory of Morrissey Hall,* Mark Hellinger, for 18 performances, 1971. PRINCIPAL STAGE WORK, DIRECTOR—American Conservatory, San Francisco, CA: *The National Health,* 1977, *Travesties,* 1978, *Hay Fever,* 1979, *Cat Among Pigeons,* 1982; other directing at Old Globe, San Diego, CA, Seattle Repertory, WA, Intiman, Seattle, WA, Hartford Stage Company, CT, Loretto-Hilton Repertory Company (now the Repertory Company of St. Louis), MO.

THEATRE-RELATED CAREER: Resident Director, American Conservatory Theatre, San Francisco, CA, 1967–70; Artistic Director, Milwaukee Repertory Theatre Company, Milwaukee, WI, 1971–77; Artistic Director, McCarter Theatre Company, Princeton, NJ, 1979–present.

WRITINGS: PLAYS, PRODUCED—adaptation, *A Christmas Carol,* Milwaukee Repertory Company, since 1977 (annual production); *Chamber Piece,* Court Steel, Milwaukee, WI, 1976; with Clark Gesner, *The Utter Glory of Morrissey Hall,* 1979; *At This Evening's Performance,* McCarter Theatre, Princeton, NJ, 1983.

AWARDS: Fulbright Fellowship, Paris, France, 1958.

SIDELIGHTS: MEMBERSHIPS—Dramatists Guild; Society of Stage Directors and Choreographers.

ADDRESS: Home—206 Hendrickson Drive, Princeton Junction, NJ 08550. Office—c/o McCarter Theatre Company, 91 University Place, Princeton, NJ 08540.

* * *

JACOBI, Derek, actor

PERSONAL: Born October 22, 1938, in London, England; son of Alfred George (a store manager) and Daisy Gertrude (a secretary; maiden name Masters) Jacobi. EDUCATION: Leyton County High School; St. John's College, Cambridge.

CAREER: DEBUT—(at age six) Both title roles, *The Prince and the Swineherd,* local library drama group, 1944. LONDON DEBUT—Laertes, *Hamlet,* Old Vic, 1963. NEW YORK DEBUT—*The Suicide,* ANTA, 1980. PRINCIPAL STAGE APPEARANCES—*Hamlet,* English National Youth Theatre, Ediburgh Festival, 1955; *Edward II,* Marlowe Society, Cambridge, 1959; Stanley Honeybone, *One Way Pendulum,* Birmingham Repertory, 1960; *Henry VIII,* Birmingham, 1960; Brother Martin, *St Joan* and P.C. Liversedge, *The Workinghouse Donkey,* Chichester Festival, 1963; Fellipillo, *The Royal Hunt of the Sun,* Cassio, *Othello,* Simon Bliss,

Hay Fever, National Theatre Company, Old Vic, 1964; Don John, *Much Ado About Nothing,* Chichester, 1965; Brindsley Miller, *Black Comedy,* Chichester, 1965 and Old Vic then Queen's, London, 1966; Tusenbach, *The Three Sisters,* Touchstone, *As You Like It,* NTC, Old Vic, 1967; King of Navarre, *Love's Labours Lost,* Old Vic, 1968; Edward Hotel, *Macrune's Guevara,* Adam, *Back to Methuselah,* Old Vic, 1969; Myshkin, *The Idiot,* Lodovico, *The White Devil,* Old Vic, 1970; Sir Charles Mountford, *A Woman Killed with Kindness,* Old Vic, 1971; Orestes, *Electra,* Greenwich, 1971; title role, *Oedipus Rex,* Mr. Puff, *The Critic,* Birmingham Repertory Company, 1972; title role, *Ivanov,* Prospect, 1972; Buckingham, *Richard III,* 1972; Sir Andrew Aguecheek, *Twelfth Night, Pericles,* Prospect Theatre Company, 1973; *The Grand Tour,* Goldsmith's Hall, 1973; *Pericles,* Her Majesty's, London, 1974; Rakitin, *A Month in the Country,* Chichester Festival, 1974; Will Mossop, *Hobson's Choice,* Guildford, 1975; Rakitin, *A Month in the Country,* Cecil Vyse, *A Room with a View,* Prospect, Albert, London, 1975; *Hamlet,* Octavius Casear, *Antony and Cleopatra,* Prospect, Old Vic, London, 1977; Thomas Mendip, *The Lady's Not for Burning, Ivanov,* Prospect, 1978; *The Lunatic, the Lover and the Poet, The Grand Tour,* Old Vic, 1978; *Hamlet,* Prospect, Old Vic, 1979.

MAJOR TOURS—*Twelfth Night, Pericles,* Europe and Middle East tour, 1973; *The Hollow Crown, Pleasure and Repentance,* tour, 1975; *The Grand Tour, Hamlet,* Scandinavia, (including Elsinore), Australia, Japan and China (first Western tour of China).

FILM DEBUT—Cassio, *Othello,* 1965. FILM APPEARANCES—*Blue Blood,* 1973; *The Day of Jackall,* 1973; *The Odessa File,* 1974; *The Three Sisters,* 1974; Townley, *The Medusa Touch,* 1978; Davis, *The Human Factor,* 1979; *The Man Who Went Up in Smoke,* 1980; *Charlotte,* 1980; *The Hunchback of Notre Dame,* 1981.

TELEVISION APPEARANCES—*Man of Straw,* 1971–72; *Budgie,* 1972; *The Strauss Family,* 1973; *Markheim,* 1973; *Affairs of the Heart,* 1973; *The Pallisers,* 1975–76; Claudius, *I, Claudius,* 1977; *Paths of the Future,* 1978; *Skin,* 1979; *Richard II,* 1979; Burgess, *Philby, Burgess and MacLean,* 1979–80; *Tales of the Unexpected (Angela's Skin),* 1980; *Hamlet,* 1980; *A Stranger in Town,* 1982; Hitler, *Inside the Third Reich,* 1982.

AWARDS: British AFTA Award, 1977; *I, Claudius,* 1977; Antoinette Perry Nomination, 1980: *The Suicide.*

SIDELIGHTS: RECREATION—Music and reading.

ADDRESS: Agent—ICM Ltd, 22 Grafton Street, London, W1, England.*

* * *

JACOBS, Jim, actor, composer, writer

PERSONAL: Born December 7, 1942, in Chicago, IL; son of Harold James (a factory foreman) and Norma Virginia (Mathisen) Jacobs; married Denise Nettleton (a singer/actress); children: Kristine. EDUCATION: Attended Chicago City College. NON-THEATRICAL CAREER—advertising copywriter, Chicago Tribune, 1964–71.

CAREER: DEBUT—actor, *Don't Drink the Water*, Candlelight Playhouse, Chicago, IL, 1969. NEW YORK DEBUT—Shanty, *No Place to Be Somebody*, Morosco, 1971, 30 performances. LONDON DEBUT—playwright/lyricist/composer, *Grease*, New London Theatre, 1973, 150 performances. MAJOR TOURS—Shanty, *No Place to Be Somebody*, U.S. cities, 1971.

FILM DEBUT—actor, *Medium Cool*, 1968. PRINCIPAL FILM APPEARANCES—Sam, *Love in a Taxi*, 1977–78. TELEVISION DEBUT—*Open All Night*.

WRITINGS: PLAYS, PRODUCED—*Grease* (musical, with Warren Casey), 1972.

AWARDS: Antoinette Perry Award Nominations (7): *Grease;* ASCAP Award, Cue Magazine Award, Longest-Running Broadway Show, Grammy Nomination, Best Cast Album: *Grease.*

SIDELIGHTS: MEMBERSHIPS—AEA; SAG; AFTRA; ASCAP; Authors' League of America; Dramatists Guild.

ADDRESS: Agent—c/o Bridget Aschenberg, ICM, 40 W. 57th Street, New York, NY 10019.

* * *

JACOBS, Rusty (ne Marc), actor

PERSONAL: Born July 10, 1967, in New York City; son of Alan P. (a stockbroker) and Lori (an editor; maiden name, Schwartz) Jacobs. EDUCATION: Attended McBurney School.

CAREER: DEBUT—Tim, *Wanting*, Wonderhorse, 1979. PRINCIPAL STAGE APPEARANCES—Twin, *Peter Pan*, Lunt-Fontanne, 1979–80, 418 performances; Boy, *Memory of Whiteness*, American Place, NY, 1981; Clayton, *Glory Hallelujah*, Spectrum, NY, 1981; Henry Aldrich, *What a Life*, Manhattan Punchline, NY, 1982.

FILM DEBUT—Rusty Snyder, *Taps*, 1982. PRINCIPAL FILM APPEARANCES—Young Max/David Bailey, *Once Upon a Time in America*, 1984.

ADDRESS: Home—28 Irene Lane East, Plainview, NY 11803; Agent—c/o Cuzzins Management, 250 W. 57th Street, New York, NY 10019.

* * *

JAFFE, Sam, actor

PERSONAL: Born March 8, 1893, in New York City; died March 24, 1984; son of Bernard and Ada (Steinberg) Jaffe; married Lillian Taiz 1926 (deceased 1941); Bettye Lousie Ackerman, June 7, 1956. EDUCATION: New York City College, B.S.; Columbia University. MILITARY: U.S. Army, 1919.

CAREER: DEBUT—*The Clod*, Washington Square Players, Bandbox, NY, 1915. PRINCIPAL STAGE APPEARANCES—*The Minister in Youth*, Comedy, NY, 1918; Rev. Samuel Gardner, *Mrs. Warren's Profession*, Comedy, NY, 1918; Kristensen, *Samson and Delilah*, Greenwich Village, NY, 1920; Liebush, *The Idle Inn*, Plymouth, NY, 1921; Reb Ali, *The God of Vengeance*, Provincetown, NY, 1922; Izzy Goldstein, *The Main Line*, Klaw, 1924; Eli Iskovitch, *Izzy*, Broadhurst, NY, 1924; Lum Crowder, *Ruint*, Provincetown, NY, 1925; Yudelson, *The Jazz Singer*, Fulton, NY, 1925; Kringelein, *Grand Hotel*, National, NY, 1930; Herchkowitz, *The Bride of Torozko*, Henry Miller's, NY, 1934; Adversary, *The Eternal Road*, Manhattan Opera House, NY, 1937; Nils Krogstad, *A Doll's House*, Morosco, NY, 1937; Shylock, *The Merchant of Venice*, Penn State University, 1938; Jonah Goodman, *The Gentle People*, for the Group Theatre, Belasco, NY, 1939;

King Lear, New School, NY, 1941; Hymie, *Cafe Crown*, Cort, NY, 1942; Svoboda, *Thank You Svoboda*, Mansfield, NY, 1944; *The Greatest of These*, Chicago, 1946–47; Wouterson, *This Time Tomorrow*, Barrymore, NY, 1947; title-role, *Tartuffe*, Brattle, VT, 1950, Ivor, Hollywood, CA, 1952; Paul Virag, *Blue Danube*, summer theatres, 1952; Gourette, *Mademoiselle Colombe*, Longacre, NY, 1954; Peter Sorin, *The Sea Gull*, Phoenix, NY, 1954; title-role, *Tartuffe*, Kauffman Auditorium, 1956; Zero, *The Adding Machine*, Phoenix, NY, 1956; Dr. Waldersee, *Idiot's Delight*, Ahmanson, Los Angeles, 1970; Shylock, *The Merchant of Venice*, Dickinson State College, ND, 1971; Shaddick, *Storm in Summer*, Off-Broadway Theatre, San Diego, CA, 1972; Tarun Maharaj, *A Meeting by the River*, Palace, NY, 1979.

MAJOR TOURS—in repertory with Kearn's–Sommes Shakespeare Company, 1915–16; Rosenbaum, *The King's Maid*, 1941; the Inquistor, *Saint Joan*, 1954; Cauchon, *The Lark*, 1956.

FILM DEBUT—*The Scarlet Empress*, 1934. PRINCIPAL FILM APPEARANCES—*Lost Horizon; Gunga Din; The Day the Earth Stood Still; Asphalt Jungle*, 1954; *Under the Gun; I Can Get It for You Wholesale; Gentleman's Agreement*, 1947; *13 Rue Madeleine*, 1950; *The Barbarian and the Geisha*, 1958; *Ben Hur*, 1959; *Les Espions; Rope of Sand; Guns for San Sebastian*, 1968; *The Great Bank Robbery; Dunwich Horror*, 1971; *Bedknobs and Broomsticks*, 1971; *Foul Play*, 1980; *Battle Beyond the Stars*, 1980; *Jayne Mansfield, an American Tragedy*, 1981.

PRINCIPAL TELEVISION APPEARANCES—Dr. Zorba, *Ben Casey*, 1961–65; *Bonanza; Daniel Boone; Play of the Week; The Lovers; Quarantine; Night Gallery; The Old Man Who Cried Wolf; Enemies; Ghost Story; Love, American Style; Owen Marshall; QB VII; Streets of San Francisco; S.W.A.T.; Harry O; Medical Story; Bionic Woman; Naked City; Alias Smith and Jones; The Snoop Sisters; The Oath; Kojak; Flying High; Buck Rogers*, 1980; *Hour Magazine*, 1980; *Good Morning America*, 1981; *Love Boat*.

THEATRE-RELATED CAREER: with George Freedley founded the Equity Library Theatre, 1944.

AWARDS: Paul Robeson Award, 1978; Special Honor, Equity Library Theatre, 1977; 125th Anniversary medal City College of New York, 1973; James K. Hacket award, 1971;

Townsend Harris Award, 1962; Emmy Award Nomination, 1961–62; Academy Award Nomiantion, 1950; Edgar Allan Poe Award, 1950; Venice International Award, Best Performance, 1950.

SIDELIGHTS: Mr. Jaffe was a curator in the theatre section of the New York Public Library.*

* * *

JAGLOM, Henry, actor, director, writer

PERSONAL: Born January 26, 1943; son of Simon M. and Marie (Stadthagen) Jaglom; married Patrice Townsend, May, 1977 (divorced 1982). EDUCATION: Attended University of Pennsylvania; trained for the stage at the Actors Studio with Lee Strasberg.

CAREER: PRINCIPAL FILM WORK—Editor, *Easy Rider,* 1969; writer/director, *A Safe Place,* 1971; producer, *Hearts and Minds,* 1974; writer/director, *Tracks,* 1976; writer/director, *Sitting Ducks,* 1980; writer/director, *Can She Bake a Cherry Pie,* 1983; writer/director, *A Lovely Ride,* 1984.

AWARDS: Academy Award, Best Documentary, 1974: *Hearts and Minds.*

ADDRESS: Office: Office—International Rainbow Pictures, 933 N. Labrea, Los Angeles, CA 90038.

* * *

JAMES, Clifton, actor

PERSONAL: Born May 29, 1923; married Laurie (a writer); children: five. EDUCATION: University of Oregon; studied with the Actors Studio in New York.

CAREER: NEW YORK DEBUT—*The Cave Dwellers,* 1956. PRINCIPAL STAGE APPEARANCES—*J.B.,* NY; *All the Way Home,* NY; *The Time of Your Life,* NY; *Cat on a Hot Tin Roof,* NY; *The Shadow Box,* NY; *Total Abandon,* Booth, NY; *American Buffalo,* Circle in the Square, NY; Willie Stark, *All the King's Men,* NY; Casca, *Julius Caesar,* Toby Belch, *Twelfth Night,* Stephano, *The Tempest,* Bottom, *A Midsummer Night's Dream,* Ajax, *Troilus and Cressida,* Enobarbus, *Anthony and Cleopatra,* New York Shakespeare Festival.

PRINCIPAL FILM APPEARANCES—*David and Lisa,* 1963; *Cool Hand Luke,* 1967; *The Chase,* 1966; *Will Penny,* 1968; *The New Centurions,* 1972; *Rancho Deluxe,* 1975; *The Last Detail,* 1974; *Juggernaut,* 1974; *The Reivers,* 1969; *Superman II,* 1981; *The Iceman Cometh,* 1975; *Silver Streak,* 1976; played J. W. Pepper, the sheriff in James Bond films.

PRINCIPAL TELEVISION APPEARANCES—Striker Bellman, *Texas,* for two years.

SIDELIGHTS: MEMBERSHIPS—Actors Studio.

JARVIS, Graham, actor

PERSONAL: Born August 25, 1930 in Toronto, Canada; son of William Henry Reginald (a stocks and bonds salesman) and Margaret Biddulph (Scatcherd) Jarvis; married JoAnna Rader (a ballet teacher) on October 24, 1970; children: Matthew Graham, Alexander Charles. EDUCATION: Bishop Ridley College, St. Catherine's, ON, Canada, 1942–47; Williams College, 1947–50; studied at the American Theatre Wing with Will Lee, Graham Bernard, and others, 1955–57.

CAREER: DEBUT—Alonzo, *The Tempest,* Barter, Abingdon, VA, 1956. NEW YORK DEBUT—Townsman/understudy, *Orpheus Descending,* Martin Beck, 1957; PRINCIPAL STAGE APPEARANCES—Sheldon Marcus, *The Best Man,* Morosco, NY, 1960–61; Member of Lincoln Center Repertory Company at Washington Square: *After the Fall, Incident at Vichy, Tartuffe, Marco Millions, The Changeling,* 1964–65; Witness #5, *The Investigation,* Ambassador, NY, 1966; Vicar, *Halfway Up The Tree,* Brooks Atkinson, NY, 1967; Gamesmaster, *Adaptation—Next.* Greenwich Mews, NY, 1969, Stockbridge, MA, 1968; Narrator, *The Rocky Horror Show,* Roxy, Los Angeles, 1974, Belasco, NY, 1975.

FILM DEBUT—Man on the bus, *Bye Bye Braverman,* 1967. PRINCIPAL FILM APPEARANCES—Hold-up man, *The Out of Towners,* 1969; Beau, *A New Leaf,* 1970; Amos Bush, *Cold Turkey,* 1970; Doc, *The Travelling Executioner,* 1970; J. D., *Middle Age Crazy,* 1980. President of Schooner Tuna, *Mr. Mom,* 1983; Nuclear Medical Doctor, *Silkwood,* 1983; Guard Prescott, *The Big House,* 1984.

TELEVISION DEBUT—*The Sergeant Bilko Show.* PRINCIPAL TELEVISION APPEARANCES—Charlie Haggers, *Mary Hartman, Mary Hartman,* 1976–77, and *Forever Fernwood,* 1977–78; John Ehrlichman, *Blind Ambition,* 1980; Jack Feldspar, Vice Principal, *Making the Grade,* 1983.

SIDELIGHTS: MEMBERSHIPS—Co-Chairman, Southern California Coalition for Handgun Control, 1981 and "continue to be involved in that case."

"I got into acting by lucky accident. I had performed in school plays etc., but had never given the theatre serious consideration as a career. In the early 50's, I was working at different jobs in New York and got employed as night-time penny arcade attendant working on the 2 a.m. to 10 a.m. shift. There I met another employee named John Darley, who spent his evenings directing an off off-Broadway group before coming up to the arcade to earn his living. He was the son of Otis Skinner's stage manager, had spent all his life in the theatre and was very knowledgeable about it. I asked if he needed an actor. He said yes, and as soon as I attended my first rehearsal I made the fatal judgement; 'I can do that.' . . . But I am aware of how lucky I've been. I try to respect my craft, and the people who care about it, and the people who hopefully and patiently watch us and celebrate with us if we get it right."

ADDRESS: Agent—McCartt, Oreck, Barrett-Lionel Larner, 9200 Sunset Blvd. Los Angeles, CA 90069.

JASON, David (ne White), actor, director, writer

PERSONAL: Born February 2, 1940, in London, England;

DAVID JASON

son of Arthur (a fishmonger) and Olwen (a charlady; maiden name, Jones) White.

CAREER: DEBUT—Sanymo, *Bubble,* South Sea, England, 1965. LONDON DEBUT—*No Sex Please, We're British,* 1972. PRINCIPAL STAGE APPEARANCES—*The Relapse, The Norman Conquests; Look No Hands; The Mating Game; The Rivals.* MAJOR TOURS—3 world tours with Derek Himmo's Company.

FILM DEBUT—*Royal Flash.* PRINCIPAL FILM APPEARANCES—Title-role, *Odd Job.*

TELEVISION DEBUT—*Do Not Adjust Your Set.* PRINCIPAL TELEVISION APPEARANCES—*Porridge; A Sharp Intake of Breath; Open All Hours; Top Secret Life of Edgar Briggs; Only Fools and Horses.*

AWARDS: Mitsubishi Award, Best Situation Comedy, 1984.

ADDRESS: Home—20 Lancaster Court, 36 Newman St. London, WT England. Agent—Richard Stone, 18-20 York Buildings, Aldwych, London, England.

JEAKINS, Dorothy, costume designer

PERSONAL: Born January 11, 1914, in San Diego, CA; children: Stephen Sydney Dane, Peter Jeakins Dane. EDUCATION: Attended Otis Art Institute, 1931–34. NON-THEATRICAL CAREER: Art Students League, Los Angeles, 1935; WPA Federal Art Project, 1935–36; assistant to Ernst Dryden, 1938; Photo Research, *Voyage to America,* documentary for U.S. Pavilion, New York World's Fair, 1964; Curator of costume and textiles, Los Angeles County Museum of Art, 1968.

CAREER: PRINCIPAL STAGE WORK—New York: *King Lear; Affairs of State; Winesburg, Ohio; World of Suzy Wong; Too Late the Phalarope; My Father, My Mother and Me; Major Barbara; A Taste of Honey.* UCLA Theatre Group, Los Angeles: *Murder in the Cathedral,* 1960; *Three Sisters,* 1960; *Comedies of Despair,* 1960; *The Prodigal,* 1960; *Six Characters in Search of an Author,* 1961; *The Iceman Cometh,* 1961; *Burlesque,* 1963; *The Seagull,* 1964; *King Lear,* 1964; *Yeats and Company,* 1965. Los Angeles Civic Light Opera: *Carousel,* 1953; *Peter Pan,* 1954; *Kiss Me, Kate,* 1955; *Rosalinda,* 1956; *South Pacific,* 1957; *Annie Get Your Gun,* 1957; *Oklahoma,* 1959; *Show Boat,* 1960; *The Sound of Music,* 1961; *Oliver!,* 1962; *Carousel,* 1963. Mark Taper Forum, Los Angeles: *Who's Happy Now?,* 1967; *Crystal and Fox,* 1970; *Othello,* 1971; *Juno and the Paycock,* 1974; *Duchess of Malfi,* 1975. American Shakespeare Theatre, Stratford, CT: *Taming of the Shrew,* 1956; *Winter's Tale,* 1958; *Romeo and Juliet,* 1959; *All's Well That Ends Well,* 1959.

FIRST FILM WORK—*Dr. Rhythm,* 1938. PRINCIPAL FILM WORK—*Joan of Arc,* 1948; *Samson and Delilah,* 1949; *Cyrano de Bergerac,* 1950; *Belles on Their Toes,* 1952; *The Big Sky,* 1952; *The Greatest Show on Earth,* 1952; *Les Miserables,* 1952; *My Cousin Rachel,* 1952; *The Outcasts of Poker Flat,* 1952; *Stars and Stripes Forever,* 1952; *High Noon,* 1952; *Treasure of the Golden Condor,* 1953; *Titanic,* 1953; *Niagara,* 1953; *White Witch Doctor,* 1953; *Beneath the 12-Mile Reef,* 1953; *Three Coins in the Fountain,* 1954; *Prince Valiant,* 1954; *Friendly Persuasion,* 1956; *The Ten Commandments,* 1957; *The Young Stranger,* 1957; *South Pacific,* 1958; *Desire Under the Elms,* 1959; *Green Mansions,* 1959; *Elmer Gantry,* 1960; *Let's Make Love,* 1960; *The Unforgiven,* 1960; *The Children's Hour,* 1961; *The Music Man,* 1961; *All Fall Down,* 1962; *The Best Man,* 1964; *Ensign Pulver,* 1964; *The Night of the Iguana,* 1964; *The Fool Killer,* 1965; *The Sound of Music,* 1965; *Any Wednesday,* 1966; *Hawaii,* 1966; *The Flim-Flam Man,* 1967; *Reflections in a Golden Eye,* 1967; *Finian's Rainbow,* 1968; *The Fixer,* 1968; *The Stalking Moon,* 1968; *True Grit,* 1969; *The Molly Maguires,* 1969; *Little Big Man,* 1970; *Fat City,* 1972; *Fuzz,* 1972; *When the Legends Die,* 1972; *The Way We Were,* 1973; *Young Frankenstein,* 1974; *The Iceman Cometh,* 1974; *The Savage Is Loose,* 1974; *The Hindenberg,* 1975; *Audrey Rose,* 1977; *The Betsy,* 1978; *Love and Bullets,* 1979; *North Dallas Forty,* 1979; *The Postman Always Rings Twice,* 1980; *On Golden Pond,* 1981.

AWARDS: Academy Award—1948: *Joan of Arc,* 1950: *Samson and Delilah,* 1964: *Night of the Iguana;* Academy Award Nominations, 1952: *My Cousin Rachel,* 1956: *The Ten Commandments,* 1961: *The Children's Hour,* 1962: *The Music Man,* 1965: *The Sound of Music,* 1966: *Hawaii,* 1973: *The Way We Were.*

ADDRESS: 2926 Torito Road, Santa Barbara, CA 93108.

* * *

JENNINGS, Ken, actor

PERSONAL: Son of Thomas Joseph (a quality control inspector) and Grace Louise (a librarian; maiden name Bowe) Jennings; married Christine Orzepowski (an actress), November 7, 1975. EDUCATION: St. Peter's College, B.A., 1971. RELIGION: Roman Catholic.

CAREER: PRINCIPAL STAGE APPEARANCES—Tobias, *Sweeney Todd*, New York, 1979; Roland Maule, *Present Laughter*, Circle in the Square, New York; Shorty, *All God's Chillun Got Wings*, Circle in the Square, New York; Toad, *Wind in the Willows*, Folger Theatre; Arpad, *She Loves Me*, Goodspeed Opera House; Charlie, *Tintypes*, South Coast Repertory Theater; Planchet, *Three Musketeers*, Hartman Theatre; Artful Dodger, *Oliver!*, Pittsburgh Civic Light Opera, Papermill Playhouse, and Chateau de Ville; Chimp, *Ho! Ho! Ho!*, Berkshire Theatre Festival; Nicely Nicely Johnson, *Guys and Dolls*, Coachlight Dinner Theatre, and Lazy Susan Dinner Theatre. Appeared in numerous productions at the Halfpenny Playhouse. MAJOR TOURS—Tobias, *Sweeney Todd*.

TELEVISION APPEARANCES—Tobias, *Sweeney Todd*.

AWARDS: Theatre World Award, Outstanding Newcomer of 1979; Drama Desk Award, Outstanding Featured Actor in a Musical, 1979: *Sweeney Todd*.

SIDELIGHTS: Appeared as Earl in *The Astuter Computer Review*, a one-man musical featured at Epcot Computer Central, Walt Disney World, Orlando, FL.

ADDRESS: Agent c/o Dulcina Eisen, 154 E. 61st Street, New York, NY 10021.

* * *

JENSEN, John, stage designer

PERSONAL: Born December 20, 1933, in Weiser, ID; son of John Theodore (an educator) and Dorothy Ellen (Curtis) Jensen. EDUCATION: University of Oregon, B.S., 1955; served as assistant to Jo Mielziner, 1966–68. RELIGION: Episcopalian. MILITARY: U.S. Army, 1956–58.

CAREER: FIRST STAGE WORK—set designer, *Ardèle*, Anouilh, Guthrie Theatre Company at Croford Livingston Theatre, St. Paul, MN, 1969. FIRST NEW YORK STAGE WORK—scenic designer, *Cyrano* (the musical), Palace Theatre, 1973. PRINCIPAL STAGE WORK—set designer for *Ceremonies in Dark Old Men*, Guthrie Theatre, Minneapolis, MN, 1970; *The Thurber Carnival* and *The Lion in Winter*, Actors Theatre of Louisville, KY, 1970; *Cyrano de Bergerac* and *Taming of the Shrew*, Guthrie, 1971; *A Touch of the Poet*, Guthrie, 1971; *The Diary of a Scoundrel*, Guthrie, 1971; *The White House Murder Case*, Milwaukee Repertory, 1971; *A Midsummer Night's Dream*, Guthrie, 1972; *The Government Inspector*, Guthrie, 1973; *La Turista*, Milwaukee Repertory,

JOHN JENSEN

1974; *King Lear*, Guthrie, 1974; *Love's Labour Lost*, Guthrie, 1974; *Street Scene*, American Conservatory Theatre, San Francisco, CA, 1975; *The Ruling Class*, American Conservatory Theatre, 1975; *Mourning Becomes Electra*, Goodman, Chicago, 1976; *This Is . . . An Entertainment*, American Conservatory Theatre, 1976; *Uncle Vanya*, Pittsburgh Public Theatre, 1977; *Richard III*, Goodman, Chicago, 1977; *Travesties*, American Conservatory Theatre, 1977; *The Sea Plays*, Long Wharf, New Haven, CT, 1978; *The Philadelphia Story*, Long Wharf, 1978; *Romeo and Juliet*, Acting Company, New York, 1978; *Antigone*, Acting Company, New York, 1978; *Of Mice and Men*, Pittsburgh Public, 1978; *Vanities* and *Ashes*, Pittsburgh Public, 1979; *Rosmersholm*, Long Wharf, 1979; *Hillbilly Women*, Long Wharf, 1979; *Of Mice and Men*, American Stage Festival, 1979; *The Visions of Smone Machard, All the Way Home, The Miser, Jumpers*, and *1959 Pink Thunderbird*, McCarter, Princeton, NJ, 1979–80; *Watch on the Rhine*, Long Wharf, 1979, and Golden Theatre, New York, 1980; *Damn Yankees*, Hartford State Company, 1979; *He and She*, Brooklyn Academy of Music Theatre Company, 1980; *Cassatt*, Playhouse 46, 1980; *The Lion in Winter* and *Private Lives*, Long Wharf, 1980–81; *Zapata*, Goodspeed Opera House, 1980; *Black River*, Minnesota Opera House, 1980; *The Play's the Thing*, McCarter, 1981; *In the Jungle of Cities*, Brooklyn Academy of Music, 1981; *Arms and the Man*, Williamstown Theatre Festival, 1981; *Just Between Ourselves*, McCarter, 1981; *Constance and the Musician*, Geva, 1982; *Tartuffe*, Pittsburgh Public, 1982; *The Front Page*, Long Wharf, 1982; *Talley's Folly* and *Inherit the Wind*, Cincinnati Playhouse, OH, 1982; *The Man Who Had Three Arms*, Goodman, Chicago, 1982.

Sets and costumes for *The Tempest*, and *A Play by Alexander Solzhenitsyn*, Guthrie, 1970; *Guys and Dolls*, Dartmouth College, 1972; *Of Mice and Men*, Guthrie, 1972; *The Crucible*, Guthrie, 1974; *Loot*, Guthrie, 1975; *The Cherry Orchard*, Center Stage, Baltimore, 1976; *The Rise and Fall of the City of Mahagonny*, Minnesota Opera, St. Paul, 1977. Sets and lighting for *An Italian Straw Hat*, Guthrie, 1972; *La Traviata*, Music Associates of Aspen, 1975; *The Millionairess*, Shaw Festival, Niagara-on-the-Lake, ON, Canada; *Uncle Vanya*, and *Present Laughter*, Royal Alexandra Theatre Company, Toronto, 1978. With Desmond Heeley and Robert Scales, designed the stage for the international tour of the Stratford Festival Theatre of Canada, 1972. Created an ''environment for children'' based on *Willy Wonka's Chocolate Factory*, part of the Christmas festivities at Dayton's Department Store, Minneapolis, 1976. For the American Ballet Theatre's 1981 production of *Carmen*, Mr. Jensen reconstructed the scenery and costumes from the original 1949 designs by Antonio Clave.

THEATRE-RELATED CAREER: Teacher of design, Carnegie-Mellon University; head of design department, Mason Gross School of the Arts, Rutgers University.

SIDELIGHTS: MEMBERSHIPS—United Scenic Artists L.U. 829 (board of trustees, 1981–83); Theatre Communications Group (Board of Directors, 1983–87); League of Professional Training Programs (Steering Committee).

''I am among a group of fortunate people who have had a career thanks to the regional theatre movement in America. The regional theatres, particularly the Tyrone Guthrie Theatre, gave me an extraordinary place to work at my craft in an atmosphere and amongst other craftsmen where one could not help but learn and grow. I started in the theatre as a performer—even had my equity card—before making a decision, rather late, to put all my energy into design—something I hadn't done since high school. Working with Jo Mielziner, an extraordinary two years, mostly because of the man as a person, gave me my first look at Broadway close up. It was not what I was looking for in the theatre. Odd circumstances brought me to the Guthrie to work in the property department. Here I found rich soil for my growth. With the help of generous people—Tanya Moiseiwitch, Peter Zisler, Michael Langham—I discovered the sort of theatre where serious exploration is built on respect, trust, honesty, and great good humor. . . . Our work was, of course, flawed at times, but it never lacked for serious pursuit of fine, honest theatre. That read through it all. Here I learned what my goal in all the work should be: an authentic visual extension of the playwright. There is no question in my mind that art is craft practiced with perception. Most of us who work as commissioned, commercial artists are first and foremost craftsmen. On occasion, when we are allowed to look beyond the horizon for a glimpse of what is there, our well-oiled craft lets us share it with others. . . . I'm no athlete at all, but love to swim. Traveling is a great pleasure. I've spent a lot of time in Europe, particularly Italy—lived in Florence for four months. Favorite city there: Naples. Theatre is a way of life. Birth certificates are written on the backs of Equity cards, I believe. I love mountains. Would have been a sculptor. Shape is the most telling visual thing in the theatre. I came into design through the theatre, not through art or architecture. Because of this, I constantly wage an inner battle over my painting and drawing skills—always wanting to improve my communication ability. As a result, some of my happiest hours away from the theatre are in life drawing sessions.''

ADDRESS: Home and office—51 Fifth Ave., New York, NY 10003.

JEWISON, Norman, film and television producer, director

PERSONAL: Born July 21, 1926, in Toronto, ON, Canada; son of Percy Joseph (ran the general store and post office) and Dorothy Irene Jewison; married Margaret (Dixie) Dixon (a former model); children: Kevin, Michael, Jenny. EDUCATION: Studied piano and music theory at the Royal Conservatory; attended Malvern Collegiate Institute; University of Toronto, B.A., 1949. MILITARY: Royal Canadian Navy, WWII.

CAREER: FILM DEBUT—Director, *Forty Pounds of Trouble*, 1962. PRINCIPLE FILM WORK—Director: *The Thrill of It All*, 1963, *Send Me No Flowers*, 1964, *The Art of Love*, 1964, *The Cincinnati Kid*, 1965; co-producer/director, *The Russians Are Coming, the Russians Are Coming*, 1966, *In The Heat of the Night*, 1967; producer/director, *The Thomas Crown Affair*, 1968; director, *Gaily, Gaily;* producer, *The Landlord*, 1970; producer/director, *Fiddler on the Roof*, 1971; producer/director, *Jesus Christ Superstar*, 1973, *Rollerball*, 1975, *F.I.S.T.*, 1978, . . . *And Justice for All*, 1979; executive producer, *The Dogs of War*, 1980; director, *Best Friends*, 1982.

PRINCIPAL TELEVISION WORK—Director: *Your Hit Parade*, 1958; *The Andy Williams Show; Tonight With Harry Belafonte; General Electric's 50th Anniversary; The Broadway of Lerner and Lowe;* specials with Frank Sinatra, Judy Garland, Jackie Gleason.

AWARDS: 9 Academy Awards for his films, 29 Academy Award Nominations; Emmy Award for *Tonight With Harry Belafonte*, and *General Electric's 50th Anniversary* and for specials with Frank Sinatra and Judy Garland; officer of the Order of Canada, by the Governor General the Queen's representative in Ottawa.

SIDELIGHTS: ''Mr. Jewison's films have covered a wide range of subjects and styles, from the angry irony of . . . *And Justice for All* and the satire of *The Russians Are Coming, the Russians Are Coming* to the gamesmanship of *The Thomas Crown Affair* and the mystery of *In the Heat of the Night*, the one common denominator—in each of them the main characters in conflict predominated. 'I'm more concerned with people than with action for its own sake . . . Whatever happens in any of my films grows out of who and what its characters are and what motivates them.'''

ADDRESS: Home—18 Glouster Street, 4th Floor, Toronto, ON, Canada M4Y ILS.

* * *

JHABVALA, Ruth Prawer, writer

PERSONAL: Born 1927, in Cologne, Germany; married C. S. H. Jhabvala, 1951; children: three daughters. EDUCATION: Queen Mary College, London, England.

WRITINGS: BOOKS—(novels) *Amita, The Nature of Passion, Esmond in India, The Householder*, 1955–60; *Get Ready for Battle, A Backward Place, Travelers, In Search of Love and Beauty*. SHORT STORIES—*An Experience of India; A Stronger*

Climate; Like Birds, Like Fishes; How I Became a Holy Mother. PLAYS, PRODUCED—*A Call from the East,* Manhattan Theatre club, NY. SCREENPLAY—*The Householder,* 1962; *Shakespeare Wallah,* 1965; *The Guru,* 1969; *Bombay Talkie,* 1970; *Autobiography of a Princess,* 1975; *Roseland,* 1977; *Hullabaloo over Georgie and Bonnie's Pictures,* 1978; *The Europeans,* 1979; *Jane Austen in Manhattan,* 1980; *The Wild Party,* 1981; *Quartet,* 1981; *Heat and Dust,* 1982; *The Bostonians,* 1984.

ADDRESS: Office—Merchant Ivory Productions, Ltd., 250 W. 57th Street, Suite 1913A, New York, NY 10107.

* * *

JILLIAN, Ann (Ann Jura Nauseda Murcia), singer, dancer, and actress

PERSONAL: Born January 29, 1951; daughter of Joseph (a pilot) and Margaret Nauseda; married Andrew L. Murcia (a police sergeant and personal manager). EDUCATION: Pierce Junior College, AA degree; trained for the musical theatre with the Los Angeles Civic Light Opera and studied with Len Bledso and Paul Gleason. RELIGION: Catholic. NON-THEATRICAL CAREER: Before and between acting jobs, worked as a saleslady, answering-service employee, and cocktail waitress.

CAREER: DEBUT—Dainty June, *Gypsy,* Melodyland, Anaheim, CA, 1963. NEW YORK DEBUT—Soubrette, *Sugar Babies,* Mark Hellinger, 1979–80. PRINCIPAL STAGE APPEARANCES—Daughter, *Anniversary Waltz,* Pasadena Playhouse, CA 1964; Tintinabula, *A Funny Thing Happened on the Way to the Forum,* Ahmanson, Los Angeles, 1970; Torch Singer, *Sammy Cahn's Words and Music,* 1976; Madam Labouche, *Goodnight, Ladies,* Drury Lane, Chicago, 1977. MAJOR TOURS: *Sugar Babies,* San Francisco, Los Angeles, Chicago, Detroit, Philadelphia, 1979; *I Love My Wife,* Chicago, 1979.

FILM DEBUT—Little Bo Peep, *Babes in Toyland,* 1961. PRINCIPAL FILMS—Dainty June, *Gypsy,* 1962; Joan, *Mr. Mom,* 1983.

TELEVISION DEBUT—*Art Linkletter's House Party.* TELEVISION APPEARANCES—*Sammy the Way-Out Seal,* 1963; Millie, *Hazel;* Cassie, *It's a Living* (later, *Making a Living*); Joan, *Malibu;* three Bob Hope specials; *Perry Como Special; Night of 100 Stars,* 1982; *Battle of the Network Stars,* 1980, 1981, 1982; *Mae West,* 1982; *Jennifer Slept Here,* 1983; *Parade of Stars,* 1983; *Magic Skates,* 1983; *Black Achievement Awards Special,* 1983; *Tonight Show; Merv Griffin Show; Mike Douglas Show; Good Morning, America; Today Show; Nightline; Love Boat; Fantasy Island; Ben Casey; Twilight Zone; Wagon Train; Partridge Family.*

WRITINGS: Song—"Most Beautiful Ghost," theme song for television series *Jennifer Slept Here.*

AWARDS: Dramalogue Award, 1979: *Sugar Babies;* Emmy Nomination, Best Actress in a Limited Series or Special, 1982: *Mae West;* Golden Globe Nomination, Best Actress in a Miniseries or Motion Picture made for television, 1982: *Mae West;* Bronze Halo Award, 1982: *Mae West.*

SIDELIGHTS: MEMBERSHIPS—SAG; AFTRA; AEA.

Miss Jillian co-hosts the United Cerebral Palsy Telethon yearly. "I am most proud of my three films, my Broadway debut in *Sugar Babies,* my television movies *Mae West* and *Death Rides to Osaka,* and my television situation comedies *It's a Living* and *Jennifer Slept Here.*"

ADDRESS: Agent—c/o Eddie Bondy/Jerry Katzman, William Morris Agency, 151 El Camino Drive, Beverly Hills, CA 90212.

* * *

JOHNS, Stratford, actor

PERSONAL: Born February 22, 1925 in P.M.B, South Africa; son of Sidney Alan (an engine driver) and Dorothy Ada (Stratford) Johns; married Nanette Parsons (an actress) on March 21, 1955; children: Frith, Peta, Alan, Lissa. EDUCATION: St. Charles College; Oxford, Cambridge entrance. RELIGION: Roman Catholic. MILITARY: S.A. Navy.

CAREER: DEBUT—Langford, *White Cargo,* Southend Hippodrome. LONDON DEBUT—Mayer, *Sgt. Musgrave's Dance,* Royal Court, 1957. PRINCIPAL STAGE APPEARANCES—Pratt, *Who Saw Him Die,* Haymarket, London; Daddy Warbucks, *Annie,* Victoria Palace, London, 1978; Porterhouse, *Run for Your Wife,* Criterion, London, 1984. MAJOR TOURS—Pratt, *Who Saw Him Die,* six-week tour.

FILM DEBUT—Fireman, *Burnt Evidence,* 1954. TELEVISION DEBUT—*You Were There,* BBC. PRINCIPAL TELEVISION APPEARANCES—Barlow, *Police Chief,* 14 years, BBC; Peachum, *Beggars Opera.*

AWARDS: BBC Variety Club Personality of the Year Award, 1974.

SIDELIGHTS: Mr. Johns has appeared in over 40 films and 240 television shows; he writes in his spare time.

ADDRESS: Agent—Leading Artists, 60 St. James Street, London SW1, England.

* * *

JOHNSON, Linda Lee, actress

PERSONAL: Born June 20, in Chicago, IL; daughter of Edward Harold Sr. (a naval aviator) and Willena Kathryn (a model before marriage; maiden name, Smith) Johnson; married Douglas A. Johnson on June 24, 1972 (divorced 1984). EDUCATION: University of California, Berkeley, CA, A.B. (English); studied acting with Henrietta Harris, John Argue, and Paul E. Richards. POLITICS: Democrat. RELIGION: Methodist. NON-THEATRICAL CAREER: Jewelry Designer.

CAREER: DEBUT—Psyche, *Eros & Psyche,* Acting Openhand, Berkeley, CA, 1970. NEW YORK DEBUT—Bunny, *Afternoon in Vegas,* St. Malachys, for 20 performances, 1979. PRINCIPAL STAGE APPEARANCES—Maggie, *After the Fall,*

Arena Stage, Washington, DC, 1979; Skye, *Geniuses*, Playwrights Horizons, NY, Arena Stage, Washington, DC, 1982–83; Sarah, *A Different Moon*, W.P.A., NY, 1983.

TELEVISION DEBUT—*Changing Marriage*, PBS, California.

AWARDS: San Francisco Bay Area Critics Award, Cast member of Best Production, 1978: *Private Lives*.

SIDELIGHTS: MEMBERSHIPS—AEA: SAG.

ADDRESS: Home—Greenwich Village, New York; Agent—J. Michael Bloom, 400 Madison Avenue, New York, NY 10017.

* * *

JOHNSON, Mary Lea, producer

PERSONAL: Born August 20, 1926 in New Jersey; daughter of John Seward (an industrialist) and Ruth R. (Dill) Johnson; married (2nd marriage) Martin Richards (a producer) on August 11, 1978; children: (first marriage) Quentin, Eric, Seward, Roderick, Hillary, Alice. EDUCATION: The Masters School, Dobbs Ferry, NY; American Academy of Dramatic Arts, NY; studied costume design at La Sorbonne, Paris, France. NON-THEATRICAL CAREER: Owner, Merriwold Art Gallery, Far Hills, NJ, 1971–76.

CAREER: PRINCIPAL STAGE WORK, Produced—*The Norman Conquests*, Morosco, NY, 1976; *On the Twentieth Century*, St. James, NY, 1978; *Sweeney Todd*, Uris, NY, 1979; *Goodbye Fidel*, Ambassador, NY, 1980; *Crimes of the Heart*, Golden, NY, 1981; *March of the Falsettos*, Westside Arts, 1981; *A Doll's Life*, Mark Hellinger, 1982; *Foxfire*, Barrymore, NY, 1982.

PRINCIPAL FILM WORK, Produced—*The Boys from Brazil*, 1978; *The Shining*, 1980; *Fort Apache, The Bronx*, 1981.

THEATER-RELATED CAREER: Mary Lea joined her husband Martin Richards in 1976 to form The Producer Circle Company to produce theatre and major feature films.

AWARDS: Antoinette Perry Award, Best Musical, 1979: *Sweeney Todd;* Citizen of the Year Honoree, Mental Health Association of New Jersey; as of 1982, her productions have won thirteen other Antoinette Perry Awards, as well as New York Drama Critics Awards.

SIDELIGHTS: MEMBERHIPS—Past Board of Directors, Somerset Hospital, Somerset, New Jersey; Board of Directors, Easton Hospital, Easton, MD; League of New York Theatres and Producers; Past Board of Directors, Second Stage, NY, Phoenix, NY.

ADDRESS: Office—c/o The Producer Circle Company, 1350 Avenue of the Americas, New York, NY 10019.

* * *

JOHNSON, Mike, playwright

See SHARKEY, Jack

JOHNSTON, Justine, actress, singer

PERSONAL: Born June 13, in Evanston, IL; daughter of Joseph E. (a salesman) and Alice Justine (a pianist and clerical worker; maiden name, Schleicher) Johnston. EDUCATION: Emerson High School, Gary, IN; trained for the theatre with the Gary Civic Repertory Company and at the Goodman Theatre in Chicago. MILITARY: USO Campshows (overseas unit #860—mid-Pacific).

CAREER: DEBUT—*Stephen Foster*, Cape, Cape May, NJ, 1943. NEW YORK DEBUT—Mabel, *The Pajama Game*, St. James, 1956. PRINCIPAL STAGE APPEARANCES—Miss Jones, *How to Succeed in Business without Really Trying*, NY City Center, 1966; Heidi Schiller, *Follies*, Winter Garden, NY 1971–72; *Sondheim: A Musical Tribute*, Shubert, NY, 1973; Mrs. O'Dare (standby), *Irene*, Minskoff, NY, 1973; Mrs. Frazini, *Molly*, Alvin, NY, 1973; *James Joyce's Dubliners*, Roundabout, NY, 1975; Mrs. Philip Phillmore, *The New York Idea*, BAM Theatre Company, Brooklyn Academy of Music, NY, 1977; Mrs. Clatt, *Angel*, Minskoff, NY, 1978; Martine, *Sganarelle*, Main Street, 1980; Big Mama, *Cat on a Hot Tin Roof*, Caldwell Playhouse, NJ, 1983; stock/dinner theatre/rep. MAJOR TOURS—Mrs. Weinstein, *Milk and Honey*, first national company, (also final three weeks on Broadway), 1963; Domina, *A Funny Thing Happened on the Way to the Forum*, first national company, 1964.

FILM DEBUT—Bakery Clerk, *Sisters*, 1972. FILM APPEARANCES—Aunt Pearl, *Arthur*, 1980. TELEVISION APPEARANCES—Mrs. Sampson, *Love, Sidney*.

AWARDS: Clio, Fotomat Commercial, "Grandmothers."

SIDELIGHTS: MEMBERSHIPS—AEA (councilor, 1969–84, three consecutive five-year terms); AFTRA; SAG; Ziegfeld Club; National Academy of Television Arts and Sciences.

ADDRESS: Home—35–48 75th Street, Jackson Heights, NY 11372.

* * *

JOHNSTONE, Anna Hill, costume designer

PERSONAL: Born April 7, 1913, in Greenville, SC; daughter of Albert Sidney (a banker) and Anna Hill (Watkins) Johnstone; married Curville J. Robinson (an engineer), May 8, 1937. EDUCATION: Barnard College, B.A., 1934.

CAREER: FIRST STAGE WORK—Costume designs for the Columbia University Laboratory Players, 1935–36. FIRST NEW YORK STAGE WORK—Costume designs for *Temper the Wind*, Playhouse Theatre, 1946. PRINCIPAL STAGE WORK—Costume designs for *For Love or Money*, Henry Miller, New York, 1947; *Lost in the Stars*, Music Box, New York, 1949; *The Curious Savage*, Martin Beck, New York, 1950; *The Country Girl*, Lyceum, New York, 1950; *Bell, Book and Candle*, Ethel Barrymore, New York, 1950; *The Autumn Garden*, Coronet, New York, 1951; *Flight into Egypt*, Music Box, New York, 1952; *The Children's Hour*, Coronet, New York, 1952; *Tea and Sympathy*, Ethel Barrymore, New York, 1953; *All Summer Long*, Coronet, New York, 1954; *The Tender Trap*, Longacre, New York, 1954; supervised the costuming for *The Chalk Garden,* Ethel Barrymore, New York, 1955; designed costumes for *A Quiet Place,* Shubert, New Haven, CT, 1955; *The Hidden River,* Playhouse, New York, 1957; *The Sin of Pat Muldoon,* Cort, New York, 1957; *The Egghead,* Ethel Barrymore, New York, 1957; *This Is Goggle,* McCarter, Princeton, NJ, 1958; *The Man in the Dog Suit,* Coronet, New York, 1958; *Whoop-Up,* Shubert, New York, 1958; *Sweet Bird of Youth,* Martin Beck, New York, 1959; *Triple Play,* Playhouse, New York, 1959; *One More River,* Ambassador, New York, 1960; *After the Fall,* ANTA Washington Square, New York, 1964; *The Investigation,* Ambassador, New York, 1966.

FIRST FILM WORK—Designed costumes for *Portrait of Jenny,* 1948. PRINCIPAL FILM WORK—Designed costumes for *On the Waterfront,* 1954; *East of Eden,* 1955; *Baby Doll,* 1956; *Edge of the City,* 1957; *A Face in the Crowd,* 1957; *Odds Against Tomorrow,* 1959; *Wild River,* 1960; *Splendor in the Grass,* 1961; *David and Lisa,* 1963; *America, America,* 1963; *Ladybug, Ladybug,* 1964; *The Pawnbroker,* 1964; *Fail Safe,* 1964; *The Group,* 1966; *Bye Bye Braverman,* 1968; *The Night They Raided Minsky's,* 1968; *Alice's Restaurant,* 1969; *The Subject Was Roses,* 1969; *Me, Natalie,* 1969; *There Was a Crooked Man,* 1970; *Cotton Comes to Harlem,* 1970; *Who Is Harry Kellerman?,* 1971; *The Godfather,* 1972; *Play It Again, Sam,* 1972; *Come Back, Charleston Blue,* 1972; *The Effect of Gamma Rays on Man-in-the-Moon Marigolds,* 1973; *Summer Wishes, Winter Dreams,* 1973; *The Taking of Pelham One, Two, Three,* 1974; *Gordon's War,* 1973; *The Stepford Wives,* 1975; *Dog Day Afternoon,* 1975; *The Last Tycoon,* 1975; *The Next Man,* 1976; *King of the Gypsies,* 1978; *Going in Style,* 1979; *Prince of the City,* 1980; *Ragtime,* 1981; *Daniel,* 1983; *Heaven,* 1983.

AWARDS: Academy Award Nomination, 1972: *The Godfather;* Academy Award Nomination, 1981: *Ragtime.*

ADDRESS: Home—2501 Palisade Ave., Riverdale, NY 10463.

* * *

JOLLY, Peter, actor

PERSONAL: Born October 25, 1951; son of Richard Hayes (a manufacturer's representative) and Hope Carolyn (a retail buyer; maiden name Cassell) Jolly. EDUCATION: Marietta College, B.A.; studied Shakespeare with Bob Smith.

CAREER: DEBUT—Unknown Man, *The Bat,* Worthington High School, 1967. NEW YORK DEBUT—Harry, *The Sea Horse,* Direct Theater's Actors Festival, 1975. PRINCIPAL STAGE APPEARANCES—Max Dupree, *Knuckle,* Hudson Guild, New York; Mr. Gill, *The Show-Off,* Playwrights Horizons, New York; Man in Black, *Goose and Tom-Tom,* Public Theatre, New York; Bucky, *Earthworms,* Playwrights Horizons, New York; Woodcutter/Count, *Miss Julie,* Hudson Guild, New York; Mark, *Bhutan,* William Redfield, New York; Seth Edward, *Man in the House,* William Redfield, New York; Frank Marrant, *Street Scene,* Moonlight Conspiracy, New York; Nojd, *The Father,* Gene Frankel MCPA, New York; Sampson, *Romeo and Juliet,* York Players, New York; Ivan, *Long Voyage Home,* Washington Market Players, New York; Jean, *L'Atelier,* Trinity Square Theatre;

PETER JOLLY

Photograph by Diane Gorodnitzki

Antonio, *Twelfth Night,* Folger Theatre Group, Washington, DC; Larry Toms, *Boy Meets Girl,* Hartford Stage Company, CT; First Officer, *Twelfth Night,* Yale Repertory; Harold Parmalee, *Merton of the Movies,* Milwaukee Repertory; Invisible Man/Tarzan/Television Announcer, *The Secret Affairs of Mildred Wild,* Totem Pole Playhouse; Henry Lodge, *Move Over, Mrs. Markham,* Totem Pole Playhouse; John Buchanan, Jr., *Summer and Smoke,* Otterbein Theatre; Jean, *Miss Julie,* Trotwood Circle Theatre. As a participant in the Dawn Project at the No Smoking Playhouse, a group "dedicated to the development and nurturance of new work by American playwrights," Mr. Jolly played Mac in *Mothers and Daughters,* Tom Howard in *Reflected Glory,* Henry David Thoreau in *Walden Pond,* and the Centurion in *Androcles and the Lion.*

PRINCIPAL FILMS—Jackson, *Four Friends;* Joe, *Gellerman.* TELEVISION APPEARANCES—Joey, *Another World;* Flint, *Search for Tomorrow.*

SIDELIGHTS: MEMBERSHIPS—AFTRA, AEA, SAG. FAVORITE ROLES—Seth Edward in *Man in the House;* Larry Toms in *Boy Meets Girl;* Jean in *Miss Julie;* Ivan in *Long Voyage Home.* HOBBIES: Golf, photography, reading, swimming. Six years in the Broadway Show League.

"I have traveled extensively throughout Europe with the People to People Student Ambassador Program." AIMS: "The continued development of new American works for an audience willing to accept and want the spontaneity of the theatrical experience. Respect for the stage actor as a member of the artistic community.''

ADDRESS: 35 Bedford Street, #13, New York, NY 10014.

* * *

JONES, Brooks, director and producer

PERSONAL: Born October 23, 1934; son of Edwin A. (an industrialist) and Katherine (McKee) Jones. EDUCATION: Princeton University, B.A., 1956.

CAREER: FIRST STAGE WORK—Director, *Dark of the Moon*, McCarter, Princeton, NJ, 1960. PRINCIPAL STAGE WORK—Associate producer and producer of Princeton's McCarter Theatre, 1958–60; producer and artistic director of Cincinnati's Playhouse in the Park; directed 35 productions, 1962–70; artistic director, Center for the Arts at Purchase, NY, 1979–date.

DIRECTED: (Plays)—*The Resistible Rise of Arturo Ui*, Long Wharf, New Haven, CT, *Enrico IV*, Trinity Square Repertory; *L'Histoire du Soldat*, Long Wharf, *The Balcony* and *The Birthday Party*, Center Stage, Baltimore; *Knight of the Burning Pestle*, Long Wharf. (Regional Theatre) *The Good Woman of Setzuan; Endgame; He Who Gets Slapped; Man Is Man; The Zoo Story; Escurial; The Fantastics; The Threepenny Opera; Oh Dad, Poor Dad . . . ; Anatol; Benito Cereno*, et al. (Television) Irish Triple Bill, *Calvary Act, Act without Words, How She Lied to Her Husband*, Esso Theatre U.S.A., 1963.

PRODUCED: Center for the Arts, Purchase, NY—*The Queen and the Rebels* (moved to New York); *Man Is Man; Dario Fo Plays* (moved to New York); *The Ruling Class; Sally and Marsha* (moved to New York); *Booth Is Back in Town; Mrs. Farmer's Daughter; Shakespeare and the Indians*. Regional Theatre—Over 200 plays, including *The Cavern, Sodome et Gomorrhe, Eh?*, and *Honor and Offer*.

WRITINGS: PLAYS, PRODUCED—*Knight of the Burning Pestle*, Long Wharf, New Haven, CT.

THEATRE-RELATED CAREER: Adjunct professor, Conservatory of Music, Cincinnati, 1965–71; president, ViceVersaVision (television production), 1978–83.

SIDELIGHTS: MEMBERSHIPS—ANTA (board, 1964), Third World Board, ITI, ASCAP, TCG board, American Federation of Musicians, National Theatre Conference, AEA.

ADDRESS: Home—142 Goodwives Road, Noroton, CT 06820. Office—ViceVersaVision, Box 3239, Noroton, CT 06820.

* * *

JONES, L. Q. (ne Justice Ellis McQueen), actor, writer, director, producer

PERSONAL: Born August 19, 1927; son of Justice Ellis (a railroad worker) and Jessie Paralee (Stephens) McQueen;

married Neta Sue Lewis October 8, 1950 (divorced 1979); children: Marlin, Marily, Stephen. EDUCATION: Lamar Junior College (Beaumont, TX), 1944; Lon Morris Junior College (Jacksonville, TX), 1946; University of Texas, 1947–50. POLITICS: Republican. RELIGION: Methodist. MILITARY: U.S. Navy, Lt. Commander, 1945.

CAREER: FILM DEBUT—L.Q. Jones, *Battle Cry*, 1954. PRINCIPAL FILM APPEARANCES—*Love Me Tender*, 1956; *Between Heaven and Hell*, 1956; *The Naked and the Dead*, 1958; *The Young Lions*, 1958; *The Wild Bunch; Warlock*, 1959; *Ride the High Country*, 1962; *Ballad of Cable Hogue*, 1970; *White Line Fever*, 1975; *Time Rider; Lone Wolf McQuade*, 1983; has appeared in over 75 other films.

TELEVISION DEBUT—*Cheyenne*. PRINCIPAL TELEVISION APPEARANCES—*Playhouse 90; Charlie's Angels; Cannon; Voyagers; Yellow Roses; Chips; Standing Tall;* and over 500 other TV shows.

WRITINGS: NOVELS—*Brotherhood of Satan*. SCRIPT—*A Boy and His Dog*.

AWARDS: Hugo Award, 34th World Science Fiction Convention—Mid American, 1976: *A Boy and His Dog;* three Emmy Nominations; Cowboy Hall.

SIDELIGHTS: MEMBERSHIPS—SAG, Directors Guild, Writers Guild of America, West.

''I love the business. 'Nough said.''

ADDRESS: Office—2144 N. Cahuenga, Hollywood, CA 90068. Agent—Mike Greenfield, Charter Management, 9000 Sunset Blvd., Suite 1112, Los Angeles, CA 90069.

* * *

JONES, Tommy Lee, actor

PERSONAL: Born September 15, 1946 in San Saba, TX; son of Clyde L. and Lucille Marie (Scott) Jones; married Kimberlea Gayle Cloughley (a photojournalist), May 30, 1981; children: Austin Leonard. EDUCATION: Harvard University, B.A. (English), 1969.

CAREER: DEBUT—Harvard Drama Club, 1965–1969. NEW YORK DEBUT—Chorus, *A Patriot for Me*, 1970. PRINCIPAL STAGE APPEARANCES—*Four on a Garden; Ulysses in Nighttown; Fortune and Men's Eyes*.

FILM DEBUT—*Love Story*, 1970. PRINCIPAL FILM APPEARANCES—*Jackson County Jail; Rolling Thunder*, 1977; *The Betsy*, 1978; *Eyes of Laura Mars*, 1978; *Coalminer's Daughter*, 1980; *Black Roads*, 1981. PRINCIPAL TELEVISION APPEARANCES—*The Amazing Howard Hughes*, 1982.

AWARDS: Emmy Award, Prime Time Outstanding Lead Actor in a Special, 1983: *The Amazing Howard Hughes*.

SIDELIGHTS: MEMBERSHIPS—SAG, AEA, AFTRA, Academy of Television Arts and Sciences.

JOSELOVITZ, Ernest A. playwright

PERSONAL: Born June 18, 1942 in Danbury, CT; son of Sydney and Minnie (Kayser) Joselovitz; married Elaine Sharon Zvonkin (works in film) on September 26, 1967. EDUCATION: UCLA, B.A. (English); University of Minnesota, M.F.A..

WRITINGS: PLAYS, PRODUCED—*Parable,* (one-act) Greyfriars' Society Theatre, Pasadena, CA, 1971; *The Inheritance,* University of Minnesota, 1973; *Hagar's Children,* American Conservatory, San Francisco, CA, 1975, Changing Scene, Denver, CO, 1975, New Playwrights, Washington, DC, 1976, New York Shakespeare Festival, Public, NY, for 80 performances, 1977; *The Bubble,* (one-act) One-Act Theatre of San Francisco, 1977–78; *Sammi & Triptych,* (one-acts) Jewish Repertory, NY, 1978; *Splendid Rebels,* New Playwrights, Washington, DC, 1978–79, Corner, Baltimore, MD, 1980, Theatre Three, Dallas, TX, 1982; *Holding On,* New Playwrights, Washington, DC, 1980; *There Is No John Garfield* (one-act), Dubuque Fine Arts Society, IA, 1982; *Jesse's Land,* New Playwrights, Washington, 1982; *Flesh Eaters,* New Playwrights, Washington, 1983.

PLAYS, PUBLISHED—*Sammi,* 1975; *The Inheritance,* 1975; *Hagar's Children,* 1977; *Righting,* 1977.

THEATRE-RELATED CAREER: Playwright in Residence, New Playwrights, Washington DC, 1978–81; Dramaturg/Literary Advisor, New Playwrights, Washington, DC, 1981–present; Playwrighting Instructor, New Playwrights, George Mason University 1979–81.

AWARD: Larry Neal Writer's Award, Drama, Washington, DC, 1983; Artist-in-Education Grant, D.C. Commission for the Arts and Humanities, 1982–83; Playwright Project Grants, D.C. Commission for the Arts and Humanities, 1980–83; Guest Artist, Millay Colony for the Arts, NY, and Dorset Colony, VT, 1981–83; Individual Writer's Grant, National Endowment for the Arts/Literature, 1980; Theatre Communications Group Travel/Residency Grants; Rockefeller Foundation Grant, Office of Advanced Drama Research; Starr Playwrighting Prize, University of California, Santa Barbara; Dubuque National One-Act Competition Prize; Shubert Playwriting Fellowship, University of Minnesota; John Golden Travelling Fellowship; Phi Beta Kappa.

ADDRESS: Home—1717 Riggs Place N.W. #2, Washington, DC 20009. Office—1742 Church Street, c/o New Playwrights Theatre, Washington, DC 20036. Agent—Freedman, Brandt & Brandt, 1501 Broadway, Suite 3201, New York, NY 10036.

* * *

JOSLYN, Betsy, actress

PERSONAL: Born April 19, 1954; daughter of Frederic M. (a sales manager) and Marielouise (a teacher; maiden name, Sidnam) Joslyn. EDUCATION: Wagner College, M.A., 1975.

CAREER: DEBUT—Kitty, *Where's Charley?,* Heinz Hall, Pittsburgh, PA, 1975. NEW YORK DEBUT—Luisa, *The Fantasticks,* Sullivan Street Playhouse, 1975. PRINCIPAL STAGE

APPEARANCES—Johanna, *Sweeney Todd,* Uris, NY, 1980; Nora, *A Doll's Life,* Mark Hellinger, NY, 1982; Maria, *West Side Story,* Zurich Opernhaus, Zurich, Switzerland, 1983. MAJOR TOURS—Johanna, *Sweeney Todd,* U.S. cities, 1980–81.

PRINCIPAL TELEVISION APPEARANCES—Merv Griffin Show.

SIDELIGHTS: MEMBERSHIPS—AEA, SAG, AFTRA.

ADDRESS: Agent—c/o Baldwin-Scully, 501 Fifth Avenue, New York, NY 10019.

* * *

JULIA, Raul, actor

PERSONAL: Born March 9, 1940, in San Juan, PR; son of Raul (a restaurateur) and Olga (Arcelay) Julia; married Merel Poloway (a dancer), June 28, 1976. EDUCATION: University of Puerto Rico; studied for theatre with Wynn Handman. NON-THEATRICAL CAREER: Member of Puerto Rican singing group, "The Lamplighters," in Puerto Rico.

CAREER: NEW YORK DEBUT—Astolfo, *La Vida Es Sueno,* acting in Spanish, Astor Play Playhouse, 1964. PRINCIPAL STAGE APPEARANCES—Birdie, *Bye, Bye Birdie, The Four Poster,* Alfred, *The Happy Time,* title role, *Macbeth,* Rodrigo, *Othello,* Tapia, San Juan, PR, 1963; the suitor, *The Marriage Proposal,* 1966; Macduff, *Macbeth,* New York Shakespeare Festival, Delacorte, 1966; Luis, *The Ox Cart,* Greenwich Mews, NY, 1966; Demetrius, *Titus Andronicus,* Delacorte, NY, 1967; Cradeau, *No Exit,* Bouwerie Lane, NY, 1967; Birdie, *Bye Bye Birdie,* Dallas, 1967; *A Clerk in the Memorandum,* Anspacher, 1968; *The Hide and Seek Odyssey of Madelain Gimple,* O'Neill Theatre Center, CT, 1968; Orson (took over) *Your Own Thing,* Orpheum, NY, 1968; Chan, *The Cuban Thing,* Henry Miller's, NY, 1968; Workman, *Paradise Gardens East* and Jesus, *Conrico Was Here to Stay,* (double bill, *Frank Gagliano's City Scene*), Fortune, 1969; Grand Duke Alexis, Uncas, *Indians,* Arena Stage, Washington, DC, 1969 and then Brooks Atkinson, NY, 1969;

Persian Elder, *The Persians,* St. George's Church, NY, 1970; Paco Montoya, *The Castro Complex,* Stairway, NY, 1970; Consequently Joy, *Pinkville,* St. Clement's Church, NY, 1971; Proteus, *Two Gentemen of Verona* (musical), New York Shakespeare Festival, Delacorte, later St. James, NY, 1971; Osric, *Hamlet,* Delacorte, 1972; Gabriel Finn, *Via Galactica,* Uris, NY, 1972; Orlando, *As You Like It,* Edmund, *King Lear,* Delacorte, 1973; Commissioner, *The Emperor of Late Night Radio,* Other Stage, NY, 1974; Jaimie Lockhart, *The Robber Bridegroom,* St. Clement's Church, NY, 1974; Charles Wykeham, *Where's Charley?,* Circle in the Square, NY, 1974; Mack the Knife, *The Threepenny Opera,* Vivian Beaumont, NY, 1976; Lopatkin, *The Cherry Orchard,* Vivian Beaumont, NY, 1977; title role, *Dracula,* Baltimore, 1978, then took over at Martin Beck, NY, 1979; Petruchio, *The Taming of the Shrew,* Delacorte, NY, 1978; title role, *Othello,* Delacorte, 1979; *Betrayal,* Trafalgar, NY, 1980; Guido Contini, *Nine,* 46th Street Theatre, NY, 1982; *Design for Living,* Circle in the Square, NY, 1984. MAJOR TOURS—*Illya, Darling,* 1968.

FILM APPEARANCES—*Panic in Needle Park*, 1971; *The Organization Man*, 1971; *Been Down So Long It Looks Like Up to Me*, 1971; *Gumball Rally*, 1976; *The Eyes of Laura Mars*, 1978; Kalibanos, *Tempest*, 1980; *The Escape Artist*, 1982; *One from the Heart*, 1982.

TELEVISION APPEARANCES—(Running role), *Sesame Street*; *King Lear*; *The National Health*; *McCloud* (TV film); *Love of Life*; *Aces Up*, 1974; *Death Scream*, 1975.

AWARDS: Antoinette Perry Award Nominations, 1982: *Nine*, 1976: *The Threepenny Opera*, 1974: *Where's Charley?*, 1971: *Two Gentlemen of Verona.**

K

KAIKKONEN, Gus, actor, director, writer

PERSONAL: Born May 7, 1951; son of Gus Alexander (a millwright) and Eva Mary (a demonstrator; maiden name Caradonna) Kaikkonen. EDUCATION: Georgetown University, 1969–73. POLITICS: Democrat.

CAREER: DEBUT—Chorus, *Babes in Toyland*, Cobo Hall, Detroit, MI, 1964. NEW YORK DEBUT—Horse, *Equus*, Plymouth, 1976. PRINCIPAL STAGE APPEARANCES—Griffith, *Henry VIII*, Captain, *King Lear*, Lysimachus, *Pericles*, Horatio, *Hamlet*, Colorado Shakespeare Festival; Hobhouse, *Natural and Unnatural Acts*, Antonio, *Twelfth Night*, Benvolio, *Romeo and Juliet*, Folger Theatre, Washington, DC; Fast Eddie, *Senior Prom*, Washington Theatre Club; ensemble, *Scenes from American Life*, Richard, *Chinese Viewing Pavilion*, Frederick Treaves, *The Elephant Man*, Boarshead Theatre; Amos, *The Runner Stumbles*, Damis, *Tartuffe*, Jimmy Porter, *Look Back in Anger*, Cohoes Music Hall; Mark, *The Shadow Box*, Richie, *Streamers*, Cassio, *Othello*, Players State; Don Carlos, *Don Juan*, Benito, *Benito Cereno*, Goodman Theatre, Chicago; Brissailles, *Cyrano de Bergerac*, Long Wharf, New Haven, CT, chorus, *Dionysus Wants You!*, James Lee, *Private Hicks*, New York Shakespeare Festival Public Theatre; Lysander, *A Midsummer Night's Dream*, Gene Frankel Theatre, New York; Estragon, *Waiting for Godot*, Westend, New York; Surgeon, *Female Transport*, Performing Garage, New York; Prince, *Breakfast at Schlankenwald*, St. Luke's—YMHA, New York; Mark, *Casualties*, St. Clement's, New York; Joshua/Kathy, *Cloud 9*, Lucille Lortel, New York, 1983.

PRINCIPAL FILMS—Pogo, *Next Stop Greenwich Village;* Young Bear, *Touch the Earth.* TELEVISION DEBUT—Charlie Edwards, *Paul's Case*, 1980. TELEVISION APPEARANCES—Carlo, *Big Blue Marble;* Johnny, *Death Be Not Proud;* Sebastian, *Twelfth Night.*

DIRECTED—Assistant to director, *The Rise and Fall of the City Mahagonny*, *The Rake's Progress*, *Cosi Fan Tutte*, *Poppea*, Washington Opera Society, 1972–73; directed and adapted, *The Massacre at Paris*, Folger Theatre Group, Washington, DC, 1972; directed, *Love's Labour's Lost*, Greenwich Mews, New York, 1974; *Ivanov*, City Playworks at ETC, New York, 1975; *Brontosaurus Tales*, Cohoes Music Hall, Cohoes, New York, 1980; *Holy Mary, The Palace of Amateurs*, Playwrights Horizons, 1980; *The Chinese Viewing Pavilion*, Playwrights Horizons, 1980; *Letters from Bernice*, Boarshead, Lansing, MI, 1981; *Fridays*, Boarshead, 1981; *The Promise*, Northlight Repertory, Evanston, IL, 1982; *Eulogy*, Off-Off Television on Manhattan Cable, New York, 1982; *Mass Appeal*, Geva, Rochester,

New York, 1982; *Second Prize: Two Months in Leningrad*, Perry Street, New York, 1983

WRITINGS: PLAYS, ADAPTATIONS—Christopher Marlowe's *Massacre at Paris*. PLAYS, ONE-ACT—*What Are Friends For?*, *Potholes*, *Eulogy*. PLAYS, FULL-LENGTH—*Ramblings*, *Brontosaurus Tales*, *Time Steps*, *Fool of Hearts*, *The Chinese Viewing Pavilion*. SCREENPLAYS—*Present Losses*.

AWARDS: leCompte du Novy Award for Playwrighting, 1981; CAPS Award for Playwrighting, 1977; Theatre Critics Association award for *Time Steps* as one of the ten best plays to open outside New York City, 1979.

SIDELIGHTS: MEMBERSHIPS—AEA.

ADDRESS: Home—124 MacDougal Street, New York, NY 10012. Office—c/o Dale Davis, 1650 Broadway, New York, NY 10019. Agent—Esther Sherman, William Morris, 1350 Avenue of the Americas, New York, NY 10019.

* * *

KALCHEIM, Lee, playwright

PERSONAL: Born June 27, 1938, in Philadelphia, PA; son of Norman (a lawyer) and Beatrice (Berger) Kalcheim. EDUCATION: Trinity College, Hartford, CT, B.A., 1960; Yale Drama School, 1961–62.

WRITINGS: PLAYS, PRODUCED—*A Party for Divorce; Match Play*, 1967; *The Boy Who Came to Leave*, 1973; *The Prague Spring*, 1977; *Win with Wheeler*, 1976–78; *Breakfast with Les and Bess*, 1983; "*Friends*", 1983.

AWARDS: Emmy Award, Best Comedy Writing, *All in the Family*, 1973; Writers Guild Award, Best Children's Program, ABC After School Special 1978 Christopher Award.

ADDRESS: Office—38 W. Ninth Street, New York, NY 10012; Agent—Jeannine Edwards, J. Michael Bloom, Inc., 400 Madison Avenue, New York, NY 10017.

* * *

KANIN, Michael, writer and producer

PERSONAL: Born February 1, 1910, in Rochester, NY;

married Fay Kanin (a writer); children: Josh. EDUCATION: Art Students League; New York School of Design. EARLY CAREER: Worked as a commercial and scenic artist, musician, and entertainer before becoming a writer.

WRITINGS: PLAYS, PUBLISHED—*His and Hers* (with Fay Kanin); *Rashomon* (with Fay Kanin); *The Gay Life* (with Fay Kanin). FILMS—*They Made Her a Spy; Panama Lady; Anne of Windy Poplars; Woman of the Year* (with Ring Lardner, Jr.); *The Cross of Lorraine* (with Ring Lardner, Jr.); *Centennial Summer; Honeymoon; When I Grow Up; Sunday Punch* (with Fay Kanin); *My Pal Gus* (with Fay Kanin); *The Right Approach* (with Fay Kanin); *Rhapsody* (with Fay Kanin); *The Swordsman of Sienna* (with Fay Kanin); *The Opposite Sex* (with Fay Kanin); *Teacher's Pet* (with Fay Kanin); *The Outrage; How to Commit Marriage* (with Benn Starr).

CAREER: PRODUCED: PLAYS—*Goodbye My Fancy*, New York (with Aldrich and Myers); *Seidman and Son*, New York (with the Theatre Guild). FILMS—*A Double Life*.

DIRECTED: FILMS—*When I Grow Up*.

AWARDS: Academy Award, Best Original Screenplay, 1942: *Woman of the Year;* Academy Award Nomination, 1958: *Teacher's Pet;* Writers Guild Award Nomination, 1958: *Teacher's Pet.* Playwriting Awards Plaque, Amoco Silver Medallion, Los Angeles Film Critics Award, and citation from the city of Los Angeles for originating national Playwriting Awards program.

SIDELIGHTS: MEMBERSHIPS—Writers Guild (Board Member, 1943–44; Treasurer, 1944–45), Dramatists Guild, American National Theatre and Academy, American Theater Association, American College Theatre Festival, Academy of Motion Picture Arts and Sciences, International Sculpture Center. RECREATION—Painting, sculpture, music.

* * *

KARRAS, Alex, actor

PERSONAL: Born July 13, 1935, in Gary, IN; married Susan Clark. EDUCATION: Attended Iowa University.

CAREER: PRINCIPAL FILM APPEARANCES—*Nobody's Perfect*, 1968; *Blazing Saddles*, 1974; *Another Day at the Races; Jacob Two-Two Meets the Hooded Fang; Win, Place or Steal*, 1977; *FM*, 1978; *Victor/Victoria*, 1982.

PRINCIPAL TELEVISION APPEARANCES—(movies) *Mulligan Stew*, 1977; *When Time Ran Out*, 1980; *Hardcase; The 500-Pound Jerk; Babe; Mad Bull; Centennial.* Special—host, *NFL Preview*.

SIDELIGHTS: Mr. Karras is a former professional football player with the National Football League's Detroit Lions.

ADDRESS: Office—c/o Press Relations, Warner Brothers, 4000 Warner Blvd., Burbank, CA 91522.*

KASS, Jerome, writer

PERSONAL: Born April 21, 1937, in Chicago, IL; son of Sidney J. and Celia (Gorman) Kass; married Artha F. Schwartz, August 6, 1961; married Delia Ephron, May 21, 1982; children: Julie, Adam. EDUCATION: New York University, A.B., A.M., 1954–59; Brandeis University, postgraduate work, 1959–61; studied playwriting with Herbert Berghof.

WRITINGS: PLAYS, PUBLISHED—*Monopoly* (four short plays), 1965; *Saturday Night*, 1967; *Ballroom*, 1978. FILMS—*The Black Stallion Returns*, 1983. TELEVISION FILMS—*A Brand New Life*, 1973; *Queen of the Stardust Ballroom*, 1975; *My Old Man*, 1978; *The Fighter*, 1983.

THEATRE-RELATED CAREER: Formerly an instructor of English at Queens College, New York (1962–64) and Brandeis University, New York (1959–61). Has taught screenwriting at the American Film Institute since 1983.

AWARD: Writers Guild of America, Best Original Teleplay, 1975: *Queen of the Stardust Ballroom;* Emmy Nomination, 1975: *Queen of the Stardust Ballroom;* Antoinette Perry Nomination, Best Book for a Musical, *Ballroom:* 1978.

SIDELIGHTS: MEMBERSHIPS—Writers Guild of America, Dramatists Guild, Authors League, Academy of Television Arts and Sciences. Phi Beta Kappa.

''From 1962 to 1965, I was a student in a playwriting seminar presided over by Herbert Berghof at the HB Studio in New York. Each student was required each week to write a two-character one-act play of about ten pages. The plays would be read at each of our weekly meetings by actors from scene-study classes at the Studio. Each play was then criticized by anyone who had something to say. We'd then take the plays home and rework them. The plays were then made available to acting students at the Studio. The playwright was notified when a play of his (or hers) was to be performed. He'd see the play done and he'd have another opportunity to rework it. I saw some of my plays done dozens of times by different actors. In some cases, I'd rework a play every time I saw it done. This was how I learned the craft of playwriting. It was the most valuable education of my professional life.''

ADDRESS: c/o Robinson-Luttrell and Associates, 141 El Camino Drive, Beverly Hills, CA 90210.

* * *

KASSIN, Michael B., actor, director, writer

PERSONAL: Born September 10, 1947, in Chicago, IL; son of Irving O. (an accountant) and Shirley R. (an opera singer) Kassin. EDUCATION: University of Minnesota, B.A., 1969, M.A., 1978. MILITARY: U.S. Army Reserve, SSG. RELIGION: Jewish. NON-THEATRICAL CAREER—Taught high school in Illinois and Minnesota for six years befor returning, in 1974, to work for his M.A.

CAREER: As an actor, he has appeared at the Guthrie,

Minneapolis, the Guthrie Two, the Mixed Blood Theatre and the Richard Allen Center, NY.

WRITINGS: PLAYS, PRODUCED—*No Mourning After Dark,* Centre Stage, Minneapolis, 1975; *Brother Champ,* Mixed Blood Theatre, Minneapolis, 1976, Shirtsleeve, NY, 1978; *Sophie and Willa,* Center Stage, Baltimore, 1980; *Today a Little Extra,* Actors Theatre of Louisville, 1980. TELEVISION SCRIPTS—*Great Stone Balloon,* PBS. REVIEWS—for Minneapolis *Star,* Minnesota *Daily.* ARTICLES—*Dramatists Guild Quarterly.* PLAYS, PUBLISHED—*Today a Little Extra* in *Best Short Plays of '82.*

AWARDS: Guthrie Theatre Award; Minnesota Playwrights Lab, Grant; Oscar Firkins Scholarship; commissions from Actors Theatre of Louisville and Cricket Theatre, Minneapolis.

SIDELIGHTS: MEMBERSHIPS—Dramatists Guild.

''I write for people who don't go to the theatre and I believe in the triumph over the impossible. I believe that if I reach out to them, with all my heart, they'll reach back.''

ADDRESS: Home—776 Bronx River Road, Bronxville, NY 10708. Agent—Robert Freedman, Brandt and Brandt, Suite 2310, 1501 Broadway, New York, NY 10036.

* * *

JUDY KAYE

KAYDEN, William, producer and writer

PERSONAL: Born December 31, 1929, in New York City; son of Philip and Anna (Nadler) Kayden; children: Philip, John, Matthew. EDUCATION: University of Southern California, B.A. MILITARY: U.S. Marine Corps Reserve.

CAREER: PRODUCED: TELEVISION SCREENPLAYS—*Missing Children: A Mother's Story; Crazy Times; To Race the Wind; Lady of the House; Cops and Robin; Computercide; Yesterday's Child; The Family Nobody Wanted; I Heard the Owl Call My Name; Dead Men Tell No Tales; Daughter of the Mind.* TELEVISION DRAMATIC SERIES—*Matt Lincoln; Felony Squad; Boy and the Bear.* TELEVISION DAYTIME SERIES—*Here's Hollywood; On the Go.* TELEVISION SPECIALS—*Bicentennial Minutes; Hawaii-Ho; Turn On;* numerous *Annual Emmy Awards* presentations; numerous *Annual Academy Awards* presentations; *Operation Entertainment; World Championship Rodeo.*

WRITINGS: TELEVISION DRAMATIC SERIES—*Matt Lincoln; Felony Squad; Boy and the Bear.* TELEVISION DAYTIME SERIES—*Here's Hollywood; On the Go.*

SIDELIGHTS: MEMBERSHIPS—Writers Guild of America West, Producers Guild of America.

ADDRESS: Office—W K Productions, Inc., 999 N. Doheny Drive, Los Angeles, CA 90069.

KAYE, Judy, actress

PERSONAL: Born December 11, 1948; daughter of Jerome Joseph (a physician) and Shirley Edith (Silverman) Kaye. EDUCATION: Attended University of California at Los Angeles. POLITICS: Independent. RELIGION: Jewish.

CAREER: DEBUT—chorus, season, Melodyland, Anaheim, CA, 1967. NEW YORK DEBUT—Rizzo, *Grease,* Royale, 1977, 72 performances. PRINCIPAL STAGE APPEARANCES—(Broadway) Lily Garland, *On the Twentieth Century,* St. James, 1978; principal, *Moony Shapiro Songbook,* Morosco, 1980; Saroyana, *Oh Brother!,* Majestic, 1980; (Regional) Dorothy, *Wizard of Oz,* Arizona State University; Barbara, *Apple Tree,* Los Angeles; Henny, *Awake and Sing,* Los Angeles; Flor, *Half a Sixpence,* Martha, *1776,* Civic Light Opera; Sheila, *Hair,* Sacramento Music Circus; Agnes, *I Do, I Do,* Dallas Civic Opera; Leah, *The Dybbuk,* Arizona Civic Theatre; Kate, *Kiss Me Kate,* Cleveland Opera; Maria, *Sound of Music,* Cincinnati Opera; Julie Jordan, *Carousel,* Candlelight Dinner Theatre; Pistache, *Can-Can,* St. Louis MUNY Opera.

MAJOR TOURS—Hodel, *Fiddler on the Roof,* Los Angeles Civic Light Opera; Judy, *Godspell,* U.S. cities; Lucy, *You're A Good Man Charlie Brown,* U.S. cities, 1968; Mary Magdalene, *Jesus Christ Superstar,* U.S. cities, 1972; Betty Rizzo, *Grease,* U.S. cities, 1973; Lilly Garland, *On the Twentieth Century,* U.S. cities, 1979.

FILM DEBUT—Baby, *Just Tell Me What You Want,* 1980.

TELEVISION DEBUT—running role, *Mr. Deeds Goes to Town,* 1969. PRINCIPAL TELEVISION APPEARANCES—*The Doctors; Today Show; Merv Griffin Show; Gift of the Magi; Insight; Donald O'Connor Show; Matt Lincoln; Arte Johnson Special; Fol-De-Rol; This Week in Nemtin; The Songwriters.*

AWARDS: Theater World Award, Los Angeles Drama Critic's Circle Award, Drama Desk Nomination: *On the Twentieth Century;* Natalie Wood Award (U.C.L.A.), 1969; Frank Sinatra Award (U.C.L.A.), 1968.

SIDELIGHTS: RECREATION—golf, tennis.

ADDRESS: Agent—c/o Bret Adams, Ltd., 448 W. 48th Street, New York, NY 10036.

* * *

KEAGY, Grace, actress, singer

PERSONAL: Surname pronounced "KAY-ghee, hard 'g';" born December 16 in Youngstown, OH; daughter of David Henry (a salesman) and Clarice (a singer and pianist; maiden name, Sparrow) Stambaugh; married Hector Bethart on December 18, 1943 (divorced 1949); married Robert B. Keagy (an electrical engineer) on June 23, 1950; children: Katherine, Michael, Elizabeth, Claudia, David. EDUCATION: New England Conservatory of Music, five years; associate fellow, Morse College, Yale University, ten years; studied opera acting with Boris Goldovsky at the Minnesota Opera Company. POLITICS: "Democrat—(mostly)." RELIGION: Protestant.

CAREER: DEBUT—Dame Margery, *Shoemakers Holiday,* Guthrie, Minneapolis, MN, 1967. NEW YORK DEBUT—Queen Isabella, *Goodtime Charley,* Palace, for 120 performances, 1975. PRINCIPAL STAGE APPEARANCES: (Broadway)—Madame Bouffier, *The Grand Tour,* Palace, 1979; Rosa, *Carmelina,* St. James, 1979; Aunt Jenny, *I Remember Mama,* Majestic, 1979; Roberta, *Musical Chairs,* Rialto, 1980; Helga, *Woman of the Year,* Palace, 1983. (Regional)—Frau Schill, *The Visit,* Guthrie, Minneapolis, MN, 1967; Mrs. Huffmaster, *Harper's Ferry,* Guthrie, 1967; Leocadia Begbick, *The Rise and Fall of the City of Mahagonny,* Yale Repertory, New Haven, CT, 1974; Meme, *Saturday, Sunday, Monday,* Arena Stage Washington, DC, 1976; Mrs. Peachum, *The Threepenny Opera,* Cincinnati Playhouse in the Park, 1977; Grand Duchess, *The Student Prince,* Papermill Playhouse, NJ, 1979; Makina, *The Caucasian Chalk Circle,* Denver Center Theatre Company, CO, 1979–80; Philaminthe, *The Learned Ladies,* Denver Center Theatre Company, 1979–80; Lady Bountiful, *The Beaux Stratagem,* Hartford Stage Company, CT, 1980; Mrs. Hill, *Booth Is Back in Town,* SUNY, Purchase, NY, 1983. MAJOR TOURS—Aunt Eller, *Oklahoma,* national tour, 1979.

PRINCIPAL TELEVISION APPEARANCES—*As the World Turns; One Life to Live; The Doctors; Ryan's Hope; Search for Tomorrow.*

THEATRE-RELATED CAREER—Taught piano and voice, Minneapolis, MN, 1964–68.

AWARDS: Drama Desk Award Nomination: Rosa, *Carmelina,* 1979.

GRACE KEAGY

SIDELIGHTS: "After a full life of opera, concert work, marriage, five children, travels all over the world with a career Army husband, at the age of forty-plus, I fell into the theatre, a dream nurtured since early childhood. A few years to learn my craft in Minnesota and then an all-or-nothing try in New York. I owe it all to the Equity Library Theatre, which gave me my big break as Sally Adams in *Call Me Madam.* To my everlasting joy, it has been constant work and many rewards. Many TV commercials afford me the chance to sometimes take a role for "art's sake" like the Nurse in *Romeo and Juliet.* Where else but in New York can one fulfill all of her dreams? I look forward to many more roles and shall always be grateful for the opportunities accorded me to pursue my acting career with such positive and rewarding stimulation."

ADDRESS: Home—70 Riverside Drive, New York, NY 10024. Agent—Hesseltine, Baker Associates Ltd., 165 W. 46th Street, Suite 409, New York, NY 10036.

* * *

KEAN, Jane, actress and singer

PERSONAL: Born April 10, 1928, in New York, NY; daughter of Robert (an insurance executive) and Helen (Hansen) Kean; married Richard Linkroum, 1962 (divorced 1970); married Joe Hecht (a personal manager and actor), March 21, 1970. EDUCATION: Attended New York City public schools; trained for the stage with Sandy Meisner at the Neighborhood Playhouse.

CAREER: DEBUT—*Hi Ya, Gentlemen*, Colonial Theater, Boston. NEW YORK DEBUT—*Early to Bed*, Broadhurst, 1943. LONDON DEBUT—*Betty and Jane Kean* (vaudeville act), Palladium, 1956. PRINCIPAL STAGE APPEARANCES—*Pajama Game*, New York; *Call Me Mister*, New York; *Will Success Spoil Rock Hunter?*, New York; *Ankles Aweigh*, New York; *Mind with the Dirty Man*, Las Vegas; *Last of the Red Hot Lovers*, Las Vegas. MAJOR TOURS—*Mind with the Dirty Man*, Australia; *Follies; Light Up the Sky*.

FILM DEBUT—*Pete's Dragon*, 1976. TELEVISION DEBUT—*The Ed Sullivan Show*, 1948. TELEVISION APPEARANCES—*Days of Our Lives;* Trixie, *The Jackie Gleason Show; The Dean Martin Show; Cannon; Love, American Style.*

SIDELIGHTS: MEMBERSHIPS—AFTRA, SAG, AEA.

ADDRESS: Agent—c/o Diane Davis, 13273 Ventura Blvd., Studio City, CA 91604.

* * *

KEATON, Diane, actress

PERSONAL: Born 1949, in Santa Ana, CA. EDUCATION: Attended Santa Ana College; trained for the stage at the Neighborhood Playhouse.

CAREER: NEW YORK STAGE DEBUT—*Hair*, 1968 PRINCIPAL STAGE APPEARANCES—*Play It Again Sam*, 1971; *The Primary English Class*, 1976. PRINCIPAL FILM APPEARANCES—*Lovers and Other Strangers*, 1970; *Play It Again Sam*, 1972; *The Godfather*, 1972; *Sleeper*, 1973; *The Godfather, Part II*, 1974; *Love and Death*, 1975; *I Will I Will, For Now*, 1975; *Harry and Walter Go to New York*, 1976; *Annie Hall*, 1977; *Looking for Mr. Goodbar*, 1977; *Interiors*, 1978; *Manhattan*, 1979; *Reds*, 1981; *Shoot the Moon*, 1982.

WRITINGS: BOOKS—*Reservations* (photographs), 1980.

AWARDS: Golden Globe Award, 1978; Academy Award, Best Actress, British Academy Award, Best Actress, New York Film Critics Circle Award, National Society of Film Critics Award, 1977: *Annie Hall*.

SIDELIGHTS: Ms. Keaton is an accomplished artist and singer.

ADDRESS: Office—c/o Arlyne Rothberg, Inc., 145 Central Park W., New York, NY 10023.*

* * *

KEITH, Paul, actor, singer, and dancer

PERSONAL: Born June 1, 1944, in Chicago, IL; son of Aron (a tailor) and Ruth (Levin) Keith. EDUCATION: University of California at Los Angeles, B.A.; trained for the stage with Uta Hagen, Maria Gobett, and Amelia Haas. NON-THEATRICAL CAREER: Drama teacher, Fairfax High School, Los Angeles, CA, 1966–67.

PAUL KEITH

CAREER: DEBUT—Santa Claus, *Santa Wants New Boots*, Ardmore Playground, Los Angeles, CA. NEW YORK DEBUT—Standby, *Unfair to Goliath*, Cherry Lane, 1972. PRINCIPAL STAGE APPEARANCES—Standby, *Look Me Up*, Cherry Lane, NY, 1971; Detective Christopher, *Private Ear and Public Eye*, Warwick Playhouse, NY, 1971; Buzz, *Applause*, Pittsburgh Civic Light Opera, 1972; Bottom, *Midsummer Night's Dream*, Caesar, *Julius Caesar*, Northshore Theater, MA, 1973; gangster, *Kiss Me Kate*, Marcellus, *Music Man*, Pittsburgh Civic Light Opera, 1973; Uncle Jimmy, *No No Nanette*, Northshore, MA, 1973; lead, *Look Me Up*, Plaza, NY, 1973; Harry Berlin, *Luv*, Arena Stage, WV, 1974; Wilson, *Harvey*, Meadowbrook Dinner Theater, NJ, 1974; Jemmy, *Beggar's Opera*, McAlpin Rooftop, NY, 1974; Hysterium, *Funny Thing Happened on the Way to the Forum*, Westbury Music Fair, NY, 1974; lead, *Mixed Nuts*, Coronet, Los Angeles, CA, 1980; Frank, *Showboat*, Gershwin, NY, 1983.

MAJOR TOURS—Feldman, *Magic Show*, U.S. cities, 1975; Cornellius, *Hello, Dolly!*, East Coast cities, 1976; Ali Hakim, *Oklahoma*, West Coast cities, 1978; Frank, *Showboat*, U.S. cities, 1983.

FILM DEBUT—Paul, *Funny Girl*, 1966. PRINCIPAL FILM APPEARANCES—Joe, *Happy Hooker Goes to Hollywood*, 1978; photographer, *Frances*, 1981; Hal, *Last American Virgin*, 1981.

TELEVISION DEBUT—1st Lieutenant, *The Loner*, 1967. PRINCIPAL TELEVISION APPEARANCES—*The Fourth Network; Alice; Foul Play; Alan King Special;* Prince Edward, *The Perfect Woman;* Mr. Gompers, *Chips;* Headwaiter, *Steve*

Martin Special; Paul Lasky, *Sirota's Court;* Mr. Elkins, *Side by Side;* Bill Morison, *General Hospital;* Jacob, *Gift of the Magi;* Jerry Financio, *Maude.*

SIDELIGHTS: MEMBERSHIPS—AEA, SAG, AFTRA. RECREATION—Reading, collecting musical comedy albums.

"Striving is at the heart of an actor's craft. Constant study of acting, voice, speech, dance, and watching people are the essential tools of an artist. Also, one must constantly participate in the process of living."

ADDRESS: Agent—c/o I.C.M., 40 W. 57th Street, New York, NY 10019.

* * *

KELLY, Brian, actor and dancer

PERSONAL: Born November 2, 1956, in Chicago, IL; son of John T. (an accountant) and Reta C. (a travel agent, maiden name, Streeff) Kelly; married Terri Lees, December 7, 1981. EDUCATION: Attended University of Illinois and the National Academy of Arts; trained for the stage with Ruth Page and Larry Long.

CAREER: DEBUT—chorus, *Funny Girl,* Starlight, Indianapolis, IN, 1974. NEW YORK DEBUT—chorus, *The American Dance Machine,* Paramount, 1980, 100 performances. PRINCIPAL STAGE APPEARANCES—Prince Chulolonghorn, *The King and I,* Candlelight, Chicago, 1981; Mike Costa, *A Chorus Line,* Shubert, NY, 1982; Francis, *La Cage Aux Folles,* Palace, NY, 1983.

MAJOR TOURS—Mike Costa, *A Chorus Line,* Chicago, Los Angeles, Boston, Philadelphia, San Francisco.

TELEVISION DEBUT—"Chicagoland New Performers," 1972.

SIDELIGHTS: "I am very interested and concerned with all ecological problems that face America today."

ADDRESS: Home—171 E. 89th Street, New York, NY 10028.

* * *

KELLY, Kevin, critic

PERSONAL: Born August 5, 1934; son of St. Clair and Joan (Sinnott) Kelly. EDUCATION: Boston University, College of Liberal Arts, B.A., 1952, M.A., 1953.

CAREER: Drama critic, interviewer, *Boston Globe,* 1958–present; same, Channel 7, Boston, 1982–present.

AWARDS: Herbert Bayard Swope Award for Excellence in Journalism, 1979; Boston University, Honorary Phi Beta Kappa, 1973.

SIDELIGHTS: MEMBERSHIPS—American Theatre Critics Association; National Society of Film Critics, 1973–present;

Tony Nominating Committee, 1979–83; Pulitzer Prize Committee (Drama), 1983–84.

ADDRESS: Office—*Boston Globe,* Boston, MA 02107.

* * *

KELLY, Tim, playwright

PERSONAL: Born October 2, 1937 in Saugus, MA; son of Francis and Mary (Fury) Kelly. EDUCATION: Emerson College, Boston, MA, B.A., 1956, M.A., 1957.

WRITINGS: PLAYS, PUBLISHED—*Toga! Toga! Toga!; Krazy Kamp; Airline; Sherlock Holmes; Pecos Bill and Slue-Foot Sue Meet the Dirty Dan Gang; The Brothers O'Toole; Lizzie Borden of Fall River; Cry of the Banshee; The Time Machine; Lady Dracula; Not Far from the Gioconda Tree; Marsha; Reunion on Gallows Hill; Happily Never After; Mark Twain in the Garden of Eden; Memorial; It's a Bird! It's a Plane! It's Chickenman!; A Marriage Proposal; The Keeping Place; The Natives Are Restless; The Eskimos Have Landed; The Shame of Tombstone; Hawkshaw the Detective; Alias Smedley Pewtree; Seven Wives for Dracula; The Gift and The Giving; Raggedy Dick and Puss; Beau Johnny; Jack the Ripper; Yankee Clipper; Under Jekyll's Hyde; Terror By Gaslight; The Adventure of the Clouded Crystal; Sherlock Holmes and the Adventure of the Speckled Band; Ten Weeks with the Circus; Dark Deeds at Swan's Place; The Lalapalooza Bird; Nicholas Nickleby; Nicholas Nickleby, Schoolmaster; The Green Archer; Mystery of the Black Abbot; First on the Rope; Little Miss Christie.*

AWARDS: Theatre Americana Best Play Award, 1983: *The Man With a Buffalo Robe,* Theatre American Best Play Award, 1982: *The Tattooed Sailor;* Southern Illinois University Playwriting Award, 1982: *Charming Sally;* Playwriting Commission, Actors Theatre of Louisville, 1981: *Adventure of the Clouded Crystal;* Weisbroad Playwriting Award, 1981: *The Lalapalooza Bird;* San Diego Old Opera House Best Play Award, 1980: *Dark Deeds at Swan's Place;* Nederlander Playwriting Award, 1980: *Bloody Jack;* Forest A. Roberts Playwriting Award, Northern Michigan University, 1980: *The Ripper;* Aspen Playwrights Conference Award, 1980: *Raggedy Dick and Puss;* Playwrights Award, Colonial Players, MD, 1980: *Whitchapel Horrors;* Texas Community Theatre Stage Center Award, 1979: *Lantern in the Wind;* Playwriting Award, Santa Fe Theatre Corporation, 1978: *Pecos Bill and Slue-Foot Sue Meet The Dirty Dan Gang;* Bicentennial Playwriting Award, University of Utah, 1976: *Beau Johnny;* International Thespian Society Award, 1976: *The Tale That Wagged the Dog;* Sergel Drama Prize, University of Chicago, 1973: *Yankee Clipper;* California Festival of Religious Arts Award, 1973: *The Gift and the Giving;* New England Theatre Conference Award, 1969: *The Natives Are Restless;* Pioneer Drama Service Playwriting Award, 1964: *Not Far from the Giaconda Tree.* GRANTS—Office of Advanced Drama Research, 1978; Creative Writing Award, National Endowment for the Arts, 1977; American Broadcasting Company Fellowship, Yale University, 1967.

THEATRE-RELATED CAREER: Journalist and drama critic,

TIM KELLY

Phoenix, Arizona, 1957–67; screen and television writer, 1968–78.

SIDELIGHTS: MEMBERSHIPS—Dramatists Guild; Writers Guild of America, West.

"My plays fall into three catagories: adaptation; works I do under commission; and wholly personal, creative efforts, which are always the toughest to promote. Where do I get my ideas? Nowhere. Everywhere. What we need are not so many young playwrights—they're all over the place—but some young producers. Old ones, too. Essentially, I'm a storyteller. To a certain extent, I suppose, I do favor plot over character. What advice would I give to the aspiring playwright? Don't let anyone put you or your play down. If you don't believe in your play, no one else will. And remember—there are no creative absolutes. Don't let anyone tell you differently."

ADDRESS: Home—8730 Lookout Mountain Avenue, Hollywood, CA 90046. Agent—Bill Talbot, c/o Samuel French Inc., 25 W. 45th Street, New York, NY 10036.

* * *

KENNEDY, George, actor

PERSONAL: Born February 18, 1926, in New York City. MILITARY: U.S. Army, W. W. II.

CAREER: PRINCIPAL FILM APPEARANCES—*Jolly Pink Jungle; Little Shepard of the Kingdom Come,* 1961; *Lonely Are the Brave,* 1962; *The Man from the Diners Club,* 1963; *Strait-Jacket,* 1964; *The Silent Witness; Island of the Blue Dolphins,* 1964; *McHale's Navy,* 1964; *Charade,* 1964; *See How They Run; In Harm's Way,* 1965; *The Sons of Katie Elder,* 1965; *Shenandoah,* 1965; *Hush . . . Hush Sweet Charlotte,* 1965; *The Dirty Dozen,* 1967; *Hurry Sundown,* 1967; *The Ballad of Josie,* 1968; *Cool Hand Luke,* 1967; *Bandolero,* 1968; *Boston Strangler,* 1968; *Guns of the Magnificent Seven,* 1969; *Gaily Gaily,* 1969; *The Good Guys and the Bad Guys,* 1969; *Airport,* 1969; *Tick . . . Tick . . . Tick,* 1970; *Zigzag,* 1970; *Dirty Dingus Magee,* 1970; *False Witness; Fool's Parade,* 1971; *Lost Horizon,* 1973; *Cahill,* 1973; *Thunderbolt and Lightfoot,* 1974; *Earthquake,* 1974; *Airport 1975,* 1974; *The Eiger Sanction,* 1975; *The Human Factor,* 1975; *Airport '77,* 1977; *Mean Dog Blues; Death on the Nile,* 1978; *Brass Target,* 1979; *The Concorde: Airport '79,* 1979; *Death Ship.*

PRINCIPAL TELEVISION APPEARANCES—(movies) *The Priest Killer,* 1971; *Deliver Us from Evil,* 1973; *A Cry in the Wilderness,* 1974; *The Blue Knight;* (series) *Sarge; The Blue Knight,* 1975–76; (episodic) *Sugarfoot; Cheyenne.*

AWARDS: Academy Award, Best Supporting Actor, 1967: *Cool Hand Luke;* Bronze Star (2, military).

ADDRESS: Agent—c/o Chasin-Park-Citron Agency, 9255 Sunset Blvd., Los Angeles, CA 90069.*

* * *

KENNEDY, Laurie, actress

PERSONAL: Daughter of John Arthur (an actor) and Mary Elizabeth (Cheffey) Kennedy; married D. Keith Mano (a novelist), July 18, 1980. EDUCATION: Attended the Solebury School and Sarah Lawrence College; trained for the stage with Michael Howard.

CAREER: DEBUT—Irina, *Three Sisters,* Williamstown Summer Theatre, Williamstown, MA. 1970. NEW YORK DEBUT—Violet, *Man and Superman,* Circle-in-the-Square, 1979. PRINCIPAL STAGE APPEARANCES—Grusha, *Caucasian Chalk Circle,* Roxanne, *Cyrano,* Sonya, *Uncle Vanya,* Williamstown Theatre, Williamstown, MA, 1973; Essie, *You Can't Take It with You,* Edinburgh Festival, Scotland, 1973; Joan, *St. Joan,* Arena Stage, Washington DC, 1976; Major Barbara, *Major Barbara,* Circle-in-the-Square, NY, 1982; Ann, *He and She,* Brooklyn Academy of Music, NY, 1980; Sylvia, *Recruiting Officer,* Brooklyn Academy of Music, NY, 1981; Hilda, *Master Builder,* Roundabout, NY, 1983; (Off-Broadway) Helen, *Ladyhouse Blues;* Harriet, *Isn't It Romantic;* Sheila, *Joe Egg;* Paula, *End of Summer;* Esther/Anna, *Rememberances;* (Regional) Marianne, *Tartuffe,* Long Wharf, New Haven, CT; Sophie, *Autumn Garden,* Arena Stage, Washington, DC; Irina, *Three Sisters,* Mark Taper Forum, Los Angeles; Nancy, *The Knack,* Buffalo Studio Arena, Buffalo, NY; Mrs. Malloy, *The Matchmaker,* Iphigenia, *Iphigenia in Aulis,* Elaine, *Last of the Red Hot Lovers,* Avonia, *Trelawny of the Wells,* Williamstown Theatre Festival.

TELEVISION DEBUT—Phoebe, *Edge of Night*. PRINCIPAL TELEVISION APPEARANCES—Pat Kennedy Lawford, *President Kennedy;* Alice Faulkner, *Sherlock Holmes*.

AWARDS: Theatre World Award: *Man and Superman;* Clarence Derwent Award: *Man and Superman*.

SIDELIGHTS: MEMBERSHIPS—AEA; SAG; AFTRA. MAJOR INTERESTS—animals, travel, foreign languages.

"I am concerned about the influx of British actors, directors, and playwrights into America without a complementary reciprocity in England."

ADDRESS: Agent—c/o Lionel Larner, Ltd., 850 Seventh Avenue, New York, NY 10019.

* * *

KEPROS, Nicholas, actor, director, producer, and writer

PERSONAL: Born November 8, 1932, in Salt Lake City, UT; son of George Nicholas (a food importer) and Maria Panagiotis (Deliezas) Kepros. EDUCATION: University of Utah, B.A., 1953, M.A., 1955; RADA, London, 1956–58; studied French Classical Theatre in Paris with Cours Jean Perimony.

CAREER: NEW YORK DEBUT—Slave, *The Golden Six*, York, 1958. LONDON DEBUT—Lorenzo, *The Merchant of Venice*, Southwark Festival, 1958. PRINCIPAL STAGE APPEARANCES—Julius Apocalypse, *The Redemptor*, Cricket, NY, 1959; John of Lancaster, *Henry IV, Parts 1 and 2*, Phoenix, NY, 1960; Osric, *Hamlet*, Phoenix, NY, 1961; Richard II, *Richard II*, Cleveland, 1962; Starveling, *A Midsummer Night's Dream*, 1963, Octavius Caesar, *Antony and Cleopatra*, 1963, Malcolm, *Macbeth*, 1964, Angelo, *Measure for Measure*, 1964, Old Globe, San Diego; Arnolphe, *School for Wives*, 1965, Macbeth, *Macbeth*, 1965, McCarter, Princeton, NJ; Henry VI, *Henry VI*, NY Shakespeare Festival, 1970; Basho, *Narrow Road to the Deep North*, Charles, Boston, 1971; Hadrian, *Hadrian VII*, American Conservatory Theatre, Seattle, 1971; Schlink, *In the Jungle of Cities*, Charles, Boston, 1972; Prospero, *The Tempest*, McCarter, Princeton, 1974; Guthrie, Minneapolis: Don Armado, *Love's Labours Lost*, 1975, the Fool, *King Lear*, 1975, Joseph Surface, *The School for Scandal*, 1975, the Chaplain, *Mother Courage*, 1976, Angelo, *Measure for Measure*, 1976, Guthrie, Minneapolis; Mobius, *The Physicists*, McCarter, Princeton, 1977; Iago, *Othello*, Roundabout, NY, 1979; Basho, *The Bundle*, Yale Repertory, New Haven, 1979; Old Jew, *The Irish Hebrew Lesson*, NY, 1980; Emperor Joseph II and stand-by for Salieri, *Amadeus*, NY, 1980–83. MAJOR TOURS—Hamlet, *Hamlet*, New York State Arts Council Tour by the Phoenix Theatre, 1961.

FILM DEBUT—Archbishop Coloredo, *Amadeus*, 1984. PRINCIPAL FILMS—Funeral director, *The Ultimate Solution of Grace Quigley*, 1984.

TELEVISION DEBUT—*The Russians: Self Impressions*, 1963. TELEVISION APPEARANCES—Betrand Russell, *Lamp unto My Feet*, 1970; Joseph Surface, *School for Scandal*, 1974;

Aaron Burr, *The Trial of Aaron Burr*, 1976; the Employer, *Bartleby, the Scrivener*, 1977.

THEATRE-RELATED CAREER—Make-up artist in Juilliard Opera department, 1960–64; taught voice and movement, Rutgers University, 1968; taught acting, University of Minnesota, 1974; taught at the Juilliard School, 1981–82.

WRITINGS: Co-translator with Françoise Kourilsky of *Far from Harrisburg*, produced at La Mama in 1980; published as *Far from Hagondange* in 1983. Article: "Understanding Make-up," *The Theatre Crafts Book of Make-up, Masks, and Wigs*, 1974.

AWARDS: Golden Globe Award, San Diego Shakespeare Festival, 1964; Best Director Award, RADA, London, 1958; Award for Verse Speaking, RADA, London, 1958.

SIDELIGHTS: Mr. Kepros speaks fluent Greek, French, and Italian. "I believe in musical training (especially learning an instrument) as a prerequisite to verse speaking."

ADDRESS: Agent—c/o Monty Silver, 200 W. 57th Street, New York, NY 10019.

* * *

KERCHEVAL, Ken, actor, singer

PERSONAL: Born July 15, 1935 in Woolcottville, IN; son of John Marine (an M.D.) and Christine Reiber (a nurse) Kercheval; divorced; children: Aaron, Liza, Caleb. EDUCATION: Attended University of Indiana, College of the Pacific and the Neighborhood Playhouse in New York City.

CAREER: PRINCIPAL STAGE APPEARANCES—*Dead End*, 41st Street Theatre, NY, 1959; *Young Abe Lincoln*, O'Neill, York, NY, 1959; *23 Pat O'Brien Movies*, American Place Theatre, NY, 1962; *A Man's a Man*, Masque, NY, 1962–63; *Who's Afraid of Virginia Woolf*, Billy Rose, NY, 1962–63; *Fiddler on the Roof*, Imperial, NY; *Happily Never After*, O'Neill, NY, 1966; *The Apple Tree*, Shubert, NY, 1966; *Father Uxbridge Wants to Marry*, American Place, NY, 1967; *Here's Where I Belong*, Billy Rose, NY, 1968; *Cabaret*, Broadhurst, NY, 1966; Broadway Theatre, 1968; *Horseman, Pass By*, Fortune, NY, 1969; *Who's Happy Now*, Village South, NY, 1969; *Father's Day*, Golden, NY, 1971; *Berlin to Broadway*, Theatre de Lys, NY, 1972.

FILM DEBUT—*Pretty Poison*, 1966. PRINCIPAL FILM APPEARANCES—*The Seven Ups*, 1973; *Network*, 1977. TELEVISION DEBUT—*The Defenders*, 1959. PRINCIPAL TELEVISION APPEARANCES—*Judge Horton and the Scottsboro Boys; The Coming Asunder of Jimmy Bright; Gypsy House; The Patricia Neal Story;* Cliff Barnes, *Dallas*.

AWARDS: Fanny Kemble Award for Best Supporting Actor, Philadelphia, 1963: *Who's Afraid of Virginia Woolf*.

SIDELIGHTS: MEMBERSHIPS—AEA; SAG; AFTRA; Masons.

ADDRESS: Agent—8899 Beverly Blvd., Los Angeles, CA 90048.

KEN KERCHEVAL

E. KATHERINE KERR

KERR, E(laine) Katherine, actress and writer

PERSONAL: Born April 20, 1937, in Indianapolis, IN; daughter of John Francis (a doctor) and Beatrice Mae (Westfall) Kerr; married James Joseph Mapes (a hypnotist, producer, and actor), May 31, 1980. EDUCATION: Indiana University, B.A., 1960; trained for the stage at the Neighborhood Playhouse and the actors' Institute with Sanford Meisner and Michael Howard.

CAREER: DEBUT—Chorus, *Trojan Women*, Circle-in-the-Square, NY, 1963. PRINCIPAL STAGE APPEARANCES—Ellen/ Mrs. Saunders/Betty, *Cloud 9*, Lucille Lortel, 1981–82; Nell, *Passion*, NY, 1983.

FILM DEBUT—Wife, *Tattoo*, 1980. PRINCIPAL FILM APPEARANCES—Gilda Schultz, *Silkwood*, 1983; Lucille Haxby, *Reuben, Reuben*, 1983.

TELEVISION DEBUT—Loretta Simpson, *Another World*, 1978.

WRITINGS: PLAYS, PRODUCED—*Juno's Swans*, PAF Playhouse, Long Island, NY. PLAYS, UNPRODUCED—The God Play.

AWARDS: Obie Award, Drama Desk Nomination, Villager Citation, 1982: *Cloud 9*.

SIDELIGHTS: MEMBERSHIPS—Ensemble Studio Theater; Artist's Workshop of Westport (board of directors).

''I am a searcher and will continue to be, because I'm discovering so much 'gold' in the world.''

ADDRESS: Telephone Service—(212) 757-6300.

* * *

KERR, Jean (nee Collins), playwright, humorist

PERSONAL: Born July 10, 1923, in Scranton, PA; daughter of Thomas J. (a contractor) and Kitty (O'Neill) Collins; married Walter Kerr (author and critic), August 16, 1943; children: Christopher, (twins) John, Colin, Gilbert, Gregory, Kitty. EDUCATION: Marywood College, Scranton, PA; Catholic University, Washington, DC.

CAREER: PLAYS, PRODUCED—(with Walter Kerr) *The Song of Bernadette*, Booth, NY, 1946; *Jenny Touched Me*, Hudson, NY, 1948; (with Walter Kerr) *Thank You, Just Looking*, Catholic University, 1949; (with Walter Kerr) *Touch and Go* (substantially the same as previous entry), NY, 1949; two sketches, *John Murray Anderson's Almanac*, 1953; (with Eleanor Brooke) *King of Hearts*, 1954; (with Walter Kerr) *Goldilocks*, 1958; *Mary, Mary*, Helen Hayes, NY, 1961; *Poor Richard*, 1964; *Finishing Touches*, 1973; *Lunch Hour*, NY, 1980.

BOOKS—non-fiction: *Please Don't East the Daisies, The Snake has All the Lines;* adapted for film and TV series, *Please Don't Eat the Daisies*, 1965; *Penny Candy*, 1970; *How I Got to Be Perfect*, 1978; novels: *Angels on a Pin*, 1982; adapted *The Good Fairy*, for a television production, 1955.

AWARDS: LHD degree, *honoris causa,* from Northwestern University, 1960.

ADDRESS: Home—One Beach Avenue, Larchmont, NY.*

* * *

KERRY, Anne, actress

PERSONAL: Born June 8, 1958, in Fort Wayne, TX; daughter of Henry Eugene (a lawyer) and Elizabeth (a real estate agent; maiden name, Ladon) Kerry. EDUCATION: Juilliard Theatre Center, B.F.A., 1979. RELIGION: Buddhist.

CAREER: DEBUT—Miranda, *The Tempest,* American Shakespeare Theatre, Stratford, CT, 1979. NEW YORK DEBUT—Grace Farrell, *Annie,* 1981. PRINCIPAL STAGE APPEARANCES—Ilse, *Spring Awakening,* NY Public Theatre; Judith, *Gemini,* Charles Playhouse, Boston, MA, 1980; Desdemona, *Othello,* StageWest, Springfield, MA, 1981; Roxanne, *Cyrano de Bergerac,* Milwaukee Repertory, 1981; Sophie Western, *Tom Jones,* 1982, Stella, *A Streetcar Named Desire,* 1982, Jodie, *Quilters,* 1983, Pittsburgh Public; ensemble, *Harry Chapin, Lies and Legends,* Milwaukee Repertory, 1984.

FILM DEBUT—Katie Benjamin, *Lovesick,* 1982. TELEVISION DEBUT—Joanna Kelly, *Nurse.* TELEVISION APPEARANCES—Janet Singleton, *Another World.*

ADDRESS: Agent—Hesseltine-Baker Associates, Ltd., 165 W. 46th Street, New York, NY 10036.

* * *

KETRON, Larry, actor and writer

PERSONAL: Born July 27, 1947, in Kingsport, TN. EDUCATION: Attended University of Tennessee and East Tennessee State University. MILITARY: U.S. Army.

WRITINGS: PLAYS, PRODUCED—*Cowboy Pictures,* Playwrights Horizons, NY, 1974; *Augusta,* Playwrights Horizons, Theatre de Lys, NY, 1975; *Stormbound,* Playwrights Horizons, NY, 1975; *Patrick Henry Lake Liquors,* Manhattan Theatre Club, NY, 1976; *Quail Southwest,* Manhattan Theatre Club, NY, 1977; *Rib Cage,* Stage West, W. Springfield, MA, 1978; *The Frequency,* American Conservatory Theatre, San Francisco, CA, 1978; *The Frequency,* WPA, NY, 1979; *Character Lines,* WPA, NY, 1979, St. Nicholas, Chicago, 1980, The Show Room, Los Angeles, CA, 1982; *The Trading Post,* WPA, NY, 1981, Odyssey, Los Angeles, CA, 1983; *A Tinker's Damn,* Hershel Zohn, New Mexico State University, Las Cruces, NM, 1981; *Ghosts of the Loyal Oaks,* WPA, NY, 1981; *Asian Shade,* WPA Theatre, NY, 1983. PLAYS, PUBLISHED—*Patrick Henry Lake Liquors,* 1977; *Quail Southwest,* 1977; *Rib Cage,* 1978; *Character Lines,* 1980; *The Trading Post,* 1981; *Ghosts of the Loyal Oaks,* 1982; *Asian Shade,* 1983.

AWARDS: The Villager Award, Excellence in Playwriting, 1979: *The Frequency;* Show Business Newspaper Award, Best New Play, 1977: *Patrick Henry Lake Liquors.*

THEATRE-RELATED CAREER: Playwright-in-Residence, WPA Theatre, New York, 1979–82; Peer Review Panelist, New York Creative Artists Public Service Program, 1981–82; Guest Artist, Aspen Playwrights Conference, Aspen, CO, 1982.

SIDELIGHTS: MEMBERSHIPS—Dramatists Guild.

ADDRESS: Agent—c/o Gilbert Parker, William Morris Agency, 1350 Avenue of the Americas, New York, NY 10019.

* * *

KEYLOUN, Mark Anthony, actor

PERSONAL: Born December 20, 1960; son of Elias (a manufacturer) and Joan (Fuentevilla) Keyloun; married Jennifer Dixon, September 5, 1982. EDUCATION: Attended Georgetown University.

CAREER: DEBUT—Buzz Gunderson, *Rebel without a Cause,* New York Theatre Ensemble, NY, 1979–80. PRINCIPAL STAGE APPEARANCES—Nicky, *Monsieur Amilcar,* Chelsea Westside, NY, 1979; Sloan (understudy), *Entertaining Mr. Sloan,* Cherry Lane, NY, 1980; Blow, *Forty-Deuce,* Perry Street, 1981.

FILM DEBUT—Blow, *Forty Deuce,* 1981. PRINCIPAL FILM APPEARANCES—Mike, *Mike's Murder,* 1984; Officer Bennett, *Sudden Impact,* 1983.

ADDRESS: Agent—c/o The Lantz Office, 888 Seventh Avenue, New York, NY 10106.

* * *

KIDDER, Margot, actress

PERSONAL: Born October 17, 1948, in Yellow Knife, Canada; married Tom McGuane (divorced); married John Heard (divorced); children: (first marriage) Maggie. EDUCATION: Attended University of British Columbia.

CAREER: FILM DEBUT—*Gaily Gaily,* 1969. PRINCIPAL FILM APPEARANCES—*Quackser Fortune Has a Cousin in the Bronx,* 1970; *Sisters,* 1972; *Gravy Train,* 1974; *The Great Waldo Pepper,* 1975; *The Reincarnation of Peter Proud,* 1975; *92 in the Shade,* 1977; *Superman,* 1978; *The Amityville Horror,* 1979; *Superman II,* 1981; *Some Kind of Hero,* 1981; *Mr. Mike's Mondo Video; Willy and Phil.*

PRINCIPAL TELEVISION APPEARANCES—(series) *Nichols,* 1972; (movies) *Honky Tonk,* 1974; (episodic) *Switch; Baretta; Barnaby Jones; Hawaii Five-0, Mod Squad.* *

* * *

KILEY, Richard, actor, singer

PERSONAL: Born March 31, 1922, in Chicago, IL; son of

Leo Joseph and Leonore (McKenna) Kiley; married Mary Bell Wood (divorced); Patricia Ferrier; EDUCATION: Studied for the stage at the Barnum Dramatic School, Chicago.

CAREER: DEBUT—title role, *Mikado*, Mt. Carmel High School, Chicago, 1938. NEW YORK DEBUT—Poseidon, *The Trojan Women*, Equity Library, 1947. LONDON DEBUT—Cervantes/Don Quixote, *Man of La Mancha*, Piccadilly, 1969. PRINCIPAL STAGE APPEARANCES—Jacob, *The Sun and I*, New Stages, 1949; Joe Rose, *A Month of Sundays*, Shubert, Boston, 1951; Percival, *Misalliance*, NY City Center, Barrymore, NY, 1953; the Caliph, *Kismet*, Ziegfeld, NY, 1953; Ben Collinger, *Sing Me No Lullaby*, Phoenix, NY, 1954; Major Harry Cargill, *Time Limit!*, Booth, NY, 1956; James Tyrone, *A Moon for the Misbegotten*, Spoleto Festival, Italy, 1958; Tom Baxter, *Redhead*, 46th Street, NY, 1959; Brig Andeson, *Advise and Consent*, Cort, NY, 1960; David Jordan, *No Strings*, 54th Street, NY, 1962; leading role, *Here's Love*, Shubert, NY, 1964; Stan the Shpieler, *I Had a Ball*, Martin Beck, NY, 1964; musical version of *Purple Dust* and Cervantes/Don Quixote, *Man of La Mancha*, Goodspeed Opera House, East Haddam, CT, 1965; Cervantes/Don Quixote, *Man of La Mancha*, ANTA, Washington Square, NY, 1965; Caesar, *Her First Roman*, Lunt-Fontanne, NY, 1968; *Man of La Mancha*, Concert Theatre, Honolulu, HI, 1970; Enoch Somes, A. V. Laider, *The Incomparable Max*, Royale, NY, 1971; Robert, *Voices*, Barrymore, NY, 1972; revival, *Man of La Mancha*, Vivian Beaumont, NY, 1972; title role, *Tartuffe*, Walnut, Philadelphia, 1972; Cervantes/Don Quixote, play version, *Man of La Mancha*, American Theatre, Washington, DC, 1973; Ronald, *Absurd Person Singular*, Music Box, NY, 1974; Mr. Sloper, *The Heiress*, Kennedy Center, Broadhurst, NY, 1976; *The Master Builder*, Kennedy Center, 1977; revival, *Man of La Mancha*, Palace, NY, 1977; poetry recital, with HSH Princess Grace of Monaco, Edinburgh Festival, 1979.

MAJOR TOURS—Stanley Kowalski, *A Streetcar Named Desire*, U.S. tour, 1950; Cervantes/Don Quixote, *Man of La Mancha*, California tour, 1967–68, U.S. tour, 1978–79; *Ah! Wilderness*, U.S. tour, 1975; *Mass Appeal*, national tour, 1983; *Absurd Person Singular*, national tour, 1984.

PRINCIPAL FILM APPEARANCES—*The Blackboard Jungle*, 1955; *Pickup on South Street; The Mob; The Little Prince*, 1974; *Looking for Mr. Goodbar*, 1979; *Endless Love*, 1982. PRINCIPAL TELEVISION APPEARANCES—*Patterns; Arrowsmith; POW; Medical Center; The Andros Targets; George Washington, A.D.; The Thornbirds*, 1983.

AWARDS: Emmy Award, 1984; Antoinette Perry Award, 1965: Cervantes/Don Quixote, *Man of La Mancha;* Antoinette Perry Award, 1959: Tom Baxter, *Redhead.*

SIDELIGHTS: MEMBERSHIPS—The Players Club. FAVORITE ROLE—*Man of La Mancha.* RECREATIONS—Writing and carpentry.

ADDRESS: Agent—c/o Stephen Draper, 37 W. 57th Street, New York, NY 10019.

KINDLEY, Jeffrey, writer

PERSONAL: Born June 2, 1945, in Portland, OR; son of Robert Clarkson and Blanche Hayes (Bowman) Kindley; married Louise Ellen Sinnard, May 15, 1971; children: Evan Sinnard, Colin Bowman. EDUCATION: Columbia University, B.A., 1967, M.A., 1968, Ph.D. 1971.

WRITINGS: PLAYS, PRODUCED—*Among Adults*, Manhattan Theatre Club, NY, 1973, Galaxy Theatre Company, NY, 1974; *The Counterpart Cure*, New Dramatists, NY, 1977; *St. Hugo of Central Park*, University of Texas, 1976, New Jersey Institute of Technology, 1977, BBC Third Programme, London, 1979, University of Wisconsin, 1980; *Is There Life After High School?*, Ethel Barrymore, NY, 1982.

FILMS—*No Big Deal*, 1983; *Dear Lola*, 1983. TELEVISION—*Make-Believe Marriage*, 1979; *Rocking-Chair Rebellion*, 1980; *Family of Strangers* (with Len Jenkin), 1981; *The Electric Grandmother* (with Ray Bradbury), 1982.

AWARDS: George Foster Peabody Award, 1982: *The Electric Grandmother;* Emmy Nomination, 1981–82: *The Electric Grandmother;* Christopher Award, 1981: *Family of Strangers;* Emmy Nomination, 1980–81: *Family of Strangers;* Emmy Nomination, 1979–80: *Rocking-Chair Rebellion;* Emmy Nomination, 1978–79: *Make-Believe Marriage;* E.P. Conkle Theatre Award (University of Texas), 1976.

SIDELIGHTS: MEMBERSHIPS—Dramatists Guild; Writers Guild of America, East; New Dramatists.

ADDRESS: Home—27 W. 96th Street, #2C, New York, NY 10025. Agent—c/o Gilbert Parker, William Morris Agency, 1350 Avenue of the Americas, New York, NY 10019.

* * *

KINGSLEY, Ben, actor

PERSONAL: Born December 31, 1943, in Snaiton, Yorkshire, England; son of Rahimtulla Harji and Anna Lyna Mary Bhanji; married Gillian Alison Macauley Sutcliffe (a theatre director); children: a son. EDUCATION: Manchester Grammar School.

CAREER: DEBUT—On a schools-tour for Theatre Centre, 1964. LONDON DEBUT—The Wigmaker, *The Relapse*, Royal Shakespeare Company, Aldwych, 1967. NEW YORK DEBUT—Title role, *Edmund Kean*, 1983. PRINCIPAL STAGE APPEARANCES—Doolittle, *Pygmalion*, Rep, Stoke-on-Trent, 1965; Narrator, *A Smashing Day*, Arts, 1966; First Murderer, *Macbeth*, Party Guest, *The Cherry Orchard*, Chichester, 1966; Amiens, *As You Like It*, Royal Shakespeare Company (RSC), Stratford, 1967; Oswald, *King Lear*, Aeneas, *Troilus and Cressida*, Conrade, *Much Ado About Nothing*, Stratford, 1968, also the last two at the Aldwych, 1969; the Croucher, *The Silver Tassie*, Winwife, *Bartholomew Fair*, Aldwych, 1969; Ratcliff, *Richard III*, Claudio, *Measure for Measure*, Demetrius, Peter Brook's *A Midsummer Night's Dream*, Ariel, *The Tempest*, Stratford, 1970; Demetrius, *A Midsummer Night's Dream*, Aldwych, 1971; Sinsov, *The Enemies*, Aldwych, *1971;* Gramsci, *Occupations*, Ippolit, *Subject to Fits*, Place, 1971; Puck, *The Faery Queen*, Newcastle, 1972;

289

Johnnie, *Hello and Goodbye,* Kings Head, then Place, 1973; Fritz, *A Lesson in Blood and Roses,* Place, 1973; Errol Philander, *Statements,* Royal Court, 1974; Slender, *The Merry Wives of Windsor,* Bonze Wang, *Man Is Man,* Hamlet, *Buzz Goodbody's Other Place Production of Hamlet,* RSC, Stratford, 1975; played the last two later at the Round House, 1976; Danilo, *Dimetos,* Nottingham Playhouse, then Comedy, London, 1976; Mosca, *Volpone,* Vukhov, *Judgement,* Trofimov, *The Cherry Orchard,* RSC, Stratford, 1979; Frank Ford, *The Merry Wives of Windsor,* Iachimo, *Cymbeline,* Brutus, *Julius Caesar,* title role, *Baal,* (this last also at Other Place), RSC, Stratford, 1979; *Baal,* Warehouse, 1980; Squeers, *Nicholas Nickleby,* Aldwych, 1980; title role, *Dr. Faustus,* Manchester Royal Exchange; title role, *Edmund Kean,* Harrogate, 1981, Lyric, Hammersmith, Haymarket, London, 1983, Brooks Atkinson, NY, 1984.

FILM DEBUT—*Fear is the Key,* 1972. PRINCIPAL FILMS—title role, *Gandhi,* 1981; Robert, *Betrayal,* 1982. TELEVISION APPEARANCES—Rossetti, *The Love School; Barbara of Grebe House; Thank You, Comrades; Every Good Boy Deserves Favour; Feel Free; Edmund Kean; The Merry Wives of Windsor;* title role, *Silas Marner,* 1984.

MAJOR TOURS—Demetrius, *A Midsummer Night's Dream,* U.S., 1971; Errol Philander, *Statements,* Europe, 1974.

AWARDS: London Standard Award, Best Actor, 1983: *Betrayal;* Academy Award, Best Actor, BAFTA, Best Actor, Best Newcomer, Golden Globe Award-Best Actor, Variety Club, Best Newcomer and Best Screenactor, 1982: *Gandhi;* Honorary M.A., Safford University; Padma Shree, Government of India.

SIDELIGHTS: FAVORITE PARTS: Ariel, Hamlet, Ford, Mosca, Gandi.

ADDRESS: New Pebworth House, Pebworth, Stratford-Upon-Avon, Warwickshire, England.

* * *

KINSKI, Natassia, actress

PERSONAL: Born January 24, 1960, in Berlin, Germany; daughter of Klaus Kinski (an actor); children: Aljosha Nakzynski.

CAREER: PRINCIPAL FILM APPEARANCES—*To the Devil a Daughter; Passion Flower Hotel; Stay As You Are,* 1979; *Tess,* 1981; *Cat People,* 1982; *Exposed,* 1983; *The Moon in the Gutter; Unfaithfully Yours,* 1983; *Hotel New Hampshire,* 1984.

ADDRESS: Agent—c/o G. Beaume, Three Quai Malaquais, Paris 75006, France.*

* * *

KIRKLAND, James R. III, director, producer, actor, writer

PERSONAL: Born February 8, 1947, in Burlington, IA; son of James R. (career military service) and Dolores Helen (department store manager; maiden name, Welch) Kirkland, Jr.; married Sally Sommer, 1966 (divorced 1970); married Kathleen Krizner (business manager), September 10, 1980; children: Michael James. EDUCATION: University of Texas at El Paso, 1964–66; studied directing with Dr. Keith Fowler at the Virginia Museum Theatre, Richmond, VA. POLITICS: Humanitarian. RELIGION: Seeker. MILITARY: 62nd U.S. Army Band (trumpet), 1966–69.

CAREER: FIRST STAGE WORK, ACTOR—Sakini, *Teahouse of the August Moon,* Festival Theatre, El Paso, TX, 1964. NEW YORK DEBUT—Sasha, *Our Father,* Manhattan Theatre Club, 1974. PRINCIPAL STAGE APPEARANCES—Malcolm, *Macbeth,* Festival, El Paso, TX; Laertes, *Hamlet,* Festival, El Paso; Flavius/Titinius, *Julius Caesar,* Claudio, *Much Ado About Nothing,* Sebastian, *Twelfth Night,* Lenny, *The Homecoming,* Young Man, *Summertree,* Charlie, *Purlie,* Ben Franklin, *The Common Glory,* Williamsburg, VA.

PRINCIPAL STAGE WORK, DIRECTOR—*Saint Joan,* Virginia Museum Theatre; *Hamlet,* Virginia Museum Theatre; *Riverwind,* Barter, Abingdon, VA; *A Christmas Carol,* Arizona Theatre Company, Virginia Museum Theatre, Wayside Theatre, Lakewood, Theatre; *Merton of the Movies,* Arkansas Repertory; *Tobacco Road,* Virginia Museum Theatre; *The Caretaker,* Virginia Museum Theatre; *Side by Side by Sondheim,* Wayside Theatre, Middletown, VA; *Harvey,* Wayside Theatre; *Talley's Folly,* Lakewood Theatre Company; *The Winslow Boy,* Asolo State Theatre, FL; *The Elephant Man,* Lakewood Theatre Company; *The Crucible,* Virginia Museum Theatre; *Hamlet,* Wayside Theatre; *The Brigadier,* Actors Alliance (reading), NY; *The Miracle Worker,* Opera House, Charleston, WV; *Bye Bye Broadway,* Worcester Foothills Theatre, MA; *Charley's Aunt,* Wayside Theatre; *South Pacific,* Lakewood Theatre Company; *The Mousetrap,* Virginia Museum Theatre.

PRINCIPAL STAGE WORK, PRODUCER—*Round and Round the Garden, Vanities, Ring Round the Moon, Volpone, Bells Are Ringing, Side by Side by Sondheim, Angel Street, A Streetcar Named Desire, Harvey, Hamlet, Ghost Stories of the Civil War, Shakes & Company,* Wayside Theatre, Middletown, VA; *The Old One Two, Scenes from Shakespeare, Commedia del 'Arte,* Virginia Museum Theatre; *Talley's Folly, Chapter Two, Of Mice and Men, The Gin Game, Deathtrap, Tintypes, Chicago, The Elephant Man,* Lakewood Theatre Company.

THEATRE-RELATED CAREER: Associate artistic director, Virginia Museum Theatre, 1970–77; producing/artistic director, Wayside Theatre, Middletown, VA, 1978–80; producing director, Lakewood Theatre Company (State Theatre of Maine), 1981–83.

WRITINGS: PLAYS, PRODUCED—*Bye Bye Broadway,* Worcester Foothills Theatre, 1979. PLAYS, UNPRODUCED—Interviewers, The Nearness of You.

SIDELIGHTS: MEMBERSHIPS—AEA; SSD&C; served on the Theatre Advisory Panels for the Virginia Commission on the Arts and the Maine State Commission for the Arts and Humanities.

''As the electronics technology becomes more and more sophisticated, I am troubled by a recurring dream of taking my son to a 'specialized museum' to view a live theatre performance. Trying to explain to him just what I did all my life as he watches the robots perform a scene from some famous play written back in the eighties. How do we keep the theatre from slipping away into oblivion?''

ADDRESS: Home—Ten Old Road, South Amboy, NJ 08879.

* * *

KLAR, Gary (ne Klahr), actor

PERSONAL: Born March 24, 1947, in Bridgeport, CT; son of Benjamin (a glazier) and Marjorie Marion (Brenner) Klahr; married Carolyn Blackburn, December 20, 1980; children: Benjamin Zachary, Rachel Sara. EDUCATION: University of Arizona, B.S., 1971.

CAREER: NEW YORK DEBUT—Big Henry Black, *Chainsaws,* St. Clements, 1981. PRINCIPAL STAGE APPEARANCES—Hugo Broonzy, *The Guys in the Truck,* New Apollo, NY, 1983; Earl MacMillan, *Brothers,* Music Box, NY, 1983.

FILM DEBUT—Chuck, *Hero at Large,* 1979. TELEVISION DEBUT—Buddy Fuquar, *Ryan's Hope,* 1983.

SIDELIGHTS: MEMBERSHIPS—AEA; SAG; AFTRA; Theatre Artists Workshop of Westport.

ADDRESS: Agent—c/o Robert Kass, 156 Fifth Avenue, New York, NY 10010.

* * *

KLARIS, Harvey J. (ne Klaristenfeld), producer

PERSONAL: Born June 21, 1939, in New York City; son of William (a manufacturer) and Viola (Zeidman) Klaristenfeld; married Alice Amster, September 10, 1960 (marriage ended 1972); children: Lorin, Edward, Joshua. EDUCATION: Emory University, 1956–58; Brooklyn College, 1958–61, B.A.; Brooklyn Law School, 1961–63, L.L.B.

CAREER: Produced—*Nine,* 1982.

AWARDS: Antoinette Perry Award, Best Musical, *Nine,* 1982; Drama Desk Award, *Nine,* 1982.

ADDRESS: Home—One University Place, New York, NY 10003; Office—99 Park Avenue, New York, NY 10016; Agent—Sam Cohn, I.C.M., 40 W. 57th Street, New York, NY 10019.

* * *

KLEISER, Randal, director

CAREER: FILM DEBUT—Director, *Grease,* 1978. PRINCIPAL FILM WORK—Director, *The Blue Lagoon,* 1980, director,

writer, *Summer Lovers,* 1982; director, *Grandview U.S.A.,* 1983.

PRINCIPAL TELEVISION WORK—Director: *Marcus Welby, M.D.* episodes: "Fear of Silence," 1973, "Designs," "A Fevered Angel," "To Father a Child," 1974, "The Strange Behavior of Paul Kelland," 1975; *Foot Fetish,* (short), 1974; *Lucas Tanner* series, episode: "Bonus Baby," 1974; *All Together Now,* 1975; *The Rookies* series, episode: "From Out of the Darkness," 1976; *Starsky & Hutch* series, episodes: "Nightmare," "Terror on the Docks," 1976; *Dawn: Portrait of a Teenage Runaway,* 1976; *The Boy in the Plastic Bubble,* 1976; *Family,* series, episodes: "A Special Kind of Love," "A Right and Proper Goodbye," 1977; *Portrait of Grandpa Doc,* 1977; *The Gathering,* 1977.

AWARDS: Emmy Award Nomination, Best Direction, 1977: *The Gathering,* 1977.

ADDRESS: Agent—Creative Artists Agency, 1888 Century Park E., Suite 1400, Los Angeles, CA 90067.

* * *

KLIBAN, Ken, actor

PERSONAL: Born July 26, 1943; son of Louis (a manufacturer) and Sophia (Tove) Kliban. EDUCATION: Oberlin College, University of Miami, B.A.; New York University, M.A.; trained for the stage with Uta Hagen, Herbert Berghof, and Lee Strasberg.

CAREER: DEBUT—*Elizabeth the Queen,* City Center, NY, 1966. PRINCIPAL STAGE APPEARANCES—American Shakespeare Festival, Stratford, CT, 1966; *War and Peace,* APA-Phoenix production, Lyceum, NY, 1967; Phillip, *The Lion in Winter,* Actors Theatre of Louisville, 1970; Tybalt in *Romeo and Juliet* and Horatio in *Hamlet,* North Shore Music Theatre, 1972; Paris, *Troilus and Cressida,* Washington, DC Shakespeare Festival, 1972; Demetrius, *A Midsummer Night's Dream,* Paper Mill Playhouse, NJ, 1973; Ralph, *Butterflies Are Free,* Chateau de Ville, 1974; *In the Boom Boom Room,* New York Shakespeare Festival, 1974; Milt, *Luv,* Provincetown Playhouse, Cape Cod, MA, 1976; *Passion,* Longacre, NY, 1983; Steve, *Ulysses in Traction,* 1977, Lord Burleigh, *Mary Stuart,* 1979, Guildenstern, *Hamlet,* 1979, Julius, *Beaver Coat,* 1980, Leon, *Jedediah Kohler,* 1982, Circle Repertory Company, NY.

SIDELIGHTS: Mr. Kliban has been a recording artist at Talking Book Studio for seven years, requiring knowledge of French, Russian, German, Greek, and Hebrew.

ADDRESS: Home—170 West End Avenue, New York, NY 10023.

* * *

KLIEWER, Warren, writer, actor, director

PERSONAL: Surname pronounced *Klee*-ver; born September 20, 1931, in Mountain Lake, MN; son of John G. (a businessman) and Elizabeth (a nurse; maiden name, Kroeker) Kliewer; married Darleen Alseike, June 4, 1960 (divorced 1969); married Michele LaRue (an actress and artist), May 23, 1971. EDUCATION: University of Minnesota, B.A. (magna cum laude), 1953, M.F.A., 1967; University of Kansas, M.A., 1959. MILITARY: Conscientious objector.

CAREER: PRINCIPAL STAGE APPEARANCES—(New York) Alexander Hamilton, *Aaron Burr;* Legendre/General Dillon, *Danton's Death;* Cutbeard, *Epicoene,* 1975; Witness #1, *The Investigation,* 1980; (Regional) Bishop of Lax, *See How They Run* and *Pool's Paradise;* First Guard/Chorus, *Antigone;* Henry Peabody, *Tobacco Road,* Fulton Opera House, 1975; Reverend John Hale, *The Crucible,* Fulton Opera House, 1975; Dr. Bonfant, *The Waltz of the Toreadors,* New Jersey Shakespeare Festival, 1980; (Stock) Queeg, *Caine Mutiny Court Martial;* Gordon Lowther, *The Prime of Miss Jean Brodie;* Keller, *The Miracle Worker;* Gordon Miller, *Room Service.* MAJOR TOURS—Dr. Mayberry, *I Never Sang for My Father;* Judge/Major, *Inherit the Wind;* Faustus (one-man show); *The Seven Ages of an American* (one-man show); *Dissenters* (one-man show).

DIRECTED: PLAYS—*Bell, Book and Candle,* Wichita Summer Theater; *Our Town,* Eagles Mere Playhouse; *Antigone, Woman, Mark the Humor in Twain,* Carolina Readers' Theatre, 1974; *Under Milkwood, The Skin of Our Teeth,* Actors' Company of Pennsylvania; *Ah, Wilderness!,* Little Theatre of Winston-Salem; *Halfway up the Tree,* Playhouse on the Hill; *Ever So Humble,* Stage Directors and Choreographers Workshop Foundation, Lincoln Center, John Drew, Old Sturbridge Village, Smithsonian Institution, 1975; *Charles the Second,* Classic, 1977; *The Divided Bed,* Equity Library, 1978; *A New England Legend, La Ronde,* Equity Library, 1979; *Paterson,* Equity Library, 1980; *The Yellow Wallpaper,* Stage Directors and Choreographers Workshop, Lincoln Center, Jersey City, New Rochelle, Chicago, Philadelphia, 1980; *Hypocrites, Frauds, and Cheats,* college tour, 1981.

PRINCIPAL FILM APPEARANCES—*Hair; Ragtime; Svengali.* PRINCIPAL TELEVISION APPEARANCES—*The Adams Chronicles.*

WRITINGS: PLAYS, PRODUCED—*The Summoning of Everyman,* Bethany College, KS, 1961; *In the Suburbs of Nineveh,* Earlham College, 1962; *A Bird in the Bush,* University of Southern California, 1962; *The Harrowing of Hell,* Professional Institute, Richmond, VA, 1962; *Philip Melanchthon,* Religious Arts Festival Theater, Rochester, NY, 1963; *The Wounded,* Taylor University, 1964; *A Trial Can Be Fun, If You're the Judge,* Firehouse Theater, Minneapolis, MN, 1965; *Seventy Times Seven,* Eagles Mere Playhouse, PA, 1965; *The Wrestler,* Cobo Hall, Detroit, MI, 1964; *The Offering,* Hamline University, 1964; *In the Beginning Was Eve,* United Theological Seminary, Minneapolis, MN, 1966;

What Do You Care? It's Beyond Repair, University Theatre, Wichita, KS; *Madame Cleo Here, At Your Service,* Wichita State University, 1970, Washington Theatre Club, 1971, Princeton Inn College, 1979; *The Great Debate,* Kaleidoscope Players, midwestern cities, 1971–74; *From Ten to Twenty,* Kaleidoscope Players, midwestern cities, 1974–75; *A Lean and Hungry Priest,* Scorpio Rising Theatre, Los Angeles, 1973; *Meet Ben Franklin,* Kaleidoscope Players,

midwestern cities, 1973; *Half Horse, Half Cockeyed Alligator,* Fulton Opera House American Heritage Festival, 1974, East Lynne Company, Jersey City, 1981; *Heroes and Failures,* Hamden Hall Theatre, 1976, Gettysburg College, 1977; *The Berserkers,* New Dramatists, NY, 1977; *The Booth Brothers,* New Dramatists, 1978; *Hypocrites, Frauds and Cheats,* Brown University, Providence, RI, 1981.

PLAYS PUBLISHED—*The Summoning of Everyman,* 1961; *A Bird in the Bush,* 1962; *The Harrowing of Hell,* 1962; *The Prodical Son,* 1962; *The Devil Comes to Claim His Own,* 1963; *Seventy Times Seven,* 1965; *The Wrestling,* 1967; *A Trial Can Be Fun, If You're the Judge,* 1969; *What Are We Going to Do with All These Rotting Fish?,* 1970; *A Lean and Hungry Priest,* 1975; *How Can You Tell the Good Guys from the Bad Guys,* 1975; *The Doubting Saint,* 1975.

BOOKS—*Red Rose and Gray Cowl,* 1960; *Kansas Renaissance: An Anthology of Contemporary Kansas Writing,* 1961; *Moralities and Miracles,* 1962; *The Violators,* 1964; *Liturgies, Games, Farewells,* 1974. FICTION IN PERIODICALS—''With Fear and Trembling,'' *Mennonite Life,* 1958; ''The Hermitage,'' *Descant,* 1959; ''The Sibyl,'' *Kansas Magazine,* 1959; ''The Homecoming,'' *Mennonite Life,* 1960; ''UHF,'' *Descant,* 1960; ''The Barn-Climber,'' *Kansas Magazine,* 1961; ''War and Rumors of War,'' *Mennonite Life,* 1962; ''The Voices,'' *Descant,* 1962; ''Of Mercy and Judgment,'' *Kansas Magazine,* 1962; ''Madeleine d'Evereaux, the Whole Earth Must Know I Love You So,'' *Kansas Magazine,* 1968; ''The Prince of Egypt,'' *Kansas Magazine.*

THEATRE-RELATED CAREER—Bethany College, Lindsborg, KS, instructor in English and drama, 1959–61; Earlham College, Richmond, IN, assistant professor English, 1961–65; Wichita State University, Wichita, KS, associate professor of English and Theatre, 1966–69; National Humanities Series, Woodrow Wilson National Fellowship Foundation, Princeton, NJ, production director, 1970–73; Artistic director of Carolina Readers' Theatre, 1974; director of productions, Wichita State University Experimental Theatre, Wichita Summer Theatre, 1968, Eagles Mere Playhouse, PA, 1969, Kaleidoscope Players, Raton, NM, American Heritage Festival, Fulton Opera House; artistic director, East Lynne Company, 1980–present.

SIDELIGHTS: MEMBERSHIPS—AEA, SAG, Society of Stage Directors and Choreographers.

Mr. Kliewer is also a widely published writer of poetry. ''For me everything has a history. When I write a piece for the theater and it is performed, it takes place in the present: a performance takes place right now, this very moment. But I'm always conscious that any event is originated in a previous time to which it is still related. I'm sure this is why I'm drawn to historical or traditional subjects, which on stage can convey presentness and pastness simultaneously.''

ADDRESS: Home—281 Lincoln Avenue, Secaucus, NJ 07094.

* * *

KLINE, Kevin, actor

PERSONAL: Born October 24, 1947, in St. Louis, MO; son

of Robert Joseph (toy and record store owner and singer) and Peggy (Kirk) Kline. EDUCATION: St. Louis Priory; Indiana University; studied the theater at Juilliard School Drama Center and with Harold Guskin.

CAREER: DEBUT—*The Living Newspaper*, Indiana University, late '60s. NEW YORK DEBUT—Minor role, *Henry VI, Parts I and II, Richard III*, New York Shakespeare Festival, Delacorte, 1970. PRINCIPAL STAGE APPEARANCES—Charles Surface, *The School for Scandal*, Vaskal Pepel, *The Lower Depths*, IRA officer, *The Hostage*, Guardiano, *Women Beware Women*, Acting Company, Good Shepherd–Faith Church, NY, 1972; Vershinin, *The Three Sisters*, MacHeath, *The Beggars Opera*, Friar Peter, *Measure for Measure*, Leandre, *Scapin*, Acting Company, Billy Rose, NY, 1973; Jaime Lockhart, *The Robber Bridegroom*, McCarthy, *The Time of Your Life*, Harkness, Los Angeles, 1975; Clym Yeobright, *Dance on a Country Grave*, Hudson Guild, NY, 1977; *The Promise*, Bucks County, 1977; Bruce Granit, *On the Twentieth Century*, St. James, NY, 1978; Paul, *Loose Ends*, Circle in the Square, NY, 1979; Pirate King, *The Pirates of Penzance*, New York Shakespeare Festival, Delacorte, then Uris, NY, 1980; *Richard III*, New York Shakespeare Festival, Delacorte, NY, 1983; *Henry V*, Delacorte, 1984; also accepted understudy/standby duties for MacHeath, *The Three Penny Opera*, New York Shakespeare Festival, Vivian Beaumont, New York, 1978. MAJOR TOURS—Tony Lumpkin, *She Stoops to Conquer*, Tom, *The Knack*, Acting Company, 1974.

FILM DEBUT—Nathan Landau, *Sophie's Choice*, 1982. FILM APPEARANCES—Pirate King, *The Pirate of Penzance*, 1983; *The Big Chill*, 1983.

TELEVISION APPEARANCES—*Search for Tomorrow*, 1976–77; *The Time of Your Life*, PBS.

AWARDS: Antoinette Perry Award, Best Actor in a Musical, 1980: *The Pirates of Penzance;* Best Supporting Actor in a Musical, 1978: *On the Twentieth Century.*

SIDELIGHTS: RECREATION—Musical composition, travel, sports. "Playing piano is my therapy."

As a graduate of the first class of the Juilliard Drama Center in 1972, Mr. Kline was invited to be one of the founding members of the Acting Company.*

* * *

KLUGMAN, Jack, actor

PERSONAL: Born April 27, 1922, in Philadelphia, PA; son of Max and Rose Klugman; married Brett Somers, 1966 (separated); children: David, Adam. EDUCATION: Attended Carnegie Institute of Technology; trained for the stage at the American Theatre Wing.

CAREER: NEW YORK STAGE DEBUT—*Stevedore*, Equity Library Theatre, 1949. LONDON DEBUT—Oscar Madison, *The Odd Couple*, Queen's, 1966. PRINCIPAL STAGE APPEARANCES—*Saint Joan*, NY, 1949; *Bury the Dead*, NY, 1950; Frank Bonaparte, *Golden Boy*, ANTA, NY, 1952; Citizen/Volscian Servant, *Coriolanus*, Phoenix, NY, 1954; Carmen,

A Very Special Baby, Playhouse, NY, 1956; Herbie, *Gypsy*, Broadway, NY, 1959; Caesario Grimaldi, *Tchin-Tchin*, Plymouth, NY, 1963; Oscar Madison, *The Odd Couple*, Plymouth, NY, 1977; Horse Johnson, *The Sudden and Accidental Re-education of Horse Johnson*, Belasco, NY, 1968; Oscar Madison, *The Odd Couple*, Maddox Hall, Atlanta, GA, 1972, Miami, FL, Houston, TX, 1973.

MAJOR TOURS—Dowdy, *Mister Roberts*, U.S. cities, 1950–51; Oscar Madison, *The Odd Couple*, U.S. cities, 1974, U.S. and Canadian cities, 1975; one man show about Lyndon B. Johnson, 1983–present.

FILM DEBUT—*Time Table*, 1956. PRINCIPAL FILM APPEARANCES—*Twelve Angry Men*, 1957; *Cry Terror*, 1958; *Days of Wine and Roses*, 1962; *Act One*, 1963; *Yellow Canary*, 1963; *Hail, Mafia*, 1964; *The Detective*, 1968; *The Split*, 1968; *Goodbye Columbus*, 1969; *Who Says I Can't Ride a Rainbow*, 1971; *Two Minute Warning*, 1976.

PRINCIPAL TELEVISION APPEARANCES—*Suspicion; Studio One; Kiss Me, Kate; The Time of Your Life;* (series) *Harris Against the World*, 1964–65; *The Odd Couple*, 1970–75; *Quincy*, 1976–present; (movies) *Fame Is the Name of the Game*, 1966; *The Underground Man*, 1974; *One of My Wives Is Missing*, 1976.

AWARDS: Emmy Award, 1973, 1971: *The Odd Couple;* Emmy Award, 1964: *The Defenders*, "Blacklist."

SIDELIGHTS: MEMBERSHIPS—AFTRA, AEA, SAG.

ADDRESS: Office—c/o NBC Press Department, 30 Rockefeller Plaza, New York, NY 10020.*

* * *

KLUNIS, Tom (ne Thomas W.), actor

PERSONAL: Surname rhymes with "Loonis"; born April 29, 1930; son of William (a master welder) and Despena (Chapralis) Klunis. EDUCATION: Attended San Francisco State College; studied at the San Francisco Actors Workshop; trained for the stage with C. A. Miller. RELIGION: Greek Orthodox. MILITARY: U.S. Navy, four years.

CAREER: DEBUT—Recruiting Sergeant, *Mother Courage*, San Francisco Actors Workshop. NEW YORK DEBUT—Greek/Judge, *The Man Who Never Died*, Jan Hus Theatre. PRINCIPAL STAGE APPEARANCES—Soldier, *Gideon*, Plymouth, New York; Richelieu, *The Devils*, Broadway Theatre, New York; Gentleman, *Ivanov*, Shubert, New York; Montague, *Romeo and Juliet*, Circle-in-the-Square, New York; Tremouille, *Saint Joan*, Circle-in-the-Square, New York; John Bart, *Hide and Seek*, New York; Tiresias, *The Bacchae*, Circle-in-the-Square, New York; Sam Craig, *Our Town*, Circle-in-the-Square, New York; Robert/Michel, *The Immoralist*, Bowery Lane, New York; Trigorin, *The Seagull*, Roundabout, New York; Guard/Deaf Man/Man with Transistor, *Museum*, Public Theatre, New York; Pontius Pilate, *The Master and Margarita*, Public Theatre, New York; Dukes Frederick, *As You Like It*, LaMama, New York; Arnold Rubek, *When We Dead Awaken*, Open Space, New York; Nightingale, *Vieux*

TOM KLUNIS

Carré, WPA, New York; Dr. Herdal, *The Master Builder,* Roundabout, New York. With the New York Shakespeare Festival: Norfolk/Grey/York, *Richard III;* Montague, *Romeo and Juliet;* Montjoy, *Henry V;* Horatio, *Hamlet;* Provost, *Measure for Measure.* With the Yale Repertory Company: Ferryman, *The Bundle;* Provost, *Measure for Measure.* Old Man, *The Leper,* Spoleto Festival, Charleston, SC; Agamemnon, *Iphigenia in Aulis,* McCarter, Princeton, NJ; Gonzalo, *The Tempest,* Shakespeare and Company, Lenox, MA; Creon, *Antigone,* Advent Theatre, Nashville, TN; Jaques, *As You Like It,* Northshore Playhouse, Beverly, MA; Juan, *Not in the Book,* Palm Beach; Reuter's Man, *Inherit the Wind,* Arena Stage, Washington, DC; Lieutenant Harris, *Pueblo,* Washington Arena Stage; Player King, *Hamlet,* American Shakespeare Festival, Stratford, CT; Angelo, *Crime on Goat Island,* Cincinnati Playhouse; Prospector, *Madwoman of Chaillot,* Cincinnati Playhouse. As artist-in-residence, Gettysburg College, PA: Thomas More, *A Man for All Seasons;* Joe, *The Time of Your Life;* Caesar, *Caesar and Cleopatra.* MAJOR TOURS—Reuter's Man, *Inherit the Wind,* U.S.S.R.; Narrator, *The Play of Daniel.*

PRINCIPAL FILMS—*The Day the Fish Came Out; The Next Man; Taps.* TELEVISION APPEARANCES—Walter Pace, *Search for Tomorrow; The Guiding Light; As the World Turns; Ryan's Hope; Our Story.*

SIDELIGHTS—MEMBERSHIPS—AEA, SAG, AFTRA.

ADDRESS: Agent—c/o Monty Silver, 200 W. 57th Street, New York, NY 10019.

KNAPP, Eleanore, actress and singer

PERSONAL: Born March 9; daughter of Lester (a railroad executive) and Verna (Steinman) Knapp; married Lloyd Harris (an actor/singer), May 30, 1941. EDUCATION: Case Western Reserve University, B.A., 1937.

CAREER: NEW YORK DEBUT—chorus, *Everywhere I Roam,* National, 1938. PRINCIPAL STAGE APPEARANCES—Housekeeper, *Man of La Mancha,* ANTA, Martin Beck, Mark Hellinger, NY, 1965–70; Housekeeper, *Man of La Mancha,* Vivian Beaumont, NY, 1971; (Off-Broadway) Grand Duchess Anastasia, *Student Prince,* Dame Hannah, *Ruddigore,* Lady Blanche, *Princess Ida,* Light Opera of Manhattan, E. 74th Street Theater, NY, 1981–82; (Off-Off Broadway) Miss Mackay, *The Prime of Miss Jean Brodie,* Manhattan Theatre Club, NY, 1975; Mary, *Angels,* Theatre for the New City, New York, 1982; Gertrude Stein, *Sunsets,* Isabel, *c/o Penn Station,* Troupe Theater, 1982–83; (Regional) *Romeo and Juliet,* San Francisco Opera, CA, 1946; *Norma,* Philadelphia La Scala, PA, 1948; *Amahl and the Night Visitors,* Cincinnati Opera Company, Central City Opera Company, CO. MAJOR TOURS—Marie, *The Most Happy Fella,* U.S. cities, 1949; *Footlight Favorites,* East coast cities. 1983.

SIDELIGHTS: MEMBERSHIPS—AEA; SAG; AFTRA; American Guild of Musical Artists; Twelfth Night Club. FAVORITE ROLES—Carmen.

ADDRESS: Home—80 Lincoln Avenue, Rutherford, NJ 07070. Office—c/o Green Room, 330 W. 45th Street, New York, NY 10036.

ELEANORE KNAPP

KNIGHT, Ted (ne Tadeus Wladyslaw Konopka), actor

PERSONAL: Born December 7, 1923, in Terryville, CT; son of Charles Walter and Sophia (Kovaleski) Konopka; married Dorothy May Clarke, September 14, 1948; children: Ted, Elyse, Eric. EDUCATION: Trained for the stage at Randall School of Dramatic Arts, Hartford, CT. MILITARY: U.S. Army, 1942–44.

CAREER: PRINCIPAL TELEVISION APPEARANCES—Ted Baxter, *Mary Tyler Moore Show*, 1970–77; *Ted Knight Show*, 1977; *Too Close for Comfort*, 1980–present; *Ted Knight Musical-Comedy Special Special.*

PRINCIPAL FILM APPEARANCES—*Caddy Shack*, 1980. NEW YORK STAGE DEBUT—*My Best Friends*, 1977. PRINCIPAL STAGE APPEARANCES—Player's Ring Theatre; Omnibus Theater; Pasadena Playhouse.

PRODUCED—Television Specials—*Ted Knight Musical-Comedy Special Special.* RELATED CAREERS—Formed Kono Productions, Inc., 1976.

AWARDS: Emmy Award, Best Supporting Actor in a Comedy Series, 1972–73, 1975–76: *Mary Tyler Moore Show;* TV Father of the Year, National Fathers Day Committee, 1975.

SIDELIGHTS: MEMBERSHIPS—SAG, AFTRA, AEA.

ADDRESS: Office—P.O. Box 642, Pacific Palisades, CA 900272.*

* * *

KNOBELOCH, Jim, actor

PERSONAL: Born March 18, 1950, in Belleville, IL; son of Lester I. (a farmer) and Ruth M. (Fields) Knobeloch; married Eileen Sams (an exercise instructor), June 4, 1983. EDUCATION: Southern Illinois University, B.A. 1973; Ohio State University, M.F.A., 1976. NON-THEATRICAL CAREER: Audio Consultant, American Audiophile, New York, NY, 1981–83.

CAREER: DEBUT—Captain Keller, *Miracle Worker,* Mascoutah High School, Mascoutah, IL, 1967. NEW YORK DEBUT—Albert, *Count of Monte Cristo,* Meat and Potatoes/ Alvina Krauss, 1981, 30 performances. PRINCIPAL STAGE APPEARANCES—Schnabel, *Paradise Lost,* Mirror, NY, 1983; Tremoile, *Joan of Lorraine,* Mirror, NY, 1983. MAJOR TOURS—*Jesus Christ Superstar,* U.S. cities, 1971; Yam, *Fam and Yam,* Musician, *Sandbox,* Priest, *Box-Mao-Box,* Albee Directs Albee Repertory Tour, International cities, 1978–79.

FILM DEBUT—George Kopestonsky, *Heaven's Gate,* 1980.

SIDELIGHTS: MEMBERSHIPS—AEA; SAG; Mirror Theatre. RECREATION—motorcycling, pool, audio, equestrian, fencing.

ADDRESS: Office—c/o American Audiophile, 716 Madison Avenue, New York, NY 10022.

JIM KNOBELOCH

KNOTT, Frederick, playwright, screenwriter, television writer

PERSONAL: Born August 28, 1916, in China; son of Cyril Wakefield and Margaret Caroline (both missionaries to China; mother's maiden name, Paull) Knott; married Ann Margaret Francis (an actress; stage name, Ann Hillary); children: Anthony Frederick. EDUCATION: Oundle School, England; Cambridge University, B.A., 1938, M.A. 1942. MILITARY: Royal Artillery, 1939–46 (Major).

WRITINGS: PLAYS, PUBLISHED—*Dial M for Murder,* 1952; *Write Me a Murder,* 1961; *Wait Until Dark,* 1966.

PLAYS, PRODUCED—*Mr. Fox of Venice* (adaptation, *The Evil of the Day* by Thomas Sterling).

SCREENPLAYS, PRODUCED—*Last Page,* 1950; *Dial M for Murder,* 1953. TELEVISION PLAYS, PRODUCED—*Dial M for Murder,* (BBC) 1952, (Hallmark) 1958, (BBC) 1961, (Talent Associates) 1967.

AWARDS: Mystery Writers of America, Special Edgar Allan Poe Award, *Dial M for Murder,* 1953, *Write Me a Murder,* 1962.

SIDELIGHTS: MEMBERSHIPS—The Dramatists Guild; The Writer's Guild of America; Mystery Writers of America; The British Screenwriters' Association (Chairman, 1950); The Dramatists Club; The Players.

ADDRESS: Agent—Bridget Aschenberg, I.C.M., 40 W. 57th Street, New York, NY 10019.

KOCH, Howard W., film and television producer

*PERSONAL:*Born April 11, 1916, in New York City; married Ruth; children: Melinda, Howard Jr. EDUCATION: Attended public schools in New York City and the Peddie Preparatory School in Hightstown, NJ.

CAREER: PRINCIPAL FILM WORK, executive producer—*X-15*, 1961, *Sergeants Three*, 1962, *Manchurian Candidate*, 1962, *Come Blow Your Horn*, 1963, *Robin and the Seven Hoods*, 1964, *None but the Brave*, 1965, *For Those Who Think Young*, 1964, *The President's Analyst*, 1967, *Dragonslayer*, 1981; producer—*Warpaint, Beachead, Yellow Tomahawk, Desert Sands*, 1955, *Fort Yuma*, 1955, *Quincannon: Frontier Scout*, 1956, *Ghost Town*, 1956, *Broken Star*, 1956, *Crimes Against Joe*, 1956, *Three Bad Sisters*, 1956, *Emergency Hospital*, 1956, *Rebel in Town*, 1956, *The Black Sleep*, 1956, *Pharaoh's Curse*, 1957, *Tomahawk Train*, 1957, *Revolt at Fort Laramie*, 1957, *War Drums*, 1957, *VooDoo Island*, 1957, *Hellbound*, 1957, *The Dalton Girls*, 1957, *The Odd Couple*, 1968, *On a Clear Day, You Can See Forever*, 1970, *Plaza Suite*, 1971, *Star Spangled Girl*, 1971, *The Last of the Red Hot Lovers*, 1972, *Jacqueline Susann's Once Is Not Enough*, 1975, *Some Kind of Hero*, 1982, *Airplane II: The Sequel*, 1982.

Howard W. Koch Productions—*A New Leaf*, 1971; *Airplane*, 1980; *Airplane II: The Sequel;* producer/director—*Badge 373*, 1973; director—*Big House USA*, 1955, *Shield for Murder, Jungle Heat*, 1957, *Fort Bowie*, 1958, *Violent Road*, 1958, *Untamed Youth*, 1957, *Frankenstein 1970*, 1958, *Andy Hardy Comes Home*, 1958, *Girl in Black Stockings*, 1957, *The Last Mile*, 1959, *Born Reckless*, 1959.

PRINCIPAL TELEVISION WORK—Directed segments—*Miami Undercover, Hawaiian Eye, Cheyenne, Maverick, Lawman, The Untouchables;* produced specials—*The Academy Awards*, 1972, 73, 75, 76, 78, 80, 82, 83, *Ol' Blue Eyes is Back*, 1973, *Oscar's Best Actors, Oscar's Best Movies, Who Loves Ya Baby*, 1976, *On the Road with Bing*, 1977, *The Pirate*, (movies for television), 1978.

RELATED-CAREER: Second assistant director, *The Keys of the Kingdom*, Universal Pictures, followed by first assistant directorships with Joseph Mankiewicz, Mervyn Leroy, William Wellman, Tay Garnett and Clarence Brown; assistant director at United Artists, with Aubrey Schenck formed Bel Air Productions; vice-president production for Frank Sinatra, 1961–64; head of production, Paramount Studios, 1964–66.

AWARDS: Nominated for Best Director of the Year, Directors Guild of America, *The Untouchables;* Producer of the Year, National Association of Theatre Owners, 1980.

SIDELIGHTS: MEMBERSHIPS—Director, Southern California Theatre Association; director, Security Pacific Bank; chairman, Directors Guild of America Educational & Benevolent Foundation; council, Directors Guild of America; director, KCET; board of governors, Academy of Motion Picture Arts and Sciences; trustee, executive board and case committee, Motion Picture and Television Fund; vice-president, executive committee, Hollywood Park, Inc., director, Hamburger Hamlet; Producers Guild of America.

ADDRESS: Office—Howard Koch Productions, 5555 Melrose Avenue, Los Angeles, CA 90048.

KOCH, Howard W., Jr., producer

PERSONAL: Born December 14, 1945; son of Howard W. (a producer) and Ruth Koch; children: Billy, Emily, Robby.

CAREER: PRINCIPAL FILM WORK: Associate producer, *Once Is Not Enough*, 1975; associate producer, *The Drowning Pool*, 1975; executive producer, *The Other Side of Midnight*, 1977; *Heaven Can Wait*, 1978; *The Frisco Kid*, 1979; co-producer (with Dan Boyd), *Honky Tonk Freeway*, 1981; co-producer (with Gene Kirkwood), *The Idolmaker*, 1980, *Gorky Park*, 1983, *Heaven*, 1983.

RELATED CAREER—President, Rastar.

ADDRESS: Office—Columbia Plaza West-19, Burbank, CA 91505.

* * *

KOPYC, Frank, actor

PERSONAL: Surname pronounced *Ko*-peck; born August 6, 1948, in Troy, NY; son of Frank William (a restaurateur) and Mary Veronica (Marshall) Kopyc. EDUCATION: Yankton College, B.A., 1971; studied advanced acting with Alvina Krause, voice with Douglas Decatur.

FRANK KOPYC

CAREER: DEBUT—Artie, *House of Blue Leaves*, Nebraska Repertory, Lincoln, 1970. NEW YORK DEBUT—Pop, *Pop*, Players, 1974 for one performance. PRINCIPAL STAGE APPEARANCES—Louis, *Pal Joey*, Long Wharf, New Haven, CT; Paul Whiteman, *Hoagy Bix*, Indiana Repertory; Horatio Alger, *Son of Myself*, Pennsylvania Stage; Banquo, *Macbeth*, Golfer, *We Bombed in New Haven*, Major Petkoff, *Arms and the Man*, Nicely-Nicely, *Guys and Dolls*, M.C., *Cabaret*, Nebraska Repertory; Fiorello La Guardia, *Fiorello*, Equity Library, NY, 1976; H. Jackson, *Happy End*, Martin Beck, NY, 1977; Chorus/Pirelli, *Sweeney Todd*, Uris, NY, 1979; Magruder, *Anyone Can Whistle*, Berkshire Theatre Festival, Stockbridge, MA, 1981; Father Tucker, *El Bravo*, Entermedia, New York, 1982; Sancho, *Man of La Mancha*, Lake George Opera; General Understudy, *Chaplin* (Pre-Broadway), 1983.

TELEVISION DEBUT—*Steve Martin's Best Special Ever*. TELEVISION APPEARANCES—*One Life to Live*.

SIDELIGHTS: MEMBERSHIPS—AEA; SAG; AFTRA. Mr. Kopyc also plays piano and clarinet.

ADDRESS: Agent—Don Buchwald & Associates, 10 E. 44th Street, New York, NY 10036.

* * *

KORTY, John Van Cleave, director

PERSONAL: Born June 22, 1936, in Lafayette, IN; son of Richard Marshall and Mary Elizabeth (Van Cleave) Korty; married Beulah Chang, January 16, 1966; children: Jonathan, David. EDUCATION: Antioch College, B.A., 1959.

CAREER: DIRECTED: FILMS—*The Crazy Quilt*, 1966; *Funnyman*, 1967; *Riverrun*, 1969; *Alex and the Gypsy*, 1976; *Oliver's Story*, 1978; *Twice Upon a Time*, 1983.

TELEVISION FILMS—*The People*, 1972; *Go Ask Alice*, 1973; *Class of '63*, 1974; *Autobiography of Miss Jane Pittman*, 1974; *Farewell to Manzanar*, 1976; *Forever*, 1977; *A Christmas without Snow*, 1980; *Who Are the DeBolts?*, 1978; *The Haunting Passion*, 1983; *Second Sight, a Love Story*, 1984.

AWARDS: Academy Award, Best Feature-Length Documentary, Emmy Award, Outstanding Achievement, DGA Award, 1978: *Who Are the Debolts?*; Humanitas Award, Christopher Award, 1976: *Farewell to Manzanar*; Emmy Award, Best Director of a Dramatic Special, Directors Guild Award, Best Television Director, 1974: *Autobiography of Miss Jane Pittman*.

SIDELIGHTS: MEMBERSHIPS—Directors Guild of America, Writers Guild of America.

ADDRESS: Office—200 Miller Avenue, Mill Valley, CA 94941. Agent—c/o Sam Adams, Adams, Ray and Roseberg, 9200 Sunset Blvd., Penthouse 25, Los Angeles, CA 90069.

JERZY KOSINSKI

KOSINSKI, Jerzy, writer

PERSONAL: Born June 14, 1933, in Lodz, Poland; son of Mieczyslaw and Elzbieta (Liniecka) Kosinski; married Mary H. Weir January 11, 1962 (died 1968). EDUCATION: University of Poland, M.A. (Political Science), 1953, M.A. (History) 1955; Ph.D. canidate, Columbia University, NY, 1958–65. NON-THEATRICAL CAREER: Assistant professor and research fellow, Institute of Sociology and Cultrual History, Political Sciences Academy, Warsaw, Poland, 1955–57; fellow, Center for Advanced Studies, Wesleyan University, CT, 1968–69; Council of Humanities, fellow, visiting lecturer, English, Princeton University, NJ, 1969–70; visiting professor, English Prose and Davenport College Fellow, Yale University School of Drama, 1970–73.

WRITINGS: BOOKS—*The Future Is Ours, Comrade*, 1960; *No Third Path*, 1962; *The Painted Bird*, 1965; *Steps*, 1968; *Being There*, 1971; *The Devil Tree*, 1973; *Cockpit*, 1975; *Blind Date*, 1977; *Passion Play*, 1979; *Pinball*, 1982. SCREENPLAYS—*Being There*, 1978; *Passion Play*, 1980.

ACTING CAREER: FILM DEBUT—Grigori Zinoviev, *Reds*, 1982. PRINCIPAL TELEVISION APPEARANCES—Guest, *The To-*

night Show, The Merv Griffin Show, Today Show, A.M. America, CBS Nightly News, Signature, 60 Minutes, The David Frost Show, The Dick Cavett Show, Entertainment Tonight; presenter, *Academy Award Show,* 1982; *Panorama,* Washington, DC.

AWARDS: Spertus College International Award, 1982; Ph.D. Hon. C. Hebrew Letters, Spertus College of Judaica, 1982; British Academy of Film and Television Arts Award, Screenplay, 1981: *Being There;* ACLU First Amendment Award, 1980; Best Screenplay Award, Writers Guild of America, 1979: *Being There;* Brith Sholom Humanitarian Freedom Award, 1974; American Academy of Arts and Letters Award in Literature, 1970; National Book Award, 1969: *Steps;* Guggenheim Lit. Fellow, 1967.

SIDELIGHTS: MEMBERSHIPS—Executive board and president, 1973–75, P.E.N.; executive board, National Writers Club; director, International League for Human Rights; ACLU chairman of Artists and Writers Committee and member of the National Advisory Committee; the Century Association, NYC, Authors Guild, AFTRA, SAG, Writers Guild.

ADDRESS: Office—c/o Scientia-Factum, Inc., Suite 18-k, 60 W. 57th Street, New York, NY 10019.

* * *

KRAMER, Stanley E., producer and director

PERSONAL: Born September 29, 1913, in New York City; married Ann Pearce, 1950 (divorced); married Karen Sharpe, 1966; children: (first marriage), Casey, Larry; (second marriage), Katharine, Jennifer. EDUCATION: New York University, B.S., 1933. MILITARY: U.S. Army.

CAREER: PRINCIPAL FILM WORK—Producer: *Moon and Sixpence,* 1942; *So This Is New York,* 1948; *Home of the Brave,* 1949; *Champion,* 1949; *The Men,* 1950; *Cyrano de Bergerac,* 1950; *Death of a Salesman,* 1951; *High Noon,* 1952; *The Happy Time,* 1952; *The Sniper,* 1952; *My Six Convicts,* 1952; *Eight Iron Men,* 1952; *The Four Poster,* 1952; *The 5000 Fingers of Dr. T.,* 1952; *The Wild One,* 1953; *Member of the Wedding,* 1953; *The Juggler,* 1953; *The Cain Mutiny,* 1954.

PRODUCER/DIRECTOR: *Not As a Stranger,* 1955; *The Pride and the Passion,* 1957; *The Defiant Ones,* 1958; *On the Beach,* 1959; *Inherit the Wind,* 1960; *Judgement at Nuremberg,* 1961; *It's a Mad, Mad, Mad, Mad World,* 1963; *Ship of Fools,* 1965; *Guess Who's Coming to Dinner,* 1967; *The Secret of Santa Vittoria,* 1969; *R.P.M.,* 1970; *Bless the Beasts and the Children,* 1971; *Oklahoma Crude,* 1973; *The Domino Principle/The Domino Killings,* 1977; *The Runner Stumbles,* 1979.

RELATED CAREERS: Researcher, MGM Films; film cutter; film editor; writer, radio and film; formed Stanley Kramer Productions, 1949; formed Stanley Kramer Company, 1950 (merged with Columbia Pictures, 1951).

AWARDS: Irving Thalberg Award, 1962; Gallatin Medal, New York University, 1968; New York Film Critics Award,

Best Director, 1958: *The Defiant Ones;* Academy Award (4), 1952: *High Noon; Look* Achievement Award, Best Director, 1950.

ADDRESS: Office—c/o Stanley Kramer Productions, P.O. Box 158, Bellevue, WA 90889.*

* * *

KRAUSS, Marvin A., producer, manager

PERSONAL: Born October 11, 1928, in New York City; son of Ernest (a dress manufacturer) and Anna (Daniels) Krauss; married Elaine Tanenbaum (an interior designer), January 25, 1953; children: Anne, Robin, Nina, Seth. EDUCATION: City College of New York, B.S. and one-year fellowship (speech department). MILITARY: Sergeant, U.S. Signal Corps.

CAREER: FIRST NEW YORK STAGE PRODUCTION—*The Poison Tree.* PRINCIPAL STAGE PRODUCTIONS—*Ain't Misbehavin';* *American Buffalo; An Unpleasant Evening with H. L. Mencken; Beatlemania; Broadway Follies; Butterflies Are Free; Can-Can; Carnival; Catch Me If You Can; Children of a Lesser God* (national company); *Children! Children!; Comedy a Musical Commedia; Dancin'; Dreamgirls; Find Your Way Home; Frankenstein; Gabrielle; Godspell; Gypsy; Happiest Girl in the World; Jockeys; King of Hearts; L'il Abner; La Cage Aux Folles; Little Johnny Jones; Master Harold . . . and the Boys* (national company); *Mayflower; Merlin; Minnie's Boys; No Hard Feelings; Parade; Platinum; Richard III; Ride the Winds; Rock and Roll; Saturday, Sunday, Monday; Seven Brides for Seven Brothers; Seventy Girls Seventy; Sherry; Snoopy; Something's Afoot; Summer Brave; Sunset; Teibele and Her Demon; The Andersonville Trial; The Eccentricities of a Nightingale; The Gingerbread Lady; The Madwoman of Central Park West; The Magic Show; The Merchant; The National Lampoon Show; The Neighborhood Playhouse at 50; The Night That Made America Famous; The Pleasure of His Company; The Poison Tree; The Rocky Horror Show; The Sudden and Accidental Re-education of Horse Johnson; The Watering Place; The Women; Thoughts; Thurber Carnival; Tommy; Wally's Cafe; What's a Nice Country Like You Doing in a State Like This?; Woman of the Year; You're a Good Man, Charlie Brown.*

BROADWAY CONCERTS—*Al Jarreau with David Sanborn; Bette Midler—Clams on the Half-Shell; Bette Midler—Divine Madness; Bing Crosby—On Broadway; Charles Aznavour; Cleo Laine; Count Basie, Ella Fitzgerald, Frank Sinatra; Diana Ross; Englebert Humperdinck; George Benson; Gilda Radner; LaBelle; Lily Tomlin; Liza; Los Muchachos; Lou Rawls; Mr. Words—A Tribute to Ira Gershwin; Natalie Cole; Neil Diamond; Paul Anka; Peter Allen—Up in One; Shirley Bassey; Shirley MacLaine.*

SIDELIGHTS: MEMBERSHIPS—League of New York Theatres and Producers (Board of Governors); Association of Theatrical Press Agents and Managers. President of Marvin A. Krauss Associates, Inc., a theatrical producing/management concern.

ADDRESS: Home—25 Central Park West, New York, NY

Photograph by Peter Cunningham

MARVIN A. KRAUSS

10023; Office—250 West 52nd Street, New York, NY 10019.

* * *

KUBRICK, Stanley, producer, director and writer

PERSONAL: Born July 26, 1928, in New York City.

CAREER: PRINCIPAL FILM WORK—Writer/producer/director, *Day of the Fight;* writer/producer/director, *Flying Padre;* producer/director, *Fear and Desire,* 1953; producer/director, *Killer's Kiss,* 1955; director, *The Killing,* 1956; writer/director, *Paths of Glory,* 1958; director, *Spartacus,* 1960; director, *Lolita,* 1962; writer/producer/director, *Dr. Strangelove,* 1964; writer/producer/director, *2001: A Space Odyssey,* 1968; writer/producer/director, *A Clockwork Orange,* 1971; writer/producer/director, *Barry Lyndon,* 1975; writer/producer/director, *The Shining,* 1980.

AWARDS: Academy Award, Best Special Visual Effects, 1968: *2001: A Space Odyssey;* New York Critics Award, 1964: *Dr. Strangelove.*

ADDRESS: Office—c/o Louis C. Blau, Loeb and Loeb, 10100 Santa Monica Blvd., Suite 2200, Los Angeles, CA 90067.*

KURTZ, Swoosie, actress

PERSONAL: Born September 6, in Omaha, NE; daughter of Frank (an Air Force colonel and three-time Olympic diver) and Margo (a writer) Kurtz. EDUCATION: Attended the University of Southern California; trained for the stage at the London Academy of Dramatic Arts.

CAREER: DEBUT—*Charley's Aunt* and *Skin of Our Teeth,* Cincinnati Playhouse in the Park, Cinncinati, OH, 1966. NEW YORK DEBUT—*The Effect of Gamma Rays on Man-in-the-Moon Marigolds,* Mercer Arts and New Theatre, 1970. PRINCIPAL STAGE APPEARANCES—Muriel, *Ah, Wilderness!,* Circle in the Square, NY, 1975; Mariane, *Tartuffe,* Circle in the Square, NY, 1977; Rita, *Uncommon Women and Others,* Phoenix, NY, 1977; Bette, *A History of American Film,* ANTA, NY, 1978; Gwen, *Fifth of July,* New Apollo, NY, 1980–81.

FILM DEBUT—*Slapshot,* 1977. PRINCIPAL FILM APPEARANCES— Hooker, *The World According to Garp,* 1981; Edie, *Against All Odds,* 1983. PRINCIPAL TELEVISION APPEARANCES—*Love, Sidney,* 1982; *A Caribbean Mystery,* 1983.

AWARDS: Antoinette Perry Award, Outer Critics Circle Award, Drama Desk Award, 1981: *Fifth of July;* Antoinette Perry Award Nomination, 1978: *Tartuffe;* Obie Award, 1978: *Uncommon Woman and Others;* Drama Desk Award, 1978: *A History of American Film;* Emmy Award Nominations, 1982, 1983: *Love, Sidney.*

ADDRESS: Agent—c/o Creative Artists Agency, 1888 Century Park East, Suite 1400, Los Angeles, CA 90067.

SWOOSIE KURTZ

L

LACHMAN, Morton, director, producer, writer

PERSONAL: Born March 20, 1918, Seattle, WA; son of Sol and Rose (Bloom) Lachman; married Elaine, June 23, 1984; children: (former marriage) Joanne, Diane, Robert. EDUCATION: University of Washington, B.A., 1939. MILITARY: U.S. Army Signal Corp.

CAREER: PRINCIPAL TELEVISION WORK—Director/producer/ writer, *Bob Hope Specials:* Morocco, Moscow, Near East, Europe, Vietnam, Korea and Thailand; director/producer, Chrysler Theater; producer, *Kraft Music Hall* (Des O'Connor from London); director, *ABC Playbreak;* director, *That's My Mama;* director, *The Girl Who Couldn't Lose;* executive producer: *All in the Family, Sanford and Son, One Day at a Time, Gimme a Break* (also co-creator), *No Soap Radio, Book of Lists* (also co-creator), *Kate & Allie.*

AWARDS: Emmy Award, directing, *The Girl Who Couldn't Lose.*

SIDELIGHTS: MEMBERSHIPS—Directors Guild of America, Writers Guild of America, AFTRA.

ADDRESS: Office—4115 B. Warner Blvd. Burbank, CA 91505. Agent—Bernie Weintraub, Robinson-Weintraub, 8428 Melrose Place, Los Angeles, CA 90069.

* * *

DIANE LADD

LADD, Diane, actress

PERSONAL: Born November 29, 1939, in Meridian, MS; daughter of Preston P. (a poulterer) and Mary Bernadette (Anderson) Ladner; married Bruce Dern (an actor, divorced); children: Laura Elizabeth. EDUCATION: Graduated from St. Aloysius Academy; trained for the stage with Frank Corsaro in New York.

CAREER: DEBUT—*The Verdict,* Meridian, MS. PRINCIPAL STAGE APPEARANCES—(Broadway) Lu Ann, *Texas Trilogy; Carry Me Back to Morningside Heights;* (Off-Broadway) *One Night Stands of a Noisy Passenger; Orpheus Descending;* (Regional and Stock) *Women Speak; The Medium Rare Review; The Fantasticks; The Wall; The Goddess; Toys in the Attic; The Deadly Game; Hamlet.* MAJOR TOURS—*A Hatful of Rain,* U.S. cities.

PRINCIPAL FILM APPEARANCES—*Wild Angels,* 1966; *The Reivers,* 1969; *Macho Calahan,* 1970; *W.U.S.A.,* 1970; *White Lightning,* 1973; Flo, *Alice Doesn't Live Here Anymore,* 1974; *Chinatown,* 1974, *Embryo,* 1976; *All Night Long,* 1981; *Something Wicked This Way Comes,* 1983.

PRINCIPAL TELEVISION CREDITS—Belle, *Alice;* Thaddeus, *Rose and Eddie; Addie and the King of Hearts; Willa; Black Beauty;* Kitty Styles, *The Secret Storm; Love Boat.*

WRITINGS: God Give Me One More Minute (autobiography), 1982.

AWARDS: Golden Globe Award, Best Supporting Actress: *Alice;* Academy Award nomination, Golden Globe Award nomination, British Academy Award, Best Supporting Actress, 1974: *Alice Doesn't Live Here Anymore;* Broadway Tour Award: *Texas Trilogy;* UCLA Favorite Actress Award: *Texas Trilogy;* Eleanore Duse Mask Award.

ADDRESS: Agent—c/o Sherry Carlin, Key Enterprises, P.O. Box 1616, Suite 138, Studio City, CA 91604.

* * *

LAHTI, Christine, actress

PERSONAL: Born April 4, 1950, in Detroit, MI; daughter of Paul Theodore (a surgeon) and Elizabeth Margaret (an artist; maiden name, Tabar) Lahti; married Thomas Schlamme (a director), September 4, 1983. EDUCATION: University of Michigan, M.F.A.; trained for the stage at the Herbert Berghof Studios with William Esper and Uta Hagen.

CAREER: DEBUT—*The Zinger.* NEW YORK DEBUT—Ruth, *The Woods*, Public Theatre, 1978. PRINCIPAL STAGE APPEARANCES—*Division Street*, Ambassador, NY, 1980; *Loose Ends*, Circle in the Square, NY, 1981; *Present Laughter*, Circle in the Square, NY, 1983.

FILM DEBUT—*And Justice for All*, 1980. PRINCIPAL FILM APPEARANCES—Dr. Scott, *Whose Life Is It Anyway?*, 1982; *Swing Shift*, 1984. PRINCIPAL TELEVISION APPEARANCES—*The Last Tenant; The Executioner's Song.*

AWARDS: Theatre World Award, 1978: *The Woods.*

SIDELIGHTS: MEMBERSHIPS—Ensemble Studio Theater.

ADDRESS: Agent—c/o Jeff Hunter, D.H.K.P.R., 165 W. 46th Street, New York, NY 10036.

* * *

LAIRD, Jack, actor, director, writer, producer, orchestra leader

PERSONAL: Born May 8, 1923 in Bombay, India; son of Leonard (a journalist) and Thelma (an actress; maiden name, Laird) von Schultheis; married Cicely Browne (an actress) on January 1, 1948 (divorced 1954); children: Sean, Persephone. EDUCATION: Studied at the Dramatic Workshop of New School for Social Research with Irwin Piscator, 1946–47; also studied at the Actor's Lab, in Hollywood CA, 1958–49. POLITICS: Democrat. MILITARY: U.S. Army Air Force, 1st Lieutenant, Eastern Theatre of Operations, World War II, 1943–45.

CAREER: DEBUT—Willie, *East Lynne*, Foothill Playhouse, Monrovia, CA, 1934. NEW YORK DEBUT—Chris Miller, *The Barker*, Abbe Playhouse, 1946. PRINCIPAL STAGE APPEARANCES—Ficsur, *Liliom*, Abbe Playhouse, NY, 1946; Heavy, *Here Come the Clowns*, Abbe Playhouse, NY, 1946; *Let Us Be Gay, Chicken Every Night*, Worcester Playhouse, MA, 1946; *Joan of Lorraine, Dark of the Moon*, Hilltop Playhouse, Baltimore, MD, 1947; *Room Service, The Milky Way*, Tiverton Playhouse, Tiverton, RI, 1948; *Androcles and the Lion, Street Scene, Once in a Lifetime*, Player's Ring, Hollywood, CA, 1949–50; *Phaedra, Shadow of a Gunman*, Actor's Lab, Hollywood, CA, 1950; *Detective Story*, Sombrero Playhouse, Phoenix, AZ, 1951; *Stalag 17*,

Las Palmas, Hollywood, CA, 1952. MAJOR TOURS—*Made in Heaven*, National Company, 1947–48.

FILM DEBUT—child, *The Circus Clown*, 1934. PRINCIPAL FILM APPEARANCES—Dr. Phillips, *Mr. Belvedere Goes to College*, 1949; Sgt. McGuire, *Francis*, 1950; Digges, *Sword in the Desert*, 1950; Worms, *Jouney into Light*, 1951.

TELEVISION DEBUT—*Rebound*, 1950. PRINCIPAL TELEVISION APPEARANCES—*Colgate Comedy Hour; Fireside Theatre; Ed Wynn Show; Ben Casey; Armchair Detective; Ironside; Hauser's Memory; Hollywood Playhouse; The Protectors; Night Gallery; Destiny of a Spy.*

PRINCIPAL TELEVISION WORK, PRODUCER—*Ben Casey; Channing; See How They Run; Chrysler Theatre; The Jane Wyman Show; The Dark Intruder; Perilous Voyage; The Protectors; Night Gallery; Kojak; How I Spent My Summer Vacation; Destiny of a Spy; Trial Run; The Movie Murderer; Charlie Chan: Happiness Is a Warm Clue; Testimony of Two Men; Harvest Home; Switch; Beggarman, Thief; One of Our Own; Doctors Hospital; Shadow over Elveron; Hauser's Memory; The Crime Club; The Ganster Chronicles.* PRINCIPAL TELEVISION WORK, DIRECTOR—*Night Gallery; Kojak.*

WRITINGS: PLAYS, PRODUCED—*Monsieur Jules*, Stage Society, 1952; *The Game*, Stage Society, 1953. TELEVISION SHOWS—*Fireside Theatre; The Trouble with Father; Private Secretary; My Three Sons; The Millionaire; Highway Patrol; Have Gun—Will Travel; Code Three; M Squad; Ford Theatre; Man With a Camera; Dragnet; The Lineup; China Smith; The Brothers Brannigan; The Fugitive; The Wild Wild West; Bronco; The Martian Files; The Hanged Man; Bus Riley's Back in Town; Perilous Voyage; Night Gallery; Kojak; One of Our Own; Doctors Hospital.*

AWARDS: Writers Guild of America Nomination for Outstanding Script in the Category of Anthological Drama written Originally for TV, 1976: "One of Our Own," U.S. Treasury Department Award for Patriotic Public Service, 1976; Academy of Television Arts and Sciences Nomination for Outstanding Drama Series, 1975: *Kojak;* 40th Annual Fame Award, 1971: *Night Gallery;* Grand Prize, Golden Asteroid, 9th International Festival of Science Fiction Films, 1971: *Hauser's Memory;* Academy of Television Arts and Sciences Nomination for Outstanding Single Program, Comedy or Drama, 1971: "They're Tearing Down Tim Riley's Bar," *Night Gallery;* Academy of Television Arts and Sciences, Nomination for Outstanding Writing Achievement in Drama, 1962: "I Remember a Lemon Tree," *Ben Casey;* Writers Guild of America Award Nomination for Outstanding Writing Achievement, TV Episodic Drama, 1962: "I Remember a Lemon Tree," *Ben Casey;* Purple Heart Medal and Bronze Star Medal, U.S. Army.

SIDELIGHTS: MEMBERSHIPS—Writers Guild of America; Dramatists Guild; Common Cause; ACLU; Southern Poverty Law Center Klanwatch Project; Oxfam America; Nuclear Control Institute; National Lawyers Guild Fund Capp Street Foundation; NOW; Environmental Defense Fund; Center for Law in the Public Interest.

"Motivation: I am compulsively driven . . . there is nothing in this world which cannot be improved upon . . . Broadway is a disaster area . . . the motion picture industry is in the grips of corporate giants and their Wall Street equivalents and their art will be sacrificed in the name of fiscal responsibility, and audiences will be doomed to an unending succession of xeroxed entertainment . . . television languishes in the grip of statisticians and research consultants . . . network programming executives with an axe poised perpetually above their heads are afraid to be bold, daring and innovative . . . and so it goes. I am a true film buff, a self-educated scholar in the 'history of the cinema' as both art and entertainment. I collect films, both sound and silent, as well as lobby cards, window cards, inserts and one-sheets and books on this eternally fascinating subject. I am an amateur photographer and a gourmet cook and am well travelled, but not nearly so well as I'd like to be. I have recently completed a mini-series for a major network which deals with the relationship between Louis B. Mayer and Irving Thalberg and the history of MGM. It was a labor of love.''

ADDRESS: Office—Universal Studios, Universal City, CA 91608. Agent—Marvin Moss, Marvin Moss, Inc., 9200 Sunset Blvd., Los Angeles, CA 90069.

* * *

LAMOS, Mark, actor and director

PERSONAL: Born March 10, 1946, in Melrose Park, IL; son of Gustav (a horticulturalist) and Ruth (an office manager; maiden name, Oechslin) Lamos; married Sharon Anderson, 1970 (divorced, 1977). EDUCATION: Northwestern University, B.S., 1969.

CAREER: DEBUT—Joe, *Lovers*, Academy Festival Theater, Lake Forest, IL, 1969. NEW YORK DEBUT—Private Bowers, *Love-Suicide at Schofield Barracks*, ANTA, 1971, 12 performances. PRINCIPAL STAGE APPEARANCES—Hamlet, *Hamlet*, Old Globe, San Diego, CA, 1977; leading roles, Guthrie, Minneapolis, MN, 1974–77; Feste, *Twelfth Night*, Stratford, CT, 1978; Octavius, *Man and Superman*, Circle in the Square, NY, 1978.

DIRECTED: Plays—*Don Giovanni*, St. Louis Opera, MO, 1983; *Arabella*, Santa Fe Opera, NM, 1983; *Merchant of Venice*, Stratford, Canada, 1984.

THEATRE-RELATED CAREER: Artistic Director, Arizona Theater Company, Tucson, AZ, 1978; Artistic Director, California Shakespearean Festival, Visalia, CA, 1978–80; Artistic Director, Hartford Stage Company, Hartford, CT, 1980–present.

ADDRESS: Office—Hartford Stage Company, 50 Church Street, Hartford, CT 06103. Agent—c/o Milton Goldman, ICM, 40 W. 57th Street, New York, NY 10019.

* * *

LAMPERT, Zohra, actress

PERSONAL: Born May 13, 1937, in New York City; daughter of Morris (an ironworker and architect) and Rachil (a hatmaker and draper; maiden name, Eriss) Lampert. EDUCA-

TION: High School of Music and Art, New York; University of Chicago; studied for the theatre with Mira Ristova (''Still, I continue studying with her'').

CAREER: DEBUT—Conchita, *Dancing in the Chequered Shade*, McCarter, Princeton, NY, 1955. NEW YORK DEBUT—*Venice Preserv'd*, Phoenix, ''Side Show,'' Phoenix, 1955–56. PRINCIPAL STAGE APPEARANCES—Mashenka, *Diary of a Scoundrel*, Phoenix, NY, 1956; Maid to Lady Britomart, *Major Barbara*, Martin Beck, NY, 1956, later Rummy Michens in the same production; Adele, *Maybe Tuesday*, Playhouse, NY, 1958; Jennifer Lewison, *Look: We've Come Through*, Hudson, NY, 1961; Illyona, *First Love*, Morosco, NY, 1961; Member, *Second City*, Square East, NY, 1962–63; Kattrin, *Mother Courage and Her Children*, Martin Beck, NY, 1963; Felice, *After the Fall*, Lincoln Center Repertory, ANTA Washington Square, NY, 1964; Princess Kukachin, *Marco Millions*, Lincoln Center Repertory, ANTA Washington Square, NY, 1964; Rachel, *Nathan Weinstein, Mystic, Connecticut*, Brooks Atkinson, NY, 1966; Jane, *The Natural Look*, Longacre, NY, 1967; Brenda, *Lovers and Other Strangers*, Brooks Atkinson, NY, 1968; Iris, *The Sign in Sidney Brustein's Window* (musical), Longacre, 1972; others.

FILM DEBUT—*Pay or Die*, 1960. FILM APPEARANCES—Angelina, *Splendor in the Grass*, 1961; *A Fine Madness*, 1966; *Bye Bye Braverman*, 1968; Jessica, *Let's Scare Jessica to Death*, 1971.

TELEVISION APPEARANCES—*Doctor Kildare, The Defenders, Sam Benedict, Alfred Hitchcock Presents*, Leonard Bernstein's ''Carmen'' on *Omnibus; The Reporter*, 1964; Jenny, *Better Luck Next Time*, 1964; *The F.B.I.*, 1970; Ellie, *Where the Heart Is*, 1970–71; *Love, American Style*, 1972–73; Hannah, *The Connection*, 1972; Janine, *The Bob Newhart Show*, 1973; Anne, *The Girl with Something Extra*, 1973–74; Dr. Norah Purcell, *Doctors' Hospital*, 1975–76; Woman, *The Cafeteria*, 1984.

AWARDS: Variety NY Drama Critics Poll, Kattrin, *Mother Courage and Her Children*, 1963; Antoinette Perry Award nominations, *Look, We've Come Through*, 1961, *Mother Courage and Her Children*, 1963; Andy Awards, *Banker's Trust Radio Commercials, Enkasheer Television Commercial—Girl in Lobby*, 1970.

SIDELIGHTS: MEMBERSHIPS—AEA; SAG; AFTRA; AGVA.

Ms. Lampert's early stage name was Zohra Alton. She began using the name Lampert in 1956 in the production of *Major Barbara* at the Phoenix. Her uncle, Samuel Iris, is an actor.

ADDRESS: Agent—Sheila Robinson, I.C.M. 40 W. 57th Street, New York, NY 10019.

* * *

LANCASTER, Burt (Stephen), actor

PERSONAL: Born November 2, 1913, in New York, NY; son of James Lancaster; married Norma Anderson, December 26, 1946 (divorced 1969); children: James Stephen,

William Henry, Susan Elizabeth, Joanne Mari. EDUCATION: Attended New York University. MILITARY: U.S. Army. NON-FILM CAREER: Circus acrobat, 1932–39; floor walker, Marshall Field, Chicago, 1939.

CAREER: PRINCIPAL FILM APPEARANCES—*Desert Fury*, 1946; *The Killers*, 1947; *I Walk Alone*, 1947; *Brute Force*, 1948; *All My Sons*, 1948; *Sorry, Wrong Number*, 1948; *Kiss the Blood Off My Hands*, 1948; *Criss-Cross*, 1949; *Rope of Sand*, 1949; *Vengeance Valley*, 1951; *Jim Thorpe—All American*, 1951; *Ten Tall Men*, 1951; *The Crimson Pirate*, 1952; *Come Back Little Sheba*, 1953; *South Sea Woman*, 1953; *From Here to Eternity*, 1953; *The Big Top: His Majesty O'Keefe*, 1954; *The Kentuckian*, (also directed), 1954; *The Rose Tatoo*, 1955; *Trapeze*, 1956; *The Rainmaker*, 1957; *Gunfight at the OK Corral*, 1957; *Sweet Smell of Success*, 1957; *Run Silent, Run Deep*, 1958; *Separate Tables*, 1958; *Mister 880*, 1959; *Flame and the Arrow*, 1959; *The Devil's Disciple*, 1959; *The Unforgiven*, 1960; *Elmer Gantry*, 1960; *The Young Savages*, 1961; *Judgement at Nuremberg*, 1961; *Birdman of Alcatraz*, 1962; *The Leopard*, 1963; *A Child Is Waiting*, 1963; *Seven Days in May*, 1964; *The Halleujah Trail*, 1965; *The Professionals*, 1966; *The Swimmer*, 1968; *The Scalphunters*, 1968; *Castle Keep*, 1969; *The Gypsy Moths*, 1969; *Airport*, 1970; *Lawman*, 1971; *Valdez Is Coming*, 1971; *Ulzana's Raid*, 1972; *Executive Action*, 1973; *Scorpio*, 1973; *The Midnight Man* (also produced and directed), 1974; *Buffalo Bill and the Indians*, 1976; *The Midnight Crossing*, 1977; *1900*, 1977; *The Island of Dr. Moreau*, 1977; *Twilight's Last Gleaming*, 1977; *Go Tell the Spartans*, 1978; *Atlantic City*, 1980; *Cattle Annie and Little Britches*, 1981; *Local Hero*, 1982; *Apache; Vera Cruz; Conversation Piece*.

AWARDS: Venice Film Award, Best Actor, 1962: *Bird Man of Alcatraz;* Academy Award, Best Actor, 1960: *Elmer Gantry*.

ADDRESS: Office —c/o AVCO Embassy Pictures Company, 956 Seward Street, Los Angeles, CA 90038.*

* * *

LANDAU, Martin, actor, director, producer, writer, and teacher

PERSONAL: Born June 20, in New York, NY; son of Morris (a machinist) and Selma (Buchman) Landau; married Barbara Bain (an actress), January 31, 1957; children: Susan Meredith, Juliet Rose. EDUCATION: Attended James Madison High School, Brooklyn, NY; trained for the stage at the Actors Studio with Lee Strasberg.

CAREER: DEBUT—Charley Gennini, *Detective Story*, Peaks Island Playhouse, Peaks Island, ME, 1951. NEW YORK DEBUT—Nick, *First Love*, Provincetown Playhouse, 1951, 18 performances. PRINCIPAL STAGE APPEARANCES—Lally, *The Penguin*, Current Stages, NY, 1952; Juvan, *Goat Song*, Equity Library Theatre, NY, 1953; Husband, *Middle of the Night*, ANTA, NY, 1957. MAJOR TOURS—*Stalag 17*, Eastern U.S. cities, 1952; Husband, *Middle of the Night*, U.S. and Canadian cities, 1957–58.

FILM DEBUT—Leonard, *North by Northwest*, 1958. PRINCIPAL

FILM APPEARANCES—Rufio, *Cleopatra*, 1961–62; Caiaphus, *Greatest Story Ever Told*, 1963; Jesse Coe, *Nevada Smith*, 1964; Chief Walks-Stooped-Over, *The Hallelujah Trail*, 1964; Logan Sharp, *They Call Me Mr. Tibbs*, 1969. TELEVISION DEBUT—*Crime Syndicated*, 1951. PRINCIPAL TELEVISION APPEARANCES—Rollin Hand, *Mission: Impossible;* Commander John Koenig, *Space: 1999;* *Playhouse 90;* *Studio One; Kraft; Goodyear Playhouse*.

AWARDS: Emmy Award Nominations, Best Television Actor, 1966, 1967, 1968; Golden Globe Award, Best Television Actor, 1967; Bravo Award (Germany); Belgian Viewers Award; SACI Award (Brazil).

SIDELIGHTS: MEMBERSHIPS—AEA; SAG; AFTRA; Academy of Motion Picture Arts and Sciences; Academy of Television Arts and Sciences; Actors' Studio West (executive director); Actors' Studio (board of directors). RECREATION—painting, photography, writing.

ADDRESS: Agent—c/o Stanley Bushell, 415 N. Crescent Drive, #320, Beverly Hills, CA 90210.

* * *

LANDIS, John Davis, film director, writer

PERSONAL: Born August 30, 1950, Chicago, IL; married Deborah Nadoolman (a costume designer).

CAREER: PRINCIPAL FILM WORK—Director/writer/actor,

JOHN LANDIS

Schlock, 1971; director/writer, *Kentucky Fried Movie,* 1977; director/writer, *National Lampoon's Animal House,* 1977; director/co-writer, *The Blues Brothers,* 1980; director/writer, *An American Werewolf in London,* 1981; director/co-writer/ co-producer, *Twilight Zone—The Movie,* 1983; director, *Trading Places,* 1983; director/co-writer/producer, Michael Jackson's *Thriller,* 1983; director/co-writer/actor, *Into the Night,* 1984.

ADDRESS: Agent—Mike Marcus, Contemporary Artists Agency, 1888 Century Park E., Los Angeles, CA 90069.

* * *

LANG, Charley, actor

PERSONAL: Born December 24, 1955, in Passaic, NJ; son of Charles Edward (an accountant) and Joan Teresa (Blanc) Lang. EDUCATION: Catholic University, B.F.A. (Acting).

CAREER: DEBUT—James Keller, *The Miracle Worker,* Olney Theatre, Olney, MD, 1978. NEW YORK DEBUT—Young Charlie, *Da,* Morosco, 1978, 300 performances. PRINCIPAL STAGE APPEARANCES—Cuthbert, *Once a Catholic,* Helen Hayes, NY, 1979; Skylight, *Class Enemy,* Players Theatre, NY, 1980; Mark Dolson, *Mass Appeal,* Booth, NY, 1982. MAJOR TOURS—Richard Miller, *Ah, Wilderness,* international cities, 1976; Mark Dolson, *Mass Appeal,* U.S. cities, 1982.

FILM DEBUT—Dave, *The Late Great Me,* 1979. TELEVISION

CHARLEY LANG

DEBUT—costar, *Footsteps* (series). PRINCIPAL TELEVISION APPEARANCES—*Ohms,* 1979; *Kent State,* 1980; *The Gentleman Bandit,* 1981; *First Affair,* 1983.

WRITINGS: SCREENPLAYS—*The Growing Season* (with Todd Robinson).

SIDELIGHTS: "Look for light and freedom and do not ponder too deeply over the evil in life."

ADDRESS: Agent—c/o D.H.K.P.R., 165 W. 46th Street, New York, NY 10036.

* * *

LANG, Pearl, dancer, choreographer, actress

PERSONAL: Born May, 1922 in Chicago, IL; daughter of Jacob and Frieda (Feder) Lack; married Joseph Wiseman, November 22, 1963. EDUCATION: Attended Wright Junior College and the University of Chicago.

CAREER: PRINCIPAL STAGE APPEARANCES—Soloist, Martha Graham Dance Company, 1944–54; featured roles in Broadway productions—*Carousel,* 1945–47; *Finian's Rainbow,* Solveig, *Peer Gynt,* ANTA.

PRINCIPAL CHOREOGRAPHY, DANCE WORKS—*Song of Deborah, Moonsung and Windsung,* 1952; *Legend, Rites,* 1953; *And Joy Is My Witness, Nightflight,* 1954; *Sky Chant,* 1957; *Persephone,* 1958; *Black Marigolds,* 1959; *Shirah,* 1960; *Apasionada,* 1961; *Broken Dialogues,* 1962; *Shore Bourne,* 1964; *Dismembered Fable,* 1965; *Pray for Dark Birds,* 1966; *Tongues of Fire,* 1967; *Piece for Brass,* 1969; *Moonways and Dark Tides,* 1970; *Sharjuhm,* 1971; *At That Point in Place and Time,* 1973; *The Possessed,* 1974; *Prairie Steps,* 1975; *Bach Rondelays, I Never Saw Another Butterfly, A Seder Night, Kaddish,* 1977; *Icarus, Cantigas Ladino,* 1978; *Notturno,* 1980; *Gypsy Ballad, Hanele the Orphan, The Tailor's Megilleh,* 1981; (staged chorus), *Oedipus Rex,* Tanglewood Festival, 1981; *Paslm* and *Song of Songs,* 1983.

PRINCIPAL CHOREOGRAPHY, TELEVISION—*Omnibus; Frontiers of Faith; Look Up and Live; ABC Directions; CBC Folio; The Dybbuk* for CBC.

PRINCIPAL TELEVISION APPEARANCES—Three Mary's, *El Penitente;* Emily Dickinson, *Letter to the World,* 1970; *Clytemnestra,* 1973; Jocasta, *Night Journey* for Martha Graham Dance Company. ADDITIONAL STAGE WORK—co-directed, *Murder in the Cathedral,* Stratford, CT; numerous Israel Bond programs.

THEATRE-RELATED CAREER: Founder, Pearl Lang Dance Company, 1953, and Pearl Lang Dance Foundation; teacher and lecturer on Dance, Yale University Faculty, 1954–68, Juilliard School of Music, NY, 1953–69, Jacob's Pillow, Connecticut College, Neighborhood Playhouse, 1963–68, also aboard in Israel, Sweden, and the Netherlands.

AWARDS: Two Guggenheim Fellowships.

SIDELIGHTS: MEMBERSHIPS—American Guild of Musicians and Artists.

ADDRESS: Home—382 Central Park West, New York, NY 10025. Studio—c/o American Dance Center, 1515 Broadway, New York, NY 10036.

* * *

LANG, Philip J., orchestrator

PERSONAL: Born April 17, 1911; son of Philip H. (an executive) and Irene V. (Coleman) Lang; married Ruth E. Foote, August 4, 1942; children: Roger, Marcia, Bruce. EDUCATION: Ithaca College, B.S. (Music); Juilliard Institute (advanced study, no degree). RELIGION: Catholic. MILITARY: U.S. Maritime Service (ensign). NON-THEATRICAL CAREER: Associate Professor, Orchestration, University of Michigan, Summer Sessions, 1949–51; Associate Professor of Orchestration, University of Colorado, Summer Sessions, 1955–56; Guest Conductor, Adjudicator, and lecturer for clinics and festivals; former partner and editor Lawson-Gould Music, Inc.

CAREER: ORCHESTRATOR—THEATER: *Billion Dollar Baby,* 1945; *Annie Get Your Gun,* 1946; *Barefoot Boy with Cheek,* 1947; *Bonanza Bound,* 1947; *High Button Shoes,* 1947; *Arms and the Girl,* 1950; *Make a Wish,* 1951; *Two on the Aisle,* 1951; *Can-Can,* 1953; *Maggie,* 1953; *Fanny,* 1954;

PHILIP J. LANG

Plain and Fancy, 1955; *Bells Are Ringing,* 1956; *My Fair Lady,* 1956; *Shangri-La,* 1956; *Jamaica,* 1957; *New Girl in Town,* 1957; *Goldilocks,* 1958; *Portofino,* 1958; *Destry Rides Again,* 1959; *Saratoga,* 1959; *Take Me Along,* 1959; *Christine,* 1960; *Camelot,* 1960; *Subways Are for Sleeping,* 1961; *Carnival,* 1961; *Kean,* 1961; *Mr. President,* 1962; *Jennie,* 1963; *Tovarich,* 1963; *Ben Franklin in Paris,* 1964; *I Had a Ball,* 1964; *Hello, Dolly!,* 1964; *Hot September,* 1965; *Pleasures and Palaces,* 1966; *The Roar of the Greasepaint, etc.,* 1966; *I Do! I Do!,* 1966; *Mame,* 1966; *How Now, Dow Jones,* 1967; *Sherry,* 1967; *George M.,* 1968; *Maggie Flynn,* 1968; *Dear World,* 1969; *Applause,* 1970; *Ari,* 1971; *Sugar,* 1972; *Lorelei,* 1973; *Mack and Mabel,* 1974; *Cyrano,* 1975; *One Night Stand,* 1976; *Annie,* 1977; *A Musical Jubilee,* 1978; *I Remember Mama,* 1979; *The Grand Tour,* 1979; *42nd Street,* 1980; *Charlie and Algernon,* 1981.

FILMS—*Li'l Abner,* 1959; *The Night They Raided Minsky's,* 1968; *Hello, Dolly!,* 1969; *The Molly McGuires,* 1970. TELEVISION SHOWS—*Hallmark Productions, David Susskind Productions, Omnibus Productions, Ballet de Marseille, Tonight Show.*

WRITINGS: BOOKS, PUBLISHED—*Scoring for the Band,* Mills Music.

AWARDS: Grammy Award, *My Fair Lady,* Original Cast Album, 1956; Commander, U.S. Maritime Service (honorary), 1981; Doctor of Music, Ithaca College (honorary), 1983.

SIDELIGHTS: MEMBERSHIPS—ASCAP; Kappa Gamma Psi; Oracle (Ithaca College Honor Society).

RECREATION—Golf, fishing, Egyptology.

ADDRESS: Home—231B Agawam Drive, Stratford, CT 06497. Agent—Deborah Coleman, 667 Madison Ave., New York, NY 10021.

* * *

LANGELLA, Frank, actor

PERSONAL: Born January 1, 1940, in Bayonne, NJ; son of Frank (president, barrel & drum company) and his wife; married Ruth Weil (a magazine editor), June 14, 1977. EDUCATION: Syracuse University, 1959; trained for the stage with Sawyer Falk; studied acting with Wynn Handman, dance with Anna Sokolow, voice at Kersting Studios.

CAREER: NEW YORK DEBUT—Michel, *The Immoralist,* Bouwerie Lane, 1963. PRINCIPAL STGE APPEARANCES—Apprentice, Pocono Playhouse, 1954; in summer stock (pre-1964): First Man, *A Thurber Carnival,* Paul Verrall, *Born Yesterday,* New Playhouse, Syracuse; Caesar, *Caesar and Cleopatra,* title role, *George Dandin,* Mr. Martin, *The Bald Soprano,* Choubert, *Victims of Duty,* Syracuse Repertory; Professor, *The Lesson,* Jack, *Jack, or the Submission,* Tuft's Arena, Medford, MA; Joe Pond, *Charm,* Milkman, *Under the Yum Yum Tree,* Cape Playhouse, Dennis, MA; Eugene, *Look Homeward, Angel,* Malcolm, *Macbeth,* Hines, *The Pajama Game,* Erie Playhouse, Erie, PA; Tom, *The Glass Menagerie,* Rudolpho, *A View from the Bridge,* Donald

Gresham, *The Moon Is Blue*, Charles Playhouse, Boston, MA; Richard Rich, *A Man for All Seasons*, Rudolpho, *A View from the Bridge*, Old Actor, *The Fantasticks*, Williamstown, MA; Son (flier), *The Good Woman of Setzuan*, Caesar, *Caesar and Cleopatra*, Iago, *Othello*, Directors Workshop, Sheridan Square Playhouse, NY; title role, *Telemachus*, New Dramatists, NY; Valentine, *Love for Love*, Maidman, NY; Cliff, *Look Back in Anger*, Key Playhouse, NY; Satan/Cain, *Man*, Key; Benito Cereno, *The Old Glory*, American Place, NY, 1964; Young man, *Good Day*, Cherry Lane, NY, 1965; Flamineo, *The White Devil*, Circle in the Square, NY, 1965; Jamie, *Long Day's Journey Into Night*, Long Wharf, New Haven, CT, 1966; Juan, *Yerma*, Vivian Beaumont, NY, 1966; title role, *Dracula*, Berkshire Theatre Festival, Stockbridge, MA, 1967; Urbain Grandier, *The Devils*, Mark Taper Forum, Los Angeles, 1967; with Long Island Festival Repertory Theatre, April–June, 1968; Will, *A Cry of Players*, Berkshire Theatre Festival, 1968, then Vivian Beaumont, NY, 1968; title role, *Cyrano de Bergerac*, Williamstown, MA, 1971; appeared with Yale Repertory, 1971–72; lead, *The Tooth of Crime*, McCarter, Princeton, NJ, 1972; Oberon, *A Midsummer Night's Dream*, Loveless, *The Relapse*, Guthrie Theatre Company, Minneapolis, MN, 1972; Petruchio, *The Taming of the Shrew*, Studio Arena, Buffalo, NY, 1973; *The Seagull*, Williamstown, MA, 1974; Leslie, *Seascape*, Shubert, NY, 1975, later, Shubert, Los Angeles; *Ring Around the Moon*, Williamstown, MA, 1975; title role, *The Prince of Homburg*, Chelsea Theater Center, 1976; title role, *Dracula*, Martin Beck, NY, 1977; title role, *Cyrano de Bergerac*, Williamstown, MA, 1980; Salieri, *Amadeus*, Broadhurst, NY, 1982; *Passion*, Morrosco, 1983; *Design for Living*, Circle in the Square, NY, 1984.

DIRECTED—Plays: *John and Abigail*, Berkshire Theatre Festival, MA, 1979; *Passion*, Morosco, NY, 1980.

PRINCIPAL FILMS—George Prager, *Diary of a Mad Housewife*, 1970; Ostap Bender, *The Twelve Chairs*, 1970; *House Under the Trees*, 1971; *The Deadly Trap*, 1971; *Wrath of God*, 1972; *Dracula*, 1979; Harry Crystal, *Those Lips, Those Eyes*, 1980; *Sphinx*, 1981.

TELEVISION APPEARANCES—Jesus, *CBS Easter Sunday Special*, 1965; *Trials of Brian*, 1965; *Good Day*, 1966; an episode of *Ben Franklin*; Don Diego, *Mark of Zorro*, 1974; Konstantine, *The Sea Gull*, 1975; John, *Eccentricities of a Nightingale*, 1976; title role, *The Prince of Homburg*, 1977.

RECORDINGS—Narration for performance by Daniel Nagrin Company, *The Peloponnesian War*.

THEATRE-RELATED CAREER—Toured Europe with a Folksinging Group, 1959–60.

AWARDS: Antoinette Perry Award, 1975: *Seascape;* 3 Obies, *The Old Glory, The White Devil, Good Day;* Syracuse Critics Award, Best Actor, 1959; National Society of Film Critics Award, 1970: *Diary of a Mad Housewife;* Antoinette Perry Award Nomination, 1978: *Dracula*, 1978; Drama League Award, 1978: *Dracula; Cosmopolitan's* Bachelor of the Month Award, January 1975.

SIDELIGHTS: MEMBERSHIPS—Board of the Berkshire Theatre Festival since 1970.

ADDRESS: Agent—William Morris Agency, 1350 Sixth Avenue, New York, NY 10019.*

* * *

LANSBURY, Angela, actress

PERSONAL: Born October 16, 1925, in London, England; naturalized U.S. citizen, 1951; daughter of Edgar Isaac (a lumber merchant) and Moyna (an actress; maiden name, Macgill) Lansbury; married Richard Cromwell (an actor) 1945 (divorced 1946); married Peter Pullen Shaw (an agent) August 1949; children: Anthony Peter, Deirdre Angela; stepson, David. EDUCATION: South Hampstead High School for Girls, 1934–39; Webber-Douglas School for Dramatic Arts, 1940; studied for the stage at the Feagin School of Drama, NY, 1942. NON-THEATRICAL CAREER—Clerk, then saleswoman, Bullocks, Wilshire.

CAREER: DEBUT—Singer, Samovar Club, Montreal, Canada, 1942. NEW YORK DEBUT—Marcelle, *Hotel Paradiso*, Henry Miller's, 1957. LONDON DEBUT—Mistress, *All Over*, Royal Shakespeare Company, Aldwych, 1972. PRINCIPAL STAGE APPEARANCES—Helen, *A Taste of Honey*, Lyceum, NY, 1960; Cora Hoover Hooper, *Anyone Can Whistle*, Majestic, NY, 1964; Mame Dennis Burnside, *Mame*, Winter Garden, NY, 1966; Countess Aurelia, *Dear World*, Mark Hellinger, NY, 1969; Prettybelle Sweet, *Prettybelle*, Shubert, Boston, 1971; Mame Dennis, *Mame*, Westbury Music Fair, Long Island, NY, 1972; *Sondheim: A Musical Tribute*, Shubert, NY, 1973; Rose, *Gypsy*, Piccadilly, London, 1973, also Shubert, Los Angeles, Winter Garden, NY, 1974; Gertrude, *Hamlet*, Old Vic, National, London, 1975, also for the opening of the Lyttelton, 1976; Anna, *The King and I*, Uris, NY, 1978; Mrs. Lovett, *Sweeny Todd*, Uris, NY, 1979; *Counting the Ways, Listening*, Hartford Stage, CT; Lillian, *A Little Family Business*, Ahmanson, Los Angeles, Martin Beck, NY, 1982; Mame, *Mame*, Uris, NY, 1983.

FILM DEBUT—Maid, *Gaslight*, 1944. FILM APPEARANCES—*National Velvet*, 1944; Sybil, *The Picture of Dorian Gray*, 1945; *The Harvey Girls*, 1946; *The Hoodlum Saint*, 1946; *The Private Affairs of Bel Ami*, 1946; *Till the Clouds Roll By*, 1946; *Tenth Avenue Angel*, 1946; *If Winter Comes*, 1947; *State of the Union*, 1948; M'Lady, *The Three Musketeers*, 1948; *The Red Danube*, 1948; *Samson and Delilah*, 1949; *Kind Lady*, 1951; *Mutiny*, 1952; *Remains to be Seen*, 1952; *Key Man*, 1954; *The Purple Mask*, 1955; *The Court Jester*, 1955; *A Lawless Street*, 1955; *Please Murder Me*, 1956; *The Long, Hot Summer*, 1958; *The Reluctant Debutante*, 1958; *The Summer of the Seventeenth Doll*, 1959; *Season of Passion*, 1959; *The Dark at the Top of the Stairs*, 1960; *A Breath of Scandal*, 1960; *Hawaii*, 1961; *All Fall Down*, 1961; *The Four Horsemen of the Apocalypse*, (voice only) 1962; *The Manchurian Candidate*, 1962; *In the Cool of the Day*, 1963; *The World of Henry Orient*, 1964; *Dear Heart*, 1964; *The Greatest Story Ever Told*, 1965; *Harlow*, 1965; *The Amorous Adventures of Moll Flanders*, 1965; *Mister Buddwing*, 1966; *Woman without a Face*, 1966; *Something for Everyone*, 1970; *Bedknobs and Broomsticks*, 1971; *Death on the Nile*, 1978; *The Lady Vanishes*, 1980; *The Mirror Crack'd*, 1980; *The Pirates of Penzance*, 1982.

TELEVISION APPEARANCES—*Kraft Theatre; Studio One; Play-*

house 90; Gertrude Vanderbilt Whitney, *Little Gloria, Happy at Last,* 1982; *Lace,* 1983; *The Gift of Love,* 1983; Jessica Fletcher, *The Death of Sherlock Holmes,* 1984.

RECORDINGS—In addition to the Original Cast recordings of *Mame, Dear World, Sweeney Todd* and *Anyone Can Whistle,* Miss Lansbury played a role on the new *The Beggars Opera,* recorded 1982.

AWARDS: Antoinette Perry Award, Best Actress in a Musical, 1979: Sweeney Todd, 1974: Gypsy, 1969: Dear World, 1966: Mame; Academy Award nominations, Best Supporting Actress, 1945: *The Picture of Dorian Gray,* 1944: Gaslight; Hollywood Foreign Correspondent's Gold Globe, *Dorian Gray,* 1945; Chicago's Sarah Siddons Award, *Gypsy,* 1974; After Dark's Ruby Award, Performer of the Year, *Sweeney Todd,* 1979.

SIDELIGHTS: Ms. Lansbury once considered a political career, before she began in show business.

ADDRESS: c/o Edgar Lansbury, 1650 Broadway, Suite 501, New York, NY 10019.*

* * *

LANSING, Sherry Lee, film executive

PERSONAL: Born July 31, 1944, in Chicago, IL; daughter of Norton and Margo Lansing. EDUCATION: Northwestern University, B.S, 1966. NON-FILM CAREER: Teacher, Los Angeles Public Schools, 1966–69; model, Max Factor Company, 1969–70, Alberto-Culver Company, 1969–70.

CAREER: PRINCIPAL FILM WORK—Actress, *Loving,* 1970; *Rio Lobo,* 1970; executive story editor, Wagner International, 1970–73; vice-president of production, Heyday Productions, Universal City, CA, 1973–75; executive story editor, vice-president, creative affairs, MGM Studios, Culver City, CA, 1975–77; senior vice-president production, Columbia Pictures, Burbank, CA, 1977–80; president of production, 20th Century Fox Productions, Beverly Hills, CA 1980–83; president, Jaffe-Lansing Productions, 1983–present.

ADDRESS: Office—Jaffe-Lansing Productions, Paramount Studios, 5555 Melrose Avenue, Los Angeles, CA 90038.*

* * *

LANTZ, Robert, literary and talent representative, playwright, producer

PERSONAL: Born July 20, 1914, in Berlin, Germany; son of Adolf (a screenwriter) and Ella (Schloessinger) Lantz; married Sherlee Weingarten (a writer) February 24, 1950; children: Anthony R. EDUCATION: University of Berlin, 1932–33.

CAREER: PRINCIPAL STAGE WORK, Producer—*The Nervous Set,* Henry Miller's, NY, 1959; *Kean,* Broadway, NY, 1961.

WRITINGS: PLAYS, PRODUCED (in Vienna, Austria)—*L'Inconnue de la Seine, Das Geliebte Leben, Voegelchen,* 1933–35.

THEATRE-RELATED CAREER: Mr. Lantz was head of the New York office of Berg-Allenberg, artists representatives, 1948–49; head of the stage and movie departments of the Gale Agency, Inc., New York City, 1949–50; since 1950, head of his own agency, the Lantz Agency, representing literary artists and others in the performing arts. He served as story editor in London for 20th Century Fox, 1936–41 and for Columbia Pictures, 1941–46; as literary and talent representative in London for Universal International Pictures, 1946–47; executive vice-president of Figaro, Inc., New York City, 1955–58.

SIDELIGHTS: MEMBERSHIPS—International P.E.N., London.

ADDRESS: Office—Lantz Office, 888 Seventh Avenue, New York, NY 10106.

* * *

LASSICK, Sydney, actor

PERSONAL: Born July 23, 1922, in Chicago, IL; son of Alex (operator fruit and vegetable produce store) and Anna (Gershfield) Lassick. EDUCATION: Attended public schools in Chicago and 2 years at De Paul University as a Drama major; received a certificate of drama from the Pasadena Playhouse, 1954. RELIGION: Jewish. MILITARY: U.S. Navy.

CAREER: FILM DEBUT—Cheswick, *One Flew Over the Cuckoo's Nest,* 1975. PRINCIPAL FILM APPEARANCES—Mr. Fromm, *Carrie,* 1976; Hymie Stiglitz, *Hot Stuff,* 1978; apple core vendor, *The History of the World, Part I,* 1981.

PRINCIPAL TELEVISION APPEARANCES—*Baretta; Barney Miller; Heroes of the Bible.*

ADDRESS: Agent—Kaplan/Witkin Agency, 3518 W. Cahuenga Blvd., Hollywood, CA 90068.

* * *

LASZLO, Andrew, cinematographer

PERSONAL: Born January 12, 1926, in Hungary; son of Laszlo and Elizabeth Laszlo; married Ann Granger, 1952; children: Andrew, Jr., Jeffrey, James, Elizabeth. MILITARY: U.S. Army, Signal Corps, Sergeant, 1950–52.

CAREER: FIRST FILM WORK—Apprentice at the Motion Picture Studios, Budapest. PRINCIPAL FILM WORK, cinematographer/director of photography—*One Potato,* 1964; *You're a Big Boy Now,* 1967; *The Night They Raided Minsky's,* 1968; *Popi,* 1969; *The Out of Towners,* 1970; *Lovers and Other Strangers,* 1970; *The Owl and the Pussycat,* 1970; *Jennifer on My Mind,* 1971; *To Find a Man,* 1972; *Class of '44,* 1973; *Countdown at Kusini,* 1976; *Thieves,* 1977; *Somebody Killed Her Husband,* 1978; *The Warriors,* 1979; *Southern Comfort,* 1981; *Angela; Funhouse;*

I, The Jury; First Blood, 1982; *Comeback; Streets of Fire,* 1984; *Thief of Hearts,* 1984.

PRINCIPAL TELEVISION WORK (mini-series)—*Shogun; Top of the Hill; The Dain Curse; Washington, Behind Closed Doors;* (features/pilots) *Thin Ice; Spanner's Key; Give Me Your Poor; The Man without a Country; Blue Water Gold; Teacher, Teacher; Daphne; The Cliffdwellers; The Happeners;* (specials) *Bell Telephone Hour Special, Easter Sunrise Services,* Denver Symphony, Mormon Tabernacle Choir; *Ed Sullivan, Vietnam Veterans Easter Special,* 1970; *Ed Sullivan in Cuba; Ed Sullivan in Ireland; Ed Sullivan in Alaska; Ed Sullivan in Portugal; The Beatles at Shea Stadium; New York, New York;* (series) *Coronet Blue; Doctors and Nurses; The Nurses; Naked City; Brenner; Mama; Joe and Mabel; Phil Silvers Show;* (documentaries) *The Twentieth Century; High Adventure.*

AWARDS: Emmy Award Nominations: 1980: *Shogun,* 1973: *The Man without a Country.*

SIDELIGHTS: MEMBERSHIPS—American Society of Cinematographers, Directors Guild of America, Academy of Motion Picture Arts and Sciences; served two terms as Governor of National Academy of Television Arts and Sciences. HOBBIES—Photography, writing, flying, wood and metal working.

Mr. Laszlo lectures extensively at such institutions as Brown University, Dartmouth Collee, Ithaca College, New York University, and the American Film Institute.

ADDRESS: Home—Three Locust Lane, Glen Head, NY 11545. Agent—Kendall Giler, Creative Technicians Agency, 1923½ Westwood Blvd., Los Angeles, CA 90025.

* * *

LAUGHLIN, Sharon, actress

PERSONAL: Born March 12, 1949, in OR; daughter of Dale (a clothing store owner) and Virginia (Morehouse) Laughlin. EDUCATION: University of Washington, B.A.; trained for the stage with Nick Miller.

CAREER: PRINCIPAL STAGE APPEARANCES—(Broadway) Cathy, *One by One;* Maria/understudy lead, *The Heiress;* (Off-Broadway) lead, *Subject to Fits,* Public Theatre; lead, *Huui-Huui,* Public Theatre; lead, *Mod Donna,* Public Theatre; Lady Mortimer, *Henry IV, Parts I and II,* New York Shakespeare Festival, Delacorte; (Off-Off Broadway) Isabel, *Ring Round the Moon,* Olivia, *Twelfth Night,* lead, *Declassee,* Charlotte, *For the Use of the Hall,* Lion Theatre Company; (Regional) Portia, *Julius Caesar,* American Shakespeare Festival, Stratford, CT; Kate, *Old Times,* Goodman, Chicago, IL; Rosalind, *As You Like It,* Center Stage, Baltimore, MD; Marion, *Father's Day,* Pittsburgh Playhouse, PA; lead, *Derelict,* Studio Arena, Buffalo, NY; Joanna, *Present Laughter,* Repertory Theatre of St. Louis, MO. MAJOR TOURS—Hedda, *Hedda Gabler,* East Coast cities.

PRINCIPAL FILM APPEARANCES—*Three Hundred Year Weekend; The Happy Hooker.*

SIDELIGHTS: MEMBERSHIPS—AEA; SAG.

ADDRESS: Agent—c/o Arthur Shafman International, Ltd., 723 Seventh Avenue, New York, NY 10019.

* * *

LAURO, Shirley (nee Shapiro Mezvinsky), writer

PERSONAL: Born November 18, 1933, in Des Moines, IA; daughter of Phillip (a businessman) and Helen (a legal secretary; maiden name, Davidson) Shapiro; married Dr. N. Mezvinshky, July 22, 1956 (divorced, 1966); married Dr. Louis Lauro (a psychoanalyst), August 18, 1973; children: Andrea Lynn (first marriage). EDUCATION: Northwestern University, B.S. (cum laude), 1955; University of Wisconsin, M.S., 1957. POLITICS: Democrat. RELIGION: Jewish.

WRITINGS: PLAYS, PRODUCED—*The Contest,* Alley, Houston, TX, 1975, Ensemble Studio Theatre, NY, 1976, Philadelphia Drama Guild, PA, 1982; *Nothing Immediate,* Actors Theater of Louisville, 1980; *The Coal Diamond,* Circle Repertory, NY, 1980, Actors Theatre of Louisville, KY, 1980; *Open Admissions,* Ensemble Studio, NY, 1981, Long Wharf, New Haven, CT, 1982, Broadway, NY, 1984. PLAYS, PUBLISHED—*The Coal Diamond,* 1979; *Nothing Immediate,* 1980; *Open Admissions,* 1980; *I Don't Know Where You're Coming from at All!,* 1982; *In the Garden of Eden,* 1982. PLAYS, UNPRODUCED—Margaret and Kit. BOOKS— *The Edge,* 1965 and 1967. THEATRE-RELATED CAREER:

SHIRLEY LAURO

Photograph by Catherine Kitzer

Teacher—City College of New York, Yeshiva University, Marymount Manhattan College, Manhattan Community College, NY.

AWARDS: New York Dramatists Guild Hull-Warriner Award, Best Play on a Controversial Theme, 1981: *Open Admissions;* National Foundation for Jewish Culture Award, Best Play on a Jewish Theme, 1981: *The Contest;* Actors' Theatre of Louisville, Best One-Act Play, 1980: *The Coal Diamond;* Samuel French Award, Best Short Play, 1979: *Nothing Immediate* and *Open Admissions*.

SIDELIGHTS: MEMBERSHIPS—American Place Theater Women's Project; Ensemble Studio Theater; Actor's Studio; League of Professional Theater Women.

Plays have been produced also at People's Light and Theater Company, PA, The Company of Angels, CA, and throughout U.S., Canada, and Europe.

"I began as a fiction writer and actress, but as part of a mainstream of American women who came to maturity during the women's revolution, I began to feel that I could communicate better in a more direct, dynamic and assertive way—[writing for] the stage!"

ADDRESS: Agent—c/o Gilbert Parker, William Morris Agency, 1350 Avenue of Americas, New York, NY 10022.

* * *

LAWRENCE, Eddie (ne Lawrence Eisler), actor, director, writer, lyricist

PERSONAL: Born March 2, 1921 in New York, NY; son of Benjamin Daniel (a banker) and Bess (a designer; maiden name, Garbow) Eisler; married Eunice Norma Davidson in 1948 (divorced 1967); married Marilyn Bligh-White (a designer), November 26, 1968; children: Garrett Bligh. EDUCATION: Brooklyn College, B.A.; studied at the Atelier Léger and the Académie de la Grande Chaumière in Paris France. POLITICS: Independent. MILITARY: U.S. Army, 1941–45, WWII.

CAREER: DEBUT—Crookfinger Jake, *Threepenny Opera,* Theatre de Lys, NY, 1955. PRINCIPAL STAGE APPEARANCES—Sandor, *Bells Are Ringing,* Shubert, NY, 1956–59; Banjo, *Sherry,* Alvin, NY; Baldwin, *Oh Kay!,* Royal Alexandria, Toronto, Canada, Opera House, Washington, DC; *One Man Show,* Paris, France.

MAJOR TOURS—Sandor, *Bells Are Ringing,* national tour.

FILM DEBUT—Wisecracking GI, *Act of Love,* 1953. PRINCIPAL FILM APPEARANCES—Scratch Wallace, *The Night They Raided Minsky's; The Wild Party; Blade; Who Killed Mary Whatsername; Abner the Baseball; Somebody Killed My Husband;* 25 other "shorts" for Paramount.

TELEVISION DEBUT—Comedian, *Kay Kyser Kollege of Musical Knowledge.* PRINCIPAL TELEVISION APPEARANCES—*Johnny Carson Show* (over 40 appearances); *Mike Douglas Show* (25 appearances); *Steve Allen Show; Jack Paar Show; Merv Griffin Show; David Frost Show; Victor Borge Specials;*

Chevrolet Show; Garry Moore Show; Soupy Sales Show; The Today Show; The Eddie Lawrence Show (daily); *Robert Montgomery Presents; Mr. Peepers*.

WRITINGS: PLAYS, PRODUCED—*The Beautiful Mariposa,* NY, 1952, 1971, 1981; *Sort of an Adventure,* NY, 1952, 1971, 1981; *Louie and the Elephant,* NY, 1971, 1981; *Kelly* (book and lyrics), 1965; PLAYS, UNPRODUCED—Jonas; The Expressionist (musical). BOOKS—*Actors Auditions,* 1955; *67 Original Auditions for Actors,* 1983. RECORDINGS—*25 Years of Comedy;* 7 albums and 40 singles featuring his original "The Old Philosopher."

SIDELIGHTS: "Eddie Lawrence has enjoyed a colorful and adventurous career; after returning from directing and writing a series of shows for the American Expeditionary Stations in World War II, he teamed up with Marley to form the *Lawrence and Marley* comedy radio show. He has also written comedy material for Bert Lahr, Jack E. Leonard, and Sid Caesar. Lawrence did a nightly newscast during the Second World War from a hut near Caserta, Italy. In 1945, it was the only English news that came in loud and clear in Yalta. One night, Mr. Churchill lit up his after-dinner cigar and beckoned to Mr. Roosevelt, mumbling, 'Well, let's see what Sergeant Lawrence has to say to us tonight.' There were witnesses."

ADDRESS: Home—435 E. 57th Street, New York, NY 10022.

* * *

LAWRENCE, VICKI, actress

PERSONAL: Born March 26, 1949, in Los Angeles, CA; daughter of Howard Axelrad (a C.P.A.) and Ann Alene (Loyd) Lawrence; married Al Schultz (a businessman), November 16, 1974; children: Courtney Allison, Garrett Lawrence. EDUCATION: Attended U.C.L.A. for two years. POLITICS: Republican. RELIGION: Lutheran.

CAREER: DEBUT—Carrie Pipperidge, *Carousel,* Dallas Music Hall, Dallas, TX, 1968. TELEVISION DEBUT—*The Carol Burnett Show,* 1967. TELEVISION APPEARANCES—*The Carol Burnett Show,* 1967–78; Mama, *Mama's Family,* 1983–84.

AWARDS: Emmy Award, Outstanding Supporting Actress, Music-Comedy-Variety Show, 1976: *The Carol Burnett Show;* Gold Record, 1972: *The Night the Lights Went Out in Georgia*.

SIDELIGHTS: MEMBERSHIPS—SAG, AFTRA, AEA. ACTIVITIES—sailing, needlepoint.

"I love spending lots of time with my family. I work with a lot of charities—haven't zeroed in on one that's my favorite . . . possibly children's hospitals."

ADDRESS: Office—Emerald Leasing, 3350 Barham Blvd., Los Angeles, CA 90068. Agent—Tony Fantozzi, William Morris Agency, 151 El Camino, Beverly Hills, CA 90210.

LEACHMAN, Cloris, actress

PERSONAL: Born June 30, 1930, in Des Moines, IA; married George England, 1953 (divorced 1979); children: 5 children. EDUCATION: Attended Northwestern University.

CAREER: PRINCIPAL FILM APPEARANCES—*Kiss Me Deadly*, 1955; *Butch Cassidy and the Sundance Kid*, 1969; *W.U.S.A.*, 1970; *The Last Picture Show*, 1971; *The Steagle*, 1971; *Dillinger*, 1973; *Daisy Miller*, 1974; *Young Frankestein*, 1974; *Crazy Mama*, 1975; *High Anxiety*, 1977; *The North Avenue Irregulars*, 1979; *Scavenger Hunt*, 1979; *Herbie Goes Bananas; History of the World, Part I*, 1981.

PRINCIPAL TELEVISION APPEARANCES—Lassie, 1957; *Twilight Zone; Route 66, Laramie; Trials of O'Brien; Mary Tyler Moore Show; Phyllis*, 1975–77; (movies) *Brand New Life; The Migrants; Death Scream*, 1975; *A Girl Named Sooner*, 1975; *The New Original Wonder Woman*, 1975; *The Love Boat*, 1976; (plays) *Ladies of the Corridor*, 1975.

AWARDS: Academy Award, Best Supporting Actress, 1971: *The Last Picture Show;* Emmy Award (4): *Mary Tyler Moore Show.**

* * *

LEAR, Norman (ne Norman Milton Lear), television and film producer, writer, director

PERSONAL: Born July 22, 1922 in New Haven, CT; son of Herman (a salesman) and Jeanette Lear; married (second marriage) Frances (a consultant for women's employment with Women's Place); children: (first marriage) Ellen; (second marriage) Kate, Maggie. EDUCATION: Attended Emerson College, Boston, MA. MILITARY: U.S. Army Air Force, Technical Sergeant, WW II, 1942–45. NON-THEATRICAL CAREER: Worked in publicity firm of George and Dorothy Ross; furniture salesman; sidewalk photographer (specializing in baby pictures); free-lance comedy writer.

CAREER: PRINCIPAL TELEVISION WORK—Writing (with Ed Simmons), *The Ford Star Review, Colgate Comedy Hour;* Writing/Directing—*The Martha Raye Show, Tennessee Ernie Ford Show, The George Gobel Show;* Writing/Producing—*All in the Family,* 1971, *Sanford and Son,* 1972, *Maude,* 1972, *Good Times,* 1974, *The Jeffersons,* 1975, *Hot L Baltimore,* 1975, *One Day at a Time,* 1975, *Mary Hartman, Mary Hartman,* 1976, *Forever Fernwood,* 1977, *All That Glitters,* 1977, *America 2Night.* 1978, *Fernwood 2Night,* 1978, *The Baxters,* 1980, *Palmerstown,* 1980, *a.k.a. Pablo,* 1984. PRINCIPAL FILM WORK—Producer/Writer—*Come Blow Your Horn,* 1963, *Never Too Late,* 1965, *Divorce: American Style,* 1967, *The Night They Raided Minsky's,* 1968, *Start the Revolution without Me, Cold Turkey,* 1971.

RELATED CAREER: Co-founder, Tandem Productions, 1959; Co-Founder, T.A.T. Communications Company, now Embassy Communications Company, 1974.

AWARDS: The Gold Medal, International Radio and Television Society, for "his profound effect on a medium which has itself profoundly affected this nation," 1982; William O. Douglas Award, Public Counsel, for his efforts toward the

preservation of First Amendment rights and the First Amendment Lectureship Award in memory of Justice William O. Douglas from the Ford Hall Foundation, 1981; George Foster Peabody Award for "establishing (with *All in the Family*) the right to express social comment in a social comedy, for devising the technique of humor as a bridge to better understanding of national issues, for providing excellent production in every way and for providing the public with the greatest of all healers—humor", 1977; Mark Twain Award, International Platform Association, selected as "Mark Twain's successor as America's most delightful humorist, gentle depictor of the virtues and weaknesses of humanity with humor's paintbrush", 1977; Valentine Davies Award, Writers Guild of America, 1977; Humanitarian Award, National Conference of Christians and Jews, 1976; Man of the Year Award, Hollywood Chapter, National Academy of Television Arts and Sciences, 1973; Broadcaster of the Year Award, International Radio and Television Society, 1973; Showman of the Year Awards, Publicists Guild, 1971 and 1977; Academy Award Nomination, Best Screenplay, *Divorce: American Style;* 3 Emmy Awards, Academy of Television Arts and Sciences, for *All in the Family.*

SIDELIGHTS: Board of Directors: Constitutional Rights Foundation, Helsinki Watch, Los Angeles Urban League, Mexican-American Legal Defense and Educational Fund, National Women's Political Caucus, Co-Founder of People for the American Way. In answering if he thought shows like *All in the Family* have had any effect on bigotry, Mr. Lear says: "If the Judeo-Christian ethic has had no effect on prejudice over the last 2,000 years, I'd be an awful fool to think we could do it in a half-hour of comedy. I do what I do, not because I expect to change the world, but because I love it. The entertainment business is a tough business and it can be incredibly frustrating, but there's nothing in the world I'd rather be doing. If there's anybody anywhere having a better time, you'll have to point him out to me."

ADDRESS: c/o of Embassy Communications Company, 100 Universal City Plaza, Universal City, CA 91608.

* * *

LEARNED, Michael, actress

PERSONAL: Born April 9, 1939, in Washington, DC; married Peter Donat (divorced); married William Parker, December 18, 1979; children: (first marriage) Caleb, Christopher, Lucas. EDUCATION: Attended schools in Austria and England.

CAREER: PRINCIPAL TELEVISION APPEARANCES—*Gunsmoke; Police Story;* (movies) *Hurricane,* 1974; *It Couldn't Happen to a Nicer Guy,* 1974; *Widow,* 1976; *Little Mo,* 1978; *Off the Minnesota Strip,* 1980; (series) *The Waltons,* 1972–79; *Nurse,* 1980–81; (special) *Christmas without Snow,* 1980.

PRINCIPAL FILM APPEARANCES—*Apocalypse Now,* 1977; *Touched by Love,* 1980.

PRINCIPAL STAGE APPEARANCES—*The Three Sisters,* Fourth Street, NY, *A God Slept Here;* Cleopatra, *Antony and Cleopatra; Under Milkwood; Tartuffe; Rose Tattoo, Adap-*

tion/Next, Deedle Dumpling, My Son, God, American Conservatory Theatre (ACT), San Francisco; *The Merchant of Venice,* ACT, then Old Globe, San Diego; Amanda, *Private Lives; Importance of Being Earnest; Miss Margarida's Way; Dear Liar;* Queen Elizabeth, *Mary Stuart,* Ahmanson, Los Angeles; *Actors and Actresses,* Hartman, Stanford, CT; Natalya, *A Month in the Country,* Mark Taper, Los Angeles.

AWARDS: Emmy Award, 1981: *Nurse,* 1973, 1974, 1976: *The Waltons;* Photoplay Award, 1974.

ADDRESS: Agent—c/o Henderson/Hogan Agency, Inc., 247 S. Beverly Drive, Beverly Hills, CA 90212.

* * *

LEDERER, Francis (ne Franz), actor, dancer, director, producer, writer, teacher

PERSONAL: Born November 6, 1899, Prague, Czechoslovakia; son of Josef (a leather merchant) and Rose (a business woman; maiden nane, Ornstein) Lederer; married Ada Nejedly (divorced); Margarita Bolando (divorced); Marion Irvine (Commissioner of Cultural Affairs, Los Angeles, CA), July 10, 1941. EDUCATION: Attended the Gymnasium, Prague; Handelsacademie, Prague; graduate, Academie Fuer Musik und Darstellende Kunst, Prague; studied with Leopold Kramer at the New German Theatre, Prague; studied with Elia Kazan at the Actors Studio in New York City, 1951. RELIGION: Jewish. MILITARY: Served in WWI with the Czechoslovakian artillery, corporal. NON-THEATRICAL CAREER: Apprentice and salesman; shop window decorator in Prague.

CAREER: DEBUT—a walk on in *Burning Heart,* while apprenticing at the New German Theatre, Prague, 1919–22. NEW YORK DEBUT—Andreas Steiner, *Autumn Crocus,* Morosco, 1932. LONDON DEBUT—Fleuriot, *My Sister and I,* Streatham Hill, 1931. PRINCIPAL STAGE APPEARANCES— Joined a touring repertory company as an actor, stage manager, property man and prompter, performing throughout Moravia, Silesia and Hungary, 1922; various German theatres in Brno, Olmutz and Marienbad in Czechoslovakia, played Romeo in the Mex Reinhardt production of *Romeo and Juliet,* Prince Henry, *Henry IV, Part 1,* and *Wonder Bar,* 1928–30; Mosca, *Volpone,* Garrick, London, 1932; Andreas Steiner, *Autumn Crocus,* Lyric, London, 1931; Victor Florescu, *The Cat and the Fiddle,* Palace, NY, 1932; *Autumn Crocus,* El Capitan, Los Angeles, 1934; Joe Bonaparte, *Golden Boy,* Curran, San Francisco, 1937; Chico, *Seventh Heaven,* Civic, Chicago, IL, 1939; succeeded Laurence Oliver as Gaylord Esterbrook, *No Time for Comedy,* Barrymore, NY, 1939; appeared at the Wilmington Playhouse, DE: General Bonaparte, *The Man of Destiny,* Kenneth Dovey, *The Old Lady Shows Her Medals,* Old Master, *Playgoers,* 1942; Lafont, *Parisienne,* Fulton, NY, 1950; Captain Bluntschli, *Arms and the Man,* Edison, NY, 1950; Adrian Van Dyck, *Collector's Item,* Palace, Manchester, England, 1951; *Relative Values* and *Nina,* Berlin, Germany, 1951; Jacques Devallee, *Wedding in Paris,* Hippodrome, London, 1954; Paul Delville, *The Marriage-Go-Round; The Pleasure of His Company; Three Curtains; Watch on the Rhine.*

FRANCIS LEDERER

MAJOR TOURS—Max Christman, *The Pursuit of Happiness,* 1941; *The Play's the Thing,* 1942; *A Doll's House,* 1944; *The Silver Whistle,* summer theatres, 1950; Prince Regent, *The Sleeping Prince,* opened Huntington Hartford, 1956; Mr. Frank, *The Diary of Anne Frank,* 1958.

PRINCIPAL FILM APPEARANCES—*Refuge,* 1929; *Pandora's Box,* 1929; *Wonderful Lies of Nina Petrova,* 1930; *Man of Two Worlds,* 1934; *The Pursuit of Happiness,* 1934; *Romance in Manhattan,* 1934; *The Gay Deception,* 1935; *One Rainy Afternoon,* 1936; *My American Wife,* 1936; *It's All Yours,* 1938; *Confessions of a Nazi Spy,* 1939; *The Man I Married,* 1940; *Voice of the Wind,* 1944; *The Madonna's Secret,* 1946; *The Diary of a Chambermaid,* 1946; *Million Dollar Weekend,* 1948; *Captain Carey, U.S.A.,* 1950; *Stolen Identity,* 1953; *The Ambassador's Daughter,* 1956; *Lisbon,* 1956; *Maracaibo,* 1958. PRINCIPAL TELEVISION APPEARANCES—*Turn the Key Deftly,* Breck Showcase, CBS, 1959.

THEATRE-RELATED CAREER: Founder, American National Academy of Performing Arts, Los Angeles, CA 1973; founder, International Academy of Performing Arts, Washington, DC, 1975.

AWARDS: Honorary Mayor of Canoga Park, many civic awards.

SIDELIGHTS: MEMBERSHIPS—SAG, Directors Guild, AEA, AFTRA, Recreation and Parks Commissioner, City of Los Angeles, founding member, Hollywood Museum and has served on various committees to beautify Los Angeles and the surrounding area.

ADDRESS: Home—Box 32, Canoga Park, CA 91305.

* * *

LEE, Anna (nee Joan Boniface Winnifrith), actress

PERSONAL: Born January 2, 1913, in Ightham, Kent, England; daughter of Bertram Thomas (rector of Ightham) and Edith Maude (Digby) Winnifrith; married Robert Stevenson (a director), June 1936 (d. 1940); married Robert Nathan (author, poet) April 5, 1970; children: Venetia Stevenson, Caroline Stevenson, John Stafford, Stephen Stafford, Jeffrey Byron. EDUCATION: Granville House, Eastbourne; trained for the stage by Elsie Fogerty and at the Central School of Speech Training and Dramatic Art. POLITICS: Republican. RELIGION: Catholic.

CAREER: DEBUT—Various parts, London Repertory Company, England. MAJOR TOURS—Tessa, *The Constant Nymph;* also: *The Last Hour, Jane Eyre,* London Repertory Company, 1933; *Miranda,* Summer Tour, 1950.

FILM DEBUT—*The Camels Are Coming,* 1934. PRINCIPAL FILMS—*Passing of the Third Floor Back,* 1935; *Young Man's Fancy,* 1936; *Non-Stop New York,* 1937; Kathy, *King Solomon's Mines,* 1938; *The Four Just Men,* 1939; *Return to Yesterday,* 1940; *Seven Sinners,* 1940; *My Life with Caroline,* 1941; Bronwen, *How Green Was My Valley,* 1941; *Flying Tigers,* 1942; *Commandoes Strike at Dawn,* 1942; *Flesh and Fantasy,* 1943; *Hangmen Also Die,* 1943; *Summer Storm,* 1944; *Bedlam,* 1946; *The Ghost and Mrs. Muir,* 1947; *High Conquest,* 1947; *G.I. War Brides,* 1948; *Fort Apache,* 1948; *Prison Warden,* 1949; *Gideon of Scotland Yard (Gideon's Day),* 1958; *The Last Hurrah,* 1958; *The Crimson Kimono,* 1959; *This Earth Is Mine,* 1959; *The Horse Soldiers,* 1959; *Whatever Happened to Baby Jane?,* 1962; *The Prize,* 1963; *The Sound of Music,* 1965; *Seven Women,* 1965; *In Like Flint,* 1967.

TELEVISION DEBUT—Dora Foster, *A Date with Judy* (Saturday daytime version) June 2, 1951–July, 1952. TELEVISION APPEARANCES—Panelist, *It's News to Me,* 1951–54; *Maverick, Dr. Kildare, The Loretta Young Show, The F.B.I., Mr. Novak, Mission Impossible, Perry Mason, Mannix, Family Affair, Baretta, Gunsmoke, Knight Rider, Eleanor and Franklin; The Beasts are Loose, Scruples,* Lila Quartermaine, *General Hospital,* 1978–present.

WRITINGS: Television script, produced—episode for *The Loretta Young Show,* 1955.

AWARDS: Two "Soapy" Awards, 1982, 1983: *General Hospital;* Dawson Milward Award, Central School, Royal Albert Hall, London; awarded M.B.E. by Queen Elizabeth, July, 1983.

SIDELIGHTS: MEMBERSHIPS—Royal Oak Foundation of California, Inc. (chairman). ACTIVITIES—Gardening, embroidery, music, reading, collecting antiques and British Commonwealth Coins.

Miss Lee's favorite charity is the Royal Oak Foundation of California, which is dedicated to the preservation of places of historical interest and beauty throughout the United Kingdom. She is very proud of her Scottish heritage and is a member of the MacFarlane Clan.

ADDRESS: Home—1240 N. Doheny Drive, Los Angeles, CA 90069. Agent—Henderson-Hogan, 247 S. Bevery Drive, Beverly Hills, CA 90212.

* * *

LEE, Jack, musical director and conductor

PERSONAL: Born July 30, 1929, in Lakewood, OH; son of David Joseph (a train dispatcher) and Mary Ellen Lee; married Charlotte Fairchilde, February 17, 1962 (divorced 1964). EDUCATION: Baldwin Wallace College, B.A., 1952; B.M., 1952; trained for the stage at Cleveland Playhouse with Dr. Benno Frank. RELIGION: Catholic.

CAREER: DEBUT—Newsboy, *The Old Homestead,* Cain Park, Cleveland Heights, OH, 1944–45. NEW YORK DEBUT—conductor, *Best Foot Forward,* Equity Library, 1956. LONDON DEBUT—conductor, *My One and Only,* Drury Lane, November 7, 1983, 1 performance. PRINCIPAL STAGE WORK—conductor, *Sweet Charity,* Palace, NY, 1966; conductor, *Irene,* Minskoff, NY, 1973; conductor, *Peter Pan,* Lunt-Fontaine, NY, 1978. REGIONAL: Conductor, Kansas City Starlite Theatre, Kansas City, MO, 1956–58, Kenley Players, Warren, OH, 1961–65, Dallas Summer Musical Theatre, Dallas, TX, 1974–78; conductor, *My One and Only,* St. James, NY, 1983. MAJOR TOURS—Conductor, *Sweet Charity, Irene, Annie Get Your Gun, George M, Applause, Funny Girl, No Strings, Peter Pan,* U.S. cities.

FILM WORK—Vocal coach, *Sweet Charity,* 1968. PRINCIPAL TELEVISION APPEARANCES—Conductor, *Ed Sullivan Show, Mike Wallace, Calamity Jane, Mike Douglas, Merv Griffin, Jerry Lewis, Bob Hope, Antoinette Perry Awards Show.*

SIDELIGHTS: MEMBERSHIPS—Phi Mu Alpha Sinfonia; Alpha Sigma Phi; Phi Kappa Gamma.

ADDRESS: Office—c/o Gigi Hilge, 25 Central Park West, New York, NY 10023. Agent—c/o Bret Adams, 448 W. 44th Street, New York, NY 10036.

* * *

LEE, Lance, writer

PERSONAL: Born August 25, 1942 in New York, NY; son of David (a television producer) and Lucile (Wilds) Levy; married Jeanne Barbara Hotchings (a medical technologist) on August 30, 1962; children: Heather, Alyssa. EDUCATION: Boston University, 1960–62; Brandeis University, B.A., 1964; Yale University School of Drama, M.F.A., 1967.

WRITINGS: PLAYS, PRODUCED—*Time's Up*, Goodman, Chicago, IL, New Playwrights Project, 1976, Theatre Upstairs, Los Angeles, 1977, Mercury Theatre Cafe, Denver, CO, 1981; *Gambits*, O'Neill Playwrights Conference, 1975, ANTA-West Playwrights Unit (reading), 1975, Victory Gardens, Chicago, IL, 1979; *Fox, Hound & Huntress*, Odyssey, Los Angeles, 1971; *Rasputin*, Yale School of Drama, 1967, O'Neill Playwrights Conference, 1969, Impossible Ragtime Theatre, NY (reading), 1977. PLAYS PUBLISHED—*Time's Up, Fox, Hound & Huntress*. PLAYS, UNPRODUCED—Life Scenes, Hearts. NOVEL UNPUBLISHED—Falling for Eden. POETRY published in *Glass Onion, The Journal, England: Voices International, POEM, Lake Superior Review, Midwest Poetry Review, Cottonwood Review, San Fernando Poetry Journal, Poetry Project One, Whiskey Island Quarterly*. SHORT STORIES published in *Riverside Quarterly, Literary Quarterly*. ARTICLES published in *Coast Magazine, Chicago Review, Los Angeles Times*. SCREENPLAYS—Two of a Kind.

THEATRE-RELATED CAREER: Lecturer, Speech, Bridgeport University, CT, 1967–68; instructor, Creative Writing, Southern Connecticut State College, New Haven, CT, 1968; assistant professor, Playwriting, University of Southern California, senior lecturer in Playwriting, 1968–71; lecturer, Playwriting, UCLA, 1971–73; lecturer, Screenwriting, California State University at Northridge, 1981.

AWARDS: F. T. Wells Scholarship to Squaw Valley Community of Writers, 1982–83; National Endowment for the Arts Fellowship, 1976; Theatre Development Fund Fellowship, 1976; Fellowship, Rockefeller Foundation, Office for Advanced Drama Research, 1971; Arts of Theatre Foundation Fellowship, 1967; Theron Bamberger Award in Playwriting, Brandeis University, 1964.

SIDELIGHTS: MEMBERSHIPS—Dramatists Guild; Authors League; member, Citizens Advisory Committee for Topanga State Park; chairman, ad hoc coalition for the establishment of State Parks in Topanga and Pacific Palisades and Malibu; founding chairman and general consultant to the Steering Committee, Pacific Palisades Comminity Council Center Committee; member, Delegate Assembly, Community Relations Conference of Southern California; environmental delegate, Pacific Palisades Community Council; founding president, Temescal Canyon Association and Board Chairman.

ADDRESS: Agent—Alleen Hussung, c/o Samuel French, Inc. 25 W. 45th Street, New York, NY 10036.

* * *

LEE, Michele (nee Michele Lee Dusick), actress

PERSONAL: Born June 24, 1942 in Los Angeles, CA; daughter of Jack (a make-up artist) and Sylvia Helen (Silverstein) Dusick; married James Farentino (an actor) on February 20, 1966 (divorced 1983); children: David Michael. EDUCATION: Studied acting with Jeff Corey.

CAREER: DEBUT—*Vintage '60*, Review, Ivar Theatre, Hollywood, CA, 1960. NEW YORK DEBUT—*Vintage '60*, Brooks Atkinson for eight days, 1960. PRINCIPAL STAGE APPEAR-ANCES—Miranda, *Bravo Giovanni*, NY, 1962; Rosemary, *How to Succeed in Business without Really Trying*, 46th Street, 1963; Gittle Mosca, *Seesaw*, Uris, NY, 1973, St. Louis, MO, 1974; *The Big Knife*, Chicago, 1976; Nellie, *South Pacific*, Atlanta, GA, 1977; Lola, *Damn Yankees*, Kansas, St. Louis, MO, 1978. DIRECTED—*Oliver*, San Jose Civic Light Opera, 1978.

FILM DEBUT—Rosemary Pilkington, *How to Succeed in Business without Really Trying*, 1967. PRINCIPAL FILM APPEAR-ANCES—Carole Bennett, *The Love Bug*, 1969; *The Comic*, 1969; *Nutcracker Fantasy*, 1979.

TELEVISION DEBUT—*The Danny Kaye* Show, 1963. PRINCIPAL TELEVISION APPEARANCES—Romp, 1968; *The World of Pizzazz*, 1969; *John Dos Passos, U.S.A.*, 1970; *The First Nine Months Are the Hardest*, 1970; *Of Thee I Sing*, 1972; *Laugh-In*, 1972; *Make Mine Red, White, and Blue*, 1972; *Norman Rockwell Special*, 1973; *The Glen Campbell Special*, 1974; *The Antoinette Perry Award Show*, 1974; *The Michele Lee Show* (pilot), 1974; *The Perry Como Special*, 1974; *Only with Married Men*, 1974; *The Don Rickles Special*, 1975; *Lights, Camera, Monty Special*, 1975; *Dark Victory*, 1976; Host, *Antoinette Perry Award Show*, 1976; *Hollywood Diamond Jubilee*, 1977; *Bud and Lou*, 1978; *The Love Boat*, 1978–80; Karen Fairgate Mackenzie, *Knot's Landing*, 1979–; *NBC Mother's Day Special*, 1981; *Bonnie and the Franklins*, 1982; *Night of 100 Stars*, 1982; *Kraft Salutes Walt Disney World's 10th Anniversary Special*, 1982; *Perry Como Christmas Special*, 1983; *David Copperfield Special*, 1983; *Parade of the Stars*, 1983; *Antoinette Perry Award Show*, 1983.

AWARDS: Emmy Award Nomination, Lead Actress in a Dramatic Series, 1981–82: *Knot's Landing;* Antoinette Perry Award Nomination, 1974: *Seesaw;* Drama Desk Award, Outer Circle Critics Award, 1973: *Seesaw;* Motion Picture Herald Fame Award, 1967; Motion Picture Exhibitors Top Star of Tomorrow Award, 1967.

SIDELIGHTS: RECREATIONS—Painting, sculpture, piano, writing, riding, swimming.

ADDRESS: Office—8447 Wilshire Boulevard, Beverly Hills, CA 90211. Agent—William Morris Agency, 151 El Camino Drive, Beverly Hills, CA 90212.

* * *

LeFEVRE, Adam, actor, writer

PERSONAL: Surname sounds like "fever;" born August 11, 1950 in Albany, NY; son of Ira Deyo (a physician) and Helen Tate (an administrator; maiden name, Rhodes) LeFevre; married Cora Ann Bennett (a business administrator) on November 3, 1979; children: Tate Augusta. EDUCATION: Williams College, B.A., 1972; University of Iowa, M.F.A., 1976; studied at the National Theatre Institute. NON-THEATRICAL CAREER: Instructor in English, Northeastern University, 1979–80; instructor in English, Bernard Baruch College, City University of New York, 1981.

CAREER: DEBUT—Tilden, *Buried Child*, Victory, Dayton, OH. NEW YORK DEBUT—Sam, *Turnbuckle*, Manhattan Punchline Theatre. PRINCIPAL STAGE APPEARANCES—Balthazar, *Romeo and Juliet,* Long Wharf, New Haven, CT, 1981; Willie Wayne, *The Wake of Jamey Foster,* Hartford Stage Company, CT, 1982; Bingo, *Goose & Tom Tom,* New York Shakespeare Festival, 1982.

FILM DEBUT—J.T., *Return of the Secaucus 7,* 1978. PRINCIPAL FILM APPEARANCES—Haskell, *Reckless,* 1983.

WRITINGS: PLAYS, PRODUCED—*Yucca Flats,* Manhattan Theatre Club, NY, 1973; *The Crashing of Moses Flying-By,* Theatre Three, Dallas, TX, 1983. POETRY, PUBLISHED—*Everything All at Once,* 1978.

SIDELIGHTS: MEMBERSHIPS—Dramatists Guild.

ADDRESS: Home—Two Hummel Road, New Paltz, NY 12561. Agent—Don Buchwald & Associates, Ten E. 44th Street, New York, NY 10017.

* * *

LeFRAK, Francine, producer

PERSONAL: Born October 18, 1950; daughter of Samuel I. (a real estate developer) and Ethel (Stone) LeFrak. EDUCATION: Finch College, B.A., 1970. NON-THEATRICAL CAREER: Vice president, Sotheby Parke Bernet Auction Galleries, 1970–74; guest lecturer, New School for Social Research, 1970–74; art appraiser/advisor, 1974–77; guest instructor, Hunter College: ''The Art of the Creative Process,'' 1978.

CAREER: PRINCIPAL STAGE WORK, Producer/co-producer— *They're Playing Our Song,* London, 1980; *March of the Falsettos,* NY, 1981; *Crimes of the Heart,* NY, 1981; *Nine,* NY, 1982; *My One and Only,* NY, 1983.

PRINCIPAL FILM WORK, Production associate—*The Eyes of Laura Mars,* 1977.

PRINCIPAL TELEVISION WORK, Producer—*This Year in Jerusalem:* ''Americans Living in Israel,'' *Eyewitness News; If There's a Cure for This?,* *Midday Live;* co-ordinator, segments— *Bob Hope's 80th Birthday,* 1983; *Royal Variety Show,* London, 1983; consultant, projects—WNET Channel 13.

AWARDS: Outer Critics Circle Award, 1982: *March of the Falsettos;* Outer Critics Circle Award, Best New Broadway Musical, 1982: *Nine;* Drama Desk Award, Best Musical, 1982: *Nine;* Antoinette Perry Award, Best Musical, 1982: *Nine.*

SIDELIGHTS: MEMBERSHIPS—League of New York Theatres and Producers; board of advisors, Healthy America, National Coalition on Health in America; Art Appraisers Association of America; president, The Whole Picture Company Ltd.; president, LeFrak Productions, Inc. Ms. Lefrak was instrumental in bringing a number of productions to the Broadway stage, including *Ain't Misbehavin'* and *Children of a Lesser God.* She teaches a private aerobics class and is currently developing new projects.

ADDRESS: Office—LeFrak Productions Inc., 40 W. 57th Street, New York, NY 10019.

LE GALLIENNE, Eva, actress, director, manager, producer, writer

PERSONAL: Born January 11, 1899, in London, England; daughter of Richard (a poet and editor) and Julie (a journalist; maiden name, Norregaard) Le Gallienne. EDUCATION: Privately educated in Paris, Collège de Sevigny. RELIGION: Protestant.

CAREER: DEBUT—Small role, *Monna Vanna,* Queen's, London, 1914. NEW YORK DEBUT—Maid, *Mrs. Boltay's Daughter,* Comedy, 1915. PRINCIPAL STAGE APPEARANCES— *The Laughter of Fools,* Prince of Wales, London, 1915; *Peter Ibbetson,* His Majesty's, London, 1915; *Bunny,* Hudson, NY, 1916; *The Melody of Youth,* Fulton, NY, 1916; *Mr. Lazarus,* Shubert, NY, 1916; *Saturday to Monday,* Bijou, NY, 1917; *Lord and Lady Algy,* Broadhurst, NY, 1917; *The Off-Chance,* Empire, NY, 1918; *Belinda,* Empire, NY, 1918; *Lusmore,* Henry Miller's, NY, 1919; *Elsie Janis and Her Gang,* George M. Cohan, NY, 1919; *Not So Long Ago,* Booth, NY, 1920; Julie, *Liliom,* Garrick, NY 1921; *Sandro Botticelli,* Provincetown, NY, 1923; *The Rivals,* 48th Street, NY, 1923; Princess Alexandra, *The Swan,* Cort, NY, 1923; The Child, *Hannele* (matinees only), Cort, NY, 1924; *La Vièrge Folle,* Gaiety, NY, 1924; *The Call of Life,* Comedy, NY, 1925; Hilda, *The Master Builder,* Maxine Elliott's NY, 1925; Ella, *John Gabriel Borkman,* Booth, NY, 1926.

In 1926 Miss Le Gallienne founded the Civic Repertory Theatre; there she staged and directed productions as well as acting in them. They include Imperia, *Saturday Night,* Masha, *The Three Sisters,* Hilda, *The Master Builder,* Ella, *John Gabriel Borkman,* Mirandolina, *La Locandiera,* Viola, *Twelfth Night,* Sister Joanna, *The Cradle Song,* Aunt Isabel, *Inheritors,* Jo, *The Good Hope,* Peri, *The First Stone,* Princell Orloff, *Improvisations in June,* Hedda, *Hedda Gabler,* Marie Louise, *L'Invitation au Voyage,* Varya, *The Cherry Orchard,* Peter, *Peter Pan,* Masha, *The Sea Gull,* Anna Karenina, *The Living Corpse,* Juanita, *The Woman Have Their Way,* Lady Torminster, *The Open Door,* Juliet, *Romeo and Juliet,* Genevieve, *Siegfried,* Elsa, *Alison's House,* Marguerite, *Camille,* Julie, *Liliom,* Cassandra Austen, *Dear Jane,* White Queen, *Alice in Wonderland.*

Directed and starred in *L'Aiglon, Hedda Gabler, The Cradle Song,* Broadhurst, NY, 1934; Rebecca West, *Rosmersholm,* Shubert, NY, 1935; Donna Laura, *A Sunny Morning,* Broadway Theatre, NY, 1935; Angelica, *Love for Love,* Westport Country Playhouse, Westport, CT, 1936; Mathilda Wesendonk, *Guild,* NY, 1935; Mirandolina, *The Mistress of the Inn,* Mt. Kiscoe, NY, 1937; Hamlet, *Hamlet,* Cape Playhouse, Dennis, MA, 1937; Marie Antoinette, *Madame Capet,* Cort, NY, 1938; Juliet, *Frank Fay's Music Hall,* 44th Street Theatre, NY, 1939; directed and played Mrs. Malaprop, *The Rivals,* Guild, NY, 1942; Lettie, *Uncle Harry,* Broadhurst, NY, 1942; directed and played Andreyevna, *The Cherry Orchard,* National, NY, 1944; Thérèse, *Thérèse Raquin,* Biltmore, NY, 1945.

In 1946, with Margaret Webster and Cheryl Crawford, Miss Le Gallienne founded the American Repertory Theatre; at the International Theatre she appeared in the following: Katherine, *Henry VIII,* Comtesse de La Bière, *What Every Woman Knows,* directed and played Ella, *John Gabriel Borkman,* directed and played White Queen, *Alice in Wonderland.*

Other roles—Mrs. Alving, *Ghosts,* Cort, NY, 1948; Signora Amaranta, *Fortunato,* Woodstock, NY, 1950; Lady Starcross, *The Starcross Story,* Royale, NY, 1954; Marcia Elder, *The Southwest Corner,* Holiday, NY, 1955; solo reading, *An Afternoon with Oscar Wilde,* Theatre de Lys, NY, 1957; Queen Elizabeth, *Mary Stuart,* Phoenix, NY, 1957.

With the National Repertory Theatre, Miss Le Gallienne appeared as: Queen Elizabeth, *Mary Stuart,* 1959–60, Queen Elizabeth, *Elizabeth the Queen,* 1959–60; Madame Arkadina, *The Sea Gull,* 1963–64, Mme. Desmermortes, *Ring Around the Moon,* 1963–64. Other roles—Queen Marguerite, *Exit the King,* APA, Lyceum, NY, 1968; Countess, *All's Well That Ends Well,* American Shakespeare Festival, Stratford, CT, 1970; Mrs. Woodfin, *The Dream Watcher,* White Barn, Westport, CT, 1975, Seattle Repertory, 1977; Fanny Cavendish, *The Royal Family,* Helen Hayes, NY, 1975–76; Grandmother, *To Grandmother's House We Go,* Alley Theatre, Houston, TX, 1980, Biltmore, NY, 1980–81; White Queen, *Alice in Wonderland,* Virginia, NY, 1982–83.

MAJOR TOURS—*Rio Grande,* 1916–17; *Alice in Wonderland, The Master Builder, Romeo and Juliet, Hedda Gabler,* 1933; Amanda, *Private Lives,* summer theatres, 1939; Miss Moffatt, *The Corn Is Green,* national, 1949–50; Lavinia, *Listen to the Mockingbird,* national, 1958; Fanny Cavendish, *The Royal Family,* national, 1977.

DIRECTED—(in addition to those already noted above), *Ah, Wilderness,* Guild, NY, 1941; *Liliom, Hedda Gabler,* National Repertory Theatre tour, 1964–65; and translated, *The Cherry Orchard,* A.P.A., Lyceum, 1968; *A Doll's House,* Seattle Repertory Theatre, Seattle, WA 1975.

PRODUCED—(in addition to those already noted above) co-produced with Lucille Lortel at the White Barn Theatre, Westport, CT: *Come Slowly, Eden, Seven Ages of Bernard Shaw, Israeli Mime Theatre, The Effect of Gamma Rays on Man-in-the-Moon Marigolds,* 1966.

FILM DEBUT—*Prince of Players,* 1955. PRINCIPAL FILMS—Grandmother, *Resurrection,* 1979. TELEVISION APPEARANCES—Fanny Cavendish, *The Royal Family,* 1978.

WRITINGS: PLAYS, PUBLISHED—*Alice in Wonderland* (with Florida Friebus), Samuel French, 1932; *The Strong Are Lonely,* Samuel French, 1953; *Six Plays of Henrik Ibsen;* translations and critical preface, Modern Library, 1957; *The Wild Duck and Other Plays;* translations and critical preface, Modern Library, 1961; Preface to *Hedda Gabler,* Faber, 1953; *The Master Builder,* with a prefatory study, Faber, 1955. BOOKS, PUBLISHED—*At 33,* a memoir, Longman's, 1934; *Flossie and Bossie Harper,* 1949, Faber, 1950; *With a Quiet Heart,* a memoir, Viking, 1957; *Seven Tales of Hans Christian Andersen,* translations, Harper, 1959; *The Nightingale,* translation, Harper, 1959; *The Nightingale,* translation, Harper, 1965, Collins, 1966; *The Mystic in the Theatre,* a study of Eleonora Duse, Farrar Straus & Giroux, 1966; *The Little Mermaid,* translation, Harper, 1971; *The Spider & Other Stories,* translations, Harper, 1980. Also numerous articles and book reviews including "Ibsen, the Shy Giant," *Saturday Review,* August 14, 1971; "Sarah Bernhardt," *Forum,* Winter, 1974.

AWARDS: Pictorial Review Award, 1926; Town Hall Club Award, Society of Arts & Sciences Gold Medal, Gold Medal

for Speech: American Academy of Arts & Letters, 1934; Women's National Press Club: Outstanding Woman of the Year, 1947; Norwegian Grand Cross of the Royal Order of St. Olaf, 1961; ANTA Award, Special Antoinette Perry Award, 1964; Brandeis University Award, 1966; Handel Medallion from New York City, Drama League Award, Episcopal Actors' League Award, 1976; Special ANTA Award, Theatre World Award, 1977; Emmy, *The Royal Family,* Woman of Achievement Award: National Conference of Christians and Jews, 1978; Achievement in Arts Awards, Connecticut Commission on the Arts, 1980.

HONORARY DEGREES—M.A., Tufts, 1927; D.H.L., Smith, Litt. D, Russell Sage College, 1930; Litt. D., Brown, 1933; Litt. D., Mt. Holyoke, 1937; D.H.L., Ohio Wesleyan, 1953; Litt. D., Goucher College, 1961; D.H.L., University of North Carolina, 1964; D.H.L., Bard, 1965; D.H.L., Fairfield University, 1966.

SIDELIGHTS: MEMBERSHIPS—AEA, SAG, AFTRA, Dramatists Guild, SSD&C. RECREATION—Gardening.

Miss LeGallienne became a star in 1921 when she played the lead in the first American production of Ferenc Molnar's *Liliom.* She was a prime mover in establishing repertory theatre in the United States. She speaks fluent French, Danish, and Russian; she loves birds and animals of all kinds.

ADDRESS: Home—Weston, CT 06883. Agent—Mitch Douglas, I.C.M., 40 W. 57th Street, New York, NY 10019.

* * *

LEIDER, Jerry, producer

PERSONAL: Born May 28, 1931, in Camden, NJ; son of Myer and Minnie L. Leider; married Susan Trustman; children: Matthew, Kenneth. EDUCATION: Syracuse University, B.A., 1953; University of Bristol (England) M.A., 1954.

CAREER: THEATER DEBUT—Producer, *Ages of Man,* NY and London, 1956–59. TELEVISION DEBUT—Executive producer, *And I Alone Survived,* 1978. FILM DEBUT—Producer, *The Jazz Singer,* 1980. PRODUCED: Plays—*The Visit,* NY; *Shinbone Alley,* NY. TELEVISION FILMS—*Willa; Hostage Tower; Skeezer; Jane Doe; The Scarlet and the Black; The Haunting Passion; Sunset Limousine.* FILMS—*Sophie's Choice,* 1982; *Dark Crystal,* 1982; *The Last Unicorn,* 1982; *The Evil That Men Do,* 1983; *Trenchcoat,* 1983; *Where the Boys Are,* 1984. RELATED CAREERS: Director of special programs, CBS Television, 1960–61; director of program sales, CBS Television, 1961–62; vice-president of television operations, Ashley Famous Agency, Inc., 1962–69; president, Warner Brothers Television, 1969–74; vice-president of foreign production, Warner Brothers Films, 1975–76; president, GJL Productions, 1977–82; president, ITC Productions, 1982–present.

AWARDS: Arents Alumni Medal, Syracuse University, 1979.

SIDELIGHTS: MEMBERSHIPS—American Film Institute, Academy of Television Arts and Sciences, Hollywood Radio

JERRY LEIDER

and Television Society (board of directors, president 1975–76), Academy of Motion Picture Arts and Sciences.

ADDRESS: Office—ITC Productions, Inc., 12711 Ventura Blvd., Studio City, CA 91604. Agent—c/o Tony Fantozzi, William Morris Agency, 151 El Camino, Beverly Hills, CA 90212.

* * *

LEIGH, Mitch, composer, producer

PERSONAL: Born January 30, 1928. EDUCATION: High School of Music and Art; Yale University, B.A./M.A.

CAREER: COMPOSER, SCORES—*Man of La Mancha,* 1964; *Cry for Us All,* 1969; *Sarava,* 1978; *Once in Paris,* 1978. COMPOSER, INCIDENTAL MUSIC—*Too True to Be Good; Never Live over a Pretzel Factory.*

PRODUCER/DIRECTOR—*The King and I,* 1980 (Yul Brynner Package), still touring.

AWARDS: Antoinette Perry; Drama Critics Circle; Variety Poll; Yale School of Music Certificate of Merit; Spanish Pavillion Award; song, "The Impossible Dream" awarded the Contemporary Classic Award by the Songwriters Hall of Fame.

ADDRESS: Office—200 Central Park S., Room 8B, New York, NY 10019.

* * *

LEMAY, Harding, playwright, scriptwriter

PERSONAL: Born March 16, 1922, in North Bangor, NY; son of Henry James (a farmer) and Eva Mary (a schoolteacher; maiden name, Gorrow) Lemay; married Priscilla Amidon, October 1947 (marriage ended 1953); married Dorothy Shaw (a librarian), September 19, 1953; children: Stephen, Susan. EDUCATION: Chateaugay High School, Chateaugay, NY, 1935–39; trained for the stage with Sanford Meisner, Martha Graham, Herbert Berghof and at the Neighborhood Playhouse in New York. POLITICS: Liberal. MILITARY: U.S. Army, 1943–46 (Corporal). NON-THEATRICAL CAREER: New York Public Library, special assignments, 1952–56; television liaison, American Book Publishers Council, 1956–58; publicity manager, Alfred A. Knopf, 1958–61; assistant to chairman and to president, 1961–63; vice-president, 1963–67; lecturer, Hunter College, C.U.N.Y, 1968–72; lecturer, New School for Social Research, 1983–84.

WRITINGS: PLAYS, PRODUCED—*Look at Any Man,* 1963; *The Little Birds Fly,* 1965; *From a Dark Land,* 1967; *Return Upriver,* 1968; *The Death of Eagles,* 1970; *The Joslyn Circle,* 1971 (all originally produced at the New Dramatists, NY); *The Off Season,* 1973; *Escape Route,* 1981. TELEVISION SCRIPTS—*They* (with Marya Mannes), NBC, 1970; *Whose Life?,* NBC, 1970; head writer, *Another World,* NBC, 1971–79. BOOKS—*Inside, Looking Out,* 1971; introduction, *Introduction to an Assassin's Diary,* 1973; *Eight Years in Another World,* 1981.

AWARDS: Emmy, Best Writing, Daytime Serial, 1975: *Another World,* 1980: *The Guilding Light;* National Book Award Nomination in Biography, 1972: *Inside, Looking Out.*

SIDELIGHTS: MEMBERSHIPS—Dramatists Guild; New Dramatists; PEN; Writers Guild of America East; Author's League; Players. RECREATION—Reading, tennis, music.

"You write for what's in your head, to get it out of your head."

ADDRESS: c/o The Players, 16 Gramercy Park South, New York, NY 10003.

* * *

LENTHALL, Franklyn (ne S. Franklyn Leinthall), actor, director, producer, curator

PERSONAL: Born July 14, 1919 in Nanticoke, PA; son of Samuel Franklyn (an electrician) and Lena (a welfare worker; maiden name, Fraunfelter) Leinthall. EDUCATION: Graduate, Wyoming Seminary, Kingston, PA, 1938; studied at Cornell University, 1942–44; graduate, American Academy of Dramatic Arts, NY, 1946; studied theatre in New York City with Frances Robinson Duff, two years, Katherine Tyndal Dryer, one year, Fanny Bradshaw, one year and Dr. Stein at Hunter College for one year. POLITICS: Republican. RELIGION: Methodist, licensed lay preacher in the United Methodist Church. MILITARY: U.S. Army, Technical Sergeant, 1942–45.

CAREER: DEBUT—Vane, *Easy Virtue*, Harvey's Lake Theatre, Alderson, PA, 1937. PRINCIPAL STAGE APPEARANCES—Owen Turner, *Light up the Sky*, Weston Playhouse, VT, 1950; Dr. Paul Stronberg, *Flow to the Meadow*, and Sheriff Weeks, *Sun-Up*, Gateway Summer Theatre, Gatlinburg, TN, 1951; Elyot Chase, *Private Lives*, Boothbay Playhouse, ME, 1970.

PRINCIPAL FILM APPEARANCES—*Carnegie Hall*, 1947; *Kiss of Death*, 1947; *Portrait of Jenny*, 1948; *Naked City*, 1948; *The West Point Story*, 1950; *The Marrying Kind*, 1952.

PRINCIPAL STAGE WORK—Producer/Director—(three one-acts) *Finders Keepers, The Happy Journey, A Pair of Lunatics*, Pilgrim, NY, 1951; *Personal Appearance*, Gray Gables, Kitchman, NY, 1953; founded and produced for Lenthall Players in NY: *Trespass, Daphne Laureola, The Mousetrap, The Holly and the Ivy, Castle in the Air, Down Came a Blackbird, Papa Is All, Don't Listen Ladies, High Ground, Black Chiffon, The Sign of Jonah, Hay Fever, Sun-Up, Monique*, St. Paul and St. Andrew Methodist Church, NY, 1956–58; in 1957, he purchased the Boothbay Playhouse in Boothbay, ME and produced and directed plays, 1957–74, including: *The Reluctant Debutante*, 1957; *Holiday for Lovers*, 1958; *Dear Delinquent*, 1959; *Fashion*, 1960; *Sound of Murder*, 1961; *The Man in the Dog Suit*, 1962; *Come Blow Your Horn*, 1963; *Under the Yum Yum Tree*, 1964; *Light up the Sky*, 1965; *Ready When You Are C.B.*, 1966; *Barefoot in the Park*, 1967; *Black Comedy*, 1968; *Blithe Spirit*, 1969; *Another Language*, 1970; *Plaza Suite*, 1971; *The Royal Family*, 1972; *Norman Is That You?*, 1973; *End of Summer*, 1974. Maine State Touring Theatre, with *Hedda Gabler* and *Don't Listen Ladies*, toured 7,000 miles through state of Maine.

WRITINGS: Contributor to book *Autographs and Manuscripts; Collector's Manual*, section on American Theatre, 1978; contributor to *Maine: A Guide Downeast*, 1970. ARTICLES IN *The Boothbay Theatre Museum, Down East Magazine, Hobbies Magazine, Spinning Wheel Magazine, The Maine Teacher Magazine, Playbill Magazine*.

THEATRE-RELATED CAREER: Teacher/faculty member, American Academy of Dramatic Arts, five years; teacher/faculty member, American Theatre Wing, two years; faculty member, Katherine Long School at the Metropolitan Opera, NY; theatre consultant to Governor of Maine, six months; founder, Boothbay Theatre Museum.

AWARDS: Wyoming (PA) Seminary Distinguished Service Award in recognition of unselfish and dedicated service in his chosen career, 1979.

SIDELIGHTS: MEMBERSHIPS—Maine State Commission on the Arts and Humanities, six months; advisory board of the Drama League of New York; executive board of the Theatre Library Association, three years; Mr. Lenthall was acting

curator of and consultant to the Theatre and Music Collection at the Museum of the City of New York for one year.

"The preservation of American Theatre memorabilia, in comparison with other countries, is a new venture. It should be on our list of priorities!"

ADDRESS: c/o Boothbay Theatre Museum, Corey Lane, Boothbay, ME 04537.

* * *

LEONARD, Lu, actress

PERSONAL: Born June 5, 1932, in Long Beach, CA; daughter of Hal F. (an actor) and Amy F. (an actress; maiden name, Goodrich) Price. EDUCATION: Attended Los Angeles City College; trained for the stage with Mary Tarcai in New York. RELIGION: Protestant.

CAREER: DEBUT—Rachel, *Plain and Fancy*, National Tour, U.S. cities, 1955. NEW YORK DEBUT—Mae, *The Pajama Game*, St. James, 1951. PRINCIPAL STAGE APPEARANCES—(Broadway) *The Happiest Girl in the World; The Gay Life; Bravo Giovanni; Drat the Cat;* (Off-Broadway) Mrs. Peachum, *Threepenny Opera;* (Regional and Stock) Luce, *Boys from Syracuse*, Goodman Theatre, Chicago; Miss Tweed, *Something's Afoot*, A.C.T., San Francisco; *Home*, Company of Angels Theater, Los Angeles, CA; Matron, *Women Behind Bars*, Roxy, Los Angeles, CA; *Thumbelina*, Faerie Tale Theater, Los Angeles, CA.

FILM DEBUT—*Ma and Pa Kettle*, 1950's. PRINCIPAL FILM APPEARANCES—*Silent Movie; Pete's Dragon; Leo and Loree;* Mrs. Pugh, *Annie; Johnny Dangerously*. TELEVISION DEBUT—*Ray Milland Show*. PRINCIPAL TELEVISION APPEARANCES—*Studio One; Omnibus; The Red Skelton Show; Police Woman; Laverne and Shirley; Mork and Mindy*.

AWARDS: Dramalogue Award, 1980: *Home;* Sarah Siddons Award nomination: *Boys from Syracuse*.

SIDELIGHTS: MEMBERSHIPS—Company of Angels.

ADDRESS: Agent—c/o Honey Sanders, 229 W. 42nd Street, New York, NY 10036.

* * *

LESLIE, Don, actor, producer, teacher

PERSONAL: Born November 23, 1948; son of John (a seaman) and Sylvia (Duker) Leslie. EDUCATION: University of California at Berkeley, B.A.; University of Oregon, M.F.A.

CAREER: DEBUT—Governor, *Convention*, Drama Ensemble, NY, 1976. PRINCIPAL STAGE APPEARANCES—Mr. Stokes, *Rose*, Cort, NY, 1980; Oxenby, *The Dresser*, Brooks Atkinson, NY, 1980–81.

PRINCIPAL FILM APPEARANCES—Louis D'Amato, *Prince of*

the City. PRINCIPAL TELEVISION APPEARANCES—Jim Bouton, *Ball Four.*

THEATRE-RELATED CAREER: Teaches acting in own studio in New York City. Producing on off-Broadway *Losing It* scheduled for 1984 production.

ADDRESS: Home—609 Columbus Avenue, New York, NY 10024.

* * *

LESTER, Mark L. film director, producer, writer

PERSONAL: Born November 26, 1946, in Cleveland, OH.

CAREER: PRINCIPAL FILM WORK—Writer/producer, *Tricia's Wedding,* 1972; producer, *Twilight of the Mayas,* 1972; writer/producer/director, *Steelarena,* 1973, writer/producer/ director, *Truck Stop Women,* 1974; producer/director, *The Way He Was,* 1975; producer/director, *Bobbie Jo and the Outlaw,* 1976; director, *Stunts,* 1977; producer/director, *Roller Boogie,* 1979; executive producer, *The Funhouse,* 1981; director/writer/executive producer, *The Class of 1984,* 1982; director/writer; *Firestarter,* 1984. PRINCIPAL TELEVISION WORK—Director, *Gold of the Amazon Women,* 1978.

ADDRESS: Agent—c/o ICM, 8899 Beverly, Los Angeles, CA 90048.

* * *

Le VIEN, Jack, director, producer

PERSONAL: Surname has accent on second word "Vienne;" born July 18, 1918; son of Christopher Luke (a journalist) Le Vien; married Countess of Shaftesbury in 1956 (divorced 1960). MILITARY: U.S. Army, Colonel, World War II.

CAREER: PRINCIPAL FILM WORK, DIRECTED—*Black Fox; The Finest Hours; A King's Story.*

WRITINGS: BOOKS —*The Valiant Years; The Finest Hours.*

AWARDS: Academy Award Nomination, Best Feature-Length Documentary, 1965: *A King's Story;* Academy Award Nomination, Best Feature-Length Documentary, 1964: *The Finest Hours;* Academy Award, Best Feature-Length Documentary, 1963: *Black Fox.*

SIDELIGHTS: MEMBERSHIPS—British Academy of Film and Television Arts; Overseas Press Club.

ADDRESS: Home—15 Chesterfield Hill, London W1, England.

* * *

LEWINE, Richard, composer, producer, writer

PERSONAL: Born July 28, 1910; son of Irving (in real estate) and Jane Lewine; married (first marriage) Mary Haas; (second marriage) Elizabeth Rivers, November 27, 1971; children: Peter, Cornelia. EDUCATION: Attended Franklin School in New York; studied Music at Columbia University. MILITARY: U.S. Army, Signal Corps, Captain.

CAREER: PRINCIPAL STAGE WORK, COMPOSER—*Make Mine Manhattan,* NY, 1947–48; *The Girls Against the Boys,* NY, 1959; *Naughty-Naughty; The Fireman's Flame; The Girl from Wyoming,* 1936–38; songs for reviews—*The Ziegfeld Follies; Fools Rush In; Tis of Thee* and others.

FILM SCORE—*The Days of Wilfred Owen.* PRINCIPAL TELEVISION WORK, PRODUCER—*Wonderful Town; The Fabulous Fifties; New York Philharmonic Young People's Concerts* (three seasons); *Hootenanny* (two seasons); *Blithe Spirit; Aladdin; Noel Coward–Mary Martin Special; Cinderella; My Name Is Barbra.*

WRITINGS: BOOKS—*Encyclopedia of Theater Music,* with Alfred Simon; *Songs of the American Theatre,* with Alfred Simon.

AWARDS: Emmy Award and Screen Producer's Award, Best Produced Program, 1965: *My Name Is Barbra.*

SIDELIGHTS: MEMBERSHIPS—Council member, Dramatists Guild; AGAC; ASCAP; secretary, Dramatists Guild Fund; Author's League; Coffee House Club, NY.

ADDRESS: Home—352 E. 69th Street, New York, NY 10021.

* * *

LEWIS, Marcia, actress

PERSONAL: Born August 8, 1938 in Boston, MA; daughter of Edwin Parker (an engineer) and Bernice Phyllis (Lamb) Lewis; married Richard Alan Woody (a theatrical agent) November 19, 1966. EDUCATION: Jewish Hospital School of Nursing, R.N., 1959; attended University of Cincinnati; trained for the stage with Kenneth MacMillan at Herbert Berghof Studios.

CAREER: DEBUT—General Cartwright, *Guys and Dolls,* University of Cincinnati Theatre, Cincinnati, 1961. NEW YORK DEBUT—Ernestina Money, *Hello Dolly,* St. James, New York, 1969, 416 performances. PRINCIPAL STAGE APPEARANCES—Miss Hannigan, *Annie,* Alvin, New York, 1981–82; *The Time of Your Life,* Lincoln Center Repertory Company, New York. STOCK—Miss Hannigan, *Annie;* Mrs. Schinn, *Music Man;* Dolly Tate, *Annie Get Your Gun;* Aunt Eller, *Oklahoma;* Ernestina Money, *Hello Dolly;* Ellie, *Showboat;* Rose, *Gypsy.*

FILM DEBUT—Margie, *Night Warning,* 1981. PRINCIPAL FILM APPEARANCES—"Froglady," *Ice Pirates,* 1983. TELEVISION DEBUT—*Bob Newhart Show,* 1974. PRINCIPAL TELEVISION APPEARANCES—*All My Children; Legs; The Good Time Girls; Who's Watching the Kids; The Bionic Woman; Happy Days; Mr. Moon's Magic Circus; The Good Book.*

SIDELIGHTS: MEMBERSHIPS—Women in Film Society.

ADDRESS: Home—2048 Lewis Terrace, Los Angeles, CA 90046. Agent—c/o The Gage Group, 1650 Broadway, New York, NY 10019 and 9229 Sunset Blvd., Los Angeles, CA 90069.

* * *

LIM, Paul Stephen, writer, director, and critic

PERSONAL: Born January 5, 1944, in Manila; son of Ignacio (a businessman) and Patricia (Na) Lim. EDUCATION: University of Kansas, B.A., 1970, M.A., 1974. RELIGION: Roman Catholic.

CAREER: FIRST STAGE WORK—playwright, *Conpersonas,* William Inge Memorial Theater, Lawrence, KS, 1975. NEW YORK DEBUT—playwright, *Woeman,* Marquee, New York, 1982, 21 performances. BRITISH DEBUT—playwright/director/ actor, *Homerica,* Attenborough Theater, Leicester, England, 1983, 2 performances. PRINCIPAL ENGAGEMENTS—playwright, *Conpersonas,* Kennedy Center, Washington, DC, 1976; playwright, *Points of Departure,* East West Players Theater, Los Angeles, CA, 1980.

WRITINGS: PLAYS, PUBLISHED—*Conpersonas: A Recreation in Two Acts,* 1977. PLAYS, UNPUBLISHED—Homerica: A Trilogy On Sexual Liberation, 1977; Points of Departure, 1977; Woeman, 1978; Chambers, 1979; Flesh, Flash and Frank Harris, 1980; Hatchet Club, 1983. BOOKS—*Some Arrivals, but Mostly Departures* (collection of stories), 1982. THEATRE-RELATED CAREER: Lecturer on Theater, University of Kansas, presently.

AWARDS: Palanca Memorial Awards for Literature (Philippines), 1978: *Hatchet Club;* 1977: ''Victor and Other Issues''; 1977: *Points of Departure;* 1976: ''Taking Flight''; 1975: *Password;* Kenneth Rockwell Award, General Excellence, University of Kansas, 1976; Shubert Fellowship in Playwriting, 1976; American College Theater Festival Award, Best Original Script, 1976: *Conpersonas;* James B. Kennedy Award, General Excellence, University of Kansas, 1973.

SIDELIGHTS: MEMBERSHIP: Phi Beta Kappa, Dramatists Guild, American Association of University Professors.

''I want to write plays which do more than just entertain.''

ADDRESS: Home—934 Pamela Lane, Lawrence, KS 66044. Office—English Department, University of Kansas, Lawrence, KS 66045.

* * *

LINDFORS, Viveca (nee Elsa Viveka Torsten), actress, writer

PERSONAL: Born December 29, 1920, in Upsala, Sweden; daughter of Torsten (a Major and publisher) Karin (a painter; maiden name, Dymling) Lindfors; married Folke Rogard, 1941 (divorced 1949); married Donald Siegal (a director), 1949 (divorced 1953); married George Tabori (a writer), July

VIVECA LINDFORS

4, 1954 (divorced 1972); children: (first marriage) Lena; (second marriage) Kristoffer; (third marriage) John. EDUCATION: High school; Royal Dramatic Theatre School, 1937–40, Stockholm.

CAREER: DEBUT—*Ann Sophie Hedvig,* Lyceum School for Girls, Stockholm, 1937. NEW YORK DEBUT—Inez Cabral, *I've Got Sixpence,* Ethel Barrymore, 1952. LONDON DEBUT—Sophia, *The White Countess,* Saville, 1954. PRINCIPAL STAGE APPEARANCES—*French without Tears,* Royal Dramatic Theatre, Stockholm, 1940; the Bride, *Blood Wedding,* Royal Dramatic Theatre, 1943; Olivia, *Twelfth Night,* Royal Dramatic, 1945; Anna, *Anastasia,* Lyceum, NY, 1954; Cordelia, *King Lear,* City Center, NY, 1956; title role, *Miss Julie,* Missy, *The Stronger,* Phoenix, NY, 1956; Anna, *The Rose Tatoo,* stock, 1956; Livia, *The Golden Six,* Playhouse, NY, 1958; Frieda, *I Rise in Flames, Cried the Phoenix,* Theatre de Lys, NY, 1959; Sultana of Ilyuwatyat, *Brouhaha,* East Broadway Playhouse, NY, 1960; *Brecht on Brecht,* Theatre de Lys, NY, 1962; Vera Simpson, *Pal Joey,* City Center, NY, 1963; *Brecht on Brecht,* Stockholm, Sweden, 1963; various roles, *Postmark Zero,* Brooks Atkinson, NY, 1965; *Brecht on Brecht,* Gateway, St. Louis, MO, 1966; Portia, *The Merchant of Venice,* Theatre Festival, Berkshire, MA, 1966; Angela, *The Demonstration,* The Dog, *Man and Dog,* double bill called *The Nigger-Lovers,* Orpheum, NY, 1967; Cuba, *Cuba Si,* Teresa Carrar, *The Guns of Carrar,* Theatre de Lys, NY, 1968; title role, *Mother Courage and Her Children,* Arena Stage, Washington, DC, 1970; Alice, *Dance of Death,* Arena Stage, 1970; Alice, *Dance of Death,* Ritz, NY, 1971; in her own play *I Am a Woman,* Theatre in

Space, 1974; *Scream,* Alley, Houston, 1978; *I Am a Woman,* Paf Playhouse, NY, 1979; *Are You Now or Have You Ever Been. . . ?,* Promenade, NY; with her son Kristoffer, *My Mother . . . My Son.*

MAJOR TOURS—*An Evening with Will Shakespeare,* 1952–53; Gillian, *Bell, Book, and Candle,* 1953; *Anastasia,* national tour, 1955; Catherine, *Suddenly, Last Summer,* Princess del Lago, *Sweet Bird of Youth,* Natalia, *I Am a Camera, Miss Julie,* U.S and South Ameica, 1961; Elizabeth von Ritter, *A Far Country,* national, 1962–63; *I Am a Woman,* 1972–74.

FILM DEBUT—Naked girl (Swedish film), 1936. PRINCIPAL FILMS—*Think If I Marry the Minister,* (Sweden) 1940; *The Crazy Family,* (Sweden) 1941; *Anna Lens,* (Sweden) 1941; *The Two Brothers,* (Sweden) 1941; *In Death's Waiting Room,* (Sweden) 1942; *To the Victor,* 1947; *The (New) Adventures of Don Juan,* 1948; *Night unto Night,* 1949; *Backfire,* 1950; *No Sad Songs for Me,* 1950; *This Side of the Law,* 1950; *Dark City,* 1950; *Gypsy Fury,* 1951; *The Flying Missile,* 1951; *Four in a Jeep,* 1951; *Journey into Light,* 1951; *The Raiders,* 1952; *No Time for Flowers,* 1952; *Run for Cover,* 1953; *Moonfleet,* 1953; *Weddings and Babies,* 1956; *I Accuse!/Captain Dreyfuss,* 1958; *The Tempest,* 1959; *The Story of Ruth,* 1960; *King of Kings,* 1962; *No Exit,* 1962; *These Are the Damned,* 1962; *An Affair of the Skin,* 1964; *Brainstorm,* 1965; *Sylvia,* 1965; *The Witness* (voice only), 1967; *The Stronger; The Jewish Wife; An Actor Works; The Way We Were,* 1973; *Welcome to L.A.,* 1975; *Tabu,* 1975; *The Wedding,* 1977; *Creepshow,* 1983.

TELEVISION APPEARANCES—*The Bridge of San Luis Rey,* 1958; *The Idiot,* 1958; scenes from *Anasatsia; The Last Tycoon; The Defenders,* 1963; *Naked City,* 1963; *Ben Casey,* 1964; *The Nurses,* 1964; others.

WRITINGS: PLAYS—*I Am a Woman* (with Paul Austin), 1972; *My Mother, My Son* (with Kristoffer Tabori). MEMOIRS—*Viveka . . . Viveca.*

AWARDS: Berlin Festival Film Award, 1960: *No Exit,* 1951: *Four in a Jeep;* Drama League Award, *Anastasia.*

SIDELIGHTS: MEMBERSHIPS—(and co-founder with George Tabori) The Strolling Players, 1966; co-founder, *Berkshire Theatre Festival,* Stockbridge, MA; (artistic director, 1966–69); founder, Berkshire Children's Theatre.

ADDRESS: Home—172 E. 95th Street, New York, NY 10028.

* * *

LINN, BAMBI (nee Linnemeier), actress, dancer, choreographer

PERSONAL: Born April 26, 1926, in Brooklyn, NY; daughter of Henry William (a surveyor and accountant) and Mary (Tweer) Linnemeier; married Rod Alexander (dancer, choreographer) 1950 (divorced 1959); married Joseph G. De Jesus (a dancer, teacher, and builder), July 10, 1960; children: Belinda, Elisa, Joseph, Jennifer. EDUCATION: Professional

Children's School, NY, professional training with Vera Nemchinova, Edward Caton, Nimura, Mikhael Mordkin, Hanya Holm, Charles Weidman, Madame Anderson, Luigi, Agnes DeMille; studied acting with Sanford Meisner at the Neighborhood Playhouse, also with Bobby Lewis and Uta Hagen.

CAREER: DEBUT—*Hell on Wheels,* Agnes DeMille Ballet Co., Jacob's Pillow, MA, 1942. NEW YORK DEBUT—Aggie, *Oklahoma!,* St. James, 1943. LONDON DEBUT—Louise, *Carousel,* Drury Lane, London, 1950. PRINCIPAL STAGE APPEARANCES—*Carmen,* San Carlo Opera, 1942; soloist, Charles Weidman Modern Dance Co., 1945; Louise, *Carousel,* Majestic, NY, 1945; Alice, *Alice in Wonderland,* American Repertory Theatre International/Majestic, NY, 1947; Sally, *Sally,* Martin Beck, NY, 1948; soloist, Ballet Theatre: *Petrushka; Les Patineurs, Peter and the Wolf, Jardin aux Lilas,* 1949; lead dancer, choreographer, *Green Mansion Summer Theatre,* 1950; Bonnie, *It's Great to Be Alive,* Broadway, NY, 1950; ballerina, *Song of Norway,* Louisville, KY, 1951; Louise, *Carousel,* City Center, NY, 1954; lead act, *Danny Kaye Show,* Philadelphia, 1955; soloist, Buffalo Philharmonic Orchestra, 1958; Eve, *In the Beginning,* Metropolitan Opera Ballet Company, Opera House, NY, 1959; Laurie, *Oklahoma!,* Dayton, OH, 1959; Blanch, *I Can Get It for You Wholesale,* Shubert, NY, 1962; guest artist, *Benefit,* Shakespeare Festival Theatre, Stratford, CT, 1963; *Women of Ireland,* Brick Church, NY, 1979; Mary Magdalene, *Family Portrait,* Brick Church, 1981; One-Woman Show, *Hattie,* Westport Playhouse, CT (was also co-author), 1981.

MAJOR TOURS—Lead, *All the Way Home,* New England Company, 1947; *Bloomer Girl,* Los Angeles and San Francisco Opera, 1951; Dance Jubilee Co. starring Bambi Linn and Rod Alexander, East Coast, 1958; soloist, American Ballet Co., Spoleto World Festival, Italy, 1959; Elsie, *Redhead,* north east tour, 1960.

FILM DEBUT—Dance-Laurie, *Oklahoma!,* 1956. TELEVISION APPEARANCES—*Kate Smith Show, Peter Potter Show, Seven Lively Arts,* 1949; lead dancer, *Your Show of Shows,* 1953–56; guest dancer (alternate weeks), *N.B.C. Special,* 1956–58; *Ed Wynn Special, Benny Goodman Special, General Motors Fiftieth Anniversary Show, Ding Dong School,* 1957; *The Verdict Is Yours,* 1959; *Jerome Kern Special, Dave Garroway Show,* 1959; *Andy Williams Special, Music for a Spring Night,* 1960.

AWARDS: Theatre World Award, 1945; Donaldson Award, 1945.

SIDELIGHTS: MEMBERSHIPS—AEA, AFTRA, SAG, AGVA.

In addition to theatre, film and dance companies, Ms. Linn has performed in nightclubs in New York, Las Vegas, and Los Angeles. She worked as a dance critic for the *Westport News,* 1980–82, and has lectured on dance in dance schools, public high schools, and colleges since 1957, when she organized the dance department of the Bronx House Music School. Her one-woman show, *Women of Ireland,* written for her in 1979, has been performed around the East Coast and has been expanded to a two-women presentation featuring Susan Reed. It was performed in various towns in Connecticut in 1982.

ADDRESS: Home—45 S. Compo Road, Wesport, CT 06880.

* * *

LITHGOW, John, actor, director

PERSONAL: Born June 6, 1945 in Rochester, NY; son of Arthur W. (a producer) and Sarah Jane (a teacher; maiden name, Pride) Lithgow; married Jean Taynton (divorced 1980); married Mary Yeager (a professor); children: Ian, Phoebe, Nathan. EDUCATION: Graduate, Harvard College; London Academy of Music and Dramatic Arts. NON-THEA-TRICAL CAREER: Printmaker, founded Lithgow Graphics.

CAREER: DEBUT—Mustardseed, *A Midsummer Night's Dream*, Antioch Shakespeare Festival, OH, 1953. NEW YORK DEBUT—Kendall, *The Changing Room*, Morosco, 1973. PRINCIPAL STAGE APPEARANCES—James, *My Fat Friend*, Brooks Atkinson, NY, 1973; George, *Once in a Lifetime*, Circle in the Square, NY; Frank, *Spokesong*, Circle in the Square; Treva, *Bedroom Farce*, Brooks Atkinson; Joe Hill, *Salt Lake City Skyline*, Public Theatre, NY; Chris, *Division Street*, Ambassador, NY; Bruce, *Beyond Therapy*, Brooks Atkinson; Gethin, *Comedians*, Music Box, NY; 1974; Burke, *Anna Christie*, Imperial, NY, 1974; Great Lakes Shakespeare Festival, OH: appeared in fifteen Shakespearean roles, 1963–64; Bunthorne, *Patience*, Peachum, *Threepenny Opera*, Don Andres, *La Perichole*, Lord Chancellor, *Iolanthe*, Highfield Theatre, Falmouth, MA, 1965; Henry Higgins, *Pygmalion*, Lennie, *Of Mice and Men*, Achilles, *Troilus and Cressida*, McCarter, Princeton, NJ, 1969–70; Sir, *The Roar of the Greasepaint, the Smell of the Crowd*, Dr. Talacryn, *Hadrian VII*, Captain Vale, *The Magistrate*, Bucks Country Playhouse, New Hope, PA, 1970; Kendall, *The Changing Room*, Kiper, *What Price Glory*, Arthur, *Trelawney of the Wells*, Long Wharf, New Haven, CT, 1972.

PRINCIPAL STAGE WORK, Director—*As You Like It, Much Ado About Nothing, The Way of the World*, McCarter, Princeton, NJ, 1970; *The Magistrate, Barefoot in the Park*, Bucks County Playhouse, New Hope, PA, 1970; *Abduction from the Seraglio*, Princeton, NJ Opera Theatre, 1970; *Beaux Strategem*, Center Stage, Baltimore, MD, 1972; *A Pagan Place*, Long Wharf, 1973.

FILM DEBUT—LaSalle, *Oppression*, 1976. PRINCIPAL FILM APPEARANCES—*All That Jazz*, 1977; *Rich Kids*, 1977; *The World According to Garp*, 1981; *Twilight Zone*, 1983; *Terms of Endearment*, 1983; *Footloose*, 1984. TELEVISION DEBUT—"The Country Girl," *Hallmark Hall of Fame*, 1973.

AWARDS: Academy Award Nomination, Best Supporting Actor, 1983: *Terms of Endearment;* Antoinette Perry Award, Best Supporting Actor, 1973: *The World According to Garp; The Changing Room;* Fulbright Study Grant, London, 1967–69; magnum cum laude, Harvard College, 1967.

SIDELIGHTS: MEMBERSHIPS—AEA; SAG; AFTRA. REC-REATION—Music, guitar, banjo, art and painting, drawing, and "my family."

ADDRESS: Agent—Contemporary Artists Agency, 1888 Century Place, Los Angeles, CA 90048.

LIVINGSTON, Harold, screenwriter, producer

PERSONAL: Born September 4, 1924, in Haverhill, MA; son of Myron (a physician) and Betty (Segal) Livingston; married Lois Leavitt, August 31, 1958; children: Myra, Leah, Eve, David. EDUCATION: Brandeis University, 1950–53. MILITARY: U.S. Air Force, 1942–45; Israeli Air Force 1948–49; U.S. Air Force, 1950–51.

WRITINGS: SCREENPLAYS—*The Street Is My Beat*, 1966; *The Hell with Heroes*, 1968; *Star Trek-The Motion Picture*, 1979. TELEVISION—(scripts for, with inclusive dates) *Banacek* (1972–74); *Barbary Coast* (1975–76); *Mannix* (1963–75); *Mission Impossible* (1966–72); *Star Trek* (1966–69); *Destination Mindanao*. PLAYS, PRODUCED—*The Recruiting Officer*, Royal Playhouse, NY, 1958. NOVELS—*The Coasts of the Earth*, 1954; *The Detroiters*, 1958; *The Climacticon; Summer Colony*, 1961; *The Heroes Are All Dead*.

AWARDS: Houghton Mifflin Literary Fellowship, 1954: *The Coasts of the Earth*.

SIDELIGHTS: MEMBERSHIPS—Writers Guild of America, West.

ADDRESS: Home—273 N. Layton Drive, Los Angeles, CA 90049.

* * *

LIVINGSTON, Jay, composer, lyricist

PERSONAL: Born March 28, 1915 in McDonald, PA; son of Maurice and Rose (Wachtel) Livingston; married Lynne Gordon on March 19, 1947; children: Travilyn, Laura. EDUCATION: University of Pennsylvania, B.A. (Journalism), 1937; studied piano and harmony with Harry Archer in Pittsburgh, PA. MILITARY: U.S. Army, Private, 1942–43.

CAREER: DEBUT—rehearsal pianist and contributor of songs for Olsen & Johnson's *Hellzapoppin'*, 46th Street, NY, 1938. PRINCIPAL STAGE WORK, SONGWRITER—*Sons o' Fun*, Winter Garden, 1941; *I Love Lydia*, Players Ring, Hollywood, CA, 1952; *Oh Captain* (music and lyrics with Ray Evans), Alvin, NY, 1958; *Let It Ride*, Eugene O'Neill, 1961; *Sugar Babies* (two songs), Mark Hellinger, NY 1979.

PRINCIPAL FILM WORK, SONGWRITER—*Swing Hostess*, 1944; *I Accuse My Parents*, 1944; *Why Girls Leave Home*, 1944; *Crime, Inc.*, 1945; *Stork Club*, 1945; *Kitty*, 1945; *To Each His Own*, 1946; *Monsieur Beaucaire*, 1946; *Imperfect Lady*, 1947; *My Favorite Brunette*, 1947; *Golden Earrings*, 1947; *Isn't It Romantic*, 1948; *The Paleface*, 1948; *Streets of Laredo*, 1949; *Sorrowful Jones*, 1949; *Song of Surrender*, 1949; *My Friend Irma*, 1949; *The Great Lover*, 1949; *Samson and Delilah*, 1949; *Copper Canyon*, 1950; *Paid in Full*, 1950; *Captain Carey, U.S.A.*, 1950; *Fancy Pants*, 1950; *My Friend Irma Goes West*, 1950; *The Furies*, 1950; *The Lemon Drop Kid*, 1951; *The Mating Season*, 1951; *The Cowboy and the Redhead*, 1951; *Ace in the Hole*, 1951; *Here Comes the Groom*, 1951; *Aaron Slick from Pumpkin Crick*, 1951; *A Place in the Sun*, 1951; *Crosswinds*, 1951; *When Worlds Collide*, 1951; *My Favorite Spy*, 1951; *Rhubarb*, 1951; *That's My Boy*, 1951;

JAY LIVINGSTON

Anything Could Happen, 1952; *Somebody Loves Me*, 1952; *Son of Paleface*, 1952; *The Great Houdini*, 1952; *What Price Glory*, 1952; *Thunder in the East*, 1953; *Off Limits*, 1953; *Sangaree*, 1953; *Here Come the Girls*, 1953; *The Stars Are Singing*, 1953; *Three Ring Circus*, 1954; *Red Garters*, 1954; *Casanova's Big Night*, 1954; *Lucy Gallant*, 1955; *Second Greatest Sex*, 1955; *The Scarlet Hour*, 1956; *The Man Who Knew Too Much*, 1956; *Istanbul*, 1957; *Tammy and the Bachelor*, 1957; *The James Dean Story*, 1957; *Raw Wind in Eden*, 1958; *The Big Beat*, 1958; *Saddle the Wind*, 1958; *This Happy Feeling*, 1958; *Another Time, Another Place*, 1958; *Once Upon a Horse*, 1958; *Houseboat*, 1958; *Vertigo*, 1959; *Take a Giant Step*, 1959; *A Private's Affair*, 1959; *All Hands on Deck*, 1961.

PRINCIPAL TELEVISION WORK, SONGWRITER—*Satins and Spurs*, 1957; theme song—*Bonanza, Mister Ed, To Rome with Love.*

AWARDS: Aggie Award, American Guild of Authors and Composers, 1982; elected to Songwriters Hall of Fame, 1973; Academy Award Nominations: "Dear Heart," 1964, "Almost in Your Arms," from *Houseboat*, 1958; Academy Awards: "Que Sera Sera (What Ever Will Be Will Be)" from *The Man Who Knew Too Much*, 1956, "Mona Lisa," from *Captain Carey, U.S.A.*, 1950, "Buttons and Bows," from *The Paleface*, 1948.

SIDELIGHTS: MEMBERSHIPS—Executive Board, Motion Picture Academy (Music Branch), 1960's and 70's; Executive Board, Record Academy, 1960's; Dramatists Guild; ASCAP; West Coast Executive Committee, AGAC.

Mr. Livingston's best-known songs are: *G'bye Now, To Each His Own, Buttons and Bows, Golden Earrings, Almost in Your Arms, Tammy, Que Sera Sera, Never Let Me Go, Silver Bells, I'll Always Love You, As I Love You, A Thousand Violins, Dear Heart, Wish Me a Rainbow*, themes from *Bonanza*, and *Mister Ed, All the Time, Through Children's Eyes*. Mr. Livingston has performed his songs and music at the 92nd Street YMHA in New York City as well as on various cruise ships and at Duke University.

ADDRESS: c/o ASCAP, One Lincoln Plaza, New York, NY 10023.

* * *

LLOYD, Christopher, actor

PERSONAL: Born October 22, 1938 in Stamford, CT; married Kay (an actress). EDUCATION: Studied at the Neighborhood Playhouse, NY.

CAREER: PRINCIPAL STAGE APPEARANCES—*Happy End*, NY; *Red White and Maddox*, NY; *Macbeth*, New York Shakespeare Festival; *Hot L Baltimore*, Mark Taper Forum, Los Angeles, CA; *The Possessed*, Yale Repertory, New Haven, CT; *A Midsummer Night's Dream*, Yale Repertory; *Kaspar*, NY.

PRINCIPAL FILM APPEARANCES—*One Flew over the Cuckoo's Nest*, 1975; *Another Man, Another Chance*, 1977; *Three Warriors*, 1978; *Goin' South*, 1978; *The Onion Field*, 1979; *The Black Marble*, 1980; *The Postman Always Rings Twice*, 1981; *Mr. Mom*, 1983; *Star Trek III, The Search for Spock; Buckaroo Banzai; National Lampoons Highjinks; To Be or Not to Be*, 1983; *The Lone Ranger; Pilgrim Farewell; The Lady in Red; Acts of a Young Man; The Early Adventures of Butch Cassidy and the Sundance Kid.*

PRINCIPAL TELEVISION APPEARANCES—*Barney Miller; The Word; Lacy and the Mississippi Queen; Visions; Stunt Seven; Jim, Taxi.*

AWARDS: Obie Award, Kaspar, *Kaspar;* Drama Desk Award, Kaspar, *Kaspar.*

SIDELIGHTS: Mr. Lloyd has also performed extensively in summer stock and off-Broadway productions in addition to his Broadway, film, and television performances.

ADDRESS: Agent—c/o Phil Gersh, Gersh Agency Inc., 222 Canon Drive, Beverly Hills, CA 90210.

* * *

LLOYD WEBBER, Andrew, composer

PERSONAL: Born March 22, 1948, in London, England; son of William Southcombe (CBE) and Jean Hermione (Johnstone) Lloyd Webber; married Sarah Jane Tudor (Hugill); children: one son. EDUCATION: Westminster School.

CAREER: WRITINGS: STAGE SCORES—*Joseph and the*

Amazing Technicolor Dreamcoat, 1968; *Jesus Christ Superstar,* 1970; *Jeeves,* 1975; *Evita,* 1976; *Tell Me on a Sunday,* 1980; *Cats,* 1981; *Song and Dance,* 1982. FILM SCORES—*Gumshoe,* 1971; *The Odessa File,* 1974. COMPOSITION—*Variations* (based on A minor Caprice No. 24 by Paganini), 1977.

AWARDS: Antoinette Perry Award: *Evita;* Antoinette Perry Award: *Cats.*

SIDELIGHTS: MEMBERSHIPS—The Savile Club. RECREATION—Architecture.

ADDRESS: 11 W. Eaton Place, SW1, London, England.*

* * *

LOBEL, Adrianne, designer

PERSONAL: EDUCATION: Yale University, School of Drama.

CAREER: PRINCIPAL STAGE WORK, DESIGNED—*My One and Only,* St. James Theatre, NY, 1983; *The Mikado,* Chicago Lyric Opera; *Dwarfman,* Goodman Theatre, Chicago; *Play Mas,* Goodman Theatre, Chicago; *Lulu,* American Repertory Theatre, Cambridge, MA; *The Inspector General,* American Repertory Theatre, Cambridge, MA; *La Traviata,* Julliard School of Music and Drama, NY; *The Visions of Simone Machard,* La Jolla Playhouse, CA; Ms. Lobel's design work has also been seen at Arena Stage, Washington, DC, Guthrie, Minneapolis, MN, Yale Repertory, New Haven, CT, Hartford Stage Company, CT, Manhattan Theatre Club, NY, American Place, NY, Phoenix, NY.

AWARDS: Joseph Jefferson Award, *Play Mas,* Goodman Theatre, Chicago.

ADDRESS: Home—50 E. 80th Street, New York, NY 10021.

* * *

LOCKHART, June, actress

PERSONAL: Daughter of Gene (an actor) and Kathleen (an actress) Lockhart; children: Anne Kathleen, June Elizabeth. EDUCATION: graduated from Westlake School for Girls.

CAREER: DEBUT—*Peter Ibbetson,* Metropolitan Opera House, New York. BROADWAY DEBUT—ingenue, *For Love or Money.* PRINCIPAL STAGE APPEARANCES—*The Pleasure of His Company,* San Antonio, TX; *Forty Carats; Bedroom Farce,* Ahmanson, Los Angeles; *Butterflies Are Free; Once More with Feeling,* Lawrence Welk Village Theatre; *No Sex Please, We're British,* Stage West, Los Angeles, CA; *Murder at the Howard Johnson's,* Union Plaza, Las Vegas, NV. MAJOR TOURS—*Bedroom Farce,* U.S. cities; *Once More with Feeling,* U.S. cities.

PRINCIPAL FILM APPEARANCES—*All This and Heaven Too; Sergeant York; Adam Had Four Sons; The White Cliffs of Dover; Meet Me in St. Louis; The Yearling; Son of Lassie;*

JUNE LOCKHART

Strange Invaders; Peter No Tail. PRINCIPAL TELEVISION APPEARANCES—*Lassie; Lost In Space; Petticoat Junction; Magnum P.I.; The Greatest American Hero; Quincy—The Wedding; Grizzly Adams; Knots Landing; Braking the Habit; Take My Word for It.*

AWARDS: Anoinette Perry Award, Best Debut Performance: *For Love or Money;* Donaldson Award, Theatre World Award, Woman of the Year in Drama (Associated Press): *For Love or Money;* Emmy Award Nomination: *Lassie.*

SIDELIGHTS: "June has ridden a camel in New Delhi, an elephant in the circus, and cuddled gorillas, orangutans, and tigers. She is a 'zoo freak.' She has owned and driven a 1923 Seagrave fire engine, flown a blimp, is an antique car buff, a member of the Teamsters Union, flown in a hot air balloon, driven the Army's largest tank, and recently sat at the throttle of the Canadian VIARAIL. She is actively involved in Hearing Dog Inc., a new program in which dogs are rescued from the Animal Shelter and trained to hear for the deaf. She writes limericks."

ADDRESS: Agent—c/o Patricia Newby Management, 9021 Melrose Ave., #207, Los Angeles, CA 90069.

* * *

LOEWENSTERN, Tara, actress

PERSONAL: Daughter of Hugo (a musician) and Mary Lou (an artist; maiden name, Parr) Loewenstern. EDUCATION:

Attended Southern Methodist University, University of Texas and the Royal Academy of Dramatic Art; trained for the stage at Herbert Berghof Studios with Uta Hagen.

CAREER: DEBUT: *Patrick Henry Lake Liquors,* Performing Arts Foundation, Huntington, NY, 1977. LONDON DEBUT— Wendla, *Spring Awakening,* Vanbrugh, 1977. PRINCIPAL STAGE APPEARANCES—Abigail, *The Crucible,* Equity Library, 1977; Ismene, *Oedipus the King,* Cathedral of St. John the Divine, NY, 1977; women, *The Black, the Blue, and the Gray,* Hartford Stage Company, CT, 1978; Juliet, *Romeo and Juliet,* Ophelia, *Hamlet,* Belle/Mrs. Fred, *A Christmas Carol,* Mrs. Finter, *Right of Way,* Georgia, *Vienna Notes,* Lucy Lockit, *The Beggar's Opera,* Lucy, *The Rivals,* Guthrie, Minneapolis, MN, 1978–80; Tink Solheim, *Museum,* Kennedy Center, Washington, DC; Billye Harmony, *Progress!,* Westbeth, NY, 1981; Antigone, *Antigone,* Denver Center Theater, CO, 1982; Witch/understudy Lady Macbeth, *Macbeth,* Circle in the Square, NY, 1982; Janice, *Weapons of Happiness,* Studio Arena, Buffalo, NY, 1983; Carol, *Family Friends,* Gramercy Arts, NY, 1983; Lupe, *Action,* Actors and Directors Lab, 1983.

AWARDS: Honours Diploma, Royal Academy of Dramatic Art; Kendal Prize; Sir Emile Littler's Award; Caryl Brahms Award; William Poel Memorial; Bryan Mosley Prize.

SIDELIGHTS: MEMBERSHIP—AEA. FAVORITE ROLES—Janice, *Weapons of Happiness;* Juliet, *Romeo and Juliet.*

"I need to act, to create. The role of Juliet was important because it taught me how to sink or swim: circumstances important to my career."

ADDRESS: Telephone Service—(212) 799-9099.

* * *

LOGGIA, Robert, actor

PERSONAL: Surname pronounced "low-jah;" born January 3, 1930 in New York, NY; son of Benjamin (a shoe designer) and Elena (Blandino) Loggia; married (2nd marr.) Audrey O'Brien (a business executive), December 27, 1982; children: (first marriage) Tracey, John, Kristina. EDUCATION: University of Missouri, Bachelor of Journalism, 1951; studied with Stella Adler at the Actors Studio. RELIGION: Catholic. MILITARY: U.S. Army, Panama Caribbean Forces Network.

CAREER: DEBUT—Petruchio, *The Taming of the Shrew,* Wagner College, Staten Island, NY, 1948. NEW YORK DEBUT—Frankie Machine, *Man with the Golden Arm,* Cherry Lane, 1955. LONDON DEBUT—Solyony, *The Three Sisters,* World Theatre Festival, Aldwych, 1964. PRINCIPAL STAGE APPEARANCES—Julian, *Toys in the Attic,* Hudson Guild, 1960; Solyony, *The Three Sisters,* Morosco, 1963; *In the Boom Boom Room,* 1973–74.

FILM DEBUT—Frankie Peppo, *Somebody Up There Likes Me,* 1956. PRINCIPAL FILM APPEARANCES—Joseph, *The Greatest Story Ever Told;* Tulio Renata, *The Garment Jungle,* 1956; Byron Mayo, *An Officer and a Gentleman,* 1982; Dr. Ray-

ROBERT LOGGIA

mond, *Psycho II,* 1982; Frank Lopez, *Scarface,* 1983. PRINCIPAL TELEVISION APPEARANCES—*The Nine Lives of Elfego Baca,* Walt Disney series, 1957–59; *T.H.E. Cat,* title role, 1966–68.

ADDRESS: Agent—Blake Edwards Entertainment, 1888 Century Park E., Suite 1616, Los Angeles, CA 90067.

* * *

LONDON, Roy, actor, writer, director

PERSONAL: Born March 3, 1943 in New York, NY; son of Robert Lincoln (an attorney) and Frances (a teacher; maiden name Abes) London. EDUCATION: Antioch College, B.A., 1963. RELIGION: Jewish.

CAREER: DEBUT—Christy Mahon, *Playboy of the Western World,* Trotwood Circle, Dayton, OH, 1959. LONDON DEBUT—Trinculo, *The Tempest,* Royal Shakespeare Company, 1968. PRINCIPAL STAGE APPEARANCES—(Broadway) *Little Murders; The Gingham Dog; The Birthday Party;* (Off-Broadway) *America Hurrah; Viet-Rock; Monopoly; Once in a Lifetime.* MAJOR TOURS—*Lovers and Other Strangers; The Two of Us.* DIRECTED (Off-Broadway): *Sweeney Agonistes,* Circle Repertory Company (New York) and *The Lesson,* Manhattan Theatre Club.

FILM DEBUT—Rucker, *Hardcore,* 1979. TELEVISION DEBUT— Holden Caulfield, *Catcher in the Rye, Revisted,* 1965. PRINCIPAL TELEVISION APPEARANCES—*Botticelli;* district attorney,

ROY LONDON

The Trial of the New York Thirteen; Jeffrey Kleinblatt, *House Calls; Hill Street Blues; Newhart.*

WRITINGS: PLAYS, PUBLISHED—*The Amazing Activity of Charley Contrare and the Ninety-Eighth Street Gang,* 1974; *Mrs. Murray's Farm,* 1976; *Disneyland On Parade,* 1984. PLAYS, UNPUBLISHED—Bicentennial show, Museum of the City of New York, 1976; In Connecticut, 1980; Here Wait, 1980; Kiss Me, 1983. RADIO PLAY—*Chinaman's Chance,* 1977. TELEVISION SHOWS—*The California Gold Rush* (movie, with Tom Chapman) 1981; *Devil's Food* (movie).

AWARDS: National Endowment for the Arts Award for Playwriting, 1975: *The Amazing Activity of Charley Contrare and the Ninety-Eighth Street Gang:* Grants—New York State Creative Arts Program, 1975.

ADDRESS: Office—c/o Paul Diaz, 6430 Sunset Blvd., #701, Los Angeles, CA 90028. Agents—c/o Bret Adams Ltd., 440 W 44th Street, New York, NY 10036 and c/o Peggy Hadley Enterprises, 119 W. 57th Street, New York, NY 10019.

* * *

LONEY, Glenn, writer and educator

PERSONAL: Born December 24, 1928; son of David Merton (a farmer) and Marion Gladys (a teacher; maiden name Busher) Loney. EDUCATION: University of California at Berkeley, A.B., 1950; University of Wisconsin, M.A.,

1951; Stanford University, Ph.D., 1954. POLITICS: Democrat. RELIGION: Protestant. MILITARY: U.S. Army, 1953–55.

WRITINGS: BOOKS—*Briefing and Conference Techniques,* 1959; *Tragedy and Comedy* (two anthologies, with Robert Corrigan), 1971; *The Forms of Drama* (with Robert Corrigan), 1972; *Peter Brook's RSC Production of "A Midsummer Night's Dream,"* 1974; *Authorized Production Book of Young Vic's "Scapino,"* 1975; *The Shakespeare Complex* (with Pat MacKay), 1975; *Your Future in the Performing Arts,* 1980; *The House of Mirth/The Play of the Novel,* 1981; *Twentieth Century Theatre* (2 vols), 1983; *California Gold-Rush Drama,* 1983; *American Musical Theatre,* 1984; *Staging Shakespeare,* 1984. CRITIQUES, ESSAYS, AND REPORTAGE—*Educational Theatre Journal; Quarterly Journal of Speech; Opera News; High Fidelity/Musical America; Opera* (Holland); *Modern Drama; Craft Horizons; Progressive Architecture; Theatre Crafts; After Dark; Dance; Rundschau; Life; Reporter; Signature; Saturday Evening Post; Scandinavian Times; Cue; Show; Theatre Arts; Theatre Design and Technology; Music Journal; Smithsonian; Architectural Forum; Commonweal; American Scholar; Variety; Players; Theatre Annual; American Artist; NAEB Journal; American-German Review; Theatre Today; Dramatists Guild Quarterly; INTER/View; Performing Arts Journal.* NEWSPAPER REVIEWS AND REPORTAGE—*Christian Science Monitor; New York Herald-Tribune; New York Times; New York Daily News/Weekly Column; Los Angeles Times.* THEATRE-RELATED CAREER: Educator—instructor, San Francisco State University, 1955–56; instructor, University of Nevada/Las Vegas, 1956; professor, University of Maryland (Europe), 1956–59; instructor, Hofstra University, 1959–61; instructor, Adelphi University, 1959–61; professor, Brooklyn College and CUNY Graduate Center, 1961–present.

AWARDS: Fellow, American-Scandinavian Foundation.

SIDELIGHTS: MEMBERSHIPS—Phi Beta Kappa, Alpha Mu Gamma, AAUP, American Society for Theatre Research, Theatre Library Association, IFTR, Theatre Historical Society; League of Historic American Theatres; Drama Desk; New Drama Forum; Outer Critics Circle; American Theatre Critics Association; Ibsen Society of America.

"Even before going to teach in Europe (and North Africa and the Middle East) in 1956, I was fascinated by theatre history's surviving monuments. During my European tour of duty, and subsequently each summer vacation, I have been able to study many famed theatres and sites, as well as to report on foreign theatre activity and personalities. I have reviewed major music and drama festivals, always relating drama, dance and opera to the theatre tradition."

ADDRESS: Home—3 E. 71st Street, New York, NY 10021. Office—Ph.D. Program in Theatre, City University Graduate Center, 33 W. 42nd Street, New York, NY 10036. Agent—c/o Sally Wecksler, 170 West End Avenue, New York, NY 10023.

* * *

LONG, Jodi, actress

PERSONAL: Born January 7; daughter of Lawrence K. (an

JODI LONG

ex-vaudvillian and golf professional) and Kimiye T. (an ex-vaudvillian; maiden name, Tsunemitsu) Leung. EDUCATION: State University of New York at Purchase, B.F.A., 1976; trained for the stage with Joseph Anthony, Robert Lewis, and Norman Ayrton.

CAREER: NEW YORK DEBUT—Hop Daughter, *Nowhere to Go But Up,* Winter Garden, 1962. PRINCIPAL STAGE APPEARANCES—Rossignol, *Marat/Sade,* Changing Space, NY, 1976; Blue, *Strippers,* Everyman, NY, 1977; Monica Chin Lee, *The Verandah,* Gene Frankel Theater, NY, 1978; Ophelia, *Hamlet,* Everyman, NY, 1978; Blossom Springfield, *Fathers and Sons,* New York Shakespeare Festival, 1978; Seline, *Loose Ends,* Arena Stage, Washington, DC, Circle in the Square, NY, 1979–80; Sumi, *Monkey Music,* Pan Asian Repertory, NY, 1980; Bacchae Woman, *The Bacchae,* Circle in the Square, NY, 1980; Joanne, *Family Devotions,* New York Shakespeare Festival, 1981; Commentator, *Rowher,* Pan Asian Repertory, NY, 1982; Titania, *A Midsummer Night's Dream,* Pittsburgh Public Theatre, PA, 1982; Becky Lou, *The Tooth of Crime,* Syracuse Stage, NY, La Mama, NY, 1983; Titania, *A Midsummer Night's Dream,* Pan Asian Repertory, NY, 1983; Alice, *I'm Getting My Act Together and . . . ,* Cincinnati Playhouse in the Park, Cincinnati, OH, 1983; Cherie, *Bus Stop,* Byrdcliff, Woodstock, NY, 1983.

FILM DEBUT—Betsy Okamoto, *Rollover,* 1981. PRINCIPAL FILM APPEARANCES—Reporter, *Splash,* 1984. TELEVISION DEBUT—Jade Precious Stone, *Jade Snow,* 1976. PRINCIPAL TELEVISION APPEARANCES—Gail, "Nurse," *CBS Movie of the Week,* 1980.

SIDELIGHTS: MEMBERSHIPS—AEA; SAG; AFTRA. FA-

VORITE ROLES—Cherie, *Bus Stop;* Becky Lou, *The Tooth of Crime;* Titania, *A Midsummer Night's Dream.*

"I believe that if one is emotionally true to a part, and with the proper classical training, one can transcend typecasting and yet not deny what one is. I am an actress foremost who happens to also be an American of Chinese and Japanese descent."

ADDRESS: Home—450 Greenwich Street, New York, NY 10013. Telephone Service—(212) 757-6300.

* * *

LONGENECKER, John, producer, screenwriter

PERSONAL: Born February 12, 1947; son of C. Robert (a talent agent and television producer) and Ruth Hussey (the actress) Longenecker. EDUCATION: Attended UCLA, Motion Picture Department and the University of Southern California, Cinema Department. RELIGION: Catholic.

CAREER: PRINCIPAL FILM WORK—Producer/co-writer, *The Resurrection of Bronco Billy,* 1970; production assistant, *The Sting,* 1973; production assistant/casting director, *The Trial of Billy Jack,* 1973; producer, *Prior Commitment* (upcoming); co-producer, *Boy Wonders* (with Randy Carter; upcoming); writer, *The Executive Woman* (upcoming); producer/owner, John Longenecker Pictures; producer/partner, Carter-Longenecker-Glennon Productions.

PRINCIPAL TELEVISION WORK—Producer/host, *Take One: Student Films,* 1971.

AWARDS: Academy Award, Best Short Film, Live Action, 1970: *The Resurrection of Bronco Billy.*

WRITINGS: BOOK—*Sanctuary* (co-author). ARTICLES—"Hollywood Tributes," *Premiere* Magazine.

SIDELIGHTS: MEMBERSHIPS—Academy of Motion Pictures Arts & Sciences, Producers Guild, USC Cinema-Television Alumni Association, Community Legal Assistance (board of directors), Beverly Hills Citizen Committee.

"Mr. Longenecker holds the distinction of having been the youngest producer (23 years old) to ever win the Academy Award."

ADDRESS: Office—John Longenecker Pictures, P.O. Box 5155, Beverly Hills, CA 90210.

* * *

LORD, Jack (ne John Joseph Patrick Ryan), actor, director, producer, and writer

PERSONAL: Born December 30, 1930 in New York, NY; son of William Lawrence (a steamship executive) and Ellen Josephine (a farmer; maiden name O'Brien) Ryan; married Marie de Narde (a fashion designer), April 1, 1952. EDUCA-

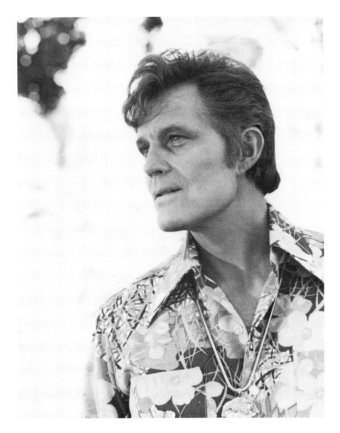

JACK LORD

TION: New York University, B.S., 1954; trained for the stage at the Neighborhood Playhouse with Sanford Meisner.

CAREER: DEBUT—*The Illegitimist*, ANTA New York, 1954. PRINCIPAL STAGE APPEARANCES—Slim Murray, *The Traveling Lady*, 1954; Brick, *Cat on a Hot Tin Roof*, Morosco, New York, 1955. MAJOR TOURS—*Flame Out*, Cleveland, OH Washington, DC, Philadelphia, 1953; *The Little Hut*, 1954; *The Savage*, Boston, Marblehead, MA.

FILM DEBUT—*The Court Martial of Billy Mitchell*. PRINCIPAL FILM APPEARANCES—*God's Little Acre; Dr. No; Williamsburg, the Story of a Patriot; Tip on a Dead Jockey; Man of the West; The Hangman; Walk Like a Dragon; Ride to Hangman's Tree; Doomsday Flight*. TELEVISION DEBUT—*Man Against Crime* (series). PRINCIPAL TELEVISION APPEARANCES—Stoney Burke, *Stoney Burke* (series); Steve McGarrett, *Hawaii Five-O* (series); *Omnibus; Studio One; U.S. Steel Hour; Goodyear Playhouse; Playhouse 90; The Untouchables; Alcoa Theatre; Bonanza; Loretta Young Show; The Millionaire; Checkmate; Have Gun, Will Travel; The Greatest Show on Earth; Climax; Kraft; Philco; Danger; Suspense; The Web; You Are There; Rawhide; Lineup; Naked City; Route 66; Dr. Kildare; Grand Hotel; The Virginian; The FBI; The Loner; Kraft Suspense Theatre; Combat; 12 O'Clock High; The Bob Hope Chrysler Theatre*. DIRECTED: FILMS—*M Station: Hawaii*, 1979. TELEVISION SHOWS—*Death with Father; How to Steal a Masterplace; Honor is an Unmarked Grave; Top of the World; Why Won't Linda Die; Who Says Cops Don't Cry; Hawaii Five-O*

(multiple episodes). PRODUCED: TELEVISION SHOWS—*Hawaii Five-O* (series).

WRITINGS: TELEVISION SCREENPLAYS—*Melissa*, 1968

AWARDS: Theatre World Award, 1954: *Traveling Lady;* Cowboy Hall of Fame Award, 1963; Fame Award, 1963; St. Gaudens Plaque for Fine Arts; 1948.

SIDELIGHTS: MEMBERSHIPS—Screen Actors Guild, Actors Equity Association, AFTRA, AGVA, DGA.

Mr. Lord's paintings are displayed in over thirty major galleries and universities around the world. "Hawaii Five-O was a huge and successful plateau in my life, but now it is time to climb some new mountains. Capricorn goats are always doing that anyway."

ADDRESS: Office—c/o Hawaii Five-O Studio, Honolulu, HI 96816. Agent—c/o J. William Hayes, 132 S. Rodeo Drive, Beverly Hills, CA.

* * *

LOREN, Bernice (nee Bernice Levine), actress, director, and writer

PERSONAL: Born in Montreal, Canada; daughter of Sam (a businessman) and Gertrude (Goldfine) Levine; married Duncan Tulk, November 29, 1951 (divorced 1953); married Roland Frederick Bernhagen (a designer/technical director), July 25, 1967. EDUCATION: McGill University, Montreal, B.A.; trained for the stage at the New School for Social Research with Erwin Piscator; also Lee Strasberg, Reiken Ben-Ari, Valerie Bettis, and Marian Rich.

CAREER: DEBUT—Karen André, *Night of January 16th*, Center Stage, East Jordan, MI, 1948. NEW YORK DEBUT—Calpurnia, *Julius Caesar*, Everyman's Theatre, 1951. PRINCIPAL STAGE APPEARANCES—Ruth, *Blithe Spirit*, 1948; Judith, *Hay Fever*, 1949; Toinette, *The Imaginary Invalid*, 1949; Tracy, *The Philadelphia Story*, 1949; Marian, *Parlor Story*, Miriam, *Guest in the House*, 1949—all at Center Stage, East Jordan, MI; Mrs. Brown, *Claudia*, Centre Playhouse, Rockville Centre, NY, 1950; Veta Louise, *Harvey*, Palm Tree Playhouse, Sarasota, FL, 1952; Anne, The *Milky Way*, Palm Tree Playhouse, Sarasota, FL, 1952; Sue, *All My Sons*, Palm Tree Playhouse, Sarasota, FL 1952; Tatiana, *The Anniversary*, Contemporary, New York, 1955; Marguerite Ida/Helena Annabel, *Doctor Faustus Lights the Lights*, Carnegie Chapter Hall, New York, 1958; Aunt Sarah, *One Foot in America*, Brooklyn Academy of Music, 1959; Chorus of Women, *Electra*, IASTA, New York, 1961; Eurydice, *Antigone*, Stage 73, New York, 1966. DIRECTED: *All My Sons*, 1948; *Voice of the Turtle*, 1948; *Arsenic and Old Lace*, 1948; *Angel Street*, 1949; *Home of the Brave*, 1949; *My Sister Eileen*, 1949; *The Importance of Being Earnest*, 1949; *Guest in the House*, 1949—all at Center Stage, East Jordan, MI; *Hello Out There*, Equity Library, New York, 1954; *The Enchanted Forest*, Stage 73, New York, 1962; *Aspects of Theatre*, Expressions Theatre, New York, 1964; *Theatre Offerings*, Expressions Theatre, New York, 1976.

TELEVISION DEBUT—*The Marble Faun*.

RELATED THEATRICAL CAREER: Teaching theatre—City College of New York, 1955–68; School for Creative Communication, New York, 1982–present; Expressions, School for Theatre Arts, New York, 1972–present.

WRITINGS: BOOKS—*Toward Greater Theatre Appreciation,* 1954; *Effective Speaking,* 1963.

SIDELIGHTS: MEMBERSHIPS—Actors Equity Association, Dramatists Guild.

With Roland F. Bernstein and Marilyn Lief Kramberg, Ms. Loren co-founded *Expressions,* a not-for-profit theatre school. ''I developed something of a crusading spirit about the quality of theatre and of theatre practice. I think acting is at its most exciting and rewarding when, along with the ability to communicate with and affect the audience, there is a characterization so full and true that the actor may not even be recognizable from role to role.''

ADDRESS: Office—250 W. 55th Street, New York, NY 10019.

* * *

LOUDON, Dorothy, actress

PERSONAL: Born September 17, 1933, in Boston, MA; daughter of James E. (advertising manager for a machine company) and Dorothy Helen (sheet music demonstrator at Filene's department store; maiden name, Shaw) Loudon, Jr., married Norman Paris (a composer and music arranger/conductor), December 18, 1971 (died 1977). EDUCATION: Syracuse University; American Academy of Dramatic Arts; studied for the theatre with Sawyer Falk, Lola Allbee, Gertrude Binley Kay.

CAREER: DEBUT—Passionella, *The World of Jules Feiffer,* pre-Broadway tryout, 1962. NEW YORK DEBUT—Wilma Risque, *Nowhere to Go But Up,* Winter Garden, 1962, for two weeks. PRINCIPAL STAGE APPEARANCES—*Noel Coward's Sweet Potato,* Ethel Barrymore, NY, 1968; Lillian Stone, *The Fig Leaves Are Falling,* Broadhurst, NY, 1969; Mabel, *Three Men on a Horse,* Lyceum, NY, 1969; Charlotte Haze, *Lolita, My Love,* Shubert, Philadelphia, 1971; Beatrice, *The Effect of Gamma Rays on Man-in-the-Moon Marigolds,* ACT, Marines, San Francisco, 1972; Edith Potter, *The Women,* 46th Street Theatre, NY, 1973; Miss Hannigan, *Annie,* Alvin, NY, 1977; Bea Asher, *Ballroom,* Majestic, NY, 1978; Mrs. Lovett (replacing Angela Lansbury), *Sweeney Todd,* Uris, NY, 1980; Cara Varnum, *West Side Waltz,* Ethel Barrymore, NY, 1981; Dottie Otley, *Noises Off,* Brooks Atkinson, NY, 1983–84.

MAJOR TOURS—title role, *The Unsinkable Molly Brown,* stock, 1963; Reno Sweeney, *Anything Goes,* stock, 1964; Ellen Manville, *Luv,* national, 1965; Eve, Bar-bara, Passionella, *The Apple Tree,* national, 1970; *You Know I Can't Hear You When the Water's Running,* national, 1970; Karen Nash, Muriel Tate, Norma Hubley, *Plaza Suite,* national, 1971; Beatrice, *The Effect of Gamma Rays on Man-in-the-Moon Marigolds,* 1972; Cara Varnum, *West Side Waltz,* national, 1981–82.

FILM DEBUT—*Garbo Talks,* 1984. TELEVISION APPEARANCES—*The Gary Moore Show,* 1962; *The Ed Sullivan Show; The Kraft Music Hall; The Dinah Shore Show; Those Ragtime Years,* 1960; *Music of the Thirties,* 1961; *Regards to George M. Cohan,* 1962; celebrity panelist, *Laugh Line,* 1969; *Dorothy,* 1979.

RECORDINGS: In addition to cast albums of *Annie* and *Ballroom,* there is *Dorothy Loudon at the Blue Angel,* Decca, 1960 and others.

THEATRE-RELATED CAREER—Nightclub singer and satirist, Ruban Bleu, Blue Angel, Mister Kelly's, others; ''cover'' records singer for RCA.

AWARDS: Sarah Siddons, Actress of the Year, 1982; *West Side Waltz;* Antoinette Perry Award, Drama Desk, Outer Critics Circle, 1977: *Annie;* Antoinette Perry Award Nomination, Drama Desk Nomination, 1979; *Ballroom;* Drama Desk, 1970: *Three Men on a Horse,* 1969: *The Fig Leaves Are Falling;* Theatre World, Most Promising Newcomer, 1962: *Nowhere to Go But Up;* Woman of the Year, Yeshiva University's Albert Einstein College of Medicine, 1979.

SIDELIGHTS: Ms. Loudon can be heard singing the best songs of the great masters of theatre music on the series of Ben Bagley ''Revisited'' albums, many conducted by her late husband, Norman Paris. RECREATIONS—Writing, painting, sewing (she makes most of her own clothes), playing the piano.

''I'm happiest when I'm onstage. I think that's probably why most people act: it's because they get to be somebody else. I find a strength onstage that I don't have offstage. It's when I have my confidence.''

ADDRESS: Agent—Lionel Larner, Ltd, 850 Seventh Avenue, New York, NY 10019.

* * *

LOWRY, Jane, actress

PERSONAL: Born February 11, 1937, in Minneapolis, MN; daughter of Goodrich (a banker) and Louise (Moyer) Lowry. EDUCATION: Northwestern University, B.A.; trained for the stage with Alvina Krause.

CAREER: NEW YORK DEBUT—Beatrice Blaine, *This Side of Paradise,* Sheridan Square Playhouse, 1963. PRINCIPAL STAGE APPEARANCES—(Broadway) Lila, *Poor Bitos,* Cort; standby, *A Delicate Balance,* Martin Beck; (Off-Broadway) Sophie Gluck, *A Lovely Sunday for Creve Coeur,* Hudson Guild; Irene, *Cracks,* Theatre de Lys; Vicky, *The Dodge Boys,* Hudson Guild; Marion, *Father's Day,* Van Dam; Suzy, *Hot L Baltimore,* Circle in the Square; Olga, *The Three Sisters,* Circle Repertory; Eve, *And He Made a Her,* Cherry Lane; *The Zykovs,* Manhattan Theatre Club; (Regional) Julie Cavendish, *The Royal Family,* Faye, *Chapter Two,* Meadow Brook, MI; Flo, *The Summer People,* Coconut Grove Playhouse; Miss Gilchrist, *The Hostage,* Cincinnati Playhouse, OH; Lily, *Ah, Wilderness,* Stage West, Suzy, *Hot L Baltimore,* Center Stage, Baltimore, MD; Julia, *A Delicate Balance,* Pittsburgh Playhouse, PA; Kitty DuVal, *The Time*

JANE LOWRY

of Your Life, Loretto-Hilton, St. Louis, MO; Laura, *The Glass Menagerie,* Ivanhoe; Hannah Jelke, *The Night of the Iguana,* Clinton, CT; Miss Alma, *Summer and Smoke,* Wayside.

FILM DEBUT—Aunt Annie, *Alice, Sweet Alice,* 1975. PRINCIPAL FILM APPEARANCES—Susan Harding, *Believe in Me.* PRINCIPAL TELEVISION APPEARANCES—Esther, "My Mother Was Never a Kid," *ABC Afterschool Special;* Pat Broer, *Ryan's Hope;* Anne Bingham, *Adams Chronicles;* "The Gang that Stole Manhattan," *McCloud;* Gloria, *Run, Valerie, Run;* Nurse Galbraith, *Love of Life.*

SIDELIGHTS: MEMBERSHIPS—AEA; SAG; AFTRA.

ADDRESS: Telephone Service—(212) 757-6300.

* * *

LOWRY, W. (Wilson) McNeil, writer and patron

PERSONAL: Born February 17, 1913; son of Benedict Harrison (a businessman) and Helen (a teacher; maiden name, Graham) Lowry; married Elsa Koch, August 31, 1936; children: Elsa. EDUCATION: University of Illinois, A.B., 1934; Ph.D., 1941. POLITICS: Democrat. MILITARY: U.S. Navy Reserve (active duty, 1943–46). NON-THEATRICAL CAREER: Associate editor, Dayton, OH, *Daily News,* 1946–47; chief, Washington bureau, Cox newspapers, 1947–

52; associate director, International Press Institute, Zurich, Switzerland, 1952–53; director, Ford Foundation, 1953–64, vice president, 1964–75; director, American Council of Learned Societies, 1976–present.

THEATRE-RELATED CAREER: Vice president, Ford Foundation, Humanities and Arts Program, 1964–present; director American Assembly on Performing Arts, 1977.

AWARDS: Antoinette Perry Award, Distinguished Support of the American Theater, 1963; ANTA Award, 1961; American Association Dance Companies Award, Distinguished Service in Dance; National Council Arts Administrators Award, Leadership in Visual Arts; American Association of University Press Award, Distinguished Services to Higher Education.

SIDELIGHTS: MEMBERSHIPS—Century Club, Phi Beta Kappa, Sigma Delta Chi, National Press Club (Washington, DC), Art Students League.

ADDRESS: Home—1161 York Avenue, New York, NY 10021. Office—104 E. 40th Street, New York, NY 10016.

* * *

LUCAS, George, producer, director, writer

PERSONAL: Born 1944, in Modesto, CA; married Marcia Griffin, 1969. EDUCATION: University of Southern California, B.A.

CAREER: PRINCIPAL FILM WORK—Assistant to director, *The Rain People,* 1969; director, documentary on making *The Rain People;* director/co-author, *THX-1138,* 1971, *American Graffiti,* 1973; director/writer, *Star Wars,* 1977; executive producer, *More American Graffiti,* 1979, *Empire Strikes Back,* 1980, *Raiders of the Lost Ark,* 1981; *Return of the Jedi,* 1982; *Indiana Jones and the Temple of Doom,* 1984.

AWARDS: Grand Prize for Film, National Student Film Festival, 1967: *THX.*

ADDRESS: Office—P.O. Box 2009, San Rafael, CA 94912.*

* * *

LUCKINBILL, Laurence (George), actor, director

PERSONAL: Born November 21, 1934, in Fort Smith, AR; son of Laurence Benedict and Agnes (Nulph) Luckinbill; married Robin Strasser (actress, divorced); Lucie Arnaz (actress), June 23, 1980; children: (first) Nicholas, second son, step-daughter, Jennifer; (second) Simon. EDUCATION: University of Arkansas, B.A., 1955; Catholic University of America, M.F.A., 1957; trained for the theatre with Uta Hagen at HB Studios; George Kernodle, University of Arkansas. RELIGION: Roman Catholic. MILITARY: Army Chemical Corps. 1956. NON-THEATRICAL CAREER: Cannery worker; studied medicine.

CAREER: DEBUT—China, *Pageant of All Nations,* St. Boniface Parish Hall, Fort Smith, AR, 1939. NEW YORK DEBUT—Old Shepherd, *Oedipus Rex,* Carnegie Playhouse, 1959. LONDON DEBUT—Hank, *The Boys in the Band,* Wyndham's, 1969. PRINCIPAL STAGE APPEARANCES—George Fabry, *There Is a Play Tonight,* Theatre Marquee, 1961; Iago, *Othello,* Hotspur, *Henry IV, Part 1,* Justice Swallow, *Henry IV, Part 1,* Great Lakes Shakespeare Festival, Cleveland, OH, 1962; title role, *Caligula,* McCarter, Princeton, NJ, 1962; William Roper, *A Man for All Seasons,* ANTA, NY, 1963; *Faces in the American Mirror,* 1963; William Roper, *A Man for All Seasons,* ANTA, NY, 1963; Simon Holt, *Beekman Place,* Morosco, NY, 1964; Damis, *Tartuffe,* ANTA Washington Square, NY, 1965; title role, *Galileo,* McCarter, Princeton, NJ, 1965; *Arms and the Man,* 1965;

Sodom and Gomorrah, Playhouse in the Park, Cincinnati, OH, 1966–67 season; Biff Loman, *Death of a Salesman,* Edmund, *King Lear,* American Conservatory Theatre, San Francisco, 1966, Orestes, *The Flies,* APA Repertory, NY, 1966; Hank, *The Boys in the Band,* Theatre Four, NY, 1968; Sensuality, *Horseman, Pass By,* Fortune, 1969; Ted, *The Electric Map* (in a double bill called *The Memory Bank*), Tambellini's Gate, NY, 1970; Dr. Prentice, *What the Butler Saw,* McAlpin Rooftop, NY, 1970; Patrick, *A Meeting by the River,* New Theater for Now, Los Angeles, CA, 1972, also Edison, NY, 1972; *Tadpole,* New Theatre for Now, 1973; Frank Elliot, *Alpha Beta,* Eastside Playhouse, NY, 1973; Brian, *The Shadow Box,* Mark Taper Forum, Los Angeles, 1975; Hamlet, *Poor Murderer,* Ethel Barrymore, NY, 1976; *The Shadow Box,* Morosco, NY, 1977; Simon, *A Prayer for My Daughter,* Public/Anspacher, NY, 1977; title role, *Galileo,* New York Actors Theatre, Havemeyer Hall, Columbia, NY, 1978; (replacement) George Schneider, *Chapter Two,* Imperial, NY, 1979; *Past Tense,* Circle in the Square, NY, 1980; Ken Harrison, *Whose Life Is It Anyway?,* Los Angeles, 1980; Vernon Gersch, *They're Playing Our Song,* St. Louis Municipal Opera, 1982; *The Guardsman,* U. of Arkansas, 1983.

MAJOR TOURS—William Roper, *A Man for All Seasons,* national, 1963–64; *Educating Rita,* stock tour, 1981; He, *I Do, I Do,* stock tour, 1983.

DIRECTED: Plays—As State Department Drama Advisor to Sudan in 1961, directed *Macbeth* in Arabic; *Our Town,* Rome (in Italian), 1961; *Old Aquaintance,* Paramus, NJ, 1967.

PRINCIPAL FILMS—Hank, *The Boys in the Band,* 1970; *Such Good Friends,* 1971; *The Money; The Promise,* 1979.

PRINCIPAL TELEVISION APPEARANCES—Pabundren, *As I Lay Dying;* Frank Carver, *The Secret Storm;* Glenn Garth Gregory, *The Delphi Bureau,* 1972–73; *Eisenhower,* 1978; *The Mating Season,* 1980; *One More Try,* 1982; *Death Sentence; Panic on the 5:22; Winner Take All; The Lindbergh Kidnapping Case.*

THEATRE-RELATED CAREER: Stage carpenter; founding director, *New York Actors Theatre,* 1978.

WRITINGS: BOOKS—*Feature People.* PLAYS—*Roy Brightswood* (also known as *Roy Hurd*); *The Golden Gate.* ARTICLES—"The Irrelevance of Being an Actor," *New York Times,* 1970.

SIDELIGHTS: FAVORITE PART—Galileo. HOBBY—Writing articles about the theatre and films.

ADDRESS: Office—c/o Richard M. Rosenthal, 445 Park Avenue, New York, NY 10022.*

* * *

LUMET, Sidney, director

PERSONAL: Born June 25, 1924, in Philadelphia, PA; son of Baruch and Eugenia (Wermus) Lumet; married Rita Gam (divorced); Gloria Vanderbilt, August 27, 1956 (divorced 1963); married Gail Jones, November 23, 1963 (divorced 1978); married Mary Gimbel, October, 1980; children: Amy, Jenny. EDUCATION: Attended Columbia University. MILITARY: U.S. Army, 1942–46.

CAREER: DIRECTOR—Films: *Twelve Angry Men,* 1957; *Stage Struck,* 1958; *That Kind of Woman,* 1959; *The Fugitive Kind,* 1960; *A View from the Bridge,* 1961; *Long Days Journey into Night,* 1962; *Fail Safe,* 1964; *The Pawnbroker,* 1965; *The Hill,* 1965; *The Group,* 1966; *The Deadly Affair,* 1967; *Bye, Bye Braverman,* 1968; *Last of the Mobile Hot Shots,* 1970; *Child's Play,* 1972; *Serpico,* 1974; *Lovin' Molly,* 1974; *Murder on the Orient Express,* 1974; *Dog Day Afternoon,* 1975; *Network,* 1977; *Equus,* 1977; *The Wiz,* 1978; *Just Tell Me What You Want,* 1980; *Prince of the City,* 1981; *Deathtrap,* 1982; *The Verdict,* 1982; *Daniel,* 1983.

TELEVISION—*Mama; Danger; You Are There; Alcoa; Goodyear Playhouse; Best of the Broadway; Omnibus; Playhouse 90; Kraft Television Theater; Studio One.* PLAYS—Summer Stock, 1947–49; *Caligula,* 1960.

PRINCIPAL STAGE APPEARANCES—(Child actor) *Dead End,* 1935; *My Heart's in the Highlands,* 1939; *George Washington Slept Here,* 1940–41.

ADDRESS: Office—c/o LAH Film Corporation, 156 W. 56th Street, 2nd Floor, New York, NY 10019.*

* * *

LU PONE, Patti, actress

PERSONAL: Born April 21, 1949, in Northport, NY. EDUCATION: Trained for the stage at the Juilliard School.

CAREER: DEBUT—Title role, *Iphegenia,* student company at Young Vic, Europe, 1970. NEW YORK DEBUT—Lady Teazle, *The School for Scandal,* Kathleen, *The Hostage,* Natasha, *The Lower Depths,* the Acting Company (first season), Good Shepherd Faith Church, 1972. PRINCIPAL STAGE APPEARANCES—Irina, *The Three Sisters,* Lucy Lockit, *The Beggar's Opera,* Lizzie, *Next Time I'll Sing to You,* Acting Company (second season), Billy Rose, NY, 1973; Rosamund, *The Robber Bridegroom,* Prince Edward, *Edward II,* Kitty Duval, *The Time of Your Life,* Acting Company, Harkness, NY, 1975; Genevieve, *The Baker's Wife,* Kennedy Center, Washington, DC, 1976; Ruth, *The Woods,* St. Nicholas,

Chicago, 1977; Rita/Lily La Pon, *The Water Engine*, Plymouth, NY, 1978; Call Girl, *Working*, 46th Street, NY, 1978; Monagh, *Catchpenny Twist*, Hartford Stage, CT, 1979; title role, *Evita*, Broadway Theatre, NY, 1979; Rosalind, *As You Like It*, Guthrie, Minneapolis, 1981; Ruth, *The Woods*, Second Stage, NY, 1981; Moll, *The Cradle Will Rock*, NY, 1982; *Stars of Broadway*, Colonie Coliseum, Albany, NY, 1983, *Edmond*, NY, 1983; Nancy, *Oliver!*, Mark Hellinger, 1984. MAJOR TOURS—Title role, *Evita*, pre-Broadway national tour, 1979.

FILM APPEARANCES—*King of the Gypsies*, 1978; *1941*, 1980; *Striking Back*, 1981. TELEVISION APPEARANCES—Kitty, *The Time of Your Life*.

AWARDS: Antoinette Perry Award, 1980: *Evita;* Antoinette Perry Award Nomination, 1976: *The Robber Bridegroom.*

SIDELIGHTS: In addition to her stage work, Ms. LuPone has lead an active nightclub and concert life, performing in major venues. Both her brothers are also in the theatre.

ADDRESS: Agent—DHKPR, 165 W. 46th Street, New York, NY 10036.*

* * *

LUPUS, Peter, actor

PERSONAL: Born June 17, 1943 in Indianapolis, IN; son of Peter Sr. (a businessman) and Mary I. (Lambert) Lupus; married Sharon M. Hildenbrand (a fitness consultant). EDUCATION: Butler University, Indianapolis, IN, three years; studied with Robert Montgomery, Lurene Tuttle, Jeff Corey, Eric Morris, Al Morganstern, and Martin Landau at Jordon College in Indianapolis. MILITARY: U.S. Army. NON-THEATRICAL CAREER: Executive Vice-President and Part Owner, Family Fitness Centers of Southern California.

CAREER: DEBUT—*Will Success Spoil Rock Hunter?*, Indianapolis Starlight Musical Series. PRINCIPAL STAGE APPEARANCES—*Cactus Flower; Accommodations; Boeing, Boeing; Love in E Flat; Saving Grace; Arsenic and Old Lace; Any Wednesday; Wake up Darling; The Paisley Convertible; Agatha Sue, I Love You; The Only Game in Town; A Streetcar Named Desire.*

TELEVISION DEBUT—*I'm Dickens, He's Fenster.* PRINCIPAL TELEVISION APPEARANCES—Willy Armitage, *Mission Impossible* (seven seasons); *The Red Skelton Show; Jack Benny Show; Dobie Gillis; Joey Bishop Show; Danny Kaye Show; Mike Douglas Show; Johnny Carson Show; Merv Griffin Show; Donald O'Connor Show; Woody Woodbury Show; Lucky Paris; Movie Game; Skitch Henderson Show; Tom Kennedy Show.* PRINCIPAL FILM APPEARANCES—*Muscle Beach Party.*

WRITINGS: *Peter Lupus' Guide to Radiant Health and Beauty*, with Dr. Samuel Homola; *Peter Lupus' Celebrity Body Book*, with Dr. Samuel Homola.

AWARDS: Winner, New Male Star of the Year Award, Southern California Symphony; Man of the Year, *Playgirl*

PETER LUPUS

Magazine; Best Built Actor, World Body Building Guild; The Bronze Halo, Southern California Motion Picture Council, for Outstanding Contributions to Entertainment.

SIDELIGHTS: MEMBERSHIPS—USO National Council; past Honorary Mayor of Studio City; CA; past National Chairman of Cystic Fibrosis; Salute to Youth program; past King Pin for National "Bowl Down Cancer;" past member L.A. Mayor's Citizens Narcotics Commission; past Grand Marshal of the Christmas Lane Parade.

ADDRESS: Agent—Ruth Webb Agency, 9229 Sunset Boulevard, Los Angeles, CA 90069.

* * *

LYMAN, Dorothy, actress, director, and producer

PERSONAL: Born April 18, 1947 in Minneapolis, MN; daughter of Hector H. (a stockbroker) and Violet E. (Brightwell) Lyman; married Joachim Tillinger, December 1, 1971 (divorced 1978); children: Emma, Sebastian. EDUCATION: Attended Sarah Lawrence College.

CAREER: PRINCIPAL STAGE APPEARANCES—*Niagara Falls*, Mark Taper Forum, Los Angeles, 1968; *The Serpent*, Open Theatre's European tour, 1968; *Shrivings*, London, 1969; *Rosencrantz and Guildenstern Are Dead*, Florida, 1970; *Action*, American Place, New York, 1976; *House of Mirth*, Long Wharf, New Haven, CT, 1977; *On the Outside—On the Inside*, Long Wharf, New Haven, CT, 1977; *Fefu and*

CONTEMPORARY THEATRE, FILM, AND TELEVISION • Volume 1

Her Friends, American Place, New York, 1978; *Later,* Phoenix, New York, 1979; *Coupla White Chicks Sitting Around Talking,* Astor Place Theatre, New York, 1980.

DIRECTED: PLAYS—*Coupla White Chicks Sitting Around Talking,* Astor Place Theatre, 1980; *Frugal Repast,* New York Theatre Studio, 1982; *Loving Reno,* New York Theatre Studio, 1983. PRINCIPAL TELEVISION APPEARANCES—Gwen Frame, *Another World,* 1976–80; Opal Gardner, *All My Children;* Naomi Oates Harper, *Mama's Family.*

AWARDS: Emmy Award, Best Actress, 1983: *All My Children;* Emmy Award, Best Supporting Actress, 1982: *All My Children.*

SIDELIGHTS: MEMBERSHIPS—League of Professional Theatre Women.

ADDRESS: Agent—c/o Jacksina and Freedman, 1501 Broadway, New York, NY 10036.

* * *

LYNDECK, Edmund (ne Mellendick), actor

PERSONAL: Son of George Henry and Rose Ann (Tennyson) Mellendick. EDUCATION: Montclair State College, B.A.; Fordham University, M.F.A. POLITICS: Republican. RELIGION: Roman Catholic. MILITARY: U.S. Air Force, 1943–46.

CAREER: DEBUT—chorus, Paper Mill Playhouse, Millburn, NJ. NEW YORK DEBUT—Reverend John Witherspoon, *1776,* 46th Street Theater, New York, 1969. PRINCIPAL STAGE APPEARANCES—(New York) Louis Leplee, *Piaf, A Remembrance,* Playhouse Theater, 1977; Judge Turpin, *Sweeney Todd,* Uris, 1979; Eric Didrickson, *A Doll's Life,* Mark Hellinger, 1982; The Wizard, *Merlin,* Mark Hellinger, 1983; (Regional) Praed, *Mrs. Warren's Profession;* The Coach, *That Championship Season;* Angelino, *A Yard of Sun;* Deeley, *Old Times;* Claudius, *Hamlet;* Vincentio, *Taming of the Shrew;* Reverend Anderson, *The Devil's Disciple;* Con Melody, *A Touch of the Poet;* Fagin, *Oliver;* Noirtier, *The Count of Monte Cristo;* Walter Burns, *The Front Page.* MAJOR TOURS—Judge Turpin, *Sweeney Todd,* U.S. cities, 1980–81.

TELEVISION DEBUT—Dr. Hendryx, *The Doctors,* 1972. THEATRE-RELATED CAREER: Teaching—(English) St. Peter's College; Jersey City State College; St. Francis College.

ADDRESS: Home—24 Willow Street, Bayonne, NJ 07002. Agent—c/o J. Michael Bloom, Ltd., 200 Madison Ave., New York, NY 10017.

M

MABLEY, Edward (Howe), playwright, director, educator
(John Ware)

PERSONAL: Born March 7, 1906 in Binghampton, NY; son of Clarence Ware (a film technician) and Mabelle (a musician; maiden name, Howe) Mabley. EDUCATION: Attended Wayne State University, Detroit, MI, 1923. MILITARY: U.S. Army, Signal Corps, Sergeant, 1942–43. NON-THEATRICAL CAREER—Mayor of Pomona, NY, 1971; U.S. Navy civilian employee, New York, 1944–45; research writer for Walter Dorwin Teague, (an industrial designer), New York, NY, 1937–42.

CAREER: PLAYS, PRODUCED—*Temper the Wind,* with Leonard Mins, Playhouse Theatre, NY, 1946; *Glad Tidings* (original title: *Sacred and Profane*) Somerset Playhouse, MA, 1951, Lyceum, NY, 1951; *Red Sky at Morning,* with Joanna Roos, Olney Theatre, MD, 1953. MUSICAL PLAYS, PRODUCED—*The Mermaid in Lock No. 7* (jazz opera), music by Elie Siegmeister, American Wind Symphony, PA, 1958; *Dick Whittington and His Cat* (symphonic story for narrator and orchestra), music by Elie Siegmeister, Philadelphia Orchestra, 1967; *I Have a Dream,* (cantata based on speech by Martin Luther King), music by Elie Stiegmeister, New York, 1967; *The Plough and the Stars* (grand opera, based on the play by Sean O'Casey), music by Elie Siegmeister, Louisiana State University, 1969, Grand Théâtre, Bordeaux, France, 1970; *Dublin Song,* music by Elie Siegmeister, Washington University, St. Louis, MO, 1963; *Night of the Moonspell* (grand opera based on *A Midsummer Night's Dream*), music by Elie Siegmeister, Shreveport, LA, 1976; *Bon Voyage,* book and lyrics (adapted from play by Labiche), music by Vera Brodsky Lawrence, York Players, NY, 1977.

PLAYS, UNPRODUCED—The Feathered Serpent; Doubleplay; Cross-Currents.

MUSICAL PLAYS UNPRODUCED—Piggy Bank Rag; The Twin Musicals; Monsieur Choufleuri.

PLAYS, PUBLISHED—*Glad Tidings,* 1952; *Discrimination for Everybody* (from his radio play, *Created Equal*), 1948; *Spring Journey,* with Joanna Roos, 1950; *June Dawn,* with Dorothy Evans, 1949. MUSICAL PLAYS, PUBLISHED—*Dick Whittington and His Cat; I Have a Dream; The Mermaid in Lock No. 7; Monsieur Chofleuri.* MUSICAL PLAYS UNPUBLISHED—The Plough and the Stars; Night of the Moonspell.

TELEVISION SHOWS—*The Silver Cord* (adaptation of Sidney Howard's play of the same title), 1949; *Laburnum Grove* (adaptation of J. B. Priestley's play), 1949; *Borderline of Fear,* with Joanna Roos, 1950; *The Box Supper,* with music by Otis Clements, 1950; *Jasper,* with music by Otis Clements, 1950; *The O'Neills,* with Ruth Friedlich, 1949–50; *The Woman at High Hollow,* 1958. TELEVISION SHOWS, PUBLISHED—*Borderline of Fear, The Best Television Plays of 1951.* RADIO SHOWS—*Borderline of Fear* (beamed behind the Iron Curtain by U.S. State Department), 1951; *Created Equal,* 1947; author of more than 50 produced plays for radio and television.

BOOKS, PUBLISHED—*The Motor Balloon "America;" Dramatic Construction.*

THEATRE-RELATED CAREER: Manager/Puppeteer, Tatterman Marionettes, Cleveland, OH; free-lance writer and director, New York, 1945–52; television director, CBS, 1952–69, NBC, 1969; Instructor, Playwriting, under John Gassner, New School for Social Research, 1946–present.

AWARDS: National Theatre Conference Playwriting Fellowships, 1947–48; Naval Ordinance Development Award for exceptional service, 1945.

SIDELIGHTS: MEMBERSHIPS—Dramatists Guild; American Society of Composers, Authors and Published; Directors Guild of America; Charter member, Writers Guild of America, East.

"In 1947, Mabley bought a 200-year-old farmhouse in northern Rockland County, where he lived until 1973. His hobby is travelling, and he has visited many remote parts of the world. In 1937, when he joined the staff of Walter Dorwin Teague, to work on exhibits for the New York World's Fair of 1940, he wrote and staged half a dozen major exhibits including the Ford Motor Company's *A Thousand Times Neigh,* which told the story of the coming of the automobile from the point of view of the horse. The dancers assembled for this production became the nucleus of The New York City Ballet."

ADDRESS: Home—15 W. 72nd Street, New York, NY 10023. Agent—Bertha Klausner, International Literary Agency, 71 Park Avenue, New York, NY 10016.

* * *

MACK, Carol K., writer

PERSONAL: Born Nov. 20, daughter of Edwin A. (a manufacturer) and Sylvia (Levy) Klein; married Peter R. Mack;

CAROL MACK

children: Joshua, Melissa, Dinah. EDUCATION: Mount Holyoke College, B.A.; studied acting at the Herbert Berghof Studios with Uta Hagen. RELIGION: Jewish. NON-THEATRICAL CAREER: Lecturer, Wagner College, Hampshire College; writer of educational film strips; reader for a film company.

WRITINGS: PLAYS, PRODUCED—*Esther,* New Dramatists, 1975, White Barn Theatre Foundation, 1976, Promenade, NY, 1977; *Survival Games,* Berkshire Theatre Festival (Unicorn Stage), MA, 1980; *Postcards,* University of Jacksonville and Daytona Playhouse, FL, 1982, Ensemble Studio Theatre, 1983; *A Safe Place,* Berkshire Theatre Festival in association with the Kennedy Center for the Performing Arts, 1981; *Territorial Rites,* American Place, NY, 1983. PLAYS, PUBLISHED—*Territorial Rites,* Women's Project Anthology, Vol. 2, 1984. BOOKS—*The Chameleon Variant* (novel, with Dr. David Ehrenfeld), 1980.

AWARDS: Susan Smith Blackburn Prize finalist and FDG/CBS Award finalist, 1983: *Territorial Rites;* University of Jacksonville One Act Award, 1982: *Postcards;* John Gassner One-Act Memorial Award (second place), 1982: *Gazebo;* Stanley Drama Award, 1976: *A Safe Place.*

SIDELIGHTS: MEMBERSHIPS—Dramatists Guild, League of Professional Theatre Women/NY, The Women's Project.

ADDRESS: Agent—c/o Susan Schulman, 454 W. 44th Street, New York, NY 10036.

MACKAY, Lizbeth, actress

PERSONAL: Born March 7, 1951 in Buffalo, NY; daughter of Robert J. (a salesman) and Alice F. (a dancer; maiden name, Steurnagel) Mackay. EDUCATION: Adelphi University, B.A. (Acting); Yale School of Drama, M.F.A. (Acting).

CAREER: DEBUT—American Shakespeare Festival, Fellowship Actress, Stratford, CT, 1970. NEW YORK DEBUT—Lenny Magrath, *Crimes of the Heart,* Manhattan Theatre Club, 1980. PRINCIPAL STAGE APPEARANCES—Cleveland Playhouse, Cleveland, OH, 1975–78—Anne Whitefield, *Man and Superman,* Cora Flood, *Dark at the Top of the Stairs,* Ginny, *Relatively Speaking,* Curley's Wife, *Of Mice and Men,* Estella, *Great Expectations,* Alexandra, *Little Foxes;* Henriette, *The Learned Ladies,* Elena, *The Romantics,* Zerbinetta, *Scapino;* Alice, *You Can't Take It with You,* Center Stage, Baltimore, 1979; Miss Fancy, *Sly Fox,* Alaska Repertory, 1980; Lenny, *Crimes of the Heart,* Golden, NY 1981–82. MAJOR TOURS—Lenny, *Crimes of the Heart,* Ahmanson, Los Angeles, 1983.

TELEVISION DEBUT—Leora Sanders, *All My Children,* 18 months. TELEVISION APPEARANCES—*P.M. Magazine.*

AWARDS: Theatre World Award, Lenny, *Crimes of the Heart,* 1982; Outer Critics Circle Award for Outstanding Debut, Lenny, *Crimes of the Heart,* 1981–82.

SIDELIGHTS: MEMBERSHIPS—AEA, AFTRA.

ADDRESS: Agent—Sheila Robinson, International Creative Management, 40 W. 57th Street, New York, NY 10019.

* * *

MACKINTOSH, Cameron, producer

PERSONAL: Born October 17, 1946, in Enfield Middlesex, England; son of Ian Robert (a jazz trumpeter and timber merchant) and Diana Gladys (a production secretary; maiden name, Tonna) Mackintosh. EDUCATION: Attended Prior Park College (Somerset, England); studied for the stage at the Central School of Speech and Drama. RELIGION: Roman Catholic.

CAREER: FIRST STAGE WORK—Stage manager, *Oliver!.* tour, British cities, 1965. NEW YORK DEBUT—Producer/deviser, *Tomfoolery,* Top of the Gate, 1981. LONDON DEBUT—Producer, *Little Woman,* Jeanetta Cochrane, 1967. PRODUCED: Plays—(London) *Anything Goes,* Saville, 1969; *Trelawney,* Sadler's Wells, Prince of Wales, 1972; *The Card,* Queens, 1973; *Winnie the Pooh,* Phoenix, 1974, 1975; *Owl and the Pussycat Went to See,* Westminster, 1975; *Side by Side by Sondheim,* Wyndhams, Garrick, 1976; *Oliver!,* Albery, 1977–80, Aldwych, 1983; *Godspell,* Phoenix, 1975, Her Majesty's P.O.W., 1977, Shaftsbury, Duke of York, 1978; *Diary of a Madam,* Phoenix, 1977; *After Shave,* Apollo, 1977; *Out on a Limb,* Vaudeville, 1977; *Gingerbread Man,* Old Vic, 1978; *My Fair Lady,* Adelphi, 1979; *Gingerbread Man,* Old Vic, 1979, Royalty, 1980, Westminster, 1981; *Tomfoolery,* Criterion, 1980; *Jeeves Takes Charge,* Fortune, 1981; *Cats,* New London, 1981; *Song and Dance,* Palace, 1982; *Blondel,* Old Vic, Aldwych,

Photograph by John Haynes

CAMERON MACKINTOSH

1983; *Little Shop of Horrors,* Comedy, 1983; *Abbacadabra,* Lyric Hammersmith, 1983; *The Boyfriend,* Old Vic, 1984.

INTERNATIONAL: *Relatively Speaking,* Canada, 1974; *Little Whiff of Windsor,* South Africa, 1975; *Side by Side by Sondheim,* Canada, 1976, Ireland, 1977; *Lauder,* South Africa, 1976; Australia, New Zealand, 1977; *Tomfoolery,* Ireland, 1981, NY, Village Gate, 1981; *Little Shop of Horrors,* Orpheum, NY, 1982, South Africa, 1984; *Cats,* Winter Garden, NY, 1982; *My Fair Lady,* Canada, 1982; *Oklahoma,* Australia, 1982; *Tomfoolery,* South Africa, 1982; *Oliver!,* Scandinavia, 1982, Canada, 1983, Australia, 1984; *Song and Dance,* Australia, 1983.

MAJOR TOURS (BRITAIN) *Little Woman,* 1967; *Murder at the Vicarage,* 1969; *Rebecca,* 1969; *At Home with the Dales,* 1970; *Salad Days,* 1972; *Butley,* 1973; *Winnie the Pooh,* 1973–74; *Time and Time Again,* 1974; *Godspell,* 1974–80; *The Owl and the Pussycat Went to See,* 1974, 1975, 1976; *Relatively Speaking,* 1974–75; *An Inspector Calls,* 1974; *Private Lives,* 1974; *Bell, Book and Candle,* 974; *A Merry Whiff of Windsor,* 1975; *Beyond the Fringe,* 1975; *Rock Nativity,* 1975; *So Who Needs Marriage,* 1975; *John, Paul, George and Ringo,* 1975–76; *Touch of Spring,* 1976; *Virginia Woolf,* 1976; *Lauder,* 1976; *Oliver!,* 1977, 1983; *Side by Side by Sondheim,* 1978–79; *My Fair Lady,* 1978, 1981–82; *Rocky Horror Show,* 1979–80; *Gingerbread Man,* 1979; *Oklahoma,* 1980.

WRITINGS: *Tomfoolery* (deviser); *Robin Ray* (co-deviser).

SIDELIGHTS: MEMBERSHIPS—Society of West End Theatres (executive officer), Dramatist League.

ADDRESS: Office—46 Museum Street, London WC1, England.

* * *

MACKLIN, Albert, actor

PERSONAL: Born November 18, 1958, in Los Angeles, CA; son of Dr. Sherman Mussoff (dean, UCLA School of Medicine) and June Bernice (O'Connell) Mellinkoff. EDUCATION: Stanford University, B.A., 1979; trained for the stage at the American Conservatory Theatre, San Francisco.

CAREER: DEBUT—Mr. Mell, *The Play's the Thing,* California Actor's Theatre, Los Gatos, CA, 1979. NEW YORK DEBUT—Ricky Hocheiser, *Poor Little Lambs,* Theatre at St. Peter's, 1982. PRINCIPAL STAGE APPEARANCES—Menzies, *Another Country,* Long Wharf, New Haven, CT, 1983; Zonker, *Doonesbury,* Biltmore, New York, 1983.

FILM DEBUT—Martin, *Streamers,* 1983. TELEVISION DEBUT— The Angel, *Amy and the Angel,* ABC Afternoon Special, 1982.

ADDRESS: Agent—c/o Leaverton-Sames Associates, Ltd., 1650 Broadway, New York, NY 10019.

* * *

MACLAINE, Shirley, actress

PERSONAL: Born April 24, 1934, in Richmond, VA; daughter of Ira O. and Kathlyn (MacLean) Beaty; married Steve Parker, September 17, 1954; children: Stephanie Sachiko. EDUCATION: Attended Washington and Lee High School, Arlington, VA.

CAREER: FILM DEBUT—*Trouble with Harry,* 1956. PRINCIPAL FILM APPEARANCES—*Artists and Models,* 1956; *Around the World in 80 Days,* 1956; *Hot Spell,* 1957; *The Matchmaker,* 1958; *The Sheepman,* 1957; *Some Came Running,* 1958; *Ask Any Girl,* 1959; *Career,* 1959; *Can-Can,* 1960; *The Apartment,* 1960; *Two Loves,* 1961, *The Loudest Whisper,* 1962; *My Geisha,* 1962; *Children's Hour,* 1962; *Two for the Seesaw,* 1963; *Irma La Douce,* 1963; *What a Way to Go,* 1964; *The Yellow Rolls Royce,* 1964; *John Goldfarb Please Come Home,* 1965; *Gambit,* 1966; *Woman Times Seven,* 1967; *Sweet Charity,* 1968; *The Bliss of Mrs. Blossom,* 1968; *Two Mules for Sister Sara,* 1969; *Desperate Characters,* 1970; *The Possession of Joel Delaney,* 1971; *The Turning Point,* 1977; *Being There,* 1979; *A Change of Seasons,* 1980; *Loving Couples,* 1980; *Terms of Endearment.* 1983.

PRINCIPAL TELEVISION APPEARANCES—*Shirley's World,* 1971–72; *Shirley McLaine at the Lido,* 1979; *Shirley McLaine . . . Every Little Movement,* 1980.

PRINCIPAL STAGE APPEARANCES—*Me and Juliet,* 1953; *Pajama Game,* 1954.

WRITINGS: BOOKS—*Don't Fall Off the Mountain,* 1970; *The New Celebrity Cookbook,* 1973; *You Can Get There from Here,* 1975; *Out on a Limb,* 1983; (editor) *McGovern: The Man and His Beliefs,* 1972.

AWARDS: Venice Film Festival Award, Best Actress, 1959: *The Apartment;* Silver Bear Award, Best Actress, International Berlin Film Festival, 1959: *Ask Any Girl;* Foreign Press Award, 1959: *Some Came Running.*

ADDRESS: Office—c/o Chasin-Park-Citron Agency, 9255 Sunset Blvd., Los Angeles, CA 90069.*

* * *

MACLEOD, Gavin, actor

PERSONAL: Born February 28, 1931, in Mt. Kisco, NY; married Patti Steele; children: Keith, David, Julie, Meghan; (stepchildren) Tommy, Stephanie, Andrew. EDUCATION: Ithaca College, B.F.A. MILITARY: U.S. Air Force.

CAREER: PRINCIPAL TELEVISION APPEARANCES—(series) *McHale's Navy,* 1962–64; *The Mary Tyler Moore Show,* 1970–77; *The Love Boat,* 1977–present; (episodic) *To Catch a Thief; Hawaii Five-O; Run for Your Life; The Hollywood Squares; The Mike Douglas Show;* (movies) *Only with Married Men,* 1974; *The Intruders; Ransom for Alice; Murder Can Hurt You; Scruples.*

PRINCIPAL FILM APPEARANCES—*I Want to Live,* 1958; *Compulsion,* 1959; *Operation Petticoat,* 1959; *High Time,* 1960; *War Hunt,* 1962; *McHale's Navy,* 1964; *Sand Pebbles,* 1966; *Deathwatch,* 1967; *The Party,* 1968; *Kelly's Heroes,* 1970.

PRINCIPAL STAGE APPEARANCES—*A Hatful of Rain; Middle of the Night; The Egg; An Evening of the Absurd; Lullabye; The Webb and the Rock; Carousel; A Funny Thing Happened on the Way to the Forum; Gypsy; The Seven-Year Itch; Annie Get Your Gun.*

SIDELIGHTS: MEMBERSHIPS—AFTRA.

ADDRESS: Agent—c/o William Morris Agency, 151 El Camino, Beverly Hills, CA 90212.*

* * *

MACNEE, Patrick, actor

PERSONAL: Born February 6, 1922, in the United Kingdom; son of Daniel and Dorothea (Henry) Macnee; children: Rupert and Jennifer. EDUCATION: Attended Summerfields, Oxford, England. MILITARY: Royal Navy, 1942–46.

CAREER: PRINCIPAL STAGE APPEARANCES: *Secretary Bird,* Australia; *Sleuth,* New York, 1972–73.

FILM DEBUT—*Life and Death of Colonel Blimp,* 1942. PRINCIPAL FILMS: *Hamlet; The Fatal Night; Dick Barton; All over*

the Town; The Elusive Pimpernel; The Girl Is Mine; Flesh and Blood; Small Back Room; Scrooge; Three Cases of Murder; Battle of the River Plate; Les Girls; Doctors Wear Scarlet, 1969; *Mr. Jericho,* 1970; *King Solomon's Treasure,* 1977; *The Sea Wolves,* 1980; *Dick Turpin; The Howling; A Stroke of Luck.* TELEVISION APPEARANCES—Starred in 30 television plays in Canada, 1952–58; featured in three episodes of *Playhouse 90,* two episodes of *Alfred Hitchcock Presents,* and more than fifty other television programs, including *The Avengers,* 1960–70; *The New Avengers,* 1976–79; *Thriller; Beyond Reasonable Doubt* (Australia); *Return of the Man from UNCLE,* 1983.

* * *

MACY, Bill (ne William Macy Garber), actor

PERSONAL: Born May 18, 1922, in Revere, MA; son of Michael (a manufacturer) and Mollie (Friedopfer) Garber; married Samantha Harper (an actress). EDUCATION: New York University School of Education, B.S., 1954; trained for the stage at New York University and studied with Lee Strasberg. MILITARY: U.S. Army Engineers, 1943–46.

CAREER: PRINCIPAL STAGE APPEARANCES—*Once More with Feeling,* New York; *And Miss Reardon Drinks a Little,* New York; *The Roast,* New York; *I Ought to Be in Pictures,* New York; *The Tempest,* London; *America Hurrah,* New York and London; *Oh! Calcutta!,* New York and London; *The Balcony,* New York; *The Cannibals,* New York; *Awake and Sing,* New York; *An American Comedy,* Mark Taper Forum, Los Angeles.

PRINCIPAL FILMS—*The Late Show; The Jerk; Serial; My Favorite Year.* TELEVISION APPEARANCES—Walter Findlay, *Maude;* Myron Selznick, *The Scarlett O'Hara Wars;* Mr. Goldberger, *The Day the Bubble Burst.*

SIDELIGHTS: HOBBIES—Photography, tennis, and reading.

ADDRESS: Agent—c/o The Artists Agency, 10000 Santa Monica Blvd., Los Angeles, CA 90067.

* * *

MADEIRA, Marcia, lighting designer

PERSONAL: Born January 25, 1945, in Boston, MA; daughter of Albert Pierpont (a college professor) and Beatrice (vom Baur) Madeira. EDUCATION: Carnegie-Mellon University, B.F.A., 1969.

CAREER: PRINCIPAL STAGE WORK (LIGHTING DESIGNER)—*The Boys from Syracuse,* Equity Library, NY, 1977; *The Music Man,* City Center, NY, 1979–80; *The Elephant Man,* Theatre of the Stars, Atlanta, GA, 1980; *Merton of the Movies,* Hartman, Stamford, CT, 1981; *Hedda Gabler,* Hartman, 1981; *Cloud 9,* Theatre de Lys, NY, 1981; *A Streetcar Named Desire,* Hartman, CT, 1982; *Lullabye and Goodnight,* NY Shakespeare Festival, 1982; *Outrage!,* Kennedy Center, Washington, DC, 1982; *Nine,* 46th Street, NY, 1982; *The Caine Mutiny,* Hartman, CT, 1983; *Actors and*

Actresses, Hartman, CT, 1983; *My One and Only*, St. James, NY, 1983; *Marilyn, an American Fable*, Minskoff, NY, 1983; *Lyndon*, NY, 1984. MAJOR TOURS (LIGHTING DESIGNER)—*The Big Broadcast of 1944*, 1979–80; *West Side Story*, European cities, 1981.

NIGHT CLUBS (LIGHTING DESIGNER)—*Ann-Margret Show*, 1980–83; *The Copa Girls*, Atlantic City, NJ, 1982. SPECIAL EFFECTS (LIGHTING DESIGNER)—Hal Prince 50th Birthday Party, Phoenix Movie Studios, 1978; The American Book Awards, Park Avenue Armory, NY, 1980; Giorgio Armani Fashion Show, Rockefeller Center, NY, 1980; Beverly Sills Recital, Crystal Cathedral, Garden Grove, CA, 1980.

AWARDS: Antoinette Perry Award, Drama Desk Award, Outstanding Lighting Design, 1982: *Nine*.

ADDRESS: Home—305 W. 72nd Street, New York, NY 10023.

* * *

MAHAFFEY, Valerie, actress

PERSONAL: Born in Sungei Gerong, Indonesia; daughter of Lewis Deweese (a petroleum consultant) and Jean Viola (Coates) Mahaffey. EDUCATION: University of Texas, B.F.A., 1975. RELIGION: Episcopalian.

CAREER: DEBUT—Florry, *The Princess of Schenk Avenue*, E. P. Conkle Playwright's Workshop, Austin, TX, 1974. NEW YORK DEBUT—Catherine Howard, *Rex*, Lunt-Fontanne, 1976. PRINCIPAL STAGE APPEARANCES—(Broadway) Lucy, *Dracula*, 1979; Secretary/Jessie, *Fearless Frank*, 1980; Rebecca, *Scenes and Revelations*, 1981; Sarah, *Translations*, Manhattan Theatre Club, 1981; Banton, *Twelve Dreams*, Public Theatre, 1982; Griselda/Kit/Shona, *Top Girls*, 1983; (Regional) Hermia, *A Midsummer Night's Dream*, 1975; Angel, *I Married an Angel*, Berkshire Theatre, MA, 1977; Juliet, *Romeo and Juliet*, Milwaukee Repertory, 1978; Mattie, *Ethan Frome*, Long Wharf Theatre, New Haven, CT, 1982; Desdemona, *Othello, All's Well That Ends Well*, Dallas Shakespeare Festival, 1982; Anabella, *The Keeper*, Philadelphia, 1982; Cecily, *The Importance of Being Earnest*, 1983; Jean, *Play Memory*, McCarter, Princeton, NJ, and Philadelphia, PA, 1983.

TELEVISION DEBUT—"Tell Me My Name," *G.E. Theater*, 1976. PRINCIPAL TELEVISION APPEARANCES—Ashley Bennett, *The Doctors;* "The Leather Stocking Tales," *Once Upon a Classic;* "The Open Window," *Tales of the Unexpected*.

AWARDS: Obie Award, 1983: *Top Girls;* Emmy Award Nomination, Best Supporting Actress, 1980: *The Doctors*.

SIDELIGHTS: MEMBERSHIPS—AEA; SAG; AFTRA.

ADDRESS: Agent—c/o Jeff Hunter, D.H.K.P.R., 1560 Broadway, New York, NY 10036.

MAHER, Joseph, actor and director

PERSONAL: Born December 29, 1933, in Westport, Ireland; son of Joseph (a school teacher) and Delia A. (O'Malley) Maher. EDUCATION: Attended Christian Brothers High School, Ireland.

CAREER: DEBUT—Biondello, *Taming of the Shrew*, Canadian Players Theater, Toronto, Canada, 1959. NEW YORK DEBUT—I.R.A. Officer, *The Hostage*, One Sheridan Square Theater, 1962. PRINCIPAL THEATER APPEARANCES—(New York) *Eh?*, 1966; *The Chinese Prime Minister*, 1968; *The Prime of Miss Jean Brodie*, 1968; *The Local Stigmatic*, 1969; *The Contractor*, 1973; *Who's Who in Hell*, 1974; *Henry the Fifth*, 1974; *The Royal Family*, 1975; *Days in the Trees*, 1976; *Savages*, 1977; *Spokesong*, 1979; *Night and Day*, 1980; *Entertaining Mr. Sloane*, 1981; *Live Like Pigs*, 1981; *84 Charing Cross Road*, 1982–83; (Regional) Theatre Company of Boston, 1965; Guthrie Theatre, Minneapolis, MN, 1971; *Juno and the Paycock*, Long Wharf Theater, New Haven, CT, 1973; *Forget-Me-Not-Lane*, Long Wharf, 1973; *National Health*, Long Wharf, 1974; *Afore Night Come*, Long Wharf, 1975; *Savages*, Mark Taper Forum, Los Angeles, CA, 1975; *Richard III*, Long Wharf, 1976; *Black Angel*, Mark Taper Forum, Los Angeles, 1976; *Absent Friends*, Long Wharf, 1977; *Spokesong*, Long Wharf, 1978; *Tales from Hollywood*, Mark Taper Forum, Los Angeles, 1982; *The Hostage*, Long Wharf, 1983.

DIRECTED: *The Hostage*, Long Wharf, New Haven, CT, 1983.

FILM DEBUT—*For Pete's Sake*. PRINCIPAL FILM APPEARANCES—*Heaven Can Wait; Under the Rainbow; Just Tell Me What You Want; Those Lips, Those Eyes; The Evil That Men Do*, 1983. TELEVISION DEBUT—*Little Moon of Alban: Hallmark Hall of Fame*. PRINCIPAL TELEVISION APPEARANCES—*M*A*S*H*: Wonder Woman; Little Gloria, Happy at Last; Will There Really Be a Morning; My Old Man*.

WRITINGS: PLAYS, PRODUCED—*Dance for Me, Simeon*, A.T.A., New York.

AWARDS: Antoinette Perry Award nomination, 1980: *Night and Day;* Antoinette Perry Award nomination, 1979: *Spokesong;* Obie Award, 1977: *Savages;* Los Angeles Critics nomination, 1975: *Savages*.

SIDELIGHTS: FAVORITE PARTS—Captain, *Juno and the Paycock;* Alan West, *Savages*.

"I would someday like to play James Tyrone in *Long Day's Journey into Night*."

ADDRESS: Agent—c/o Writers and Artists Agency, 162 W. 56th Street, Suite 404, New York, NY 10019.

* * *

MALDEN, Karl (ne Mladew Sekulovich), actor and director

PERSONAL: Born March 22, 1914, in Chicago, IL; son of Peter and Minnie (Sebera) Sekulovich; married Mona

Graham, December 18, 1938; children: Mila, Carla. EDUCATION: Attended Emerson School, Gary, IN; studied at Art Institute, Chicago, 1933–36; trained for the stage at the Goodman Theatre School, Chicago. MILITARY: U.S. Air Force, 1943–45.

CAREER: NEW YORK DEBUT—Barker, *Golden Boy,* Belasco, 1937. PRINCIPAL STAGE APPEARANCES—(New York)—Joe, *How to Get Tough About It,* Martin Beck, 1938; Charlie Johnson, *Missouri Legend,* Empire, 1938; Magruder, *The Gentle People,* Belasco, 1939; Hunk, *Key Largo,* Ethel Barrymore, 1939; Captain George McNab, *Flight to the West,* Guild, 1940; Ben, *Uncle Harry,* Broadhurst, 1942; Giltzparer, *Counterattack,* Windsor, 1943; Matthew Graves, *Sons and Soldiers,* Morosco, 1943; Adams, *Winged Victory,* 44th Street, 1943; André Vauquin, *The Assassin,* National, 1945; Stag, *Truckline Cafe,* Belasco, 1946; George Deever, *All My Sons,* Coronet, 1947; Mitch, *A Streetcar Named Desire,* Ethel Barrymore, New York, 1947; Buttonmolder, *Peer Gynt,* ANTA, 1951; Ephraim Cabot, *Desire Under the Elms,* ANTA, 1952; Dan Hilliard, *The Desperate Hours,* Ethel Barrymore, 1955; Hank Parsons, *The Egghead,* Ethel Barrymore, 1957.

FILM DEBUT—*Boomerang,* 1947. PRINCIPAL FILMS—*The Kiss of Death,* 1947; *Where the Sidewalk Ends,* 1950; *The Gunfighter,* 1950; *The Halls of Montezuma,* 1950; *A Streetcar Named Desire,* 1951; *Diplomatic Courier,* 1952; *The Sellout,* 1952; *Operation Secret,* 1952; *Ruby Gentry,* 1952; *Take the High Ground,* 1953; *I Confess,* 1953; *On the Waterfront,* 1954; *Baby Doll,* 1956; *Fear Strikes Out,* 1957; *Bombers B-52,* 1957; *The Hanging Tree,* 1959; *Parrish,* 1960; *Pollyanna,* 1960; *One-Eyed Jacks,* 1961; *The Great Imposter,* 1961; *Birdman of Alcatraz,* 1962; *All Fall Down,* 1962; *Gypsy,* 1962; *How the West Was Won,* 1962; *Come Fly with Me,* 1963; *Dead Ringer,* 1964; *Cheyenne Autumn,* 1964; *The Cincinnati Kid,* 1965; *Nevada Smith,* 1966; *Hotel,* 1967; *The Adventures of Bullwhip Griffin,* 1967; *Billion Dollar Brain,* 1967; *Hot Millions,* 1968; *Patton,* 1970; *Cat O'Nine Tails,* 1971; *Wild Rovers,* 1971; *Summertime Killer,* 1973. TELEVISION APPEARANCES—Lieutenant Mike Stone, *Streets of San Francisco,* 1972–77; Skag, *Skag,* 1980.

DIRECTED: Films—*Time Limit,* 1957.

AWARDS: Drama Critics Circle Award, 1948: *A Streetcar Named Desire;* Donaldson Award, 1950; Critics Award, 1950; Academy Award, 1952: *A Streetcar Named Desire;* Academy Award Nomination, 1954: *On the Waterfront.*

SIDELIGHTS: MEMBERSHIPS—AEA, SAG, (Board Member, 1963–66; Director, 1966–69), SDG, AFTRA.

ADDRESS: Agent—c/o Creative Artists Agency, 1888 Century Park East, Suite 1400, Los Angeles, CA 90028.

* * *

MALICK, Terrence, producer, director, writer

PERSONAL: Born 1943, in Waco, TX. EDUCATION: Graduated from Harvard University; also attended Oxford University; studied film at American Film Institute, CA. NON-FILM

CAREERS: Reporter, *Time, Newsweek, New Yorker;* lecturer, philosophy, M.I.T.

CAREER: PRINCIPAL FILM WORK—Writer, *The Gravy Train,* 1974; producer/writer/director, *Badlands,* 1974; writer/director, *Days of Heaven,* 1978.

ADDRESS: Office—Evarts Ziegler Associates, Inc., 9255 W. Sunset Blvd., Los Angeles, CA 90069.*

* * *

MALLE, Louis, director

PERSONAL: Born 1932, in Thumeries, France; married Candace Bergen, September 27, 1980.

CAREER: DIRECTOR—Films: (co-director with J. Y. Cousteau) *The World of Silence,* 1956; (assistant to director) *A Man Escaped,* 1957; *Elevator to the Gallows,* 1957; *The Lovers,* 1960; *Zazie in the Metro,* 1962; *Private Life,* 1963; *Vive Le Tour; Bon Baisers de Bangkok; Viva Maria,* 1966; *The Thief; The Fire Within,* 1968; *William Wilson,* 1968; *Phantom India,* 1968; *Murmur of the Heart,* 1971; *Humain; Trop Humain; Lacombe Lucien,* 1973; *Black Moon,* 1975; *Pretty Baby,* 1978; *Atlantic City,* 1981; *My Dinner with Andre,* 1982; *Crackers,* 1983.

ADDRESS: Office—92 Champs Elysees, Paris, France 75008.*

* * *

MALTZ, Albert, playwright, novelist, screenwriter

PERSONAL: Born October 28, 1908 in Brooklyn, NY; son of Bernard (a builder) and Lena (Sherry) Maltz; married Margaret Larkin, 1937 (divorced 1963); married Rosemary Wylde, 1964 (died 1968); married Esther Goldstein, 1969; children; Peter, Katherine. EDUCATION: Columbia College, A.B., 1930; attended Yale School of Drama, 1930–32.

WRITINGS: PLAYS, PRODUCED—*Merry-Go-Round,* with George Sklar, Provincetown Playhouse, NY, 1922; *Peace on Earth,* with George Sklar, Theatre Union Inc. (Civic Repertory Theatre), 1933; *Black Pit,* Theatre Union Inc. (Civic Repertory Theatre), 1935. PLAYS, PUBLISHED—one-acts—*Private Hicks,* 1935; *Rehearsal,* 1937; *The Morrison Case,* 1952. FILMS—*This Gun for Hire,* with W. R. Burnett, 1942; *Moscow Strikes Back* (documentary), 1942; *Destination Tokyo,* with Delmer Daves, 1943; *Pride of the Marines,* 1945; *Cloak and Dagger,* with Ring Lardner, Jr., 1946; *The Naked City,* 1948; *Two Mules for Sister Sara,* 1970.

SHORT STORIES—*The Way Things Are,* 1938; *Off-Broadway,* 1960; *Afternoon in the Jungle,* 1971. NOVELS—*The Underground Stream,* 1940; *The Cross and the Arrow,* 1944; *The Journey of Simon McKeever,* 1949; *A Long Day in a Short Life,* 1956; *A Tale of One January,* 1964. ESSAYS—*The Citizen Writer,* 1950. Articles and stories published in *The New Yorker, Harper's, New Masses, Southern Review, Scholastic.*

AWARDS: Silver Medal, The Commonwealth Club, *The Journey of Simon McKeever,* 1949; O. Henry Memorial Award for Short Story, *The Happiest Man on Earth,* 1938.

SIDELIGHTS: MEMBERSHIPS—Phi Beta Kappa; Authors League of America; Screenwriters Guild of America, West. RECREATION—Swimming, walking, chess, study of American History.

ADDRESS: c/o Authors League of America, 234 W. 44th Street, New York, NY 10036. Agent—Roslyn Targ Literary Agency, 250 W. 57th Street, New York, NY 10019.

* * *

MANCINI, Henry, composer

PERSONAL: Born April 16, 1924, in Cleveland, OH; son of Quinto and Anna (Pece) Mancini; married Virginia O'Connor, September 13, 1947; children: Christopher, Monica and Felice (twins). EDUCATION: Studied at Julliard Institute of Music.

CAREER: PRINCIPAL FILM WORK—Composer: *Glenn Miller Story; Benny Goodman Story,* 1956; *Touch of Evil,* 1960; *High Time,* 1960; *Breakfast at Tiffany's,* 1961; *Bachelor in Paradise,* 1961; *Hatari,* 1962; *The Pink Panther,* 1964; *Charade,* 1964; *A Shot in the Dark,* 1964; *Dear Heart,* 1965; *What Did You Do in the War, Daddy?,* 1966; *Two for the Road,* 1967; *The Hawaiians,* 1970; *Visions of Eight,* 1973; *Oklahoma Crude,* 1973; *99 44/100% Dead,* 1974; *The White Dawn,* 1974; *The Girl from Petrovka,* 1974; *The Great Waldo Pepper,* 1975; *Return of the Pink Panther,* 1975; *W.C. Fields and Me,* 1976; *The Pink Panther Strikes Again,* 1976; *Silver Streak,* 1976; *Revenge of the Pink Panther,* 1978; *Who Is Killing the Great Chefs of Europe?,* 1978; *Prisoner of Zenda,* 1979; *Nightwing,* 1979; *"10,"* 1979; *Little Miss Marker,* 1980; *Change of Seasons,* 1980; *Back Roads,* 1981; *S.O.B.,* 1981; *Mommie Dearest,* 1981; *Whose Little Girl Are You?,* 1982; *Trail of the Pink Panther,* 1982.

PRINCIPAL TELEVISION WORK—Composer: *Peter Gun,* 1958; *Mr. Lucky,* 1959.

RECORDINGS—*The Blues and the Beat; Mr. Lucky Goes Latin; Breakfast at Tiffany's; Combo; Experiment in Terror; Hatari; Our Man in Hollywood; Uniquely Mancini; Days of Wine and Roses.*

AWARDS: Academy Award (3): *Days of Wine and Roses, Breakfast at Tiffany's;* Grammy Award (20); Honorary Doctorate of Music, Duquesne University, 1977.

SIDELIGHTS: MEMBERSHIPS—Composers and Lyricists Guild of America (executive board), ASCAP.

ADDRESS: Office—Regency Artists Ltd. 9200 Sunset Blvd., Suite 823, Los Angeles, CA 90069.*

MANDELKER, Philip, producer, director

PERSONAL: Died March 26, 1984.

CAREER: PRINCIPAL FILM WORK: Producer—*Amber Waves,* 1980; *The Women's Room,* 1980; *Freedom,* 1981; co-produced with Len Hill—*Dream House,* 1981, *Mae West,* 1982; *Having It All,* 1983.

* * *

MANN, Delbert, director

PERSONAL: Born January 30, 1920, in Lawrence, KS; son of Delbert, Sr. (a college professor) and Ora (a teacher and civic worker; maiden name, Patton) Mann; married Ann Caroline Gillespie (a writer), January 13, 1942; children: David, Frederick, Susan, Steven. EDUCATION: Vanderbilt University, A.B., 1941; Yale Drama School, M.F.A., 1947. MILITARY: Army Air Corps, 1942–45.

CAREER: FIRST STAGE WORK—production stage manager, Wellesley Summer Theatre, Wellesley, MA, 1947. NEW YORK DEBUT—director, *Speaking of Murder,* Royale, 1956. DIRECTED: PLAYS—*A Quiet Place; Zelda; The Glass Menagerie.* OPERA—*Wuthering Heights,* NY City Center Company.

FILMS—*Marty; The Bachelor Party; Desire Under the Elms; Separate Tables; Middle of the Night; The Dark at The Top of the Stairs; The Outsider; Lover, Come Back; A Gathering of Eagles; Dear Heart; Mister Buddwing; The Pink Jungle; Kidnapped; Birch Interval; Night Crossing.* TELEVISION SHOWS—More than 100 live shows for *Philco-Goodyear Playhouse, Omnibus, Playhouse 90, Ford Star Jubilee, DuPont Show of the Month, Playwrights '56,* and *Lights Out,* including *Marty; The Bachelor Party; Middle of the Night; What Makes Sammy Run?; Darkness at Noon; The Day Lincoln Was Shot; Yellow Jack; The Petrified Forest; Our Town* (musical); *The Plot to Kill Stalin;* and *The Rich Boy;* (Television Specials) *Heidi; David Copperfield; Jane Eyre; The Man without a Country; The First Woman President; A Girl Named Sooner; The Francis Gary Powers Story; Breaking Up; Tell Me My Name; Home to Stay; All Quiet on the Western Front; To Find My Son; All the Way Home; the Member of the Wedding; Bronte; The Gift of Love.*

THEATRE-RELATED CAREER: Professional Lecturer in Film Art at Claremont-McKenna College, 1974 to date.

AWARDS: Academy Award, Best Director, 1955: *Marty;* Directors Guild Award: *Marty;* Christopher Awards: *Jane Eyre, The Man without a Country;* Emmy Award Nominations: *Our Town, Breaking Up, All Quiet on the Western Front;* Directors Guild Award Nominations: *The Dark at the Top of the Stairs, Heidi, David Copperfield, All Quiet on the Western Front, The Member of the Wedding;* Look Magazine Award: *The Plot to Kill Stalin;* LL.D., Northland College, 1959; Distinguished Flying Cross; Air Medal.

SIDELIGHTS: MEMBERSHIPS—Directors Guild of America (president, 1967–71); Producers Guild; Board of Trust, Vanderbilt University, 1962–date.

DELBERT MANN

ADDRESS: Agent—c/o Leonard Hirshan, William Morris Agency, 151 El Camino, Beverly Hills, CA 90212.

* * *

MANN, Emily, playwright, director

PERSONAL: Born April 12, 1952; daughter of Arthur (a professor of American History) and Sylvia B. (a remedial reading specialist) Mann; married Gerry Bamman (an actor and playwright) on August 12, 1981; children: Nicholas Issac. EDUCATION: Harvard/Radcliffe University, B.A., 1974; University of Minnesota, M.F.A. (Directing); studied at the Guthrie Theatre on a Bush Fellowship.

CAREER: DIRECTED—Resident director, Guthrie, Minneapolis, *The Glass Menagerie; Annulla Allen: Autobiography of a Survivor; Reunion; Ashes,* Guthrie 2. *He and She,* Brooklyn Academy of Music (BAM), Brooklyn; *Oedipus the King,* BAM; *Still Life,* American Place, NY; *Dwarfman,* Goodman, Chicago; *Master of a Million Shapes,* Goodman, Chicago; *Through the Leaves,* Empty Space; *Value of Names, A Tantalizing, A Weekend Near Madison,* Actors Theatre of Louisville.

WRITINGS: PLAYS, PRODUCED—*Still Life,* American Place, NY, 1981; *Annulla Allen: Autobiography of a Survivor,* Guthrie, Minneapolis, Goodman, Chicago. PLAYS UNPUBLISHED—Execution of Justice. SCREENPLAY—Fanny Kelly.

AWARDS: Guggenheim Fellowship in Playwriting, 1983; National Endowment for the Arts Associate Artists Grant, 1983; Rosamond Gilder Award for Outstanding Creative Achievement in the Theatre, 1983; Obie Award, Best Play, Best Direction, Best Production, *Still Life,* 1981; Lucy Alan

Paton Prize for Distinguished Achievement in the Arts, Radcliffe College, 1974, Phi Beta Kappa.

SIDELIGHTS: MEMBERSHIPS—SSD&C, Dramatists Guild, Executive Board, Theatre Communications Group, Actors Studio, writers and directors unit, League of Professional Theatre Women.

ADDRESS: Agent—George Lane, c/o William Morris Agency Inc., 1350 Avenue of the Americas, New York, NY 10019.

* * *

MANULIS, John Bard, director, producer

PERSONAL: Born September 8, 1956; son of Martin (a television, film and theatrical producer) and Katharine (an actress; maiden name, Bard) Manulis. EDUCATION: Harvard University, A.B., M.A. POLITICS: Democrat. RELIGION: Episcopalian.

CAREER: FIRST STAGE WORK, Assistant Stage Manager: *Twelfth Night, The Butler Did It, Serenading Louie, After the Season,* Academy Festival Theatre, Lake Forest, IL, 1978 season. NEW YORK DEBUT, Directed—*The Deserter,* Circle Repertory Company, 1979. PRINCIPAL STAGE WORK, Directed—*Seduction Duet,* Circle Repertory Company, NY, 1981, *Foxtrot By the Bay,* Circle Repertory Company and White Barn, CT, 1982, *The Great Grandson of Jedediah Kohler,* Circle Repertory Company, 1982; Assistant Director—*The Suicide,* NY, 1981, *Fifth of July,* Mark Taper Forum, Los Angeles, CA, 1981, *Talley's Folly,* Mark Taper Forum, Los Angeles, CA, 1981, *A Tale Told,* Circle Repertory Company, NY, 1982.

PRINCIPAL FILM WORK, Production Assistant—*All the President's Men,* 1975. PRINCIPAL TELEVISION WORK, Executive Producer—*The Comedy Zone,* 1984.

THEATRE-RELATED CAREER: Assistant to Marshall W. Mason, Circle Repertory Company, New York, NY, 1978–80; Casting Director, Circle Repertory Company, New York, NY, 1980–82.

SIDELIGHTS: MEMBERSHIPS—Directors Unit, The New Dramatists, 1983; Playwright's/Directors Unit, The Actors Studio, 1981–83; President, Harvard Dramatic Club, 1977.

"I entered college as a pre-med with a love of working with people, emerged with a passion for theatre and a love of working with people. Have a fascination with humanity, our repetitive evolution and our methods. Love sports and comedy, can struggle through French. I am deeply indebted to Marshall W. Mason and Circle Repertory Company as artistic and professional mentors."

ADDRESS: Home—511 W. 20th Street, New York, NY 10011. Office—Nederlander Television Productions, 1650 Broadway, New York, NY 10019.

MANULIS, Martin, producer, director

PERSONAL: Born May 30, 1915; son of Abraham Gustave and Anne (Silverstein) Manulis; married Katharine Bard (an actress), June 14, 1939; children: Laurie, Karen, John Bard. EDUCATION: Columbia University, B.A., 1935. RELIGION: Episcopal. MILITARY: U.S. Naval Reserve.

CAREER: PRINCIPAL STAGE WORK: Director—*Made in Heaven*, John Golden, NY, 1946; *Private Lives*, NY; *The Men We Marry*, NY; *Laura*, NY; *The Show Off*, NY; *The Philadelphia Story*, NY; *Pride's Crossing*, NY; *The Hasty Heart*, NY.

PRINCIPAL FILM WORK: Producer—*The Days of Wine and Roses*, 1963; *Dear Heart*, 1965; *Luv*, 1967; *Duffy*, 1968; *The Out of Towners*, 1970.

PRINCIPAL TELEVISION WORK: Producer—*Playhouse 90; Climax; Suspense; Studio One; Best of Broadway; Chiefs; Space; The Fighter.*

RELATED CAREER—Head of production, John C. Wilson, 1941–49; managing director, Westport Country Playhouse, 1945–50; staff producer and director, CBS-TV, 1951–58; head of production, Twentieth Century Fox Television; currently president, Martin Manulis Productions, Ltd.

SIDELIGHTS: MEMBERSHIPS—Academy of Motion Pictures; Academy of Television; Producers Guild; board of directors, Center Theatre Group, Music Center, Los Angeles; board of directors, St. John's Hospital, Santa Monica, CA.

ADDRESS: Office—P.O. Box 818, Beverly Hills, CA 90213. Agent—Bill Haber, Creative Artists Agency, 1888 Century Park E., Suite 1400, Los Angeles, CA 90067.

* * *

MANUS, Willard, writer, playwright

PERSONAL: Born September 28, 1930 in New York City; son of Isidore (a merchant) and Henriette (Lewine) Manus; married Mavis Ross (a cookbook writer) on May 26, 1960; children: Lisa, Ross. EDUCATION: Adelphi College, Garden City, NY, B.A., 1952. POLITICS: Independent. RELIGION: Jewish. NON-THEATRICAL CAREER: Reporter, *Yonkers Daily Times*, NY, 1953; writer, CBS, *John Henry Faulk Show*, 1953–54; managing editor, *Bounty*, NY, 1955; publicity director, Macmillan Publishing Company, NY, 1962–64; free-lance writer in Lindos, Rhodes, Greece, 1965–70; foreign correspondent in the Mediterranean, *Financial Post*, Ontario, Canada, 1970–78.

WRITINGS: PLAYS, PRODUCED—*The Bleachers* (one-act), Public Theatre, NY, 1975; *Junk Food* (new version of *Creatures of the Chase*), Actors Theatre of Los Angeles, CA, 1981, revised second production, 1982; *The Kendo Master*, Company of Angels Theatre, Los Angeles, CA, 1981; *Bon Appetit*, Group Repertory Theatre, Hollywood, CA, 1983. PLAYS UNPRODUCED—"The Deepest Hunger"; "The Second God"; "The Yard"; "Man in the Sun"; "The Love Boutique." TELEVISION SCRIPTS—*Secrets of Midland*

Heights, 1980; *Shannon*, 1981; *Too Close for Comfort*, 1983. PLAYS, PUBLISHED—*Creatures of the Chase*, 1967. BOOKS (novels)—*The Fixers*, 1957; *Mott the Hoople*, 1967; *The Fighting Men*, 1982; (non-fiction)—*This Is Lindos*, 1974; (children's)—*The Proud Rebel*, 1959; *Sea Treasure*, 1962; *The Mystery of the Flooded Mine*, 1964; *The Island Kids*, 1974.

ARTICLES, STORIES PUBLISHED—*Argosy* (United Kingdom), *Blackwood's Magazine*, *Holiday*, *Nation*, *New Leader*, *Observer*, *Quest*, *Venture*, *Chicago Tribune*, *Denver Post*, *New York Times*, *San Francisco Chronicle*, *Washington Post*.

THEATRE-RELATED CAREER: Publicity Director, Cecilwood Summer Playhouse, Fishkill, NY, 1956–59; Film and Theatre Critic, Century City News, Los Angeles, CA, 1980.

SIDELIGHTS: MEMBERSHIPS—Los Angeles Film Critics Association; Playwrights Unit, Los Angeles Actors Theatre, Group Repertory Theatre, N. Hollywood, CA; Writers Guild of America, West.

'My plays look radically unlike each other. Their settings range from the bleachers of the old Polo Grounds to a dirt farm in Oklahoma to a garbage dump in Pittsburgh. In the future I hope to change gears even more and write a series of short stories, or perhaps a novel, dealing with my experiences living on a Greek island from 1965 to 1978. Enough though, I shouldn't go on talking about my work because, to paraphrase Samuel Beckett, I doubt whether I'm qualified to do so.'' Speaks Greek and owns a home on a Greek island where he enjoys ''freediving'' and spearfishing.

ADDRESS: Home—248 Lasky Drive, Beverly Hills, CA 90212.

* * *

MARCHAND, Nancy, actress

PERSONAL: Born June 19, 1928, in Buffalo, New York; daughter of Raymond L. (a physician) and Marjorie (Freeman) Marchand; married Paul Sparer (actor, writer, director); children: David, Kathryn, Rachel. EDUCATION: Carnegie Institute of Technology.

CAREER: DEBUT—*The Late George Apley*, Ogunquit, ME, 1946. NEW YORK DEBUT—Hostess of the Tavern, *The Taming of the Shrew*, City Center, 1951. PRINCIPAL STAGE APPEARANCES—Princess of France, *Love's Labours Lost*, Mrs. Dudgeon, *The Devil's Disciple*, Tibuiena, *The Critic*, Regan, *King Lear*, Brattle Theatre, Cambridge, MA, 1950–52; Princess of France, *Love's Labours Lost*, City Center, NY, 1953; Nerissa, *The Merchant of Venice*, City Center, NY, 1953; Kate, *The Taming of the Shrew*, Nurse, *Romeo and Juliet*, Amelia, *Othello*, Shakespeare Festival, Antioch, OH, 1954; Mrs. Grant, *Teach Me How to Cry*, Theatre de Lys, NY, 1955; Mrs. Mi Tzu, *The Good Woman of Setzuan*, Phoenix, NY, 1956; *Antigone*, Carnegie Hall Playhouse, NY, 1956; Miriam Ackroyd, *Miss Isobel*, Royale, NY, 1957; Paulina, *The Winter's Tale*, Shakespeare Festival, Stratford, CT, 1958; Lady Capulet, *Romeo and Juliet*, Mistress Page, *The Merry Wives of Windsor*, Shakespeare Festival, Stratford, CT, 1959; Ursula, *Much Ado About Nothing*, Lunt-Fontanne, NY, 1959; Madame Irma, *The Balcony*, Circle in the Square, NY, 1960; Jane Peyton, *Laurette*, Shubert, New Haven, CT, 1960; Lady Sneerwell, *The School for Scandal*, Madame Arkadina, *The Seagull*, APA, Folksbiene Playhouse, NY, 1962; Beatrice, *Much Ado About Nothing*, Amalia, *Right Your Are . . .*, Vaisilissa Karpovna, *The Lower Depths*, APA, Ann Arbor, MI, 1963; last two roles plus the Woman, *The Tavern*, in repertory, APA, Phoenix, NY, 1964; Prostitute, *Judith*, Ann Whitefield, *Man and Superman*, APA, Phoenix, 1965; the Old Lady, *Good Day*, Cherry Lane, NY, 1965; Genevieve, *3 Bags Full*, Henry Miller's, NY, 1966; A Woman of Canterbury, *Murder in the Cathedral*, American Shakespeare Festival, Stratford, CT, 1966; Dol Common, *The Alchemist*, Dolores, *Yerma*, Lincoln Center Repertory Theatre, Vivian Beaumont, NY, 1966; *The Sorrows of Frederick*, Mark Taper Forum, Los Angeles, 1967; Gertrude Forbes-Cooper, *After the Rain*, John Golden, NY, 1967; Duenna (Sister Clare), *Cyrano de Bergerac*, Vivian Beaumont, NY, 1968; Mrs. Latham, *Forty Carats*, Morosco, NY, 1968; Queen Elizabeth, *Christmas Dinner*, Berkshire Theatre Festival, Stockbridge, MA, Ceil Adams, *And Miss Reardon Drinks a Little*, Morosco, NY, 1971; *Mary Stuart*, Vivian Beaumont, NY, 1971; Tatiana, *Enemies*, Vivian Beaumont, NY, 1972; Mrs. Gogan, *The Plough and the Stars*, Vivian Beaumont, NY, 1973; Myra Power, *Patrick's Day*, Long Wharf, New Haven, CT, 1973; Vera Simpson, *Pal Joey*, Goodman, Chicago, 1974; Madame Ranevskaya, *The Cherry Orchard*, Goodman, Chicago, 1974; Ruth Chandler, *Taken in Marriage*, Public/Newman, NY, 1979; Ida Bolton, *Mornings at Seven*, Lyceum, NY, 1980; title role, *Sister Mary Ignatius Explains It All for You*, Westside Arts, NY, 1982; Bessie, *Awake and Sing*, Circle in the Square, NY, 1984; also stand-by for the leads in *Tchin-Tchin* and *Strange Interlude* in 1962 and 1963.

FILM DEBUT—*Bachelor Party*, 1957. FILM APPEARANCES—*Ladybug, Ladybug*, 1963; *Me, Natalie*, 1969; Julie, *Tel Me That You Love Me, Junie Moon*, 1969; *The Hospital*, 1970.

TELEVISION APPEARANCES—"Little Women," *Studio One*, 1950; "Of Famous Memory," *Kraft Theatre*, 1951; "The Hospital," *Studio One*, 1952; "The Peaceful Warrior," *Kraft Theatre*, 1952; the Girl, "Marty," *Kraft Theatre*, 1953; "The Old Maid," *Kraft Theatre*, 1954; "The Office Dance," *Kraft Theatre*, 1954; *The Catered Affair*, 1954; "Career," *Kraft Theatre*, 1954; "A Child Is Born," *Kraft Theatre*, 1954; "The Renaissance," *Omnibus*, 1955; "The Trial of Captain Kidd," *Omnibus*, 1957; "Rudy," *(Studio One)*, 1957; "Mayerling," *Producer's Showcase*, 1957; "Material Witness," *Kraft Theatre*, 1958; "The Sleeping Beauty," *Shirley Temple's Story Book*, 1958; "The Miracle at Spring Hill," *Armstrong Circle Theatre*, 1958; "Free Weekend," *Playhouse 90*, 1959; "The Hidden Image," *Playhouse 90*, 1959; *The Indestructible Mr. Gore*, 1959; *A Piece of Blue Sky*, 1960; Angustias, *The House of Bernarda Alba*, 1960; "The Long Echo," *The Law and Mr. Jones*, 1960; "The Attack," *Defenders*, 1960; *Don Juan in Hell*, 1965; *The Statesman*, 1966; *The Lower Depths*, 1966; *Dark Lady of the Sonnets*, 1966; "What's a Nice Girl Like You . . . ," *N.Y.P.D.*, 1968; Lady Judge, *The Edge of Night*, 1970; Mary Lassiter, *Beacon Hill*, 1975; Mrs. Smith, *The Adams Chronicles*, 1975; Margaret Pynchon, *Lou Grant*, 1977; also *Search for Tomorrow;* Vinnie Phillips *Love of Life*.

AWARDS: Emmy Awards, 1979, 1980, 1981, 1982: *Lou Grant;* Obie, 1960: *The Balcony*, 1960.

SIDELIGHTS: RECREATION—Needlework, reading.

ADDRESS: Home—205 W. 89th Street, New York, NY 10025.

* * *

MARGOLIS, Mark, actor

PERSONAL: Born November 26, 1939 in Philadelphia, PA; son of Isidore (an aircraft worker) and Fanya (a decorator; maiden name Fried) Margolis; married Jacqueline Petcove (an actress), June 3, 1962; children: Morgan. EDUCATION: Attended Temple University. POLITICS: Liberal. RELIGION: Jewish.

CAREER: DEBUT—Dude, *Tobacco Road*, Philadelphia Civic Theatre, Philadelphia, PA, 1958. NEW YORK DEBUT—Casca, *Infidel Caesar*, Music Box, 1962, five performances. PRINCIPAL STAGE APPEARANCES—Moishe, *Second Avenue Rag*, Phoenix, New York, 1980; tutor, *Sholom Aleichem*, Rialto, New York, 1982; Old Sam, *My Uncle Sam*, Public Theater, New York, 1983; Sarge, *Kid Twist*, Soho Repertory, New York; Francisco, *Hamlet;* Jim Fitch, *Terrible Jim Fitch;* Joe Easter, *Days to Come*, WPA, New York; Martin, *Child of Clay Country*, Circle Repertory Company, New York; Shamanov, *Last Summer in Chulimsk;* Ametistov, *Zoya's Apartment*, Gene Frankel Theater, New York; Hetman, *Days of the Turbins*, Billymunk, New York; Smiley Coy, *The Big Knife*, AMAS Repertory, New York; Diamond Louis, *The Front Page*, Baltimore Centre Stage; Cyrano, Santa Fe Festival Theatre, NM; Virgil, *Bus Stop*, Meadowbrook Theatre, MI; Dracula, *Count Dracula*, Commonwealth Stage, MA; Macbeth, *Macbeth*, Camden Shakespeare Festival Theatre, ME. MAJOR TOURS—Blue Dome Theatre Ensemble, U.S. cities, 1967–72.

FILM DEBUT—Flamboyant man, *Deathwish*, 1975. PRINCIPAL FILM APPEARANCES—*Eddie Macon's Run*, 1982; Adam Zarevski, *Far From Poland*, 1983; Alberto, *Scarface*, 1983; Sergeant Morrison, *Short Eyes;* Quintana, *Josiah; Santa Claus*. TELEVISION DEBUT—*Kojak*, 1976. PRINCIPAL TELEVISION APPEARANCES—Jemmy, *The Other Side of Victory*, 1979; Lewis Hale, *A Jury of Her Peers*, 1981; Adam Zarevski, *Far from Poland*, 1983; *As the World Turns;* Dinty, *One Life to Live; The White Shadow;* Myers, *Muggable Mary;* Ricky Nichols, *Rage of Angels*.

WRITINGS: PLAYS—*A Cry for Joshua*, Shubert, New York, 1961.

SIDELIGHTS: MEMBERSHIPS—AEA, SAG, AFTRA.

ADDRESS: Home—40 Harrison Street, New York, NY 10013. Agent—c/o Dulcina Eisen Associates, 154 E. 61st Street, New York, NY 10021.

MARGULIES, David, actor and director

PERSONAL: Surname pronounced Mar-gyoo-lies; born February 19, 1937; son of Harry David (a lawyer) and Runya (a nurse and Guggenheim Museum employee; maiden name Zeltzer) Margulies; married Carol Grant, March 17, 1969; married Lois Smith (an actress); children: Jonathan. EDUCATION: City College of New York, B.A., 1958; trained for the stage with the American Shakespeare Festival and studied with Morris Carnovsky, Phoebe Brand, and William Hickey. MILITARY: U.S. Army, 1961–62. THEATER-RELATED CAREER: Has taught acting at various schools since 1968.

CAREER: DEBUT—Member of Venetian Army, *Othello*, New York Shakespeare Festival, Belvedere Lake Theatre, New York, and Playhouse in the Park, Philadelphia, 1958. PRINCIPAL STAGE APPEARANCES—Posthumus, *The Golden Six*, York Playhouse, New York, 1958; Grimaldi, *'Tis a Pity She's a Whore*, Orpheum Theatre and Player's Theatre, New York, 1958; *Romeo and Juliet*, *A Midsummer Night's Dream*, and *All's Well That Ends Well*, American Shakespeare Festival, Stratford, CT, 1959; *The Winter's Tale*, American Shakespeare Festival, Stratford, 1960; Freddie, *The Disenchanted*, Tenthouse Theatre, Highland Park, IL, 1960; Orlov, *Who Was That Lady I Saw You With?*, Tenthouse Theatre, IL, 1960; *Under Milkwook*, Circle in the Square, New York, 1961; *The Second City*, Chicago, 1962; David, *Six Characters in Search of an Author*, Martinique Theatre, New York, 1963; Benjamin, *Thistle in My Bed*, Gramercy Arts Theatre, New York, 1963; Sol Stern, *The Tender Trap*, Paper Mill Playhouse, NJ, and Mineola Playhouse, Mineola, NY, 1964; Clarin, *Life Is a Dream*, Astor Place Playhouse, New York; the Girl's Father, *The Fantasticks*, Westport Playhouse, Coconut Grove Playhouse, and Tappan Zee Playhouse, 1964; Pope and Second Scholar, *The Tragical Historie of Dr. Faustus*, Phoenix Theatre, New York, 1964; Lorenzaccio, *Lorenzaccio*, Equity Library Theatre, New York, 1965.

With The American Conservatory Theatre, Pittsburgh Playhouse, 1965, the Director, *Six Characters in Search of an Author*, Apollo, *Apollo of Bellac*, Bernard, *Death of a Salesman*, Truffaldino, *The Servant of Two Masters*, *Under Milkwood*, Eisenring, *The Firebugs*, Studio Arena, Buffalo, NY, 1966; Elbow, *Measure for Measure*, NY Shakespeare Festival, Delacorte, 1966; Christoforu, *The Public Eye*, and Berenger, *The Rhinoceros*, Academy Playhouse, Wilmette, IL, 1967; Davies, *The Caretaker*, Theatre of the Living Arts, Philadelphia, 1967; Arthur, *Tango*, Pocket Theatre, New York, 1969; the Man, *The Man with the Flower in His Mouth*, Sheridan Square Playhouse, New York, 1969; Reverend Dupas, *Little Murders*, Circle in the Square, New York, 1969; Feivel Leishik, *Seven Days of Mourning*, Circle in the Square, New York, 1969; Bertram, Rat Catcher, *The Last Analysis*, Circle in the Square, New York, 1971; Dr. Rance, *What the Butler Saw*, Academy Playhouse, Lake Forest, IL, 1971; Norman, *The Opening*, Tappan Zee Playhouse, New York, 1972; *The Revue*, Moon Theatre, East Hampton, New York, 1972; Liphitz, *Happy Days Are Here Again*, Manhattan Theatre Club, New York, 1972; Aaron Silver, *An Evening with the Poet Senator*, Playhouse 2, New York, 1973; Harvey Appleman, *Kid Champion*, New York Shakespeare Festival, 1975; co-directed (with Jack Gelber)

and played the Director, *Rehearsal*, American Place, New York, 1975; the Doctor, *Zalmen or the Madness of God*, Lyceum, New York, 1976; Sammy Samuels, *Comedians*, Music Box, New York, 1976–77; *Hold Me*, Chelsea Westside, New York, 1977; Harry Metzger, *The Prince of Grand Street*, Forrest Theatre, Philadelphia and Shubert, Boston, 1978; Teddy, *Every Place Is Newark*, First Aspen Playwrights Conference, Aspen, CO, 1978; *A Special Evening*, Ensemble Studio, New York, 1979; Imre Laszlo, *Break a Leg*, Palace, New York, 1979; First Player and Player King, *Hamlet*, Sanctuary, New York, 1979; Norbe/Gregory, *Walter and the Flatulist*, Sanctuary, New York, 1980; Serge Barrescu, *The Westside Waltz*, Barrymore, New York, 1981–82; David Ben-Gurion, *David and Paula*, American Jewish Theatre, New York, 1982; King Lear, *King Lear*, Shakespeare in Delaware Park, Buffalo, NY, 1983. MAJOR TOURS—Philostrate, *A Midsummer Night's Dream*, American Shakespeare Festival production, Boston, Baltimore, Cleveland, 1960; Serge Barrescu, *The Westside Waltz*, San Diego, Denver, Los Angeles, San Francisco, Philadelphia, Seattle, Washington, DC, Boston, Chicago, December 1980 to June 1981, October 1981, March 1982 to June 1982.

FILM DEBUT—Doorman, *A New Leaf*, 1969; PRINCIPAL FILMS—*Sunday Breakfast* (short subject shown at New York Film Festival), 1971; the Acting Teacher, *Scarecrow in a Garden of Cucumbers*, 1971; Bill Phelps, *The Front*, 1976; Detective, *Hide in Plain Sight;* Larry Goldie, *All That Jazz*, 1979; *Rabbi Joshua Drexel*, Last Embrace, *1979;* Dr. Levy, *Dressed to Kill;* Dr. Jack Zimansky, *Times Square;* Dr. Duberstein, *Daniel*, 1983; Mayor of New York, *Ghostbusters*. TELEVISION DEBUT—Pete, *A Mother for Janek*, 1965. TELEVISION APPEARANCES—*Kojak*, 1977; Brother-in-Law, *The Death of Ivan Ilyich*, 1978; Chubby, *My Old Man*, 1979; *A Doctor's Story; Ryan's Hope; One Life to Live; All My Children*.

DIRECTED—Plays: *The Oresteia*, Theatre of the Living Arts, Philadelphia, 1968; *Next*, Berkshire Theatre Festival, Stockbridge, MA, 1968; *The Christmas Dinner*, Berkshire Theatre Festival, Stockbridge, MA, 1970; *The Complete Works of Studs Edsel*, Folger Theatre Group, Folger Museum, Washington, DC, 1972; *Where Do We Go from Here?*, State College, Johnson, VT, 1973; *Actors*, Ensemble Studio Theatre, Johnson, VT, 1973; *The Merry Wives of Windsor*, New York Shakespeare Festival, Delacorte, 1974; *Where Do We Go from Here?*, New York Shakespeare Festival, Newman Theatre of the Public Theatre, 1974; *End of the War*, Ensemble Studio Theatre, New York, 1978.

SIDELIGHTS: MEMBERSHIPS—AEA, SAG, AFTRA, Society of Stage Directors and Choreographers, Ensemble Studio Theatre (executive board, 1973–77), Actors Studio, Loft Theatre (artistic director, 1967).

''I am now directing and playing Moliere in rehearsals of Michael Bulgakov's *A Cabal of Hypocrites* at the Actors Studio. I have never been happier and I hope that I will continue in the future to do my own work.''

ADDRESS: Agent—c/o Bret Adams Ltd., 448 W. 44th Street, New York, NY 10036.

MONTE MARKHAM

MARKHAM, Monte, actor

PERSONAL: Born June 21, 1938, in Manatee, FL; son of Jesse Edward (a merchant) and Millie Content (Willbur) Markham; married Klaire Keevil Hester, June 1, 1961; children: Keevil Lee Ford (daughter), Jason Morgan. EDUCATION: University of Georgia, M.F.A., 1960. MILITARY: U.S. Coast Guard Reserve, 1958–67. NON-THEATRICAL CAREER: Instructor, Stephens College, MO, 1960–62.

CAREER: DEBUT—Morris, *The Heiress,* Priscilla Beach Theatre, White House Beach, MA, 1954. NEW YORK DEBUT—Donald Marshall, *Irene,* Minskoff, 1973, 200 performances. PRINCIPAL STAGE APPEARANCES—*Same Time Next Year,* Brooks Atkinson, Ambassador, NY, 1978; *The Last of Mrs. Cheyney,* Kennedy Center, Washington, DC, 1978; Hamlet, *Hamlet,* University of California (guest artist); Old Globe Shakespeare Festival, CA; Ashland Shakespeare Festival, OR; Actors Theatre of San Francisco, CA; Directors Unit, Actors Studio. MAJOR TOURS—Aaron Burr, *Together Tonight: Jefferson, Hamilton and Burr,* U.S. cities, 1976; *The Last of Mrs. Cheyney,* U.S. cities, 1978–79.

FILM DEBUT—McMasters, *The Hour of the Gun,* 1967. PRINCIPAL FILM APPEARANCES—Keno, *Guns of the Magnificent*

Seven, 1968; *One Is a Lonely Number,* 1972; *Midway; Airport '77;* Joe, *Ginger in the Morning.*

TELEVISION DEBUT—*Mission Impossible,* 1966. PRINCIPAL TELEVISION APPEARANCES—*The Second Hundred Years,* 1967; *Mr. Deeds Goes to Town,* 1968; *The New Perry Mason,* 1972; *Death Takes a Holiday; The Astronaut; Hustling; Relentless; Drop Out Father; Hotline,* 1983; *Jack Holborn,* 1984.

AWARDS: Theatre World Award, 1972; *Irene.*

ADDRESS: Agent—c/o David Shapira and Associates, 15301 Ventura Blvd., Sherman Oaks, CA 91403. Agent—c/o Lionel Larner, Ltd., 850 Seventh Avenue, New York, NY 10019.

* * *

MARKINSON, Martin, theatre owner, producer

PERSONAL: Born December 23, 1931 in Brooklyn, NY; son of Abraham and Dora (Rose) Markinson; married Arlene Gelfand, April 15, 1962; children: Brett, Keith, Sydney. EDUCATION: Attended Pace College. MILITARY: U.S. Air Force, Sargeant 1st Class, 1950–53.

CAREER: PRODUCED—*Torch Song Trilogy,* 1982. THEATRE-RELATED CAREER—Owner, Helen Hayes Theatre, NY.

MARTIN MARKINSON

AWARDS: Antoinette Perry Award, Best Play, *Torch Song Trilogy,* 1982–83.

SIDELIGHTS: MEMBERSHIPS—Friars Club.

ADDRESS: Home—144 Haviland Lane, Stamford, CT, 06903. Office—245, Great Neck Road, Great Neck, NY, 11021.

* * *

MARLEY, John, actor and director

PERSONAL: Born October 17, in New York City; died May 22, 1984; married Sandra Lilosevich (a producer); children: Alexis; by previous marriage: Peter, Julia, Ben. EDUCATION: attended City College of New York. MILITARY: signal corps, sergeant, 1942–45.

CAREER: DEBUT—FBI Agent, *Sing Me No Lullaby.* NEW YORK DEBUT—*Stop Press.* PRINCIPAL STAGE APPEARANCES—*The Strong Are Lonely; Gramercy Ghost; Enemy of the People.* MAJOR TOURS—Punch Drunk Fighter, *Hope Is a Thing with Feathers.*

FILM DEBUT—*Kiss of Death,* 1948. PRINCIPAL FILMS—Frankie Ballou, *Cat Ballou;* Jack Woltz, *The Godfather,* 1972; Phil, *Love Story; Faces; A Man Called Sledge,* 1970; *Framed,* 1975; *W. C. Fields and Me,* 1976; *The Car,* 1977; *The Greatest,* 1977; *Hooper,* 1978; Phil, *Oliver's Story,* 1978; *Tribute,* 1980; *America, America; Blade; On the Edge.* TELEVISION APPEARANCES—Professor Falcon, *Falcon's Gold; Three Steps to Heaven; Moviola; Telethon;* plus roles in numerous daytime dramas, series, and live television shows.

DIRECTED: Plays—*Galileo; The Tavern; The Strong Are Lonely.* Directed productions for the Cleveland Playhouse, OH; Center Stage, Baltimore, MD; Civic Playhouse, CA; Pasadena Playhouse, CA.

AWARDS: Best Actor, Venice Film Festival: *Faces;* Academy Award Nomination and Golden Globe Award Nomination: *Love Story.*

SIDELIGHTS: MEMBERSHIPS—AFI, SAG, AEA, AFTRA.

ADDRESS: Agent—c/o Merrit Blake, Harold Cohen Management.

* * *

MARLOWE, Joan, publisher and writer

PERSONAL: Born January 7, 1920, in Ithaca, NY; daughter of Lionel E. (editor of *Ithaca Journal News*) and Mildred (Cole) Mintz; married Ward Morehouse (an author/critic), January 24, 1941 (divorced 1947); married Roderic Warren Rahe (a chemist), September 13, 1952; children: (first marriage) one son; (second marriage) two sons. EDUCATION: Stephens Junior College, A.B., 1938; attended Cornell University, 1938–39. NON-THEATRICAL CAREER: Member of the editorial board at *Newsweek* magazine, 1943.

CAREER: Editor and publisher (with Betty Blake) of *Theatre Information Bullitin* and *New York Theatre Critics' Reviews,* 1964 to date.

WRITINGS: BOOKS—*Broadway—Inside the Last Decade,* 1943 (with Betty Blake); *The Keys to Broadway,* 1951 (with Betty Blake).

SIDELIGHTS: MEMBERSHIPS—Drama Desk (treasurer, 1958–60); Outer Circle (recording secretary, 1957–75); New Drama Forum, Inc (co-president, 1980–83).

Appeared as Jane Wilson in *Mr. and Mrs. North* at the Belasco Theatre in New York City in 1941.

RECREATION: Tennis, cooking, boats.

ADDRESS: Home—18 Tory Hole Road, Darien, CT 06820. Business—c/o Proscenium Productions, Two Park Ave., Suite 21-D, New York, NY 10016.

* * *

MARRIOTT, Anthony, playwright, actor

PERSONAL: Born January 17, 1931, London, England; son of Leslie William (a colonel in regular army) and Monica Mary (Hill) Marriott; married Heulwen Margaret Roberts, December 10, 1956; children: Shân, Sally, Simon. EDUCATION: Felsted School, Essex, 1945–49, Higher Certificate, Cambridge; Central School of Speech and Drama, 1949–51. POLITICS: Labour Party Member. RELIGION: Church of England. NON-THEATRICAL CAREER: Justice of the Peace (Greater London), appointed, February 1977.

CAREER: DEBUT—*Laburnum Grove,* Horsham Repertory Co., 1950. PRINCIPAL STAGE APPEARANCES—In various repertory seasons, 1951–54, including Horsham, Worthing, Warrington, Manchester Library Theatre, Dundee, Bridgewater, Redcar, Norwich, Yeovil, Saltburn, Salisbury. PRINCIPAL RADIO BROADCASTS—BBC Drama Repertory Company, 1954–56, including starring in *Journey into Space* series; *Dan Dare* and *Film Time,* Radio Luxembourg series.

WRITINGS: PLAYS, PUBLISHED—With Alistair Foot, *Uproar in the House,* Garrick and Whitehall Theatres, 1967–69; with Alistair Foot, *No Sex Please—We're British,* Strand and Garrick Theatres, 1971; with Alistair Foot, *I Want to Be a Father, Madam,* Eastbourne, and national tour, 1973; with Bob Grant, *Darling Mr. London,* Billingham, and three national tours, 1974; with Bob Grant, *No Room for Sex,* Brighton, and national tour, 1974; with John Chapman, *Shut Your Eyes and Think of England,* Apollo, 1977; with John Chapman, *Anything You Say, The Wrong Mr. Right, Divided We Stand,* 1977; with Bob Grant, *Home Is Where Your Clothes Are* and *Spoof;* with Jonathan Daly, *A Matter of Style.*

SCREENPLAYS—Contract writer for the Rank Organisation, worked on: *Waltz of the Toreadors, Gypsy and the Gentleman, Operation Amsterdam, Doctor,* 1958–60; *Ouch,* 1965; *Divorce British Style* (re-titled *Sex and the British*), 1967; *The Intrepid Mr. Twigg,* 1969; *No Sex Please—We're British,* 1974. TELEVISION—Story editor, *Ghost Squad* series; contract writer BBC Radio Light Entertainment created and wrote *Roundabout* series and BBC TV Light Entertainment, *Archie Andrews* series; with Roger Marshall, *Public Eye*, ABC, 1965–66; contributor, *Avengers, No Hiding Place, This Man Craig, Fireball XL5, Supercar*, 1965–66; documentaries, *Britain and the Common Market, The Meaning of Ecumenism, Life of William the Conqueror, Everyday's a Holiday;* children's film, *The Ghost of Monks Island;* series, with Bob Grant, *Meals and Wheels, Now That Mother's Gone, September People, Getting It Right, Petticoat Cash*, 1984. BOOKS—*Marker Calls the Tune*, 1967.

AWARDS: Society of West End Theatre, Best Comedy Nomination, 1979: *Shut Your Eyes and Think of England.*

SIDELIGHTS: MEMBERSHIPS—Writers Guild of Great Britain, Garrick Club, Green Room Club, Honorary Secretary, Dramatists Club, 1984, London Welsh Rugby Football Club, Wyke Green Golf Club. HOBBIES—Golf, animal welfare, Welsh rugby.

''*No Sex Please—We're British* has been performed in 52 countries and on February 21, 1979 became the Longest Running Comedy in the History of World Theatre.''

ADDRESS: Home—168 Wood Lane, Osterley Middlesex, TW 75EH. Agent—Douglas Rae, 28 Charing Cross Road, London, WC 2, England.

* * *

MARRIOTT, B. Rodney, director

PERSONAL: Born June 16, 1938; son of Bertram Henry (a contractor) and Sara Durfee (a Girl Scout executive; maiden name, Cook) Marriott. EDUCATION: Yale University, B.A. (magna cum laude), 1960; University of California at Berkeley, 1961–62.

CAREER: NEW YORK DEBUT—Directed—*The Runner Stumbles*, Circle Repertory, 1979. PRINCIPAL STAGE WORK—Directed—Circle Repertory, NY—*Innocent Thoughts, Harmless Intentions*, 1980, *Threads*, 1981, *The Diviners*, 1981, *Confluence*, 1982, *The Holdup*, 1982. Workshop productions—*Breakfast Play, Cat and Mouse, Comeback, Screaming Eagle, Elm Circle, Skirmishers, American Options, Harry the Thief, American Welcome; The Rodeo Stays in Town for At Least a Week*, Ensemble Studio Theatre, NY; *K-2*, Theatre by the Sea, Portsmouth, NH, 1982; *Clara's Play*, Boarshead Theatre, MI, 1981; *Joe Egg*, Capital Repertory, Albany, NY; St. Mary's Summer Festival—*The Rivals, Talley's Folly, Twelfth Night, A Streetcar Named Desire; Union City Thanksgiving*, INTAR Stage Two, NY; *A View from the Bridge*, Yale University; *The Rimers of Eldritch*, Yale University; *Growing Pains*, Fordham University; *The Serpent*, Fordham University.

THEATRE-RELATED CAREER: Instructor, Advanced Acting, Theatre History, Fordham University; Instructor, Playwriting, 92nd Street YMCA, NY; Instructor, Text Analysis, New York University Graduate Writing Program; Instructor, New Plays and Playwrights, New School for Social Research; Director of Theatre Program, New York State Summer School of the Arts; Carnegie Teaching Fellow, Yale University; Drama Department, Phillips Exeter Academy; Instructor, Theatre, Brearley School.

AWARDS: Scholar of the House, Yale University; Phi Beta Kappa; Woodrow Wilson Fellow, Masters Program, U.C. at Berkeley.

SIDELIGHTS: MEMBERSHIPS—Dramatists Guild, SSD&C, The Players Club.

Mr. Marriott is currently serving as Acting Artistic Director of New York's award-winning Circle Repertory Company and is developing a number of new plays including: *Levitation, Dysan, Family Planning, Nightsong, The Bicycle Man, Defender of the Faith, Banjo, On Wayward Wings*. He has served as dramaturg on numerous new play projects and has directed over one hundred productions in academic and regional theaters prior to coming to New York City. He served with the U.S. Peace Corps in Nigeria, West Africa.

ADDRESS: Home—12 E. 22nd Street, New York, NY 10010. Office—161 Avenue of the Americas, New York, NY 10013. Agent—Luis Sansurso, International Creative Management, 40 W. 57th Street, New York, NY 10019.

* * *

MARSHALL, Garry, producer, director, writer

PERSONAL: Born November 13, 1934, in New York City. EDUCATION: Northwestern University, B.S.

CAREER: PRINCIPAL TELEVISION WORK—Writer, *Jack Paar Show, Joey Bishop Show, Danny Thomas Show, Dick Van Dyke Show, Spy;* writer/creater, *Hey Landlord;* executive producer, *The Odd Couple;* creator/exective producer, *The Little People, Happy Days, Laverne and Shirley, Mork and Mindy, Angie, Sitcom-The Adventures of Garry Marshall, Beane's of Boston, Who's Watching the Kids, Evil Roy Slade.*

PRINCIPAL FILM WORK—Writer/producer, *How Sweet It Is*, 1968; *The Grasshopper*, 1970.

ADDRESS: Office—c/o Paramount Pictures, 5555 Melrose Avenue, Los Angeles, CA 90038. Agent—c/o The Sy Fischer Company, 10100 Santa Monica Blvd., Suite 2440, Los Angeles, CA 90067.*

* * *

MARSHALL, Penny, actress

PERSONAL: Born October 15, 1943, in New York City; daughter of Anthony W. and Marjorie Irene (Ward) Marshall; married Rob Reiner, April 19, 1971; children: Tracy Lee (a daughter). EDUCATION: Attended University of New Mexico.

CAREER: TELEVISION DEBUT—*Danny Thomas Hour*. PRINCIPAL TELEVISION APPEARANCES—*The Odd Couple*, 1972–74; *Friends and Lovers*, 1974; *Let's Switch*, 1974; *Wives* (pilot), 1975; *Chico and the Man,* 1975; *Mary Tyler Moore,* 1975; *Heaven Help Us,* 1975; *Saturday Night Live,* 1975–77; *Happy Days,* 1975; *Battle of the Network Stars,* 1976; *Barry Manilow Special,* 1976; *The Tonight Show,* 1976–77; *Dinah,* 1976–77; *Mike Douglas Show,* 1975–77; *Merv Griffin Show,* 1976–77; *Blansky's Beauties,* 1977; *$20,000 Pyramid,* 1976–77; *Network Battle of the Sexes,* 1977; *Laverne and Shirley,* 1976; *More Than Friends* (movie), 1978.

PRINCIPAL FILM APPEARANCES—*How Sweet It Is,* 1968; *The Savage Seven,* 1968; *The Grasshopper,* 1970; *1941,* 1979.

ADDRESS: Agent—c/o Creative Artists Agency, 1888 Century Park E., Suite 1400, Los Angeles, CA 90067.*

* * *

MARX, Arthur, writer

PERSONAL: Born July 21, 1921; son of Groucho (a comedian) and Ruth (Johnson) Marx; married Lois Goldberg (an interior decorator), May 27, 1961; children: Steve and Andy. EDUCATION: Attended University of Southern California. MILIARY: U.S. Coast Guard, 1942–45.

WRITINGS: PLAYS, PUBLISHED— *The Impossible Years,* 1965 (with Bob Fisher); *Minnie's Boys,* 1970 (with Bob Fisher); *Chic Life,* also known as *My Daughter's Rated X,* 1970 (with Bob Fisher); *Sugar and Spice,* 1974; *Groucho,* 1983 (with Bob Fisher). FILMS—with Bob Fisher; *Global Affair; Eight on the Lam; I'll Take Sweden; Cancel My Reservation; The Impossible Years* (story only). TELEVISION SHOWS—segments for many situation comedies, including *All in the Family, Maude,* and *The Jeffersons.* STORY CONSULTANT: *Alice* for four years and wrote 42 segments (with Bob Fisher). BOOKS—*The Ordeal of Willie Brown,* 1950; *Life with Groucho,* 1954; *Not as a Crocodile,* 1958; *Son of Groucho* (autobiography), 1972; *Everybody Loves Somebody Sometime—Especially Himself,* 1974; *Goldwyn,* 1976; *Red Skelton,* 1979. Magazine articles for *Saturday Evening Post; Colliers; Redbook; Sport; Good Housekeeping; Woman's Home Companion; Esquire; Saturday Review; L.A. Magazine; Saga; Parade; New York Times Magazine.*

AWARDS: Straw Hat Award for Best Play of the 1970 Summer Stock Season: *Chic Life.*

SIDELIGHTS: MEMBERSHIPS—Dramatists Guild; Authors Guild; Writers Guild of America.

ADDRESS: Agent—c/o Scott Meredith, 845 Third Ave., New York, NY 10022.

* * *

MASAK, Ron, actor, director, writer, entertainer

PERSONAL: Surname pronounced May-Sack; born July 1, 1936, in Chicago, IL; son of Floyd Lewis (a salesman and musician) and Mildred Alice (a buyer, also in management; maiden name, Rudy) Masak; married Kay Frances Knebes,

September 23, 1961; children: Tammy, Debbie, Kathy, Mike, Bobby, Christine. EDUCATION: Chicago City College and C.T.C., A.A.; studied for the theatre with H. Adrian Rehner at the Drama Guild. MILITARY: U.S. Army.

CAREER: DEBUT—Shapiro, *Stalag 17,* Drama Guild, Chicago, 1954. PRINCIPAL STAGE APPEARANCES—Sakini, *Teahouse of the August Moon,* Will, *No Time for Sergeants,* title role, *Mr. Roberts,* Alan, *Enter Laughing,* Stanley, *A Streetcar Named Desire,* Mortimer, *Arsenic and Old Lace,* Sam, *Photo Finish,* all as resident leading man with the Candelight Dinner Theatre, Summit, IL, 1962–66; played over thirty-five leads, twelve-hundred consecutive performances in all.

MAJOR TOURS—Headline Act (comedy, impressions, songs, etc.), *Rolling Along,* World Tour, 1960–61.

FILM DEBUT—Zabrinski, *Ice Station Zebra,* 1967. FILM APPEARANCES—*Daddy's Gone A-Hunting,* 1968; *Diary of a Young Stockbroker,* 1969; *Tora! Tora! Tora!,* 1970; *Evel Knievel,* 1971; Claude, *The Man from Clover Grove,* 1974; Herbie, *Harper Valley, P.T.A.,* 1979.

TELEVISION DEBUT—*The Twilight Zone,* 1959. TELEVISION APPEARANCES—Charlie Wilson, *Love Thy Neighbor,* 1973; *Police Story; The Neighborhood,* over one hundred T.V. shows and movies of the week; Vince Lombardi's *Second Effort.*

WRITINGS: ADDITIONAL DIALOGUE AND LYRICS—*The Man from Clover Grove.* LYRICS—(disco hit) *Hey Wake Up and Listen.* SCREENPLAY—*Ya Gotta Believe* (motivational drama), 1983.

AWARDS: Best Actor Award, Chicago, 1955–56; Vince Lombardi Inspiration Appreciation Award, 1980; Man of the Year for M.D.A., 1983.

SIDELIGHTS: MEMBERSHIPS—Theta Alpha Phi; the Masquers; American Cancer Stricken Families (life member and chairman); M.D.A. Board; chosen as Special Olympics announcer, 1984.

Mr. Masak has appeared in over eighteen-hundred television commercials, his first thirty-two being for Budweiser. He is preparing to star on Broadway as Lou Costello in *Lou's on First.*

ADDRESS: Office—RAMKAY, 5440 Shirley, Tarzana, CA. Agent—Sam Goras, S.G.A., 12750 Ventura Blvd., Studio City, CA 91606.

* * *

MASON, James, actor

PERSONAL: Born May 15, 1909, in Huddersfield, Yorkshire, England; died July 27, 1984; son of John and Mabel Hattersley (Gaunt) Mason; married Pamela Kellino (divorced); Clarissa Kaye. EDUCATION: Marlborough College and Peterhouse College, Cambridge.

CAREER: DEBUT—Prince Ivan, *The Rascal,* Theatre Royal,

Aldershot, UK, 1931. LONDON DEBUT—Oliver Brown, *Gallows Glorious*, Arts Theatre, 1933. NEW YORK DEBUT—David, *Bathsheba*, Barrymore, 1947. PRINCIPAL STAGE APPEARANCES—Old Vic-Sadler's Wells company: Valentine, *Twelfth Night*, Yasha, *The Cherry Orchard*, Cromwell, *Henry VIII*, Claudio, *Measure for Measure*, Jeremy *Love for Love;* Earl of Arran/Paris, *Queen of Scots*, New Theatre, 1924; with the Dublin Gate Theatre company, 1934–37; Captain O'Shea, *Parnell*, Gate, London, 1936; Hannibal, *The Road to Rome*, Embassy and Savoy, 1937; Antoine, *A Man Who Has Nothing*, Q, 1937; Christopher Carson, *Bonnet Over the Windmill*, New, 1937; Byron, *The Heart Was Not Burned*, Gate, 1938; Henri Jouval, *Sixth Floor*, St. James, 1939; Paul Venner, *Jupiter Laughs*, New, 1941; with Stratford, Ontario Shakespeare Festival: Angelo, *Measure for Measure*, title-role, *Oedipus Rex*, 1954; Constantine Chase, *Paul and Constantine*, La Jolla Playhouse, CA, 1957; *Mid-Summer*, Ivoryton Playhouse, 1958; Frank, *Faith Healer*, Longacre, NY, 1979.

FILM DEBUT—*Late Extra*, 1935. PRINCIPAL FILM APPEARANCES—*Twice Branded*, 1936; *Troubled Waters*, 1936; *Prison Breaker*, 1936; *Secret of Stamboul*, 1936; *Mill on the Floss*, 1937; *Fire over England*, 1937; *High Command*, 1937; *Catch as Catch Can*, 1937; *Return of the Scarlet Pimpernel; I Met a Murder* (also wrote and produced), 1939; *This Man Is Dangerous; Hatter's Castle*, 1941; *Hotel Reserve; They Were Sisters; The Night Has Eyes*, 1942; *The Man in Gray*, 1943; *Fanny by Gaslight*, 1944; *Seventh Veil*, 1945; *The Wicked Lady*, 1945; *Odd Man Out*, 1947; *Upturned Glass; Patient Vanishes; Man of Evil; Place of One's Own; Caught*, 1948; *Madame Bovary*, 1949; *Reckless Moment*, 1949; *Pandora and the Flying Dutchman*, 1951; *Lady's Possessed; Rommel: The Desert Fox; Five Fingers*, 1952; *Botany Bay; Story of Three Lovers; Prisoner of Zenda*, 1952; *Face to Face (Secret Share); Julius Caesar*, 1953; *Desert Rats*, 1953; *Man Between*, 1955;

Forever Darling, 1956; *Bigger Than Life* (also produced), 1956; *Island in the Sun*, 1957; *Cry Terror*, 1958; *The Decks Ran Red*, 1958; *North by Northwest*, 1959; *Journey to the Center of the Earth*, 1959; *A Touch of Larceny*, 1960; *Marriage-Go-Round*, 1961; *Lolita*, 1962; *Hero's Island*, 1962; *Fall of the Roman Empire*, 1964; *The Pumpkin Eater*, 1964; *Lord Jim*, 1965; *The Blue Max*, 1966; *Georgy Girl*, 1966; *The Deadly Affair*, 1967; *The Sea Gull*, 1968; *Duffy*, 1968; *Spring and Port Wine*, 1969; *Mayerling*, 1969; *Age of Consent*, 1970; *Kill*, 1971; *Child's Play*, 1972; *Frankenstein: The True Story*, 1973; *The Last of Sheila*, 1973; *The Mackintosh Man*, 1973; *The Marseille Contract*, 1974; *11 Harrowhouse*, 1974; *The Autobiography of a Princess*, 1975; *Inside Out*, 1975; *Great Expectations*, 1975; *Mandingo*, 1975; *Voyage of the Damned*, 1977; *Cross of Iron*, 1977; *Heaven Can Wait*, 1978; *The Boys from Brazil*, 1979; *The Water Babies*, 1979; *Murder by Decree*, 1979; *The Passage*, 1979; *ffolkes*, 1980; *Evil under the Sun*, 1982; *The Verdict*, 1982; *Yellowbeard*, 1983; *The Shooting Party.*

WRITINGS: BOOKS—with former spouse, Pamela Mason, *The Cats in Our Lives*, 1949; *Favorite Cat Stories of James and Pamela Mason*, 1957.

ADDRESS: Agent—c/o Al Parker Ltd., 55 Park Lane, London W1, England.

MASON, Marsha, actress

PERSONAL: Born April 3, 1942, in St. Louis, MO; daughter of James and Jacqueline Mason; married Gary Campbell, 1964 (divorced); married Neil Simon, October 25, 1973 (divorced). EDUCATION: Graduated from Webster College, MO.

CAREER: FILM DEBUT—*Blume in Love*, 1973. PRINCIPAL FILM APPEARANCES—*Cinderella Liberty*, 1973; *Audrey Rose*, 1977; *The Goodbye Girl*, 1977; *The Cheap Detective*, 1978; *Promises in the Dark*, 1979; *Chapter Two*, 1979; *Only When I Laugh*, 1981; *Max Dugan Returns*, 1983.

PRINCIPAL STAGE APPEARANCES—(New York) *The Deer Park*, 1967; *Cactus Flower*, 1968; *The Indian Wants the Bronx*, 1968; *Happy Birthday, Wanda June*, 1970; *Private Lives*, 1971; *You Can't Take It with You*, 1972; *Cyrano de Bergerac*, 1972; *A Doll's House*, 1972. MAJOR TOURS—*Cactus Flower*, U.S. cities, 1968; *The Crucible*, 1972; *The Good Doctor*, 1973; *King Richard III*, 1974.

PRINCIPAL TELEVISION APPEARANCES—(series) *Love of Life; Brewsie and Willie; Cyrano de Bergerac.*

AWARDS: Golden Globe Award, 1978: *The Goodbye Girl;* Golden Globe Award, 1974: *Cinderella Liberty.*

SIDELIGHTS: MEMBERSHIPS—American Conservatory Theater, San Francisco, CA.

ADDRESS: Agent—c/o William Morris Agency, 1350 Avenue of the Americas, New York, NY 10019.*

* * *

MASON, Marshall W., director

PERSONAL: Born February 24, 1940, in Amarillo, TX; son of Marvin Marshall and Lorraine Chrisman (Hornsby) Mason; married Zita Litvinas (deceased). EDUCATION: Northwestern University; studied for the theatre at the Actors' Studio.

CAREER: DEBUT—(as an actor) Malvolio, *Twelfth Night*, Eagles Mere, PA, 1959. PRINCIPAL STAGE APPEARANCES—Claudius, *Hamlet*, Circle Repertory, NY, 1979; Malvolio, *Twelfth Night*, Circle Repertory, NY, 1980.

DIRECTED: Plays—*The Wild Duck, The Trojan Women, Cat on a Hot Tin Roof*, Northwestern University, 1959; *Medea, An Evening of Love, The Clown, The Rue Garden*, Cafe Cino, 1962; assistant director, *One Way Pendulum*, Phoenix, NY, 1962; *Little Eyolf*, Actors' Playhouse, NY, 1964; *Home Free*, off-Broadway, 1965, Mercury, London, 1968 with *The Madness of Lady Bright;* in July 1969 became the Artistic Director of the Circle Repertory Company. His work since includes: *The Hot L Baltimore*, Circle Rep, 1973; *When We Dead Awaken*, 1973; *Battle of Angels, The Sea Horse*, Circle Rep, 1974; *Come Back, Little Sheba*, Queens Playhouse, NY, 1974; *Harry Outside, The Mound Builders*, Circle Rep, 1975; *Knock, Knock, Serenading Louie*, co-director, *Mrs. Murray's Farm*, director, *The Farm, A Tribute to Lili Lamont*, Circle Rep, 1976; *My Life, Ulysses in*

Traction, Circle Rep, 1977; (supervised) *Gemini*, Litle Theatre, NY, 1977; *The Fifth of July, In the Recovery Lounge*, Circle Rep, 1978; *Winter Signs, Talley's Folly*, Circle Rep, 1979; *Murder at the Howard Johnson's*, John Golden, NY, 1979; *Slugger*, Paf Playhouse, NY, 1979; *Talley's Folly*, John Golden, NY, 1980; *The Fifth of July*, New Apollo, 1980; *Foxfire*, Guthrie, Minneapolis, 1981; *Richard II*, Circle Rep, 1982; *Angels Fall*, Longacre, NY, 1982; *The Great Grandson of Jedediah Kohler*, Entermedia, NY, 1982; *Passion*, Longacre, NY, 1983; also *Tally's Folly*, London; productions at Mark Taper Forum, Los Angeles, Academy Festival Theatre, Lakewood, IL, etc. TELEVISION SHOWS—*Kennedy's Children*, 1982; *The Fifth of July*, 1983.

AWARDS: Obie Awards, *Hot L Baltimore, Battle of Angels, The Mound-Builders, Serenading Louie, Knock, Knock;* Antoinette Perry Award Nominations, *Knock, Knock, Talley's Folly, The Fifth of July;* also the recipient of the Drama Desk Award, the Margo Jones Award, the Outer Critics Circle Award, the Theatre World Award, a Shubert Foundation Award, and the Arts and Business Council for the Circle Repertory's consistent searching out and producing works by new American talent.

SIDELIGHTS: RECREATION—Archaeology, travel.

Mr. Mason relinquished the position of Artistic Director of the Circle Repertory Company in 1980 to allow himself the freedom of directing in other venues.

ADDRESS: Home—165 Christopher Street, New York, NY 10014.*

* * *

MASON, Pamela, actress, writer

PERSONAL: Born March 10, 1918, South End on the Sea, England; daughter of Isadore and Helen Spear (Morgan) Oster; married Roy Kellino, 1936 (divorced); married James Mason (an actor) 1940 (divorced 1964); children: Portland, Morgan. EDUCATION: Attended private schools in England.

CAREER: DEBUT—*The Luck of the Devil*, London, England, 1936. PRINCIPAL STAGE APPEARANCES—*Bathsheba*, NY, 1969, and others.

PRINCIPAL FILM APPEARANCES—*I Met a Murderer*, London, England, 1938; *They Were Sisters*, 1944; *The Upturned Glass*, 1946; *Pandora and the Flying Dutchman*, 1946; over 20 other film appearances. PRINCIPAL TELEVISION APPEARANCES—*The Pamela Mason Show*, London, England, 1960–68; *The Weaker Sex*, 1969; featured on talk shows.

WRITINGS: BOOKS, NOVELS—*This Little Hand*, 1942; *Del Palma*, 1944; *The Blinds Are Down*, 1946; *Ignoramus Ignoramus*, 1950; *Marriage Is the First Step Toward Divorce*, 1950; *The Female Pleasure Hunt*, 1972; *Favorite Cat Stories of Pamela and James Mason*, 1976.

SIDELIGHTS: Lectures at women's clubs, nationwide.

ADDRESS: Agent—Bettye McCartt, NcCartt, Oreck & Barret, 9200 Sunset Blvd., Los Angeles, CA 90069.

MASTERSON, Peter (ne Carlos Bee Masterson, Jr.), actor, writer, and director

PERSONAL: Born June 1, 1934, in Houston, TX; son of Carlos Bee (a lawyer) and Josephine (Smith) Masterson; married Carlin Glynn (an actress), December 29, 1960; children: Alexandra, Mary Stuart, Peter Carlos. EDUCATION: Rice University, Houston, B.A., 1957; trained for the stage with Stella Adler at the Stella Adler Theatre School.

CAREER: DEBUT—*Call Me by My Rightful Name*, One Sheridan Square, New York, 1961. PRINCIPAL STAGE APPEARANCES—*Marathon '33*, ANTA, 1963; *Blues for Mr. Charlie*, 1964, Lee Harvey Oswald, *The Trial of Lee Harvey Oswald*, ANTA, 1967, *The Great White Hope*, ANTA, New York, 1968–70; Tom, *That Championship Season*, Booth, New York, 1973–74; DeSantis, *The Poison Tree*, Ambassador, New York, 1975.

FILM DEBUT—*Ambush Bay*, 1965. PRINCIPAL FILMS—*Counterpoint*, 1967; *In the Heat of the Night*, 1967; *Tomorrow*, 1969; *The Exorcist*, 1971; *Man on a Swing*, 1972; *The Stepford Wives*, 1974. TELEVISION DEBUT—*Camera Three*, 1959. TELEVISION APPEARANCES—*Pueblo; The Quinns; A Question of Guilt.* DIRECTED: PLAYS—*The Best Little Whorehouse in Texas*, 46th Street Theatre, New York, 1978; *The Best Little Whorehouse in Texas*, Theatre Royal Drury Lane, London, 1981; *The Last of the Knucklemen*, New York, 1983.

WRITINGS: PLAYS, PUBLISHED—*The Best Little Whorehouse in Texas*, 1978 (with Carol Hall and Larry King). FILMS—*The Best Little Whorehouse in Texas* (with Larry King). TELEVISION FILMS—*City in Fear* (story only).

AWARDS: Drama Desk Award, Best Director, 1978: *The Best Little Whorehouse in Texas;* Antoinette Perry Award Nominations for Best Director and Best Writer, 1979: *The Best Little Whorehouse in Texas.*

SIDELIGHTS: MEMBERSHIPS—Actors Studio.

ADDRESS: Home—1165 Fifth Avenue, New York, NY 10029.

* * *

MASTRANTONIO, Mary Elizabeth, actress, singer

PERSONAL: Born November 17, in Lombard, IL; daughter of Frank A. (a foundryman/owner) and Mary D. (Pagone) Mastrantonio. EDUCATION: Attended University of Illinois, 1976–78; studied in New York City.

CAREER: DEBUT—Lady Sybil, *Camelot*, Marriot Lincolnshire, IL, 1979. NEW YORK DEBUT—Understudy, Maria, *West Side Story*, 1980. PRINCIPAL STAGE APPEARANCES—Dore Spenlow, *Copperfield*, ANTA, NY, 1981; Musica, *Oh Brother*, ANTA, NY, 1981; Katerina Cavalieri, Constanza, *Amadeus*, 1982; Katharine, *Henry V*, Delacort, NY, 1984.

FILM DEBUT—Gina Montana, *Scarface*, 1983.

ADDRESS: Agent—J. Michael Bloom, 400 Madison Avenue, New York, NY 10019.

MATHESON, Murray, actor

PERSONAL: Born July 1, 1912, in Casterton, Australia; son of Kenneth Murray (a grazier) and Ethel Sunderland (Barret) Matheson. EDUCATION: Attended public schools in Sandford, Australia; trained for the stage at the Melbourne Little Theatre and with Ada Reeve. MILITARY: Royal Air Force, 1940–45.

CAREER: DEBUT—Chorus, *High Jinks*, His Majesty's Theatre, Melbourne, Australia, 1934. NEW YORK DEBUT—Captain Worthy, *The Relapse*, Theatre Guild, 1950. LONDON DEBUT—*Band Wagon*, Palladium, 1939. PRINCIPAL STAGE APPEARANCES—*Roberta*, His Majesty's Theatre, Melbourne, Australia, 1934; *Billie*, Apollo Theatre, Melbourne, Australia, 1935; appeared with the Bournemouth Repertory Company, England, 1936; *And on We Go*, Savoy, London, 1937; Blenderband, *The Millionairess*, Théâtre Michel, Paris, France, 1937; *George and Margaret*, Charles Theatre, London, 1937; Eric, *The Human Element*, Théâtre de l'oeuvre, Paris, 1939; *Swinging the Gate*, Ambassadors Theatre, London, 1940; *Lights Up*, Savoy, London, 1940; *Better Late*, Garrick, London, 1946; Peter Henderson, *Escapade*, 48th Street Theatre, New York, 1953; *Down Came a Blackbird*, John Drew Theatre, East Hampton, NY, 1955; Felix Callender, *Third Person*, President, New York, 1955; *Dead on Nine*, John Drew Theatre, 1956; *You Never Can Tell*, John Drew Theatre, 1956; Simon, *Simon and Laura*, John Drew Theatre, 1957; Aegisthos, *Electra*, Rita Allen Theatre, New York, 1959; Gosport, *Harliquinade*, Rita Allen Theatre, New York, 1959; Argan, *The Imaginary Invalid*, Goodman, Chicago, 1959; Earl of Blandings, *Oh, Kay!*, East 74th Street Theatre, New York, 1960; Sandor Turai, *The Play's the Thing*, Bucks County Playhouse, New Hope, PA, 1964; Charles, *Blithe Spirit*, La Jolla Playhouse, California, 1964; Denny, *Janus*, Paper Mill Playhouse, Millburn, NJ, 1965; Dirk Winston, *Mary, Mary*, Bucks County Playhouse, 1965; Mr. Applegate, *Damn Yankees*, Melodyland, Berkeley, CA, 1965; *Yeats and Company: The Prose, Poetry and Plays of W. B. Yeats*, Theatre Group, UCLA, California, 1965; *Dial "M" for Murder*, California; Captain Hook, *Peter Pan*, California; *Heaven Can Wait*, California; Sir, *The Roar of the Greasepaint . . .*, California; Von Mark, *The Student Prince*, Dorothy Chandler Pavilion, Los Angeles, 1966; Caesar, *Caesar and Cleopatra*, Goodman, Chicago, 1968; *Lock up Your Daughters*, Pasadena Playhouse, CA, 1968; Tucker, *The Ruling Class*, Goodman, Chicago, 1972; Dr. Theodore Holley, *The Charlatan*, Mark Taper Forum, Los Angeles, 1974; *Misalliance*, Globe Theatre, San Diego, CA, 1982.

MAJOR TOURS—*Ten Minute Alibi*, Australia; *Tons of Money*, Australia; *While Parents Sleep*, Australia; Charlie Parker in *Oscar Wilde* and Marchbanks in *Candida*, Berlin, Vienna, Brussels, Prague, Warsaw, Budapest, 1937–39; *New Faces*, England, 1940; *There Goes Yesterday*, Canada, 1948–50; *The Drunkard; The Cocktail Party; Tonight at 8:30;* Henry Higgins, *My Fair Lady*, 1960–61.

FILM DEBUT—*Way to the Stars*, 1940. PRINCIPAL FILMS—*Journey Together*, 1945; *The Fool and the Princess*, 1946; *School for Secrets*, 1946; *Hurricane Smith*, 1952; *Plymouth Adventure*, 1952; *Botany Bay*, 1953; *Flight to Tangier*, 1953; *King of the Khyber Rifles*, 1953; *Jamaica Run*, 1953; *The Bamboo Prison*, 1954; *Love Is a Many Splendid Thing*, 1955; *Wall of Noise*, 1963; *Signpost to Murder*, 1965;

Assault on a Queen, 1966; *How to Succeed in Business Without Really Trying*, 1967; *In Enemy Country*, 1968; *Star!*, 1968; *Twilight Zone*, 1983. TELEVISION DEBUT—Unidentified guest, *The Cocktail Party* (CBC), 1949. TELEVISION APPEARANCES—*Adventures in Paradise*, 1959; *Alfred Hitchcock Presents:* Bunthorne, *Patience* (CBC), 1960; *Thriller; U.S. Steel Hour; Alcoa Theater;* King Magnus, *The Apple Cart* (CBC); *The Fugitive; Suspense; Twilight Zone; Sam Benedict; Naked City; Route 66; The Islanders; Laramie; Tall Man; The Tiger at the Gates* (CBC); *Studio One; Kraft Theatre; Omnibus; The Man from UNCLE; Get Smart; Perry Mason; Twelve O'Clock High; The Defenders; Profiles in Courage; My Favorite Martian; One Step Beyond; The FBI; The Invaders; The Girl from UNCLE; Banacek; Famous Jury Trials* (Toronto, 1968).

ADDRESS: Agent—c/o I.C.M., 8899 Beverly Blvd., Beverly Hills, CA 90048; 40 W. 57th Street, New York, NY 10019.

* * *

MATHESON, Richard (Burton), screenwriter

PERSONAL: Born February 20, 1926, in Allendale, NJ; son of Bertolf (a tile floor installer) and Fanny (Mathieson) Matheson; married Ruth Ann Woodson, July 1, 1952; children: Richard, Alison, Christian, Bettina. EDUCATION: University of Missouri, B.A., 1949. MILITARY: U.S. Army, ETO, 1944–45.

WRITINGS: SCREENPLAYS—*The Incredible Shrinking Man*, 1957; *The Beat Generation*, 1959; *The House of Usher*, 1960; *The Pit and the Pendulum*, 1961; *Master of the World*, 1961; *Tales of Terror, Facts in the Case of M. Valdemar, Morella, The Black Cat, Cask of Amantillado*, 1962; with Charles Beaumont and George Baxt, *Burn Witch Burn*, 1962; *The Raven*, 1963; *The Comedy of Terrors*, 1964; *Die! Die! My Darling*, 1965; *The Young Warriors*, 1967; *The Devil's Bride*, 1968; *de Sade*, 1969; *Legend of Hell House*, 1973; *Somewhere in Time*, 1980; *Twilight Zone—The Movie*, 1983; *Jaws 3-D*, 1983. TELEPLAYS—*Duel*, 1971; *Ghost Story*, 1972; *The Night Stalker*, 1972; *The Night Strangler*, 1973; *Dying Room Only*, 1973; *Scream of the Wolf*, 1973; *Dracula*, 1974; *Trilogy of Terror*, 1974; *The Stranger Within*, 1974; *The Morning After*, 1974; *Dead of Night*, 1975; *The Strange Possession of Mrs. Oliver*, 1977; *The Martian Chronicles*, (mini-series), 1980. SERIES—*Lawman; Twilight Zone; Star Trek; Girl from U.N.C.L.E.; Chrysler Playhouse.* SHORT STORIES—*Born of Man and Woman*, 1954, abridged edition *Third From the Sun*, 1970; *The Shores of Space*, 1957; *Shock: Thirteen Tales to Thrill and Terrify*, 1961, reprinted as *Shock I*, 1979; *Shock II*, 1964, reprinted, 1979; *Shock III*, 1966, reprinted 1979; *Shock Waves*, 1970. NOVELS—*Fury on Sunday*, 1954; *I Am Legend*, 1954; reprinted as *The Omega Man: I Am Legend*, 1971; *Someone Is Bleeding*, 1954; *The Shrinking Man*, 1956 reprinted, 1979; *A Stir of Echoes*, 1958, reprinted 1979; *Ride the Nightmare*, 1959; *The Beardless Warriors*, 1960; *Hell House*, 1971; *Bid Time Return*, 1975; *What Dreams May Come*, 1978.

AWARDS: World Fantasy award, Best Novel, 1976: *Bid Time Return;* Writers Guild award, for best anthology adapted from another medium, 1973; guest of honor at the World

Science Fiction Convention, 1958, 1976; Hugo Award, World Science Fiction Convention, for best motion picture, 1958: *The Incredible Shrinking Man.*

SIDELIGHTS: MEMBERSHIPS—Writers Guild, Dramatists Guild.

''Matheson has been largely concerned with the occult and tales of fright in his screenplays. He was Hollywood's dean of Edgar Allan Poe adapters in the early sixties and afterwards developed macabre stories on his own. His teleplays too, explored the eerie and mysterious including one that he based on personal experience, *Duel.*''

ADDRESS: Agent—Don Congdon Associates, Inc., 177 E. 70th Street, New York, NY 10021.

* * *

MATTHEWS, Francis, actor

PERSONAL: Born September 2, 1927 in York, England; son of Henry Ernest (Trades Union Secretary, O.B.E.) and Kathleen Mary (Empson) Matthews; married Angela Browne (an actress) on February 23, 1963; children: Paul, Dominic, Damien. EDUCATION: St. Michael's Jesuit College, Leeds, England, 1938–45. RELIGION: Catholic. MILITARY: Royal Navy, amenities writer, 1945–47.

CAREER: DEBUT—Young Miner, *The Corn Is Green,* Princes, Bradford, England, 1945. NEW YORK DEBUT—Stuart, *Help Stamp Out Marriage,* Booth, for 40 performances, 1966. LONDON DEBUT—Martin, *The Devil Was Sick,* Fortune, 1956. PRINCIPAL STAGE APPEARANCES—Guy Stevens, *How Say You,* Aldwych, London, 1959; Mr. Darcy, *First Impressions,* Birmingham, England, 1971; Mr. White, *Who's Who?,* Fortune, London, 1971; Eric, *Trinity Tales,* Birmingham, England, 1975; Alex Clayborne, *Touch of Spring,* Comedy, London, 1975; Reg, *Middle Age Spread,* Lyric, Apollo, London, 1980; Mr. Stone, *Business of Murder,* Duchess, London, 1981; Willie, *Aren't We All?,* Haymarket, London, 1984.

MAJOR TOURS—Bob Peasley, *No Escape,* British Isles; Pat, *That's No Lady, That's My Husband,* British Isles, 1972–73; Cowardly Custer, O'Keefe, Toronto, Canada, 1974; Andrew, *Signs of the Times,* British Isles; Henry Higgins, *My Fair Lady,* Holland and Belgium; Noel Coward, *Noel and Gertie,* Monaco.

FILM DEBUT—Ranjit, *Bhowani Junction,* 1955. PRINCIPAL FILM APPEARANCES—Dr. Kleve, *Revenge of Frankenstein,* 1958; Jonathan, *Corridors of Blood,* 1958; Auclair, *Treasure of Monte Cristo,* 1960; Charles, *Dracula, Prince of Darkness,* 1965; Kessnikoff, *Rasputin,* 1965; Lewis, *Just Like a Woman,* 1966; Jason, *Champagne Rose Is Dead,* 1968; Giorgio, *Two Eyes of Crystal Water,* 1974.

TELEVISION DEBUT—Ensign Trefusis, *Prelude to Glory,* 1954. PRINCIPAL TELEVISION APPEARANCES—Ken Palmer, *My Friend Charles,* 1956; Esme, *Esme Divided,* 1957; Lt. Lamb, *Triton,* 1961; Grant, *Dark Island,* 1962; Capt. Tenbro, *Last Man Out,* 1963; Simon, *Little Big Business,* 1963–64; Lord Hansford, *My Man Joe,* 1967; Paul Temple,

FRANCIS MATTHEWS

Paul Temple 1969–71; Eric, *Trinity Tales,* 1975; Stanley, *Middlemen,* 1977; Tom, *Don't Forget to Write,* 1977–78; Noel Coward, *Ike—The War Years,* 1978; Jack Askew, *A Roof Over My Head,* 1977; Geoffrey, *Tears Before Bedtime,* 1983.

WRITINGS: RADIO SHOWS—*Local Time,* weekly anthology series, BBC. Numerous humorous articles for magazines.

AWARDS: Most Popular Actor, Italian TV Poll, 1974: *Paul Temple* series.

SIDELIGHTS: ''At the age of sixteen I rushed headlong, and untutored, into the only thing I had ever wanted to do by bombarding the local theatre in Leeds to take me on backstage. And so since leaving school, I have known no other life. Back in 1945 my inspirations were Robert Donat, Olivier, Noel Coward, Cary Grant . . . the sort of actors who seemed to have a clarity of purpose and a high degree of perfectionism. I also believed deeply that the job should be fun above all. If it was not that, it was not worth doing. That does not mean that an actor should not take his work seriously, but actors who take themselves seriously are a different matter.

''I also believe that the most important thing an actor should do is work—to be open to the possibility of trying anything, because no experience at our job, however horrendous, is wasted. Favorite roles, as most actors know, are not necessarily the most important ones, professionally. For me, the film *Bhowani Junction* and the international television series *Paul Temple* opened the most doors, but *Trinity Tales, Little Big Business* and *Middlemen* on television and *Who's Who* and *Help Stamp Out Marriage, That's No Lady, That's My Husband* and *My Fair Lady,* gave me the sort of satisfaction that makes the role difficult to say goodbye to. I have sung with swing bands, hosted comedy shows on radio, provided the voice of Captain Scarlet, sung and danced in revues, played high drama and low comedy and kept all my options open, because that is what I believe an actor is, or at least used to be, about. My pastimes are tennis, cricket, trying to write all the time and lending support to the Stars Organization for Crippled Children.''

ADDRESS: Home—Old Field, New Road, Esher, Surrey, KT10 9PG. Agent—Richard Stone, 18–20, York Buildings, London WC2N6JU, England.

* * *

MAXWELL, Ronald, F., director, writer

PERSONAL: Born January 5, 1947. EDUCATION: New York University, College of Arts and Sciences; New York University Graduate School of the Arts, Institute of Film and Television.

CAREER: PRINCIPAL FILM WORK, Director—*The Guest,* 1964; *Little Darlings,* 1980; *The Night the Lights Went out in Georgia,* 1981; *Kidco.* TELEVISION, DIRECTOR—*Verna: USO Girl,* 1977; *Sea Marks.*

AWARDS: Emmy Award Nomination, Best Director, 1977–78: *Verna: USO Girl;* Grand Prize, Chicago Film Festival, *Verna: USO Girl.*

SIDELIGHTS: MEMBERSHIPS—Directors Guild of America.

ADDRESS: Agent—Jeff Berg, c/o I.C.M., 8899 Beverly Blvd., Los Angeles, CA 90048.

* * *

MAY, Beverly (nee Wilson), actress

PERSONAL: Born August 11, 1927, in East Wellington, BC, Canada; daughter of Joseph (a coalminer) and Mona (Quayle) Wilson; married William Francis May (a professor); children: Catherine, Theodore, David, Elisabeth. EDUCATION: University of British Columbia, B.A., 1948; Yale School of Drama, M.F.A., 1950.

CAREER: DEBUT—Unborn Child, *The Bluebird,* Nanaimo, British Columbia, 1934. NEW YORK DEBUT—Dora Strang, *Equus,* Helen Hayes, 1976. PRINCIPAL STAGE APPEARANCES—(Broadway) Mrs. Walker, *Once in a Lifetime,* Circle in the Square, 1978; Sister Anderson, *Whose Life Is It Anyway?,* Royale, 1979; Mrs. Smale, *Rose,* Cort, 1981; Gert, *The Curse of an Aching Heart,* Little, 1982; Sadie, *Slab Boys,* Playhouse, 1983; (Off-Broadway) Albertine, *Bonjour, La Bonjour,* Phoenix, 1980; Madame, *My Sister in This House,*

Second Stage, 1981; Peggy, *And a Nightingale Sang,* Mitzi Newhouse, 1983.

TELEVISION DEBUT—party guest, *Father Brown.* PRINCIPAL TELEVISION APPEARANCES—*As the World Turns, Another World, Ryan's Hope.*

AWARDS: Obie Award, 1981: *My Sister in This House.*

ADDRESS: Agent—c/o Smith Freedman and Associates, 870 Seventh Avenue, New York, NY 10019.

* * *

MAYO, Virginia (nee Virginia Clara Jones), actress and dancer

PERSONAL: Born November 30, 1920, in St. Louis, MO; daughter of Luke Ward (a newspaperman) and Martha Henrietta (Rautenstrauch) Jones; married Edward Francis Michael O'Shea (an actor), July 5, 1947 (died December 3, 1973); children: Mary Catherine. EDUCATION: Attended St. Louis public schools; studied drama with Alice Jones Wientge. POLITICS: Republican. RELIGION: Catholic.

CAREER: DEBUT—dancer with St. Louis Municipal Opera Company, Summer 1937. NEW YORK DEBUT—vaudeville act called *Pansy the Horse,* Strand Theatre, 1937. PRINCIPAL STAGE APPEARANCES—*Banjo Eyes,* New York, 1940; *Mrs. Astor's Pet Horse,* Paramount Hotel, New York, 1941–42; *Good News; Hello Dolly; Forty Carats; The Loving Couch; That Certain Girl,* Thunderbird Hotel, Las Vegas, 1967; *How the Other Half Loves; Cactus Flower; Butterflies Are Free; Fiorello!; George Washington Slept Here; Tunnel of Love.* MAJOR TOURS—*No, No Nanette,* San Francisco, Chicago; *Barefoot in the Park,* United States and Canada, 1968–69; *Too Many for the Bed* (originally titled *Move Over, Mrs. Markham*), Denver, CO, Texas, Arizona, Minneapolis, MN, Millburn, NJ, Hyannis, MA, Sacramento, CA, Florida, Chicago, Louisiana.

FILM DEBUT—Princess, *Princess and the Pirate,* 1944. PRINCIPAL FILMS—*Up in Arms; The Best Years of Our Lives; Smart Girls Don't Talk; Flaxy Martin; The Girl from Jones Beach; Backfire; Colorado Territory; White Heat; Always Leave Them Laughing; The Flame and the Arrow; South Sea Woman; Captain Horatio Hornblower; The West Point Story; Along the Great Divide; Painting the Clouds with Sunshine; Starlift; She's Working Her Way Through College; The Iron Mistress; She's Back on Broadway; King Richard and the Crusaders; The Silver Chalice; Great Day in the Morning; Congo Crossing; Kid from Brooklyn; Wonder Man; A Son is Born; Out of the Blue; Seven Days Ashore; Proud Ones; Big Land; Fort Utah; Young Fury; Fort Dobbs; Devil's Canyon; Tall Stranger; Jack London; Westbound; Red Light; The Haunting; French Quarter; Won Ton Ton, the Dog Who Saved Hollywood.* TELEVISION APPEARANCES—*Police Story; The Outsider; Night Gallery; Bob Hope Specials; Daktari; Dinah Shore Show; A.M. New York; Mike Douglas Show; Castle of Evil; Lannigan's Rabbi; Merv Griffin Show.*

AWARDS: National Film Award, 1980.

SIDELIGHTS: MEMBERSHIPS—SAG, AEA, AFTRA, Daughters of the American Revolution. HOBBIES: Painting.

ADDRESS: Agent—c/o Ruth Webb, 7500 De Vista, Los Angeles, CA 90046.

* * *

MAYRON, Melanie, actress and writer

PERSONAL: Born October 20, 1952, in Philadelphia, PA; daughter of David (a pharmaceutical chemist) and Norma (a real estate agent; maiden name Goodman) Mayron. EDUCATION: Graduate of American Academy of Dramatic Arts, 1972; trained for the stage with Sandra Seacat and John Lehne.

CAREER: DEBUT—Gilmer, Godspell, bus and truck tour, 1972–73. NEW YORK DEBUT—The Goodbye People, Belasco, 1979. PRINCIPAL STAGE APPEARANCES—Gilmer, Godspell, Marines Memorial Theatre, San Francisco, CA, 1974; Shulamith, Gethsemane Springs, Mark Taper Forum, Los Angeles, 1976; Gilmer, Godspell (10-year anniversary revival), La Mama, New York, 1982.

FILM DEBUT—Ginger, Harry and Tonto, 1974. PRINCIPAL FILMS—The Great Smokey Roadblock, 1974; You Light Up My Life, 1975; Marsha, Car Wash, 1975; Susan, Girl Friends, 1978; Heartbeeps, 1980; Terry, Missing, 1981. TELEVISION APPEARANCES—Playing for Time; Will There Really Be a Morning?; Hustling; The Best Little Girl in the World; Lily Tomlin; Sold Out; Rhoda.

WRITINGS: TELEVISION FILMS—Tunes for a Small Harmonica; The Pretend Game (both co-authored with Catlin Adams).

AWARDS: Best Actress, Lucarno Film Festival, 1979: Girl Friends. Best Newcomer Nominee, British Academy Awards, 1979.

SIDELIGHTS: MEMBERSHIPS—Actor's Studio.

ADDRESS: Agent—c/o DHKPR, 7319 Beverly Blvd., Suite 11, Los Angeles, CA 90036.

* * *

MAZURSKY, Paul, director, producer, writer, actor

PERSONAL: Born April 25, 1930, in Brooklyn, NY; son of David and Jean (Gerson) Mazursky; married Betsy Purdy, March 12, 1953; children: Meg, Jill.

PRINCIPAL FILM WORK—actor, Blackboard Jungle, 1955; actor, Deathwatch; writer (with Larry Tucker), I Love You, Alice B. Toklas, 1968; writer/director, Bob & Carol & Ted & Alice, 1969; writer/director/actor, Alex in Wonderland, 1970; producer/director/writer/actor, Blume in Love, 1972; producer/director/writer, Harry and Tonto, 1973; producer/director/writer, Next Stop, Greenwich Village, 1976; producer/director/writer/actor, Unmarried Woman, 1978; actor, A Man, a Woman and a Bank; producer/director/writer,

Willie and Phil, 1980; producer/director/writer/actor, Tempest, 1982.

RELATED CAREERS—Nightclub comedian, 1954–60; producer/director/writer/performer, Second City Improvisational Revue.

WRITINGS: TELEVISION—Danny Kaye Show; Monkees Show (also created).

ADDRESS: Office—c/o Columbia Pictures, Burbank Studios, 4000 Warner Blvd., Burbank, CA 91522. Agent—c/o ICM, 8899 Beverly Blvd., Los Angeles, CA 90048.*

* * *

MAZZOLA, John W., executive

PERSONAL: Born January 20, 1928, in Bayonne, NJ; son of Roy Stephen (an attorney) and Eleanor Burnett (Davis) Mazzola; married Sylvia Drulie (a producer), March 7, 1959; children: Alison, Amy. EDUCATION: Tufts University, A.B., 1949; Fordham University, LL.D., 1952. MILITARY: Agent, Counter-Intelligence Corps, U.S. Army, 1953–55. NONTHEATRICAL CAREER: Admitted to NY bar, 1956; member of law firm Milbank, Tweed, Hadley & McCloy, 1953–64.

CAREER: Lincoln Center for the Performing Arts, New York City: secretary, executive vice-president, 1964–68; general manager, 1969–70; managing director, 1970–77; president, 1977–.

AWARDS: Decorated Cavaliere Ufficiale Ordine al Merito della Repubblica Italiana (Italy); Ordre des Arts et des Lettres (France); Benjamin Franklin Fellow, Royal Society of Arts (Great Britain).

SIDELIGHTS: MEMBERSHIPS—Red Cross (Board of Directors); boards of many community and civic organizations; Century Club, NY; Misquamicut Club, RI; Watch Hill Yacht Club, RI.

Consultant to performing arts centers in the United States and abroad.

ADDRESS: Office—Lincoln Center, 132 West 65th Street, New York, NY 10023.

* * *

MCBAIN, Diane, actress, producer, writer

PERSONAL: Born May 18, 1941; daughter of Walter G. and Cleo L. (Ferguson) McBain; married Rodney L. Burke, 1971 (divorced 1974); children: Andrew Evan. EDUCATION: Attended Pierce College and the University of California, Los Angeles; studies acting with Harry Mastrogeorge.

CAREER: FILM DEBUT—Ice Palace, 1959. PRINCIPAL FILM APPEARANCES—Parrish, 1960; title role, Claudelle Inglish,

DIANE MCBAIN

1960; *Black Gold*, 1961; *A Distant Trumpet*, 1962; *The Caretakers*, 1963; *Mary, Mary*, 1963; *Fly from the Hawk*, 1964; *Spinout*, 1965; *I Sailed to Tahiti*, 1966; *Thunder Alley*, 1966; *Savage Season*, 1967; *The Delta Factor*, 1967; *Wicked, Wicked*, 1969.

TELEVISION DEBUT—*Surfside Six*, 1960–62. PRINCIPAL TELE-VISION APPEARANCES—*Barbary Coast*; *Police Story*; *Hawaii Five-O*; *Grizzly Adam's Christmas Special*; *Marcus Welby, M.D.*; *ABC's Wonderful World of Entertainment*; *Eight Is Enough*; *Donner Pass* (television movie); *Dallas*; *Days of Our Lives*, 1982–84.

PRINCIPAL STAGE APPEARANCES—*Who's Happy Now?*; *The Tender Trap*; *Hedda Gabler*; *Star Spangled Girl*; *Bell, Book and Candle*; *A Streetcar Named Desire*; *The Glass Menagerie*, 1983.

RELATED CAREER—Producer, Pied Piper Productions, 1980–present.

SIDELIGHTS: MEMBERSHIPS—SAG, AFTRA, AEA.

Miss McBain received the Special Service Award from the USO for visits made to Vietnam in 1966 and 1967.

ADDRESS: Agent—Allen Goldstein and Assoc., 9000 Sunset Blvd., Suite 910, Los Angeles, CA 90069.

McCALL, Nancy, actress

PERSONAL: Born January 12, 1948; daughter of James Ira (a textile management consultant) and Susan Moore (Self) Teat. EDUCATION: Northwestern University, B.M., 1970; trained for the stage by Michael Shurtleff, Alan Savage, Larry Moss, and Paul Odvert.

CAREER: DEBUT—Fruma Sarah, *Fiddler on the Roof*, Candlelight Dinner Playhouse, Chicago, IL, 1971. NEW YORK DEBUT—Peggy, *Godspell*, Promenade, 1975. PRINCIPAL STAGE APPEARANCES—Connee Boswell, *The Heebie Jeebies*, Westside Arts, NY, 1981; Annabella, *Nine*, 46th Street, NY, 1982–82. MAJOR TOURS—Robin, *Godspell*, U.S. cities, 1973–74; Annabella, *Nine*, U.S. cities, 1984.

SIDELIGHTS: MEMBERSHIPS—Delta Delta Delta sorority.

ADDRESS: Service—(212) 840-1234.

* * *

McCALLUM, David, actor and director

PERSONAL: Born September 19, 1933, in Scotland; married Katherine Carpenter; children: Peter, Sophie; three sons by previous marriage. EDUCATION: Royal Academy of Dramatic Art, London, 1949–51.

CAREER: PRINCIPAL STAGE APPEARANCES—*After the Prize*; *Alfie*; *California Suite*, New York; *Camelot*; *Crown Matrimonial*; *Deathtrap*; *Donkey's Years*; *The Flip Side*; *The Mousetrap*; *Night Must Fall*; *Outward Bound*; *The Philanthropist*; *Romantic Comedy*; *Salome*; *Sleuth*; *Signpost to Murder*.

PRINCIPAL FILMS—*A Night to Remember*; *Billy Budd*; *Critical List*; *The Diamond Hunters*; *Dogs*; *Freud*; *The Great Escape*; *Hell Drivers*; *La Cattura*; *The Long and the Short and the Tall*; *Mosquito Squadron*; *Three Bites of the Apple*; *The Secret Place*; *Watcher in the Woods*; *Robbery Under Arms*; *Violent Playground*; *The Greatest Story Ever Told*; *Around the World Under the Sea*. TELEVISION APPEARANCES—Illya Kuryakin, *The Man From UNCLE*; 1964–67; *Teacher, Teacher*; *Hauser's Memory*; *Invisible Man*; *The Colditz Story*; *The File on Devlin*; *Frankenstein*; *Kidnapped*; *Profiles in Courage*; *Sapphire and Steel* (ATV, England). Appeared as a child actor on BBC.

DIRECTED: Plays—productions for the British Army. Television—an episode of the BBC series, *Ten Who Dared*, 1974.

SIDELIGHTS: MEMBERSHIPS—enjoys working with his computer and playing golf.

ADDRESS: Agent—c/o Don Buchwald, 10 E. 44th Street, New York, NY 10017.

* * *

McCARTHY, Mary, author, drama critic

PERSONAL: Born June 21, 1910 in Seattle, WA; daughter of Roy Winfield (a lawyer) and Therese (Preston) McCarthy;

married Harold Johnsrud (a playwright and actor) on June 21, 1933 (divorced 1936); married Edmund Wilson (a writer) on February 8, 1938 (divorced 1946); married Bowden Broadwater (a teacher) in 1947 (divorced 1961); married James Raymond West (U.S. Foreign Service officer) on April 15, 1961; children: (second marriage) Reuel Wilson. EDUCATION: Vassar College, A.B., 1933.

WRITINGS: CRITIC—*The Partisan Review*, 1937–48. BOOKS OF DRAMATIC CRITICISM—*Sights and Spectacles*, 1956; *Mary McCarthy's Theatre Chronicles*, 1963. OTHER BOOKS—*The Company She Keeps*, 1942; *The Oasis*, 1949; *Cast a Cold Eye*, 1950; *The Groves of Academe*, 1952; *A Charmed Life*, 1955; *Memories of a Catholic Girlhood*, 1957; *Venice Observed*, 1956; *The Stones of Florence*, 1959; *On the Contrary*, 1961; *The Group*, 1963; *Vietnam*, 1967; *Hanoi*, 1968; *The Writing on the Wall*, 1970; *Birds of America*, 1971; *Medina*, 1972; *The Mask of State*, 1974; *The Seventeenth Degree*, 1974.

AWARDS: Stony Brook Award, 1983; Honorary Degrees, D. Litt., University of Maine, Orono, 1982, Bowdoin College, 1981, University of Aberdeen (Scotland), 1979, Bard College, 1976, Hull (England), 1974, Syracuse University, 1973; President's Distinguished Visitor, Vassar College, 1982; Guggenheim Fellow, 1959–60; National Institute Grant, 1957; Horizon Prize, 1949; Phi Beta Kappa.

SIDELIGHTS: MEMBERSHIPS—National Institute of Arts and Letters.

ADDRESS: Home—Castine, Maine, 04421. Agent—A. M. Heath and Co. Ltd., London, England WC2N 4DD.

* * *

McCLURE, Michael, poet, playwright, educator

PERSONAL: Born October 20, 1932 in Marysville, KS; son of Thomas and Marian Dixie (Johnston) McClure; married Joanna Keera Kinnison (a poet and teacher) on October 10, 1954; children: Katherine Jane. EDUCATION: University of Wichita, 1951–53; University of Arizona, 1953–54; San Francisco State College, B.A. 1955.

WRITINGS: PLAYS, PRODUCED—*The Blossom*, Poets Theatre, NY, 1960; *The Beard*, Evergreen, NY, 1967, Royal Court, London, England, 1968; *Gargoyle Cartoons*, 1970; *General Gorgeous*, A.C.T. San Francisco, 1974, Yale Repertory, New Haven, CT, 1975; *Gorf*, 1975; *The Grabbing of the Fairy*, 1978; *The Mammals* (three plays), 1978; *Josephine the Mouse Singer*, 1980; *The Red Snake*, 1982. BOOKS OF POETRY—*Hymns to St. Geryon*, 1959; *Dark Brown*, 1961; *The New Book*, 1961; *Ghost Tantras*, 1964; *Little Odes*, 1967; *Star*, 1970; *Rare Angel*, 1974; *September Blackberries*, 1974; *Jaguar Skies*, 1975; *Antechamber*, 1981. OTHER PUBLICATIONS—*Meat Science Essays*, 1963; *Freewheelin Frank, Secretary of the Angels—as told to Michael McClure*, 1969; *The Mad Cub*, 1970; *The Adept*, 1971; *Hail Thee Who Play*, 1974.

THEATRE-RELATED CAREER—Professor, Humanities and Sciences, California College of Arts and Crafts, 1962–present; Poetry readings and lecturer U.S. and abroad, 1955–present.

AWARDS: Obie, Best Play, *Josephine the Mouse Singer*, 1979; Rockefeller Fellowship, 1974; Guggenheim Fellowship, 1971; Obie, *The Beard*, 1968.

SIDELIGHTS: MEMBERSHIPS—AAAS, Sons of Anacreon.

"Beginning with *The Beard*, McClure's plays have stirred controversy and elicited sometimes extreme reactions. *The Beard* has been called a 'classic', but it was closed by the Los Angeles police at fourteen performances. In addition to his plays and poetry, McClure has published essays and articles on topics ranging from art and censorship to liberation; his song, 'Mercedes Benz,' was made popular by the late Janis Joplin. He describes himself as a 'mammal patriot' and is dedicated to the survival of the environment. He believes biology can improve our understanding of life and of poetry and literature."

ADDRESS: Home—264 Downey Street, San Francisco CA 94117. Office—Caiifornia College of Arts and Crafts, 5212 Broadway, Oakland, CA 94618. Agent—Helen Merrill, 337 W. 22nd Street, New York, NY 10011.

* * *

JEFF McCRACKEN

McCRACKEN, Jeff, actor

PERSONAL: Born in Chicago, IL; son of Robert E. (an architect) and Joan H. McCracken; married Janet Taylor (an actress and teacher), December 31, 1982. EDUCATION: Trained for the stage at the Neighborhood Playhouse with Sanford Meisner and Bill Alderson. MILITARY: U.S. Air Force, 1971–74.

CAREER: DEBUT—Ernie, *One Hundred Percent Alive,* Westwood Playhouse, Los Angeles, CA, 1979. NEW YORK DEBUT—Louis, *In Connecticut,* Circle Repertory, 1980, 60 performances. PRINCIPAL STAGE APPEARANCES—The Hope, *The Great White Hope,* Inner City Cultural Center, NY; Bob, *At Home,* Beverly Hills Playhouse, CA; Ivan, *The Marriage Proposal,* Beverly Hills Playhouse, CA; Joey, *The Indian Wants the Bronx,* Beverly Hills Playhouse, CA; Cal, *The Team,* Circle Repertory, NY; Chris, *Penitents,* Circle Repertory, NY; LA Joe, *Thymus Vulgaris,* Circle Repertory, NY; John Polk, *Am I Blue,* Hartford Stage, CT, Circle Repertory, NY, 1982; Roger, *Breakfast with Les and Bess,* Broadway, NY, 1983.

FILM DEBUT—Billie Joe, *One Man Jury,* 1978. PRINCIPAL FILM APPEARANCES—*Stranger in Our House,* 1980; Bill, *Kent State,* 1981; *Family Reunion,* 1982; Dennis, *Running Brave,* 1983. TELEVISION DEBUT—Vic Kresky, *Bay City Blues,* 1983.

WRITINGS: FILMS—Screenplay *Self-Portrait* (with Michael Jacobs), 1983–84.

ADDRESS: Agent—c/o Hesseltine/Baker Associates Ltd., 165 W. 46th Street, Suite #409, New York, NY 10036; c/o Sandy Bresler and Associates, 15760 Ventura Blvd., Suite # 1730, Encino, CA 91436.

* * *

McCRANE, Paul, actor

PERSONAL: Born January 19, 1961, in Philadelphia, PA; son of James J. (a writer and actor) and Eileen C. (a nurse; maiden name, Manyak) McCrane, Jr. EDUCATION: Holy Ghost Preparatory School; studied for the theatre with Uta Hagen at H.B. Studio, NY; studied stage fighting with B. H. Barry.

CAREER: DEBUT—Bert, *Landscape of the Body,* NY Shakespeare Festival, Public Theatre, 1977. PRINCIPAL STAGE APPEARANCES—Ensemble, *Dispatches,* NY Shakespeare Festival, 1978; Eddie, *Runaways,* Plymouth, NY, 1978; Jeff/Waiter, *Split,* Second Stage, NY, 1979; Christopher, *Sally's Gone, She Left Her Name,* Center Stage, Baltimore, MD, 1981; Ronnie, *The House of Blue Leaves,* Berkshire Theatre Festival, Stockbridge, MA, 1981; Rovo, *Hunting Scenes from Lower Bavaria,* Manhattan Theatre Club, NY, 1981; Carlo, *Crossing Niagrara,* Manhattan Theatre Club, NY, 1981; Alvin Coolidge, *The Palace of Amateurs,* Berkshire Theatre Festival, Stockbridge, MA, 1982; Ricky, *Hooters,* Hudson Guild, NY, 1982; Wishy Burke, *The Curse of an Aching Heart,* Little, NY, 1982; Leslie, *The Hostage,* Longwharf, New Haven, CT, 1983.

PAUL McCRANE

Photograph by Jack Mitchell

FILM DEBUT—Young Patient, *Rocky II,* 1979. FILM APPEARANCES—Montgomery, *Fame,* 1980; Brenner, *Purple Hearts,* 1984; Frank Berry, *The Hotel New Hampshire,* 1984. TELEVISION DEBUT—Joey Rodick, *Death Penalty,* 1979. TELEVISION APPEARANCES—Bobby Moore, *And Baby Comes Home,* 1980; Preacher, *We're Fighting Back,* 1981; Iggy Vile, *Moving Right Along,* 1982; George Nicholas, *Nurse—Fevers,* 1982.

AWARDS: Joseph Jefferson Award nomination, Best Supporting Actor, *Landscape of the Body,* 1977; Youth in Entertainment Award, Best Young Disc Artist, 1980; Grammy Award nomination, Best Motion Picture Album, *Fame,* 1981.

SIDELIGHTS: MEMBERSHIPS—AEA; SAG; AFTRA; Amnesty International.

"My favorite role, to date, is Leslie Alan Williams in Brendan Behan's *The Hostage;* my motivation: Uta Hagen and her book, *Respect for Acting.*"

ADDRESS: Agent—Hesseltine-Baker, 165 W. 46th Street, New York, NY 10036; The Artist's Agency, 10,000 Santa Monica Boulevard, Los Angeles, CA 90067.

* * *

McDONALD, Tanny, actress and singer

PERSONAL: Born February 13, 1940, in Princeton, IN;

TANNY MCDONALD

daughter of Douglas Hewitt (a lawyer) and Irene Elizabeth (Codding) McDonald; married Robert David Currie, March 5, 1966. EDUCATION: Vassar College, B.A.; Ecole de Beaux Arts, Fontainebleau, France; Hunter College Opera Workshop; trained for the stage at H/B Studio with Uta Hagen.

CAREER: Member of American Savoyards, performing complete Gilbert and Sullivan repertoire, Jan Hus Theatre, New York, 1960. BROADWAY DEBUT—Fredel, *Fiddler on the Roof,* Imperial, 1964. PRINCIPAL STAGE APPEARANCES—Gypsy Mother, *Carricknabauna,* Greenwich Mews Theater, New York, 1967; Ruth, *The Homecoming,* Hudson Valley Repertory, 1968; Rosemary, *How to Succeed in Business Without Really Trying,* Williamstown, MA, 1968; Agnes, *Brand,* Cubicle, New York, 1971; Jenny Diver, *The Beggars' Opera,* Chelsea Theatre Center, New York, 1972; Elizabeth Edwards, *The Lincoln Mask,* Plymouth, 1972; Constance Fletcher, *The Mother of Us All,* Lenox Art Festival, 1972; Isabelle Rimbaud, *Total Eclipse,* Chelsea Theatre Center, New York, 1974; Penelope, *Happy Birthday, Wanda June,* Baltimore Center Stage, 1974; Sharon, *Finian's Rainbow,* Penn State Festival Theatre, 1974; Lili Vanesi, *Kiss Me, Kate,* Penn State Festival Theatre, 1974; Whore Mother, *Gorky,* American Place, New York, 1975; Betty Dullfeet, *Arturo Ui,* Clarisse, *When You Comin' Back, Red Ryder?,* A Contemporary Theatre, Seattle, 1975; Abbie, *Desire Under the Elms,* A Contemporary Theatre, Seattle, 1976; Cyprienne, *Let's Get a Divorce,* Virginia Museum Theatre, 1978; Desiree, *A Little Night Music,* Penn State Festival Theatre, 1977; Agnes, *The Fourposter,* Alaska Repertory, 1978; Hadley Hemingway, *Clothes for a Summer Hotel,* Cort, New York, 1979; Widowed Mother, *Don Juan Comes Back from*

the War, Manhattan Theatre Club, New York, 1979; Pirate Jenny, *Threepenny Opera,* Penn State Festival Theatre, 1979; Woman II, *Side by Side by Sondheim,* Virginia Museum Theatre, 1979; Anna Held, *Tintypes,* Cincinnati Playhouse, 1981, and Actors' Theatre of Louisville, 1982; Gladys, *A Lesson from Aloes,* Cincinnati Playhouse, 1982; Mrs. Saunders/Betty, *Cloud Nine,* Alley Theatre, Houston, TX, 1983; Vera, *Pal Joey,* Penn State Festival Theatre; Chelsea, *On Golden Pond,* Alaska Repertory; Louka, *Arms and the Man,* Loretto-Hilton Theatre, St. Louis, MO; *The Dining Room,* Huntington Theatre, Boston; *Gogol,* New York Shakespeare Festival; worked with Counterpoint Theatre, 1976–79. MAJOR TOURS—Grandma Tzeitel, *Fiddler on the Roof,* 1966; Sally Thomas, *Signpost to Murder,* 1970; Mrs. Malloy, *Hello Dolly,* 1972.

FILM DEBUT—Juno, *Hercules in New York,* 1969. PRINCIPLE FILMS—*The Father; The Gardner.* TELEVISION DEBUT—Iris Fonteyn, *The Doctors.* TELEVISION APPEARANCES—Lydia Wilton, *Duty Bound;* Lady Macbeth, *Macbeth;* Lady Bird Johnson, *Kennedy.*

AWARDS: Reid Hall Fellowship for study of music in Paris, France, 1959.

SIDELIGHTS: MEMBERSHIPS—AEA, AFTRA, SAG.

''My early years were spent training as a classical pianist (Nadia Boulanger, Jean Doyen, Jean Casadesus; master classes under Artur Rubenstein and Robert Casadesus), culminating in two Paris recitals. Vocal study in New York (Hunter College Opera Workshop, William Weibel of Metropolitan Opera, Olga Ryss) led to New York performances as Pamina and Papagena in *The Magic Flute,* and as Musetta in *La Boheme.* I went into theatre to do the classics. I would read a play and say to myself, 'I know that person. I can show you who she is.' I believe in the joy of live theatre: of actually being out there doing it; of developing the skills to do it—body, voice, intellect, experience. Whenever I don't get a part I covet, I go back to the drawing board, and I take pride and pleasure in moving back and forth between straight drama and musicals, applying the techniques and skills of one to the other.''

ADDRESS: Home—125 W. 96th Street, New York, NY 10025; Agent—c/o Jim Wilhelm, 35 W. 96th Street, New York, NY 10025.

* * *

McDONOUGH, Jerome, writer, composer, and director

PERSONAL: Born November 2, 1946, in Seguin, TX; son of Jerome Charles (a college professor) and Dorothy Ann (a draftsman; maiden name Munson) McDonough; married Raenell Roberts (a keyboard performer), December 21, 1969; children: Brian Christopher. EDUCATION: West Texas State University, B.S., 1968, M.A., 1972. POLITICS: Democrat. RELIGION: Catholic. MILITARY: U.S. Army reserve, 1968–74. NON-THEATRICAL CAREER: Worked for the Pioneer Corporation 1969–71 as editor of *The Jet* and assistant to the director of publications and information. Teacher/coordinator of creative writing workshops at Amarillo College, TX,

1970–81. Teacher of theatre arts and English at Caprock School since 1970.

WRITINGS: PLAYS, PUBLISHED—*The Betrothed*, 1972; *Filiation*, 1973; *Transceiver*, 1974; *Fables*, 1974; *The Old Oak Encounter*, 1974; *A Short Stretch at the Galluses* (adapted from the musical *A Stretch at the Galluses* co-authored with John Gibson), 1974; *Asylum*, 1975; *Dirge*, 1975; *The Noble's Reward*, 1975; *Requiem*, 1977; *Eden*, 1978; *O, Little Town*, 1978; *Stages*, 1979; *It's Sad, So Sad When an Elf Goes Bad*, 1979; *Plots*, 1981; *The Nearest Star*, 1981; *Juvie*, 1982; *Roomers*, 1983; *The Least of These*, 1983; *A Christmas Carol* (adapted from Charles Dickens) 1976. Contributor to periodicals, including *Writer's Digest, The Dramatists Guild Quarterly*, and *Prolog*.

AWARDS: Winner, Texas Educational Theatre Association Playwriting Contest, 1977 (*Asylum*) and 1979 (*Eden*); *Asylum* named number five, International Thespian Society List of Most-Produced Short Plays; *Juvie* included in *The Best Short Plays of 1984*.

SIDELIGHTS: MEMBERSHIPS—Dramatists Guild. HOBBIES—Music performance (voice, guitar, drums, synthesizers) and composition (some theatre pieces, some Praise, rock, pop, country, and folk), multi-track recording, and computers (word processing).

''I suppose I love theatre because I believe in the shortest possible distance between cause and effect. I want to help create an emotion and feel it bounce off another human being with no time and very little space intervening. Theatre can create a marvelous closeness. . . . My influences or, more accurately, my heroes range from Thornton Wilder to Tennessee Williams to Arthur Miller to Kaufmann and Hart to Mary Chase to Samuel Beckett to Grotowski and Schechner to Brecht to Edward Albee to Neil Simon to Jack Douglas. If there is some commonality in that list, I fail to perceive it. People who have personally touched my career include my teachers, Loula Grace Erdman, Kathleen Cook, Dr. A. K. Knott, and William Angus Moore; my parents, classical theatre man Jerome Charles McDonough and all-time compassion model Dorothy Ann Munson McDonough; editors William Talbot, Kay Myerly, and Shubert Fendrich and, perhaps most critically of all, editor/publisher/stupidity detector I. E. Clark, a close, close friend. . . . Composer/buddy John Gibson has alternately helped and distorted my perspective, whichever was needed at the time. John's wife, Dana Adams Gibson, and my wife, Raenell McDonough, have inspired me with both encouragement and occasional astonishing observations. Dr. Daniel Schwartz knows more about Broadway than I will ever learn, but he has been willing to share. A recently met friend, director Jane Armitage, promises to be a lifelong wonder. . . . More and more I now aspire toward commercial professional productions. I would very much like to be part of the Broadway/Off-Broadway/Regional Theatre realm and am attempting steps in those directions. . . . Mostly, I never want to be far from a space where theatre is actively evolving. If the words keep coming, perhaps I'll be allowed to help mold that theatre.''

ADDRESS: Home—6106 Dartmouth, Amarillo, TX 79109.

McGILL, Everett Charles, III, actor

PERSONAL: Born October 21, 1945, in Miami Beach, FL; son of Everett Charles and Ollie Dell (McKinzie) McGill, Jr. EDUCATION: University of Missouri at Kansas City, graduated 1968; attended Kansas City Conservatory of Music, 1966, 1967, 1968; prepared for the stage at the Royal Academy of Dramatic Art, London, with June Kemp, Robert Palmer, and Eve Shapiro; studied at HB Studios, New York City, with Uta Hagen.

CAREER: DEBUT—Isaac, *The Father*, New York, 1971. PRINCIPAL STAGE APPEARANCES—Sandy, *Brothers*, Theatre Four, 1972; Ryabsov, *Enemies*, Repertory Theatre of Lincoln Center, New York, 1972; Nugget, *Equus*, Plymouth, New York, 1974; Dale Laverty, *A Texas Trilogy*, John F. Kennedy Center for the Performing Arts, Washington, DC, 1976, and Broadhurst, New York, 1976; Alfred, *Home*, Long Wharf, New Haven, CT, 1976; Dunois, *St. Joan*, Long Wharf, 1977; Lorenzo, *The Merchant*, Forrest Theatre, Philadelphia, John F. Kennedy Center, Washington, DC, and Plymouth, New York, 1977; Riverton, *Rosa*, St. Clement's, New York, 1978; Butterworth, *Dracula*, Martin Beck, New York, 1978–79; David Scott, *Whose Life Is it Anyway?*, Golden, New York, 1980.

FILM DEBUT—*Yanks*, 1979. PRINCIPAL FILMS—*Brubaker*, 1980; *Quest for Fire*, 1982; *Dune*. TELEVISION APPEARANCES—Ryabsov, *Enemies* (for NET's *Theatre in America* series), 1974; Chad Richards, *The Guiding Light*, 1975–76.

SIDELIGHTS: Leader of Dell-Shays Rhythm and Blues Band, Kansas City, KS, 1964–67.

* * *

McGUIRE, Mitch (ne Walter), actor, director, and producer

PERSONAL: Born December 26, 1936, in Chicago, IL; son of James Edward (a cab driver) and Ruth (a bookeeper; maiden name, Casserly) McGuire; married Linda Fowler, October 31, 1971 (divorced 1975); married Cathryn Williams (a dancer and teacher), September 25, 1982; children: Michael Kelli and Lauri. EDUCATION: Attended Santa Monica City College and Goodman Memorial Drama School. POLITICS: Democrat. RELIGION: Protestant. MILITARY: U.S. Coast Guard, 1956–58.

CAREER: DEBUT—Manager, *Six Characters in Search of an Author*, Old Globe Theater, San Diego, CA, 1963. NEW YORK DEBUT—Ernst, *The Rapist*, Gate Theater, 1965, 36 performances. PRINCIPAL STAGE APPEARANCES—Major Domo, *Tom Paine*, Stage 73, New York, 1968; Ben, *Waiting for Lefty*, Roundabout, New York, 1968; Poet, *La Ronde*, Syracuse Stage, 1973; Conventioneer, *Red Devil Battery Sign*, Shubert, Boston, MA, 1975; at the Manhattan Punch line—Frank Feelings, *Flagship*, Snooks, *The Vegetable*, 1979; Tommy, *The Male Animal*, 1980; Mack, *The Butter and Egg Man*, 1982; Mike Crowbar, *What's So Funny?*, 1983. MAJOR TOURS—Bill, *Natural Ingredients*, East Coast cities, 1971; Ben, *Sunshine Boys*, Ohio and Arizona cities, 1976.

MITCH MCGUIRE

FILM DEBUT—Horace William, *Too Far to Go*, 1981. TELEVISION DEBUT—Anesthetist, *The Doctors and Nurses*, 1966. PRINCIPAL TELEVISION APPEARANCES—Agent, *FBI Today; Ritz Newsiola; The Guiding Light; Search for Tomorrow; All My Children; One Life to Live; The Doctors.*

RELATED THEATRICAL CAREER—Co-Founder and Executive Director, Manhattan Punch Line Theater, New York, 1979–present.

SIDELIGHTS: MEMBERSHIPS—Players Club. HOBBIES—"Fixing things."

ADDRESS: Office—Manhattan Punch Line, 410 W. 42nd Street, New York, NY 10036. Agent—c/oTRH, 2 Dag Hamarskjold Plaza, New York, NY 10017.

* * *

McHENRY, Don (ne Donald Evan McHenry, Jr.), actor

PERSONAL: Born February 25, 1908, in Paterson, NJ; son of Donald Evan (an engineer) and Elizabeth Ellen (Evans) McHenry. EDUCATION: Rutgers University College of Pharmacy, Ph.G., 1926; Carleton College, B.A., 1929; prepared for the stage at the New York School of Theatre and studied with Elizabeth B. Grimball. POLITICS: Independent. MILITARY: U.S. Army, 1942–45.

NON-THEATRICAL CAREER: Worked as a pharmacist before becoming an actor.

CAREER: DEBUT—Summer productions at the Maverick Theatre, Woodstock, NY, 1935–37. NEW YORK DEBUT—Murray Tserk, *Don't Throw Glass Houses*, Vanderbilt, 1938. PRINCIPAL STAGE APPEARANCES—Porter, *The Tower Beyond Tragedy*, ANTA, New York, 1950; for the Broadway Chapel Players, 1951–53: Fool, *The Hour Glass*, Tobit, *Tobias and the Angel*, Captain, *Thunder Rock*, *In April Once;* Captain Fox Reddleman, *Venus Observed*, New Century, 1952; Herbert Reedbeck, *Venus Observed*, Ann Arbor Drama Festival, 1952; Ezekiel Cheever, *The Crucible*, Martin Beck, New York, 1953; M. Brun, *Fanny*, Majestic, New York, 1954; Mayor Slade, *Destry Rides Again*, Imperial, New York, 1959; Mr. Perpetua, *The Cantilevered Terrace*, 41st Street Theatre, New York, 1962; Girl's Father, *The Fantasticks*, Goodspeed Opera House, East Haddam, CT, 1963; Senator Canfield, *The Child Buyer*, Professional Theatre Program, University of Michigan, 1964; Harold Haskell, *Watch the Birdie*, 1964; Ulysses, *Tiger at the Gates*, Theatre of the Living Arts, Philadelphia, 1965; with Pennsylvania State University Festival of Professional Theatre, 1965: Lord Hastings in *Richard III*, the Doctor in *The Skin of Our Teeth*, and Monsewer in *The Hostage;* Mr. Lundy, *Brigadoon*, Pabst Theatre, Milwaukee, WI, 1965–66; Tutor, *Medea*, Music Theatre, Houston, 1966; Lord Burleigh, *Elizabeth the Queen*, City Center, New York, 1966; Old John, *A Cry of the Players*, Berkshire Theatre Festival, Stockbridge, MA, 1968, and at the Vivian Beaumont Theatre, New York, 1968–69; Gentleman/Brother Superior, *Hunger and Thirst*, Berkshire Theatre Festival, 1969; *A Passage to E. M. Forster*, Berkshire Theatre Festival, 1970; Lord Bishop of Durham, *Vivat! Vivat Regina!*, Broadhurst, New York, 1972; Sen. Thaddeus Jones, *A Conflict of Interest*, U.R.G.E.N.T. Theatre, 1973. Tutor, *Medea:* National Theatre, 1947, City Center, New York, 1949, U.S. State Department Productions, Hebbel Theatre, Berlin, Germany, 1951, Sarah Bernhardt Theatre, Paris, France, 1956, Clarence Brown Theatre, University of Tennessee, 1982, Kennedy Center, Washington, D.C., 1982, and Cort Theatre, New York, 1982. MAJOR TOURS—Ashley, *White Cargo*, 1941; M. Brun, *Fanny*, 1957; Karl Miller, *Kind Sir*, 1963–64; Mr. Brownlow, *Oliver!*, 1966; Tragic Gentleman, *Jacobowsky and the Colonel*, 1967; Justice Worthy, *Lock Up Your Daughters*, 1968; Polonius, *Hamlet*, 1970–71.

PRINCIPAL FILMS—Dr. Lappe, *The Three Days of the Condor*, 1974. TELEVISION DEBUT—*The Milton Berle Show*, 1948. TELEVISION APPEARANCES—*Skylark*, 1950; *Abe Lincoln in Illinois*, 1950; *Berkeley Square*, 1950; *Return of Edward Bernard*, 1952; *Hallmark Hall of Fame*, 1954; *Robert Montgomery Presents*, 1954; *U.S. Steel Hour*, 1954; *Studio One*, 1954; *Excursion*, 1954; *Medea*, 1954; *Bernadette*, 1960; *The Secret Storm*, 1960–63; *Route 66*, 1963; *The Nurses*, 1964; *The Defenders*, 1964; *The Edge of Night*, 1966–69; *The Crucible*, 1967; *Directions*, 1967–70; *Neither Are We Enemies (Hallmark Hall of Fame)*, 1970; *The Guiding Light*, 1974; Bent, *The Chinese Prime Minister (Hollywood Television Theatre)*, 1974; Sir Cotterell Dormen, *The Adams Chronicles*, 1975; Tutor, *Medea*, Kennedy Center Tonight, 1982.

SIDELIGHTS: MEMBERSHIPS—AEA; AFTRA; SAG.

ADDRESS: Home—247 W. Tenth Street, New York, NY 10014.

* * *

McINERNEY, Bernie , actor

PERSONAL: Born December 4, 1936, in Wilmington, DE; son of Bernard (an auditor) and Kathryn (Gallagher) McInerney; married Leilani Johnson (an actress and singer); children: Kathleen Clare, Bernard Joseph. EDUCATION: University of Delaware, B.A.; Catholic University of America, M.F.A. RELIGION: Catholic.

CAREER: DEBUT—Russian Ambassador, *Romanoff and Juliet*, Adelphi Summer Playhouse, Garden City, NY, 1960. NEW YORK DEBUT—James, *That Championship Season*, Booth, 1972. LONDON DEBUT—James, *That Championship Season*, Garrick, 1974. PRINCIPAL STAGE APPEARANCES— JoJo, *Curse of an Aching Heart*, New York; Ted Quinn, *The American Clock*, Clurman Theatre and Spoleto Festival, Charleston, SC; Sergeant Cokes, *Streamers*, New York; *How He Lied to Her Husband*, Roundabout, New York; *Winners*, Roundabout, New York; Wally, *Losing Time*, Manhattan Theatre Club; Fran Hogan, *Father Dreams*, Ensemble Studio Theatre, New York; Petruchio, *The Taming of the Shrew*, The White House, Washington, D.C. (invitational performance). Appeared in summer stock productions for 10 seasons at the Olney Theatre, Olney, MD; for five seasons at the Nutmeg Playhouse, Storrs, CT; and at the Wagon Wheel Playhouse, Warsaw, IN. MAJOR TOURS— Harry, *Company;* James, *That Championship Season;* toured the United States, Europe, and Canada for three seasons with the National Players, performing the works of Shakespeare.

FILM DEBUT—Dick Lederhouse, *So Fine*, 1982. PRINCIPAL FILMS—Johnson, *Trading Places;* Dr. Weber, *King of the Gypsies;* Dr. Neuman, *The Natural.* TELEVISION DEBUT— Mark Faraday, *Edge of Night*, 1975. TELEVISION APPEARANCES—*Police Story; Hustling; One Life to Live; Ryan's Hope; Johnny We Hardly Knew Ye; Eischied; O'Malley; As the World Turns; The Andros Targets; All My Children; Sanctuary of Fear; Rocking-Chair Rebellion; Fighting Back; Guiding Light; Today's FBI; Search for Tomorrow; Another World; Ethel Is an Elephant.*

THEATRE-RELATED CAREER: Actor-in-residence, director, and teacher at Holy Cross College, 1968–70.

ADDRESS: Agent—c/o Henderson/Hogan, 200 W. 57th Street, New York, NY 10019.

* * *

McKAYLE, Donald, choreographer, director

PERSONAL: Born July 6, 1930 in New York, NY; son of Philip Augustus and Eva Wilhelmina (Cohen) McKayle; married Esta Beck in 1955 (divorced 1964); married Lea Levin (nee Lea Vivante; a designer) on May 9, 1965. EDUCATION: City College of New York, 1947–49.

CAREER: PRINCIPAL STAGE WORK, DIRECTOR/CHOREOGRAPHER—*Free and Easy*, NY, 1961; *Trumpets of the Lord*, NY, 1963; *Black New World*, London, England, 1967; *Raisin*, Arena Stage, Washington, DC, 1973; *Raisin*, NY, 1974; *Dr. Jazz*, NY, 1975; *The Last Minstrel Show*, NY, 1978; *Evolution of the Blues*, Westwood Playhouse, LA/Drury Lane, Chicago, 1978–79; *My Heart Belongs to Daddy*, Israel, 1979; *Sophisticated Ladies*, NY, 1981.

CHOREOGRAPHER—*The Tempest, Anthony and Cleopatra, As You Like It*, NY Shakespeare Festival, 1963–64; *Golden Boy*, NY, 1964; *A Time for Singing*, NY, 1966; *The Four Musketeers*, London, England, 1967; *I'm Solomon*, NY, 1968; *Mass*, Mark Taper Forum, Los Angeles, CA. 1972.

PRINCIPAL FILM WORK, CHOREOGRAPHER—*The Great White Hope*, 1968; *Bed Knobs and Broomsticks*, 1970; *Charlie and the Angel*, 1972; *The Minstrel Man*, 1975–76; *Cindy*, 1977; *The Jazz Singer*, 1980. PRINCIPAL TELEVISION WORK, CHOREOGRAPHER—*The Fred Waring Show*, (Jungle Drums), 1952; *Rainbow Round My Shoulder*, 1959; *Her Name Was Moses*, 1960; *District Storyville* (Toronto), 1963; *Exploring*, 1964; *Amahl and the Night Visitors*, 1964; *Dance USA*, 1965; *Sounds of Summer*, 1965; *Fanfare*, 1965; *The Strolling Twenties*, 1965; *Ten Blocks on the Camino Real*, 1966; *Black New World*, 1967; *The Bill Cosby Special*, 1967; *The Ed Sullivan Show*, 1967–68; *The Second Bill Cosby Special*, 1968; *T.C.B.* (Motown Special), 1968; *Soul*, 1968; *And Beautiful*, 1969; *The Leslie Uggams Show*, 1969; *Dick Van Dyke and the Other Woman*, 1969; *The Hollywood Palace*, 1969; *The 43rd Annual Academy Awards Show*, 1970; *The Super Comedy Bowl*, 1971; *A Funny Thing Happened on the Way to a Special*, 1972; *The New Bill Cosby Show*, 1972–73; *The Grammy Award Show*, 1973; *Black Omnibus*, 1973; *Good Times* (director), 1974; *Free to Be You and Me*, 1974; *The 49th Annual Academy Awards Show*, 1976; *The Minstrel Man*, 1976; *The Mad, Mad, Mad, Mad, World of the Super Bowl*, 1977; *The Richard Pryor Special*, 1977; *Komedy Tonight*, 1977; *Cindy*, 1978; *The Annual Emmy Awards Show*, 1979.

PRINCIPAL BALLET AND CONCERT WORK, CHOREOGRAPHER— *Out of Chrysalis*, Julliard Dance Theatre, 1958; *One-Two-Three, Follow Me*, Merry-Go-Rounders, 1962; *Daughters of the Garden*, Bat-Sheva Company (Israel), 1964; *Nocturn*, Bat-Sheva Company, 1965; *Daughters of the Garden*, Harkness Ballet Company of NY, 1965; *Nocturn*, Repertory Dance Theatre, 1968; *Games*, Gloria Newman Dance Company, 1970; *Rainbow Round My Shoulder*, Alvin Ailey City Center Dance Theatre, 1972; *Games*, Ballet Hispanico, 1975; *Games*, Repertory Dance Theatre, 1975; *Games*, Alvin Ailey City Center Dance Theatre, 1975; *Blood Memories*, Alvin Ailey City Center Dance Theatre, 1976; *Album Leaves*, Bat-Sheva Company, 1977; *Variations on a Summer's Theme*, Dancemakers (Toronto), 1979; *District of Storyville*, Alvin Ailey City Center Dance Theatre, 1979. PRINCIPAL REVIEW WORK, CHOREOGRAPHER—*Harry Belafonte*, 1957; *Rita Moreno*, 1958/1978; *Helen Gallagher*, 1960; *The Supremes*, 1972; *The Temptations*, 1974; *Robert Decormier Singers*, 1957; *Aretha Franklin*, 1979/1980.

THEATRE-RELATED CAREER: Faculty Member—Julliard School of Music, Bennington College, Sarah Lawrence College, California Institute of the Arts, Martha Graham School of Contemporary Dance, Neighborhood Playhouse, Bard College, Connecticut College, University of Oregon, Inner City

Cultural Center, International Sommerakademie Destanz, Rubin Academy of Music (Jerusalem), University of Washington; Founder/Director, Donald McKayle Dance Company, 1951–68.

WRITINGS: BOOKS—*The Dance Has Many Faces: Modern Dance—7 Points of View*.

SIDELIGHTS: MEMBERSHIPS—Board of Directors: The New Dance Group, NY, Clarke Center for the Performing Arts, NY, Society of Stage Directors and Choreographers, Modern Dance Foundation, Hackensack, NJ, The Dance Circle, Boston, MA, National Center for Afro-American Artists, Roxbury, MA, National Endowment for the Arts Dance Panel; National Arts Awards, Dance Panel; The Dramatists Guild; Association of American Dance Companies; Black Academy of Arts and Letters; Directors Guild of America; ASCAP; AEA; AGMA; AFTRA; AGVA.

ADDRESS: Home—3839 Davana Road, Sherman Oaks, CA 91423.

* * *

McKELLEN, Ian, actor, director

PERSONAL: Born May 25, 1939, in Burnley, England; son of Denis Murray (a civil engineer) and Margery Lois (Sutcliffe) McKellen. EDUCATION: Bolton School, Lancashire; St. Catherine's College, Cambridge, B.A., 1961.

CAREER: DEBUT—Roper, *A Man for All Seasons*, Belgrade, Coventry, 1961. LONDON DEBUT—Godfrey, *A Scent of Flowers*, Duke of York's, 1964. NEW YORK DEBUT—Leonidik, *The Promise*, Henry Miller's, 1967. PRINCIPAL STAGE APPEARANCES—Repertory, including title roles in *Henry V* and *Luther*, 1962–63; repertory, including Aufidius, *Coriolanus*, Arthur Seaton, *Saturday Night and Sunday Morning*, title role, *Sir Thomas More*, Nottingham, U.K. 1963–64; Claudio, *Much Ado About Nothing*, Protestant Evangelist, *Armstrong's Last Goodnight*, Capt. de Foenix, *Trelawny of the Wells*, National Theatre Company, Chichester Festival, U.K. 1965; Alvin, *A Lily in Little India*, Hampstead, then St. Martin's, U.S. 1965–66; Andrew Cobham, *Their Very Own* and *Golden City*, Royal Court, U.K. 1966; title role, *O'Flaherty*, Mermaid, U.K. 1966; title role, *VC* and Bonaparte, *The Man of Destiny*, Mermaid, U.K. 1966; Leonodik, *The Promise*, Oxford Playhouse, 1966, then Fortune, U.K. 1967; Tom, *The White Liars* and Harold Gorringe, *Black Comedy*, Lyric, London, 1968; Pentheus, *The Bacchae*, Liverpool Playhouse, 1969; Darkly, *Billy's Last Stand*, Theatre Upstairs, U.K. 1970; title role, *Hamlet*, Prospect Theatre Company, Cambridge, U.K. 1971; Svetovidov, *Swan Song*, Crucible, Sheffield (inaugural production), U.K. November 1971; Michael, *The Wood Demon*, Footman, *The Way of the World, Knots*, Edgar, *King Lear*, Edinburgh Festival, U.K., and Brooklyn Academy of Music, NY, 1973; same plays plus *Giovanni*, Wimbledon, U.K., 1974; title role, *Dr. Faustus*, Royal Shakespeare Company, Edinburgh Festival then Aldwych, London, 1974; title role, *The Marquis of Keith*, Aldwych, U.K., 1974;

Philip the Bastard, *King John*, Aldwych, U.K., 1975; Colin, *Ashes*, Young Vic, U.K., 1975; Aubrey Bagot, *Too True to*

Be Good, Royal Shakespeare Company (RSC), Globe, U.K., 1975; Romeo, *Romeo and Juliet*, Leontes, *The Winter's Tale*, title role *Macbeth* (The Other Place), Stratford, U.K., 1976; solo show, *Words, Words, Words*, Edinburgh Festival, 1977; title role, *Macbeth*, RSC, Face, *The Alchemist* (The Other Place), Stratford, U.K., 1977; Alex, *Every Good Boy Deserves Favor*, Festival Hall, U.K., 1977; solo show, *Acting Shakespeare*, Edinburgh Festival, 1977; Romeo, Karsten Bernick, *Pillars of the Community*, Face, Langevin, *Days of the Commune*, Aldwych, U.K., 1977–78; Sir Toby, *Twelfth Night*, Andrei, *The Three Sisters*, RSC, 1978; Max, *Bent*, Royal Court, then Criterion, U.K., 1979; Salieri, *Amadeus*, Broadhurst, NY, 1980; *Cowardice*, Ambassadors, 1983; Pierre, *Venice Preserv'd*, Platonov, *Wild Honey*, title role, *Coriolanus*, National Theatre, 1984.

MAJOR TOURS—Title role, *Richard II*, Prospect Theatre, 1968; *Richard II*, title role, *Edward the Second*, Prospect, including the Mermaid and the Picadilly (both London), 1969; Capt. Plume, *The Recruiting Officer*, Cpl. Hill, *Chips with Everything*, Cambridge Theatre Company, 1971; Giovanni, *'Tis Pity She's a Whore*, Page-Boy, *Ruling the Roost*, Prince Yoremitsu, *The Three Arrows*, Actors Company, Edinburgh Festival and subsequent tour, 1972; *Acting Shakespeare*, Israel, Scandinavia, Spain, France, Cyprus, Romania, Los Angeles and the Ritz, NY, 1980–83.

DIRECTED—Plays: *The Prime of Miss Jean Brodie*, Liverpool Playhouse, 1969; *The Erpingham Camp*, Palace, Watford, U.K., 1972; *A Private Matter*, Vaudeville, London, 1973; *The Clandestine Marriage*, Savoy, London, 1975; RSC small-scale tour, including *Twelfth Night* and *The Three Sisters* in which he also appeared, 1978.

FILM APPEARANCES—*Alfred the Great*, 1969; *A Touch of Love*, 1969; *The Promise*, 1969; *Prince of Love*, 1981; *The Scarlet Pimpernel*, 1982; *The Keep*, 1983.

TELEVISION APPEARANCES—*David Copperfield; Ross; Hedda Gabler; Macbeth; Every Good Boy Deserves Favor; Walter; Acting Shakespeare*, 1982.

AWARDS: Antoinette Perry Award, New York Drama League Award, Outer Critics Circle Award, 1981: *Amadeus;* Antoinette Perry Award Nomination, 1984: *Acting Shakespeare;* Drama Desk Award, 1983: *Acting Shakespeare;* Clarence Derwent Award, 1964: *The Promise;* "Plays and Players" Award for most promising actor, 1976; Actor of the Year, *Macbeth*, 1976; Society of West End Theatres Awards for *Pillars of the Community*, 1977, *The Alchemist*, 1978 and Max in *Bent*, 1979.

SIDELIGHTS: Mr. McKellen was awarded the C.B.E. in 1979 and was made an Honorary Fellow of St. Catherine's College, Cambridge, 1982. His one-man show, *Acting Shakespeare*, was scripted by himself.

ADDRESS: Agent—James Sharkey, 90 Regent Street, London W1, England.

* * *

McKENZIE, Julia, actress, director, singer

PERSONAL: Married Jerry Harte (an actor), 1972. EDUCA-

TION: Trained for the theatre at the Guildhall School of Music in London.

CAREER: LONDON DEBUT—*Maggie May,* Adelphi, 1966. NEW YORK DEBUT—*Side by Side by Sondheim,* Music Box, 1977. PRINCIPAL STAGE APPEARANCES—Gloria, *Mame,* Drury Lane, London, 1969; April, *Company,* Her Majesty's, London, 1971; Girl in Owl Coat, *Promises, Promises,* Prince of Wales, London, 1970; Principal Woman, *Cowardly Custar,* Mermaid, London, 1973; Principal Woman, *Cole,* Mermaid, 1974; Lily, *On the Twentieth Century,* Her Majesty's, London, 1980; Adelaide, *Guys and Dolls,* National, London, 1982; others.

TELEVISION DEBUT—*Fame Is the Spur,* BBC. TELEVISION APPEARANCES—*Song by Song. . .,* NET.

SIDELIGHTS: Because of a conflict of names with an American actress, registered with Actors Equity Association, Ms. McKenzie was billed in the United States as Julie N. McKenzie.

ADDRESS: Agent—April Young, 31 Kings Road, London, SW 3, England.

* * *

McMAHON, Ed, announcer, actor

PERSONAL: Born March 6, 1923 in Detroit, MI; son of Edward Leo (a fund-raiser) and Eleanor (Russell) McMahon; married Alyce Furrel on July 5, 1945 (divorced 1976); married Victoria Valentine, on March 6, 1976; children: Claudia, Michael, Linda, Jeffrey. EDUCATION: Catholic University, Washington, DC, B.A. (Speech and Drama). RELIGION: Roman Catholic. MILITARY: Naval Aviation Cadet, U.S. Marine Corps Avaition, retired Colonel.

CAREER: DEBUT—College productions at Catholic University. NEW YORK DEBUT—*The Impossible Years,* 1965.

FILM DEBUT—*The Incident,* 1966. PRINCIPAL FILM APPEARANCES—*Fun with Dick and Jane; Slaughter's Big Rip Off; The Great American Traffic Jam; Starmaker: The Golden Moment; The Kid from Left Field.*

TELEVISION DEBUT—*Take Ten,* WCAU, 1949. PRINCIPAL TELEVISION APPEARANCES—Announcer, *Who Do You Trust?,* 1958; joined Johnny Carson on *The Tonight Show Starring Johnny Carson,* 1962; host, *Monitor;* host, *Star Search;* many guest appearances on major networks and commercials.

WRITINGS: BOOKS PUBLISHED—*The Bartender's Companion; Slimming Down; Here's Ed.*

AWARDS: Man of the Year, Bedside Network; Man of the Year, Marine Corps Scholarship Fund; Spirit of Life, City of Hope; Humanitarian Award, Myasthenia Gravis Foundation; Spirit of Truth Award, Advertising Club; Six Air Medals and numerous theatre of war awards.

SIDELIGHTS: MEMBERSHIPS—National VP MDA (on board of directors); board of directors, Young Musicians Foundation; board of governors, Veterans Bedside Network; honorary chairman, Myasthenia Gravis Foundation; AFTRA, SAG, AGVA. HOBBIES—boating and reading.

"My work is my avocation. I thrive on being busy. My favorite role was the aerospace chief in *Fun with Dick and Jane.* Favorite lifetime role is Johnny Carson's sidekick. Favorite TV role is host of *Star Search.*"

ADDRESS: Office—c/o Carson Productions, 3000 W. Alameda Avenue, Burbank, CA 91523. Agent—Madeline Kelly, same address.

* * *

McMILLAN, Kenneth, actor

PERSONAL: Born July 2, 1932, in Brooklyn, son of Harry (a truck driver) and Margaret McMillan; married Kathryn McDonald, June 20, 1969; children: Alison. EDUCATION: High School of the Performing Arts; trained for the theatre with Uta Hagen and Irene Dailey at HB Studios, NY. NON-THEATRICAL CAREER: Salesman, section manager, floor superintendent, Gimbel's Department Store.

CAREER: DEBUT—*Sweet Bird of Youth,* touring company, 1962. PRINCIPAL STAGE APPEARANCES—*Weekends Like Other People,* Phoenix, NY; *Red Eye of Love,* Provincetown Playhouse, NY; *King of the Whole Damned World,* Jan Hus, NY; *Little Mary Sunshine,* Players, NY; *Babes in the Wood,* Orpheum, NY; *Moonchildren,* Theatre de Lys, NY; *Henry IV, Part I,* Festival Theatre, Central Park, NY; *The Merry Wives of Windsor,* Festival Theatre, Central Park, NY; *Where Do We Go from Here?,* Public, NY; *Kid Champion,* Public, NY; *Streamers;* Mitzi Newhouse, Lincoln Center, NY; *Borstal Boy,* Lyceum, NY; *American Buffalo,* Ethel Barrymore, NY; *In the Boom Boom Room,* Long Beach, CA, 1979; *The Odd Couple,* Tiffany's Attic, Kansas City, Meadowbrook Dinner Theatre, NJ; Luther Billis, *South Pacific,* stock; Alfred Doolittle, *My Fair Lady,* stock; Charlie, *DuBarry Was a Lady,* stock; *You Never Know, A Connecticut Yankee, Oh Boy!, Oh Lady, Lady,* Goodspeed Opera House, East Haddam, CT. Also: one year Milwaukee Rep, WI, 1963; three years, Studio Arena Theatre, Buffalo, NY, 1965–69. MAJOR TOURS—*Last of the Red Hot Lovers,* five-month tour.

FILM APPEARANCES—*Serpico,* 1974; *The Taking of Pelham 1, 2, 3,* 1974; *The Stepford Wives,* 1975; *Oliver's Story,* 1978; *Blood Brothers,* 1979; *Hide in Plain Sight,* 1980; *Little Miss Marker,* 1980; *Carny,* 1980; *Borderline,* 1980; *Eyewitness,* 1981; *Whose Life Is It Anyway?,* 1981; *True Confessions,* 1981; *Ragtime,* 1981; *Heartbeeps,* 1981; *The Killing Hour; Blue Skies Again, Head Over Heels (Chilly Scenes of Winter),* 1983; *Reckless,* 1983; *Dune,* 1984; *Pope of Greenwich Village,* 1984. TELEVISION APPEARANCES—Bill Connor, *King;* Jack Doyle, *Rhoda; The Hustler of Muscle Beach; Breaking Up; Johnny We Hardly Knew Ye; Joe Dancer; Salem's Lot; A Death in Canaan; Lou Grant; The Rockford Files; Starsky and Hutch; Kojak; In the Custody of Strangers; Packin' It In; Implied Force;* Walter, *Maggie Briggs,* 1984.

ADDRESS: Agent—Henderson-Hogan, 247 S. Beverly Drive, Beverly Hills, CA 90212.

* * *

McNALLY, Terrence, playwright

PERSONAL: Born November 3, 1939, in Corpus Christi, TX; son of Hubert Arthur (a beer distributor) and Dorothy Katharine (Rapp) McNally. EDUCATION: Columbia University, 1960. NON-THEATRICAL CAREER—tutor for John Steinbeck's children on a world cruise; newspaper reporter.

CAREER: DEBUT—Le Renaud, *Le Petit Prince,* Minor Latham, Columbia University, NY, 1958; Mr. McNally also worked as a stage manager for the Actor's Studio, New York.

WRITINGS: PLAYS, PRODUCED—*Columbia Varsity Show,* 1960; *This Side of the Door,* New York Drama Workshop, 1962; *And Things That Go Bump in the Night,* Tyrone Guthrie, Minneapolis, MN, Royale, NY, 1965; *Sweet Eros, Witness, Tour, Noon, Cuba Si,* NY, 1968; *Here's Where I Belong,* Billy Rose, NY, 1968; *Next,* 1969; *Bringing It All Back Home,* LaMama, NY, 1969; *Where Has Tommy Flowers Gone?,* Yale Repertory, also in NY, 1971; *Bad Habits,* John Drew, Easthampton, NY, 1971; *Botticelli,* Old Post Office, Easthampton, NY, 1972; *Bringing It All Back Home,* Provincetown, NY, 1971; *Whiskey,* St. Clements, NY, 1973; *The Tubs,* Yale Repertory, New Haven, CT, 1974; *Bad Habits (Ravenswood/Dunelawn),* Off-Broadway, then Broadway, 1974; *The Ritz,* (revised version of *The Tubs*), Royale, NY, 1975; *Broadway, Broadway,* John Drew, Shubert-Philadelphia, Eugene O'Neill, NY, (closed in previews), 1978; *Actors and Directors,* closed out-of-town, 1982; *It's Only a Funny Play,* (revised version of *Broadway, Broadway*), Manhattan Punch Line, NY, 1983; *The Rink,* Martin Beck, NY, 1984. First-produced plays in London were *Sweet Eros* and *Next* in a double bill at the Open Space, 1971.

SCREENPLAYS—*Noon,* 1970; *The Ritz,* 1976. TELEVISION PLAYS—*Apple Pie,* 1966; *Last Gasps,* 1966; *The Five-Forty-Eight* (adaptation), 1979; *Mama Malone,* 1984. RADIO PLAYS—*The Lisbon Traviata,* 1979. BOOKS—*Five in Hand,* collection of plays, 1969. NEWSPAPER COLUMN, "Terrence McNally's Letters," published in *Wisdom's Child,* 1979.

AWARDS: Antoinette Perry Award Nominations, 1984: *The Rink,* 1975: *The Ritz;* Obie, 1974: *Bad Habits,* 1974; CBS Fellowship-Teacher at Yale; Stanley Award, NYC Writers Conference for Drama, 1962; Guggenheim Fellowship.

SIDELIGHTS: MEMBERSHIPS—Dramatists Guild (Vice-President, counsel, 1982).

ADDRESS: 218 W. Tenth Street, New York, NY 10014.*

* * *

McNAUGHTON, Stephen (ne Stephen Scott), actor

PERSONAL: Born in Denver, CO; son of Robert Ernest and

Rose Frances (Ferris) Scott; married Susan Elizabeth Scott (an actress) May 29, 1971. EDUCATION: University of Denver, B.A., 1971; trained for the stage with Uta Hagen and Wynn Handman.

CAREER: DEBUT—Joseph, *The Christmas Story,* St. Mary Magdelene Cafeteria Theater, Denver, CO, 1959. NEW YORK DEBUT—Patron from Sheridan Square, *The Ritz,* Longacre Theater, 1975, 500 performances. PRINCIPAL STAGE APPEARANCES—Levi, *Joseph and the Amazing Technicolor Dreamcoat,* New York; Narrator, *The Best Little Whorehouse in Texas,* New York; Henry Anderson, *Shenandoah,* New York; Duff/Tiger, *The Ritz,* New York; *Da,* New York; *Cheaters,* New York; Francisco/Cornelius, *Hamlet,* New York Shakespeare Festival, New York; Jeffrey, *Monsters,* Astor Place Theatre, New York; Bobby Joe, *Chase a Rainbow,* Theatre Four, New York; Joker, *Summer Brave,* Equity Library Theater, New York; Regional—Tybalt, *Romeo and Juliet;* Arviragus, *Cymbeline;* Stock—Bassanio, *The Merchant of Venice;* Valere, *Tartuffe;* Swiss Cheese, *Mother Courage and Her Children;* Geoffrey, *Something's Afoot;* Wally, *I Love My Wife.*

TELEVISION DEBUT—Brian Madison, *The Edge of Night.* PRINCIPAL TELEVISION APPEARANCES—Daniel Doggett, *Jake's Way;* Host, *Sign-On;* Gil Barrett, *All My Children.*

SIDELIGHTS: MEMBERSHIPS—Actors Equity Association, SAG, AFTRA.

"The theatre must entertain, but we working within its

STEPHEN McNAUGHTON

confines will be dilettantes until we begin to strive to enlighten.''

ADDRESS: Agent—c/o Associated Artists, 311 W. 43rd Street, New York, NY 10036.

* * *

MCQUEEN, Steve (ne Terence Stephen), actor

PERSONAL: Born March 24, 1930, Indianapolis, IN; died November 7, 1980. MILITARY: U.S. Marine Corps, 1948–50, tank driver.

CAREER: PRINCIPAL STAGE WORK—summer stock; replacement, *A Hatful of Rain.*

PRINCIPAL FILM APPEARANCES—*Somebody Up There Likes Me,* 1956; *Never Love a Stranger,* 1958; *The Great St. Louis Bank Robbery,* 1958; *The Blob,* 1958; *Never So Few,* 1959; *The Magnificent Seven,* 1960; *Hell Is for Heroes,* 1962; *The War Lover,* 1962; *Love with the Proper Stranger,* 1963; *The Great Escape,* 1963; *Baby, the Rain Must Fall,* 1965; *The Cincinnati Kid,* 1965; *Nevada Smith,* 1966; *The Sand Pebbles,* 1966; *Bullitt,* 1968; *The Thomas Crown Affair,* 1968; *The Reivers,* 1969; *Le Mans,* 1970; *Junior Bonner,* 1972; *The Getaway,* 1972; *Papillon,* 1973; *The Towering Inferno,* 1974; *Enemy of the People.*

PRINCIPAL TELEVISION APPEARANCES—star, *Wanted—Dead or Alive.**

* * *

MEACHAM, Paul (Thomas, Jr.), actor, producer

PERSONAL: Born August 5, 1939 in Memphis, TN; son of Paul Thomas, Sr. (a used car dealer) and Jessie Elizabeth (a teacher; maiden name, McDaniel) Meacham; married Lynda Patterson in November, 1962 (divorced 1970); married Patricia Anne Livesay (Assistant to Director of Subscription Department, New York City Opera/Ballet) on May 15, 1982; children: (first marriage) Katherine, (second marriage) Sarah. EDUCATION: University of Tennessee, Knoxville, B.S. (Education), M.A. (Speech and Theatre), 1958–66; Doctoral studies in Theatre, Michigan State University, 1967–69. POLITICS: Democrat. RELIGION: Methodist (inactive).

CAREER: DEBUT—Charlie Davenport, *Annie Get Your Gun,* East High School, Memphis, TN, 1958. NEW YORK DEBUT—Boss, *The Adding Machine,* WPA, for 12 performances, 1971. PRINCIPAL STAGE APPEARANCES—Menelaus, *Troilus and Cressida,* NJ Shakespeare Festival; Dr. Seward, *Count Dracula,* George Street Playhouse, New Brunswick, NJ; Paul Sycamore, *You Can't Take It with You,* Barter, VA; two seasons at Cohoes Music Hall in Cohoes, NY, roles include Charlie, *Death of a Salesman,* Father Day, *Life with Father,* Carlson, *Of Mice of Men;* Fezziwig, *A Christmas Carol,* Virginia Stage Company; Parris, *The Crucible,* Virginia Stage Company; three seasons with Milwaukee Repertory, WI, roles include Hedges, *Born Yesterday,* Fezziwig, *A Christmas Carol,* Fireman, *Lakeboat,* Ligniere, *Cyrano de*

PAUL MEACHAM

Bergerac; O'Neill Theatre Center, National Playwrights Conference—Powerman, *Ghost Dancing,* Gene, *First Draft,* Col. Troop, *Proud Flesh;* Lineman, *Lineman and Sweet Lightnin',* Kennedy Center, Washington, DC; two seasons with the Classic Stage Company, NY, roles include Antonio, *Revenger's Tragedy,* Hebble Tyson, *The Lady's Not for Burning,* Teddy, *The Homecoming,* Stubb, *Moby Dick,* Toby Belch, *Twelfth Night;* Teddy Roosevelt, *Fighting Bob,* Astor Place, NY; Dr. Seward, *The Passion Of Dracula,* Cherry Lane.

FILM DEBUT—Bill Donnelly, *Hoodlums,* 1981. PRINCIPAL FILM APPEARANCES—*Prince of the City.* PRINCIPAL TELEVISION APPEARANCES—Pete, *All My Children;* Chief Murphy, *One Life to Live;* Room Clerk, *Edge of Night;* Dr. Roberts, *The Doctors.*

WRITINGS: PLAYS, PRODUCED—*Charlatans,* a musical, WPA, NY, 1972.

THEATRE-RELATED CAREER: Television producer and director, University of Tennessee Knoxville, 1964–66; assistant director, Department of Conferences, University of Tennessee, 1966–67; instructor/director, Department of Speech/Theatre, University of Tennessee, 1969–70; instructor, Plainfield High School, NJ, 1971–75.

SIDELIGHTS: MEMBERSHIPS—Sigma Alpha Epsilon; AEA; SAG; AFTRA.

''I became a producer in 1981 with *Fighting Bob,* by Tom Cole at the Astor Place Theatre in NY; it closed after 8 previews and 8 performances.''

ADDRESS: Home—604 Jefferson Street, Hoboken, NJ 07030.

* * *

MEARA, Anne, actress, comedienne

PERSONAL: Raised on Long Island, NY; married Jerry Stiller (an actor and comic); children: Amy. EDUCATION: Apprenticed at Southold, Long Island and Woodstock, NY; studied at the Herbert Berghof Studios in New York.

CAREER: PRINCIPAL STAGE WORK—Performed with the New York Shakespeare Festival in Central Park; *Ulysses in Nighttown,* NY; *A Month in the Country,* NY; *Maedchen in Uniform,* NY; Bunny, *The House of Blue Leaves,* NY.

Principal Stiller and Meara Appearances—Compass Players, Crystal Palace, St. Louis, MO; Happy Medium, Chicago; New York—Phase Two, Village Gate, Village Vanguard, Bon Soir, The Blue Angel, the Royal Box, the Persian Room, Plaza Hotel; the Establishment, London, England; the Sands, Las Vegas, NV; Harrah's Lake Tahoe and Reno, NV; the hungry i, San Francisco; the Crescendo, Los Angeles.

PRINCIPAL FILM APPEARANCES—*Boys from Brazil; The Out-Of-Towners; Lovers and Other Strangers; Fame; Nasty Habits.*

PRINCIPAL TELEVISION APPEARANCES—*Merv Griffin Show; Ed Sullivan Show; The Corner Bar; Medical Center; The Male Menopause; Kate McShane; Rhoda;* Veronica, *Archie Bunker's Place; The Other Woman.*

WRITINGS: Television script—*The Other Woman.*

AWARDS: Emmy Nomination, (4th) Veronica, the cook, *Archie Bunker's Place;* The Voice Imagery Award, Radio Advertising Bureau.

SIDELIGHTS: "At first glance, the Stillers are a contrast: Jerry is short, pensive and retiring. Anne is tall, bubbly and beautiful. Jerry was raised in Brooklyn and his family once won the Irish Sweepstakes. Anne grew up on Long Island. She hoped from a very young age to become a Shakespearean actress. Jerry and Anne both loved acting and met on mutual territory—an agent's office. . . . They continue to sell and entertain with their hilarious commercials . . . and were recently honored by the Marketing Communications Executives International for their outstanding contributions in advertising and promotion. . . . When they discovered that ushers were making more money than themselves and the fact that they wanted to have children, and that their comedic talents were surfacing, they left the legitimate theatre to form the comedy team of Stiller and Meara."

ADDRESS: Agent—Morgan Communications, 301 W. 53rd Street, New York, NY 10019.

STEPHEN MENDILLO

MENDILLO, Stephen W., actor

PERSONAL: Born October 9, 1943; son of John C. (an M.D. and a surgeon) and Emily W. (a nurse; maiden name, Wetmore) Mendillo; married Caroline Lexow in 1964 (divorced 1972); children: Stephen, Kristen. EDUCATION: Colorado College, Colorado Springs, B.A.; Yale University, School of Drama, M.F.A.

CAREER: DEBUT—Prince Myshkin, *Subject to Fits,* Yale Repertory, New Haven, CT, 1970. NEW YORK DEBUT—Tyler, *The National Health,* Circle in the Square, for 120 performances, 1973. PRINCIPAL STAGE APPEARANCES—George, *Ah Wilderness,* Circle in the Square, NY, 1976; Marco, *A View from the Bridge,* Ambassador, NY, 1983; Martin, *Fool for Love,* Circle Repertory Company at Douglas Fairbanks, NY, 1983–84; Long Wharf, New Haven, CT: *Journey's End, The Seagull, Afore Night Come, Arturo Ui, Streamers, Cyrano de Bergerac, The Workroom;* Williamstown Theatre Festival: *Children of the Sun, Caucasian Chalk Circle, The Three Sisters, The Cherry Orchard, The Good Woman of Szechuan, Operation Sidewinder, We Bombed in New Haven;* Yale Repertory Theatre, New Haven, CT: *Macbeth, Dance of Death, Julius Caesar; All the Way Home,* McCarter Theatre Company, Princeton, NJ; *Loot,* Hartford Stage Company, CT; *Rocket to the Moon,* Indiana Repertory; *Loose Ends,* Arena Stage, Washington, DC; *Subject to Fits,* Theatre Company of Boston; *A Streetcar Named Desire,* Hartman Theatre Company; *Benefit of a Doubt,* Folger Theatre Company; Dallas Shakespeare Festival: *The Tempest, Henry IV, A Midsummer Night's Dream.*

FILM DEBUT—George, *Key West*, 1973. PRINCIPAL FILM APPEARANCES—Ahearn, *Slapshot;* football coach, *Lianna;* Adolf, *King of the Gypsies;* Babe Ruth, *The Cotton Club; Rollercoaster; The Great Gatsby; Across 110th Street; Remember My Name; Big Wednesday; Harry and Tonto.*

TELEVISION DEBUT—*Beacon Hill.* PRINCIPAL TELEVISION APPEARANCES—*Serpico;* Fred Krebs, *Another World; Delvecchio; Soap; Today's FBI;* Billy, *The Story of a Street Kid; Trackdown; Ah Wilderness.*

THEATRE-RELATED CAREER: Speech and voice teacher, Connecticut School of Broadcasting, Stratford, CT, 1980–83.

AWARDS: Oliver Thorndike Acting Award, Yale University, School of Drama, 1970.

SIDELIGHTS: MEMBERSHIPS—SAG; AEA; AFTRA; Yale Club of New York City.

ADDRESS: Home—24 Seaview Avenue, Milford, CT 06460. Agent—Bob Waters, 510 Madison Avenue, New York, NY 10019.

* * *

MERCHANT, Ismail, producer, director

PERSONAL: Born 1936, Bombay, India. EDUCATION: St. Xavier's College, Bombay; New York University M.A. (business administration). NON-FILM CAREER: Messenger, United Nations; McCann Erickson advertising agency.

CAREER: FIRST FILM WORK—*The Creation Of Woman,* NYU. PRINCIPAL FILM WORK—Formed Merchant Ivory Productions, 1961, produced: *The Householder,* 1962; *Shakespeare Wallah,* 1965; *The Guru,* 1969; *Bombay Talkie,* 1970; *Savages,* 1972; *Autobiography of a Princess,* 1975; *The Wild Party,* 1975; *Roseland,* 1977; *Hullabaloo Over Georgie and Bonnie's Pictures,* 1978; *The Europeans,* 1979; *Jane Austen in Manhattan,* 1980; *Quartet,* 1981; *Heat and Dust,* 1982; *The Bostonians,* 1984.

ADDRESS: Office—Merchant Ivory Productions Ltd., 250 W. 57th Street, Suite 1913A, New York, NY 10107.

* * *

MEREDITH, Don, sportscaster, actor

PERSONAL: Born April 10, 1938 in Mt. Vernon, TX; son of Jeffery and Hazel Meredith; married Susan S. in July 1971; children: Mary, Michael, Heather. EDUCATION: Southern Methodist University, Dallas, TX. NON-THEATRICAL CAREER: Principal quarterback, Dallas Cowboys football team.

CAREER: PRINCIPAL TELEVISION APPEARANCES—*McCloud,* 1975; *Police Story,* 1976, 1977; *Supertrain,* 1978; Movies for Television—*Banjo Jackett,* 1974; *Terror on the 40th Floor,* 1974; *Sky Heist,* 1975; *Mayday at 40,000 Feet,* 1975;

Power and Passion, 1978; *Kate Bliss and the Ticker Tape Kid,* 1978; *KKK (My Undercover Years),* 1978; *John Denver Special,* 1980; *Dinah and Friends,* 1980; *The Night the City Screamed,* 1980; *Omnibus,* 1980; *Legends of the West,* 1980; *Terror Among Us,* 1980; *Superstars,* 1981; *Country Music Awards,* 1981; *Weekend Heroes,* 1981.

THEATRE-RELATED CAREER: Co-host, *CBS Monday Night Football.*

ADDRESS: c/o Meredith Productions, Inc., P.O. Box 597, Santa Fe, NM 87501.

* * *

MERMAN, Ethel, actress, singer

PERSONAL: Born January 16, 1909, in Astoria, NY; died February 15, 1984; daughter of Edward and Agnes Zimmerman; married William B. Smith, November 16, 1940 (divorced 1941); Robert D. Levitt, (divorced); Robert F. Six, (divorced 1961); Ernest Borgnine, July 1964, (divorced). EDUCATION: Attended public schools in Long Island City, NY. NON-THEATRICAL CAREER: Secretary to President, B.K. Vacuum Booster-Brake Company.

CAREER: NEW YORK DEBUT—*Girl Crazy,* 1930. PRINCIPAL STAGE APPEARANCES—*George White's Scandals,* 1931–32; *Take a Chance,* 1932; *Anything Goes,* 1934; *Red, Hot and Blue,* 1936; *Stars in Your Eyes,* 1939; *Dubarry Was a Lady,* 1939; *Panama Hattie,* 1940; *Something for the Boys,* 1943; *Annie Get Your Gun,* 1946; *Call Me Madam,* 1950; *Happy Hunting,* 1956; *Gypsy,* 1959; *Hello Dolly,* 1970.

PRINCIPAL FILM APPEARANCES—*We're Not Dressing,* 1934; *Kid Millions,* 1934; *The Big Broadcast,* 1935; *Strike Me Pink,* 1936; *Anything Goes,* 1936; *Happy Landing,* 1938; *Alexanders Ragtime Band,* 1938; *Straight; Place and Show; Stage Door Canteen,* 1943; *Call Me Madam,* 1953; *No Business Like Show Business,* 1954; *Gypsy,* 1963; *It's a Mad, Mad, Mad, Mad World,* 1963; *Won Ton Ton,* 1976; *Airplane!,* 1980.

PRINCIPAL TELEVISION APPEARANCES—*Merv Griffin's Salute to Irving Berlin,* 1976; numerous other appearances.

WRITINGS: BOOKS—*Merman, an Autobiography,* 1978.

AWARDS: Antoinette Perry Award, 1972, 1951; Drama Desk Award, 1969–70; New York Drama Critics Award, 1943, 1946, 1959; Barter Theatre of Virginia Award, 1957; Donaldson Award, 1947.*

* * *

MERRIAM, Eve, writer, playwright

PERSONAL: Born July 19, 1916 in Philadelphia, PA; married, Leanord C. Lewin (a writer); Waldo Salt (a screenwriter); children: (first marriage) Guy, Dee. EDUCATION: Attended Cornell University; University of Pennsylvania,

A.B., 1937; graduate studies at the University of Wisconsin and Columbia University. NON-THEATRICAL CAREER: Copywriter, 1939–42; radio writer, documentaries, scripts in verse, CBS, 1942–46; conductor of weekly radio program on modern poetry, WQXR, New York, 1942–46; daily verse column in *PM*, NY, 1945; feature editor, *Deb*, 1946; fashion copy editor, *Glamour*, 1947–48; free-lance magazine and book writer, 1949–present.

WRITINGS: PLAYS, PUBLISHED—*The Club; Street Dreams, the Inner City Musical; Out of Our Fathers' House; At Her Age; Dialogue for Lovers; And I Ain't Finished Yet.* POETRY—*Family Circle*, 1946; *Tomorrow Morning*, 1953; *Montgomery Alabama: Money, Mississippi and Other Places*, 1957; *The Double Bed: From the Feminine Side*, 1958; *The Trouble with Love*, 1960; *There Is No Rhyme for Silver*, 1962; *It Doesn't Always Have to Rhyme*, 1964; *Catch a Little Rhyme*, 1966; *Independent Voices*, 1968; *The Inner City Mother Goose*, 1969; *The Nixon Poems*, 1970; *Finding a Poem*, 1970; *I Am a Man: Ode to Martin Luther King, Jr.*, 1971. OTHER BOOKS—*The Real Book about Franklin D. Roosevelt*, 1952; *The Real Book about Amazing Birds*, 1954; *Woman with a Torch*, 1956; *The Voice of Liberty: The Story of Emma Lazarus*, 1963; *A Gaggle of Geese*, 1960; *Mommies at Work*, 1961; *Basics: An I-Can-Read-Book for Grownups*, 1962; *Funny Town*, 1963; *What's in the Middle of a Riddle*, 1963; *After Nora Slammed the Door*, 1964; *American Women in the 1960's*, 1964; *The Unfinished Revolution*, 1964; *What Can You Do with a Pocket?* 1964; *Small Fry*, 1965; *Don't Think About a White Bear*, 1965; *The Story of Benjamin Franklin*, 1965; *Do You Want to See Something?*, 1965; *Miss Tibbett's Typewriter*, 1966; *Andy All Year Round*, 1968; *Epaminondas*, 1968.

THEATRE-RELATED CAREER: Teacher, School of Dramatic Writing, Playwriting course, New York University, 1984; Playwright-in-residence, Ithaca College, 1979.

AWARDS: Obie Award, *The Club;* Yale Younger Poets Prize; National Council of Teachers of English Award for Excellence in Poetry for Children; YWCA Award of merit for outstanding contribution to women.

SIDELIGHTS: MEMBERSHIPS—Council of Dramatists Guild; Young Playwrights Festival Committee; Authors League Council.

"I am fortunate in that my work is my main pleasure, and, while I find all forms of writing absorbing, I like poetry as the most immediate and richest form of communication. My favorite non-writing pursuits are frequenting public libraries and second-hand bookstores, and travel travel travel. I also enjoy riding a bike, swimming (in temperate waters only!) and walking. In my dreams I am a proficient ice-skater—in real life, I am wobbly but willing. I expect to be the last living inhabitant of Manhattan when everyone else has quit for sub- or exurbia. The city in winter is my delight, as the ocean is in summer."

ADDRESS: Home—101 W. 12th Street, New York, NY 10011.

MERRILL, Dina, actress

PERSONAL: Born December 29, in New York City; married Cliff Robertson (an actor) on December 21, 1966; children: Heather. EDUCATION: American Academy of Dramatic Arts; studied with Uta Hagen, Sandford Meisner, and David Craig. POLITICS: Republican.

CAREER: DEBUT—June, *The Man Who Came to Dinner*, Bucks County Playhouse, PA, 1944. NEW YORK DEBUT—understudy for lead role, *Mermaids Sleeping*, Empire, 3 months, 1946. PRINCIPAL STAGE APPEARANCES—Mrs. Manningham, *Angel Street*, Lyceum, NY, 1975; Jillian Hellmar, *Are You Now, or Have You Ever Been*, Century, NY, 1979; Peggy Porterfield, *On Your Toes*, Virginia Theatre, NY, 1983.

FILM DEBUT—*Desk Set*, 1957. PRINCIPAL FILM APPEARANCES—*Don't Give up the Ship*, 1959; *Butterfield 8*, 1960; *The Sundowners*, 1961; *The Young Savages*, 1961; *Operation Petticoat*, 1962; *The Courtship of Eddie's Father*, 1962; *A Wedding*, 1975; *Just Tell Me What You Want*, 1980. TELEVISION DEBUT—*Playwright's '56*, 1956. PRINCIPAL TELEVISION APPEARANCES—*Playhouse 90; Westinghouse Presents; Alcoa Circle Theatre; Matinee Theatre; Bob Hope Specials.*

SIDELIGHTS: MEMBERSHIPS—Vice Chairman, Republican Party, County of Manhattan; President, New York Mission Society; Board Member, Juvenile Diabetes Foundation. Miss Merrill has served on the Board of Directors of E. F. Hutton and Continental Telecom since 1980–81.

ADDRESS: Agent—Stark Hesseltine, c/o Hesseltine Baker Associates Ltd., 165 W. 46th Street, New York, NY 10036.

* * *

MERRILL, Gary, actor

PERSONAL: Born August 2, 1915, in Hartford, CT; son of Benjamin Gary (a businessman) and Hazel May (a teacher; maiden name, Andrews) Merrill; married Barbara Leeds (divorced 1950); Bette Davis (an actress) 1950 (divorced 1960); children (adopted) Michael, Margot. EDUCATION: Loomis School; Bowdoin College; Trinity College; trained for the stage at the Hilda Spong School and with Arnold Berke and Benno Schneider. POLITICS: Independent. MILITARY: Army and Air Force (four and a half years).

CAREER: DEBUT—*Squaring the Circle*, Brighton Beach, NY, 1936. NEW YORK DEBUT—Extra, *The Eternal Road*, Manhattan Center, December, 1936 for 128 performances. PRINCIPAL STAGE APPEARANCES—*Born Yesterday*, Lyceum, NY, 1946; *At War with the Army*, Booth, NY, 1948; *The World of Carl Sandburg*, 1959–60; *Morning's at Seven*, Lyceum, NY, 1980. MAJOR TOURS—*Brother Rat*, National, 1937–38; *This Is the Army; Winged Victory.*

FILM DEBUT—*Winged Victory*, 1944. FILM APPEARANCES—*Slattery's Hurricane*, 1948; Col. Davenport, *12 O'Clock High*, 1949; *All About Eve*, 1950; *Decision Before Dawn*, 1951; *Another Man's Poison*, 1951; *Phone Call from a Stranger*, 1953; *Night without Sleep*, 1953; *Blueprint for Murder*, 1953; *The Human Jungle*, 1954; *The Black Dako-*

GARY MERRILL

tas, 1956; *The Pleasure of His Company*, 1961; *The Woman Who Wouldn't Die*, 1965; *Around the World Under the Sea*, 1966; *Destination Inner Space*, 1966; *Catacombs*, 1966; *The Power*, 1968. TELEVISION DEBUT—*Danger*, 1953. TELEVISION APPEARANCES—*U.S. Steel Hour*, 1953; *The Mask*, 1954; *Justice*, 1954–55; *Alcoa Theatre*, 1958; *Alfred Hitchcock Presents; Playhouse 90; Winston Churchill—The Valiant Years*, 1960–63; *The Reporter*, 1964.

SIDELIGHTS: MEMBERSHIPS—Portland Country Club; Portland Yacht Club.

ADDRESS: Home—P.O. Box 6097 Falmouth Foreside, ME; Agent—Don Buchwald, Ten E. 44th Street, New York, NY 10017.

* * *

MEYER, Nicholas, screenwriter, director

PERSONAL: Born December 24, 1945; son of Bernard C. (a psychoanalyst) and Elly (a concert pianist; maiden name, Kassman) Meyer; married Lauren Leigh Taylor, June 6, 1984. EDUCATION: University of Iowa, B.A., 1968. POLITICS: Democrat. RELIGION: Jewish.

CAREER: PRINCIPAL FILM WORK—Unit publicist, *Love Story*, 1969; screenwriter, *The Seven-Per-Cent Solution*, 1975; screenwriter/director, *Time After Time*, 1979; director, *Star Trek II: The Wrath of Khan*, 1982.

PRINCIPAL TELEVISION WORK—Screenwriter, *Judge Dee*, 1974; screenwriter, *The Night That Panicked America*, 1975; director, *The Day After*, 1983.

WRITINGS: SCREENPLAYS—*Judge Dee*, 1974; *The Night That Panicked America*, 1975; *The Seven-Per-Cent Solution*, 1975; *Time After Time*, 1979. BOOKS—*Target Practice*, 1974; *The Seven-Per-Cent Solution*, 1975; *The West End Horror*, 1975; *Black Orchid* (with Barry Jap Kaplan), 1978; *Confessions of a Homing Pigeon*, 1981.

AWARDS: Academy of Science Fiction, Fantasy, and Horror Films, Best Director, 1982: *Star Trek II: The Wrath of Khan;* George Pal Memorial Award from the Academy of Science Fiction, Fantasy, and Horror Films; Academy Award Nomination, Best Screenplay Adaption, 1975: *The Seven-Per-Cent Solution.*

SIDELIGHTS: MEMBERSHIPS—Academy of Motion Picture Arts and Sciences; Writers Guild of Amerca; Directors Guild of America; Academy of Science Fiction, Fantasy, and Horror Films; Baker Street Irregulars.

ADDRESS: Office—183 N. Martel Avenue, Suite 270, Los Angeles, CA 90036. Agent—Stan Kamen, William Morris, 151 El Camino Drive, Beverly Hills, CA 90212.

* * *

MEYERS, Timothy, actor

PERSONAL: Born August 31, 1945 in New Orleans, LA; son of Christopher Doyle and Adelaide DeVendel (Hull) Meyers. EDUCATION: Louisiana State University at New Orleans, B.A. (Theatre), 1968. POLITICS: Democrat. RELIGION: Episcopalian.

CAREER: DEBUT—Crookfinger Jake, *Threepenny Opera*, Repertory, New Orleans, LA, 1970. NEW YORK DEBUT— Kenickie, *Grease*, Eden, 1972. PRINCIPAL STAGE APPEARANCES—Oscar, *Sidewalkin'*, Manhattan Theatre Club; Blackbeard, *Hot Grog*, Phoenix, NY; Tim, *The Foursome*, Astor Place, NY; Shanty, *No Place To Be Somebody*, national company, NY; Wally, *Rock Island*, No Smoking Playhouse, NY; Pinky, *The Sugar Bowl*, New Dramatists, NY; Lucien, *Romeo and Jeanette*, Floating Theatre, NY; Lusk, *Jack the Ripper*, Manhattan Punchline, NY; Harry Roat, *Wait Until Dark*, Ernst, *Cabaret*, Henry, *The Fantasticks*, Bowers, *Terra Nova*, Geoffrey Thornton, *The Dresser*, Sol, *True West*, Weston, *Curse of the Starving Class*, Scanlon, *One Flew over the Cuckoo's Nest*, Sportscaster, *Lady of the Diamond*, Sturrock, *Write Me a Murder*, Stingo, *She Stoops to Conquer*, McComber, *Ah Wilderness*, Meadows, *Loot*, Studio Arena Theatre, Buffalo, NY; Damis, *Tartuffe;* Mike, *The Caretaker;* Morty, *Steambath;* Phil Murray, *Comedians;* Oswald, *King Lear;* Puck, *A Midsummer Night's Dream;* Pompey, *Measure for Measure;* Odysseus, *The Greeks*. Additional stage work includes performances at Kennedy Center, Washington, DC, Arena Stage, Washington, DC, Hartford Stage Company, CT, Folger Theatre, Washington, DC, Seattle Repertory Theatre, WA, New Jersey Shakespeare Festival, Berkshire Theatre Festival, MA.

PRINCIPAL FILM APPEARANCES—*The Taking of Pelham 1-2-3; The Night of the Juggler; To Smithereens*. PRINCIPAL TELEVISION APPEARANCES—*Ryan's Hope; Kojak*.

TIMOTHY MEYERS

WRITINGS: PLAYS, PRODUCED—*Little Tips*, Lincoln Center Library, 1980.

AWARDS: New Jersey Drama Critics and the *New York Daily News,* Best Actor, 1974; Morty, *Steambath;* Antoinette Perry Award Nomination, 1972; Kenickie, *Grease.*

ADDRESS: Home—409 W. 50th Street, New York, NY 10019. Agent—Beverly Chase, 162 W. 54th Street, New York, NY 10019.

* * *

MICHAELS, Richard, director

PERSONAL: Born February 15, 1936; children: Gregory, Meredith. EDUCATION: Attended Cornell University.

CAREER: DIRECTED—(television) *Bewitched* (54 episodes), 1968; *Sadat; Scared Straight; Another Story; Silence of the Heart;* . . . *And Your Name Is Jonah; Homeward Bound; The Children Nobody Wanted; Berlin Tunnel 21; Once an Eagle.*

AWARDS: Christopher Award: . . . *And Your Name Is Jonah;* Christopher Award: *Homeward Bound;* Scott Newman Drug Abuse Prevention Award: *Scared Straight;* Television Festival Special Award: *Homeward Bound.*

ADDRESS: Agent—c/o David Gersh, 222 N. Canon Drive, Beverly Hills, CA 90210.

* * *

MILES, Joanna, actress, producer

PERSONAL: Born March 6, 1940; daughter of Johannes (an artist) and Jeanne (an artist; maiden name, Miles) Schiefer; married William Burns in 1970 (divorced 1977); married Michael Brandman (a TV studio executive producer) on April 29, 1978; children: (second marriage) Miles. EDUCATION: Putney Prep School, Putney, VT; Actors Studio, NY; Neighborhood Playhouse, NY; studied with Lee Strasberg.

CAREER: PRINCIPAL STAGE APPEARANCES—*Lorenzo,* NY; *Dancing for the Kaiser,* Circle Repertory Company, NY; *Drums in the Night,* Circle in the Square, NY; *Dylan,* NY; *One Night Stands of a Noisy Passenger,* NY; *The Wakefield Tragedies; So Much of Heaven, So Much of Earth; Dracula; Once in a Lifetime; The Cave Dwellers; Kramer,* Mark Taper Forum, Los Angeles; *Goodbye My Fancy.*

PRINCIPAL FILM APPEARANCES—*Cross Creek; Fragments; Bug; The Ultimate Warrior; The Way We Live Now.* PRINCIPAL TELEVISION APPEARANCES—*All My Children; The Secret Storm; The Nurses; The Defenders; Caribe; Flame in the Wind; The Edge of Night; Search for Tomorrow; Barnaby Jones; The Incredible Hulk; Mannix; NYPD; The Magician; Barney Miller; Trapper John, M.D.; The Sound of Murder; Promise of Love; Born Innocent; A Fire in the Sky; Harvest Home; The Glass Menagerie; Aloha Means Goodbye; Sophisticated Gents; Turn the Key Deftly; In What America; The Trial of Captain Jensen; My Mother's House.*

WRITINGS: PLAY, MUSICAL BOOK—Feathers. PICTURE BOOK WITH INTERVIEWS—*Strippers.*

THEATRE-RELATED CAREER: Producer, The Miles Company, 1982–83.

AWARDS: Actors Studio Award, 1980; Woman in Radio and TV Award, 1974; Emmy Award, Best Supporting Actress, *The Glass Menagerie,* 1974.

SIDELIGHTS: MEMBERSHIPS—Academy of Motion Picture Arts and Sciences; Actors Studio; Women in Film and TV. RECREATION—Photograpy, travel, writing, producer developer.

ADDRESS: Office—2062 N. Vine Street, Hollywood, CA 90068. Agent—c/o STE Representation, 211 South Beverly Drive, Beverly Hills, CA 90212.

* * *

MILES, Julia, producer, manager

PERSONAL: Born in Pelham, GA; daughter of John Cornelius (a farmer) and Saro Priscilla (Jones) Hinson; married William Miles in June, 1950 (divorced 1958); married

Samuel C. Cohn (an agent), August 11, 1982; children: Stacey, Lisa, Marya. EDUCATION: Northwestern University, B.S., 1950.

CAREER: CO-PRODUCED—*Theatre Current*, St. Ann's Church, Brooklyn, NY, 1957–61; PRODUCED—*Red Eye of Love; George Washington Crossing the Delaware; Not Enough Rope; Fortuna*, 1961–64, Off-Broadway; Production Coordinator/General Manager, American Place Theatre, 1964–67; Associate Director, American Place Theatre, 1967–present; Artistic Director, Special Project, the Women's Playwriting and Directing Project at the American Place Theatre, 1978–present; FILMS PRODUCED—*Four Friends*, 1981; Four Women Productions, *The Living* (currently in pre-production.)

SIDELIGHTS: MEMBERSHIPS—Board Member/Secretary, The American Place Theatre; Board Member, The Bridge, U.S.A./France Musical Theatre Festival St. Chinian, France; Advisory Board, Omega Liturgical Dance Co., St. John The Divine Cathedral; Founding Member, American Theatre Association Committee for Women in Theatre; National Theatre Conference; Theatre Communications Group, NY; former member and chairman, New York State Council on the Arts—Theatre Panel; Women in the Theatre Industry Panel, NY; Networking for Women in the Performing Arts, YWCA, NY; Women's Playwriting Conference for the Mid-West, Minneapolis; Founder, League of Professional Theatre Women/New York; Steering Committee, Performing Artists for Nuclear Disarmament; Bellagio Study and Conference Center, Bellagio, Italy.

ADDRESS: Home—25 Central Park West, New York, NY 10023. Office—American Place Theatre, 111 W. 46th Street, New York, NY 10036.

* * *

MILES, Sylvia, actress

PERSONAL: Born in New York City. EDUCATION: Pratt Institute, graduate; studied with Erwin Piscator at the Dramatic Workshop of the New School for Social Research; studied four years with Harold Clurman and the Group Theatre, three years with N. Richard Nash; also studied with Lee Strasberg at the Actors Studio and Stella Adler and Frank Corsaro.

CAREER: NEW YORK DEBUT—*Riot Act*, Cort, 1963. PRINCIPAL STAGE APPEARANCES—*A Stone for Danny Fisher*, Downtown National, NY, 1956; Maggie, *The Iceman Cometh*, Circle in the Square, 1957–58; Thief, *The Balcony*, Circle in the Square, 1960–62; *A Chekhov Sketchbook*, Gramercy Arts, 1962; Stella, *Matty and the Moron and Madonna*, Orpheum, 1965; *Luv, The Owl and the Pussycat*, Hampton Playhouse, 1967; Monique, *The Kitchen*, 81st Street, 1966–67; *The Killing of Sister George*, Santa Fe Theatre Co., 1969; Sylvie, *Rose Bloom*, Eastside Playhouse, NY, 1971–72; *Who's Afraid of Virginia Woolf?*, Pittsburgh Playhouse, 1972; Nellie Toole, *Nellie Toole and Company*, Theatre Four, NY, 1973; *Night of the Iguana*, Circle in the Square, NY, 1977; *Employment Agency*, Chichester Festival, Sussex, England, 1978; *Before Breakfast*, Chichester Festival,

1978; *Vieux Carre*, Piccadilly Theatre, Nottingham Playhouse, England, 1978.

FILM DEBUT—*Parrish*, 1961. PRINCIPAL FILM APPEARANCES—*Murder Inc.*, 1961; *Psychomania*, 1964; *The Truant*, 1965; *Midnight Cowboy*, 1970; *The Last Movie*, 1970; *Who Killed Mary Whatser Name*, 1971; *Heat*, 1972; *92 in the Shade*, 1975; *Farewell My Lovely*, 1976; *The Great Scout and Cathouse Thursday*, 1977; *The Sentinel*, 1977; *Zero to Sixty*, 1978; *Shalimar*, 1978; *Fun House*, 1981; *Hammett*, 1981; *Evil Under the Sun*, 1982.

PRINCIPAL TELEVISION APPEARANCES—*The Sid Caesar Show; The Steve Allen Show; Car 54, Where Are You?; Play of the Week; Route 66; The Defenders; Naked City; Girl Talk; The Doctors; Love of Life; Search for Tomorrow; The Mike Douglas Show; The Tonight Show; The Merv Griffin Show; The David Frost Show; All My Children; 51st State* series (one-hour PBS documentary on her life), "I Was Always Sylvia," 1974.

AWARDS: Actress of the Year in a New Play, nomination, S.W.E.T. Awards, England, 1978: *Vieux Carre*; Academy Award nominations, Best Supporting Actress, 1976: *Farewell My Lovely*, 1970: *Midnight Cowboy*.

SIDELIGHTS: MEMBERSHIPS—Actors Studio since 1968. "Ms. Miles is a rated chess player, having played in numerous tournaments. Several of her games have been published in *The New York Times* chess column."

ADDRESS: Agent—c/o Milton Goldman 40 W. 57th Street, New York, NY 10019.

* * *

MILGRIM, Lynn, actress

PERSONAL: Born March 17, 1940; daughter of Hans (a government worker and salesman) and Esther Ruth (Goldman) Milgram; married Leonard Phillips on February 17, 1963 (divorced 1972); married Richard Greene (an actor) on June 30, 1980; children: (second marriage) Jocelyn Milgrim Greene. EDUCATION: Swarthmore College, B.A. (with Honors) 1960; Harvard University, Ed. M. 1961; studied at the Hedgerow Theatre with Jasper Deeter and Rose Shulman, and at the H.B. Studios with Uta Hagen. NON-THEATRICAL CAREER: Teacher, 6th Grade, Arlington Public Schools, MA, 1961–64.

CAREER: DEBUT—Lucinda, *Physician in Spite of Himself*, Hedgerow, Moylan, PA, 1956. NEW YORK DEBUT—Sis/Girl with the cello, *City Scene*, Fortune, 16 performances, 1969. PRINCIPAL STAGE APPEARANCES—Eileen, *Crimes of Passion*, Astor Place, NY, 1969; Amy, *Charley's Aunt*, Brooks Atkinson, NY, 1970; Lady Macbeth, *Macbeth*, Mercer O'Casey, NY, 1971; Thelma, *After Magritte*, Theatre Four, NY, 1972; Cynthia, *The Real Inspector Hound*, Theatre Four, 1972; Tilda, *Echoes*, Bijou, NY, 1973; Davina, *Otherwise Engaged*, Plymouth, NY, 1977; Barbara/Harriet/Maggie, *Museum*, NY Shakespeare Festival, 1978; Carolyn, *Ribcage*, Manhattan Theatre Club, 1978; Jan, *Bedroom Farce*, Brooks Atkinson, NY, 1979; Jane, *Short-Change*

LYNN MILGRIM

Review, Second Stage, NY, 1980; Alice/Mrs. Eberly, *Bits and Pieces*, Second Stage, NY, 1980; Jenny, *Close of Play*, Manhattan Theatre Club, 1981; Cathy Bridges, *What Would Jeanne Moreau Do?*, WPA, NY, 1982; Alain ("Marks"), *Talking With*, Manhattan Theatre Club, 1982; Doris/Mary/ Delia, *Win/Lose/Draw*, Provincetown Playhouse, NY, 1983; Miranda, *Sand Dancing*, Hudson Guild, NY, 1983.

FILM DEBUT—Gina Holt, *Tell Me That You Love Me, Junie Moon*, 1969. PRINCIPAL FILM APPEARANCES—Faith, *Enormous Changes at the Last Minute*, 1984. TELEVISION DEBUT—Mother, *Nightmare*, 1976. PRINCIPAL TELEVISION APPEARANCES—Sister Agatha, *One Life to Live*, 1977; Susan Shearer, *Another World*, 1978–79, 1982; Deborah Charles, "A Matter of Privacy", *Nurse*, 1982; Mother, *My Mother the Witch*, 1983.

AWARDS: Villager Downtown Theatre Award, *What Would Jeanne Moreau Do?*, 1982.

SIDELIGHTS: "I have also played major roles at the following theatres: Actors Theatre of Louisville, Arena Stage, Washington, DC, Charles Playhouse, Boston, MA, Cincinnati Playhouse in the Park, Long Wharf Theatre, Syracuse Stage, Michigan Theatre Ensemble and the Hartford Stage Company."

ADDRESS: Agent—Bret Adams Ltd., 448 W. 44th Street, New York, NY 10036.

MILLER, Arthur, playwright

PERSONAL: Born October 17, 1915, in New York City; son of Isadore and Augusta (Barnett), Miller; married Mary Grace Slattery, August 5, 1940 (divorced); Marilyn Monroe (an actress) June, 1956 (divorced); Ingeborg Morath, February, 1962; children: (first marriage) Jane Ellen, Robert. EDUCATION: University of Michigan, A.B., 1938. NON-THEATRICAL CAREER: Journalist for the Michigan Daily.

WRITINGS: PLAYS PUBLISHED/PRODUCED—*The Man Who Had All the Luck*, 1944; *Situation Normal*, 1944; *All My Sons*, 1947; *Death of a Salesman*, 1948; *The Crucible*, 1953; *A View from the Bridge*, 1955; *A Memory of Two Mondays*, 1955; *After the Fall*, 1964; *Incident at Vichy*, 1964; expanded one-act, *A View from the Bridge*, into a full-length play, 1965; *The Price*, 1968; *The Creation of the World and Other Business*, 1972; *Up for Paradise*, (musical), 1977; *The Archbishop's Ceiling*, 1977; *The American Clock*, 1980; *Elegy for a Lady*, 1984; *Some Kind of Love*, 1984. ADAPTATIONS—*An Enemy of the People*, 1950. SCREENPLAYS—*The Misfits*, 1961; *Playing for Time*, 1981. BOOKS—*Focus* (novel), 1946; *Salesman Beijeng*, 1984. SHORT STORIES—*I Don't Need You Anymore* (collection), 1967. ARTICLES, ESSAYS AND STORIES contributed to *Harpers, Saturday Evening Post, The New York Times Magazine*.

PRINCIPAL STAGE WORK, Director, *The Price*, Duke of York's, London, 1969; appeared in and directed *Up for Paradise*, University of Michigan, 1974. RELATED CAREER: Associate professor of Drama, University of Michigan, 1973–74.

ADDRESS: Agent—Katharine Brown, ICM, 40 W. 57th Street, New York, NY 10019.

* * *

MILLER, Buzz (ne Vernal Philip Miller), choreographer, dancer, teacher

PERSONAL: Born December 23, 1923 in Snowflake, AZ; son of Allen K. (a rancher) and Philena (Hunt) Miller. EDUCATION: Arizona State University at Tempe, B.A. (Music); studied Ballet with Mia Slavenska in Los Angeles, CA. MILITARY: U.S. Army, World War II, Europe.

CAREER: PRINCIPAL STAGE APPEARANCES, Dancer—*Magdalena*, Ziegfeld, NY, 1948; *Pal Joey*, NY, 1951; *Two's Company*, NY, 1952; *Me and Juliet*, NY, 1953; *Pajama Game*, NY, 1954; *Anything Goes*, NY, 1955; *Bells Are Ringing*, NY, 1957; *Redhead*, NY, 1959; *Hot Spot*, NY, 1963; *Funny Girl*, NY, 1964–66.

PRINCIPAL FILM APPEARANCES, Dancer—*On the Riviera*, 1951; *No Business Like Show Business*, 1954; *Anything Goes*, 1955; *Pajama Game*, 1956; *Justine*, 1968;

PRINCIPAL TELEVISION APPEARANCES, Dancer—*All About Music*, 1957; *The Big Record*, 1958; *Arthur Godfrey Special*, 1959; *Saul and the Witch of Endor* (Ballet), 1959; *Ernie Kovacs Special*, 1960; *Home for the Holidays*, 1961; *The Broadway of Lerner and Loewe*, 1961; *Brief Dynasty*, 1962;

BUZZ MILLER

Music for the Young, 1962; *Arias and Arabesques,* 1962; *Psalms,* 1963; *Arts—USA,* 1965; *Bell Telephone Hour,* 1965; *Jephtha's Daughter,* 1966; *Lincoln Center—Stage 5,* 1967; *Gunther Schuller Special,* 1968. *Camera 3,* 1968; *Portrait of Billie,* 1970; *The Dick Cavett Show,* 1980; *The Merv Griffin Show,* 1980.

PRINCIPAL STAGE APPEARANCES, BALLETS AND DANCE COMPANIES—Jack Cole Dancers (touring) 1949–51; *Arabian Nights,* 1955; Ballets de Paris, *La Chambre,* 1955; *The Unicorn, The Gorgon and the Manticore,* 1957; Festival of Two Worlds, Spoleto Festival, Italy, 1958; *Schola Cantorum* of New York, Carnegie Hall, NY, 1960; Roland Petit Ballet, London, England, 1960; *Bartok Concerto, Catulli Carmina,* Caramoor Festival, 1964; *The Captive Lark,* 1966; *Chu Chem,* 1966; Charmen deLavallade Company, 1968; *Banda,* Israel Festival, 1968; *Songs of Catullus,* Lincoln Center, NY, 1969; *Dracula,* 1969; Guest Artist, American Dance Machine, 1979–80.

PRINCIPAL CHOREOGRAPHY—(Assistant) *Oldsmobile Announcement Show,* TV, 1956; *Ionization,* Savero Company, Detroit Symphony Orchestra, 1961; *Postures,* for TV program *Look Up and Live,* 1961; (Assistant) *Bravo Giovanni; Moondreamers,* La Mama E.T.C., NY, 1968; *Patterns,* Zina Bethune Company, 1971; *Aida,* State Opera, Berlin, Germany, 1972; *Credo,* National Council of Churches, 1972; *Conversations about the Dance,* Hunter College, 1975; (Co-choreographed) National Academy Ballet; *Kew Drive,* City College of New York, 1978; *Satin Doll,* American Dance Machine, 1978; *Kew Drive,* Les Ballets Jazz de

Montreal, 1979; *Steam Heat,* American Dance Machine, 1979; *Me And My Shadow,* Leonard Davis School of the Performing Arts at City College of New York, 1981.

THEATRE-RELATED CAREER: Associate Director to Julie Bovasso at La Mama E.T.C., NY, 1970, 1975; Teacher: George Balanchine's School of American Ballet, The National Academy of Dance, Champaign, IL, American Dance Machine, University of Illinois at Urbana (Guest), Staten Dansskola, Stockholm, Harkness School of Ballet, City College of New York, American University, Washington, DC (Guest), Connecticut College (Guest), Jack Garfein's Actors and Directors Lab, NY; Teacher: Pittsburgh Ballet Theatre, Cambridge School of Ballet, Master Classes, Southern Methodist University.

AWARDS: U.S. Army, Purple Heart Medal, Bronze Star Medal, World War II.

SIDELIGHTS: MEMBERSHIPS—AEA; SAG; AFTRA.

In Mr. Miller's distinguished career he had the honor of being a soloist at the Inauguration of Presidents Kennedy and Johnson. He has also devoted much time and energy to teaching and passing on a tradition in dance to young students.

ADDRESS: Home—8 W. Ninth Street, New York, NY 10011. Office—The American Dance Machine, 115½ E. 61st Street, New York, NY 10021.

* * *

MILLER, Susan (nee Figlin), playwright

PERSONAL: Born April 6, 1944 in Philadelphia, PA; daughter of Isaac (a musician and business executive) and Thelma (a singer and artist; maiden name, Freifelder) Figlin; married Bruce Miller (an attorney) on June 13, 1965 (divorced 1976); children: Jeremy. EDUCATION: Pennsylvania State University, B.A., 1965; Bucknell University, M.A. 1970; (16 credits toward M.F.A.) Pennsylvania State University, 1973. RELIGION: Jewish. NON-THEATRICAL CAREER: English Teacher, public schools, Carlisle, PA, 1965–68.

WRITINGS: PLAYS, PRODUCED—*No One Is Exactly 23,* Pennsylvania State University, 1967, Dickinson College, 1968; *Daddy and a Commotion of Zeras,* Alice Theatre Company, NY, 1970; *Denim Lecture,* Pennsylvania State University, 1970, Mark Taper Forum, Los Angeles, CA, 1974; *Confessions of a Female Disorder,* Universities of Washington, North Carolina, Vassar College, Connecticut College, O'Neill Playwrights National Conference, 1973, Mark Taper Forum, Los Angeles, CA, 1973; *Flux,* Phoenix Repertory Company, NY, 1975, American Repertory Company in London, England, 1977, New York Shakespeare Festival, 1977, Second State Company, NY, 1982; *Arts and Leisure,* American Theatre Association Conference, 1982; *Cross Country,* Brooklyn College, University of California at Riverside, Trinity College, Interart Theatre, NY, 1977, Mark Taper Forum, Los Angeles, CA, 1976; *Nasty Rumors and Final Remarks,* St. Nicholas, Chicago, IL, 1981, New York Shakespeare Festival, 1979.

THEATRE-RELATED CAREER: Director of Drama, Pennsylvania State University, 1969–73; Instructor of English, Literature, Theatre Arts, Pennsylvania State University, 1969–73; Lecturer (playwriting seminar) Department of English, UCLA, 1975–76.

AWARDS: National Endowment for the Arts Fellowship in Creative Writing, 1983 and 1976; finalist, Susan Blackburn Smith Prize in Playwriting, 1980; Obie Award for excellence in playwriting, 1978: *Nasty Rumors and Final Remarks;* Rockefeller Grant in Playwriting, 1975; O'Neill National Playwrights Contest, 1973.

SIDELIGHTS: MEMBERSHIPS—Dramatists Guild; Writers Guild of America; ACLU; Authors League of America.

ADDRESS: Agent—Flora Roberts, 157 W. 57th Street, New York, NY 10019.

* * *

MILLIGAN, Tuck, actor

PERSONAL: Born in Kansas City, MO; son of William Finley (an attorney) and Louise (Rule) Milligan. EDUCATION: University of Missouri at Kansas City, B.A., 1971; studied acting with Wynn Handman in New York. POLITICS: Democrat. RELIGION: Episcopalian.

CAREER: DEBUT—Friedrich Von Trapp, *The Sound of Music,* Starlight Music Theatre, Kansas City, MO, 1967. NEW YORK DEBUT—Alan Strang, *Equus,* Plymouth, for more than 50 performances, 1975–76. PRINCIPAL STAGE APPEARANCES—Ronnie, *The House of Blue Leaves,* Westport (NY) Country Playhouse, Falmouth (MA) Playhouse, and Bucks County (PA) Playhouse, 1976; Wali-Dad/Birdy Johnson, *The Crucifier of Blood,* Helen Hayes, NY, 1978; Romeo, *Romeo and Juliet,* Seattle Repertory Company, WA, 1982.

TELEVISION DEBUT—*The Doctors.* PRINCIPAL TELEVISION APPEARANCES—*Kojak; Andros Targets;* Theo Whiting, *The Doctors,* 1981–82; *Anatomy of an Illness.*

SIDELIGHTS: MEMBERSHIPS—ACLU, president of Conestoga Productions, Eagle Scout, Boy Scouts of America.

ADDRESS: Agent—STE Representation Ltd., 888 Seventh Avenue, New York, NY 10019; 211 S. Beverly Drive, Beverly Hills, CA 90212.

* * *

MILTON, David Scott, playwright

PERSONAL: Born September 15, 1934 in Pittsburgh, PA; son of S. I. (in the bakery business) and Gertrude Bertha (Osgood) Milton; married Sheila Kvester (a nurse) on May 24, 1981. EDUCATION: Attended public schools in Pittsburgh, PA.

WRITINGS: PLAYS, PRODUCED—*Metaphysical Cop* (one-

act), Off Center, NY, 1967; *Scraping Bottom* (one-act), New York Theatre Ensemble, 1968; *Duet for Solo Voice* (one-act), American Place, NY, 1970; *Bread,* American Place, 1974; *Duet,* Golden, NY, 1975; *Skin,* Odyssey, Los Angeles, CA, 1981. SCREENPLAYS—*Born To Win,* 1971. SCREENPLAYS, UNPRODUCED—Kool-Aid Kelly, Cat in the Bag, Get the Police. TELEVISION—*Notes on a Passport: Peggy Stuart Coolidge in Asia,* 1969; Adaptation of David Hare's *Knuckle,* 1975. NOVELS—*The Quarterback,* 1970; *Paradise Road,* 1974; *Kabbalah,* 1980; *Skyline,* 1982.

THEATRE-RELATED CAREER: Senior lecturer in Drama, University of Southern California, 1977–83.

AWARDS: Neil Simon Playwright's Award, 1981: *Skin;* Mark Twain Journal Award, 1974: *Paradise Road;* film *Born To Win* featured at the New York Film Festival.

SIDELIGHTS: MEMBERSHIPS—Writers Guild of America; Dramatists Guild; Author's Guild. RECREATIONS—weight lifting, racquetball, crossword puzzles, modern Russian history, arborculture.

"I am obsessed by man and his condiiton: his dreams, his frailties, his bravery, his foolishness. I loathe ideologues, shy away from systems, dislike technocrats, shun those intellectuals possessing thought without wisdom. We are all here for a pathetically short span; we are dust. Greatness is fleeting; deeds are transitory. We must respect and acknowledge each other on this short ride from dark into dark. It is a funhouse ride and we only take it once."

ADDRESS: Home—Star Route 3 Box 101, Tehachapi, CA 93561. Office—1235 24th Street, Santa Monica, CA 90404. Agent—Robert Stein, Berkus-Cosay-Stein, 1900 Avenue of the Stars, Los Angeles, CA 90067.

* * *

MINKUS, Barbara, actress

PERSONAL: Born August 15, 1943, in Chicago; daughter of Leslie David (a merchant) and Bernice H. (Hyman) Minkus; married Arnold Barron (an eye surgeon), December 10, 1972; children: Benjamin, Jennifer. EDUCATION: Immaculate Heart, Los Angeles, B.A., 1979; California Family Study Center, M.A., 1981.

CAREER: PRINCIPAL STAGE APPEARANCES—*Julius Monk's Bits and Pieces,* Plaza Nine, NY, 1966–67; Rose Mitnick, *Education of Hyman Kaplan,* Imperial, NY, 1969; Fanny, *Funny Girl,* Coconut Grove, FL and tour of Eastern states, 1967–69.

PRINCIPAL TELEVISION APPEARANCES—*Danny Kaye Show; Merv Griffin Show; Love, American Style* (seven seasons); *Curiosity Shop; Pac Man.*

PRINCIPAL FILM APPEARANCES—*What's So Bad About Feeling Good?,* 1968; *Lady Sings the Blues,* 1972; *Love at First Bite,* 1979.

AWARDS: Television Academy, Most Promising Entertainer, 1967.

SIDELIGHTS: MEMBERSHIPS—Women in Film.

ADDRESS: Agent—Dade-Rosen, 9172 Sunset Blvd., Los Angeles, CA 90069.

* * *

MINNELLI, Liza May, actress, singer, dancer

PERSONAL: Born March 12, 1946, in Los Angeles, CA; daughter of Vincente (a designer and stage and film director) and Judy Garland (the actress, singer; original name, Frances Gumm) Minnelli; married Peter Allen (the singer), 1967 (divorced 1972); John Joseph "Jack" Haley, Jr. (producer), 1974 (divorced); Mark Gero (sculptor and producer). EDUCATION: Studied for the theatre with Uta Hagen and Herbert Berghof.

CAREER: DEBUT—*Take Me Along, Flower Drum Song,* Cape Cod Melody Tent, Hyannis, MA, July, 1962. NEW YORK DEBUT—Ethel Hofflinger, *Best Foot Forward,* Stage 73, 1963. LONDON DEBUT—In concert with her mother, Palladium, 1964. PRINCIPAL STAGE APPEARANCES—Title role, *The Diary of Anne Frank,* summer stock and subsequent U.S. and European tour, 1962; Lili, *Carnival,* Mineola Playhouse, Mineola, NY, 1964; in revue, 1964; Flora, *Flora, the Red Menace,* Alvin, NY, 1965; in variety. Olympia, Paris, 1971; also in London at the Royal Festival Hall and the Rainbow; *Liza with a Z,* Winter Garden, NY, 1974; Roxie Hart (vacation replacement), *Chicago,* 46th Street Theatre, NY, 1975; *A Star-Spangled Gala,* Metropolitan Opera House, NY, 1976; Michelle Craig, *The Act,* Majestic, NY, 1977; Lillian Hellman, *Are You Now or Have You Ever Been. . . ?,* Promenade, NY, 1979; in concert, Carnegie Hall, NY, 1979; Angel, *The Rink,* Martin Beck, NY, 1984.

FILM DEBUT—Child, *In the Good Old Summertime,* 1949. PRINCIPAL FILMS—*Charlie Bubbles,* 1968; Pookie, *The Sterile Cuckoo,* 1969; title role, *Tell Me That You Love Me, Junie Moon,* 1969; Sally Bowles, *Cabaret,* 1972; *A Matter of Time,* 1973; *That's Entertainment,* 1974; *Lucky Lady,* 1975; *New York, New York,* 1977; Linda, *Arthur,* 1981.

TELEVISION APPEARANCES—*The Ed Sulivan Show; The Judy Garland Show; Liza with a Z; Liza at the Winter Garden; Liza and Goldie;* others.

CONCERTS—Extensive work in Las Vegas at Riviera, Lake Tahoe's Harrahs, the Torre del Duque in Nueva Andalucia, Spain as well as major concert halls around the world; Miss Minnelli made a major world tour in 1975 with her show *Liza with a Z.*

AWARDS: Antoinette Perry Award, 1977: *The Act,* 1974: *Liza with a Z,* 1965: *Flora, the Red Menance;* Antoinette Perry Award Nomination, 1984: *The Rink,* Academy Award, 1972: *Cabaret;* Las Vegas Entertainment Female Star of the Year, 1972, 1974.

SIDELIGHTS: Her close friends, who helped shape her personna and career, John Kander and Fred Ebb, have written most of her successes on Broadway and in the movies, including, *Flora. . . , Cabaret, The Act, New York, New York, Chicago,* and special material; they discuss their long relationship in a taped dialogue on file with the T.O.F.T. Collection in the Theatre Collection of the Performing Arts Research Center, N.Y. Public Library at Lincoln Center.

ADDRESS: Agent—Creative Management Associates, 40 W. 57th Street, New York, NY 10019; PMK Public Relations, 545 Madison Avenue, New York, NY 10022.

* * *

MINNELLI, Vincente, film director

PERSONAL: Born February 28, 1903; son of Vincente and Mina (an actress; maiden name, Genelle) Minnelli; married Judy Garland (an actress and singer) (divorced); married Lee M. Anderson (writer) on April 2, 1982; children: (previous marriage) Liza Minnelli, Tina Nina Minnelli. RELIGION: Catholic.

CAREER: FIRST STAGE WORK—Designed the curtain for *Earl Carroll's Vanities,* 1930. PRINCIPAL STAGE WORK—Designed *Earl Carroll's Vanities,* 1931–32; *Dubarry Was a Lady;* Chief Costume and Set Designer, Radio City Music Hall, NY: *Scheherazade, Coast to Coast,* etc., 1933–35; Designed/Directed—*At Home Abroad, The Show Is On, The Ziegfeld Follies of 1936, Hooray For What?.*

PRINCIPAL FILM WORK—Directed—*Cabin in the Sky, Meet Me in St. Louis, The Clock, Yolanda and the Thief, Ziegfeld Follies, The Pirate, Madame Bovary, Father of the Bride, The Bad and the Beautiful, An American in Paris, The Band Wagon, Brigadoon, Kismet, The Cobweb, Lust for Life, Gigi, The Reluctant Debutante, Some Came Running, Four Horsemen of the Apocalypse, The Sandpiper, The Undercurrent, Designing Woman, On a Clear Day, A Matter of Time.*

WRITINGS: Illustrations and drawings for the book *Casanova's Memoirs,* 1930.

AWARDS: Academy Award: *Gigi,* Order of Arts and Letters

VINCENTE MINNELLI

by the French Government for his contribution to French Culture.

SIDELIGHTS: MEMBERSHIPS—Directors Guild of America; Academy of Motion Picture Arts and Sciences. RECREATIONS—painting and international travel.

"Mr. Minnelli's sketches and water colors are in the Metropolitan Museum of Art in New York City and the Museum of the City of New York as well as the files of the Radio City Music Hall. The Museum of Modern Art in New York is compiling a large book covering his work to be brought out in 1984 under the title *Vincente Minnelli, the Man and His Movies.*"

ADDRESS: Agent—Walter and Paul Kohner, Sunset Blvd., Hollywood, CA 90060.

* * *

MISCHER, Don, producer, director

EDUCATION: University of Texas, B.A., 1963, M.A., 1965.

CAREER: PRINCIPAL TELEVISION WORK—Producor/director: specials, Goldie Hawn, Shirley Maclaine, Barry Manilow, Cheryl Ladd, John Denver, Mikhail Baryshnikov; directed for six consecutive years, *The Kennedy Center Honors; Motown 25: Yesterday, Today, Forever,* 1982; *Donahue and Kids,* 1981; *Ain't Misbehavin,* 1982; *Making Television Dance with Twyla Tharp; The Great American Dream Machine,* 1972; *Shirley Maclaine . . . Illusions,* 1982; *An Evening with Robin Williams; Marlo Thomas Special,* 1982; *Famous Lives; Happy Birthday Bob* (Bob Hope's 80th birthday special); specials—*Goldie and Liza Together; Donna Summer Special;* in association with Barbara Walters, packaged *Barbara Walters Specials.*

RELATED CAREER—Founder, Don Mischer Productions, 1978.

AWARDS: Emmy Award, Outstanding Variety and Music Program, and the Directors Guild of America Award for Outstanding Directorial Achievement, 1983: *Motown 25: Yesterday, Today, Forever;* Directors Guild Award for Outstanding Directorial Achievement, 1982: *Shirley Maclaine . . . Illusions;* Emmy Award Nominations, Best Program, Best Director, *Marlo Thomas Special;* DGA Awards for Outstanding Directorial Achievement, *The Kennedy Center Honors;* Emmy Award for Directing, 1981: *The Kennedy Center Honors;* Emmy Award, Best Children's Program, 1981: *Donahue and Kids;* Emmy Award Nominations, 1981–82: *Barbara Walters Specials;* Emmy Award Nomination, Best Variety Program, 1980: *Goldie and Liza Together,* 1980.

SIDELIGHTS: MEMBERSHIPS—Directors Guild of America, Academy of Television Arts and Sciences.

ADDRESS: Office—9350 Wilshire Blvd., Beverly Hills, CA 90212. Agent—The Brillstein Company, 9200 Sunset Blvd., Beverly Hills, CA 90212.

MITCHELL, James, actor, dancer, director

PERSONAL: Born February 29, 1920; son of John A. and Edith (Burne) Mitchell. EDUCATION: Los Angeles City College, A.A., 1939; State University of New York, Empire State College, New York City, B.A., 1974; Goddard College, Plainfield, VT, M.A., 1976; studied dance with Don Farnsworth, Igor Youskevitch, Anna Sololow, Nanette Charisse, Eugene Loring, Valentina Pereyaslavic, Edward Caton, Carmelita Maracci, Aubrey Hitchins, Helene Platova, Bella Lewitzky, Lester Horton; studied theatre with Sondra Lee, Michael Egan, George Shdanoff, Elsa Schrieber, Robert Lewis, Jerry Blunt.

CAREER: PRINCIPAL STAGE APPEARANCES—*Bloomer Girl,* Shubert, NY, 1945; *Billion Dollar Baby,* Alvin, NY, 1946; *Brigadoon,* Ziegfeld, NY, 1947; performed with Agnes de Mille Dance Theatre, 1953–54; *The Threepenny Opera,* Theatre de Lys, NY, 1956; *Winkleberg,* Renata, NY, 1956; *First Impressions,* Alvin, NY, 1957; *Carnival,* Imperial, NY, Civic Light Opera, Los Angeles and San Francisco, CA, Lyric Theatre, London, England, 1961–62; *Tonight at 8:30,* Coconut Grove Playhouse, FL, 1963; *The Deputy,* Brooks Atkinson Theatre, NY, 1964; *L'Histoire du Soldat,* American-Israel Cultural Foundation, Waldorf Astoria Hotel, NY, 1966; *Fallen Angels,* Papermill Playhouse, NJ, 1966; *The Threepenny Opera,* Mineola Playhouse, NY, 1966; member of the company, American Laboratory Theatre, L.A., 1967–68; *The Father,* Roundabout, NY, 1973; *Mack and Mabel,* Majestic, NY, 1975; *True Romances,* Mark Taper Forum, Los Angeles, 1977; *The American Nightmare,* Phoenix, NY, 1977; *Big Fish, Little Fish,* Megaw Theatre, Los Angeles, 1978.

MAJOR TOURS—*Funny Girl,* Guber-Gross summer circuit tour, 1967; Agnes de Mille Dance Theatre, Hurok Attractions, U.S. Tour, 1953–54.

DIRECTED—*L'il Abner,* Papermill Playhouse, NJ, 1968; *The Merry Widow* and *Brigadoon,* St. Louis Municipal Opera, 1968; *The Fantasticks,* North Shore Music Theatre, Beverly, MA, 1968; *The Threepenny Opera,* Drake University, Des Moines, IO, 1968.

PRINCIPAL FILM APPEARANCES—*Colorado Territory; House Across the Street; Toast of New Orleans; Border Incident; Stars in My Crown; Devil's Doorway,* 1945–50; *The Bandwagon; The Prodigal; Deep in My Heart,* 1954; *Oklahoma,* 1955; *The Silence,* 1975; *The Turning Point,* 1976. PRINCIPAL TELEVISION APPEARANCES—*The Edge of Night,* 1964–65; *The Academy Awards Show,* 1965; *Cyd Charisse Specials,* 1966; *Where the Heart Is,* 1969–73; *Lou Grant,* 1978; *Charlie's Angels,* 1978; *All My Children,* 1979–present.

THEATRE—RELATED CAREER: Teacher, movement for actors, American Labratory Theatre, 1966–67; teacher, movement for actors and directors, Yale University, School of Drama, 1974; visiting critic in acting, Yale University, School of Drama, 1974; teacher, movement for actors and directors, Juilliard School of Drama, 1976.

AWARDS: Donaldson Award, Best Dancer, *Brigadoon,* 1947.

SIDELIGHTS: MEMBERSHIPS—Founder and board member, Lewitzky Dance Foundation, Los Angeles.

ADDRESS: Agent—c/o Agency for the Performing Arts, 888 Seventh Avenue, New York, NY 10023.

* * *

MITCHELL, Julian, writer

PERSONAL: Born May 1, 1935 in Epping, England; son of William (a lawyer) and Christine Mary (Browne) Mitchell. EDUCATION: attended Winchester College, 1948–53; Wadham College, Oxford University, B.A., 1958; St. Antony's College, Oxford University, M.A., 1962.

WRITINGS: PLAYS—*A Heritage and Its History,* adapted from novel by I. Compton-Burnett, 1965; *A Family and a Fortune,* adapted from novel by I. Compton-Burnett, 1966; *Half-Life,* 1977; *The Enemy Within,* 1980; *Another Country,* 1982; *Francis,* 1983. TELEPLAYS—*A Question of Degree; Rust; Abide with Me;* (series)—*Jennie, Lady Randolph Churchhill; Staying On; The Good Soldier.* SCREENPLAYS—*Arabesque,* 1965; *Another Country,* 1984.

NOVELS—*Imaginary Toys,* 1961; *A Disturbing Influence,* 1962; *As Far As You Can Go,* 1963; *The White Father,* 1964; *A Circle of Friends,* 1966; *The Undiscovered Country,* 1968.

AWARDS: BAFTA Best Play Award, 1982: *Another Country;* International Critics Award, Christopher Award, 1977: *Abide with Me;* Somerset Maugham Award of The Library Association, 1966: *A Circle of Friends;* John Llewellyn Rhys Memorial Prize, British Library Association, 1964: *The White Father.*

SIDELIGHTS: Mr. Mitchell is also the author of the radio series *Life and Death of Dr. John Donne,* and has contributed many articles and poems and reviews to periodicals.

ADDRESS: Office—16 Ovington Street, London SW3 2JB, England. Agent—A. D. Peters, 10 Buckingham Street, London WC2, England.

* * *

MITCHELL, Lauren, actress

PERSONAL: Born May 5, 1957; daughter of Thomas B. (an advertising photographer) and Carole Jo (an interior designer; maiden name, Beall) Mitchell. EDUCATION: Graduate of the Neighborhood Playhouse, where she studied with Wynn Handman.

CAREER: DEBUT—understudy/pit singer, *Changes,* Lucille Lortel Theatre, NY, 1980. PRINCIPAL STAGE APPEARANCES—Grace Farrell, *Annie,* Uris, 380 performances, 1982; Claudia, *Nine,* 46th Street, 1983; *Some Enchanted Evening,* St. Regis, NY, 1983; Sonia, *They're Playing Our Song,* Melody Top, Milwaukee, WI, 1983; MAJOR TOURS: Sonia, understudy, *They're Playing Our Song,* national tour, 1981; Grace Farrell, *Annie,* national tour, 1981.

TELEVISION DEBUT—*Search for Tomorrow,* 1978.

ADDRESS: Agent—Hesseltine-Baker Associates, 165 W. 46th Street, New York, NY 10036.

* * *

MOLNAR, Robert, actor, mime

PERSONAL: Born June 22, 1927; son of Theodore R. C. (a musician) and Emma (a dancer; maiden name, Young Molnar) Menge; married Hilary Ostlere (a writer and dance critic), February 12, 1972. EDUCATION: Ohio Northern University, B.A.; University of Cincinnati, M.A. (English Literature); studied with Bobby Lewis and Marcel Marceau. RELIGION: Episcopalian. MILITARY: U.S. Navy, Pharmacist's Mate.

CAREER: DEBUT—David Greenhill, *It Can't Happen Here,* WPA, Emery Auditorium, Cincinnati, OH, 1937. NEW YORK DEBUT—Sol Siegal, *Hamlet of Stepney Green,* Cricket, 1957. PRINCIPAL STAGE APPEARANCES—Old actor, *The Fantasticks,* Sullivan Street, NY, for over 600 performances, 1978–80; Merlin, *Camelot,* Winter Garden, 1980–82; Fagin, *Oliver,* Beef n' Boards Dinner Theatre, 1982; Hebbie Tyson, *The Lady's Not for Burning,* Equity Library, 1983. MAJOR TOURS—Stephen Hopkins, *1776,* bus and truck tour, 1975–77, bicentennial summer engagement in Philadelphia, 1976–77.

ROBERT MOLNAR

PRINCIPAL TELEVISION APPEARANCES—*The Littlest Circus; Something New.*

SIDELIGHTS: MEMBERSHIPS—Concerned Citzens of Montauk; Off-Broadway Committee, AEA.

ADDRESS: Home—P.O. Box 1050, Montauk, NY 11954. Office—401 First Avenue, #22 C, New York, NY 10010.

* * *

MONTGOMERY, Robert, writer, composer

PERSONAL: Born 1946 in Cincinnati, OH: son of William Donton and Elizabeth Ann (Mischenko) Montgomery; married Nancy Lee Sheridan, 1968; children: Esme Alain. EDUCATION: Dartmouth College, B.A., 1968; Yale School of Drama, M.F.A. in playwrighting, 1971. POLITICS: Internationalist. RELIGION: American Catholic.

WRITINGS: PLAYS—*Subject to Fits,* Public Theatre, NY, 1971, Royal Shakespeare Company, 1972, Theater Matrix, NY, 1979, Soho Repertory, NY, 1982; *Lotta,* Public Theatre, NY, 1973; *Electra* (a three-character "response to the versions of Aeschylus, Sophocles, Euripides, and Hofmannsthal"), 1974 and 1976 (tour); *Green Pond* (book and lyrics; music by Mel Marvin), Stage South, 1977 Spoleto Festival, Chelsea, NY, 1977; words and music for *Oedipus at the Holy Place* (based on Sophocles' *Oedipus at Colonus*), Indianapolis Repertory, 1981; words and music for *Passion Play,* Woodstock–St. Paul's Church, Columbia University, NY, 1982; words and music for *Joan,* Indianapolis Repertory, 1984. PLAYS, PUBLISHED—*Subject to Fits; Green Pond* (music and lyrics only).

THEATRE-RELATED CAREER: Taught at the Eugene O'Neill Theatre Institute, Fordham University, and New York University. Guest lecturer at Smith College, State University of New York at Buffalo, Yale School of Drama, and Connecticut College.

AWARDS: Drama Desk Award, Most Promising Playwright: 1971.

SIDELIGHTS: MEMBERSHIPS—Writers Guild. Performed as a singer for two Manhattan Theatre Club shows.

ADDRESS: Agent—c/o Joyce Ketay, 320 W. 90th Street, New York, NY 10024.

* * *

MOONEY, William, actor, director

PERSONAL: Born May 2, 1936 in Bernie, MO; son of Lowell E. (a lumberman) and Louise S. Mooney; married Valorie Goodall (an opera singer and professor) on January 13, 1962; children: Sean, William. EDUCATION: University of Colorado, five years; American Theatre Wing, two years.

CAREER: PRINCIPAL STAGE APPEARANCES—*Lolita,* NY; *The Truth* and *The Brownsville Raid,* Negro Ensemble Company,

NY; *A Man for All Seasons,* NY; (one-man show) *Half Horse, Half Alligator;* (one-man show) *Damn Everything But the Circus,* U.R.G.E.N.T., NY; *Poor Richard; The Prime of Miss Jean Brodie; Golden Rainbow; The Black Terror,* Public Theatre, NY; *Strike Heaven on the Face,* Phoenix, NY; *Crossing the Bar,* Center Stage, Baltimore. MAJOR TOURS—*The Tender Trap; Period of Adjustment; The Secretary Bird.*

PRINCIPAL FILM APPEARANCES—*Flash of Green; Network; The Next Man.* PRINCIPAL TELEVISION APPEARANCES—Paul Martin, *All My Children; One Life to Live; Plaza Suite.* DIRECTED—*Jam,* AMAS Repertory Company, NY; *Candide, Robber Bridegroom, Threepenny Opera, Merry Widow,* "Plays in the Park," Edison, NJ.

AWARDS: Emmy Nominations (two) Paul Martin, *All My Children.*

SIDELIGHTS: MEMBERSHIPS—The Players Club. Mr. Mooney has served as a director at the AMAS Repertory Company in New York for over five productions.

ADDRESS: Agent—Schumer-Oubré Management, 1697 Broadway, New York, NY 10036.

* * *

MOOR, Bill (ne William H. Moor III), actor

PERSONAL: Born July 13, 1931 in Toledo, OH; son of William Hendrickson, Jr. (a real estate broker) and Lucille (Prestler) Moor. EDUCATION: Northwestern University, School of Speech, 1½ years; Denison University, Theatre Department, B.A.; studied acting with Frank Corsaro and Lee Strasberg in New York. RELIGION: Roman Catholic.

CAREER: DEBUT—Brazilian sailor, *My Sister Eileen,* Arlington Little Theatre, VA, 1946. NEW YORK DEBUT—Hatcham, *Dandy Dick,* Cherry Lane, 1956. LONDON DEBUT—Oray Sparks, *Sparkin,* Islington, London, 1953. PRINCIPAL STAGE APPEARANCES—Interviewer, *The Days and Nights of Beebe Fenstermaker,* Sheridan Square Playhouse, NY, 1963; Gus, Bill, *The Dumbwaiter* and *The Collection,* Pocket, NY, 1963–64; Wolf, *The Sweet Enemy,* Actor's Playhouse, NY, 1965; Escalus, *Measure for Measure,* New York Shakespeare Festival, 1966; Queenie, *Fortune and Men's Eyes,* Actors Playhouse, NY, 1967; Reverend Phelps, *Blues for Mr. Charlie,* ANTA, NY, 1964; Sandells, *A Cry of Players,* Vivian Beaumont, NY, 1968–69; Burgundy, *King Lear,* Vivian Beaumont, NY, 1968–69; Harold, *The Boys in the Band,* Theatre Four, NY, 1970; New Phoenix Repertory Company, NY: Draftsman, *The Great God Brown,* Lyceum, 1972–73, Don Luis, *Don Juan,* Lyceum, 1972–72, Henry, *Holiday,* Barrymore, 1973–74, Station Master, *The Visit,* Barrymore, 1973–74, Germal, *Chemin De Fer,* Barrymore, 1973–74; Johannes Rosmer, *Rosmersholm,* Roundabout, NY, 1974; Wendell, *P.S. Your Cat Is Dead,* Golden, 1975; Clark, *The Resistable Rise of Arturo Ui,* Theatre Company of Boston, 1975; Scrooge, Vancouver Symphony Orchestra, Queen Elizabeth, 1975 and 1980; Narrator, *Dandelion Wine,* Arena Stage, Washington, DC, 1976; Frank Elgin, *The Country Girl,* Meadowbrook, Rochester, MI, 1976;

BILL MOOR

Lawrence Oberman and the Chain Letter, *The Water Engine*, Plymouth, NY, 1978; Van Rensburg, *The Biko Inquest*, Theatre Four, NY, 1978; Edward IV, *Richard III*, Cort, NY, 1979; Brooklyn Academy of Music Theatre Company, 1979–80: Cleomenes, *The Winter's Tale*, Col. Wigmore, *Johnny on a Spot*, Dr. Makrov, *Barbarians*, Chouilloux, *The Purging*; John Healy, *The Potsdam Quartet*, Lion, NY, 1982; Gavin, *Requiem for a Nun*, Guthrie, Minneapolis, MN, 1982; Sir Andrew Charleson, *Plenty*, Plymouth, NY, 1982–83; Father, *The Birthday Present*, Young Playwrights Festival at the Circle Repertory Company, 1983; Randall Utterword, *Heartbreak House*, Circle in the Square, NY, 1983–84.

MAJOR TOURS—Henry Jeanigan, *Quare Medicine*, Edinburgh Festival and tour of Scotland and England, 1953; Harold, *The Boys in the Band*, national tour, 1979–70; Queenie, *Fortune and Men's Eyes*, Toronto, Montreal, and San Francisco, 1967–68; Dundas, *Mourning in a Funny Hat*, 1972; toured with the New Phoenix Repertory Company in four plays, 1972–73.

FILM DEBUT—Auctioneer, *The Legend of Nigger Charlie*, 1972. PRINCIPAL FILM APPEARANCES—Barry Traynor, *The Seduction of Joe Tynan*, 1979; Gresson, *Kramer vs. Kramer*, 1979; Terence Martin, *(Traces) Hanky Panky*, 1982.

TELEVISION DEBUT—Pastor, *Duty Bound*, 1972. PRINCIPAL TELEVISION APPEARANCES—Cosgrove, Sr., "A Shield for Murder," *Kojak*, 1974; Jonathan Dodge, *Strangers in the Homeland*, 1976; Reverand Van Buskirk, *Woman of Valor*,

1977; Cornell, *A Queen's Destiny*, 1977; *Search for Tomorrow; The Guiding Light; Love of Life; Ryan's Hope.*

AWARDS: Drama Desk Award Nomination for Outstanding Featured Actor, 1981–82: *The Potsdam Quartet;* Notable New Face of the Year, Harold, *The Boys in the Band;* Roger Dettmer Citation in the newspaper *Chicago Today*, 1969.

SIDELIGHTS: MEMBERSHIPS—The Actors Studio, 1964–present.

"One role which influenced my acting enormously was Queenie in *Fortune and Men's Eyes*. With the help of the director Michael Nestor and the willing, open and considerable talents of my fellow cast members, they taught me how far you can go in a characterization, how really indomitably character must be portrayed. I was encourged continually to go further. What I finally discovered was that the farther I went, [I released] all myself into the character without my knowing it at first. It was a wonderful experience to play the role for a year and a half. During that time I believed that I could do anything. That's a good faith to develop for an actor. It's certainly exhilarating. After being in New York for 12 years I had finally reached the phase where I no longer had to take outside jobs, and was able to make my living by acting. That's one of the many personal rewards for having played that role."

ADDRESS: Agent—Marilyn Szatmary, c/o J. Michael Bloom, Ltd., 400 Madison Avenue, New York, NY 10019.

* * *

MOORE, Christopher, actor

PERSONAL: Born January 20, 1952 in Hillburn, NY; son of Bill and Kay (DeFreece) Moore. EDUCATION: Northeastern University, Boston, MA, B.A. (Drama and Speech), 1974.

CAREER: DEBUT—Leonardo, *Blood Wedding*, Carl Ell Center, Boston, MA, 1973. NEW YORK DEBUT—William Lewis, *Mulatto*, American Folk Theater, 1980. PRINCIPAL STAGE APPEARANCES—Sir Thurio, *Two Gentlemen of Verona*, Potters Field, NY, 1980; Pvt. Wilkie, *A Soldiers' Play*, Theatre Four, NY, 1982–83; Buddy, *Terrain*, Ensemble Studio, NY, 1983. MAJOR TOURS—Pvt. Wilkie, *A Soldiers' Play*, Cincinnati Playhouse in the Park, OH, 1984.

TELEVISION DEBUT—Officer Barry Rydell, *As the World Turns*, 1983–84.

WRITINGS: PLAYS—The Last Season, 1984.

THEATRE-RELATED CAREER: Radio sportscaster/writer/producer, National Black Network, 1974–present; member, Negro Ensemble Company, 1982–present.

SIDELIGHTS: MEMBERSHIPS—AEA.

DUDLEY MOORE

MOORE, Dudley, actor and composer

PERSONAL: Born April 19, 1935, in London; son of John and Ada Francis (Hughes) Moore; married Suzy Kendall (divorced); Tuesday Weld (divorced). EDUCATION: Attended Dagenham County High School, Guildhall School of Music, and Magdalen College, Oxford.

CAREER: STAGE DEBUT—*Beyond the Fringe*, Lyceum, Edinburgh, Scotland, 1960. LONDON DEBUT—*Beyond the Fringe*, Fortune, 1961. NEW YORK DEBUT—*Beyond the Fringe*, John Golden, 1962. PRINCIPAL STAGE APPEARANCES—Allan Felix, *Play It Again, Sam*, Globe, 1969. MAJOR TOURS—*Beyond the Fringe (Good Evening)*, Australia, New Zealand, 1971, New York, 1973, U.S. cities, 1975. PRINCIPAL FILM APPEARANCES—*Bedazzled*, 1967; *Thirty Is a Dangerous Age*, 1968; *Cynthia: The Hound of the Baskervilles*, 1978; *Foul Play*, 1979; *"10"*, 1979; *Wholly Moses*, 1980; *Arthur*, 1981; *Six Weeks*, 1982; *Lovesick*, 1983; *Romantic Comedy*, 1983; *Unfaithfully Yours*, 1983, *Best Defense*, 1984.

WRITINGS: COMPOSITIONS (musical scores)—*Serjeant Musgraves' Dance*, Royal Court, London, 1959; *The Caucasian Chalk Circle*, Aldwych, London, 1962; *England, Our England*, Princes, London, 1962.

SIDELIGHTS: RECREATION—Music.

ADDRESS: Office—c/o Mary Walker, 21 Hasker Street, London, SW3.

MOORE, Judith, actress

PERSONAL: Born February 12, 1944 in Princeton, WV; daughter of Wilbert Wesley (a greenhouse manager) and Gladys Lorene (an elementary school teacher; maiden name, Lyons) Smith; married J. Kenneth Moore (curator, Metropolitan Museum of Art), June 9, 1973. EDUCATION: Concord College, Athens, WV, B.S. (Music), 1969; studied musical comedy at the H.B. Studios with Kenneth McMillan. POLITICS: Republican. RELIGION: Methodist.

NON-THEATRICAL CAREER: Lifeguard, Princeton Municipal Pool, Princeton, WV, 1960–62; music teacher, Collins High School, Oak Hill, WV, 1969; service manager, Saks Fifth Avenue, NY, 1969–70; service manager, Henri Bendel's, NY, 1971; registration assistant, New School for Social Research, NY, 1972–73.

CAREER: DEBUT—Chorus member, *Honey in the Rock*, Beckley, WV, 1961. NEW YORK DEBUT—Mrs. Wilson/Salvation Army leader, *The Drunkard*, 13th Street, for 312 performances, 1971. PRINCIPAL STAGE APPEARANCES—Marge, *Promises, Promises!*, Bergen Mall, Paramus, NJ, 1972; Gen. Cartwright, *Guys and Dolls*, Kenley Players, Warren OH, 1973; Luce, *Boys from Syracuse*, Equity Library, NY, 1973; Algy, *The Club*, A Contemporary Theatre, Seattle, WA, 1977, Coconut Grove Playhouse, Miami, FL, 1980; Beverly, *The Shadow Box*, Concord College, Athens, WV, 1978; Lily Sedgewick, *Ten by Six*, Wonderhorse, NY, 1980; Anna Kopecka, *Schweik in the Second World War*, Westside Arts, NY, 1981; Mathilda, *The Evangelist*, Wonderhorse, NY, 1982; Hattie, *Laundry and Bourbon*, Network, NY,

JUDITH MOORE

1982; Nurse/Mrs./Harriet, *Sunday in the Park with George*, Playwrights Horizons, NY, 1983; Domina, *A Funny Thing Happened on the Way to the Forum*, Coconut Grove Playhouse, Miami, FL, 1983. MAJOR TOURS—Algy, *The Club*, national tour, 1980; Ruth, *The Pirates of Penzance*, U.S. tour, 1983.

PRINCIPAL FILM WORK—Singer in Chinatown elevator/singer on rooftop, *Siren Island*, 1982.

AWARDS: Second place medal, Best Actress, West Virginia Forensic Competition, 1962.

SIDELIGHTS: MEMBERSHIPS—AEA. RECREATION—Crossword puzzles, murder mysteries. "My work has taken me all over the U.S., and vacation travel includes England, Scotland, Jamaica, and Nassau."

"As a child, I saw a production of *Tom Sawyer* and realized that I'd rather be acting than watching. My mother was the driving force at the outset, making sure that I auditioned for an outdoor drama that was beginning production 30 miles from my home. I began working professionally in the summer months and attending high school in the winter. I was sixteen. My favorite role is that of Marge in *Promises, Promises!*, and the pivotal role of my career so far has been Nurse/Mrs./Harriet in *Sunday in the Park with George* at Playwrights Horizons."

ADDRESS: Agent—Roxy Horen, Horen/Allen Management, 1650 Broadway, New York, NY 10019.

* * *

MOORE, Maureen, actress

PERSONAL: Born August 12, 1952; daughter of John Francis (a steelworker) and Mary Ann (Risk) Moore; married Barry M. Vener (a stockbroker), March 27, 1978. EDUCATION: Carnegie-Mellon University, B.A.

CAREER: DEBUT—singer, Inkspots, New Haven, CT. NEW YORK DEBUT—Dainty June, *Gypsy*, Winter Garden, 1974. PRINCIPAL STAGE APPEARANCES—Ophelia, *Hamlet*, and Polly Peachum, *Beggars' Opera*, Great Lakes Shakespeare Festival, Cleveland, OH, 1972; *Godspell*, Wilbur Theater, Boston, MA, 1973; comedienne, *Unsung Cole*, Circle Repertory, New York, 1977; Margo, *By Strouse*, Manhattan Theatre Club, 1978; Cleo, *I Love My Wife*, Barrymore, New York, 1979; *The Moonie Shapiro Songbook*, Morosco, New York, 1981; Becky, *Do Black Patent Leather Shoes Really Reflect Up?*, Alvin, New York, 1982; Constanza Weber, *Amadeus*, Broadhurst, New York, 1983; Lady Anne, *Richard III*, Anne Page, *Merry Wives of Windsor*, chorus leader, *Electra*, Elma, *Bus Stop*, Great Lakes Shakespeare Festival; Stock—Josie, *George M!*; Jenny *Shenandoah*; Sally Bowles, *Cabaret*; Ado Annie, *Oklahoma*; Julie, *The New Moon*; Ruby, *Al Jolson Tonight*; Maureen, *Broadway Baby*. MAJOR TOURS—*Godspell*, U.S. cities, 1972–73; June, *Gypsy*, U.S. cities, 1973–74; Ruby Keeler, *Al Jolson Tonight*, U.S. cities, 1980.

FILM DEBUT—Elizabeth, *The Goodbye Girl*, 1978. PRINCI-

MAUREEN MOORE

PAL FILMS APPEARANCES—*Pope of Greenwich Village*, 1984.

ADDRESS: Home—26 W. 88th Street, New York, NY 10024. Office—c/o Barry Vener, E. F. Hutton, 950 3rd Ave., New York, NY 10022. Agent—c/o Leaverton/Sames Ltd., 1640 Broadway, New York, NY 10019.

* * *

MOORE, Tom (ne H. Thomas Moore), director

PERSONAL: Born August 6, 1943; son of Heustis Thomas and Maryanne Francis (Moody) Moore. EDUCATION: Purdue University, B.A. 1965; Yale University, School of Drama, M.F.A., 1968.

CAREER: PRINCIPAL STAGE WORK—DIRECTED—(New York:) *Grease*, Eden, Broadhurst, Royale, Majestic (two national companies, bus and truck companies, two London companies), 1972–80; *Over Here*, Shubert, 1974–75; *Once in a Lifetime*, Circle in the Square (uptown), 1978; *Division Street*, Ambassador, 1980; *Frankenstein*, Palace, 1980; *'Night Mother*, Golden, 1983.

REGIONAL THEATRE—American Conservatory Theatre, San Francisco, CA—*Knock Knock*, 1977, *Hotel Paradiso*, 1978–79, *The Little Foxes*, 1979–81, *The Three Sisters*, 1981–82; Williamstown Theatre Festival, MA—*Hay Fever*, 1979, *Our Town*, 1976; Mark Taper Forum, Los Angeles, CA—*Division Street*, 1980, *A Flea in Her Ear*, 1982, *A Month in the Country*, 1983; *The Boys in Autumn*, Marines Memorial,

San Francisco, CA, 1981; *The Importance of Being Earnest*, Old Globe, San Diego, CA, 1982; *'night Mother*, American Repertory, Cambridge, MA, 1982–83; *Hay Fever*, Ahmanson, Los Angeles, CA, 1983. *Ex-Miss Copper Queen on a Set of Pills*, Martinique, NY, 1967; *Welcome to Andromeda*, American Place, 1969, Cherry Lane, 1973; *Oh What a Lovely War*, State University of New York, Buffalo, 1968; *Loot*, Brandeis University, 1968, Guthrie, Minneapolis, MN, 1975–76; *Once in a Lifetime*, Arena Stage, Washington, DC, 1975–76; as Artistic Director, Peterborough Players, NH—*The Night Thoreau Spent in Jail, You Can't Take It with You, The Hostage*.

THEATRE-RELATED CAREER: Lecturer, Seminar in American Studies, Salzburg, Austria, 1974; Teacher, American Dramatic Institute Abroad, London University, England, 1968; Teacher, Vocal Workshop, Yale School of Music, 1969; Assistant Director, Journeyman Program, Mark Taper Forum, Los Angeles, CA, 1969.

PRINCIPAL FILM WORK—Directed—*Journey*, 1972. PRINCIPAL TELEVISION WORK—Directed—*Fridays*, 1981–82.

AWARDS: Antoinette Perry Award Nomination, Best Director, 1983: *'night Mother;* Designated Old Master, Purdue University, 1981; Antoinette Perry Award Nomination, Best Director of a Musical, 1974: *Over Here;* Golden Eagle Award, Cine, for film, 1972: *Journey;* Golden Knight Award, Malta Film Festival, 1972: *Journey;* RCA/NBC, Fellowship, Yale School of Drama, 1968.

SIDELIGHTS: MEMBERSHIPS—SSD&C; Writers Guild; Directors Guild.

Mr. Moore's production of *Grease* on Broadway was the longest-running show in the history of Broadway until *A Chorus Line* surpassed it in 1984.

ADDRESS: Agent—Samuel Liff, c/o William Morris Agency, 1350 Avenue of the Americas, New York, NY 10019.

* * *

MORENO, Rita (nee Rosa Dolores Alverio), actress, dancer

PERSONAL: Born December 11, 1931, in Humacao, PR; married Leonard I. Gordon, June 18, 1965; children: Fernanda Lu.

CAREER: NEW YORK DEBUT—Angelina, *Skydrift*, Belasco, 1945. LONDON DEBUT—Ilona Ritter, *She Loves Me*, Lyric, 1964. PRINCIPAL STAGE APPEARANCES—Iris Parodus Brustein, *The Sign in Sidney Brustein's Window*, Longacre, NY, 1964; Sharon Falconer, *Gantry*, George Abbott, NY, 1970; Elaine Navazio, *Last of the Red Hot Lovers*, O'Neill, NY, 1970; Shoplifter, *Detective Story*, Shubert, Philadelphia, 1973; Staff Nurse Norton, *The National Health*, Long Wharf, New Haven, CT, 1973–74, Circle in the Square, NY, 1974; Googie Gomez, *The Ritz*, Longacre, NY, 1975; Serafina, *The Rose Tattoo*, Long Wharf, New Haven, CT, 1977; Louise, *Wally's Cafe*, Brooks Atkinson, NY, 1981.

FILM DEBUT—*So Young, So Bad*, 1950. PRINCIPAL FILM APPEARANCES—*Pagan Love Song; Toast of New Orleans; Singin' in the Rain; Cattle Town; Latin Lovers; Jivaro; Yellow Tomahawk; Garden of Evil; Fort Vengeance; Untamed*, 1955; *Seven Cities of Gold*, 1955; *The Lieutenant Wore Skirts*, 1956; *The King and I*, 1956; *The Deerslayer*, 1957; *This Rebel Breed*, 1960; Anita, *West Side Story*, 1961; *Summer and Smoke*, 1962; *The Little Sister; Cry of Battle*, 1963; *The Night of the Following Day*, 1969; *Popi*, 1969; *Marlowe*, 1969; *Carnal Knowledge*, 1971; *The Ritz*, 1976; *Happy Birthday Gemini*, 1980; *The Boss' Son; The Four Seasons*, 1981.

PRINCIPAL TELEVISION APPEARANCES—*The Electric Company*.

AWARDS: Guinness Book of World Records as only person to win Academy Award, Grammy Award, Antoinette Perry Award, Emmy Award; Emmy Award, 1977–78; Antoinette Perry Award, Best Supporting Actress, 1975: *The Ritz;* Grammy Award, Best Recording, 1973; Academy Award, Best Supporting Actress, 1962: *West Side Story*.

ADDRESS: Agent—c/o William Morris Agency, 151 El Camino, Beverly Hills, CA, 90212.*

* * *

MOREY, Charles (ne Charles L. Morey, III), actor and director

PERSONAL: Born June 23, 1947 in Oakland, CA; son of Charles L. (Jr., a businessman) and Mozelle Kathleen (Milliken) Morey; married Joyce Cohen (an actress), May 29, 1982. EDUCATION: Dartmouth College, B.A., 1969; Columbia University, M.F.A., 1971. RELIGION: Episcopalian.

CAREER: DEBUT—The Gentleman Caller, *The Glass Menagerie*, Theatre by the Sea, Portsmouth, NH, 1969. NEW YORK DEBUT—C. Maynes, *Jungle of Cities*, New York Shakespeare Festival Public Theatre, New York, 1971, 20 performances. PRINCIPAL STAGE APPEARANCES—Resident actor, season of plays, Theatre by the Sea, Portsmouth, NH, 1969; resident actor, season of plays, Peterborough Players, Peterborough, NH, 1969, 1970, 1971; resident actor, season of plays, Syracuse Repertory Theatre, Syracuse, NY 1972; resident actor, season of plays, Peterborough Players, 1973, 1974; Stephano, *The Tempest*, Folger Theater, Washington, DC, 1976; resident actor, season of plays, Peterborough Players, 1976; Osip, *Idle Hands*, Ark Theatre Company, 1979; Ross, *Macbeth*, Ark Theatre Company, 1983. MAJOR TOURS—Actor 2, *An Evening with George Bernard Shaw*, 1972–73.

DIRECTED: Plays—*Of Men and of Angels*, Ensemble Studio Theatre, New York, 1978; *Vivien*, McCarter Theatre Company, Princeton, NJ, 1980; *Arsenic and Old Lace*, Pioneer Memorial Theatre, 1981; *Unheard Songs*, Ark Theatre Company, 1982; *Charley's Aunt*, Pioneer Memorial Theatre, 1982; *Life with Father*, Pioneer Memorial Theatre, 1983; *Eminent Domain, Bing and Walker, Ragged Mountain Elegies, An Evening's Frost, Of Men and of Angels, Unheard Songs, Our Town, A Flea in Her Ear, The Time of Your Life, Scapino, Of Mice and Men, The Philadelphia Story, The Playboy of the Western World, A Streetcar Named*

CHARLES MOREY

pany, Minneapolis, 1966–67; chorus, *The House of Atreus,* Ted Ragg / Charles Fish / Ignatius Dullfeet, *The Resistible Rise of Arturo Ui,* Minnesota Theatre Company, Minneapolis, MN, 1968, Billy Rose, NY, 1968; Charles Playhouse, Boston, MA, 1969–70; Man, *Peanut Butter and Jelly,* University of the Streets, NY, 1970; Thoreau, *The Night Thoreau Spent in Jail,* Alley, Houston, TX, 1970; George Mische, *The Trial of the Catonsville Nine,* Faith Church, NY, 1971, Lyceum, NY, 1971; Julian Weston, *Find Your Way Home,* Brooks Atkinson, NY, 1974; Richard III, *Richard III,* Mitzi E. Newhouse, NY, 1974; Edmund Tyrone, *Long Day's Journey into Night,* Brooklyn Academy, NY, 1976; Chorus, *Henry V,* Delacorte, NY, 1976; Scoutmaster Hennessey, *Dirty Jokes,* Lake Forest, Chicago, IL, 1976; Micah, *G R Point,* Playhouse, NY, 1979; Kenneth Harrison, *Whose Life Is It Anyway,* Kennedy Center, Washington, DC; *The Ballad of Dexter Creed,* Public, NY, 1982; *Uncle Vanya,* Public, NY, 1982; Captain Queeg/Barney Greenwald, *Caine Mutiny Court Martial,* Circle in the Square, NY, 1983.

PRINCIPAL FILM APPEARANCES—*Bang the Drum Slowly,* 1973; *The Last Detail,* 1974; *Report to the Commissioner,* 1975; *Who'll Stop the Rain,* 1978; *Shoot It: Black, Shoot It: Blue; Reborn,* 1982; *Winged Serpent,* 1982; *The Link,* 1982.

PRINCIPAL TELEVISION APPEARANCES—Dorf, *Holocaust;* Wilbur Wright, *The Winds of Kitty Hawk; Too Far to Go;* Gentleman Caller, *The Glass Menagerie.*

DIRECTED: Plays—*Love's Labour's Lost, Psalm to the Son of*

Desire, The Runner Stumbles, Knock-Knock, Ah Wilderness, Peterborough Players, 1977–83.

THEATRE-RELATED CAREER: Guest director—Benedictine College, Atchison, KS, 1974–75; University of Pittsburgh, Johnstown, PA, 1978; Franklin Pierce College, Rindge, NH, 1979; Sarah Lawrence College, Bronxville, NY, 1979; artistic director, Peterborough Players, 1977–present.

SIDELIGHTS: MEMBERSHIPS—AEA, SAG, AFTRA.

ADDRESS: Home—718 W. 171st Street, #51, New York, NY, 10032. Office—Peterborough Players, Box 1, Peterborough, NH, 03458.

* * *

MORIARTY, Michael, actor, composer, writer

PERSONAL: Born April 5, 1941, in Detroit, MI; children: Matthew. EDUCATION: Attended Dartmouth College; trained for the stage at London Academy of Music and Dramatic Art.

CAREER: STAGE DEBUT—Octavius Caesar, *Antony and Cleopatra,* Delacorte, NY, 1963. PRINCIPAL STAGE APPEARANCES—Jack, *As You Like It,* Delacorte, NY, 1963; Floritzel, *The Winter's Tale,* Delacorte, NY, 1963; Longaville, *Love's Labour's Lost,* Delacorte, NY, 1965; Helenus, *Troilus and Cressida,* Delacorte, NY, 1965; Minnesota Theatre Com-

MICHAEL MORIARTY

Man, St. John's Cathedral, NY, 1979. PRODUCED: Plays—*What Everywoman Knows*, Public, NY, 1982.

WRITINGS: PLAYS, PRODUCED—*Flight to the Fatherland*, Geva, Rochester, NY 1979; *The Ballad of Dexter Creed*, Public, NY, 1982. MUSIC—*Symphony for String Orchestra*, Greenwich House Orchestra, NY, 1984.

AWARDS: Antoinette Perry Award, Theatre World Award, Drama Desk Award, 1974: *Find Your Way Home;* Emmy Award; *The Glass Menagerie;* "en homenaje" Award (Spain), 1982: *Reborn* and *Too Far to Go;* Certificate of Achievement, Yeshiva University.

ADDRESS: Agent—c/o Robert Lantz Office, 888 Seventh Avenue, New York, NY 10019.

* * *

MORIYASU, Atsushi, scenic designer

PERSONAL: Born January 16, 1956, in Kobe, Japan; son of Tadashi and Koko (Nishiyama) Moriyasu. EDUCATION: State University of New York at Purchase, B.F.A., 1978.

CAREER: NEW YORK DEBUT—Scenic designer, *Station J*, Pan Asian Repertory Theatre, 1982. PRINCIPAL STAGE WORK—(scenic designer) *Teahouse*, Greek Theatre of New York, 1983; *A Midsummer Night's Dream*, Greek Theatre of New York, 1983; *A Song for a Nissei Fisherman*, Actor's Outlet Center, New York, 1983.

AWARDS: Villager Downtown Theater Award, Outstanding Set Design, 1983: *Teahouse*.

SIDELIGHTS: "I am a sculptor in New York City. I love sky."

ADDRESS: Office—39 White Street, New York, NY 10013.

* * *

MORRIS, Aldyth, writer

PERSONAL: Born August 24, 1901, in Logan, UT; daughter of Weston (a college professor) and Frances M. (a college professor) Vernon; married Raymond L. Morris, June 28, 1929; children: Richard V. EDUCATION: Utah State College, A.B., 1921.

WRITINGS: PLAYS, PRODUCED—*Fourth Son*, Phoenix Theatre, 1955, Chinese Civic Association Theatre, 1955; *Secret Concubine*, Princeton Festival Players, 1956; Blue Masque Players, Catawba College, 1959, Carnegie Theatre, NY, 1960, Chinese Civic Association, Honolulu, HI, 1960; *RLS*, Hawaii Performing Arts Company, Honolulu, 1977, Hawaii Public Theatre, 1978; *Captain Cook*, Kennedy Theatre, University of Hawaii, Honolulu, Monomoy Theatre, Cape Cod, Detroit University, MI, 1978; *Damien*, Honolulu Community Theatre, Honolulu, 1963, Monomoy Theatre, Cape Cod, 1964, Kennedy Theatre, University of Hawaii, 1976,

Performing Arts Foundation, Huntington, Long Island, NY, 1980, Open Eye Theatre, NY, 1981, Intiman Theatre, NY, 1981, Berkeley Stage, CA, 1982, Stratford Shakespearean Festival, Ontario, Canada, 1982 and 1983, Redlands Summer Festival, CA, 1982. PLAYS, UNPRODUCED—Liliuokalani. TELEVISION PLAYS—*Damien*, 1978, 1979 and 1980. BOOKS—*Damien*.

AWARDS: Peabody Award: *Damien;* Christopher Award, Best Play Showing Man in Ethical Crisis: *Secret Concubine*.

SIDELIGHTS: MEMBERSHIPS—Dramatists Guild, National League of American Pen Women, National Society of Arts and Letters.

ADDRESS: Home—1028 15th Avenue, Honolulu, HI 96816. Agent—c/o Sheila Lemon, Ltd., Assets House, 17 Elverton Street, London SW1P 20G.

* * *

MORRIS, Edmund, writer and actor

PERSONAL: Born September 22, 1912, in Odessa, Russia; son of William (a furniture dealer) and Nessie (Bittman) Stein; married Estelle Davis, June 13, 1944; children: Steven. EDUCATION: University of San Fernando College of Law, L.L.B.; trained for the stage at the American Theatre Wing with Lee Strasberg. MILITARY: U.S. Army Air Force.

CAREER: DEBUT—Mac, *Having a Wonderful Time*, East Coast cities, 1937. PRINCIPAL STAGE APPEARANCES (1937–42)—Joe Bonaparte, *Golden Boy;* Mr. Prince, *Rocket to the Moon;* Moe Axelrod/Ralph Berger, *Awake and Sing;* Larry Ormand, *Two on an Island;* German Consul, *Margin for Error;* Elevator Man, *He*.

WRITINGS: PLAYS, PRODUCED—*The Wooden Dish*, Phoenix, London, U.K. cities, 1954; *The Wooden Dish*, Booth, NY, 1955. PLAYS, PUBLISHED—*The Wooden Dish*. SCREENPLAYS—*Walk on the Wild Side*, 1961; *Savage Guns*, 1962; *Project X*, 1967. TELEVISION PLAYS—*The Wooden Dish*, 1961. EPISODIC TELEVISION SCRIPTS—*By-Line; Danger; Man Who Never Was; Man Behind the Badge; Ford Theatre; Charley Wilde; Philco Playhouse; Suspense; Rifleman; DA's Man; The Texan; Lawman; Courtsmartial; Littlest Hobo; Man without Gun; The Clock; Armstrong Circle Theatre; Zane Grey Theatre; Channing; Sugar Foot; Casey Crime Photographer; Tarzan; Richard Diamond; Colonel Flack; Wells-Fargo; Checkmate; Frontier Circus; Rat Patrol; Medical Center*.

THEATRE-RELATED CAREER: Associate Professor of Theatre, University of Denver, 1972–73.

AWARDS: Television-Radio Writers Award Nomination, 1963–64: *Channing*.

ADDRESS: Home—1122 18th Street, Santa Monica, CA 90403.

JOAN MORRIS

MORRIS, Joan, actress, director, singer

PERSONAL: Born February 10, 1943, in Portland, OR; daughter of Joseph Ellis (U.S. Marines) and Katherine Emma (a teacher; maiden name, Fleck) Morris; married William Eldon Bolcom (a composer), November 28, 1975. EDUCATION: Gonzaga University for two years; trained for theatre at American Academy of Dramatic Arts, diploma 1968; studied speech with Clifford Jackson, voice with Frederica Schmitz-Svevo, and acting with Julie Bovasso.

CAREER: DEBUT—Polly Peachum, *The Threepenny Opera*, Portland Civic, Portland, OR, 1961. NEW YORK DEBUT—Daughter, *The Drunkard*, 13th Street, 1966–67, 50 performances. PRINCIPAL STAGE APPEARANCES—Polly Peachum, *The Beggars' Opera*, Guthrie, Minneapolis, MN, 1979.

DIRECTED: PLAYS—*Three Dollar Revue* and *Four Dollar Revue*, University of Michigan Theatre Department, 1981, 1982.

TELEVISION DEBUT—*The Dick Cavett Show* (two evenings), 1979. TELEVISION APPEARANCES—*Evening with the Boston Pops; Fascinating Rhythms* (Rochester, NY, TV, WXXI), 1983.

THEATRE-RELATED CAREER: Assistant adjunct professor, Vocal Interpretation, American Popular Songs, University of Michigan, 1981–present.

WRITINGS: BOOKS, PUBLISHED—Entry on Charles K. Harris, for *Grove's Dictionary of American Music and Musi-*cians. Phonograph Record Liner Notes, *After the Ball* and *Vaudeville*, both for Nonesuch Records.

AWARDS: Grammy Nomination, *After the Ball*, 1975.

SIDELIGHTS: With her husband, Ms. Morris has toured extensively performing American and English popular songs from the mid-nineteenth century to the present. They have concertized in Bath, England; LaRochelle, France; Stuttgart and Cologne, Germany; and Rome, Italy; other European cities are on their agenda as well. They have recorded eleven albums for Nonesuch, Columbia, and RCA Red Seal Records.

ADDRESS: Home—3080 Whitmore Lake Road, Ann Arbor, MI 48103. Agent—Mr. Lee Walter, c/o Shaw Concerts, Inc., 1995 Broadway, New York, NY 10023.

* * *

MORRIS, John, composer

PERSONAL: Born October 18, 1926; son of Thomas Arthur (an engineer) and Helen (Sherratt) Morris; married Francesca Bosetti (a writer and editor) on October 10, 1949; children: Evan Bosetti, Bronwen Helen. EDUCATION: University of Washington; Juilliard School, New School, 1948–51.

CAREER: PRINCIPAL STAGE WORK, ORIGINAL MUSIC FOR PLAYS—New York Shakespeare Festival productions: *Peer Gynt, Richard III, Love's Labour's Lost, Electra, As You Like It, Comedy of Errors, Titus Andronicus, Henry IV, Pt. I, Henry IV Pt. II, Romeo and Juliet, Hamlet* (two productions), *The Cherry Orchard;* American Shakespeare Festival, Stratford, CT: *The Tempest, Julius Caesar, Antony and Cleopatra, Measure for Measure, Twelfth Night; My Mother, My Father and Me*, NY; *Camino Real*, Acting Company, NY; musicial with Gerald Freedman, *A Time for Singing*, NY; *Take One Step* and *Young Andy Jackson*, NY (children's musicals).

PRINCIPAL FILM WORK, Original Music—*The Producers; The Twelve Chairs; The Gamblers; Blazing Saddles; The Bank Shot; Young Frankenstein; Sherlock Holmes' Younger Brother; Silent Movie; The Last Remake of Beau Geste; The In-Laws; The World's Greatest Lover; In God We Trust; High Anxiety; The Elephant Man; History of the World, Part One; Yellowbeard; To Be or Not to Be; Johnny Dangerously; The First One In.* PRINCIPAL DANCE AND BALLET MUSIC, Broadway Productions—*Mack and Mabel; Nash at Nine; Much Ado about Nothing; Look to the Lillies; Dear World; Baker Street; All-American; Kwamina; Wildcat; Bye, Bye Birdie; Bells Are Ringing; Pipe Dreams; Peter Pan; Hair; Tap Dance Kid.*

PRINCIPAL TELEVISION WORK, Original Music—*Splendor in the Grass; The Electric Grandmother; The Scarlet Letter; The Adams Chronicles; Georgia O'Keefe; The Franken Project; The Firm; The Tap Dance Kid; Make Believe Marriage; After School Special Time; French Chef Theme* for Julia Child's show; *Making Things Grow* theme; *The Desperate Hours; The Skirts of Happy Chance; Infancy and Childhood;* Musical Specials—*Anne Bancroft Specials* 1 and 2; *'S Lemmon, S' Gershwin, S' Wonderful; The Music World of Harold Arlen; The Music of Cole Porter; The Littlest Angel; Hallmark Christmas Specials; The Canterville Ghost.*

AWARDS: Emmy Award, *The Tap Dance Kid;* Academy Award Nomination, *Blazing Saddles;* Academy Award Nomination, *The Elephant Man.*

SIDELIGHTS: MEMBERSHIPS—ASCAP; Academy of Motion Picture Arts and Sciences.

''After attending the Juilliard School as a scholarship piano major under the aegis of Alfred Mirovitch, the first part of Mr. Morris's career led him to Broadway where he began as assistant to Lehman Engel.''

ADDRESS: Agent—Sam Schwartz of Gorfaine/Schwartz, Los Angeles, CA.

* * *

MOSHER, Gregory, director, producer

PERSONAL: Born January 15, 1949; son of Thomas (a physician) and Florence (Moessner) Mosher; EDUCATION: Oberlin College, OH, 1967–69; State University of New York at Ithaca, B.F.A., 1971; Juilliard School, 1971–74.

CAREER: PRINCIPAL STAGE WORK, DIRECTED—Goodman, Chicago, IL: *The Son*, Stage 2, 1974–75, *American Buffalo*, Stage 2, 1975–76, *Statues/The Bridge at Belharbour*, Stage 2, 1975–76, *Streamers*, Mainstage, 1976–77, *Sizwe Bansi Is Dead*, Stage 2, 1976–77, *A Life in the Theatre*, Stage 2, 1976–77, *The Seagull*, Mainstage, 1977–78, *Battering Ram*, Stage 2, 1977–78, *Native Son*, Mainstage, 1978–79, *Lone Canoe or The Explorer*, Mainstage, 1978–79, *Emigrés*, Stage 2, 1978–79, *The Island*, Stage 2, 1978–79, *Bal*, Mainstage, 1979–80, *The Suicide*, Mainstage, 1980–81, *Plenty*, Mainstage, 1980–81, *Panto*, Mainstage, 1981–82, *Lakeboat*, Mainstage, 1981–82, *Edmond*, Mainstage, 1981–82, *Gardenia*, Mainstage, 1983–83, *Disappearance of the Jews*, Mainstage, 1982–83, *Glengarry Glen Ross*, Mainstage, 1983–84.

PRODUCED—Goodman, Chicago, IL: *Winnebago, Once and for All, Three Women*, Stage 2, 1974–75; *Three Plays of the Yuan Dynasty, Chicago/The Local Stigmatic, Dandelion Wine*, Stage 2, 1975–76; *Steamers*, Mainstage, 1976–77; *The Sport of My Mad Mother, A Life in the Theatre, Kaspar, George Jean Nathan in Revue*, Stage 2, 1976–77; *The Seagull*, Mainstage, 1977–78; *Hail Scrawdyke, Annulla Allen, The Prague Spring*, Spring 2, 1977–78; *A Christmas Carol, Two-Part Inventions, Bosoms and Neglect, Holiday*, Mainstage, 1978–79; *Curse of the Starving Class, Scenes and Revelations*, Stage 2, 1978–79; *Death and the King's Horseman, A Christmas Carol, An Enemy of the People, Talley's Folly, Cyrano de Bergerac*, Mainstage, 1979–80; *Betrayal, Plenty, Play Mas, Dwarfman, Master of a Million Shapes*, Mainstage, 1980–81; *Still Life, Endgame/Krapp's Last Tape, The Frosted Glass Coffin/A Perfect Analysis Given by a Parrot/Some Problems for the Moose Lodge, Kukla and Ollie Live, A House Not Meant to Stand*, Stage 2, 1980–81; *The Front Page, A House Not Meant to Stand, Sganarelle*, Mainstage, 1981–82; *The Man Who Had Three*

Arms, The Comedy of Errors, The Dining Room, Red River, A Soldiers Play, Mainstage, 1982–83; *Kukla and Ollie Live/The Theatre of Burr Tillstrom, The Beckett Project: Ohio Impromptu, Eh Joe, A Piece of Monologue, A Spalding Grey Retrospective, Jungle Coup, Gorilla, Hotline*, Stage 2, 1982–83; *A Raisin in the Sun, Candida, The Road, The Time of Your Life, The Three Musketeers*, Mainstage, 1983–84; *Diagonal Man/Theory and Practice*, Bread and Puppet Theatre, Stage 2, 1983–84.

DIRECTED, New York—*American Buffalo*, 1975; *Edmond*, 1982.

THEATRE-RELATED CAREER: Associate Director/Director Stage 2, Goodman, Chicago, IL, 1974–78; Director, Goodman, Chicago, IL, 1978–present.

AWARDS: Obie Award, Best Direction, 1983: *Edmond.*

SIDELIGHTS: MEMBERSHIPS—The Players Club.

ADDRESS: Home—649 West Deming No. 2, Chicago, IL 60614. Office—Goodman Theatre, 200 S. Columbus Drive, Chicago, IL 60603.

* * *

MOSSE, Spencer, lighting designer

PERSONAL: Surname sounds like ''Moss-ah;'' born October 17, 1945; son of Ernest Goodman and Ruth Marion Mosse. EDUCATION: Bard College, 1963–1967; Yale University, School of Drama, 1967–69 apprenticed to John Robertson and Martin Aronstein at the New York Shakespeare Festival; continued training working with lighting designers: Jules Fisher, John Gleason, Gilbert Hemsley, Joan Larkey, Tharon Musser, H. R. Poindexter, Jennifer Tipton, Jean Rosenthal, and Lee Watson.

CAREER: PRINCIPAL STAGE WORK—New York Productions—*Rainbow Jones*, 1974; *Short Eyes*, Vivian Beaumont, 1974; *Mourning Pictures*, 1974; *Lamppost Reunion*, 1975; *Godspell*, 1971–76; *After the Season*, 1980; Off-Broadway—*Bloomers*, Equity Library, 1974; *Studs Edsel*, Ensemble Studio Theatre, 1974; *Magritte Skies*, Playwrights Horizons, 1976; Theatre at the Riverside Church: *The Shoeshine Parlor, Straight from the Ghetto, Cruxifiction, One Last Look, The Dolls, Street Sounds, The Blacks, Clara's Old Man, The Marriage Proposal, Looking for Tomorrow*, 1975–77; *Alfred Dies*, Actors Studio, 1977; *In the Wine Time*, Manhattan Theatre Club, 1976; *Transformations*, Manhattan Theatre Club, 1977; *Boseman and Lena*, Manhattan Theatre Club, 1977; *The Wayside Motor Inn*, Manhattan Theatre Club, 1977; *Lady House Blues*, Playwrights Horizons, Queens Playhouse, 1979; *Eternal Love*, South Street, 1981; New York Shakespeare Festival: *Puerto Rican Festival, The Hunter, Rosalyn Tureck Conducts, The Happiness Cage, Burning, The Time Trial, The Shoeshine Parlor, Crack, Sleeparound Town, Remembrance, The Tempest, Don Juan, Egyptology*, 1966–83.

REGIONAL THEATRE COMPANIES—Hartford Stage Company, CT: *Joe Egg, The Farce of Scapin, Mackeral, Beau Stra-*

tegem, Is There Life After High School?, 1969–81; Philadelphia Drama Guild: *The Royal Family, The Glass Menagerie, The Birthday Party, Hedda Gabler, The Miser, Heartbreak House, Enter a Free Man, Five Finger Exercise, Blithe Spirit, Hamlet, The Show-Off, Travesties, Saint Joan, Hobson's Choice, Uncle Vanya, The Au Pair Man, Arms and the Man, Private Lives, The Blood Knot, Night of the Iguana, The Last Few Days of Willie Callandar, You Never Can Tell, Summer, Twelfth Night, Thark*, 1975–80; Milwaukee Repertory Theatre: *Namesake, Island, A Christmas Carol, Merton of the Movies, Fridays, The Recruiting Officer, Dance of Death, On the Road to Babylon, Cyrano de Bergerac, Julius Caesar, Secret Injury, Secret Revenge, Miss Lulu Bett, The Glass Menagerie, Uncle Vanya*, 1979–83; Cincinnati Playhouse in the Park: *The Diary of Anne Frank, The Man Who Came to Dinner, Tintypes, Talley's Folly*, 1979–82; Syracuse Stage: *The Blood Knot, Cat on a Hot Tin Roof*, 1979–82; Alaska Repertory: *The Man Who Came to Dinner, Major Barbara*, 1981–82; Seattle Repertory: *Awake and Sing, The Ballad of Soapy Smith*, 1983.

SIDELIGHTS: MEMBERSHIPS—United Scenic Artists.

ADDRESS: 350 W. 51st Street, New York, NY 10019.

* * *

MOSTEL, Joshua, actor and director

PERSONAL: Born December 21, 1946; son of Zero (ne Sammuel Joel, an actor) and Kathryn Celia (an actress, dancer, and writer; maiden name, Harken) Mostel; married Peggy Rajski (a producer and director), June 24, 1983. EDUCATION: Brandeis University, B.A., 1970.

CAREER: DEBUT—Joey, *The Homecoming*, Boy, *The Hostage, Lysistrata*, Provincetown Playhouse, MA, 1968. NEW YORK DEBUT—*Unlikely Heroes*, Broadway, 1971. PRINCIPAL STAGE APPEARANCES—*The Proposition*, MA and NY, 1971; *An American Millionaire*, Circle in the Square, NY, 1975; Milo, *A Texas Trilogy*, Kennedy Center, Washington, DC and NY, 1976; Hirschel, *Gemini*, Arena Stage, Washington, DC, 1978; Bottom, *A Midsummer Night's Dream*, Kenyon Theatre Festival, OH, 1980.

FILM DEBUT—Borrelli, *Going Home*, 1971. PRINCIPAL FILM APPEARANCES—King Herod, *Jesus Christ Superstar*, 1973; Morris Fink, *Sophie's Choice*, 1982; private investigator, *Star 80*, 1983; Sol, *Windy City*, 1983. PRINCIPAL TELEVISION APPEARANCES—*Seventh Avenue*, 1975; *Delta House*, 1979; *At Ease*, 1982. DIRECTED—*Ferocious Kisses*, Manhattan Punchline, 1982.

WRITINGS: Television Special—*Media Probes: The Language Show* (with Mickey Lemle).

ADDRESS: Agent—c/o Jeff Hunter, D.H.K.P.R., 165 W. 46th Street, New York, NY 10036.

MOULTON, Robert, choreographer, director, educator

PERSONAL: Born July 20, 1922 in Dodge Center, MN; son of Edwin D. (a butcher) and Ethel Jane (a teacher; maiden name, Pendergast) Moulton; married Marion Skowland (a librarian), June 19, 1948; children: Miranda, Charles. EDUCATION: University of Minnesota, B.A., 1947, M.A., 1949, Ph.D., 1956; studied Dance with Madame Risk, Cuban Ballet; studied at the Connecticut College of Dance, 1951; choreography with Louis Horst, NY, 1951–53; at Martha Graham School of Dance, NY, 1952–53; choreography with Audrey de Vos, London, England, 1962; also with Gertrude Lippincott, José Limon, Hilde Holgar; and Alexander Technique with Margery Barstow, environmental movement with Anna Halprin. POLITICS: Democrat. RELIGION: Episcopalian. MILITARY: U.S. Army, Pfc, European Theater of Operations, 1942–46.

CAREER: DEBUT—Vaudeville Dancer, Fargo, ND, 1930. PRINCIPAL STAGE WORK, CHOREOGRAPHY—Royal Winnipeg Ballet Company: *Grassland*, 1958, *Brave Song*, 1959, *Beggar's Ballet*, 1963; Canadian Contemporary Dancers: *Rondo ad Absurdum*, 1967, *True Believer*, 1968, *Bach Is Beautiful*, 1970, *7 Rituals*, 1972; Calgary Dance Theatre: *Nickel Dances*, 1971, *Bachanelle*, 1972; Duluth Civic Ballet: *Turned on Bach*, 1973; Stage Coach Opera Company (adapted, directed, choreographed): *Geisha, Belle of New York, Merry Widow, Black Crook, Floradora, Forty-five Minutes from Broadway, The Last Days of Pompeii, The Count of Monte Cristo, The Three Musketeers*, 1962–72. PRINCIPAL STAGE WORK, DIRECTED AND CHOREOGRAPHED—*El Capitan*, Minnesota Opera Company, 1973 and 1975; *Die Fledermaus*, Duluth Civic Opera, 1974; *Pirates of Penzance, Merry Widow*, Minnesota Opera Company, 1980. OPERA CHOREOGRAPHY—*Patience, Amahl and the Night Visitors, L'enfant prodigue, Down in the Valley, The Consul*. STAGE CHOREOGRAPHY—*Camille*, Guthrie, Minneapolis, MN, 1980, *The Emperor's New Clothes*, Rainbow, Winnipeg, Canada, 1979.

THEATRE-RELATED CAREER: Professor of Theatre Arts, University of Minnesota, 1949–84; artistic director, University of Minnesota Theatre, 1980–84.

WRITINGS: PLAYS, PRODUCED—Musical (book), *Jesse James*, 1976.

AWARDS: Distinguished Teacher Award, University of Minnesota, 1983; dance fellowship, Minnesota Arts Council, 1973; master teacher, National Endowment for the Arts, 1972; University of Minnesota Fellowship to study dance in Sweden and England, 1961–62; One of the Ten Outstanding Young Men in American Educational Theatre, AETA, 1957; fellowship, School of American Dance at Connecticut College, 1951; University of Minnesota, Gopher Award, 1950; Charles Nichols Service Award, University of Minnesota Theatre, 1943; Three Battle Stars, Royal Canadian Army for service in the Eastern Theatre of Operations, World War II.

SIDELIGHTS: MEMBERSHIPS—Society of Stage Directors and Choreographers; AETA; C.O.R.D.; AAUPHER; Phi Epsilon Delta.

Mr. Moulton has served as a teacher of stage movement at the American Conservatory Theatre in San Francisco and has conducted workshops throughout the U.S. and Canada. He was the artistic director of the Stage Coach Opera Company, 1962–72, specializing in melodramas and 19th-century operettas.

ADDRESS: Home—48 Melbourne Avenue, S.E., Minneapolis, MN 55414. Office—110 Rarig Center, 330 21st Avenue S., University of Minnesota, Minneapolis, MN 55455.

* * *

MULGREW, Kate, actress

PERSONAL: Born April 29, 1955; daughter of Thomas James (a contractor) and Joan Virginia (an artist/painter; maiden name, Kiernan) Mulgrew; married Robert Harry Egan (a director), July 31, 1982; children: Ian Thomas. EDUCATION: New York University; studied for the theatre with Stella Adler. RELIGION: Roman Catholic.

CAREER: DEBUT—Blanche, Widower's Houses, Cyrano Repertory, NY, 1974. PRINCIPAL STAGE APPEARANCES— Emily, Our Town, American Shakespeare, Stratford, CT, 1975; Desdemona, Othello, Hartman, Stamford, CT, 1977; Regina, Another Part of the Forest, Seattle Repertory, WA, 1981; Barbara, Major Barbara, Seattle Repertory, 1982; Tracy, The Philadelphia Story, Alaska Repertory, 1983.

FILM DEBUT—Isolt, Lovespell, 1978. PRINCIPAL FILMS—A Stranger Is Watching, 1980.

TELEVISION DEBUT—Mary Ryan, Ryan's Hope, 1975–77. TELEVISION APPEARANCES—Mrs. Columbo, Mrs. Columbo, 1977–78; Tony, The Word, 1978; Rachel, The Manions of America, 1979–80; Mother Seton, Mother Seton, 1981.

THEATRE-RELATED CAREER: Teacher, Audition Technique, Cornish Institute, Seattle, WA, 1982.

AWARDS: Golden Globe Nomination, Best Dramatic Actress in a Series, 1978: Mrs. Columbo.

SIDELIGHTS: MEMBERSHIPS—AEA; AFTRA; SAG; Committee for Right to Life (board member).

Ms. Mulgrew is featured in a chapter of the book They Came from Dubuque and has a featured interview in a book by Karen Kalli on fame and spirit.

"Regina Hubbard introduced me to my husband—but Richard Burton taught me power in Lovespell."

ADDRESS: Home—2580 Fifth Avenue W., Seattle, WA 98119. Office—950 Third Avenue, New York, NY 10022. Agent—Hesseltine/Baker, 165 W. 46th Street, No. 409, New York, NY 10036.

* * *

MUNDY, Meg, actress

PERSONAL: Born in London, England; daughter of John (a cellist and conductor) and Clytie (a singer and voice teacher;

maiden name, Hine) Mundy; children: Sotos Yannopoulos. EDUCATION: Institute of Musical Art (two years); studied for the theatre with Sanford Meisner and Marc Daniels and at the American Theatre Wing. NON-THEATRICAL CAREER: Beauty editor, Condé Nast Publications: Vogue, 1962–68, Mademoiselle, 1968–70; market editor, Condé Nast Publications, House and Garden, 1976–77; fashion director, Klopman Hills–Burlington Industries, 1970–75.

CAREER: DEBUT—A Cloud, Artistophanes' The Clouds, Mt. Kisco Theatre, NY. PRINCIPAL STAGE APPEARANCES— Ten Million Ghosts, 1936; Chorus, Hooray for What!, Winter Garden, NY, 1937; The Fabulous Invalid, 1938; Chorus, Three to Make Ready, 1938; How I Wonder; Lead, The Respectful Prostitute, 1948; Mary McLeod, Detective Story, Hudson, NY, 1949; Love's Labours Lost, 1951; Love Me Little, 1953; in stock and regional theatres appeared in the following: The Winslow Boy, The Gioconda Smile, Epitaph for George Dillon, The Time of Your Life, Summer and Smoke, Misalliance, The Rainmaker, The Rope Dancers, 1948–58; Mrs. Lord, The Philadelphia Story, Vivian Beaumont, NY, 1981; Mrs. Kirby, You Can't Take It with You, Papermill Playhouse, NJ, then NY, 1983.

FILM APPEARANCES—Oliver's Story, 1980; Ordinary People, 1980; The Bell Jar, 1981.

TELEVISION APPEARANCES—Playhouse 90, Omnibus, Suspense, U.S. Steel Hour, Philco TV Playhouse, Theatre Guild, Ford Hour, Kraft Television Theatre, Naked City, Play of the Week, G.E. Theatre, Alfred Hitchcock Presents, Purex Summer Specials, 1948–58; The Doctors, 1976–present.

AWARDS: Theatre World Award, 1948: The Respectful Prostitute.

SIDELIGHTS: Memberships—AEA (National Board Member and Delegate to AFTRA, 1980–83); SAG; AFTRA.

ADDRESS: Agent—Jeff Hunter, DHKPR, 165 W. 46th Street, New York, NY 10036.

* * *

MURPHY, Michael, actor

PERSONAL: Born May 5, 1938, in Los Angeles; son of Bearl Banton (a salesman) and Georgia Arlyn (a teacher; maiden name, Money) Murphy. EDUCATION: University of Arizona, 1957–61, B.A. NON-THEATRICAL CAREER: Teacher, English/Drama, Los Angeles City School System/University High School, 1962–64.

CAREER: DEBUT—Take Her, She's Mine, Valley Music Theatre, Los Angeles, 1966. NEW YORK DEBUT—Director, Rat's Nest, Vandam, then Grove Street Theatre, 1978–79 for six-month run. PRINCIPAL STAGE APPEARANCES—Our Town, Huntington Hartford, Los Angeles, 1970; The Hotel Play, La Mama, NY, 1981; Playing in Local Bands, Yale Repertory, New Haven, CT, 1982–83.

PRINCIPAL FILMS—The Legend of Lylah Clare, 1968; The Arrangement, 1969; Brewster McCloud, 1970; M*A*S*H,

1970; *McCabe & Mrs. Miller,* 1971; *What's Up, Doc?,* 1972; *Nashville,* 1975l; *An Unmarried Woman,* 1977; *The Front,* 1977; *Manhattan,* 1980; *The Year of Living Dangerously,* 1983; *Strange Behavior; Cloak and Dagger.*

TELEVISION DEBUT—*Saints and Sinners,* 1962. TELEVISION APPEARANCES—*Ben Casey; Dr. Kildare; Bonanza; Combat!; The Autobiography of Miss Jane Pittman; John Cheever's "Oh Youth, and Beauty;" Two Marriages,* 1984.

ADDRESS: Agent—Creative Artists Agency, 1888 Century Park East, Los Angeles, CA 90067.

* * *

MURRAY, Bill, actor and writer

PERSONAL: Born September 21, 1950, in Evanston, IL; married Margaret Kelly, 1980; children: Homer. EDUCATION: Graduated from Loyola Academy and attended Regis College, Denver, CO.

CAREER: PRINCIPAL TELEVISION APPEARANCES—*Saturday Night Live with Howard Cosell; Saturday Night Live* (also writer), 1977–80; *TVTV; Things We Did Last Summer.*

PRINCIPAL FILM APPEARANCES—*Meatballs,* 1977; *Mr. Mike's Mondo Video,* 1979; *Where the Buffalo Roam,* 1980; *Caddyshack,* 1980; *Stripes,* 1981; *Tootsie,* 1982; *Ghostbusters,* 1984; *The Razor's Edge,* 1984.

PRINCIPAL STAGE APPEARANCES—Second City, Chicago; *National Lampoon Revue,* Off-Broadway. RADIO—*National Lampoon Radio Hour.*

AWARDS: Emmy Award, Best Writing for a Comedy Series, 1977: *Saturday Night Live.*

ADDRESS: Office—Agency for the Performing Arts, 888 Seventh Avenue, New York, NY 10106.*

* * *

MURRAY, Don, actor, director, producer, writer

PERSONAL: Born July 31, 1929 in Hollywood, CA; son of Dennis A. (a dance director and stage manager) and Ethel (a singer and former Ziegfeld girl; maiden name, Cook) Murray; married Hope Lange (divorced); married Elizabeth C. Johnson; children: Christopher, Patricia, Colleen, Sean, Michael. EDUCATION: Studied at the American Academy of Dramatic Arts in New York and with Paton Price. RELIGION: Church of the Brethren.

CAREER: DEBUT—An ant, *The Insect Comedy,* City Center, NY, 1948. PRINCIPAL STAGE APPEARANCES—Broadway productions: sailor, *The Rose Tattoo,* 1951, Henry, *The Skin of Our Teeth,* 1955, Tom, *The Norman Conquests,* 1975, George, *Same Time Next Year,* 1977; John Proctor, *The Crucible,* American Shakespeare Festival, Stratford, CT, 1975.

DON MURRAY

MAJOR TOURS—*California Suite,* national tour, 1978; Billy Flynn, *Chicago,* eastern states tour, 1979.

FILM DEBUT—Bo, *Bus Stop,* 1956. PRINCIPAL FILM APPEARANCES—*Bachelor Party,* 1956; *Hatful of Rain,* 1957; *From Hell to Texas,* 1957; *Shake Hands with the Devil,* 1958; *The Hoodlum Priest,* 1960; *Advise and Consent,* 1961; *Escape from East Berlin,* 1962; *One Man's Way,* 1962; *Baby, the Rain Must Fall,* 1963; *Confessions of Tom Harris,* 1966; *Conquest of the Planet of the Apes,* 1971; *The Cross and the Switchblade,* 1970; *Happy Birthday, Wanda June,* 1972; *Deadly Hero,* 1975; *Damien,* 1976; *Endless Love,* 1981. TELEVISION DEBUT—Principal Dancer, *The Art Ford Show,* 1948. PRINCIPAL TELEVISION APPEARANCES—*For I Have Loved Strangers,* 1958; *The Hasty Heart,* 1958; *Billy Budd,* 1958; *Winterset,* 1959; *Alas Babylon,* 1960; *The Borgia Stick,* 1967; *Rainbow,* 1978; *The Boy Who Drank Too Much,* 1979; *Knot's Landing,* 1980–82; *The Return of the Rebels,* 1982; *Thursday's Child,* 1983; *Quarterback Princess,* 1983; *License to Kill,* 1984.

WRITINGS: TELEVISION STORY—*For I Have Loved Strangers.* SCREENPLAYS—*The Hoodlum Priest, Confessions of Tom Harris, The Cross and the Switchblade, Damien* (also served as producer and director for *The Cross and the Switchblade* and *Damien;* produced *Hoodlum Priest* and *Confessions of Tom Harris*).

AWARDS: Best Actor, Brussels Film Festival, 1961: *The Hoodlum Priest;* Best Film Award, *The Hoodlum Priest,* Mexico, San Sebastian Spain, Cannes Film Festival, Coronado California; Academy Award Nomination, Bo, 1956: *Bus Stop.*

SIDELIGHTS: MEMBERSHIPS: The Lambs Club.

Co-founder of the Homeless Land Program, a refugee resettlement project on Sardinia, Italy. "Mr. Murray was a social worker in Germany for the Church of the Brethren, 1952, in Italy for the Congregation Christian Church, 1954–55. He worked with refugees in barbed wire camps near Naples with his former wife, Hope Lange, and social worker Belden Paulson and Brethren Service Volunteers, and bought land on Sardinia and took refugees in from the camps and founded a free community in Simaxis, Sardinia."

ADDRESS: Agent—Blake-Glenn, 409 N. Camden, Beverly Hills, CA 90212.

* * *

MURRAY, Mary Gordon, actress

PERSONAL: Born November 13, 1953, in Ridgewood, NJ; daughter of Arthur Edwin (a certified public accountant) and Eileen Catherine (a personnel coordinator; maiden name, White) Murray. EDUCATION: Attended Ramapo College for two years; trained for the stage at the Juilliard Theatre Center and with Wynn Handman and Word Baker.

CAREER: DEBUT—Mary, *Godspell,* touring company. NEW YORK DEBUT—Queenie, *The Robber Bridegroom,* Biltmore, 1976–77. PRINCIPAL STAGE APPEARANCES—Monica/Cleo, *I Love My Wife,* NY; Sandy, *Grease,* NY; Ellen, *Play Me a Country Song,* NY; Belle, *Little Me,* NY; Mary, *Cowboy,*

MARY GORDON MURRAY

New York Shakespeare Festival; Connie Sue, *Blue Plate Special,* Manhattan Theatre Club; Rachel, *Ludlow Fair;* Sabina, *The Skin of Our Teeth;* Irma, *The Madwoman of Chaillot;* Barbara Allen, *Dark of the Moon;* Catherine, *A View from the Bridge;* Actress One, *Spoon River Anthology; Merry Go Round.*

TELEVISION APPEARANCES—*One Life to Live.*

AWARDS: Antoinette Perry Award Nomination, Best Actress in a Musical, 1982: *Little Me.*

SIDELIGHTS: MEMBERSHIPS—Television Academy.

ADDRESS: Agent—c/o Robert Duva Enterprises, 277 W. Tenth Street, New York, NY 10014.

* * *

MUSANTE, Tony (ne Anthony P. Musante, Jr.), actor, director, writer

PERSONAL: Born June 30 in Bridgeport, CT; son of Anthony Peter (an accountant) and Natalie Anne (a schoolteacher; maiden name, Salerno) Musante; married Jane Sparkes (a writer) on June 2, 1962. EDUCATION: Northwestern University, 1957; Oberlin College, B.A. 1958; studied with Walt Witcover, Will Geer, and Tucker Ashworth at the H.B. Studios in New York.

CAREER: NEW YORK DEBUT—Assistant Stage Manager and understudy, *Borak,* Martinque, 1960. PRINCIPAL STAGE APPEARANCES—Off-Broadway: *Zoo Story; Pinter Plays; The Balcony; Match-Play; Kiss Mama; Night of the Dunce; L'Histoire du Soldat,* 1967; *A Gun Play,* 1971; *Cassatt,* 1981; *A Streetcar Named Desire,* Hartford Stage Company, 1972; Broadway: *P.S. Your Cat Is Dead,* 1975; *27 Wagons Full of Cotton, Memory of Two Mondays,* Phoenix, 1976; *The Lady from Dubuque,* 1980.

REGIONAL: *Souvenir,* Shubert, Los Angeles, 1975; *The Archbishop's Ceiling,* Kennedy Center, Washington, DC, 1977; *Two Brothers,* Long Wharf, New Haven, CT, 1978; *Grand Magic,* Manhattan Theatre Club, 1979; *Falling Man,* 1981; *The Taming of the Shrew,* Old Globe Theatre, San Diego, 1982; *The Big Knife,* Berkshire Theatre Festival, MA, 1983.

FILM DEBUT—Cleve Schoenstein, *Once a Thief,* 1964. PRINCIPAL FILM APPEARANCES—*The Incident,* 1967; *The Detective,* 1967; *The Mercenary, 1968; One Night at Dinner,* 1968; *The Bird with the Crystal Plumage,* 1969; *The Grissom Gang,* 1970; *The Anonymous Venetians,* 1970; *The Last Run,* 1971; *The Pisciotta Case,* 1972; *Goodbye and Amen,* 1977; *Break Up,* 1978; *Nocturne,* 1981; *The Pope of Greenwich Village,* 1984.

TELEVISION DEBUT—Joe Ferrone, *Ride with Terror,* 1963. PRINCIPAL TELEVISION APPEARANCES—*The DuPont Show; Chrysler Theatre; Alfred Hitchcock Presents; The Fugitive; Trails of O'Brien,* 1967; *Toma* series, 22 episodes, 1973–74; *Police Story,* 1974; *Judgement: The Court Martial of Lt. William Calley,* 1974; *Medical Story,* 1975; *Desperate Miles,* 1975; *The Quality of Mercy,* 1975; *Legend of the*

Photograph by Christopher Brown

TONY MUSANTE

August 26, 1978; children: (first marriage) Leland Hallie. EDUCATION: Michigan State University; Columbia University, B.S.; studied acting with Uta Hagen, Herbert Berghof, Michael Howard, Philip Burton and Allan Miller. POLITICS: Liberal Democrat. RELIGION: Jewish.

CAREER: PRINCIPAL STAGE APPEARANCES—Broadway: Jean McCormack and Mimsey, *Plaza Suite;* standby, 4A, pregnant woman, *6 Rms Riv Vu;* standby Josie, *A Moon for the Misbegotten,* Circle in the Square; leader of the chorus, understudy Irene Papas, *Iphigenia in Aulis,* Circle in the Square; Vivie Warren, *Mrs. Warren's Profession,* Lincoln Center Library; Nadya, *Our Father,* Manhattan Theatre Club; the Girl, *Rocking Chair,* LaMama E.T.C.; Silvia, *Two Gentlemen of Verona,* Theatre Four; Lydia Languish, *The Rivals,* Playwright's Horizons; Rosalind, *As You Like It,* Equity Library Theatre; A Contemporary Theatre, Seattle, WA: Ruth, *The Homecoming,* Maggie, *After the Fall,* Ruth, *The Great Divide;* Virginia Museum Theatre, Richmond, VA: Barbara, *Children,* Esther, *Democracy,* Beatrice, *Much Ado About Nothing,* Katherine, *The Taming of the Shrew;* Mary, *Serenading Louie,* Asolo Stage Two, Sarasota, FL; *Artichoke,* A Contemporary Theatre, Seattle, WA.

MAJOR TOURS—Andromache, *The Trojan Women,* national; Vittoria, *The White Devil,* national.

PRINCIPAL TELEVISION APPEARANCES—Sally Fairfax, *The World Turned Upside Down;* Jenny, *American Lifestyles;* Jean Atwater, *The Guiding Light.*

Black Hand, 1976; *Nowhere to Hide,* 1977; *My Husband Is Missing,* 1978; *The Story of Esther,* 1979; *Breaking Up Is Hard to Do,* 1979; *High Ice,* 1980; *Weekend, American Playhouse,* 1982.

WRITINGS: Television—episodes of *TOMA* with Jane Sparkes; screenplays in collaboration with Jane Sparkes.

AWARDS: Emmy Nomination, 1976: *The Quality of Mercy;* Drama Desk Award Nomination, Best Actor, 1975: *P.S. Your Cat Is Dead;* Photoplay Gold Medal Award, 1974: *TOMA* series; Best Actor, South America International Film Festival, 1968: *The Incident.*

SIDELIGHTS: MEMBERSHIPS—President of the Jury of International Film Festival, La Coruna, Spain, 1983.

ADDRESS: Agent—Don Wolff c/o The Artists Agency, 10,000 Santa Monica Boulevard, Los Angeles, CA 90067.

* * *

MYLES, Lynda, playwright, actress

PERSONAL: Born July 22, 1939, in New York City; daughter of Lee (a bandleader, later owner automatic transmission business) and Rose (Schor) Myles; married Jan Leighton, 1968 (divorced 1974); Mel Cobb (an actor, director, writer)

LYNDA MYLES

WRITINGS: PLAYS PRODUCED—*Wives,* O'Neill Playwright's Conference, 1979, Lion Theatre, NY, 1983, produced on *Earplay* by National Public Radio as *Dinner Roll Scandal,* 1982; *Thirteen,* reading, Hudson Guild, NY, 1982, Stage Arts Theatre Company, NY, 1983. TELEVISION—*As the World Turns;* contributor to *New York* Magazine.

SIDELIGHTS: MEMBERSHIPS—AEA, SAG, AFTRA, Dramatists Guild.

"I knew one actress who turned to playwriting and then I heard of another. That's what did it: just hearing that there were other actresses—women—who had done it. Here I have been acting in men's plays all my life and it never occured to me that I could be a playwright. It really was a little astonishing. So I started to write."

ADDRESS: Agent—Sandra Landau c/o Sy Fischer Company, One E. 57th Street, New York, NY 10022.

N

NADELL, Carol L., actress

PERSONAL: Born August 19, 1944 in New York, NY; daughter of Emmanuel K. (a dentist) and Ruth Raphael (a guidance counselor) Nadell (divorced). EDUCATION: Graduate of High School of Performing Arts, NY, 1962; Hunter College, B.A. 1966; studied acting with Sanford Meisner and Eve Collyer, NY, in New York City.

CAREER: DEBUT—Jennie, *Portrait of Jennie*, Bristol Valley Playhouse, Naples, NY, 1967. PRINCIPAL STAGE APPEARANCES—Millie/Sybil/Jackie/Francine, *All Over Town;* Isabel, *East Lynne*, Sharon Playhouse, CT; Laura, *Laura*, Sharon Playhouse, CT; Natasha, *The Three Sisters*, Princeton Ensemble, Princeton University, NJ; Hannah, *A Day Out of Time*, NY; Paulette, *Powder*, NY; various roles, *Other People's Tables*, NY; Selma, *Red Eye of Love*, NY; Laurie, *The Meek*, NY.

MAJOR TOURS—*You Know I Can't Hear You When the Water's Running*, national tour; *Boeing-Boeing*, national tour; *America Hurrah*, national tour; *Adaptation/Next*, national company.

PRINCIPAL FILM APPEARANCES—Mrs. Kline, *Kramer vs. Kramer;* Desk Clerk, *Blue Skies Again*.

PRINCIPAL TELEVISION APPEARANCES—*Siege; District Health Office; Prince of Central Park; The Edge of Night*.

THEATRE-RELATED CAREER: Project director, Joseph Jefferson Theatre Company, 1974–75; lecturer, American Academy of Dramatic Arts, 1979–present; artist in residence, Princeton University, NJ, 1978.

AWARDS: Francis Bergman Award, Best Actress, Hunter College, NY; Outstanding Talent in Acting, High School for the Performing Arts.

SIDELIGHTS: MEMBERSHIPS—AEA; SAG; AFTRA; Episcopal Actors Guild.

* * *

NAUGHTON, James, actor

PERSONAL: Born December 6, 1945, in Middletown, CT; son of James Joseph (a teacher) and Rosemary (a teacher; maiden name, Walsh) Naughton; married Pamela Parsons; children: Gregory, Keira. EDUCATION: Brown University, A.B., 1967; Yale, Drama, M.F.A., 1970.

CAREER: DEBUT—Narcissus, *Olympian Games*, Yale Repertory at John Drew, E. Hampton, NY, June 1970. NEW YORK DEBUT—Edmund, *Long Day's Journey into Night*, Promenade, 1971, three-month limited engagement. PRINCIPAL STAGE APPEARANCES—Wally, *I Love My Wife*, Barrymore, NY, 1977–78; Doctor, *Whose Life Is It Anyway?*, Royale, NY, 1980; Nick, *Who's Afraid of Virginia Woolf?*, Long Wharf, New Haven, CT, 1980.

FILM DEBUT—Kevin Brooks, *The Paper Chase*, 1972. TELEVISION DEBUT—Ben, *Look Homeward, Angel*, CBS, 1972. TELEVISION APPEARANCES—*Faraday and Co.*, 1973; *Planet of the Apes*, 1974; *Making the Grade*, 1982; *Trauma Center*, 1983.

AWARDS: Theatre World, Vernon Rice, NY Drama Critics Circle Awards, 1971: *Long Day's Journey into Night*.

ADDRESS: Agent—STE, 888 Seventh Avenue, New York, NY 10106.

* * *

NEGRO, Mary-Joan, actress

PERSONAL: Daughter of Dante Antonio (a professor and concert manager) and Ardemia (Dalliongaro) Negro; married Norman O. Snow (an actor), July 18, 1982. EDUCATION: University of Michigan, B.A.; trained for the stage and graduate from Juilliard School.

CAREER: PRINCIPAL STAGE APPEARANCES—(Broadway) *Scenes and Revelations; Wings;* (Off-Broadway) *Modigliani; Ladyhouse Blues; Canadian Gothic/American Modern; Rebel Women;* (Regional) McCarter Theatre Company, Princeton, NJ; San Diego Shakespeare Festival, CA; O'Neill Theatre Center; (The Acting Company) *The Three Sisters, Edward II, The Time of Your Life, The Beggars Opera, The Hostage, Lower Depths, She Stoops to Conquer, Love's Labors Lost*.

PRINCIPAL TELEVISION APPEARANCES—*Ryan's Four; Wings; Remington Steele; Another World; Richard II; The Neighborhood* (pilot); *The Family Man; Best of Families; Kojak; The Time of Your Life; The New Actors for the Classics; The Andros Targets; Rafferty*.

SIDELIGHTS: Ms. Negro was a founding member of John Houseman's Acting Company.

ADDRESS: Agent—c/o Writers and Artists Agency, 162 W. 56th Street, New York, NY 10019.

* * *

NELLIGAN, Kate, actress

PERSONAL: Born March 16, 1951, in London, Ontario, Canada; daughter of Patrick Joseph (a municipal employee) and Josephine Alice (a school teacher; maiden name, Dier) Nelligan. EDUCATION: Attended York University (Canada); trained for the stage at the Central School of Speech and Drama.

CAREER: STAGE DEBUT—Corrie, *Barefoot in the Park*, Little Theater, Bristol, U.K., 1972. LONDON DEBUT—Jenny, *Knuckle*, Comedy, 1974. PRINCIPAL STAGE APPEARANCES—Hypatia, *Misalliance*, Stella, *A Streetcar Named Desire*, Pegeen Mike, *The Playboy of the Western World*, Grace Harkaway, *London Assurance*, Lulu, *Lulu*, Sybil Chase, *Private Lives*, Little Theater, Bristol, Theatre Royal, Bristol, Old Vic, 1972–73; Ellie Dunn, *Heartbreak House*, Old Vic,

KATE NELLIGAN

London, 1975; Marianne, *Tales from the Vienna Woods*, National, London, 1977; Rosalind, *As You Like It*, Royal Shakespeare Company, Stratford, U.K., 1977; Susan Traherne, *Plenty*, National, London, 1978; Susan Traherne, *Plenty*, Public, New York, 1982, Broadway, 1983; Josie, *Moon for the Misbegotten*, American Repertory, Cambridge, MA, Cort, NY, 1984.

PRINCIPAL FILM APPEARANCES—*The Romantic Englishwoman*, 1975; *Dracula*, 1979; *Eye of the Needle*, 1980; *Without a Trace*, 1982. PRINCIPAL TELEVISION APPEARANCES—*Licking Hitler; Measure for Measure; Dreams of Leaving; Therese Raquin.*

AWARDS: Evening Standard Award, Best Actress, 1978: *Plenty.*

SIDELIGHTS: RECREATION—Reading, cooking, gardening. FAVORITE ROLE—Josie, *Moon for the Misbegotten.*

ADDRESS: Agent—c/o Sam Cohn, I.C.M., 40 W. 57th Street, New York, NY 10019.

* * *

NELSON, Novella, actor and singer

PERSONAL: Born December 17, 1938; daughter of James A. and Evelyn H. (Hines) Nelson; married George Blanchard, 1969; children: Alesa. EDUCATION: Brooklyn College, B.A., 1959; trained for the stage at the American Mime Theatre. RELIGION: Israelite.

CAREER: DEBUT—Essie, *To Follow the Phoenix*, Schubert, Chicago, IL, 1961. NEW YORK DEBUT—*In White America*, Circle in the Square, 1964–65. LONDON DEBUT—Addie, *The Little Foxes*, Victoria Palace, 1982. PRINCIPAL STAGE APPEARANCES—Madame Tongo, *House of Flowers*, Theatre de Lys, NY, 1967; Vandy, *Horseman Pass By*, Theatre de Lys, NY, 1969; Missy, *Purlie*, Broadway, NY, 1970; Ftatateeta, *Caesar and Cleopatra*, Palace, NY, 1977; Addie, *The Little Foxes*, Martin Beck, NY, 1981; Calpurnia, *Julius Caesar*, New York Public Theatre; Vicky, *Passing Games*, American Place; (Repertory) Alliance, Atlanta, GA; Theatre Company of Boston, MA; ACT, Seattle, WA.

FILM DEBUT—Jean Starret, *An Unmarried Woman*, 1977. PRINCIPAL FILM APPEARANCES—Claire Goode, *The Seduction of Joe Tynan*, 1978; Lizzie, *Sweet Ginger Brown*, 1983; Mrs. Rice, *The Harlem Six;* Stephanie St. Clair, *The Cotton Club.*

PRINCIPAL TELEVISION APPEARANCES—Birana, *UN*, "Birana,"; Obedia, *One Life to Live;* Mrs. Jones, *Watch Your Mouth/Chicago Red;* Harriet Tubman, *You Are There; Camera Three; Soul; VD Blues; Women Alive; Inside Bed Stuy; Like It Is.*

DIRECTED: Plays—*Runners*, Pilgrim Playhouse; *Les Femmes Noire*, New York Public Theatre; *Black Visions*, New York Public Theatre; *Sweet Talk*, New York Shakespeare Festival; *Nigger Nightmare*, Manhattan Theatre Club, New York Public Theatre; *Where We At*, Negro Ensemble Company, NY; *Perfection in Black*, Negro Ensemble Company. PRO-

DUCED: *There's Still Free Music in Central Park*, NY; *Music and Poetry at Reno's.*

THEATRE-RELATED CAREERS: Consultant—New York Shakespeare Festival, 1970–75; CAPS, 1972–76. Lecturer—Bennington; Goddard; State University of New York; Smithsonian Institute; Brooklyn College; American Mime Theatre; American Academy of Dramatic Arts.

ADDRESS: Agent—c/o ICM 40 W. 57th Street, New York, NY 10019.

* * *

NELSON, Ralph, director, actor, producer, writer, lyricist

PERSONAL: Born August 12, 1916; son of Carl Leo (a chauffeur) and Elsa (Lagergreen) Nelson; married Celeste Holm (an actress) September 11, 1936 (divorced 1938); married Barbara Powers on February 6, 1954 (deceased); children: Theodor, Ralph, Peter, Meredith. EDUCATION: Attended public schools in Long Island City, NY. MILITARY: Captain, U.S. Army Air Corps. 1941.

CAREER: DEBUT—*Ticket of Leave Man*, Wharf Theatre, Provincetown, MA, 1933. NEW YORK DEBUT—Cabin boy, *False Dreams, Farewell*, Little Theatre, for 24 performances, 1934. PRINCIPAL STAGE APPEARANCES—*Romeo and Juliet*, Martin Beck, NY, 1935; *The Taming of the Shrew*, Guild, NY, 1936; radio operator, *There Shall Be No Night*, Alvin, NY. MAJOR TOURS—Rosencrantz, *Hamlet*, U.S. tour; Mr. Cherry, *Idiot's Delight*, U.S. tour.

PRINCIPAL TELEVISION APPEARANCES—*Kraft Theatre; Berkeley Square; Outward Bound; She Stoops to Conquer.*

PRINCIPAL FILM WORK, DIRECTED—*Requiem for a Heavyweight*, 1962; *Soldier in the Rain*, 1963; *Lilies of the Field*, 1963 (also produced); *Fate Is the Hunter*, 1964; *Father Goose*, 1965; *Duel at Diablo*, 1966; *Charly*, 1968; *Soldier Blue*, 1970; *Wilby Conspiracy*, 1975; PRINCIPAL TELEVISION WORK, DIRECTED—*Playhouse 90; Climax; Omnibus; Mama* series.

WRITINGS: PLAYS, PRODUCED—*Mail Call*, NY, 1943; *Angels Weep*, NY, 1944; *The Wind Is 90*, NY. SCREENPLAYS—*The Wrath of God; Flight of the Doves*. ADAPTATIONS—*Hamlet*, Old Vic Theatre Company, London, England.

AWARDS: Academy Award, Best Picture of the Year, and 5 Award Nominations for Producing and Directing, *Lilies of the Field;* Emmy Award, *Requiem for a Heavyweight;* Honorary Doctor of Humane Letters, Columbia College.

THEATRE-RELATED CAREER:Guest Lecturer, UCLA, USC, San Francisco State College, New York University, Columbia University, University of Michigan.

SIDELIGHTS: MEMBERSHIPS—AEA; SAG; AFTRA; Dramatists Guild; Author's League (Life Member); Writers Guild of America, West; Directors Guild of America; Producers Guild; ASCAP.

ADDRESS: Office—c/o Kaufman & Bernstein, 1900 Avenue of the Stars, Los Angeles, CA 90067. Agent—Chason-Park-Citron, 9255 Sunset Blvd., Los Angeles, CA 90069.

* * *

NEUFELD, Mace, producer

PERSONAL: Born July 13, 1928; son of Philip (a stockbroker) Neufeld; married Helen Katz (a designer), February 28, 1954; children: Brad, Glenn, Nancy. EDUCATION: Yale University, B.A., 1949; New York Law School, 1962.

CAREER: PRINCIPAL TELEVISION WORK—Producer: *Angel on My Shoulder*, 1980; *American Dream*, 1981; *Cagney and Lacy*, 1981; *Juarez; The Far Pavilions*, 1984; executive producer, *East of Eden.*

AWARDS: Golden Globe: *East of Eden.*

SIDELIGHTS: MEMBERSHIPS—ASCAP, Motion Picture Academy, Television Academy, Producers League, American Film Institute (executive committee, trustee), Yale Club, Regency Club.

ADDRESS: Home—624 N. Arden Drive, Beverly Hills, CA 90210.

* * *

NEUFELD, Peter, manager, producer

PERSONAL: Born December 12, 1936 in Brooklyn, NY; son of Syndey (a furniture manufacturer) and Anita (Voit) Neufeld. EDUCATION: College of William and Mary, Williamsburg, VA, B.F.A., 1958. MILITARY: U.S. Army, Specialist 4th Class, 1958–61.

CAREER: PRINCIPAL STAGE WORK, ASSISTANT COMPANY MANAGER—*Kismet, Carousel*, Music Theatre of Lincoln Center, 1963–64; *A Time for Singing*, Broadway Theatre, NY, 1965–66; *Annie Get Your Gun*, Music Theatre of Lincoln Center, NY, 1965–66; *The Impossible Years*, Playhouse, NY, 1966–67; *The Investigation*, Ambassador, NY, 1966–67; *Under the Weather*, Cort, NY, 1966–67; *Those That Play the Clowns*, ANTA, NY, 1966–67; *Ilya Darling*, Mark Hellinger, NY, 1966–67.

COMPANY MANAGER—*A Minor Adjustment*, Brooks Atkinson, NY, 1967–68; *Something Different*, Cort, NY, 1967–68; *Here's Where I Belong*, Billy Rose, NY, 1967–68; *I Never Sang for My Father*, Longacre, NY, 1967–68; *Ilya Darling*, Mark Hellinger, NY, 1967–68; *The Chinese and Dr. Fish*, Barrymore, NY, 1969–70; *Park*, Golden, NY, 1969–70; *Little Boxes*, New Theatre, NY, 1969–70.

GENERAL MANAGER—*The Local Stigmatic*, Actors Playhouse, 1969–70; *The Unseen Hand, Forensic, The Navigators*, Astor Place Playhouse, NY, 1969–70; *How Much, How Much?*, Provincetown Playhouse, NY, 1969–70; *Awake and Sing*, Bijou, NY, 1969–70; *No, No, Nanette*, 46th

Street, NY, 1970–71; *The Candyapple,* Edison, NY, 1970–71; *Foreplay,* Bijou, NY, 1970–71; City Center American Dance Season, NY, 1970–71; *The Sign in Sidney Brustein's Window,* Longacre, 1971–72; *Don't Bother Me I Can't Cope,* Playhouse, NY, 1971–72; *The World Famous Steel Pier Big Band,* Shubert, NY, 1972–73; *The Contrast, Blue Boys,* Eastside Playhouse, NY, 1972–73; *The American Revolution,* Ford's Theatre Society, Washington, DC, 1973–74; *Rachael Lily Rosenblum,* Broadhurst, NY, 1973–74; *Fashion,* McAlpin Rooftop, NY, 1973–74; *Music, Music,* City Center, 55th Street, NY, 1973–74; *Sgt. Pepper's Lonely Hearts Club Band on the Road,* Beacon, NY, 1974–75; *Manhattan Follies,* Persian Room, Plaza Hotel, NY, 1974–75; *See America First,* Upstairs at Jimmy's, NY, 1974–75; *The Hashish Club,* Bijou, NY, 1974–75; *Augusta,* Theatre de Lys, NY, 1975–76; *Legend,* Barrymore, NY, 1975–76; *Starting Here, Starting Now,* Barbarann Theatre Restaurant, 1976–77; *Annie,* Alvin, NY, 1975–76; *Working,* 46th Street, NY, 1977–78; *Timbuktu!,* Mark Hellinger, NY, 1978–79; *Sweeney Todd,* Uris, NY, 1978–79; *Break a Leg,* Palace, NY, 1978–79; *Evita,* Broadway Theatre, NY, 1979–80; *Once a Catholic,* Helen Hayes, NY, 1979–80; *Talley's Folly,* Brooks Atkinson, NY, 1979–80; *Goodbye Fidel,* New Ambassador, 1979–80; *The Suicide,* ANTA, NY, 1979–80; *Kaufman at Large,* Perry Street, NY, 1980–81; *March of the Falsettos,* Westside Arts, NY, 1980–81; *The First,* Martin Beck, NY, 1981–82; *Beyond Therapy,* Brooks Atkinson, NY, 1981–82; *Upstairs at O'Neals,* O'Neal's Time Square Restaurant, NY, 1982–83; *Cats,* Winter Garden, NY, 1982–83.

MAJOR TOURS, GENERAL MANAGER—*You Know I Can't Hear You When the Water's Running,* national tour, 1968–69; *The Student Prince, The Desert Song,* national tour, 1973–74.

GENERAL MANAGER/ASSOCIATE PRODUCER—*Jesus Christ Superstar,* Mark Hellinger, NY, 1971–72. PRODUCER—*Murder Among Friends,* Biltmore, NY, 1975–76; *Night Games,* Park Royal, NY, 1978–79; *Evita,* Broadway Theatre, NY, 1979–80; *Cats,* Winter Garden, NY, 1982–83.

THEATRE-RELATED CAREER: Managing director, O'Neill Foundation Playwrights Conference, 1968–69; partnership with R. Tyler Gatchell to manage and produce commercial theatre, Gatchell & Neufeld, Ltd., 1969–present.

SIDELIGHTS: MEMBERSHIPS—Association of Theatrical Press Agents and Managers.

Mr. Neufeld has served as a guest lecturer on commercial theatre and careers within it at the College of William and Mary, Columbia University, Yale University, New York University, and for the Foundation for the Development of the American Professional Theatre (FEDAPT).

ADDRESS: Office—165 W. 46th Street, New York, NY 10036.

* * *

NEUFELD, Sigmund Jr., director, editor

PERSONAL: Born May 12, 1931, in Los Angeles, CA; son of Sigmund (a film producer) and Ruth (Auld) Neufeld. EDUCATION: Los Angeles City College, 2½ years.

CAREER: PRINCIPAL TELEVISION WORK—Editor/director, *Lassie, Kojak;* director: *Doctors Hospital, The Invisible Man, City of the Angels, Baretta, Serpico, Eddie Capra Mysteries, Switch, Project UFO, The Incredible Hulk, Wonder Woman, Flying High, Kate Loves a Mystery, Buck Rogers, The Chisholms, Galactia 1980, Here's Boomer, Simon & Simon, T.J. Hooker, Scarecrow & Mrs. King, Me & Mr. Stenner* (ABC *Afterschool Special*).

SIDELIGHTS: MEMBERSHIPS—DGA, AFI, ATAS.

ADDRESS: Home—1867 Rising Glen Rd., Los Angeles, CA 90069. Agent—Herb Tobias & Associates, 1901 Avenue of the Stars, Suite 840, Los Angeles, CA 90067.

* * *

NEUMAN, Joan (nee Daniel)

PERSONAL: Born October 4, 1926, in New York City; daughter of James (a sales manager) and Harriet (Durlacher) Daniel; married Herbert J. Neuman, October 28, 1948 (marriage ended 1963). EDUCATION: New York University, B.S. (Drama), 1948; studied acting with Stella Adler and singing with Sue Seton.

CAREER: PRINCIPAL STAGE APPEARANCES—*Journey to the Wall,* Community, San Francisco, 1964; Lady Caroline, *A*

JOAN NEUMAN

Woman of No Importance, 17th Street Theatre, NY, 1964; Mme. Pernelle, *Tartuffe,* Repertory Company at Lincoln Square, NY, 1967; Madrecita, *Camino Real,* Comedy Club, NY, 1967; Lucy, *All the King's Men,* Comedy Club, NY, 1968; *Telemachus Clay,* Theatre for the Forgotten, Rikers Island, NY, 1968; Maggie, *The Gamblers,* 1969; Martha, *Arsenic and Old Lace,* Comedy Club, NY, 1970; Mrs. Nijinski, *Little Blue Stars,* 18th Street Playhouse, NY, 1979; Marge, *Chance Meeting in Luna,* 1981; Katina, *Happy Sunset Inc.,* Greek, NY, 1982; Hazel, *Hazel's Girl,* Nat Home, NY, 1983.

PRINCIPAL FILM APPEARANCES—Miss Molina, *The Lords of Flatbush,* 1974; the mother, *Annie Hall,* 1977; talkative woman, *The First Deadly Sin,* 1980; the mother, *Stardust Memories,* 1980.

* * *

NEVINS, Claudette (ne Claudette Weintraub), actress

PERSONAL: Born April 10; daughter of Joseph Weintraub (a fur salesman) and Anna (a garment worker; maiden name, Lander) Weintraub; married (first marriage) Elliot Nevins (divorced); married Benjamin L. Pick (real estate investments); children: Jessica, Sabrina. EDUCATION: New York University, B.A.; studied acting with Michael Howard. RELIGION: Jewish.

CAREER: DEBUT—*Middle of the Night, Waltz of the Toreadors,* Woodstock Playhouse, Woodstock, NY, 1958. NEW YORK DEBUT—Halinka, *The Wall,* Billy Rose, NY, 1960–61. PRINCIPAL STAGE APPEARANCES—*In White America,* Sheridan Square Playhouse, NY, 1963–64; *Danton's Death,* Lincoln Center, Vivian Beaumont, NY, 1965; *Plaza Suite,* Plymouth, NY, 1968; *King Arthur, The Hostage, The Homecoming, The Little Foxes, Major Barbara, Twelfth Night, You Can't Take It With You,* Atlanta Repertory Theatre, GA, 1968–69; *Major Barbara, Ring Round the Moon, The Cherry Orchard, The Iceman Cometh,* Arena Stage, Washington, DC, 1959–60; *Old Times, The Death and Life of Jesse James,* Mark Taper Forum, Los Angeles. MAJOR TOURS—*Invitation to a March,* 1961; *A Shot in the Dark,* 1962; *The Great White Hope,* national tour, 1969–70; *Blithe Spirit,* 1982–83.

FILM DEBUT—*All the Marbles,* 1981.

TELEVISION DEBUT—*Love of Life,* 1965–68. PRINCIPAL TELEVISION APPEARANCES—Series, *Headmaster, Husbands and Wives, + Lovers, Married: The First Year, Over Here Mr. President, Hart to Hart, Magnum P.I., Family;* Movies of the Week—*Jacqueline Bouvier Kennedy, Mrs. Sundance, Take Your Best Shot, Sam Shepherd Murder Trial, Love Me and I'll Be Your Best Friend, The Possessed, The Hancocks (The Dark Side of Innocence);* Guest Appearances—*Barnaby Jones, Lou Grant, The Rockford Files, Three's Company, One Day at a Time, Police Story, Police Squad, Harry-O, M*A*S*H, Knot's Landing, C.H.I.P.S., Cassie and Co., Mississippi.*

AWARDS: Phi Beta Kappa.

ADDRESS: Agent—Irv Schechter, 9300 Wilshire Blvd., Beverly Hills, CA 90212.

* * *

NEWMAN, Paul, actor, director, producer

PERSONAL: Born January 26, 1925, in Cleveland, OH; son of Arthur S. and Theresa (Fetzer) Newman; married Jacqueline Witte, December 1949; Joanne Woodward, January 1958; children: (first marriage) Scott, Susan, Stephanie; (second marriage) Elinor, Melissa, Clea. EDUCATION: Kenyon College, 1949; Yale School of Drama, 1951, postgraduate. MILITARY: U.S. Naval Reserve, 1943–46.

CAREER: PRINCIPAL STAGE APPEARANCES—*Picnic,* NY, 1953–54; *Desperate Hours,* 1955; *Sweet Bird of Youth,* 1959; *Baby Want a Kiss,* 1964. PRINCIPAL TELEVISION APPEARANCES—*Philco; U.S. Steel; Playhouse 90.* PRINCIPAL TELEVISION WORK—Director, *The Shadow Box,* 1979.

PRINCIPAL FILM APPEARANCES—*The Silver Chalice,* 1955; *The Rack,* 1956; *Somebody Up There Likes Me,* 1957; *Until They Sail,* 1957; *The Helen Morgan Story,* 1957; *The Long, Hot Summer,* 1958; *Cat on a Hot Tin Roof,* 1958; *The Left Handed Gun,* 1958; *Rally 'Round the Flag Boys!,* 1959; *The Young Philadelphians,* 1959; *From the Terrace,* 1960; *Exodus,* 1960; *The Hustler,* 1961; *Sweet Bird of Youth,* 1962; *Adventures of a Young Man,* 1962; *Hud,* 1963; *A New Kind of Love,* 1963; *The Prize,* 1963; *The Outrage,* 1964; *What a Way to Go!,* 1964; *Lady L,* 1966; *Torn Curtin,* 1966; *Harper,* 1966; *Hombre,* 1967; *Cool Hand Luke,* 1967; *The Secret of Harry Frigg; Winning,* 1969; *Butch Cassidy and the Sundance Kid,* 1969; *WUSA,* 1970; *Sometimes a Great Notion,* 1971; *Pocket Money,* 1972; *The Life and Times of Judge Roy Bean,* 1972; *The Mackintosh Man,* 1973; *The Sting,* 1973; *The Towering Inferno,* 1974; *The Drowning Pool,* 1975; *Buffalo Bill and the Indians,* 1976; *Slap Shot,* 1977; *Quintet,* 1979; *Ran Out,* 1980; *Fort Apache, the Bronx,* 1981; *Absence of Malice,* 1981; *The Verdict,* 1982; *Harry and Son,* 1983. In addition, director, *Rachel, Rachel,* 1968; producer, *WUSA,* 1970; co-director (with Richard Colla), *Sometimes a Great Notion,* 1971; director, co-writer, *Harry and Son,* 1983.

RELATED CAREER—Formed First Artists Production Co. Ltd. in 1969.

AWARDS: Academy Award Nominations, 1983: *The Verdict,* 1963, 1961, 1959; Producers Guild of America, Best Motion Picture Producer of the Year, 1968; Harvard University, Hasty Pudding Theatrical, Man of the Year, 1968; Golden Globe, 1967.

ADDRESS: Office—2048 Century Park E., Suite 2500, Los Angeles, CA 90067.*

* * *

NEWMAR, Julie (nee Newmeyer), actress, dancer, choreographer

PERSONAL: Born August 16, 1933, in Hollywood, CA;

daughter of Donald Charles (head of Physical Education Department of Los Angeles City College) and Helene (Ziegfeld Follies girl; maiden name, Jesmer) Newmeyer; married: J. Holt Smith (a lawyer), divorced 1984; children: John Jewl Smith. EDUCATION: U.C.L.A. (continuing); trained for the theatre with Lee Strasberg at the Actor's Studio. NON-THEATRICAL CAREER: management of (family-held) real estate.

CAREER: DEBUT—Alice, *Alice in Wonderland,* Broadway Department Store, Hollywood, CA, 1940. PRINCIPAL STAGE APPEARANCES—Vera, *Silk Stockings,* Imperial, NY, 1955; Stupefyin' Jones, *L'il Abner,* St. James, NY, 1956; Katrin, *The Marriage-Go-Round,* Imperial, NY, 1958; Lola, *Damn Yankees,* summer stock, 1965; Irma, *Irma La Douce;* Adelaide, *Guys and Dolls;* Mona, *Dames at Sea; Ziegfeld Follies; In the Boom Boom Room,* Los Angeles. MAJOR TOURS—Eve, *Stop the World . . . I Want to Get Off,* national tour.

FILM DEBUT—*Just for You,* 1952. FILM APPEARANCES—Dorcas, *Seven Brides for Seven Brothers,* (as Julie Newmeyer) 1954; *The Rookie,* 1959; Katrin, *The Marriage-Go-Round,* 1960; *For Love or Money,* 1963; Heski, *MacKenna's Gold,* 1969; *The Maltese Bippy,* 1969; *Hysterical,* 1983. TELEVISION DEBUT—Rhoda Miller/AF 709/Rhoda, the Robot, *My Living Doll,* 1964–65. TELEVISION APPEARANCES—Catwoman, *Batman,* 1966; *The Danny Kaye Show; Omnibus; Route 66; The Jonathan Winters Show; Chips; Hart to Hart; Wide World of Sports* (sky diving); *Love, American Style; Colombo; Fantasy Island; The Powers of Mathew Star;* Ultra Witch, *Monster Squad,* 1983.

JULIE NEWMAR

AWARDS: Antoinette Perry Award, Best Supporting Actress, 1958: *The Marriage-Go-Round.*

SIDELIGHTS: MEMBERSHIPS—Actors Studio. RECREATION—designing clothing, gardening, writing, playing piano, sky diving, swimming, skiing, watching TV (especially ". . . news and informational shows and some musical/variety shows . . . and I adore movies made especially for television)", reading, excluding fiction ("I'm from Hollywood—that's fiction enough!")—her favorite authors are I. F. Stone and James Reston.

ADDRESS: Agent—H. David Moss, 113 N. San Vicente Blvd., Los Angeles, CA 90211.

* * *

NEWTON, John (ne Reeds), actor

PERSONAL: Born November 11, 1925 in Grand Juncton, CO; son of Frank Haynes (a newspaperman) and Ruth (Newton) Reeds; married Donamarie (Dusty) Krause (a professor at San Jose State University), June 11, 1950; children: Robin Lee (ne Robin Haynes), John Michael. EDUCATION: University of Washington, Seattle, B.A. (Drama) 1952; Colorado College, 1946–49; UCLA (Cinematography), 1960. MILITARY: U.S. Air Force, Aviation Radioman, First Class, 1942–46.

CAREER: DEBUT—Managed and starred in a melodrama company while attending Colorado College, 1946–49. PRINCIPAL STAGE APPEARANCES—*Othello,* Cherry Lane, NY, 1951; *Weekend,* NY, 1969; Cheever, *The Crucible,* Lincoln Center Repertory Company; Mitch, *A Streetcar Named Desire,* Lincoln Center Repertory Company, and the 25th *Streetcar* Anniversary production in NY; Marshall of the Court, *First Monday in October,* NY; *Best Little Whorehouse in Texas,* two years, NY; Henry, *Present Laughter,* Circle in the Square (uptown), NY, 1982; *The Rivals,* Roundabout, NY; *Candaules Commissioner,* Chelsea Theatre Center, NY; *Cyrano de Bergerac,* York Players, NY; *Glass Menagerie; Command Decision; Send Me No Flowers; Point of No Return.*

MAJOR TOURS—*Best Little Whorehouse in Texas,* national company, 1982.

PRINCIPAL FILM APPEARANCES—*The Sentinel; The Satan Bug; This Rebel Breed; Man from the Diner's Club.*

PRINCIPAL TELEVISION APPEARANCES—*Camera 3; Robert Montgomery Presents; Kaiser Aluminum Hour; Kraft Mystery Theatre; The Doctors; Gunsmoke; The Fugitive; That Girl; Voyage; F.B.I.*

SIDELIGHTS: Mr. Newton, in addition to his Broadway and Off-Off Broadway roles, has performed with the major regional theatre companies including Pittsburgh Public Theatre, Actors Theatre of Louisville, Hartford Stage Company, Alley Theatre in Houston, TX, Virginia Stage Company, Seattle Repertory Company, and Great Lakes Shakespeare Festival. He is a licensed pilot, a chess buff, a compulsive reader and a doting grandfather. Both of his sons are pursuing careers in the theatre.

ADDRESS: Home—34 W. 65th Street, New York, NY 10023. Agent—Hesseltine Baker & Associates, 165 W. 46th Street, New York, NY 10036.

* * *

NICHOLS, Mike, director, author, actor

PERSONAL: Born November 6, 1931, in Berlin, Germany; son of Nicholaievitch (Dr. Paul Nichols) and Brigitte (Landauer) Peschowsky; married Patricia Scot (divorced); married Margot Callas (divorced). EDUCATION: Attended University of Chicago; trained for the stage with Lee Strasberg.

CAREER: DIRECTED—PLAYS—*Barefoot in the Park*, Biltmore, NY, 1963; *The Knack*, NY, 1964; *Luv*, NY, 1964; *The Odd Couple*, NY, 1965; *The Apple Tree*, NY, 1966; *The Little Foxes*, NY, 1967; *Plaza Suite*, NY, 1968; *The Prisoner of Second Avenue*, NY, 1971; *Uncle Vanya*, NY, 1973; *Streamers*, NY, 1976; *Comedians*, NY, 1976; *The Gin Game*, NY, 1977; *Drinks Before Dinner*, NY, 1978; *The Gin Game*, London, 1979; *The Real Thing*, NY, 1983; *Hurlyburly*, NY, 1984.

DIRECTOR: FILMS—*Who's Afraid of Virginia Woolf?*, 1965; *The Graduate*, 1968; *Catch 22*, 1970; *Carnal Knowledge*, 1971; *The Day of the Dolphin*, 1973; *The Fortune*, 1975; *Silkwood*, 1983.

STAGE DEBUT—Playwrights Theater Club, Compass, Chicago, IL. NEW YORK DEBUT—*An Evening with Mike Nichols and Elaine May*, John Golden, 1960. PRINCIPAL STAGE APPEARANCES—Howard Miller, *A Matter of Position*, Walnut, Philadelphia, PA, 1962; Inaugural Gala, Washington, D.C., 1965; George, *Who's Afraid of Virginia Woolf?*, Long Wharf, New Haven, CT, 1980.

PRODUCED: Plays—*Annie*, 1977; *The Gin Game*, 1977.

AWARDS: Antoinette Perry Award, Best Director, 1971: *The Prisoner of Second Avenue;* Antoinette Perry Award, Best Director, 1968: *Plaza Suite;* Antoinette Perry Award, Best Director, 1965, 1964: *Luv* and *The Odd Couple;* Antoinette Perry Award, Best Director, 1963: *Barefoot in the Park;* Academy Award, New York Film Critics Award, Best Director, 1968: *The Graduate.*

SIDELIGHTS: Movies, horses.

ADDRESS: Office—c/o Marvin B. Meyer, Rosenfeld, Meyer and Sussman, 9601 Wilshire Blvd., Beverly Hills, CA 90210.*

* * *

NICHOLSON, Jack, actor, director, producer, writer

PERSONAL: Born April 28, 1937, in Neptune, NJ; son of John and Ethel May Nicholson; married Sandra Knight, 1961 (divorced 1966); children: Jennifer.

CAREER: THEATRE DEBUT—*Tea and Sympathy*, Hollywood, CA.

FILM DEBUT—*Cry Baby Killer*, 1958. PRINCIPAL FILM APPEARANCES—*Too Young to Live; Studs Lonigan*, 1960; *Hell's Angels on Wheels; Little Shop of Horrors; Little Raven; Flight to Fury; Ensign Pulver*, 1964; *The Trip*, 1967; *The Shooting*, 1968; *Head*, 1968; *Psych Out*, 1968; *Easy Rider*, 1969; *Five Easy Pieces*, 1970; *Carnal Knowledge*, 1971; *The Last Detail*, 1974; *Chinatown*, 1974; *Tommy*, 1975; *The Passenger*, 1975; *The Fortune*, 1975; *One Flew Over the Cuckoo's Nest*, 1975; *The Missouri Breaks*, 1976; *The Last Tycoon*, 1977; *Goin South*, 1978; *The Shining*, 1980; *The Postman Always Rings Twice*, 1981; *The Order; Reds*, 1981; *Terms of Endearment*, 1983. In addition, producer, *Ride the Whirlwind*, 1968; director, *Drive, He Said*, 1971; director *Goin' South*, 1978.

WRITINGS: SCREENPLAY—*A Safe Place*, 1971.

AWARDS: Best Supporting Actor, 1984: *Terms of Endearment;* Academy Award, Best Actor, New York Film Critics Circle, Golden Globe, 1975: *One Flew Over the Cuckoo's Nest;* Academy Award, New York Film Critics Circle, 1974: *Chinatown;* Cannes Film Festival Prize, 1974: *The Last Detail;* Academy Award, Best Supporting Actor, 1969: *Easy Rider.**

* * *

NIMOY, Leonard, actor

PERSONAL: Born March 26, 1931, in Boston; son of Max and Dora (Spinner) Nimoy; married Sandra Zober (an actress), February 21, 1954; children: Julie, Adam. EDUCATION: Boston College, B.A.; Antioch, M.A.; studied for the theatre with Jeff Corey. MILITARY: U.S. Army, 1954. NONTHEATRICAL CAREER: cab driver, pet shop clerk, soda jerk, movie usher.

CAREER: DEBUT—*Hansel and Gretel*, Elizabeth Peabody Playhouse, Boston, 1939. NEW YORK DEBUT—*Full Circle*, ANTA, 1973. PRINCIPAL STAGE APPEARANCES—*Awake and Sing*, Elizabeth Peabody Playhouse, Boston, 1948; *Dr. Faustius*, Orchard Gables Repertory, Los Angeles, 1950; *Stalag 17*, Pasadena Playhouse, CA, 1951; Stanley, *A Streetcar Named Desire*, Atlanta Theatre Guild, 1955; Brick, *Cat on a Hot Tin Roof*, Town and Gown Repertory, Birmingham, AL, 1959; *Deathwatch*, Cosmo Alley Gallery, Los Angeles, 1960; *Monserrat*, Los Angeles, 1963; *Irma La Douce*, Valley Music Theatre, Woodland Hills, CA, 1965; *Man in the Glass Booth*, Old Globe, San Diego, 1971; *Full Circle*, Kennedy Center, Washington, DC, 1973; Arthur, *Camelot*, North Shore Music Theatre, Beverly, MA, 1973; *One Flew Over the Cuckoo's Nest*, Little Theatre on the Square, Sullivan, IL, 1974; the King, *The King and I*, Melody Top, Milwaukee, WI, 1974; Tevya, *Fiddler on the Roof*, Opera House, Atlanta, GA, 1974; *Caligula*, St. Edward's University, Austin, TX, 1975; He, *The Fourposter*, Drury Lane North, Chicago, 1975; *Twelfth Night*, Pittsburgh Public

Theatre, PA, 1975; Higgins, *My Fair Lady*, Melody Top, Milwaukee, 1976; Dysart, *Equus*, Helen Hayes, NY, 1977. MAJOR TOURS—Tevya, *Fiddler on the Roof*, 1971; *Oliver*, 1972, 1973; *Six Rms Riv Vu*, 1973; *Sherlock Holmes*, national tour, 1976; Vincent, *Vincent: The Story of a Hero*, 1978, 1979, 1980 (also wrote, produced, and directed by Mr. Nimoy).

FILM DEBUT—*Queen for a Day*, 1950. PRINCIPAL FILMS— *Rhubarb*, 1951; *Kid Monk Baroni*, 1952; *Point*, 1952; *Francis Goes to West Point*, 1952; *The Old Overland Trail*, 1953; *The Balcony*, 1963; *Deathwatch*, 1966; *Valley of Mystery*, 1967; *The Missing Are Deadly*, 1975; *The Invasion of the Body Snatchers*, 1978; *Star Trek*, 1979; *A Woman Called Golda*, 1980; *Star Trek II: The Wrath of Khan*, 1982; *Star Trek III: The Search for Spock*, 1984.

TELEVISION APPEARANCES—*Matinee Theatre*; *Cain's Hundred*; *Sea Hunt*; *Rawhide*; *Eleventh Hour*; *Kraft Theatre*; *Wagon Train*; *Perry Mason*; *Twilight Zone*; *Dragnet*; *Gunsmoke*; *The Man from U.N.C.L.E.*; *Dr. Kildare*; *Bonanza*; *The Virginians*; *Profiles in Courage*; *Get Smart*; Mr. Spock, *Star Trek*, 1966–69; Paris, *Mission: Impossible*; *The Coral Jungle*; *Assault on the Wayne*, 1970; *Baffled*, 1972; *Three Faces of Love*, 1972; *The Alpha Caper*, 1973; *Vincent: The Story of a Hero*, 1980; *The Adventures of Marco Polo*, 1982; Host/Narrator, *In Search of . . .*; *Seizure: The Story of Kathy Morris*; *T.J. Hooker*.

DIRECTED: Films—*Star Trek III: The Search for Spock*, 1984; Television Shows—*Night Gallery*; *The Powers of Matthew Star*; *T.J. Hooker*.

RECORDINGS: *Leonard Nimoy Presents Spock's Music from Outer Space*, 1967; *Two Sides of Leonard Nimoy*; *The Way I Feel*; *The Touch of Leonard Nimoy*; *The New World of Leonard Nimoy*; *The Martian Chronicles*; *The Illustrated Man*; *War of the Worlds*; *The Green Hills of Earth*; *Gentlemen, Be Seated*.

WRITINGS: BOOKS, PUBLISHED—*You and I*, 1973; *Will I Not Think of You*, 1974; *I Am Not Spock*, 1975; *We Are All Children Searching for Love*, 1977; *Come Be with Me*, 1978; *These Words Are for You*, 1981; *Warmed by Love*, 1983.

SIDELIGHTS: RECREATION—Photography, writing poetry.

''Mr. Nimoy lectures on entertainment, reads and discusses his poetry, and does his own film processing.''

ADDRESS: Public Relations Agent—c/o Freeman and Doff, 9034 Sunset Blvd., Suite 100, Los Angeles, CA 90069.

* * *

NIVEN, David, actor

PERSONAL: Born March 1, 1910, in Kirriemuir, Scotland; died July 29, 1983; son of William Graham and Lady (Cmyn Platt) Niven; married Primula Rollo (deceased, 1946); Hjordis Tersmeden; children: (first marriage) two sons. EDUCATION: Attended Sandhurst College. MILITARY: British Army, Highland Light Infantry, Second Lieutenant to Colonel,

1939–45. NON-FILM CAREER: Lumberman, Canada; newspaper writer; laundry messenger; representative of a London wire firm; gunnery instructor to revolutionists in Cuba.

CAREER: FILM DEBUT—*Without Regret*, 1935. PRINCIPAL FILM APPEARANCES—*Splendor*, 1935; *Barbary Coast*, 1935; *Feather in Her Hat*, 1935; *Rose Marie*; *Dodsworth*, 1936; *The Charge of the Light Brigade*, 1936; *Dinner at the Ritz*; *Four Men and a Prayer*; *Three Blind Mice*; *The Prisoner of Zenda*, 1937; *Beloved Enemy*, 1937; *The Dawn Patrol*, 1938; *Bluebeard's Eight Wife*, 1938; *Wuthering Heights*, 1939; *Bachelor Mother*, 1939; *The Real Glory*, 1939; *Eternally Yours*, 1939; *Raffles*, 1940; *The First of the Few*, 1942; *The Way Ahead*, 1944; *Magnificent Doll*, 1946; *The Perfect Marriage*, 1946; *A Matter of Life and Death*, 1946; *The Other Love*, 1947; *The Bishop's Wife*, 1947; *Bonnie Prince Charlie*, 1948; *Enchantment*, 1948; *A Kiss in the Dark*, 1948; *The Elusive Pimpernel*, 1950; *A Kiss for Corliss*, 1950; *Happy Go Lovely*, 1951; *Soldiers Three*, 1951; *Toast of New Orleans*; *Lady Says No*; *Island Rescue*; *The Moon Is Blue*, 1953; *Happy Ever After*, 1954; *Love Lottery*, 1954; *The King's Thief*, 1955; *O'Leary Night (Tonight's the Night)*; *Carrington V.C.*, 1956; *Around the World in 80 Days*, 1956; *The Birds and the Bees*, 1956; *The Little Hut*, 1957; *Oh Men! Oh Women!*, 1957; *My Man Godfrey*, 1957; *The Silken Affair*, 1957; *Separate Tables*, 1958; *Bonjour Tristesse*, 1958; *Ask Any Girl*, 1959; *Happy Anniversary*, 1959; *Please Don't Eat the Daisies*, 1960; *Guns of Navarone*, 1961; *Guns of Darkness*, 1962; *The Best of Enemies*, 1962; *Fifty-Five Days at Peking*, 1963; *The Pink Panther*, 1964; *Bedtime Story*, 1964; *Island of Blue Dolphins*, 1964; *Lady L*, 1965; *King of the Mountain*; *Captive City*; *Eye of the Devil*, 1967; *Casino Royale*, 1967; *The Impossible Years*, 1968; *Before Winter Comes*, 1968; *The Extraordinary Seaman*, 1969; *Prudence and the Pill*, 1969; *The Brain*, 1969; *King, Queen, Knave*, 1972; *Vampira*, 1974; *Paper Tiger*; *No Deposit, No Return*; *Murder by Death*, 1976; *Candleshoe*, 1978; *Death on the Nile*, 1978; *Escape to Athena*, 1979; *Rough Cut*, 1980; *The Sea Wolves*, 1981; *Whose Little Girl Are You?*.

PRINCIPAL TELEVISION APPEARANCES—Host/actor, *The David Niven Show*, 1959–64; star, *The Rogues*, 1964–65; formed Four Star TV, 1952.

WRITINGS: BOOKS—*Round the Rugged Rocks*, 1951; *The Moon Is a Balloon*, 1971; *Bring on the Empty Horses*, 1975; *Go Slowly, Come Back Quickly*, 1981.

AWARDS: New York Film Critics Award, 1960; Academy Award, New York Film Critics Award, 1958: *Separate Tables;* Legion of Merit.*

* * *

NOLAN, Lloyd, actor

PERSONAL: Born August 11, 1902, in San Francisco, CA; son of James Charles (a shoe manufacturer) and Elizabeth (Shea) Nolan; married Mary Mell Efird (an actress), May 23, 1933; children: Jay Benedict, Melinda Joyce. EDUCATION: Attended Stanford University; trained for the stage at the Pasadena Playhouse with Gilmore Brown. POLITICS: Republican.

LLOYD NOLAN

CAREER: FILM DEBUT—the heavy, *Stolen Harmony*, 1934. PRINCIPAL FILM APPEARANCES—*Texas Rangers*, 1936; *Big Brown Eyes*, 1937; *House Across the Bay; Bataan*, 1943; *Captain Eddie*, 1945; *The House on 92nd Street*, 1945; *Circumstantial Evidence*, 1945; *A Tree Grows in Brooklyn*, 1945; *Somewhere in the Night*, 1946; *Two Smart People*, 1946; *Lady in the Lake*, 1946; *Wild Harvest*, 1947; *Green Grass of Wyoming*, 1948; *Street with No Name*, 1948; *Bad Boy*, 1949; *Easy Living*, 1949; *The Sun Comes Up*, 1949; *The Lemon Drop Kid*, 1951; *We Joined the Navy*, 1952; *Island in the Sky*, 1953; *Crazy Legs*, 1953; *Last Hunt*, 1956; *Santiago*, 1956; *Peyton Place*, 1956; *Abandon Ship!*, 1957; *A Hatful of Rain*, 1957; *Portrait in Black*, 1960; *Susan Slade*, 1961; *Circus World*, 1964; *Never Too Late*, 1965; *The Double Man*, 1968; *Sergeant Ryker*, 1958; *Ice Station Zebra*, 1969; *Airport*, 1970; *Earthquake*, 1974.

TELEVISION DEBUT—*The Barker*. PRINCIPAL TELEVISION APPEARANCES—Captain Queeg, *The Caine Mutiny Court-Martial*, 1955; *Ah, Wilderness!;* Martin Kane, *Private Eye*, 1952–53; *Julia*.

STAGE DEBUT—(vaudeville) *The Radio Robot*, Keith-Albert Circuit, Worcester, MA, 1925.

NEW YORK DEBUT—*The Cape Cod Follies*, Bijou, 1928, 80 performances. LONDON DEBUT—Captain Queeg, *The Caine Mutiny Court Martial*, Hippodrome, 1956, 182 performances. PRINCIPAL STAGE APPEARANCES—*The Lower Road, Romeo and Juliet, You Never Can Tell*, Cape Cod Playhouse, Dennis, MA; *The Blue and the Gray or War Is Hell*, Old

Rialto, Hoboken, NJ, 1929; Holloway, *Sweet Stranger*, Cort, NY, 1930; Emil, *Reunion in Vienna*, Martin Beck, NY, 1931; *Americana*, Shubert, NY, 1932; Biff Grimes, *One Sunday Afternoon*, Little, NY, 1933; Geoffrey Carver, *Ragged Army*, Selwyn, NY, 1934; Rudy Flannigan, *Gentlewoman*, Cort, NY, 1934; Queeg, *The Caine Mutiny Court-Martial*, Plymouth, NY, 1954; Johnny Condell, *One More River*, Ambassador, NY, 1960. MAJOR TOURS—Oliver Erwenter, *Silver Whistle*, U.S. cities, 1950; Samuel Rilling, *Courtin' Time*, Boston, MA, Philadelphia, PA, 1951; Queeg, *The Caine Mutiny Court-Martial*, U.S. cities, 1955.

AWARDS: Donaldson Award, New York Critics Award, 1954: *The Caine Mutiny Court-Martial;* Emmy Award, 1955: *The Caine Mutiny Court-Martial.*

SIDELIGHTS: MEMBERSHIPS—SAG, AEA, AFTRA. RECREATION—Golf, archaeology.

ADDRESS: Agent—c/o Mark Levin, 328 S. Beverly Drive, Suite E, Beverly Hills, CA 90210. Office—c/o E.B.M., 132 S. Rodeo Drive, Beverly Hills, CA 90212.

* * *

NOLTE, Nick, actor

PERSONAL: Born 1942, in Omaha, NE. EDUCATION: Five colleges in four years on football scholarships including Pasadena City College and Phoenix City College.

CAREER: PRINCIPAL STAGE APPEARANCES—Several plays at Actors Inner Circle, Phoenix, AZ; stock in Colorado; Old Log Theatre, Minneapolis, 1968–71; *The Last Pad*, Hollywood, CA.

PRINCIPAL TELEVISION APPEARANCES—*Winter Kill*, 1974; *The California Kid*, 1974; *Death Sentence*, 1974; *Adams of Eagle Lake*, 1975; *The Treasure Chest Murder*, 1975; *The Runaways*, 1975; *Feather Farm;* Tom Jordache, *Rich Man, Poor Man*, 1976; *Medical Center; Gunsmoke.*

PRINCIPAL FILM APPEARANCES—*Return to Macon County Line*, 1975; *The Deep*, 1977; *Who'll Stop the Rain*, 1978; *North Dallas Forty*, 1979; *Heart Beat*, 1980; *Cannery Row*, 1982; *48 Hours*, 1982; *Under Fire*, 1983.

ADDRESS: Agent—c/o ICM, 40 E. 57th Street, New York, NY 10019.*

* * *

NORMAN, Marsha, playwright, producer

PERSONAL: Born September 21, 1947; daughter of Billie Lee and Bertha Mae (Conley) Williams; married Dann Byck (a producer) on November 23, 1978. EDUCATION: Agnes Scott College, B.A. (Philosophy); University of Louisville, M.A. (Teaching). NON-THEATRICAL CAREER: Teacher, Kentucky Department of Health, 1969–70; Teacher, Gifted Program, Jefferson County Public Schools, KY, 1970–72; Filmmaker-in-the-Schools, Director of Special Project, Kentucky Arts Commission, 1972–76; writer, Book Section, Children's Section, *Louisville Times,* 1974–79.

WRITINGS: PLAYS, PRODUCED/PUBLISHED—*Getting Out,* Actors Theatre of Louisville, Theatre de Lys, NY, 1979–80; *Third & Oak: The Laundromat;* '*night Mother,* Golden, NY, 1983–84; *Traveller in the Dark,* American Repertory, Cambridge, MA, 1984.

AWARDS: Pulitzer Prize in Drama, 1983: '*night Mother; Newsday* Oppy Award: *Getting Out;* John Gassner Medallion: *Getting Out.*

SIDELIGHTS: MEMBERSHIPS—Dramatists Guild; Writers Guild; PEN.

ADDRESS: Agent—Biff Liff, c/o William Morris Agency, 1350 Avenue of the Americas, New York, NY 10019.

* * *

NORTH, Edmund H., writer

PERSONAL: Born March 12, 1911; son of Robert (an actor and producer) and Eleanor (an actress; maiden name, Hall) North; married Collette Ford, December 11, 1947; children: Susan, Bobbie. EDUCATION: Attended Stanford University. MILITARY: U.S. Army 1941–45.

WRITINGS: FILMS—*One Night of Love,* 1934; *I Dream Too Much,* 1935; *Young Man with a Horn,* 1950; *The Day the Earth Stood Still,* 1951; *Cowboy,* 1958; *Sink the Bismarck!,* 1960; *Patton* (with Francis Coppola), 1970; *Meteor,* 1979.

AWARDS: Morgan Cox Award, 1975; Academy Award, Writers' Guild Award, Best Screenplay, 1970: *Patton;* Valentine Davies Award, 1967.

SIDELIGHTS: MEMBERSHIPS—Writers Guild of America West (past president), Motion Picture Academy of Arts and Sciences.

ADDRESS: Agent—c/o Robert Eisenbach, 760 N. La Cienega, Los Angeles, CA 90069.

* * *

NOTO, Lore(nzo), actor, producer

PERSONAL: Married Mary; children: Janice, Tony, Thad, Jody.

CAREER: PRINCIPAL STAGE APPEARANCE—Boy's Father, *Fantasticks,* 1971–present. PRINCIPAL STAGE WORK, PRODUCED—*Fantasticks,* 1960–present; *The Yearling,* Alvin, NY.

SIDELIGHTS: MEMBERSHIPS—AEA.

ADDRESS: Home—24 Ascan, Forest Hills, NY 11325. Office—181 Sullivan Street, New York, NY 10012.

NOURI, Michael, actor

PERSONAL: Born December 9, 1945, in Washington, DC; son of Edward and Gloria (Montgomery) Nouri. EDUCATION: Avon Old Farms; Rollins College; Emerson College; studied for the theatre with Larry Moss, Lee Strasberg, Bill Alderson, Bob Modica.

CAREER: NEW YORK DEBUT—Peter Latham, *Forty Carats,* Morosco, New York, 1969–71. PRINCIPAL STAGE APPEARANCES—*Nefertiti,* Blackstone, Chicago, 1977; *Booth,* Playwright's Horizon, New York, 1982. MAJOR TOURS—*Forty Carats,* Kenley Players, Ohio, 1970.

FILM DEBUT—Don Farber, *Goodbye, Columbus,* 1969. PRINCIPAL FILMS—*Contract on Cherry Street,* 1977; Nick, *Flashdance,* 1982. TELEVISION DEBUT—Giorgio Bellonci, *Beacon Hill,* 1975. TELEVISION APPEARANCES—*The Gangster Chronicles.*

AWARDS: Emmy Nomination, Best Actor, 1976.

ADDRESS: Office—c/o Lazarow & Co., 119 W. 57th Street, New York, NY 10019. Agent—D.H.K.P.R., 165 W. 46th Street, New York, NY 10036.

* * *

NUGENT, Nelle, producer

PERSONAL: Born May 24, 1939 in Jersey City, NJ; daughter of John Patrick and Evelyn Adelaide (Stern) Nugent; married Jolyon Fox Stern on April 7, 1982. EDUCATION: Skidmore College, B.S., 1960.

CAREER: PRINCIPAL STAGE WORK, PRODUCED—Broadway productions: *Dracula, The Elephant Man, Morning's at Seven, Home, Amadeus, Piaf, Rose, Nicholas Nickleby, The Dresser, Mass Appeal, Pilobolus, All's Well That Ends Well, Good, Total Abandon, The Glass Menagerie, The Lady and the Clarinet, Painting Churches.*

AWARDS: Antoinette Perry Awards: *Dracula, The Elephant Man, Morning's at Seven, Amadeus, Nicholas Nickleby;* New York Drama Critics Awards: *The Elephant Man, Nicholas Nickleby;* Drama Desk Awards: *Amadeus, The Elephant Man, Nicholas Nickleby;* Entrepreneurial Woman of the Year, Los Angeles Critics Award.

THEATRE-RELATED CAREER: Stage manager, off-Broadway, 1960–63; stage manager, Broadway, 1964–69; vice president, production services, Theatre Now, Inc. 1968–70; associate managing director, Nederlander Organization, 1970–76; chairman, McCann and Nugent Productions Inc., 1976–present.

SIDELIGHTS: MEMBERSHIPS—Voting member, Blue Cross-Blue Shield; board of visitors, Syracuse University; board of directors, League of New York Theatres.

ADDRESS: Office—1501 Broadway, New York, NY 10036.

FRANCE NUYEN

NUYEN, France, actress

PERSONAL: Born July 31, 1939, in Marseilles, France; daughter of Louis and Julie (Mazaut) Nuyen; children: Fleur Morell. EDUCATION: Antioch, B.A.; studied for the theatre with Lee Strasberg at the Actors Studio in New York.

CAREER: NEW YORK DEBUT—Suzie, *The World of Suzie Wong,* 1958.

FILM DEBUT—Liat, *South Pacific,* 1958. PRINCIPAL FILMS— *In Love and War,* 1958; *The Last Time I Saw Archie,* 1961; *Satan Never Sleeps,* 1962; *Diamondhead,* 1963; *A Girl Named Tamiko,* 1963; *The Man in the Middle,* 1963; *Dimension 5;* 1965; *Black Water Gold,* 1969; *Last Train to Rob,* 1970; *The Great Game,* 1972; *Planet of the Apes,* 1973.

TELEVISION APPEARANCES—*Ed Sullivan Show,* 1958; *Perry Como Show; Jack Parr Show; Merv Griffin Show; Hong Kong; Wild, Wild West; Burke's Law; Man from U.N.C.L.E.; I Spy; Gunsmoke; The Magician; Chopper One; Police Story; Fantasy Island; Columbo; Charlie's Angels; Trapper John, M.D.; Medical Center; Star Trek.*

AWARDS: Daniel Blum Award, 1959: *The World of Suzie Wong;* Volunteer of the Year, San Fernando Valley Directors of Volunteers, 1981; Commendation from the Board of Supervisors of Los Angeles County, 1982.

SIDELIGHTS: MEMBERSHIPS—Board of Directors, The Free Art Clinic; Board of Directors, William O'Douglas Outdoor Classroom.

''Concurrent with Miss Nuyen's acting career has been a profound interest in and ongoing study of holistic healing and psychology. She has studied with Paul Richard, the French mystic, physicist, philosopher, author and diplomat, Rev. Eunice Jean Hurt and Pir Villayat Khan. She has been very active with various groups and in various ways, teaching, choreographing celebratory masses and working in the fields of self-awareness, stress management, meditation and healing programs in institutions for young drug abusers, abused and battered children, a state prison, and the drug control center of Veteran's Hospital. She became aware of her cosmic values at a very early age and conscious of her healing ability at age ten. . . . Of her performing career she notes, ''*Suzie Wong, South Pacific, Diamondhead* . . . all significant theatrical projects on racial equalization . . . and pioneers in the subject.''

ADDRESS: Office—P.O. Box 5022, Beverly Hills, CA 90210. Agent—Bob Kenneally ATI, 8816 Burton Way, Beverly Hills, CA 90211.

O

OAKLAND, Simon, actor

PERSONAL: Born 1922, in New York City; died August 29, 1983. EDUCATION: Studied at the Americn Theatre Wing. NON-THEATRICAL CAREER: Former professional violinist. MILITARY: Served during World War II.

CAREER: NEW YORK DEBUT—*Skipper Next to God.* PRINCIPAL FILM APPEARANCES—*The Brothers Karamazov,* 1958; *I Want to Live,* 1958; *Who Was That Lady?,* 1960; *The Rise and Fall of Legs Diamond,* 1960; *Psycho,* 1960; *Murder, Inc.,* 1960; *West Side Story,* 1961; *Follow That Dream* 1962; *Third of a Man,* 1963; *Wall of Noise,* 1963; *The Satan Bug,* 1965; *The Plainsman,* 1966; *The Sand Pebbles,* 1966; *Tony Rome,* 1967; *Chubasco,* 1968; *Scandalous John,* 1971; *Chato's Land,* 1972; *Emperor of the North,* 1973; *Happy Mother's Day . . . Love George,* 1973.

PRINCIPAL TELEVISION APPEARANCES—Series, *Toma,* 1973–74; *The Night Stalker,* 11974–75; *Baa Baa Black Sheep,* 1976–77; *Black Sheep Squadron,* 1977–78.*

* * *

OATES, Warren, actor

PERSONAL: Born July 5, 1928, in Depoy, KY; died April 3, 1982. EDUCATION: Attended University of Louisville, KY.

CAREER: PRINCIPAL FILM APPEARANCES—*Up Periscope,* 1958; *Yellowstone Kelly,* 1959; *The Rise and Fall of Legs Diamond,* 1960; *Private Property,* 1960; *Ride the High Country,* 1962; *Hero's Island,* 1962; *Mail Order Bride,* 1963; *The Rounders,* 1965; *Major Dundee,* 1965; *The Shooting,* 1966; *Return of the Seven,* 1966; *Welcome to Hard Times,* 1967; *In the Heat of the Night,* 1967; *The Split,* 1968; *Crooks and Coronets,* 1969; *The Wild Bunch,* 1969; *Smith,* 1969; *Barquero,* 1970; *Two-Lane Blacktop,* 1970; *There Was a Crooked Man,* 1970; *The Hired Man,* 1971; *92 in the Shade,* 1972; *The Thief Who Came to Dinner,* 1973; *Tom Sawyer,* 1973; *Kid Blue,* 1973; *Dillinger,* 1974; *Cockfighter,* 1974; *Badlands,* 1974; *Bring Me the Head of Alfredo Garcia,* 1974; *The White Dawn,* 1974; *Race with the Devil,* 19756; *Drum,* 1976; *Dixie Dynamite,* 1976; *China 9, Liberty 37,* 1978; *The Brink's Job,* 1978; *Sleeping Dogs,* 1978; *Stripes,* 1981.

PRINCIPAL TELEVISION APPEARANCES—*And Baby Makes Six; True Grit; My Old Man; Baby Comes Home.**

O'BRIEN, Jack, director

PERSONAL: Born June 18, 1939, in Saginaw, MI; son of J. George (a business representative) and Evelyn Mae (MacArthur [O'Brien-Martens]) O'Brien. EDUCATION: University of Michigan, 1957–61, A.B., 1962, M.A.; trained for the theatre with Ellis Rabb and John Houseman; spent six years with APA Repertory.

CAREER: NEW YORK DEBUT—Director, *Cock-a-Doodle Dandy,* APA Repertory Company, 1969. PRINCIPAL ENGAGEMENTS: DIRECTOR—*Porgy and Bess,* Houston Grand Opera, 1976 (moved to Broadway); *Street Scene,* New York City Opera, 1977–78; *The Most Happy Fella,* New York and Public Broadcasting, 1979; *The Skin of Our Teeth,* American Playhouse (live on Public Broadcasting), 1983; *Porgy and Bess,* Radio City Music Hall, New York, 1983. MAJOR TOURS—*Porgy and Bess,* National and Europe, 1977–78.

Also: Assistant/Associate Director, *APA Repertory Co.,* 1964–69; Associate Artistic Director, *The Acting Company,* New York, 1974–75; Artistic Director, *The Old Globe Theatre,* San Diego, 1981–present.

THEATRE-RELATED CAREER—Instructor, theatre, Hunter College (NYC), 1963–64.

SIDELIGHTS: MEMBERSHIPS—AEA; S.S.D.C.; Directors Guild.

ADDRESS: Office—Old Globe Theatre, P.O. Box 2171, San Diego, CA 92112. Agent—Phyllis Wender, Rosenstone/ Wender, Three E. 48th Street, New York, NY 10017.

* * *

O'CONNOR, Carroll, actor, writer, producer

PERSONAL: Born August 2, 1924, in New York, NY; son of Edward Joseph and Elise Patricia (O'Connor) O'Connor. Married Nancy Fields, July 27, 1951; children: Hugh. EDUCATION: National University of Ireland, B.A., 1952; University of Montana, M.A., 1956.

CAREER: PRINCIPAL STAGE APPEARANCES—*Ulysses in Nighttown,* NY, 1958; *The Big Knife,* NY, 1959; *Playboy of the Western World,* NY, *The Egg, Heartbreak House, Candide, Ladies of Hanover Tower,* Los Angeles Theatre Group; *Brothers,* NY, 1983.

PRINCIPAL FILM APPEARANCES—*Lad Had a Dog*, 1961; *Fever in the Blood*, 1961; *By Love Possessed*, 1961; *Lonely Are the Brave*, 1962; *Cleopatra*, 1963; *In Harm's Way*, 1965; *What Did You Do in the War Daddy?*, 1966; *Hawaii*, 1966; *Not with My Wife You Don't*, 1966; *Warning Shot*, 1967; *Waterhole No. 3*, 1967; *The Devil's Brigade*, 1968; *For Love of Ivy*, 1968; *Marlowe*, 1969; *Death of a Gunfighter*, 1969; *Kelley's Heroes*, 1970; *Doctors' Wives*, 1971; *Law and Disorder*, 1974.

PRINCIPAL TELEVISION APPEARANCES—*The Sacco and Vanzetti Story*, 1960; *U.S. Steel Hour; Kraft Theatre; Armstrong Circle Theater; All in the Family*, 1971–79; *The Funny Papers*, 1972; *Of Thee I Sing*, 1972; *The Carroll O'Connor Special*, 1973; *The Last Hurrah*, 1973; *Archie's Place*, 1979–82.

WRITINGS: PLAYS, PRODUCED—*Ladies of Hanover Tower*, Los Angeles Theater Group, CA. SCREENPLAYS—*Little Anjie Always; The Great Robinson.*

AWARDS: George Foster Peabody Award, Broadcasting Excellence, 1980; Emmy Award, Best Actor, 1973, 1977, 1978, 1979: *All in the Family;* Golden Globe Award: *All in the Family.*

SIDELIGHTS: MEMBERSHIPS—The Players Club, Sigma Phi Epsilon.

ADDRESS: P.O. Box 49935, Los Angeles, CA 90049-0935.

* * *

O'DONNELL, Mark, playwright

PERSONAL: Born July 19, 1954 in Cleveland, OH; son of Hubert John (a welder) and Frances (Novak) O'Donnell. EDUCATION: Harvard University, B.A. (magna cum laude) 1976; studied with Jorie Wyler at the American Academy of Dramatic Art.

WRITINGS: PLAYS, PRODUCED—*Hasty Pudding Theatricals*, Harvard University, 1974–76; *That's It Folks*, Playwrights Horizons, 1983; *Fables for Friends*, Playwrights Horizons, 1980 and 1984. TELEVISION—*Saturday Night Live* (writer and performer), 1981–82. BOOKS—*Tools of Power* with Kurt Andersen and Roger Parloff.

AWARDS: LeComte de Nuoy Prize, 1980; BMI Varsity Show Award for Lyrics, 1976; Academy of American Poets Prize, 1976.

THEATRE-RELATED CAREER: Teacher, New York University, 1982; teacher, New School for Social Research, NY, 1983–84.

SIDELIGHTS: MEMBERSHIPS—Dramatists Guild.

Mr. O'Donnell has written humor for *Esquire Vanity Fair, The New York Times*, and the *Saturday Review*, in addition to writing poetry and lyrics.

ADDRESS: Home—202 Riverside Drive, New York, NY

10025. Agent—Luis Sanjurjo c/o ICM, 40 W. 57th Street, New York, NY 10019.

* * *

OLIANSKY, Joel, director, producer

PERSONAL: Born October 11, 1935, in New York City; son of Albert (a pharmacist) and Florence (a teacher; maiden name, Shaw) Oliansky; married Patricia, June 21, 1960 (divorced 1977); children: Ingrid, Adam. EDUCATION: Hofstra University, B.A., 1959; Yale University, M.F.A., 1962.

CAREER: FILM DEBUT—Director, writer, *The Competition*, 1980. PRINCIPAL TELEVISION WORK—Writer, *The Law*, 1976, *Masada*, 1981, director, *Cagney and Lacey*, etc.

WRITINGS: BOOKS—novel, *Shame, Shame on the Johnson Boys*, 1966.

AWARDS: Writers Guild of America Awards, 1981: *Masada*, 1979: *The Law;* Emmy Award, 1971: *The Senator.*

ADDRESS: Agent—Adams/Rosenberg, 9200 Sunset Blvd., Los Angeles, CA 90069.

* * *

OLIM, Dorothy, manager, producer

PERSONAL: Born October 14, 1934, in New York City; daughter of Sol (a merchant) and Esther (Kessel) Olim; married Gerald S. Krone, April 5, 1965 (divorced February 26, 1970). EDUCATION: Juilliard School of Music, 1949–50; St. John's College, Annapolis, MD, 1951–53; Neighborhood Playhouse School of the Theatre, Summer, 1953; Columbia University, School of Dramatic Arts, B.F.A., 1955, M.F.A., 1956.

CAREER: DEBUT—Sorceress, *The Boys from Syracuse*, Lambertville Music Circus, NJ, 1953 (also served as assistant treasurer). NEW YORK DEBUT—The Signora, *Tonight We Improvise*, Living Theatre, 1954. PRODUCER: Plays—*The One-Eyed Man Is King*, Theatre East, NY, 1956; (associate with Lore Noto and Sheldon Baron) *The Fantasticks*, Sullivan Street Playhouse, NY, 1960; (with Gerald Krone) *A Worm in Horseradish*, Maidman Playhouse, NY, 1961; (with Gerald Krone) *The Golden Apple*, York Playhouse, NY, 1962; *The Lion in Love*, One Sheridan Square, NY, 1963; *Pimpernal*, Gramercy, NY, 1964; (with St. John Terrell and Gerald Krone), *I Must Be Talking to My Friends*, NY, Orpheum, 1967; also, forty-five plays at the Saranac Lake Summer Theatre, 1956–60.

MANAGER: General Manager, St. John Terrell's Music Circus, Sterling Forest Gardens, Tuxedo, NY, 1960; General Manager, E. 11th Street Theatre, NY, 1961–62. As Dorothy Olim Associates, Inc., has been the General Manager of *The River Niger, Bob and Ray—The Two and Only, Your Own Thing, America Hurrah, MacBird, Fortune and Men's Eyes, Vietrock, Collision Course, Red Cross & Mu-*

zeeka, Tom Paine, Happy Ending & Day of Absence, We Bombed in New Haven, You Never Know, Rosebloom, Big Time Buck White, Father's Day, Curse of an Aching Heart, Solomon's Child, Poppie Nongena, A Weekend Near Madison, Piano Bar, others. Her firm also represents Theatre Four, a 299-seat Off-Broadway theatre.

AWARDS: Drama Critics Circle Award, 1968: *Your Own Thing;* Antoinette Perry Award, 1974: *The River Niger.*

SIDELIGHTS: MEMBERSHIPS—Association of Theatrical Press Agents and Managers (Member of Board of Governors); League of Professional Theatre Women, New York; League of Off-Broadway Theatre Owners and Producers (Secretary-Treasurer); The Negro Ensemble Company (Board of Directors, 1967–71).

Miss Olim has lectured around the country on the subjects of "How to produce Off-Broadway" and "economics of the theatrical industry." She is a former president and current board member of the League of Advertising Agencies, of which her agency, Krone-Olim Advertising, Inc., is a member.

ADDRESS: Office—1540 Broadway, New York, NY 10036.

* * *

OLIVIER, Laurence Kerr (Baron, created 1970; Knight, 1947) actor, director, manager

PERSONAL: Born May 22, 1907, in Dorking, U.K.; son of Reverend Gerard Kerr and Agnes Louise (Crookenden) Olivier; married Jill Esmond 1930, (divorced 1940); married Vivien Leigh, 1940 (divorced 1960); married Joan Plowright, March 17, 1960; children: Richard Kerr, Tamsin Agnes Margaret, Julie Kate. EDUCATION: Attended St. Edward's School, Oxford; studied for the stage with Elsie Fogerty.

CAREER: STAGE DEBUT—Katherine, *The Taming of the Shrew,* Shakespeare Festival Theatre, Stratford-on-Avon, U.K., 1922. NEW YORK DEBUT—Hugh Bromilow, *Murder on the Second Floor,* Eltinge, 1929. PRINCIPAL STAGE APPEARANCES—Suliot Officer, *Byron,* Century, U.K., 1924; Thomas of Clarence/Snare, *Henry IV, Part II,* Regent, U.K., 1925; *Henry VIII, The Cenci,* Empire, U.K., 1925; Birmingham Repertory Company, 1926–28; Minstrel, *The Marvellous History of Saint Bernard,* Kingsway, U.K., 1926; Young Man, *The Adding Machine,* Malcolm, *Macbeth,* Martellus, *Back to Methuselah,* Harold, *Harold,* The Lord, *Taming of the Shrew,* Court, U.K., 1928; Gerald Arnwood, *Bird in Hand,* Royalty, U.K., 1928; Captain Stanhope, *Journey's End,* Apollo, U.K., 1928; Michael Geste, *Beau Geste,* His Majesty's, U.K., 1929; Prince Po, *The Circle of Chalk,* New, U.K., 1929; Richard Parish, *Paris Bound,* Lyric, U.K., 1929; John Hardy, *The Stranger Within,* Garrick, London, 1929; Jerry Warrender, *The Last Enemy,* Fortune, London, 1929; Ralph, *After All,* Arts, London, 1930; Victor Prynne, *Private Lives,* Phoenix, London, 1930, Times Square, NY, 1931; Steven Beringer, *The Rats of Norway,* Playhouse, NY, 1933; Julian Dulcimer, *The Green Bay Tree,* Cort, NY, 1933; Richard Kurt, *Biography,*

Globe, London, 1934; Bothwell, *Queen of Scots,* New, London, 1934; Anthony Cavendish, *Theatre Royal,* Lyric, London, 1934; Peter Hammond, *Ringmaster,* Shaftesbury, London, 1935; Richard Harben, *Golden Arrow,* Whithall, London, 1935; Romeo, *Romeo and Juliet,* New, London, 1935; Mercutio, *Romeo and Juliet,* New, London, 1935;

Robert Patch, *Bees on the Boatdeck,* Lyric, London, 1936; Hamlet, *Hamlet,* Old Vic, London, 1937; Sir Toby Belch, *Twelfth Night,* King Henry, *Henry V,* Macbeth, *Macbeth,* Old Vic, London, 1937; Hamlet, *Hamlet,* Old Vic Company, Kronborg Castle, Elsinore, 1937; Macbeth, *Macbeth,* New, London, 1937; Iago, *Othello,* Vivaldi, *The King of Nowhere,* Caius Marcius, *Coriolanus,* Old Vic, London, 1938; Gaylord Easterbrook, *No Time for Comedy,* Ethel Barrymore, NY, 1939; Romeo, *Romeo and Juliet,* 51st Street Theatre, NY, 1940; Button Moulder, *Peer Gynt,* Old Vic, London, 1944; Sergius Saranoff, *Arms and the Man,* Duke of Gloster, *Richard III,* Astrov, *Uncle Vanya,* Old Vic, London, 1944; Hotspur, *Henry IV, Part I,* Justice Shallow, *Henry IV, Part II,* Oedipus, *Oedipus Rex,* Puff, *The Critic,* Old Vic, London, 1945–46; *Peer Gynt, Arms and the Man, Richard III,* Comedie Francaise, France, 1945; in repertory, Century, NY, 1946; King Lear, *King Lear,* New, London, 1946; Richard III, *Richard III,* Sir Peter Teazle, *The School for Scandal,* Chorus, *Antigone,* New London, 1949;

Duke of Altair, *Venus Observed,* St. James, London, 1950; Caesar, *Caesar and Cleopatra,* Antony, *Antony and Cleopatra,* St. James, London, 1951; Caesar, *Caesar and Cleopatra,* Antony, *Antony and Cleopatra,* Ziegfeld, NY, 1951; Grand Duke, *The Sleeping Prince,* Phoenix, London, 1953; Macbeth, *Macbeth,* Titus, *Titus Andronicus,* Malvolio, *Twelfth Night,* Shakespeare Memorial, Stratford-upon-Avon, 1955; Archie Rice, *The Entertainer,* Royal Court, Palace, London, 1957, Royale, NY, 1958; Coriolanus, *Coriolanus,* Memorial, Stratford-on-Avon, UK, 1959; Berenger, *Rhinoceros,* Royal Court, London, 1960; Becket, *Becket,* St. James, NY, 1960; Henry II, *Becket,* Hudson, NY, 1961; Prologue/Bassanes, *The Broken Heart,* Astrov, *Uncle Vanya,* Chichester Festival, U.K., 1962; Fred Midway, *Semi-Detached,* Saville, London, 1962; Astrov, *Uncle Vanya,* Old Vic, London, 1963; Astrov, *Uncle Vanya,* Captain Brazen, *The Recruiting Officer,* National, London, 1963; Othello, *Othello,* Halvard Solness, *The Master Builder,* National, London, 1964; Tattle, *Love for Love,* Old Vic, London, 1965; Edgar, *The Dance of Death,* National, London, 1967; A. B. Raham, *Home and Beauty,* National, London, 1969; Shylock, *The Merchant of Venice,* National, London, 1970; James Tyrone, *Long Days Journey into Night,* National, London, 1971; Antonio, *Saturday, Sunday, Monday,* John Tagg, *The Party,* National, London, 1973.

MAJOR TOURS—Richard Coaker, *The Farmer's Wife,* U.K. cities, 1926; *The School for Scandal, Richard III,* Mr. Antrobus, *The Skin of Our Teeth,* Australia, New Zealand, 1948; Titus, *Titus Andronicus,* European cities, 1957; Henry II, *Becket,* UK and US cities, 1961; Othello, *Othello,* Moscow, Berlin, 1965; *Love for Love, The Dance of Death,* Plucheux, *A Flea in Her Ear,* Canadian cities, 1967.

FILM DEBUT—*Too Many Crooks,* 1927. PRINCIPAL FILM APPEARANCES—*Wuthering Heights; Rebecca; Pride and Prejudice; Lady Hamilton; Henry V* (also produced and directed); *The Beggar's Opera; Richard III; The Prince and the Show-*

girl (also directed); *The Devil's Disciple; Spartacus; The Entertainer; Term of Trial; Othello; Khartoum; Oh! What a Lovely War; The Battle of Britain; Dance of Death; Three Sisters* (also directed); *David Copperfield; Nicholas and Alexandra; Lady Caroline Lamb; Sleuth; The Betsy; The Boys from Brazil; A Little Romance; Dracula; Inchon; The Jazz Singer; The Bounty.*

PRINCIPAL TELEVISION APPEARANCES—John Gabriel Borkman, *John Gabriel Borkman*, 1958; *The Moon and Sixpence*, 1960; *Long Day's Journey into Night*, 1973; *The Merchant of Venice; Love Among the Ruins; Cat on a Hot Tin Roof; King Lear; Brideshead Revisited.*

DIRECTED: Plays—*King Lear*, Old Vic, London, 1946; *The School for Scandal, Antigone, The Proposal*, Old Vic, London, 1949; *Venus Observed*, New Century, NY, 1952; *The Chances, The Broken Heart, Uncle Vanya*, Chichester Festival, UK, 1962; *Hamlet*, National, London, 1963; *The Crucible*, National, London, 1965; *Juno and the Paycock*, National, London, 1966; *The Three Sisters*, National, London, 1967; *The Advertisement, Love's Labour's Lost*, National, London, 1968; *Amphitryon 38*, National, London, 1971; *Eden End*, National, London, 1974; *Filumena*, New York, 1980.

PRODUCED: Plays—*Golden Arrow*, 1935; *Bees on the Boatdeck* (with Ralph Richardson), Lyric, London, 1936; *The Skin of Our Teeth*, Phoenix, London, 1945; *Born Yesterday*, Barrick, London, 1947; *A Streetcar Named Desire*, Aldwych, London, 1949; *Venus Observed*, St. James, London, 1950; *Captain Carvallo*, St. James, London, 1950; *Caesar and Cleopatra, Antony and Clepatra*, St. James, London, 1951; *Othello*, St. James, London, 1951; *The Happy Time* (with Gilbert Miller), St. James, London, 1952; *Anastasia*, St. James, London, 1953; *Waiting For Gillian*, St. James, London, 1954; *Meet a Body*, Duke of York, London, 1954; *Double Image*, London, 1956; *Summer of the Seventeenth Doll, Titus Andronicus*, London, 1957; *The Shifting Heart*, London, 1959; *The Tumbler*, New York, *A Lodging for a Bride, Over the Bridge*, London, 1960.

AWARDS: Academy Award, Special, 1979; Order of the Yugoslav Flag with Golden Wreath, 1971; Olympus Award, Taormina Film Festival, 1962; Selznick Golden Laurel Trophy, 1956; British Film Academy Award, 1956: *Richard III;* Grand Officer of the Ordine al Merito della Republica, 1954; Officer of the Legion d'Honneur, 1953; Commander of the Order of Dannebrog, 1949; Academy Award, 1948–49: *Hamlet.* Honorary Degrees—HonDLitt, Oxon, 1957; HonLLD, Edinburgh, 1964; LLD, Manchester, DLitt, London, 1968; HonDLitt, Sussex, 1978.

SIDELIGHTS: MEMBERSHIPS—Garrick Club, Green Room Club. RECREATION—Tennis, swimming, gardening.

ADDRESS: Office—33-4 Chancery Lane, London, WC2.*

* * *

OLSON, James, actor

PERSONAL: Born October 8, 1930, in Evanston, IL; son of LeRoy (an engineer) and Florence (Nelson) Olson. EDUCATION: Northwestern, 1948–52, B.S. in Speech; studied for the theatre with Alvina Krause and Lee Strasberg. MILITARY: U.S. Army, 1952–54 (an M.P.)

CAREER: DEBUT—Hans Brinker, *Hans Brinker and the Silver Skates*, Evanston Children's Theatre, IL, 1942. NEW YORK DEBUT—Captain Dick Dicer, *The Young and Beautiful*, Longacre, 1955. LONDON DEBUT—Tusenbach, *The Three Sisters*, Aldwych, 1964. PRINCIPAL STAGE APPEARANCES—American Shakespeare Festival, Stratford, CT, 1954–56; *The Sin of Pat Muldoon*, Cort, NY, 1957; *J.B.*, ANTA, NY, 1959; *Romulus*, Music Box, NY, 1962; *The Chinese Prime Minister*, Royale, NY, 1964; Tusenbach, *The Three Sisters*, Morosco, NY, 1965; *The Glass Menagerie*, Huntington Hartford, Los Angeles, CA, 1966; *Slapstick Tragedy*, Longacre, NY, 1966; *Of Love Remembered*, ANTA, NY, 1967; *The Crucible*, Ahmanson, Los Angeles, CA, 1973; *A Safe Place*, Berkshire Theatre Festival, MA, 1981; *Twelve Dreams*, Public Theatre, 1981; *Winterplay*, Second Stage, NY, 1983.

PRINCIPAL FILMS—*The Strange One*, 1957; *Rachel, Rachel*, 1968; *The Andromeda Strain*, 1970; *Ragtime*, 1982.

TELEVISION DEBUT—Mickey Mantle, *Kraft TV Playhouse—Life of Mickey Mantle.* TELEVISION APPEARANCES—TV films: *A Tree Grows in Brooklyn; Someone I Touched; The Spell; The New Land; The Court-Martial of George Armstrong Custer; Vince Lombardi Story; The Missiles of October; Moviola.*

ADDRESS: Agent—Bauman & Hiller, 9220 Sunset Blvd., Hollywood, CA 90069.

* * *

O'MORRISON, Kevin, playwright, actor

PERSONAL: Born in St. Louis, MO; son of Sean E. (a farmer) and Dori Elizabeth (a saleswoman; maiden name, Adams) O'Morrison; married Linda Soma (a playwright's agent) on April 30, 1966. EDUCATION: Illinois Military School, 1927–30; privately tutored for university degree; studied playwriting, acting, directing with Robert Lewis and Harold Clurman at the American Theatre Wing, NY; studied European theatre for two years in England, 1971–72. MILITARY: USAF, Corporal, 1943–46.

CAREER: DEBUT—Firk, *Shoemakers' Holiday*, Little Theatre, St. Louis, MO, 1936. NEW YORK DEBUT—Walk-on, *Julius Caesar*, Mercury, 1938. PRINCIPAL STAGE APPEARANCES—Ed, *Winged Victory*, 44th Street, NY, 1943–44; Fergus, *Deirdre of the Sorrows*, Gate, NY, 1959; Doctor, *The Rose Tattoo*, City Center, Billy Rose, NY, 1966.

MAJOR TOURS—Ed, *Winged Victory*, national tour, 1944–45; *Second Helping*, east coast tour, 1940; stage manager for *Sing, Man, Sing*, east coast tour, 1956.

FILM DEBUT—Sgt. Chuck Vincent, *Dear Ruth*, 1946. PRINCIPAL FILM APPEARANCES—Moore, *The Set Up*, 1949; Red Dawson, *The Young Lovers*, 1950; Bob Gilmore, *The Golden Gloves Story*, 1950; Bank Manager, *The Friends of Eddie Coyle*, 1973.

TELEVISION DEBUT—Charlie Wild, *Charlie Wild, Private Detective*, 1950–51. PRINCIPAL TELEVISION APPEARANCES— *US Steel Hour; Philco Playhouse; Treasury Men In Action; Rocky King; Man Against Crime;* Judge Sirica, *Watergate Coverup Trial.*

WRITINGS: PLAYS, PUBLISHED/PRODUCED—*The Long War*, 1967; *The Morgan Yard*, O'Neill Theatre Center National Playwrights Conference, 1971, Cleveland Playhouse, 1973–74, Mercury Theatre, Colchester, England, 1974, Olympia, Dublin Theatre Festival, Ireland, 1974, Missouri Repertory Company, 1976, University of Utah, 1981; *A Party for Lovers*, 1982; *Ladyhouse Blues*, O'Neill Theatre Center National Playwrights Conference, 1976, Phoenix, NY, Dallas Theatre Center, TX, 1976, Playwrights Horizons, Queens Festival Playhouse, NY, 1979, St. Clements, NY, 1979–80, American Stage Festival, NH, 1983, Norwegian National Theatre, Norway, 1981; *Dark Ages* (two one-acts) *On Line/ On Ice*, Impossible Ragtime Theatre, NY, 1979–80.

PLAYS, UNPRODUCED/UNPUBLISHED—The Mutilators; The Old Missouri Jazz. TELEPLAYS—*The House of Paper*, 1959; *And Not a Word More*, 1960; *A Sign for Autumn*, 1962.

THEATRE-RELATED CAREER: Artist in residence at more than 30 colleges and universities including University of Minnesota, Trinity University in San Antonio, TX, University of Montana, Kansas City Regional Council for Higher Education. Visiting Professor of Professional Theatre, University of Missouri at Kansas City, MO, 1976.

AWARDS: NRT National Play Award, *A Party for Lovers*, 1981.

SIDELIGHTS: MEMBERSHIPS—PEN: Freedom to Write Program; Dramatists Guild; Writers Guild of America East; Authors League; AEA; AFTRA; SAG; Lambs Club; Fellow, National Endowment for the Arts, 1979–80; O'Neill Theatre Center, Playwrights Conference selection, *Ladyhouse Blues*, 1976; Fellow, Creative Arts Public Service, 1975; O'Neill Theatre Center Playwrights Conference selection, *The Morgan Yard*, 1971.

''I began to write in an attempt to impose a moment's order upon the disorderly time and circumstance I live in. The attempts have not always succeeded in illuminating the material at hand the first time out. Sometimes not the second time out. Nor, sometimes, the third. Being stubborn, I keep at the material, which produces lots of paper, no end of copyrights, and re-establishes confusion, by making hash of play-chronology: i.e. to the question: 'What was your first play?'—the only honest answer is, 'I can't really answer that.' The reason being, my first play was also something like my third play, my fifth, my seventh, and just lately, is my 'latest'. Two drafts of those attempts at harnessing historical material have had productions: one amateur (academic), one professional. A totally obsolete text was nicely published, and except as a literary curiosity—has no dramatic relevance to the material as it now stands (although the latest version contains—in addition to new characters—all of the ones in the first version). If this is confounding, all I can say is that, to me, it is fun. As well as being my profession and my calling.''

ADDRESS: Office—Brevoort-East, 20 E. Ninth Street, New York, NY 10003. Agent—Janet Roberts, c/o William Mor-

ris Agency, 1350 Avenue of the Americas, New York, NY 10019.

* * *

O'NEAL, (Patrick) Ryan, actor

PERSONAL: Born April 20, 1941, in Los Angeles, CA; son of Charles and Patricia (Callaghan) O'Neal;married Joanna Moore, April 1963 (divorced February 1967); Leigh Taylor-Young, February 1967; children: (first marriage) Tatum Beatrice, Griffin Patrick; (second marriage) Patrick.

CAREER: PRINCIPAL TELEVISION APPEARANCES—*Tales of the Vikings*, German, 1959; *Screen Gems Pilots; Donny Dru; Our Man Higgins; Empire; Dobie Gillis; Two Faces West; Perry Mason; G.E. Theatre; The Virginian; This Is the Life; The Untouchables; My Three Sons; Bachelor Father; June Allyson Show; Peyton Place*, 1964–69; *The Driver*, 1978.

PRINCIPAL FILM APPEARANCES—*The Big Bounce*, 1969; *The Games*, 1970; *Love Story*, 1970; *The Wild Rovers*, 1971; *What's Up, Doc?* 1972; *The Thief Who Came to Dinner*, 1973; *Paper Moon*, 1973; *Barry Lyndon*, 1975; *Nickelodeon*, 1976; *A Bridge Too Far*, 1977; *Oliver's Story*, 1978; *The Main Event*, 1979; *Green Ice; So Fine*, 1981; *Partners*, 1982.

AWARDS: Donatello, 1970: *Love Story.*

ADDRESS: Agent—c/o ICM, 8899 Beverly Blvd., Los Angeles, CA 90048.*

* * *

ORBACH, Jerry, actor

PERSONAL: Born October 20, 1935, in Bronx, NY; son of Leon and Emily (Olexy) Orbach; married Marta Curro (divorced); married Elaine Cancilla; children: Anthony Nicholas, Christopher Ben. EDUCATION: Attended University of Illinois and Northwestern University; trained for the stage with Herbert Berghof, Mira Rostova and Lee Strasberg, singing with Hazel Schweppe.

CAREER: STAGE DEBUT—Typewriter man, *Room Service*, Chevy Chase Tent Theatre, Wheeling, IL, 1952. NEW YORK DEBUT—Streetsinger/Mack the Knife, *Threepenny Opera*, Theatre de Lys, 1955. PRINCIPAL STAGE APPEARANCES— *Show Case*, Evanston, IL, 1953–54; *Picnic, The Caine Mutiny Court Martial*, Grist Mill Playhouse, Andover, NJ, 1955; *The King and I, Harvey, Guys and Dolls, The Student Prince*, stock, 1955–59; El Gallo, *The Fantasticks*, Sullivan Street Playhouse, NY, 1960; Paul, *Carnival!*, Imperial, NY, 1961, Shubert, Chicago, IL, 1963; Larry Foreman, *The Cradle Will Rock*, Theatre Four, NY, 1964; Sky Masterson, *Guys and Dolls*, City Center, NY, 1965; Jigger Craigin, *Carousel*, State, NY, 1965; Charlie Davenport, *Annie Get Your Gun*, State, Broadway, NY, 1966; Malcolm, *The Natural Look*, Longacre, NY, 1967; Harold Wonder, *Scuba Duba*, New, NY, 1967; Chuck Baxter,

Promises, Promises, Imperial, NY, 1968; Paul Friedman, *6 Rms Riv Vu,* Helen Hayes, NY, 1972; *The Rose Tattoo,* Walnut Street, Philadelphia, 1973; *The Trouble with People,* Coconut Grove, Miami, FL, 1974; Billy Flynn, *Chicago,* 46th Street, NY, 1975; *42nd Street,* Winter Garden, NY, 1980–81, Majestic, NY, 1984–present.

MAJOR TOURS—Paul Friedman, *6 Rms Riv Vu,* U.S. cities, 1973; Billy Flynn, *Chicago,* U.S. cities, 1977–78; George Schneider, *Chapter Two,* U.S. cities, 1978–79.

PRINCIPAL FILM APPEARANCES—*Please Come Home,* 1964; *The Gang That Couldn't Shoot Straight,* 1971; *A Fan's Notes,* 1974; *Sentinel,* 1977. PRINCIPAL TELEVISION APPEARANCES—*Shari Lewis Show; Jack Paar; Bob Hope Presents; Love, American Style.*

AWARDS: Antoinette Perry Award, 1968: *Promises, Promises.*

ADDRESS: Agent—Contemporary-Korman, 132 Lasky Drive, Beverly Hills, CA 90212.*

* * *

ORDWAY, Sally, playwright

PERSONAL: Born in Lafayette, AL; daughter of Charles B. (a chemical engineer) and Mary (a teacher; maiden name, Tucker) Ordway. EDUCATION: Hollins College, B.A.; Hunter College, M.A. (Theatre); also studied at Yale University School of Drama. POLITICS: Democrat.

WRITINGS: PLAYS, PRODUCED—*Free! Free! Free!,* Theatre Genesis, NY, 1965, Hunter College Playwrights Project, NY, 1969; *There's a Wall Between Us, Darling,* Theatre Genesis, NY, 1965, Actors Place, St. Luke's Church, NY, 1969; *A Desolate Place Near a Deep Hole,* Cafe Cino, NY, 1965, Loeb Drama Center, Cambridge, MA, 1966, Playbox, NY, 1966, University of Wisconsin, 1967; *A Passage Through Bohemia,* O'Neill Theatre Center, Playwrights Conference, 1966, Theatre for the New City, NY, 1976; *Movie, Movie on the Wall,* O'Neill Theatre Center, Playwrights Conference, 1968, Mark Taper Forum, Los Angeles, CA, 1968, Peace Festival, Westbeth Center, NY, 1970, Company Theatre, Los Angeles, CA, 1972; *We Agree,* Westbeth Center, NY, 1970, New York Theatre Ensemble, 1971; *Allison,* Music Barn, Stockbridge, MA, 1970, Peace Festival, Westbeth Center, NY, 1970; *Crabs,* Assembly, NY, 1971, Company, Los Angeles, CA, 1972, Almost Free Theatre, London, England, 1973; *San Fernando Valley* and *Australia Play,* New York Theatre Ensemble, 1971, Company, Los Angeles, CA, 1972, Academy, Atlanta, GA, 1973, Stagelights II, NY, 1973, Joseph Jefferson, NY, 1973, Bear Republic, Santa Cruz, CA, 1975; *Family Family,* Westbeth Playwrights' Feminist Collective, NY, 1972, Joseph Jefferson, NY, 1973, Benefit for N.O.W. Town Hall, NY, 1974, Southhampton College, NY, 1975, Women in the Performing Arts Festival, Lincoln Center, NY, 1975; *Playthings, The Chinese Caper,* Theatre for the New City, NY, 1973;

Sex Warfare, Westbeth Playwrights' Feminist Collective, NY, 1974; *War Party* and *Memorial Day,* Theatre-at-St.

Clements, NY, 1974; *The Hostess,* Westbeth Playwrights' Feminist Collective, NY, 1975; *S.W.A.K. (Sealed with a Kiss),* Phoenix, NY, 1977 (staged reading), Williamstown Theatre Festival (staged reading), 1977, Playwrights Horizons, 1977, Woman's Project, American Place, 1979, Fort Lewis College, Durango, CO, 1982; *Once Upon a Woman,* Royal Court, NY, 1978; *Film Festival,* Playwrights Horizons (staged reading), 1979; *Promise Her Anything,* Columbia University Theatre, NY, 1980; *No More Chattanooga Choo Choo,* Woman's Project, American Place, 1981; *A Pretty Passion,* Women's Interart, NY, 1982; *Binoculars,* Amateur Comedy Club, NY, 1982.

PLAYS, PUBLISHED—*There's a Wall Between Us, Darling,* 1968; *Crabs,* 1971; *San Fernando Valley,* 1971; *Movie, Movie, on the Wall,* 1971; *Family, Family,* 1974. PRINCIPAL SCREENPLAY—Adaptation of novel *Wait 'Til the Sun Shines Nellie,* 1969.

AWARDS: Finalist, Great American Play Contest, Actors Theatre of Louisville, 1978; National Endowment of the Arts Grant, 1978; Creative Arts Service Grant, 1978; ABC Grant, Writing for the Camera, Yale School of Drama, 1967–68.

SIDELIGHTS: MEMBERSHIPS—Actors Studio, 1966–70; O'Neill Playwrights Conference, 1966–68; Westbeth Playwrights Feminist Collective, 1971–75; Woman's Project at the American Place Theatre, 1978–present; PEN; Dramatists Guild; League of Professional Theatre Women, NY; Women in Film.

ADDRESS: Office—334 W. 38th Street, New York, NY 10018. Agent—Charles Hunt, c/o Fifi Oscard Associates, 19 W. 44th Street, New York, NY 10036.

* * *

O'ROURKE, Robert, stage manager, producer, director

PERSONAL: Born August 20, 1947; son of Charles M. (a store manager) and Flora E. (an artist; maiden name, Ottes) O'Rourke. EDUCATION: Hunter College, B.A., 1968; Ohio State University, M.F.A., 1971; attending Graduate school at City University of New York. NON-THEATRICAL CAREER: Substitute teacher, New York public schools, 1969–71.

CAREER: PRINCIPAL STAGE WORK, Stage Managed—*We Interrupt This Program,* Ambassador, NY; *Kennedy's Children,* Golden, NY; *My Fair Lady,* St. James, NY; *Sarava,* Broadway, NY; *Gilda Radner, Live from New York,* Winter Garden, NY; *Loose Ends,* Circle in the Square; *Major Barbara,* Circle in the Square; *Past Tense,* Circle in the Square; *The Man Who Came to Dinner,* Circle in the Square; *One Night Stand,* Nederlander, NY; *Bring Back Birdie,* Martin Beck, NY; *Oh Brother,* ANTA, NY; *Oh Johnny,* Players, NY.

MAJOR TOURS—*Oh Kay,* Kennedy Center, Royal Alexandria; *Come Blow Your Horn,* New England tour; *My Fat Friend,* New England tour; *Send Me No Flowers,* New England tour; *The Seven Year Itch,* Palm Beach, FL.

PRINCIPAL STAGE WORK. Directed—*The Suicide*, Festival Theatre Foundation; *Let's Get a Divorce*, Festival Theatre Foundation; *The Happy Hunter*, Festival Theatre Foundation; *Three Sons*, Playwrights Horizons; *From Here Inside My Head*, Clark Center for the Performing Arts.

THEATRE-RELATED CAREER: Office manager/advance director, Charles Forsythe Productions, 1975 and 1977; founder/director, Festival Theatre Foundation, Inc., NY, 1977–present; acting instructor, New York Community College, 1974; treasurer, Eastside Playhouse, NY, 1973–74; assistant treasurer/house manager, New Theatre, NY; resident stage manager, Cherry County Playhouse, 1973; resident stage manager, Millbrook Playhouse, 1971; instructor, introduction to Theatre, Ohio State University, 1969–71.

SIDELIGHTS: In addition to his directing and stage managing, Mr. O'Rourke has extensive experience in the production and management of fashion shows, industrial commercial films and shows as well as benefit performances.

ADDRESS: Home—170 W. 74th Street, New York, NY 10024.

* * *

OSUNA, Jess, actor

PERSONAL: Born May 28, 1928, in Berkeley, CA; son of Jesus P. (a longshoreman) and Gaudencia (Villanueva); married Sydney Sloane (a fashion coordinator) on February 17, 1952; children: Tracy. EDUCATION: Elizabeth Holloway School of the Theatre, San Francisco, CA; studied with Herbert Berghof and Uta Hagen at the H.B. Studios in New York City. POLITICS: Registered Democrat. RELIGION: Catholic. MILITARY: U.S. Army, Corporal, 1946–48.

CAREER: DEBUT—British soldier, *The Devil's Disciple*, Curran, San Francisco, CA, 1949–50. NEW YORK DEBUT—The Robber/The Father, *Bugs and Veronica*, Pocket, 1965. PRINCIPAL STAGE APPEARANCES—*The Goodbye People*, Barrymore, NY, 1968; *The Infantry*, NY; *The Biko Inquest*, NY; *Monopoly*, NY; *Hamp*, NY; *Blood Wedding*, NY; *A Cry of Players*, Berkshire Theatre Festival, MA; *The Merchant of Venice*, Berkshire Theatre Festival, MA; *Happy Birthday, Wanda June*, Edison, NY, 1971; *Keep Off the Grass*, NY; *An Almost Perfect Person*, NY; *The American Clock*, Harold Clurman, NY, Spoleto Festival, 1980; *The Roads to Home*, Manhattan Punchline Theatre, NY, 1981.

JESS OSUNA

MAJOR TOURS—*That Championship Season*, national tour, 1974; *An Almost Perfect Person*, summer tour, 1978.

FILM DEBUT—Frank, *A New Leaf*, 1969. PRINCIPAL FILM APPEARANCES—Sonny, *The Effect of Gamma Rays on Man-in-the-Moon Marigolds*, 1971; The Major, *Three Days of the Condor*, 1975; Joe, FBI, *All the President's Men*, 1975; Mr. Ackerman, *Kramer vs. Kramer*, 1979; Dean, *Taps*, 1981.

PRINCIPAL TELEVISION APPEARANCES—Dr. Willis, *Who Will Love My Children*, 1982; The Uncle, *Old Man*; *Kojak*; *Colombo*. THEATRE-RELATED CAREER: Teacher/Counselor, Acting and Scene Study, H.B. Studios, NY, 1970–83.

AWARDS: Obie Award for Distinguished Performance, *Bugs and Veronica*, 1966.

ADDRESS: Home—463 West Street, New York, NY 10014. Agent—Henderson/Hogan Agency, 200 W. 57th Street, New York, NY 10019.

P

PACINO, Al, actor

PERSONAL: Born April 25, 1940, in New York City; son of Salvatore and Rose Pacino. EDUCATION: High School of the Performing Arts, NY; trained for the stage at the Actors Studio.

CAREER: FILM DEBUT—*Panic in Needle Park,* 1971. PRINCIPAL FILM APPEARANCES—*The Godfather,* 1972; *Scarecrow; Serpico,* 1974; *Godfather II,* 1974; *Dog Day Afternoon,* 1975; *Bobby Deerfield,* 1977; *And Justice for All,* 1979; *Crusing,* 1980; *Author! Author!,* 1982; *Scarface,* 1983.

PRINCIPAL STAGE APPEARANCES—(Off-Broadway) *Why Is a Crooked Letter; The Peace Creeps;* Charles Playhouse, Boston, MA, 1967–68; Murps, *The Indian Wants the Bronx,* Astor Place, NY, 1968; Bickham, *Does a Tiger Wear a Necktie?,* Belasco, NY, 1969; Graham, *The Local Stigmatic,* Actors Playhouse, NY, 1969; Kilroy, *Camino Real,* Vivian Beaumont, NY, 1970; Pavlo, *The Basic Training of Pavlo Hummel,* Theatre Company of Boston, MA, 1972; Richard, *Richard III,* Theatre Company of Boston, MA, 1973; Arturo, *Arturo Ui,* Charles Playhouse, Boston, MA, 1975; Richard, *Richard III,* Cort, NY, 1979; (Regional) *Hello Out There, The Connection, American Buffalo,* Circle in the Square Downtown, NY, 1981, Booth, NY, 1983–84. MAJOR TOUR—*American Buffalo,* Washington, DC, Boston, San Francisco, London.

AWARDS: National Society of Film Critics Award, Academy of Motion Picture Arts and Sciences Nomination, Best Actor, 1972: *The Godfather;* Antoinette Perry Award, Best Supporting Actor, 1969: *Does a Tiger Wear a Necktie?;* Obie, Best Actor, 1967–68: *Indian Wants the Bronx.*

ADDRESS: Agent—William Morris, 1350 Sixth Avenue, New York, NY 10019.

* * *

PAGANO, Giulia, actress

PERSONAL: First name pronounced Julia; born July 8, 1949 in New York; daughter of Bartolomeo (Bert) Diego (a photographer) and Gloria (a model; maiden name, Gulledge) Pagano. EDUCATION: Studied at the American Academy of Dramatic Arts and with Uta Hagen, at the H. B. Studios, NY. POLITICS: "Depends on who's running." RELIGION: None organized.

GIULIA PAGANO

CAREER: DEBUT—Ophelia, *Hamlet,* Theatre Intime, Princeton, NJ, 1967. NEW YORK DEBUT—Wilhelmina, *The Passion of Dracula,* Cherry Lane, 1977. PRINCIPAL STAGE APPEARANCES—Sonia, *After the Rain,* Loretto Hilton Repertory Theatre, St. Louis, MO, 1972; Singer, *The Ecstasy of Rita Joe,* Washington Theatre Club, Washington, DC, 1973; Ruth, *Moonchildren,* Charles Playhouse, Boston, MA, 1974; standby, *Kennedy's Children,* NY, 1974; Kate, *She Stoops to Conquer,* Syracuse Stage, NY, 1978; Daisy, *Animal Kingdom,* Hartman, Stamford, CT, 1978; Hedda, *Hedda Gabler,* Cincinnati Playhouse in the Park, 1979, George Street Playhouse, New Brunswick, NJ, 1980; Ellie Dunn, *Heartbreak House,* Roundabout, NY, 1980; Catherine, *The Winslow Boy,* Roundabout, 1980–81 and on tour of U.S.; Julie, *Miss Julie,* Roundabout, NY, 1981–82; Kerstin, *Playing with Fire,* Roundabout, NY, 1981–82; Third Woman of Corinth/standby for lead, *Medea*, NY, 1982; Claudia Faith, *Nuts*, Birmingham, MI, 1983; Mrs. Manning, *Day Six*, Philadelphia Festival, PA, 1983; Barbara, *Major Barbara*, Yale Repertory, New Haven, CT, 1983.

PRINCIPAL FILM APPEARANCES—*Endymion*.

PRINCIPAL TELEVISION APPEARANCES—Mrs. Chapman, *All My Children; Masada; Medea.*

AWARDS: Jehlinger Award, American Academy of Dramatic Arts, 1971.

SIDELIGHTS: MEMBERSHIPS—AEA; SAG; AFTRA.

"My motivation comes from a deep-rooted love of the ability to create and the job and fulfillment that enactment makes me feel. . . . I am not out to 'entertain,' I do what I do because it gives me pleasure. And my pleasure comes from sharing an experience with people, with the hope that they are moved in some way, that they experience something new, something that makes them feel and question and most importantly, think. I guess, in a word, I'd like to raise consciousnesses. As Nietzsche said, 'The higher its nature, the seldomer a thing succeedeth.' That doesn't stop me from trying."

FAVORITE ROLES: *Hedda Gabler*, Wilhelmina Murray in *Passion of Dracula*, Kate Winslow, *The Winslow Boy* and Claudia Draper, *Nuts*. Least favorite: Ellie Dunn in *Heartbreak House*, Julie in *Miss Julie*, and Barbara in *Major Barbara.*

ADDRESS: Home—205 W. 86th Street, New York, NY 10024. Agent—Bret Adams Ltd., 448 W. 44th Street, New York, NY 10036.

* * *

PAGE, Geraldine, actress

PERSONAL: Born November 22, 1924, in Kirksville, MO; daughter of Leon Elwin and Edna Pearl (Maize) Page; married Alexander Schneider (divorced); Rip Torn; children: two sons, one daughter. EDUCATION: Studied at the Goodman Theatre School, Chicago, IL, 1942–45; studied acting at the Herbert Berghof Studios in New York City and at the American Theatre Wing, studied voice with Alice Hermes.

CAREER: DEBUT—*Excuse My Dust*, Englewood Methodist Church, Chicago, 1940. NEW YORK DEBUT—Sophomore, *Seven Mirrors*, Blackfriars Guild, 1945. LONDON DEBUT—Lizzie Curry, *The Rainmaker*, St. Martins, 1956. PRINCIPAL STAGE APPEARANCES—Summer stock productions at Lake Zurich Summer Playhouse, 1945–48, Woodstock Winter Playhouse, 1947–49, Shadylane Summer Theatre, 1950–51; Pagan Crone, *Yerma*, Alma, *Summer and Smoke*, Circle in the Square, NY, 1951–52; Lily Barton, *Midsummer*, Vanderbilt, NY, 1953; Marcelline, *The Immoralist*, Royale, NY, 1954; Lizzie Curry, *The Rainmaker*, Cort, NY, 1954; Amy McGregor, *The Innkeepers*, Golden, NY, 1956; Abbie Putnam, *Desire under the Elms*, Natalia Islaev, *A Month in the*

Country, Marcelline, *The Immoralist* repertory at the Studebaker, Chicago IL, 1956, Mrs. Shankland,/Miss Railton-Bell, double-bill, *Separate Tables*, Music Box, NY, 1957; Alexandra del Lago, *Sweet Bird of Youth*, Martin Beck, NY, 1959; Sister Bonaventure, *The Umbrella*, Locust, Philadelphia, 1962; Nina Leeds, *Strange Interlude*, Hudson, NY, 1963; Olga, *Three Sisters*, Morosco, NY, 1964; Julie Cunningham, *PS I Love You*, Henry Miller's, NY, 1964;

Oriane Brice, *The Great Indoors*, O'Neill, NY, 1966; Baroness Lemberg, *White Lies*, Clea, *Black Comedy*, Barrymore, NY, 1967; Angela Palmer, *Angela*, Music Box, NY, 1969; *The Marriage Proposal* and *The Boor*, Playhouse in the Park, Philadelphia, 1971; Mary Todd Lincoln, *Look Away*, Playhouse, 1973; a Benefit Gala at Circle in the Square, 1974; Regina Giddens, *The Little Foxes*, Academy Festival, Lake Forest, IL, Walnut, Philadelphia, 1974; Marion, *Absurd Person Singular*, Music Box, NY, 1974; Blanche DuBois, *A Streetcar Named Desire*, Academy Festival, Lake Forest, IL, 1976; Tekla, *Creditors*, Hudson Guild, Public/Newman, NY, 1977; *Clothes for a Summer Hotel*, 1980–81; Mother Miriam Ruth, *Agnes of God*, Music Box, NY, 1982; with the Mirror Theatre company, *Paradise Lost, Rain, Inheitors, Ghosts*, 1983–84.

MAJOR TOURS—*The Rainmaker*, 1955; *Separate Tables*, 1957; *Sweet Bird of Youth*, 1959; *Marriage and Money*, 1971; *Slightly Delayed*, 1979.

FILM DEBUT—*Out of the Night*, 1947. PRINCIPAL FILM APPEARANCES—*Taxi*, 1953; *Hondo; Summer and Smoke*, 1961; *Sweet Bird of Youth*, 1962; *Toys in the Attic*, 1963; *Dear Heart*, 1964; *The Happiest Millionaire*, 1966; *You're a Big Boy Now*, 1966; *Monday's Child*, 1966; *Trilogy*, 1969; *Whatever Happened to Aunt Alice?*, 1969; *Beguiled*, 1971; *J.W. Coop*, 1972; *Pete 'n Tillie*, 1972; *Day of the Locust*, 1974; *Abbess of Crewe*, 1976; *Nasty Habits*, 1977; *Interiors*, 1978; *Honky Tonk Freeway*, 1980; *Harry's War*, 1980; *I'm Dancing as Fast as I Can*, 1982.

TELEVISION DEBUT—*Easter Story*, 1946. PRINCIPAL TELEVISION APPEARANCES—*A Christmas Memory*, 1967; *The Thanksgiving Visitor*, 1969.

AWARDS: British Academy of Film and Television Arts, 1979: *Interiors;* Emmy Award, Best Actress, 1967: *A Christmas Memory*, 1969: *A Thanksgiving Visitor;* Donatello, Best Foreign Actress, 1960: *Sweet Bird Youth;* Theatre World, 1952–53; Drama Critics Circle, 1952–53 season and 1960: *Sweet Bird of Youth;* Three Golden Globes; Cinema Nuova Plaque, Venice; National Board of Review of Motion Pictures, Academy Award Nomination, Best Supporting Actress, *Hondo.*

SIDELIGHTS: MEMBERSHIPS—AEA, SAG, AFTRA, Phi Beta. FAVORITE ROLES—Alma, *Summer and Smoke*, Sadie Thompson, *Rain*, Blanche, *Streetcar Named Desire*, Mama, *Papa Is All*. RECREATIONS—Studying acting.

ADDRESS: Agent—Stephen Draper, 37 W. 57th Street, New York, NY 10019.

PAKULA, Alan J., producer, writer

PERSONAL: Born April 7, 1928, in New York City. EDUCATION: Yale University.

CAREER: PRINCIPAL STAGE WORK—Producer: *Comes a Day; Laurette; There Must Be a Pony.*

PRINCIPAL FILM WORK—Producer: *Fear Strikes Out*, 1957, *To Kill a Mockingbird*, 1963, *Love with the Proper Stranger*, 1964, *Baby the Rain Must Fall*, 1965, *Inside Daisy Clover*, 1966, *Up the Down Staircase*, 1967, *The Stalking Moon*, 1969; director: *The Sterile Cuckoo*, 1969, *Klute*, 1971, *Love, Pain and the Whole Damn Thing*, 1972, *The Parallax View*, 1974, *All the President's Men*, 1976, *Comes a Horseman*, 1978; co-producer/director, *Starting Over*, 1979; director, *Rollover*, 1981; director/writer, *Sophie's Choice*, 1983.

AWARDS: Academy Award, Best Screenplay, 1982: *Sophie's Choice.*

ADDRESS: Agent—William Morris Agency, 151 El Camino Blvd., Beverly Hills, CA 90212. Business—Gus Productions, 10889 Wilshire Blvd., Los Angeles, CA 90024.*

* * *

PALMIERI, Joe, actor

PERSONAL: Born August 1, 1939, in Brooklyn, NY; son of Frank and Dorothy (Rubinate) Palmieri. EDUCATION: Mount

JOE PALMIERI

St. Mary's College, B.F.A., 1961; trained for the stage with Philip Burton. RELIGION: Roman Catholic.

CAREER: DEBUT—Baseball player, *Our Town*, Barnstormers Summer Theatre, Tamworth, NH, 1955. NEW YORK DEBUT—Gower, *Henry V*, New York Shakespeare Festival Mobile Theatre, 1965. PRINCIPAL STAGE APPEARANCES—Waiter, *The Butter and Egg Man*, Cherry Lane, NY, 1965; Rageneau, *Cyrano de Bergerac*, Vivian Beaumont, NY, 1968; Emory, *Boys in the Band*, Theatre Four, NY, 1970; Beggar/Lockit, *The Beggar's Opera*, Chelsea Theatre Center, NY, 1973; Omega, *Lysistrata*, Brooks Atkinson, NY, 1973; Baron/Grand Inquisitor, *Candide*, Broadway Theatre, NY, 1974–75; Bernard, *Umbrellas of Cherbourg*, New York Shakespeare Festival, 1978–79; *Plenty*, Mr. DePinna, *You Can't Take It with You*, Chairman, *After the Fall*, Arena Stage, Washington, DC, 1979–80; *On the Razzle*, Bart Keeley, *Geniuses*, Baron/Brand Inquisitor, *Candide*, Arena Stage, Washington, DC, 1982–83.

MAJOR TOURS—Thomas, *The Rivals*, Dr. Jardin, *The Madwoman of Chaillot*, National Repertory Theatre, U.S. cities; Mr. DePinna, *You Can't Take It with You*, chairman, *After the Fall*, Hong Kong, 1980.

ADDRESS: Agent—c/o Dorothy Scott, Marje Fields, Inc., 15 W. 46th Street, New York, NY 10036.

* * *

PAPE, Joan, actress

PERSONAL: Married Bradford S. Uhle; children: a son, Dagan. EDUCATION: Purdue University, B.A. 1965; Yale University, School of Drama, M.F.A. 1968.

CAREER: NEW YORK DEBUT—Sister Cecilia, *The Secret Affairs of Mildred Wild*, 1972. PRINCIPAL STAGE APPEARANCES—Eve, *A History of the American Film*, NY; Sister Woman, *Cat on a Hot Tin Roof*, NY; Gina, *The Wild Duck*, Daisey, *He and She*, Brooklyn Academy of Music Repertory; Ruby, *Getting Out*, NY; *Funeral Games*, South Street, NY; *Museum*, Public Theatre; May, *Once in a Lifetime*, Arena Stage, Washington, DC; April, *Hot L Baltimore*, Cincinnati Playhouse in the Park; *Cat on a Hot Tin Roof, Macbeth, Measure for Measure*, American Shakespeare Festival, Stratford, CT; Magistrate, *Equus*, Williamstown Theatre Festival, MA; Rossignnol, *Marat/Sade*, Williamstown Theatre Festival; Maria, *Twelfth Night*, Yale Repertory, New Haven, CT; Mary, *Saved*, Yale Repertory; Natasha, *The Three Sisters*, Yale Repertory; *Prometheus Bound*, Yale Repertory.

PRINCIPAL TELEVISION APPEARANCES—Molly Backus, *The Doctors;* Beth McGrew, *Texas;* Mrs. Cox, *The Man That Corrupted Hadleyburg; Story Theatre.*

ADDRESS: Agent—Fifi Oscard Associates, 19 W. 44th Street, New York, NY 10036.

PAPP, Joseph (ne Papirofsky), founder, producer, director of New York Shakespeare Festival

PERSONAL: Born June 22, 1921, in Brooklyn NY; son of Samuel and Yetta (Miritch) Papirofsky; married Peggy Marie Bennion (divorced); married Gail Bovard Merrifield, January 18, 1976; children: Susan, Barbara, Michael, Miranda, Anthony. EDUCATION: Attended Eastern District High School (Brooklyn); trained for the stage at the Actors Laboratory, Hollywood. MILITARY: U.S. Navy Reserve, 1942–46.

CAREER: FIRST STAGE WORK—*Telegram from Heaven,* Actors Laboratory, Hollywood, CA, 1948. PRINCIPAL STAGE WORK—Lake Arrowhead, NY, 1951; producer/director, One-Act Play Company; producer, *Bedtime Story, Hall of Healing, Time to Go,* Yugoslav Hall, NY, 1952; director, *Deep Are the Roots,* Equity Library, NY, 1952; founder, New York Shakespeare Workshop, 1953; produced and directed, New York Shakespeare Festival, Delacorte, Central Park, NY: *Cymbeline,* 1955, *The Changeling,* 1956, *Twelfth Night,* 1958, *Antony and Cleopatra,* 1959, *King Henry V,* 1960, *Romeo and Juliet,* 1961, *Much Ado About Nothing,* 1961, *Julius Caesar,* 1962, *The Merchant of Venice,* 1962, *King Lear,* 1962, *Antony and Cleopatra,* 1963, *Twelfth Night,* 1963; *Hamlet,* 1964; *Troilus and Cressida,* 1965, *Henry V,* 1965, *The Taming of the Shrew,* 1965, *All's Well That Ends Well,* 1966, *King John,* 1967, *Hamlet,* 1968, *Romeo and Juliet,* 1968, *Twelfth Night,* 1969.

PRODUCED: Plays—*An Evening with Shakespeare and Marlowe,* 1954; *Shakespeare's Women, Much Ado About Nothing, As You Like It, Romeo and Juliet, Two Gentlemen of Verona,* 1955; *Much Ado About Nothing, Titus Andronicus, Julius Caesar, The Taming of the Shrew,* 1956; *Romeo and Juliet, Two Gentlemen of Verona, Macbeth, King Richard III,* 1957; *As You Like It, Othello,* 1958; *Julius Caesar,* 1959; *Measure for Measure, The Taming of the Shrew,* 1960; *A Midsummer Night's Dream, King Richard II, The Tempest, Macbeth,* 1962; *As You Like It, The Winter's Tale,* 1963; *Othello, Electra, A Midsummer Night's Dream,* 1964; *Love's Labour's Lost, Coriolanus, Romeo and Juliet,* 1965; *Measure for Measure, Macbeth,* 1966; *The Comedy of Errors, Titus Andronicus, Volpone,* 1967; *Henry IV, Part I and Part II, Richard III,* 1970; *Timon of Athens, Two Gentleman of Verona* (also on Broadway), *Cymbeline,* 1971; *Hamlet, TiJean and His Brothers, Much Ado About Nothing,* 1972; *As You Like It* (also directed), *King Lear, Two Gentlemen of Verona,* 1973; *Pericles, The Merry Wives of Windsor, What the Wine-Sellers Buy,* 1974; *Hamlet, The Comedy of Errors,* 1975; *Henry V, Measure for Measure,* 1976; *Threepenny Opera, Agamemnon, An Unfinished Woman,* 1977; *All's Well That Ends Well, The Taming of the Shrew,* 1978; *Julius Caesar, Coriolanus,* 1979; *The Pirates of Penzance,* 1980; *Don Juan,* 1982; *Don Pasquale,* 1983.

At the Public Theater, NY: *Hair, Hamlet,* 1967; *Ergo,* (also directed) *The Memorandum,* (also directed) *Hui, Hui, The Expressway, Romania . . . That's the Old Country, Untitled,* 1968; *Cities in Bezique, Invitation to a Beheading, No Place to Be Somebody, Sambo, Stomp, The Wonderful Years, Kumaliza, Play on the Times,* 1969; *Mod Donna, The Happiness Cage, Trelawny of the "Wells," Jack MacGowran in the Works of Samuel Beckett, X Has No Value, Willie, Fuga, Coocooshay,* 1970; *Subject to Fits, Slag, Here Are Ladies, Blood, Candide, Underground, Life and Times of J. Walter Smintheus/Jazznite, The Basic Training of Pavlo*

Hummel, Dance wi' Me or The Fatal Twitch, Nigger Nightmare, Sticks and Bones, The Black Terror, The Wedding of Iphigenia, Iphigenia in Concert, 1971; *Black Visions, That Championship Season, Older People, The Hunter, The Corner, Wedding Band, The Children, The Cherry Orchard,* 1972; *Siamese Connections, The Orphan, Lotta,* 1973; *More Than You Deserve, Barbary Shore, Short Eyes, The Emperor of Late Night Radio, Les Femmes Noires, The Killdeer, The Measures Taken, Where Do We Go From Here?, Sweet Talk, The Last Days of British Honduras, In the Boom Boom Room, Kid Champion,* (also directed) *Fishing, Time Trial, Ghosts, A Chorus Line, Jesse and the Bandit Queen, So Nice, They Named It Twice,* 1975;

Jinx Bridge, Rich and Famous, Apple Pie, Woyzeck, For Colored Girls . . . , Rebel Women, 1976; *Marco Polo Sings a Solo, Ashes, Museum, Hagar's Children, On the Lock-In, The Stronger/Creditors, Miss Margarida's Way, Landscape of the Body, The Misanthrope, Tales of the Hasidim, The Mandrake, Where the Mississippi Meets the Amazon, The Dybbuk, A Photograph, The Water Engine,* 1977; *A Prayer for My Daughter, Curse of the Starving Class, Runaways, Sganarelle, I'm Getting My Act Together . . . , Spring Awakening, Fathers and Sons, The Master and Margarita, Drinks Before Dinner,* 1978; *Julius Caesar, The Umbrellas of Cherbourg, New Jerusalem, Taken in Marriage, Coriolanus, Sancocho, Dispatches, The Woods, Happy Days, Leave It to Beaver Is Dead, Nasty Rumours/Final Remarks, Remembrance, Spell No. 7, The Art of Dining, The Sorrows of Stephen, Salt Lake City Skyline, Marie and Bruce,*

JOSEPH PAPP

413

Tongues, 1979; *Alice in Concert, Texts, Penguin Touquet*, 1980; *The Dance and the Railroad, Family Devotions, Twelve Dreams, Lullabye and Goodnight, Specimen Days*, 1981; *The Death of Von Richtohfen as Witnessed from Earth, Plenty, Top Girls, Egyptology, Buried Inside Extra*, 1982; *Orgasmo Adulto, Escapes from the Zoo, Sound and Beauty, A Private View, Lenny and the Heartbreakers, Cinders, Fen, The Human Comedy, The Nest of the Woodgrouse, Found a Peanut*, 1983–84.

New York Shakespeare Festival at Lincoln Center: *In the Boom Boom Room* (also directed), *Troilus and Cressida, The Au Pair Man*, 1973; *The Tempest, What the Wine-Sellers Buy, The Dance of Death, Macbeth, Short Eyes, Richard III, Mert and Phil* (also directed), 1974; *Black Picture Show, A Midsummer Night's Dream, A Doll's House, The Taking of Miss Janie, Little Black Sheep, Trelawny of the "Wells," Hamlet*, 1975; *The Shortchanged Review, Mrs. Warren's Profession, Streamers, Threepenny Opera*, 1976; *The Cherry Orchard, Agamemnon*, 1977. Broadway: *Two Gentlemen of Verona*, 1971; *Sticks and Bones*, 1972; *A Chorus Line*, 1975; *The Leaf People*, 1975; *For Colored Girls Who Have Considered Suicide/When the Rainbow Is Enuf*, 1976; *Miss Margarida's Way*, 1977; *The Water Engine, Mr. Happiness*, 1978; *Paul Robeson*, 1978; *Runaways*, 1978; *The Pirates of Penzance*, 1981; *Plenty*, 1982; *The Human Comedy*, 1984.

Television and Film—*The Merchant of Venice*, 1962; *Antony and Cleopatra*, 1963; *Hamlet*, 1964; *Much Ado About Nothing*, 1973; *Sticks and Bones*, 1973; *Wedding Band*, 1974; *Kiss Me, Petruchio*, 1978; *The Haggadah*, 1981; *Alice at the Palace*, 1982; *The Pirates of Penzance*, 1982; *The Dance and the Railroad*, 1982; *Swan Lake, Minnesota*, 1982; *A Midsummer Night's Dream*, 1982; *Rehearsing Hamlet*, 1983.

RELATED CAREERS: Producer, Rebekah Harkness Foundation Dance Festival, 1962–65; producer, Robert Joffrey Ballet, 1965; producer, Newport Folk Festival, 1965; adjunct professor of play production, Yale University Drama School, 1966.

AWARDS: Antoinette Perry Awards, 1981, 1976, 1973, 1972, 1958, 1957; Antoinette Perry Award, Special, Professional Excellence, Distinguished Achievement in Theater, 1979, 1973; Antoinette Perry Award, Special, Longest Running Show in Broadway History, 1984: *A Chorus Line;* New York Drama Critics Circle Award, 1983, 1981, 1975, 1974, 1972, Obie Award, 1979, 1977, 1976, 1975, 1956, 1955; Pulitzer Prize, 1976, 1973, 1970; Outer Critics Circle Citations, 1972, 1971, 1968; 1958, 1957; The Virginia Museum Theater Award, 1984; Richard L. Coe Award, 1983; American Academy and Institute of Arts and Letters Gold Medal Award, Distinguished Service to the Arts, 1981; Common Wealth Award of Distinguished Service, 1979; Myrtle Wreath Award, 1979; Distinguished Achievement Award, 1979; Actors' Fund Medal, 1977; New York State Award, 1972; Albert S. Bard Award, 1968; Award of Merit Lotos Club, 1973, 1968; Shakespeare Club Award (New York), 1958. Honorary Doctor of Fine Arts—Northwestern University, 1972; City University of New York, 1974; Villanova University, 1976; Kalamazoo College, 1977; New York University, 1978; Princeton University, 1979.

SIDELIGHTS: MEMBERSHIPS—ANTA (president, 1969),

Directors Guild of America, International Theater Institute, AEA, Sigma Alpha Delta.

ADDRESS: Office—c/o New York Shakespeare Festival, 425 Lafayette Street, New York, NY 10003.

* * *

PARKS, Hildy de Forrest, actress, producer, writer

PERSONAL: Born March 12, 1926 in Washington, DC; daughter of Steve McNeil (a high school principal) and Cleo Lenore (a concert singer; maiden name, Scanland) Parks; married Sidney Morse (a talent representative) in March, 1946 (divorced 1949); married Jackie Cooper (an actor; divorced 1951); married Alexander Cohen (a producer) on February 24, 1956; children: Gerry and Christopher Cohen. EDUCATION: University of Virginia, Mary Washington College, B.A., 1945.

CAREER: DEBUT—Curley's Wife, *Of Mice and Men*, Dramatic Workshop, New School for Social Research, NY, 1945. PRINCIPAL STAGE APPEARANCES—Shari, *Bathsheba*, Barrymore, 1947; Girl, *Summer and Smoke*, Music Box, NY, 1948; Joadie, *Magnolia Alley*, Mansfield, NY, 1949; Lt. Ann Girard, *Mister Roberts*, Coliseum Theatre, London, England, 1950; Alice, *To Dorothy, a Son*, Golden, NY, 1951; Gwendolyn Holly, *Be Your Age*, 48th Street Theatre, NY, 1953; Alice Pepper, *The Tunnel of Love*, Royale, NY, 1957; *The Time of Your Life*, Brussels World's Fair, Belgium, 1958.

PRINCIPAL FILM APPEARANCES—Wife, *The Night Holds Terror*, 1955; *Seven Days in May*, 1964; *Fail Safe*, 1964; *The Group*, 1966. PRINCIPAL TELEVISION APPEARANCES—*Studio One*, 1946–47; *Armstrong Circle Theatre; Philco Television Playhouse; Kraft Television Theatre; Danger; The Defenders; Suspense; The Web;* a panelist, *To Tell The Truth; Down You Go; Love of Life*, five years.

PRINCIPAL STAGE WORK, PRODUCTION ASSOCIATE—*Baker Street*, Broadway, NY, 1965; *The Devils*, Broadway, 1965; *Ivanov*, Shubert, NY, 1966; *A Time for Singing*, Broadway, 1966; *Black Comedy*, Barrymore, NY, 1967; *White Lies*, Barrymore, 1967; *Little Murders*, Broadhurst, NY, 1967. ASSOCIATE PRODUCER—*The Unknown Soldier and His Wife*, Vivian Beaumont, Lincoln Center, NY, 1967; *Halfway Up the Tree*, Brooks Atkinson, NY, 1967; *Dear World*, Mark Hellinger, NY, 1969. PRODUCTION ASSOCIATE—*Home*, Morosco, NY, 1970; *Prettybelle*, Shubert, Boston, 1971; *Fun City*, Morosco, NY, 1972; *6 Rms Riv Vu*, Helen Hayes, NY, 1972. PRODUCER—*The Unknown Soldier and His Wife*, London, England, 1973. PRODUCTION ASSOCIATE—*Ulysses in Nighttown*, Winter Garden, NY, 1974; *Who's Who in Hell*, Lunt-Fontanne, NY, 1974; *We Interrupt This Program*, Ambassador, NY, 1975.

WRITINGS: Antoinette Perry Award Shows from their inception, producer/writer 1977–present; *CBS: On the Air; William Shakespeare* for kids; *Parade of Stars; Night of 100 Stars; The 30th Emmy Awards Show*.

AWARDS: Emmy Award, *Night of 100 Stars;* Emmy Award, *30th Annual Antoinette Perry Award Show*.

SIDELIGHTS: MEMBERSHIPS—AEA; AFTRA; SAG; Writers Guild; Dramatists Guild; Board of Govenors, League of New York Theatres; Community Board #5 Manhattan, New York City.

ADDRESS: Office—225 W. 44th Street, New York, NY 10036.

* * *

PARNELL, Peter, playwright

PERSONAL: Born August 21, 1953; son of Sol (a businessman) and Pearl (a dental hygienist; maiden name, Bogen) Parnell. EDUCATION: Dartmouth College, B.A. (Theatre and English), 1975.

WRITINGS: PLAYS, PRODUCED/PUBLISHED—*Scooter Thomas*, O'Neill Theatre Center, National Playwrights Conference, 1977; *Sorrows of Stephen*, Shakespeare Festival, 1979–80; *The Rise and Rise of Daniel Rocket*, Playwrights Horizons, NY, 1982.

THEATRE-RELATED CAREER: Playwright in residence, Denver Center Theatre Company, Denver, CO, 1983–84.

AWARDS: Nicholas Gagarin Fellowship, Playwrights Horizons, 1983; National Endowment for the Arts Grant (Playwriting), 1983–84.

SIDELIGHTS: MEMBERSHIPS—Dramatists Guild; Writers Guild of America, East; Artistic Board of Directors, Playwrights Horizons, NY.

ADDRESS: Home—79 Irving Place, New York, NY 10003. Agent—Luis SanJurjo, International Creative Management, 40 W. 57th Street, New York, NY 10019.

* * *

PATTERSON, Raymond, actor

PERSONAL: Born December 1, 1955; son of Floyd Tyler (a technician) and Evelyn Marie (a computer technician; maiden name, Lemons) Patterson. EDUCATION: University of Maryland, B.A.

CAREER: DEBUT—Jesus, *Jesus Christ Superstar*, University of Maryland, 1977. NEW YORK DEBUT—Soloist, *Hair*, Biltmore, 1977, 100+ performances. PRINCIPAL STAGE APPEARANCES—Ariel, *The Tempest*, La Mama, NY, Annenberg Center, Philadelphia, 1978; Old Witch, *Faust*, La Mama, 1978; *Arturo Ui*, Annenberg Center, Philadelphia, 1979; principal, *Black Theatre Festival at Lincoln Center*, Mitzi Newhouse, NY, 1979; principal, *Broadway Soul at Lincoln Center*, NY, 1979; singer/dancer, *Comin' Uptown*, Winter Garden, NY, 1980–81; General Trujillo, *Battle of the Giants*, Studio 19, NY, 1980; *GI Hero*, American Heroes, Studio 19, NY, 1981; Jesse, *Child of the Sun*, Henry Street Settlement, NY, 1981; Chubby Checker/Jackie Wilson, *Rock 'n' Roll, the First 5,000 Years*, St. James, NY, 1982; principal, *Camptown*, Ensemble Studio, NY, 1983; *Mrs.*

RAYMOND PATTERSON

Farmer's Daughter, Pepsico Summer Festival, Purchase, NY, 1983; principal, *Dancin' in the Street*, Ford's Theater, Washington, DC, 1983. MAJOR TOURS—The Architect, *The Architect and the Emperor of Assyria*, Caracas, Venezuela, 1979, Taormina, Sicily, 1980.

FILM DEBUT—Ron, *The First Time*, 1983. TELEVISION DEBUT—''Bernstein's *Mass*'' (special). PRINCIPAL TELEVISION APPEARANCES—*Jerry Lewis Telethon*, 1977; *Entertainment Tonight*, 1982.

THEATRE-RELATED CAREER: Theater columnist, *Routes Magazine*, 1980–81.

AWARDS: Man of the Year Award, Phi Beta Kappa, 1976.

SIDELIGHTS: MEMBERSHIPS—Phi Eta Sigma, Delta Kappa, Zodiac Club of Zeta, AEA, AFTRA, SAG.

''My motivation for the theatrical pursuit is my quest for self-expression, exchange of ideas and views with others and a quest for knowledge.''

ADDRESS: Agent—c/o Renee Jennett, Henderson-Hogan, 200 W. 57th Street, Suite 304, New York, NY 10019.

* * *

PEASLEE, Richard, composer

PERSONAL: Born June 13, 1930; son of Amos J. and

Dorothy Q. Peaslee; married Dixie Palmer (a painter), November 10, 1962; children: Jessica, Richard, Jr. EDUCATION: Yale University, B.A. 1952; Juilliard School of Music, B.S., 1956. POLITICS: Democrat. RELIGION: Quaker. MILITARY: U.S. Army, Artillery, 1952–54.

CAREER: PRINCIPAL STAGE WORK—COMPOSER: *The Theatre of Cruelty,* Royal Shakespeare Company, London, England, 1963; *An Evening's Frost,* NY; *Marat/Sade,* Royal Shakespeare Company, 1964 and 1966; *A Midsummer Night's Dream,* Royal Shakespare Company, 1970; *Oedipus Rex,* National Theatre, London, 1965; *Us,* Royal Shakespeare Company; *The Serpent,* Open Theatre, NY; *Terminal,* Open Theatre; *Indians,* Broadway production, NY; *Songs of Love and War,* Lenox Arts Center, MA; *Boccaccio,* Broadway production, NY; *Antony and Cleopatra,* Royal Shakespeare Company, London; *Frankenstein,* Broadway production; *The Children's Crusade,* First All Children's Theatre, NY; *The Marriage of Figaro,* Guthrie, Minneapolis, MN.

FILM COMPOSITION—*Where Time Is a River,* 1965. PRINCIPAL FILM WORK—*Tell Me Lies,* 1966; *Marat/Sade,* 1965. TELEVISION DEBUT—*The 51st State.* PRINCIPAL TELEVISION WORK—*Wild, Wild World of Animals.*

SIDELIGHTS: MEMBERSHIPS—BMI; Affiliated Federation of Musicians, Local 802. RECREATIONS—Backpacking, white-water canoeing with the family.

ADDRESS: Home/Office—90 Riverside Drive, New York, NY 10024.

* * *

PECK, Gregory, actor, producer

PERSONAL: Born April 5, 1916, in La Jolla, CA; married Veronique Passani; children: four. EDUCATION: University of California; Neighborhood Playhouse School, dramatics.

CAREER: PRINCIPAL STAGE APPEARANCES—*The Doctor's Dilemma; The Male Animal; Once in a Lifetime; The Play's the Thing; You Can't Take It with You; The Morning Star; The Willow and I; Sons and Soldiers.*

PRINCIPAL FILM APPEARANCES—*Days of Glory,* 1944; *Keys of the Kingdom,* 1944; *Valley of Decisions,* 1945; *Spellbound,* 1945; *Duel in the Sun,* 1946; *The Yearling,* 1946; *The Macomber Affair,* 1947; *Gentleman's Agreement,* 1947; *The Paradine Case,* 1947; *Yellow Sky,* 1948; *The Great Sinner,* 1949; *Twelve O'Clock High,* 1949; *The Gunfighter,* 1950; *Captain Horatio Hornblower,* 1951; *Only the Valiant,* 1951; *David and Bathsheba,* 1951; *World in His Arms,* 1952; *Snows of Kilimanjaro,* 1952; *Roman Holiday,* 1953; *Night People,* 1954; *Man with a Million,* 1954; *Purple Plain,* 1955; *Moby Dick,* 1956; *Man in the Grey Flannel Suit,* 1956; *Designing Woman,* 1957; *The Big Country,* 1958; *The Bravados,* 1958; *Pork Chop Hill,* 1959; *On the Beach,* 1959; *Beloved Infidel,* 1959; *Guns of Navarone,* 1961; *Cape Fear,* 1961; *How the West Was Won,* 1962; *To Kill a Mockingbird,* 1963; *Captain Newman, M.D.,* 1964; *Behold a Pale Horse,* 1964; *Mirage,* 1965; *Arabesque,* 1966; *Mackenna's Gold,* 1969; *The Chairman,* 1969; *The Stalking Moon,* 1969; *Marooned,* 1969; *I Walk the Line,* 1970; *Shootout,* 1971;

Billy Two Hats, 1972; *The Dove,* 1974; *The Omen,* 1976; *MacArthur,* 1977; *The Boys from Brazil,* 1979; *The Sea Wolves,* 1981. In addition, co-producer, *The Big Country,* 1958; producer, *The Trial of the Catonsville Nine,* 1972.

PRINCIPAL TELEVISION APPEARANCES—Abraham Lincoln, *The Blue and the Gray,* 1982; *The Scarlet and the Black,* 1983.

AWARDS: Academy of Motion Picture Arts and Sciences Jean Hersholt Humanitarian Award, 1968; Academy Award, Best Actor, 1962: *The Kill a Mockingbird;* Presidential Medal of Freedom; voted on of the Ten Best Money-Making Stars, Motion Picture Herald-Fame Poll, 1947.

SIDELIGHTS: MEMBERSHIPS—Academy of Motion Picture Arts and Sciences (governor; president, 1967–70); National Council on the Arts, 1965–present; American Film Institute (founding chariman, board of trustees, 1967–69); National Chairman, American Cancer Society, 1966.*

* * *

PECKINPAH, (David) Sam, director, screenwriter

PERSONAL: Born February 21, 1925, in Fresno, CA; son of David Edward and Fern (Chruch) Peckinpah; married Cecilia M. Selland, July 17, 1947 (divorced March 1962); children: Sharon, Kristen, Melissa, Matthew. EDUCATION: Fresno State College, B.A., 1947; University of California, M.A., 1949. MILITARY: Served with U.S. Marine Corps, Reserves, 1943–46.

CAREER: PRINCIPAL FILM WORK—Director, *The Deadly Companions,* 1961; director, *Ride the High Country,* 1962; director/co-writer, *Major Dundee,* 1965; director, *The Glory;* writer, *Guys;* writer, *Villa Rides;* director/co-writer, *The Wild Bunch,* 1969; director, *The Ballad of Cable Hogue,* 1970; director/co-writer, *Straw Dogs,* 1971; director, *The Getaway,* 1972; director, *Junior Bonner,* 1972; director, *Pat Garrett and Billy the Kid,* 1973; director/writer, *Bring Me the Head of Alfredo Garcia,* 1974; director/writer, *The Killer Elite,* 1975; director/writer, *Cross of Iron,* 1977; director, *Convoy,* 1978; director, *The Osterman Weekend,* 1983.

PRINCIPAL TELEVISION WORK—Writer, *Gunsmoke;* writer, *20th Century Fox Hour;* writer for Dick Powell's *Zane Gray Theatre,* the pilot for *The Westerner;* writer/director/producer, *The Westerner,* 1958; writer, *Rifleman,* 1960; director, *Rifleman* (first five shows); writer/director, *Klondike.*

PRINCIPAL STAGE WORK—Writer, director, *Noon Wine,* 1967.

AWARDS: Madrid Best Film Award, 1970: *Ballad of Cable Hogue;* Belgian Best Film Award, 1962: *Ride the High Country;* Writers Guild Nomination, Best Writing Achievement in Television for Specific Segment, *Gunsmoke;* Writers Guild Nomination, Best Achievement in Television: *20th Century Fox Hour;* Producers Guild Nomination, Best Filmed Series: *The Westerner;* Screen Directors Guild Award.

SIDELIGHTS: MEMBERSHIPS—Directors Guild of America; Writers Guild of America, Academy Motion Picture Arts and Sciences.

ADDRESS: Office—88 Calle Galeana, San Angel, Mexico.*

* * *

PERRY, Roger, actor, choreographer, composer

PERSONAL: Born May 7, 1933, in Davenport, IA; married Jo Anne; children: Dana (previous marriage). EDUCATION: Grinnell College, B.A.; trained for the stage at Raiken Ben-Ari's Actor's Workshop. MILITARY: U.S. Air Force.

CAREER: TELEVISION DEBUT—*Harrigan and Son.* PRINCIPAL TELEVISION APPEARANCES—*Arrest and Trail; The FBI; Love, American Style; Ironsides; Barnaby Jones; Star Trek; The Feminist and the Fuzz; BJ and the Bear; Quincy; Chips;* Councilman Costello, *Falcon Crest;* Mr. Parker, *Facts of Life.*

WRITINGS: PLAYS, PRODUCED—*Bundy Drive,* Tremont Theater, Catalina Island, CA, Gallery Theater (aboard the Queen Mary), Long Beach, CA.

SIDELIGHTS: Writer of popular songs.

ADDRESS: Agent—Fred Amsel & Assoc., 291 S. La Cienega Blvd., Suite 307, Los Angeles, CA 90069.

* * *

PERSKY, Lester, producer

PERSONAL: Born July 6, 1927, in New York; son of Louis (a businessman) and Dora (Linden) Persky. EDUCATION: Brooklyn College, B.A. MILITARY: U.S. Coast Guard, Staff Officer.

CAREER: PRINCIPAL FILM WORK: Producer—*Fortune and Men's Eyes,* 1971; *The Last Detail,* 1974; *For Pete's Sake,* 1974; *Bite the Bullet,* 1975; *The Killer Elite,* 1975; *The Front,* 1976; *The Missouri Breaks,* 1976; *Bound for Glory,* 1977; *Equus,* 1977; *Yanks,* 1979; *Hair,* 1979; *Lone Star,* 1983; *Handcarved Coffins,* 1984. Financing/Production services—*Shampoo,* 1975; *The Man Who Would Be King,* 1976; *Taxi Driver,* 1976.

RELATED CAREER—President, Persky-Bright Organization (film financing), 1973–present; owner, Lester Persky Productions, 1980–present; member New York City Mayor's Office of Motion Pictures and Television.

SIDELIGHTS: MEMBERSHIPS—Academy of Motion Picture Arts and Sciences, 1978–present; National Finance Council, Democratic National Committee, 1977–80.

ADDRESS: Office—Lester Persky Productions, 485 Madison Avenue, New York, NY 10022.

PETERS, Bernadette (nee Lazzara), actress and singer

PERSONAL: Born February 28, 1948, in Ozone Park, Long Island, NY; daughter of Peter and Marguerite (Maltese) Lazzara. EDUCATION: Attended Quintano School for Young Professionals, NY.

CAREER: STAGE DEBUT—Tessie, *The Most Happy Fella,* City Center, NY, 1959. PRINCIPAL STAGE APPEARANCES—Cinderella, *The Penny Friend,* Stage 73, NY, 1966; understudy, *The Girl in the Freudian Slip,* Booth, NY, 1967; Bettina, *Johnny No-Trump,* Cort, NY, 1967; Alice, *Curley McDimple,* Bert Wheeler, NY, 1967; Josie Cohan, *George M!,* Palace, NY, 1968; Ruby, *Dames at Sea,* Bouwerie Lane, NY, 1968; Gelsomina, *La Strada,* Lunt-Fontanne, NY, 1969; Consuelo, *Nevertheless They Laugh,* Lambs Club, NY, 1971; Hildy, *On the Town,* Imperial, NY, 1971; Dorine, *Tartuffe,* Walnut Street, Philadelphia, PA, 1972; Mabel Normand, *Mack and Mable,* Majestic, New York, 1974; *Sunday in the Park with George,* Booth, NY, 1984.

PRINCIPAL FILM APPEARANCES—*The Longest Yard,* 1974; *Silent Movie,* 1976; *Vigilante Force,* 1976; *W.C. Fields and Me,* 1976; *The Jerk,* 1979; *Tulips,* 1980; *Pennies from Heaven,* 1981; *Heartbeeps,* 1981; *Annie,* 1982.

PRINCIPAL TELEVISION APPEARANCES—*The Carol Burnett Show,* 1970–75; *All's Fair; The Martian Chronicles,* 1980.

AWARDS: Drama Desk Award, 1968: *Dames at Sea.*

SIDELIGHTS: RECREATION—Piano, guitar, old songs, old jewellery.

ADDRESS: Agent—Agency for the Performing Arts, 888 Seventh Avenue, New York, NY 10106.*

* * *

PETERSON, Lenka (nee Betty Ann Isacson), actress

PERSONAL: Born October 16, 1925, in Omaha, NE; daughter of Sven Edward (a physician) and Lenke (Leinweber) Isacson; married Daniel Patrick O'Connor (a manager of special news programs), May 8, 1948; children: Kevin, Brian, Darren, Glynnis, Sean. EDUCATION: Attended Northwestern University and State University of Iowa; trained for the stage with Lee Strasberg, David Mann, and Etienne DeCroux. POLITICS: Liberal Democrat. RELIGION: Catholic.

CAREER: DEBUT—Corliss Archer, *Kiss and Tell,* USO Tour, Pacific Theater of War, 1945–46. NEW YORK DEBUT—Orphie, *Bathsheba,* Barrymore, 1946. PRINCIPAL STAGE APPEARANCES—(Broadway) Rose Kirk, *Nuts;* Mary Follett, *All the Way Home;* Laura, *Look Homeward Angel;* Kitty, *The Time of Your Life;* Ella, *Sundown Beach;* Maude, *The Grass Harp;* Selma, *The Young and the Fair;* Binnie, *The Girls of Summer; Harvest of Years; Years Ago;* (Off-Broadway) Mrs. Krekelberg, *El Bravo; Leaving Home,* Theatre of the Riverside Church; *Brecht on Brecht,* Theatre de Lys; (Regional) Sarah, *Quilters,* Pittsburgh Public Theatre, PA; Kate, *All My Sons,* Philadelphia Drama Guild; Mrs. Hardcastle, *She Stoops to Conquer,* Studio Arena, Buffalo, NY;

Ethel, *On Golden Pond,* Abbie, *Arsenic and Old Lace,* Henny, *Bosoms and Neglect,* Trinity Square, Providence, RI; Mrs. Stilson, *Wings,* Michigan Ensemble Theatre; Beline, *Imaginary Invalid, Detective Story, By Grand Central Station,* Loretto-Hilton Theatre, St. Louis, MO; Sally, *Threads,* Playmakers Repertory, NC; Eleanor, *A Lion in Winter,* Westchester Regional Theatre; Candida, *Candida,* Long Wharf, New Haven, CT; Mme. Pernell, *Tartuffe, Arsenic and Old Lace,* Hartman Theatre, Stamford, CT; Mrs. Light, *Dynamo.*

FILM DEBUT—*Take Care of My Little Girl,* 1950. PRINCIPAL FILM APPEARANCES—*Panic in the Streets,* 1950; *The Phoenix City Story,* 1955; Mrs. Griffin, *Black Like Me; Life Guard,* 1976.

TELEVISION DEBUT—*Hollywood Screen Test.* PRINCIPAL TELE-VISION APPEARANCES—*Someone I Touched; Visions; Ryan's Hope; Love, Sidney; One Life to Live; Another World; Kojak; Quincy; Lucas Tanner; Hallmark Hall of Fame; Playhouse 90; Kraft Theatre; Pulitzer Prize Playhouse.*

AWARDS: Dorothy McGuire Acting Award, Omaha Community Playhouse.

SIDELIGHTS: MEMBERSHIPS—AEA, SAG, AFTRA, Actors' Sudio, New Rochelle Council of the Arts.

''I am filled with gratitude that I was able to have a large and wonderful family and keep working almost continuously as an actress. It was difficult, but very, very much worth it. I recommend it to young actresses. The work enriches creative mothering, and all the stresses and the joys and the love feed the acting.''

ADDRESS: Agent—c/o Smith-Freedman, 850 Seventh Avenue, New York, NY 10019.

* * *

PETRIE, Daniel, director, actor, screenwriter

PERSONAL: Born November 26, 1920 in Glace Bay, Nova Scotia, Canada; son of William M. (a businessman) and Mary Anne (Campbell) Petrie; married Dorothea Grundy (a producer) on October 27, 1946; children: Daniel Jr., Donald, Mary, June. EDUCATION: St. Francis Xavier University, Nova Scotia, B.A., 1942; Columbia University, M.A., 1945; attended Northwestern University, 1947–48. MILI-TARY: Royal Canadian Army, Lieutenant, Artillery, 1942–43. NON-THEATRICAL CAREER: Assistant professor, Creighton University, 1948–49.

CAREER: PRINCIPAL STAGE WORK—ACTOR, DEBUT: Charlie, *Kiss Them for Me,* Belasco, NY, 1945. PRINCIPAL STAGE APPEARANCES—Understudy/and role of Nels in national tour, *I Remember Mama,* 1946–47. PRINCIPAL STAGE WORK—DIRECTOR—*The Cherry Orchard,* Sombrero Playhouse, Phoenix, AZ, Royal Poinciana Playhouse, Palm Beach, FL, 1959; *A Shadow of My Enemy,* ANTA, NY, 1957; *Who'll Save the Ploughboy,* Phoenix, NY, 1962; *Morning Sun,* Phoenix, NY, 1963; *Conversations in the Dark,* Walnut Street, Philadelphia, 1963 and 1972; *Monopoly; Volpone; A Lesson from Aloes.*

PRINCIPAL FILM WORK—Director: *The Bramble Bush,* 1960; *A Raisin in the Sun,* 1961; *The Main Attraction,* 1962; *Stolen Hours,* 1962; *The Idol,* 1965; *The Spy with a Cold Nose,* 1966; *The Neptune Factor,* 1972; *Buster and Billie,* 1973; *Lifeguard,* 1974; *The Betsey,* 1978; *Resurrection,* 1980; *Fort Apache, The Bronx,* 1981; *Six Pack,* 1982. PRINCIPAL TELE-VISION WORK, Director—*Studs Place* and *Hawkins Falls,* 1950; *The Billy Rose Show,* 1950–51; *Somerset Maugham Theatre,* 1951; *Treasury Men in Action,* 1952; *Excursion,* 1953; *Omnibus,* 1953; *Revlon Mirror Theatre,* 1953; *Justice,* 1954; *Armstrong Circle Theatre,* 1954; *Elgin Theatre Hour,* 1955; *Alcoa Goodyear Theatre,* 1956; *US Steel Hour,* 1955–58; *DuPont Show of the Month,* 1958–61; *The Defenders, The Benefactor,* 1962; *East Side/West Side,* 1963; *One Day in the Life of Ivan Denisovich, Bob Hope Chrysler Show,* 1963. TELEVISION MOVIES—*Silent Night, Lonely Night,* 1969; *Big Fish, Little Fish,* 1970; *The City* (a pilot), 1971; *A Howling in the Woods,* 1971; *A Stranger in Town,* 1972; *Moon of the Wolf,* 1972; *Hec Ramsey* (a pilot), 1973; *Mousey,* 1973; *The Gun and the Pulpit,* 1974; *Returning Home,* 1975; *Sybil,* 1976; *Eleanor and Franklin,* 1976; *Eleanor and Franklin: The White House Years,* 1977; *Harry Truman, Plain Speaking.*

THEATRE-RELATED CAREER: Faculty, American Film Institute, 1979–83; guest lecturer, University of Southern California, University of Iowa.

WRITINGS: SCREENPLAYS—*The Bay Boy,* 1983.

AWARDS: Emmy Award, Outstanding Special, 1977: *Sybil;* Emmy Award, 1977: *Eleanor and Franklin: The White House Years;* Peabody Award, 1977: *Sybil;* Emmy Award, Outstanding Drama, 1976: *Eleanor and Franklin;* Critics Circle Award, 1976: *Eleanor and Franklin;* Peabody Award, 1976: *Eleanor and Franklin;* Outstanding Film Award, London Film Festival, 1974: *Buster and Billie;* Honorary L.H.D., St. Francis Xavier University, Antigonish, Nova Scotia, 1973; Western Heritage Award, Outstanding Western Fiction Television, 1972: *Hec Ramsey;* Television Director's Guild of America Awards: *Hands of Love,* 1970, *Silent Night, Lonely Night,* 1969, *The Benefactor,* 1963; Christopher Award for Direction, *The Prince and the Pauper, The DuPont Show of the Month;* Directors Guild of America Award for Direction, *A Raisin in the Sun,* 1961; Cannes Film Festival Humanitarian Award, *A Raisin in the Sun,* 1960.

SIDELIGHTS: MEMBERSHIPS—Academy of Motion Picture Arts and Sciences; Writers Guild of America; Directors Guild of America; Academy of Television Arts and Sciences.

ADDRESS: Agent—Jack Gilardi, c/o ICM, 9255 Sunset Blvd., Los Angeles, CA 90069.

* * *

PIELMEIER, John, playwright

PERSONAL: Born February 23, 1949 in Altoona, PA; son of Len J. and Louise (Blackburn) Pielmeier; married Irene O'Brien (a writer and artist) on October 9, 1982. EDUCATION: Catholic University, Washington, DC, B.A. (Speech and

Drama), 1970; Pennsylvania State University, M.F.A. (Playwriting), 1978.

WRITINGS: PLAYS, PRODUCED—*Agnes of God*, O'Neill Theatre Center's National Playwright's Conference, Music Box, NY; *A Chosen Room*, Guthrie Two, Minneapolis, MN; *Soledad Brothers*, Pennsylvania State University; *Jass*, New Dramatists, NY; *A Ghost Story*, Actors Theatre of Louisville. PLAYS, UNPRODUCED—*Song of Myself*; *Sleight-of-Hand*. TELEPLAYS—*Choices of the Heart*, 1983.

AWARDS: Grant, National Endowment for the Arts, 1982; co-winner, Festival of New American Plays, Actors Theatre of Louisville, 1980: *Agnes of God;* Shubert Fellowship in Playwriting, 1971–72; Special Mention, Playbill Award.

SIDELIGHTS: MEMBERSHIPS—Playwrights Lab of the Actors Studio; New Dramatists Inc. Mr. Pielmeier has worked extensively in regional theatre.

ADDRESS: Agent—Jeannine Edmunds, c/o J. Michael Bloom, Ltd., 400 Madison Avenue, New York, NY 10017.

* * *

PINTAURO, Joseph T., playwright, novelist, poet

PERSONAL: Born November 22, 1930 in Ozone Park, NY;

Photograph by Rameshwar Das

JOSEPH PINTAURO

son of Aniello (a cabinet maker) and Carmela (Yovino) Pintauro. EDUCATION: Manhattan College, B.B.A.; Fordham University, M.A. (English Literature); St. Jerome's College, Ontario, B.A., (Philosophy); Niagara University, completed Theological Studies; studied at the H.B. Studios and with Warren Robertson in New York. POLITICS: Democrat. RELIGION: Roman Catholic. MILITARY: U.S. Marine Corps, Pfc. NON-THEATRICAL CAREER: Copywriter, Young and Rubicam Advertising Company, eight years.

WRITINGS: PLAYS, PRODUCED—*A, My Name Is Alice*, Circle in the Square Workshop, NY; *The Interviewer*, Cubiculo, NY; *Holy Communion*, Cubiculo, NY; *Cacciatore (Vito and Charlie, Flywheel and Anna, Uncle Zepp)*, Actors Repertory Company, NY, 1977, University of Rhode Island, 1979, Hudson Guild, NY, Edinburgh Festival, Scotland; *Snow Orchid*, Circle Repertory, NY, 1982. BOOKS—(novels): *Cold Hands*, 1980; *State of Grace*, 1983; and ten books of poetry.

THEATRE-RELATED CAREER: Professor, fiction writing, Sarah Lawrence College, 1981–82; teacher, playwriting, Southampton College, 1981; playwright in residence, Circle Repertory Company, NY, 1980.

SIDELIGHTS: MEMBERSHIPS—PEN; Dramatists Guild; Poets and Writers.

ADDRESS: Home—Box 531, Sag Harbor, NY 11963. Agent—Luis Sanjurjo, c/o ICM, 40 W. 57th Street, New York, NY 10019.

* * *

PIPPIN, Donald, composer, musical director, vocal arranger

PERSONAL: Born November 25, 1931, in Macon, GA; son of Earl C. (a retail businessman) and Irene L. (Ligon) Pippin; married Marie Santell (an actress-singer), January 27, 1973. EDUCATION: University of Alabama (two years); University of Chattanooga (two years), B.A.; Juilliard School of Music; private musical studies with George Shick. MILITARY: Infantry Medical Corps, technical services.

CAREER: NEW YORK DEBUT—Musical director, *Oliver*, Imperial, 1962–63. PRINCIPAL STAGE WORK—Musical director/vocal arranger—*110 in the Shade*, Broadhurst, NY, 1963; *Mame*, Winter Garden, NY, 1966; *Dear World*, Mark Hellinger, NY, 1969; *Applause*, Palace, NY, 1970; *Seesaw*, NY, 1973; *A Chorus Line*, Shubert, NY, 1975; *Woman of the Year*, Palace, NY, 1981; *La Cage aux Folles*, Palace, NY, 1983.

TELEVISION DEBUT—ABC Staff Musician, three years. TELEVISION APPEARANCES—Beethoven, in TV commercial for Scotch Recording Tape.

WRITINGS: PLAYS, PUBLISHED—*The Contrast* (with Steve Brown and Tony Stimac), Samuel French; *Fashion* (with Steve Brown and Tony Stimac), Samuel French. SONGS—many written with Sammy Cahn and Carolyn Leigh.

AWARDS: Antoinette Perry Award, Best Musical Direction, 1962: *Oliver;* Gold Record: *A Chorus Line;* military—two Bronze Stars.

SIDELIGHTS: MEMBERSHIPS—B.M.I.; Dramatists Guild; A.F. of M. Locals 802 and 47. RECREATION—Do-it-yourself home projects; camera studies.

ADDRESS: Home—Rt. 5, Miltown Road, Brewster, NY 10509.

* * *

PITONIAK, Anne, actress

PERSONAL: Born March 30, 1922; daughter of John and Sophie (Porubovic) Pitoniak; married on June 17, 1950 (divorced 1969); children: Christian Milord, Susan Milord Gorman. EDUCATION: Woman's College of the University of North Carolina, Greensboro, B.A.; Lee Strasberg and Ernie Martin at the Lee Strasberg Institute, 1975–76. POLITICS: Democrat.

CAREER: DEBUT—*What a Life,* U.S.O. tour of U.S., 1945. PRINCIPAL STAGE APPEARANCES—*All The Way Home,* NY; *The Duel,* NY; *The Cage,* NY; member, Actors Theatre of Louisville for five seasons playing principal roles in: *Getting Out, The Gin Game,* created role of Mother Superior, *Agnes of God, On Golden Pond, Full Hookup, The New Girl, Talking With;* Emily Stilson, *Wings,* Santa Fe Theatre Festival; *Talking With,* Manhattan Theatre Club; Thelma, *'night Mother,* American Repertory Theatre, Cambridge, MA, Golden, NY; she has appeared in principal roles at the following theatres: American Stage Festival, Milford, NH; Guthrie, Minneapolis, MN; Center Stage, Baltimore MD; O'Neill National Playwrights Conference, New London, CT; Cincinnati Playhouse in the Park, OH.

PRINCIPAL FILM APPEARANCES—*The Survivors.*

AWARDS: Outer Critic's Circle Award, Best Actress, 1983: Thelma, *'night Mother;* Antoinette Perry Award Nomination, 1983: Thelma, *'night Mother;* Theatre World Award, 1983: *'night Mother.*

SIDELIGHTS: Ms. Pitoniak spent two years as a civilian actress technician in the South Pacific, the Philippines, and Japan and following her tour of duty, she worked in New York in radio and television soap operas and commercials for over twenty-five years.

ADDRESS: Agent—Bret Adams Ltd., 448 W. 44th Street, New York, NY 10036.

* * *

PLESHETTE, Suzanne, actress

PERSONAL: Born January 31, in New York, NY; daughter of Eugene (a television producer and marketing company

SUZANNE PLESHETTE

executive) and Geraldine (Rivers) Pleshette; married Thomas Joseph Gallagher III, March 16, 1968. EDUCATION: Attended Syracuse University, NY, and Finch College, New York City.

CAREER: PRINCIPAL STAGE APPEARANCES, BROADWAY PRODUCTIONS, NY: *Compulsion; Cold Wind and the Warm; The Golden Fleecing; Two for the Seesaw; The Miracle Worker; Special Occasions.*

PRINCIPAL FILM APPEARANCES—*Rome Adventure,* 1962; *The Birds,* 1963; *Youngblood Hawke,* 1964; *The Power,* 1968; *If It's Tuesday, This Must Be Belgium,* 1969; *Suppose They Gave a War and Nobody Came,* 1969; *Support Your Local Gunfighter,* 1971; *The Shaggy D.A.,* 1976; *Hot Stuff,* 1979; *Oh God! Book II,* 1980. PRINCIPAL TELEVISION APPEARANCES—*The Bob Newhart Show,* 1972–78; *Movie of the Week: Flesh and Blood,* 1979; *If Things Were Different,* 1979; *Maggie,* 1983.

ADDRESS: Agent—c/o ICM, 8899 Beverly Blvd., Los Angeles, CA 90048.

* * *

PLUMLEY, Don, actor

PERSONAL: Born February 11, 1934; son of Jacob Earl (a foreman for a large tire company) and Franzisca (Merz-

DON PLUMLEY

weiler) Plumley; children: Devon. EDUCATION: Pepperdine College, B.A. (Speech and Drama), 1959; trained for the stage with Estelle Harman. MILITARY: U.S. Army, 1954–56.

CAREER: DEBUT—Jorgson, *Submerged,* Manual Arts High School, Los Angeles, CA, 1951. NEW YORK DEBUT—Pavel/General Berianko, *Doomsday,* Jan Hus, 1958, 16 performances. PRINCIPAL STAGE APPEARANCES—Village idiot, *The Cage,* Theatre of Today, NY, 1961; *A Midsummer Night's Dream,* New York Shakespeare Festival, 1961; Bardolph, *Merry Wives of Windsor,* Equity Library, NY, 1962; Jenkins/Trevelyan, *The Saving Grace,* Writer's Stage, NY, 1963; Harry Baker, *Come Blow Your Horn,* Sir Stephen Spettigue, *Charley's Aunt,* Sidney Black, *Light up the Sky,* Dr. Lyman, *Bus Stop,* Wayside, VA, 1963; Gooper, *Cat on a Hot Tin Roof,* Manitoba Theater Center, 1964; Le Bret, *Cyrano de Bergerac,* Equity Library, NY, 1964; Antonio, *Twelfth Night,* Hartford Stage, CT, 1966; Coulmier, *Marat/Sade, Armstrong's Last Goodnight,* Theater Company of Boston, 1966–67; Alderdice Midget, *Amen to a Mantis,* Red Barn, Long Island, NY, 1967; *The Balcony, The Threepenny Opera, The Firebugs, A View from the Bridge, The Miser,* Hartford Stage Company, CT, 1966–68; Philosopher, *Bourgeois Gentleman,* Philharmonic Hall, NY, 1969;

William Blore, *Ten Little Indians,* Gendarme, *Scuba Duba,* Krojack, *Don't Drink the Water,* Bucks County Playhouse, PA, 1969; Iggy Carney, *A Whistle in the Dark,* Mercury, NY, 1969–70; Captain Horster, *An Enemy of the People,* Lincoln Center, NY, 1970; Pisanio, *Cymbeline,* Delacorte, NY, 1971; Mickey Free, *Operation Sidewinder,* Lincoln Center, NY, 1971; Slim, *Back Bog Beast Bait,* American

Place, NY, 1971; Bartender/the Colonel, *The Kid,* American Place, 1972; Sgt. Coyne, *Poison Tree,* Playhouse in the Park, Philadelphia, Westport Country Playhouse, CT, 1973; Harold Ryan, *Happy Birthday, Wanda June,* Center Stage, Baltimore, MD, 1974; Stable Owner/Father, *Equus,* Plymouth, NY, 1975; Captain MacMorris, *Henry V,* New York Shakespeare Festival, 1976; Mr. Jefferson, *Salt Lake City Skyline,* Public Theater, NY, 1979; *On Borrowed Time,* Hartford Stage, CT, 1982; Peter Shirley, *Major Barbara, Richard II,* Yale Repertory, New Haven, CT, 1983; Bailey, *Barnum's Last Tape,* La Mama, NY, 1983. MAJOR TOURS—Mad Animal, *Marat/Sade,* U.S. cities, 1967; Iago, *Othello,* U.S. cities, colleges, and universities, 1968–69.

FILM DEBUT—Minister, *The Hospital,* 1971. PRINCIPAL FILM APPEARANCES—*The Senator,* 1979; Inspector McNeil, *Ragtime,* 1981.

TELEVISION DEBUT—*Robert Taylor's Detectives,* 1960. PRINCIPAL TELEVISION APPEARANCES—Ranger Captain, *You Are There,* 1972; Burne, *Adams Chronicles,* 1973; Billings, *Give Me Liberty,* 1975; Whispering Wally, *Runaway Barge,* 1975; Texas Kid, *Starsky and Hutch,* 1976; Captain Olley, *Captains Courageous,* 1977; Dr. Warner, *One Life to Live,* 1979; Sheriff Parker, *Seventeenth Summer,* 1980; Frank Craven, *Lou Grant,* 1981.

AWARDS: Show Business Award, 1977: *Patrick Henry Lake Liquors;* Obie Nomination, Best Supporting Actor, 1970: *Whistle in the Dark.*

ADDRESS: Agent—c/o D.H.K.P.R., 165 W. 46th Street, New York, NY 10036.

* * *

POGGI, Gregory, manager, producer

PERSONAL: Born April 12, 1946; son of Joseph (an electrician) and Marie (a school teacher; maiden name, Bersani) Poggi; married Margery Klain (a producer and management consultant), June 16, 1973. EDUCATION: Iona College, B.A. (English Literature, Theatre and Communications Arts), 1968; Indiana University, M.A. (Theatre Arts), 1969, Ph.D. (Dramatic Literature, Theory and Criticism), 1977.

CAREER: PRINCIPAL STAGE WORK—Co-Founder and General Manager, Indiana Repertory Theatre, Indianapolis, 1971–74, created a working board of directors from within the community; developed a funding base (both public and private) and implemented a city-wide annual fundraising effort; created grass-roots community participation and audience involvement for a new theatre company; established touring and educational programs. Managing Director and General Manager, Manitoba Theatre Center, Winnipeg, Canada, 1974–79; MTC is English-speaking Canada's oldest and largest resident professional theatre. Artistic Director and Managing Director, Philadelphia Drama Guild, Philadelphia, PA, 1979–present, produced twenty plays in four seasons, several world premieres and a North American premiere; The Drama Guild is Philadelphia's thirteen-year-old resident professional theatre company.

AWARDS: Study grant, Association for Cultural Exchange, to study British theatre, at Oxford University and University of London, England; received a full scholarship to college and a four-year doctoral teaching fellowship to graduate school; magna cum laude, Iona College, 1968.

THEATRE-RELATED CAREER: Guest Lecturer, Wharton School of Finance, Arts Management Program, University of Pennsylvania, 1981–present.

SIDELIGHTS: MEMBERSHIPS—Trustee, Hospital Audiences, Inc., 1973–74; Theatre Advisory Panel, Indiana Arts Commission, 1973–74; Metropolitan Arts Council, Indianapolis, IN, 1973–74; chairman, Board of Governors, Association of Canadian Theatres, 1975–78; Board of Governors, Canadian Conference of the Arts, Toronto, Canada, 1978–79.

ADDRESS: Home—2107 Locust Street, Philadelphia, PA 19103. Office—220 S. 16th Street, Philadelphia, PA 19102.

* * *

POIRET, Jean (ne Jean Gustave Poiré), actor, writer, director, singer

PERSONAL: Surname pronounced "Puaray"; born August 17, 1926 in Paris; son of Georges and Anne-Marie (Maistre) Poiré; married Françoise Dorin, October 2, 1958; children: Sylvie, Nicolas. EDUCATION: Drama School of the Rue Blanche, Paris.

CAREER: DEBUT—actor and singer, Parisian theatres, 1948–54, wrote and appeared in sketches with Michel Serrault. PRINCIPAL STAGE APPEARANCES—Monsieur Masun, *L'Ami de la famille la Coquine; Pour avoir Adrienne, le Train pour Venise; Vive de Sacré Léonard; Fleur de cactus; Operation Lagrelèche,* 1967; *Le Canard à l'orange,* 1971.

PRINCIPAL FILM APPEARANCES—*Cette Sacrée Gamine,* 1955; *Assassins et Voleurs,* 1956; *La Terreur des Dames,* 1956; *Adorables Demons,* 1956; *La Vie est Belle,* 1956; *Clara et Les Méchants,* 1957; *Le Naïf aux Quarante Enfants,* 1957; *Nina,* 1958; *Oh Que Mambo,* 1958; *Messieurs les Ronds de Cuir,* 1959; *Vous n'avey Rien à Declarer,* 1959; *La Française et l'Amour—Le Divorce,* 1960; *Candide ou l'optimisme à xxème siècle,* 1960; *La Gamberge,* 1961; *Auguste,* 1961; *Les Parisiennes—Antonia,* 1961; *Les Snobs,* 1961; *C'est Pas Moi, C'est L'Autre,* 1962; *Les Quatre Vérités—Le Corbeau et le Renard,* 1962; *Comment Réussir en Amour,* 1962; *Un Drôle de Paroissien,* 1962; *Les Vierges,* 1962; *La Foire aux Cancres,* 1963; *La Grande Frousse,* 1964; *Jaloux Comme un Tigre,* 1964; *Le Petit Monstre,* 1964; *La Tête du Client,* 1965; *Les Baratineurs,* 1965; *La Bourse et la Vie,* 1965; *Le Grande Bidule,* 1967; *Ces Messieurs de la Famille,* 1968; *La Grande Lessive,* 1969; *Trois Hommes sur un Cheval,* 1969; *Ces Messieurs de la Gachette,* 1969; *Le Mur de L'Atlantique,* 1970; *La Gueule de l'Autre,* 1979; *Le Dernier Metro,* 1980; *Que les Fros Salaires Levent le Doigt,* 1982. PRINCIPAL TELEVISION APPEARANCES—numerous programs including: *On Purge Bébé, Pour avoir Adrienne,* 1976.

WRITINGS: PLAYS, PRODUCED—*Le Vison Voyageur,* 1969; *Douce Amère,* Renaissance Theatre, 1970; also played

principal roles in *La Cage aux Folles,* Théâtre du Palais Royal, Paris, 1973, Théâtre Variétés, 1977, Théâtre Montparnasse, produced as a musical in the United States at the Colonial Theatre in Boston, 1983 and at the Palace Theatre, New York, NY, 1983; also two films, *La Cage Aux Folles #1* and *#2; Féfé de Broadway,* Théâtre de la Michodière, 1982, Théâtre Edouard VII, 1983.

ADDRESS: Agent—Martonplay, 14 Rue des Sablons, 75116 Paris, France.

* * *

POLANSKI, Roman, director, writer, actor

PERSONAL: Born August 18, 1933, in Paris, France; married Sharon Tate (deceased); EDUCATION: Art School, Cracow, Poland; State Film College, Lodz, Poland, five years.

CAREER: PRINCIPAL FILM WORK—Director/actor, *Two Men and a Wardrobe,* 1958; director, *When Angels Fall;* director, *Le Gros et le Maigre;* director, *The Mammals;* director/writer, *The Fearless Vampire Killers,* 1967; director/writer, *Rosemary's Baby,* 1968; director/writer, *Macbeth,* 1972; director/actor/writer, *What?,* 1973; director/actor/writer, *Chinatown,* 1974; director/actor/co-writer, *The Tenant,* 1976; director/writer, *Tess,* 1981; also, acted in *A Generation, The End of the Night, See You Tomorrow, The Innocent Sorcerer.*

PRINCIPAL STAGE WORK—Director/actor, *Amadeus,* Warsaw, Poland, 1981.

ADDRESS: Office—c/o Carlin Levy & Co., 265 N. Robertson Blvd., Beverly Hills, CA 90211.*

* * *

POLLACK, Sydney, director, producer, actor

PERSONAL: Born July 1, 1934, in Lafayette, IN; son of David and Rebecca (Miller) Pollack; married Claire Griswold, October 22, 1958; children: Steven, Rebecca, Rachel. EDUCATION: Neighborhood Playhouse Theatre School, NY. MILITARY: U.S. Army, 1957–59.

CAREER: PRINCIPAL STAGE APPEARANCES—Broadway: *The Dark Is Night Enough,* 1954; *A Stone for Danny Fisher,* 1955. MAJOR TOURS—*Stalag 17.* PRINCIPAL STAGE WORK—Assistant to Sanford Meisner, Neighborhood Playhouse Theatre, 1954; director, UCLA, *P.S. 193.*

PRINCIPAL TELEVISION APPEARANCES—*Playhouse 90; Kraft Television Theatre; Goodyear Playhouse; Alcoa Presents; Shotgun Slade; Ben Casey; A Cardinal Act of Mercy.* PRINCIPAL TELEVISION WORK—Director: *Naked City; Route 66; The Defenders; Ben Casey, Dr. Kildare, The Chrysler Theatre,* 1960–65; *Two Is the Number.*

PRINCIPAL FILM WORK—Director: *The Slender Thread,* 1965, *This Property Is Condemned,* 1966, *The Scalphunters,* 1968,

Castle Keep, 1968, *The Swimmer*, 1968, *They Shoot Horses, Don't They?* 1969, *Jeremiah Johnson*, 1972, *The Way We Were*, 1973, *Three Days of the Condor*, 1975, *The Yakuza*, 1975, *The Electric Horseman*, 1979; director/producer, *Absence of Malice*, 1981; director/co-producer/actor, *Tootsie*, 1982.

RELATED CAREER: Instructor, acting, Neighborhood Playhouse Theatre, 1954–60; executive director, West Coast Branch, Actors Studio.

AWARDS: Academy Award Nomination, Best Director, Best Picture, 1982: *Tootsie;* 5 Emmy Nominations: *Playhouse 90;* Emmy Award, Director: *The Game on Bob Hope—Chrysler Theatre.*

ADDRESS: Business—Mirage Enterprises, 4000 Warner Blvd., Burbank, CA 91522.*

* * *

POMPIAN, Paul, producer, writer

PERSONAL: Born November 15, 1944, in Chicago, IL; son of Lillian (a writer; maiden name, Busch) Pompian. EDUCATION: Loyola University, Chicago, IL, B.A.; Northrop University School of Law, J.D. MILITARY: U.S. Army, Captain, Distinguished Service Medal. NON-THEATRICAL CAREER: Teacher, University of Alberta, Edmonton Alberta, 1978–84; guest lecturer, Loyola, USC, UCLA.

CAREER: FIRST FILM WORK—Producer, *Crime in America*, 1969. PRINCIPAL FILM WORK—Producer/writer, *Chesty Anderson, USN*, 1975; writer, *Supermarket*. PRINCIPAL TELEVISION WORK—Producer, *Death of a Centerfold: The Dorothy Stratten Story;* producer, *Hear No Evil;* producer, *I Want to Live;* producer, *Through Naked Eyes.*

WRITINGS: SCREENPLAYS—*Chesty Anderson, USN; Crime in America; Supermarket.*

SIDELIGHTS: MEMBERSHIPS—Producers Guild, Writers Guild.

ADDRESS: Agent—Jeff Cooper, 1900 Avenue of the Stars, Los Angeles, CA 90067.

* * *

POOLE, Roy, actor

PERSONAL: Born March 31, 1924 in San Bernardino, CA; son of Roy Warren (a merchant) and Isabel (a dental nurse; maiden name, Trudeen) Poole; married Marie Blanche Côte on September 6, 1946. EDUCATION: University of Redlands, 1940–42; Stanford University, B.A., 1948. MILITARY: U.S. Army, World War II, 1943–46.

CAREER: DEBUT—Professor Scallop, *The Dark House*, San Bernardino High School, CA, 1939. NEW YORK DEBUT—Jean and 1st Ecuadorian Indian, *Now I Lay Me Down to Sleep*, Broadhurst, 1949. PRINCIPAL STAGE APPEARANCES—

Various roles, *Under Milkwood*, Kaufmann Auditorium, NY, 1953; Messenger, *Cretan Woman*, Provincetown Playhouse, NY, 1954; Mr. Sterling, *Clandestine Marriage*, Provincetown Playhouse, NY, 1954; Tremouille, *St. Joan*, NY, 1956; O'Dempsey, *Purple Dust*, Cherry Lane, NY, 1956; various roles, *I Knock at the Door*, Belasco, NY, 1957; Macbeth, *Macbeth*, Shakespeare in the Park, NYSF, 1957; Prisoner A, *Quare Fellow*, Circle in the Square, NY, 1958; David Bowman, *Flowering Cherry*, Lyceum, NY, 1959; Ray Knox, *Face of a Hero*, O'Neill, NY, 1960; Chief of Police, *The Balcony*, Circle in the Square, NY, 1960; Dobelle, *Moon in the Yellow River*, East End, NY, 1961; Starbuck, *Moby Dick*, Barrymore, NY, 1962; the Baron, *Witches Sabbath*, Madison Avenue Playhouse, NY, 1962;

Gloucester, *King Lear*, Shakespeare in the Park, NYSF, 1962; Julian/Danton, *Poor Bitos*, Cort, NY, 1964; Kent, *King Lear*, American Shakespeare Festival, Stratford, CT, 1965; Stephen Hopkins, *1776*, 46th Street, NY, 1969; Seth Petersen, *Scratch*, St. James, NY, 1971; Ben, *Death of a Salesman*, Circle in the Square, NY, 1975; Jake, *27 Wagons-ful of Cotton*, Phoenix, NY, 1976; Gus, *A Memory of Two Mondays*, Phoenix, NY, 1976; General Randolph, *Secret Service*, Phoenix, NY, 1976; C. F. Friday, *Boy Meets Girl*, Phoenix, NY, 1976; Dan McCorn, *Broadway*, Wilbur, Boston, MA, 1978; Krapp, *Krapp's Last Tape*, Pittsburgh Public, 1979; Father Mullarkey, *Once a Catholic*, Helen Hayes, NY, 1979; Harding, *The Villager*, Lion, NY, 1981; Eddie Loomis, *Quartermaine's Terms*, Playhouse 91, NY, 1983.

MAJOR TOURS—Leroy, *The Bad Seed*, national tour, 1954–55; Jamie, *Long Day's Journey Into Night*, national tour, 1957–58.

FILM DEBUT—Owen Bradley, *Experiment in Terror*, 1961. PRINCIPAL FILM APPEARANCES—McHabe, *Up the Down Staircase*, 1965; editor, *Gaily, Gaily*, 1967; union boss, *Sometimes a Great Notion*, 1970; doctor, *Mandingo*, 1975; union lawyer, *Network*, 1976; doctor, *Brubaker*, 1976; John Duncan, *The Betsy*, 1977; doctor, *Awakening of Edna*, 1980; lawyer, *A Stranger Is Watching*, 1981.

TELEVISION DEBUT—Bit player, *Kay Kyser's Kollege of Musical Knowledge*, 1948. PRINCIPAL TELEVISION APPEARANCES—Co-Star, *The Autobiography of Miss Jane Pittman, Carl Sandburg's Lincoln, The Andros Targets, The Winds of War;* guest appearances—*The Guiding Light, Search for Tomorrow, Ryan's Hope, Edge of Night, Another World, Somerset, A Time for Us, Love Is a Many Splendored Thing, One Life to Live, Where the Heart Is.*

AWARDS: Obie Award for performance, 1983: *Quartermaine's Terms.*

SIDELIGHTS: MEMBERSHIPS—The Lambs Club.

ADDRESS: Agent—Don Buchwald Associates, 10 E. 44th Street, New York, NY 10024.

* * *

POPE, Peter, director and producer

PERSONAL: Born February 10, 1955, in Houston, TX; son

of Hal (an optometrist) and Christine (a salesperson; maiden name, Reeves) Pope; married Karen MacIntyre (a dancer and choreographer), July 18, 1981. EDUCATION: University of Texas, B.A., 1979. MILITARY: U.S. Air Force, 1973–75.

CAREER: FIRST STAGE WORK—Production manager/assistant stage manager/multiple understudy, *T-Shirts,* Glines, NY, 1980. PRINCIPAL STAGE WORK—Associate producer, *Last Summer in Bluefish Cove,* Actors Playhouse, NY, 1980–81; Director, *Torch Song Trilogy,* Glines, 1981; producer, *Sports Czar,* Empire Stage Players, NY, 1981; coproducer, *My Blue Heaven,* Glines, NY, 1981; producer, *Held Over,* Greene Street Studio, NY, 1981; director, *Torch Song Trilogy,* Actors Playhouse, Helen Hayes, NY, 1982; director, *Punchy,* Westside Mainstage, NY, 1983. MAJOR TOURS—Director, *Torch Song Trilogy,* U.S. and Australian cities, 1983.

FILM DEBUT—Tod Norman Dorman, *Data Hex,* 1979.

SIDELIGHTS: MEMBERSHIPS—AEA; SSD&C.

ADDRESS: Agent—c/o Robert Lantz, The Lantz Office, 888 Seventh Avenue, New York, NY 10106.

* * *

POTTS, David, set designer

PERSONAL: Born July 29, 1949 in Cleveland, OH; son of Edward Eugene (a mechanical engineer) and JoAnne (Allanson) Potts. EDUCATION: Purdue University, 1967–71; Brandeis University, 1974–76.

CAREER: PRINCIPAL STAGE WORK—Set Designer: *Early Warnings,* Manhattan Theatre Club, NY; *Domestic Issues,* Circle Repertory, NY; *Philadelphia Story,* Alaska Repertory, Anchorage; *Goodnight Grandpa,* Entermedia, NY; *Talley's Folley,* Merrimack Regional, Lowell, MA; *Translations,* Missouri Repertory, Kansas City; *The Dresser,* Cincinnati Playhouse in the Park, OH; *Shim Sham,* Pennsylvania Stage Company; *Price of Genius,* Lamb's, NY; *Isle Is Full of Noises,* Hartford Stage Company, CT; *Threads,* Circle Repertory; *Moon for the Misbegotten,* Victory, Dayton, OH; *Hobson's Choice,* American Stage Festival, Milford, NH; *House of Blue Leaves,* Berkshire Theatre Festival, Stockbridge, MA; *In Connecticut,* Geva, Rochester, NY; *Childe Byron,* Circle Repertory; *Rocket to the Moon,* Indiana Repertory, Indianapolis; *She Loves Me,* Playwrights Horizons, NY; *Album,* Cherry Lane, NY; *Arms and the Man,* Playwrights Horizons, NY; *These Men,* Clurman, NY; *Toys in the Attic,* Indiana Repertory; *Primary English Class,* St. Nicholas, Chicago; *Petrified Forest,* Berkshire Theatre Festival, MA; *Carnival,* Berkshire Theatre Festival; *Winter Signs,* Circle Repertory, NY; *Slugger,* PAF Playhouse, Huntington, NY; *The Runner Stumbles,* Circle Repertory, NY; *A Delicate Balance,* Indiana Repertory; *Nongogo,* Manhattan Theatre Club; *Dodsworth,* Berkshire Theatre Festival; *Rib Cage,* Manhattan Theatre Club; *Statements After an Arrest Under the Immortality Act/Soweto,* Manhattan Theatre Club; *The Birthday Party,* Indiana Repertory; *The Last Street Play,* Manhattan Theatre Club; *Exiles,* Circle Repertory, NY; *My Life,* Circle Repertory, NY; *The Sea Horse,*

Westside Arts, NY; *Big Maggie,* Douglas Fairbanks, NY; *Full Hook Up,* Circle Repertory, NY; *Ah, Wilderness,* McCarter, Princeton, NJ.

PRINCIPAL TELEVISION WORK, SET DESIGN—*Kennedy's Children; Fifth of July* (PBS).

THEATRE-RELATED CAREER: Adjunct professor, State University of New York at Purchase, 1979–81; resident designer, Circle Repertory Theatre, 1981–83; design consultant, Berkshire Theatre Festival, 1979–83.

AWARDS: ACE Nominee, Art Director, 1983: *Fifth of July,* 1983; renderings exhibited at Touchstone Gallery, 1981.

SIDELIGHTS: MEMBERSHIPS—United Scenic Artists.

Mr. Potts supports the Bronx Zoo, the National Audubon Society, the Museum of Natural History, Smithsonian Institution, and the National Geographic Society.

ADDRESS: Home—188 Sixth Avenue, New York, NY 10013.

* * *

PRESSMAN, Michael, director

PERSONAL: Born July 1, 1950, in New York City; son of David (a theater and television director) and Sasha (a dancer; maiden name, Katz) Pressman; EDUCATION: California Institute of the Arts, B.F.A.

CAREER: FILM DEBUT—Director, *Great Texas Dynamite Chase,* 1976. PRINCIPAL FILM WORK—Director, *The Bad News Bears in Breaking Training,* 1977; director, *Boulevard Nights,* 1979; director, *Those Lips, Those Eyes,* 1980; director, *Some Kind of Hero,* 1982; director, *Dr. Detroit,* 1983. TELEVISION DEBUT—Director, *Like Mom, Like Me,* 1978.

ADDRESS: Agent—c/o Rick Nicita, Creative Artists Agency, 1888 Century Park East, Suite 1400, Los Angeles, CA 90067.

* * *

PRICE, Lonny, actor

PERSONAL: Born March 9, 1959, in New York, NY; son of Murray A. (an owner of a car-leasing company) and Edie L. (a merchandise manager; maiden name, Greene) Price. EDUCATION: Graduated from the Performing Arts High School; trained for the stage at the Juilliard School. RELIGION: Jewish.

CAREER: DEBUT—Young Amshel, *The Rothschilds,* Camden County Music Fair, Camden, NJ. NEW YORK DEBUT—Racks, *Class Enemy,* Players, 1979. PRINCIPAL STAGE APPEARANCES—Rudy, *The Survivor,* Morosco, NY, 1981; Charley Kringas, *Merrily We Roll Along,* Alvin, NY, 1981; Hally, *Master Harold . . . and the Boys,* Lyceum, NY, 1982.

LONNY PRICE

FILM DEBUT—Steven Levy, *Headin' for Broadway*, 1980. PRINCIPAL FILM APPEARANCES—David, *The Chosen*, 1981; Ronnie Crawford, *Muppets Take Manhattan*, 1984. TELEVISION DEBUT—*Make-Believe Marriage*, 1979.

AWARDS: Theatre World Award, 1980.

ADDRESS: Agent—c/o Lionel Larner, Ltd., 850 Seventh Avenue, New York, NY 10019.

* * *

PRICE, Michael P., producer

PERSONAL: Born August 5, 1938; son of William (hotel management) and Sylvia (Stein) Price; married Jo-Ann Nevas (an educator), February 14, 1971; children: Daniel Charles, Rebecca Sara. EDUCATION: Michigan State University, B.A., 1960; University of Minnesota, M.A., 1961; Yale University, M.F.A., 1963.

CAREER: PRINCIPAL STAGE WORK—PRODUCER: Productions first produced at the Goodspeed Opera House in East Haddam, CT, and subsequently transferred to Broadway— *Shenandoah, Very Good Eddie, Something's Afoot, Going Up, Annie, Whoopee, The Five O'Clock Girl, Little Johnny Jones;* producer, Valley Music Hall, Salt Lake City, Utah, 1965–66; executive director, Goodspeed Opera House, East Haddam, CT, 1967–present.

Photograph by Brownell

MICHAEL P. PRICE

AWARDS: Antoinette Perry Award, Special Award for the Goodspeed Opera House Theatre, 1980.

SIDELIGHTS: MEMBERSHIPS—Founder, League of Historic American Theatres; Connecticut Commission on the Arts; Panel for Opera and Musical Theatre, National Endowment for the Arts.

''Mr. Price has been executive director of the Goodspeed Opera House for sixteen years, during which time it has been the only theatre in America dedicated to the preservation of the American musical and the development of new works to add to the repertoire.''

ADDRESS: Office—c/o Goodspeed Opera House, East Haddam, CT 06423.

* * *

PRINZ, Rosemary, actress

PERSONAL: Born January 1, in New York, NY; daughter of Milton (a cellist) and Virginia (D'Elia) Prinz; married Michael Thoma, 1951 (divorced, 1957); married Joseph Patti, December 17, 1967. EDUCATION: Trained for the stage with Sanford Meisner. POLITICS: Democrat.

CAREER: DEBUT—Usher, *Dream Girl,* Cragsmoor Summer Theatre, 1947. NEW YORK DEBUT—Girl Scout, *The Grey Eyed People,* Martin Beck, 1953. PRINCIPAL STAGE APPEARANCES—(Broadway) *Tribute; Prisoner of Second Avenue; Three Men on a Horse; Tonight in Samarkand; Late Love;* (Regional) *Glass Menagerie,* Milwaukee Repertory; *Buried Child,* Milwaukee Repertory; *Long Day's Journey into Night,* Cohoes Music Hall, NY; *Importance of Being Earnest,* Sharon, CT; *In Connecticut,* Circle Repertory, NY; *My Husband's Wild Desires,* Studio Arena, Buffalo, NY; *A Little Night Music, Studio Arena,* Buffalo, NY; (Stock) *Gypsy; Twigs; Mame; Applause; I Do, I Do; 13 Rue de L'Amour; Last of the Red Hot Lovers; Lovers and Other Strangers; Cat on a Hot Tin Roof; Marriage Go Round; Annie Get Your Gun; A Girl Could Get Lucky; Lullaby; Mary, Mary; Two for the Seesaw; Kind Sir; The Unsinkable Molly Brown; Voice of the Turtle; Paint Your Wagon;* (Dinner Theatre) *40 Carats; Peterpat; Ninety Day Mistress; Mary, Mary; Kiss Me, Kate; A Girl Could Get Lucky; Irma La Douce; Two for the Seesaw; The Owl and the Pussycat.* MAJOR TOURS—*Tribute; California Suite; Prisoner of Second Avenue; Last of the Red Hot Lovers; The Apple Tree; Glad Tidings; Joan of Lorraine; Same Time, Next Year; Absurd Person Singular; Any Wednesday; A Girl Could Get Lucky.*

PRINCIPAL TELEVISION APPEARANCES—*Archie Bunker's Place; The Mickey Rooney Show; Hart to Hart; Knot's Landing; Laverne and Shirley; As the World Turns; All My Children; How to Survive a Marriage; Courtroom One.*

ADDRESS: Agent—c/o Michael Hartig Management, Ltd., 527 Madison Avenue, New York, NY 10022.

STEVE PUDENZ

* * *

PUDENZ, Steve, actor

PERSONAL: EDUCATION: University of Northern Iowa, B.A., 1969; University of Iowa, M.F.A., 1975.

CAREER: PRINCIPAL STAGE APPEARANCES—Lt. Charles, *The Adding Machine,* Winchester, *Edward II,* Banquo, *Macbeth,* Lion Theatre Company, 1983; Richard, *Dick Deterred,* William Redfield Theatre, West Bank Cafe, NY; Papa Belliarti, *Hijinks!,* Chelsea Theatre Center, NY; *Old Fashioned,* Colonnades Theatre Lab, NY; *Dona Rosita While She Waits,* Chelsea Theatre Center, NY; Oberon, *A Midsummer Night's Dream,* No Smoking Playhouse, NY; *Cat on a Hot Tin Roof,* Michigan Ensemble; *The Ponder Heart,* New Stage, Jackson, MS; Captain Donahoe, *The Failure to Zig-Zag,* Indiana Repertory; *Ah! Wilderness,* Indiana Repertory; Ragg/O'Casey/Defense, *The Resistible Rise of Arturo Ui,* Hartman Theatre Company; *Saints,* Musical Theatre Lab; Lycus, *A Funny Thing Happened on the Way to the Forum,* Coconut Grove Playhouse, FL.

PRINCIPAL TELEVISION APPEARANCES—*Search for Tomorrow; Ryan's Hope.*

SIDELIGHTS: MEMBERSHIPS—AEA; AFTRA.

ADDRESS: Home—305 W. 45th Street, No. 6H, New York, NY 10036. Agent—Jean Thomas Agency, New York, NY.

DAVID PURDHAM

PURDHAM, David, actor

PERSONAL: Surname pronounced PUR-dam; born June 3, 1951, in San Antonio, TX; son of Bert W. (stepfather; a psychologist) and Doris E. (Sanders) Hudson. EDUCATION: University of Maryland, B.A., 1972; University of Washington, M.F.A., 1976.

CAREER: DEBUT—Pompey, *Antony and Cleopatra*, Oregon Shakespeare Festival, Ashland, OR, 1976. NEW YORK DEBUT—Stanhope, *Journey's End*, Classic, 1980, 100 performances. PRINCIPAL STAGE APPEARANCES—Theo Sarapo, *Piaf*, Plymouth, NY, 1981; George/Fennec, *The Little Prince and the Aviator*, Alvin, NY, 1982; Tartuffe, *Tartuffe*, Pittsburgh Public Theatre, PA, 1982; Petruchio, *Taming of the Shrew*, Huntington, NY, 1983; Henry, *Henry V*, Nicholas, *Life and Adventures of Nicholas Nickelby*, Great Lakes Shakespeare Festival, 1983. MAJOR TOURS—Nicholas, *Nicholas Nickelby*, Chicago, 1982–83.

FILM DEBUT—Student Actor, *Playin' for Keeps*, 1983. TELEVISION DEBUT—*Nurse* (first episode). PRINCIPAL TELEVISION APPEARANCES—Father Emmerich, *Ryan's Hope;* Indian Narrator, *Light in the West.*

SIDELIGHTS: ''First American actor to play Nicholas in *The Life and Adventures of Nicholas Nickelby,* Chicago, 1982.'' RECREATION—Rock climbing, canoeing. ''In 1972 I crossed the Sahara Desert and in 1973 I rode a bicycle across the United States.''

ADDRESS: Agent—c/o Michael Thomas Agency, 22 E. 60th Street, New York, NY 10022.

Q

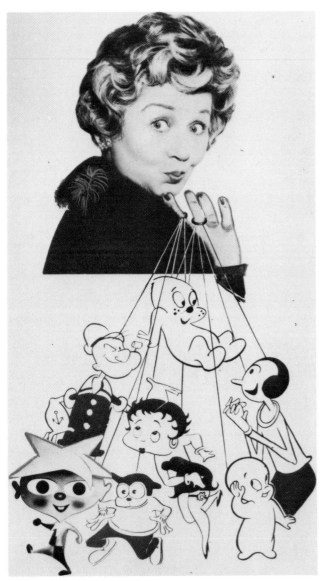

MAE QUESTEL

QUESTEL, Mae, actress

PERSONAL: Born September 13, 1908, in the Bronx, NY; daughter of Simon and Frieda (Glauberman) Questel; married Leo Balkin, December 22, 1930; Jack E. Shelby, November 19, 1970; children: (first marriage) Richard, Robert (deceased). EDUCATION: Student of drama, J.G. Geiger, NYC, (scholar) Theatre Guild, New York City, Columbia University, 1949, American Theatre Wing.

CAREER: DEBUT—Appeared in vaudeville, Palace Theatre, 1930. PRINCIPAL STAGE APPEARANCES—*Dr. Social*, 1948; *A Majority of One*, 1959–60; *Come Blow Your Horn*, 1963; *Enter Laughing*, 1963; *Bajour*, 1964; *The Warm Peninsula*, 1966; *Walk Like a Lion*, 1969; *Where Have You Been, Billy Boy*, 1969; *Barrel Full of Pennies*, 1970.

PRINCIPAL FILM APPEARANCES—*A Majority of One*, 1962; *It's Only Money*, 1962; *Funny Girl*, 1968; *Move*, 1970; sang Betty Boop theme song, "Chameleon Days" in *Zelig*, 1983; *Hot Resorts*, 1984.

PRINCIPAL TELEVISION APPEARANCES—*Somerset*, 1976–77; *All My Children*, 1983; commercials: spokeswoman for Scott Paper Co. as Aunt Bluebell, 1971–78; Playtex, 1970–72; Romilar, 1970–72; Folger's Coffee, 1970–72; Speidel, 1981–82; S.O.S., 1982; Parker Brothers Video Game, Popeye, voice of Olive Oyl, 1983.

PRINCIPAL RADIO WORK—*Betty Boops Frolics*, 1932; cartoon voices: Betty Boop, 1931–present; Olive Oyl, *Popeye*, 1933–present; *Mr. Bugs Goes to Town*, 1934; *Little Audrey*, 1946.

AWARDS: Annie Award International, Animated Film Society, 1979; Troupers Award for outstanding contribution to entertainment, 1979; named Living Legend, New York University School of Social Work, 1979; National Academy of Television Arts and Sciences Award, 1978; Mae Questel Day named by City of Indianapolis, 1968; Troupers Award, 1963.

SIDELIGHTS: MEMBERSHIPS—AEA, SAG, AFTRA, Hadassah. Miss Questel has recorded numerous songs including "Good Ship Lollipop" and served as cartoon voices on the early television animated show *Winky Dink and You*.

ADDRESS: Home—27 E. 65th Street, New York, NY 10021. Agent—c/o Fred Amsel & Associates, 215 LaCienega Blvd. Suite 200, Beverly Hills, CA 90211; Michael Thomas Agency, 22 E. 60th Street, New York, NY 10022.

*　*　*

QUINN, Anthony, actor

PERSONAL: Born April 21, 1915, in Chihuahua, Mexico; son of Frank and Manuela (Oaxaca) Quinn; married Katherine de Mille (divorced); married Yolanda Addolari. EDUCATION: Attended Polytechnic High School, Los Angeles, CA.

CAREER: FILM DEBUT—*Parole*, 1936. PRINCIPAL FILM APPEARANCES—*The Plainsman*, 1937; *Daughter of Shanghai*, 1937; *The Buccaneer*, 1937; *Dangerous to Know*, 1938; *King of Alcatraz*, 1938; *Union Pacific*, 1939; *Television Spy*, 1939; *Emergency Squad*, 1940; *Road to Singapore*, 1940; *Parole Fixer*, 1940; *City for Conquest*, 1940; *The Ghost Breakers*, 1940; *Blood and Sand*, 1941; *The Black Swan*, 1942; *Larceny, Inc.*, 1942; *Road to Morocco*, 1942; *Ox Bow Incident*, 1943; *Roger Touhy, Gangster*, 1944; *Guadalcanal Diary*, 1944; *Buffalo Bill*, 1944; *Irish Eyes Are Smiling; China Sky*, 1945; *Back to Bataan*, 1945; *Where Do We Go from Here?*; *Black Gold*, 1947; *California*, 1947; *Tycoon*, 1948; *The Brave Bulls*, 1951; *Mask of the Avenger*, 1951; *They Died with Their Boots On; The Brigand; World in His Arms*, 1952; *Viva Zapata*, 1952; *Against All Flags*, 1952; *Ride, Vaquero*, 1953; *City Beneath the Sea*, 1953; *Seminole*, 1953; *Blowing Wild*, 1953; *East of Sumatra*, 1953; *Long Wait*, 1954; *Attila the Hun*, 1954; *Magnificent Matador*, 1955; *Ulysses*, 1955; *Naked Street*, 1955; *Seven Cities of Gold*, 1955;

La Strada, 1956; *Lust for Life*, 1956; *Wild Party*, 1956; *Man from Del Rio*, 1956; *Ride Back*, 1957; *Hunchback of Notre Dame*, 1957; *The River's Edge*, 1957; *Wild Is the Wind*, 1957; *Hot Spell*, 1958; *Black Orchid*, 1959; *Last Train from Gun Hill*, 1959; *Warlock*, 1959; *Heller with a Gun; Heller in Pink Tights*, 1960; *Savage Innocents*, 1961; *Guns of Navarone*, 1961; *Barabbas*, 1962; *Lawrence of Arabia*, 1962; *Requiem for a Heavyweight*, 1962; *The Visit*, 1964; *Behold a Pale Horse*, 1964; *Zorba the Greek*, 1965; *High Wind in Jamaica*, 1965; *The Happening*, 1967; *Guns for San Sebastian*, 1968; *Secret of Santa Vittoria*, 1969; *Dream of Kings*, 1969; *Flap*, 1970; *The Last Warrior*, 1970; *Walk in the Spring Rain*, 1970; *RPM**, 1970; *Across 110th Street*, 1972; *Deaf Smith and Johnny Ears*, 1973; *The Don Is Dead*, 1973; *Los Amigos*, 1973; *Mohammed: Messenger of God*, 1977; *The Greek Tycoon*, 1978; *Caravans*, 1978; *Children of Sanchez*, 1978; *The Passage*, 1979; *Lion in the Desert*, 1981.

NEW YORK STAGE DEBUT—Stephen S. Christopher, *The Gentleman from Athens*, Mansfield, NY, 1947. PRINCIPAL STAGE APPEARANCES—Stanley Kowalski, *A Streetcar Named Desire*, Harris, Chicago, IL, 1948–49, City Center, NY, 1950; Texas, *Borned in Texas*, Fulton, NY, 1950; Alvin Connors, *Let Me Hear the Melody*, Playhouse, Wilmington, DE, 1951; Henry II, *Becket*, St. James, NY, 1960; Caesario Grimaldi, *Tchin-Tchin*, Plymouth, NY, 1962; King Del Rey, *The Red Devil Battery Sign*, Shubert, Boston, MA, 1975; Zorba, *Zorba!*, Forrest, Philadelphia, PA, Broadway Theater, NY, 1983.

PRINCIPAL TELEVISION APPEARANCES—*Jesus of Nazareth*.

WRITINGS: BOOKS—*The Original Sin*, 1972.

AWARDS: Academy Award, Best Actor, 1956: *Lust for Life;* Academy Award, Best Actor, 1952: *Viva Zapata!*

SIDELIGHTS: Mr. Quinn is also a sculptor and painter. His works were unveiled at the Center Art Galleries in Honolulu, Hawaii in 1982.

ADDRESS: Agent—c/o William Morris Agency, 1350 Avenue of the Americas, New York, NY 10019.

* * *

QUINN, Patrick, actor

PERSONAL: Born February 12, 1950 in Philadelphia, PA; son of James William II (a funeral director) and Elizabeth Jane (Remy) Quinn. EDUCATION: Temple University, B.S. 1971, M.F.A., 1973. RELIGION: Roman Catholic.

CAREER: DEBUT—Chorus, *Man of La Mancha*, Valley Forge Music Fair, Devon, PA, 1970. NEW YORK DEBUT—Perchik, *Fiddler on the Roof*, for 390 performances, Winter Garden, 1976. PRINCIPAL STAGE APPEARANCES—Bruce Granit, *On the 20th Century*, St. James, NY, 1979; Constantine, *A Day in Hollywood, A Night in the Ukraine*, Royale, NY, 1981; Star, *Forbidden Broadway*, Palsson's Supper Club, NY, 1983–84; *It's Better with a Band*, Don't Tell Mama Supper Club; *Can't Help Lovin 'Dat Man*, St. Regis Hotel, NY; *By Strouse*, Ballroom, NY; Cardinal Richelieu, *The Three Musketeers*, Hartman Theatre, Stamford, CT; Cleante, *The Miser*, Philadelphia Drama Guild; Alain, *The Amorous Flea*, Philadelphia Drama Guild; J.D. Carter, *Rotunda*, American Theatre, Washington, DC; Dr. Morris Ritz, *The Grass Harp*, Tomlinson Theatre; Billy Crocker, *Anything Goes*, Northstage; Tommy Albright, *Brigadoon*, Pocono Playhouse, PA; Wally, *I Love My Wife*, Cape Playhouse. MAJOR TOURS—Bruce Granit, *On the 20th Century*, national tour, 1979; Cornelius, *Hello Dolly*, national tour, 1982.

PATRICK QUINN

TELEVISION DEBUT—Marty Bursky, *Bosom Buddies,* 1980–82.

AWARDS: San Francisco Drama Critics Award, 1980: *On the 20th Century;* Joseph Jefferson Award Nomination, 1980: *On the 20th Century;* Los Angeles Drama Critics Award, Nomination, 1980: *On the 20th Century.*

SIDELIGHTS: MEMBERSHIPS—voting member, Antoinette Perry Awards, 1978–present; AEA, Council, 1978–present; SAG; AFTRA; Players Club.

ADDRESS: Agent—Hesseltine, Baker Ltd., 165 W. 46th Street, New York, NY 10036.

R

RABE, David, playwright

PERSONAL: Born March 10, 1940, in Dubuque, IA; son of William and Ruth (McCormick) Rabe; married Elizabeth Pan (divorced); married Jill Clayburgh. EDUCATION: Loras College, B.A.

WRITINGS: PLAYS, PRODUCED—*The Basic Training of Pavlo Hummel*, New York Shakespeare Festival, 1971; *Sticks and Bones*, 1971; *The Orphan, Boom Boom Room*, 1973; *In the Boom Boom Room, Burning*, 1974; *Streamers*, 1976; *Hurlyburly*, 1984. TELEVISION PLAYS—*Sticks and Bones*.

AWARDS: Antoinette Perry Award, Best Play, 1971: *Sticks and Bones;* Outer Circle Critics, New York Drama Critics Citation: *Sticks and Bones;* Obie, Drama Desk, Variety Critics Poll: *The Basic Training of Pavlo Hummel*.

ADDRESS: Office—c/o Public Theater, 425 Lafayette Street, New York, NY 10003.*

* * *

RADNITZ, Robert B., producer

PERSONAL: Born in Great Neck, NY. EDUCATION: University of Virginia. NON-THEATRICAL CAREER: Taught for two years at the University of Virginia.

CAREER: PRINCIPAL FILM WORK: Producer—*A Dog of Flanders*, 1960; *Misty*, 1961; *Island of the Blue Dolphins*, 1964; *And Now Miguel*, 1966; *My Side of the Mountain*, 1969; *The Little Ark*, 1972; *Sounder*, 1972; *Where the Lilies Bloom*, 1974; *Birch Interval*, 1976; *Sounder II*, 1976; *A Hero Ain't Nothin' but a Sandwich*, 1977; *Cross Creek*, 1982.

PRINCIPAL STAGE WORK—Co-producer, *The Frogs of Spring*, NY; producer, *The Young and the Beautiful*.

RELATED CAREER—Reader for Harold Clurman, worked at United Artists, story consultant for Twentieth Century Fox, producer of the first three years of film retrospectives at the Museum of Modern Art.

AWARDS: Academy Award Nomination, Best Picture, 1972: *Sounder*.

SIDELIGHTS: MEMBERSHIPS—Board of directors, vice-president (1982): Producers Guild of America.

''Mr. Radnitz was the first producer honored by a joint resolution of both houses of Congress in 1973.'' He is president of Robert B. Radnitz Productions, Ltd.

ADDRESS: Office—10182½ Culver Blvd., Culver City, CA 90630. Agent—Ben Benjamin, ICM, 8899 Beverly Blvd., Los Angeles, CA 90048.

* * *

RAMPLING, Charlotte, actress

PERSONAL: Born February 5, 1946, in Stumer, England; daughter of Godfrey Lionel (an athlete) and Anne Isabelle (a painter; maiden name, Gurteen) Rampling; married Jean Michel Jarre (a composer), October 7, 1978; children; Barnaby, Emile, David-Alexis. EDUCATION: Jeanne D'Arc Academie pour Jeune Filles, Versailles; St. Hilda's, Bushey, England; studied with William Gaskill and George Devine at the Royal Court Theatre in London.

CAREER: PRINCIPAL FILM APPEARANCES—*The Knack*, 1965; *Rotten to the Core*, 1965; *Georgy Girl*, 1966; *The Long Duel*, 1967; *Sequestro di Persona; Three*, 1969; *The Damned*, 1970; *Ski Bum*, 1971; *Corky; Asylum*, 1972; *Zardoz*, 1974; *Tis Pity She's a Whore*, 1974; *The Night Porter*, 1975; *Giordano Bruno; Farewell, My Lovely*, 1975; *Yuppi Dui, La Chair De L'orchidee; Caravan to Vaccares*, 1976; *Foxtrot; Orca*, 1977; *The Mauve Taxi; Stardust Memories*, 1980; *The Verdict*, 1982.

PRINCIPAL TELEVISION APPEARANCES—*Six More*, BBC; *The Superlative Seven*, Avenger series, *Mystery of Cader Iscom; The Fantasists; What's in It for Henry Zinotchka; Sherlock Holmes*.

ADDRESS: Agent—Jean Diamond, London Management, Regent Street, London, W1 England.

* * *

RANDALL, Tony (ne Leonard Rosenberg), actor

PERSONAL: Born February 26, 1920, in Tulsa, OK. EDUCATION: Attended Northwestern University and Columbia University; trained for the stage at the Neighborhood Playhouse. MILITARY: U.S. Army, 1942–46.

CAREER: STAGE DEBUT—Upper Ferndale Country Club, NY, 1939. PRINCIPAL STAGE APPEARANCES—The Brother, *The Circle of Chalk*, New School for Social Research, 1941; Marchbanks, *Candida*, North Shore Players, Marblehead, MA, 1941; Scarus, *Anthony and Cleopatra*, Martin Beck, NY, 1947; Adam, *To Tell the Truth*, New Stages, NY, 1948; Major Domo, *Caesar and Cleopatra*, National, NY, 1949; Arthur Turner, *Oh Men! Oh Women!*, Henry Miller's, NY, 1954; E. K. Hornbeck, *Inherit the Wind*, National, NY, 1955; Captain Henry St. James, *Oh, Captain!*, Alvin, NY, 1958; J. Francis Amer, *UTBU*, Helen Hayes, NY, 1966.

MAJOR TOURS—Miner, *The Corn Is Green*, New York City Theatres, 1942; Octavius Moulton-Barrett, *The Barretts of Wimpole Street*, U.S. cities, 1947; *Arms and the Man*, 1960; *Goodbye Again*, 1961; Felix Ungar, *The Odd Couple*, 1970–76; *The Music Man*, 1978.

TELEVISION DEBUT—*One Man's Family*, 1949. PRINCIPAL TELEVISION APPEARANCES—*TV Playhouse; Max Liebman Spectacular; Sid Caesar; Mr. Peepers*, 1952–55; *Dinah Shore; Playhouse 90;* Felix Ungar, *The Odd Couple*, 1970–75; *The Tony Randall Show*, 1976; *Love, Sidney*, 1981–83.

FILM DEBUT—*Oh Men!, Oh Women!*, 1957. PRINCIPAL FILM APPEARANCES—*Will Success Spoil Rock Hunter?*, 1957; *No Downpayment*, 1957; *The Mating Game*, 1959; *Pillow Talk*, 1959; *The Adventures of Huckleberry Finn*, 1960; *Let's Make Love*, 1960; *Boys' Night Out*, 1962; *Lover Come Back*, 1962; *Send Me No Flowers*, 1964; *Seven Faces of Dr. Lao*, 1964; *The Alphabet Murders*, 1966; *Fluffy; Bang, Bang, You're Dead*, 1966; *Hello Down There*, 1969; *Everything You Always Wanted to Know About Sex But Were Afraid to Ask*, 1972; *Scavenger Hunt*, 1979; *Foolin' Around*, 1980; *King of Comedy*, 1983.

AWARDS: Emmy Award, 1975: *The Odd Couple*.

SIDELIGHTS: MEMBERSHIPS—Association of the Metropolitan Opera Company. RECREATION—Opera.

ADDRESS: Office—145 Central Park West, New York, NY 10023.*

* * *

RAUCHER, Herman, screenwriter

PERSONAL: Born April 13, 1928; married Mary Kathryn Martinet (a dancer and choreographer), April 20, 1960; children: Jacqueline Leigh, Jennifer Brooke. EDUCATION: New York University, School of Commerce, B.S., 1949. MILITARY: U.S. Army, 1950–52.

WRITINGS: SCREENPLAYS—*Sweet November*, 1968; *Hieronymus Merkin*, 1969; *Watermelon Man*, 1970; *Summer of '42*, 1972; *Class of '44*, 1973; *Ode to Billy Joe*, 1976; *The Other Side of Midnight*, 1977; PLAYS—*Harold; Two Weeks Somewhere Else;* TV PLAYS FOR—*Studio One; Alcoa Hour; Goodyear Playhouse; Matinee Theatre;* NOVELS—*Summer of '42; Ode to Billy Joe, A Glimpse of Tiger; There Should Have Been Castles; Maynard's House;* Television mini-series (under pseudonym Paul Yurick; co-writer)— *Master of the Game, Part One.*

SIDELIGHTS: MEMBERSHIPS—Writers Guild of America, Dramatists Guild, Authors League, Academy of Motion Picture Arts and Sciences, American Film Institute.

ADDRESS: Agent—Arthur B. Green, 101 Park Avenue, New York, NY 10178.

* * *

RAY, Aldo, (ne DaRe), actor

PERSONAL: Born September 25, 1926, in PenArgyle, PA; son of Silvo M. and Marie T. (a bingo player; maiden name, De Pizzol) DaRe; married Shirley Green, August, 1951; married Jean Marie (Jeff) Donnell (an actress), September 30, 1954 (divorced 1956); married Johanna Bennett (a casting director), 1960 (divorced March, 1967); children: Paul, Eric. EDUCATION: University of California, Berkeley, 1946–50. POLITICS: Republican. MILITARY SERVICE: U.S. Navy, 1944–46.

CAREER: THEATRICAL DEBUT—Sefton, *Stalag 17*, La Jolla Playhouse, La Jolla, California, June 1983.

FILM DEBUT—Hausler, *Saturday's Hero*, 1950. PRINCIPAL FILMS—*My True Story*, 1951; Keefer, *The Marrying Kind*, 1952; Boxer, *Pat and Mike*, 1952; O'Hara, *Sadie Thompson*, 1952; *Let's Do It Again*, 1953; Lead, *We're No Angels*, 1954; *Battle Cry*, 1955; *The Naked and the Dead*, 1958; *Sylvia*, 1968; *The Green Berets*, 1968; many others. TELEVISION APPEARANCES—*Desilu Playhouse—K.O. Kitty*, 1958; *The Virginian; Bonanza;* others.

SIDELIGHTS: MEMBERSHIPS—SAG; AFTRA; American Legion.

Mr. Ray was a constable of the twelfth township, Contra Costa County, California, in 1951.

ADDRESS: Office—1765 N. Highland Avenue, Hollywood, CA 90028. Agent—Robert Hussong Agency, 721 N. La Brea, Suite 201, Los Angeles, CA 90038.

* * *

REARDON, Dennis J., playwright

PERSONAL: Born September 17, 1944, in Worcester, MA; son of William Robert (professor of theatre, University of California at Santa Barbara) and Margaret Regina (Terry) Reardon; married Georgia Wooldridge (a flight attendant) on June 9, 1971; children: daughter, Siobhan. EDUCATION: University of Kansas, Lawrence, 1966. MILITARY: U.S. Army, Specialist 5th Class, 1968–69.

WRITINGS: PLAYS, PRODUCED—*The Happiness Cage*, Public Theatre, New York Shakespeare Festival, 1970, Brandeis University, Temple University, Cricket, Minneapolis, MN, Toneelgroep Globe, the Netherlands (toured), Performing Arts Company, Silverton, South Africa; *Siamese Connections*, University of Michigan, 1971, Actors Studio, NY,

1972, Public Theatre, New York Shakespeare Festival, 1973, P.A.C.T., Los Angeles; *The Leaf People,* Booth, NY, 1975; *The Incredible Standing Man and His Friends,* Hartwick College, Oneonta, NY, 1980; *Steeple Jack,* reading, Portland Stage Company, Portland ME, 1983; *Subterranean Homesick Blues Again,* Actors Theatre of Louisville, 1983. PLAYS UNPRODUCED—Unauthorized Entries (*Security, Club Renaissance*).

PRINCIPAL FILM WORK—Screen adaptation of *Happiness Cage,* 1972.

THEATRE-RELATED CAREER: Teacher, composition and literature, Indiana University, 1966–67; playwright in residence, lecturer in playwrighting, University of Michigan, 1970–71; playwright in residence, teacher playwrighting, Hartwick College, 1980.

AWARDS: National Education Association Grant, writer in residence, Hartwick College, 1980; first prize (Major Drama), Avery Hopwood Award, 1971: *Siamese Connections;* Shubert Fellowship in Playwriting, 1970; teaching fellowship, Indiana University, 1966–67; Hopkins Award, University of Kansas, 1965–66; graduated cum laude, University of Kansas, 1966.

SIDELIGHTS: Active Member Dramatists Guild.

ADDRESS: Agent—Susan Shulman Agency, 165 West End Avenue, New York, NY 10023.

* * *

REDEKER, Quinn K., actor, screenwriter

PERSONAL: Born May 2, 1936; son of Herman Fredrick (a banker) and Jacquelyn Mae (in real estate; maiden name, Smith) Redeker; children: Brennen C., Arianne D., Glaen C., Quinn K. EDUCATION: Two years of college; studied with Sanford Meisner at Twentieth Century Fox. POLITICS: Democrat. MILITARY: U.S. Marines, U.S. Air Force.

CAREER: PRINCIPAL FILM APPEARANCES—*North to Alaska,* 1959; *Marriage-Go-Round,* 1961; *The Three Stooges Meet Hercules,* 1962; *Airport,* 1970; *Christine Jorgensen Story,* 1970; *Andromeda Strain,* 1971; *Where the Buffalo Roam; The Candidate,* 1972; *The Electric Horseman,* 1979; *Coast-to-Coast,* 1980; *Ordinary People,* 1980.

PRINCIPAL TELEVISION APPEARANCES—*Lock-up,* 1959; *Police Story; Barnaby Jones; The Rockford Files; Kojak; The Days of Our Lives.*

STAGE DEBUT—*Sunday in New York,* Civic, Los Angeles, 1963.

WRITINGS: SCREENPLAYS—*The Deer Hunter* (originator and one of four writers), 1978; *Shanghi Tango,* 1985; *Siramon,* 1985.

AWARDS: Academy Award Nomination, Best Screenplay, 1978: *The Dear Hunter.*

SIDELIGHTS: MEMBERSHIPS—Motion Picture Academy, 1979–present, Television Academy, 1982–present.

ADDRESS: Agent—Leading Artists, 1900 Avenue of the Stars, Suite 1530, Los Angeles, CA 90067.

* * *

REDFORD, Robert, actor, director

PERSONAL: Born August 18, 1937, in Santa Barbara, CA; married Lola Van Wangemen. EDUCATION: University of Colorado; Pratt Institute, NY; American Academy of Dramatic Arts, NY.

CAREER: PRINCIPAL STAGE APPEARANCES—*Tall Story,* 1959; *Sunday in New York; Barefoot in the Park.*

PRINCIPAL FILM APPEARANCES—*Warhunt,* 1962; *Situation Hopeless, But Not Serious,* 1965; *Inside Daisy Clover,* 1966; *The Chase,* 1966; *This Property Is Condemned,* 1966; *Barefoot in the Park,* 1967; *Downhill Racer,* 1967 (also produced); *Butch Cassidy and the Sundance Kid,* 1969; *Big Fauss and Little Halsey,* 1970; *Tell Them Willy Boy Is Here,* 1970; *The Crow Killer; Jeremiah Johnson,* 1972; *The Hot Rock,* 1972; *The Candidate,* 1972; *The Way We Were,* 1973; *The Sting,* 1973; *The Great Gatsby,* 1974; *The Great Waldo Pepper,* 1975; *Three Days of the Condor,* 1975; *All the President's Men,* 1976; *A Bridge Too Far,* 1977; *The Electric Horseman,* 1979; *Brubaker,* 1980; *The Natural,* 1984 (also produced). DIRECTED—*Ordinary People,* 1980.

AWARDS: Academy Award, Golden Globe, Best Director, 1981: *Ordinary People.*

ADDRESS: Office—Wildwood Enterprises, 4000 Warner Blvd., Burbank, CA 91522. Agent—c/o Rogers & Cowan, 122 E. 42nd Street, New York, NY 10168.*

* * *

REDGRAVE, Lynn, actress

PERSONAL: Born March 8, 1943, in London, U.K.; daughter of Sir Michael Scudemore and Rachel (Kempson) Redgrave; married John Clark, April 2, 1967; children: Benjamin, Kelly, Annabelle. EDUCATION: Attended Queensgate School (London); trained for the stage at London's Central School of Speech and Drama.

CAREER: STAGE DEBUT—Helena, *A Midsummer Night's Dream,* Royal Court, London, 1962. PRINCIPAL STAGE APPEARANCES—Sarah Elliott, *The Tulip Tree,* Haymarket, London, 1962; Court Lady, *Hamlet,* National, London, 1963; Court Lady, *Saint Joan,* Rose, *The Recruiting Officer,* National, London, 1963; Barblin, *Andorra,* Jackie Coryton, *Hay Fever,* National, London, 1964; Margaret, *Much Ado About Nothing,* Kattrin, *Mother Courage,* Miss Prue, *Love for Love,* National, London, 1965; Carol Melkett, *Black Comedy,* Ethel Barrymore, NY, 1967; Mave, *Zoo, Zoo Widdershins Zoo,* Edinburgh Festival, 1969; *The Two of Us,*

Garrick, London, 1970; Joanne, *Slag*, Royal Court, London, 1971; *A Better Place*, Gate, Dublin, 1972; Billie Dawn, *Born Yesterday*, Greenwich, London, 1973; Vicky, *My Fat Friend*, Brooks Atkinson, NY, 1974; Vivie, *Mrs. Warren's Profession*, Beaumont, NY, 1976; Joan, *Knock Knock*, Biltmore, NY, 1976; *Misalliance*, Lake Forest, IL, 1976; Joan, *St. Joan*, Goodman, Chicago, IL, Circle-in-the-Square, NY, 1977; Viola, *Twelfth Night*, American Shakespeare Festival, Stratford, CT, 1978.

MAJOR TOURS—National Theater Company, Moscow, Berlin, 1965; Vicky, *My Fat Friend*, U.S. cities, 1974; *The Two of Us*, U.S. cities, 1975; *Hellzapoppin*, U.S. cities, 1976.

FILM DEBUT—*Tom Jones*, 1963. PRINCIPAL FILM APPEARANCES—*Girl with Green Eyes*, 1964; *Georgy Girl*, 1966; *The Deadly Affair*, 1967; *Smashing Time; The Virgin Soldiers*, 1970; *The Last of the Mobile Hot-Shots*, 1970; *Viva la Muerta; Don't Turn the Other Cheek; Tua; Every Little Crook and Nanny*, 1972; *Everything You Always Wanted to Know About Sex*, 1972; *The National Health; The Happy Hooker; The Big Bus*, 1976; *Sunday Lovers*, 1981.

PRINCIPAL TELEVISION APPEARANCES—*Pretty Polly; Ain't Afraid to Dance; The End of the Tunnel; I Am Osango; What's Wrong with Humpty Dumpty; Egg on the Face of the Tiger; Blank Pages; A Midsummer Night's Dream; Pygmalion; Turn of the Screw; William; Vienna 1900; Daft as a Brush;* host, *Not for Women Only*, 1977–present; *Centennial*, 1978; *The Muppets; Gaugin the Savage; Beggarman Thief; The Seduction of Miss Leona; Housecalls;* 1979.

AWARDS: Sarah Siddons Award, Chicago's Best Stage Actress, 1977, 1978; All American Favorites Award, Runner-Up Actress, 1975; Academy Award Nomination, Best Actress, Golden Globe Award, New York Film Critics Award, 1967: *Georgy Girl*.

ADDRESS: Office—Box 1207, Topanga, CA 90290. Agent—c/o International Clients' Servicing, Balscadden Bay, Howth, Dublin, Eire and 200 W. 57th Street, New York, NY 10019.*

* * *

REDGRAVE, Vanessa, actress

PERSONAL: Born January 30, 1937, in London; daughter of Sir Michael and Rachel (Kempson) Redgrave; married Tony Richardson, April 29, 1962; children: Natasha Jane, Joely Kim. EDUCATION: Attended Queensgate School; trained for the stage at London's Central School of Speech and Drama.

CAREER: STAGE DEBUT—Clarissa, *The Reluctant Debutante*, Frinton Summer Theatre, U.K., 1957. LONDON DEBUT—Carokine Lester, *A Touch of the Sun*, Saville, 1958. PRINCIPAL STAGE APPEARANCES—Mrs. Spottsworth, *Come On, Arts*, Cambridge, U.K., 1957; Sarah Undershaft, *Major Barbara*, Royal Court, London, 1958; Principal Boy, *Mother Goose*, Leatherhead, U.K., 1958; Helena, *A Midsummer Night's Dream*, Valeria, *Coriolanus*, Memorial Stratford-on-Avon, 1959; Rose Sinclair, *Look on Tempests*, Comedy, London, 1960; Stella Dean, *The Tiger and the Horse*, Queen's, London, 1960; Boletta, *The Lady from the Sea*, Queen's London, 1961; Rosalind, *As You Like It*, Royal

Shakespeare Company, Stratford-on-Avon, Aldwych, London, 1961; Katharina, *The Taming of the Shrew*, Imogen, *Cymbeline*, Stratford-on-Avon, U.K., 1962; Nina, *The Sea Gull*, Queen's, London, 1964; Jean Brodie, *The Prime of Miss Jean Brodie*, Wyndham's, London, 1966; Gwendolen Harleth, *Daniel Deronda*, University, Manchester, U.K., 1969; Susan Thistlewood, *Cato Street*, Young Vic, London, 1971; Polly Peachum, *The Threepenny Opera*, Prince of Wales, London, 1972; Viola, *Twelfth Night*, Shaw, London, 1972; Cleopatra, *Anthony and Cleopatra*, Bankside Globe, London, 1973; Gilda, *Design for Living*, Phoenix, London, 1973; Ellida, *The Lady from the Sea*, Circle-in-the-Square, NY, 1976; Ellida, *Lady from the Sea*, Royal Exchange, Manchester, 1978, Round House, U.K., 1979.

PRINCIPAL FILM APPEARANCES—Leonie, *Morgan, A Suitable Case for Treatment*, 1965; Sheila, *Sailor from Gibraltar*, 1965; Anne-Marie, *La Musica*, 1965; Jane, *Blow Up*, 1967; *A Man for All Seasons*, 1966; *Red and Blue;* Guinevere, *Camelot*, 1967; Isadora, *Isadora Duncan*, 1968; *Charge of the Light Brigade*, 1968; *The Sea Gull*, 1968; *A Quiet Place in the Country*, 1968; Daniel Deronda, *Dropout*, 1969; *The Trojan Women*, 1970; *The Devils*, 1970; *The Holiday*, 1971; *Mary Queen of Scots*, 1971; *La Vacanza; Murder on the Orient Express*, 1974; *Winter Rates*, 1974; *Seven Percent Solution*, 1975; *Julia*, 1976; *Agatha*, 1978; *Yanks*, 1978; *Bear Island; The Bostonians*, 1984.

PRINCIPAL TELEVISION APPEARANCES—*A Farewell to Arms; Katherine Mansfield;* Helena, *A Midsummer Night's Dream*, Rosalind, *As You Like It*, 1962; Maggie, *Sally*, 1964; *Bear Island*, 1979; *Playing for Time*, 1980; *My Body, My Child*, 1981.

WRITINGS: BOOKS—*Pussies and Tigers*, 1964.

AWARDS: Golden Globe Award, 1978; Academy Award, Best Supporting Actress, 1977: *Julie;* British Guild of TV Producers and Directors Award, 1966; Variety Club of Great Britain Award, Best Actress, 1966, 1961; Evening Standard Drama Award, 1961; Commander, Order of the British Empire.

ADDRESS: Agent—c/o Marina Martin Management, Ltd., Seven Windmill Street, London, W1P 1HF.*

* * *

REDINGTON, Michael, producer, actor

PERSONAL: Born May 18, 1927, in Leicester, England; son of Toby (a surveyor) and Kathleen (Mawby) Redington; married Ann Connel (a garden designer), July 28, 1950; children: Mandy, Simon.

CAREER: DEBUT—Ghost of Christmas Past, *A Christmas Carol*, Theatre Royal, Leicester, England, 1942. LONDON DEBUT—*Richard III, Antigone, School for Scandal*, Old Vic, 1949. NEW YORK DEBUT—Snug the Joiner, *A Midsummer Night's Dream*, Metropolitan Opera, 1953.

PRODUCED: PLAYS—*Heartaches of an English Pussycat*, Old Vic, London, 1980; *The Flying Karamazov Brothers*, May Fair Theatre, London, 1981; *84 Charing Cross Road*, Ambassadors, London, 1981, Nedlerlander, NY, 1982; *This Thing Called Love*, Ambassadors, London, 1983; *Pack of Lies*, Lyric, London, 1983.

ADDRESS: Office—c/o Mrs. Julia Kuney, 79 W. 12th Street, New York, 10011.

* * *

REES, Roger, actor

PERSONAL: Born May 5, 1944, in Aberystwyth, Wales, U.K.; son of William John and Doris Louise (Smith) Rees. EDUCATION: Attended Balham Secondary Modern School; Camberwell School of Art; Slade School of Fine Art.

CAREER: STAGE DEBUT—Alan, *Hindle Wakes*, Wimbledon, U.K., 1964. PRINCIPAL STAGE APPEARANCES—Yasha, *The Cherry Orchard*, Pitlochry, 1965; *The Taming of the Shrew*, *As You Like It*, Royal Shakespeare Company, Stratford, U.K., 1967; Volumnius, *Julius Caesar*, Fenton, *The Merry Wives of Windsor*, Royal Shakespeare Company, Stratford, U.K., 1968; Patchbreech, *Pericles*, Curio, *Twelfth Night*, Guildford, *Henry VIII*, *The Winter's Tale*, Royal Shakespeare Company, Stratford, U.K., 1969; *The Winter's Tale*, *Twelfth Night*, Damaschke, *The Plebeians Rehearse the Uprising*, Stephen Undershaft, *Major Barbara*, Royal Shakespeare Company, Stratford, U.K., 1970; Claudio, *Much Ado About Nothing*, Roderigo, *Othello*, Royal Shakespeare Company, Stratford, U.K., 1971, Aldwych, London, 1971–72; Gratiano, *The Merchant of Venice*, Balin, *The Island of the Mighty*, Aldwych, London, 1971–72; Marchbanks, *Candida*, Neptune, Halifax, Nova Scotia, 1973; Vosco, *Paradise*, Q, *Moving Clocks Go Slow*, Theatre Upstairs, London, 1975; Benvolio, *Romeo and Juliet*, Young Shepherd, *The Winter's Tale*, Malcolm, *Macbeth*, Antipholus, *The Comedy of Errors*, Royal Shakespeare Company, Stratford, U.K., 1976; Ananias, *The Alchemist*, Other Place, U.K., 1977, Aldwych, London, 1977; Malcolm, *Macbeth*, Nazzer, *Factory Birds*, Warehouse, London, 1977; Petulant, *The Way of the World*, Aldwych, London, 1978; Posthumus, *Cymbeline*, Royal Shakespeare Company, Stratford, U.K., Other Place, U.K., 1979; Semyon Podsekalnikov, *The Suicide*, Other Place, U.K., Newcastle, The Warehouse, 1980; Nicholas, *Nicholas Nickleby*, Aldwych, London, 1980, Plymouth, NY, 1981; *The Real Thing*, Strand, London, 1983; David, *Cries from the Mammaz House*, Royal Court, London, 1983.

MAJOR TOURS—Fabian, *Twelfth Night*, Pierre, *Aunt Sally or the Triumph of Death*, Young Marlowe, *She Stoops to Conquer*, Brother, *Fear and Misery in the Third Reich*, Simple Simon, *Jack and the Beanstalk*, Cambridge Theatre Company, U.K. cities, 1973–74; Charles Courtly, *London Assurance*, Royal Shakespeare Company, U.S. cities, 1974–75; Algernon, *The Importance of Being Earnest*, Stanley, *The Birthday Party*, Cambridge Theatre Company, U.K. cities, 1975; Sir Andrew, *Twelfth Night*, Tusenbach, *The Three Sisters*, *Is There Honey Still for Tea?*, Royal Shakespeare Company, U.K. cities, 1978.

PRINCIPAL FILM APPEARANCES—*Star 80*, 1983. PRINCIPAL TELEVISION APPEARANCES—*Place of Peace*; *Under Western Eyes*; *Bouquet of Barbed Wire*; *Saigon*; *Imaginary Friends*;

Nicholas Nickleby; *The Comedy of Errors*; *Macbeth*; *The Voysey Inheritance*; *The Ebony Tower*.

AWARDS: Antoinette Perry Award, Best Actor, 1982: *Nicholas Nickleby*.

SIDELIGHTS: RECREATION—Horse riding, tap dancing.

ADDRESS: c/o I.C.M., 22 Grafton Street, London W1 England.

* * *

REEVE, Christopher, actor

PERSONAL: Born September 25, 1952, in New York City; son of F.D. and Barbara Reeve. EDUCATION: Cornell University, B.A.; Julliard School, NY, Herbert Berghof Studios; studied with Uta Hagen, Marian Seldes, Austin Pendleton.

CAREER: PRINCIPAL STAGE APPEARANCES—Boothbay Theatre, ME; Williamstown Theatre; San Diego Shakespeare Festival; Loeb Drama Center; *A Matter of Gravity*, NY, 1976; *My Life*, 1977; *Fifth of July*, 1980; *The Greeks*, Williamstown Theatre Festival, 1981. MAJOR TOURS—*Irregular Verb to Love*, national tour;

PRINCIPAL TELEVISION APPEARANCES—*Love of Life*; *Enemies*; *The American Revolution*.

PRINCIPAL FILM APPEARANCES—*Gray Lady Down*, 1978; *Superman*, 1978; *Somewhere in Time*, 1980; *Superman II*, 1980; *Deathtrap*, 1982; *Monsignor*, 1982; *Superman III*, 1983; *The Bostonians*, 1984. RELATED CAREER—Backstage work at Old Vic, London.*

* * *

REID, Kate, actress

PERSONAL: Born November 4, 1930, in London; daughter of Walter C. and Helen Isabel (Moore) Reid; married Austin Willis, July 13, 1953 (divorced 1962); children: Reid, Robin. EDUCATION: Attended Havergal College and University of Toronto; trained for the stage at the Herbert Berghof Studio with Uta Hagen.

CAREER: STAGE DEBUT—Daphne, *Damask Cheek*, Hart House, University of Toronto. LONDON DEBUT—Lizzie, *The Rainmaker*, St. Martin's, 1956. NEW YORK DEBUT—Martha, *Who's Afraid of Virginia Woolf?*, 1962. PRINCIPAL STAGE APPEARANCES—*Years Ago*, Gravenhurst, Ontario, Canada, 1948; Catherine Ashland, *The Stepmother*, St. Martin's, London, 1958; Celia, *As You Like It*, Emilia, *Othello*, Stratford Shakespeare Festival, Ontario, Canada, 1959; Nurse, *Romeo and Juliet*, Helena, *A Midsummer Night's Dream*, Stratford Shakespeare Festival, Ontario, Canada, 1960; Katherine, *Henry VIII*, Jacquenetta, *Love's Labour's Lost*, Elly Cassidy, *The Canvas Barricade*, Stratford, 1961; Lady Macbeth, *Macbeth*, Katharine, *The Taming of the*

Shrew, Stratford, 1962; Cassandra, *Troilus and Cressida,* Adriana, *The Comedy of Errors,* Lisa/Sister Marthe, *Cyrano de Bergerac,* Stratford, 1963; Portia, *Julius Caesar,* Madame Ranevsky, *The Cherry Orchard,* Stratford, 1965; Caitlin Thomas, *Dylan,* Plymouth, NY, 1964; Martha, *Who's Afraid of Virginia Woolf?,* Manitoba Theatre Centre, Winnipeg, Canada, 1965; Portia, *Julius Caesar,* Stratford Shakespeare Festival, Ontario, Canada, 1965;

Celeste, *The Mutilated,* Moyla, *The Gnadiges Fraulein, (Slapstick Tragedy),* Longacre, NY, 1966; Medical Officer, *The Adventures of Private Turvey,* The Mayor's Wife, *The Ottawa Man,* Confederation Memorial Centre, Charlottetown, Prince Edward Island, Canada, 1966; Writer's Wife, *What Do You Really Know About Your Husband?,* Shubert, New Haven, CT, 1967; Esther Franz, *The Price,* Morosco, NY, 1968, Duke of York's, London, 1969; Gertrude, *Hamlet, The Three Sisters,* Stratford, Ontario, Canada, 1970; Juno Boyle, *Juno and the Paycock,* Walnut, Philadelphia, PA, 1973; *Leaving Home,* Vancouver, 1973; Lily, *The Freedom of the City,* Alvin, NY, 1974; Nurse, *Romeo and Juliet,* Big Mama, *Cat on a Hot Tin Roof,* Stratford, CT, 1974; Big Mama, *Cat on a Hot Tin Roof,* ANTA, NY, 1974; *Mrs. Warren's Profession, The Apple Cart,* Shaw Festival, Niagra-on-the-Lake, Canada, 1976; *The Corn Is Green,* Alley, Houston, TX, 1977; Rummy Mitchens, *Major Barbara,* Shaw Festival, Niagra-on-the-Lake, Canada, 1978; Gwyneth Price, *I Sent a Letter to My Love,* Long Wharf, New Haven, CT, 1978; Henny, *Bosoms and Neglect,* Longacre, NY, 1979, Stratford, Ontario, Canada, 1980; *Twelfth Night,* Fonsia, *The Gin Game,* Stratford, Ontario, Canada, 1980; *Mornings at Seven,* NY, Linda, *Death of a Salesman,* NY, 1984.

PRINCIPAL FILM APPEARANCES—*One Plus One; This Property Is Condemned,* 1966; *The Andromeda Strain,* 1971; *The Rainbow Boys; A Delicate Balance,* 1973; *Atlantic City,* 1981.

PRINCIPAL TELEVISION APPEARANCES—*Candida; A Month in the Country; The Three Sisters; Salt of the Earth; Queen after Death; Hamlet;* Aunt Lil, *Dallas.*

AWARDS: Office of the Order of Canada, 1976; Hon PhD, York University.

SIDELIGHTS: FAVORITE ROLES—All played.

ADDRESS: Agent—c/o Contemporary-Korman Artists, Ltd., 132 Lasky Drive, Beverly Hills, CA 90212. Office—14 Binscarth Road, Toronto, Canada.*

* * *

REID, Tim, actor

PERSONAL: Born December 19, 1944 in Norfolk, VA; married (second marriage) Daphne Maxwell (an actress); children: (first marriage) Tim, Jr., Tori, (second wife's first marriage) Christopher. EDUCATION: Norfolk State College, B.S. (Business and Marketing). NON-THEATRICAL CAREER: Sales representative, DuPont Corp.

CAREER: DEBUT—*Oedipus Rex,* Norfolk State College.

PRINCIPAL STAGE APPEARANCES—Comedy Team, *Tim and Tom,* with Tom Dreesen, Chicago, IL, and tours throughout Midwest, 1971–75.

PRINCIPAL TELEVISION APPEARANCES—*Easy Does It; Rhoda; Maude; Lou Grant; What's Happening?; Fernwood 2Night; The Richard Pryor Show;* Venus Flytrap, *WKRP in Cincinnati,* 1978–82; Downtown Brown, *Simon and Simon,* 1983–84: *You Can't Take It with You; Teachers Only.*

PRINCIPAL FILM APPEARANCES—*Mother, Jugs and Speed; Uptown Saturday Night; The Union.*

WRITINGS: TELEVISION—Several episodes of *WKRP in Cincinnati;* POETRY—*As I Feel It.*

ADDRESS: c/o The Garrett Company, 6922 Hollywood Blvd., Los Angeles, CA 90028.

* * *

REISNER, Allen, director

CAREER: PRINCIPAL FILM WORK—Director: *St. Louis Blues; The Day They Gave Babies Away.*

PRINCIPAL TELEVISION WORK—Director: *The Girl in the Gold Bathtub; The Gentleman from Seventh Avenue; Sorry, Wrong Number; Epitaph for a Spy; The Dance; Escape of Pierre Mendes-France; Deliverance of Sister Ceclia; The Prowler; The Sound of Silence.* LIVE TELEVISION PRODUCTIONS—*Playhouse 90; Climax; Studio One; Schlitz Playhouse of Stars; United States Steel Hour; Pursuit; Suspense; Danger; Prudential Family Playhouse; Ford Theatre; Claudia; City Hospital.*

SERIES—*Hawaii Five-O; Mannix; Kojak; Barnaby Jones; The Untouchables; Streets of San Francisco; Naked City; Ironsides; Cannon; I Spy; Search; It Takes a Thief; City of Angels; O'Hara, U.S. Treasury; Felony Squad; NYPD; Five Fingers; Burke's Law; Shaft; Jigsaw John; Gunsmoke; Rawhide; Branded; High Chaparrel; The Outcasts; Lancer; The Loner; Cowboy in Africa; The Rounders; The Outlaws; The Defenders; Twilight Zone; Marcus Welby; Ben Casey; Owen Marshall; The Greatest Show On Earth; Night Gallery; Kung Fu; The Interns; The City; Tales of the Unexpected; Mr. Novak; The Eleventh Hour; Slattery's People; Empire; Matt Lincoln; San Francisco International; Going My Way; Route 66; East Side, West Side; Movin' On; Bracken's World.*

MOVIES FOR TELEVISION—*Mary Jane Harper Cried Last Night; Your Money or Your Wife; To Die in Paris; The Cliff; Cops and Robin; They're Playing Our Song; Skag; The Captains and the Kings.*

SIDELIGHTS: MEMBERSHIPS—Directors Guild of America, Academy of Motion Picture Arts and Sciences.

ADDRESS: Office—c/o Perry & Neidorf, 315 S. Beverly Dr., Beverly Hills, CA 90212. Agent—Contemporary-Korman, 132 Lasky Drive, Beverly Hills, CA 90212.

REPOLE, Charles, actor, director

PERSONAL: Surname pronounced REP-o-lee; son of Herbert and Minola Repole. EDUCATION: Hofstra University, B.A. (Speech/Theatre), M.A. (Directing).

CAREER: PRINCIPAL STAGE APPEARANCES—Eddie, *Very Good Eddie; Whoopee!;* Og, *Finian's Rainbow; I Love My Wife; How to Succeed in Business without Really Trying; Images.*

DIRECTED: Plays—*The Sunshine Boys,* Kennedy Center, Washington, DC; *The Sound of Music,* Kennedy Center; *They're Playing Our Song; A Day in Hollywood, a Night in the Ukraine; Whoopee! Babes in Arms; Once Upon a Mattress,* Penn State Summer Festival; *Spoon River Anthology; The Glass Menagerie; The Great Houdini.*

AWARDS: Antoinette Perry Award Nomination, Theatre World Award, Outstanding New Performer, *Very Good Eddie.*

ADDRESS: Agent—John Peel, Producers Association, 2095 Broadway, Suite 405, New York, NY 10023.

* * *

RESNICK, Patricia, screenwriter, actress

PERSONAL: Born February 9, 1953 in Miami, FL; daughter of Edward (a lawyer) and Phyllis Resnick. EDUCATION: University of Southern California, B.A. (Cinema), 1975.

CAREER: PRINCIPAL FILM APPEARANCES—Neighbor, *Three Women,* 1977; secretary, *Welcome to L.A.,* 1977; Redford, *A Wedding,* 1978.

WRITINGS: SCREENPLAYS—*A Wedding* (with R. Altman, Considine and Nicholls), 1978; *Quintet* (with Altman and Chetwynd), 1979; *Nine to Five* (with C. Higgins), 1980. PLAYS—*Ladies in Waiting,* PBS, 1977, Chicago, IL, 1982.

AWARDS: Writers Guild Nominations: *Nine to Five, A Wedding;* British Academy Award Nomination: *A Wedding.*

SIDELIGHTS: MEMBERSHIPS—Writers Guild, Academy of Motion Picture Arts and Sciences.

ADDRESS: Office—Laventhol and Horwath, 2049 Century Park E., Suite 3700, Los Angeles, CA 90067. Agent—William Morris, 151 El Camino Drive, Beverly Hills, CA 90212.

* * *

REYNOLDS, Burt, actor, director

PERSONAL: Born February 11, 1936, in Waycross, GA; son of Burt Reynolds; married Judy Carne (divorced 1965). EDUCATION: Florida State University, Palm Beach Jr. College.

CAREER: PRINCIPAL STAGE APPEARANCES—*Mister Roberts; Look, We've Come Through; The Rainmaker.*

PRINCIPAL TELEVISION APPEARANCES—*M Squad; Riverboat; Pony Express; Branded; Gunsmoke,* 1962–65; *Hawk,* 1966; *Dan August,* 1970–71.

PRINCIPAL FILM APPEARANCES—*Angel Baby,* 1961; *Armored Command,* 1961; *Operation CIA,* 1965; *Navajo,* 1967; *Sam Whiskey,* 1968; *Impasse,* 1968; *Caine,* 1968; *Shark; 100 Rifles,* 1969; *Fade-In; Skullduggery,* 1969; *Deliverance,* 1972; *Fuzz,* 1972; *Everything You Always Wanted to Know About Sex But Were Afraid to Ask,* 1972; *Shamus,* 1972; *White Lightening,* 1973; *The Man Who Loved Cat Dancing,* 1973; *The Longest Yard,* 1974; *At Long Last Love,* 1975; *Hustle,* 1975; *W.W. and the Dixie Dance Kings,* 1975; *Lucky Lady,* 1975; *Silent Movie,* 1976; *Nickelodeon,* 1976; *Gator,* 1976 (also directed); *Smokey and the Bandit,* 1977; *Semi-Tough,* 1977; *The End,* 1977 (also directed); *Starting Over,* 1979; *Rough Cut,* 1980; *Smokey and the Bandit II,* 1980; *Cannonball Run,* 1981; *Paternity,* 1981; *Sharkey's Machine,* 1981 (also directed); *The Best Little Whorehouse in Texas,* 1982; *Best Friends,* 1982; *Stroker Ace,* 1983; *The Man Who Loved Women,* 1983; *Cannonball Run II,* 1984.

SIDELIGHTS: MEMBERSHIPS—Directors Guild of America.

ADDRESS: 8730 Sunset Blvd., Suite 201, Los Angeles, CA 90069.*

* * *

RICHARDS, Lloyd, director, educator, actor

PERSONAL: Born Toronto, Canada. EDUCATION: Wayne State University.

CAREER: PRINCIPAL STAGE APPEARANCES—(Broadway) *The Egghead; Freight;* (Off-Broadway) *Othello; Oedipus Rex; Respectful Prostitute; Home of the Brave; Little Foxes; Hedda Gabler; Stevedore.*

PRINCIPAL TELEVISION APPEARANCES—*Hallmark Hall of Fame; Studio One; The Web; Search for Tomorrow; The Guiding Light; Famous Jury Trials.* RADIO—*Hotel for Pets; Helen Trent; Inheritance; Theatre Guild of the Air; Greatest Story Ever Told; Up for Parole; Jungle Jim; My True Story.*

DIRECTED: PLAYS—(Broadway) *A Raisin in the Sun,* 1958; *The Long Dream,* 1960; *The Moon Besieged,* 1962; *I Had a Ball,* 1964; *The Yearling,* 1966; *Paul Robeson,* 1977–78; (Off-Broadway) *Lower than the Angels,* 1965; *Who's Got His Own,* 1966; *The Ox Cart,* 1966; *The Great I Am,* 1972; *The Past Is the Past, Goin' Thru Changes,* Billie Holiday Theatre, 1974; *The Lion and the Jewel,* Richard Allen Center, 1977; (Regional) *That's the Game Jack,* Tanglewood Writers Conference, 1967; *Rainless Sky, Bedford Forest, A Man Around the House, Just Before Morning, Valentine's Day, Summertree,* O'Neill Theater Center, 1966–68; *Ghosts,* Cincinnati Playhouse in the Park, OH; *Timon of Athens,* Yale Repertory, New Haven, CT, 1980; *Hedda Gabler, Uncle Vanya,* Yale Repertory, 1981; *Johnny Bull, A Doll's House,* Yale Repertory, 1982; *A Touch of the Poet,* Yale Repertory, 1983; (Educational) *The Crucible,*

Boston University, 1962; *Richard III,* Boston University; *The Rose Tattoo,* Hunter College, NY, 1973; *Eight Ball,* University of North Carolina, 1973; *The Sign in Sidney Brustein's Window,* Hunter College, 1976; *Night Must Fall,* Hunter College, 1978.

DIRECTED: TELEVISION—*Miss Black America,* 1960–70; *You Are There,* "Harriet Tubman," "Galileo," 1971–72; *ABC Wide World of Entertainment,* "The Last Chapter,"; "Eight Ball," 1973; *Visions,* "Gold Watch," 1976; *Vision,* "Freeman," 1977; *Bill Moyers Journal,* "No Easy Walk to Freedom," 1979; *Roots: The Next Generation* (segment #6), 1979; *Paul Robeson,* 1979; *Medal of Honor Rag,* 1982.

THEATRE-RELATED CAREER: Resident director—Actors Company Repertory Theatre, Detroit, MI; Greenwich Mews, NY; Great Lakes Drama Festival, 1954; Northland Playhouse, Detroit, MI, 1955–58; Australian National Playwrights Conference, 1974; artistic director, Eugene O'Neill Theater Center, National Playwrights Conference; dean and artistic director, Yale School of Drama/Repertory Theater.

AWARDS: New England Theatre Conference Award, Outstanding Creative Achievement in the American Theatre, 1983; Downtown New Haven Arts Award, 1983; Connecticut Commission on the Arts Award, 1982; National Theatre Conference Person of the Year Award, 1981; Doctor of Humane Letters, Wayne State University, 1980; Christopher Award, Direction, 1980: *Paul Robeson;* Honorary Doctorate, Yale University, 1979.

SIDELIGHTS: MEMBERSHIPS—Theater Communications Group (board of directors); Connecticut Commission on the Arts; Rockefeller Foundation; Public Broadcasting Service (board of directors); Society of Stage Directors and Choreographers (president, 1970–80); Ford Foundation; International Theatre Institute; New York State Council on the Arts.

ADDRESS: Office—Yale Repertory Company, Yale University, New Haven, CT 06520.

* * *

RICHARDS, Martin (ne Morton Richard Klein), producer

PERSONAL: Born March 11, 1932; son of Sidney (a stockbroker) and Shirley (Mandel) Klein; married Mary Lea Johnson (a producer) on August 11, 1978. EDUCATION: Attended New York University.

CAREER: PRINCIPAL STAGE WORK—Producer, Broadway productions, NY: *Chicago,* 1975; *The Norman Conquests,* 1975; *On the Twentieth Century,* 1978; *Sweeney Todd,* 1979; *Goodbye Fidel,* 1980; *Crimes of the Heart,* 1981; *A Doll's Life,* 1982; *La Cage Aux Folles,* 1983. OFF-BROADWAY—*Dylan,* 1972; *March of the Falsettos,* 1981.

PRINCIPAL FILM WORK, PRODUCER—*Some of My Best Friends Are . . . ,* 1971; *The Boys from Brazil,* 1978; *The Shining,* 1980; *Fort Apache, the Bronx,* 1981.

THEATRE-RELATED CAREER: Casting director, major motion pictures, 1968–75; with Mary Lea Johnson, formed the Producer Circle Company in 1975 to produce theatre and major feature films.

AWARDS: As of 1982, Mr. Richards' productions have won 12 Antoinette Perry Awards and various other awards including New York Drama Critics Awards.

SIDELIGHTS: MEMBERSHIPS—The League of New York Theatres and Producers; Academy of Motion Picture Arts and Sciences.

"Mr. Richards was a child actor, appearing on Broadway in *Mexican Hayride* and late in second company of *West Side Story.* During the fifties, he performed in various nightclubs, on television on the *Arthur Godfrey's Talent Scouts* and *Chance of a Lifetime.* He also sang with the Paul Whiteman Orchestra and recorded for ASCOT and Capitol records."

ADDRESS: Office—c/o The Producer Circle Company, 1350 Avenue of the Americas, New York, NY 10019, and 9200 Sunset Blvd., Los Angeles, CA 90069.

* * *

RICHARDSON, Claibe (ne Clairborne F.), composer

PERSONAL: Claibe rhymes with "Abe;" born November 10, 1929, in Shreveport, LA; son of George Norman (a

CLAIBE RICHARDSON

banker) and Effie Irene (Eisler) Richardson. EDUCATION: Louisiana State University, B.A.; Stephen F. Austin University, work on Master's Degree. RELIGION: Methodist. MILITARY: Air Force (four years).

CAREER: DEBUT—Composer, *Shoestring Revue,* Barbizon Plaza, NY, 1957. PRINCIPAL STAGE WORK—*The Grass Harp,* Martin Beck, NY, 1971; *The Royal Family,* Helen Hayes, NY, 1976; *The Curse of an Aching Heart,* Little, NY, 1982.

TELEVISION WORK—Theme (also associate producer) *Show Street,* 1964.

AWARDS: ASCAP Awards, numerous; International Broadcasters Award, Show Album of the Year Awards, *The Grass Harp.*

SIDELIGHTS: MEMBERSHIPS—ASCAP; AGAC; Dramatist Guild; York Theatre Company Board. RECREATION: Swimming, cooking, walking.

Mr. Richardson is an animal lover, with two cherished cats, ''Never'' and ''Li'l Boss.'' He speaks a little Spanish. He is also the president, since 1977, of Thackery Falls Music Company in New York City.

ADDRESS: Home—115 W. 71st Street, New York, NY 10023. Agent—Gilbert Parker, William Morris Agency, 1350 Avenue of the Americas, New York, NY 10019.

* * *

RIGDON, Kevin, lighting designer

PERSONAL: Born February 17, 1956; son of Donald Lee (a market analyst) and Arlene Mae (a personnel manager; maiden name, Rybak) Rigdon; married Elizabeth Anne Shepherd (a writer) on April 23, 1983. EDUCATION: Drake University, 1974–75; served as an intern with the Guthrie Theatre in Minneapolis, MN, 1975–76. RELIGION: Episcopalian.

CAREER: PRINCIPAL STAGE WORK—LIGHTING DESIGNER (New York)—*Glengarry Glen Ross,* Golden, 1984; *And a Nightingale Sang,* Mitzi Newhouse, Lincoln Center, 1983; *True West,* Cherry Lane, 1983; *Edmond,* Provincetown Playhouse, 1982; (Regional) Goodman, Chicago, IL: *Glengarry Glen Ross, Gardenia, Jungle Coup, Eh Joe, Edmond, The Woolgatherer;* Remains Theatre, Chicago, IL: *Traps, Moby Dick, The Tooth of Crime; The Hiding Place,* Virginia Museum Theatre, Richmond, VA; Williamstown Theatre Festival, MA (set also): *Gideon's Point, The Melody of The Glittering Parrot, Theatre of the Film Noir;* Steppenwolf Theatre Company, Chicago, Set and Lighting Design—*True West, Loose Ends, Waiting for the Parade, Of Mice and Men, No Man's Land, Savages, Arms and the Man, Absent Friends, Balm in Gilead, The Quiet Jeanie Green, Death of a Salesman, Bonjour, La, Bonjour, The Glass Menagerie, Our Late Night, The Caretaker, Sandbar Flatland, Exit the King, Rosencrantz and Guildenstern Are Dead, The Dumb Waiter, The Sea Horse.*

THEATRE-RELATED CAREER: Resident designer, Steppenwolf, Chicago, IL, 1976–82; assistant production manager, Goodman, Chicago, IL, 1982–83; lighting designer, Mordine and Company Dance Company, 1983–84.

AWARDS: Joseph Jefferson Awards, Lighting and Scenic Design, 1983: *Moby Dick,* Lighting Design, 1982: *Tooth of Crime,* 1981: *Balm in Gilead.*

SIDELIGHTS: MEMBERSHIPS—United Scenic Artists.

ADDRESS: Home—89 N. Sixth Street, Brooklyn, NY 11211.

* * *

RIVERA, Chita (nee Concita del Rivero), actress, singer, and dancer

PERSONAL: Born January 23, 1933, in Washington, D.C.; daughter of Pedro Julio Figueroa del Rivero; married Anthony Mordente; children: Lisa. EDUCATION: Attended New York City public schools; trained for the stage at the American School of Ballet.

CAREER: NEW YORK DEBUT—*Call Me Madam,* Imperial, 1952. LONDON DEBUT—Anita, *West Side Story,* Her Majesty's, 1958. PRINCIPAL STAGE APPEARANCES—Chorus, *Guys and Dolls,* 46th Street, NY, 1953; *Can-Can,* Shubert, NY, 1954; *Shoestring Revue,* President, NY, 1955; Fifi, *Seventh Heaven,* ANTA, NY, 1955; Rita Romano, *Mr. Wonderful,* Broadway Theatre, NY, 1956; *Shinbone Alley,* Broadway Theatre, NY, 1957; Anita, *West Side Story,* Winter Garden, NY, 1957; Rose Grant, *Bye Bye, Birdie,* Martin Beck, NY, 1960. Rose, *Bye Bye Birdie,* Her Majesty's, London, 1961; Athena Constantine, *Zenda,* Curran, San Francisco, CA, 1963; Anyanka, *Bajour,* Shubert, NY, 1964; Jenny, *The Threepenny Opera,* Mineola, Long Island, NY, 1966; *Flower Drum Song,* Melody Top, Milwaukee, WI, 1966; *Zorba,* Westbury Music Fair, NY, 1970; Billie Dawn, *Born Yesterday,* Walnut Street, Philadelphia, PA, 1972; *Milliken Breakfast Show,* Waldorf-Astoria, NY, 1972; *Sondheim: A Musical Tribute,* Shubert, NY, 1973; *Father's Day,* Ivanhoe, Chicago, IL, 1974; Velma Kelly, *Chicago,* 46th Street, NY, 1975; *Hey Look Me Over,* Avery Fisher, NY, 1981; Anna, *The Rink,* Martin Beck, NY, 1984.

MAJOR TOURS—Principal dancer, *Call Me Madam,* U.S. cities, 1952; Rose, *Bye Bye, Birdie,* U.S. cities, 1962; Charity, *Sweet Charity,* U.S. and Canadian cities, 1967–68; *Jacques Brel Is Alive and Well . . . ,* U.S. cities, 1972; Lilli Vanessi/Katherine, *Kiss Me, Kate,* U.S. cities, 1974.

PRINCIPAL FILM APPEARANCES—Charity, *Sweet Charity,* 1969. PRINCIPAL TELEVISION APPEARANCES—Neighbor, *The New Dick Van Dyke Show,* 1973–74.

AWARDS: Antoinette Perry Award, Best Actress in a Musical, 1984: *The Rink.*

SIDELIGHTS: RECREATIONS—Cooking, bowling, riding, tennis, swimming.

ADDRESS: Office—c/o Armando Rivera, 91 Clinton Street, New York, NY 10002.*

RIVERS, Joan (nee Joan Molinsky), comedienne, writer, director

PERSONAL: Born 1937 in Brooklyn, NY; daughter of Meyer C. (a doctor) Molinsky; married Edgar Rosenberg (a writer and producer), July 15, 1965; children: Melissa. EDUCATION: Barnard College, NY, B.A., 1958. NON-THEATRICAL CAREER: Fashion co-ordinator, Bond Clothing Stores.

CAREER: PRINCIPAL APPEARANCES, COMEDIENNE—appeared in many cabarets and coffee houses in Greenwich Village, NY; *Bon Soir*, NY; *Second City*, Improvisational group, Chicago; *Upstairs at the Downstairs*, five years, NY; star headliner in Las Vegas and Atlantic City, NJ Clubs and Casinos. PRINCIPAL APPEARANCES, TELEVISION—debut on *Tonight Show, Starring Johnny Carson*, 1965; guest host, *Tonight Show*, a record number of performances for a single host; *That Show*, 260 original programs, 1969–71; co-host, *Emmy Awards Show*, 1983.

PRINCIPAL FILM WORK, DIRECTING—*Rabbit Test*, 1978. RECORDINGS: Comedy—*What Becomes a Semi-Legend Most?*

WRITINGS: PLAYS, PRODUCED—Co-author, *Fun City*, NY. TELEVISION—*That Show*, 1969–71; *Candid Camera; Husbands and Wives.* SCREENPLAYS—*Rabbit Test*, 1978. BOOKS—*Having a Baby Can Be a Scream*, 1974; *Can We Talk?*, 1983.

AWARDS: Woman of the Year, Hadassah, 1983; Clio, Best Performance in a Television Commercial, 1976 and 1982; Jimmy Award for Best Comedian, 1981; Las Vegas Comedienne of the Year Award, 1976 and 1977; Georgie Award, Best Comedienne of 1975, American Guild of Variety Artists; Phi Beta Kappa, Barnard College.

SIDELIGHTS: Chairman, National Cystic Fibrosis Foundation.

''Miss Rivers attended Adelphi Academy, Connecticut College for Women, and graduated Phi Beta Kappa from Barnard College while secretly envisioning herself as a great dramatic actress, and longing to be cast as a tragic Shakespearean heroine. While waiting for that glorious moment, she supported herself as a neophyte comedienne. After her stint with the *Second City* improvisational group, she returned to New York and landed a job writing for the television show *Candid Camera*—the rest, as they say, is history.''

ADDRESS: Agent—c/o Bill Sammeth, 9200 Sunset Blvd., Los Angeles, CA 90069.

* * *

ROBARDS, Jason, Jr., actor

PERSONAL: Born July 26, 1922, in Chicago, IL; son of Jason Sr. and Hope Maxine (Glancille) Robards; married Eleanor Pitman, 1948 (divorced); Rachel Taylor (divorced); Lauren Bacall, 1961 (divorced); Lois O'Connor; children: (first marriage) Jason III, Sarah Louise, David; (third marriage) Sam; (fourth marriage) Shannon, Jake. EDUCATION: Hollywood High School; studied for the theatre at the American Academy of Dramatic Arts. MILITARY: U.S. Navy, 1939–46.

CAREER: DEBUT—*Out of the Frying Pan*, Delyork Theatre, Rehoboth Beach, DE, 1947. NEW YORK DEBUT—Rear end of the Cow, *Jack and the Beanstalk*, Children's World Theatre, 1947. PRINCIPAL STAGE APPEARANCES—Walk-on, *The Mikado*, Century, 1947; also in *Iolanthe* and *The Yeoman of the Guard*, Century, 1947; understudy and assistant stage manager, *Stalag 17*, 48th Street Theatre, NY, 1951; assistant stage manager, *The Chase*, Playhouse, NY, 1952; Ed Moody, *American Gothic*, Circle in the Square, NY, 1953; Hickey, *The Iceman Cometh*, Helen Hayes, NY, 1956; Jamie, *Long Day's Journey into Night*, Helen Hayes, NY, 1956; Hotspur, *Henry IV, Part I*, Polinexes, *The Winter's Tale;* Stratford, Ontario Shakespeare Festival, 1958; Manley Halliday, *The Disenchanted*, Coronet, NY, 1958; title-role, *Macbeth*, Cambridge, MA, 1959;

Julian Berneirs, *Toys in the Attic*, Hudson, NY, 1960; William Baker, *Big Fish, Little Fish*, ANTA, NY, 1961; Murray Burns, *A Thousand Clowns*, O'Neill, NY, 1962; two plays in repertory, Quentin, *After the Fall* and Seymour Rosenthal, *But for Whom Charlie*, Washington Square, NY, 1964; Erie Smith, *Hughie*, Royale, NY, 1964; Vicar of St. Peters, *The Devils*, Broadway, NY, 1965; Capt. Starkey, *We Bombed in New Haven*, Ambassador, NY, 1968; Frank Elgin, *The Country Girl*, Billy Rose, NY, 1972; James Tyrone, Jr. *A Moon for the Misbegotten*, Morosco, NY, 1973, Ahmanson, Los Angeles, 1974; Erie Smith, *Hughie*, Zellerbach, Los Angeles, 1975; James Tyrone, *Long Day's Journey into Night*, Brooklyn Academy of Music, NY, 1975; Erie Smith, *Hughie*, Lake Forest, IL, 1976; Cornelius Melody, *A Touch of the Poet*, Helen Hayes, NY, 1977; *O'Neill and Carlotta*, Public, NY, 1979; *You Can't Take It With You*, Plymouth, NY, Kennedy Center, 1983.

FILM DEBUT—*The Journey*, 1958. PRINCIPAL FILM APPEARANCES—*Long Day's Journey into Night; By Love Possessed*, 1961; *Tender Is the Night*, 1962; *Act One*, 1963; *A Thousand Clowns*, 1966; *Any Wednesday*, 1966; *Divorce: American Style*, 1967; *The Ballad of Cable Hogue*, 1970; *Pat Garrett and Billy the Kid*, 1973; *All the President's Men*, 1976; *Julia*, 1977; *Comes a Horseman*, 1978; *Hurricane*, 1979; *Raise the Titanic*, 1980; *Melvin and Howard*, 1980; *Something Wicked This Way Comes*, 1983; *Max Dugan Returns*, 1983.

PRINCIPAL TELEVISION APPEARANCES—Hickey, *The Iceman Cometh;* Dr. Rank, *The Doll House;* Robert Jordan, *For Whom the Bell Tolls; You Can't Take It with You; Hughie; The Day After; Sakharov; The Atlanta Child Murders; FDR: The Last Year; Washington: Behind Closed Doors.*

AWARDS: Academy Award, Best Supporting Actor, 1977: *Julia*, 1976: *All the President's Men;* New York Drama Critics Award, 1959–60: Julian Berneirs, *Toys in the Attic;* Antoinette Perry Award and the New York Critics award, 1958–59: Manley Halliday, *The Disenchanted.*

SIDELIGHTS: MEMBERSHIPS—The Players Club. FAVORITE ROLES: Hickey, Macbeth, Jamie, Hotspur, Halliday. RECREATIONS—Guitar, banjo, photography.

ADDRESS: Agent—STE Representation, 888 Seventh Avenue, New York, NY 10019.

JASON ROBARDS, JR.

ROBBINS, Jana (nee Marsha Eisenberg), actress

PERSONAL: Born April 18, in Johnstown, PA; daughter of Phillip (a businessman) and Edythe Elaine (Stept) Eisenberg; married Richard Rosenwald (a personal manager), January 26, 1969; children: Eric. EDUCATION: Stephens College, Columbia, MO, B.F.A., 1967; studied for the theatre with Warren Robertson and Larry Moss, at the Warren Robertson Workshop; studied voice with Paul Gauert.

CAREER: DEBUT—Aldonza, *Man of La Mancha,* national tour, 1968–69. NEW YORK DEBUT—Patricia Bingham, *Good News,* St. James, December 1974. PRINCIPAL STAGE APPEARANCES—Tzeitel, *Fiddler on the Roof,* 1973; Maxie, *Johnny Manhattan,* 1975; Young Woman, *Tickles by Tucholsky,* Theatre Four, NY, 1976; Louise, *Gypsy,* Papermill Playhouse, NJ, 1976; Cleo/Monica, *I Love My Wife,* Biltmore, NY, 1977; Leader, *Zorba,* 1978; Rosie, *Bye, Bye, Birdie,* North Shore Music Theatre, Beverely, MA, 1978; Martirio, *The House of Bernarda Alba,* Cincinnati, 1978; Polly, *Does Anybody Here Do the Peabody?,* NY, 1978; Sally, *Cabaret,* Evening Dinner Theatre, 1979; Woman II, *Side by Side by Sondheim,* Seattle Repertory, 1979; Sylvia Metcalfe, *Tip-Toes,* Brooklyn Academy of Music, NY, 1979; Rosalie, *Carnival,* MUNY, 1980; Lady Sneerwell, *The School for Scandal,* Cincinnati, 1980; Soprano, *The All Night Strut,* NY, 1980; Anita, *West Side Story,* Milwaukee Melody Top, WI, 1982; Jennie, *Chapter Two,* Waldo Astoria, Kansas City, 1982; Olivia, *Twelfth Night,* NY, 1982; Cleo, *The Most Happy Fella,* Kansas City Lyric Opera, 1983; Lenny, *Crimes of the Heart,* NY, 1983; Colette,

Colette Collage, NY, 1983; Lead, *Circus Gothic,* Douglas Fairbanks, NY, 1984.

MAJOR TOURS—Patricia Bingham, *Good News,* nine months pre-Broadway, 1974; Melba, *Pal Joey,* summer package, 1983; other summer stock tours.

AWARDS: New Jersey Drama Critics Award, Best Supporting Actress in a Musical, 1976: *Gypsy.*

SIDELIGHTS: MEMBERSHIPS—AEA; SAG; AFTRA.

''My favorite roles are highly diversified. They would be Lenny in *Crimes of the Heart,* Jennie in *Chapter Two,* Louise in *Gypsy,* Rosie in *Bye, Bye, Birdie* and the Leader in *Zorba.* I also greatly enjoyed Martirio in *House of Bernarda Alba.*''

ADDRESS: Office—Rosenwald Associates, 250 W. 57th Street, New York, NY 10019. Agent—Hesseltine-Baker, 165 W. 46th Street, New York, NY 10036.

* * *

ROBINSON, Martin P., actor and puppeteer

PERSONAL: Born March 9, 1954, in Dearborn, MI; son of Harold L. (a sales executive) and Patricia A. (Mains) Robinson. EDUCATION: American Academy of Dramatic Arts, A.A., 1974.

CAREER: DEBUT—Balthazar, *Romeo and Juliet,* North Shore Music Theatre, Beverly, MA, 1974. NEW YORK DEBUT—Frank, *The Yellow Wallpaper,* Encompass, 1976, 30 performances. LONDON DEBUT—Puppet designer, *Little Shop of Horrors,* Comedy, 1983. PRINCIPAL STAGE APPEARANCES—Puppeteer, *Bil Baird's Marionettes,* Williamsburg, VA, 1977; ensemble, *The Haggadah,* Public Theatre, NY, 1980–81; Audrey Two Manipulation/puppet designer, *Little Shop of Horrors,* Orpheum, NY, 1982–84.

MAJOR TOURS—Puppeteer, *Nicolo Marionettes,* U.S. cities, 1975, 1978; ensemble, *Claude Kipnis Mime Theatre,* U.S., Canadian, Carribean cities, 1975–76.

FILM DEBUT—Puppeteer, *Muppets Take Manhattan,* 1984. TELEVISION DEBUT—Mr. Snuffleupagus, *Sesame Street.* PRINCIPAL TELEVISION APPEARANCES—Puppeteer, *Sesame Street,* 1981–84.

AWARDS: Drama Desk Award, Special Effects, 1982–83: *Little Shop of Horrors;* Villager Award, Puppet Design, 1982: *Little Shop of Horrors.*

SIDELIGHTS: MEMBERSHIPS—AEA; SAG; AFTRA; Mime Guild.

''With a background in sculpture and a taste for the bizarre in my acting, I feel I've found the perfect combination of the two in the design and performing of puppets.''

ADDRESS: Agent—c/o Esther Sherman, William Morris Agency, 1350 Avenue of the Americas, New York, NY 10019.

ROGERS, Gil (ne John V. Jr.), actor

PERSONAL: Born February 4, 1934; son of John Veach (a thoroughbred horse breeder, farmer, real estate, and rural appraiser) and Betty (King) Rogers; married Juliet Ribet, February 31, 1964 (divorced, 1969); married Margaret Hall (an actress), January 12, 1970; children: Amanda. EDUCATION: Transylvania University, B.A., 1955; trained for the stage with Nola Chilton. POLITICS: Liberal Republican. RELIGION: Episcopalian. MILITARY: U.S. Army, 1957–58.

CAREER: DEBUT—Perry, *Five Little Peppers*, Lexington Children's Theatre, KY, 1941. NEW YORK DEBUT—*The Thorntons*, Provincetown Playhouse, 1958. PRINCIPAL STAGE APPEARANCES—(Broadway) Brady, *The Great White Hope*, Alvin, NY, Arena Stage, Washington, DC, 1967; Ed Earl Dodd, *Best Little Whorehouse in Texas*, 46th Street, NY, 1980–82; Squire, *The Corn Is Green*, Lunt-Fontanne, NY, 1983; (Off-Broadway) Doc, *Come Back Little Sheba*, Queens Playhouse; *Mecca*, Quaigh; *The Memory Bank*, Gate; *The Jew Who Defended Hitler*, Manhattan Theatre Club; *Yucca Flats*, Manhattan Theatre Club; *Remembrance*, New York Shakespeare Festival; (Regional) Front Street, Memphis, TN, 1965; Arena Stage, Washington, DC, 1967–68; San Diego Shakespeare Festival, 1968; Playhouse in the Park, Cincinnati, OH, 1970; O'Neill Theatre Center, Waterford, CT, 1971, 1975; Seattle Repertory, WA, 1976, 1978; Washington Theatre Club; Mineola Playhouse. MAJOR TOURS—*Andersonville Trial*, 1960–61; *The Great Sebastians; Forty Carats; The World of Carl Sandburg.*

FILM DEBUT—Foreman, *Nothing But a Man*, 1959. PRINCIPAL FILM APPEARANCES—Father, *A Fan's Note*, 1970; Lt. Parks, *Panic in Needle Park*, 1970; Sheriff Hart, *The Children*, 1978; Eddie, *Eddie Macon's Run*, 1982; *W. W. and the Dixie Dance Kings; Pretty Poison; The Line; The Bell Jar.*

TELEVISION DEBUT—Doctor, *Another World*, 1971. PRINCIPAL TELEVISION APPEARANCES—Dr. Brandt, *The Doctors*; Ray Gardner, *All My Children*; Brent Kenwood, *Search for Tomorrow; Rodeo Red and the Runaway; Nova*, "The Trial of Denton Cooley"; *Eyewitness*, "Deathwish"; *Our Story:* Governor Prence, "The Peach Gang," Theodore Sedgewick, "The Last Ballot," Reverend Scanlon, "The Devil's Work," Cornelius Vanderbilt, "The Erie War."

SIDELIGHTS: MEMBERSHIPS—Players Club, Merriewold Club (board of directors).

ADDRESS: Agent—Barna Ostertag, 501 Fifth Avenue, New York, NY 10017.

* * *

ROMAN, Lawrence, playwright

PERSONAL: Son of Irving (a grocer) and Bessie Dora (Roud) Roman; married Evelyn Mildred Zirkin (an artist); children: Steven Mark, Catherine Ann. EDUCATION: UCLA, B.A.

WRITINGS: PLAYS, PRODUCED—*Under the Yum Yum Tree*, Broadway production, 1961. SCREENPLAYS—(adaptation)

Paper Lion, 1967; *A Warm December; McQ*. TELEPLAYS—*Anatomy of an Illness*, 1984.

ADDRESS: Office—9157 Sunset Blvd., #202, Los Angeles, CA 90069. Agent—The Literary Group, Ken Gross, 9220 Sunset Blvd., #318, Los Angeles, CA 90069.

* * *

ROMERO, Cesar, actor, dancer

PERSONAL: Born February 15, 1907, in New York; son of Cesar Julio (an exporter) and Maria Mantilla (a singer; maiden name, Martí) Romero. EDUCATION: Collegiate School, NY, 1923–26. MILITARY: U.S. Coast Guard, 1943–46 (chief bosun's mate).

CAREER: DEBUT—Dancer, *Lady Do*, Brooklyn, NY, 1927. NEW YORK DEBUT—Ricci, *Dinner at Eight*, Music Box, 1932, for more than 300 performances. PRINCIPAL ENGAGEMENTS—Nightclub dancer with partner Liz Higgins, 1926–29; *Stella Brady*, Globe, NY; *All Points West; Spring in Autumn*, New York, 1933; *Ten Minute Alibi*, 1934; *Mr. Barry's Etchings*, 1975. MAJOR TOURS—Count di Ruvo, *Strictly Dishonorable*, 1930–31; *Social Register*, 1931; *My Three Angels*, Dinner Theatre Tour, 1976; *Never Get Smart with an Angel*, Dinner Theatre Tour, 1977; *Goodbye, Tiger, Goodbye Fifi*, 1980–81; *A Dash of Spirits*, 1981–82; *The Max Factor*, Dinner Theatre Tour, 1983.

FILM DEBUT—Jorgensen, *The Thin Man*, 1934. FILM APPEARANCES—*British Agent*, 1934; *Show Them No Mercy*, 1935; *Metropolitan*, 1935; *Love Before Breakfast*, 1936; *Wee Willie Winkie*, 1937; *Happy Landing*, 1938; *My Lucky Star*, 1938; *The Return of the Cisco Kid* (and others in that series), 1939; *The Gay Caballero*, 1940; *Weekend in Havana*, 1941; *Springtime in the Rockies*, 1942; *Tales of Manhattan*, 1942; *Orchestra Wives*, 1942; *Coney Island*, 1943; *Wintertime*, 1943; *Carnival in Costa Rica*, 1947; *Captain from Castille*, 1947; *That Lady in Ermine*, 1948; *Deep Waters*, 1948; *Love That Brute*, 1950; *Happy Go Lovely*, 1951; *Lost Continent*, 1951; *FBI Girl*, 1951; *Prisoners of the Casbah*, 1953; *Vera Cruz*, 1954; *The Americano*, 1955; *The Racers (Such Men Are Dangerous)*, 1955; *Around the World in Eighty Days*, 1956; *The Leather Saint*, 1956; *The Story of Mankind*, 1957; *Villa*, 1958; *Oceans 11*, 1960; *Pepe*, 1960; *The Castilian*, 1963; *Two on a Guillotine*, 1964; *Sergeant Deadhead*, 1964; *Marriage on the Rocks*, 1965; *Batman*, 1966; *Hot Millions*, 1968; *Crooks and Coronets*, 1969; *The Midas Run*, 1969; *A Talent for Loving*, 1969; *Now You See Him, Now You Don't*, 1972; also: *The Runaway, Sophy's Place, The Computer Wore Tennis Shoes, The Strongest Man in the World, Soul Soldier, The Spectre of Edgar Allan Poe, The Timber Tramps, Carioca Tiger, The Story of Father Kino.*

TELEVISION DEBUT—*The Jack Carter Show: Gravediggers of 1950: A Musical Extravaganza*, 1950. TELEVISION APPEARANCES—*The Bigelow Theatre—The Big Hello*, 1950; *Campbell Soundstage—The Cavorting Statue*, 1952; host, *Your Chevrolet Showroom*, 1953–54; *Passport to Danger*, 1955; panelist, *Take a Good Look*, 1959–61; the Joker, *Batman*, 1966–67; Sr. Rodriguez, *Chico and the Man*, 1976; also: *The Milton Berle Show; The Martha Raye Show; Zane Grey*

Theatre; The Dinah Shore Show; Wagon Train; The Red Skelton Show; The Betty Hutton Show; Playhouse 90; Stage Coach West; Pete and Gladys; Ben Casey; Dr. Kildare; Night Gallery; Alias Smith and Jones; Nanny and the Professor; The Mod Squad; Julia; The Jimmy Stewart Show; Ironside; Vegas; Fantasy Island; The Love Boat; Matt Houston, others.

SIDELIGHTS: ''In 1972, Mr. Romero opened a restaurant in Los Angeles called 'Cappucino.' His three feature films made in 1951 for RKO in England brought him a percentage of the company. He is the grandson of José Martí, the great Cuban patriot and martyr for whom Havana's airport is named. In 1965 he was the honored guest at the unveiling of the Martí statue in New York's Central Park.''

ADDRESS: Agent—Beakle & Jennings, 9615 Brighton Way, Beverly Hills, CA 90210.

* * *

ROSENTHAL, Rick (ne Richard L., Jr.), director

PERSONAL: Born June 15, 1949, New York City; married Nancy Stephens (an actress) May 23, 1981. EDUCATION: Harvard University, 1971.

CAREER: FILM DEBUT—*Halloween II,* 1981. PRINCIPAL FILM WORK—*Bad Boys,* 1983; *American Dreamer,* 1984. TELEVISION DEBUT—*Secrets of Midland Heights.*

PRINCIPAL TELEVISION WORK—pilot, *Darkroom.*

ADDRESS: Office—c/o Whitewater Films, 7471 Melrose Avenue, #17, Los Angeles, CA 90046. Agent—The Gersh Agency, 202 N. Canon, Beverly Hills, CA 90201.

* * *

ROSENWALD, Richard S., producer, writer, personal manager

PERSONAL: Born August 30, 1943; son of Robert E. (an attorney-at-law) and Dorothy (Shubart) Rosenwald; married Jana Robbins (an actress), January 26, 1969; children: Robert Eric. EDUCATION: Washington University, B.S., 1967, M.B.A., 1969. POLITICS: Former elected Democratic Party official. RELIGION: Jewish.

CAREER: PRODUCER: Co-founder (with Bruce Wall) and namer of the American Shaw Festival, Mt. Gretna, PA, 1981 (first season, 1982), which continues in operation. PERSONAL MANAGEMENT: Richard Rosenwald Associates, founded 1981.

SIDELIGHTS: MEMBERSHIPS—National Academy of Television Arts and Sciences.

''While I don't consider myself particularly prominent at this time in the business, I do believe that what I have done in the three short years that I have had my office would seem to be

sufficient . . . to take notice . . .I fully expect to be heavily involved in production within the next three years.''

ADDRESS: Office: 250 W. 58th Street, Suite 1432, New York, NY 10107.

* * *

ROSS, Justin (ne Ira Ross Cohen), actor, dancer, choreographer, writer

PERSONAL: Born December 15, 1954, in Brooklyn, NY; son of Manny (an auctioneer) and Beatrice Shirley (a dance teacher; maiden name, Kravitz) Cohen; EDUCATION: High School of the Performing Arts, 1968–72 (ballet major).

CAREER: DEBUT—Corps de Ballet, Houston Ballet Company, TX, 1972. NEW YORK DEBUT—Spooky (tap dancing Vietnam War casualty), *More Than You Deserve,* New York Shakespeare Festival, 1973. PRINCIPAL ENGAGEMENTS—Neuron, *Brainchild,* Forrest, Philadelphia, 1974; Steve (Doug Henning's assistant), *The Magic Show,* Cort, NY, 1974; Lewis, *Pippin,* Imperial, NY, 1974; Greg, *A Chorus Line,* Shubert, NY, 1976; multiple roles, *On the Road to Babylon,* Milwaukee Rep, WI, 1978; Dr. Frank N'futer, *The Rocky Horror Show,* Westbury Music Fair, NY, 1978; Pete, the King of Disco, *Got Tu Go Disco,* Minskoff, NY, 1979; Roscoe, *Fourtune,* Actors Playhouse, NY, 1980; Dickon, *Feathertop,* American Stage Festival, NH, 1981; principal,

JUSTIN ROSS

Encore, Radio City Music Hall, NY, 1982; Justin, *Weekend,* Theatre-at-the-Church, St. Peters, NY, 1983. CHOREOGRAPHED: (with Baayork Lee) *Lissette,* night club act, 1983; *EBN-OZN,* MTV Video, 1983; *Lovesong,* Studio Arena, Buffalo/Indiana Rep, 1983.

FILM DEBUT—Dancer, *The Fan,* 1980. PRINCIPAL FILMS—Zimmer, *Wunderkind,* 1983.

WRITINGS: Night-club act (with Bill Russell), *At Your Service* (Mr. Ross's own act); comedy material.

AWARDS: Sergei Denham Award, most promising ballet student, High School of Performing Arts.

SIDELIGHTS: MEMBERSHIPS—AEA; SAG; AGVA; AGMA.

''The arts are what I understand. I have no head for numbers or facts, but I do understand color and movement, essence and feeling. I've been incredibly lucky. For many years I went from one show to the next, extremely fortunate that such roles were available.''

ADDRESS: Agent—Lionel Larner Ltd., 850 Seventh Avenue, New York, NY 10019.

* * *

RUBINSTEIN, John, actor and composer

PERSONAL: Born December 8, 1946, in Los Angeles, CA; son of Arthur (a concert pianist) and Aniela (a dancer and writer; maiden name Mlynarski) Rubinstein; married Judi West (an actress and dancer), December 15, 1971; children: Jessica Anne, Michael John. EDUCATION: Attended the University of California at Los Angeles.

CAREER: DEBUT—Tom of Warwick, *Camelot,* Circle Star, San Carlos, CA, 1965. NEW YORK DEBUT—Pippin, *Pippin,* Imperial, 1972, 820 performances. PRINCIPAL STAGE APPEARANCES—Billy, *Streamers,* Westwood Playhouse, Los Angeles, CA; Ariel, *The Tempest,* University of California at Los Angeles, CA; Marchbanks, *Candida,* Massachusetts Repertory, Boston, MA; *Picture,* Mark Taper Forum, Los Angeles, CA; James Leeds, *Children of a Lesser God,* NY, 1980; *Fools,* NY, 1981; Barney Greenwald, *The Caine Mutiny Court-Martial,* Circle in the Square, NY, 1983. MAJOR TOURS—Warren Smith, *On a Clear Day You Can See Forever,* U.S. cities, 1968.

FILM DEBUT—Confederate soldier, *Journey to Shiloh,* 1966. PRINCIPAL FILM APPEARANCES—Zachariah, *Zachariah;* Jesus, *In Search of Historic Jesus; The Trouble with Girls; Getting Straight; The Wild Pack; The Car; The Boys from Brazil; Daniel.*

TELEVISION DEBUT—*The Virginian,* 1966. PRINCIPAL TELEVISION APPEARANCES—*Ironside; Dragnet; Room 222; The Psychiatrist; The Protectors; The Young Lawyers; The Storefront Lawyers; Matt Lincoln; The Mary Tyler Moore Show; Cannon; The Mod Squad; Nichols; Hawaii Five-O; Barnaby Jones; Policewoman; Barbary Coast; The Rookies; The Streets of San Francisco; Harry O; Vega$; The Class of '65; Movin' On; Stop the Presses; The Love Boat; Wonder*

Woman; Lou Grant; Fantasy Island; The Quest; Quincy; Trapper John, M.D.; Emerald Point; (TV movies) *The Marriage Proposal; God Bless the Children; A Howling in the Woods; Something Evil; All Together Now; The Gift of the Magi; Roots: The Next Generations; Just Make Me an Offer; The French Atlantic Affair; Corey: For the People; Happily Ever After; Moviola; Skokie; The Mr. and Ms. Mysteries; Killjoy; Freedom to Speak; Someone's Killing the High Fashion Models; I Take These Men; M.A.D.D.: Mothers Against Drunk Drivers.*

WRITINGS: MUSICAL SCORES—(films) *Paddy; Jeremiah Johnson; The Candidate; Kid Blue; The Killer Inside Me;* (television) *All Together Now; Emily, Emily; Stalk the Wild Child; Champions: A Love Story; To Race the Wind; The Ordeal of Patty Hearst; Amber Waves; Johnny Belinda; Secrets of a Mother and Daughter; Choices of the Heart; The Dollmaker; Family; The Fitzpatricks; The Mackenzies of Paradise Cove; The New Land; For Heaven's Sake, The Lazarus Syndrome.*

AWARDS: Drama Desk Award Nomination, 1983: *The Caine Mutiny Court-Martial;* Antoinette Perry Award, Drama Desk Award, Los Angeles Drama Critics Award, Best Actor, 1980: *Children of a Lesser God;* Theatre World Award, 1972–73: *Pippin;* BMI Varsity Show Award, 1966: *The Short and Turbulent Reign of Roger Ginzburg;* Emmy Award Nomination, 1978: *Family.*

SIDELIGHTS: MEMBERSHIPS—AEA; SAG; AFTRA, American Federation of Musicians, Composers and Lyricists Guild of America, ASCAP, Players Club.

ADDRESS: Office—c/o Bernstein, Fox and Goldberg, Suite 1630, 1900 Avenue of the Stars, Los Angeles, CA 90067. Agent—c/o Bruce Savan, Agency for the Performing Arts, 888 Seventh Avenue, New York, NY 10019.

* * *

RUDD, Enid, playwright, actress, producer

PERSONAL: Born April 19, 1934; married Bernard Rudd (a judge); children: Matthew, Charles. EDUCATION: American Academy of Dramatic Arts.

CAREER: WRITINGS: PLAYS, PRODUCED—*Peterpat,* 46th Street Theatre, NY, toured under new title: *The Marriage Gambol,* U.S. tour; *The Ashes of Mrs. Reasoner,* Hollywood Television Theatre; *Does Anybody Here Do the Peabody?* Actors Theatre of Louisville, KY, Wonderhorse Theatre, NY, Los Angeles production; *Step Out of Line,* Showcase production; *What a Lot of Barney,* Augustana College, S.D. TELEVISION—Staff writer for *Adam's Rib, One Life to Live, The Edge of Night.*

PRINCIPAL STAGE WORK, ACTING—*Signor Chicago; Mr. Roberts,* Palm Beach Playhouse; *I Remember Mama; King John,* Equity Library Theatre; *Hamlet,* Cherry Lane Theatre.

PRINCIPAL FILM APPEARANCES—*So Young So Bad; Crowded Paradise.* PRINCIPAL TELEVISION APPEARANCES—*Kraft Television Theatre; Philco Playhouse, The Goldbergs.* THEATRE-

RELATED CAREER: Instructor of Playwriting, Upsala College, East Orange, NJ.

SIDELIGHTS: MEMBERSHIPS—AEA; SAG; AFTRA; Dramatists Guild; Screen Writers Guild.

ADDRESS: Home—13 Glenside Drive, West Orange, NJ 07052.

* * *

RUDOLPH, Louis, producer, writer

PERSONAL: Born February 14, 1942, in Los Angeles, CA; son of Richard Rudolph; married Barbara Gottfried; children: Lisa, Amanda. EDUCATION: University of California, Los Angeles, B.A., 1962.

CAREER: FIRST TELEVISION WORK—Producer: *In Concert, Credence Clearwater Revival,* and *Blood, Sweat and Tears*

Behind the Iron Curtain, 1968. PRINCIPAL TELEVISION WORK—Producer: also writer, *The Dr. Sam Shepherd Murder Case,* 1971; *A Case of Rape;* supervised development and production of *Rich Man, Poor Man; Roots; Washington: Behind Closed Doors; Hustling; The Boy in the Plastic Bubble; Young Joe, the Forgotten Kennedy;* executive producer, *Ike; The Comeback Kid; Attica; Jacqueline Bouvier Kennedy.*

RELATED CAREER—Director of Development for National General Television, 1968–71; writer/producer/director, Universal Television, 1971–74; director of Motion Pictures and Miniseries/vice-president of division, ABC Television Network, 1974–78; producer for ABC Circle Films, 1978.

SIDELIGHTS: MEMBERSHIPS—The City of Hope, Braille Institute, United Jewish Welfare Fund, United Way; Exceptional Children's Foundation.

ADDRESS: Office—c/o Columbia Pictures Television, Columbia Plaza E., No. 129, Burbank, CA 91505.

S

SABIN, David, actor

PERSONAL: Surname pronounced "SAY-bin; born April 24, 1937, in Washington, DC; son of Arthur (a salesman) and Abigail (a government clerk; maiden name, Cooper) Sabin; married Sharon, May 24, 1969 (divorced, 1981); children: Portia. EDUCATION: Catholic University of America, B.A., 1959. RELIGION: Episcopalian.

CAREER: DEBUT—Uncle Louis, *The Happy Time*, high school. NEW YORK DEBUT—Boy's father, *The Fantasticks*, Sullivan Street Playhouse, 1965, 500 performances. PRINCIPAL STAGE APPEARANCES—(Broadway) Brabantio, *Othello*; Hartog, *Dance a Little Closer*; Morton Gross, *The Water Engine*; Sir Toby Belch, *Music Is*; Pugachov, *The Suicide*; Tiger Brown, *The Threepenny Opera*; Edgar Allan Rich, *Celebration*; Alastair Waymarsh, *Ambassador*; Lord Duveen, *Jimmy Shine*; Virgil Gunch, *Gantry*; Maxie, *Slapstick Tragedy*; Captain Joyner, *The Yearling*; the senator, *Miss Moffat*; the clown, *Gabrielle*; (Off-Broadway) Endicott, *Preppies*, Promade; Berlioz, *The Master and Margarita*, New York Shakespeare Festival; Albert McKinley, *Now Is the Time*, Theater de Lys; Bohun, *You Never Can Tell*, Roundabout; Boss Mangan, *Heartbreak House*, Roundabout; Boniface, *Rogues to Riches*, Apple Corps; Storyteller, *Prairie Du Chien*, New York Shakespeare Festival; (Regional) Tevye, *Fiddler on the Roof*, Artpark; Phil, *That Championship Season*, Seattle Repertory, WA; Pozzo, *Waiting for Godot*, Cincinnati Playhouse, OH; Joe, *The Shadow Box*, Charles Playhouse, Boston, MA; Stormy, *Summer*, Philadelphia Drama Guild; Oscar Madison, *The Odd Couple*, Mummers', Oklahoma; Agazzi, *Right You Are*, Meadowbrook, MI; Igo, *An Attempt at Flying*, Yale Repertory, New Haven, CT; Mayor, *The Front Page*, Dr. Waldersee, *Idiot's Delight*, Ernest, *Design for Living*, Williamstown Theater Festival, MA; Shamraev, *The Sea Gull*, Eddie, *After the Fall*, Manitoba Theater Company.

MAJOR TOURS—Mr. Dobitch, *Promises, Promises*, U.S. cities; Beaurevers, *A Shot in the Dark*, U.S. cities.

PRINCIPAL TELEVISION APPEARANCES—Little John, *When Things Were Rotten*; Dr. Peck, *Love of Life*; *Kojak*; *The Rockford Files*; *Switch*; *The Rookies*.

SIDELIGHTS: MEMBERSHIPS—The Players Club.

"I am in incessant pursuit of one sub-par round of golf."

ADDRESS: Agent—c/o Hesseltine-Baker Associates, 165 W. 46th Street, New York, NY 10036.

SACHS, Andrew, actor

PERSONAL: Born in Berlin, Germany; son of Hans Emil (an insurance broker) and Katharina (Schrott-Fiecht) Sachs; married Melody Good (a fashion designer) 1962; children: William, John, Katie. EDUCATION: William Ellis School for six years, London, England. MILITARY: National Service, Royal Armoured Corps.

CAREER: DEBUT—Tony, *Frieda*, Delawarr Pavilion, Bexhill-on-Sea, 1947. LONDON DEBUT—Grobhchick, *Simple Spymen*, Whitehall, 1958–61, over 1200 performances. PRINCIPAL STAGE APPEARANCES—Performed in repertory at Worthing and Liverpool, 1951–53; *Voyage Round My Father*, Haymarket, London, 1971–72; *Habeas Corpus*, Lyric, London, 1973–74; *No Sex Please—We're British*, Strand, London, 1975; Andrew Aguecheek, *Twelfth Night*, Armaud, *M. Perrichon's Travels*, Chichester Festival, 1976; Arnold Crouch, *Not Now Darling*, Savoy, London, 1980. MAJOR TOURS—Morgan, *Reluctant Heroes*, U.K., 1955; Polignac, *Dry Rot*, U.K., 1956; Arnold Crouch, *Not Now Darling*, South Africa, 1969, Australia, Toronto, 1981; Augustin Jedd, *Dandy Dick*, U.K., 1981.

FILM DEBUT—Dotheby Hall Boy, *Nicholas Nickleby*, 1946. PRINCIPAL FILM APPEARANCES—*Hitler, the Last Ten Days*, 1972; *Are You Being Served?*, 1977; *History of the World, Part I*, 1980.

TELEVISION DEBUT—*Six Proud Walkers*, BBC. PRINCIPAL TELEVISION APPEARANCES—*Buddenbrooks*, 1965; Manuel, *Fawlty Towers*, 1975, and 1979; Trinculo, *The Tempest*, 1980; Mr. Polly, *The History of Mr. Polly*, 1980; Ernest, *Dead Ernest*, 1982; *Discovery of Animal Behaviour*, series, *Flight of the Condor*, series, *World About Us*, *Rainbow Safari*, BBC Natural History unit, 1981–84; subject of *This Is Your Life*, 1980; *There Comes a Time*, 1984; *Tom O'Connor* series, 1984.

WRITINGS: RADIO PLAYS—*The Revenge*, and others for BBC, 1962–84.

PLAYS PRODUCED—*Made in Heaven*, Chichester Festival, 1975; *The Stamp Collectors*, Worthing, 1977. PLAYS PUBLISHED—*Three Melodramas*, 1977.

AWARDS: Gold Record: *Fawlty Towers*, Album One, 1984; Variety Club of Great Britain Award, 1976.

ADDRESS: Agent—Richard Stone, 18 York Buildings, London WC2N, England.

ST. JOHNS, Richard R., producer and lawyer

PERSONAL: Born January 20, 1929, in Los Angeles, CA; son of Adela (a journalist; maiden name, Rogers) St. Johns; married Susan Parker; children: Kathleen, Tracey, Sean. EDUCATION: Stanford University, B.A., 1953; Stanford Law School, Doctorate of Jurisprudence, 1954.

CAREER: PRINCIPAL FILM WORK: Produced—(executive producer) *The Uncanny; Matilda,* 1978; *The Silent Flute (Circle of Iron); Nightwing,* 1979; *The Wanderers,* 1979; *The Mountain Men,* 1980; *The Final Countdown,* 1980; *A Change of Seasons,* 1980; *Dead and Buried; Death Hunt,* 1981; *American Pop,* 1981; *Venom,* 1982.

RELATED CAREERS: Entertainment lawyer, O'Melveny and Meyers, 1954; senior vice-president, Filmways Inc., 1968; president, Filmways Inc., 1969; formed Richard R. St. Johns and Associates, 1972; formed Guinness Film Group, 1975.

ADDRESS: Office—MGM, 10202 W. Washington Blvd., Culver City, CA 90230.

* * *

SALTZ, Amy, director

PERSONAL: Born August 31; daughter of Jerome (budget director, Federation of Jewish Philanthropies) and Florence (administrator, Jewish Family Services; maiden name, Zunser) Saltz. EDUCATION: University of Wisconsin, B.A.; workshops with Peter Brook, William Ball, Robert Wilson, Ellen Thompson. RELIGION: Jewish.

CAREER: PRINCIPAL STAGE WORK, DIRECTED—*Touch,* off-Broadway production, was also co-author; *Romania, That's the Old Country,* New York Shakespeare Festival; *Play on the Times,* New York Shakespeare Festival; *And Miss Reardon Drinks a Little,* American Academy of Dramatic Arts, 1978–79; *The Stronger,* Juilliard School, NY, 1978–79; *Threads,* Playmakers Repertory, NC, 1978–79; *Funeral March for a One Man Band,* St. Nicholas Theatre Company, Chicago, 1978–79; *A Voice of My Own,* Acting Company, 1978–79; *Spoon River Anthology,* Whole Theatre Company, NJ, 1979–80; *The Gin Game,* Playmakers Repertory, NC, 1979–80; *The Shadow of Heroes,* St. Nicholas Theatre Company, Chicago, 1979–80; *Dusa, Fish, Stas & Vi,* Juilliard School of Drama, NY, 1980–81; *I'm Getting My Act Together and Taking It on the Road,* Pittsburgh Public Theatre, Ford's Theatre, Washington DC, 1980–81; *Loose Ends,* Cincinnati Playhouse in the Park, 1980–81; *Chocolate Cake,* and *The Final Placement,* Actors Theatre of Louisville, 1980–81; *Fishing,* The Second Stage, NY, 1980–81; *How Women Break Bad News,* Circle Repertory, NY, 1981–82; *Propinquity* and *Star Gazing,* New York University, 1981–82; *Ghosts of the Loyal Oak,* WPA Theatre, NY, 1981–82; *Billy Bishop Goes to War,* Actors Theatre of Louisville, 1981–82; *Medea,* Cincinnati Playhouse in the Park, 1983; *Win/Lose/Draw,* Provincetown Playhouse, O'Neill Playwrights Conference, 1983. Also directed productions at the Napa Valley Theatre and with the Plowright Playhouse.

WRITINGS: PLAYS, PRODUCED—co-author, *Touch,* NY; *The*

Minstrel Show, Interart Theatre, NY, 1977; *Play On the Times,* New York Public Theatre, 1970.

THEATRE-RELATED CAREER: Assisted Gerald Freedman in productions at New York Shakespeare Festival, the San Francisco Opera, and Lincoln Center. Assisted Joseph Papp at New York Shakespeare Festival and Stuart Vaughn at the Delacorte Theatre. Spent six years with the New York Shakespeare Festival in various capacities including work on 15 Shakespearean productions. Teacher, Lincoln Center Institute, 1978–79; acting teacher, New York State Summer School for the Arts, 1976–80; teacher/co-ordinator, Acting Company National Tour program; directing seminar, Georgia Council on the Arts.

AWARDS: Joseph Jefferson Award, Best Direction, 1979: *Funeral March for a One-Man Band;* Grammy Award Nomination, Best Musical, 1971: *Touch.*

SIDELIGHTS: MEMBERSHIPS—SSD&C; Actor's Studio Playwrights & Directors Unit; League of Professional Theatre Women.

ADDRESS: Agent—c/o Jonathan Sand, Writers and Artists Agency, 162 W. 56th Street, New York, NY 10019.

* * *

SANDA, Dominique (nee Varaigne), actress

PERSONAL: Born March 11, 1951; daughter of Gerard and Lucienne (Pichon) Varaigne; children: Marquand Yann. EDUCATION: Saint Vincent de Paul, Paris. RELIGION: Catholic.

CAREER: PRINCIPAL FILM APPEARANCES—*Une Femme Douce,* 1968; *First Love,* 1969; *Il Conformista,* 1970; *Il Giardino dei Finzi-Contini,* 1970, *La Notte Dei Fiori,* 1970; *Sans Mobile Apparent,* 1971; *Impossible Object,* 1972, *Mackintosh Man,* 1972; *Steppen Wolf,* 1973; *Conversation Piece,* 1974; *Novecento,* 1975; *L'Eredita Ferramonti,* 1976; *Damnation Alley,* 1977; *Aldila dil Bene e dil Male,* 1977; *La Chanson De Roland,* 1978; *Utopia,* 1978; *Le Navire-Night,* 1979; *Cabo Blanco,* 1979; *Le Voyage en Douce,* 1979; *Les Ailes de la Colombe,* 1980; *L'Indiscretion,* 1981; *Une Chambre en Ville,* 1982; *Poussiere d'Empire,* 1983.

AWARDS: Prix d' interpretation Feminine, Cannes, 1978.

SIDELIGHTS: MEMBERSHIPS—Art Media, Paris. FAVORITE ROLES—Ada, *1900,* Anna Conformiste, *Une Femme Douce,* Nicol, *Garden of Finzi-Contini,* Catherine Croy, *The Wings of the Dove.* HOBBIES—Gardening, piano, traveling.

ADDRESS: Agent—Art Media, Ten Avenue Georges X, Paris, France 75008.

* * *

SANDRICH, Jay, director

PERSONAL: Born February 24, 1932, Los Angeles, CA; son

of Mark (a director) and Freda (Wirtschater) Sandrich; married Nina, 1953 (divorced 1976); children: Eric, Tony, Wendy. EDUCATION: UCLA, B.A., 1953. MILITARY: U.S. Army Signal Corps, 1st Lieutenant, 1953–55.

CAREER: FILM DEBUT—Director, *Seems Like Old Times,* 1980. PRINCIPAL TELEVISION WORK—Producer, *Get Smart,* 1965; director—*He & She,* 1967; *Bill Cosby Show,* 1969; director, *The Mary Tyler Moore Show,*1970–77; *Soap,* 1977–79.

AWARDS: Emmy Award, 1971, 1973: *The Mary Tyler Moore Show.*

SIDELIGHTS: MEMBERSHIPS—Directors Guild of America.

ADDRESS: Agent—Ron Meyer, Creative Artists Agency, Century City, Los Angeles, CA 90069.

* * *

SANGER, Jonathan, producer

PERSONAL: Born April 21, 1944; son of Abbe (a lawyer) and Belle (Haim) Sanger; married Carla Galperin (executive director, Los Angeles Child Care and Development Council); children: David, Christopher. EDUCATION: University of Pennsylvania, B.A., 1965; Annenberg School of Communications, M.A., 1967.

CAREER: PRINCIPAL FILM WORK: Producer—*The Elephant Man,* 1980; *Frances,* 1982.

AWARDS: British Academy Award, Best Picture, Christopher, *Scholastic* Magazine Bell Ringer, First Prize, Cesare Award, 1980: *The Elephant Man.*

SIDELIGHTS: MEMBERSHIPS—Directors Guild of America; American Film Institute; board of directors, Independent Feature Project; board of directors, Pasadena Film Forum.

ADDRESS: Office—10201 W. Pico Blvd., Suite 247, Los Angeles, CA 90035.

* * *

SANTONI, Reni, actor

CAREER: FILM DEBUT—*The Pawnbroker,* 1965. PRINCIPAL FILM APPEARANCES—*The Return of the Magnificent Seven,* 1966; *Enter Laughing,* 1967; *Anzio,* 1968; *Dirty Harry,* 1972; *I Never Promised You a Rose Garden,* 1977; *They Went That a Way and That a Way; Dead Men Don't Wear Plaid,* 1982; *Bad Boys,* 1983.

PRINCIPAL TELEVISION APPEARANCES—*Charlie's Angels; Rockford Files; Merv Griffin Show; Owen Marshall; The Psychiatrist; Indict and Convict; Panic on the 5:22; Report to Murphy; Chips.*

PRINCIPAL STAGE APPEARANCES—*The Third Ear,* NY, 1964.

ADDRESS: Agent—c/o Shiffrin Artists, Inc., 7466 Beverly Blvd., Suite 205, Los Angeles, CA 90036.

* * *

SAPHIER, Peter, producer, executive

PERSONAL: Born August 5, 1940, in Los Angeles, CA; son of James L. (an agent) and Arna F. Saphier; married Liliane Moreau (a fashion designer), October 2, 1964; children: Nathalie, Peter D. EDUCATION: Antioch College, B.A., 1963. MILITARY: U.S Army, 1963, reserves, 1964–69.

CAREER: PRINCIPAL FILM WORK: Producer—*Eddie Macon's Run,* 1983; *Scarface,* 1983.

RELATED-CAREER—Programmer, subscription television, Santa Monica, CA, 1964; Universal Studios/Universal Pictures, Los Angeles, 1964–81 (vice-president, 1972–81); president, Martin Bregman Productions, Los Angeles, 1981–83; senior vice-president in charge of motion picture activity, Taft Entertainment, Los Angeles, 1983–present.

SIDELIGHTS: MEMBERSHIPS—Academy of Motion Picture Arts and Sciences, Filmex, American Film Institute.

ADDRESS: Office—Taft Entertainment, 10960 Wilshire Blvd., Los Angeles, CA 90024.

* * *

SATO, Isao, actor

PERSONAL: Born June 27, 1949, in Tokyo, Japan; son of Toshio Hirai (a real estate salesman) and Kyoko Sato; married Shizue Kanemitsu, October 17, 1976 (divorced 1979). EDUCATION: Attended Keio University (Japan); trained for the stage at Toho Musical Academy and Shiki Theatrical Company.

CAREER: DEBUT—Soldier, *The Wizard of Oz,* Nissei Theatre, Tokyo, 1970. NEW YORK DEBUT—Kayama, *Pacific Overtures,* Winter Garden, 1976, 193 performances. PRINCIPAL STAGE APPEARANCES—Servant, *Nobunaga-ki,* Nissei, Tokyo, 1971; Lelio, *Lelio,* Tokyo Bunka Kaikan, Tokyo, 1971; Theo, *Piaf,* Nissei, Tokyo, 1971; Narrator, *Soldier's Tale,* Tokyo Bunka Kaikan, 1972; servant, *Marriage of Figaro,* Dai-ichi Seimei Hall, Tokyo, 1972; Theo, *Piaf,* Yubin-chokin Hall, 1972; Fox, *Animal Conference,* Nissei, Tokyo, 1972; 1st Player/Player Queen, *Hamlet,* Nissei, Tokyo, 1972; Balthazar, *Much Ado About Nothing,* Dai-ichi Seimei Hall, 1973; Patrick Dennis, *Mame,* Nissei, Tokyo, 1973; Theo, *Piaf,* Nissei, Tokyo, 1974; Yukichi Fukuzawa, *John Manjiro,* Nissei, Tokyo, 1974; Kayama, *Pacific Overtures,* Shubert, Boston, MA, Opera House, Washington, D.C., 1975, Winter Garden, NY, Music Center, Los Angeles, CA, Curran, San Francisco, CA, 1976; Sup-tai, *Genghis Khan,* Imperial, Eiko, *Utamaro,* Imperial, Tokyo, 1977; Aladdin, *Aladdin,* Orpheum, Vancouver, BC, Canada, Concert Hall, Winnipeg, Canada, 1978; Chan Ch'uer/Fa-lian, *Fanshen,* A Contemporary Theatre, Seattle, WA, 1979; Wenging, *Peking Man,* Horace Mann, NY, 1980; Dr. Peng/

ISAO SATO

Bailiff, *Extenuating Circumstances*, Perry Street, NY, 1981; China Joe/Mrs. Smith, *Shot Thru the Heart*, Birmingham, MI, 1983.

MAJOR TOURS—Indian/Pirate, *Peter Pan*, Northern Japanese cities, 1971; 1st Player/Lucianus, *Hamlet*, Northern Japanese cities, 1971; Theo, *Piaf*, Nagoya, Osaka, Japan, 1972; Young Man, *A Girl from the Star*, Northern Japanese cities, 1972; Watchmaker, *Intermezzo*, Northern Japanese cities, 1973; Balthazar, *Much Ado About Nothing*, Western Japanese cities, 1973; Old Man, *Twin Lotte*, Northern Japanese cities, 1974; Fisherman, *John Manjiro*, Kobe, Osaka, Japan, 1974; Aladdin, *Aladdin*, New Jersey and Iowa cities, 1978–79.

AWARDS: Antoinette Perry Award Nomination, Best Featured Actor in a Musical, 1976: *Pacific Overtures;* Shiki Theatre Award, Most Promising Actor, 1971.

SIDELIGHTS: MEMBERSHIPS—AEA; SAG; AFTRA. RECREATION—personal computing, theatre going, skiing, video-film collecting.

ADDRESS: Home—295 Park Avenue S., New York, NY 10010.

* * *

SAUNDERS, Nicholas (ne Nikita Soussanin), actor

PERSONAL: Born June 2, 1914, in Kiev, Russia; son of Nicholas (an actor) and Suzanne (Strormer) Soussanin; mar-

ried Gedda Petry (an actress), December 22, 1938; children: Lanna, Theodore. EDUCATION: Graduated from Hollywood High School; trained for the stage with Andrey Zhilinsky, Vera Solovieva, Leo and Barbara Bulgakov. RELIGION: Russian Orthodox.

CAREER: DEBUT—Father, *Lady in the Dark,* U.S. tour, 1942. NEW YORK DEBUT—Father, *Lady in the Dark*, Broadway Theatre, 1943. PRINCIPAL STAGE APPEARANCES—(Broadway) Secretary Mason, *Magnificent Yankee*, Royale, NY, 1946; Counselor Drivinitz, *Anastasia*, Lyceum, NY, 1955; Mr. Whitmyer, *Take Her She's Mine*, Biltmore, NY, 1962; *Passion of Joseph D; A Call on Kuprin; A Highland Fling; A New Life; Scenes and Revelations,* Circle in the Square; (Off-Broadway) Curtis Metcalf, *My Great Dead Sister*, Playhouse 46; Mulka, *The Investigation;* John O'Connor, *After the Rise*, Astor Place; Gregory, *Blood Moon*, Actors and Directors; (Off-Off-Broadway) General Ivoglin, *Subject to Fits*, Soho Repertory; Major Volkov, *Zeks*, Theatre for the New City; Ralph Michaelson, *Past Tense*, Harbor Repertory; Joe Keller, *All My Sons*, Veterana Ensemble; Dr. Samoylenko, *The Duel*, Manhattan Punchline; *Celimare, The Spider's Web, Unicorn in Captivity*, Impossible Ragtime Theater; Ybsgrubber, *The Raspberry Picker*, American Jewish Theatre; Uncle Dvoyetochiyr, *Summer Frolic*, 1983; (Regional/Stock) Matthew Brady, *Inherit the Wind;* H.S., *The Rainmaker*, George Street Playhouse, NJ; *Never Too Late*, Woodstock Playhouse, NY. MAJOR TOURS—Owen Wister, *The Magnificent Yankee*, U.S. cities; Fairchild, *Sabrina Fair.*

FILM DEBUT—Air Force Major, *Fail Safe*, 1964. PRINCIPAL FILM APPEARANCES—*Bananas; The Next Man; Paradise Alley; Arthur;* prison doctor, *Daniel*, 1983.

TELEVISION DEBUT—Walter Craig, *Craig's Wife*, 1947. PRINCIPAL TELEVISION APPEARANCES—Captain Barker, *Sergeant Bilko;* Sergeant Ross, *Martin Kane, Private Eye;* Judge, *The Defection of Simas Kudirka;* Governor, *Equal and Orderly Justice; As the World Turns; Edge of Night; Ryan's Hope, Jack Leary, The Doctors; Love of Life; Secret Storm.*

SIDELIGHTS: MEMBERSHIPS—Lambs Club.

ADDRESS: Home—175 W. 72nd Street, New York, NY 10023.

* * *

SAUNDERS, Sir Peter (Kt. 1982), producing manager, theatre owner

PERSONAL: Born November 23, 1911, in London, England; son of Ernest Saunders; married Ann Stewart (deceased); Catherine Baylis (nee Katie Boyle). EDUCATION: Oundle. MILITARY: British Army for six years during the war, rising through the ranks to Captain. NON-THEATRICAL CAREER: Film cameraman, film director, journalist, press agent.

CAREER: PRINCIPAL STAGE WORK—Produced alone or in association with others: *Fly Away Peter*, St. James, London, 1947; *The Perfect Woman*, Playhouse, London, 1948;

PETER SAUNDERS

Breach of Marriage, Duke of York's, London, 1949; administrator for the Dunfermline Festival, *The Saxon Saint*, 1949; *My Mother Said*, Fortune, London, 1949; *The Hollow*, Fortune, London, 1951; *The Mousetrap*, Ambassadors', London, 1952, and after 8 years at the same theatre, on August 25, 1960 achieved the "Long Run Record" (in London and New York) of 3214 performances; on December 23, 1970, became the "World's Longest Runing Play," March 25, 1974 transferred to the St. Martin's and still continues, 1984; *Witness for the Prosecution*, Winter Garden, London, 1953, NY, 1954; *The Manor of Northtstead*, Duchess, London, 1954; *Spider's Web*, Savoy, London, 1954; *The Water Gipsies*, Winter Garden, London, 1956; *The Bride and the Bachelor*, Duchess, London, 1956; *Subway in the Sky*, Savoy, London, 1957; *Verdict*, Strand, London, 1958; *The Trial of Mary Dugan*, Savoy, London, 1958; *And Suddenly It's Spring*, Duke of York's, London, 1959; *Go Back For Murder*, Duchess, London, 1960; *You Prove It*, St. Martins, London, 1961; *Fit to Print*, Duke of York's, London, 1962; *Rule of Three*, Duchess, London, 1962; *Alfie*, Duchess, London, and NY, 1963; *The Reluctant Peer*, Duchess, London, 1964; *Hostile Witness*, Haymarket, London, and NY, 1964; *Every Other Evening*, Phoenix, London, 1964; *Return Ticket*, Duchess, London, 1965; *Arsenic and Old Lace*, Vaudeville, London, 1966; *Justice Is a Woman*, Vaudeville, London, 1966; *As You Like it*, Vaudeville, London, 1967; *Oh Clarence!*, Lyric, London, 1968; *On a Foggy Day*, St. Martin's, London, 1969; *The Jockey Club Stakes*, Vaudeville, London, 1970; *Move Over Mrs.*

Markham, Vaudeville, London, 1971; *Lover*, St. Martin's, London, 1973; *Cockie*, Vaudeville, London, 1973; *Double Edge*, Vaudeville, London, 1975; in 1971, acquired Volcano Productions Ltd., whose productions include: *No Sex Please, We're British*, Strand, London, 1971; *The Mating Game*, Apollo, London, 1971; *Lloyd George Knew My Father*, Savoy, London, 1972; *Parents' Day*, Globe, 1972; *Stand and Deliver*, Roundhouse, 1972; *At the End of the Day*, Savoy, London, 1973; *Signs of the Times*, Vaudeville, London, 1973; *Birds of Paradise*, Garrick, 1973; *Touch of Spring*, Comedy, London, 1975; *Betzi*, Haymarket, London, 1975; *Out on a Limb*, Vaudeville, London, 1976; *Cause Celebre*, Her Majesty's, London, 1977; *The Family Reunion*, Vaudeville, London, 1979; *Cards on the Table*, Vaudeville, London, 1981.

MAJOR TOURS—Producer: *Wanted on Voyage, The Ex-Mrs. Y*, 1949; *The Poison Belt, Murder at the Vicarage, Flowers for the Living, Castle in the Air, Black Coffee*, 1950; *Daddy Wore Velvet Gloves, Say It with Flowers*, 1951; *To Dorothy a Son*, 1952; *Murder on Arrival*, 1959; *The More the Merrier*, 1960; *Milk and Honey*, 1961; *No Room for Sex*, 1975; *In the Red*, 1977.

PRINCIPAL RADIO WORK—Over 1500 programs for Radio Luxembourg. PRINCIPAL TELEVISION WORK—Series of plays of his own choice including, *The Manor of Northstead* on A.E. Matthews' 90th Birthday, 1959.

THEATRE-RELATED CAREER: Operated repertory at the Royal Artillery Theatre, Woolwich, 1951; also at the Prince of Wales Theatre, Cardiff, 1956; in 1958, took over a long lease of the Ambassadors'; bought the freehold of the Duchess Theatre, 1961, and sold it in 1968; acquired a long lease on the St. Martin's Theatre, 1968; bought the freehold of the Vaudeville Theatre, 1969, and of the Duke of York's, 1976, selling it in 1979 to Capital Radio on condition that it remained a live theatre in perpetuity; chairman and managing director of Peter Saunders Ltd., Peter Saunders Group Ltd., Volcano Productions Ltd., and Hampdale Ltd.; director of Dominfast Investments Ltd., West End Theatre Managers Ltd., Kroy Investments Ltd., Theatre Investment Fund Ltd., Theatre Investment Finance Ltd., and the Duke of York's Theatre Ltd.; member and director on board, consortium owners of Yorkshire Television, 1967.

WRITINGS: AUTOBIOGRAPHY—*The Mousetrap Man*, 1972. PLAYS, PRODUCED—*Scales of Justice*, 1978.

AWARDS: Varity Club of Great Britain, Silver Heart for the Theatrical Manager of the Year, 1955.

SIDELIGHTS: MEMBERSHIPS—Executive Council of the Society of West End Theatre, 1954–present (president, 1961–62 and 1967–69); Council of the Theatrical Managers Association, 1958–64; president of the Stage Golfing Society, 1963; president of the Stage Cricket Club, 1956–65; editorial board, of *Who's Who in the Theatre*, 1970–present; Board of advisors, *Contemporary Theatre, Film & Television*, 1984; vice-president, Actors' Benevolent Fund, 1972–present; vice-president, Theatres Investment Fund, 1973–present; member of the consortium awarded London General Radio Station by IBA, 1973; served on the board of the U.S. Bicentennial World Theatre Festival, 1976; board of advisors, *Night of 100 Stars II*. RECREATIONS—Cricket, bridge, the music of George Gershwin, and telephoning.

ADDRESS—Office—c/o The Vaudeville Theatre, Strand, London, WC2R 7NA England.

* * *

SAXON, John (ne Carmine Orrico), actor

PERSONAL: Born August 5, 1936; son of Antonio and Anna (Protettore) Orrico; children: Antonio. EDUCATION: Attended public schools in Brooklyn, NY; studied with Michael Chekhov and Stella Adler.

CAREER: DEBUT—Danny, *Night Must Fall,* Fort Lee Playhouse, NJ, 1959. PRINCIPAL STAGE APPEARANCES—*The Glass Menagerie,* Oakland CA, 1966; *Another Part of the Forest,* Ivanhoe, Chicago, IL, 1971; *Guys and Dolls,* Long Beach Civic Theatre, CA, 1973; *The Price,* Solari, Beverly Hills, CA, 1981.

FILM DEBUT—Leonard, *Unguarded Moment,* 1956. PRINCIPAL FILM APPEARANCES—*Reluctant Debutante,* 1958; *Crytough,* 1958; *The Unforgiven,* 1959; *Warhunt,* 1960; *Mr. Hobbs Takes a Vacation,* 1961; *The Cardinal,* 1963; *The Appaloosa,* 1965; *Joe Kidd,* 1971; *Enter the Dragon,* 1972; *Black Christmas,* 1975; *Electric Horseman,* 1979; *Battle Beyond the Stars,* 1980; *Wrong Is Right,* 1981; *Prisoner of the Lost Universe,* 1982. PRINCIPAL TELEVISION APPEARANCES—*The Bold Ones,* 1969–72; 150 guest appearances.

WRITINGS: Episodes for *Fantasy Island.*

ADDRESS: Agent—Jack Fields & Assoc., 9255 Sunset Blvd., Suite 1105, Los Angeles, CA 90069.

* * *

SAYLES, John, writer, director

PERSONAL: Born September 28, 1950, in Schnectady, NY. EDUCATION: Williams University.

CAREER: PRINCIPAL FILM WORK—Director: *The Return of the Secaucus Seven,* 1980; *Lianna,* 1982; *Baby It's You,* 1983; *Matewan,* 1984.

WRITINGS: BOOKS—(novel), *Pride of the Bimbos,* 1975; (novel), *Union Dues,* 1978; (short stories), *The Anarchist's Convention.* SCREENPLAYS—*Alligator,* 1977; *Piranha,* 1978; *The Lady in Red,* 1979; *Return of the Secaucus Seven,* 1980; *The Howling,* 1980; *Battle Beyond the Stars,* 1980; *The Challenge,* 1982; *Lianna,* 1982; *Baby It's You,* 1983.

ADDRESS: Agent—Maggie Field c/o Robinson-Weintraub & Associates, 554 S. San Vicente Blvd. Suite 3, Los Angeles, CA 90048.*

* * *

SCHAFER, Natalie, actress

PERSONAL: Born November 5, in New York, NY; daughter of Charles (a stockbroker) and Jane (Tim) Schafer; married Louis Calhern (an actor) on April 20, 1934 (divorced, 1942, died, 1956). EDUCATION: Attended Oaksmere School in Mamaroneck, NY.

CAREER: DEBUT—playing stock in Atlanta, GA, Stock Company. NEW YORK DEBUT—Eleanor, *Trigger,* Little Theatre, 1927. PRINCIPAL STAGE APPEARANCES—Ethel, *March Hares,* Little Theatre, NY, 1928; Edith Major, *These Few Ashes,* Booth, NY, 1928; Helen Bent, *The Nut Farm,* Biltmore, NY, 1929; Marjorie Kellam, *The Rhapsody,* Cort, NY, 1930; Annabelle Barrington, *The Great Barrington,* Avon, NY, 1931; Viva North, *Perfectly Scandalous,* Hudson, NY, 1931; Constance Carroll, *New York to Cherbourg,* Forrest, NY, 1932; Margaret Kenny Brown, *So Many Paths,* Ritz, NY, 1934; The Princess of the Western Regions, *Lady Precious Stream,* Booth, NY, 1936; Irene Burroughs, *Susan and God,* Plymouth, NY, 1937; Alison Du Bois, *Lady in the Dark,* Alvin, NY, 1941; Sylvia, *The Doughgirls,* Lyceum, NY, 1942; Allora Eames, *A Joy Forever,* Biltmore, NY, 1946; Mrs. Marion Gibbs, *Forward The Heart,* 48th Street Theatre, NY, 1949; Leading Lady, *Six Characters in Search of an Author,* Phoenix, NY, 1955; Beulah Moulsworth, *Romanoff and Juliet,* Plymouth, NY, 1957; Susan Ashe, *The Highest Tree,* Longacre, NY, 1959; *The Front Page,* Huntington-Hartford, Los Angeles; Lady Kitty, *The Circle,* Roundabout, NY, 1974. MAJOR TOURS—*The Killing of Sister George,* six-month national tour, 1968.

FILM DEBUT—*Marriage Is a Private Affair,* 1944. PRINCIPAL FILM APPEARANCES—*Keep Your Powder Dry,* 1945; *Wonder Man,* 1945; *Molly and Me,* 1945; *Repeat Performance,* 1947; *Dishonored Lady,* 1947; *Secret Beyond the Door,* 1948; *The Time of Your Life,* 1948; *The Snake Pit,* 1948; *Caught,* 1949; *Callaway Went Thataway,* 1951; *Take Care of My Little Girl,* 1951; *The Law and the Lady,* 1951; *Payment on Demand,* 1951; *Anastasia,* 1956; *Oh Men! Oh Women!,* 1957; *Forty Carats,* 1973; *The Day of the Locust,* 1975.

PRINCIPAL TELEVISION APPEARANCES—*Kraft Television Theatre; Philco Television Playhouse; Lux Video Playhouse; Schlitz Playhouse of the Stars; Mr. and Mrs. North; Robert Montgomery Presents; I Love Lucy; Armstrong Circle Theatre; Ann Sothern Show; Topper; Studio One;* original cast, Mrs. Thurston Howell, *Gilligan's Island; Canterville Ghost; Mannix; The Brady Bunch; Simon & Simon; CHiPs; Trapper John, M.D.; Matt Houston; McMillan and Wife; Vegas; Three's Company; Boomer; The Love Boat.*

WRITINGS: TELEPLAY—*The Love Boat* (episode).

ADDRESS: Office—P.O. Box 5522, Beverly Hills, CA 90210. Agent—Stark Hesseltine, Hesseltine, Baker Ltd., 165 W. 46th Street, New York, NY 10036.

* * *

SCHAFFEL, Robert, producer

PERSONAL: Born March 2, 1944; son of Edward and Rita (Lewiston) Schaffel; children: Jill.

CAREER: FIRST FILM WORK—Producer, *Gordon's War,*

1973. PRINCIPAL FILM WORK—Producer, *Lookin to Get Out*, 1982; producer, *Table for Five*, 1983.

SIDELIGHTS: MEMBERSHIPS—Academy of Motion Picture Arts and Sciences.

ADDRESS: Office—c/o Tri Star Pictures, 1875 Century Park East, Los Angeles, CA 90067. Agent—Michael Ovitz, Creative Artists Agency, 1888 Century Park East, Los Angeles, CA 90067.

* * *

SCHMIDT, Marlene, producer, writer

PERSONAL: Born September 7; married Howard Avedis (film director, writer, producer). EDUCATION: University of Washington, B.A. (Communications); studied Cinema and Law at University of California at Los Angeles and University of Southern California; studied acting with Jeff Corey.

CAREER: PRINCIPAL FILM WORK—Producer, *The Stepmother*, 1972; *The Teacher*, 1974; *Scorchy*, 1976; *Texas Detour*, 1977; *The Fifth Floor*, 1978; *Separate Ways*, 1979; *Mortuary*, 1982; *Playing with Fire*, 1984. FILM-RELATED CAREER: Casting department, Columbia Pictures Television; producer, CBS-TV affiliate talk show, five years.

AWARDS: Academy Award Nomination, 1972: *The Stepmother*.

SIDELIGHTS: MEMBERSHIPS—Screen Actors Guild.

ADDRESS: Home—13521 Rand Drive, Sherman Oaks, CA 91423. Office—c/o Hickmar Productions, Burbank Studios, PB4 Room 105, Burbank, CA 91505. Agent—Mike Greenfield, Charter Management, 9000 Sunset Blvd., Los Angeles, CA 90069.

* * *

SCHMOELLER, David L., writer, director, producer

PERSONAL: Born December 8, 1947, in Louisville, KY; son of Nora Elizabeth George (a painter); children: Shailar Cobi. EDUCATION: University of Texas at Austin, B.A., M.A., 1974; trained for film work with the American Film Institute. POLITICS: Democrat.

CAREER: FILM DEBUT—Writer/director, *Tourist Trap*, 1979. PRINCIPAL FILM WORK—Writer/director, *The Seduction*, 1982. TELEVISION DEBUT—Writer, *James at 15*, 1979.

WRITINGS: SCREENPLAYS—*The Day Time Ended*, 1980; *Last Chance Romance*, 1984.

AWARDS: Student Academy Award, 1975; La Toque Film Festival Award (France), Best Dramatic Film.

ADDRESS: Office—Schmoeller Corporation, 2244 Stanley Hills Drive, Los Angeles, CA 90046. Agent—c/o Shapiro-

Lichtman, 1800 Avenue of the Stars, Los Angeles, CA 90067.

* * *

SCHNEIDER, Alan, director

PERSONAL: Born December 12, 1917, in Kharkov, Russia; died May 3, 1984 in London; son of Leo Victor and Rebecka (Malkin) Schneider; married Eugenie Muckle. EDUCATION: University of Wisconsin B.A.; Cornell University, M.A. and studied at Johns Hopkins University. NON-THEATRICAL CAREER: Journalist, teacher.

CAREER: FIRST STAGE WORK—Director, *Jim Dandy*, Catholic University Theatre, Washington, DC, 1941. PRINCIPAL STAGE WORK—Director: Catholic University Theatre, 1941–52; Cain Park Theatre, Cleveland Heights, OH, 1947–48; *A Long Way from Home*, Maxine Elliott's, NY, 1948; *My Heart's in the Highlands*, Dartington Hall, England, 1949; *Pullman Car Hiawatha*, Neighborhood Playhouse, NY, 1952; *Hide and Seek*, Neighborhood Playhouse, NY, 1952; *The Remarkable Mr. Pennypacker*, 1953; *All Summer Long*, 1954; *Anastasia*, 1954; *The Skin of Our Teeth* (also in the *Salute to France* program) Paris, 1955; *Tonight in Samarkand*, 1955; *Waiting for Godot*, Miami, 1956; *Little Glass Clock*, 1956; *The Trip to Bountiful*, London, 1956; *The Glass Menagerie*, (revival), 1956; *The Circus of Dr. Lao*, Chicago, 1957; *Miss Lonelyhearts*, 1957; *Endgame*, 1958; *Kataki, Summer of the Seventeenth Doll* (revival), 1959; *Krapp's Last Tape*, 1960; *Measure for Measure*, New York Shakespeare Festival, 1960; *The American Dream, Happy Days, The Caucasian Chalk Circle*, Arena Stage, Washington, DC, 1961; *Endgame, Uncle Vanya*, Arena Stage, Washington, DC, 1962; *Who's Afraid of Virginia Woolf?*, 1962; *The Pinter Plays*, 1962; *The Threepenny Opera*, Arena, Washington, DC, 1963; *The Ballad of the Sad Cafe*, 1963; *Play and the Lover* (double-bill), 1964; *Who's Afraid of Virginia Woolf?*, London, 1964; *The Glass Menagerie*, Guthrie Theatre, Minneapolis, MN, 1964; *Tiny Alice*, 1964;

Do Not Pass Go, The Zoo Story, Krapp's Last Tape, The Mutilated, The Gnadiges Fraulein, Entertaining Mr. Sloane, Herakles, Happy Days, 1965; *Malcolm, Slapstick Tragedy, The Cherry Orchard*, Tel Aviv, 1966; *A Delicate Balance*, 1966; *You Know I Can't Hear You When the Water's Running, The Birthday Party*, 1967; *I Never Sang for My Father, Box, Quotations from Chairman Mao Tse-Tung, Krapp's Last Tape, Happy Days*, 1968; *The Watering Place, The Gingham Dog, La Strada*, 1969; *Blood Red Roses, Inquest, Saved*, 1970; *Waiting for Godot*, 1971; *The Foursome*, Arena, Washington, DC, 1972; *The Sign in Sidney Brustein's Window, Moonchildren, Happy Days, Act without Words I, Not I, Krapp's Last Tape, Our Town*, Arena, Washington, DC, (toured the USSR), 1972; *The Madness of God*, Arena, Washington, DC, 1974; *A Texas Trilogy*, Arena Stage, and NY, 1975; *Footfalls/That Time*, 1978; *Loose Ends*, Circle in the Square, NY, 1979; *Rockaby*, Studio Arena, Buffalo, NY, 1980; *The Lady from Dubuque*, Booth, NY, 1980; *Ohio Impromtu, Catastrophe, What When*, Harold Clurman, NY, 1983; *Our Town*, La Jolla Playhouse, CA, 1983; *Rockaby*, Harold Clurman, NY, 1983; *Pieces of Eight*, 1984; was directing *The War at Home* for the National Theatre in London when he died.

PRINCIPAL FILM WORK—Directed NY Film with *Samuel Beckett's Film,* 1964. PRINCIPAL TELEVISION WORK—Director: *Pullman Car Hiawatha,* 1951; *Oedipus the King; The Life of Samuel Johnson; Waiting for Godot; The Years Between.*

THEATRE-RELATED CAREER—Director of Drama Division, Juilliard School, 1976–79; professor of Drama, University of California, San Diego, 1979–82; University of Wisconsin, lecturer, ''Perspectives on Directing,'' 1983.

WRITINGS: MEMOIRS—*Entrances,* 1983. CRITICISM—*The New Leader;* contributor to *Saturday Review, Theatre Arts, The New York Times.*

AWARDS: Honorary Doctor of Fine Arts, Williams College, 1983; Obie 1962–63: *The Pinter Plays;* Antoinette Perry Award, 1962–63: *Who's Afraid of Virginia Woolf?.*

SIDELIGHTS: MEMBERSHIPS—President, Theatre Communications Group, 1982; Quinn Martin Professor of Drama, University of California, San Diego; executive vice president, SSD&C, 1976.*

* * *

SCHOENBAUM, Donald, managing director

PERSONAL: Born January 3, 1926, in Yonkers, NY; son of Irving (a banker) and Beatrice (Rubin) Schoenbaum; married Geraldine Cain, 1947 (divorced 1982); married Patricia Nygaard (a controller), 1983; children: Mark, Andrew, Robert (first marriage). EDUCATION: Attended New York University and University of Southern California; trained for the stage with William DeMille. MILITARY: U.S. Army, 1944–46.

CAREER: DEBUT—Petruchio, *The Taming of the Shrew,* University of Southern California, 1946. PRINCIPAL STAGE APPEARANCES—Stanley, *A Streetcar Named Desire,* Mr. Roberts, *Mr. Roberts,* Sakini, *The Teahouse of the August Moon,* Haemon, *Antigone,* Archy, *Archy and Mehitabel,* Jack Jordan, *Say Darling,* various theatres, 1948–60. PRODUCTION ACTIVITY—Producer/director, Repertory Players, Omaha, NB, 1960–64; managing director, Trinity Square Repertory, Providence, RI, 1964–65; executive vice president and managing director, Guthrie, Minneapolis, MN, 1965–present.

AWARDS: GRANTS—Ford Foundation, 1963, 1965.

SIDELIGHTS: MEMBERSHIPS—AEA; Office of Advanced Drama Research (executive committee, 1966–present); League of Resident Theatres (executive committee, secretary, president, 1977–81); Theatre Communications Group (director), National Endowment for the Arts (chairman, Theater Policy Panel); American Arts Alliance (founder, Executive Committee).

ADDRESS: Office—Guthrie Theater, 725 Vineland Place, Minneapolis, MN 55403.

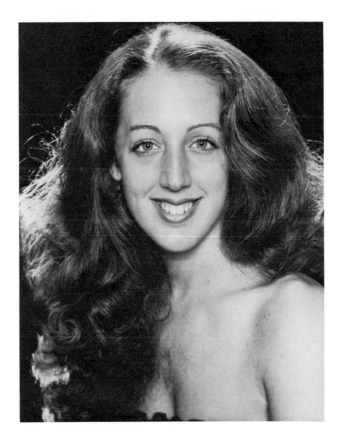

BARBARA SCHOTTENFELD

SCHOTTENFELD, Barbara, actress, playwright, composer, lyricist

PERSONAL: Surname sounds like Sha-tin-feld; born January 5, in Newark, NJ; daughter of Milton (owner of retail floor covering firm) and Mina (Dorndeld) Schottenfeld. EDUCATION: Princeton University, B.A. (English Literature) and certificate in Theatre.

WRITINGS: PLAYS, PRODUCED—*I Can't Keep Running in Place,* wrote book, music, lyrics and vocal arrangements and orchestrations, original title, *A Woman Suspended,* 1978, Princeton University, La Mama ETC, 1980, Westside Arts Theatre, 1981, St. Louis, MO, Westport Playhouse, West Palm Beach, FL, Actor's Workshop and Repertory Company, NJ, Foothills Players, Bergen Players, Chicago, Los Angeles etc; *Hello . . . I'm Not in Right Now,* reading, Ensemble Studio Theatre, produced, Off-Center Theatre, 1982 with author performing lead role, White Barn Theatre, 1983; *Camptown,* reading at Ensemble Studio Theatre. PLAYS, PUBLISHED—*I Can't Keep Running in Place,* 1982; also wrote songs for *One More Song, One More Dance,* Joyce Theatre, NY, 1983.

AWARDS: National Endowment for the Arts, Opera-Musical Producer Grant, 1984; Playwright-in-Residence Grant, National Endowment for the Arts, 1980; University Scholar, Princeton University.

THEATRE-RELATED CAREER: Artistic Director, Musical Theatre Workshop, Ensemble Studio Theatre.

SIDELIGHTS: MEMBERSHIPS—Playwright member, Ensemble Studio Theatre; ASCAP; Dramatists Guild; Authors League.

"When I write, I aspire to move an audience and entertain them at the same time. When I see great theatre, I feel intensely about the characters and come away with a feeling of elation."

ADDRESS: Agent—Don Buchwald, Don Buchwald and Associates, Ten E. 44th Street, New York, NY 10036.

* * *

SCORSESE, Martin, writer, director

PERSONAL: Born November 17, 1942, Flushing, NY; son of Charles and Catherine (Cappa) Scorsese; married Laraine Marie Brennan, May 15, 1965; (divorced); Julia Cameron (divorced); Isabella Rosellini, September 29, 1979; children: (first marriage) Catherine Terese; (second marriage) Dominica Elizabeth. EDUCATION: New York University, B.S. (Film Communications), 1964, M.A., 1966.

CAREER: PRINCIPAL FILM WORK—Director/screenwriter: *What's a Nice Girl Like You Doing in a Place Like This?*, 1963, *It's Not Just You, Murray,* 1964, *Who's That Knocking at My Door,* 1968, *The Big Shave,* 1967–68; supervising editor, assistant director, *Woodstock,* 1970; associate producer, post production supervisor, *Medicine Ball Caravan,* 1971; director/screenwriter: *Box Car Bertha,* 1972, *Mean Streets,* 1973; director: *Alice Doesn't Live Here Anymore,* 1974, *Taxi Driver,* 1976, *New York, New York,* 1977, *Raging Bull,* 1980; film appearances: *Taxi Driver,* 1976; *Cannonball,* 1976, director, *The Last Waltz,* 1978, *The King of Comedy,* 1983.

AWARDS: Brown University Film Festival, 1965; first Prize, Screen Producers Guild, 1965; first Prize, Rosenthal Foundation awards Society of Cinemetologists, 1964; Edward L. Kingsley Foundation award, 1963–64.

ADDRESS: Agent—Harry Ufland, Ufland Agency, Inc., 190 N. Canon Drive, Suite 202, Beverly Hills, CA 90210.*

* * *

SCOTT, George C(ampbell), actor, director

PERSONAL: Born October 18, 1927, in Wise, VA; married Colleen Dewhurst (divorced); married Colleen Dewhurst (second time; divorced); married Trish Van Devere, 1972. EDUCATION: Attended University of Missouri. MILITARY: U.S. Marine Corps, 1945–49.

CAREER: FILM DEBUT—*The Hanging Tree,* 1959. PRINCIPAL FILM APPEARANCES—*Anatomy of a Murder,* 1959; *The Hustler,* 1961; *The List of Adrian Messenger,* 1963; *Dr. Strangelove,* 1964; *The Bible,* 1966; *Flim-Flam Man,* 1967; *Patton,* 1970; *Jane Eyre,* 1971; *The Hospital,* 1971; *The Last Run,* 1971; *They Might Be Giants,* 1971; *The New Centurions,* 1972; *Rage* (also directed), 1972; *The Day of the*

Dolphin, 1973; *Oklahoma Crude,* 1973; *The Savage Is Loose* (also produced and directed), 1974; *The Hindenburg,* 1975; *Beauty and the Beast,* 1976; *Islands in the Stream,* 1977; *Crossed Swords,* 1978; *Movie, Movie,* 1978; *Hardcore,* 1979; *The Changeling,* 1980; *The Formula,* 1980; *Taps,* 1981.

NEW YORK DEBUT—Richard, *Richard III,* Heckscher, New York Shakespeare Festival, 1957. LONDON DEBUT—Vershinin, *The Three Sisters,* Aldwych, 1965.

PRINCIPAL STAGE APPEARANCES—Jacques, *As You Like It,* New York Shakespeare Festival, 1958; Lord Wainwright, *Children of Darkness,* Circle in the Square, NY, 1958; Tydings Glenn, *Comes a Day,* Ambassador, NY, 1958; Antony, *Antony and Cleopatra,* Heckscher, NY, 1959; Lt. Col. N. P. Chipman, *The Andersonville Trial,* Henry Miller's, NY, 1959; Shylock, *The Merchant of Venice,* Salt Lake City, UT, 1960; Dolek Berson, *The Wall,* Billy Rose, NY, 1960; Seeger, *General Seeger,* Lyceum, NY, 1962; Shylock, *The Merchant of Venice,* NY Shakespeare Festival, 1962; Ephraim Cabot, *Desire Under the Elms,* Circle in the Square, NY, 1963; Benjamin Hubbard, *The Little Foxes,* Vivian Beaumont, NY, 1967; Sam Nash/Jesse Kiplinger/Roy Hubley, *Plaza Suite,* Plymouth, NY, 1968; Michael Astrov, *Uncle Vanya,* Circle in the Square, NY, 1973; Willy Loman, *Death of a Salesman,* Circle in the Square, NY, 1975; Foxwell J. Sly, *Sly Fox,* Broadhurst, NY, 1976; *Present Laughter,* Circle in the Square, NY.

PRINCIPAL TELEVISION APPEARANCES—*East Side/West Side,* 1964–65; *Kraft Mystery Theater; Omnibus; Playhouse 90; Play of the Week; Hallmark Hall of Fame; The Price; Fear on Trial; Dupont Show of the Month; Armstrong Theatre; NBC Sunday Showcase; Dow Hour of Great Mysteries; The Crucible.*

DIRECTED: Plays—*General Seeger,* Lyceum, NY, 1962; *Death of a Salesman,* Walnut Street, Philadelphia, PA, 1974; *All God's Chillun Got Wings,* Circle in the Square, NY, 1975; *Death of a Salesman,* Circle in the Square, NY, 1975, *Present Laughter,* Circle in the Square, NY; *Design for Living,* Circle in the Square, NY, 1984. Television Plays—*The Andersonville Trial.*

AWARDS: Genie Award (Canada), 1980; Emmy Award, 1971: *The Price;* Academy Award (refused), 1971: *Patton;* Golden Globe, 1970; Obie Award, 1963, 1958; Theatre World Award, 1958; Vernon Rice Award, 1958.

SIDELIGHTS: MEMBERSHIPS—AEA, SAG, AFTRA, Directors Guild of America, Society of Stage Directors and Choreographers.

ADDRESS: Agent—c/o Jane Deacy Agency, Inc., 300 E. Seventh Street, New York, NY 10021.*

* * *

SCOTT, John, playwright, director

PERSONAL: Born July 20, 1937; son of George John and Beauta Blanch (Capito) Scott; married Sharon A. on September 26, 1981; children: Jon-Jama, Jasmin. EDUCATION:

JOHN SCOTT

South Carolina State College, B.A. 1961; Bowling Green State University, OH, M.A. 1966, Ph.D., 1972. MILITARY: U.S. Army, 1961–64.

WRITINGS: PLAYS—*After Work,* produced at Joe E. Brown Theatre, Bowling Green State University, OH, 1966; *Ride a Black Horse,* produced at the St. Mark's Playhouse, NY, 1971; *Karma,* produced by the Negro Ensemble Company in New York; *The Good Ship Credit,* produced at the Negro Ensemble Company, NY; other plays—*The Zaire Mark, Time Turns Black, I Talk with the Spirits, The Alligator Man, Black Sermon Rock, Shades, Reflections: An Anthology.* TELEPLAYS—*Ovet and Tevo, Pieces of a Man.*

AWARDS: Best Musical, Audelco Award Nomination, 1979: *Karma,* Off-Broadway.

THEATRE—RELATED CAREER: Playwright-in-Residence and artistic director of Ethnic Cultural Arts Program, Bowling Green State University in Ohio.

SIDELIGHTS: Mr. Scott has directed plays and given lectures and workshops at universities and regional theatre in the United States and abroad.

ADDRESS: Home—2589 W. Village Drive, Toledo, OH 43614. Office—Theatre Department, Bowling Green State University, Bowling Green, OH 43403. Agent—Ms. Vicki McLaughlin-Cowell, Buttonwood Road, Peekskill, NY 10566.

* * *

SCULLY, Anthony, writer

PERSONAL: Born May 28, 1942, in Hartford, CT; son of James Henry (a surgeon) and Marietta Cashen (Maguire) Scully. EDUCATION: Boston College, B.A., 1966; Yale School of Drama, M.F.A., 1969.

WRITINGS: PLAYS, PRODUCED—*The Great Chinese Revolution,* Yale Repertory, New Haven, CT, 1969; *All Through the House,* Manhattan Theatre Club, NY, 1972; *Little Black Sheep,* Vivian Beaumont, NY, 1975; *Dracula King of the Night,* Palace of Tine Arts, San Francisco, CA, 1979. RELATED CAREERS: co-director, Woodstock Center for Religion and Worship (developer for Performance Group, NY), 1970–75.

SIDELIGHTS: MEMBERSHIPS—Drama Guild; Dramatists' Guild.

ADDRESS: Office—318 W. 101st Street, #7, New York, NY 10025.

* * *

SCULLY, Joe, casting director

PERSONAL: Born March 1, 1926, in Kearny, NJ; son of Joseph B. and Helen A. (Peters) Scully; married Penelope J. Gillette (an actress and teacher); children: Samantha. EDUCATION: Goodman Theatre of the Art Institute of Chicago. RELIGION: Roman Catholic.

CAREER: PRINCIPAL FILM WORK—Casting director: *The Flim Flam Man,* 1967; *In Like Flint,* 1967; *The Secret Life of an American Wife,* 1968; *The Planet of the Apes,* 1968; *The Valley of the Dolls; Hello, Dolly!,* 1969; *Lady Sings the Blues,* 1972; *Play It as It Lays,* 1972; *Journey Through Rosebud,* 1972; *Sounder,* 1972; *Stone Killer,* 1973; *The Parralex View,* 1974; *Mixed Company,* 1974; *Where the Lilies Bloom,* 1974; *Framed,* 1975; *The Man in the Glass Booth,* 1975; *Lifeguard,* 1976; *A Man, a Woman, and a Bank,* 1979; *Middle Age Crazy,* 1980; *Death Wish II,* 1982; *Breakfast in Paris.*

PRINCIPAL TELEVISION WORK—Casting director: TV Movies—*Along Came a Spider, Doug Selby, D.A., Here We Go Again, Murder Once Removed, The Forgotten Man, Men of the Dragon, Get Cristie Love, Earth II, A Tattered Web, She Waits, Second Chance, Thief; The Morning After, The President's Plane Is Missing, The Missiles of October,* 1970–75; *Beyond Westworld, Side Show, Strangers: The Story of a Mother and Daughter, The Day the Loving Stopped, Secrets of a Mother and Daughter, Gone Are the Days,* 1978–83. Series—Casting Director: *You Are There, Rod Brown of the*

Rocket Rangers, The Web, Danger, Omnibus, 1951–56; *Julia* (pilot), *The Ghost and Mrs. Muir* (pilot), *Peyton Place, Judd for the Defense, Room 222,* 1965–70; *Bonanza, Nichols, Search, The Bill Cosby Show, Faraday & Company, The Snoop Sisters, McMillan and Wife,* 1970–75; *James at 15/16, The Paper Chase, 240 Robert, Tales of the Unexpected.*

ADDITIONAL TELEVISION AND FILM WORK—Associate producer: *The Time of Your Life, Dupont Show of the Month, Studio One, Buick Electra Playhouse, Studio One in Hollywood, Playhouse 90,* CBS-TV, 1956–60; associate producer, Four Star Television, 1960–62; producer, *Repertoire Workshop,* CBS-TV, 1962–65; casting director, Twentieth Century Fox, 1965–70; manager of talent and casting, NBC, 1975–78; casting director, Disney Pictures, 1983–present.

RELATED CAREER—Instructor, UCLA Extension of Arts, 1983–84.

WRITINGS: SCREENPLAYS—"The Little Woman," Danger, CBS, 1954; "The Young, the Talented and Hopeful," "The Powder Room," "In the Thurber Room," *Repertoire Workshop,* 1963.

AWARDS: National Association for Better Radio and Television, 1963–64: *Repertoire Workshop.*

SIDELIGHTS: MEMBERSHIPS—Academy of Motion Picture Arts and Sciences, Casting Society of America.

ADDRESS: Office—Walt Disney Pictures, 500 S. Buena Vista, Burbank, CA 91521.

* * *

SEAMON, Edward, actor

PERSONAL: Born April 15, 1932, in San Diego, CA; son of Thomas B. (a businessman) and Ocie B. (a telephone operator; maiden name, Taylor) Seamon. EDUCATION: Attended San Diego State College; trained for the stage at Herbert Berghof Studios with Herbert Berghof. MILITARY: U.S. Navy, 1951–53.

CAREER: DEBUT—Owens, *Light up the Sky,* Hilltop Theatre, Edgartown, Martha's Vineyard, MA, 1961. NEW YORK DEBUT—Edward/Manager, *Life and Times of J. Walter Sminthons,* Public Theatre, 1971. PRINCIPAL STAGE APPEARANCES—Fitzpatrick, *The Contractor,* Chelsea Westside, NY, 1973; Will Horvath, *The Trip Back Down,* Longacre, NY, 1976; Kelly, *Feedlot,* Circle Repertory, NY, 1977; Harold, *Cabin 12,* Circle Repertory, NY, 1978; Stanley, *The Rear Column,* Manhattan Theatre Club, NY, 1978; Dodge, *Buried Child,* Theatre de Lys, Circle Repertory, NY, 1979; Bill Foster, *Devour the Snow,* Golden, NY, 1979; Taylor/Tony/Duggen, *The American Clock,* Biltmore, NY, 1979; Duke of York, *Richard II,* Jedediah, *The Great Grandson of Jedediah Kohler,* Entermedia, NY, 1982; Les, *Full Hookup,* Circle Repertory, NY, 1983;

(Regional) Stanley, *A Streetcar Named Desire,* Hilltop Playhouse, Edgartown, Martha's Vineyard, MA, 1961; Frederick, *A Far Country,* Woodstock Playhouse, NY, 1963; Willis,

Moonchildren, Charles Playhouse, Boston, MA, 1974; Sydney, *The Private Secretary,* Lakewood Theater, ME, 1975; actor, Eugene O'Neill Playwright's Conference, Waterford, CT, 1975; Old Mahon, *Playboy of the Western World,* Almady, *The Play's the Thing,* Oronte, *Misanthrope,* Andrew, *Sleuth,* State University of New York at Stony Brook, NY 1977; Dodge, *Buried Child,* Playhouse in the Park, Philadelphia, 1979; Weller Martin, *Gin Game,* Theatre by the Sea, Portsmouth, NH, 1980; Oates, *Terra Nova,* Allegheny, Pittsburgh, PA, 1981; Outlaw, *The Holdup,* Little Theatre SPAC, Saratoga, NY, 1982; Red Pewsy, *Coyote Ugly,* Yale Repertory, New Haven, CT, 1983; Dr. Jim Bayliss, *All My Sons,* Zellerback, Philadelphia, 1983; Dr. Dorn, *The Sea Gull,* Little Theatre SPAC, Saratoga, NY, 1983. MAJOR TOURS—Various roles, *To Be Young, Gifted and Black,* U.S. cities, 1972.

FILM DEBUT—Mike O'Brian, *Mystery at Fire Island,* 1981. PRINCIPAL FILM APPEARANCES—Hawkins, *Further Adventurers of Tom Sawyer and Huckleberry Finn,* 1982. TELEVISION DEBUT—Malcolm Granger, *The Guiding Light,* 1976.

SIDELIGHTS: MEMBERSHIPS—Circle Repertory Company.

ADDRESS: Agent—c/o Pat Baldwin, Baldwin Scully, Inc., 501 Fifth Avenue, New York, NY 10017.

* * *

SEARS, Joe, actor, director, playwright

PERSONAL: Born August 23, 1949 in Bartlesville, OK; son of Duel J. (a rancher) and June Lawrence (a restaurant manager; maiden name, Waddell) Sears. EDUCATION: Northeastern Oklahoma State University, Tahleguah, OK, B.E.A., Theatre and Art, 1972; studied at the New York Performing Arts Repertory Theatre with Marvin Gordon and Jay Harnick. POLITICS: Democrat. RELIGION: Christian Church.

CAREER: PRINCIPAL STAGE WORK, ACTING—Debut—Sir Toby Belch, *Twelfth Night,* Bartlesville High School, OK, 1967. PRINCIPAL STAGE APPEARANCES—Doctor, *Three Sisters;* Buffalo Bill, *Indians;* has appeared in eight Shakespearean roles. MAJOR TOURS—*Ethan Allen and the Green Mountain Boys,* New York Performing Arts Repertory Theatre, 1973.

FILM DEBUT—High School Principal, *See the Man Die,* 1974. TELEVISION DEBUT—*Eyewitness News* commercials, San Antonio, TX. PRINCIPAL TELEVISION APPEARANCES—Late night host for horror films, San Antonio, TX.

WRITINGS: PLAYS, PRODUCED—*Greater Tuna,* Circle in the Square, NY, Los Angeles, CA; *The Kansas Open.*

AWARDS: Most Outstanding Mental Health Center Specialist, National Award, 1980; Best Actor Awards, Northeastern Oklahoma State University, 1969, 1970.

THEATRE-RELATED CAREER: Preventive Mental Health Specialist in Drama and Art for the San Antonio Mental Health Units, seven years. Affiliated with the Hartford Stage Company, CT; The Alley Theatre, Houston, TX; Nexus Theatre, Atlanta, GA.

SIDELIGHTS: MEMBERSHIPS—AEA; World Vision (Health Care); Cherokee National Historical Society.

ADDRESS: Home—1202 College Street, Austin, TX. Agent—Gilbert Parker, c/o The William Morris Agency, 1350 Avenue of the Americas, New York, NY 10019.

* * *

SECREST, James, actor

PERSONAL: Surname is pronounced "Seacrest;" born November 17, in Thomasville, NC; son of Frances Savannah Koontz. EDUCATION: University of North Carolina, B.A., 1957; trained for the stage at the Herbert Berghof Studio with Uta Hagen. RELIGION: Dutch Reform. NON-THEATRICAL CAREER: Private detective, 1958–59.

CAREER: DEBUT—Slippery Sam, *The Angel of Red Canyon,* Fair Grove High School, Thomasville, NC, 1950. NEW YORK DEBUT—Clay Wingate, *John Brown's Body,* Manhattan Theatre Club, 1972. PRINCIPAL STAGE APPEARANCES—Johnny, *I Knock at the Door,* Arena Stage, Washington, DC, 1961; police captain, *Incident at Vichy,* Playhouse in the Park, Cincinnati, OH, 1973; Tom, *The Glass Menagerie,* Alliance, Atlanta, GA, 1973; Noah, *The Rainmaker,* Indiana Repertory, Indianapolis, 1974; Tesman, *Hedda Gabler,* Syracuse Stage, Syracuse, NY, 1975; Alex, *Serenading*

JAMES SECREST

Louie, Stage West, Springfield, MA, 1976; Biff, *Death of a Salesman,* Milwaukee Repertory, Milwaukee, WI, 1976; Tom, *Norman Conquests Trilogy,* Actors Theatre of Louisville, KY, 1977; Oats, *Terra Nova,* Alaska Repertory, Anchorage, Ak, 1979; Michael, *The Fourposter,* Virginia Museum, Richmond, VA, 1980; Daniel Berrigan, *Trial of the Catonsville 9,* Van Dam, NY, 1981. MAJOR TOURS—*A Whitman Portrait,* U.S. cities, 1971.

FILM DEBUT—Dr. Farrow, *Fate Is the Hunter,* 1964. TELEVISION DEBUT—*Rawhide,* 1962. PRINCIPAL TELEVISION APPEARANCES—*Dr. Kildare; Cannon; Going My Way; Gallant Men; Another World; Search for Tomorrow; The Edge of Night.*

SIDELIGHTS: AEA; SAG; AFTRA.

ADDRESS: Home—484 W. 43rd Street, #15Q, New York, NY 10036.

* * *

SEFF, Richard, actor, playwright

PERSONAL: Born September 23, 1927 in New York; son of Chester (a businessman) and Henrietta (Levy) Siff. EDUCATION: New York University, B.A., 1947; studied with Stella Adler.

CAREER: DEBUT—George Bigelow, *What a Life,* Newport Casino Theatre, Newport, RI, 1946. NEW YORK DEBUT—Prisoner 302, *Darkness at Noon,* Alvin, 1950. PRINCIPAL STAGE APPEARANCES—Jimmy Luton, *Big Fish, Little Fish,* U.R.G.E.N.T., NY, 1975; Baron de Hirsch, *Herzl,* Palace, NY, 1977; Father Doherty, *Angels Fall,* S.P.A.C. Saratoga, NY, State Theatre, Miami, FL; Cheron, *Modigliani,* Astor Place, NY, 1979–80; Shamraev, *The Seagull,* American Place, 1983. MAJOR TOURS—Prisoner 302, *Darkness at Noon,* national tour, 1952; Father Doherty, *Angels Fall,* national tour, 1982–83.

FILM DEBUT—Travis's customer, *Taxi Driver,* 1977. PRINCIPAL FILM APPEARANCES—*The One and Only,* 1979; *A Different Story,* 1979; *Being There,* 1980; *A Stranger Is Watching,* 1981; *Two Minute Warning,* 1981; *The Onion Field,* 1981.

TELEVISION DEBUT—*Kraft Television Theatre,* 1950. PRINCIPAL TELEVISION APPEARANCES—*The Rockford Files; Rage of Angels; Charlie's Angels; Adams Chronicles; Best of Families; Washington Behind Closed Doors; Lou Grant;* and major soap operas.

WRITINGS: PLAYS, PRODUCED—*The Whole Ninth Floor,* Playhouse-on-the-Mall, Paramus, NJ, 1966; *Paris Is Out,* Brooks Atkinson, NY, 1970; *Shine* (co-author book), Virginia Museum Theatre, Richmond, 1983.

AWARDS: Carbonell Award for Best Supporting Performance by an actor, *Angels Fall,* Miami State Theatre, World Festival of the Arts.

THEATRE-RELATED CAREER: Theatrical representative for writers and directors, Music Corporation of America, Hesseltine, Bookman & Seff Ltd, Creative Management Association, 1954–75.

SIDELIGHTS: MEMBERSHIPS—AFTRA; SAG; AEA; Dramatists Guild.

''I have worked in many phases of legit theatre; spent many happy years discovering, nurturing and representing talent. Since 1975, I have enjoyed the ''other'' side—acting and writing for the stage.''

ADDRESS: Agent—(Acting) Bret Adams, Ltd. 448 W. 44th Street, New York, NY 10036. (Writing) c/o William Morris Agency, 1350 Avenue of the Americas, New York, NY 10019.

* * *

SEGAL, Erich, writer, lyricist

PERSONAL: Born June 16, 1937, in Brooklyn, NY; son of Samuel Michael (a rabbi) and Cynthia (Shapiro) Segal; married Karen James (an editor) June 10, 1975; children: Francesca. EDUCATION: Harvard University, A.B., 1958, A.M., 1959, Ph.D., 1965. POLITICS: Democrat. RELIGION: Jewish. NON-THEATRICAL CAREER: Professor of Classical Literature, Yale University, 1964–present.

WRITINGS: SCREENPLAYS—*Yellow Submarine,* 1968; *The Games,* 1969; *Love Story,* 1970; *RPM*,* 1971; *Oliver's Story,* 1978; *A Change of Seasons,* 1982; *Man, Woman and*

ERICH SEGAL

Child, 1983. PLAYS—*Odyssey* (book and lyrics), 1974. NOVELS—*Love Story,* 1970, *Oliver's Story,* 1977, *Man, Woman and Child,* 1980, *The Class,* 1985.

AWARDS: Golden Globe Award, Academy Award nomination, Best Screenplay, Writers Guild nomination Best Dramatic Screenplay, 1970: *Love Story.*

SIDELIGHTS: MEMBERSHIPS—Dramatists Guild, ASCAP, WGA-West, Academy of Literary Studies, Harvard Club, Yale Club, NY.

Dr. Segal has a simultaneous full-time academic career. He appeared in *Without Apparent Motive,* 1972.

ADDRESS: Office—119 W. 57th Street, Rm. 1106, New York, NY 10019. Agent—Albert Rettig, Esq. 9454 Wilshire Blvd., Rm. 302, Beverly Hills, CA 90212.

* * *

SELLECK, Tom, actor

PERSONAL: Born January 29, in Detroit, MI. EDUCATION: University of Southern California.

CAREER: PRINCIPAL FILM APPEARANCES—*Myra Breckenridge,* 1970; *Daughters of Satan,* 1972; *Seven Minutes,* 1971; *Coma,* 1978; *High Road to China,* 1983; *Lassiter,* 1984.

PRINCIPAL TELEVISION APPEARANCES—*The Rockford Files; Bracken's World; Countdown of the Superbowl; The Sacketts; Gypsy Warriors; Boston and Kilbride; The Concrete Cowboys;* lead, *Magnum P.I.*

ADDRESS: c/o Press Information CBS Entertainment, 51 W. 52nd Street, New York, NY, 10019.*

* * *

SELLERS, Peter, actor

PERSONAL: Born September 8, 1925, in Southsea, England; died July 23, 1980; son of William and Agnes (Marks) Sellers; married Anne Howe, August 15, 1951 (divorced); Britt Ekland (divorced); Miranda Louise Quarry, August 24, 1970 (divorced); Lynne Frederick, 1977; children: (first marriage) Michael, Sarah; (second marriage) one daughter. EDUCATION: St. Aloysius College, Highgate, England. MILITARY: Royal Air Force, World War II. RELIGION: Jewish.

CAREER: PRINCIPAL STAGE APPEARANCES—at London Palladium, 1948; pantomime debut, *Mother Goose,* 1954–55; royal command variety performance, 1954; *Brouhaha,* 1958.

PRINCIPAL FILM APPEARANCES—*Let's Go Crazy,* 1950; *John and Julie,* 1955; *Orders are Orders,* 1955; *The Ladykillers,* 1955; *The Smallest Show on Earth,* 1956; *The Naked Truth,* 1957; *Tom Thumb,* 1958; *Up the Creek,* 1958; *I'm Alright Jack,* 1959; *Carleton Browne of the F.O.,* 1959; *Battle of the*

Photograph by Edouard Boubat

Sexes, 1959; *The Mouse That Roared*, 1959; *The Running, Jumping, and Standing Still Film*, 1960; *Two-Way Stretch*, 1960; *Never Let Go*, 1960; *The Millionairess*, 1960; *Mr. Topaze* (also directed), 1961; *Only Two Can Play*, 1961; *Lolita*, 1961; *The Wrong Arm of the Law*, 1962; *Waltz of the Toreadors*, 1962; *Dr. Strangelove*, 1963; *Heavens Above*, 1963; *The World of Henry Orient*, 1964; *The Pink Panther*, 1964; *A Shot in the Dark*, 1964; *Kiss Me Stupid*, 1964; *What's New Pussycat?*, 1965; *After the Fox*, 1966; *Casino Royale*, 1966; *The Wrong Box*, 1966; *The Bobo*, 1967; *Woman Times Seven*, 1967; *The Party*, 1967; *I Love You Alice B. Toklas*, 1968; *The Magic Christian*, 1969; *Hoffman*, 1969; *There's a Girl in My Soup*, 1970; *Where Does It Hurt?*, 1972; *Alice in Wonderland*, 1972; *The Blockhouse; The Optimists of Nine Elms*, 1973; *Soft Beds, Hard Battles*, 1973; *The Great McGonagall*, 1974; *The Return of the Pink Panther*, 1974; *The Pink Panther Strikes Again*, 1976; *Ghost in the Noonday Sun; The Revenge of the Pink Panther*, 1978; *Murder by Death*, 1977; *The Prisoner of Zenda*, 1979; *Being There*, 1980; *The Fiendish Plot of Dr Fu Manchu*, 1980.

PRINCIPAL TELEVISION APPEARANCES—BBC: *Gently Bentley, Idiot Weekly, A Show Called Fred, Son of Fred, The Cathode Ray Tube Show; The Muppet Show*, 1979. RADIO PERFORMANCES—BBC: *The Goon Show*, 1951–60, *Ray's a Laugh, Crazy People.*

AWARDS: Honorary Degree, Mannheim Festival, 1959–60; Silver Miqueldi statuette Bilboa, 1960; Golden Gate Award for best fiction still San Francisco, 1960; Best British Actor Award, 1959: *I'm Alright Jack.**

* * *

SELZNICK, Daniel, producer, writer

PERSONAL: Born May 18, 1936, in Los Angeles; son of David O. (a film producer) and Irene (a theatre producer; maiden name, Mayer) Selznick; married Joan Keller (a film maker). EDUCATION: Harvard University, B.A., 1958; graduate work at Brandeis; studied with Stella Adler and Lee Strasberg.

CAREER: PRINCIPAL THEATRE WORK—Stage manager, *The Highest Tree*, NY; stage manager, *The Tumbler*, NY; stage manager, *The Complaisant Lover*, NY; director, *Bouboroche*, IASTA, NY; associate director, American Tent Theatre, Spoleto, Italy, 1962.

PRINCIPAL FILM WORK—Associate producer, *Targets*, 1968; former production executive, MCA-Universal. PRINCIPAL TELEVISION WORK—Co-producer, *Night of Terror;* co-produced, *Blood Feud*, 1983.

WRITINGS: ARTICLES—"Moguls, Executives and Other Types," Sunday New York *Herald-Tribune;* "Wreck of the Brokaw Mansions," Sunday New York *Herald-Tribune;* "An Old Pro on the Go Again," *New York Times Sunday Magazine;* numerous pieces for the International *Herald-Tribune.* BOOKS—*The Coming of Christ; A Tanglewood Dream.*

SIDELIGHTS: MEMBERSHIPS—Trustee, Motion Picture Relief Fund; American Cinematheque; various panels, National Endowment for the Arts; Craft and Folk Art Museum; president, Louis B. Mayer Foundation.

Mr. Selznick is currently working on productions for Columbia Pictures, Rastar Productions, and Motown Productions.

ADDRESS: Office—9441 Wilshire Blvd., Beverly Hills, CA 90212. Attorney— Joel Behr, Silverberg, Rosen, Leon and Behr, 2029 Century Park E., Los Angeles, CA 90067.

* * *

SEYMOUR, Anne (nee Eckert), actress

PERSONAL: Born September 11, 1909, in New York, NY; daughter of William Stanley (a copper expert) and May Davenport (an actress and museum curator; maiden name, Seymour) Eckert. EDUCATION: Trained for the stage at the American Laboratory Theatre School with Richard Boleslavsky and Maria Ouspenskaya. POLITICS: Democrat. RELIGION: Episcopalian.

CAREER: DEBUT—The Jitney Players, New England tour, 1928. NEW YORK DEBUT—*Mr. Moneypenny*, 1928. PRINCIPAL STAGE APPEARANCES—(Broadway) *At the Bottom*, 1930; Maria, *A School for Scandal*, 1931; Sara, *Sunrise at Campobello*, 1958; (Regional) first woman of Corinth, *Medea*, Valley Music Theatre, CA, 1965; Gertrude, *After the Rain*, Schoenberg Hall, Los Angeles, 1965; Capulet, *Ring Round the Moon*, Ahmanson, Los Angeles, 1975; Josephine Whitaker, *Close Ties*, Coronet, Los Angeles, CA, 1982; (Stock) The Elverhoj Theatre; Falmouth Playhouse; Berkshire Playhouse; Westchester Playhouse; Millbrook Theatre; Ogonquit Theatre; Copley Theatre, Boston, MA.

FILM DEBUT—Lucy Stark, *All the King's Men*, 1949. PRINCIPAL FILM APPEARANCES— *Man on Fire*, 1957; *Gift of Love*, 1958; *Home from the Hill*, 1960; *Pollyanna*, 1960; *The Subterraneans*, 1960; *All the Fine Young Cannibals*, 1960; *Misty*, 1961; *Good Neighbor, Sam*, 1964; *Where Love Has Gone*, 1964; *Stay Away Joe*, 1968; *Triumphs of a Man Called Horse.*

PRINCIPAL TELEVISION APPEARANCES—*Studio One; Robert Montgomery Presents; Kraft Television Theatre; Lux Television Playhouse; Alcoa Presents; Climax; The Jackie Gleason Show; Mama; Steve Allen's Tonight Show; Gunsmoke; Hawaiian Eye; Rawhide; Ben Casey; My Three Sons; Eleventh Hour; Mr. Novak; Empire*, 1962; *The Tim Conway Show*, 1970; *Policewoman; Police Story; Sandburg's Lincoln; Planet of the Apes; Portrait of Grandpa Doc; Ironside; Emergency; Marcus Welby; Bewitched; Bonanza; Another World; General Hospital; One Day at a Time; The Tony Randall Show; Tough Girl; Angel on my Shoulder; Beatrice; Mr. Merlin; Gloria; Cagney and Lacey.* RADIO—*Grand Hotel; The Story of May Marlin; Lights Out; Inner Sanctum; Against the Storm; The Magnificent Montague; Studio One; Portia Faces Life; Armstrong Theatre of Today.*

SIDELIGHTS: MEMBERSHIPS—Actors' Fund (chairman, West Coast Committee Board); Motion Picture Television Fund (board); Episcopalian Actors Guild; AFTRA (national and local boards); SAG (national board); Theatre Authority. Ms. Seymour is the seventh generation of a theatrical family that begins with Jack Johnstone in Belfast, Ireland in 1740 and includes Fanny Davenport, an actress/manager, Harry Davenport (*Gone with the Wind* and *Meet Me in St. Louis*), and James Seymour, the writer of *Forty-Second Street.*

ADDRESS: Agent—c/o Writers and Artists Agency, 450 N. Roxbury Drive, Beverly Hills, CA 90210. Agent—c/o Abrams-Rubaloff, 2106 Live Oak Drive E., Los Angeles, CA 90068.

* * *

SEYMOUR, Jane, actress

PERSONAL: Born February 15, 1951, Hillingdon, Middlesex, England; daughter of John Benjamin and Mieke (Frankenberg) Seymour; married David Flynn, July 18, 1981. EDUCATION: Attended Arts Educational School, London, England.

CAREER: PRINCIPAL FILM APPEARANCES—*Oh! What a Lovely War,* 1968; *The Only Way,* 1968; *Young Winston,* 1969; *Live and Let Die,* 1971; *Sinbad and the Eye of the Tiger,* 1973; *Somewhere in Time,* 1979; *Oh Heavenly Dog,* 1979.

PRINCIPAL TELEVISION APPEARANCES—*Frankenstein, the True Story,* 1972; *Captains and the Kings,* 1976; *Seventh Avenue,* 1976; *The Awakening Land,* 1977; *The Four Feathers,* 1977; *Battlestar Galactia; The Dallas Cowboy Cheerleaders,* 1979; *Our Mutual Friend,* 1975; *Killer on Board; Las Vegas Undercover; Benny and Barney; Love's Dark Ride; East of Eden,* 1980.

PRINCIPAL STAGE APPEARANCES—*Amadeus,* Constanze, Broadhurst, NY, 1980–81.

AWARDS: Named Honorary Citizen of Illinois, 1977; Emmy nomination, 1976: *Captains and The Kings.*

SIDELIGHTS: MEMBERSHIPS—SAG, AEA, British AEA, AFTRA.

ADDRESS: Agent—William Morris Agency, 151 El Camino Drive, Beverly Hills, CA 90212.*

* * *

SHARKEY, Jack, playwright, composer, writer, director (Rick Abbot, Mike Johnson, Monk Ferris)

PERSONAL: Born May 6, 1931 in Chicago; son of John Patrick (a superintendent, city mail, Chicago, IL) and Mary Jane (a schoolteacher; maiden name, Luckey) Sharkey; married Patricia Arlene Walsh (a linguist) on July 14, 1962; children: Beth Eileen, Carole Lynn, Susan Kathleen, Michael Joseph. EDUCATION: St. Mary's College, Winona, MN, B.A. (Creative Writing), 1953. POLITICS: "no party affiliation." RELIGION: Roman Catholic. MILITARY: U.S. Army, 1955–56.

WRITINGS: PLAYS, PUBLISHED—first publishing date, 1968, all titles are subsequent—*Here Lies Jeremy Troy; Spinoff;*

Roomies; How Green Was My Brownie; Dream Lover; Take a Number, Darling; Who's on First; Once Is Enough; The Creature Creeps; Honestly, Now; M Is for the Million; Meanwhile, Back on the Couch; Saving Grace; Kiss or Make Up; The Murder Room; Rich Is Better; A Gentlemen and a Scoundrel; Double Exposure; Par for the Course; Your Flake or Mine; The Second Lady; June Groom; Play On; A Turn for the Nurse; But Why Bump Off Barnaby; Return of the Maniac; The Clone People; This Must Be the Place; Let's Murder Marsha; My Son the Astronaut; Turkey in the Straw; Dracula: The Musical; Beauty and the Beast, Really; Pushover; Turnabout; What a Spot; Woman Overboard; Operetta; The Picture of Dorian Grey; Hope for the Best; The Saloonkeeper's Daughter; Not the Count of Monte Cristo; Slow Down, Sweet Chariot; And on the Sixth Day; My Husband the Wife.

NOVELS PUBLISHED—*The Secret Martians; Ultimatum in 2050 A.D.; Murder Maestro, Please; Death for Auld Lang Syne.* SHORT STORIES AND ARTICLES PUBLISHED IN *Playboy Magazine; Dude; Gent; Alfred Hitchcock's Mystery Magazine; Fantastic; Amazing; Magazine of Fantasy and Science; Galaxy; Worlds Beyond; Rogue; Sir Kay.*

AWARDS: Key to the City of Garden Grove, CA, by mayor for work in the theatre and the honor of premiering *Honestly Now* at theatre in the city's Arts Complex.

SIDELIGHTS: MEMBERSHIPS—Dramatists Guild; Writers League of America.

"I wrote my first novel at the age of 10 in 1941 and sold my first short story at age 18 in 1949. After serving in the Army, I moved to New York City and into full-time writing, creating hundreds of short stories and seven novels sold. Once my career was established, I moved back to Chicago, got married and submitted my first play, *Here Lies Jeremy Troy* to New York producer Elliot Martin in 1965; it was optioned and produced that summer. There are now over 47 plays and musicals. . . . My musical instincts stem from childhood, when I was a piano-playing prodigy doing Chopin, Liszt, et al. with easy abandon, and slated to become a concert pianist before I was out of my teens—but I found the daily practicing a drag, and much preferred composing my own music. . . . Writing a play tailored to a particular talent is always challenging—but definitely a lot of fun."

ADDRESS: Agent—M. Abbott Van Nostrand, 25 W. 45th Street, New York, NY 10036.

* * *

SHATNER, William, actor

PERSONAL: Born March 22, 1931, in Montreal, Canada; son of Joseph and Anne Shatner; married Gloria Rand, August 12, 1956 (divorced 1969); Marcy Lafferty, October 20, 1973; children: 3 daughters. EDUCATION: McGill University, B.A., 1952.

CAREER: PRINCIPAL TELEVISION APPEARANCES—*Omnibus; Studio One; U.S. Steel Hour; Alfred Hitchcock Presents; Naked City; Alcoa Premiere; Twilight Zone; Bob Hope Chrysler Theatre; Name of the Game; Mission: Impossible;*

Testimony of Two Men; The Tenth Level; The Andersonville Trial; Star Trek, 1966–69; *Star Trek* (animated), 1973–75; *Barbary Coast,* 1975–76; *T. J. Hooker;* (movies) *The Bastard,* 1978; *Disaster on the Coastliner,* 1979; *The Baby-sitter,* 1979; *The Kidnapping of the President.*

PRINCIPAL FILM APPEARANCES—*The Brothers Karamazov,* 1958; *The Intruder; The Outrage,* 1964; *Big Bad Mama; Dead of Night; Star Trek,* 1979; *Star Trek II: The Wrath of Khan,* 1982; *Star Trek III: The Search for Spock,* 1984.

STAGE DEBUT—Tom, *Tom Sawyer,* Montreal, Canada, 1952. NEW YORK DEBUT—Usumcasame, *Tamburlaine the Great,* Winter Garden, 1956.

PRINCIPAL STAGE APPEARANCES—Montreal Playhouse, 1952–53; Canadian Repertory Theatre, Ottawa, Canada, 1952–53; Young Lord, *Measure for Measure, Lucentio, The Taming of the Shrew; Chorus, Oedipus Rex,* Stratford Shakespeare Festival, Ontario, Canada, 1954; Lucius, *Julius Caesar,* Gratiano, *The Merchant of Venice,* Chorus, *King Oedipus,* Stratford Shakespeare Festival, Ontario, Canada, 1955; Fenton, *The Merry Wives of Windsor,* Duke of Gloucester, *Henry V,* Stratford Shakespeare Festival, Ontario, Canada, 1956; Robert Lomax, *The World of Suzie Wong,* Broadhurst, NY, 1958; Paul Sevigne, *A Shot in the Dark,* Booth, NY, 1961; Tom, *Remote Asylum,* Ahmanson, Los Angeles, CA, 1971.

MAJOR TOURS—Canadian Repertory Theatre, Canadian cities; *The Tricks of the Trade,* U.S. cities, 1977.

AWARDS: Theatre World Award, 1958; Tyrone Guthrie Award, 1956.

SIDELIGHTS: MEMBERSHIPS—AEA, SAG, AFTRA. RECREATION—Riding, archery, photography, writing.

ADDRESS: Agent—c/o William Morris Agency, 151 El Camino, Beverly Hills, CA 90212.*

* * *

SHAVELSON, Melville, writer, producer, director

PERSONAL: Born April 1, 1917; son of Joseph (a store owner) and Hilda (Chanin) Shavelson; married Lucille Meyers; children: Richard, Carol-Lynn. EDUCATION: Cornell University, B.A.

CAREER: PRINCIPAL FILM WORK—Writer/producer/director: *Princess and the Pirate; Wonder Man; The Kid from Brooklyn; Sorrowful Jones; It's a Great Feeling; Daughter of Rosie O'Grady; Always Leave Them Laughing; Where There's Life; On Moonlight Bay; Room for One More; I'll Be Seeing You in My Dreams; April in Paris; Trouble Along the Way; Living It Up; The Seven Little Foys,* 1955; *Beau James,* 1957; *Houseboat,* 1958; *The Five Pennies,* 1959; *It Started in Naples,* 1960; *On the Double,* 1961; *The Pigeon That Took Rome,* 1962; *A New Kind of Love,* 1963; *Cast a Giant Shadow,* 1966; *Yours, Mine, and Ours,* 1968; *The War Between Men and Women,* 1972; *Mixed Company,* 1974.

PRINCIPAL TELEVISION WORK—Creator, *Make Room for Daddy, My World, and Welcome to It;* writer/producer/director: *The Legend of Valentino, The Great Houdinis, Ike, The Other Woman, Deception* (forthcoming).

WRITINGS: In addition to screenplays above: BOOKS—*How to Make a Jewish Movie* (non-fiction); *Lualda* (novel); *The Great Houdinis* (biography, based on screenplay); *Ike* (biography, based on screenplay); *The Eleventh Commandment* (novel). PLAYS, PRODUCED—*Jimmy* (book), NY.

AWARDS: Writers Guild of America, Laurel Award for Screenwriting; Screen Writers Guild, 1959: *The Five Pennies;* Academy Award Nominations, 1958: *Houseboat,* 1955: *The Seven Little Foys;* seven Screen Writers Guild Nominations; *Fame* Magazine Award; San Sebastian Film Festival Award; Taormini Festival Award; four *Box Office* Blue Ribbon Awards; three Southern California Motion Picture Council Awards.

SIDELIGHTS: MEMBERSHIPS—Writers Guild of America, West (past president); Screen Writers (past president); president, Writers Guild Foundation.

ADDRESS: Agent—William Morris, 151 El Camino Drive, Beverly Hills, CA 90212.

* * *

SHAWN, Wallace, playwright, actor

PERSONAL: Born November 12, 1943; son of William (editor, *New Yorker*) and Cecille (Lyon) Shawn. EDUCATION: Dalton; Putney; Harvard; Oxford. NON-THEATRICAL CAREER—Taught English in India on a Fulbright.

CAREER: DEBUT—Prologue/Fawning Servant, *The Mandrake,* Public Theatre's Other Stage, NY, 1977. PRINCIPAL STAGE APPEARANCES—The Cat, *The Master and Margerita,* Public Theater's LuEsther Hall, NY, 1978; Ilya, Theatre Manager, *Chinchilla,* Phoenix, Marymount Manhattan, NY, 1979; Julius Goldfarb, *The First Time,* 1983; *Ode to Napoleon Bonaparte,* Symphony Space, NY, 1984.

FILM DEBUT—"Sexual Beast Husband", *Manhattan,* 1979. FILM APPEARANCES—*Starting Over,* 1979; *All That Jazz,* 1979; *Simon,* 1980; *My Dinner with Andre,* 1982; *Lovesick,* 1982; *Strange Invaders,* 1983; *Crackers,* 1983; *The Deal of the Century,* 1983; Freud, *The Hotel New Hampshire,* 1984.

WRITINGS: PLAYS, PRODUCED—*Our Late Night,* Public Theatre, NY, 1975; translation of Machiavelli's *The Mandrake,* 1977; *A Thought in Three Parts,* first seen in London; *Marie and Bruce; The Hotel Play; The Music Teacher,* LaMama Annex, NY, 1983; *Ode to Napoleon Bonaparte.* SCREENPLAYS, PRODUCED—*My Dinner with Andre.* PLAYS, PUBLISHED—*Marie and Bruce, The Hotel Play, The Mandrake, My Dinner with Andre.*

AWARDS: Obie, *Our Late Night,* 1975; Academy Award Nomination, 1983: *My Dinner with Andre.*

ADDRESS: Agent—c/o Luis Sanjurjo, I.C.M., 40 W. 56th Street, New York, NY 10019.

SHEINESS, Marsha, playwright and director

PERSONAL: Born November 20, 1940, in Corpus Christi, TX; daughter of Lewis (a merchant) and Sylvia Betty (a community service volunteer; maiden name, Krasner) Sheiness. EDUCATION: Los Angeles State College, B.A.

CAREER: DEBUT—Crazy Agnes, *The Drunkard*, Knox Street Theater, Dallas, TX. MAJOR TOURS—National Repertory Theater Company, U.S. cities, 1965–66. DIRECTED: PLAYS—*Professor George*, Playwrights Horizons, NY, 1975; *The Spelling Bee*, Westbeth Theater Center, NY, 1977; *Bus Stop*, St. Clement's, NY, 1978; *Dr. Kneal*, New York Stage Works, NY, 1978; *Professor George*, New York Stage Works, 1978; *Monkey Monkey Bottle of Beer, How Many Monkeys Have We Here*, New York Stage Works, NY, 1979; *Play Golem*, Jewish Repertory, NY, 1980; *Best All 'Round*, New York Stage Works, NY, 1981; *Reception*, 18th Street Playhouse, NY, 1982.

WRITINGS: PLAYS, PRODUCED—*Pancho Pancho*, The Angels Company Theater, Los Angeles, CA, 1968, Little Room, NY, 1969; *Clair and the Chair*, Clark Center, NY, 1971, Queens Festival Theater, NY, 1975, Playwrights Horizons, NY, 1975; *Stop the Parade*, Clark Center, NY, 1973, Queens Festival, NY, 1976, Playwrights Horizons, 1976; *Dealers' Choice*, Clark Center, NY, 1973, Queens Festival, NY, 1978, Playwrights Horizons, 1978; *New York, New York "Pick-Up," "No Way,"*, Queens Festival, NY, Playwrights Horizons, 1975; *The Spelling Bee*, Eugene O'Neill Playwrights Conference, Waterford, CT, 1975; Queens Festival, NY, 1976, Playwrights Horizons, NY, 1976, Westbeth, NY, 1977; *Monkey, Monkey Bottle of Beer, How Many Monkeys Have We Here?*, New Theater, NY, 1971, Walpole Footlighters, MA, 1974, Cincinnati Playhouse in the Park, OH, 1974, NY, 1979; *Professor George*, Eugene O'Neill Playwrights Conference, Waterford, CT, 1972, University of North Carolina, Chapel Hill, NC, 1972, Drake University, Des Moines, IA, 1973, Fairleigh Dickinson University, NJ, 1975, ASTA, Washington, D.C., 1975, George Street Playhouse, NJ, 1975, Queens Festival Theater, New York, 1975, Playwrights Horizons, NY, 1975, New York Stage Works, NY, 1978; *Reception*, 18th Street Playhouse, NY, 1982; *Best All 'Round*, Perry Street Theater, NY, 1982.

PLAYS, PUBLISHED—*Professor George; Monkey, Monkey Bottle of Beer, How Many Monkeys Have We Here?; Reception*. SCREENPLAYS—*Have a Nice Weekend*, 1975. TELEVISION PLAYS—*Monkey, Monkey Bottle of Beer, How Many Monkeys Have We Here?*, 1975. BOOKS—*Two Swallows in No Time*, 1970.

AWARDS: National Endowment for the Arts Award, 1979–80; *Dramatics* Magazine Award (second place), 1974: *Professor George*; Exxon Award, 1974: *Monkey, Monkey Bottle of Beer, How Many Monkeys Have We Here?*

SIDELIGHTS: MEMBERSHIPS—Dramatists Guild; Writers Guild East, PEN; AEA; SAG.

ADDRESS: Agent—Fifi Oscard Agency, 19 W. 44th Street, New York, NY 10036.

REID SHELTON

SHELTON, Reid, actor

PERSONAL: Born October 7, 1924, in Salem, OR; son of Roy Van (a real estate broker) and Jennie (an income tax auditor; maiden name, White) Shelton; married Mari Leslie, October 31, 1959 (divorced 1964). EDUCATION: Willamette University, B.M.; University of Michigan, M.M.

CAREER: NEW YORK DEBUT—*Wish You Were Here*, Imperial. LONDON DEBUT—Theseus, *Phèdre*, American Embassy, 1966, 12 performances. PRINCIPAL STAGE APPEARANCES—(Broadway) Daddy Warbucks, *Annie; 1600 Pennsylvania Avenue; The Rothschilds; Canterbury Tales; Oh, What a Lovely War!; My Fair Lady; The Saint of Bleecker Street; Carousel;* (Off-Broadway) *The Contractor*, Chelsea Theatre Center; *The Beggar's Opera*, Chelsea Theatre Center; *Man with a Load of Mischief; Phèdre*, Greenwich Mews; *Butterfly Dream*, Greenwich Mews; *Duchess of Malfi*. MAJOR TOURS—*Annie*, U.S. cities; *The Rothschilds*, U.S. cities; *1776*, U.S. cities; *My Fair Lady*, U.S. cities, USSR; *Phèdre*, British cities.

PRINCIPAL TELEVISION APPEARANCES—*Too Good to Be True; Tales of the Gold Monkey; Remington Steele; Cheers; Knight Rider; The Annie Christmas Special; The Tony Awards Special; Merv Griffin Show; Mike Douglas Show; Lottery; Three's Company; Webster*.

AWARDS: Antoinette Perry Award Nomination, Best Actor in a Musical: *Annie*.

SIDELIGHTS: MEMBERSHIPS—Player's Club.

ADDRESS: Agent—c/o Gage Group, 9229 Sunset Blvd., Suite 306, Los Angeles, CA 90069.

* * *

SHELTON, Sloane, actress

PERSONAL: Born March 17, 1934 in Hahira, GA; daughter of Clarence Duffie (an insurance salesman) and Ruth Evangeline (Davis) Shelton. EDUCATION: Attended Berea College, KY, and the Royal Academy of Dramatic Art, London, England for two years, 1957–59. POLITICS: Democrat.

CAREER: DEBUT—*The Curtain Rises*, Flat Rock Playhouse, Flat Rock, NC, 1952. NEW YORK DEBUT—Miss Metcalf, *Dark of the Moon*, Equity Library Theatre, 1960. PRINCIPAL STAGE APPEARANCES—Christian, *Androcles and the Lion*, Phoenix, NY; *The Basic Training of Pavlo Hummel*, Public Theatre, NY; *I Never Sang for My Father*, Longacre, NY; *Sticks and Bones*, Golden, NY; *The Runner Stumbles*, Little Theatre, NY; *Shadow Box*, Morosco, NY; *Passione*, Morosco, NY.

MAJOR TOURS—Cassandra, *The Trojan Women*, Madame Josephine, *Madwoman of Chaillot*, National Repertory Theatre, 1965–67; *Exit the King*, APA tour.

PRINCIPAL FILM APPEARANCES—*All the President's Men*, 1976; *All That Jazz*, 1979. PRINCIPAL TELEVISION APPEARANCES—*F.D.R.: The Last Year; Concealed Enemies; Summer Switch, Afternoon Special*.

WRITINGS: Documentary film, *Millay at Steepletop*, 1976.

AWARDS: Honors Graduate at the Royal Academy of Dramatic Art in London, England.

SIDELIGHTS: MEMBERSHIPS—Served for three years on the Theatre Advisory Panel of the New York State Council on the Arts; Actors Fund of America; AEA; SAG; O'Neill Foundation, Waterford, CT.

Miss Shelton has begun her directing career with a production of *Kudzu* at Playwrights Horizons in New York and is a member of the Directors Lab at the Circle Repertory Company.

ADDRESS: Home—49 Grove Street, New York, NY 10014. Agent—The Spylios Agency, 250 W. 57th Street, New York, NY 10107.

* * *

SHEPARD, Sam (ne Samuel Shepard Rogers), actor, playwright

PERSONAL: Born November 5, 1942, in Ft. Sheridan, IL; son of Samuel Shepard and Jane Ekaine (Schook) Rogers; married O-Lan Johnson Dark, November 9, 1969; children: Jesse Mojo. EDUCATION: Attended Mt. San Antonio Junior College.

CAREER: PRINCIPAL FILM APPEARANCES—*Days of Heaven*, 1978; *Resurrection*, 1980; *Raggedy Man*, 1981; *Frances*, 1982; *The Right Stuff*, 1983.

WRITINGS: PLAYS—*Cowboys, Rock Garden, Up to Thursday, Dog, Rocking Chair*, 1964; *Chicago, Icarus's Mother, 4-H Club*, 1965; *Fouteen Hundred Thousand, Red Cross, La Turista*, 1966; *Forensic and the Navigators, Melodrama Play*, 1967; *Shaved Splits*, 1968; *True West, Operation Sidewinder, The Unseen Hand*, 1970; *Mad Dog Blues, Cowboy Mouth* (with Patti Smith), *Back Bog Beast Bait, The Holy Ghostly*, 1971; *The Tooth of Crime*, Open Space, London, 1972; *Blue Bitch, Nightwalk* (with Jean-Claude Van Itallie and Megan Terry), 1973; *Little Ocean, Geography of a Horse Dreamer, Action*, 1974; *Killer's Head*, 1975; *Angel City, Curse of the Starving Class, Suicide in B Flat*, 1976; *Seduced, Buried Child*, 1978; *Tongues/Savage Love*, 1979. SCREENPLAYS—*Zabriski Point*, 1969; *Me and My Brother*.

AWARDS: Pulitzer Prize, Obie Award, 1979: *Buried Child;* Obie Award, 1977: *Curse of the Starving Class, Action, La Turista;* Obie Award, 1973: *The Tooth of Crime;* Obie Award, 1968: *True West;* Obie Award, 1966: *Icarus' Mother;* National Society of Arts and Letters Award, 1974. Fellowships—Rockefeller, Guggenheim.

ADDRESS: Office—c/o Magic Theatre Building D, Fort Mason Center, San Francisco, CA 94123. Agent—c/o Toby Cole, 234 W. 44th Street, New York, NY 10036.*

* * *

SHEROHMAN, Tom, actor, director, producer

PERSONAL: Born April 12, 1945, in Minneapolis, MN; son of Thomas C. (a factory worker) and Patricia F. (a cook; maiden name, Andrews) Sherohman. EDUCATION: Attended University of Minnesota, Minneapolis, 1964–67.

CAREER: PRINCIPAL STAGE WORK—Actor, *Son of Miss America*, Brave New Workshop, Minneapolis, 1967; artistic director, Sweetness and Light, Omaha, NE, 1970–71; artistic director, Dudley Riggs Etc., Minneapolis, 1973–75; writer/director, *The Limbo Lounge*, Olios, Los Angeles, 1984.

PRINCIPAL STAGE WORK—Screenwriter/actor, *Modern Problems*, 1981; screenwriter, *New Magic*, 1984. PRINCIPAL TELEVISION WORK—Player/sketchwriter, *The Redd Foxx Show*.

WRITINGS: SCREENPLAYS—*Modern Problems* (with Arthur Sellers and Ken Shapiro), 1981; *New Magic*, 1984. PLAYS—*The Limbo Lounge*.

SIDELIGHTS: MEMBERSHIPS—Writers Guild West, AFTRA, SAG, AEA.

ADDRESS: Agent—Leading Artists Inc., 445 N. Bedford Drive, Beverly Hills, CA 90210.

MADELEINE SHERWOOD

SHERWOOD, Madeleine (nee Thornton), actress and director

PERSONAL: Born November 13, 1922, in Montreal, Canada; daughter of Laurence H. and Yvonne M. (Villard) Thornton; married Robert Sherwood (divorced); children: Chloe. EDUCATION: Attended Yale Drama School; trained for the stage at the Montreal Repertory Theatre and the Actors Studio.

CAREER: THEATER DEBUT—Bessie Walty, *Corn Is Green,* Montreal Repertory, Canada. NEW YORK DEBUT—Abigail, *The Crucible,* Martin Beck, 1953. PRINCIPAL STAGE APPEARANCES—Mae, *Cat on a Hot Tin Roof,* Morosco, NY, 1955; Miss Lucy, *Sweet Bird of Youth,* Martin Beck, NY, 1959; Lily Brown, *Invitation to a March,* Music Box, NY, 1960; Ida, *The Garden of Sweets,* ANTA, NY, 1961; Morgan la Fay, *Camelot,* Majestic, NY, 1961; Lula Roca, *Hey, You, Light Man!,* Mayfair, NY, 1962; *Brecht on Brecht,* Theatre de Lys, NY, 1962; Maxine Faulk, *Night of the Iguana,* Royale, NY, 1962; Betty Dullfeet, *Arturo Ui,* Lunt-Fontanne, NY, 1963; Mrs. McIlhenny, *Do I Hear a Waltz?,* 46th Street Theater, NY, 1965; Mrs. Garnsey, *Inadmissible Evidence,* Belasco, NY, 1965; The Daughter, *All Over,* Martin Beck, NY, 1971; Teresa, *Friends,* Nita Moon, *Relations,* Provincetown Playhouse, NY, 1971; *Older People,* Anspacher, NY, 1972; Epic, *O Glorious Tinntinnabulation,* Actors Studio, NY, 1974; Mother, *Getting Out,* Marymount, Theatre de Lys, NY, 1978; *The Suicide,* (Broadway); (Off-Broadway) *Alfred Dies; Hamlet; Medea; The Secret Thighs of New England Women; The Music Keeper; Rain, Paradise Lost,* Mirror Theatre Repertory, NY, 1983.

DIRECTED: Plays—*A Taste of Honey, Noisy in the Nursery, Sundown Beach,* Actors Studio, NY; *Suddenly, Last Summer,* Cubiculo, NY; *Zoo Story, Class Reunion,* Ensemble Studio, NY; (Regional) *Artichoke; Glass Menagerie.*

FILM DEBUT—*Baby Doll,* 1956. PRINCIPAL FILM APPEARANCES—*Cat on a Hot Tin Roof,* 1958; *Sweet Bird of Youth,* 1962; *Parrish,* 1961; *Hurry Sundown,* 1967; *Pendulum,* 1969; *Until She Talks; Mr. Preble Gets Rid of His Wife; The Changeling,* 1980; *Resurrection,* 1980; *Teachers; Wicked, Wicked; The 91st Day.*

TELEVISION DEBUT—*Westinghouse Summer Theatre,* 1952. PRINCIPAL TELEVISION APPEARANCES—Mother Superior, *The Flying Nun,* 1966–70; *Studio I; Playhouse 90; The Defenders; Rich Man, Poor Man; Bonanza; The Waltons; The Electric Grandmother; Winslow House; One Life to Live; Guiding Light.*

RELATED CAREERS: Teacher—Circle in the Square Theatre School, NY; New York University; Madeleine Thornton-Sherwood Theatre Workshop.

AWARDS: Obie Award, 1962: *Hey, You, Light Man!*

SIDELIGHTS: MEMBERSHIPS—AEA, AFTRA, SAG, Actors Studio, Ensemble Studio Theatre, American Film Institute, Eugene O'Neill Theater Center, Esalen Institute, The Fortune Society.

ADDRESS: Agent—c/o Susan Smith, 850 Seventh Avenue, New York, NY 10019.

*   *   *

SHIRE, Talia (Rose), actress

PERSONAL: Born April 25, 1946, Jamaica, NY; daughter of Carmine (an arranger and composer) and Italia (Pennino) Coppola; married David Lee Shire, March 29, 1970 (divorced); Jack Schwartzman, August 23, 1980. children: (first marriage), Matthew, (second marriage), Jason. EDUCATION: attended Yale University School of Drama, 2 years.

CAREER: PRINCIPAL FILM APPEARANCES—*The Dunwich Horror,* 1971; *Gas-s-s; The Christian Licorice Store,* 1971; *The Godfather,* 1972; *The Outside Man,* 1973; *The Godfather Part II,* 1974; *Rocky,* 1976; *Old Boyfriends,* 1977; *Rocky II,* 1979; *Windows,* 1980; *Rocky III,* 1982.

PRINCIPAL TELEVISION APPEARANCES—*Rich Man, Poor Man,* 1976; *Kill Me If You Can,* 1977.

AWARDS: Academy Award Nomination, Best Actress, 1976: *Rocky;* Best Actress, New York Film Critics, 1976: *Rocky;* Academy Award Nomination, Best Supporting Actress, 1974: *The Godfather Part II.*

ADDRESS: Agent—Creative Artists Agency, 1888 Century Park E., Los Angeles, CA 90067.

RICHARD SHULL

SHULL, Richard B., actor, production stage manager

PERSONAL: Born February 24, 1929 in Evanston, IL; son of U. Homer (a manufacturing executive) and Zana Marie (a court stenographer; maiden name, Brown) Shull; married Marilyn Swartz, July 6, 1969 (divorced 1984). EDUCATION: State University of Iowa, B.A. (Drama), 1950. POLITICS: Populist. RELIGION: Pantheist. MILITARY: U.S. Army, 1950–53.

CAREER: NEW YORK DEBUT—Maxie, *Minnie's Boys*, Imperial, 110 performances, 1970. PRINCIPAL STAGE APPEARANCES—Broadway productions of *Goodtime Charley*, 1974, *Fools*, 1981, *Oh, Brother*, 1981; Stephano, *The Tempest*, Mark Taper Forum, Los Angeles, 1979; Frimbo, *Frimbo*, NY, 1980; Ephraim Cabot, *Desire Under the Elms*, NY, 1982; (Stock)—*The Petrified Forest, The Contrast, Luv, Ring 'Round the Moon, High Tor, The Odd Couple*.

PRINCIPAL STAGE WORK, PRODUCTION STAGE MANAGER—*Black-Eyed Susan*, Playhouse, NY, 1954; *Red Roses for Me*, Booth, NY, 1955; *Wake Up Darling*, Barrymore, NY, 1956; *I Knock at the Door*, Belasco, NY, 1957; *Pictures in the Hallway*, Playhouse, NY, 1958; (Off-Broadway) *Coriolanus*, Phoenix, NY, 1953; *Purple Dust*, Cherry Lane, 1957; *Journey to the Day*, Theatre de Lys, 1963; *Mr. Ferris and the Model*, Warner Playhouse, Hollywood, CA, 1967; (Others)—*Night of Stars*, Madison Square Garden, 1960; (Film) *Tears Are for Tomorrow*; English Panto, *Dame Wiggins Dilemna*; worked at Fred Miller Theatre, Hyde Park Playhouse, Lake Luzerne Playhouse, Hilltop Theatre, Music Circle Theatre, Shady Lane Playhouse.

FILM DEBUT—Werner, *The Anderson Tapes*, 1971. PRINCIPAL FILM APPEARANCES—*B.S. I Love You; Such Good Friends*, 1972; *Slither*, 1972; *Hail to the Chief*, 1972; *The Black Bird*, 1974; *Cockfighter*, 1975; *Hearts of the West*, 1975; *SSSSSSSSSS*, 1976; *The Fortune*, 1976; *Dreamer*, 1978; *Wholly Moses*, 1980; *Heartbeeps*, 1980; *Spring Break*, 1982; *Lovesick*, 1982; *Will There Really Be a Morning*, 1982; *Unfaithfully Yours*, 1983; *Splash*, 1984. TELEVISION DEBUT—Howard Tollbrook, *Diana*, 1974. PRINCIPAL TELEVISION APPEARANCES—*Holmes & Yoyo*, 1975; *Rockford Files*, 1975; *Good Times*, 1975; *Love, American Style*, 1975; *Ironside*, 1975; *Hart to Hart*, 1978, 1979; *Lou Grant*, 1979, 1980; *The Ropers*, 1980.

WRITINGS: SCREENPLAYS—*Pamela, Pamela You Are; Aroused; The Abortion*. ARTICLES—Lead article on entertainment in the People's Republic of China, *Variety*, 1977.

AWARDS: Scarlet Mask Award, State University of Iowa, 1949; Antoinette Perry Award Nomination, 1975: *Goodtime Charley*.

SIDELIGHTS: MEMBERSHIPS—University Club, NY; Friars Club; Players Club; Lambs Club; Dutch Treat Club; Academy of Motion Picture Arts and Sciences; Episcopal Actors Guild; Pennsylvania-German Society.

"I went to China to view theatre and film and television studios in 1977 and since then I have studied Chinese extensively. I am a 'railroad fan' and an antique automobile enthusiast, a member of Orders and Medals Society of America."

ADDRESS: Office—130 W. 42nd Street, New York, NY 10036. Agent—Belson & Klass, 211 S. Beverly Drive, Los Angeles, CA 90212.

* * *

SHULTZ, Tony, actor

PERSONAL: Born August 8, 1947, in Los Angeles, CA; son of Max (an aircraft parts business owner) and Evelyn (a real estate broker; maiden name, Kahn) Shultz. EDUCATION: University of California at Berkeley, B.A. (Drama), 1969; studied with Joan Darling, Mary Tarcai, Michael Howard, Milton Kasselas; dance with Jorma Strassborg and Geoff Moore, voice with Carlo Menotti, speech with Lynn Masters.

CAREER: DEBUT—Kodally, *She Loves Me*, Karamu, Cleveland, OH, 1967. NEW YORK DEBUT—Danny Zuko, *Grease*, Royale, 1974, 50 performances. LONDON DEBUT—Froines, *The Chicago Trials*, Open Space, 1969, 30 performances. PRINCIPAL STAGE APPEARANCES—Raoul, *The Baker's Wife*, Martin Beck, NY, 1977; Shultzie, *Platinum*, Mark Hellinger, NY, 1978; (Off-Broadway) Tom, *Resting Place*, Theater for the New City; Stephen, *Seminary Murder*, Lion Theatre Company; Vito, *Virgin Territory*, St. Clements; O.J., *Jass*, New Dramatists; Tom, *Holding Patterns*, Encompass; Doug, *Badgers*, Jewish Repertory; Peter, *Winterlude*, Cubiculo; Anthony, *Ketchup*, New Dramatists; (Regional) Romeo, *True Romances*, Mark Taper Forum, Los Angeles, CA; Dracula, *The Passion of Dracula*, Dorset Theater Festival; Haemon, *Antigone*, Company of Angels,

Los Angeles, CA; Touchstone, *As You Like It,* Romeo, *Romeo and Juliet,* Theatricum Botanicum, Los Angeles, CA; Joey, *Ferry Boat,* Oxford, Los Angeles, CA; (Europe) Monk, *Noonday Demons,* Open Space, London; company, *Stage 2,* Hampstead Theater Club, London; Green, *The Sapping,* Southtown, London. MAJOR TOURS—*Moving Being Company,* European cities.

FILM DEBUT—Corporal, *Executive Action,* 1975. PRINCIPAL FILM APPEARANCES—Bob Thompson, *A Stranger Is Watching,* 1981; Bud Remmington, *Girl's Night Out,* 1981; Bob, *Writing for Work.*

TELEVISION DEBUT—*Review (London),* 1970. PRINCIPAL TELEVISION APPEARANCES—Sal Brooks, *Ryan's Hope,* 1981; Tommy Geraci, *Hill Street Blues,* 1982; Lou, *One Life to Live;* intern, *The Guiding Light.*

SIDELIGHTS: MEMBERSHIPS—AEA; SAG; AFTRA; New York Writers Bloc. ACTIVITIES—Singer, composer, plays piano, guitar, harmonica, drums. Fences, rides motorcycles.

ADDRESS: Office—110 W. 40th Street, Suite #501, New York, NY 10018. Agent—c/o ATM Associates, 8282 Sunset Blvd., Los Angeles, CA 90046; c/o Bret Adams, Ltd., 448 W. 44th Street, New York, NY 10036.

* * *

SIEGEL, Arthur, composer, pianist, performer

PERSONAL: Born December 31, 1923 in Lakewood, NJ; son of Nathan (a fruit and vegetable wholesaler) and Fanny (Kahn) Siegel. EDUCATION: Studied at the American Academy of Dramatic Arts, 1942 and at the Juilliard School of Music, NY.

CAREER: FIRST STAGE WORK—Musical director and actor, Stamford Playhouse, Stamford, CT, 1943–44.

WRITINGS: MUSICAL COMPOSITIONS—(revue) *Wish You Were Here,* Greenwich Playhouse, CT, 1945; *Lovely Me,* Adelphi, NY, 1946; *Curtain Going Up,* Forrest, Philadelphia, 1952; *New Faces of 1952,* Royale, NY, 1952; *Shoestring Revue,* President, NY, 1955; *New Faces of 1956,* Barrymore, NY, 1956; *Mask and Gown,* Golden, NY, 1957; *New Faces of 1962,* Alvin, NY, 1962; *Not While I'm Eating,* Madison Avenue Playhouse, NY, 1961; *New Faces of 1968,* Booth, NY, 1968; *The American Hamburger League,* New Theatre, NY, 1969; incidental music for *Hay Fever,* Helen Hayes, NY, 1970; *A Quarter for the Ladies Room,* Village Gate, NY, 1972; *Tallulah,* NY, 1983. Songs include *Love Is a Simple Thing, Monotonous, Penny Candy;* special arrangements/pianist, *Eddie Cantor Show,* Carnegie Hall, NY, 1950; also for Imogene Coca, Hermione Gingold.

PRINCIPAL TELEVISION/RADIO COMPOSITION—(Radio revue) *New Faces,* 1948; television: wrote song for remake of *Miracle on 34th Street,* 1973. PRINCIPAL NIGHT CLUB WORK—Composer and pianist, *New Faces,* Persian Room, Plaza Hotel, NY, 1948; (revue) *Come As You Are,* Versailles Restaurant, NY, 1955; musical director, Kaye Ballard's club and television appearances. PRINCIPAL FILM WORK, COMPOSITION—Songs for *New Faces,* 1954. RECORDINGS—With

Kaye Ballard, readings from the comic strip, *Peanuts,* 1962; composed music for children's record, *Learn to Tell Time,* 1963; as a performer on *Rodgers and Hart Revisited,* 1964; singer/pianist, Ben Bagley's Painted Smiles records "Revisited Series"—Cole Porter, Jerome Kern, etc.

AWARDS: Grammy Award for children's albums of Rosemary Rice.

SIDELIGHTS: MEMBERSHIPS—ASCAP; Local 802, Musicians Union; AGAC. RECREATION—collecting phonograph records, books, theatre programs, old sheet music, and old magazines.

ADDRESS: Home—29 W. 65th Street, New York, NY 10023.

* * *

SILVER, Ron, actor

PERSONAL: Born July 2, 1946, in New York, NY; son of Irving Roy and May (Zimelman) Silver; married Lynne Miller, December 24, 1975. EDUCATION: University of Buffalo, B.A.; St. John's University (Taiwan), M.A.; trained for the stage at Herbert Berghof Studios with Uta Hagen and the Actors Studio with Lee Strasberg.

CAREER: DEBUT—*Kaspar* and *Public Insult,* City Center, NY, 1971. PRINCIPAL STAGE APPEARANCES—Pepe Hernandez, *El Grande de Coca-Cola,* Mercer Arts Center, NY, 1972; *Lotta,* New York Shakespeare Festival, 1973; *More Than You Deserve,* New York Shakespeare Festival, 1973; Pepe Hernandez, *El Grande de Coca-Cola,* Los Angeles, CA, 1975; Ralphie, *Awake and Sing,* Hollywood, CA, 1976; Lanx, *Angel City,* Mark Taper Forum, Los Angeles, 1977; Guy, *In the Boom Boom Room,* Long Beach Shakespeare Festival, CA, 1979; Charlie, *Gorilla,* Goodman, Chicago, 1983; Mel, *Friends,* Manhattan Theater Club, 1983–84.

FILM DEBUT—Vlada, *Semi-Tough,* 1977. PRINCIPAL FILM APPEARANCES—Dr. Tom Halman, *Silent Rage,* 1981; Larry Weisman, *Best Friends,* 1982; Dr. Phil Schneiderman, *The Entity,* 1982; Ted Caruso, *Lovesick,* 1983; Paul Stone, *Silkwood,* 1983; Eddie Bergson, *Goodbye People,* 1984.

TELEVISION DEBUT—*Rhoda,* 1976. PRINCIPAL TELEVISION APPEARANCES—*Rhoda; Hill Street Blues; Stockard Channing Show; Mac Davis Show; Bakers Dozen; Dear Detective;* (TV movies) *Betrayal; Word of Honor.*

AWARDS: Joseph Jefferson Award Nomination, Best Actor, 1983: *Gorilla.*

SIDELIGHTS: MEMBERSHIPS—AEA; SAG; AFTRA; Actors Studio; Actors Fund; Academy of Motion Picture Arts and Sciences.

ADDRESS: Agent—c/o Litke-Grossbart Management, 8500 Wilshire Blvd., Beverly Hills, CA; c/o Phil Gersh Agency, 222 N. Canon, Beverly Hills, CA 90210.

SILVERSTEIN, Elliot, director

PERSONAL: Surname sounds like "Silverstine"; born August 3, 1927, in Boston, MA; son of Maurice Louis (a physician) and Esther (Ostrofsky) Silverstein; married Alana King (an actress) July 18, 1982. EDUCATION: Boston College, B.S. (Social Sciences), 1949; Yale University, M.F.A., 1952. MILITARY: U.S. Coast Guard, Reserves.

CAREER: PRINCIPAL FILM WORK—Director: *Cat Ballou,* 1965; *The Happening,* 1967; *A Man Called Horse,* 1970; *The Car,* 1976.

PRINCIPAL TELEVISION WORK—Director: Staff director, *Omnibus,* 1953; many live prime time shows, 1953–59.

PRINCIPAL STAGE WORK—Director, *Maybe Tuesday.*

AWARDS: Directors Guild Nomination, Best Director, 1966: *Cat Ballou.*

SIDELIGHTS: MEMBERSHIPS—Directors Guild of America, chairman creative rights negotiating committee, first vice-president, 1982–84.

ADDRESS: Agent—Harold Cohen, Associated Management, 9200 Sunset Blvd., Los Angeles, CA 90069.

* * *

SIMON, Neil (ne Marvin Neil Simon), writer

PERSONAL: Born July 4, 1927, in New York, NY; son of Simon and Mamie Simon; married Joan Bain, September 30, 1953 (deceased); married Marsha Mason (divorced); children: (first marriage) two daughters. EDUCATION: Attended New York University. MILITARY: U.S. Army Air Force, 1945–46.

WRITINGS: PLAYS, PRODUCED—*Come Blow Your Horn,* Brooks Atkinson, NY, 1961; (Broadway) *Little Me* 1962; *Barefoot in the Park,* 1963; *The Odd Couple,* 1965; *Sweet Charity, The Star-Spangled Girl,* 1966; *Plaza Suite,* 1968; *Promises, Promises,* 1968; *Last of the Red Hot Lovers,* 1969; *The Gingerbread Lady,* 1970; *The Prisoner of Second Avenue,* 1971; *The Sunshine Boys,* 1972; *The Good Doctor,* 1973; *God's Favorite,* 1974; *California Suite,* 1976; *Chapter Two,* 1977; *They're Playing Our Song,* 1978; *I Ought to Be in Pictures,* 1980; *Fools,* 1981; *Little Me,* 1982; *Brighton Beach Memoirs,* 1983.

SCREENPLAYS—*After the Fox,* 1966; *The Out-of-Towners,* 1970; *The Heartbreak Kid,* 1972; *Murder by Death,* 1976; *The Goodbye Girl,* 1977; *The Cheap Detective,* 1978; *Only When I Laugh* (also produced and directed), 1981. TELEVISION—*Phil Silvers Arrow Show,* 1948; *The Tallulah Bankhead Show,* 1951; *Sid Caesar Show,* 1956–57; *Gary Moore Show,* 1959–60. REVUES AND SKETCHES—*Tamiment (PA) Revues,* 1952–53; *Catch a Star,* NY, 1955.

AWARDS: Antoinette Perry Award, Special Award, 1975; Antoinette Perry Award, 1965: *The Odd Couple;* Antoinette Perry Award Nomination, 1963: *Little Me, Barefoot in the*

Park; Sam S. Shubert Award, 1968; Writers Guild Screen Award, 1975, 1970, 1968.

ADDRESS: Office—c/o Eugene O'Neill Theatre, 230 W. 49th Street, New York, NY 10019. Office—c/o Dramatists Guild, 234 W. 44th Street, New York, NY 10036.*

* * *

SLADE, Bernard (ne Newbound), playwright, actor

PERSONAL: Born May 2, 1930, St. Catherines, ON, Canada; son of Frederick (a mechanic) and Bessie Harriet (Walbourne) Newbound; married Jill Hancock (nee Jill Foster, an actress and family therapist), July 25, 1953; children: Laurel, Christopher. EDUCATION: Caernarvon Grammar School, Croydon, England.

CAREER: PRINCIPAL STAGE APPEARANCES—Actor with Garden Center Theatre, Vineland, ON, Canada, Crest Theatre, Toronto, Citadel Theatre, Edmonton, AB, and appeared on CBC Television in Canada. Produced 25 plays at the Garden Center Theatre in Vineland, ON, 1954.

WRITINGS: PLAYS PRODUCED/PUBLISHED—*Simon Says, Get Married,* Crest, Canada, 1959; *A Very Close Family,* Manitoba Theatre Center, Winnipeg, 1961; *Same Time Next Year,* 1975; *Tribute,* 1978; *Romantic Comedy,* 1979; *Special Occasions,* 1982; *Fling!.* SCREENPLAYS—*Stand Up and Be Counted,* 1972; *Same Time Next Year,* 1979; *Tribute,* 1980; *Romantic Comedy,* 1983. TELEVISION—fifteen hour and half-hour anthologies for CBC, 1957–62; four plays for the *U.S. Steel Hour,* 1957–62; plays for *Matinee Theatre* and *Chrysler Theatre;* created and wrote series, *Love on a Rooftop, The Flying Nun, The Partridge Family, the Girl with E.S.P.;* episodes for series, *Bewitched* and for Movie of the Week.

RELATED CAREER: Screenwriter for CBC, CBS, ABC, NBC, 1957–present.

AWARDS: Academy Award Nomination, Best Screenplay, 1979: *Same Time Next Year;* Drama Desk Award, Best American Play, 1975: *Same Time Next Year;* Antoinette Perry Award Nomination, 1975; *Same Time Next Year.*

SIDELIGHTS: MEMBERSHIPS—Dramatists Guild, Writers Guild of America, West, Academy of Motion Picture Arts and Sciences, Society of Authors and Artists (France).

Mr. Slade's plays, *Same Time Next Year, Tribute* and *Romantic Comedy,* have been internationally produced in London, Paris, Canada and have toured the U.S. In 1978, he and his wife appeared on stage in *Same Time Next Year* at the Citadel Theatre in Edmonton, ON. "I am a prisoner of a childhood dream: to write for the theatre. The fulfillment of that dream has lived up to all my expectations. I believe the theatre should be a celebration of the human condition and that the artist's job is to remind us of all that is good about ourselves. I feel privileged to be given a platform for my particular vision of life, and, whether my plays succeed of fail, I am always grateful for the use of the hall."

ADDRESS: Office—650 Park Avenue, New York, NY, 10021. Agent—Jack Hutto, 405 W. 23rd Street, New York, NY 10011; Murray Neidorf, 315 S. Beverly, Beverly Hills, CA 90212.

* * *

SMITH, (Joseph) Cotter, actor

PERSONAL: Born May 29, 1949; son of John Lewis, Jr. (a federal judge) and Madeline (Cotter) Smith. EDUCATION: Trinity College, B.A., 1972; trained for the stage with the Actors Studio and Stella Adler.

CAREER: DEBUT—James, *The Collection*, Woods Hole Theatre Festival, Woods Hole, MA, 1974. NEW YORK DEBUT—Morris, The *Bloodknot*, Roundabout, 1980, 100 performances. PRINCIPAL STAGE APPEARANCES—Lt. Byrd, *A Soldier's Play*, Negro Ensemble Company, NY 1981–82; Jack, *The Death of a Miner*, American Place, NY, 1982; Victor/Tony, *The Last Carnival*, Trinidad, West Indies, 1982.

MAJOR TOURS—Lt. Byrd, *A Soldier's Play*, Mark Taper Forum, Los Angeles, CA, 1982.

TELEVISION DEBUT—Robert Kennedy, *Blood Feud*, 1983.

AWARDS: Outstanding Young Men of America, 1982.

SIDELIGHTS: MEMBERSHIPS—AEA; SAG; AFTRA.

ADDRESS: Agent—c/o Writers and Artists, 162 W. 56th Street, New York, NY 10019.

* * *

SMITH, Maggie, CBE, actress

PERSONAL: Born December 28, 1934, Ilford, U.K.; daughter of Nathaniel and Margaret (Hutton) Smith; married Robert Stephens, 1967 (divorced 1974); Beverley Cross, 1974; children: (first marriage) two sons. EDUCATION: Oxford High School for Girls; studied for the stage at the Oxford Playhouse School.

CAREER: DEBUT—Viola, *Twelfth Night*, OUDS, 1952. NEW YORK DEBUT—a comedienne, *New Faces '56 Revue*, Barrymore, 1956. LONDON DEBUT—comedienne, *Share My Lettuce*, Lyric, Hammersmith, Comedy, London, 1957. PRINCIPAL STAGE APPEARANCES—Vere Dane, *The Stepmother*, St. Martin's, London, 1958; with the Old Vic Company, 1959–60: Lady Playant, *The Double Dealer*, Celia, *As You Like It*, Queen, *Richard II*, Mistress Ford, *The Merry Wives of Windsor*, Maggie Wylie, *What Every Woman Knows;* Daisy, *Rhinoceros*, Strand, London, 1960; Lucile, *The Rehearsal*, Royal, Bristol, Globe, London, Queen's, Apollo, London, 1961; double-bill, Doreen, *The Private Ear*, Belinda, *The Public Eye*, Globe, London, 1962; reading, *Pictures in The Hallway*, Mermaid, London, 1962; Mary, *Mary, Mary*, Queen's, London, 1963; with the National Theatre Com-

pany, Old Vic: Silvia, *The Recruiting Officer*, 1963, Desdemona, *Othello*, also at the Chichester Festival, 1964, Hilde Wangel, *The Master Builder*, 1964, Myra, *Hay Fever*, 1964, Beatrice, *Much Ado About Nothing*, 1964, Clea, *Black Comedy*, 1965, title-role, *Miss Julie*, 1965–66, Marcela, *A Bond Honoured*, 1966, Margery Pinchwife, *The Country Wife*, 1969, Mrs. Sullen, *The Beaux' Stratagem*, Masha, *The Three Sisters*, in Los Angeles, CA, and London, 1970, Hedda, *Hedda Gabler*, 1970; Amanda Prynne, *Private Lives*, Queen's, London, 1972; title-role, *Peter Pan*, Vaudeville, London, 1974, 46th Street, NY, 1975; Stratford Ontario, Shakespeare Festival season, 1976: Cleopatra, *Antony and Cleopatra*, Millamant, *The Way of the World*, Masha, *The Three Sisters;* the Actress, *The Guardsman*, Ahmanson, Los Angeles, CA, 1976; Stratford Ontario Shakespeare Festival, 1977–78: Titania/Hippolyta, *A Midsummer Night's Dream*, Queen Elizabeth, *Richard III*, the Actress, *The Guardsman*, Judith Bliss, *Hay Fever*, Rosalind, *As You Like It*, Lady Macbeth, *Macbeth*, Amanda, *Private Lives;* Ruth Carson, *Night and Day*, Phoenix, London, ANTA, NY, 1979; Stratford Ontario Shakespeare Festival, 1980 season: Virginia Woolf, *Virginia*, Beatrice, *Much Ado About Nothing*, Masha, *The Sea Gull;* Virginia Woolf, *Virginia*, Haymarket, London, 1981.

PRINCIPAL FILM APPEARANCES—*Othello*, 1966; *The Honey Pot*, 1967; *Oh! What a Lovely War*, 1968; *Hot Millions*, 1968; *The Prime of Miss Jean Brodie*, 1968; *Love and Pain, and the Whole Damn Thing*, 1971; *Travels with My Aunt*, 1972; *Murder by Death*, 1976; *Death on the Nile*, 1977; *California Suite*, 1978; *Quartet*, 1978; *Clash of the Titans*, 1981; *Evil under the Sun*, 1981.

PRINCIPAL TELEVISION APPEARANCES—*Much Ado about Nothing*, *Man and Superman*, *On Approval*, *Home and Beauty*.

AWARDS: Evening Standard, Best Actress, 1981: *Virginia;* Academy Award, Best Supporting Actress, 1979: *California Suite;* Golden Globe, 1979: *California Suite;* Variety Club's Best Actress, 1972: Amanda, *Private Lives; Evening Standard*, Best Actress, 1970: *Hedda Gabler;* received the CBE in the New Year Honours, 1970; Academy Award, Best Actress, 1969: *The Prime of Miss Jean Brodie;* Film Critics Guild Award, 1968; Best Film Actress Award, Society of Film and Television Arts, UK, 1968; Variety Club Award, Best Actress, 1963: *Mary, Mary;* Evening Standard Award, Best Actress, 1962: *The Private Ear* and *The Public Eye*, 1962.

ADDRESS: Agent—ICM, 388 Oxford Street, London, W1N 9HE.

* * *

SMITH, Sheila, actress and singer

PERSONAL: Born April 3, 1933, in Conneaut, OH; daughter of Edward R. (a comptroller for a railroad) and Margaret Fitzgerald (a teacher; maiden name, Tinney) Smith. EDUCATION: Attended Kent State University; trained for the stage at the Cleveland Playhouse. NON-THEATRICAL CAREERS: Feature writer, *Cleveland Plain Dealer* (newspaper), 1965–75; president, Meese Smeese, Inc. (fashion designers).

CAREER: DEBUT—Corps de ballet, *The Merry Widow*, Cleveland Music Hall, 1947. NEW YORK DEBUT—Minerva, *Best Foot Forward*, Equity Library Theatre, 1956. PRINCIPAL STAGE APPEARANCES—Mitzi, *Fiorello*, City Center, NY, 1962; Remo, *Anything Goes*, Orpheum, NY, 1962; Miani, *Sweet Miani*, Players, NY, 1962; Allison, *Hot Spot*, Majestic, NY, 1963; *To Broadway with Love*, World's Fair, NY, 1964; Mame/Vera, *Mame*, Winter Garden, NY, 1966–69; Meredith Lane, *Follies*, Winter Garden, NY, 1971; Joanne, *Company*, Alvin, NY, 1971; Sweet Sue, *Sugar*, Majestic, NY, 1972–73; Mme. Irene, *Five O'Clock Girl*, Helen Hayes, NY, 1981; Dorothy/Maggie, *42nd Street*, Majestic, NY, 1981–83; Janet, *Taking My Turn*, Entermedia, NY, 1983–84.

MAJOR TOURS—*The Ziegfeld Follies*, Boston, MA, Philadelphia, PA, 1956; Hope, *Fade Out, Fade In*, Australian cities, 1965; Mame, *Mame*, U.S. and Canadian cities, 1969–70; Mrs. Latham, *Forty Carats*, East Coast cities, 1974; Lucille, *No, No Nanette*, East Coast and Midwest cities, 1974; Hesther Salomon, *Equus*, U.S. cities, 1975–76; Elsa, *Sound of Music*, U.S. cities, 1977; Golde, *Fiddler on the Roof*, East Coast and southern cities, 1978; Carlotta, *Follies*, Chicago, IL, 1980.

TELEVISION DEBUT—*Omnibus*, ''Leonard Bernstein Salute to Musical Comedy.'' PRINCIPAL TELEVISION APPEARANCES—*Ray Bolger Series*, ''Washington Square,'' 1956–57; *Love Is a Many-Splendored Thing; The Young and the Restless; Charley's Angels; Great Performances*, ''Taking My Turn, 1984.

WRITINGS: PLAYS, PRODUCED—*An Operetta Nosegay*, Chelsea, NY, 1980; *From Broadway with Love*, High Falls, NY, 1982 and 1983; *An American Operetta Soirée*, John Street, NY, 1983; *A Viennese Operetta Soirée*, John Street, NY, 1983.

AWARDS: Theatre World Award, 1967; *Mame*; Key to the City of New York, 1961.

SIDELIGHTS: MEMBERSHIPS—Gamma Phi Beta.

ADDRESS: Agent—c/o Martin Gage, The Gage Group, 1650 Broadway, New York, NY 10019.

* * *

SOBIESKI, Carol (nee O'Brien), screenwriter

PERSONAL: Born March 16, 1939, in Chicago, IL; daughter of Frank Thomas (a lawyer and rancher) and Emeline (a painter, politician, and teacher; maiden name, Bush) O'Brien; married James Louis Sobieski (a lawyer), November 22, 1964; children: Emeline, Mona, James. EDUCATION: Smith College, B.A., 1960; Trinity College (Ireland), Masters of Literature, 1961. RELIGION: Episcopalian.

WRITINGS: EPISODIC TELEVISION—*Mr. Novak; The Mod Squad; Peyton Place; Fame Is the Name of the Game*. TELEVISION MOVIES—*The Neon Ceiling; A Little Game; Where the Ladies Go; Sunshine; Sunshine Christmas; Reflections of Murder; Amelia Earhart; Harry Truman: Plain Speaking*. TELEVISION PILOTS—*Dial Hot Line; Paper Moon;*

Sunshine; Two Marriages. FILMS—*Honeysuckle Rose; Casey's Shadow; Annie; The Toy*.

AWARDS: Writers Guild Awards: *Sunshine, Sunshine Christmas, The Neon Ceiling*; Writers Guild Award Nominations; *Amelia Earhart, Where the Ladies Go, Two Marriages, Harry Truman: Plain Speaking*; Emmy Award Nomination: *Harry Truman: Plain Speaking*; Women in TV and Film Awards: *Amelia Earhart, The Women's Room*; San Francisco Film Festival Award: *The Neon Ceiling*.

SIDELIGHTS: MEMBERSHIPS—Writers Guild of America West.

ADDRESS: Agent—c/o Adams, Ray and Rosenberg, 9200 Sunset Blvd., Los Angeles, CA 90069.

* * *

SOHMERS, Barbara, actress

PERSONAL: Born July 7, in New York, NY; daughter of Phillip Harry (singer then dress manufacturer) and Ethel (a retail dress buyer; maiden name, Grossman) Sohmers; married Claude Nicot (an actor) June 30, 1961 (divorced 1976). EDUCATION: Graduate of High School of Music and Art, New York City; attended Antioch College, one year; studied at Ohio Dramatic Workshop with Erwin Piscator and others for two years. RELIGION: Jewish.

CAREER: DEBUT—As the resident leading/character actress, Loon Lake Playhouse, Loon Lake, NY, 1950's. NEW YORK DEBUT—Ilsa, *Spring's Awakening*, Provincetown Playhouse. PARIS DEBUT—Janet, *Boeing, Boeing*, Comédie Caumartin. PRINCIPAL STAGE APPEARANCES—Sarah, *Table Manners*, Meadow Brook, Rochester, MI, 1977; Essie, *Ah! Wilderness*, Arena Stage, Washington, DC, 1978; Beverly, *The Shadow Box*, Gilda, *Design for Living*, Asolo State Theatre, Sarasota, FL, 1979; Hermione, *A Winter's Tale*, Arena Stage, Washington, DC, 1979; Linda, *No Time for Comedy*, Playmakers Repertory, Chapel Hill, NC, 1980; Ethel Barrymore, *Ned and Jack*, Little Theatre, NY, 1981; Giselle, *The Workshop*, Long Wharf, New Haven, CT, 1982; Mme. Knorr, *On the Razzle*, Arena Stage, Washington, DC, 1982; Lete, *Elba*, Manhattan Theatre Club, 1983; Titania, *A Midsummer Night's Dream*, Actors Theatre of Louisville, KY, 1983; Hesione Hushabye, *Heartbreak House*, Indiana Repertory Company, 1983. MAJOR TOURS—Amanda, *Private Lives*, Eleanor, *Lion in Winter*, Long Wharf Theatre tour of U.S.; Mitzi, *Madame Princesse*, France, Belgium, Switzerland, Morocco, Tunisia, Lebanon.

FILM DEBUT—Daisy, *La Vérité*, 1959. PRINCIPAL FILM APPEARANCES—*Hold-up à 'St. Trop'; Nick Carter Ça Tout Casser; A la Française; L'Ombre dans la Glace; What's New, Pussycat?*, 1965; *L'Enfer; L'Aîné des Ferchaux; Marseille Contract*.

TELEVISION DEBUT—*Rien Que La Vérité*. PRINCIPAL TELEVISION APPEARANCES—*L'Abonné de la ligne; Anna; L'Etonnante Découverte du Professeur Delalune; Saute-Mouton;*

BARBARA SOHMERS

La Bonne Education; Le Chevalier d'Eon; La Duchesse d'Algues; L'Ecureuil; La Vie Privée de Percy; Shulmeister; Le Mutant.

THEATRE-RELATED CAREER: Has dubbed hundreds of foreign films into English.

WRITINGS: SHORT STORY—"The Adventuress," *Playgirl* Magazine, 1980. ARTICLE—"Les Maisons de Rendezvous of Paris," *Cosmopolitan* Magazine.

SIDELIGHTS: "I left the U.S. in 1957 and spent most of the 20 following years in Paris working in French theatre, films, television and radio. I speak fluent French. As a singer, I created a one-woman 'Jazz Show,' which ran for six weeks in a Café-théâtre in Paris and in concerts outside of Paris, and sang in several jazz clubs in Paris. Before going to Paris, I spent six months in Dublin, where I played in a production of de Ghelderode's *Pantagleize*, and toured the South and West of Ireland in a variety show and modeled for Irish fashion magazines. Even before leaving for Europe, I was a working actress, having appeared in John Van Drutens' last play and in the Theatre de Lys's production of *The Three-penny Opera* with the late Lotte Lenya."

ADDRESS: Home—484 W. 43rd Street, New York, NY 10036. Agent—Peggy Hadley Enterprizes, Suite 2317, 250 W. 57th Street, New York, NY 10107.

SOKOL, Marilyn, actress

PERSONAL: Daughter of Sidney S. (a commissioner of the U.S. Treasury) and Evelyn Sylvia (Gold) Sokol.

CAREER: DEBUT—Belly dancer, *Man of La Mancha*, national tour, U.S. cities, 1966–67. NEW YORK DEBUT—*The Year Boston Won the Pennant*. PRINCIPAL STAGE APPEAR-ANCES—(New York) *The Beggar's Opera*, 1972. MAJOR TOURS—*San Francisco Mime Troupe*, U.S. cities, 1967–69.

FILM DEBUT—*Zabriskie Point*, 1969. PRINCIPAL FILM AP-PEARANCES—*The Hospital*, 1971; *The Front*, 1975; *Foul Play*, 1976; *The Last Married Couple in America*, 1978; *Can't Stop the Music*, 1980. PRINCIPAL TELEVISION APPEAR-ANCES—*The Tonight Show*.

AWARDS: Obie Award, Variety Critics Award, 1972: *The Beggar's Opera*.

SIDELIGHTS: MEMBERSHIPS—AEA, SAG, AFTRA.

ADDRESS: Office—The Shukat Company, 340 W. 55th Street, New York, NY 10019. Agent—c/o Agency for the Performing Arts, 888 Seventh Avenue, New York, NY 10019.

* * *

SOKOLOW, Anna, choreographer, teacher

PERSONAL: Born February 9, 1910 in Hartford, CT; daughter of Samuel and Sara (Cohen) Sokolow. EDUCATION: Studied at the Neighborhood Playhouse; member of Martha Graham Dance Company. RELIGION: Jewish.

CAREER: PRINCIPAL STAGE WORK, CHOREOGRAPHY—*The Great Campaign*, Princess, NY, 1947; *Street Scene*, Adelphi, NY, 1947; *Sleepy Hollow*, St. James, NY, 1948; *Regina*, 46th Street, NY, 1949; *Happy as Larry*, Coronet, NY, 1950; *The Dybbuk*, Studio, NY, 1951; *Madam, Will You Walk*, Phoenix, NY, 1953; *Session for Eight, L'Histoire du soldat*, Kaufmann Auditorium, 92nd Street YM-YWHA, NY, 1954; *Rooms*, Anna Sokolow Dance Company, 92nd Street Y, 1955; *Red Roses for Me*, Booth, NY, 1955; designed choreography for New York City Opera Company productions of *La Traviata, Carmen, die Fledermaus, The Tempest, Susannah, Orpheus in the Underworld*; choreographed *Copper and Brass*, Martin Beck, NY, 1957; *Pinkville*, American Place, NY, 1971; *The Merry Wives of Windsor*, American Shakespeare Festival, Stratford, CT, 1971.

ORIGINAL WORKS FOR DANCE—*Strange American Funeral*, Dance Unit, NY, 1935; *Slaughter of the Innocents*, Guild, NY, 1937; *Opening Dance*, Guild, 1937; *Ballad in a Popular Style*, Alvin, NY, 1939; *A Short Lecture and Demonstration on the Evolution of Ragtime as Presented by Jelly Roll Morton*, Danny Daniels and Group, 92nd Street Y, NY, 1952; *Lyric Suite*, New Dance Group, 92nd Street Y, 1954; *Poem*, Anna Sokolow Theatre Dance Company, Brooklyn Academy of Music, 1956; *Le grand spectacle*, Phoenix, NY, 1957; *Session '58*, Julliard Dance Ensemble, NY, 1958;

Dreams, 92nd Street Y, 1961; *Suite No. 5 in C Minor*, New Dance Group, 92nd Street Y, 1963; *Opus '63*, Julliard Dance Ensemble, 1963; *The Question*, Juilliard Dance Ensemble, 1964; *Forms*, Anna Sokolow Dance Company, 1964; *Odes and Ballade*, Juilliard Dance Ensemble, 1965; *Opus '65*, Joffrey Ballet, Delacorte, NY, 1965;

Time + 6, Boston Ballet, 1966; *Night*, Juilliard Dance Ensemble, 1966; *Deserts*, Anna Sokolow Dance Company, 1968; *Steps of Silence*, Repertory Dance Theatre, University of Utah, 1968, Anna Sokolow Dance Company, Brooklyn Academy of Music, 1968; *Tribute*, Anna Sokolow Dance Company, Brooklyn Academy of Music, 1968; *Echoes*, Juilliard Dance Ensemble, 1969; *Magritte, Magritte*, and *Act Without Words No. 1*, Anna Sokolow Dance Company, Lyric, Edison, NY, 1970; *The Dove*, Juilliard Dance Ensemble, 1970; *Scenes from the Music of Charles Ives*, Juilliard Dance Ensemble, 1971; *Three Poems*, Juilliard Dance Ensemble, 1973; *Homage to Federico Garcia Lorca*, José Limon Dance Company, 1974; *Come, Come Travel with Dreams*, Juilliard Dance Ensemble, 1974; *Ecuatorial*, Paul Sanasardo Dance Company, 1974; *A Cycle of Cities*, Wolf Trap Farm Park, Vienna, VA, 1974.

DIRECTED—*The Moon*, New York City Opera, 1956; *Bugs and Veronica*, Pocket, NY, 1965; (with her Players Project) *Metamorphosis*, Loeb, Harvard, Cambridge, MA, 1971; (as assistant director)—*Camino Real*, National, NY, 1953.

PRINCIPAL TELEVISION WORK. Choreographer—''Esther, The Queen,'' *Lamp Unto My Feet*, 1960.

AWARDS: Dance Magazine Award; American Israel Alliance Foundation; Ohio State University; Brandeis University.

THEATRE-RELATED CAREER: Teacher, Dance, Movement for Actors, Juilliard School of Drama, NY; organized own dance company, 1939; guest choreographer for dance companies in U.S. and abroad.

SIDELIGHTS: MEMBERSHIPS—Society of Stage Directors and Choreographers.

ADDRESS: Home—71 W. 55th Street, New York, NY 10019. Office—Juilliard School of Dance, Lincoln Center, New York, NY 10023.

* * *

SOMMER, Josef (ne Maximilian Josef Sommer), actor

PERSONAL: Born June 26, 1934 in Greifswald, Germany; son of Clemons (Professor of History, University of North Carolina) and Elisebeth Sommer; children: Maria. EDUCATION: Carnegie-Mellon University, B.F.A. 1957; studied at the American Shakespeare Festival in Stratford, CT, 1962–64. MILITARY: U.S. Army, 1958–60.

CAREER: DEBUT—Bodo, *Watch on the Rhine*, Carolina Playmakers, Chapel Hill, NC, 1943. NEW YORK DEBUT—Brabantio, *Othello*, ANTA, 1970. PRINCIPAL STAGE APPEARANCES—*The Trial of the Catonsville Nine*, NY, 1971; *Children, Children*, NY, 1971; *Enemies*, Lincoln Center

Repertory, NY, 1972; *The Merchant of Venice*, Lincoln Center Repertory, 1973; *Full Circle*, NY, 1973; *Who's Who in Hell*, NY, 1974; *The Shadow Box*, Morosco, NY, 1977; *Drinks Before Dinner*, NY, 1978; *The 1940's Radio Hour*, Golden, NY, 1979; *Spokesong*, Circle in the Square, NY, 1979; *Whose Life Is It Anyway?*, Trafalgar, NY, 1980; *Black Angel*, NY, 1982; *Lydie Breeze*, NY, 1982; *The Lady and the Clarinet*, NY, 1983. Has appeared with San Diego Shakespeare Festival, 1967, American Conservatory Theatre, San Francisco, 1970–71, American Shakespeare Festival, Stratford, CT, 1962–66, 1968–70, and 1972–76, Seattle Repertory Company, 1967–71, Hartford Stage Company, 1975, Mark Taper Forum, Los Angeles, 1980, Long Wharf Theatre, New Haven, CT, 1976–79 and 1983, also at the Kennedy Center for the Performing Arts, Washington, DC, in *The Archbishop's Ceiling*, 1977. MAJOR TOURS—George, *Who's Afraid of Virginia Woolf*, with the Seattle Repertory Theatre Company at the Bergen Norway International Theatre Festival, 1969.

FILM DEBUT—District Attorney, *Dirty Harry*, 1971. PRINCIPAL FILM APPEARANCES—*The Front*, 1976; *Close Encounters of the Third Kind*, 1977; *Oliver's Story*, 1978; *Hide in Plain Sight*, 1980; *Reds*, 1981; *Independence Day*, 1981; *Absence of Malice*, 1981; *Hanky Panky*, 1982; *Still of the Night*, 1982; *Rollover*, 1982; *Sophie's Choice* (narration), 1982; *Silkwood*, 1983; *Iceman*, 1984. PRINCIPAL TELEVISION APPEARANCES—*Morning Becomes Electra*; *The Scarlet Letter*; *Saigon*; *Sparkling Cyanide*.

AWARDS: Obie Award, *Lydie Breeze*, 1982; Fulbright Grant to study professional theatre in Germany, 1960–61.

SIDELIGHTS: MEMBERSHIPS—AEA; AFTRA; SAG.

ADDRESS: Office—c/o Lazarow & Company, 119 W. 57th Street, New York, NY 10019. Agent—Jeff Hunter, c/o DHKPR Agency, 165 W. 46th Street, New York, NY 10036.

* * *

SONDHEIM, Stephen, composer and lyricist

PERSONAL: Born March 22, 1930, in New York City; son of Herbert and Janet (Fox) Sondheim. EDUCATION: Graduated from Williams College.

CAREER: FIRST STAGE WORK—Composer incidental music, *Girls of Summer*, Longacre, NY, 1956. PRINCIPAL STAGE WORK—Lyricist, *West Side Story*, 1957; lyricist, *Gypsy*, 1959; composer incidental music, *Invitation to a March*, 1960; composer/lyricist, *A Funny Thing Happened on the Way to the Forum*, 1962; composer/lyricist, *Anyone Can Whistle*, 1964; lyricist, *Do I Hear a Waltz?*, 1965; composer/lyricist, *Company*, 1970; composer/lyricist, *Follies*, 1971; composer/lyricist, *A Little Night Music*, 1973; composer/lyricist, *Sonheim: A Musical Tribute*, Shubert, NY, 1973; composer incidental music, *The Enclave*, 1973; composer/lyricist, *The Frogs*, Yale Repertory, New Haven, CT, 1974; co-lyricist, *Candide* (revival), 1974; composer/lyri-

STEPHEN SONDHEIM

cist, *Sweeney Todd*, 1979; composer/lyricist, *Merrily We Roll Along;* composer/lyricist, *Sunday in the Park with George*, 1983. ANTHOLOGIES—(musicals of collected songs)—*Side by Side by Sondheim; Marry Me a Little*.

PRINCIPAL FILM WORK—Composer, *Stavisky*, 1974; composer, *Reds*. PRINCIPAL TELEVISION WORK—Composer/lyricist, *Evening Primrose*, 1966.

WRITINGS: EPISODIC TELEVISION—*Topper*, 1953. SCREENPLAYS—*The Last of Sheila* (with Anthony Perkins), 1973.

AWARDS: Antoinette Perry Award, Best Composer and Lyricist, 1970: *Company*, 1971: *Follies*, 1973: *A Little Night Music*, 1979: *Sweeney Todd;* New York Drama Critics Circle Award, 1970: *Company*, 1971: *Follies*, 1973: *A Little Night Music, Pacific Overtures*, 1979: *Sweeney Todd;* Hutchison Prize for Musical Composition, Williams College.

SIDELIGHTS: MEMBERSHIPS—Dramatists Guild (council), National Association of Playwrights, Composers and Lyricists (president, 1973–81), American Academy, Institute of Arts and Letters.

ADDRESS: Agent—c/o Flora Roberts, 157 W. 57th Street, Penthouse A, New York, NY 10019.

SPACEK, Sissy (nee Mary Elizabeth), actress

PERSONAL: Born December 25, 1950, Quitman, TX; daughter of Edwin A. and Virginia Spacek; married Jack Fisk, 1974. EDUCATION: Attended Lee Strasberg Theatre Institute.

CAREER: FILM DEBUT—*Prime Cut*, 1972. PRINCIPAL FILM APPEARANCES—*Ginger in the Morning*, 1972; *Badlands*, 1974; *Carrie*, 1976; *Three Women*, 1977; *Welcome to L.A.*, 1977; *Heart Beat*, 1980; *Coal Miner's Daughter*, 1980; *Raggedy Man*, 1981; *Missing*, 1982; *Violets Are Blue* (forthcoming).

PRINCIPAL TELEVISION APPEARANCES—Movies for television, *The Girls of Huntington House*, 1973; *The Migrants*, 1973; *Katherine*, 1975; *Verna: USO Girl*, 1978; guest host, *Saturday Night Live*, 1977; series, two episodes of *The Waltons*.

AWARDS: Academy Award, Best Actress, 1980: *Coal Miner's Daughter;* Best Actress, New York Film Critics, Los Angeles Film Critics, Foreign Press Association award, National Film Critics award, 1980; Album of the Year, Country Music Association, 1980: *Coal Miner's Daughter;* Best Supporting Actress, New York Film Critics, 1977: *Three Women;* Best Actress, National Society of Film Critics, 1976: *Carrie;* Academy Award Nomination, Best Actress, 1976: *Carrie*.

ADDRESS: Agent—Creative Artists Agency, 1888 Century Park E., Los Angeles, CA 90067.*

* * *

SPELLING, Aaron, executive producer

PERSONAL: Born April 22, 1928, in Dallas, TX; son of David and Pearl (Wall) Spelling; married Carole Gene Marer, November 23, 1968; children: Victoria, Randall. EDUCATION: Studied at the Sorbonne, University of Paris, France, 1945–46; Southern Methodist University, B.A., 1950. MILITARY: USAAF, 1942–45.

CAREER: PRINCIPAL TELEVISION WORK—Producer: *Zane Grey Theatre, Honey West, Smothers Brothers Show, Dick Powell Show, Danny Thomas Hour, Burke's Law, Mod Squad, The Rookies, Starsky and Hutch, Family, The Beach Bums, The Love Boat, Vegas, Charlie's Angels, Fantasy Island, Hart to Hart, The B.A.D. Cats, Aloha Paradise, Dynasty, Strike Force;* movies for television—*The Legend of Valentino*, 1975; *The Boy in the Plastic Bubble*, 1976; *One of My Wives Is Missing*, 1976; *Little Ladies of the Night*, 1977; *The Users*, 1978; *Murder Can Hurt You*, 1980; *The Best Little Girl in the World*, 1981; *Sizzle*, 1981; *Matt Houston*, 1982; *Masserati and the Brain*, 1982; *Wild Women of Charity Gulch*, 1982; *Don't Go to Sleep*, 1982; *Shooting Stars*, 1983; *Hotel*, 1983.

PRINCIPAL FILM WORK—Executive producer, *Mr. Mom*, 1983.

AWARDS: NAACP Image Awards, 1970, 71, 73, 75; Man of the Year, Publicists of America, 1971; B'nai B'rith Man of the Year, 1972; Eugene O'Neill Awards, 1947–48; Purple

Heart with oak leaf cluster, Bronze Star Medal; Writers Guild of America, 1962.

SIDELIGHTS: MEMBERSHIPS—Writers Guild of America, Producers Guild of America, the Caucus, Hollywood Radio and Television Society, Hollywood Television Academy of Arts and Sciences, Friars Club, Big Brothers of America.

ADDRESS: Office—Aaron Spelling Productions, 1041 N. Formosa, Los Angeles, CA 90046.*

* * *

SPIELBERG, David, actor

PERSONAL: Born March 6, 1939; son of George (a merchant) and Manuela (Benitez) Spielberg; married Barbara Gladtone (an executive) June 13, 1965; children: Daniel. EDUCATION: Attended University of Texas for 2 years; studied with Ben Iden Payne at Ben Iden Payne School. MILITARY: U.S. Naval Reserve, two years active service, 1957–59.

CAREER: DEBUT—King, *Ondine*, Hogg Auditorium, Austin, TX, 1959. NEW YORK DEBUT—Jesse, *A Man's a Man*, Masque, 1963. PRINCIPAL STAGE APPEARANCES—Gordon, *Thieves*, Broadhurst, NY, 1971; Larry Parks, *Are You Now or Have You Ever Been?*, Cast Theatre, 1974–75; *The Trial of the Catonsville Nine*, NY; *Macbird*, NY; *Funnyhouse of a Negro*, NY; Gil, *Sleep*, American Place Theatre, NY; *Story Theatre*, Chicago, IL; Mr. Spielberg has performed with Long Wharf Theatre, Yale Repertory Theatre, Williamstown Theatre Festival, and Stockbridge Festival Theatre. MAJOR TOURS—Mickey, *After the Fall*, national tour.

FILM DEBUT—Goodman, *The Effect of Gamma Rays on Man-in-the-Moon Marigolds*, 1972. PRINCIPAL FILM APPEARANCES—*Law and Disorder*, 1974; *Hustle*, 1975; *Winterkills*, 1976; *The Choirboys*, 1977; *Real Life*, 1978; *The Hunter*, 1980; *Christine*, 1983; *The Children's War*, 1983. TELEVISION DEBUT—Walberg, D.A., *The Bold Ones*. PRINCIPAL TELEVISION APPEARANCES—Wilentz, *The Lindbergh Kidnapping Trial*; Max, *Jessica Novak*; Bob, *Bob/Carol/Ted & Alice*; David, *The Practice*; Peter Pan, *Mork & Mindy*; *Two Brothers*; *Games Your Mother Taught You*; *Maid in America*, 1982; over 100 additional appearances.

AWARDS: Obie Award for Distinguished Performance, 1971: Gil, *Sleep*; L.A. Critics Circle Award, Best Performance, Larry Parks, *Are You Now or Have You Eve Been?*; Emmy Award Nomination, *The Lindbergh Kidnapping Trial*.

THEATRE-RELATED CAREER: Associate Instructor of Acting, Yale School of Drama, 1968–69; founding member, Open Theatre; company member, Long Wharf Theatre, 1965–80.

SIDELIGHTS: MEMBERSHIPS—Academy of Television Arts and Sciences; Academy of Motion Picture Arts and Sciences.

ADDRESS: Agent—The Artists Agency, 10000 Santa Monica Blvd., Los Angeles, CA 90069.

SPIELBERG, Steven, film director, producer

PERSONAL: Born December 18, 1947, in Cincinnati, OH. EDUCATION: California State College, B.A., 1970.

CAREER: PRINCIPAL FILM WORK—Director: *The Sugarland Express*, 1974; *Jaws*, 1975; *Close Encounters of the Third Kind*, 1977; *1941*, 1979; *Raiders of the Lost Ark*, 1981; *E.T.: The Extra-Terrestrial*, 1982; *Poltergeist*, 1982; *Twilight Zone—The Movie*, 1983; *Indiana Jones and the Temple of Doom*, 1984. Producer: *I Wanna Hold Your Hand*, 1978; *1941*, 1979; *Used Cars*, 1980; *Poltergeist*, 1982; *E.T.: The Extra-Terrestrial*, 1982; *Twilight Zone—The Movie*, 1983; *Indiana Jones and the Temple of Doom*, 1984; *Gremlins*, 1984; Screenwriter: with Patrick Mann, *Close Encounters of the Third Kind*, 1977.

PRINCIPAL TELEVISION WORK—Director: segments, *Night Gallery*, *Marcus Welby, M.D.*, *Columbo*; movies for television—*Duel*, 1971, *Something Evil*, 1972.

AWARDS: Has received several Academy Awards.

RELATED CAREER: Television director, Universal Pictures; formed own production company, Amblin Productions.

SIDELIGHTS: Mr. Spielberg made home movies as a child; at 12 he made his first film with actors and a story. When he reached 13, he won a film contest with a 40 minute war movie, *Escape to Nowhere*. At 16, he made a 140 minute film *Firelight*. At California State College, he made five films and his first professional work, *Amblin*, which led to his working at Universal Pictures.

ADDRESS: Office—Amblin Productions, Burbank Studios, 4000 Warner Blvd., Burbank, CA 91522.*

* * *

SPOTA, George, producer, writer

PERSONAL: Born September 27, 1917, in New York City; son of Thomas D. (a builder) and Esther A. (De Fies) Spota; married Marie Carletti, October 12, 1940; children: Georgeann.

CAREER: PRINCIPAL STAGE WORK—Producer, *Will Rogers' U.S.A.*, with James Whitmore, 1970, ten national tours; *Eleanor*, with Eileen Heckert; *Bully*, an adventure with Theodore Roosevelt, with James Whitmore.

PRINCIPAL TELEVISION WORK—Producer/creator, *You and the Law*, *When I Grow Up*, *Faye Emerson's Women Want to Know*, *Readers Review Theatre*; executive producer, Jonathan Winters and Arlene Francis specials; *Jonathan Winters Specials*, 1964;

RELATED CAREER: Writer, Kramer Productions Inc, NY, 1947–49; writer, associate producer, Robert Jennings Productions, NY, 1950–52; producer, writer, Martin Goodman Productions, NY, 1952–70; producer, George Spota Productions, NY, 1970–present; co-personal manager for 10 years or longer: Jonathan Winters, Bill Cullen, Carol Burnett, Arlene Francis, Bess Myerson, Donald Woods, Hugh Downs.

WRITINGS: PLAYS, PRODUCED—*Walls Come Tumbling Down*, with William Storm, Company of Angels Theatre, Los Angeles, CA, 1975.

ADDRESS: Office—11151 Ophir Drive, Los Angeles, CA 90024.

* * *

SPRINGER, Ashton Jr., producer, manager

PERSONAL: Born November 1, 1930 in New York, NY; son of Ashton and Julia Euphenia (Horsham) Springer; married Myra Louise Burns (a teacher) November 6, 1956; children: Mark, Chesley. EDUCATION: Ohio State University, B.S., 1954, M.A., 1955. RELIGION: Episcopalian. NON-THEATRI-CAL CAREER: Director, Richard Lawrence Youth Center, Bronx, NY 1955–57; partner, A&M Laundromats and Coin Equipment Maintenance, NY, 1956–60; president, Motor Car Associates, Inc. New Rochelle, NY, 1960–67.

CAREER: PRINCIPAL STAGE WORK, PRODUCED—*No Place to Be Somebody*, NY, 1970; *My Sister, My Sister*, NY, 1974; *Bubbling Brown Sugar*, NY, 1975; *Going Up*, NY, 1976; *Cold Storage*, NY, 1977; *Eubie*, NY, 1978; *Whoopee*, NY, 1978; *A Lesson from Aloes*, NY, 1981; *Inacent Black*, 1981; *The Apollo—Just Like Magic*, NY, 1981.

AWARDS: Drama Critics Circle Award, Best Play, 1981: *A Lesson from Aloes;* Antoinette Perry Award Nomination, Best Play Producer, 1975: *Bubbling Brown Sugar.*

THEATRE-RELATED CAREER: Chesmark Productions Inc., 1967–70; Theatre Management Associates, Inc., New York City, 1970–present; managing partner, Little Theatre, New York, NY, 1979–present.

SIDELIGHTS: MEMBERSHIPS—Board of Governors, Good-speed Opera House, East Haddam, CT; League of New York Theatres and Producers.

ADDRESS: Office—240 W. 44th Street, New York, NY 10036.

* * *

STALLONE, Sylvester (Enzio), actor, writer, director, producer

PERSONAL: Born July 6, 1946, in New York City; son of Frank and Jacquline (Labofish) Stallone; married Sasha Czack, December 28, 1974; children: Sage, Seth. EDUCA-TION: Attended the American College in Switzerland, 1965–67; University of Miami, 1967–69. NON-RELATED CAREER: Usher, fish salesman, horse trainer, delicatessen worker, truck driver, bouncer, zoo attendant, bookstore detective, short order cook, pizza demonstrator, motel superintendent, physical education teacher, teacher, American College Switzerland.

CAREER: FILM DEBUT—Lead role, *The Lords of Flatbush*, 1973. PRINCIPAL FILM APPEARANCES—*Capone*, 1974; *Rocky*,

1976; *F.I.S.T.*, 1978; *Paradise Alley*, 1978; *Rocky II*, 1979; *Nighthawks*, 1980; *Escape to Victory*, 1980; *Rocky III*, 1981; *First Blood*, 1983; *Staying Alive*, 1983; *Rhinestone*, 1984. SCREENWRITER/PRODUCER—*Rocky*, 1976; *F.I.S.T.*, 1977; *Paradise Alley*, 1978; *Rocky II*, 1979; *First Blood*, 1983; *Staying Alive*, 1983. DIRECTOR—*Paradise Alley*, *Rocky II*, *Rocky III*, *Staying Alive*.

WRITINGS: BOOKS—*The Rocky Scrapbook*, 1977; *Rocky II*.

AWARDS: Show West Actor of the Year, 1979; Star of the Year, 1977; Academy Award, Best Picture, 1976: *Rocky;* Golden Globe, Best Picture, 1976; Donatello for Best Actor in Europe, 1976; National Theatre Owners, 1976; Chris-topher, 1976; Scholastic Magazine Bell Ringer, 1976.

SIDELIGHTS: MEMBERSHIPS—SAG, Writers Guild, Stunt-mans Association (hon), Directors Guild.

Mr. Stallone was nominated for two Academy Awards for acting and writing for his work in *Rocky* in 1976, which has only occurred three times in the history of the Academy Awards.

ADDRESS: Agent—Creative Artists Agency, 1888 Century Park E., Los Angeles, CA 90067.*

* * *

STANLEY, Gordon, actor, writer, and singer

PERSONAL: Born December 20, 1951, in Boston, MA; son of Malcolm McClain (a medical research scientist; maiden name, Dumoff) Stanley; married Renée Lutz (a stage man-ager), May 18, 1980. EDUCATION: Brown University, A.B., 1973; Temple University, M.F.A., 1976.

CAREER: DEBUT—First Murderer, *Richard III*, Court, Chi-cago, IL, 1969. NEW YORK DEBUT—Singer, *Lyrical and Satirical*, Joseph Jefferson, 1977, 14 performances. PRINCI-PAL STAGE APPEARANCES—(Broadway) Fleming, *Onward Victoria*, 1980; Jacob, *Joseph and the Amazing Technicolor Dreamcoat*, 1981–83; (Off-Broadway) Charlie, *Allegro*, Equity Library, 1978; Doc, *The Tooth of Crime*, 1979; Cecil, *Elizabeth and Essex*, 1980; Mr. Erlanson, *A Little Night Music*, 1981; Rodney, *Two on the Isles*, 1981; Sid el Kar, *The Desert Song*, Light Opera of Manhattan, 1981; (Stock/Dinner Theater) First Voice, *Under Milk Wood*, Court, Chicago, IL, 1970; Allan Felix, *Play it Again, Sam*, Ben-volio, *Romeo and Juliet*, Gangster #2, *Kiss Me, Kate*, Boss Mangan, *Heartbreak House*, Weathervane Theatre, 1971; multiple roles, *Bullshot Crummond*, Grendel's Lair, Phila-delphia, 1977; Morris, *1776*, Carter-Barron, 1980; Mr. Snow, *Carousel*, Coachlight, 1980; Motel, *Fiddler on the Roof*, Artpark, 1981; Freddy, *My Fair Lady*, Theatre of the Stars, Atlanta, GA, 1983.

AWARDS: GRANTS—National Endowment for the Arts, De-sign Demonstration, 1981.

SIDELIGHTS: MEMBERSHIPS—AEA; SAG; National Trust for Historic Preservation.

ADDRESS: Office—330 W. 45th Street, Lobby J, New York, NY 10036. Agent—c/o Jeff Lowenthal, Monty Silver Agency, 200 W. 57th Street, New York, NY 10019.

* * *

STAPLETON, Jean (nee Jeanne Murray), actress

PERSONAL: Born in New York City; daughter of Joseph E. and Marie (Stapleton) Murray; married William Putch (a producer and director). EDUCATION: Studied with Carli Laklan at the American Apprentice Theatre, with Jane Rose and William Hansen at the American Actors Company, with Joseph Anthony and Peter Frye at the American Theatre Wing, and with Harold Clurman; attended Hunter College in New York. NON-THEATRICAL CAREER: Secretary.

CAREER: DEBUT—at the Greenwood Playhouse, Peaks Island, Maine, 1941. NEW YORK DEBUT—Mrs. Watty, *The Corn Is Green*, Equity Library Theatre, 1948. PRINCIPAL STAGE APPEARANCES—Sang with the *Robert Shaw Chorale* touring women's clubs performing *Double Dozen Double Damask Dinner Napkins*, 1940; stock at Peterborough Playhouse, NH, Whitefield Playhouse, NH, and Chase Barn Playhouse, 1947–48; Mother, *America Gothic*, Circle in the Square, NY, 1953; Inez, *The Summer House*, Playhouse, NY, 1953; Sister, *Damn Yankees*, 46th Street, NY, 1955; Sue, *Bells Are Ringing*, Shubert, NY, 1956; at her husband's theatre, the Totem Pole Playhouse, Fayettesville, PA: Woody, *Goodbye My Fancy*, Miss Cooper, *Separate Tables*, Mother, *Charm*, Grace, *Bus Stop*, Mme. St. Pe, *The Waltz of the Toreadors*, 1958; Swart Petry, *A Swim in the Sea*, Walnut Street, Philadelphia, 1958; Maisie Madigan, *Juno*, Winter Garden, NY, 1959; Sally Adams, *Call Me Madam*, Totem Pole Playhouse, 1959; Laura Partridge, *The Solid Gold Cadillac*, Totem Pole Playhouse, 1960; Mrs. Ochs, *Rhinoceros*, Longacre, NY, 1961;

Totem Pole Playhouse: Mrs. Keller, *The Miracle Worker*, Emma, *Apple in the Attic*, revue, *A Thurber Carnival*, Opal, *Everybody Loves Opal*, Mrs. Baker, *Come Blow Your Horn*, Mrs. Spofford, *Gentleman Prefer Blondes*, Nannie, *All for Mary*, 1962; Aunt Eller, *Oklahoma!*, 1963; Mrs. Strakosh, *Funny Girl*, Winter Garden, NY, 1964; Totem Pole Playhouse: Brewster, *A Rainy Day in Newark*, Rosemary, *Picnic*, Annabelle, *George Washington Slept Here*, Mrs. Walworth, *Speaking of Murder*, Mrs. Pearce, *My Fair Lady*, Mrs. Yoder, *Papa Is All*, Mother Abbess, *The Sound of Music*, 1964, Anna Leonowens, *The King and I*, Bloody Mary, *South Pacific*, Lottie, *The Dark at the Top of the Stairs*, 1964, Dolly Gallagher Levi, *Hello Dolly!*, 1971, Mrs. Baer, *Butterflies Are Free*, Lola, *Come Back Little Sheba*, Opal, *Everybody Loves Opal*, 1972; *The Time of the Cuckoo*, Ahmanson, Los Angeles, 1974; Totem Pole Playhouse: title-role, *The Secret Affairs of Mildred Wild*, *Hay Fever*, *The Late Christopher Bean*, 1976, *The Reluctant Debutante*, *The Show-Off*, 1977, *The Great Sebastian's*, title-role, *Daisy Mayme*, *Little Mary Sunshine*, 1978, Miss Marple, *A Murder Is Announced*, *Papa Is All*, 1979, Miss Marple, *Murder at the Vicarage*, Aunt Eller, *Oklahoma!*, 1981, *The Curious Savage*, *Butterfly Days*, 1981, *The Corn Is Green*, 1982, *Ernest in Love*, 1983; *The Late Christopher Bean*, Kennedy Center, Washington, DC, 1983; *The Show-Off*, Syracuse Stage, Syracuse, NY, 1983; Old Woman, *Candide*, Balti-

JEAN STAPLETON

more Opera Company, 1984; *The Italian Lesson*, Baltimore Opera Company, 1985.

MAJOR TOURS—Mrs. Watty, *The Corn Is Green*, 1948–49; Myrtle Mae, *Harvey*, 1948–49 and 1949–50; Mrs. Coffman, *Come Back Little Sheba*, 1950–51; Mrs. Ochs, *Rhinoceros*, tour of California, 1961; Aary, *Mornings at Seven*, national tour, 1976; title-role, *Daisy Mayme*, 1979–80; *The Show-Off*, tour of Florida ending at the Papermill Playhouse, NJ, 1983; *Clara's Play*, New England tour, 1983.

FILM DEBUT—*Damn Yankees*, 1958. PRINCIPAL FILM APPEAR-ANCES—*Bells Are Ringing*, 1960; *Something Wild*, 1961; *Cold Turkey*, 1971; *Klute*, 1971; *The Buddy System*.

PRINCIPAL TELEVISION APPEARANCES—*Omnibus; Camera Three; Naked City; You Can't Take It with You; Aunt Mary*; played Edith Bunker on *All in the Family* series from 1971; for cable tv, Ms. Tweed, *Something's Afoot*; Ogress, *Jack and the Beanstalk* and Fairy Godmother, *Cinderella*, Faerie Tale Theatre; movies for television—*Isobel's Choice, Angel Dusted, Eleanor: First Lady of the World, A Matter of Sex*.

AWARDS: Three Emmy Awards for Edith Bunker, *All in the Family;* honorary degrees from Emerson College, Boston, Hood College, Frederick, MD, Monmouth College, NJ.

SIDELIGHTS: MEMBERSHIPS—President, advisory board, Women's Research & Institute, Washington, DC; board, Eleanor Roosevelt's Val-Kill, Hyde Park, NY; board, Wonder Woman Foundation, New York City. RECREATIONS: Swimming, singing, reading.

ADDRESS: Agent—Bauman and Hiller, 9220 Sunset Blvd., Los Angeles, CA 90069.

* * *

STATTEL, Robert, actor

PERSONAL: Born November 20, 1932 in Floral Park, NY; son of Raymond G. (a beverage distributor) and Elizabeth (Dubon) Stattel. EDUCATION: Manhattan College, B.A. (English Literature); studied European Theatre Style at the Institute for Advanced Studies in Theatre Arts. MILITARY: U.S. Navy, 1956–57.

CAREER: DEBUT—Lysander, *A Midsummer Night's Dream,* Oregon Shakespeare Festival, Ashland, OR, 1955. NEW YORK DEBUT—Theo, *Heloise,* Gate, 1968. PRINCIPAL STAGE APPEARANCES—Camille, *Danton's Death,* Mr. Harcourt, *The Country Wife,* Edgar, *King Lear,* Lincoln Center Repertory, 1966–69; Von Taussig, *A Patriot for Me,* NY, 1969; Robert, *Voices,* NY, 1972; understudy, *The Incomparable Max,* NY, 1971–72; Dr. Watson, *Sherlock Holmes,* NY, 1975–76; appeared at the City Stage Company (CSC) from 1978–to 1982 in the title roles in *King Lear, Oedipus Rex, Oedipus at Colonnus, Woyzeck, Dr. Faustus, Henry IV,* and leading roles in *The Cherry Orchard, Gilles de Rais,* Don

ROBERT STATTEL

Juan, *The Cavern; The Fuhrer Bunker* and *Great Days,* American Place, NY; *The Seagull* and *The Learned Ladies,* Roundabout, NY; other Off-Broadway: *Blue Boys, Ergo, Iphigenia in Aulis, The Minister's Black Veil, The Persians, Taming of the Shrew, Domestic Issues, Four Friends, The Two Character Play;* appeared at Martinique Theatre, Public Theatre, Circle in the Square, Playwrights Horizons, Phoenix, Theatre de Lys, Quaigh, in Circle Repertory; regional theatre companies include the American Shakespeare Festival, Stratford, CT (four seasons), Arena Stage, Washington, DC, Syracuse Stage Company, PAF Playhouse, Indiana Repertory, Milwaukee Repertory, McCarter. In New York, he appeared in eight productions at the New York Shakespeare Festival between 1966 and 1976.

PRINCIPAL TELEVISION APPEARANCES—*You Are There; Kojak; Love of Life; As the World Turns; All My Children; The Late Great Me; Another World; King Lear; The Fifty Years' Revolution; The Adams Chronicles.*

AWARDS: Drama Desk Award Nomination: *King Lear.*

ADDRESS: Home—377 Bleecker Street, New York, NY 10014. Agent—Kingman Ganz, 1501 Broadway, New York, NY 10036.

* * *

STEINBERG, Norman, writer

PERSONAL: Born June 6, 1939, in Brooklyn, NY; son of Morris Alex and Lillian (May) Steinberg; married Bonnie Strock (an interior designer) October 8, 1977. EDUCATION: University of Maryland, A.B. 1961; University of Pittsburgh, LLB (School of Law), 1964.

WRITINGS: SCREENPLAYS—*Blazing Saddles* (with Mel Brooks), 1972; *Yes, Giorgio,* 1982; *My Favorite Year,* 1982; *Johnny Dangerously,* 1984.

RELATED CAREER: Has written extensively for numerous TV series, pilots, specials and variety shows.

AWARDS: Writers Guild of America West Nominee, 1982; Writers Guild of America West Award, 1973: *Blazing Saddles;* Emmy Award, *Flip Wilson Show,* 1970.

SIDELIGHTS: MEMBERSHIPS—Writers Guild of America, Directors Guild of America, SAG.

ADDRESS: Office—c/o Paramount Studios, 5555 Melrose Avenue, LA, CA, 90038.

* * *

STEINER, Sherry, actress

PERSONAL: Born September 29, 1948; daughter of Jack (an accountant) and Doris (Glass) Handsman. EDUCATION: Chatham College, B.A.; studied with Kurt Cerf, Stephen Strimpell, and Irene Baird in New York City. RELIGION: Jewish.

CAREER: DEBUT—Ophelia, *Hamlet,* Walnut Street Theatre, Philadelphia Drama Guild, 1977. NEW YORK DEBUT—Understudy, *Ashes,* Manhattan Theatre Club/Public Theatre, 1977. PRINCIPAL STAGE APPEARANCES—Sonia, *Uncle Vanya,* Philadelphia Drama Guild, 1978; Hillary, *Safe House,* Manhattan Theatre Club, 1978; the daughter, *Catsplay,* Promenade, NY, 1978; Sister Rita, *The Runner Stumbles,* Actor's Theatre of Louisville, KY, 1978; New Play Festival at the Actor's Theatre of Louisville, 1979; Elizabeth, *Sorrows of Stephen,* Public Theatre, NY, 1979; member of the acting company at the Brooklyn Academy of Music, 1979–80; Nurse/Madeleine, *Piaf,* Plymouth, 1980–81; Susan, *Loose Ends,* Alliance, Atlanta, GA, 1982; Edward/Victoria, *Cloud 9,* Theatre de Lys, NY, 1982–83; member of the People's Light & Theatre Company, Malvern, PA, 1984.

FILM DEBUT—Blind girl, *The Asylum of Satan,* 1971. PRINCIPAL FILM APPEARANCES—Sherry, *Three on a Meathook,* 1972; Lost Girl, *The Devil's Express;* Victim, *The Demon.* TELEVISION DEBUT—Psychiatrist, *Ryan's Hope.*

SIDELIGHTS: MEMBERSHIPS—AEA; SAG; AFTRA.

"As a child growing up in the New York area, I attended both Broadway and Off-Broadway productions. To be an actress was a dream begun at 12 and continues into the present."

ADDRESS: Home—341 S. 25th Street, Philadelphia, PA 19103. Agent—Writers & Artists, 162 W. 56th Street, New York, NY 10019.

* * *

STENBORG, Helen, actress

PERSONAL: Born January 24, 1925 in Minneapolis, MN; daughter of John A. (a dentist) and Ida M. (Johnson) Stenborg; married Barnard Hughes (an actor) on April 19, 1950; children: Douglas, Laura. EDUCATION: Attended Hunter College, Columbia University; studied drama with Frances Robinson-Duff.

CAREER: DEBUT—Understudy, Claudia, *Claudia,* National Touring Company, 1943. NEW YORK DEBUT—Witness, *The Trial of the Catonsville Nine,* Lyceum, 1971. PRINCIPAL STAGE APPEARANCES—Wife, *Sheep on the Runway,* Helen Hayes, NY; *Fifth of July,* Circle Repertory, NY, 1978; *Da,* Morosco, NY, 1979; *A Life,* Morosco, NY, 1980. MAJOR TOURS—Understudy, *Claudia,* national tour, 1943; *Three's a Family,* national tour; *Da,* national tour, 1979–80.

PRINCIPAL FILM APPEARANCES—*Three Days of the Condor,* 1975; *The Europeans,* 1979; *Starting Over,* 1979; *Fifth of July; A Flash of Green.* TELEVISION DEBUT—*Kraft Television Theatre.*

SIDELIGHTS: MEMBERSHIPS—AEA; AFTRA; Episcopal Actors Guild; SAG; Circle Repertory Company.

ADDRESS: Agent—Milton Goldman, ICM, 40 W. 57th Street, New York, NY 10019.

STEWART, Michael, playwright, lyricist

PERSONAL: Born August 1, 1929, in New York City; son of William E. and Kate (Dunitz) Rubin. EDUCATION: Queen's College, B.A.; Yale University, M.F.A., 1953.

CAREER: WRITINGS: PLAYS—*Those That Play the Clowns,* 1966; *D,* 1980. LIBRETTOS—*Bye Bye Birdie,* 1960; *Carnival,* 1961; *Hello, Dolly!,* 1964; *George M.* (with John and Fran Pascal), 1968; *Mack and Mabel,* 1974; *I Love My Wife* (also lyrics), 1977; *The Grand Tour* (with Mark Bramble), 1979; *42nd Street* (with Mark Bramble), 1980; *How Do You Do I Love You; Harrigan and Hart,* 1984; *Treasure Island* (with Mark Bramble; forthcoming). LYRICS—*Barnum,* 1980. TELEVISION—*Caesar's Hour,* 1956–58. BOOKS—*Belle* (novel), 1977.

AWARDS: Antoinette Perry Award, 1964: *Hello, Dolly!;* Antoinette Perry Award, 1960: *Bye Bye Birdie;* New York Drama Critics Award, 1964: *Hello Dolly;* New York Drama Critics Award, 1961: *Carnival.*

ADDRESS: Office—c/o Dramatists Guild, 234 W. 44th Street, New York, NY 10036.

* * *

STILLER, Jerry, actor

PERSONAL: Born June 8, in New York; son of William and Bella Stiller; married Anne Meara (an actress) September 14, 1954; children: Amy, Benjamin. EDUCATION: Syracuse University, B.S. (Speech and Drama), 1950.

CAREER: PRINCIPAL STAGE APPEARANCES—Performed in various summer stock companies, 1951–53, and the Henry Street Settlement and the Cherry Lane Theatre, NY, Erie Playhouse, PA, Memphis Arena Theatre, TN, Phoenix, NY, Shakespeare Festival Theatre, Stratford, CT, New York Shakespeare Festival; Billy Barnes, *Showboat,* Chicago, 1950; *The Golden Apple,* NY, 1954; *Boubouroche,* NY, 1971; *The Ritz,* 1975; *Unexpected Guests,* 1977; *Hurlybury,* Promenade, then Barrymore, NY, 1984. MAJOR TOURS—*Peter Pan,* national tour, 1951.

PRINCIPAL FILM APPEARANCES—*The Taking of Pelham One, Two, Three,* 1974; *Airport '75,* 1974; *The Ritz,* 1976; *Nasty Habits,* 1976; *Those Lips, Those Eyes,* 1980. PRINCIPAL TELEVISION APPEARANCES—*Take Five with Stiller and Meara,* 1977–78; *Joe and Sons;* guest appearances on game shows, talk shows and specials. NIGHT CLUB APPEARANCES—Stiller and Meara Comedy Team, Compass Players, St. Louis, MO, 1957; Happy Medium, Chicago, 1960; Village Gate, NY; Village Vanguard, NY; The Blue Angel, NY; Bon Soir, NY; Phase Two, NY; Mr. Kelly's, Chicago; The Hungry I, San Francisco; Establishment, London, England; Sands, Las Vegas; Flamingo, Las Vegas; Harrah's, Reno; Lake Tahoe, NV.

THEATRE-RELATED CAREER: With wife, formed commercial production company in New York to aid businesses in promotion, advertising, and image building.

AWARDS: Voice Imagery Award, Radio Advertising Bureau; honored by the Marketing Communications Executives International for (their) outstanding contributions on advertising and promotion; Arents Pioneer Medal, 1979; Entertainment Father of the Year Award, 1977; Distinguished Alumnus Award, Syracuse University, 1973.

SIDELIGHTS: "After their marriage, the Stillers began acting with Joe Papp's just-formed Shakespeare Company in Central Park. Jerry was usually cast as a clown or oaf and Anne was cast as the leading lady. Their salaries were small. One day they discovered that the ushers made more. This revelation plus the two factors that they wanted to have children, and that their innate comedic talents were surfacing, led the Stillers to leave the legitimate theatre and form a comedy team. In addition to their act together, Jerry and Anne have taken time in recent years to continue their acting careers; Jerry has popped up several times on numerous television sitcoms such as *Alice, Private Benjamin, No Soap Radio* and *Amanda's*. Both hope to star in their own television special in the near future."

ADDRESS: Agent—c/o William Morris Agency, 1350 Avenue of the Americas, New York, NY 10019.

* * *

STINTON, Colin, actor

PERSONAL: Born March 10, 1947; son of Frederick M. (an engineer) and Barbara O. (Botting) Stinton. EDUCATION: Attended Northern Illinois University, three years.

CAREER: DEBUT—Ensemble, *Verbatim,* Body Politic Theatre/Dinglefest Theatre Company, Chicago, IL. NEW YORK DEBUT—Murray/Announcer, *The Water Engine,* Public Theatre, New York Shakespeare Festival, 1971 and Plymouth, NY, 1977–78. PRINCIPAL STAGE APPEARANCES—*Guessworks,* Body Politic Theatre, Chicago, IL; *Tom Swift and His . . . ,* Body Politic Theatre, Chicago, IL; Cody the Horse Dreamer, *Geography of a Horse Dreamer,* Organic Theatre, Chicago, IL; Jake, *Green Julia,* Magic Circle Theatre, Chicago, IL; Cop/Detective, *Cop-Out,* Hull House Theatre, Chicago, IL; Treetrunk Eel, *Captain Marbles,* St. Nicholas Theatre, Chicago, IL; Card Player, *Prairie du Chien,* Public Theatre, New York Shakespeare Festival; Goodman Theatre Company, Chicago, IL; Buckley, *Native Son,* Nick Potter, *Holiday,* Van Brandt, *Lone Canoe,* Walter Burns, *The Front Page,* Edmond, *Edmond;* series of plays, *The Invitational,* Ensemble Studio Theatre, NY; Glassnap, *The Beaver Coat,* Feste, *Twelfth Night,* Circle Repertory, NY, 1980–81; McGahey, *The Curse of an Aching Heart,* Little Theatre, NY; Edmond, *Edmond,* Provincetown Playhouse, NY; Angus, *Early Warnings,* Manhattan Theatre Club, NY; Derek Meadle, *Quartermaine's Terms,* Playhouse 91, NY.

FILM DEBUT—Billy, *The Verdict,* 1982. PRINCIPAL FILM APPEARANCES—Dale, *Daniel,* 1983; Sam, *Paul's Case;* Barnum, *Mr. Barnum; Telzon.* PRINCIPAL TELEVISION APPEARANCES—Elliot, *The Hamptons.*

THEATRE-RELATED CAREER: Three years as actor, writer, and associate director of the Dinglefest Theatre Company, Chicago, IL, specializing in improvisational and original satirical revues.

AWARDS: Theatre World Award, Murray/Announcer, 1978: *The Water Engine;* Joseph Jefferson Award, Jake, *Green Julia;* Joseph Jefferson Award Nomination, Nick Potter, *Holiday.*

SIDELIGHTS: MEMBERSHIPS—AEA; SAG; AFTRA.

ADDRESS: Agent—DHKPR, 165 West 46th Street, New York, NY 10036.

* * *

STONE, Ezra (ne Ezra Chaim Feinstone), actor, director, producer, writer, teacher, farmer

PERSONAL: Born December 2, 1917, in New Bedford, MA; son of Solomon (a chemist, teacher, collector, philanthropist) and Rose (Meadow), Feinstone; married Sara Seegar (an actress, director, teacher), October 5, 1942; children: Josef, Francine. EDUCATION: Graduate, Oak Lane Country Day School of Temple University, 1934; attended summer courses at CCNY, and Temple University; studied for the stage at the American Academy of Dramatic Arts with Charles Vehlinger and Philip Loeb; also studied at Columbia University. POLITICS: Independent. MILITARY: U.S. Army Special Services, Staff Sergeant, 1940–43; USAAF, M/Sgt., 1943–46; director of USO Camp shows. NON-THEATRICAL CAREER: Director of Special Events, consultant, IBM for 22 years.

CAREER: DEBUT—Young child, *Phosphorus* and *Suppressed Desires,* YMHA Players, Philadelphia, PA, 1924. NEW YORK DEBUT—Seven roles in revue, *Parade,* Guild, 1935. PRINCIPAL STAGE APPEARANCES—*The Flower Seller,* Plays and Players Club, Philedelphia, PA, 1929; Abie Applebaum, pre-Broadway tryout, *Room Service,* closed Philedelphia, 1935; Ed, *Oh Evening Star!,* Empire, 1936; Al, *Three Men on a Horse,* Playhouse, 1935; Mistol Bottome, *Brother Rat,* Biltmore, NY, 1936; Bank Messenger *Room Service,* Cort, NY, 1937; Henry Aldrich, *What a Life,* Biltmore, NY, 1938; Dromio, *The Boys from Syracuse,* Alvin, NY, 1938; Arthur Lee, *See My Lawyer,* Biltmore, NY, 1939; Joshua Winslow, *Your Loving Son,* Brattle, Cambridge, MA, 1940; Sir Epicure Mammon, *The Alchemist,* NY City Center, 1948; Tony Lumpkin, *She Stoops to Conquer,* NY City Center, 1949; Son-in-Law, *The Middle of the Night,* Bucks County Playhouse, PA, 1958; Banjo, *The Man Who Came to Dinner* Maxwell Archer, *Once More with Feeling,* Bucks County Playhouse, 1959; Capt. Andy, *Showboat,* Cape Cod Melody Ten, Hyannis, MA, 1960.

MAJOR TOURS—Incas the Younger, *The Last of the Mohicans,* Georgie, *Quality Street,* Sid Sawyer, *Tom Sawyer,* Jim Hawkins, *Treasure Island,* National Junior Theatre of Washington, DC, East Coast tour, 1931–32; vaudeville act, Steel Pier, Atlantic City, NJ, Keith's Theatre, Wilmington, DE, 1932; Studio Messinger, *Ah! Wilderness,* 1935; directed and appeared in U.S. Army Special Service productions of *We're Ready, First Year, Brother Rat, Three Men on a Horse, Six Jerks in a Jeep.*

PRINCIPAL STAGE WORK: Directed—*Brother Rat*, touring production, 1936; *Room Service*, touring production, 1937; *What a Life*, touring production, 1938; *See My Lawyer*, Biltmore, NY, 1939; with Herbert Berghof, *Reunion in New York*, Little, NY, 1940; summer tryout, *Your Loving Son*, 1940; U.S. Army Special Services touring productions: *We're Ready, First Year, Brother Rat, Three Men on a Horse, Six Jerks in a Jeep; This Is the Army*, Broadway, NY, 1942; *Salvo*, Metropolitan Opera House, NY, 1943; tours of Air Force revues: *Bonds Away, At Your Service, You Bet Your Life*, 1943; *January Thaw*, Golden, NY, 1946; *Me and Molly*, Belasco, NY, 1948; *To Tell You the Truth*, New Stages, 1948; *At War with the Army*, Booth, NY, 1949; pre-Broadway tryouts, *The Man That Corrupted Hadleyburg*, Erlanger, Philadelphia, 1951; *Count Your Blessings*, Bucks County Playhouse, 1952; *Blue Danube*, Bucks County Playhouse, PA, 1952; *The Pink Elephant*, Playhouse, NY, 1953; summer touring companies, *Loco, The Play's the Thing*, 1953; pre-Broadway tryout, *Comin' Thru the Rye*, Theatre Guild at the Olney, MD, 1953; *Blithe Spirit*, Bucks County Playhouse, PA, 1954; *Mrs. Gibbon's Boys*, Bucks County Playhouse, PA, 1955; tent ice show version of *On the Town*, Asbury Park, NJ, 1956; *Wake Up Darling*, Barrymore, NY, 1956; pre-Broadway tryout, *The Mistress of The Inn*, Bucks County Playhouse, PA, 1956; *Season in the Sun*, Bucks County Playhouse, PA, 1957; one women show of Ethel Barrymore Colt, *Curtains Up!*, ANTA, Theatre de Lys, NY, 1958; *Half in Earnest*, Bucks County Playhouse, PA, 1957; *Curtains Up!*, East 74th Street, NY, 1959; West Coast tryout, *Only Game in Town*, Ivar Theatre, Hollywood, CA, 1960; *Dear Ruth, Come Blow Your Horn*, Sombrero Playhouse, Phoenix, AZ, 1962; IBM industrial show, *100 Percent Club*, San Francisco, CA, 1963, NYC, 1964; benefit performance, *Tunnel of Love*, Biltmore, LA, CA, 1963; summer tryout, *God Bless Our Bank*, Charlotte, NC, 1963; *Fallen Angels*, La Jolla Playhouse, 1963; *Sweet Land*, tricentennial celebration, Newtown, PA, 1983.

FILM DEBUT—Ally Bangs, *Those Were the Days*, 1940. PRINCIPAL FILM APPEARANCES—*This Is the Army*, 1943; directed/staged, *The Daydreamer*, 1966, *Tammy and the Millionaire*, 1967.

PRINCIPAL RADIO AND TELEVISION APPEARANCES: debut, commercials for *Childrens Hour*, Philadelphia, 1932–34, *Young America*, 1932–34, Tasty Yeast Program, 1934–35; from 1938–40: *Rudy Vallee Show, Kate Smith Show, Eddie Cantor Show, Fred Allen Show, Walter O'Keefe Show, Jack Benny Show, Norman Corwin Show, Kay Kayser Show, Stoopnagle and Bud, We the People, Hobby Lobby, Edgar Bergen Show, Lux Radio Theatre*, created the role of Henry Aldrich, *The Aldrich Family* series, 1938–41, *The Eternal Light* series, 1951–present.

TELEVISION DEBUT—An FCC demonstration as Henry Aldrich in *The Aldrich Family*, 1940; *Deuteronomy Katz*. 1952; *Tvye*, 1953; *Faye Emerson Show*, 1954; Urial, *Trial of Urial*, 1959; Rabbit, *Kim Quixote, Hawaiian Eye*, 1960; *Flashback*, 1963.

PRINCIPAL TELEVISION WORK: Producer/director—*Olsen and Johnson Buick Show*, 1948–49; *Li'l Abner*, 1948; *The Aldrich Family*, 1949; *Danny Thomas Show*, 1950–51; *Martha Raye Show*, 1950–51; *Fred Allen Show*, 1950–51; *Ed Wynn Show*, 1950–51; *Colgate Comedy Hour*, 1950–51; *Ezio Pinza Show*, 1950–51; *Life with Father*, 1952; *Love That Guy*, 1952; *Auto Light Easter Parade*, 1953; *I Married Joan*, 1954–55; *Joe and Mabel*, 1955–56; *Ceasar's Hour*, 1956; *Command Preformance* (special), 1957 and a *Command Performance* with Ethel Barrymore, 1958; *4 and 20 Buddahs*, 1959; "Kelly and the College Man," *Bachelor Father*, 1959; *Angel*, 1960; *Affairs of Anatol*, 1961; *The Hathways*, 1961; *The Shari Lewis Show*, 1962; IBM industrials, ". . . a better way", *Area for Action*, 1963; Bob Hope Presents: *Wake Up Darling* and *Time for Elizabeth*, 1964; *My Living Doll*, 1964–65; *Take Five*, 1964; IBM Processing Division, *The Know How People; Petticoat Junction; The Phyllis Diller Show; Lost in Space; Please Don't Eat the Daises; Julia; The Flying Nun; The Debbie Reynolds Show; The Jimmy Stewart Show; Sandy Duncan Show;* Night clubs—revue, *The Roaring Twenties*, Chicago, IL, 1951.

THEATRE RELATED CAREER: Director of student productions/lecturer, University of Virginia, Temple University, University of Pennsylvania, Michigan State University, Adelphi, Brooklyn College, Boston University, The New School for Social Research, Yale University and the University of North Carolina; served as special projects consultant, Secretary of Commerce of the Commonwealth of Pennsylvania, 1952, the Fred Miller Theatre, Milwaukee, WI, the Ford Foundation Humanities Program, 1958; Fresno Community Theatre, 1960; teacher, American Academy of Dramatic Arts, 1956–59; founder and executive director of the postgraduate professional center of the AADA, since 1959, associate director of AADA, also taught at the American Theatre Wing, Professional Training Program, 1946–58.

WRITINGS: Sketches for: *Li'l Abner, The Aldrich Family, Danny Thomas Show, Martha Raye Show, Fred Allen Show, Ed Wynn Show, Colgate Comedy Hour, Ezio Pinza Show, Caesar's Hour*, (also editor); with Larry Gelbhardt, *Command Performance with Ed Wynn*, and *Command Performance with Ethel Barrymore*; with Rick Dorio, episodes of *The Hathways; Swami Chimp, A Man for Amanda*; writer: *Petticoat Junction, The Phyllis Diller Show, Lost in Space, Please Don't Eat the Daisies, Julia, The Flying Nun, The Debbie Reynolds Show, The Jimmy Stewart Show, Sandy Duncan Show*; with Weldon Nelick, *Coming Major*; contributor to magazines and newspapers, and since November, 1962, has written a monthly humor column "Actors' Glossary," for *Equity* magazine.

AWARDS: For "Real World", IBM; Grand Prize, Barcelona Film Festival, *The 40 Million;* Cine Golden Eagle Award; Golden Mike Award, Old Time Radio Association, Baltimore, MD; National Visuals, Cris, N.A.M.

SIDELIGHTS: MEMBERSHIPS—AEA, SAG, AGVA, Writers Guild, East, AFTRA, Radio and TV Directors Guild, SDG, SDIG, AADA, SSD&C, (secretary, 1960), TV Producers' Guild, Dramatists Guild, AMTA, Academy of Television Arts and Sciences, Actor's Fund of America, Radio Pioneers of America, American Legion, American Veterans' Committee, Air Force Society, Pennsylvania Association of Rescue Squads, Newton Reliance Company, Ayeshire Breeders' Association, Dairy Herd Improvement Association, Sacred Order of Old Bastards, Committee on Economic Development (Radio & TV), American Association for the UN, Trustee AADA, '84 Fellow AADA, Chairman of the Board, American National Theatre Academy West, American College Theatre Festival Regional Judge, the David Library of the American Revolution-director/president.

''Since moving back to Pennsylvania, Mr. Stone and his wife have been active in the cultural life of Newtown. Their production of *Sweet Land* included many local actors and technicians and brought the community together in celebration of their past through the theatre.''

ADDRESS: Home—Stone Meadow Farm, Box D, Newtown, PA, 18940. Office—c/o The David Library, Box 76, Washington Crossing, PA, 18977. Agent—Contemporary–Korman, 132 Lasky Drive, Los Angeles, CA, 90212; Georgia Gilley Agency, 8721 Sunset Blvd., Los Angeles, CA 90069.

* * *

STONE, Oliver, director, writer

PERSONAL: Born September 15, 1946, in New York City; son of Louis (a stockbroker) and Jacqueline (Goddet) Stone; married Majwa Sarkis, May 22, 1971 (divorced 1977); Elizabeth Burkit Cox (an assistant in film production), June 7, 1981. EDUCATION: Attended Hill School, 1964; Yale University, 1965; New York University, B.F.A., 1971. MILITARY: U.S. Army Infantry, Specialist 4th Class.

WRITINGS: SCREENPLAYS—*Seizure* (also directed), 1973; *Midnight Express,* 1978; *The Hand* (also directed), 1981; *Conan the Barbarian,* 1982; *Scarface,* 1983.

AWARDS: Academy Award, Best Screenplay Adaptation, 1978: *Midnight Express;* Writers Guild Award, 1978: *Midnight Express;* Bronze Star for Valor, Purple Heart.

SIDELIGHTS: MEMBERSHIPS—Academy of Motion Picture Arts and Sciences, Writers Guild of America, Directors Guild of America, Yale Club.

ADDRESS: Office—9025 Wilshire Blvd., #301, Beverly Hills, CA, 90211. Agent—Jim Wiatt, c/o ICM Agency, 8899 Beverly Blvd., Beverly Hills, CA 90048.

* * *

STOPPARD, Tom, CBE (cr. 1978), playwright and critic

PERSONAL: Born July 3, 1937, in Zlin, Czechoslovakia; son of Eugene Straussler and Martha Stoppard; married Jose Ingle, 1965 (divorced 1972); married Dr. Miriam Moore-Robinson, 1972. EDUCATION: Attended Pocklington, Yorkshire.

WRITINGS: PLAYS, PRODUCED—*Rosencrantz and Guildenstern Are Dead,* National, London, 1967, NY, Alvin, 1967; *Enter a Free Man,* London, 1968; *The Real Inspector Hound,* London, 1968; *After Magritte,* Ambiance, London, 1970; *Where Are They Now?,* 1970; *Dogg's Our Pet,* Ambiance, London, 1972; *Jumpers,* National, London, 1972; *Travesties,* Aldwych, London, 1974, NY, 1976; *Dirty Linen/Newfoundland,* Ambiance, London, 1976; *Every Good Boy Deserves Favour,* London, 1977; *Night and Day,* Phoenix, London, 1978; *Dogg's Hamlet and Cahoot's Macbeth,* Collegiate, London, 1979, NY; *The Real Thing,* London, 1982, Plymouth, NY, 1984. PLAYS, PUBLISHED—*Rosencrantz and Guildenstern Are Dead,* 1967; *The Real Inspector Hound,* 1968; *Albert's Bridge,* 1968; *Enter a Free Man,* 1968; *After Magritte,* 1971; *Jumpers,* 1972; *Artists Descending a Staircase,* 1973; *Where Are They Now?,* 1973; *Travesties,* 1975; *Dirty Linen/Newfoundland,* 1976; *Every Good Boy Deserves Favour,* 1978; *Professional Hamlet/Cahoots Macbeth,* 1980, *The Real Thing,* 1983; *On the Razzle,* 1984.

SCREENPLAYS—*The Romantic Englishwoman,* 1975; *Despair,* 1978; *The Human Factor,* 1979. TELEVISION PLAYS—*A Separate Peace,* 1966; *Teeth,* 1967; *Another Moon Called Earth,* 1967; *Neutral Ground,* 1968; *Boundaries,* 1975; *Squaring the Circle,* 1984. RADIO PLAYS—*The Disolution of Dominic Boot,* 1964; *M is for Moon Among Other Things,* 1964; *If You're Glad I'll Be Frank,* 1965; *Albert's Bridge,* 1967; *Where Are They Now?,* 1970; *Artist Descending a Staircase,* 1972; *The Dog It Was That Died,* 1983.

DIRECTED: Plays—*Born Yesterday,* Greenwich, London, 1973; *Every Good Boy Deserves Favour,* Metropolitan Opera, NY, 1979.

AWARDS: Antoinette Perry Award, Best Play, 1984: *The Real Thing;* Evening Standard Award, 1982: *The Real Thing;* Evening Standard Award, 1978: *Night and Day;* Antoinette Perry Award, Evening Standard Award, 1976: *Travesties;* Evening Standard Award, 1972: *Jumpers;* Antoinette Perry Award, New York Drama Critics Circle, 1968: *Rosencrantz and Guildenstern are Dead;* Evening Standard Award, Most Promising Playwright, 1968; John Whiting Award, 1967. Honorary Degrees—Bristol, 1976; Brumel, 1979; Leeds, 1980; Sussex, 1980.

SIDELIGHTS: RECREATIONS—Fishing, cricket.

ADDRESS: Agent—c/o Fraser and Dunlop, 91 Regent Street, London W1, UK.

* * *

STRANGIS, Greg, producer, writer

PERSONAL: Born January 5, 1951, in Los Angeles, CA; son of Sam J. (a producer and director) and Jane (Longuevan) Strangis; married Melissa Partridge, December 12, 1970 (divorced 1983); married Jill Jacobson (an actress), January 1, 1984; children: Walker Kellogue (first marriage). EDUCATION: California State University at Northridge, B.A., 1973.

CAREER: FIRST TELEVISION WORK—*Love, American Style.* PRINCIPAL TELEVISION WORK—Writer/producer, *Eight Is Enough;* writer/producer, *Harper Valley;* writer/producer, *Shirley;* executive producer, *Rainbow;* executive producer/co-writer, *Better Late Than Never;* executive producer, *Great Traffic Jam;* executive producer, *Not Just Another Love Affair;* executive producer, *Bulba* (pilot); executive producer/co-creator, *I Gave at the Office* (pilot).

AWARDS: People's Choice Award (2): *Eight Is Enough.*

SIDELIGHTS: MEMBERSHIPS—Writers Guild of America, West.

ADDRESS: Office—8271 Melrose Avenue, Los Angeles, CA 90046. Agent—c/o Harry Bloom Agency, 8833 Sunset Blvd., #202, Los Angeles, CA 90069.

* * *

STRASBERG, Susan (Elizabeth), actress

PERSONAL: Born May 22, 1938; daughter of Lee (drama coach, teacher, actor) and Paula (an actress and drama coach; maiden name, Miller) Strasberg; married Christopher Jones on September 25, 1965 (divorced); children: Jennifer. EDUCATION: Studied at the Actors Studio in New York.

CAREER: DEBUT—Maya, *Maya*, Theatre de Lys, NY, 1952. BROADWAY DEBUT—Anne Frank, *The Diary of Anne Frank*, Cort, 1955. PRINCIPAL STAGE APPEARANCES—Amanda, *Time Remembered*, Morosco, NY, 1957; Minnie Parnell, *Shadow of a Gunman*, Bijou, NY, 1958; *The Time of Your Life*, with the New York City Center at the Brussels World's Fair, 1958; Marguerite Gautier, *The Lady of the Camellias*, Winter Garden, NY, 1963. MAJOR TOURS—*Caesar and Cleopatra*, 1959; *A Woman's Rites* (one-woman show), Ohio and Florida, 1982–83.

FILM DEBUT—*Cobweb*, 1955. PRINCIPAL FILM APPEARANCES—Millie, *Picnic*, 1955; *Stage Struck*, 1958; *Kapo*, 1960; *Scream of Fear*, 1961; *Adventures of a Young Man*, 1962; *The Disorder*, 1964; *The Stronger*, *The High Bright Sun*, 1964; *The Trip*, 1967; *The Other Side of the Wind*; *Psyche Out*, 1968; *Chubasco*, 1968; *The Name of the Game Is Kill*, 1968; *Rollercoaster*, 1977; *The Manitou*, 1978; *In Praise of Older Women*, 1979; *Sweet Sixteen*, 1984; *The Returning*.

SUSAN STRASBERG

TELEVISION DEBUT—Goodyear Playhouse, *Catch a Falling Star*, 1953. PRINCIPAL TELEVISION APPEARANCES—*Romeo and Juliet*, 1954; "Dear Brutus," *Omnibus*, 1956; *The Cherry Orchard*, 1959; "Four Kings," *Chrysler Theatre*, 1963; "The Experiment," *CBS Playhouse*, 1969; *The Virginian*, 1966; *The F.B.I.*, 1967–68; *Name of the Game*, 1968; *Marcus Welby, M.D.*, 1969; *Men from Shiloh*, 1970; *Alias Smith and Jones*, 1971; *McCloud*, 1971; *Toma; Night Gallery*, 1971; *The Immigrants; Beggarman Thief; Mazes & Monsters; The World of Books; Terror in the Sky; Medical Center; Owen Marshall; The Mind's Eye*.

WRITINGS: AUTOBIOGRAPHY—*Bittersweet*.

THEATRE-RELATED CAREER: Lecturer: "Method or Madness: My 30 years in Acting"; "Love and Light: How to Survive in Today's World"; "Psychic Healing, Which Includes Self-Healing."

SIDELIGHTS: RECREATION—Writing, drawing, traveling.

FAVORITE ROLES: Millie in *Picnic*, *Kapo*, and Anne Frank.

ADDRESS: Office—c/o G. Hart, 1244-11th Street, Santa Monica, CA 90401. Agent—Traubner and Flynn, 1849 Sawtelle Blvd., #500, Los Angeles, CA 90025.

* * *

STREEP, Meryl, (ne Mary Louise Streep), actress

PERSONAL: Born in Summit, NJ; daughter of Harry and Mary W. Streep; married Donald J. Gummer, 1978; children: Henry. EDUCATION: Vassar College, B.A., 1971; Yale University, M.A., 1975.

CAREER: NEW YORK DEBUT—Imogen Parrott, *Trelawny of the 'Wells,'* Vivian Beaumont, 1975. PRINCIPAL STAGE APPEARANCES—Flora Meighan, *27 Wagons Full of Cotton*, Patricia, *A Memory of Two Mondays*, Jan/Edith Varney, *Secret Service*, Phoenix, NY, 1976; Katherine, *Henry V*, Jul/Isabella, *Measure for Measure*, Delacorte, NY, 1976; Dunyasha, *The Cherry Orchard*, Vivian Beaumont, NY, 1977; Lillian Holliday, *Happy End*, Chelsea Theatre Center, Martin Beck, NY, 1977; Katherina, *The Taming of the Shrew*, Delacorte, NY, 1978; Alice, *Wonderland in Concert*, Public, NY, 1978; Andrea, *Taken in Marriage*, Public, NY, 1979.

PRINCIPAL FILM APPEARANCES—*Julia*, 1977; *The Deer Hunter*, 1978; *Seduction of Joe Tynan*, 1979; *Kramer vs. Kramer*, 1980; *The French Lieutenant's Woman*, 1981; *Still of the Night*, 1982; *Sophie's Choice*, 1982; *Silkwood*, 1983.

PRINCIPAL TELEVISION APPEARANCES—(movies) *The Deadliest Season*, 1977; (mini-series) *Holocaust*, 1978; (specials) *Secret Service*, 1977; *Uncommon Women and Others*, 1978.

AWARDS: Academy Award Nomination, 1983: *Silkwood;* Academy Award, 1982: *Sophie's Choice;* New York Film Critics Award, Los Angeles Film Critics Award, Best Actress, Academy Award, Best Supporting Actress, 1980: *Kramer vs. Kramer;* National Society of Film Critics Award, Best Supporting Actress, 1978: *The Deer Hunter;* Hasty

Pudding Society Award, Harvard University, 1980; Woman of the Year Award, B'nai Brith, 1979; *Mademoiselle* Award, 1976; Honorary Ph.D., Dartmouth College, 1981, Vassar, 1983.

ADDRESS: Agent—c/o ICM, 40 W. 57th Street, New York, NY 10019.*

* * *

STREISAND, Barbra, singer, actress, producer, director

PERSONAL: Born April 24, 1942, in Brooklyn, NY; daughter of Emanuel and Diana (Rosen) Streisand; married Elliott Gould, March, 1963 (divorced); children: Jason Emanuel. EDUCATION: Attended Erasmus High School, Brooklyn, NY and Yeshiva of Brooklyn.

CAREER: NEW YORK STAGE DEBUT—*Another Evening with Harry Stoones*, Gramercy Arts, 1961. PRINCIPAL STAGE APPEARANCES—Miss Marmelstein, *I Can Get It for You Wholesale*, Shubert, NY, 1962; Fanny Brice, *Funny Girl*, Winter Garden, NY, 1964, Prince of Wales, London, 1966.

PRINCIPAL FILM APPEARANCES—*Funny Girl*, 1968; *Hello Dolly*, 1969; *On a Clear Day You Can See Forever*, 1970; *The Owl and the Pussy Cat*, 1970; *What's Up Doc?*, 1972; *Up the Sandbox*, 1972; *The Way We Were*, 1973; *For Pete's Sake*, 1974; *Funny Lady*, 1975; *The Main Event*, 1979; *A Star Is Born* (also produced), 1976; *All Night Long*, 1981; *Yentl* (also produced and directed), 1983.

PRINCIPAL TELEVISION APPEARANCES—*The Gary Moore Show; Tonight Show; Judy Garland Show; Dinah Shore Show; Ed Sullivan Show;* (specials) *My Name Is Barbra*, 1965; *Color Me Barbra*, 1966.

AWARDS: Academy Award Nomination, 1983: *Yentl;* Grammy Award, Best Female Vocalist, 1978, 1965, 1964, Best Song Writer (with Paul Williams), 1978; Georgie Award, 1977; Academy Award, Best Actress, 1968: *Funny Girl;* Emmy Award (5), 1965: *My Name Is Barbra*.

SIDELIGHTS: Ms. Streisand played in concert to 135,000 people in Central Park, New York, in 1968.

ADDRESS: Agent—c/o Solters and Sabinson, Inc., 62 W. 45th Street, New York, NY 10036. Office—c/o Press Relations, Columbia Records, Inc., 51 W. 52nd Street, New York, NY 10019.*

* * *

STRICK, Joseph, director, producer, writer

PERSONAL: Born July 6, 1923, in Braddock, PA; son of Frank (an inventor) and Rose (Abramowitz), Strick; married Anne (a publicist) May 9, 1946 (divorced 1965); Martine Rossignol (a paleobotanist) September 20, 1970; children: David, Betsy, Jeremy, Terence, Helen. EDUCATION: UCLA. NON-FILM CAREER: Chairman, Physical Sciences Corporation, 1965–75; chairman, Electrosolids Corporation, 1964–

75; founder, director, Westdale Savings & Loan Corp., 1965–74.

CAREER: FIRST FILM WORK—Director/producer, *Muscle Beach*, 1948. PRINCIPAL FILM WORK—Producer/director: *The Savage Eye*, 1959; *The Balcony*, 1963; *Legend of Boy and Eagle*, 1963; *Ulysses* (also screenwriter), 1967; *Ring of Bright Water*, 1968; *Tropic of Cancer* (also screenwriter), 1970; *Interviews*, 1971; *The Darwin Adventure*, 1972; *Road Movie*, 1974; *Portrait of the Artist as a Young Man*, 1977; producer, *Never Cry Wolf*, 1984.

PRINCIPAL STAGE WORK—Director: *Gallow's Humor*, Gaiety, Dublin, Ireland, 1965; *An Evening of Aristophanes*, Royal Shakespeare Company, Stratford-upon-Avon, Warwickshire.

RELATED CAREER: Managing director, Ulysses Film Production Ltd., 1967–present; president, Laser Film Corporation, 1970–present.

AWARDS: Academy Award Nominations: 1984: *Never Cry Wolf*, 1967: *Ulysses*, 1963: *The Balcony;* Christopher, 1972; Academy Award, 1971: *Interviews;* Venice Critics, Film Guild, 1959: *The Savage Eye;* Honorary Doctor of Humane Letters, Point Park College, 1984.

SIDELIGHTS: MEMBERSHIPS—Academy of Motion Picture Arts and Sciences, Directors Guild of America.

ADDRESS: Office—c/o TransLux Corporation, 625 Madison Avenue, New York, NY 10022.

* * *

STROUSE, Charles, composer

PERSONAL: Born June 7, 1928, in New York, NY; son of Ira and Ethel (Newman) Strouse; married Barbara Siman. EDUCATION: Eastman School of Music, B.M., 1947; studied composition with David Diamond, Aaron Copland, Nadia Boulanger and Arthur Berger.

CAREER: FIRST STAGE WORK—Composer, Green Mansions Theatre, Warrensburg, NY, 1952–55. FIRST BROADWAY WORK—Musical score, *Shoestring Reviews*, President, 1955. PRINCIPAL STAGE WORK—Musical score—*Shoestring '57*, 1956; *A Pound in Your Pocket*, 1956; *Bye, Bye Birdie*, 1960; *All American*, 1962; *Golden Boy*, 1964; *It's a Bird, It's a Plane, It's Superman*, 1966; *Applause*, 1970; book/music/lyrics, *Six*, 1971; *I and Albert*, London, 1972; *The Member of the Wedding*, 1975; *Annie*, 1977; *A Broadway Musical*, 1978; *Flowers for Algernon*, 1979; *Nightingale*, 1982; *Dance a Little Closer*, 1983; *Rags*, 1984.

PRINCIPAL FILM SCORES—*Mating Game*, 1959; *Bonnie and Clyde*, 1968; *The Night They Raided Minskys*, 1969; *There Was a Crooked Man*, 1970; *Just Tell Me What You Want*, 1979.

AWARDS: Honorary Doctor of Music, Niagra University, 1984.

ADDRESS: Agent—c/o Linden and Deutsch, 110 E. 59th Street, New York, NY 10022.

SULKA, Elaine, actress, producer, manager

PERSONAL: Born New York City; daughter of Michael (a butcher/shopkeeper) and Anna (Chehovich) Sulka; married Philip Meister in June 1967 (died 1982); children: Deirdre. EDUCATION: Queens College, Flushing, NY, B.A. (Sociology); Brown University, M.A. (Sociology); attended University of Wisconsin; studied at the Actors Workshop in San Francisco, 1957–60, also at the American Shakespeare Festival and Academy. NON-THEATRICAL CAREER: Probation officer; criminologist.

CAREER: DEBUT—with the Actors Workshop in San Francisco, 1957. PRINCIPAL STAGE APPEARANCES—Appeared with Old Globe Theatre Company, San Diego, CA, 1961 and 1963; understudy, Courtesan, *The Comedy of Errors,* understudy, Goneril, *King Lear,* American Shakespeare Festival, Stratford, CT, 1963; performed in approximately 30 productions with the National Shakespeare Company, including Rosalind, *As You Like It,* Katherine, *The Taming of the Shrew,* Gertrude, *Hamlet,* Lady Macbeth, *Macbeth,* Beatrice, *Much Ado About Nothing; Medea,* Circle in the Square, NY. Performed in over 50 classical revivals and original works at the Cubiculo, NY; *Brotherhood,* St. Mark's Playhouse, NY, 1971; Marylou, *The Brothers,* Theatre Four, NY, 1972.

PRINCIPAL STAGE WORK, PRODUCED—*Happy Ending* and *Day of Absence,* Harper Theatre, Chicago, IL, 1966; thirty-nine abbreviated and full-length Shakespearean productions for touring with the National Shakespeare Company.

THEATRE—RELATED CAREER: Co-founder with husband, and managing director, the national Shakespeare Company, 1963–present; co-founder, producer, director and performer, the Cubiculo Theatre, 1968–present; teacher, National Shakespeare Company Conservatory, 1977–present; guest artist, lecturer at colleges and universities.

WRITINGS: Short stories appeared in periodicals, *Woman, Aphra.* PLAYS PRODUCED—*Clytemnestra.*

AWARDS: Scholarship and Fellowship to Brown University and University of Wisconsin; graduated, Phi Beta Kappa and Cum Laude, Queens College.

SIDELIGHTS: MEMBERSHIPS—AEA; SAG.

"With the NSC and Cubiculo, Ms. Sulka has served as producer, director, booking agent, publicity director, bookkeeper, casting director and program coordinator. After the death of Mr. Meister in 1982, she became the organization's head."

ADDRESS: Home—35 W. 92nd Street, New York, NY 10025. Office—National Shakespeare Company, 414 W. 51st Street, New York, NY 10019.

* * *

SUROVY, Nicolas, actor

PERSONAL: Born June 30, 1946 in Hollywood, CA; son of Walter (an actor and manager) and Risë (an opera singer;

maiden name, Stevens) Surovy. EDUCATION: Studied with Sanford Meisner and at the Juilliard School of Drama in New York. MILITARY: U.S. Army, Sergeant, 1968–69; awarded Bronze Star, Air Medal with three clusters.

CAREER: PRINCIPAL STAGE APPEARANCES—Telemecus, *Helen,* Bowery Lane Theatre, NY, 1964; Mick, *The Caretaker* and Mercutio, *Romeo and Juliet,* Buffalo Studio Arena, NY, 1971; Roger, *The Balcony,* Hercules, *Alcestis,* Juilliard Theatre Center, NY, 1972; Joe, *The Time of Your Life,* NY; Mike Fink, *The Robber Bridegroom,* NY; Bassanio, *The Merchant,* NY; St. Claire, *Crucifer of Blood,* NY; Cousins, *Major Barbara,* NY; Tony Kirby, *You Can't Take It with You,* NY; Man, *Sisters of Mercy,* NY; Uncle Harry/ Martin, *Cloud Nine,* NY; at the Acting Company—Peter, *The Kitchen,* Canterbury, *Edward II,* Fedotik, *The Three Sisters,* Marlowe, *She Stoops to Conquer,* Tom, *The Glass Menagerie,* Henry IV, *Henry IV;* at the Goodman Theatre, Chicago, IL—Benedick, *Much Ado About Nothing,* Don Juan, *Don Juan,* Buckingham, *Richard III;* Hamlet, *Hamlet,* California Shakespeare Festival; man, *Sisters of Mercy,* Shaw Festival, Canada; Seymour, *Billy Budd,* Loretto-Hilton Repertory Theatre, St. Louis, MO; Steve, *Domestic Issues,* Yale Repertory Theatre, New Haven, CT.

PRINCIPAL FILM APPEARANCES—*For Pete's Sake,* 1967; Julian, *Bless em All;* Olsen, *Bang the Drum Slowly,* 1973. PRINCIPAL TELEVISION APPEARANCES—*Ben Casey; Branded; Blue Light; The Big Valley; Death Valley Days; Chrysler Theatre; The Road West; A World Apart; Mayflower: The Pilgrims' Adventure;* Ron Elsen, *Franken;* Joe, *The Time of Your Life;* Steve, *Nurse;* Billy Simmons, *Renegades;* Orsen, *Ryan's Hope;* Rudy Lavasso, *One Life to Live;* James, *Century Hill;* Mike Roy, *All My Children.*

ADDRESS: Agent—ICM, 8899 Beverly Blvd., Los Angeles, CA 90048; 40 W. 57th Street, New York, NY 10019.

* * *

SUTHERLAND, Donald, actor

PERSONAL: Born July 17, 1935 in St. John, NB, Canada; son of Frederick (a salesman) and Dorothy Isobel (McNichol) McLae; married Shirley Douglas (divorced); children: Keifer, Rachel, Roeg, Rossif Bon Bon. EDUCATION: University of Toronto, B.A.; studied at the London Academy of Dramatic Arts.

CAREER: DEBUT—Wally, *The Male Animal,* Hart House, Toronto, Canada, 1952. NEW YORK DEBUT—Humbert, *Lolita,* Brooks Atkinson, 1981. LONDON DEBUT—*August for the People,* Royal Court. PRINCIPAL STAGE APPEARANCES— *The Tempest,* Hart House, Toronto, Canada; *On a Clear Day You Can See Canterbury; The Shewing up of Blanco Posnet; The Spoon River Anthology.* Performed with the Perth Repertory Theatre, Scotland and Nottingham, Chesterfield, Bronley, and Sheffield repertory theatres, England.

PRINCIPAL FILM APPEARANCES—*Castle of the Living Dead; Dr. Terror's House of Horrors,* 1965; *The Dirty Dozen,* 1967; *Oedipus the King,* 1968; *Interlude,* 1968; *Joanna,* 1968; *The Split,* 1968; *Don't Look Now,* 1969; *Start the Revolution Without Me,* 1970; *The Act of the Heart,* 1970;

M*A*S*H*, 1970; *Alex in Wonderland*, 1970; *Kelly's Heroes*, 1970; *Little Murders*, 1971; *Klute*, 1971; *F.T.A.*, 1972; *Steelyard Blues*, 1973; *Alien Thunder*, 1973; *The Master*, 1973; *Lady Ice*, 1973; *S*P*Y*S*, 1974; *The Day of the Locust*, 1975; *1900*, 1976; *Casanova*, 1977; *The Eagle Has Landed*, 1977; *Invasion of the Body Snatchers*, 1978; *Animal House*, 1978; *The Great Train Robbery*, 1979; *Murder by Decree*, 1979; *A Man, a Woman, and a Bank*, 1979; *Ordinary People*, 1980; *Eye of the Needle*, 1981; *Nothing Personal*, 1981; *Gas*, 1981; *The Return of Max Dugan*, 1983.

PRINCIPAL TELEVISION APPEARANCES—*Marching to the Sea; The Death of Bessie Smith; Hamlet at Elsinore; The Saint; The Avengers; Gideon's Way; The Champions.*

AWARDS: Hon. D. Litt., Saint Mary's University; Officer, Order of Canada.

ADDRESS: Agent—Ron Meyer, c/o Creative Artists Agency, 1888 Century Park E., Los Angeles, CA 90067.

* * *

JANET SUZMAN

SUZMAN, Janet, actress

PERSONAL: Born February 9, 1939, in Johannesburg, South Africa; daughter of Saul and Betty Suzman; married Trevor Nunn, 1969; children: Joshua. EDUCATION: University of Witwatersand, B.A.; trained for the stage at LAMDA.

CAREER: STAGE DEBUT—Liz, *Billy Liar*, Tower, Ipswich, 1962. LONDON DEBUT—Luciana, *The Comedy of Errors*, Royal Shakespeare Company, Aldwych, 1962. PRINCIPAL STAGE APPEARANCES—Joan la Pucelle, *Henry VI*, Lady Anne, *Richard III*, Stratford, U.K., 1963; Lady Percy, *Henry IV, Part I and II*, Stratford, 1964; Lulu, *The Birthday Party*, Aldwych, London, 1964; Rosaline, *Love's Labour's Lost*, Portia, *The Merchant of Venice*, Stratford, 1965; Ophelia, *Hamlet*, Aldwych, London, 1965; Kate Hardcastle, *She Stoops to Conquer*, Carmen, *The Balcony*, Playhouse, Oxford, U.K. 1966–67; Katharina, *The Taming of the Shrew*, Celia, *As You Like It*, Royal Shakespeare Company, Stratford, U.K., Aldwych, London, 1967–68; *Pleasure and Repentance*, Royal Shakespeare Company, Edinburgh Festival, Scotland, 1970; Cleopatra, *Antony and Cleopatra*, Lavinia, *Titus Andronicus*, Royal Shakespeare Company, Stratford, King's Head, Islington, U.K., 1973; Cleopatra, *Antony and Cleopatra*, Aldwych, London, 1973; Hester, *Hello and Goodbye*, King's Head, Islington, Place, London, U.K., 1973; Masha, *Three Sisters*, Cambridge Theatre, U.K., 1976; Hedda, *Hedda Gabler*, Duke of York's, Edinburgh Festival, Scotland, 1977; Shen Te, *The Good Woman of Setzuan*, Royal Court, London, 1977; Minerva, *Boo Hoo*, Open Space, London, 1978; Clytemnestra, *The War*, Helen, *The Murders*, Chorus, *The Gods*, Royal Shakespeare Company, Aldwych, London, 1980; *Cowardice*, Ambassadors, London, 1983; *Boesman and Lena*, Hampstead, London, 1984.

MAJOR TOURS—Beatrice, *Much Ado About Nothing*, U.S. cities, 1969; *The Duchess of Malfi*, U.K. cities, 1979.

PRINCIPAL FILM APPEARANCES—*A Day in the Death of Joe Egg; Nicholas and Alexandra*, 1971; *The Draughtsman's Contract*, 1983; *And the Ship Sails On*, 1983.

PRINCIPAL TELEVISION APPEARANCES—*The Three Sisters; Hedda Gabler; Twelfth Night; Miss Nightingale; Clayhanger; The Zany Adventures of Robin Hood*, 1983; *Mountbatten, The Last Viceroy*, 1984.

AWARDS: Academy Award Nomination, Best Actress, 1971: *Nicholas and Alexandra;* Honorary Masters Degree, Open University, 1984.

SIDELIGHTS: MEMBERSHIPS—LAMDA (council member).

ADDRESS: Agent—c/o William Morris Agency, 147–149 Wardour Street, London W1.

* * *

SWADOS, Elizabeth A., writer and composer

PERSONAL: Born February 5, 1951, in Buffalo, NY; daughter of Robert O. and Sylvia (Maisel) Swados; EDUCATION: Bennington College, B.A., 1972. RELIGION: Jewish.

CAREER: WRITINGS: MUSICAL COMPOSITIONS, Theatre—Peter Brook, Paris France, Africa, U.S., 1972–73; La Mama Experimental Theater Club, NY, 1977–present; *Medea,* 1972; *Elektra,* 1973; *Conference of the Birds,* 1973; *Sylvia Plath Song Cycle,* 1973; *Trojan Women,* 1974; *Nightclub Cantata,* 1977; *Agamemnon,* 1977; *Runaways,* 1978; *Alice in Wonderland in Concert,* 1978; *Dispatches,* 1979; *NBC Too Far to Go,* 1978. Television—*CBS Camera 3 Shows,* 1973–74; *Ohms, Gauguin,* 1979; *PBS Short Story Series,* 1978–79. BOOKS—*Girl with the Incredible Feeling,* 1976.

RELATED CAREERS: Teacher, Carnegie-Mellon University, 1974, Bard College, 1976–77, Sarah Lawrence College, 1976–77.

AWARDS: Obie Awards, 1978, 1977, 1972; Outer Critics Circle Award, 1977; grants—New York State Council of the Arts; Guggenheim Fellowship.

SIDELIGHTS: AEA, Broadcast Music Inc.

ADDRESS: Office—c/o New York Shakespeare Festival, 425 Lafayette Street, New York, NY 10003.*

* * *

SWAIN, Elizabeth, actress, critic, literary manager

PERSONAL: Born August 6, 1941, in Peterborough, England; daughter of John Arthur and Eva Kathleen (Crane) Swain; married Robert Anthony, December 11, 1965 (divorced 1972); children: Katherine Rachel. EDUCATION: London School of Economics, 1960–63; City College of New York, B.S., 1978, M.A., 1979, Ph.D., 1984; studied with Michael Howard, Bobby Lewis and Herman Shumlin.

CAREER: DEBUT—Maria, *School for Scandal,* Asolo State Theatre, Sarasota, FL, 1964. NEW YORK DEBUT—Alice, *Alice Thro' the Looking Glass,* Equity Library Theatre, 1966. PRINCIPAL STAGE APPEARANCES—New York: *Epitaph for George Dillon, Witness for the Prosecution, The Crucible, Tango, Charley's Aunt,* 1970, *Crown Matrimonial,* 1973, *Sherlock Holmes,* 1975; Regional—*Hamlet, Macbeth, Othello, A Midsummer Night's Dream, As You Like It, The Lady's Not for Burning, The Deer Park, Private Lives, The Great Sebastians, Candida, The Day After the Fair,* A Contemporary Theatre, Seattle, WA, New Jersey Shakespeare Festival, American Shaw Festival.

TELEVISION DEBUT—*Dark Shadows.* PRINCIPAL TELEVISION APPEARANCES—*N.Y.P.D.; The Guiding Light,* 1978–83.

WRITINGS: TRANSLATIONS—Feydeau's *Le Systeme Ribadier,* produced at the Sharon Playhouse, CT, Hartman Theatre Company, Stamford, CT, Intiman Theatre, Seattle, WA; reviews, criticisms and interviews with playwrights in *Other Stages* and *Theatre Times.*

THEATRE-RELATED CAREER: Freelance dramaturg, literary manager, New York Theatre Studio, 1982–present; teacher,

''Introduction to Theatre,'' Hunter College, 1981–82; teacher, CCNY, ''Theatre History and Acting,'' 1982–present.

SIDELIGHTS: MEMBERSHIPS—AEA, SAG, AFTRA, ATA. Has recorded many *Talking Books* for the American Foundation for the Blind.

ADDRESS: Home—203 W. 81st Street, New York, NY 10025.

* * *

SWANSEN, Larry (Laurence T. Swanson), actor, playwright

PERSONAL: Born November 10, 1932 in Roosevelt, OK; son of James L. (a farmer) and Ethel May (a schoolteacher; maiden name, Colvin) Swanson. EDUCATION: University of Oklahoma Theatre School, B.F.A., M.F.A.

CAREER: DEBUT—Biff, *Death of a Salesman,* Norwich Summer Theatre, CT, 1950. NEW YORK DEBUT—Young man from across the sea, *Dr. Faustus Lights the Lights* (Living Theatre), Cherry Lane, 1951.

PRINCIPAL STAGE APPEARANCES—*The Unknown Soldier and His Wife,* Vivian Beaumont, Lincoln Center, NY; Captain Orton, *The King and I;* Eubanks, *The Great White Hope,* NY; *The Sound of Music,* City Center and Jones Beach, NY; Aimwill, *The Beaux Strategem;* Alonso, *The Tempest;* Sir Andrew, *Twelfth Night;* John Shand, *What Every Woman Knows;* Higgins, *Pygmalion;* Jack, *The Importance of Being Earnest;* Lear, *King Lear;* Drum, *Da;* Field Marshall Doerfling, *The Prince of Homburg,* Chelsea Theatre Center; *Those That Play the Clowns,* ANTA, NY, 1966; Pastor Holm, *Ice Age,;* Egg of Head, *MacBird;* Gilles de Rais, *A Darker Flower,* Pocket, NY; Theo Van Gogh, *Vincent,* Cricket, NY; Vicar, *Thistle in My Bed,* Gramercy Arts, NY. Mr. Swanson has performed at Seattle Repertory Company, Hartford Stage Company, Dartmouth Repertory Theatre, and Toledo Repertory Company.

MAJOR TOURS—Carr Gomm, *The Elephant Man,* national tour; Herr Zeller, *The Sound of Music,* national tour; Clive Champion-Cheney, *The Circle,* national tour.

PRINCIPAL FILM APPEARANCES—*Scream Baby Scream.* TELEVISION DEBUT—Field Marshall Doerfling, *The Prince of Homburg,* PBS; guest appearances: *The Tonight Show; To Tell the Truth; Dark Shadows.*

THEATRE-RELATED CAREER: Director of Drama, William Woods College, Fulton, MO.

WRITINGS: PLAYS, PRODUCED—*Boston 1721,* 1976; *Unfamiliar Beds,* 1981, and others since 1968.

AWARDS: First Prize, Indiana Arts Commission Playwriting Contest, 1976: *Boston 1721;* First Prize, Civic Theatre of Minneapolis, 1981: *Unfamiliar Beds.*

SIDELIGHTS: MEMBERSHIPS—AEA; SAG; AFTRA; Dramatists Guild.

''As a performer, I first earned money as a magician while in high school, with a full stage act running 1½ hours.''

ADDRESS: Office—c/o The Hayes Registry, 701 Seventh Avenue, New York, NY 10036.

* * *

SWEET, Dolph (ne Adolphus Jean Sweet), actor, director, teacher

PERSONAL: Born July 18, 1920 in New York City; son of John Walter (a master auto mechanic) and Louise Marie (Brasser) Sweet; married Reba Gillespie October 24, 1945 (divorced, 1973, died 1978); married Iris Braun (an actress) October 5, 1974; children: (first marriage) Jonathan. EDUCATION: Attended University of Alabama, 1939–40, 1942–43; Columbia University, B.A., 1948, M.A., 1949; studied voice with Peyton Hibbett, 1951–52 and with Elizabeth Howell, 1971–73, acting with Tamara Daykarhanova and Joseph Anthony at the Daykarhanova School for the Stage in New York City, 1958–70. RELIGION: Catholic. MILITARY: USAAF, ETO, WWII. USAF Reserve, Lt. Col. (Ret.); awarded the Distinguished Flying Cross, Purple Heart, and ETO Campaign Ribbon. NON-THEATRICAL CAREER: Textile foreman, truck driver, skating rink manager.

CAREER: DEBUT—While a prisoner of war during WWII, appeared as Mrs. White, *The Monkey's Paw* at the Stalag Luft III, Sagan, Germany, 1944. NEW YORK DEBUT—Grocer/Fireman, *Rhinoceros*, Longacre, 1961. PRINCIPAL STAGE APPEARANCES—Appeared in many roles at the Lakes Region Playhouse in New Hampshire, 1950–52, also at the Chautauqua Opera Association in New York State and at the Cherry County Playhouse in Traverse City, MI, 1956, Barter Theatre in Abingdon, VA, 1958; Vincent, *Legend of Lovers*, 41st Street Theatre, NY, 1959; Chef, *Romulus*, Music Box, NY, 1962; Commodore Roseabove, *Oh Dad, Poor Dad . . .*, Phoenix, NY, 1962; title role, *The Dragon*, Phoenix, 1963; Sacco, *The Advocate*, ANTA, NY, 1963; Johnson, *Too Much Johnson*, Phoenix, 1964; Max, *The Sign in Sidney Brustein's Window*, Longacre, NY, 1964; Bonnie Doon, *The Great Indoors*, O'Neill, NY, 1966; Max, *Berlin Is Mine*, Forum, Lincoln Center, NY, 1966; Bludgeon, *Serjeant Musgrave's Dance*, Theatre de Lys, NY, 1966; Edward Quinn, *Hogan's Goat*, American Place, St. Clement's, NY, 1965; Stever Kenny, *The Natural Look*, Longacre, NY, 1967; Sussex, *The Ceremony of Innocence*, American Place, NY, St. Clement's, NY, 1968; Whiskers, *Billy*, Billy Rose, NY, 1969; Frank Bishop, *The Penny Wars*, Royale, NY, 1969; King, *Exit the King*, Marymount, Tarrytown, NY, 1970; Max (revival), *The Sign in Sidney Brustein's Window*, Longacre, NY, 1972; title role, *Agamemnon*, McCarter, Princeton, NJ, 1972; Stanley, *Bread*, American Place, NY, 1974; *Streamers*, Newhouse, Lincoln Center, NY.

PRINCIPAL FILM APPEARANCES—*You're a Big Boy Now*, 1967; *The Swimmer*, 1968; *Finian's Rainbow*, 1968; *A Lovely Way to Die*, 1968; *The April Fools*, 1969; *The Lost Man*, 1969; *The Out-of-Towners*, 1970; *Colossus: The Forbin Project*, 1970; *The New Centurions*, 1972; *Cops and Robbers*, 1973; *Fear Is the Key*, 1973; *The Amazing Grace*, 1974; *Sisters*, 1974; *Bad News Bears, Part II*, 1977; *Which

Way Is Up, 1977; *Heaven Can Wait*, 1978; *The Wanderers*, 1979; *Go Tell the Spartans*, 1978; *To Smithereens*, 1980.

TELEVISION DEBUT—*The Defenders*, 1961–63. PRINCIPAL TELEVISION APPEARANCES—*The Nurses*, 1963; *East Side/West Side*, 1963; title role, ''The Dragon,'' *Dupont Show of the Week*, 1963; Sgt. Garrison, *The Trials of O'Brien*, 1966; Harry Constable, *The Edge of Night*, 1967; Sheriff Jesse Bard, *The Desperate Hours*, 1967; Morgan, ''To Confuse the Angel,'' *Prudential's Onstage*, 1970; General, *Between Time and Timbuktu*, 1972; Henry Peterson, *The Watergate Tapes*, 1974; sheriff, *The Migrants*, 1974; Gil McGowan, *Another World*, 1974–75; *Billy Peoples: Portrait of a Street Kid; Taxi; Little House on the Prairie; Spiderman; Angie; A Killing Affair;* co-star, *Gimme a Break; Hill Street Blues*.

AWARDS: The Distinguished Flying Cross; The Purple Heart; ETO Campaign Ribbon.

THEATRE-RELATED CAREER: Head of Drama Division of the English Department, Barnard College, Columbia University, 1949–1961.

SIDELIGHTS: MEMBERSHIPS—AEA; SAG; AFTRA; Life Member, Reserve Officers Association; Air Force Association; Life Member, Retired Officers Association; American Association of Retired Persons; Academy of Motion Picture Arts and Sciences; John Jay Society of Columbia University; Columbia University Alumni Association; Columbia University Alumni Association of Southern California; Actors Fund of America; Phi Beta Kappa. RECREATION: Swimming, reading, eating, and cooking.

As a navigator of B-24's during WWII, Mr. Sweet was shot down on the Ploesti raid and was a prisoner of war in Germany for two years. It was there that he made his theatrical debut performing roles in plays which the prisoners put on for their own entertainment. He became a full-time actor in 1961 and has remained so, ever since. Mr. Sweet was a semi-pro football player and a boxer, and is a skilled swimmer.

ADDRESS: Home—6709 Sunnybrae Avenue, Canoga Park, CA 91306. Agent—Richard Dickens & Company, 5550 Wilshire Blvd., Los Angeles, CA 90069.

* * *

SWINDELLS, John (ne John Rayner Harcourt Swindells), actor, director, playwright

PERSONAL: Surname is pronounced Swin-*dells;* born June 22, 1931 in Liverpool, England; dual citizen of England and Canada; son of George Hodgkiss (an accountant) and Doris Margery (a teacher and business woman; maiden name, Johnson) Swindells; married Audrey Battersby (a clerk), 1960 (divorced 1972); married Judith Ann Booty (nee Judy Leigh-Johnson, an actress) October 28, 1972. EDUCATION: Liverpool College of Art, two years. MILITARY: Royal Air Force, S.A.C. NON-THEATRICAL CAREER: Worked as a clerk for a shipping line for 12 years.

CAREER: DEBUT—Sgt. Cadwallader, *The Unexpected Guest*, Intimate Theatre, Palmers Green, North London, England,

JOHN SWINDELLS

1964. NEW YORK DEBUT—Bonno/Swieten, *Amadeus,* Broadhurst, 1983. LONDON DEBUT—Rafe, *Spring and Port Wine,* Richmond, 1969. PRINCIPAL STAGE APPEARANCES—In England appeared at: Theatre Royal, Margate, Salisbury Playhouse, Ludlow Shakespearean Open Air Festival, Grand Theatre, Wolverhampton, and the Mermaid Theatre in London, 1965–70; Saul Hodgkin, *The Ghost Train,* Atheneum, Plymouth, England, 1968; Duke of Norfolk, *A Man for All Seasons,* Opera House, Harrogate, 1969; in Canada appeared at: Shaw Festival, Ontario, Gryphon Theatre, Barrie, ON, Theatre New Brunswick, Bastion Theatre, Victoria, BC, and Stage West Regina; James Joyce, *Travesties,* St. Lawrence Center, Toronto, 1977; Deeley, *Old Times,* Phoenix, Toronto, 1978; Sidney, *Absurd Person Singular,* Theatre London, Ontario, 1979; Harry Trew, *Pantomime,* Geva, Rochester, NY, 1982; Bri, *Joe Egg;* Stephen Hench, *Other-wise Engaged;* Ernest, *Bedroom Farce;* Old Ekdal, *The Wild Duck;* Maxim, *Rebecca;* Chandebise/Poche, *A Flea in Her Ear;* Mr. Glass, *Slow Dance on the Killing Ground;* Sebastian, *The Tempest;* King of France, *All's Well That Ends Well;* one of the critics, *Fanny's First Play; Touched,* Wonderhorse, NY, 1982; *Billy Liar,* Westside Mainstage, NY, 1982; standby for co-lead, *Beethoven's Tenth,* Nederlander, 1984. MAJOR TOURS—Chandebise/Poche, *A Flea in Her Ear,* Canadian tour; Bonno, *Amadeus,* national tour, U.S., 1982–83; standby for co-lead, *Beethoven's Tenth,* national tour, U.S., 1984.

PRINCIPAL STAGE WORK: Directed—*Spider's Web,* England, 1968; in Canada: *Spring and Port Wine,* 1974; *The Gingerbread Lady,* 1975; *Pygmalion,* 1976; *The Last of the Red Hot Lovers,* 1977; *The Secretary Bird,* 1977; *Move Over Mrs. Markham,* 1978; *Time and Time Again,* 1978; *The Unexpected Guest,* 1978; *Come Blow Your Horn,* 1978; *Sleuth,* 1979; *The Bear,* 1980; *Showboat,* 1981; *Blithe Spirit,* 1981. Served as artistic director for the Red Barn Theatre, Ontario, 1978.

FILM DEBUT—First technician, *2001: A Space Odyssey,* 1969. PRINCIPAL FILM APPEARANCES—Teacher, *Ragtime Summer;* Police Sgt., *Nightmare Rally; Battle of Britain.* TELEVISION DEBUT—Sgt. Ted Bowman, *Z. Cars,* BBC (3 years). PRINCIPAL TELEVISION APPEARANCES—Sgt. Ted Bowman, *Coronation Street,* Granada TV; *Des O'Connor Show; Sidestreet,* CBC (3 years); *Swiss Family Robinson; The Frankie Howerd Show.*

AWARDS: Three SAM Awards for Best Radio Commercials in Canada; 2 National Awards for TV Commercials in Canada; RAF, merit award for Nursing.

WRITING: PLAYS—Woodbine Willie (with Robert Buck).

THEATRE-RELATED CAREER: Professor of Acting and Voice, University of Regina, SK, 1980–81.

SIDELIGHTS: MEMBERSHIPS—Chair, Disciplinary Committee, ACTRA, Toronto, committees for young people's clubs and for senior citizen clubs; Nestorian Association, Liverpool.

"My main motivation is to serve the craft of acting and have the respect of my peers. In my circumstances, Luck has served me well, being in the right place at the right time! My favorite roles are Shylock in *Merchant of Venice* (I have yet to play it however) and Bri in *Joe Egg.* The journey and quality of Life is important—acting is but a part of Life."

T

TABORI, Kristoffer (ne Christopher Donald Siegel), actor and director

PERSONAL: Born August 4; son of Donald (a film director) and Viveca (an actress; maiden name, Lindfors) Siegel. EDUCATION: Attended New York City public and private schools; trained for the stage with Diana Maddox and Ada Brown Mather.

CAREER: DEBUT—Flute, *Midsummer Night's Dream*, U.M.H.A. Children's Theatre, NY, 1960–61. NEW YORK DEBUT—*Cry of Players*, Lincoln Center, 1968. PRINCIPAL STAGE APPEARANCES—(Broadway) *Habeas Corpus; The Penny Wars; Henry V*, American Shakespeare Festival; (Off-Broadway) leads, *The Wager; Emil and the Detectives;* Brecht, *Guns of Carrar; Dreams of a Blacklisted Actor; How Much, How Much?; Treats;* (Repertory) *The Trouble with Europe*, Phoenix, NY; Hamlet *Hamlet*, Arena, Washington, DC; *The Threepenny Opera*, Berkshire Drama Festival; *A Funny Thing Happened on the Way to the Forum, Merchant of Venice, Waiting for Godot*, Berkshire Playhouse; Hal, *Henry IV, Part I*, Mark Taper Forum, Los Angeles, CA; *Much Ado About Nothing, Hamlet*, American Shakespeare Festial; *My Mother, My Son*, Boston Repertory, MA; *Scribes*, Phoenix, NY; Dauphin, *Saint Joan*, Arena, Washington, DC, Long Wharf, New Haven, CT; Orlando, *As You Like It*, Los Angeles Free Shakespeare, CA; Romeo, *Romeo and Juliet*, Buffalo Arena, NY; *Rose Tattoo*, Philadelphia Drama Guild, PA; Hamlet, *Hamlet*, North Shore; Romeo, *Romeo and Juliet*, Biondello, *Taming of the Shrew*, Macbeth, *Macbeth*, California Shakespeare Festival; Law, *Boy Meets Girl*, South Coast Repertory.

DIRECTED: Plays—*Treats, Romeo and Juliet*, Grove Shakespeare Festival; *Two Gentlemen of Verona*, Grove Shakespeare Festival.

FILM DEBUT—Title role, *Weddings and Babies*, 1958. PRINCIPAL FILM APPEARANCES—*Acts of a Young Man; Sidelong Glances of a Pigeon Kicker; Sweet Charity*, 1969; *John and Mary*, 1969; *Making It*, 1971; *Journey Through Rosebud*, 1972; *Girl Friends*, 1978.

TELEVISION DEBUT—"Neither Are We Enemies," *Hallmark Hall of Fame*, 1969. PRINCIPAL TELEVISION APPEARANCES—Dr. Max Carson, *Chicago Story;* lead, *T. J. Hooker; Rockford Files; Trapper John, M.D.; Rappaccini's Daughter; The Commandments; Brave New World; Black Beauty; Class of '65*, "A Short Swim to Catalina,"; *Baretta*, "A Fragile Monster Is Loose"; *Seventh Avenue*, "Best Sellers"; *Most Wanted*, "Urban Guerilla"; *Streets of San Francisco*, "Most Likely to Succeed"; *Barnaby Jones*, "The Deadly Orchid"; *Cannon*, "Flashpoint"; *Marcus Welby*, "The Faith of Childish Things"; *Rookies*, "Walk a Tight Rope"; *Ben Franklin; Toma*, "The Friends of Danny Beecher"; *Owen Marshall*, "A Lesson in Loving"; *Terror on the Beach; QB VII; The Glass House; A Memory of Two Mondays; Young Lawyers; Nichols; The Lady's Not for Burning; Family Flight; Noel Coward*, "Mad About the Boy"; *Medical Center*.

SIDELIGHTS: MEMBERSHIPS—Players Club.

ADDRESS: Agent—c/o Phillip B. Gittelman, 1221 N. Kings Road, #405, Los Angeles, CA 90069.

* * *

TALLY, Ted, playwright

PERSONAL: Born April 9, 1952 in Winston-Salem, NC; son of David K. and Dorothy E. (Spears) Tally; married Melinda Kahn (an art gallery director) December 11, 1977. EDUCATION: Yale University, B.A., 1974, School of Drama, M.F.A., 1977.

WRITINGS: PLAYS, PUBLISHED/PRODUCED—*Hooters*, 1978; *Terra Nova*, 1981; *Coming Attractions*, 1982; *Silver Linings*, 1983. TELEPLAYS—*Couples Only*, 1979; *Hooters*, 1983. SCREENPLAYS—*Empire* (unproduced), 1981; *Hush-a-Bye* (to be produced), 1983.

THEATRE-RELATED CAREER—Instructor, playwriting seminars, Yale College, New Haven, CT, 1977–79.

AWARDS: National Endowment for the Arts Grant in Playwriting, 1983–84; John Gassner Award in playwriting, 1981; New York Outer Critics Circle Award, 1981: *Coming Attractions;* New York State CAPS Grant, 1980; Los Angeles Drama-Logue Award, 1979: *Terra Nova;* CBS Foundation Playwriting Fellowship, Yale University, 1977; Theron Rockwell Field Prize, Yale University, 1977; Kazan Award, Yale University, School of Drama, 1977.

SIDELIGHTS: MEMBERSHIPS—Dramatists Guild, Writer's Guild of America.

ADDRESS: Agent—Helen Merrill, 337 W. 22nd Street, New York, NY 10011.

Photograph by Zoe Dominic

JESSICA TANDY

TANDY, Jessica, actress

PERSONAL: Born June 7, 1909, in London; daughter of Harry and Jessie Helen (Horspool) Tandy; married Jack Hawkins, 1932, (divorced 1940); married Hume Cronyn, 1942; children: Susan (1st marriage), Christopher Hume, Tandy. EDUCATION: University of Western Ontario, LL.D., 1974; trained for the stage at Ben Greet Academy of Acting.

CAREER: STAGE DEBUT—Sara Manderson, *The Manderson Girls,* Playroom Six, U.K., 1927. LONDON DEBUT—Lena Jackson, *The Rumour,* Court, 1929. NEW YORK DEBUT—Toni Rakonitz, *The Matriarch,* Longacre, 1930. PRINCIPAL STAGE APPEARANCES—Gladys, *The Comedy of Good and Evil,* Ginevra, *Alice Sit-by-the-Fire,* Birmingham Repertory, U.K., 1928; Typist, *The Theatre of Life,* Arts, London, 1929; Maggie, *Water,* Little, London, 1929; Aude, *The Unknown Warrior,* Haymarket, London, 1929; Olivia, *Twelfth Night,* Oxford, U.K., 1930; Cynthia, *The Last Enemy,* Shubert, NY, 1930; Fay, *The Man Who Pays the Piper,* St. Martin's, London, 1931; Audrey, *Autumn Crocus,* Lyric, London, 1931; Ruth Blair, *Port Said,* Wyndham's, London, 1931; Anna, *Musical Chairs,* Arts, London, 1931; *Below the Surface,* Repertory Players, London, 1932; *Juarez and Maximilian,* Phoenix, London, 1932; *Troilus and Cressida, See Naples and Die; The Witch; Rose without a Thorn, The Inspector General, The Servant of Two Masters,* Cambridge Festival, U.K., 1932; Carlotta, *Mutual Benefit,* St. Martin's, London, 1932; Manuela, *Children in Uniform,* Duchess, London, 1932; Alicia Audley, *Lady Audley's Secret,* Arts, London, 1932; Marikke, *Midsummer Fires,* Embassy, Lon-

don, 1933; Titania, *A Midsummer Night's Dream,* Open Air, U.K., 1933; Betty, *Ten Minute Alibi,* Haymarket, London, 1933; Rosamund, *Birthday,* Cambridge, U.K., 1934; Eva Whiston, *Line Engaged,* Duke of York's, London, 1934; Viola, *Twelfth Night,* Anne Page, *The Merry Wives of Windsor,* Hippodrome, Manchester, U.K., 1934; Ophelia, *Hamlet,* New, London, 1934;

Ada, *Noah,* U.K., 1935; Anna Penn, *Anthony and Anna,* Whitehall, London, 1935; Marie Rose, *The Ante-Room,* Queen's, London, 1936; Jacqueline, *French without Tears,* Criterion, London, 1936; Pamela March, *Honour Thy Father,* Arts, London, 1936; Viola/Sebastian, *Twelfth Night,* Katherine, *Henry V,* Old Vic, London, 1937; Ellen Murray, *Yes, My Darling Daughter,* St. James's, London, 1937; Kay, *Time and the Conways,* Ritz, NY, 1938; Leda, *Glorious Morning,* Duchess, London, 1938; Nora Fintry, *The White Steed,* Cort, NY, 1939; Viola, *Twelfth Night,* Open Air, London, 1939; Deaconess, *Geneva,* Henry Miller, NY, 1940; Cordelia, *King Lear,* Miranda, *The Tempest,* Old Vic, London, 1940; Dr. Mary Murray, *Jupiter Laughs,* Biltmore, NY, 1940; Abigail Hill, *Anne of England,* St. James, London, 1941; Cattrin, *Yesterday's Magic,* Guild, London, 1942; *Portrait of a Madonna,* Los Angeles, CA, 1946; Blanche Dubois, *A Streetcar Named Desire,* Ethel Barrymore, NY, 1947;

The Little Blue Light, Brattle, Cambridge, MA, 1950; Hilda Crane, *Hilda Crane,* Coronet, NY, 1950; Agnes, *The Fourposter,* Ethel Barrymore, NY, 1951; Mary Doyle, *Madame, Will You Walk,* Phoenix, NY, 1953; Agnes, *The Fourposter,* City Center, NY, 1955; Mary, *The Honey's,* Longacre, NY, 1955; Frances Farrar, *A Day by the Sea,* ANTA Playhouse, NY, 1955; Martha Walling, *The Man in the Dog Suit,* Coronet, NY, 1958; Mrs. Morgan, *I Spy,* Angela Nightingale, *Bedtime Story,* Innocent Bystander, *A Pound on Demand,* Palm Beach Playhouse, 1959, Playhouse, NY, 1959; Louise Harrington, *Five Finger Exercise,* Music Box, NY, 1959; Lady Macbeth, *Macbeth,* Cassandra, *Troilus and Cressida,* American Shakespeare Festival, Stratford, CT, 1961; Edith Maitland, *Big Fish, Little Fish,* Duke of York's, London, 1962; Gertrude, *Hamlet,* Olga, *The Three Sisters,* Linda Loman, *Death of a Salesman,* Tyrone Guthrie, Minneapolis, MN, 1963; Doktor Mathilde von Zahnd, *The Physicists,* Martin Beck, NY, 1964; Lady Wishfort, *The Way of the World,* Madame Ranevskaya, *The Cherry Orchard,* Mother-in-Law, *The Caucasian Chalk Circle,* Tyrone Guthrie, Minneapolis, MN, 1965; *Hear America Speaking,* White House, Washington, DC, 1965;

Agnes, *A Delicate Balance,* Martin Beck, NY, 1966; Frosine, *The Miser,* Mark Taper Forum, Los Angeles, CA, 1968; Hesione Hushabye, *Heartbreak House,* Shaw Festival, Niagara-on-the-Lake, Ontario, Canada, 1968; Pamela Pew-Pickett, *Tchin-Tchin,* Ivanhoe, Chicago, IL, 1969; Marguerite Gautier, *Camino Real,* Vivian Beaumont, NY, 1970; Marjorie, *Home,* Morosco, NY, 1971; The Wife, *All Over,* Martin Beck, NY, 1971; Winnie, *Happy Days,* Mouth, *Not I,* Forum, NY, 1972; Anna-May Conklin, *Come into the Garden,* Maude/Hilde Latymer, *A Song at Twilight,* Ethel Barrymore, NY, 1974; Lady Wishfort, *The Way of the World,* Hippolyta/Titania, *A Midsummer Night's Dream,* Eve, *Eve,* Stratford Shakespeare Festival, Ontario, Canada, 1976; Mary Tyrone, *Long Day's Journey into Night,* Theatre London, Ontario, Canada, 1977; Fonsia Dorsey, *The Gin*

Game, Golden, NY, 1977; Annie Nations, *Foxfire*, Mary Tyrone, *Long Day's Journey into Night*, Stratford Shakespeare Festival, Ontario, Canada, 1980; Mother, *Rose*, Cort, NY, 1981; Annie Nations, *Foxfire*, Guthrie, MN, 1981, Barrymore, NY, 1982–83; Amanda, *The Glass Menagerie*, O'Neill, NY, 1983–84.

MAJOR TOURS—Lydia Blake, *Yellow Sands*, U.K. cities, 1928; *Charles the King, Geneva and Tobias, The Angel*, Canadian cities, 1939; Blanche Dubois, *A Streetcar Named Desire*, U.S. cities, 1947; *Face to Face*, U.S. cities, 1954; Louise Harrington, *Five Finger Exercise*, U.S. cities, 1960; Agnes, *A Delicate Balance*, U.S. cities, 1967; *Noel Coward in Two Keys*, U.S. cities, 1974; Fonsia Dorsey, *The Gin Game*, U.S. cities, Lyric, London, U.S.S.R., 1979.

FILM DEBUT—*The Indiscretions of Eve*, 1932. PRINCIPAL FILM APPEARANCES—*Murder in the Family*, 1938; *The Seventh Cross*, 1944; *The Valley of Decision*, 1945; *Dragonwyck*, 1946; *The Green Years*, 1946; *Forever Amber*, 1946; *A Woman's Vengeance*, 1947; *September Affair*, 1950; *The Desert Fox*, 1951; *The Light in the Forest*, 1958; *Adventures of a Young Man*, 1961; *The Birds*, 1962; *Butley*, 1973; *Honky Tonk Freeway*, 1980; *Still of the Night*, 1981; *The World According to Garp*, 1981; *Best Friends*, 1982; *The Bostonians*, 1984.

PRINCIPAL TELEVISION APPEARANCES—*The Marriage*, 1953–54; *Christmas 'Til Closing*, 1955; *The Moon and Sixpence*, 1959; *Alfred Hitchcock Hour; Hallmark Hall of Fame; The Fallen Idol; Dupont Show of the Month; Tennessee Williams' South; Many Faces of Love*, 1977; *The Gin Game*, 1979.

AWARDS: Antoinette Perry Award, Drama Desk, Outer Circle Critics Best Actress, 1983: *Foxfire;* Common Wealth, 1983; Theatre Hall of Fame Award, 1979; Sarah Siddons Award, 1979; Los Angeles Critics Award, 1979; Drama Desk Award, 1978; Antoinette Perry Award, 1978: *The Gin Game;* Creative Arts Award, Brandeis University, 1978; Drama Desk Award, 1973: *Happy Days* and *Not I;* Obie Award, 1973: *Not I;* Bronze Medallion Award (with Hume Cronyn): *The Fourposter;* Delia Austria Medal, Drama League of New York; Twelfth Night Club Award, 1948; Antoinette Perry Award, 1948: *A Streetcar Named Desire*. Honorary Degrees—Hon LLD, University of Western Ontario, 1974.

SIDELIGHTS: MEMBERSHIPS—AEA (councillor), SAG, AFTRA, Cosmopolitan Club.

Ms. Tandy became a naturalized U.S. citizen in 1954.

ADDRESS: Office—63–23 Carlton Street, Rego Park, NY 11374.

* * *

TAYLOR, Elizabeth, (Rosemond), actress

PERSONAL: Born February 27, 1932 in London, England; daughter of Francis (an art dealer and historian) and Sara (an actress; maiden name, Southern) Taylor; married Conrad Nicholas Hilton, Jr., May 6, 1950 (divorced); married Michael Wilding (divorced); married Mike Todd (a pro-

ducer) February 2, 1957 (died March 1958); married Eddie Fisher (a singer/actor) May of 1959 (divorced); married Richard Burton (an actor) March 15, 1964 (divorced 1974); remarried Richard Burton, October 10, 1975 (divorced 1976); married William J. Warner, 1976, (divorced); children: second marriage, two sons; third marriage, one daughter, Liza. EDUCATION: Bryon House and the Hawthorne School, London, England; Metro-Goldwyn-Mayer School, Hollywood, CA.

CAREER: FILM DEBUT—*Lassie Come Home*, 1942. PRINCIPAL FILM APPEARANCES—*Man or Mouse; There's One Born Every Minute; Jane Eyre*, 1943; *The White Cliffs of Dover*, 1943; *National Velvet*, 1944; *The Courage of Lassie*, 1946; *Life with Father*, 1946; *Cynthia*, 1947; *A Date with Judy*, 1948; *Julia Misbehaves*, 1948; *Little Women*, 1948; *Conspirator*, 1949; *The Big Hangover*, 1949; *Father of the Bride*, 1950; *A Place in the Sun*, 1950; *Callaway Went Thataway*, 1951; *Love Is Better Than Ever*, 1951; *Ivanhoe*, 1951; *The Girl Who Had Everything*, 1952; *Rhapsody*, 1954; *Elephant Walk*, 1954; *Beau Brummell*, 1954; *The Last Time I Saw Paris*, 1955; *Giant*, 1956; *Raintree County*, 1957; *Cat on a Hot Tin Roof*, 1958; *Suddenly Last Summer*, 1960; *Butterfield 8*, 1960; *Cleopatra*, 1963; *The V.I.P.'s*, 1963; *The Sandpiper*, 1965; *Who's Afraid of Virginia Woolf?*, 1966; *The Taming of the Shrew*, 1967; *Reflections in a Golden Eye*, 1967; *The Comedians*, 1967; *Doctor Fautus*, 1968; *Boom!*, 1968; *Secret Ceremony*, 1969; *The Only Game in Town*, 1970; *Under Milkwood*, 1971; *X, Y and Zee*, 1972; *Hammersmith Is Out*, 1972; *Night Watch*, 1973; *Ash Wednesday*, 1973; *That's Entertainment*, 1974; *The Driver's Seat*, 1975; *The Blue Bird*, 1976; *Winter Kills*, 1979; *A Little Night Music*, 1979; *The Mirror Crack'd*, 1980.

PRINCIPAL STAGE APPEARANCES—Regina, *The Little Foxes*, O'Neill, NY, 1981; *Private Lives*, O'Neill, NY, 1983. PRINCIPAL TELEVISION APPEARANCES—*Victory at Entebbe; Return Engagement; Genocide* (documentary narration); *Between Friends*.

AWARDS: Theatre World Special Award, 1981: *Little Foxes;* Academy Awards, Best Actress, 1966: *Who's Afraid of Virginia Woolf*, 1960: *Butterfield 8*.

WRITINGS: BOOKS—*Nibbles and Me*, with Richard Burton; *World Enough and Time* (poetry reading), 1964.

SIDELIGHTS: ''Miss Taylor has always dedicated time and financial support to the needs of the unfortunate. The value of the goodwill she has earned throughout the years now accrues to causes to which she has lent her support both financially and through active participation. Among the many causes she has assisted was the Israeli War Victims Fund in 1976 for the Chaim Sheba Hospital, which was specifically established for the victims of all nationalities. She has also assisted the Variety Clubs International by raising money in Europe, Israel, and America for the children's wings in hospital; and the Botswana Clinics in Africa by giving contributions to health clinics in Lobaste and Gaborne . . . Miss Taylor and producer Zev Bufman have formed the Elizabeth Theatre Group which will present major productions on Broadway beginning with *Private Lives, The Corn Is Green*, and *Inherit the Wind*. She and Mr. Bufman plan to undertake other theatrical ventures in future seasons.''

ADDRESS: Agent—Chen Sam & Assoc., Inc., 315 E. 72nd Street, New York, NY 10021.

* * *

TAYMOR, Julie, designer, director, writer, actress

PERSONAL: Born December 15, 1952 in Boston, MA; daughter of Melvin Lester (a gynecologist) and Elizabeth (political science teacher; maiden name, Bernstein) Taymor. EDUCATION: Oberlin College, Ohio, B.A. (Folklore and Mythology), 1974; American Society for Eastern Arts, Seattle, WA, 1973; studied with Herbert Blau, director Oberlin Group, 1973–74; Herbert Berghof Studios (acting), 1971–72; Open Theatre, NY, 1971; Bread and Puppet Theatre, VT, 1971; Ecole du Mime de Jacques Coq, Paris, 1970; Theatre Workshop of Boston, 1967–69; Boston Children's Theatre, 1963–66.

CAREER: PRINCIPAL STAGE WORK, DESIGN: Puppetry, Masks, Set, and Costumes—Masks—The British Theatre Group, Paris, France, 1970, Bread and Puppet Theatre, VT, 1971, Robin Wood, theatre director, Boston, MA, 1972; puppets—*The Elephant Calf,* Oberlin College, 1973; costumes—*Seeds of Atreus,* Oberlin Group, 1974; production design—*Tirai,* Teatr Loh, Java, Bali, 1978, La Mama, NY, 1980, *The Odyssey,* Center Stage, Baltimore, MD, 1979, *The Haggadah,* New York Shakespeare Festival, 1980, 1981, 1982, *Way of Snow,* Teatr Loh, Java Bali, 1976, Ark, NY, 1980, World Puppet Festival, Washington, DC, 1980, *Sea Rhythms,* Smithsonian Institution, Washington, DC, 1980, *Black Elk Lives,* Entermedia, NY, 1981; sets and puppetry—*Gioconda and Si-Ya-U,* Dance Theatre Workshop, for the Talking Band, 1982, La Mama Theatre, 1982 and Europe, 1982; moving sculptures and shadows—*Savages,* Center Stage, Baltimore, MD, 1982; masks and puppets—*This Chameleon Love,* Theatre for a New Audience, NY, 1982–83; sets—*Do Lord Remember Me,* American Place, NY, 1982.

PRINCIPAL STAGE WORK, DIRECTED—*Way of Snow; Liberty's Taken; Tirai; The Haggadah* (visual concept, masks, and puppetry); *Perjuangan Suku Naga* (choreography).

FILM, TELEVISION, AND VIDEO PROJECTS—Documentaries, *Awaji Puppet Theatre,* Japan, 1977, *Kabuki Backstage,* Japan, 1977, *Chinese Temple Puppets,* Indonesia, 1978, *Cremation,* Bali, Indonesia, 1978, *Last Rites of Toraja,* Sulawesi, Indonesia, 1978; videos—*Teatr Loh, Indonesia, 1971–78,* Boston, MA, 1979; television—*Video Dream Theatre,* 1980, *The Haggadah,* PBS, 1981, *Betcha Don't Know . . . ,* Children's Television Workshop, *Songs of Innocence,* CBS cable; film—*Say No,* (puppet design).

WRITINGS: PLAYS PRODUCED—*Way of Snow* and *Tirai* (see Principal Stage Work, Theatre Design).

THEATRE-RELATED CAREER: Teacher, workshop in puppet construction, Ohio Arts Council, 1974; conducted lecturers and theatre workshops in Tokyo, Bangkok, Singapore, Manila, Sumatra, and Java for the U.S. Information Service, 1977; workshop and lecturers, Baltimore International Theatre Festival, 1979; teacher, New School for Social Research, NY, 1981–82.

AWARDS: National Endowment for the Arts Grant, Artistic Association to the American Place Theatre, 1982–83; NEA Opera/Musical production grant: for *Revolutionary,* people/puppet musical to be produced by American Place Theatre, 1982–83 season; CAPS Award, for development of a mixed media theatre piece, 1982; Peg Santvoord Foundation Grant, Script Development, 1981; Maharam Theatre Design Citations, *Way of Snow* and costumes for *Tirai,* 1981; Citation of Excellence in the Art of Puppetry, *Way of Snow, Haggadah,* American Center of the Union Internationale de la Marionette, 1980–81; Villager Theatre Award, for the art of play direction for *Way of Snow,* 1980–81; International Communications Agency, Ford Foundation and Asian Cultural Council, special funding to direct Asian/American Theatre Workshop sponsored by the La Mama Third World Institute of Theatre Art Studies, 1980; Maharam Theatre Design Award, *The Haggadah,* 1979–80; Villager Theatre Award, for distinguished prop/set design and puppets for *The Haggadah,* 1979–80; Ford Foundation Grant, complete video-tape documentary on Teatr Loh; U.S. State Department Grant to serve as consultant on Indonesian art forms, 1978; Ford Foundation Grant, to develop and direct a new international theatre company (Teatr Loh) in Indonesia, 1977–78; Thomas J. Watson Traveling Fellowship in Visual Theatre and Puppet Theatre, Eastern Europe, Indonesia and Japan, 1974; Ohio Arts Council Grant, 1974.

ADDRESS: Home—718 Broadway, New York, NY 10003.

* * *

TEER, Barbara Ann, director, actress, dancer, writer

PERSONAL: Born June 18, 1937 in East St. Louis, IL; daughter of Fred L. and Lila B. (Benjamin) Teer; children: a son, Omi, and a daughter, Folashade. EDUCATION: University of Illinois, B.A. (Dance Education), 1957; studied with Sanford Meisner, Paul Mann, Phillip Burton, and Lloyd Richards; studied dance in Berlin, Paris, and at Wigman School of Dance.

CAREER: PRINCIPAL STAGE WORK, ACTING/DANCER—*Kwamina,* 54th Street Theatre, NY, 1961; Bella Belafunky, *Raisin' Hell in the Son,* Provincetown Playhouse, NY, 1962; *The Living Premise,* Premise, NY, 1963; Violet, *Home Movies,* Provincetown Playhouse, NY, 1964; *Funnyhouse of a Negro,* Theatre Company of Boston, 1965; *Prodigal Son,* Greenwich Mews, NY, 1965; Mary, *Day of Absence,* St. Mark's Playhouse, NY, 1965; Clara, *Who's Got His Own,* American Place Theatre at St. Clement's, NY, 1966; Jean Biggs, *The Experiment,* Orpheum, NY, 1967; *Slaves,* 1968; *Angel Levine,* 1969; *Where's Daddy,* 1969. PRINCIPAL STAGE WORK, DIRECTING—Founder, executive producer, National Black Theatre, Inc. 1968; *Ritual,* National Black Theatre (NBT), 1971; *Change! Love Together! Organize! A Revival,* NBT, 1972; *A Soul Journey into Truth,* NBT, 1974; *The Believers,* off-Broadway; *Softly Comes a Whirlwind, Whispering in Your Ear,* NBT, 1978; *Five on the Black Hand Side,* 1970; (television)—*Me and My Song;* "The Ritual," *Soul,* 1970; guest lecturer, *Positively Black,* 1976; writer, co-producer, film—*Rise: A Love Song for a Love People.* MAJOR TOURS—She has toured with the National Black Theatre to Haiti, Bermuda, Trinidad, Guyana, South Africa, Nigeria.

PRINCIPAL FILM APPEARANCES—*Gone Are the Days*, 1964; *The Pawnbroker*, 1965; *The Group*, 1966; *The Slaves*, 1969. PRINCIPAL TELEVISION APPEARANCES—*A Carol for Another Christmas; Camera Three; Kaleidoscope; The Ed Sullivan Show; Black Journal.*

AWARDS: Monarch Merit Award for Outstanding Contributions to the Performing and Visual Arts, National Council for Culture and Art, 1983; National Association of Negro Business and Professional Women's Club, Inc., Riverside Club, for Contribution to the Field of the Performing Arts, 1981; Blackfrica Promotions, Harlem Week '80, for Creative Excellence, 1980; Community Service Award, Reality House, Inc., 1980; Universal Awareness Award, Toward a New Age, Inc., 1979; Cultural Arts Service Award, Black Spectrum Theatre Company, 1978; Certificate of Appreciation, Lorton Voices, Lorton Penitentiary, 1976; Best Film, National Association of Media Women's Black Film Festival, 1975: *Rise: A Love Song for a Love People;* Female Artist of the Year Award, Blackfrica Promotions, 1975; Dedication and Achievement in Theatre, Mt. Morris Church, 1975; International Benin Award, New Dimensions Associates, 1974; Certificate of Achievement, Harlem Chamber of Commerce, 1974; First Annual Audelco Recognition Award in Theatre, 1973; Token of Esteem, E. St. Louis Illinois Community Schools, 1973; New York Metropolitan Chapter of Alabama State University Alumni Association, for Dedication and Efforts in the Field of Drama, 1972; Distinguished Contribution, M. W. King Solomon Grand Lodge, 1972; Vernon Rice Drama Desk Award, Best Actress, 1965: Violet, *Home Movies.*

WRITINGS: ARTICLES PUBLISHED—"The Black Woman: She Does Exist," *New York Times*, 1967; "We Can Be What We Were Born To Be," *New York Times*, 1968.

SIDELIGHTS: "In 1973 Ms. Teer received a Ford Foundation Fellowship to visit seven African countries to further her research. She spent four months in Western Nigeria acquainting herself fully with the Yoruba culture and religion. Ms. Teer has visited Nigeria 7 times and considers it to be her 'second home.' She wanted to discover the science of spirit and the secret of Soul. She along with her performing company of 35 people continued their research in South America, the West Indies, Haiti, bars, the Apollo Theatre and numerous churches in Harlem. The National Black Theatre has performed in Trinidad, Guyana, Western Nigeria and throughout the United States. Because of [its] cultural contributions to the City and State of New York, Mayor Koch and the Government of New York State proclaimed May 7, 1979 as 'National Black Theatre Day.' . . . in Harlem . . . on the corner of 125th Street and Fifth Avenue she is developing an educational and cultural facility: The National Black Institute of Theatre Arts, dedicated to demonstrating the material wonders of high technology and the magnificence which flows from the cultural sound called Soul."

ADDRESS: Office—c/o The National Black Theatre, Nine E. 125th Street, New York, NY 10035.

HOWARD TEICHMANN

TEICHMANN, Howard Miles, playwright, writer, director, producer, educator

PERSONAL: Born January 22, 1916 in Chicago, IL; son of Jack (a businessman) and Rose (Berliner) Teichmann; married Evelyn Jane Goldstein (a writer) on April 2, 1939; children: Judith Robin Steckler. EDUCATION: University of Wisconsin, B.A., 1938. MILITARY: U.S. Army, senior editor, *OWI*, Overseas Branch, WWII, on staff of Lt. General Brehon Sommerrell. NON-THEATRICAL CAREER: Professor of English, Barnard College, Columbia University.

CAREER: FIRST STAGE WORK—Assistant stage manager, Orson Welles's Mercury Theatre, first production, *Danton's Death*, 1938; became stage manager and assistant to the president of the Mercury Theatre.

WRITINGS: PLAYS PRODUCED/PUBLISHED—Co-author with George Kaufman, *The Solid Gold Cadillac*, 1953; *Miss Lonelyhearts*, 1957; *The Girls in 509*, 1959; *Julia, Jake and Uncle Joe*, 1961; *A Rainy Day in Newark*, 1963; *Smart Aleck: Alexander Woollcott at 8:40.*

TELEVISION—*A Day in the Life of a Chorus Girl; Trio; Showtime U.S.A.; Slezak and Son; Ford 50th Anniversary*

Show; Gillette Christmas Show; Rosalind Russell's Wonderful World of Entertainment; The Jane Frohman Show; and for *Theatre U.S.A.*

RADIO SHOWS—*Orson Welles's Mercury Theatre of the Air; Twelve Crowded Months; Cavalcade of America; Texaco Star Theatre; Campbell Playhouse; Helen Hayes Theatre; Stories America Loves; CBS Workshop; The Nature of the Enemy; Enough and on Time; Tell It to the Marines; They Were Expendable; Newsreel for Thaksgiving; Many a Watchful Night; They Live Forever; We Glory in the Title; Labor for Victory; Warriors of Peace; 167th Anniversary of the U.S. Marine Corps; Opening Recruitment Drive, U.S.A.F.; Road of Life; Ford Theatre; Gertrude Lawrence's Revlon Revue; Radio Reader's Digest; Theatre USA; Great Scenes from Great Plays.*

BIOGRAPHIES—*George S. Kaufman, An Intimate Portrait; Smart Aleck: The Wit and World of Alexander Woollcott; Alice: The Life and Times of Alice Roosevelt Longworth; Fonda: My Life.*

AWARDS: Declaration of Esteem and Appreciation from the Broadway Association, 1972; Distinguished Service Award, School of Journalism, University of Wisconsin, 1959; Emmy Award, *Ford 50th Anniversary Show,* 1954; Peabody Award, 1953.

SIDELIGHTS: MEMBERSHIPS—Council of the Dramatists Guild; Dramatists Guild, treasurer, Dramatists Guild Fund; Director, Dramatists Play service; Writers Guild East; PEN; Mayor's Advisory Board, New York City.

ADDRESS: Agent—Morton Janklow, 598 Madison Avenue, New York, NY 10022.

* * *

TEWES, Lauren (nee Cynthia Tewes), actress

PERSONAL: Surname sounds like "Tweeze;" born October 26, 1953 in Trafford, PA; daughter of Joseph (a wood pattern maker) and Joanne (Woods) Tewes. EDUCATION: Attended Rio Hondo College, Whittier, CA, and the University of California at Riverside, CA; studied with Rich Walters, Rick Rizzo, and Charles Conrad.

CAREER: DEBUT—*Arsenic and Old Lace,* Pacific Conservatory Theatre, CA. PRINCIPAL STAGE APPEARANCES—Billie Dawn, *Born Yesterday,* Jacksonville Dinner Theatre, FL, 1982; Meg, *Crimes of the Heart,* Westport Country Playhouse, CT, 1983.

MAJOR TOURS—Meg, *Crimes of the Heart,* Corning Theatre, Pocono Playhouse, Cherry County Playhouse, 1983.

FILM DEBUT—*Eyes of a Stranger,* 1980. TELEVISION DEBUT—*Charlie's Angels.* PRINCIPAL TELEVISION APPEARANCES—*The Love Boat; Fantasy Island; Dallas Cowboys' Cheerleaders; Starsky & Hutch; Vegas.*

AWARDS: 1st Annual Chancellor's Award for Excellence in the Theatre at University of California at Riverside.

LAUREN TEWES

Photograph by Harry Langdon

SIDELIGHTS: "I have traveled extensively with the *Love Boat* company, Australia, South America, China, Japan, South Pacific, Mediterranean, Carribbean; my hobbies include gourmet cooking, reading, movies. *Communication* is *most* important.

ADDRESS: Agent—c/o Thomas K. Barad, Barad Entertainment Inc., 7285 Franklin Avenue, Los Angeles, CA 90046.

* * *

THOMAS, Richard, actor

PERSONAL: Born June 13, 1951, in New York, NY; son of Richard S. (a ballet instructor) and Barbara (a ballet dancer and teacher; maiden name, Fallis) Thomas; married Alma Gonzales, February 14, 1975; children: Richard F., Barbara, Gwyneth, Pilar. RELIGION: Christian.

CAREER: DEBUT—Singer, *Damn Yankees,* Sarendaga, NY, 1957. NEW YORK DEBUT—John Roosevelt, *Sunrise at Campobello,* Booth, 1958. PRINCIPAL STAGE APPEARANCES—*Member of the Wedding,* Equity Library, NY, 1959; *Strange Interlude; Playroom; Everything in the Garden; Fifth of July,* NY; *Saint Joan; Merton of the Movies; Streamers,* Los Angeles, CA. MAJOR TOURS—*Whose Life Is It Anyway?,* Eastern U.S. cities.

FILM DEBUT—*Winning*, 1969. PRINCIPAL FILM APPEARANCES—*Last Summer*, 1969; *The Todd Killings*, 1971; *Red Sky at Morning; Cactus in the Snow; You'll Like My Mother*, 1972; *9/30/55*, 1978; *Battle Beyond the Stars*.

TELEVISION DEBUT—*Hallmark Hall of Fame*, "A Christmas Tree," 1959. PRINCIPAL TELEVISION APPEARANCES—*The Waltons; The Homecoming; Silence; No Other Love; All Quiet on the Western Front; Red Badge of Courage; Getting Married; To Find My Son; Berlin Tunnel 21; Roots: The Next Generations; Johnny Belinda; Living Proof: The Hank Williams, Jr. Story; Hobson's Choice; Master of Ballantrae*.

WRITINGS: BOOKS OF POETRY—*Poems by Richard Thomas; In the Moment; Glass*.

AWARDS: Emmy Award, Best Actor in a Dramatic Series: *The Waltons;* Friends of Robert Frost Award.

ADDRESS: Agent—c/o John Gaines, APA, 9000 Sunset Blvd. Los Angeles, CA 90069.

* * *

THOMPSON, Robert, producer, director

PERSONAL: Born May 31, 1937, in Palmyra, NY; son of Roger (a farmer) and Gladys (Smith) Thompson; married Helen M. Miller, August 31, 1957 (divorced 1976); children: Mark, Peter, Patrick. EDUCATION: Ithaca College, B.S. (Radio and TV), 1960; UCLA, M.F.A. (Directing), 1961.

CAREER: PRINCIPAL FILM WORK—Producer, *The Paper Chase*, 1973. PRINCIPAL TELEVISION WORK—Producer/director, *Lanigan's Rabbi*, 1974; *The Paper Chase*, 1976; producer/director, *Bud and Lou*, 1978; *California Fever*, 1980; *The Mark of Zorro;* director—*Hill Street Blues, Fantasy Island, Dynasty, Greatest American Hero, Magnum P.I., ABC Playbreak, Fame, Dallas, The New FBI, Chicago Story*.

FILM-RELATED CAREER: Head of talent, signing of contract players, Universal Studios, 1961–68; head of talent, creative affairs, Cinema Center Films, CBS, Los Angeles, CA, 1968–72; president, Thompson-Paul Productions Inc. Sherman Oaks, CA, 1974–present.

WRITINGS: PLAYS, UNPUBLISHED—three one acts, The Preparation, It Is Only a Game, Goodbye My Son.

SIDELIGHTS: MEMBERSHIPS—Directors Guild of America.

Mr. Thompson acted and directed extensively while attending Ithaca College and UCLA. He adapted work for television while at Ithaca College and worked at local radio and television studios which produced his work.

ADDRESS: Home—4536 Mary Ellen Avenue, Sherman Oaks, CA 91423. Office—13444 Ventura Blvd., Sherman Oaks, CA 91423. Agent—Irv Schecter & Associates, 9300 Wilshire Blvd., Suite 410, Beverly Hills, CA 90212.

CHRISTOPHER TIMOTHY

TIMOTHY, Christopher, actor

PERSONAL: Born October 14, 1940, in Bala, N. Wales; son of Eifion Andrew and Marian Gwladys (Hailstone) Timothy; married Annie Veronica Swatton. EDUCATION: Central School of Speech and Drama, London, 1960–63.

CAREER: LONDON DEBUT—Corporal M.P., *Chips with Everything*, Royal Court, London. NEW YORK DEBUT—Corporal M.P., *Chips with Everything*, Booth (six months). PRINCIPAL STAGE APPEARANCES—Three years with the National Theatre at the Old Vic, Queen's Theatre, U.K. tours, and tours to Moscow and West Berlin; Sid, *Waiting for Lefty;* Hibbert, *Long Day's Journey into Night*, Cambridge Theatre, London; Alvin, *Actor's Nightmare*, Ambassador's, London; Bernard, *Happy Birthday*, Apollo, London; Clive, *See How They Run*, Shaftesbury, London; Rosencrantz, *Rosencrantz and Guildenstern Are Dead*, Young Vic, then Cambridge Theatre, London; Jesus, *The York Mystery Plays*, York Abbey, 1980; lead, *The Cure for Love*, U.K. tour; Firk, *The Shoemakers' Holiday*, Leicester; Petruchio, *Taming of the Shrew*, Farnham.

PRINCIPAL FILM APPEARANCES—lead, *Some Sunday;* Spike, *Here We Go Round the Mulberry Bush*, 1968; Cerdic, *Alfred the Great*, 1969; Corporal Brook, *The Virgin Soldiers*, 1969; *The Mind of Mr. Soames*, 1970; *Up the Chastity Belt; Spring and Port Wine;* the National Theatre's *Othello*.

PRINCIPAL TELEVISION APPEARANCES—Willis, "Murder Must Advertise," *Lord Peter Wimsy;* Kevin, *The Kitchen;* Corporal, *The Moon Shines Bright on Charlie Chaplin;* Sid Love, "Murder Most English," *The Flaxborough Chronicles;* Voyzek, "Voyzek," *All the World's a Stage;* James Herriot, *All Creatures Great and Small;* the National Theatre's *Much Ado About Nothing; Julius Caesar; Twelfth Night; Royal Command Performance of 1982; Three Sisters; Mussolini; Take Three Girls; Take Three Women; A History and Its Heritage; A Family and a Fortune;* et al.

AWARDS: BBC TV Personality of 1979: *All Creatures Great and Small* (co-winner); Variety Club of Great Britain; Outstanding Male Personality for 1978: *All Creatures Great and Small;* Screenwriters' Guild/Pye Television Ltd; Amateur Film Maker Award, Best Sound: *Some Sunday;* Laurence Olivier Award: Sid, *Waiting for Lefty;* John Gielgud Scholarship.

ADDRESS: Agent—Peter Froggatt, Plant and Froggatt Ltd., 4 Windmill Street, London W1, England.

* * *

TOLAN, Michael (ne Seymour Tuchow), actor and producer

PERSONAL: Born November 27, 1925, in Detroit, MI; son of Morris (a tool and die maker) and Gertrude (Gold) Tuchow; married Rosemary Forsyth, June 29, 1966 (divorced 1970); married Carol Hume, January 1, 1979; children: Alexandra, Jenny. EDUCATION: Wayne State University, B.A., 1947; trained for the stage with Stella Adler.

CAREER: DEBUT—(radio)—*Lone Ranger, Green Hornet, Challenge of the Yukon,* Detroit, MI, 1945. NEW YORK DEBUT—Senatorial messenger/first sentinel, *Coriolanus,* Phoenix, 1954. PRINCIPAL STAGE APPEARANCES—Dr. Astrov, *Uncle Vanya,* Rev. Morell, *Candida,* John Worthing, *The Importance of Being Earnest,* Oedipus, *Oedipus,* Actors Company of Detroit, MI, 1947–49; chauffeur, *Will Success Spoil Rock Hunter?,* Belasco, NY, 1955; Mother, *A Hatful of Rain,* Lyceum, NY, 1955; John Rivers, *The Genius and the Goddess,* Henry Miller's, NY, 1957; Igor Romanoff, *Romanoff and Juliet,* Plymouth, NY, 1957; Jerome Black, *A Majority of One,* Shubert, NY, 1959; Freud, *A Far Country,* Music Box, NY, Huntington Hartford, Hollywood, CA, Geary, San Francisco, CA, 1961; Rudd Kendall, *Old Acquaintance,* Royal Poinciana Playhouse, Palm Beach, FL, 1961; Ralph Granger, *Banderol,* Forrest, Philadelphia, 1962; Lilburn Lewis, *Brother to Dragons,* St. Clement's, NY, 1965; Nikolai Alexeevich Chulkaturin, *The Journey of the Fifth Horse,* St. Clement's, NY, 1966; Eli, *Eli the Fanatic,* Plymouth, NY, 1971.

FILM DEBUT—Duke Malloy, *The Enforcer,* 1951. PRINCIPAL FILM APPEARANCES—Lazarus, *The Greatest Story Ever Told,* 1964; *The Lost Man,* 1969; *John and Mary,* 1969; Dr. Ballinger, *All That Jazz,* 1979.

PRINCIPAL TELEVISION APPEARANCES—*Eleventh Hour; The Nurses; Dupont Show of the Week; Route 66; US Steel Hour; Play of the Week: The Dybbuk, Volpone, Lament for a*

MICHAEL TOLAN

Bulfighter, Wingless Victory, 1960–61; Dr. Tazinski, *The Nurses; Espionage; Ladies' Man; Naked City; Bob Hope Presents; Felony Squad; Wallace Stevens: A Poet's Season; The Bell Telephone Hour; Stage for Protest; Tarzan; Rat Patrol; The Invaders; Mannix; The FBI; Mission: Impossible; Journey to the Unknown; Dan August; Owen Marshall; Nichols; Medical Center; Cannon; Ghost Story; Loose Change; The Best of Families; Valley Forge; Mary Tyler Moore Show; The Senator; The Adams Chronicles; The Mountbatten Story; Robert Lowell Biography; Dance in America.* PRODUCED: Plays—*The Old Glory,* St. Clement's Church, 1964, Theater de Lys, NY, 1965; *The Outside Man,* St. Clement's, NY, 1964; *Lower Than Angels,* St. Clement's, NY, 1965; *Juana La Loca,* St. Clement's, NY, 1965. Film—*Five On the Black Hand Side; Four Friends.* PRODUCED AND ASSOCIATE DIRECTED: Plays—*A Step Away from War,* 1965, *Jonah,* 1966, *Who's Got His Own,* 1966, *Mercy Street,* 1969, *Five on the Black Hand Side,* 1970, *Two Times One,* 1970, *The Pig Pen,* 1970, *Sunday Dinner,* 1970, St. Clement's, NY; *The Carpenters,* 1970, *Pinkville,* 1971, *Bog Bay Beast Bait,* 1971, American Place, NY.

AWARDS: Broadway Show League's Most Valuable (baseball) Player, 1959; Sylvania Award Nomination, Best Television Performance in a starring role, 1957: *Teddy Bear.*

SIDELIGHTS: MEMBERSHIPS—Player's Club. RECREATION—Baseball, tennis.

ADDRESS: Agent—J. Michael Bloom, 400 Madison Avenue, New York, NY 10017.

TOSER, David, costume designer

PERSONAL: Born in Milwaukee, WI; son of Franz Carl (a businessman) and Janet Young (a social activist; maiden name, Wilson) Toser. EDUCATION: Brown University, Providence, RI, B.A.; Yale, M.F.A.; studied for the theatre at Parsons School of Design. NON-THEATRICAL CAREER—Guest lecturer, Carnegie Mellon University, 1979–80; Guest professor, Temple University, 1980–81.

CAREER: LONDON DEBUT—*Very Good Eddie.* PRINCIPAL THEATRE WORK—*Sterling Silver; Any Resemblance to Persons Living or . . .; Shoot Anything with Hair That Moves; Christopher Fish; Trixie True, Teen Detective,* Theatre de Lys, NY; *Bundle of Nerves; Noel Coward's Sweet Potato,* NY; *Does a Tiger Wear a Necktie?,* NY; *The Great White Hope,* NY, 1968; *Very Good Eddie,* Booth, NY; *Going Up,* NY; *Whoopie!,* NY; *Little Johnny Jones,* NY; *Our Town,* NY; *Status Quo Vadis,* NY; *Tip-Toes,* Brooklyn Academy of Music, NY; 46 productions at Goodspeed Opera House, East Haddam, CT, including: *Red Blue Grass Western-Flyer Show, After You, Mr. Hyde, Cowboy, Annie, Shenandoah, Hubba, Hubba, The King of Schnorrers; Rhinoceros,* Pittsburgh Playhouse, PA; *Juno's Swans,* PAF Playhouse; Pittsburgh Public: *The Importance of Being Earnest, Uncle Vanya, Ashes, Vanities, Father's Day, Medal of Honor Rag, For Colored Girls. . .;* American Conservatory Theater, San Francisco: *The Devil's Disciple, Endgame, Noah, Tiny Alice, Death of a Salesman;* Vanguard Projects: *Cyrano de Bergerac, Hamlet, The Glass Menagerie, Elizabeth the Queen, Caesar and Cleopatra, The Trial; Betrayal,* Syracuse Stage; *Blithe Spririt,* Pennsylvania Stage Company. MAJOR TOURS—*Absurd Person Singular,* national; *The Great White Hope,* national; *The Price,* bus and truck; *A Majority of One,* bus and truck; *Shenandoah,* bus and truck; *The Sound of Music,* bus and truck.

TELEVISION SHOWS—*Best of Families,* episodes 3–6; *Under Milkwood.*

SIDELIGHTS: MEMBERSHIPS—United Scenic Artists, Local 829.

ADDRESS: Home—253 E. 77th Street, New York, NY 10021. Office—Ten W. 19th Street, New York, NY 10011.

* * *

TREYZ, Russell, director, writer

PERSONAL: Born August 9, 1940; son of George Victor (a manufacturer and a banker) and Jane (Leffingwell) Treyz; married Alice Elliot (an actress) on May 15, 1971; children: Amanda Mary, Ross Denney-Elliott. EDUCATION: Princeton University, B.A., 1962; Yale University, School of Drama, M.F.A. (Directing), 1965; studied Film Production at New York University.

CAREER: FIRST STAGE WORK, DIRECTED—*Light up the Sky,* Stage West, Springfield, MA, 1970. NEW YORK DEBUT—*Whitsuntide,* Martinique, 1972. PRINCIPAL STAGE WORK, DIRECTED—*Private Lives,* Woodstock Playhouse; *Look Back in Anger,* Theatre by the Sea, Portsmouth, NH; *Man with a Load of Mischief,* Royal Poinciana Playhouse, FL; *The*

RUSSELL TREYZ

Student Prince, Pittsburgh Civic Light Opera; *The Music Man,* P.C.P.A., CA; *The Importance of Being Earnest,* McCarter, Princeton, NJ; *Play It Again Sam,* Ivoryton Playhouse; *Babes in Arms,* Goodspeed Opera House, East Haddam, CT; *Mame,* Alliance Theatre, Atlanta, GA; *Something's Afoot,* Alaska Repertory Theatre; *Comedy of Errors, Two Gentlemen of Verona, Tartuffe,* Alabama Shakespeare Festival; *Mass Appeal,* Actors Theatre of Louisville, KY; *Follies, In White America, Oklahoma,* Equity Library Theatre, NY; *The Refrigerators,* La Mama ETC, NY; *Here Be Dragons/A Knack with Horses,* Theatre at St. Clement's; *The Girls Most Likely to Succeed, Bloodsport, The Case Against Robert Guardino,* Playwrights Horizons, NY; *The Year of the Dragon,* American Place, NY; *Cottonpatch Gospel,* Lambs, NY. MAJOR TOURS—*Cottonpatch Gospel.* TELEVISION—*The Year of The Dragon; Cottonpatch Gospel.*

THEATRE-RELATED CAREER: Head of Drama Department, Interlochen Arts Academy, Traverse City, MI, 1965–66; artistic director, Ashtabula Playhouse, OH, 1966–68; artistic director, resident director, Theatre by the Sea, Portsmouth, NH, 1975–79.

WRITINGS: BOOK OF MUSICAL—*Cotton Patch Gospel,* with Tom Key and Harry Chapin.

AWARDS: Drama Desk Award, Most Promising Director, 1971; Cum Laude Graduate, Princeton University, 1962.

SIDELIGHTS: MEMBERSHIPS—Society of Stage Directors and Choreographers; Dramatists Guild.

ADDRESS: Home—107 Bedford Street, New York, NY 10014.

TUCCI, Maria, actress

PERSONAL: Born June 19, in Florence, Italy; daughter of Niccolo (a novelist) and Laura (Rusconi) Tucci; married Robert Adams Gottlieb (a publisher); children: Elizabeth and Nicholas.

CAREER: THEATER DEBUT—*Romeo and Juliet,* New York Shakespeare Festival, Delacorte, 1958. PRINCIPAL STAGE APPEARANCES—Angelina, *The Milk Train Doesn't Stop Here Anymore,* Morosco, NY, 1963; Katia, *Five Evenings,* Village South, NY, 1963; Elena, *Corruption in the House of Justice,* Cherry Lane, NY, 1963; Cassandra, *The Trojan Women,* Circle in the Square, NY, 1963; girl, *The Deputy,* Brooks Atkinson, NY, 1964; Virgilia, *Coriolanus,* Juliet, *Romeo and Juliet,* American Shakespeare Festival, Stratford, CT, 1965; Isabella, *The White Devil,* Circle in the Square, NY, 1965; Rosa, *The Rose Tattoo,* City Center, NY, 1966; Maria, *Yerma,* Vivian Beaumont, NY, 1966; Antigone, *Antigone,* Stratford, CT, 1967; Alexandra, *The Little Foxes,* Vivian Beaumont, NY, 1967; Ophelia, *Hamlet,* Stratford, CT, 1969; Teacher, *The Shepherd of Avenue B,* Fortune, NY, 1970; Agnes, *The School for Wives,* Lyceum, NY, 1971; Annie/Susan, *Sissie's Scrapbook,* Playwrights Horizon, NY, 1973; Teacher, *A Pagan Place,* Long Wharf, New Haven, CT, 1974; Ruth Atkins, *Beyond the Horizon,* McCarter, Princeton, NJ, 1974; Kattrin, *Mother Courage,* 1975; Juliet, *Romeo and Juliet,* 1975; Regan, *King Lear,* Stratford, CT, 1975; Hermione/Perdita, *The Winter's Tale,* Stratford, CT, 1975; Catherine Sloper, *The Heiress,* McCarter, Princeton, NJ, 1976; Elizabeth Proctor, *The Crucible,* Stratford, CT, 1976; title role, *Major Barbara,* McCarter, Princeton, NJ, 1976; Kitty, *Spokesong,* Long Wharf, New Haven, CT, 1978; Andrea, *Drinks Before Dinner,* Public, NY, 1978; Kitty, *Spokesong,* Circle in the Square, NY, 1979; *A Lesson from Aloes,* Playhouse, NY, 1981; *Kingdoms,* Cort, NY, 1981; *The Guardsman,* Long Wharf, New Haven, CT, 1983; *Requiem for a Heavyweight,* Long Wharf, New Haven, CT, 1984.

PRINCIPAL FILM APPEARANCES—*Daniel,* 1983; Priscilla Hiss, *Concealed Enemies,* 1984. PRINCIPAL TELEVISION APPEARANCES—*Beyond the Horizon,* 1975.

ADDRESS: Agent—c/o D.H.K.P.R., 165 W. 46th Street, New York, NY 10036.

* * *

TUNE, Tommy, director, choreographer, dancer, actor

PERSONAL: Born February 28, 1939, in Witchita Falls, TX; son of Jim P. and Eva M. (Clark) Tune. EDUCATION: University of Texas at Austin and University of Houston, B.F.A.

CAREER: NEW YORK DEBUT—Chorus, *Baker Street,* Broadway Theater, 1965. PRINCIPAL STAGE APPEARANCES—*Joyful Noise,* Mark Hellinger, NY, 1966; *How Now Dow Jones,* Lunt-Fontanne, NY, 1967; David, *Seesaw,* Uris, NY, 1973; Captain Billy Buck Chandler, *My One and Only,* NY, 1983. MAJOR TOURS—David, *Seesaw,* U.S. cities, 1974.

DIRECTED: Plays—*The Club,* Circle-in-the-Square, NY, 1976; *Sunset,* Studio Arena, Buffalo, NY, 1977; *The Best*

TOMMY TUNE

Little Whorehouse in Texas, Entermedia, NY, 1978, 46th Street Theater, 1979; *A Day in Hollywood, A Night in the Ukraine,* John Golden, NY, 1980; *Cloud 9,* Theatre de Lys, NY, 1981; *Nine* 46th Street Theater, NY, 1982; *My One and Only,* St. James, NY, 1983. CHOREOGRAPHED: Plays—*Canterbury Tales,* U.S. cities, 1969; *The Best Little Whorehouse in Texas,* Entermedia, NY, 1978, 46th Street Theater, NY, 1979; *A Day in Hollywood, A Night in the Ukraine,* John Golden, NY, 1980; *My One and Only,* St. James, NY, 1983. Films—*Hello, Dolly!,* 1969; *The Boyfriend,* 1971; *That's Dancing,* 1984.

AWARDS: Antoinette Perry Award, Best Choreography (with Thommie Walsh), 1983: *My One and Only;* Antoinette Perry Award, Best Actor in a Musical, 1983: *My One and Only;* Antoinette Perry Award, Best Director, 1982: *Nine;* Obie Award, Best Director, 1982: *Cloud Nine;* Drama Desk Award, Outstanding Choreography (with Thommie Walsh), 1982–83: *My One and Only;* Drama Desk Award, Best Director of a Musical, 1981–82: *Nine;* Drama Desk Award, Best Director of a Play, 1981–82: *Cloud Nine;* Antoinette Perry Award, Best Director of a Musical, Best Choreography, 1980: *A Day in Hollywood, A Night in the Ukraine;* Drama Desk Award, Best Choreography, Best Musical Staging, 1979–80: *A Day in Hollywood, A Night in the Ukraine;* Drama Desk Award, Best Director of a Musical, 1977–78: *The Best Little Whorehouse in Texas;* Antoinette Perry Award, Best Actor, 1974: *Seesaw.*

SIDELIGHTS: FAVORITE ROLE—Billy Buck Chandler, *My One and Only.*

ADDRESS: Office—c/o Towerhouse Productions, Inc., 890 Broadway, New York, NY 10003.

* * *

TURMAN, Lawrence, producer

PERSONAL: Born November 28, 1926; children: John, Andrew, Peter. RELIGION: Jewish.

CAREER: PRINCIPAL FILM WORK—Producer: *The Graduate,* 1967; *The Flim Flam Man,* 1967; *The Great White Hope,* 1970; *The Drowning Pool,* 1975; *Cave Man,* 1981.

ADDRESS: Office—9336 W. Washington, Bungalow G, Culver City, CA 90230.

* * *

TWAIN, Norman, producer, director

PERSONAL: Born September 13, 1930, in Atlantic City, NJ; son of Charles (a merchant) and Doris (a merchant; maiden name, Ager) Twain; married Sandra Church (an actress) 1964 (divorced); married Deanna Deignan September 27, 1981; children: (second marriage) Dena Rose. EDUCATION: Columbia University, B.A. 1952, M.A. (English) 1953. MILITARY: U.S. Army 1953–55.

CAREER: PRINCIPAL STAGE WORK—Producer, with Warner Le Roy, *The Golden Six,* York Playhouse, NY, 1958; with Bernard Miller, *Epitaph for George Dillon,* Henry Miller, NY, 1959; producer and director, *A Distant Bell,* O'Neill, NY, 1960; producer, *Roots,* Mayfair, NY, 1961; with Carroll and Harris Masterson, *The Lady of the Camellias,* Winter Garden, NY, 1963, also, *Traveller without Luggage,* ANTA, NY, 1964; with Edward Padula, Carroll and Harris Masterson, *Bajour,* Shubert, NY, 1964; *Gilbert Becaud on Broadway,* Longacre, NY, 1966; with Carroll and Harris Masterson, *The Apparition Theatre of Prague,* Cort, NY, 1966; with Edward Specter Productions, *Henry, Sweet Henry,* Palace, NY, 1967; with Marcel Akselrod by arrangement with Feliz Marouani, *Gilbert Becaud Sings Love,* Cort, NY, 1968; in association with Albert I. Fill, *Charles Aznavour,* Music Box, NY, 1970; *Lolita, My Love,* Shubert, Boston, MA, 1971; *Nicol Williamson's Late Show,* Eastside Playhouse, NY, 1973; in association with Michael Liebert, *The World of Lenny Bruce,* Players, NY, 1974; artistic director, Westwood Playhouse, *Streamers, Hold Me;* artistic director of the Long Beach Theatre Festival, *Cyrano de Bergerac, Our Town, The Man Who Came to Dinner, Eccentricities of a Nightingale, In the Boom Boom Room, As You Like It.*

PRINCIPAL TELEVISION WORK—Producer, *Vanities,* HBO: *Superman,* ABC Special; *Cheaters,* Showtime.

FILM—*Hotel New Hampshire.*

SIDELIGHTS: MEMBERSHIPS—SDG; League of New York Theatres.

ADDRESS: Office—119 W. 57th Street, New York, NY 10019.

* * *

TYSON, Cicely, actress

PERSONAL: Born December 19, 1933, in New York City; daughter of William and Theodosia Tyson; married Miles Davis, 1981. EDUCATION: Attended New York University; trained for the stage at the Actors' Studio.

CAREER: NEW YORK DEBUT—Jolly Rivers, *Jolly's Progress,* Longacre, 1959. PRINCIPAL STAGE APPEARANCES—Girl, *The Cool World,* Eugene O'Neill, NY, 1960; Stephanie Virtue Diop, *The Blacks,* St. Mark's Playhouse, NY, 1961; Mavis, *Moon on a Rainbow Shawl,* East 11th Street, NY, 1962; Celeste Chipley, *Tiger Tiger Burning Bright,* Booth, NY, 1962; Joan, *The Blue Boy in Black,* Masque, NY, 1963; Reverend Marion Alexander, *Trumpets of the Lord,* Astor Place Playhouse, NY, 1963; *A Hand Is on the Gates,* Longacre, NY, 1966; Myrna Jessup, *Carry Me Back to Morningside Heights,* John Golden, NY, 1968; Reverend Marion Alexander, *Trumpets of the Lord,* Brooks Atkinson, NY, 1969; *To Be Young, Gifted and Black,* Cherry Lane, NY, 1969; *The Blacks,* Playhouse in the Park, Cincinnati, OH, 1970–71; Abbie Putnam, *Desire Under the Elms,* Academy Festival, Chicago, IL, 1974.

PRINCIPAL FILM APPEARANCES—*Twelve Angry Men,* 1957; *Odds Against Tomorrow,* 1959; *The Last Angry Man,* 1959; *A Man Called Adam,* 1966; *The Comedians,* 1967; *The Heart Is a Lonely Hunter,* 1968; *Sounder,* 1972; *The Blue Bird,* 1976; *The River Niger,* 1976; *A Hero Ain't Nothin' but a Sandwich,* 1978; *The Concorde-Airport '79,* 1979.

PRINCIPAL TELEVISION APPEARANCES—*East Side/West Side,* 1963; *The Autobiography of Miss Jane Pittman,* 1973, 1974; *Just An Old Sweet Song,* 1976; *Roots,* 1977; *A Woman Called Moses,* 1978; *King,* 1978.

AWARDS: Emmy Award, Best Actress in a Special, 1973: *The Autobiography of Miss Jane Pittman;* Academy Award Nomination, Best Actress, 1972: *Sounder;* National Society of Film Critics Award, Atlanta Film Festival Award, Best Actress, 1972: *Sounder;* Vernon Price Award, 1962; NAACP Award; National Council Negro Women Award; Capitol Press Award. Honorary Doctorates—Atlanta University; Loyola University; Lincoln University.*

U

ULLMANN, Liv, actress

PERSONAL: Born December 16, 1939, in Tokyo, Japan; daughter of Norwegian parents; married Hans Stang (divorced); children: one daughter by Ingmar Bergman (film/stage director). EDUCATION: Studied acting in London for eight months.

CAREER: DEBUT—*Diary of Anne Frank*, Stavanger, Norway. PRINCIPAL STAGE APPEARANCES—a leading actress of classic roles in Norway; Nora, *A Doll's House*, Vivian Beaumont, NY; *Anna Christie*, Broadway, NY, 1977; *I Remember Mama*, Royale, NY, 1979; Mrs. Alving, *Ghosts*, Brooks Atkinson, NY, 1982.

FILM DEBUT—*Persona*, 1966. PRINCIPAL FILM APPEARANCES—*The Hour of the Wolf; Shame; The Passion of Anna; Cries and Whispers*, 1972; *Face to Face; Scenes from a Marriage; Serpents; Autumn Sonata; The Night Visitor; Pope Joan; The Emigrants; The New Land; Lost Horizon; 40 Carats; Zandy's Bride; The Abdication; A Bridge Too Far.*

WRITINGS: BOOKS—Autobiography, *Changing*, 1978.

AWARDS: Official Goodwill Ambassador, UNICEF, 1980; National Society of Film Critics or New York Film Critics Best Actress awards for 6 films in past 7 years; honored for performances in *Face to Face* and *Scenes from a Marriage* by NY Film critics and National Society of Film Critics; Best Actress, NY Film Critics, *Cries and Whispers.*

ADDRESS: Agent—Paul Kohner—Michael Levy Agency, 9169 Sunset Blvd., Los Angeles, CA 90069.*

* * *

USTINOV, Peter (Alexander), actor, writer, director

PERSONAL: Born April 16, 1921, in London; son of Iona and Nadia (Benois) Ustinov; married Isolde Denham, 1940 (divorced); married Suzanne Cloutier (divorced); married Helena du Lau d'Allemans; children: (first marriage) Tamara; (second marriage) Pavia, Andrea, Igor. EDUCATION: Attended Westminster School; trained for the stage at the London Theatre Studio. MILITARY: British Army, World War II.

CAREER: FILM DEBUT—*Mein Kampf, My Crimes*, 1941. PRINCIPAL FILM APPEARANCES—*Odette*, 1950; *Hotel Sahara*, 1950; *Quo Vadis*, 1951; *The Egyptian*, 1954; *We're No Angels*, 1955; *Spartacus*, 1961; *Photo Finish*, 1963; *John Goldfarb*, 1965; *Viva Max*, 1970; *One of Our Dinosaurs Is Missing*, 1975; *Logan's Run*, 1976; *Treasure of Matacumbe*, 1976; *The Last Remake of Beau Geste*, 1977; *The Mauve Taxi*, 1977; *Death on the Nile, Thief of Bagdad*, 1978; *Ashanti*, 1979; *Charlie Chan and the Curse of the Dragon Queen*, 1980; *The Great Muppet Caper*, 1981; *Evil Under the Sun*, 1982.

PRINCIPAL FILM WORK—Producer, *School for Secrets*, 1946; producer, *We're No Angels*, 1955; writer/actor, *The Way Ahead*, 1943–44; writer, *The Banbury Nose*, 1944; *Love of Four Colonels*, 1951; director/actor, *Billy Budd*, 1962; writer/director/actor, *Photo Finish*, 1963; writer/actor, *Romanoff and Juliet*, 1958; director/actor, *Hammersmith Is Out*, 1972; producer/director/actor, *Memed My Hawk*, 1984.

PRINCIPAL STAGE APPEARANCES—*Romanoff and Juliet*, New York, London; *Beethoven's Tenth*, Vaudeville, London, 1983, Nederlander, U.S. tour, 1983–84.

OPERA—Director, *The Magic Flute*, Hamburg, 1968; director/set and costume designer, *Don Quichotte*, Paris, 1973; director/set and costume designer, *Don Giovanni*, Edinburgh Festival, 1973; director, *Les Brigands*, Berlin, 1978; director/libretticist, *The Marriage*, Piccola Scala, 1981, Edinburgh Festival, 1981; director *Mavra* and *The Flood*, Piccola Scala, Milan, 1982.

WRITINGS: BOOKS—*The Loser*, 1960; *We Were Only Human*, 1961; *Add A Dash of Pity*, 1966; *Frontiers of the Sea*, 1966; *Unknown Soldier and His Wife*, 1967; *Halfway Up the Tree*, 1968; *Krumnagel*, 1971; *Dear Me*, 1977. PLAYS—*Romanoff and Juliet; Overheard*, 1981; *Beethoven's Tenth*, 1983.

AWARDS: UNICEF Award, Distinguished Service at the International Level, 1978; Emmy Award, Best Dramatic Actor in a Single Program, 1971: *A Storm in Summer;* Emmy Award, 1966: *Barefoot in Athens;* Academy Award, Best Supporting Actor, 1964: *Topkapi;* Academy Award, Best Actor, 1961: *Spartacus;* Emmy Award, 1957: *Dr. Johnson;* Commander, Order of the British Empire.

SIDELIGHTS: MEMBERSHIPS—Queens, Club, Royal Automobile Club, Arts Theatre, Garrick Savage.

ADDRESS: Agent—c/o William Morris Agency, 147–149 Wardour Street, London W1.

V

VALENTINE, James, actor, teacher

PERSONAL: Born February 18, 1930, in Rockford, IL; son of Everett Carl (a furniture salesman) and Mae Elizabeth (Swenson) Valentine. EDUCATION: Attended Beloit College in Wisconsin for one year and the Central School of Speech and Dramatic Art in London, England for three years; received diploma, 1951.

CAREER: DEBUT—House painter, *Kiss and Tell*, Shady Lane Playhouse, Maringo, IL, 1944. PRINCIPAL STAGE APPEAR-ANCES—(New York)—Regency Rake and footman, *Conversation Piece*, Barbizon, 1956; Ben, *Cloud 7*, 1956; Geoffrey Colwyn-Stuart, *Epitaph of George Dillon*, Golden and Henry Miller, 1957; Joseph, *Duel of Angels*, Helen Hayes, 1958; Flight Lt. Higgins, *Ross*, O'Neill and Hudson, 1961; Peter Cook, *Beyond the Fringe*, Golden and Barrymore, 1964–65; Brittanus, *Caesar and Cleopatra*, Palace, 1976; Jack Worthing, *The Importance of Being Earnest*, Circle in the Square, 1977; Merlyn, *Camelot*, New York State Theatre and Winter Garden, 1980; Mock Turtle, *Alice in Wonderland*, Virginia Theatre, 1982–83.

MAJOR TOURS—David Bulloch, *The Reluctant Debutante*, 1957; Gilbert Dayney, *Jane*, 1957; Eric Birley, *An Inspector Calls*, 1958; Geoffrey Cowlyn-Stuart, *Epitaph for George Dillon*, 1959; Yasha, *The Cherry Orchard*, 1960; Timothy Gregg, *Not in the Book*, 1960; narrator, *Under Milk Wood*, 1963; son, *Six Characters In Search of an Author*, Circle in the Square production, 1963; Peter Cook, *Beyond the Fringe*, U.S. and Canada, 1964–65; Andrew Hunter, *Girl in My Soup*, 1969; Almady, *The Play's the Thing*, 1978; Merlyn and King Pellinore, *Camelot*, 1980–83.

PRINCIPAL STAGE APPEARANCES (Regional)—With American Shakespeare Festival, Stratford, CT, Poins, *Henry IV, Part I*, 1962, Young Percy, *Richard III*, 1962, Andrew Agucheek, *Twelfth Night*, 1966, Duke of Warwick, *Henry IV, Part II*, 1966, Caesar, *Julius Caesar*, 1967, Egeus, Philostrate, *A Midsummer Night's Dream*, 1967, Prince of Arragon, *Merchant of Venice*, 1967; with the Shaw Festival, Niagra-on-the-Lake, Ontario, Canada, Randall, *Heartbreak House*, 1968, *Chemmy Circle*, 1968, Dr. Paramore, *The Philanderer*, 1971, General Mitchner, *Press Cuttings*, 1971, Reginald Bridgenorth, *Getting Married*, 1971, Boone, *You Never Can Tell*, 1973, Juggins, *Fanny's First Play*, 1973, Phano Cles, *The Brass Butterfly*, 1973, Major Swindun, *The Devil's Disciple*, 1974, Jack Chesney, *Charley's Aunt*, 1974, Bashville, *The Admirable Bashville*, 1974, Brittanus, *Caesar and Cleopatra*, 1975, Dean Knapp, *Leaven of Malice*, 1975, Valentine, *You Never Can Tell*, 1977, Captain Kearney, *Captain Brassbound's Conversion*, 1977; has ap-

peared with Manitoba Theatre, Edmonton, Alberta, Theatre of the Living Arts, Philadelphia, Front Street Theatre, Memphis, TN, Theatre Calgary, Neptune Theatre, Nova Scotia, Cincinnati Playhouse in the Park, Philadelphia Drama Guild, Loeb Drama Center (Harvard University), Bastion Theatre, Victoria, BC, Hartford Stage Company, Studio Arena, Buffalo, NY, Westport Country Playhouse, Coconut Grove Playhouse, FL, and University of Michigan Professional Theatre Program, Actors Company. PRINCIPAL FILM APPEARANCES—*Stolen Face*, England, 1951; *Gathering Storm*, England, 1952; Brittanus, *Caesar and Cleopatra*.

PRINCIPAL TELEVISION APPEARANCES—*Live from Manchester*, England, 1954; *ITV's Armchair Theatre*, England, 1954; Capt. Stanhope, *If This Be Treason*, 1954; *The Dupont Show of the Month:* Gilbert, *The Browing Version*, 1957, Fritz, *The Prisoner of Zenda*, 1958, Lt. Wyatt, *Billy Budd*, 1958, Noah Claypole, *Oliver Twist*, 1958; *Play of the Week*, Gaston, *Waltz of the Torreadors*, 1959, Yasha, *The Cherry Orchard*, 1959; *The Hallmark Hall of Fame*, *Shangri-la*, 1959; also *Camera Three*, *Look up and Live*, and the HBO production of *Camelot*.

AWARDS: The Laurence Olivier Prize for Best Actor, Central School of Speech and Dramatic Art, London, England, 1951.

THEATRE-RELATED CAREER: Teacher, Beloit College, WI.

SIDELIGHTS: MEMBERSHIPS—AEA, SAG, AFTRA. REC-REATION—Reading, cooking, walking, and sitting in parks.

"A Shaw Festival production of *You Never Can Tell* was given a Command Performance for Her Majesty the Queen on June 28, 1973 at the Festival Theatre, Niagra-On-The-Lake, Ontario Canada. The cast was presented to Her Majesty and Prince Philip. . . . The appreciation of the theatre lives of Sir Ralph Richardson and Sir John Gielgud are a constant and treasured inspiration to me. . . . I have acted in every state in the union except Wyoming and in all the Canadian provinces."

* * *

VALLONE, Raf, actor, director

PERSONAL: Born February 17, 1916; son of Giovanni (a lawyer) and Caterina Vallone; married Elena, July 26, 1952; children: Eleonora, Arabella, Saverio. EDUCATION: University of Turin (Italy), degrees in Law and Philosophy. RELI-GION: Catholic. NON-THEATRICAL CAREER—Journalist.

CAREER: DEBUT—Woyzeck, *Woyzeck,* Gobetti, Turin, Italy, 1946. NEW YORK DEBUT—Eddie, *A View from the Bridge.* PRINCIPAL STAGE APPEARANCES—*The Prince,* Théâtre Antoine, Paris, Eliseo, Rome; also plays by Pirandello, Ibsen, Garcia-Lorca, Valle Inclan. MAJOR TOURS—All the major cities of Europe including Paris, London, Rome, Venice, Geneva, Florence.

FILM DEBUT—*Bitter Rice,* 1948. FILM APPEARANCES—*Vendetta,* 1949; *Il Cristo Probito,* 1950; *Anna,* 1951; *Il Cammino della Speranza; Thérèse Raquin,* 1953; *The Beach,* 1953; *The Sign of Venus,* 1955; *El Cid,* 1961; *A View From the Bridge,* 1961; *Phaedra,* 1962; *The Cardinal,* 1963; *Harlow,* 1965; *Beyond the Mountains,* 1966; *The Italian Job,* 1969; *Obsession,* 1976.

TELEVISION DEBUT—Eddie, *A View from the Bridge* (live—in London). TELEVISION APPEARANCES—*All My Sons, A View from the Bridge, Il Mulino del Po;* others.

WRITINGS: PLAYS, UNPUBLISHED—''Forbidden? By Who?''; ''Repos du Guerrier'' (adapted from a French novel).

AWARDS: Golden Donatello Award; Foemina, Paris; Silver Bear, Berlin; Grand Prix, Cannes Festival; Prix ''Anna Magnani.'' Military—Commendatore, given by President Sandro Pertini, Italy.

SIDELIGHTS: MEMBERSHIPS—Academy of Motion Picture Arts and Sciences; SAG; AGMA; SIAE (Italian Authors League); British Equity.

ADDRESS: Home—Via Bacone, 14, Rome, Italy, 00197. Agent—William Morris, 1350 Avenue of the Americas, New York, Y 10019; 151 El, Camino, Beverly Hills, CA 90212; Via Nomentana 60, Rome, Italy 00161; 147/149 Wardour Street, London, W1, England.

* * *

VAN PATTEN, Dick (ne Richard Vincent Van Patten), actor

PERSONAL: Born December 9, 1928, in Kew Gardens, NY; son of Richard (an interior decorator) and Josephine (worked in advertising; maiden name, Acerno) Van Patten; married Patricia Poole (a dancer) April 25, 1954; children: Nels, Jimmy, Vincent. EDUCATION: Attended public schools in Richmond Hills, NY. RELIGION: Catholic.

CAREER: DEBUT—The child, *Tapestry in Gray,* Shubert, NY, 1935. PRINCIPAL STAGE APPEARANCES—Henry Wadsworth Benson, *Home Sweet Home,* Greenwich Guild, Theatre, CT, 1936; Isaac, *The Eternal Road,* Manhattan Opera House, 1937; Theodore, *Goodbye Again,* Pine Brook Country Club, Nichols, CT, 1937; boy, *On Borrowed Time,* Longacre, NY, 1938; Nine, *Run Sheep, Run,* Windsor, NY, 1938; Karl Gunther, *The American Way,* Center, NY, 1939; Pete Brown, *The Woman Brown,* Tommy, *Ah! Wilderness,* Wharf Theatre, Provincetown, MA, repeated role of Pete Brown in *The Woman Brown* at the Biltmore, NY, 1939; Tommy, *Ah! Wilderness,* Maplewood Theatre, NJ, 1940; Jessie, *Our Girls,* Starlight Theatre, Pawling, NY, 1940;

Moses, *Something about a Soldier,* Bucks County Playhouse, New Hope, PA, 1940; Toby, *Carriage Trade,* Stamford Playhouse, CT, 1940; Roger, *The Lady Who Came to Stay,* Maxine Elliott's, NY, 1941; Timothy Kincaid, *The Land Is Bright,* Music Box, NY, 1941; Bodo, *Watch on the Rhine,* Majestic, Boston, MA, 1942; ''Short Pants Houlihan,'' *Evening Rise,* Woodstock Playhouse, NY, 1942; telegraph boy, *The Skin of Our Teeth,* Plymouth, NY, 1942; Elwood, *The Snark Was a Boojum,* 48th Street Theatre, NY, 1943; Felix, *Decision,* Belasco, NY, 1944;

Dexter Franklin, *Kiss and Tell,* Biltmore, NY, 1943; Sgt. Walter Burrows, *Too Hot for Maneuvers,* Broadhurst, NY, 1945; Ernie Sheffield, *The Wind Is Ninety,* Booth, NY, 1945; Michael Brown, *O Mistress Mine,* Empire, NY, 1946; Toto, *Cry of the Peacock,* Locust, Philadelphia, PA, 1950; Ensign Pulver, *Mister Roberts,* Alvin, NY, 1948, Quarterdeck Theatre, Atlantic City, NJ, 1951; Nels, *Here's Mama,* Ogunquit Playhouse, ME, Cape Playhouse, Dennis, MA, 1952; Michael Barnes, *The Male Animal,* Music Box, NY, 1952; Charlie Reader, *The Tender Trap,* Pocono Playhoue, PA, 1955; Grant Cobbler, *Oh Men! Oh Women!,* Pocono Playhouse, PA, 1955; Happy, *Death of a Salesman,* Long Beach Playhouse, NY, 1955; Francis X. Dignan, *King of Hearts,* 1956; Ruby Pulaski, *Have I Got a Girl for You,* Music Box, NY, 1963; Mr. Hollender, *Don't Drink the Water,* Coconut Grove Playhouse, FL, 1968; Hon. Newton Prince, *But, Seriously. . . ,* Henry Miller's, NY, 1969; Marion Cheever, *Next, Adaptation,* Greenwich Mews, NY, 1969.

MAJOR TOURS—George Macauley, *Will Success Spoil Rock Hunter?,* 1957; Ensign Beau Gilliam, *Golden Fleecing,* 1960; Henry Greene, *Strictly Dishonorable,* Mt. Tom Playhouse, MA, Vineland Theatre, Toronto, Canada, Tappen Zee Playhouse, NY, Elitch Gardens, Denver, CO, 1964–65.

FILM DEBUT—Jimmy Dugan, *Reg'lar Fellers,* 1941. PRINCIPAL FILM APPEARANCES—Edgar Palmer, *Psychomania,* 1964; *Charly,* 1968; *Making It,* 1971; *Joe Kid,* 1972; *Dirty Little Billy,* 1972; *Snowball Express,* 1972; *Westworld,* 1973; *Soylent Green,* 1973; *Superdad,* 1974.

RADIO DEBUT—Mark Brown, *Young Widder Brown* series, 1941. PRINCIPAL RADIO BROADCASTS—Hartzell, *One Foot in Heaven;* Teddy Thompson, *Miss Hatty;* Wilfred, *Duffy's Tavern;* Toby Smith, *Henry Aldrich;* Ray, *David Harum;* Teddy, *Right to Happiness;* Jimmy Dugan, *Reg'lar Fellers; The March of Time;* Dexter Franklin, *Kiss and Tell;* Chic, *Wednesday's Child;* Michael Brown, *O Mistress Mine;* Roger, *Theatre;* Wayne, *State Fair;* Ben Banks, *Father of the Bride;* Nick Kane, *Elmer the Great;* Cadet Osborne, *The Major and the Minor;* Nat Kahn, *Good Housekeeping.*

TELEVISION DEBUT—As a child on *Story Hour,* 1936. PRINCIPAL TELEVISION APPEARANCES—Nels, series, *Mama,* 1949–58; *Final Ingredient,* 1959; Larry Renfrew, *Young Dr. Malone,* 1963; *The Kraft Television Theatre; Nurses; The Verdict Is Yours; Mike Hammer; Silent Service; Rawhide; Men in White, Dupont Show of the Month,* 1960; *Eight Is Enough; When Things Were Rotten; The Dick Van Dyke Show; Patners; Arnie; Grandpa Max; A Memory of Two Mondays; The Love Boat.*

AWARDS: The Donaldson Award 1941: *The Lady Who Came to Stay.*

SIDELIGHTS: RECREATION—Tennis, swimming, horseback riding.

ADDRESS: Office—MEW Co., 151 N. San Vicente Blvd., Beverly Hills, CA 90211.

* * *

VEGA, Jose, general/production manager, actor, producer

PERSONAL: Born November 7, 1920 in New York City; son of Manuel and Pilar (Cagancho) Vega; married Victoria Vandyke, December 21, 1933; children: one daughter.

CAREER: FIRST STAGE WORK—Dancer, *Prince Igor*, Academy of Music, Brooklyn, NY, 1937. PRINCIPAL STAGE APPEARANCES—Flamenco dancer, *Carmen*, Mecca Temple, NY, 1940; flamenco soloist, *Senia Russakof Ballet*, Jordan Hall, Boston, MA, 1940; toured U.S., *Jose Vega and His Spanish Ensemble*, 1939–42. PRINCIPAL STAGE APPEARANCES—Detective, *Mr. and Mrs. North*, Catskills, NY, 1942; sailor/consul, *My Sister Eileen*, Summer tour and with the New York Co. Subway Circuit, 1944; Guildenstern, *Hamlet*, Bridgeport Summer Theatre, CT, 1945; Croupier, *Her Cardboard Lover*, Montclair Playhouse, NJ, 1945; Count Giolio Dorse, *Within This Hour*, Corporal Resnick, *Return to Eden*, Martha's Vineyard Playhouse, Oak Bluffs MA, 1945; stage manager and understudy property man, *Lute Song*, Plymouth, NY, 1946; stage manager and general understudy, *Another Part of the Forest*, Fulton, NY, 1946, Erlanger, Chicago, IL, 1947; assistant stage manager and understudy, *A Streetcar Named Desire*, Barrymore, NY, 1947; *Bell, Book and Candle*, Barrymore, NY, 1950; *I Am a Camera*, Empire, NY, 1951; *Flight into Egypt*, Music Box, NY, 1952; *The Children's Hour*, Coronet, NY, 1952; *The Seven Year Itch*, Fulton, NY, 1955; *The Chalk Garden*, Barrymore, NY, 1955; *A Very Special Baby*, Playhouse, NY, 1956; *Anniversary Waltz*, Blackstone, Chicago, IL, 1956; *The Genius and the Goddess*, Henry Miller's, NY, 1957; *High Spirits*, Alvin, NY, 1964.

DIRECTOR—*A Streetcar Named Desire*, Princeton Summer Theatre, NJ, 1951; producer/director, Roosevelt Playhouse, Miami, FL, 1951; producer/director, Astor Theatre, Syracuse, NY, 1952; summer tour, *Bell, Book and Candle*, 1953; productions at the Lakewood Theatre, Barnsville, PA, 1955; summer tour, *The Bad Seed*, 1956; productions at the Joy Thompson's Tent Theatre, Mt. Gabriel, Canada, 1956; summer tour, *Show Girl*, 1961.

PRINCIPAL STAGE WORK: Company manager—*Mark Twain Tonight—Hal Holbrook*, 1962, *Oh Calcutta*, 1971–72, *JFK*, 1971–72, *A Doll's House* (road company), 1971–72; production manager—*Aspern Papers*, 1961, *Night Life*, 1962, *The Boys from Syracuse*, 1963, *Semi-Detached*, 1963, *Something More*, 1964–65, *High Spirits*, 1964–65, *Hello Dolly* (international company, Las Vegas company), 1965, *Oliver* (road company), 1965, *The Lion in Winter*, 1966, Eugene O'Neill Foundation Playwrights' Conference, 1966, *Those That Play the Clowns*, 1966, *Something Different*, 1967, *The Impossible Years*, 1967, *To Clothe the Naked*, 1967, *The Natural Look*, 1967, *Fire!*, 1968, *George M!*, 1968, *The Rothschilds* (national company), 1971–72, *Forum*, 1971–72.

General manager—*Paris Is Out!*, 1969–70, *Salvation* (NY and Los Angeles), 1969–70, *A Dream Out of Time*, 1970–71, *The Me Nobody Knows* (Chicago Company), 1970–71, *Earl of Ruston*, 1970–71, *W.C.* (summer tour), 1970–71, *The Sunshine Boys*, 1971–72, *The Good Doctor*, 1973–74, *Scapino*, NY and Los Angeles, 1974–75, *The Wiz*, 1974–75, *God's Favorite*, 1974–75, *Poison Tree*, 1975–76, *Me & Bessie*, 1975–76, *California Suite* (NY and national company), 1976–77, *Ain't Misbehavin'*, 1977–78, *Chapter Two* (NY and national company), 1977–78, *Whose Life Is It Anyway?*, 1978–79, *They're Playing Our Song* (NY and national company), 1978–79, *The Mighty Gents*, 1978–79, *Division Street*, 1979–80, *I Ought to Be in Pictures* (NY and national company), 1979–80, *Children of a Lesser God* (NY and national company), 1979–80, *Last Licks*, 1979–80, *Grownups*, 1980–81, *Einstein and the Polar Bear*, 1980–81, *Fools*, 1980–81, *Little Me*, 1981–82, *Duet for One*, 1981–82, *Georgia Brown and Friends*, 1982–83, *Master Harold and the Boys*, 1982–83, *Brighton Beach Memoirs* (NY and national company), 1982–83, *The Real Thing*, 1983–84.

AWARDS: Emmy Award, 1959: *Open End* (producer); Emmy Award, 1959–60: *Art Carney Special, V.I.P.* (associate producer).

SIDELIGHTS: MEMBERSHIPS—AEA, SAG, National Academy of Television Arts and Sciences.

ADDRESS: 32 King Street, New York, NY 10014. Office—1564 Broadway, New York, NY 10036.

* * *

VERHEYEN, Mariann, costume designer

PERSONAL: Born March 9, 1950; daughter of Lawrence Gerard (a mechanic) and Esther Catherine (Roob) Verheyen. EDUCATION: St. Norbert College, DePere, WI, B.A. 1972; University of Wisconsin, M.F.A. 1978; studied color theory with Margery Krelick.

CAREER: FIRST STAGE WORK—Costume design, *A Christmas Carol*, St. Norbert College, WI, 1970. NEW YORK DEBUT—Costume design, *Electra* and *Orestes*, Juilliard School of Music and Dramatic Art, 1981. PRINCIPAL STAGE WORK, Design assistant at Brooks Van Horn, Inc., 1978–80; assistant to Jane Greenwood, 1980–81, worked on *The White Devil*, Acting Company, NY, *The Ruling Class*, State University of New York at Purchase; *Summer*, Hudson Guild, NY; *Hedda Gabler*, Roundabout Theatre, NY; *Merton of the Movies*, Hartmann, Stamford, CT; *Umbrellas of Cherbourg*, Civic Light Opera of Los Angeles; *Romantic Comedy*, road company; *The Bob Hope Birthday Special at West Point*; *Hot'l Baltimore*, *The White House Murder Case*, *After the Fall*, *The Trojan Women*, *Lear*, *The Tales of Hoffman*, University of Wisconsin, Madison, 1975–78; *All's Well That Ends Well*, Colorado Shakespeare Festival, Boulder, CO, 1981; *Comedy of Errors*, Juilliard School of Music and Dramatic Art, NY, 1981; *Love's Labour Lost*, Juilliard School of Music and Dramatic Art, NY, 1981; *The Royal Family*, Missouri Repertory Theatre, Kansas City, 1982;

Emigres, Hudson Guild, NY, 1982; *Henry V,* Oregon Shakespeare Festival, Ashland, 1982; *Close Ties,* Alley, Houston, TX, 1982; *The Dining Room,* Huntington Theatre Co., Boston, MA, 1982; *Something Different,* Second Stage, NY, 1983; *Salome,* staged reading at San Antonio Festival, TX, 1983; *Wednesday, Accounts, Blood Relations,* Hudson Guild, NY, 1983; *Design for Living, Time and the Conways,* Huntington Theatre Company, Boston, MA, 1983.

PRINCIPAL TELEVISION WORK—*American Dance Machine,* Showtime, 1981.

AWARDS: The Villager, Downtown Theatre Award, Outstanding Costumes, 1983: *Wednesday, Accounts, Blood Relations,* Hudson Guild, NY.

ADDRESS: 80 N. Moore Street, New York, NY 10013.

* * *

VERNON, Anne (nee Edith Vignaud), actress, painter, writer

PERSONAL: Born January 7, 1924, in Paris, France; daughter of Georges and Raymonde (Vatasso) Vignaud. EDUCATION: Ecole des Beaux Arts, Paris, France. RELIGION: Catholic.

CAREER: DEBUT—*Huis-Clos,* Théâtre du Vieux Colombier, Paris. NEW YORK DEBUT—*La Petite Hutte,* Coronet. PRINCIPAL STAGE APPEARANCES—*L'Invitation au Chateau,* Théâtre de L'Atelier, Paris. MAJOR TOURS—*Quatre Pieces sur Jardin,* South America, 1946; France, Antilles, Tunisia, 1973.

FILM DEBUT—*Edouar et Caroline,* 1950. PRINCIPAL FILM APPEARANCES—*Shakedown; Terror on a Train; La Rue de L'Estrapade; Love Lottery; Ainsi Finit La Nuit; A Warning to Wantons; Patto Col Diavolo; A Tale of Five Cities; Song of Paris; The Umbrellas of Cherbourg; General Della Rovere.*

WRITINGS: French cookbooks, 1978–80.

SIDELIGHTS: MEMBERSHIPS—Cercle Interallié, Paris.

Miss Vernon was the subject of a 1980 French TV film detailing her work in painting, *Les Peintres Enchanteurs.* Her pseudonym is F.M.R., and her paintings have been in various exhibitions in Paris.

ADDRESS: Home—37 quai d' anjou, Paris, France. Agent—Lorcaster, 27 rue de Richelieu, 1 Paris, France.

* * *

VON ZERNECK, Frank, producer

PERSONAL: Born November 3, 1940; son of Peter (an actor) and Beatrice Francis (an agent) von Zerneck; married Julie Hawthorne Mannix (a writer) January 15, 1965; children:

FRANK VON ZERNECK

Danielle, Francis Jr. EDUCATION: Hofstra University, B.A., 1962.

CAREER: PRINCIPAL PRODUCTIONS—(with Robert Greenwald): Television Films—*Delta County U.S.A.; Escape from Bogen County; Sharon: Portrait of a Mistress; Getting Married; Katie: Portrait of a Centerfold; Flatbed Annie and Sweetpie: Lady Truckers; Anatomy of a Seduction; Portrait of a Stripper; Disaster on the Coastliner; Portrait of an Escort; The Babysitter; Miracle on Ice; Return of the Rebels; Lois Gibbs and the Love Canal; In the Custody of Strangers; Forbiddin Love; The First Time; Baby Sister; Night Partners; Policewoman Centerfold; Obsessive Love; The Club; Summer Fantasies;* Television— *Texas Rangers; Answers;* Films—*The Desperate Miles; 21 Hours at Munich;* Plays—*Me and Bessie,* NY and National Tour; *I Have a Dream,* NY and National Tour; *A Sense of Humor.*

AWARDS: Emmy Award Nomination (multiple); Golden Globe Award; Christopher Award (multiple); Certificate of Excellence Award of National Film Board of Review.

SIDELIGHTS: MEMBERSHIPS—California Theatre Council, League of Resident Theaters, Producers Guild of America, League of New York Theaters and Producers.

ADDRESS: Office—100 Universal City Plaza, Universal City, CA 91608. Agent—c/o Ziffren, Brittenham, Gullen, 2049 Century Park E., Los Angeles, CA 90067.

W

WADE, Adam, actor, director, producer, writer, singer

PERSONAL: Born March 17, 1935, in Pittsburgh, PA; son of Henry O. (a steel worker) and Pauline (Simpson) Wade; married Oscar Lewis (a dancer and choreographer), May 16, 1978; children: Sheldon, Damon, Patrice, Tanya. EDUCATION: Attended Virginia State University; trained for the stage at the Al Fann Theatrical Ensemble with Al Fann.

CAREER: DEBUT—*Hallelujah Baby.* NEW YORK DEBUT—Father, *My Sister, My Sister.* PRINCIPAL STAGE APPEARANCES—*Reflection in a Glass; Too Late; King Heroin; Masks in Black; God's Trombone; Falling Apart;* Nathan Detroit, *Guys and Dolls,* Las Vegas, NV; *Same Time Next Year,* Drury Lane, Chicago, IL, 1982. MAJOR TOURS:*Hallelujah Baby,* East Coast cities; *Adam Wade Show,* South Africa, Spain, Portugal.

FILM DEBUT—*Claudine.* PRINCIPAL FILM APPEARANCES—*The Anderson Tapes,* 1971; *Phantom of the Fillmore; Across 110th Street,* 1972; *Come Back Charleston Blue,* 1972; *Gordon's War,* 1973; *Crazy Joe,* 1974; *The Education of Sonny Carson,* 1974; *The Taking of Pelham One-Two-Three,* 1974; *Super Cops,* 1974; *Nicky's World; Street Killers.*

PRINCIPAL TELEVISION APPEARANCES—John Burroughs, *Search for Tomorrow; Kojak; Where the Heart Is; As the World Turns; Edge of Night; Love of Life; Somerset; Police Woman; Sheriff Lobo; Madigan; Adam 12; F.B.I.; Tony Orlando and Dawn; Tonight Show; Good Times; Jeffersons; B.J. and the Bear; This Is the Year That Will Be; David Frost Comedy Revue; Sammy Davis Jr. Show; Mike Douglas Show; Positively Black; Sanford and Son; Sanford Arms; Like It Is; Dukes of Hazard;* host, *Musical Chairs;* host, *Miss Teenage Black America;* host, *AM Chicago.* RADIO—*Heartbeat Theatre; Reflections in a Glass; Sounds of the City.* DIRECTED: Plays—*Guys and Dolls.*

WRITINGS: PLAYS—*The Dancer* (musical). SCREENPLAYS—*Kaanan.*

AWARDS: Actors Temple Award (Ezrath Israel Congregation); Grand Marshal Award (Virginia State University); Keys to the City (Pittsburgh, PA; Petersburg, VA); Clio Award Nomination, 1973: *Baby Sitter;* Clio Award, 1972: *Virgin Islands 50 Dollar Days.*

SIDELIGHTS: MEMBERSHIPS—AEA; SAG; AFTRA.

ADDRESS: Agent—c/o William Cunningham Agency, 261 S. Robertson, Beverly Hills, CA 90211.

WAITE, Ralph, actor

PERSONAL: Born June 22, 1928, in White Plains, NY; son of Ralph H. (a construction engineer) and Esther (Mitchell) Waite; married Beverly, 1951 (divorced 1966); married Kerry, 1972 (divorced 1980); married Linda East (an interior decorator), December 4, 1982; children: Kathleen, Suzanne, Liam. EDUCATION: Bucknell University, B.A.; Yale Divinity School, B.D.; trained for the stage with Lee Strasberg and Mary Tarchi. MILITARY: U.S. Marine Corps. 1946–48.

CAREER: DEBUT—Chief of police, *The Balcony,* Circle in the Square, NY, 1960. LONDON DEBUT—Lead, *Blues for Mr. Charley,* Aldwych, 1966. PRINCIPAL STAGE APPEARANCES—*Hogan's Goat,* NY, 1965; *Watering Place,* NY, 1969; *The Trial of Lee Harvey Oswald,* NY, 1967; Captain, *The Father,* Circle in the Square, NY, 1981; appeared in numerous productions at the Theatre Co-op, Boston and the Long Wharf, New Haven, CT.

FILM DEBUT—Harry, *Cool Hand Luke,* 1970. PRINCIPAL FILM APPEARANCES—*Five Easy Pieces,* 1970; *Grissolm Gang,* 1971; *The Lawman,* 1971; *The Sporting Club,* 1971; *Chato's Land,* 1972; *The Stone Killer,* 1973; *On the Nickel,* 1980. TELEVISION DEBUT—John, *The Waltons,* 1972–1980. PRINCIPAL TELEVISION APPEARANCES—*Roots,* 1977; *Waiting for Godot; Red Alert; The Secret Life of John Chapman; A Good Sport,* 1984.

THEATRE-RELATED CAREER: Founder, Los Angeles Actors Theater, 1975–present.

SIDELIGHTS: FAVORITE ROLE—Azdak, *Caucasian Chalk Circle.*

ADDRESS: Office—Warner Brothers Studio, 4000 Warner Blvd., Burbank, CA 91522. Agent—c/o Ron Meyer, Creative Artists Agency, 1888 Century Park E., Suite 1400, Century City, CA 90067.

* * *

WALLACE, George D., actor

PERSONAL: Born June 8, 1917 in New York, NY; son of George (a shipbuilder) and Helen (a fashion model; maiden name, Dewey) Wallace; married Lydia Tobles in 1939 (divorced 1950); married, Jane Johnston (an actress), October 19, 1964; children: Linda. EDUCATION: Attended public schools on Long Island, NY; studied with Ben Bard in

Hollywood, CA. MILITARY: U.S. Navy, 1936–40, 1942–45, Chief Boatswain Mate.

CAREER: DEBUT—*Clash By Night,* Ben Bard's Dramatic School, Hollywood, 1950. NEW YORK DEBUT—Mack, *Pipe Dream,* Shubert, 1955. PRINCIPAL STAGE APPEARANCES—Sid Sorokin, *The Pajama Game,* 46th Street, NY, 1957; Matt, *New Girl in Town,* Warwick Musical Theatre, RI, Carousel, Framingham, MA, Oakdale Musical Theatre, Wallingford, CT, 1958; Frank Butler, *Annie Get Your Gun,* Carousel Theatre, MA, 1958; Fred Graham, *Kiss Me Kate,* Sacramento Music Circus, CA, 1958; Billy Bigelow, *Carousel,* Musicarnival, Cleveland, OH, 1959; Joe Dynamite, *Wildcat,* State Fair Music Hall, Dallas, TX, 1960, Theatre under the Stars, Atlanta, GA, 1963; Randolph, James O'Connor, Omar, *Jennie,* Majestic, NY, 1963; David, *Company,* Alvin, NY, 1970. MAJOR TOURS—King Arthur, *Camelot,* national tour, 1964; David, *Company,* national tour, 1971; *Man of La Mancha,* national tour.

FILM DEBUT—Commando Cody, *Radar Men from the Moon.* PRINCIPAL FILM APPEARANCES—*Forbidden Planet,* 1955; *Six Black Horses,* 1962; *Caprice,* 1967; *Towering Inferno,* 1974; *Lifeguard,* 1976; *Billy Jack Goes to Washington; Secret Files of J. Edgar Hoover.*

PRINCIPAL TELEVISION APPEARANCES—*The Ed Sullivan Show; Fireside Theatre; Armstrong Circle Theatre; Lux Video Theatre; Gunsmoke; Maverick; Rawhide; Hill Street Blues; Remington Steele; Kojak; The Waltons; Bonanza; The Bionic Woman; Bob Newhart Show; Days of Our Lives.*

AWARDS: Drama Critic's Circle Award Nomination, Best Actor, 1957: Matt, *New Girl in Town;* Sylvania Award, "International Incident" episode of *Fireside Theatre,* 1951; Pacific Fleet's Light Heavyweight Boxing Championship and Outstanding Athlete of the Year, U.S. Navy.

ADDRESS: Agent—Henderson-Hogan Agency, 200 W. 57th Street, New York, NY 10019.

* * *

WALLACE, Lee, actor

PERSONAL: Born July 15, 1930, in Brooklyn, NY; son of Eddie and Celia (Gross) Melis; married Marilyn Chris Wallace (an actress), December 14, 1974; children: Paul Christopoulos. EDUCATION: Attended New York University; trained for the stage with Michael Howard. RELIGION: Jewish. MILITARY: U.S. Army, 1951–53.

CAREER: DEBUT—Young man, *A Flag Is Born,* Joan of Arc Theater, NY, 1949. BROADWAY DEBUT—Ted, *Unlikely Heroes,* Plymouth, 1970. PRINCIPAL STAGE APPEARANCES—(Broadway) *Some of My Best Friends; Secret Affairs of Mildred Wild; Molly; Zalman or the Madness of God;* (Off-Broadway) *Goodnight Grandpa; The Basic Training of Pavlo Hummel,* Public; *Macbeth,* Public; *Journey of the Fifth Horse,* American Place; *Booth Is Back in Town,* Lincoln Center; *Saturday Night; Awake and Sing; Curtains;* (Regional) Hickey, *The Iceman Cometh,* Long Wharf, New Haven, CT; Lopakin, *The Cherry Orchard,* Williamstown

LEE WALLACE

Theatre Festival, MA; *In the Matter of J. Robert Oppenheimer,* Atlanta Municipal Theatre, GA; *Uncle Vanya,* Yale Repertory, New Haven, CT; *Tartuffe, Servant of Two Masters, Death of a Salesman, Antigone,* American Conservatory Theater, San Francisco, CA. MAJOR TOURS—*Irene,* U.S. cities; *Laugh a Little, Cry a Little,* U.S. cities.

PRINCIPAL FILM APPEARANCES—*Klute,* 1971; *The Happy Hooker;* mayor, *The Taking of Pelham 1-2-3,* 1974; *Thieves,* 1977; *Children's War.* PRINCIPAL TELEVISION APPEARANCES—*Visions,* "Blessings"; *Child Stealers; Long Journey Back; Concealed Enemies.*

THEATRE-RELATED CAREERS—Acting teacher and coach, NY, 1978–present.

SIDELIGHTS: MEMBERSHIPS—AEA, SAG, AFTRA.

ADDRESS: Agent—c/o Henderson, Hogan Agency, 200 W. 57th Street, New York, NY 10019.

* * *

WALLACE, Tommy Lee, writer, director

PERSONAL: EDUCATION: Ohio University, B.F.A. (Design), 1971; University of Southern California, M.F.A. program in film production, 1971–74.

CAREER: PRINCIPAL FILM WORK—director, co-writer, *Starman in November*, University of Southern California, 1974; associate art director, *Dark Star*, 1974; art director, sound effects editor, *Assault on Precinct 13*, 1976; production designer, picture editor, *Halloween*, 1978; co-writer, *El Diablo*, 1979; production designer, picture editor, *The Fog*, 1980; writer, *Test Pattern*, 1980; writer, *Amityville II: The Possession*, 1981; co-writer, *The Ninja*, 1982: director, writer, *Halloween III*, 1982; director, co-writer, *Motel*, 1983; writer, *White Rabbit*, 1984.

FILM-RELATED CAREER: Animation cameraman, 1971–72; teaching assistant, USC, Cinema Division, 1973–74; story analyst/film editor, 1974–78.

AWARDS: Cum Laude graduate, Ohio University.

ADDRESS: Agent—The Gersh Agency, 222 N. Canon Drive, Beverly Hills, CA 90210.

* * *

WALLACH, Eli, actor

PERSONAL: Born December 7, 1915, Brooklyn, NY; son of Abraham and Bertha (Schorr) Wallach; married Anne Jackson (an actress), March 5, 1948; children: Peter, Roberta, Katherine. EDUCATION: Attended University of Texas and City College of New York; studied at the Neighborhood Playhouse School of Theatre and with Lee Strasberg at the Actors Studio.

CAREER: DEBUT—Boy's club performance in Brooklyn, 1930. NEW YORK DEBUT—Crew Chief, *Skydrift*, Belasco, 1945. LONDON DEBUT—Sakini, *Teahouse of the August Moon*, Her Majesty's, 1954. PRINCIPAL STAGE APPEARANCES—*Androcles and the Lion, Yellow Jack*, 1947–48, American Repertory Company, NY; Diomedes, *Antony and Cleopatra*, Martin Beck, NY, 1947; Stefanowski, *Mister Roberts*, Alvin, NY, 1949; Alvarro Mangiacavallo, *The Rose Tattoo*, Martin Beck, NY, 1951; Kilroy, *Camino Real*, National, NY, 1953; Dickson, *Scarecrow*, Theatre de Lys, NY, 1953; Julien, *Mademoiselle Colombe*, Longacre, NY, 1954; Sakini, *Teahouse of the August Moon*, Martin Beck, NY, 1955; Bill Walker, *Major Barbara*, Martin Beck, NY, 1956; Old Man, *The Chairs*, Phoenix, NY, 1958; Willie, *The Cold Wind and the Warm*, Morosco, NY, 1958; Berenger, *Rhinoceros*, Longacre, NY, 1961; Ben, *The Tiger*, Paul XXX, *The Typists*, Orpheum, NY, 1963, Globe, London, England, 1964; Milt Manville, *Luv*, Booth, NY, 1964; Charles Dyer, *Staircase*, Biltmore, NY, 1968; Ollie H and Wesley, *Promenade All!*, Alvin, NY.

General St. Pe, *The Waltz of the Toreadors*, Eisenhower Theatre, Washington, DC, 1973, and the Circle in the Square, NY, 1973; Peppino, *Saturday, Sunday, Monday*, Martin Beck, NY, 1974; Arthur Canfield, *The Sponsor*, Peachtree Playhouse, Atlanta, GA, 1975; Colin, *Absent Friends*, Long Wharf, New Haven, CT, 1977; Mr. Frank, *The Diary of Anne Frank*, Theatre Four, NY, 1978; Alexander, *Every Good Boy Deserves Favour*, Metropolitan Opera, NY, 1979; *Twice Around the Park*, Cort, NY, 1982–83 and Edinburgh Festival, Scotland, 1984; Stephan, *The Nest of the Woodgrouse*, Public, NY, 1984.

ELI WALLACH

MAJOR TOURS—Alvarro Mangiacavallo, *The Rose Tattoo*, 1951; *The Tiger* and *The Typists*, national tour, 1966; *Promenade All!*, 1971; General St. Pe, *The Waltz of the Toreadors*, 1974; Colin, *Absent Friends*, 1977; Alexander, *Every Good Boy Deserves Favour*, 1979.

FILM DEBUT—*Baby Doll*, 1956. PRINCIPAL FILM APPEARANCES—*The Magnificent Seven*, 1960; *The Misfits*, 1961; *How the West Was Won*, 1962; *The Victors*, 1963; *Lord Jim*, 1965; *Tiger Makes Out*, 1967; *Cinderella Liberty*, 1974; *Crazy Joe*, 1974; *The Sentinel*, 1977.

AWARDS: Emmy Award, *A Poppy Is Also a Flower*.

SIDELIGHTS: FAVORITE ROLES—Kilroy, *Camino Real*, Mangiacavallo, *The Rose Tatoo*. RECREATIONS—Woodwork, collecting antiques, tennis, baseball, swimming.

ADDRESS: Agent—c/o Creative Artists Agency, 1888 Century Park E., Los Angeles, CA 90067.

* * *

WALSH, Dermot, actor, director, producer, writer

PERSONAL: Born September 10, 1924, in Dublin, Ireland; son of Michael Francis (a journalist) and Josephine (Leslie) Walsh; married Hazel Court (an actress), 1949 (divorced 1963); Diana Scougall (an actress), 1968 (divorced 1972); Elisabeth Annear (nee Scott; actress, producer), 1972; children: Sally, Michael, Elisabeth, Olivia. EDUCATION: St.

Mary's College, Dublin, 1932–41 (matriculation); National University, Dublin, 1941–44; Four Courts, Dublin, 1941–44; studied at the Abbey Theatre School of Acting with Lennox Robinson. RELIGION: "Would-be Catholic."

CAREER: DEBUT—Crowd artiste, *The Strings Are False*, Olympia, Dublin. LONDON DEBUT—Firstborn, *Buoyant Billions*, Prince's, 1949. PRINCIPAL STAGE APPEARANCES—Tone, *Reluctant Heroes*, Whitehall, London, 1950–52; *Relations Are Best Apart*, Garrick, London, 1954–55; *The Kidders*, Arts Theatre, St. Martin's, London, 1957–58; *Policy For Murder*, Duke of York's, London, 1962; *Ring of Jackals*, Queen's, London, 1965; *The Man Most Likely To . . .*, Vaudeville, London, 1968–69; *Lady Frederick*, Vaudeville, Duke of York's, London, 1970; *Laburnim Grove*, Duke of York's, London, 1977; *Murder Among Friends*, Comedy, London, 1978; *Who Killed Agatha Christie?*, Mayfair, London, 1979; *The Mousetrap*, St. Martins, London, 1980–81; *No Sex, Please, We're British*, Garrick, London, 1984–85.

MAJOR TOURS—*The Doctor's Dilemma, Patrick Sarsfield, The Importance of Being Earnest, The United Brothers, The School for Scandal*, Southern Ireland, 1944; *A Trip to Scarborough, The Earl of Straw, Carmilla, Arms and the Man*, Southern Ireland, 1945; *Random Harvest*, U.K. and West Germany, 1948; *The Stars Bow Down*, Malvern Festival, 1949; *Smilin' Through*, U.K., 1952; *The Long March, The Distant Hill*, U.K., 1953; *Tropical Fever*, Ireland, 1955; *Kathleen, Love Her to Death*, U.K., 1955; *Mary, Mary*, Australia, New Zealand, 1963–64; *Person Unknown, The Morning After, Countercrime*, U.K., 1965; *The Constant Wife, Canaries Sometimes Sing, No Fear or Favour, I Wonder Who the Baddy Is?*, U.K., 1967; *Home on the Pig's Back, Jane Eyre, She Stoops to Conquer, King's Rhapsody, A Christmas Carol*, U.K., 1972; *See How They Run*, U.K., 1975; *Murder with Love*, U.K. and Ireland, 1976; *A Murder Is Announced*, U.K., Ireland, 1978; *Murder, Bloody Murder*, U.K., 1979; *Stage Stuck, Blithe Spirit*, U.K., Ireland, 1982.

FILM DEBUT—*Bedelia*, 1945. PRINCIPAL FILM APPEARANCES—*Hungry Hill*, 1946; *Jassy*, 1946; *The Mark of Cain*, 1947; *To the Public Danger*, 1947; *My Sister and I*, 1947; *Third Time Lucky*, 1948; *Sea Fury*, 1958; *Sea of Sand*, 1958; *Make Mine a Million*, 1958; *The Bandit of Zhobe*, 1958; *The Flesh and the Fiends*, 1959; *The Challenge*, 1959; *The Cool Mikado*, 1962; *The Wicked Lady*, 1982; twenty-six second-feature films from 1949–66.

PRINCIPAL TELEVISION APPEARANCES—Richard, *Richard the Lionheart*, 39 episodes, BBC; fifty-three TV films, thirty-four TV plays, 1949–79.

THEATRE-RELATED CAREER: Co-producer, *Random Harvest*, 1948–49; co-producer, *Smilin' Through*, 1952; producer, director, *The Murder Line*, 1967–68, *Stage Struck*, 1982, *Blithe Spirit*, 1982; managing director, Quillbell Ltd. Theatrical Producing Company, 1981–present.

WRITINGS: PLAYS—*The Murder Line*, 1967.

ADDRESS: Office—28 Berkeley Square, London WIX 6HD, England.

WALSH, James, manager, producer

PERSONAL: Born May 6, 1937; son of Harold F. (a doctor) and Henrietta C. (a nurse; maiden name, Sanders) Walsh; married Juliet Taylor (a casting director) June 15, 1976; children: Jason, Sam. EDUCATION: University of California at Los Angeles, B.A., 1960. MILITARY: U.S. Army Medical Corps.

CAREER: GENERAL MANAGER, NEW YORK PRODUCTIONS—*Thieves; 1600 Pennsylvania Avenue; Prince of Grand Street; Finishing Touches; The Prime of Miss Jean Brodie; The Wake of Jamey Foster; Lenny; Barnum; Lena Horne, the Lady and Her Music*, and over 30 other productions. PRODUCER—NEW YORK PRODUCTIONS—*Matty and the Moron; Madonna; The Hawk; Riot; The Deer Park; The Beard; The Watering Place; Doonesbury.*

SIDELIGHTS: MEMBERSHIPS—League of New York Theatres and Producers, ATPAM.

ADDRESS: Office—161 W. 54th Street, New York, NY 10019.

* * *

WALTER, Jessica, actress

PERSONAL: Born January 31, 1944, in New York, NY; daughter of David (a musician) and Esther (a teacher: maiden name, Groisser) Walter; married Ross Bowman, March 27, 1966 (divorced 1978); married Ron Leibman (an actor), June 26, 1983; children: Brooke (1st marriage). EDUCATION: Graduated from Performing Arts High School; trained for the stage at the Neighborhood Playhouse.

CAREER: DEBUT—Kid sister, *Middle of the Night*, Bucks County Playhouse, New Hope, PA, 1958. NEW YORK DEBUT—Liz, *Advise and Consent*, Cort, 1961. PRINCIPAL STAGE APPEARANCES—Cigarette girl, *Nightlife*, Brooks Atkinson, NY, 1962; Clarice/Ada, *Photofinish*, Brooks Atkinson, NY, 1963; mistress, *A Severed Head*, Royale, NY, 1964. FILM DEBUT—Laura, *Lilith*, 1964. PRINCIPAL FILM APPEARANCES—Libby, *The Group*, 1965; Pat Stoddard, *Grand Prix*, 1967; Leslie, *Bye Bye Braverman*, 1968; Pat, *Number One*, 1969; Evelyn, *Play Misty for Me*, 1971. TELEVISION DEBUT—*Amy Prentiss*, 1974–75; *Love of Life; The FBI; Mission: Impossible; Cannon; Medical Center; Mannix; Visions; Barnaby Jones; Hawaii Five-O; Wheels;* (TV Movies) *Hurricane*, 1974; *Having Babies*, 1976; (series) *Bare Essence*, 1983.

AWARDS: Emmy Award Nominations, 1980: *Trapper John, M.D.;* 1976: *Streets of San Francisco;* Emmy Award, Best Actress, 1975: *Amy Prentiss;* Golden Globe Award, 1971: *Play Misty for Me;* Clarence Derwent Award, 1963: *Photofinish.*

SIDELIGHTS: MEMBERSHIPS—SAG (board member, 1973–74, vice president, 1975–83); AFTRA; A.E.A.

ADDRESS: Agent—c/o Phil Gersh Agency, 222 N. Canon Drive, Beverly Hills, CA 90210.

JESSICA WALTER

WARD, David S., director and writer

PERSONAL: Born October 24, 1945, in Providence, RI; son of Robert and Miriam (Schad) McCollum; married Rosana Desoto (an actress), 1979; children: Joaquin Atwood, Sylvana Bonifacia Desoto. EDUCATION: Pomona College, B.A., 1967; University of California at Los Angeles, M.F.A., 1970.

CAREER: DIRECTED—*Cannery Row,* 1982.

WRITINGS: SCREENPLAYS—*Steelyard Blues,* 1972; *The Sting,* 1973; *Cannery Row,* 1982.

AWARDS: Academy Award, Best Original Screenplay, 1973: *The Sting.*

SIDELIGHTS: MEMBERSHIPS—Academy of Motion Picture Arts and Sciences Directors Guild; Writers Guild.

ADDRESS: Agent—c/o Jeffrey Berg, I.C.M., 8899 Beverly Blvd., Beverly Hills, CA 90048.

* * *

WARDEN, Jack (ne Lebzelter), actor

PERSONAL: Born September 18, 1920, in Newark, NJ; son of John (an engineer and technician) and Laura (Costello) Lebzelter; married Wanda Dupree, 1958 (divorced); chil-

dren: Christopher. EDUCATION: Attended Barringer High School, Newark, Our Lady of Good Counsels, Newark, graduated, DuPont Manual High School, Louisville, KY: trained for the stage with Margo Jones. POLITICS: Democrat. MILITARY: U.S. Navy, 1938–41; U.S. Maritime Service, 1941–42; U.S. Army, 1941–46.

CAREER: DEBUT—Sir Toby Belch, *Twelfth Night,* Margo Jones, Dallas, TX, 1947. NEW YORK DEBUT—Mickey, *Golden Boy,* ANTA, 1952.

PRINCIPAL FILM APPEARANCES—*Asphalt Jungle,* 1950; *From Here to Eternity,* 1953; *Edge of the City,* 1957; *Twelve Angry Men,* 1957; *Bachelor Party,* 1957; *Run Silent, Run Deep,* 1958; *That Kind of Woman,* 1959; *The Sound and the Fury,* 1959; *Wake Me When It's Over,* 1960; *Escape from Zahrain,* 1962; *Donavan's Reef,* 1962; *Thin Red Line,* 1964; *Blindfold,* 1966; *The Sporting Club,* 1971; *Welcome to the Club,* 1971; *Who Is Harry Kellerman and Why Is He Saying Those Terrible Things about Me?,* 1971; *Summertree,* 1971; *The Man Who Loved Cat Dancing,* 1973; *Billy Two Hats,* 1974; *Apprenticeship of Duddy Kravitz,* 1974; *Shampoo,* 1975; *White Buffalo; All the President's Men,* 1976; *Death on the Nile,* 1978; *Heaven Can Wait,* 1978; . . . *And Justice for All,* 1979; *Being There,* 1979; *Beyond the Poseidon Adventure,* 1979; *Dreamer,* 1979; *The Change; Used Cars; Carbon*

JACK WARDEN

Copy, 1981; *So Fine*, 1981; *The Great Muppet Caper*, 1981; *The Verdict*, 1982; *Crackers; The Aviator Pilot.*

TELEVISION DEBUT—Arthur Clary, *Philco Television Playhouse*, ''Ann Rutledge,'' 1950. PRINCIPAL TELEVISION APPEARANCES—Gorman, *Retaliation*, 1951; champ, *Assignment: Man Hunt*, ''The Champ,'' 1952; Lefty, *Kraft Television Theater*, ''Snookie,'' 1953; Teddy Merrill, *The Big Story*, ''Chester Potter of the Pittsburgh Press,'' 1953; Jerry French, *Gulf Playhouse*, ''Comeback,'' 1953; *Kraft Television Theater*, ''Old MacDonald Had a Curve,'' 1953; Brick Nelson, *Campbell Soundstage*, ''The Promise,'' 1953; Frank T. Whip, *Mister Peepers Show*, 1953; Blik, *Goodyear Television Playhouse*, ''Train to Trouble,'' 1953; Taxi Driver, *Kraft Television Theater*, ''Dream House,'' 1953; Dr. Max, *Goodyear Television Playhouse*, ''Native Dancer,'' 1954;

Pete, *The Big Story*, ''Jean Barrett of the Philadelphia Evening Bulletin,'' 1954; Sheriff Bass, *Kraft Television Theater*, ''Dr. Rainwater Goes A-Courtin','' 1954; Stamper, *Kraft Television Theater*, ''The Worried Ban Blues,'' 1954; *The Imogene Coca Show*, 1954; Hal, *Goodyear Television Playhouse*, ''Class of '58,'' 1954; Bill Foley, *The Big Story*, ''Roger Dove,'' ''Courant,'' 1954; Lt. Earl Floyd, *Justice*, ''Save Me Now,'' 1955; Ted Link, *The Big Story*, ''Ted Link of the St. Louis Post Dispatch,'' 1955; Buzz Calderone, *Philco Television Playhouse*, ''Shadow of the Champ,'' 1955; Boze, *Producers' Showcase*, ''The Petrified Forest,'' 1955; Alex Hamner, *Justice*, ''Flight from Rear,'' 1955; Harry Pomeroy, *Goodyear Television Playhouse*, ''The Mechanical Heart,'' 1955; Frank Doran, *Alcoa Hour*, ''Tragedy in a Temporary Town,'' 1956; *Home Show*, ''A Very Special Baby,'' 1956;

Sgt. Debb, *Kaiser Aluminum Hour*, ''A Real Fine Cutting Edge,'' 1957; Robert de Beaudrincourt, *Hallmark Hall of Fame*, ''The Lark,'' 1957; Newspaperman, *Suspicion*, ''The Flight,'' 1957; Jack Armstrong, *Omnibus*, ''Abraham Lincoln: The Early Years,'' 1959; Mike Wilson, *Bonanza*, The Paiute War,'' 1959; Emmet Fitzgerald, *Five Fingers*, ''The Moment of Truth,'' 1959; Ollie, *The Outlaws*, ''Starfall,'' 1960; Martin, *Wagon Train*, ''The Martin Onyx Story,'' 1962; Axton, *Tales of Wells Fargo*, ''The Traveler,'' 1962; Jubal Tatum, *The Virginian*, ''Throw a Long Rope,'' 1962; *The Trailmaster; Walt Disney's World; Dr. Kildare; Naked City; Bob Hope Presents; Slattery's People; Bus Stop; Great Adventure; The Untouchables; Desilu Playhouse; The Breaking Point; The Wackiest Ship in the Army; Twilight Zone; Route 66; Ben Casey; The Fugitive; The Invaders; N.Y.P.D.; Hobson's Choice; Topper; Jig Saw John; Bad News Bears; A.D.; The Life and Times of Robert Kennedy.*

PRINCIPAL STAGE APPEARANCES—Algernon, *The Importance of Being Earnest*, Tony Lumpkin, *She Stoops to Conquer;* Tristotin, *The Learned Ladies;* Gremio, *The Taming of the Shrew*, Yasha, *The Cherry Orchard, Front Porch* (retitled *Picnic*), *Summer and Smoke, Lear and Bough*, Margo Jones Theater Company, Dallas, TX, 1947–51; Johnny, *Lullaby*, Lyceum, NY, 1954; Mike Hertzog, *Sing Me No Lullaby*, Phoenix, NY, 1954; Marco, *A View from the Bridge*, Coronet, NY, 1955; Joey, *A Very Special Baby*, Playhouse, NY, 1956; Dave, *The Body Beautiful*, Broadway, NY, 1958; *Cages*, York, NY, 1963; *Conversations in the Dark*, Walnut Street Theater, Philadelphia, PA, 1963; *A Wen and Orange*

Souffle, Festival of Two Worlds, Spoleto, Italy, 1966; *The Man in the Glass Booth*, Royale, NY, 1969; *Stages; Actor and Actrices.*

AWARDS: Obie Award, 1963; Emmy Award, 1972.

SIDELIGHTS: MEMBERSHIPS—AEA, SAG, AFTRA, National Maritime Union, Players Club. RECREATION—Golf, swimming, walking, dancing, skiing, sailing, fishing, singing, reading, carpentry, sunset watching.

ADDRESS: Office—9000 Sunset Blvd., Los Angeles, CA 90069. Agent—c/o John Gaines, Agency for the Performing Arts, 888 Seventh Avenue, New York, NY 10106.

* * *

WARE, John, playwright, director, educator

See MABLEY, Edward (Howe)

* * *

WARREN, Lesley Ann, actress

PERSONAL: Born August 16, 1946; daughter of William (a real estate agent) and Carol (a singer; maiden name, Verb-

LESLEY ANN WARREN

low) Warren; married Jon Peters, May 3, 1967 (divorced 1977); children: Christopher. EDUCATION: Attended the Professional Children's School and Music and Art High School; trained for the stage at the Actors Studio with Lee Strasberg.

CAREER: DEBUT—Snookie, *110 in the Shade,* NY. FILM DEBUT—*Happiest Millionaire,* 1966. PRINCIPAL FILM APPEARANCES—*Race to the Yankee Zephyr,* Norma, *Victor/Victoria,* 1982; Faye, *Night in Heaven,* 1983; Eve, *Choose Me,* 1983; Gilda, *Songwriter,* 1983. TELEVISION DEBUT—Cinderella, *Cinderella,* 1964. PRINCIPAL TELEVISION APPEARANCES—Marja, *79 Park Avenue,* 1978; *Portrait of a Stripper,* 1980; Sara, *Beulahland,* 1981; Michelle, *Portrait of a Showgirl,* 1982.

AWARDS: Academy Award Nomination, Best Supporting Actress, Golden Globe Award Nomination, People's Choice Award, 1982: *Victor/Victoria;* Golden Globe Award, 1979: *79 Park Avenue.*

SIDELIGHTS: MEMBERSHIPS—SAG; AFTRA.

ADDRESS: Office—500 Sepulveda Blvd., Suite #510, Los Angeles, CA 90049. Agent—c/o Ron Meyer, Creative Artists Agency, 1888 Century Park E., Suite 1400, Los Angeles, CA 90067.

* * *

WASSERSTEIN, Wendy, writer

PERSONAL: Born October 18, 1950, in Brooklyn, NY; daughter of Morris W. (a textile manufacturer) and Lola (a dancer; maiden name, Schleifer) Wasserstein. EDUCATION: Mount Holyoke College, B.A., 1971; City College of New York, M.A., 1973; Yale Drama School, M.F.A., 1976.

WRITINGS: PLAYS, PRODUCED—*Any Woman Can't,* Playwrights Horizons, NY, 1973; *Uncommon Women and Others,* Phoenix, NY, 1977, Los Angeles Stage Company, CA, St. Nicholas, Chicago, IL, Magic, San Francisco, CA; *Isn't It Romantic,* Phoenix, NY, 1981, Playwrights Horizons, NY, 1983. SCREENPLAYS—*The House of Husbands* (with Christopher Durang—not filmed), 1981. TELEVISION SCRIPTS—*Uncommon Women and Others,* 1978; *The Sorrows of Gin,* 1980.

AWARDS: Obie Award, Joseph Jefferson Award, Dramalogue Award, Inner Boston Critics Award: *Uncommon Women and Others;* Hale Mathews Foundation Award; Guggenheim Fellowship, 1983.

SIDELIGHTS: MEMBERSHIPS—Dramatists Guild; Playwrights Horizons (artistic board); Dramatists Guild for Young Playwrights.

"I have been most inspired by the work of my colleagues and being involved on the artistic board of Playwrights Horizons. My associations with this community is vital to my work. Also, as a child, I studied at the June Taylor School of the Dance. In its own way, that too is vital."

ADDRESS: Agent—c/o Arlene Donovan, I.C.M., 40 W. 57th Street, New York, NY 10019.

WATKIN, David, cinematographer

PERSONAL: Born March 23, 1925; son of John Wilfrid (a lawyer) and Beatrice Lynda (Dadswell) Watkin.

CAREER: PRINCIPAL FILM WORK—Cinematographer, *The Knack,* 1964; *Help,* 1965; *Marat/Sade,* 1966; *The Charge of the Light Brigade,* 1967; *Catch 22,* 1969; *The Devils,* 1970; *The Boyfriend,* 1971; *The Three Musketeers,* 1974; *The Four Musketeers,* 1975; *Jesus of Nazareth,* 1975; *Endless Love,* 1981; *Chariots of Fire,* 1981; *Yentl,* 1983.

ADDRESS: Home—6 Sussex Mews, Brighton, England.

* * *

WATSON, Moray, actor

PERSONAL: First name sounds like "Murry;" born June 25, 1928, in Sunninsdale, Berks, England; son of Gerard Arthur (a ship-broker) and Jean (MacFarlane) Watson; married Pam Marmont (an actress), June 28, 1955; children: Emma Kate, Robin Guy. EDUCATION: Eton College, 1946; Webber Douglas Academy of Dramatic Art, London. RELIGION: Protestant. MILITARY: National Service, Officer in Northamptonshire Regiment, 1946–48.

CAREER: DEBUT—Repertory season, Nottingham, England. NEW YORK DEBUT—*The Public Eye,* Morosco, 1963. LONDON DEBUT—*Small Hotel,* St. Martins, 1955. PRINCIPAL STAGE APPEARANCES—London: *A River Breeze,* Phoenix, 1956; *Plaintiff in a Pretty Hat,* St. Martins, 1957; *The Grass is Greener,* St. Martins, 1958; *The Bad Soldier Smith,* Westminster, 1960; *The Doctor's Dilemma,* Haymarket, 1963; *You Never Can Tell,* Haymarket, 1966; *The Rivals,* Haymarket, 1967; *Don't Just Lie There—Say Something,* Garrick, 1972; *On Approval,* Vaudeville, 1977; *Hay Fever,* Queens, 1983; U.S.—*The Private Ear/The Public Eye,* Morosco, 1963–64; The American Shaw Festival, Mt. Gretna Playhouse, PA: *Misalliance, Hay Fever, The Browning Version,* 1983. MAJOR TOURS—*Widowers Houses, How the Other Half Loves,* English Actors Company, Latin American Tour, 1976.

FILM DEBUT—Sellars, *The Grass Is Greener,* 1959. PRINCIPAL FILM APPEARANCES—*The Valiant,* 1968; *Operation Crossbow,* 1970; *Every Home Should Have One,* 1971; *The Sea Wolves,* 1982.

TELEVISION DEBUT—*Compact.* PRINCIPAL TELEVISION APPEARANCES—*Upstairs Downstairs; Quiller, The Palissers; Rumpole of the Bailey; Churchill; Pride and Prejudice.*

THEATRE-RELATED CAREER: Director, Webber Douglas Academy of Dramatic Art.

SIDELIGHTS: MEMBERSHIPS—British Actors Equity Association, The Garrick Club, Board of Directors, Webber Douglas Academy of Dramatic Art, London, England.

"I endeavour to see life through rose-tinted glasses, whilst not missing the other grimmer realities. My constant aim is to search for the dignity in man, while endeavoring to better myself through my fellow man—and so be worthy of the

MORAY WATSON

search. A life in the Theatre lends itself to this pursuit more readily than most careers.''

ADDRESS: Home—Underwood House, Etlhingham E., Sussex, England. Agent—c/o Lending Artists, Michael Whitehall, 60 St. James Street, London W1, England.

* * *

WATT, Douglas, critic

PERSONAL: Born January 20, 1914, in New York, NY; son of Benjamin Douglas (a structural engineer) and Agnes Rita (Niemann) Watt; married Ray Mantel, November 7, 1937 (divorced 1950); married Ethel Madsen (a theatrical producer), November 5, 1951. children: Richard, James. EDUCATION: Cornell University, B.A., 1934; trained for the stage with Alexander Drummond. RELIGION: Roman Catholic. MILITARY: U.S. Army Air Force, World War II.

CAREER: New York *Daily News;* copy boy, 1936–37; radio columnist, 1937–40; drama reporter, 1940–71; senior drama critic, 1971–present; staff writer *New Yorker* Magazine, 1946–present.

WRITINGS: SONGS, PUBLISHED—*There's Not a Moment to Spare,* 1939; *After All These Years,* 1940; *I'd Do It Again,* 1941; *Man,* 1945; *Heaven Help Me,* 1968.

RELATED CAREERS: Columnist, *Small World,* 1955–70.

AWARDS: Drama Desk Award, Distinguished Drama Criticism, 1983; Silurian Society Award, Distinguished Drama Criticism, 1979.

SIDELIGHTS: MEMBERSHIPS—New York Drama Critics Circle, Dutch Treat Club, ASCAP, AGAC.

ADDRESS: Home—27 W. 86th Street, New York, NY 10024. Office—*Daily News,* 220 E. 42nd Street, New York, NY 10017.

* * *

WATTS, Robert, manager

PERSONAL: Born May 23, 1938, in London; son of Hugh Shadforth (a barrister) and Aziz Diane (Meade) Watts; married Julia James; children: Simon, Lydia, Barnaby. EDUCATION: Marlborough College (England), S.C.E.,; University de Grenoble (France), Certificat de Stides Francaises. MILITARY: Royal West African Frontier Force (Nigeria), 1958–60.

CAREER: FILM DEBUT—*A French Mistress,* 1960. PRINCIPAL FILM WORK—runner, *Fury at Smuggler's Bay,* 1960; assistant director, *The Man in the Middle, The Pumpkin Eater,* 1964; assistant director, *Hysteria, The Yellow Rolls Royce, Repulsion, Darling,* 1965; assistant director, *Thunderball,* 1965; production manager, *2001: A Space Odyssey,* 1968; location manager, *You Only Live Twice,* 1967; location manager, *Billion Dollar Brain,* 1967; location manager, *The Adventurers,* 1970; production manager, *El Condor,* 1970; production manager, *Flight of the Doves,* 1970; production manager, *The Wrath of God,* 1972; unit production manager, *Papillon,* 1973; production supervisor, *Alfie Darling,* 1973; production manager, *The Wilby Conspiracy,* 1975; production manager, *Inside Out,* 1975; production supervisor, *Star Wars,* 1977; production manager, *The Other Side of Midnight,* 1977; associate producer, *Meetings with Remarkable Men,* 1977; associate producer, *The Empire Strikes Back,* 1980; associate producer, *Raiders of the Lost Ark,* 1981; co-producer, *Return of the Jedi,* 1983; producer, *Indiana Jones and the Temple of Doom,* 1984.

SIDELIGHTS: LANGUAGES—French, Spanish, German.

ADDRESS: Office—c/o E.M.I. Studios, Boreham Wood, United Kingdom. Agent—c/o Duncan Heath, 162/170 Wardour Street, London, W1 U.K.

* * *

WEAVER, William, actor and production stage manager

PERSONAL: Born October 15, 1917, in Miamisburg, OH; son of Harry Clay (a hotel owner) and Clara (Hurst) Weaver. EDUCATION: High school graduate. POLITICS: Democrat. RELIGION: Lutheran. MILITARY: U.S. Air Force, 1941–45, Captain; awarded the Distinguished Flying Cross and two Air Medals.

CAREER: DEBUT—Officer Owens, *Pickup Girl,* national tour, U.S. cities, 1945–46. NEW YORK DEBUT—Production stage manager, *The Fourposter,* Ethel Barrymore, 1951, 631 performances. PRINCIPAL STAGE WORK—(Production stage manager/stage manager) *One Eye Closed,* Bijou, NY, 1954; *The Desperate Hours,* Barrymore, NY, 1954–55; *Red Roses for Me,* Booth, NY, 1955–56; *Happiest Millionaire,* Lyceum, NY, 1956–57; *Mighty Man Is He,* Cort, NY, 1959–60; *Kwamina,* 54th Street, NY, 1961; *An Evening's Frost,* Theatre de Lys, NY, 1965–66; *Showboat,* State, NY, 1966; *More Stately Mansions,* Broadhurst, NY, 1967–68; *Zelda,* Barrymore, NY, 1969; *Emperor Henry IV,* Barrymore, NY, 1972; *The Kingfisher,* Biltmore, NY, 1978–79; *Deathtrap,* Music Box, NY, 1979; *My Fair Lady,* Uris, NY, 1981.

MAJOR TOURS—Henry Adams, *Magnificent Yankee,* U.S. cities, 1946–47; young man, *Sabrina Fair,* U.S. cities, 1954; Hibbetts, *Take Her She's Mine,* U.S. cities, 1962–63; (production stage manager/stage manager), *Desperate Hours,* U.S. cities, 1955; *Romanoff and Juliet,* U.S. cities, 1959; *How to Succeed . . . ,* U.S. cities, 1963–64; *Oliver,* U.S. cities, 1965; *Showboat,* U.S. cities, 1966; *Forty Carats,* U.S. cities, 1970–71; *The Kingfisher,* U.S. cities, 1979–80; *My Fair Lady,* U.S. cities, 1980–81.

ADDRESS: Home—59 W. 21st Street, New York, NY 10010.

* * *

WEBB, Jack, producer, writer, director, actor

PERSONAL: Born April 2, 1920, in Santa Monica, CA; died December 22, 1982; son of Samuel Chester and Margaret (Smith) Webb; married Julie Peck, July 1947 (divorced); Dorothy Thompson, January 1955 (divorced 1957); Jackie Loughery, June 1958, (divorced 1964); children: (first marriage) Stacy, Lisa. EDUCATION: Attended public schools in California. MILITARY: U.S. Army Air Force, World War II, 1942–45.

CAREER: PRINCIPAL RADIO WORK—Star, *Pat Novak for Hire,* San Francisco, 1945; *Johnny Modero Pier 23,* 1947; created *Dragnet,* 1949; created *Pete Kelly's Blues,* 1950; created *True Series,* 1961.

PRINCIPAL TELEVISION WORK—Producer/director/actor, *Dragnet,* 1955–70; creator, producer, *Adam-12,* 1968–74; executive producer, *The D.A.,* 1970–71, *O'Hara, U.S. Treasury,* 1970–71, *Emergency, Mobile One,* 1971–75, *Chase,* 1973, *The Rangers,* 1974–75; *Mobile Two,* 1975, *Sam,* 1977, *Project UFO,* 1978, *Little Mo,* 1978; narrator, *Escape,* 1973.

PRINCIPAL FILM WORK—feature roles: *Sunset Boulevard, The Men, Halls of Montezuma, You're in the Navy Now, He Walked By Night, Dragnet, Pete Kelly's Blues, The D.I., The Last Time I Saw Archie;* producer/director, *Archie,* 1959.

AWARDS: Winner, *Look* Magazine award, Best Director, 1954; Best Mystery Show, Academy of Television Arts and Sciences, 1952–54; Best Mystery Show, TV & Radio, 1953–54; Best Mystery Show and Most Popular Star of

Tomorrow, M.P. Daily's 15th Annual Radio Poll, 1950–51. Over 100 comendations of merit awarded by radio and TV critics.

WRITINGS: BOOKS—*The Badge,* 1958.

SIDELIGHTS: MEMBERSHIPS—Honorary Chairman, United Cerebral Palsy Association; SAG, Screen Directors Guild, American Society of Cinematographers, AFTRA.*

* * *

WEILL, Claudia, director

PERSONAL: Daughter of Guy and Marie-Helene Weill. EDUCATION: Radcliffe, B.A., 1969.

CAREER: PRINCIPAL THEATRE WORK—Director: *An Evening for Merlin Finch,* Williamstown Theatre Festival, MA, 1975; *Scenes from American Life,* Williamstown Theatre Festival, MA, 1976; *Standing on My Knees,* Tacoma Actors Guild, WA 1983; *Stillife,* American Place, NY, 1983; *Digging to China,* Williamstown Theatre Festival, 1983; *'night, Mother,* Syracuse Stage, NY, 1984; *Found a Peanut,* Public, NY, 1984; *The Longest Walk,* American Place, NY, 1984.

PRINCIPAL FILM WORK—Director: *The Other Half of the Sky: A China Memoir,* 1974; *Girlfriends,* 1979; *It's My Turn,* 1981.

PRINCIPAL TELEVISION AND SHORT FILM WORK—Director: *This Is the Home of Mrs. Levant Graham,* 1970; *The 51st State,* ten segments; *Sesame Street,* twenty segments; *Joyce at 34,* 1972; *The Great Love Experiment,* 1984.

RELATED CAREER—Teacher, acting, Cornish Institute, 1983; guest lecturer on film directing, New York University and Columbia.

AWARDS: Donatello, Best Director, 1979; *Mademoiselle* Woman of the Year, 1974 (shared); American Film Institute Independent Filmmakers Grant, 1973.

ADDRESS: Office—Cyclops Films Inc., 1697 Broadway, New York, NY 10019.

* * *

WEINER, Robert, producer, critic, manager, journalist

PERSONAL: Born September 9, in New York City. EDUCATION: Columbia University, B.A.

CAREER: FIRST STAGE WORK—Production assistant, Show of the Month Club, Inc., 1950. PRINCIPAL STAGE WORK—Press promotion, management, producer, press assistant to Arthur Cantor for approximately 25 productions in New York; box office treasurer, Newport Casino Theatre, 1955; production assistant, *The Desk Set,* Broadhurst, 1955, *Shangri-La,* Winter Garden, 1956, *Auntie Mame,* Broadhurst, 1956; producer, *No Time for Sergeants* (two company tours), 1958, *Tall Story,* Belasco, NY, 1959, *Medium Rare,*

Happy Medium, Chicago, IL, 1960, *Put It in Writing,* Royal Poinciana Playhouse, Palm Beach, FL, 1962; general manager, *Double Entry,* Martinique, NY, 1961, and production supervisor for *Spoon River Anthology,* Booth, NY, 1963, *What Makes Sammy Run?* 54th Street, NY, 1964, *Her First Roman,* Lunt-Fontanne, NY, 1968, *Gantry,* George Abbott, NY, 1970, *A Day in the Death of Joe Egg,* Brooks Atkinson, NY, 1968.

PRINCIPAL FILM WORK—Production supervisor/casting director, *Who Killed Teddy Bear,* 1965; associate producer, *Bullitt,* 1968; technical advisor to director, *John and Mary,* 1969; producer, *Groupies,* 1970; production executive/casting supervisor, *The French Connection,* 1971; production executive/casting supervisor, *The Seven-Ups,* 1973. PRINCIPAL TELEVISION WORK—Production supervisor, pay-TV production of *Spoon River Anthology,* Hartford, CT, and *Electric Showcase,* ABC, 1963; associate producer, for D'Antoni/Baer Television Productions, 1965–66; associate producer, *Comedy Tonight* series, 1970; producer, *Dylan Thomas's "A Child's Christmas in Wales",* 1973; producer, *Ailey Celebrates Ellington;* executive producer, *Gianni Schicchi* (comic opera).

RELATED CAREER: Managing Director of theatre operations, executive producer, and liaison for the Yale–ABC Writing for the Camera grant, Yale University, School of Drama, 1966; consultant, Joseph E. Seagram/U.S.A. 1981–83, coordinator for special promotional events, for charities and the arts; guest lecturer, Yale School of Drama.

WRITINGS: ARTICLES/COLUMNS—Weekly columnist, *Soho Weekly News,* NY, 4 years; contributor to *New York Magazine, New York Sunday News, Daily News, Cue, People, Penthouse, US, Variety, Circus, New York Post;* contributing editor, *Inter/View Magazine, Words and Music Magazine;* weekly columnist, *Friday Morning Quarterback;* drama, film, music, dance critic, *WBLS/FM Radio,* two years.

AWARDS: Emmy Award Nomination, *Ailey Celebrates Ellington;* Christopher Award, *Dylan Thomas's "A Child's Christmas in Wales."*

SIDELIGHTS: MEMBERSHIPS—Voting member, National Academy of Recording Arts and Sciences, Drama Desk Awards Nominating Committee, 1980–83, Blue Ribbon Jury Panel, Emmy Awards, 1973–76 and 1980, League of New York Theatres and Producers, National Academy of Television Arts and Sciences, Rock Writer's Guild, AFTRA, Theatre Arts Jury, Brandeis University, 1975.

ADDRESS: 161 W. 54th Street, New York, NY 10019.

* * *

WEINTRAUB, Fred, producer

CAREER: PRINCIPAL FILM WORK—Producer: *Woodstock,* 1970, *Klute,* 1971, *Summer of '42,* 1972, *Rage,* 1972, *Enter the Dragon,* 1973, *Outlaw Blues,* 1977, *The Promise,* 1979, *Tom Horn,* 1980, *High Road to China,* 1983, *Out of Control,* 1984, *Killer Angels,* 1985.

PRINCIPAL TELEVISION WORK—created, *Hootenanny, The Dukes of Hazard.*

RELATED CAREER: In the music business, Mr. Weintraub introduced Bob Dylan, Judy Collins, Peter, Paul and Mary, and managed Joan Rivers, Neil Diamond, Bill Cosby and the Four Seasons. He owned the Bitter End club in New York City. He served as a studio executive with Warner Brothers Inc.

ADDRESS: c/o MGM/UA Entertainment Company, 10202 W. Washington Blvd., Culver City, CA 90230.

* * *

WEIR, Peter, director, writer

PERSONAL: Born August 8, 1944, in Sydney, Australia.

CAREER: FIRST FILM WORK—Director/writer, "Michael" an episode of the feature, *Three to Go,* 1970. PRINCIPAL FILM WORK—Director/writer: *The Cars That Ate Paris; The Last Wave,* 1978; *The Plumber,* 1979; director: *Picnic at Hanging Rock,* 1975, *Gallipoli,* 1981, *The Year of Living Dangerously,* 1982.

ADDRESS: Agent—Tom Patak, William Morris Agency, 151 El Camino Dr., Beverly Hills, CA 90212.*

* * *

WERTMULLER, Lina, writer, director

PERSONAL: Born in Rome, Italy.

CAREER: FIRST FILM WORK—Assistant to Federico Fellini, *8½,* 1962. PRINCIPAL FILM WORK—Writer/director: *This Time; Let's Talk about Men; The Seduction of Mimi; Love and Anarchy; All Screwed Up; Swept Away; Seven Beauties; A Night Full of Rain; The Lizards.*

PRINCIPAL TELEVISION WORK—Italian series, *Gian Burasca.*

SIDELIGHTS: "After graduating from high school, Ms. Wertmuller went to drama school and began working in the theatre in 1951. She stage managed, did puppetry, and wrote for radio shows, prior to assisting Fellini on *8½.*"*

* * *

WEST, Mae, actress, writer

PERSONAL: Born August 17, 1892, in Brooklyn, NY; died November 22, 1980; daughter of John Patrick and Matilda (Delker-Dolger) West; married Frank Wallace, 1911 (divorced 1943). EDUCATION: Privately tutored.

CAREER: PRINCIPAL STAGE APPEARANCES—On stage in vaudeville at age 5; *Little Nell the Marchioness,* 1897; *Mrs. Wiggs of the Cabbage Patch; Ten Nights in a Barroom; East*

Lynne; The Fatal Wedding; A la Broadway, 1911; *Vera Violetta,* 1911; *A Winsome Widow,* 1912; *Such Is Life,* 1913; *Sometime,* 1918; *Demi-Tasse,* 1919; *The Mimic World,* 1921; *Sex,* 1926; *The Wicked Age,* 1927; *Diamond Lil,* 1928; *The Constant Sinner,* 1931; *Catherine Was Great,* 1944; *Ring Twice Tonight,* 1946; *Diamond Lil,* 1948–51; *Come on Up . . . Ring Twice,* 1952; *Sextet,* 1961.

PRINCIPAL FILM APPEARANCES—*Night After Night,* 1932; *She Done Him Wrong,* 1933; *I'm No Angel,* 1933; *Diamond Lil,* 1933; *Belle of the Nineties,* 1934; *Going to Town,* 1935; *Klondike Annie,* 1936; *Go West Young Man,* 1936; *Every Day's a Holiday,* 1937; *My Little Chickadee,* 1940; *The Heat's On,* 1943; *Myra Breckenridge,* 1969; *Sextette,* 1978.

WRITINGS: PLAYS—*The Drag,* 1927; *Pleasure Man,* 1928. NOVEL—*Diamond Lil; The Constant Sinner.* AUTOBIOGRAPHY—*Goodness Had Nothing to Do with It,* 1959.

SCREENPLAYS—*I'm No Angel,* 1933; *Going to Town,* 1935; *Klondike Annie,* 1936; *Go West Young Man,* 1936; *My Little Chickadee* (collaborator), 1940.

AWARDS: Voted Money-Making Star, Motion Picture *Herald*-Fame Poll, 1933–34.*

* * *

WHITE, George C., director and theater executive

PERSONAL: Born August 16, 1935, in New London, CT; son of Nelson Cooke (a writer and artist) and Aida Catherine (Rovetti) White; married Elizabeth Darling (a jeweler), July 5, 1958; children: George, Caleb, Juliette. EDUCATION: Yale University, B.A., 1957; Yale School of Drama, M.F.A., 1961; trained for the stage at the Shakespeare Institute, Stratford-on-Avon, England. POLITICS: Independent. RELIGION: Protestant. MILITARY: U.S. Army.

CAREER: DEBUT—Assistant manager, International Ballet Festival, Nervi, Italy, 1955. NEW YORK DEBUT—Stage manager, *Azuma-Kabuki,* Broadway Theater, 1955, 30 performances. PRINCIPAL STAGE APPEARANCES—Various roles, *John Brown's Body,* Players, NY, 1956. MAJOR TOURS—*Azuma Kabuki,* international cities, 1955. TELEVISION DEBUT—Bruce Bennett, *Citizen Soldier,* 1958.

PRINCIPAL WORK—Production coordinator, Talent Associates, 1961–63; administrative vice-president, Paramount Pictures, 1963–65; founder/president, Eugene O'Neill Memorial Theater Center, Waterford, CT, 1965–present; advisor/director, Theatre One, Connecticut College for Women, 1967–70; regional theatre consultant, National Educational TV Network; guest lecturer, Wagner College, 1970; acting director, Hunter College, 1972–73; professor, University of North Carolina; professor of theater administration, Yale University, 1978–79.

SPECIAL POSITIONS—Co-chairman, theatre administration program, Yale Drama School; member executive committee, Theatre Library Association, 1967; board of governors, American Playwrights Theatre; board member, ANTA, 1967–68; member, Mayor's Theatre Advisory Committee, NY; advisory board, International Theatre Institute; guest

administrator, Australian National Playwrights Conference, 1973; delegate, International Theatre Institute, Moscow, 1973; member, Connecticut Commission on the Arts, 1979; co-founder, Caribbean-U.S. Theatre Exchange.

DIRECTED: Actors Theatre of St. Paul, 1979–80; Hartman Repertory Theatre, 1980.

AWARDS: Antoinette Perry Award, Special Award, 1979; National Opera Institute Award; New London Bar Association's Public Service Award; *Connecticut* Magazine Award, Special Contributions to the State, 1981; Distinguished Citizen's Award, Town of Waterford, 1976; Margo Jones Award, 1968; New England Theatre Conference Award, Special Citation, 1968.

SIDELIGHTS: MEMBERSHIPS—Arts and Business Council; International Theater Institute; Film Forum International; Eastern Connecticut Symphony; Dance Arts Council; Connecticut Opera Association; Connecticut Public TV; Operation Rescue (planning board); Rehearsal Club (board of directors); Theater of Latin America; Yale Alumni Board; National Endowment of the Arts; Yale Club; Century Club; Players Club; Cosmos (Washington, DC); Thames Club.

ADDRESS: Office—Eugene O'Neill Memorial Theater Center, 234 W. 44th Street, New York, NY 10036.

* * *

WHITEHEAD, Paxton, actor

PERSONAL: Born October 17, 1937, in East Malling, Kent, U.K.; son of Charles Parkin and Louise (Hunt) Whitehead; married Patricia Gage; children: Sarah, Charles (previous marriage). EDUCATION: Attended Rugby School; trained for the stage at Webber-Douglas School.

CAREER: STAGE DEBUT—Alphonse, *All for Mary,* Devonshire Park, Eastbourne, U.K., 1956. NEW YORK DEBUT—Dawson-Hill, *The Affair,* Henry Miller's, 1962. PRINCIPAL STAGE APPEARANCES—Francisco, *Hamlet,* Royal Shakespeare Company, Stratford, U.K., 1958; Torvald Helmer, *A Doll's House,* Theatre Four, NY, 1963; Gower, *Henry V,* King of France, *King Lear,* American Shakespeare Festival, Stratford, CT, 1963; *Beyond the Fringe,* John Golden, NY, 1964; Higgins, *My Fair Lady,* Memphis, TN, 1964; Jack Absolute, *The Rivals,* Boston, MA, 1964; Archie Rice, *The Entertainer,* Hartford, 1965; Cusins, *Major Barbara,* Cincinnati, 1965; Algernon, *The Importance of Being Earnest,* Winnipeg, 1965; Lord Summerhays, *Misalliance,* Magnus, *The Apple Cart,* Shaw Festival, Niagra-on-the-Lake, 1966; Sergius, *Arms and the Man,* Cusins, *Major Barbara,* Shaw Festival, 1967; Hector Hushabye, *Heartbreak House,* Coustilliou, *The Chemmy Circle,* Shaw Festival, 1968; Dubedat, *The Doctor's Dilemma,* the actor, *The Guardsman,* Shaw Festival, 1969; Tempest, *Forty Years On,* Shaw Festival, 1970; Charteris, *The Philanderer, Tonight at 8:30,* Shaw Festival, 1971; Valentine, *You Never Can Tell,* Savoyard, *Fanny's First Play,* Shaw Festival, 1973; Fancourt Babberley, *Charley's Aunt,* Shaw Festival, 1974; Burgoyne, *The Devil's Disciple,* Shaw Festival, 1975; Sergius, *Arms and the Man,* Magnus, *Apple Cart,* Adrian, *The Millionairess,* Shaw Festival, 1976; Ronnie Gamble, *Thark,* Shaw Festival,

1977; The Emperor, *The Brass Butterfly*, Chelsea Theater Center, NY, 1970; Reverend Alexander Mill, *Candida*, Longacre, NY, 1970; Canon Throbbing, *Habeas Corpus*, Martin Beck, NY, 1975; Sherlock Holmes, *The Crucifer of Blood*, Helen Hayes, NY, 1978; Henry Carr, *Travesties*, Manitoba Theatre Centre, Winnipeg, Canada, 1979; Oscar Wilde, *The Trials of Oscar Wilde*, Citadel, Edmonton, 1980; Ronnie Gamble, *Thark*, Malvolio, *Twelfth Night*, Philadelphia Drama Guild, PA, 1980; Pellinore, *Camelot*, State, NY, 1980; Sergeant of Police, *Pirates of Penzance*, Ahmanson, Los Angeles, CA, 1981; Harpagon, *The Miser*, Old Globe, San Diego, CA, 1982; Hector, *Heartbreak House*, Theatre Royal, London, 1983; Anthony Absolute, *The Rivals*, Old Globe, San Diego, CA, 1983; Freddy, *Noises Off*, Brooks Atkinson, New York, 1983–84.

MAJOR TOURS—Anew McMaster Company, U.K. cities, 1957; Francisco, *Hamlet*, Royal Shakespeare Company, Soviet Union, 1958; *Beyond the Fringe*, U.S. cities, 1963.

PRINCIPAL TELEVISION APPEARANCES—*Lady Windermere's Fan, The First Night of Pygmalion, Riel*, 1977; *Hart vs. Hart*, 1982, 1983; *Magnum P.I.*, 1983.

DIRECTED: Plays—*The Circle*, The Shaw Festival, Niagra-on-the-Lake, 1968; *Misalliance*, Shaw Festival, 1972; *Getting Married*, Shaw Festival, 1972; *Charley's Aunt*, Shaw Festival, 1972; *Widowers' Houses*, Shaw Festival, 1977.

RELATED CAREERS—Artistic director, Shaw Festival, Niagra-on-the-Lake, 1967–77; Playhouse, Vancouver, Canada, 1971–73.

AWARDS: Antoinette Perry Award Nomination, 1980: *Camelot*.

SIDELIGHTS: MEMBERSHIPS—Players Club. RECREATION—Tennis, Skiing, cards.

ADDRESS: Agent—c/o Barna Ostertag, 501 Fifth Avenue, New York, NY 10017.

* * *

WHYTE, Ron, writer

PERSONAL: Born in Black Eagle, MT; son of Henry A. Melville (a railroad executive) and Eva (an executive secretary; maiden name, Ranieri) Whyte. EDUCATION: San Francisco State College, B.A., 1964; Yale University School of Drama, M.F.A., 1967; Union Theological Seminary, M. Div., 1976; trained for the stage at the Actors Studio with Lee Strasberg and Harold Clurman. POLITICS: Democrat.

WRITINGS: PLAYS, PRODUCED—*Welcome to Andromeda*, American Place, NY, 1969, Cherry Lane, NY, 1973, Actors Theatre of Louisville, KY, 1975, John Jay New Theatre, NY, 1979, Toronto, Vancouver, SK, Canada, 1983; *Amerikan Shrapnel*, American Shakespeare Festival, Stratford, CT, 1971; *Horatio*, Loretto-Hilton, St. Louis, MO, American Conservatory Theatre, San Francisco, CA, 1974, Arena Stage, Washington, DC, 1975; *Funeral March for a One-Man Band*, Westbeth Theater Center, NY, 1978, St. Nicholas, Chicago, IL, 1979, San Diego Repertory, 1981, Ivan-

RON WHYTE

hoe, Chicago, IL, 1982; *Disability: A Comedy*, Arena Stage, Washington, DC, 1978, Mark Taper Forum Lab, Los Angeles, CA, 1979–80, Arena Stage, Washington, DC, 1981, Actors Theatre of St. Paul, MN, 1983, Off-Broadway, NY, 1983–84; *Counter/Cultures*, Birmingham Festival, AL, 1979; *The Hunchback of Notre-Dame*, American Stage Festival, NH, 1979, New York Shakespeare Festival, NY, 1981; *The Final Extinction of Alexander Pope*, Postus-Teatret, Copenhagen, Denmark, 1980; *Andromeda II*, The Actors Studio, New York, 1980.

PLAYS, PUBLISHED—*Welcome to Andromeda*, 1973; *Disability: A Comedy*, 1982.

SCREENPLAYS—*Valentine's Eve*, 1968; *Pigeons*, 1970; *The Happiness Cage*, 1972; *The Parents*, 1978. BOOKS—*The Flower That Finally Grew*, 1970; *Exeunt Dying: Theatrical Mysteries*, 1977; *Sign-Off Devotional*, 1978; *The Story of Film: A History of World Cinema from Its Dawn to the Present*, 1980.

AWARDS: Pulitzer Prize Nomination, 1983: *Disability: A Comedy;* Joseph Jefferson Award Nomination, 1983: *Funeral March for a One-Man Band;* Joseph Jefferson Award (4), 1979: *Funeral March for a One-Man Band;* Drama-Logue Award (3), 1978: *Welcome to Andromeda;* Best Short Plays of 1974 Award, 1974: *Welcome to Andromeda;* Time Magazine Award, Ten Best Plays of the Year, 1973–74: *Welcome to Andromeda*.

SIDELIGHTS: MEMBERSHIPS—American Association for the Advancement of the Humanities; American Society of Composers, Authors, and Publishers; The Actors Studio Playwrights and Directors Unit; The Authors League; Baker Street Irregulars; Creative Artists Public Service Program; The Dramatists Guild; National Endowment for the Arts; New York State Council on the Arts; The Riverside Church; Writers Guild of America East and West.

ADDRESS: Agent—c/o Paul William Bradley, Ruth Hagy Brod Agency, 15 Park Avenue, New York, NY 10016. Theatrical Attorney—c/o Robert N. Solomon, Frankfurt, Garbus, Klein and Selz, 485 Madison Avenue, New York, NY 10022.

* * *

WIENER, Sally Dixon, writer, composer, lyricist

PERSONAL: Born September 18, 1926; daughter of George Lane (a doctor) and Ellen S. Payson (a nurse; maiden name, Swanson) Dixon; married John A. Wiener (a lawyer), April 10, 1951; children: John, Ellen, Ann. EDUCATION: University of Arizona, B.A., 1947; at the New School studied music and theatre with Aaron Frankel and playwriting with Harold Callen and Edward Mabley. RELIGION: Episcopalian.

WRITINGS: PLAYS, PRODUCED—Book, music, lyrics, *Majorie Daw* (musical), Equity Library, NY, 1970; *Telemachus, Friend,* St. Peter's Gate, NY, 1972, Baruch College, NY, 1972; *The Blue Magi,* St. Peter's Gate, NY, 1972, The Lambs, NY, 1976; *The Pimienta Pancakes,* Theatre Off Park, NY, 1976, Double Image, NY, 1976; *Flyin' Turtles,* University of Western New Mexico, Silver City, 1976; *Show Me a Hero,* Sunset, Carmel, CA, 1979, St. Malachy's, NY, 1980. PLAYS, PUBLISHED—*Telemachus, Friend,* 1974.

AWARDS: American Song Festival Lyric Competition, Honorable Mention, Certificate of Merit, 1982: *Gonna Lock the Door and Throw Away the Key;* National Play Award, Semi-Finalist, 1981: *The Second Battle of Baltimore;* Festival of First Playwriting Award, 1979: *Show Me a Hero;* Stanley Drama Award, Semi-Finalist, 1978: *Show Me a Hero.*

SIDELIGHTS: MEMBERSHIPS—Dramatists Guild.

"Harold Prince, the producer, has said that casting is 90% of direction, and I suppose 99% of playwrighting is sweat. It's the 1%, when a character takes over the typewriter, that's the joy. Putting Act I, Scene 1, Page 1 on a piece of paper is giving over a period of your life, all too voluntarily, to discouragement and loneliness and, usually, with no promise of it becoming a reality on stage. If and when it does, there is another kind of joy—the collaborative process during which, suddenly, it is no longer your baby. It is a child who has learned to walk. And even though the monetary rewards are, for the most part, few and far between, for the average playwright, one feels in good company."

ADDRESS: Agent—c/o Robert Freedman, Brandt and Brandt Dramatic Department, 1501 Broadway, New York, NY 10036.

WILDER, Billy, producer, director, writer

PERSONAL: Born June 22, 1906, in Austria; married Audrey Young (a reporter). MILITARY: Head film section, Psychological Warfare division, U.S. Army, American Zone, Germany, 1945.

CAREER: PRINCIPAL FILM WORK—Screenwriter, *People On Sunday,* Berlin; *Emil and the Detectives;* screenwriter/director, *Mauvaise Graine,* Paris; screenwriter: *Bluebeard's Eighth Wife,* 1938, *Midnight,* 1939, *Ninotchka,* 1939, *Arise My Love,* 1940, *Hold Back the Dawn,* 1941; director/screenwriter: *Five Graves to Cairo,* 1943; *Double Indemnity,* 1944, *The Lost Weekend,* 1945, *The Emperor Waltz,* 1948, *A Foreign Affair,* 1948, *Sunset Boulevard,* 1950; producer/director/screenwriter, *The Big Carnival, (Ace in the Hole),* 1951, *Stalag 17,* 1953, *Sabrina,* 1954, *Love in the Afternoon,* 1957, *Some Like It Hot,* 1959, *The Spirit of St. Louis,* 1957, *Witness for the Prosecution,* 1957, *One, Two, Three,* 1961, *Irma La Douce,* 1963, *Kiss Me, Stupid,* 1964, *The Fortune Cookie,* 1966, *The Private Life of Sherlock Holmes,* 1970, *Avanti,* 1972, *Fedora,* 1979; director/screenwriter: *The Front Page,* 1974, *Buddy, Buddy,* 1981.

AWARDS: Academy Awards, Best Picture, co-award, Best Story/Screenplay, 1960: *The Apartment;* Academy Award, co-award, Best Story/Screenplay, 1950: *Sunset Boulevard;* Academy Award, Best Director, co-award, Best Screenplay, 1945: *The Lost Weekend.*

ADDRESS: Office—c/o Equitable Investment Corp., 6253 Hollywood Blvd., Suite 1122, Los Angeles, CA, 90048.*

* * *

WILKOF, Lee, actor and writer

PERSONAL: Born June 25, 1951, in Canton, OH; son of Darwin B. (a businessman) and Ann Louise Wilkof; married Constance Marie Grappo (a writer and director), February 2, 1984. EDUCATION: University of Cincinnati, B.A.; trained for the stage at Herbert Berghof Studio with Austin Pendelton and Ellen Sandler. RELIGION: Jewish.

CAREER: DEBUT—Dr. Kitchell, *Bells Are Ringing,* Showboat Majestic, Cincinnati, OH, 1973. NEW YORK DEBUT—Styopka, *Diary of a Scoundrel,* Theater in Space, 1974, 12 performances. PRINCIPAL STAGE APPEARANCES—*The Present Tense,* Park Royal, NY, 1977; *The Tavern,* Snowmass, CO, 1981; *Pennant Fever,* Beverly Hills Playhouse, CA, 1980; *Little Shop of Horrors,* WPA, Orpheum, Westwood Playhouse, NY, 1982–83.

FILM DEBUT—Brian, *Serial,* 1980. PRINCIPAL FILM APPEARANCES—Yussol, *Wholly Moses,* 1981. TELEVISION DEBUT—Harvey Perlstein, *W.E.B. Delta House,* 1978. PRINCIPAL TELEVISION APPEARANCES—*Einswine,* 1979; Stanley Freisen, *Hart to Hart,* 1979–1981; *Moviola,* 1981; *Prisoner without a Name, Cell without a Number,* 1983; *Newhart,* 1983; *Oh, Madeline,* 1983.

WRITINGS: PLAYS—*The Present Tense* (with Stephen Rosenfield, Jeff Sweet, Alen Menken, and Haila Strauss), Off-Broadway, 1977.

AWARDS: Dramalogue Award, 1980: *Pennant Fever;* Obie Award, 1977: *Present Tense;* Drama Desk Nomination, 1977: *Present Tense.*

SIDELIGHTS: MEMBERSHIPS—American Film Institute. REC-REATION: Banjo playing, composing, cartooning.

"I take an active interest in the cause of nuclear disarmament."

ADDRESS: Agent—c/o Abrams Artists, 420 Madison Avenue, New York, NY 10017. Agent—c/o Abrams, Harris, Goldberg Agency, 9229 Sunset Blvd, Los Angeles, CA 90046.

* * *

WILLIAMS, Bradford Cody, puppeteer, designer, director

PERSONAL: Born January 8, 1951 in White Plains, NY; son of Robert Cody and Patricia (Packard) Williams. EDUCA-TION: Hope College, Holland, MI, B.A. (Art), 1973; studied puppetry at the University of Connecticut, 1975–79 and puppet performance with Burr Tillstrom.

CAREER: FIRST STAGE WORK—Actor/designer/prop master, Hope Summer Theatre, Holland, MI, 1972–75. FILM, TV, STAGE WORK—Puppeteer/designer, *Brad Williams' Punch & Judy Theatre* (a one-man touring show), 1975–present; puppeteer/designer, *The Pandemonium Puppet Company,* tours throughout New England, 1976–79; assistant puppet, mask and set design, *Black Elk Lives,* Entermedia, NY, 1981; puppeteer/puppet design and construction, *Pinwheel,* children's cable television production (Nickelodeon), 1980–81; director, puppet and mask designer, *The Scarecrow,* Union Square, Y, 1981; puppet design and construction, *Mainly Mozart,* Story Concert Players, NY, 1982; mask builder, *Lennon,* Entermedia, NY, 1982; set designer, Story Concert Players, 1982; puppeteer, designer, *The Nickelodeon Road-show,* NY, present; mask designer, builder, *The Fantastic Toyshop,* New York Pantomime Theatre, 1983.

SIDELIGHTS: MEMBERSHIPS—Puppeteers of America, Union Internationale de la Marionette, Association of Theatrical Artists and Craftspeople, SAG.

"Puppetry can be a valuable tool in adult theatre. Like the mask, a puppet can add dimension and visual variety. Adults also need fantasy (often more than children)."

ADDRESS: Home/Office—214 Riverside Drive, #109, New York, NY 10025.

* * *

WILLIAMS, Elmo, film editor, director, writer

PERSONAL: Born April 30, 1913; son of Oscar P. (a farmer) and Audra O. (a clerk, maiden name, Etter) Williams; married Lorraine Cunningham (a writer) December 23,

1940; children: Stacy, Toby, Jody. EDUCATION: Attended public schools; studied film editing with Merrill White. RELIGION: Protestant.

CAREER: FIRST FILM WORK—Editor, *Lady for a Day,* 1933. PRINCIPAL FILM WORK—Editor: *Nell Gwyn, Peg Woffington, 60 Glorious Years, Victoria the Great, Sunny, No No Nanette, Cowboy, High Noon;* director: *Tall Texan, Apache Kid, The Cowboy;* assistant producer, *The Longest Day,* 1962; producer: *Zorba the Greek,* 1965, *Those Magnificent Men in Their Flying Machines,* 1966, *The Blue Max,* 1966, *Tora! Tora! Tora!,* 1970, *Sidewinder,* 1977, *Caravans,* 1978, *Man, Woman and Child,* 1983.

AWARDS: Academy Award, Film Editing, *High Noon;* Academy Award Nomination, Editing, *20,000 Leagues Under the Sea;* Gold Scissors Award, A.C.E.

SIDELIGHTS: MEMBERSHIPS—A.C.E., A.M.P.A.S., DGA, S.M.P.F.E., P.G.

ADDRESS: Office—Gaylord Productions, 9255 Sunset Blvd., Los Angeles, CA 90049.

* * *

WILLIAMS, Jobeth, actress

PERSONAL: Born in Texas. EDUCATION: Brown University.

CAREER: STAGE APPEARANCES—Performed with theatre companies in Washington, DC, Philadelphia, Rhode Island and Boston; *Gardenia,* Manhattan Theatre Club, 1982.

FILM DEBUT—*Kramer vs. Kramer,* 1979. PRINCIPAL FILM APPEARANCES—*Stir Crazy,* 1980; *The Dogs of War,* 1981; *Poltergeist,* 1982; *Endangered Species,* 1982; *The Big Chill,* 1983.

PRINCIPAL TELEVISION APPEARANCES—*Fun and Games; Feasting with Panthers; Jabberwocky; The Guiding Light; Somerset.**

* * *

WILLIAMS, Tennessee (ne Thomas Lanier Williams), playwright

PERSONAL: Born March 26, 1911, in Columbus, MS; died February 25, 1983 in New York City; son of Cornelius Coffin and Edwina (Dakin) Williams. EDUCATION: University of Missouri, 1931–33; Washington University, St. Louis, MO, 1936–37; State University of Iowa, B.A., 1938.

CAREER: WRITINGS: PLAYS, PUBLISHED/PRODUCED—one acts, *Candles to the Sun,* 1936, *The Fugitive Kind,* 1937, *Spring Song,* 1938, *Not About Nightingales,* 1939, produced under the title *American Blues,* 1939; *Battle of Angels,* Boston, 1940; *Stairs to the Roof,* Chicago, 1944; *The Glass Menagerie,* Chicago, 1944, NY, 1945; *You Touched Me,* 1945; *A Streetcar Named Desire,* 1947; *Summer and Smoke,* 1948; *The Rose Tattoo,* 1950; *Camino Real,* 1953; *Cat on a*

Hot Tin Roof, 1955; *Three Players of a Summer Game*, 1955; *Orpheus Descending*, 1957; *Garden District* (double bill, *Something Unspoken, Suddenly Last Summer*), 1957; *Sweet Bird of Youth*, 1959; *Period of Adjustment* (co-directed), 1959; *The Night of the Iguana*, 1961; *The Milk Train Doesn't Stop Here Anymore*, 1963; *The Mutilated* and *The Gnadiges Fraulein*, produced as *Slapstick Tragedy*, 1966; *The Two-Character Play*, 1967; *The Seven Descents of Myrtle*, 1968; *In the Bar of a Tokyo Hotel*, 1969; *Small Craft Warnings; Out Cry*, 1973; *The Latter Days of a Celebrated Soubrette*, 1974; *The Red Devil Battery Sign*, 1975; *This Is*, 1976; *The Eccentricities of a Nightingale*, 1976; *Vieux Carré*, 1976; *A Lovely Sunday for Creve Coeur*, 1979; *Clothes for a Summer Hotel*, 1980; *Kerche Hutchem, und Kinder*, 1980; *A House Not Meant to Stand*, 1981; *Something Cloudy—Something Clear*, 1981; other short plays—*The Lady of Larkspur Lotion, The Purification, This Property Is Condemned, I Rise in Flames Cried the Phoenix, Portrait of a Madonna, 27 Wagons Full of Cotton, The Last of My Solid Gold Watches, I Can't Imagine Tomorrow, Confessional, A Perfect Analysis Given by a Parrot*.

SCREENPLAYS—*The Glass Menagerie; A Streetcar Named Desire; The Rose Tattoo; Baby Doll; Suddenly Last Summer; The Fugitive Kind.*

BOOKS—*The Roman Spring of Mrs. Stone; Noise and the World of Reason;* POETRY—*Androgyne Mon Amour, In the Winter of Cities;* SHORT STORY COLLECTIONS—*One Arm; Hard Candy; The Knightly Quest; Eight Mortal Ladies; Possessed.* AUTOBIOGRAPHY—*Memoirs*, 1975.

AWARDS: Medal of Freedom, President Carter, 1980; Kennedy Center Honors, 1979; Theatre Hall of Fame, 1979; Gold Medal for Drama, National Institute of Arts and Letters, 1969; Antoinette Perry Award, New York Drama Critics Award, 1962: *The Night of the Iguana;* Pulitzer Prize for Drama, New York Drama Critics Award, 1955: *Cat on a Hot Tin Roof;* Pulitzer Prize for Drama, New York Drama Critics Award, 1947–48: *A Streetcar Named Desire;* New York Drama Critics Award, 1944–45: *The Glass Menagerie;* Honorary LHD, HHD.*

* * *

WILLISON, Walter, actor, singer, playwright, lyricist

PERSONAL: Born June 24, 1947 in Monterey Park, CA; son of Clarence Virgil (fleet sales manager for Chevrolet) and Freda Arline (McClaren) Willison. EDUCATION: Attended public schools in California.

CAREER: DEBUT—Walter, *Here's Love*, California Theatre, San Bernadino, CA, 1964. NEW YORK DEBUT—Garson Hobart, *Norman Is That You?*, Lyceum, for 20 previews and 12 performances, 1970. PRINCIPAL STAGE APPEARANCES—James Preston, *On a Clear Day You Can See Forever*, Greek, Los Angeles, CA, Geary, San Francisco, CA, 1968; Danny, *Your Own Thing*, Marines Memorial, San Francisco, CA, 1968; Prince Dauntless, *Once Upon a Mattress*, Desert Inn Hotel, Las Vegas, NV, 1969; Japheth, *Two by Two*, Imperial, NY, 1970–71; celebrant/first rock singer, *Mass*, Kennedy Center, Washington, DC, 1971; Charlie, *Wild and Wonderful*, Lyceum, NY, 1971; guest star, *A Celebration of*

WALTER WILLISON

Richard Rodgers, Imperial, NY, 1972; Prince Charming, *Snow White and the Seven Dwarfs*, St. Louis Municipal Opera, MO, 1972; Pippin, *Pippin*, Imperial, NY, 1972–73; Lt. Cable, *South Pacific*, 25th Anniversary, NY, Players Club, NY, 1974; guest star, *A Gala Tribute to Joshua Logan*, Imperial, NY, 1974; guest star, *A Tribute to George Abbott*, Shubert, NY, 1975; Carny O'Brien, *Front Street Gaieties*, Mayfair, Santa Monica, CA, 1980–81; lead, *They Say It's Wonderful, a Salute to Irving Berlin*, St. Regis Hotel, NY, 1981; Kid Kotten, *Broadway Scandals of 1928*, O'Neal's, NY, 1982.

MAJOR TOURS—James Preston, *On a Clear Day You Can See Forever*, bus and truck national tour, 1967–68; Danny, *Your Own Thing*, bus and truck national tour, 1969–70.

FILM DEBUT—Mongolian Prince, *Harry and Tonto Go to New York*, 1976. PRINCIPAL FILM APPEARANCES—Soundtrack vocals, *Fantasies*, 1980. TELEVISION DEBUT—*The Today Show*, 1970. PRINCIPAL TELEVISION APPEARANCES—*The David Frost Show*, 1970; Clyde Griffins, *An American Tragedy*, segment of *The Great Novelists*, 1975; *Celebrity Revue*, 1976; Dr. Buck Wheaton, *Days of Our Lives*, 1978; Dr. Calvin Campbell, *McDuff, the Talking Dog*, 1976–77; co-star, *Ziegfeld: The Man and His Women*, 1978.

WRITINGS: PLAYS, PRODUCED—*Front Street Gaieties*, ''Dodge City's Hottest Revue,'' Los Angeles, CA, 1980–81; *Broadway Scandals of 1928*, book and lyrics, Club Broadway, O'Neal's Times Square, NY, 1982.

AWARDS: Honorary Lifetime Citizenship of the State of Kansas, 1983; Theatre World Award, 1970–71; Antoinette Perry Award Nomination, Best Supporting Actor in a Musical, 1971: *Two by Two.*

SIDELIGHTS: MEMBERSHIPS—Board of Directors, William Inge Library, Independence Community College, Kansas, Dramatists Guild, ASCAP, SAG, AEA, AFTRA, AGMA.

ADDRESS: 123 W. 78th Street, Penthouse #4, New York, NY 10025. Agent—Luis San Jurjuro, ICM, 40 W. 57th Street, New York, NY 10019.

* * *

WILSON, Lanford, playwright

PERSONAL: Born April 13, 1937, in Lebanon, MO; son of Ralph Eugene and Violetta Careybelle (Tate) Wilson. EDUCATION: Attended University of Chicago and San Diego State College.

WRITINGS: PLAYS, PRODUCED—*So Long at the Fair,* Caffe Cino, NY, 1963; *Home Free, No Trespassing, Sandcastle, The Madness of Lady Bright,* 1964; *Ludlow Fair, Balm in Gilead, This Is the Rill Speaking, Days Ahead, Sex Is Between Two People,* 1965; *The Gingham Dog, The Rimers of Eldritch, Wandering,* 1966; *Wandering Days Ahead,* 1967; *Lemon Sky,* 1969; *Serenading Louie, The Great Nebula in Orion,* 1970; *The Hot L Baltimore, The Family Continues,* 1972; *The Mound Builders,* 1975; *Fifth of July,* 1978; *Brontasaurus,* 1978; *Talley's Folly,* 1979; *A Tale Told,* 1981. PLAYS, PUBLISHED—*Balm in Gilead and Other Plays,* 1966; *The Rimers of Eldritch and Other Plays,* 1968; *The Gingham Dog,* 1969; *Lemon Sky,* 1970; *The Hot L Baltimore,* 1973; *The Mound Builders,* 1976; *Fifth of July,* 1979; *Talley's Folley,* 1980; *A Tale Told,* 1982. TELEVISION PLAYS—*This Is the Rill Speaking,* 1967; *The Sandcastle; Stoop; The Migrants; Taxi!*

AWARDS: Pulitzer Prize, 1980; Outer Critics Circle Award, Drama Critics Circle Award, 1980, 1973; Obie Award, 1975, 1972; Vernon Rice Award, 1966–67.

SIDELIGHTS: MEMBERSHIPS—Dramatists Guild, Circle Repertory Company (founder and resident playwright).

ADDRESS: Office—P.O. Box 891, Sag Harbor, NY 11963.*

* * *

WINDSOR, Marie (nee Emily Marie Bertelsen), actress

PERSONAL: Born December 11, 1921, in Marysvale, UT; daughter of Lane Joseph (a mining investor and businessman) and Etta Marie (Long) Bertelsen; married Ted Steele, 1946 (annulled 1947); married Jack Rodney Hupp (a realtor), November 18, 1954; children: Richard Rodney. EDUCATION: Attended Brigham Young University; trained for the stage with Maria Ouspenskaya, Jeff Corey, Lee Strasberg, Peggy Fury, Harvey Lembeck, and Stella Adler. POLITICS: Independent or Republican. RELIGION: Science of Mind.

MARIE WINDSOR

CAREER: DEBUT—Miss Smith, *Forty Thousand Smiths,* Ben Bard, Los Angeles, CA, 1940. NEW YORK DEBUT—Phyllis Brent, *Follow the Girls,* 44th Street Theater, 1945. PRINCIPAL THEATRE APPEARANCES—*Once in a Lifetime,* Pasadena Playhouse, CA, 1940; *Merry-Go-Rounders,* National, Washington, DC, 1943; *Fashions of the Times,* NY, 1944; *The Would-be Gentleman,* Ritz, Los Angeles, 1959; *Fancy Meeting You Again,* La Jolla Playhouse, CA, 1960; *The Vinegar Tree,* Actors Repertory, 1983. FILM DEBUT—*All American Coed,* 1941. PRINCIPAL FILM APPEARANCES—*Weekend for Three,* 1941; *Playmates,* 1941; *Call Out the Marines,* 1942; *Smart Alecks,* 1942; *Parachute Nurse,* 1942; *Eyes in the Night,* 1942; *The Big Street,* 1942; *The Lady or the Tiger,* 1942; *Three Hearts for Julia,* 1943; *Pilot Number 5,* 1943; *Let's Face It,* 1943; *The Hucksters,* 1947; *Romance of Rosy Ridge,* 1947; *Song of the Thin Man,* 1947; *Unfinished Dance,* 1947; *On an Island with You,* 1948; *Three Musketeers,* 1948; *The Kissing Bandit,* 1948; *Force of Evil,* 1948; *Outpost in Morocco,* 1949; *Beautiful Blonde from Bashful Bend,* 1949; *Hellfire,* 1949; *The Fighting Kentuckian,* 1949; *Dakota Lil,* 1950; *The Showdown,* 1950; *Frenchie,* 1950; *Double Deal,* 1950;

Little Big Horn, 1951; *Hurrican Island,* 1951; *Two Dollar Bettor,* 1951; *Japanese War Bride,* 1952; *The Sniper,* 1952; *The Narrow Margin,* 1952; *Outlaw Women,* 1952; *The Jungle,* 1952; *The Tall Texan,* 1953; *Trouble Along the Way,* 1953; *City that Never Sleeps,* 1953; *So This Is Love,* 1953; *Cat Women of the Moon,* 1953; *The Eddie Cantor Story,* 1953; *Hell's Half Acre,* 1954; *The Bounty Hunter,* 1954; *The Silver Star,* 1955; *Abbott and Costello Meet the Mummy,* 1955; *No Man's Woman,* 1955; *Two-Gun Lady,* 1956; *The*

Killing, 1956; *Swamp Women*, 1956; *The Parson and the Outlaw*, 1957; *Unholy Wife*, 1957; *Girl in Black Stockings*, 1957; *The Story of Mankind*, 1957; *Day of the Bad Men*, 1958; *Island Women*, 1958; *Paradise Alley*, 1961; *Critic's Choice*, 1963; *The Day Mars Invaded Earth*, 1964; *Bedtime Story*, 1964; *Mail Order Bride*, 1964; *Chamber of Horrors*, 1966; *The Good Guys and the Bad Guys*, 1969; *Wild Women*, 1970; *Support Your Local Gunfighter*, 1971; *One More Train to Rob*, 1971; *Cahill—U.S. Marshall*, 1973; *Manhunter*, 1974; *The Outfit*, 1974; *Hearts of the West*, 1975; *Freaky Friday*, 1977; *Salem's Lot*, 1980; *The Perfect Woman*, 1980; *Lovely but Deadly*, 1981.

TELEVISION DEBUT—Actress-model, *Orry Kelly Fashion Show*, 1944. PRINCIPAL TELEVISION APPEARANCES—*Shultz Playhouse of the Stars; The Whistler; Ford Theater; Lux Theater; Gem Theater; Bonanza; Waterfront; Pepsi Cola Theater; Derringer; Bat Masterson; Outsider; Pursuit; Studio One;* "*Wild Women,*" *ABC Movie of the Week; City Detective; The Falcon; Science Fiction Theater; Meet McGraw; Best of the Post; Lawman; Maverick; Bridges Show; Bronco; The Rebel; Requiem of a Planet; Charlie Farrell Show; Alaskans; Screen Directors Playhouse; The Unexpected; Playhouse 90; Grand Jury; Branded; Batman; Jesse James; The Rogues; Tales of Wells Fargo; Rawhide; Lassie; Family Theater; 77 Sunset Strip; Mr. Public Defender; Cheyenne; The Eddie Cantor Comedy Hour; Wyatt Earp; This Is Your FBI; Apartment in Rome; The Verdict Is Yours; Hawaiian Eye; Little Cabbage; Trademark; Bourbon Street Beat; Grand Jury; New Comedy Showcase; Deputy; Matinee Theater; The Nicest Girl in Gomorrah; The Outsider; Bracken's World; Adam 12; Lloyd Bridges Show; Hawaii Five-O; Scared Stiff; Full Circle; Divorce Court; Perry Mason; Mannix; Key Witness; Climax; Alias Smith and Jones; Hec Ramsey; Man Hunter; Barnaby Jones; Police Story; Marcus Welby, M.D.; Stranded; Project UFO; Charlie's Angels; Incredible Hulk; Simon and Simon.*

AWARDS: Honorary Captain, U.S. Army U.S.O. (Korea), 1952.

SIDELIGHTS: MEMBERSHIPS—SAG (board), AFTRA, AEA, Academy of Motion Picture Arts and Sciences, Academy of Television Arts and Sciences, Beverly Hills Chamber of Commerce, WAIFS, THALIANS, John Tracy Clinic Womens Auxiliary, Silver Dollar Club, Actors for an Actors' Guild (steering committee), Theater East.

"I have sold over a hundred and twenty-five of my paintings and for two years had my own gallery."

ADDRESS: Office—9743 Santa Monica Blvd., Beverly Hills, CA 90210. Agent—c/o Mark Levin, 328 S. Beverly Drive, Beverly Hills, CA 90212.

* * *

WINTERS, Warrington, actor

PERSONAL: Born July 28, 1909; son of George Woodruff (a farm machinery salesman) and Annie Bell (a piano teacher; maiden name, Brown) Winters; married Helen Elveback, 1934 (divorced 1946); married Margaret Spears, 1947 (di-

vorced 1955); married Lucy Zackheim, September 27, 1958; children: Anne Kilner, Victoria Rose, George Woodruff, Juliet Halliday. EDUCATION: University of Minnesota, B.A., 1935; M.A., 1936; Ph.D., 1942; trained for the stage at the Bush Conservatory, Chicago, with Elias Day. POLITICS: Rooseveltian Democrat. RELIGION: Episcopalian. MILITARY: U.S. Army Air Corps, 1942–46.

CAREER: PRINCIPAL STAGE APPEARANCES—(New York) Match Seller, *A Slight Ache*, Classic Theater; Chorus, *Agamemmon*, Greek Theatre; Dr. Evans, *In the Matter of J. Robert Oppenheimer*, 92nd Street Y; Aegeon, *The Comedy of Errors*, Manhattan Punchline; Fred, *A Midnight Moon*, Theatre for the New City; Freeman, *The Tavern*, Meat and Potatoes; Cosme, *Phantom Lady*, New York Theatre Ensemble; Serebryakov, *Uncle Vanya*, Troupe; Duke of York, *Richard II*, American Folk; James Mayo, *Beyond the Horizon*, 78th Street Lab; Creon, *Black Medea*, New Federal; Witness #2, *The Investigation*, Friends' Meeting House; Gonzalo, *The Tempest*, Westbeth; Tom Garrison, *I Never Sang for My Father*; Vermandero, *The Changeling*, 3 Muses; Firs, *The Cherry Orchard*, 18th Street Theatre; Capulet, *Romeo and Juliet*, Riverside Shakespeare Company; Devlin, *The Movie Man*, Theatre 12; Alfred Tennyson, *Freshwater*, Gene Frankel Theatre; The Lord, *Livin' at the Racoon Lodge*, Classic; *Compulsion, Summer and Smoke, A Night at the Black Pig, The Seagull, Ivanov, The Mousetrap, Oedipus Rex*, 1974–83; (Regional) *Broadway; The Beaux Stratagem; An Enemy of the People; She Stoops to Conquer; A Marriage of Convenience; The Rivals; Volpone; The Merchant Gentleman; A Midsummer Night's Dream*, 1930–50.

PRINCIPAL FILM APPEARANCES—Sheriff Lucas, *One Down and Two to Go*. PRINCIPAL TELEVISION APPEARANCES—Dr. Cotton Tufts, *The Adams Chronicles; A Death in the Country;* Harry, *Nobody Ever Died of Old Age;* Admiral Whitley, *Murder for Two.*

SIDELIGHTS: MEMBERSHIPS—AEA, SAG, AFTRA, Players Club, American Association of University Professors.

ADDRESS: Agent—c/o Eric Ross, 60 E. 42nd Street, New York, NY 10032.

* * *

WOLPER, David (Lloyd), producer

PERSONAL: Born January 11, 1928, in New York City; son of Irving S. and Anna (Fass) Wolper; married Margaret Dawn Richard, 1958 (divorced); Gloria Hill, June 11, 1974; children: (first marriage), Mark, Michael, Leslie. EDUCATION: Attended Drake University, 1946, University of Southern California, 1949.

CAREER: PRINCIPAL FILM WORK—Producer: *The Devil's Brigade; The Bridge at Remagen; If It's Tuesday, This Must Be Belgium*, 1968; *I Love My Wife; Wattstax; Willy Wonka and the Chocolate Factory*, 1971; *The Hellstrom Chronicle*, 1971; *Visions of Eight*, 1973; *Birds Do It, Bees Do It*, 1974.

PRINCIPAL TELEVISION WORK—Producer: *Biography* series, 1962–63; *Hollywood and the Stars* series, 1963–64; *Men in*

Crisis; Race for Space; Project: Man in Space; The Rafer Johnson Story; Biography of a Rookie; Hollywood: The Golden Years; Hollywood: The Fabulous Era; Hollywood: The Great Stars; D-Day; Escape to Freedom; The Making of the President, 1960, 1964, 1968; The Yanks Are Coming; Berlin: Kaiser to Khrushchev; December 7: Day of Infamy; The American Woman in the 20th Century; The Rise and Fall of American Communism; Legend of Marilyn Monroe; Four Days in November; Kreboizen and Cancer; National Geographic Series; The Undersea World of Jacques Cousteau, 1967–68; China, Roots of Madness; The Journey of Robert F. Kennedy; Say Goodbye George; George Plimpton Series; Appointment with Destiny; American Heritage Smithsonian Specials; They've Killed President Lincoln; Sandburg's Lincoln; I Will Fight No More Forever; The March of Time Series; The Rise and Fall of the Third Reich; Primal Man, the First Woman President; Chico and the Man; Get Christie Love; Welcome Back, Kotter; Collision Course; Roots; Roots: The Next Generation; Moviola, 1979; The Thorn Birds, 1982; Murder Is Easy, 1982; Casablanca, 1982; Victory at Entebbe; Mystic Warrior, 1983; North and South, 1984.

RELATED CAREER: Vice-President, treasurer, Flamingo Films, TV sales company, 1948–50; Vice-President in charge of West Coast operations Motion Pictures for Television, 1950–54; chairman of the board, president, Wolper Television Sales Company, 1964–present; chairman of the board, Metromedia, Inc., 1965–68; president, chairman of the board, Wolper Productions, Los Angeles, 1958–present, Wolper Pictures Ltd.; president, Fountainhead International, 1960–present.

AWARDS: Academy Award and 11 nominations from the Academy of Motion Picture Arts and Sciences; Grand Prix, Television Program, Cannes Film Festival, 1964, 1971; Monte Carlo International Film Festival, 1964; 28 Emmy Awards and 93 nominations from the Academy of Television Arts and Sciences; Distinguished Service award, U.S. Jr. Chamber of Commerce, 1963; George Foster Peabody, 1963; Golden Mike of the American Legion, 1963; award for documentaries, San Francisco International Film Festival, 1960.

SIDELIGHTS: MEMBERSHIPS—National Academy of Television Arts and Sciences; Screen Producers Guild; American Rocket Society; Writers Guild of America; Manuscript Society; Chairman, board of directors, Dodger Baseball Museum; board of directors, Cedars of Lebanon-Mt. Sinai Hospital, Thalina Clinic, Emotionally Disturbed Children; founding member, Hollywood Museum; chairman, President's Advisory Council to American Revolution Bicentennial Administration; Los Angeles Olympic Organizing Committee.

ADDRESS: Office—c/o Warner Brothers Inc., 4000 Warner Blvd., Burbank, CA 91522.

* * *

WOOD, Natalie (nee Natasha Gurdin) actress

PERSONAL: Born 1938, in San Francisco, CA; died November 29, 1982, off the coast of CA; daughter of Nicholas

(a set designer and decorator) and Marci (a ballet dancer; maiden name, Kuleff) Gurdin; married Robert Wagner, 1957 (divorced 1962); Richard Gregson, May 31, 1969 (divorced); Robert Wagner, July 16, 1972; children: (second marriage) one daughter; (third marriage) Courtney.

CAREER: FILM DEBUT—*Happy Land*, 1943. PRINCIPAL FILM APPEARANCES—*Tomorrow Is Forever*, 1946; *The Bride Wore Boots*, 1946; *Miracle on 34th Street*, 1947; *The Ghost and Mrs. Muir*, 1947; *Driftwood*, 1947; *Chicken Every Sunday*, 1949; *No Sad Songs for Me*, 1950; *The Jackpot*, 1950; *Never a Dull Moment*, 1950; *Our Very Own*, 1950; *The Blue Veil*, 1951; *Just for You*, 1952; *The Star*, 1953; *Rebel without a Cause*, 1955; *The Searchers*, 1956; *Burning Hills*, 1956; *Girl He Left Behind*, 1956; *Marjorie Morningstar*, 1956; *Cry in the Night*, 1956; *No Sleep Till Dawn*, 1957; *Kings Go Forth*, 1958; *Cash McCall*, 1959; *All the Fine Young Cannibals*, 1960; *West Side Story*, 1961; *Splendor in the Grass*, 1961; *Gypsy*, 1963; *Sex and the Single Girl*, 1964; *Love with the Proper Stranger*, 1964; *The Great Race*, 1965; *Inside Daisy Clover*, 1966; *Penelope*, 1966; *This Property Is Condemned*, 1966; *Bob and Carol and Ted and Alice*, 1969; *The Affair*, 1973; *Peeper*, 1975; *Meteor*, 1979; *Brainstorm*, 1982.

PRINCIPAL TELEVISION APPEARANCES—*Cat on a Hot Tin Roof; From Here to Eternity.**

* * *

WOODWARD, Joanne (Gignilliat), actress

PERSONAL: Born February 27, 1930, Thomasville, GA; daughter of Wade and Elinor (Trimmer) Woodward; married Paul Newman (an actor) January 29, 1958; children: Elinor Terese, Melissa Stewart, Clea Olivia. EDUCATION: Attended Louisiana State University; studied at the Neighborhood Playhouse Dramatic School. POLITICS: Democrat. RELIGION: Episcopalian.

CAREER: DEBUT—understudy, *Picnic*, 1953. PRINCIPAL STAGE APPEARANCES—*Baby Want a Kiss*, 1964; *Candide*, Circle in the Square, NY, 1982.

PRINCIPAL FILM APPEARANCES—*Kiss Before Dying; Three Faces of Eve*, 1957; *Count Three and Pray*, 1955; *Long Hot Summer*, 1958; *No Down Payment*, 1957; *Sound and the Fury*, 1959; *Rally Round the Flag Boys*, 1958; *The Fugitive Kind*, 1960; *Paris Blues*, 1961; *The Stripper*, 1963; *A New Kind of Love*, 1963; *A Big Hand for the Little Lady*, 1965; *A Fine Madness*, 1965; *Rachel, Rachel*, 1968; *Winning*, 1969; *WUSA*, 1970; *They Might Be Giants*, 1971; *The Effect of Gamma Rays on Man-in-the-Moon Marigolds*, 1972; *Summer Wishes, Winter Dreams*, 1973; *The Drowning Pool*, 1975; *The End*, 1978; *Harry and Son*, 1983.

PRINCIPAL TELEVISION APPEARANCES—*All the Way Home; Sybil*, 1976; *Come Back Little Sheba*, 1977; *See How She Runs*, 1978; *Streets of L.A.*, 1979; *The Shadow Box*, 1980; narrator, *Angel Dust.**

WOUK, Herman, writer, playwright

PERSONAL: Surname rhymes with "spoke," born May 27, 1915 in New York City; son of Abraham Isaac (an industrialist in the power laundry field) and Esther (Levine) Wouk; married Betty Sarah Brown (a literary agent) December 9, 1945; children: Abraham (deceased), Nathaniel, Joseph. EDUCATION: Columbia University, A.B., 1934. MILITARY: U.S. Navy, served in Pacific aboard two destroyer minesweepers, U.S.S. *Zane*, and U.S.S. *Southard* became lieutenant, 1942–46. RELIGION: Jewish.

WRITINGS: PLAYS PRODUCED/PUBLISHED—*The Traitor*, 48th Street Theatre, NY, 1949; *The Caine Mutiny Court-Martial*, Santa Barbara, CA, 1953, Plymouth, NY, 1954; *Nature's Way*, Coronet, NY, 1957. SCREENPLAYS—*The Winds of War*, from his novel of the same title, 1983; motion pictures based on Mr. Wouk's novels include—*Slattery's Hurricane*, 1949, *Her First Romance*, based on *The City Boy*, 1951, *The Caine Mutiny*, 1954, *Marjorie Morningstar*, 1958, *Youngblood Hawke*, 1962; *Don't Stop the Carnival*, 1965; *The Winds of War*, 1971; *War and Remembrance*, 1978. NON-FICTION—*This Is My God*, 1959.

AWARDS: Ralph Waldo Emerson Award, International Platform Association, 1981; American Book Award nomination, 1981: *War and Remembrance;* Alexander Hamilton Medal, Columbia College Alumni Association, 1980; Litt.D., American International University, 1979; LL.D., Clark University, 1960; L.H.D., Yeshiva University, 1955; Columbia University Medal of Excellence, 1952; Pulitzer Prize in fiction, 1952: *The Caine Mutiny: A Novel of World War II;* four campaign stars and the presidential unit citation, for service in WWII; Richard H. Fox Prize, 1934.

THEATRE-RELATED CAREER: Radio program writer for various comedians, New York City, 1935; writer for Fred Allen, radio comedian, 1936–41; editor, Columbia University's humor magazine, *Jester* and wrote varsity musicals.

SIDELIGHTS: MEMBERSHIPS—Authors Guild, Authors League of America, P.E.N., Dramatists Guild, Reserve Officers Association of the United States, Writers Guild of America East, Century Club (New York City), Bohemian Club (San Francisco, Cosmos Club, Metropolitan Club (Washington, DC).

ADDRESS: Agent—BSW Literary Agency, Inc. 3255 N Street, N.W., Washington, DC 20007.

* * *

WYLER, GRETCHEN (nee Weinecke), actress, dancer

PERSONAL: Born February 15, 1932, in Bartlesville, OK; daughter of Louis Gustave (a gasoline engineer) and Peggy (Highley) Weinecke; married Shepard Coleman, June 18, 1956 (divorced 1968). EDUCATION: Graduated high school, Bartelsville, OK; studied dance with June Runyon in Tulsa, OK.

CAREER: DEBUT—Ballet ensemble, St. Louis Municipal Opera, 1950. NEW YORK DEBUT—Chorus dancer, *Where's Charley?* Broadway, 1951 for one year. LONDON DEBUT—

Charity, *Sweet Charity*, Prince of Wales, 1968 for ten months. PRINCIPAL ENGAGEMENTS—Chorus, *Guys and Dolls*, 1952; Janice Dayton, *Silk Sotckings*, Imperial, NY, 1955; Lola, *Damn Yankees*, 46th Street Theatre, NY, 1956; *Rumple*, NY, 1957; Rose, *Bye Bye Birdie*, 1961; *Sly Fox*, Broadhurst, NY; *The Gingerbread Lady*, University of Miami; Maggie, *The Man Who Came to Dinner*, Williamstown Theatre Festival, MA; *First Lady*, Berkshire Theatre Festival, MA, 1981; leading roles in stock productions of *Mame, Redhead, Annie Get Your Gun, Kismet, Say, Darling, 110 in the Shade, Here's Love, Bells Are Ringing, Call Me Madam, Anything Goes, Golden Rainbow, Applause, Dames at Sea, The Boy Friend, Bus Stop, A Hatful of Rain, Rattle of a Simple Man, Born Yesterday.* MAJOR TOURS—Adelaide, *Guys and Dolls*, national tour; Frenchy, *Destry Rides Again*, national tour; Viola, *Your Own Thing*, national tour; *And Miss Reardon Drinks a Little*, national tour. PRODUCED: Plays—*The Ballad of Johnny Pot*, Off-Broadway, NY, 1971.

FILM DEBUT—*Pollyanna*, 1960. FILM APPEARANCES—*The Devil's Brigade*, 1968; Aunt Kissy, *Private Benjamin*, 1979; *When the Circus Came to Town*. TELEVISION DEBUT—*Colgate Comedy Hour*, 1956. TELEVISION APPEARANCES—*Bob Crosby/Gretchen Wyler Show*, summer replacement for the Perry Como Show, 1958; *Step This Way*, 1966; Toni McBain, *On Our Own*, 1977–78; Dr. Conrad, *Dallas*, 1981; also: *Charlie's Angels, St. Elsewhere, Hart to Hart, Making a Living, The New Odd Couple, Gimme a Break,* "Portrait of an Escort—" *CBS Movie*.

AWARDS: Outer Circle Critics Award, Best Supporting Actress in a Musical, 1955: *Silk Stockings.*

SIDELIGHTS: MEMBERSHIPS—Fund for Animals (vice-chairman).

In addition to the above, Miss Wyler has toured extensively with her own night-club act and has become a "Town Hall Concert Artist" with her one-woman show, *Broadway Greats and the Songs That Made Them Famous*. Offstage, Ms. Wyler is an activist for the rights of animals. In 1968, she founded a shelter for animals in upstate New York. She is on the boards of seven humane and wildlife organizations; she has sponsored successful animal welfare legislation.

ADDRESS: Agent—Jack Fields & Assoc., 9255 Sunset Blvd., Suite 1105, Los Angeles, CA 90069. Agent—Hesseltine-Baker, 165 W. 46th Street, New York, NY 10036.

* * *

WYNN, Tracy Keenan, writer

PERSONAL: Born February 28, 1945, in Hollywood, CA; son of Keenan (an actor) and Eve (Abbott) Wynn; married Kerstin Wassgren, 1976; children: Aidan, Amanda, Brendan. EDUCATION: Le Rosey, Switzerland, 1962; UCLA, Westwood, CA, B.A., 1967 (cum laude). RELIGION: Episcopalian. MILITARY: U.S. Air Force Reserve.

WRITINGS: SCREENPLAYS—*The Deep; The Longest Yard.* MOVIES FOR TELEVISION—*Tribes*, 1970; *The Glass House*, 1972; *Autobiography of Miss Jane Pittman*, 1974.

AWARDS: Emmy Award, 1970: *Tribes;* Writers Guild Award, 1970: *Tribes;* Emmy Award, 1974; *Autobiography of Miss Jane Pittman,* and Writers Guild Award; Emmy Award Nomination, 1972: *The Glass House.*

SIDELIGHTS: MEMBERSHIPS—WGA, DGA.

Mr. Wynn teaches screenwriting, most recently at the Aspen Playwrights Conference in Colorado.

ADDRESS: Agent—Bill Haber, Contemporary Artists Agency, 1888 Century Park East, Los Angeles, CA 90067.

Y

YABLANS, Frank, executive producer

PERSONAL: Born August 27, 1935, in New York City; son of Morris and Annette Yablans; married Ruth Edelstein, December 21; children: Robert, Sharon, Edward. EDUCATION: City College of New York, University of Wisconsin. MILITARY: U.S. Army, 1954–56.

CAREER: PRINCIPAL FILM WORK—Executive producer, Frank Yablans Presentations, Inc: *Silver Streak,* 1976; *The Other Side of Midnight,* 1977; *The Fury,* 1978; *North Dallas Forty,* 1979; co-screenwriter, *Mommie Dearest,* 1982; *Monsignore,* 1982.

RELATED CAREER: Booking manager, Walt Disney Productions, 1958–66; vice-president Filmways Productions, 1966–69; vice-president sales, marketing, executive vice-president, Paramount Pictures Corporation, New York City, 1969–75; president, Frank Yablans Presentations Inc., 1975–present.

AWARDS: Decorated Commendatore Repubblica Italiana.

SIDELIGHTS: MEMBERSHIPS—Chairman, Variety Club International; director, Motion Picture Association; corporate chairman, entertainment division, Federation of Jewish Philanthropies; board of directors, Boy's Clubs of America; Will Rogers Hospital; trustee, American Film Institute; Fairview Country Club.

ADDRESS: Office—Frank Yablans Presentations Inc., MGM Studios, 10202 W. Washington Blvd., Culver City, CA 90230.*

* * *

YABLANS, Irwin, producer

PERSONAL: Born in Brooklyn, NY. MILITARY: U.S. Army, 1954–56.

CAREER: PRINCIPAL FILM WORK—Associate producer, *Badge 373,* 1972; producer: *The Education of Sonny Carson,* 1974; *Halloween,* 1978; *Roller Boogie,* 1978; *Fade to Black,* 1979; *Hell Night,* 1981; *The Seduction,* 1982; *Tank,* 1983.

RELATED CAREER: Warner Brothers, 1956 held sales posts in Washington, DC, Albany, Detroit, Milwaukee and Portland; Los Angeles manager Paramount Productions, 1962, western sales manager, 1972; president, Compass International Pictures, 1974; Executive vice-president, Lorimar Productions.

ADDRESS: Office—c/o Lorimar, 3970 Overland Avenue, Culver City, CA 90230.*

* * *

YANKOWITZ, Susan, writer

PERSONAL: Born February 20, 1941, in Newark, NJ; daughter of Irving N. (an attorney) and Ruth (Katz) Yankowitz; married Herbert Leibowitz (a writer and editor), May 3, 1977; children: Gabriel. EDUCATION: Sarah Lawrence College, B.A., 1963; Yale School of Drama, M.F.A., 1968.

WRITINGS: PLAYS, PRODUCED—*The Cage,* Omar Khayyam Café, NY, 1965; *Nightmare,* Yale University, New Haven, CT, 1967; *Slaughterhouse Play,* Public Theatre, NY, 1971; *Boxes,* Magic, Berkeley, CA, 1972; *Wooden Nickels,* Theatre for the New City, NY, 1973; *America Piece,* U.S. and Europe, 1974; *Still Life,* Interart, NY, 1977, Factory Theatre Lab, Toronto, Canada, 1977; *True Romances,* Mark Taper Lab, Los Angeles, CA, 1978; *Qui Est Anna Mark?,* TEP, Paris, France, 1979; *Who Done It?,* Interart, NY, 1982; *A Knife in the Heart,* O'Neill Theatre Center, Waterford, CT, 1982; *Baby,* Barrymore, NY, 1983. PLAYS, PUBLISHED—*Slaughterhouse Play,* 1971; *Boxes,* 1973; *Portrait of a Scientist as a Dumb Broad,* 1974; *Terminal,* 1975. BOOKS—*Silent Witness,* 1976–77. SCREENPLAYS—*Portrait of a Scientist as a Dumb Broad,* 1969; *To See the Elephant,* 1974; *Milk and Funny,* 1976; *The Prison Game,* 1977; *Charlotte Perkins Gilman: Forerunner,* 1979; *Silent Witness,* 1979; *The Amnesiac,* 1980. RADIO PLAYS—*Rats' Alley,* 1969.

AWARDS: Vernon Rice Drama Desk Award, 1969. GRANTS/FELLOWSHIPS—Joseph E. Levine, 1968; NEA Creative Writing, 1972; Rockefeller, 1973; CAPS Award, 1974; Guggenheim, 1975; NEA Creative Writing, 1979.

SIDELIGHTS: MEMBERSHIPS—Dramatists Guild, Writers Guild of America East, PEN.

ADDRESS: Agent—c/o Flora Roberts, Inc., 157 W. 57th Street, New York, NY 10107.

* * *

YATES, Peter, director

PERSONAL: Married Virginia Pope, 1960; children: three.

CAREER: PRINCIPAL FILM WORK—Assistant director, *A Taste of Honey, The Entertainer;* director: *Summer Holiday,* 1962; *One Way Pendulum,* 1964; *Robbery,* 1967; *Bullitt,* 1968; *John and Mary,* 1969; *Murphy's War,* 1971; *The Hot Rock,* 1972; *The Friends of Eddie Coyle,* 1973; *For Pete's Sake,* 1976; *Mother, Jugs and Speed,* 1976; *The Deep,* 1977; producer/director: *Breaking Away,* 1979; *Eyewitness,* 1981; *Krull,* 1982; *The Dresser,* 1983.

ADDRESS: Office—c/o Tempest Productions, Inc., 1775 Broadway, Suite 621, New York, NY 10019. Agent—c/o ICM, 40 W. 57th Street, New York, NY 10019.*

* * *

YESTON, Maury, composer, writer

PERSONAL: Born December 23, 1945; son of David (a businessman) and Frances (a businesswoman; maiden name, Haar) Yeston; married Anne Sheedy (a flutist), November 13, 1982; children: Jake. EDUCATION: Yale University, B.A., 1963–67; Clare College/Cambridge University, M.A., 1967–69; Yale University, Ph.D., 1970–74; trained for the stage with the BMI Musical Theatre workshop and Lehman Engel.

WRITINGS: PLAYS, PRODUCED—Composer/lyricist—*Nine,* 46th Street Theater, NY, 1982. BOOKS—*The Stratification of Musical Rhythm,* 1975; *Readings in Schenker Analysis,* 1976.

MAURY YESTON

Photograph by Christian Steiner

THEATRE-RELATED CAREER: Associate professor, Yale University, 1975–82; teacher, BMI Musical Theatre Workshop, 1982–present.

AWARDS: Antoinette Perry Award, Best Score, Drama Desk Award, Best Music, Best Lyrics, 1982: *Nine.*

SIDELIGHTS: MEMBERSHIPS—Dramatists Guild, Society of Music Theory, A.M.S.

ADDRESS: Agent—c/o Flora Roberts, 157 W. 57th Street, New York, NY 10019.

* * *

YORK, Michael (ne York-Johnson), actor

PERSONAL: Born March 27, 1942, in Fulmer, England; son of Joseph Gwynne (a businessman) and Florence May (Chown) Johnson; married Patricia Watson (a photographer), March 27, 1968. EDUCATION: University College, Oxford, M.A.; trained for the stage with the National Youth Theatre (England).

CAREER: DEBUT—Sergius, *Arms and the Man,* Repertory Theatre, Dundee, Scotland, 1964. LONDON DEBUT—Walk-on, *Much Ado about Nothing,* National Theatre Company, 1965. NEW YORK DEBUT—Felice, *Out Cry,* Lyceum, 1973, 16 performances. PRINCIPAL STAGE APPEARANCES—Hamlet, *Hamlet,* Thorndike, Leatherhead, England, 1970; the Twin, *Ring Round the Moon,* Ahmanson, Los Angeles, 1975; *Bent,* NY, 1980; Cyrano, *Cyrano de Bergerac,* Santa Fe, NM, 1981. FILM DEBUT—Lucentio, *The Taming of the Shrew,* 1966. PRINCIPAL FILM APPEARANCES—*Accident,* 1967; *Red and Blue,* 1967; *Smashing Time,* 1967; Tybalt, *Romeo and Juliet,* 1968; *The Strange Affair,* 1968; *The Guru,* 1969; *Alfred the Great,* 1969; *Justine,* 1969; *Something for Everyone,* 1970; *Zeppelin,* 1971; *La Poudre d'Escampette,* 1971; *Cabaret,* 1972; *England Made Me,* 1973; *Lost Horizon,* 1973; D'Artagnan, *The Three Musketeers,* 1974; *Murder on the Orient Express,* 1974; D'Artagnan, *The Four Musketeers,* 1975; *Conduct Unbecoming,* 1975; *Logan's Run,* 1976; *Seven Nights in Japan,* 1977; *Last Remake of Beau Geste,* 1977; *Island of Dr. Moreau,* 1977; *A Man Called Intrepid,* 1978; *The Riddle of the Sands,* 1978; *The White Lions,* 1979; *Fedora,* 1979; *Final Assignment,* 1980.

TELEVISION DEBUT—Young Jolyon, *The Forsyte Saga.* PRINCIPAL TELEVISION APPEARANCES—*Rebel in the Grave; Great Expectations; Jesus of Nazareth; True Patriot; Much Ado about Nothing; A Man Called Intrepid; The Phantom of the Opera; For Those I Loved.*

ADDRESS: Agent—c/o John Gaines, Agency for the Performing Arts, 9000 Sunset Blvd., Suite 315, Los Angeles, CA 90069.

* * *

YORKIN, Bud (Alan), producer, director

PERSONAL: Born February 22, 1926, in Washington, PA;

married Peg (a producing director); children: Nicole, David. EDUCATION: Carnegie-Mellon University, B.A.; Columbia University, M.A. MILITARY: U.S. Navy Air Force.

CAREER: TELEVISION DEBUT—Stage manager/director, *Colgate Comedy Hour*. DIRECTED: Television—*The Dinah Shore Show; The Tony Martin Show; The Ernie Ford Show; The George Gobel Show;* writer/director/producer, *An Evening with Fred Astaire;* producer/director, *Jack Benny Special* (2); Television Specials (with Norman Lear)—*Duke Ellington Special*, "We Love You Madly"; *Another Evening with Fred Astaire; TV Guide Awards Show; Bobby Darin and Friends; The Danny Kaye Special; Henry Fonda and the Family; The Andy Williams Special; An Evening with Carol Channing; Stage 67*, "Where It's At"; *The Many Sides of Don Rickles; Robert Young and the Family;* Television Series—*All in the Family; Sanford and Son; Maude; Good Times; Diff'rent Strokes; Archie Bunker's Place; What's Happening; Carter Country;* Films—*Come Blow Your Horn,* 1963; *Never Too Late,* 1965; *Divorce: American Style,* 1967; *Inspector Clouseau; Start the Revolution without Me,* 1970; *The Night They Raided Minsky's* (with Norman Lear); *Cold Turkey* (with Norman Lear).

AWARDS: Emmy Award (6); Peabody; Sylvania; Look; Directors Guild; Man of the Year, Television Academy, 1973; Industry Award, Publicists Guild.

SIDELIGHTS: MEMBERSHIPS—Directors Guild of America (board of governors), Academy of Television Arts and Sciences (board of governors), American Film Institute (council board), Carnegie-Mellon University (board of trustees).

ADDRESS: Office—1901 Avenue of the Stars, Suite 1600, Los Angeles, CA 90067.

Z

ZADAN, Craig, writer, director, producer

PERSONAL: EDUCATION: Hofstra University, LI, NY.

CAREER: PRINCIPAL STAGE WORK—Co-producer, *Sondheim: A Musical Tribute,* Shubert, NY; producer/writer of dialogue/director, *Broadway at the Ballroom,* a series of evening performances by songwriters using their own material; director, *The Umbrellas of Cherbourg,* New York Shakespeare Festival, workshop production; director/co-conceived, *Up in One.*

PRINCIPAL FILM WORK—Co-producer, *Footloose,* 1983; executive producer, *Bread & Circus.*

RELATED CAREER—Writer of features, and the ''Intelligencer'' column, *New York* Magazine; director of theatre projects, New York Shakespeare Festival, two years; associate producer, recording, *I'm Getting My Act Together and Taking It on the Road;* vice president of Creative Affairs, United Artists; vice president, Theatre Production/Motion Picture Development, Casablanca Records & Filmworks; head of development and production executive, Indieprod Company; associate producer original motion picture soundtrack, *Footloose;* own production company, Storyline Productions, film in development, *Parallels.*

WRITINGS: BOOKS—*Sondheim & Co.*

AWARDS: Grammy Award nomination for best Original Cast Recording: *I'm Getting My Act Together and Taking It on the Road.*

ADDRESS: Office—Tri-Star Pictures, 711 Fifth Avenue, New York, NY 10022.

* * *

ZAKS, Jerry, actor and director

PERSONAL: Born September 7, 1946, in Stuttgart, Germany; son of Sy (a butcher) and Lily (Gliksman) Zaks; married Jill P. Rose (an actress), January 14, 1979; children: Emma Rose. EDUCATION: Dartmouth College, A.B., 1963–67; Smith College, M.F.A., 1967–69; trained for the stage with Curt Dempster.

CAREER: PRINCIPAL STAGE APPEARANCES—(Broadway) *Grease,* 1974; *Once in a Lifetime,* 1977; *1940's Radio Hour,* 1978; *Tintypes,* 1980; (Off-Broadway)—Ensemble Studio,

1971–81; O'Neill Center, CT, 1975; Phoenix, 1976–78; Arena Stage, Washington DC, 1978.

PRINCIPAL TELEVISION APPEARANCES—*Tuscaloosa's Calling Me,* 1979; *Attica,* 1979; *CBS Kennedy Center Tribute to James Cagney,* 1980; *Gentleman Bandit* (movie), 1981.

DIRECTED: PLAYS—Ensemble Studio, NY, 1978–80; Phoenix Theatre, NY, 1980–81; Playwrights Horizons, NY, 1981; Philadelphia Drama Guild, 1981.

AWARDS: Drama Desk Nomination, Outstanding Actor in a Musical, 1980: *Tintypes.*

SIDELIGHTS: MEMBERSHIPS—AEA, SAG, AFTRA, SSD&C, Ensemble Studio Theatre (board of directors, 1976–present), Ark Theatre Company.

ADDRESS: Agent (directing)—c/o Helen Merrill, 337 W. 22nd Street, New York, NY 10011. Agent (acting)—c/o Monty Silver, 200 W. 57th Street, New York, NY 10019.

* * *

ZALOOM, Paul, puppeteer, political satirist

PERSONAL: Born December 14, 1951; son of Joseph Albert (an importer) and Virginia Bell (an executive; maiden name, Carson) Zaloom; married Jayne Ellen Israel (a drug and alcohol counselor) on June 6, 1981; children: Amanda. EDUCATION: Goddard College, B.A. (Puppetry), 1973; studied puppet theatre with Bread and Puppet Theatre in Vermont.

CAREER: DEBUT—Puppeteer, many different productions with the Bread and Puppet Theatre, Glover, VT, 1971. NEW YORK DEBUT—Puppeteer, *The Revenge of the Law,* and *Harvey McLeod,* with the Bread and Puppet Theatre at the New York Shakespeare Festival, Public Theatre, 1972. PRINCIPAL STAGE APPEARANCES—Created one-man shows; *The Fruit of Zaloom,* Performing Garage, NY, 1979, *Zalooming Along,* Performing Garage, NY, 1980, *Zaloominations,* Theatre for the New City, NY, 1981, *Crazy as Zaloom,* Theatre for the New City, 1982, *Creature from the Blue Zaloom,* Inroads Theatre Company, NY, 1984. MAJOR TOURS—Has toured all of his one-man shows throughout the U.S.

AWARDS: Citation of Excellence, Union Internationale de la

PAUL ZALOOM

Photograph by Jim Moore

Marionette, 1983: *Crazy as Zaloom;* Villager Theatre Award, *The Villager,* NY; 1979: *Fruit of Zaloom.*

SIDELIGHTS: MEMBERSHIPS—Puppeteers of America, Union Internationale de la Marionette, Performing Artists for Nuclear Disarmament, Puppetry Guild of Greater New York, Executive Board, 1983–84, Member of the Bread and Puppet Theatre, 1971–76 (full-time). Since 1976, he has been a part-time member of the company.

''Zaloom's work animates found-objects, debris, junk, and toys as puppets and environments in short plays, and he uses conventional hand-puppets. He also creates paper videotapes (or ''crankies''), a scroll of paper with illustrations that is unrolled with an accompanying narration. Zaloom designs and builds all of his puppets, draws all paper videotapes, and directs and performs all the work. 'Two elements can be found in all my work: first it is all funny. My primary objective is to make people laugh. Secondly, it is political. By ''political,'' I mean that the work is about real issues and events in the world today as I see them. I do not espouse any political line or suggest any solutions. I try to reduce complex issues like acid rain, deterioration of U.S. underground water supplies, book banning, the greenhouse effect, civil defense planning, nuclear war, ocean dumping, etc. into simple, clear, accurate puppet scenes. But if the audience doesn't laugh, then I have failed. Ideally, the audience *does* laugh and has a great time; then simultaneously or even the next

day, the gravity and urgency of these issues hits the audience.' ''

ADDRESS: Home—54 Franklin Street, New York, NY 10013. Agent—Arts Arcadia Associates, 853 Broadway, Rm. 1208, New York, NY 10003.

* * *

ZINNEMANN, Fred, film director

PERSONAL: Born April 29, 1907, in Austria; son of Oskar (a doctor) and Anna F. (Feiwel) Zinnemann; married Renée Bartlett, 1936; children: Tim. EDUCATION: University of Vienna, B.A., 1927; trained as a student of film at the Technical School of Cinematography in Paris, 1927–28.

CAREER: DIRECTED: Films—*The Wave,* 1934; *The Seventh Cross,* 1941; *The Search,* 1946–47; *The Men,* 1949; *Teresa,* 1950; *High Noon,* 1951; *Benjy,* 1951; *The Member of the Wedding,* 1952; *From Here to Eternity,* 1953; *Oklahoma,* 1956; *A Hatful of Rain,* 1957; *The Nun's Story,* 1958; *The Sundowners,* 1959; *Behold a Pale Horse,* 1964; *A Man for All Seasons,* 1966; *The Day of the Jackal,* 1972; *Julia,* 1976.

AWARDS: Order of Arts and Letters (France), 1982; Donatello Award, 1978: *Julia;* Fellowship Award; D. W. Griffith

FRED ZINNEMANN

Award, 1971; Gold Medal Award (Vienna), 1967; New York Film Critics Award, Best Director, Academy Award, Best Picture, Best Director, Directors Guild Award, 1966: *A Man for All Seasons;* Golden Thistle Award (Edinburgh), 1965; New York Film Critics Award, 1958: *The Nun's Story;* New York Film Critics Screen Directors Guild, Academy Award, 1951: *From Here to Eternity;* Academy Award, Best Documentary, 1951: *Benjy;* Screen Directors Guild Award, New York Film Critics Award, 1951: *High Noon;* Screen Directors Guild Award, 1947: *The Search.*

SIDELIGHTS: MEMBERSHIPS—American Film Institute, Academy of Motion Picture Arts and Sciences, Directors Guild of America (vice-president, 1961–64), Directors Guild of Great Britain (honorary president, 1982), British Academy of Film and Television Arts, Sierra Club.

ADDRESS: Agent—c/o Stan Kamen, William Morris Agency, 151 El Camino, Beverly Hills, CA 90212.

* * *

ZOLLO, Frederick M., producer, writer

PERSONAL: Born February 24, 1950 in Boston, MA; son of Carmen F. Zollo. EDUCATION: Boston University; London School of Economics and Political Science; Brandeis University. NON-THEATRICAL CAREER: Stringer, *Manchester Guardian*, Northern Ireland, 1970's.

CAREER: PRINCIPAL STAGE WORK—Producer (Broadway productions) *Guys and Dolls* (revival), *The Basic Training of Pavlo Hummel, Paul Robeson, On Golden Pond, 'night Mother, Hurlyburly, Almost an Eagle;* (Off-Broadway Productions) *Key Exchange, Funhouse;* (National Tours) *On Golden Pond, The Shadow Box, Key Exchange;* (Regional Theatre) *Bosoms and Neglect, Vanities, Sexual Perversity in Chicago* and *The Duck Variations, The Last Minstrel Show.*

WRITINGS: PLAYS, PRODUCED—*Conversations with Myself, The Last Three Rounds of Eddie Jacobs,* both produced in London, England; *Temporary Technical Difficulties,* produced off-Broadway, NY. SCREENPLAYS—*Shooting.* TELE-PLAYS—*Bicentennial Minutes.*

AWARDS: Guys and Dolls revival received five Antoinette Perry Award Nominations; *'night Mother* received the Pulitzer Prize for Drama; Emmy Award for *The Bicentennial Minutes.*

SIDELIGHTS: MEMBERSHIPS—New York League of Theatre Owner and Producers.

ADDRESS: Office—Zollo Productions, 357 W. 55th Street, New York, NY 10019.

* * *

ZUCKER, David, director, producer, electrician

PERSONAL: Born October 16, 1947, Milwaukee, WI. EDUCATION: University of Wisconsin, B.A., (Electrical Engineering), 1970; studied with Ed Gein at the Method School.

CAREER: DEBUT—Actor/writer/director, Kentucky Fried Theater: *Vegetables,* 1972, *My Nose,* 1974, *Beating a Dead Horse,* 1975.

PRINCIPAL FILM WORK—Writer, *Kentucky Fried Movie,* 1977; writer, director, *Airplane!,* 1980; *Top Secret,* 1984.

PRINCIPAL TELEVISION WORK—Writer, director, *Police Squad,* 1982.

AWARDS: Writers Guild, Best Comedy, 1980: *Airplane!*

ADDRESS: c/o Paramount Pictures, 5555 Melrose Avenue, Los Angeles, CA 90038.

Cumulative Index

To provide continuity with the last edition of *Who's Who in the Theatre*, this index interfiles references to *Who's Who in the Theatre*, 17th Edition, with references to *Contemporary Theatre, Film, and Television*, Volume 1.

References in the index are identified as follows:

Number only—*Contemporary Theatre, Film, and Television*, Volume 1
WWT-17—*Who's Who in the Theatre*, 17th Edition

531

Cumulative Index

Cumulative Index